Professional Microsoft® SQL S

Professional
Microsoft® SQL Server® 2008
Administration

Professional
Microsoft® SQL Server® 2008
Administration

Brian Knight
Ketan Patel
Wayne Snyder
Ross LoForte
Steven Wort

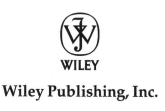

WILEY

Wiley Publishing, Inc.

Professional Microsoft® SQL Server® 2008 Administration

Published by
Wiley Publishing, Inc.
10475 Crosspoint Boulevard
Indianapolis, IN 46256
www.wiley.com

Copyright © 2009 by Wiley Publishing, Inc., Indianapolis, Indiana

Published simultaneously in Canada

ISBN: 978-0-470-24796-9

Manufactured in the United States of America

10 9 8 7 6 5 4 3 2 1

Library of Congress Cataloging-in-Publication Data

Microsoft SQL server 2008 administration / Brian Knight ... [et al.].
   p. cm.
   Includes index.
   ISBN 978-0-470-24796-9 (paper/website)
  1. SQL server. 2. Database management.   I. Knight, Brian.
   QA76.9.D3M57366 2008
   005.75'85 — dc22

                            2008037353

About the Authors

Brian Knight, SQL Server MVP, MCSE, MCDBA, is the co-founder of SQLServerCentral.com and JumpstartTV.com. Brian is a principal consultant and owner of Pragmatic Works. He runs the local SQL Server users group (JSSUG) in Jacksonville, Florida, and was on the Board of Directors of the Professional Association for SQL Server (PASS). Brian is a contributing columnist for *SQL Server Standard*, maintains a regular column for the database website SQLServerCentral.com, and does regular webcasts at Jumpstart TV. He is the author of nine SQL Server books. Brian is a speaker at numerous conferences, including PASS, SQL Connections, and TechEd, and many code camps. His blog can be found at www.pragmaticworks.com. Brian spends weekends practicing to be an amateur surgeon and proceeds from this book will help pay for the mobile CAT scan for his van.

Ketan Patel, B.E., electronics engineering, MCSE, MCDBA, is a senior development manager for the Business Intelligence Center of Excellence group at Microsoft. He has worked with SQL Server and other Microsoft technologies for nearly nine years. Ketan has also spoken at TechEd. He spends his spare time with his family and friends, playing cricket and watching NFL.

Wayne Snyder is recognized worldwide as a SQL Server expert and Microsoft Most Valued Professional (MVP), with over 25 years of experience in project management, database administration, software design, performance measurement, and capacity planning. He is a popular consultant, trainer, writer, and speaker, and produces a series of Web-based seminars on SQL Server 2005. Wayne has edited many SQL Server books, has SQL Training CDs with Learnkey, is president of PASS, the Professional Association for SQL Server (www.sqlpass.org), plays keyboard for a cover band named SoundBarrier (www.soundbarrierband.com), and is a managing consultant for Mariner, a Business Intelligence Company (www.mariner-usa.com).

Ross LoForte is a technical architect at the Microsoft Technology Center Chicago, focused on Microsoft SQL Server solutions. Ross has more than 16 years of experience in business development, project management, and designing SQL architecture solutions. For the past eight years, Ross has been working with the Microsoft Technology Centers, and has led architecture design and proof-of-concept engagements for Microsoft's largest and most strategic customers to design enterprise, mission-critical SQL Server solutions. Ross is a SQL Server instructor at DePaul University in Chicago, and regularly presents at TechEd, SQL PASS, Gartner, TDWI, and other conferences. A published author, he has been active with the Professional Association for SQL Server, the Chicago SQL Server Users Group, and the SQL Server community for many years.

Steven Wort has been working with SQL Server for the past 14 years. He spent much of that time working as a freelance application developer and database architect building VB and Web applications on SQL Server for many of London's largest financial institutions. He moved to the United States nine years ago, joining Microsoft over seven years ago. After three years working in PSS on the SIE team, he moved over to the SQL Server Product group, spending a year working on SQL Server scalability, followed by a year working with the SQL Playback team. Two years ago Steven moved to the Windows division, where he started work on the SQL Server side of the Watson system. When he is not involved with technology, Steven can be found doing something active somewhere outdoors in the Pacific Northwest.

Geoff Hiten, a Microsoft MVP, is a senior SQL Server consultant based in Atlanta. Geoff began working with SQL Server in 1992 with version 4.2 and has used every version since. He specializes in high-availability and high-performance SQL systems. Recent projects include: system upgrades, SQL Server platform migrations, performance tuning, custom reporting solutions, and database strategy implementations. Geoff is currently on the leadership team of the Atlanta area Microsoft Database Forum

Users group (AtlantaMDF) and can be found lurking in the halls at PASS (Professional Association for SQL Server) Community Summit events. In addition, Geoff has been a Subject Matter Expert for Microsoft Training Curriculum materials and has authored articles, white papers, and podcasts on SQL Server.

K. Brian Kelley (MCSE, Security+, CISA) is a systems and security architect for AgFirst Farm Credit Bank. At AgFirst he provides infrastructure and security guidance with respect to Windows-based technologies including Active Directory, Internet Information Server, and Microsoft SQL Server. Brian, author of *Start to Finish Guide to SQL Server Performance Monitoring* and contributing author for *How to Cheat at Securing SQL Server 2005*, is a regular columnist and blogger at SQLServerCentral.com focusing primarily on SQL Server security. He is also a frequent contributor for SQL Server Standard Magazine. Brian is a member of the Professional Association of SQL Server (PASS) and the Information Systems Audit and Control Association (ISACA). He is also active in the Midlands PASS chapter, an official PASS chapter for South Carolina.

Credits

Executive Editor
Robert Elliott

Development Editor
Sara Shlaer

Technical Editor
John Mueller

Production Editor
Kathleen Wisor

Copy Editor
Luann Rouff

Editorial Manager
Mary Beth Wakefield

Production Manager
Tim Tate

Vice President and Executive Group Publisher
Richard Swadley

Vice President and Executive Publisher
Joseph B. Wikert

Project Coordinator, Cover
Lynsey Stanford

Proofreader
Nancy Carrasco
Publication Services, Inc.

Indexer
Robert Swanson

Acknowledgments

As always, I must thank my wife and best friend for supporting me for the past 10 years of marriage. I've been fortunate to have found a woman who doesn't fall asleep immediately when copyediting my technical writing. Thanks to my three children, Colton, Liam, and Camille, for allowing their daddy to be distracted sometimes with this book when they wanted to play. Thanks also to all the wonderful co-authors, who truly made this book possible. Once again, I must thank the Pepsi-Cola Company for inventing Mountain Dew, which drove the late night writing. — *Brian Knight*

I would like to thank my parents, Thakorbhai and Induben, for their unwavering and selfless support and inspiration in my life, and my wife, Sweety, for her invaluable support and understanding. I would like to acknowledge Brian Knight, the lead author, for providing me with a great opportunity to co-author this book. I would also like to acknowledge Sara Shlaer, the development editor, and John Mueller, technical editor — without them this book would not exist or contain the level of depth that it has. Last but not the least, I want to thank B. J. Moore and Jim Walch, both general managers at Microsoft, for their invaluable support and encouragement. — *Ketan Patel*

Thank-you to my loving wife, Vickie, whose generosity and support make my life better each day. — *Wayne Snyder*

I'd like to thank my wife, Anna, and my daughter, Jennifer, for their support while writing this book. Additionally, I'd like to thank Adam Hecktman and Tony Surma for their support, and for making the Microsoft Technology Center Chicago a great facility to learn and experience. — *Ross LoForte*

I have to start by thanking my wife, Tracy, and two daughters, Eleanor and Caitlin, for putting up with me over the past few months of writing. They have been infinitely patient and understanding while I have spent many long hours working. I must also thank everyone in the SQL Product Group who has helped me with information about SQL Server 2008. Finally, I would like to thank everyone at Wrox Press for their help with this work over the past months. — *Steven Wort*

I would like to thank my wife Cheryl for being my other, better half, and my children; Victoria, Alexandra, and Katherine, who challenge me to do better simply by being who they are. — *Geoff Hiten*

Thanks to Kimberly, my beautiful bride and my children, James, Paul, and Faye. I love you all very much. Thanks also to Brian Knight for opening the door and to Mark Melichar for encouraging me to seize the opportunity. You guys have been great mentors and I can't thank you enough. — *K. Brian Kelly*

Contents

Contents

Contents

Contents

Contents

Contents

Contents

Contents

Contents

Contents

Contents

Contents

Contents

Introduction

SQL Server 2008 represents a sizable jump forward in scalability, performance, and usability for the DBA, developer, and business intelligence (BI) developer. It is no longer unheard of to have 20-terabyte databases running on a SQL Server. SQL Server administration used to just be the job of a database administrator (DBA), but as SQL Server proliferates throughout smaller companies, many developers have begun to act as administrators as well. Additionally, some of the new features in SQL Server are more developer-centric, and poor configuration of these features can result in poor performance. SQL Server now enables you to manage the policies on hundreds of SQL Servers in your environment as if you were managing a single instance. We've provided a comprehensive, tutorial-based book to get you over the learning curve of how to configure and administer SQL Server 2008.

Who This Book Is For

Whether you're an administrator or developer using SQL Server, you can't avoid wearing a DBA hat at some point. Developers often have SQL Server on their own workstations and must provide guidance to the administrator about how they'd like the production configured. Oftentimes, they're responsible for creating the database tables and indexes. Administrators or DBAs support the production servers and often inherit the database from the developer.

This book is intended for developers, DBAs, and casual users who hope to administer or may already be administering a SQL Server 2008 system and its business intelligence features, such as Integration Services. This book is a *professional* book, meaning the authors assume that you know the basics about how to query a SQL Server and have some rudimentary concepts of SQL Server already. For example, this book does not show you how to create a database or walk you through the installation of SQL Server using the wizard. Instead, the author of the installation chapter may provide insight into how to use some of the more advanced concepts of the installation. Although this book does not cover how to query a SQL Server database, it does cover how to tune the queries you've already written.

How This Book Is Structured

The first ten chapters of the book are about administering the various areas of SQL Server, including the developer and business intelligence features. Chapter 1 briefly covers the architecture of SQL Server and the changing role of the DBA. Chapters 2 and 3 dive into best practices on installing and upgrading to SQL Server 2008. Managing your SQL Server database instance is talked about in Chapter 4. This chapter also describes some of the hidden tools you may not even know you have.

Once you know how to manage your SQL Server, you can learn in Chapter 5 how to automate many of the redundant monitoring and maintenance tasks. This chapter also discusses best practices on configuring SQL Server Agent. Chapters 6 and 7 cover how to properly administer and automate many tasks inside of the Microsoft business intelligence products, such as Integration Services and Analysis Services.

Developers will find that Chapter 8 is very useful, as it covers how to administer the development features, such as SQL CLR. Chapter 9 explains how to secure your SQL Server from many common threats and how to create logins and users. Chapter 10 covers how to create a SQL Server project and do proper change management in promoting your scripts through the various environments. It also covers the Policy-Based Management framework in SQL Server.

Chapters 11 through 15 make up the performance tuning part of the book. Chapter 11 discusses how to choose the right hardware configuration for your SQL Server in order to achieve optimal performance. After the hardware and operating system is configured, Chapter 12 shows you how to optimize your SQL Server instance for the best performance. Chapter 13 describes how to monitor your SQL Server instance for problematic issues such as blocking and locking. Chapters 14 and 15 discuss how to optimize the T-SQL that accesses your tables and then how to index your tables appropriately.

Chapters 16 through 20 consist of the high-availability chapters of the book. Chapter 16 covers how to use the various forms of replication, while database mirroring is covered in Chapter 17. Classic issues and best practices with backing up and recovering your database are discussed in Chapter 18. Chapter 19 dives deeply into the role of log shipping in your high-availability strategy, and Chapter 20 presents a step-by-step guide to clustering your SQL Server and Windows 2008 server.

This edition of the book covers all the same great information we covered in the last book, and we've added loads of new content for SQL Server 2008, which adds numerous new features to improve the DBA's life. In short, the new version of SQL Server focuses on improving your efficiency, the scale of your server, and the performance of your environment, so you can do more in much less time, and with fewer resources and people. This means you can manage many servers at one time using Policy-Based Management, scale your I/O load using compression, and collect valuable information about your environment using data collectors, to name just a few key new features.

What You Need to Use This Book

To follow the examples in this book, you will need to have SQL Server 2008 installed. If you wish to learn how to administer the business intelligence features, you need to have Analysis Services and the Integration Services components installed. You need a machine that can support the minimum hardware requirements to run SQL Server 2008; and you also need the `AdventureWorks2008` and `AdventureWorksDW2008` databases installed. Instructions for accessing these databases can be found in the ReadMe file on this book's Web site.

Some features in this book (especially in the high-availability part) require the Enterprise or Developer Edition of SQL Server. If you do not have this edition, you will still be able to follow through some of the examples in the chapter with Standard Edition.

Conventions

To help you get the most from the text and keep track of what's happening, we've used a number of conventions throughout the book.

> **Boxes like this one hold important, not-to-be forgotten information that is directly relevant to the surrounding text.**

Tips, hints, tricks, and asides to the current discussion are offset and placed in italics like this.

As for styles in the text:

❑ We *highlight* new terms and important words when we introduce them.

❑ We show keyboard strokes like this: Ctrl+A.

❑ We show file names, URLs, and code within the text like so: `persistence.properties`.

❑ We present code in two different ways:

```
In code examples we highlight new and important code with a gray background.
```

```
The gray highlighting is not used for code that's less important in the present
context, or has been shown before; that code appears like this.
```

Source Code

As you work through the examples in this book, you may choose either to type in all the code manually or to use the source code files that accompany the book. All of the source code used in this book is available for download at `www.wrox.com`. Once at the site, simply locate the book's title (either by using the Search box or by using one of the title lists) and click the Download Code link on the book's detail page to obtain all the source code for the book.

Because many books have similar titles, you may find it easiest to search by ISBN; this book's ISBN is 978-0-470-24796-9.

Once you download the code, just decompress it with your favorite compression tool. Alternately, you can go to the main Wrox code download page at `www.wrox.com/dynamic/books/download.aspx` to see the code available for this book and all other Wrox books.

Errata

We make every effort to ensure that there are no errors in the text or in the code. However, no one is perfect, and mistakes do occur. If you find an error in one of our books, such as a spelling mistake or a faulty piece of code, we would be very grateful for your feedback. By sending in errata, you may save another reader hours of frustration and at the same time you will be helping us provide even higher quality information.

To find the errata page for this book, go to `www.wrox.com` and locate the title using the Search box or one of the title lists. Then, on the book details page, click the Book Errata link. On this page you can view all errata that has been submitted for this book and posted by Wrox editors. A complete book list, including links to each book's errata, is also available at www.wrox.com/misc-pages/booklist.shtml.

If you don't spot "your" error on the Book Errata page, go to www.wrox.com/contact/techsupport.shtml and complete the form there to send us the error you have found. We'll check the information and, if appropriate, post a message to the book's errata page and fix the problem in subsequent editions of the book.

p2p.wrox.com

For author and peer discussion, join the P2P forums at p2p.wrox.com. The forums are a Web-based system for you to post messages relating to Wrox books and related technologies and interact with other readers and technology users. The forums offer a subscription feature to e-mail you topics of interest of your choosing when new posts are made to the forums. Wrox authors, editors, other industry experts, and your fellow readers are present on these forums.

At http://p2p.wrox.com you will find a number of different forums that will help you not only as you read this book, but also as you develop your own applications. To join the forums, just follow these steps:

1. Go to p2p.wrox.com and click the Register link.

2. Read the terms of use and click Agree.

3. Complete the required information to join as well as any optional information you wish to provide and click Submit.

4. You will receive an e-mail with information describing how to verify your account and complete the joining process.

You can read messages in the forums without joining P2P but in order to post your own messages, you must join.

Once you join, you can post new messages and respond to messages other users post. You can read messages at any time on the Web. If you would like to have new messages from a particular forum e-mailed to you, click the Subscribe to this Forum icon by the forum name in the forum listing.

For more information about how to use the Wrox P2P, be sure to read the P2P FAQs for answers to questions about how the forum software works as well as many common questions specific to P2P and Wrox books. To read the FAQs, click the FAQ link on any P2P page.

SQL Server 2008 Architecture

The days of SQL Server being merely a departmental database are long gone. SQL Server can now easily scale to databases dozens of terabytes in size. (For details see the results of the Winter survey at `www.microsoft.com/sql/prodinfo/compare/wintercorp-survey.mspx`.) In this chapter, we lay some of the groundwork that will be used throughout the book. We first discuss how the role of the database administrator (DBA) has changed since some of the earlier releases of SQL Server, and then quickly jump into architecture and tools available to you as an administrator. This chapter is not a deep dive into the architecture but it provides enough information to give you an understanding of how SQL Server operates.

The Expanding Role of a DBA

The role of the database administrator has been changing slowly over the past few versions of the SQL Server product. Beginning with SQL Server 2005, this slow transition of the DBA role has been accelerated immensely. Traditionally, a DBA would fit into one of two roles: development or administration. It's much tougher to draw a line now between DBA roles in SQL Server 2008. In addition, the new role of Business Intelligence DBA is on the rise. As lines blur and morph, DBAs have to quickly prepare themselves to take on different roles. If you don't position yourself to be more versatile, you may be destined for a career of watching SQL Server alerts and backups.

Production DBA

Production DBAs fall into the traditional role of a DBA. They are a company's insurance policy that the production database won't go down. If the database does go down, the company cashes in its insurance policy in exchange for a recovered database. The Production DBA also ensures that the server is performing optimally, and he or she promotes database changes from development to quality assurance (QA) to production. Other tasks performed by a Production DBA include the following:

- ❑ Install SQL Server instances and service packs.
- ❑ Monitor performance problems.
- ❑ Install scripts from development.
- ❑ Create baselines of performance metrics.
- ❑ Configure the SQL Server optimally.
- ❑ Configure/implement high availability plans.
- ❑ Create\implement disaster recovery and scalability plans.
- ❑ Ensure that backups have been run.

Since the release of SQL Server 2000, there has been a trend away from full-time Production DBAs, and the role has merged with that of the Development DBA. The trend may have slowed, though, with laws such as Sarbanes-Oxley, which require a separation of power between the person developing the change and the person implementing the change. In a large organization, a Production DBA may fall into the operations department, which would consist of the network administrators and Windows-support administrators. Placing a Production DBA in a development group removes the separation of power that may be needed for some regulatory reasons. It may create an environment where "rush" changes are immediately put into production, without proper inspection and auditing.

Development DBA

Development DBAs also play a very traditional role in an organization. They wear more of a developer's hat and are the development staff's database experts and representatives. This administrator ensures that all stored procedures are optimally written and that the database is modeled correctly, both physically and logically. He or she also may be the person who writes the migration processes to upgrade the database from one release to the next. The Development DBA typically does not receive calls at 2:00 A.M. Other Development DBA tasks may be as follows:

- ❑ Model an application database.
- ❑ Create stored procedures.
- ❑ Develop the change scripts that go to the Production DBA.
- ❑ Performance-tune queries and stored procedures.
- ❑ Create data migration plans and scripts.
- ❑ Serve as an escalation point for the Production DBA.

The Development DBA typically would report to the development group. He or she would receive requests from a business analyst or another developer. In a traditional sense, Development DBAs should never have modification access to a production database. They should, however, have read-only access to the production database to debug in a time of escalation.

Business Intelligence DBA

The Business Intelligence (BI) DBA is a new role that has evolved due to the increased capabilities of SQL Server. In SQL Server 2005, BI grew to be an incredibly important feature set that many businesses could not live without. The BI DBA is an expert at these features.

BI DBAs may have specializations, just like normal SQL DBAs. A Production BI DBA will perform the same functions as the Production DBA: installs, service packs, deployments, high availability, performance tuning, and backups. The only difference is that the Production BI DBA will be paying closer attention to SQL Server Analysis Services (SSAS), SQL Server Integration Services (SSIS), SQL Server Reporting Services (SSRS), and perhaps Proclarity, Business Scorecard Manager, and Performance Point Servers.

Development BI DBAs specialize in the best practices, optimization, and use of the BI toolset. In a small organization, he or she may create your SSIS packages to perform Extract Transform and Load (ETL) processes or reports for users. In a large organization, developers create the SSIS packages and SSRS reports. The Development BI DBA is consulted regarding the physical implementation of the SSIS packages, and Analysis Services (SSAS) cubes. Development BI DBAs may be responsible for the following types of functions:

❑   Model\consult regardingAnalysis Services cubes and solutions.

❑   Create reports using Reporting Services.

❑   Create\consult around ETL using Integration Services.

❑   Develop deployment packages that will be sent to the Production DBA.

Organizationally, the BI DBA most often reports to the development group. In some cases, Analysis Services experts may report to the analyst group or the project management office. In some small organizations, the BI DBA may report directly to an executive such as a CFO.

Hybrid DBA

The most exciting role for a DBA is a hybrid of all the roles just mentioned. This Hybrid DBA is very typical with smaller organizations but is becoming popular with larger organizations as well. An organization with high turnover may want to spread its investment over many Hybrid DBAs instead of relying on specialized roles.

Organizationally, you may see Hybrid DBAs reporting directly to the product organization or to a specialized DBA group. No matter where these DBAs report, each typically has a slate of products that he or she supports, performing every DBA function for that product. Organizations that rely on Hybrid DBAs should have adequate backup personnel to reduce the organization's risk if a Hybrid DBA leaves the company. Also, this DBA should never install his or her own changes into production.

Ideally, for regulatory reasons and for stability, the DBA's backup DBA should install the change into production. That way, you can ensure that the DBA who installed the script didn't make ad hoc changes in order to make the change work. We cover much more about this change-management process in Chapter 10.

The only role of a Hybrid DBA that's questionable is development of stored procedures. In most organizations where we see this role, the Hybrid DBA does not develop stored procedures. Instead, he or she creates difficult stored procedures or tunes the ones causing issues. The developer working on the application develops his or her own stored procedures and then provides them to the Hybrid DBA to package and proof. The main reason for this is that the DBA is too taxed for time, working on other functions of the database.

New Things You Need to Learn

The best of us continue to learn new skills and keep up with the changing face of software. It is the business we are in. We must continue to grow and learn or risk becoming obsolete. Each new release of SQL Server since 7.0 has required DBAs to know more things that were traditional concerns of developers. As Microsoft puts more and more on the SQL Server CD, and integrates SQL Server with other development environments, programs, and tools, the breadth of our skills must also grow. Here are some reminders of items that warrant your attention:

❑ Resource Governor allows you to manage workload by setting resource limits. New in SQL Server 2008, knowledge of this feature is a must for DBAs.

❑ Certificates and Kerberos have been used in SQL Server since SQL 2005. While you do not need to be an expert, you must spend some time getting acquainted with how these things work. Kerberos will become especially important if your site uses Reporting Services (SSRS) and your Reporting Services database is on a separate server than Reporting Services Web Service.

❑ CLR Integration enables you to use .NET programming in your stored procedures, triggers, and functions. It also means you need to learn a .NET programming language, or at least the basics of one. You should become acclimated to a .NET programming language such as C# or VB.NET to remain effective. For example, if you are a DBA trying to debug a performance problem with a CLR stored procedure, then you need to know the language the stored procedure is written in to understand the performance problem. Features such as Integration Services and Reporting Services are very much tied to expressions, which are variants of VB.NET.

❑ You need to learn something about XML, including some XPath, and XQuery. These features, introduced in SQL Server 2005, are now getting use in some implementations.

❑ Get some practical experience on database mirroring.

❑ Of course, you should learn about SSRS, SSIS, and SSAS, even if your shop does not currently use those features.

Beginning with SQL Server 2005 and continuing for SQL Server 2008, these products require a leap forward in the knowledge a DBA must have to be effective. If you want to be a leader, then you must stay ahead of the game. We'll help you get it done.

SQL Server Architecture

In older editions of SQL Server, you had to use many different tools depending on the function you were trying to perform. In SQL Server 2008, the challenge for Microsoft was to avoid increasing the number of management tools while increasing the features and products that ship with SQL Server. They accomplished this by creating one tool for business-intelligence development (Business Intelligence Development Studio — BIDS) and another for management of the entire platform, including business intelligence and the database engine (SQL Server Management Studio). BIDS is based on a lightweight version of Visual Studio 2008. A new end-user report development tool is also added — Report Designer.

SQL Server envelops a large surface now. It can act as a reporting tool and store your OLAP cubes. It can also perform your ETL services through SQL Server Integration Services. Many people just use SQL Server for its classic use: to store data. SQL Server 2008 can run on Windows XP, 2000, Vista, and Windows Server 2003 and 2008. Tools such as SharePoint and Office quickly integrate on top of SQL Server and can provide an easy user interface (UI) for SQL Server data. This book covers administration on each of these tiers.

Transaction Log and Database Files

The architecture of database and transaction log files remains unchanged from prior releases. The purpose of the transaction log is to ensure that all committed transactions will be persisted in the database and can be recovered.

The transaction log is a *write-ahead* log. As you make changes to a database in SQL Server, the record is first written to the transaction log. Then, during a checkpoint and at other times, the log data is quickly transferred to the data file. This is why you may see your transaction log grow significantly in the middle of a long-running transaction even if your recovery model is set to simple. (We cover this in much more detail in Chapter 18.)

Every time SQL Server starts, it performs a recovery process on each database. The recovery process ensures that the data in the database is in a consistent state. This means that all committed transactions are recorded in the data files, and that no uncommitted data is in the data files. The recovery process reads the transaction log, looking for any committed transactions that were never added to the data file. The recovery process adds this data to the data file. This is called *rolling a transaction forward*. Recovery also looks for any uncommitted changes that may have been pre-written to the data files. Because the transaction did not commit, recovery will remove these changes from the data files. This is called *rolling a transaction back*. In SQL Server 2008 Enterprise Edition, this process can be done in parallel across all the databases on your instance. Additionally, a fast recovery feature in Enterprise Edition makes databases available after the roll-forward process is complete.

> *The recovery process also runs at the end of a restore. Although there is some confusion and misuse of terms, even in Microsoft's Books Online, Restore replaces a database from backups. This only occurs when you use the Restore T-SQL command. The recovery process runs at the end of the restore and during startup, to ensure that the database is in a consistent state.*

A database may consist of multiple filegroups. Each filegroup may contain one or more physical data files. Filegroups are used to ease administrative tasks for a collection of files. Data files are divided into

8KB data pages. You can specify how full each data page should be with the fill factor option of the create/alter index T-SQL command. (We go much more into this in Chapter 14.) In SQL Server 2008, you have the capability to bring your database partially online if a single file is corrupt. In this instance, the DBA can bring the remaining files online for reading and writing, and the user receives an error if he or she tries to access the other parts of the database that are offline. (You'll learn much more about this in Chapter 18.)

Historically, the largest row you could write has been 8060 bytes. There are two exceptions to this limit: text, ntext, image, varchar(max), varbinary(max), and nvarchar(max) columns may each be up to 2 gigabytes large, and are managed separately. Beginning with SQL 2005, the 8KB limit applies only to those columns of fixed length. The sum of fixed-length columns, and pointers for other column types, must still be less than 8060 bytes per row. However, each variable-length column may be up to 8KB in size, so the row size can be larger than 8KB in total. If your actual row size exceeds 8060 bytes, you may experience some performance degradation, as the logical row must now be split across multiple physical 8060-byte rows.

SQL Native Client

The SQL Native Client is a data-access method that ships with SQL Server 2008 and is used by both OLE DB and ODBC for accessing SQL Server. The SQL Native Client simplifies access to SQL Server by combining the OLE DB and ODBC libraries into a single access method. The access type exposes some of the new features in SQL Server:

- ❑ Database mirroring
- ❑ Multiple Active Recordsets (MARS)
- ❑ Snapshot isolation
- ❑ Query notification
- ❑ XML data type support
- ❑ User-defined data types (UDTs)
- ❑ Encryption
- ❑ Performing asynchronous operations
- ❑ Using large value types
- ❑ Performing bulk copy operations
- ❑ Table-value parameters
- ❑ Large CLR user-defined types
- ❑ Password expiration

In some of these features, you can use the feature in other data layers such as Microsoft Data Access Components (MDAC), but it will take more work. MDAC still exists, and you can use it if you don't need some of the new functionality of SQL Server 2005\2008. If you are developing a COM-based application, you should use SQL Native Client; and if you are developing a managed code application like in C#, you should consider using the .NET Framework Data Provider for SQL Server, which is very robust and includes the SQL Server 2005\2008 features as well.

System Databases

The system databases in SQL Server are crucial, and you should leave them alone most of the time. The only exception to that rule is the model database, which allows you to deploy a change such as a stored procedure to any new database created.

> If a system database is tampered with or corrupted, you run the risk that SQL Server will not start. It contains all the stored procedures and tables needed for SQL Server to remain online.

The Resource Database

SQL Server 2005 added the Resource database. This database contains all the read-only critical system tables, metadata, and stored procedures that SQL Server needs to run. It does not contain any information about your instance or your databases, because it is only written to during an installation of a new service pack. The Resource database contains all the physical tables and stored procedures referenced logically by other databases. The database can be found by default in C:\Program Files\Microsoft SQL Server\MSSQL10.MSSQLSERVER\MSSQL\Binn.mdf and .ldf, and there is only one Resource database per instance.

> *The use of drive C: in the path assumes a standard setup. If your machine is set up differently, you may need to change the path to match your setup. Additionally, the .MSSQLSERVER is the instance name. If your instance name is different, use your instance name in the path.*

In SQL Server 2000, when you upgraded to a new service pack, you would need to run many long scripts to drop and recreate system objects. This process took a long time to run and created an environment that couldn't be rolled back to the previous release after the service pack. In SQL Server 2008, when you upgrade to a new service pack or quick fix, a copy of the Resource database overwrites the old database. This enables you to both quickly upgrade your SQL Server catalog and roll back a release.

The Resource database cannot be seen through Management Studio and should never be altered unless you're under instruction to do so by Microsoft Product Support Services (PSS). You can connect to the database under certain single-user mode conditions by typing the command USE MSSQLSystemResource. Typically, a DBA runs simple queries against it while connected to any database, instead of having to connect to the resource database directly. Microsoft provides some functions which allow this access. For example, if you were to run this query while connected to any database, it would return your Resource database's version and the last time it was upgraded:

```
SELECT serverproperty('resourceversion') ResourceDBVersion,
serverproperty('resourcelastupdatedatetime') LastUpdateDate
```

> *Do not place the Resource database on an encrypted or compressed drive. Doing this may cause upgrade or performance issues.*

The master Database

The master database contains the metadata about your databases (database configuration and file location), logins, and configuration information about the instance. You can see some of the metadata stored in `master` by running the following query, which returns information about the databases that exist on the server:

```
SELECT * FROM sys.databases
```

The main difference between the `Resource` and `master` databases is that the `master` database holds data specific to your instance, whereas the `Resource` database just holds the schema and stored procedures needed to run your instance, but does not contain any data specific to your instance. You should always back up the `master` database after creating a new database, adding a login, or changing the configuration of the server.

> You should never create objects in the **master** database. If you create objects here, you may need to make more frequent master db backups.

tempdb Database

The `tempdb` database is similar to the operating system paging file. It's used to hold temporary objects created by users, temporary objects needed by the database engine, and row-version information. The `tempdb` database is created each time you restart SQL Server. The database will be recreated to be its original database size when the SQL Server is stopped. Because the database is recreated each time, there is no reason to back it up. Data changes made to objects in the `tempdb` database benefit from reduced logging. It is important to have enough space allocated to your `tempdb` database, because many operations that you will use in your database applications use the `tempdb`. Generally speaking, you should set `tempdb` to autogrow as it needs space. If there is not enough space, the user may receive one of the following errors:

- ❏ **1101 or 1105:** The session connecting to SQL Server must allocate space in `tempdb`.
- ❏ **3959:** The version store is full.
- ❏ **3967:** The version store must shrink because `tempdb` is full.

model Database

`model` is a system database that serves as a template when SQL Server creates a new database. As each database is created, SQL Server copies the `model` database as the new database. The only time this does not apply is when you restore or attach a database from a different server.

> *If a table, stored procedure, or database option should be included in each new database that you create on a server, you may simplify the process by creating the object in* model. *When the new database is created,* model *is copied as the new database, including the special objects or database settings you have added to the* model *database. If you add your own objects to* model, *model should be included in your backups, or you should maintain a script which includes the changes.*

msdb Database

`msdb` is a system database that contains information used by SQL Server agent, log shipping, SSIS, and the backup and restore system for the relational database engine. The database stores all the information about jobs, operators, alerts, and job history. Because it contains this important system-level data, you should back up this database regularly.

Schemas

Schemas enable you to group database objects together. You may wish to do this for ease of administration, as you can apply security to all objects within a schema. Another reason to use schemas is to organize objects so the consumers may find the objects they need easily. For example, you may create a schema called HumanResource and place all your employee tables and stored procedures into it. You could then apply security policies on the schema to allow appropriate access to the objects contained within it.

When you refer to an object you should always use the two-part name. The dbo schema is the default schema for a database. An Employee table in the dbo schema is referred to as dbo.Employee. Table names must be unique within a schema. You could create another table called Employee in the HumanResources schema. It would be referred to as HumanResources.Employee. This table actually exists in the AdventureWorks2008 sample database for SQL Server 2008. (All SQL Server 2008 samples must be downloaded and installed separately.) A sample query using the two-part name follows:

```
SELECT BusinessEntityID, JobTitle
FROM HumanResources.Employee
```

Prior to SQL 2005, the first part of the two-part name was the user name of the object owner. The problem with that implementation was related to maintenance. If a user who owned objects was to leave the company, you could not remove that user login from SQL Server until you ensured that all the objects owned by the user were changed to a different owner. All of the code that referred to the objects had to be changed to refer to the new owner. By separating ownership from the schema name, SQL 2005 and 2008 remove this maintenance problem.

Synonyms

A *synonym* is an alias, or alternate name, for an object. This creates an abstraction layer between the database object and the consumer. This abstraction layer enables you to change some of the physical implementation, and isolate those changes from the consumer. An example is related to the use of linked servers. You may have tables on a different server which need to be joined to tables on a local server. You refer to objects on another server using the four-part name, as shown in the following code:

```
SELECT Column1, Column2
FROM LinkedServerName.DatabaseName.SchemaName.TableName
```

For example, you might create a synonym for LinkedServerName.DatabaseName.SchemaName.Tablename called SchemaName.SynonymName. Data consumers would refer to the object using the following query:

```
SELECT Column1, Column2
FROM SchemaName.SynonymName
```

This abstraction layer now enables you to change the location of the table to another server, using a different linked server name, or even to replicate the data to the local server for better performance without requiring any changes to the code which refers to the table.

A synonym cannot reference another synonym. The object_id function returns the id of the synonym, not the id of the related base object. If you need column-level abstraction, use a view instead.

Dynamic Management Views

Dynamic management views (DMVs) and functions return information about your SQL Server instance and the operating system. DMVs simplify access to data and expose new information that was not available in versions of SQL Server prior to 2005. DMVs can provide you with various types of information, from data about the I/O subsystem and RAM to information about Service Broker.

Whenever you start an instance, SQL Server begins saving server-state and diagnostic information into DMVs. When you stop and start the instance, the information is flushed from the views and fresh data begins to be loaded. You can query the views just like any other table in SQL Server with the two-part qualifier. For example, the following query uses the `sys.dm_exec_sessions` DMV to retrieve the number of sessions connected to the instance, grouped by login name:

```
SELECT login_name, COUNT(session_id) as NumberSessions
FROM sys.dm_exec_sessions GROUP BY login_name
```

Some DMVs are functions which accept parameters. For example, the following code uses the `sys.dm_io_virtual_file_stats` dynamic management function (we use the term DMV for simplicity throughout this book) to retrieve the I/O statistics for the AdventureWorks2008 data file:

```
SELECT * FROM
sys.dm_io_virtual_file_stats(DB_ID('AdventureWorks2008'),
FILE_ID('AdventureWorks2008_Data'))
```

You'll learn much more about DMVs throughout this book, starting in Chapter 4.

SQL Server 2008 Data Types

As you create a table, you must assign a data type for each column. In this section, we cover some of the more commonly used data types in SQL Server. Even if you create a custom data type, it must be based on a standard SQL Server data type. For example, you may create a custom data type (`Address`) by using the following syntax, but notice that it based on the SQL Server standard `varchar` data type:

```
CREATE TYPE Address
FROM varchar(35) NOT NULL
```

If you are changing the data type of a column in a very large table in SQL Server Management Studio's table designer interface, the operation may take a very long time. You can observe the reason for this by scripting the change from the Management Studio interface. Management Studio creates a secondary temporary table with a name like `tmpTableName` and then copies the data into the table. Finally, the interface deletes the old table and renames the new table with the new data type. There are other steps along the way, of course, to handle indexes and any relationships in the table.

If you have a very large table with millions of records, this process can take more than ten minutes, and in some cases more than an hour. To avoid this, you can use a simple one-line T-SQL statement in the query window to change the column's data type. For example, to change the data type of the Job `Title` column in the `Employees` table to a `varchar(70)`, you could use the following syntax:

```
ALTER TABLE HumanResources.Employee ALTER COLUMN JobTitle Varchar(70)
```

> When you convert to a data type that may be incompatible with your data, you may lose important data. For example, if you convert from a numeric data type that has data such as 15.415 to an integer, the number 15.415 would be rounded to a whole number.

You may wish to write a report against your SQL Server tables which displays the data type of each column inside the table. There are dozens of ways to do this, but one method we often see is to join the sys.objects table with the sys.columns table. There are two functions that you may not be familiar with in the following code. The TYPE_NAME() function translates the data type id into its proper name. To go the opposite direction, you could use the TYPE_ID() function. The other function of note is SCHEMA_ID(), which is used to return the identity value for the schema. This is useful primarily when you wish to write reports against the SQL Server metadata.

```
SELECT  o.name AS ObjectName,
        c.name AS ColumnName,
        TYPE_NAME(c.user_type_id) as DataType
FROM    sys.objects o JOIN sys.columns c
ON      o.object_id = c.object_id
WHERE   o.name ='Department'
and o.Schema_ID = SCHEMA_ID('HumanResources')
```

This code returns the following results (note that the Name data type is a user-defined type):

```
ObjectName          ColumnName      DataType
-------------------------------------------------

Department          DepartmentID    smallint
Department          Name            Name
Department          GroupName       Name
Department          ModifiedDate    datetime
```

Character Data Types

Character data types include varchar, char, nvarchar, and nchar, text, and ntext. This set of data types stores character data. The primary difference between the varchar and char types is data padding. If you have a column called FirstName that is a varchar(20) data type and you store the value of "Brian" in the column, only five bytes will be physically stored. If you store the same value in a char(20) data type, all 20 bytes would be used. SQL will insert trailing spaces to fill the 20 characters.

If you're trying to conserve space, why would you ever use a char data type? There is a slight overhead to using a varchar data type. If you are going to store a two-letter state abbreviation, for example, you're better off using a char(2) column. Although some DBAs have opinions about this that border on religious conviction, generally speaking it's good to find a threshold in your organization and specify that anything below this size will become a char versus a varchar. Our guideline is that, in general, any column that is less than or equal to five bytes should be stored as a char data type instead of a varchar data type. Beyond that point, the benefit of using a varchar begins to outweigh the cost of the overhead.

The nvarchar and nchar data types operate the same way as their varchar and char counterparts, but these data types can handle international Unicode characters. This comes at a cost though. Data stored as

Unicode consumes 2 bytes per character. If you were to store the value of "Brian" in an `nvarchar` column, it would use 10 bytes, and storing it as an `nchar(20)` would use 40 bytes. Because of this overhead and added space, do not use Unicode columns unless you have a business or language need for them.

Next are `text` and `ntext`. The `text` data type stores very large character data on and off the data page. You should use these sparingly, as they may affect performance. They can store up to 2GB of data in a single row's column. Instead of using the `text` data type, the `varchar(max)` type is a much better alternative because the performance is better. Additionally, `text` and `ntext` data types will not be available in some future version of SQL Server, so begin using `varchar(max)` and `nvarchar(max)` instead of `text` and `ntext` now.

The following table shows the data types, with short descriptions and the amount of storage required.

Data Type	Description	Storage Space
Char(n)	N between 1 and 8,000 characters	n bytes
Nchar(n)	N between 1 and 4,000 Unicode characters	(2 x n bytes) + 2 bytes overhead
Ntext	Up to ((2 to the 30th power) - 1) (1,073,741,823) Unicode characters	2 bytes per character stored
Nvarchar(max)	Up to ((2 to the 30th power) - 1) (1,073,741,823) Unicode characters	2 x characters stored + 2 bytes overhead
Text	Up to ((2 to the 31st power) - 1) (2,147,483,647) characters	1 byte per character stored
Varchar(n)	N between 1 and 8,000 characters	1 byte per character stored + 2 bytes overhead
Varchar(max)	Up to ((2 to the 31st power) - 1) (2,147,483,647) characters	1 byte per character stored + 2 bytes overhead

Exact Numeric Data Types

Numeric data types consist of `bit`, `tinyint`, `smallint`, `int`, `bigint`, `numeric`, `decimal`, `money`, `float`, and `real`. Each of these data types stores different types of numeric values. The first data type, `bit`, stores only a 0 or a 1, which in most applications translates into true or false. Using the `bit` data type is perfect for on and off flags, and it occupies only a single byte of space. Other common numeric data types are shown in the following table.

Data Type	Description	Storage Space
bit	0, 1, or Null	1 byte for each 8 columns of this data type
tinyint	Whole numbers from 0 to 255	1 bytes
smallint	Whole numbers from −32,768 to 32,767	2 bytes
int	Whole numbers from −2,147,483,648 to 2,147,483,647	4 bytes

Data Type	Description	Storage Space
bigint	Whole numbers from −9,223,372,036,854,775,808 to	
	9,223,372,036,854,775,807	8 bytes
numeric(p,s) or decimal(p,s)	Numbers from −1,038 +1 through 1,038 −1	Up to 17 bytes
money	−922,337,203,685,477.5808 to 922,337,203,685,477.5807	8 bytes
smallmoney	−214,748.3648 to 214,748.3647	4 bytes

Numeric data types, such as decimal and numeric, can store a variable number of digits to the right and left of the decimal place. *Scale* refers to the number of digits to the right of the decimal. *Precision* defines the total number of digits, including the digits to the right of the decimal place. For example, 14.88531 would be a numeric(7,5) or decimal(7,5). If you were to insert 14.25 into a numeric(5,1) column, it would be rounded to 14.3.

Approximate Numeric Data Types

The data types float and real are included in this group. They should be used when floating-point data must be represented. However, because they are approximate, not all values can be represented exactly.

The n in the float(n) is the number of bits used to store the mantissa of the number. SQL Server uses only two values for this field. If you specify between 1 and 24, SQL uses 24. If you specify between 25 and 53, SQL uses 53. The default is 53 when you specify float(), with nothing in parenthesis.

The following table shows the approximate numeric data types, with a short description and the amount of storage required.

Data Type	Description	Storage Space
float[(n)]	−1.79E+308 to -2.23E-308,0, 2.23E-308 to 1.79E+308	N< = 24 - 4 bytes N> 24 - 8 bytes
real()	−3.40E+38 to -1.18E-38,0, 1.18E-38 to 3.40E+38	4 bytes

The synonym for real *is* float(24).

Binary Data Types

Binary data types such as varbinary, binary, varbinary(max), and image store binary data such as graphic files, Word documents, or MP3 files. The values are hexadecimal 0x0 to 0xf. The image data type stores up to 2GB outside the data page. The preferred alternative to an image data type is the `varbinary(max)`, which can hold more than 8KB of binary data and generally performs slightly better than an `image` data type. New in SQL Server 2008 is the capability to store `varbinary(max)` objects in operating system files via FileStream storage options. This option stores the data as files, and is not subject to the 2GB size limit of `varbinary(max)`.

The following table shows the binary data types, with a short description and the amount of storage required.

Data Type	Description	Storage Space
Binary(n)	N between 1 and 8,000 hex digits	n bytes
Image	Up to 231-1(2,147,483,647) hex digits	1 byte per character
Varbinary(n)	N between 1 and 8,000 hex digits	1 byte per character stored + 2 bytes overhead
Varbinary(max)	Up to 231-1(2,147,483,647) characters	1 byte per character stored + 2 bytes overhead

Date and Time Data Types

The `datetime` and `smalldatetime` types both store date and time data. The `smalldatetime` is 4 bytes and stores from January 1, 1900 through June 6, 2079 and is accurate to the nearest minute. The `datetime` data type is 8 bytes and stores from January 1, 1753 through December 31, 9999 to the nearest 3.33 millisecond.

SQL Server 2008 has four new date-related data types: `datetime2`, `dateoffset`, `date`, and `time`. You can find examples using these data types in SQL Server Books Online.

The `datetime2` data type is an extension of the `datetime` data type, with a wider range of dates. Time is always stored with hours, minutes, and seconds. You can define the `datetime2` data type with a variable parameter at the end — for example, `datetime2(3)`. The 3 in the preceding expression means to store fractions of seconds to three digits of precision, or .999. Valid values are between 0 and 9, with a default of 3.

The `datetimeoffset` data type is just like the `datetime2` data type, with the addition of the time offset. The time offset is + or - up to 14 hours, and contains the UTC offset, so that you can rationalize times captured in different time zones.

The `date` data type stores the date only, a long-requested piece of functionality. Alternately, the `time` data type stores the time only. The `time` data type also supports the `time(n)` declaration so you can control granularity of the fractional seconds. As with `datetime2` and `datetimeoffset`, n can be between 0 and 7.

The following table shows the date/time data types, with a short description and the amount of storage required.

Data Type	Description	Storage Space
Date	January 1, 1 to December 31, 9999	3 bytes
Datetime	January 1, 1753 to December 31, 9999, Accurate to nearest 3.33 millisecond	8 bytes
Datetime2(n)	January 1, 1 to December 31, 9999 N between 0 and 7 specifies fractional seconds	6 to 8 bytes
Datetimeoffset(n)	January 1, 1 to December 31, 9999 N between 0 and 7 specifies fractional seconds +- offset	8 to 10 bytes
SmalldateTime	January 1, 1900 to June 6, 2079, Accurate to 1 minute	4 bytes
Time(n)	Hours:minutes:seconds.9999999 N between 0 and 7 specifies fractional seconds	3 to 5 bytes

Other System Data Types

There are several other data types which we have not seen. They are shown in the following table for completeness.

Data Type	Description	Storage Space
Cursor	This contains a reference to a cursor and may be used only as a variable or stored procedure parameter.	Not applicable
Hierarchyid	Contains a reference to a location in a hierarchy	1 to 892 bytes + 2 bytes overhead
SQL_Variant	May contain the value of any system data type except text, ntext, image, timestamp, xml, varchar(max), nvarchar(max), varbinary(max), sql_variant, and user-defined data types. The maximum size allowed is 8,000 bytes of data + 16 bytes or metadata.	8,016 bytes
Table	Used to store a data set for further processing. The definition is like a Create Table. Primarily used to return the result set of a table-valued function, they can also be used in stored procedures and batches.	Dependent on table definition and number of rows stored

Data Type	Description	Storage Space
Timestamp or Rowversion	Unique per table, automatically stored value. Generally used for version stamping, the value is automatically changed on insert and with each update.	8 bytes
Uniqueidentifier	Can contain Globally Unique Identifier (GUID). guid values may be obtained from the Newid() function. This function returns values which are unique across all computers. Although stored as a binary 16, it is displayed as a char(36).	16 bytes
XML	Can be stored as Unicode or non-Unicode	Up to 2GB

A cursor *data type may not be used in a* Create Table *statement.*

The hierarchyid column is new to SQL Server 2008. You may wish to add a column of this data type to tables where the data in the rows can be represented in a hierarchy, as in an organizational hierarchy or manager/employee hierarchy. The value that you store in this column is the path of the row within the hierarchy. Levels in the hierarchy are shown as slashes. The value between the slashes is the numerical location of this member within the row. An example is /1/3. Special functions are available which can be used with this data type.

The XML data type stores an XML document or fragment. It is stored like a text or ntext in size depending on the use of UTF-16 or UTF-8 in the document. The XML data type allows the use of special constructs for searching and indexing. (This is covered in more detail in Chapter 15.)

CLR Integration

In SQL Server 2008, you can also create your own data types and stored procedures using the CLR (Common Language Runtime). This enables you to write more complex data types to meet your business needs in Visual Basic or C#, for example. These types are defined as a class structure in the base CLR language. (We cover the administrative aspect of these in much more detail in Chapter 8.)

Editions of SQL Server

SQL Server 2008 is available in numerous editions, and the features available to you in each edition vary widely. The editions you can install on your workstation or server also vary based on the operating system. The editions of SQL Server range from SQL Express on the lowest end to Enterprise Edition on the highest. The prices of these also vary widely, from free to more than $20,000 per processor.

> *Ted Kummert, Microsoft corporate vice president, announced at the Professional Association for SQL Server (PASS) conference in September, 2007, that prices for SQL Server 2008 would remain the same as they were for SQL 2005. No price increase — woohooo!*

Compact (32-bit Only)

SQL Compact is a free edition which is intended to be an embedded database for mobile and other compact devices with occasionally connected users.

SQL Express (32-bit Only)

SQL Express is the free version of SQL Server meant for installation on laptops or desktops to support distributed applications such as a remote sales force application. You can use this edition to store sales or inventory data for your disconnected sales force and replicate updated data to them when they become connected again. SQL Express was called Microsoft Desktop Edition (MSDE) in SQL Server 2000. It is extremely lightweight and does not occupy much hard drive space. Vendors are free to distribute SQL Express, and it can be wrapped into your application's installation as just another component.

SQL Express is not meant to scale past a few users. Key features missing from SQL Express are SQL Agent and some of the robust management tools. It does ship with a very lightweight tool for managing the database, but scheduling of backups must be done in the Windows Task Scheduler, not SQL Server.

Workgroup Edition (32-bit and 64-bit)

The Workgroup Edition of SQL Server is the lowest-cost commercial edition of SQL Server. It scales minimally up to two processors and 4GB of RAM(64-bit), but it's adequate for small and medium-sized businesses. There is no limit on the number of users or database size. This edition of SQL Server was initially introduced to compete with lower-end vendors such as MySQL, and should be used for small organizations or departmental applications. It is easily upgraded to the other, more scalable, editions.

Web Edition (32-bit and 64-bit)

The Web Editions of SQL Server are low cost options intended for web site owners or web hosting companies. These editions include the scalability and manageability features in SQL Server 2008.

Standard Edition (32-bit and 64-bit)

The Standard Edition of SQL Server contains high availability clustering features as well as business intelligence. It is intended for small to medium-sized businesses and departmental solutions.

Enterprise, Evaluation, and Developer Editions (32-bit and 64-bit)

Enterprise Edition is the best option for SQL Server if you need to use some of the more advanced business intelligence features or if the uptime of your database is very important. Although the Standard Edition of SQL Server enables you to have high-availability options, Enterprise Edition far outdoes its sister edition with higher-end clustering as well as more advanced mirroring and log-shipping options. The counter to this, of course, is cost. This edition of SQL Server will cost you about $25,000 per processor if you choose that licensing model. (We discuss licensing later in this chapter.)

The Evaluation Edition of SQL Server is a variant of SQL Server Enterprise Edition that expires after 180 days. After the allotted evaluation period, SQL Server will no longer start. This edition has the same features as the Enterprise Edition and may be upgraded for production use. It is not licensed for production use.

The Developer Edition of SQL Server is intended for development and testing of applications using SQL Server. It contains all of the features of the Enterprise Edition. This edition is not licensed for production use.

Operating System

The edition of SQL Server that you can install varies widely based on the operating system on your server or workstation, as summarized in the following table. The table is representative and does not include each version and service pack for each OS and SQL combination which are supported.

Operating System	SQL Express	Workgroup	Web	Standard	Developer	Enterprise
Windows Server 2003 Standard (with SP2+)	✓	✓	✓	✓	✓	✓
Windows Server 2003 Enterprise (with SP2+)	✓	✓	✓	✓	✓	✓
Windows Server 2008 Standard	✓	✓	✓	✓	✓	✓
Windows Server 2008 Enterprise	✓	✓	✓	✓	✓	✓
Windows Server 2008 Data Center	✓	✓	✓	✓	✓	✓
Windows 2008 Server Data Center	✓	✓	✓	✓	✓	✓
Windows Vista	✓	✓	✓	✓	✓	✓
Windows XP Professional Edition (SP2+)l	✓	✓	✓	✓	✓	

SQL Server 2008 will not run with any of the Windows Server 2008 Core Installation options because the Windows 2008 Server Core does not support the .NET Framework, which is required by SQL Server 2008. Microsoft may add this support in a future release.

Maximum Capacity of SQL Server

Memory and the number of processors is a huge contributing factor when you're scaling SQL Server. As you can imagine, the amount of memory you can scale and the number of processors will vary based on the edition of SQL Server you purchase. In some cases, your scalability is restricted only to the operating system's maximum memory or number of processors. This is where 64-bit becomes really useful. (We cover 64-bit scalability in much more detail in Chapter 15.)

Capacity	SQL Express	Workgroup	Web	Standard	Enterprise
Memory Supported 32-bit	1GB	OS Maximum	OS Maximum	OS Maximum	OS Maximum
Memory Supported 64-bit	N/A	4GB	OS Maximum	OS Maximum	OS Maximum
Maximum Database Size	4GB	No Limit	No Limit	No Limit	No Limit
Number of Processors	1	2	4	4	OS Maximum

Database Features by Edition

The main advantage offered by the higher (and more expensive) editions of SQL Server is the greater number of features available. In the following set of grids, you can see how the features line up across the various editions. These grids do not capture all the features of SQL Server but focus on those features of high consumer interest and areas that help distinguish the editions. This information was obtained from Microsoft Books Online.

Scalability

As demand for database resources increases, the ability to provide that higher scalability becomes very important. This list shows the scalability features, and as you might expect, they are all included in the Enterprise Edition only.

Feature	Express Advanced	Express	Web	Workgroup	Standard	Enterprise
Partitioning						✓
Data compression						✓
Resource governor						✓
Partition table parallelism						✓

High Availability

Keeping your data online and ready to use is of primary importance to most facilities. These are the functions and features associated with high availability.

Feature	Express Advanced	Express	Web	Workgroup	Standard	Enterprise
Multi-instance support	16	16	16	16	16	50
Online system changes	✓	✓	✓	✓	✓	✓
Backup log shipping			✓	✓	✓	✓
Database mirroring	Witness only	Witness only	Witness only	Witness only	✓ (safety full only)	✓ (full)
Failover clustering					2 nodes	OS maximum
Dynamic AWE					✓	✓
Failover without client configuration					✓	✓
Automatic corruption recovery from mirror					✓	✓
Database snapshots						✓
Fast recovery						✓
Online indexing						✓
Online restore						✓
Mirrored backups						✓
Hot add memory						✓
Online configuration of P2P nodes						✓
Hot add CPU						✓
Backup compression						✓

Security

As more data governance, auditability, and accountability is imposed, security features become more important. SQL Server 2008 included auditing, and new encryption capabilities which help meet those requirements.

Feature	Express Advanced	Express	Web	Workgroup	Standard	Enterprise
C2 compliant tracing	✓	✓	✓	✓	✓	✓
SQL auditing foundation	✓	✓	✓	✓	✓	✓
Fine grained auditing					✓	✓
Transparent database encryption						✓
ISV encryption (off-box key management)						✓

Replication

SQL Server allows you to make copies of data using replication. Depending on your data needs, you may choose periodic snapshots, transaction based replication, or replication for occasionally connected users.

Feature	Express Advanced	Express	Web	Workgroup	Standard	Enterprise
Merge replication	Subscriber only	Subscriber only	Subscriber only	Subscriber only	✓	✓
Transactional replication	Subscriber only	Subscriber only	Subscriber only	Subscriber only	✓	✓
Snapshot replication	Subscriber only	Subscriber only	Subscriber only	Subscriber only	✓	✓
Change Tracking	✓	✓	✓	✓	✓	✓
Heterogeneous subscribers					✓	✓
Oracle publishing						✓
P2P transactional replication						✓

Manageability

While SQL Server databases have historically been easy to manage, Microsoft is adding improvements in this area to allow DBAs to easily manage larger groups of servers. Particularly interesting and important in this release are the policy-based management features.

Feature	Express Advanced	Express	Web	Workgroup	Standard	Enterprise
User instances	✓	✓				
Dedicated admin connection	✓ (Under trace flag)	✓ (Under trace flag)	✓	✓	✓	✓
Policy-based configuration	✓	✓	✓	✓	✓	✓
Policy-based management	✓	✓	✓	✓	✓	✓
Performance data collection and warehouse			✓	✓	✓	✓
Standard performance reports					✓	✓
Plan guides					✓	✓
Plan freezing for plan guides					✓	✓
Policy-based best practices					✓	✓
Multi-server policy-based management					✓	✓
Distributed partitioned views						✓
Parallel index operations						✓
Automatic query-to-indexed-view matching						✓
Parallel database backup checksum check						✓

Feature	Express Advanced	Express	Web	Workgroup	Standard	Enterprise
Database mail			✓	✓	✓	✓
Database migration tools	✓	✓	✓	✓	✓	✓

Management Tools

These are the management tools which come with each edition of SQL Server 2008. SQL Express Advanced now includes SQL Server Management Studio.

Feature	Express Advanced	Express	Web	Workgroup	Standard	Enterprise
SQL management objects (SMO)	✓	✓	✓	✓	✓	✓
SQL Configuration Manager	✓	✓	✓	✓	✓	✓
SQL CMD(command prompt tool)	✓	✓	✓	✓	✓	✓
SQL Server Management Studio	✓ (Express version)		✓ (Express version)	✓	✓	✓
SQL Profiler			✓	✓	✓	✓
SQL Server Agent			✓	✓	✓	✓
Database tuning advisor			✓	✓	✓	✓
Microsoft Operations Manager Pack			✓	✓	✓	✓

The table above indicates that the Web edition contains the Express version of SQL Server Management Studio. This is the information obtained from Microsoft Books Online. However, I am unsure that is true. If this information is critical to your decision about the Web version please consult Microsoft to get a determination.

Development Tools

Tight integration of development tools with SQL Server have gotten better through the years. Intellisense was a wonderful addition to the tools, and if you use Multidimensional Expression (MDX), the MDX editor is quite helpful.

Feature	Express Advanced	Express	Web	Workgroup	Standard	Enterprise
Visual Studio Integration	✓	✓	✓	✓	✓	✓
SQL query, edit, and design tools				✓	✓	✓
Intellisense(Transact-SQL and MDX)				✓	✓	✓
Version control support				✓	✓	✓
Business Intelligence Development Studio					✓	✓
MDX edit, debug and design tools					✓	✓

Programmability

While notification services goes away in this release, service broker remains. Stronger XML support is also included in all editions. The new date/time data types, merge/upsert, and filestream support are also exciting new additions.

Feature	Express Advanced	Express	Web	Workgroup	Standard	Enterprise
Common language runtime (CLR) integration	✓	✓	✓	✓	✓	✓
Native XML support	✓	✓	✓	✓	✓	✓
XML indexing	✓	✓	✓	✓	✓	✓
MERGE and UPSERT capabilities	✓	✓	✓	✓	✓	✓
FILESTREAM support	✓	✓	✓	✓	✓	✓
Date and Time data types	✓	✓	✓	✓	✓	✓
Internationalization support	✓	✓	✓	✓	✓	✓
Full-text search	✓		✓	✓	✓	✓

Feature	Express Advanced	Express	Web	Workgroup	Standard	Enterprise
Specification of language in query	✓		✓	✓	✓	✓
Service broker(messaging)	Client only	Client only	Client only	✓	✓	✓
XML/A support					✓	✓
Web services (HTTP/SOAP endpoints)					✓	✓

Spatial and Location Services

SQL Server 2008 has added geospatial libraries and data types, included with all editions.

Feature	Express Advanced	Express	Web	Workgroup	Standard	Enterprise
Spatial indexes	✓	✓	✓	✓	✓	✓
Geodetic data type	✓	✓	✓	✓	✓	✓
Advanced spatial libraries	✓	✓	✓	✓	✓	✓
Standards-based spatial support	✓	✓	✓	✓	✓	✓

Integration Services

Integration Services allows you to extract, transform, and load data from one data source to another. Standard and Enterprise editions come with additional connectivity and transformation capabilities.

Feature	Express Advanced	Express	Web	Workgroup	Standard	Enterprise
Import/Export Wizard with basic sources/destinations and Execute SQL task	✓	✓	✓	✓	✓	✓
Integration Services runtime	✓	✓	✓	✓	✓	✓

Feature	Express Advanced	Express	Web	Workgroup	Standard	Enterprise
Integration Services API and object model			✓	✓	✓	✓
SSIS Designer including VSTA scripting					✓	✓
Basic tasks and transformations					✓	✓
Log providers and logging					✓	✓
Data profiling tools					✓	✓
Additional sources and destinations:					✓	✓
Raw File source						
XML source						
Datareader destination						
Raw File destination						
Recordset destination						
SQL Server Compact destination						
SQL Server destination						
Advanced sources and destinations:						✓
Data Mining Query transformation						
Fuzzy Lookup and Fuzzy Grouping transformations						
Term Extraction and Term Lookup transformations						
Data Mining Model Training destination						
Dimension Processing destination						
Partition Processing destination						

Data Warehouse Creation

New designers and auto-generation of staging schemas, new to 2008 are included in the Standard and Enterprise edition.

Feature	Express Advanced	Express	Web	Workgroup	Standard	Enterprise
Create cubes without a database					✓	✓
Auto-generate staging and data warehouse schema					✓	✓
Attribute relationship designer					✓	✓
Efficient aggregation designers					✓	✓

Data Warehouse Scale and Performance

As you might imagine, all of the performance and high scalability features are in the Enterprise edition. Change data capture is very exciting.

Feature	Express Advanced	Express	Web	Workgroup	Standard	Enterprise
Change data capture						✓
Star join query optimization						✓
Scalable read-only AS configuration						✓
Proactive caching						✓
Auto parallel partition processing						✓
Partitioned cubes						✓
Distributed partitioned cubes						✓

Multi-Dimensional Analytics

Special aggregations and intelligence, and semi-additive measures are available. General performance improvements are included everywhere SSAS is supported.

Feature	Express Advanced	Express	Web	Workgroup	Standard	Enterprise
SQL Server Analysis Services service					✓	✓
SQL Server Analysis Services backup					✓	✓
General performance/scale improvements					✓	✓
Dimension, attribute, relationship, aggregate and cube design improvements					✓	✓
Personalization extensions					✓	✓
Financial aggregations						✓
Partitioned customers						✓
Custom rollups						✓
Semi-additive measures						✓
Writeback dimensions						✓
Linked measures and dimensions						✓
Binary and compressed XML transport						✓
Account intelligence						✓
Perspectives						✓
Analysis Services shared, scalable databases						✓

Data Mining

Serious data-mining efforts will require the Enterprise edition of SQL Server.

Feature	Express Advanced	Express	Web	Workgroup	Standard	Enterprise
Standard algorithms					✓	✓
Data mining tools: wizards, editors, query builders					✓	✓
Cross validation						✓
Models on filtered subsets of mining structure data						✓
Time series: custom blending between ARTXP and ARIMA models						✓
Time series: prediction with new data						✓
Unlimited concurrent data mining queries						✓
Advanced configuration and tuning for algorithms						✓
Algorithm plug-in API						✓
Parallel model processing						✓
Time-series: cross-series prediction						✓
Unlimited attributes for association rules						✓
Sequence prediction						✓
Multiple prediction targets for naïve bayes, neural network and logistic regression						✓

Reporting

Reporting Services (SSRS), supported in many environments is one of the most popular SQL Server features. Particularly helpful in SQL Server 2008 is the ability to run SSRS Service outside of IIS.

Feature	Express Advanced	Express	Web	Workgroup	Standard	Enterprise
Report server	✓		✓	✓	✓	✓
Report Designer	✓		✓	✓	✓	✓
Report Manager	✓		✓	✓	✓	✓
Role-based security	✓ (Fixed roles)		✓ (Fixed roles)	✓ (Fixed roles)	✓	✓
Ad-hoc reporting (Report Builder)				✓	✓	✓
Word export and enhanced text formatting	✓		✓	✓	✓	✓
Enterprise-scale reporting engine	✓		✓	✓	✓	✓
IIS-agnostic report deployment	✓		✓	✓	✓	✓
Updated management tools	✓		✓	✓	✓	✓
Report definition customization extensions(RDCE)	✓		✓	✓	✓	✓
SharePoint integration					✓	✓
Enhanced SSRS gauges and charting	✓		✓	✓	✓	✓
Custom authentication			✓	✓	✓	✓
Export to Excel, PDF, and images	✓		✓	✓	✓	✓
Remote and non-relational data source support					✓	✓
E-mail and file share delivery					✓	✓

Feature	Express Advanced	Express	Web	Workgroup	Standard	Enterprise
Report history, scheduling, subscriptions and caching					✓	✓
Data source, delivery and rendering extensibility					✓	✓
Scale out (Web farms)						✓
Infinite click-through						✓
Data-driven subscriptions						✓
Reporting Services memory limits	4GB		4GB	4GB	Unlimited	Unlimited

Licensing

Every DBA has probably received a dreaded licensing question or two, and we hope to answer some of those common questions in this section. There is no difference in price between 32-bit and 64-bit servers. SQL Server licensing applies to all components, and to each component separately.

If you have a license on a machine, you may install all of SQL Server, Reporting Services, the SQL Server Engine, Analysis Services, and Integration Services. There are no extra licenses involved; it is a single product. However, if you wish to install only Analysis Services, or any other part of SQL Server on a difference physical server, that is another license.

Licensing can become very complicated, and licensing options are subject to change, so before you make any big commitments, it is wise to consult your Microsoft representative for an official opinion.

Licensing Options

The following list details the basic licensing models available to you:

❑ **Processor Licensing Model:** With the Processor licensing model, you pay a license fee for each processor. This model is a good choice if your SQL Server will be accessible over the Internet, or a high number of clients need to access each SQL Server. Using this model, there are no extra licensing fees to pay for each client or for Internet access, or anything else.

❑ **Server plus Device Client Access License (CAL):** The Server + Device CAL model requires you to pay a license fee for each server (instead of per processor in the processor model), plus a license fee for each device (client computer) that accesses the SQL Server functionality. This model is good when you have a small number of clients that access SQL Server, inside the firewall, and when there are many users accessing the same device. An example of multiple users on a device might be a kiosk in a shopping center, or a call center that runs around the clock. For example, suppose each device in the call center is used by three people, one person on each of three shifts. You can buy a server license for the SQL Server plus a single CAL for the device, and all three of your employees have access. Once a device has a CAL, that device may access any licensed SQL Server in your environment.

❑   **Server plus User CAL:** This model requires you to pay a license fee for each server, plus a license fee for each user. This model is commonly used when your users do not need SQL access outside of the firewall and when the ratio of users to servers is small. Depending on current pricing, as of this writing User CALs might be a good option when there are fewer than 25 users per processor for the Standard edition and fewer than 75 users per processor in the Enterprise Edition. User CALs might also be a good option, compared to the device CALs, when a user has multiple devices that need access to SQL Server. This might occur when a single user has both a desktop PC and a laptop.

❑   **Middleware, Transaction Servers, and Multi-tiered Architectures:** The device CAL must be obtained for each *unique* device which accesses SQL Server. You may have a multi-tiered environment where the data-access layer runs on a single device, and your application, which supports many users, connects to the data-access layer, which in turn connects to SQL Server. Paying the license fee for the single data-access layer will not suffice. You must still pay a CAL for each device (PC) that the users have. Using middleware, transaction servers, or multi-tiered architecture does not enable you to avoid paying the license fee for each device or user.

❑   **Hyper-Threading and Multicore Processors:** There are no extra or special charges for Hyper-Threaded or multicore processors. Although you can configure SQL Server to use a lower number of processors than are installed, you will have to pay for each processor on the motherboard, as long as the operating system can see it. As an example, if you have four processors on your server, and have configured SQL Server to use only two, you will still have to pay license fees for four processors. The only way around this is to make some of the processors unavailable to the operating system by disabling them, taking them off of the motherboard, or running SQL Server in a virtual environment with fewer processors.

Virtual Server Licensing Issues

You may run SQL Server 2008 in a virtual environment. At least one license is required for SQL in each virtual environment where SQL Server runs.

❑   **Server/CAL License Model:** The Standard and Workgroup editions require a Server license for each instance of SQL Server running in a physical or virtual environment. For a SQL Server Standard instance in each of three virtual machines, you would need a Server license for each instance — a total of three Server licenses.

If you are using the Enterprise Edition, you must have a Server license for each physical environment in which SQL Server runs. An example of this would include taking a large machine and partitioning it into several physical environments. Each physical environment running an instance of SQL Server Enterprise Edition requires a separate Server license. However, once one

Enterprise license exists for the physical server, there are no additional licensing requirements for other instances running within virtual environments on this physical server.

To recap, an Enterprise Edition requires a single license for each physical server, and includes all virtual servers. The Standard and Workgroup edition require a separate license for each virtual server.

❏ **Processor License Model:** Once a processor has a SQL Server license, it may be used for as many instances of SQL Server as you wish, in either the physical or virtual environments.

If you run SQL in a physical environment, you must have licenses for all processors. If you run SQL in a virtual environment, you must have licenses for each processor available to the environment. You pay only once for the license for a processor, however. Suppose you have a four-processor machine and you wish to pay for licenses for two of the four processors, processors 2 and 3. You may not run SQL Server on the physical environment because you have not licensed all four of the processors. However, you may set up as many virtual environments which use only processors 2 and 3 as you wish. You may also install as many named instances of SQL Server as you wish on any of the virtual machines, because you have paid the processor license for SQL Server for the processors available to these virtual machines.

You will never need more SQL Server processor licenses than there are processors on the server, regardless of the number of virtual machines or SQL Server instances.

❏ **Passive Server Licensing:** SQL Server has three features that can be used for failover support:

  ❏ Database mirroring

  ❏ Failover clustering

  ❏ Backup log shipping

  These may be used to allow another server to pick up the work from a failed server. The failover or passive server is not being used by clients, except when the primary server has failed. The passive server does not have to be licensed, unless you are using the Processor licensing model, and the passive server has more processors than the active server. In this case, you must purchase processor licenses for each of the extra processors on the passive server. The passive server may take over the duties of the active server for 30 days. Afterward, the passive server must be licensed.

❏ **Reporting Services Licensing:** Reporting Services consists of two main pieces — the Reporting Services Web Service and the Reporting Services metadata database. The metadata database stores information about the reports, security, and subscriptions. Every Reporting Services install must connect to a SQL Server metadata database. Each of the two components must have a valid SQL license. If they are installed on the same server, you need one license. One of the first things you might do to increase scalability is to place the Reporting Services database on a separate physical server than the Reporting Services Web service — that is two licenses.

❏ **Processor License Model:** This model is required if you are using Reporting Services in an extranet or intranet environment. No additional Device or User CALs are necessary.

❏ **Server/Cal License Model:** This model requires a Server license for Reporting Services, and a device or user CAL for each device/user accessing a report, either directly on indirectly, including Report Builder and Report Designer.

Summary

In this chapter, we covered the basic architecture for SQL Server, including how it stores its data and how it communicates. We also addressed the various data types and when to use one type rather than another. Last, we answered some of the many dreaded SQL Server edition and licensing questions that we often hear from users. Now that you have the groundwork down, you're ready to jump into installing SQL Server and some of the common issues that you may experience.

2

SQL Server 2008 Installation Best Practices

SQL Server is relatively easy to install. You can put the CD or DVD into the drive, in most cases click straight though, and you'll get a running, useful install. Several decisions are made by default as you click through, however. In this chapter, you learn about those decisions and discover the related gotchas and how to avoid them.

The core installation process follows these general steps:

- ❑ Plan the system.
- ❑ Get the hardware and software.
- ❑ Install the operating system and service packs.
- ❑ Set up the I/O subsystem.
- ❑ Install SQL Server and service packs.
- ❑ Burn in the system.
- ❑ Do post-install configurations if necessary.
- ❑ Clean up for deployment and go!

This chapter focuses on the plan and the actual install.

Planning the System

Pre-installation planning will pay off with happier users and time savings for you. Because it is so easy to pop in the CD or DVD and click through to install the product, it is equally easy to forego the planning process — but resist the temptation!

Your planning will involve several functions, including the funding source, network group, and infrastructure (hardware/operating systems group). The funding source or business group needs to tell you something about the dollars available and the planning period that this configuration should support. Are you building something to last for four months or two years? The business people will also have some requirements related to uptime and scalability. Incremental uptime and scalability is always more expensive as your tolerance for problems decreases. The infrastructure group will be able to advise you about your company's configuration rules, hardware-vendor recommendations, and approved levels of software. Don't forget about support as well.

Let's drill into some of the details.

Hardware Options

If you are in a growing organization, you should probably buy bigger and more than you think you need. More memory and faster or more processors are almost always preferable. At the very least, ensure that you have room to grow. For instance, if you have four memory slots and plan on buying 4GB of memory, do not buy four 1GB sticks of memory, because you will have used up all of the slots. Instead, consider buying two 2GB sticks, leaving two slots available for expansion.

Microsoft recommends some minimum configurations, and you'd better believe they mean *minimum*. Even for a small test machine, the minimum will not be enough. You should take this to heart. The minimum configuration means the product will most likely not run with fewer resources. It also means that you will need more hardware for any significant usage. The full minimum requirements can be found on Microsoft's site at `http://msdn.microsoft.com/en-us/library/ms143506(SQL.100).aspx`.

You need to do some homework here. How many concurrent connections do you expect? How many of them will actually be doing work at any given point in time? How will that translate into disk I/Os? If you have an existing system, measure it. If you are using purchased software (such as SAP, PeopleSoft, or any of a host of others), talk with the software vendor about hardware requirements. Many vendors employ staff who specialize in configuration of their application; use them.

Although we are primarily discussing the SQL Server Database Engine in this section, you may be working with other parts of SQL Server.

Processors

For SQL Server installs for which you expect many connections, more processors are better. This means that two 1.6 GHz processors will likely be better than a single 3 GHz processor. Although SQL multi-threads, having two processors instead of one (or four instead of two), helps prevent a situation in which a single connection ties up the system; it's just a safer bet. The new multicore processors are great also. While dual-core processors are not quite as fast as two separate processors, they are certainly cheaper to purchase and potentially cheaper to license software. Intel has also announced plans to develop chips with tens to hundreds of cores on a single processor chip. Most serious production systems should be 64-bit, especially Analysis Services and Reporting Services Report Manager.

One of the very customer-friendly decisions that Microsoft made in SQL Server 2005, which carries over to SQL Server 2008, is that you must only pay for the physical socket when it comes to multicore server licensing. For example, if you have a four-CPU, quad-core server, it would appear to Windows and SQL Server as 16 processors, but you would only be charged for four CPUs if you choose per-processor licensing. As you start to benchmark the machines, a quad-core CPU doesn't perform quite as well as a 4-CPU machine, but the reduction isn't severe. The reason for the slight slowdown is the overhead of the switching in the cores.

Disk Configuration

When you plan your disk drives, consider availability, reliability, space requirements, and throughput. You need to design the disk I/O subsystem to meet your needs. In particular, you need to decide how to implement availability and reliability, which usually transfers into Redundant Array of Inexpensive Disks (RAID) and Storage Area Network (SAN) decisions:

- ❏ How will the `master` and `model` databases be protected? (Probably mirrored)
- ❏ How will the data files for the database be configured? (Probably RAID 5 or RAID 10.) You learn more about the hardware configuration of your SQL Server in Chapter 11.
- ❏ How will the log files be configured? (Mirrored)
- ❏ Where will `tempdb` be placed and configured? (Away from other files and probably mirrored)

We suggest three rules for data-disk configuration to get maximum recoverability. Although these are used mostly when creating user databases, the system databases need to be on a different drive from the one you expect to use for your user databases. The rules are as follows:

- ❏ Keep the log away from data. Keep a database's log files on a different physical drive from the data.
- ❏ Keep the data away from the `master`. Keep the `user` database files on a different physical drive from `master`/`model`/`tempdb`.
- ❏ Mirror the log.

SQL Server will not know anything about your decisions regarding RAID levels and SAN or Network Attached Storage (NAS) storage. It uses only the drive letters that have been exposed to the operating system. Therefore, you need to make and implement all of these decisions before you install SQL Server.

Disk Throughput

Incorrectly estimating disk throughput is the most common mistake people make when configuring SQL Server. Suppose you've been told by an administrator, "I need to have 300GB of storage for my production database." You buy a couple of 150GB hard drives, and off you go. If this database is expected to get 300 I/Os per second of requests, though, you are going to be in trouble. Imagine an Ultra-320 SCSI with the following specifications:

- ❏ Capacity: 147GB
- ❏ Spindle speed: 10KB RPM
- ❏ Average seek: 4.5 msec
- ❏ Average latency: 3.0 msec
- ❏ Track-to-track seek time: 0.3 ms
- ❏ Max external transfer rate: 320 Mbits/sec

This is a commonly available, high-performance drive. Now consider how this performance should play into your thinking about a SQL Server install and configuration.

With no data transfer, the theoretical max random I/Os/second would be 1,000 Mbits/second / (4.5 seek + 3.0 latency) = 133 I/Os/second. The theoretical max serial I/Os/second would be 1,000 Mbits/second/(3.0 latency) = 333 I/Os/second.

For your calculations, however, you should use a more conservative capability estimate of 100 random I/Os and 200 sequential I/Os per second for this configuration. It is much more likely that you will be constrained by the I/O transfers per second than the 32 Mbytes/second the hard drive can yield (320 Mbits/second/10 bits/byte, including parity bits = 32 Mbytes/second). Now you'll find that 100 random I/Os/second * 8KB per transfer = 0.8 Mbytes/second.

This calculation is for random reads and writes to a single drive. SQL Server's lazy writer, worker threads, and other processes do 8KB random I/Os. Notice that this is well under the maximum advertised throughput of 32 Mbytes per second.

Even if you are doing sequential I/Os, 1.6 Mbytes/second is still way under the maximum throughput of 32 Mbytes/second: 100 sequential I/Os/second 8KB = 1.6 Mbytes/second.

Read-Ahead Manager does 64KB I/Os. It also tries to order the I/Os so that they become sequential I/Os, which provide much better throughput. The results are 100 random I/Os/second 64KB = 6.4 Mbytes/second and 300 sequential I/Os/second 64K = 12.8 Mbytes/second.

Even at the fastest throughput one might reasonably expect from this hard drive, the limitation will be the I/O transfer rate, not the 32 Mbytes advertised maximum throughput.

If you use RAID 5, each logical write is physically two reads and two writes. This I/O will be spread across two drives, so the throughput of each drive is divided in half. That would bring your I/O transfer rate for write operations down from 100 to 50.

In this example, you need 300 logical writes per second against a RAID 5 array, so you must have 300/50, or six, drives. Even though you need only about 300GB of disk storage, your configured RAID 5 array will contain about 600GB of usable storage (five usable drives of the six, each 150GB/drive). The bottom line is this: Do not configure only for storage; you must consider transfer-rate needs as well.

Note that the actual time to transfer the data is a small part of the overall I/O time. Transferring an 8KB chunk of data would take about 1/4 of a millisecond (32,000,000 bytes/second/8,000 bytes). Transferring 64KB bytes of data would take about 2 milliseconds. This is small when compared to the average seek and average latency time of 7.5 milliseconds for this drive (4.5 + 3.0).

Some disk drives are faster than the one we used as an example here, and disk capabilities change over time, so you must do your own research and come up with your own numbers.

Best Practices

In general, to get higher throughput, you should spread the I/Os across multiple smaller physical drives. Hardware-based arrays are faster (and more expensive) than software arrays. Consider the transfer rates necessary to support the concurrent users you expect on your system. Also note that even though you may have 500 users connected, most of them will likely be waiting, rather than active. You will have to do some research to better understand your users to get an idea of what percentage of connected users will actually be *active* at any given time. If most users are heads-down, data-entry folks, you may have nearly 90 to 100 percent of them active most of the time. If your users are a mix of inquirers and updaters who keep the application running all day but only use it occasionally, you may have as few as 10 percent of your users active. This knowledge should be part of both your research and your plan.

Because most large I/Os in SQL Server are 64KB bytes, that would be a good stripe size to choose when you are configuring your RAID arrays.

SQL does not officially support data files on NAS or network file shares but will run if you enable Trace flag 1807 (which is an override switch in SQL Server). Do not expect to get good performance from NAS or network file shares. Better advice would simply be to always use direct-connected hard drives or SAN for your SQL files. Finally, you should always use NTFS for your data files. NTFS provides better security and more fault tolerance via soft sector sparing.

> *An additional type of disk you can use is a solid-state drive (SDD). These drives have no moving parts inside of them and are similar to the flash drives inside your computer technology. They're much more expensive because the technology is still maturing, but read performance is nearly 100 percent faster on this type of system and writes nearly 150 percent faster in our testing.*

Disk Controllers

Disk controllers have a throughput limit as well. Take the maximum throughput expected from your earlier drive calculations to determine the maximum number of drives you should attach to a controller.

You need to be careful about the caching on these controllers. Disk caching can bring wonderful performance improvements to your system, but you can easily get into trouble by using it. The issue is that you must be able to guarantee that transaction-log writes will be completed under all circumstances. Controller caching works like this: When SQL Server sends a write command to the controller, the controller can save the data in cache and immediately send an I/O Complete message back to SQL Server. One of the things the hardware controller can do is attempt to batch together multiple smaller I/Os into what might become a single larger sequential I/O, instead of many smaller random I/Os. SQL Server continues to work, even though the I/O has not actually been committed to disk. As long as the I/O eventually makes it to disk, life is good; but if the I/O gets lost for any reason, SQL recovery will not work, because part of the log is missing. Then you are in big trouble.

The way to avoid this problem is to ensure that you are using a disk controller designed for use in a data-critical transactional DBMS environment. You should be able to turn off write caching and take advantage of read-only caching. Not all controllers allow this. You should be covered by a UPS, but this is not enough to ensure that the I/O will be completed. UPSs cannot cover everything, such as operating system traps, memory parity errors, or operating system errors that cause a system reset.

Another problem that can circumvent proper write caching is an operations issue. A normal server shutdown (from the operating system) will wait until all of the I/Os are complete. Operators should generally wait until disk activity is complete before rebooting a system. When you shutdown the system, cached writes can be discarded, corrupting the databases.

There are disk controllers that avoid all of these problems. They can intercept the RST (reset) bus signals to bypass resets that would discard cached writes. They also include ECC (error checking and correcting) memory, as well as onboard battery backup.

Although many controllers have a cache, most of the cache is protected by capacitors, not onboard battery backup. Capacitor-based caching cannot protect data from power failures and only ensures that the current sector is written. Onboard battery backup can protect a cached write for several days. As long as power is restored within the time limits, the controller will prevent new access, complete the pending I/Os, and then allow new access.

Some controllers also allow selective write-through, allowing transaction-log I/Os to bypass caching, while other writes are cached to improve performance.

Software and Install Options

The next step in the plan is making choices about the software and installation options, such as choosing where the files will be located, setting security options, and configuring your disks.

Collation

When you choose a collation, you choose a character set, called a code page. The code page contains the mapping between the hex digits stored in the database and the characters they represent. For instance, x20 (hex 20) is a space character. What makes it a space character is the code page you are using. You look up the hex 20 in the character-set map (code page), and you can see that it represents a space in the language (or character set) that is part of your collation.

Collation affects two other things: case sensitivity and sort order. You will learn more details about these two items in a moment.

In versions of SQL Server before SQL Server 2000, choosing the correct collation was a big deal. The collation you chose during the install was the collation used for everything on the entire server. If you needed a different collation, you had to install another server. SQL Server 2008 allows you to make collation choices at the server, database, column, and expression levels.

The collation you choose during install is the collation for the system databases, including tempdb, and the default collation for everything else. Those who add new objects to this instance of SQL Server may choose other collations for their objects.

There are two general types of collations: SQL Server collations and Windows collations.

SQL Server Collations

SQL Server collations affect the code page used to store data in char, varchar, and text columns. They also affect how comparisons and sorting is done on these data types. For example, if you were to create a SELECT statement like the following against a case-sensitive collation database, it would not return the employee named Brian (in mixed case).

```
SELECT * FROM Employees where Name = 'BRIAN'
```

SQL Server collations do not, however, affect Unicode data types. Unicode data types may compare and sort differently. This is the primary shortcoming of using SQL collations. You can set up an environment in which single-byte and double-byte character sets use different collations. You should use SQL collations for backward compatibility. All of the SQL collation names begin with SQL_. Any other collation name is a Windows collation.

Windows Collations

Windows collations use rules based on the chosen Windows locale for the operating system. The default behavior is that comparisons and sorting follow the rules used for a dictionary in the associated language. You may specify binary, case, accent, Kana, and width sensitivity. The key point is that Windows collations ensure that single-byte and double-byte character sets behave the same way in sorts and comparisons.

Case Sensitivity

Your collation is either case sensitive or not. Case sensitive means that *U* is different from *u*. This will be true for everything in the region to which the collation applies (in this case, `master`, `model`, `resource`, `tempdb`, and `msdb`). This is true for all of the data in those databases. Here is the gotcha: Think about what the data in those databases actually is. The *data* includes the data in all of the system tables, which means object names are also case sensitive. The function to list the collations supported by SQL 2008 is `fn_helpcollations()`. On a case-sensitive server, this command would give you an "invalid object name" error:

```
Select * from FN_HELPCOLLATIONS()
```

This command, however, would work correctly:

```
Select * from fn_helpcollations()
```

This returns more than 1,000 rows, but a few of the rows would look like this:

```
Name                   Description
Latin1_General_BIN     Latin1-General, binary sort
Latin1_General_BIN2    Latin1-General, binary code point comparison sort
Latin1_General_CI_AI   Latin1-General, case-insensitive, accent-insensitive,
kanatype-insensitive, width-insensitive
Latin1_General_CI_AI_WS Latin1-General, case-insensitive, accent-insensitive,
kanatype-insensitive, width-sensitive
```

Suppose you have a case-sensitive database in which all of the objects are also case sensitive, and you have a table name `Emp`, with a single column named `Firstname`, with four rows with values `Tom`, `Mary`, `tom`, and `mary`.

The following command finds no rows from our fictional table, because the objects are case sensitive:

```
SELECT * FROM  Emp WHERE Firstname = 'TOM'
```

The following command finds only one row, `Tom`:

```
SELECT * FROM  Emp WHERE Firstname = 'Tom'
```

To find all the rows regardless of case, you would have to write something like the following:

```
SELECT * FROM Emp WHERE Upper(Firstname) LIKE 'TOM'
```

Binary collations are case sensitive. If you choose a dictionary collation, you may choose the case sensitivity you need. However, as you can see, collation affects comparisons.

Sort Order

The collation you choose also affects sorting. Binary orders (Latin1_General_BIN, for instance) sort based on the bit value of the character; they are case sensitive. Using the example table from earlier and a binary order, consider the following statement:

```
SELECT * FROM Emp ORDER BY Firstname
```

The result set would be as follows:

```
Mary
Tom
mary
tom
```

If you choose a dictionary sort order (Latin1_General_CS_AI, for instance), the previous statement would yield the following result set:

```
mary
Mary
tom
Tom
```

Most business applications that contain character data types generally need a dictionary sort. Microsoft Books Online for SQL Server can provide you with a list of the extensions (_CI, _CS, and so on) and their meanings. Here you only need to understand the conceptual differences.

Collation Best Practices and Warnings

The big deal here is compatibility. If you try to compare two text fields that have different collations, which collation should be used for the comparison? You must provide the collation name in your code. This is a pain to do. Some collations are not comparable, which is even worse. Think about your use of linked servers in an environment of mixed collations. If you are using SQL replication between this instance and some other server, particularly SQL Server 2000 and SQL Server 7, you must make sure the data being shared also shares the same collation. Try to standardize a collation across the enterprise. If you don't do this, your employees will have to relearn their query patterns as they go from server to server.

Ensure compatibility with other servers where necessary. Change the default only if you need to do so for compatibility with other servers. The caveat here is that if you have an earlier version of SQL Server installed on this server, it will automatically choose a SQL collation. In this case, you must decide whether you need compatibility with that earlier version. If you do not need compatibility, choose a Windows collation.

SQL Server collations cannot be used with SQL 2008 Analysis Services. If you choose a SQL Server collation and are also installing Analysis Services, the install will choose a Windows collation that most closely matches your SQL Server collation choice. Your results, however, may be inconsistent. To guarantee consistent results between your database engine and Analysis Services, use a Windows collation.

If you have servers that have regional settings for both English (UK) and English (United States), you might be in for a surprise. The default collation for English (UK) is Latin1_General_CI_AS, whereas the default collation for English (United States) is `SQL_Latin1_General_CP1_CI_AS`. You will have to choose the proper collation for one of these to ensure consistency. They both use code page 1252, however.

In general, when you do not have to ensure compatibility with multiple servers, use the default Windows collation, and choose the case-sensitivity options to suit your needs. If you are upgrading an earlier version in place, use the default SQL Server collation chosen by the install. If you are trying to replicate with another SQL Server 2008 instance, you can discover its collation with the following statement on the existing system:

```
SELECT SERVERPROPERTY(N'Collation')
```

This would return `SQL_Latin1_General_CP1_CI_AS` on a normal default configuration of a SQL Server instance.

If you are trying to replicate with SQL Server 7.0 or SQL Server 2000, for instance, use the following command on the existing instance to get the collation information:

```
EXEC sp_helpsort
```

This would return the much more descriptive value that resembles the following:

```
Latin1-General, case-insensitive, accent-sensitive, kanatype-insensitive, width-
insensitive for Unicode Data, SQL Server Sort Order 52 on Code Page 1252 for non-
Unicode Data
```

Microsoft recommends that if you are trying to match the Windows locale of another computer (without changing your server's Windows locale), you must obtain the locale name from the other server. For Windows 2000 or Windows 2003, this can be found in Control Panel ⇨ Regional Options. On Windows XP, Vista, and Windows 2008, this is under Control Panel ⇨ Regional and Language Options. Once you have the region name, search MSDN for the topic "Collation Settings in Setup." This topic provides a mapping between locale name and default collation.

Microsoft's recommendation here does not take into account the possibility that the other server might not use the default collation. I prefer to use `serverproperty` and `sp_helpsort` to get the collation directly. I provide Microsoft's recommendation only for completeness.

System Files Location

For most servers where higher availability is a requirement, it is recommended that you mirror the C: drive where the operating system lives. You should place the SQL Server install in the default Program Files folder on the `C:` drive as well. This means that the `master`, `model`, `resource`, `msdb`, and `tempdb` databases will also be on the `C:` drive by default.

`Tempdb` might need some extra consideration, because it performs more duties in SQL Server 2008 than it did in SQL Server 2000. It contains more information related to certain locking schemes, and it supports several other new features. As a post-install item, you may wish to either move `tempdb` using the `Alter database` command or have it grow to another disk drive. To do this, turn off autogrow for the existing file, and add new files in some new location. The preferred method is simply to move it to an otherwise not busy disk drive, as `tempdb` could see a lot of I/O.

Disk Setup

Without getting into the doldrums of discussing each of the RAID types, here is some simple advice: Mirror the OS, the SQL exe files, the system databases, and all transaction logs. Data files for other databases where high availability is necessary should be protected via RAID, with duplicate disk controllers. The more disk spindles you use, the better your I/O throughput will be. If you have the money, RAID 10 or SAN will give the best performance. A less expensive option that does not provide as good performance is RAID 5. Whatever you do, use hardware RAID. For SQL Server, 64KB is a good RAID stripe size.

Security Considerations

Do not install the SQL Server Database Engine on a domain controller or on the same box as IIS. Reporting Services in SQL Server 2008 no longer requires IIS. If you're using Reporting Services often and you're exposing it to the Internet, Microsoft recommends that you move it to its own machine.

While you can get the details about service accounts on MSDN (look for "Setting Up Windows Service Accounts"), this section provides only the points that you need to know. Up to 10 services are part of SQL Server 2008, depending on what you install. If you install more than one instance, that is up to 10 per instance. For maximum security, use a different local Windows login for each account, instead of sharing a single account locally. Local Windows logins are safer than domain logins, but they are more trouble because you have to keep up with more logins.

Although Microsoft's suggestion is to use separate local accounts for each service, most companies use a single domain login account for all services, using the minimum security settings. Some things can only be done when the service is running under a domain account, for example:

❑ Remote procedure calls

❑ Replication

❑ Backing up to network drives

❑ Heterogeneous joins that involve remote data sources

❑ SQL Server Agent mail features and SQL Server Mail

As mentioned earlier, most companies use a single domain account for all services on all production servers. This makes maintenance easier; for instance, you have to set up only a single file share with permissions for backing up to a network drive. There are several kinds of service accounts you can choose from:

❑ **Domain account:** This is an active directory domain account that you create and is the preferred account type for SQL Server services needing network access.

❑ **Local System account:** This is a highly privileged account you should not use for services.

❑ **Local Service account:** This is a special, preconfigured account that has the same permissions as members of the Users group. Network access is done as a null session with no credentials.

❑ **Network Service account:** This account is the same as the Local Service Account, except that network access is allowed, credentialed as the computer account. Do not use this account for SQL Server or SQL Agent Service accounts.

❑ **Local Server account:** This is a local Windows account that you create. This is the most secure method you can use for services that do not need network access.

If you are making any changes to properties related to a SQL Server Service, do not use Windows Services dialogs. For example, suppose the password for a domain Windows account for your SQL Service has been changed. You need to change the stored password for the SQL Service. Although this can be done via Windows Administrative Tools, you should always use SQL Server Configuration Manager to manage the services associated with SQL Server.

Installing SQL Server

In this section you learn about the different types of installations: side by side, upgrade, and new. Details about upgrades are covered in Chapter 3. You can also create a script that installs SQL Server for you. This can be very useful when you need to complete many similar installations.

Each install works with a single instance. If you wish to install a named instance of the Database Engine and a default instance of Analysis Services, you must go through two separate install processes.

Side-By-Side, Upgrade, and New Installs

A new install occurs when no other SQL Server components are on the server and you have a clean slate to work with. Make sure that there are no remnants of previous SQL installs. Check the directories and the registry to ensure that you have a clean system.

If SQL Server components exist on the box, you can upgrade the existing instance. In this case, you install SQL Server on top of the existing instance. SQL Server also supports a side-by-side install. A side-by-side install occurs when you are adding another instance of SQL Server. SQL Server 2008 supports multiple instances of the Database Engine, Reporting Services, and Analysis Services on the same box. It will also run side by side with previous versions of SQL Server. If the existing instance is a default instance, of course, your new install must be a named instance. The following table indicates which versions can run side by side with SQL 2008.

Side-By-Side Support	SQL Server 2000 (32-bit)	SQL Server 2000 (64-bit)	SQL Server 2008 (32-bit)	SQL Server 2008 (64-bit) IA64	SQL Server 2008 (64-bit) X64
SQL Server 2000 (32-bit)	Yes	No	Yes	No	Yes
SQL Server 2000 (64-bit)	No	Yes	No	Yes	No
SQL Server 2008 (32-bit)	Yes	No	Yes	No	Yes
SQL Server 2008 (64-bit) IA64	No	Yes	No	Yes	No
SQL Server 2008 (64-bit) X64	Yes	No	Yes	No	Yes

The biggest issue with side-by-side installs is memory contention. Make sure you set up your memory so that each instance is not trying to acquire the entire physical memory.

Some companies who need many instances of low-usage SQL Servers are placing a single instance of SQL Server in a virtual machine and placing several virtual machines on a single server. VMWare and Microsoft's Virtual Server software support this architecture. Using Microsoft's Virtual Server or Virtual PC, you can create an image using Virtual PC and quickly transfer the virtual machine to Virtual Server. This is more often found in the development environment than production, but it depends on the load placed on the servers and the size of the physical box. This does enable you to move the instances around transparently and to provision new instances quickly.

Scripted Installation

You can install SQL Server via command prompt calls to `Setup.exe`. In our experience, this was used in the past more frequently than today. You could create a small setup script, with all of your options selected, send it to a remote site, and have someone run the script to do the installation. We include a couple of the command-line syntax examples in this section. If you wish to do a very small number of installations, you can connect to the server via a remote desktop connection and do the install as if you were local. You can also use scripting to upgrade or uninstall SQL Server.

If you are installing SQL from a remote share, you must have read and execute permissions on the share. Expect all commands to be case sensitive. In addition, make sure you note the direction of the slashes in the commands; it matters.

First, ensure that the SQL Install CD/DVD is in the disk drive. Use the following command-line prompt to install all components:

```
Start /wait <CD or DVD Drive> \setup.exe /qb INSTANCENAME=<InstanceName>
```

The Database Engine, SQL Server Agent, Reporting Server, and Analysis Services are all instance aware. To install selective components, use the following syntax:

```
Start /wait <CD or DVD Drive> \setup.exe /qb INSTANCENAME=<InstanceName>
ADDLOCAL=SQL_Engine, SQL_Replication
```

Either the `/qn` or `/qb` flag is required. Using `/qn` suppresses the user interface, and all setup messages and errors are placed in the setup log. Using `/qb` shows the user interface during install and displays messages in dialogs. You can think of `/qn` as an unattended install, and `/qb` as an attended install.

The other components, which are not instance aware, do require the INSTANCENAME token. If you are installing to the default instance, use INSTANCENAME=MSSQLSERVER.

The ADDLOCAL option describes the software you wish to install. You can get the complete list of option values in Books Online. The thing you need to know here is that there is a two-level hierarchy of software pieces. As an example, the SQL_Engine parent has three children: SQL_Data_Files, SQL_Replication, and SQL_FullText. If you include only the parent, then only the parent and none of its children is installed. Installing a child feature automatically installs the parent, however. Removing a parent automatically removes all of the child features. These features are all case sensitive and must be included in a comma-delimited list with no spaces.

PIDKEY is the software key that comes with your software. Do not include spaces or the dash (-) character in the key.

The SAPWD option is used to specify the SA password. Always use a strong password. A strong password contains at least eight characters and includes characters from at least three of the following groups: uppercase characters, lowercase characters, digits, and other special characters. (More details regarding securing your SQL Server install are covered in Chapter 9.)

You can use many other parameters in the command prompt, many of which are login passwords for service accounts, virtual names, and IP addresses for cluster installs. Check out Books Online to get the complete list.

You can also take all of the options, format them in an .ini style, and place them in a text file. Then reference the ini file as follows:

```
Start /wait <CD or DVD Drive> \setup.exe /settings C:\sqlinstall.ini /qn
```

An ini file is an "initialization" file formatted in an ini style. Microsoft provides an ini file that you can modify to meet your needs. The file name is Template.ini, *and it is located in the root directory of your install CD or DVD.*

Remote Installation

Remote installations are not supported; you need to use Remote Desktop Connections instead. In previous editions of SQL Server, you could sit at one machine and do an install directly to another machine. This is called a *remote install*. It is beneficial if you are in one city and need to install SQL Server on a machine in another city. However, because the operating system now allows Remote Desktop Connections, there is no need for the SQL Server product to include this capability. You can make a Remote Desktop Connection by selecting Start ⇨ All Programs ⇨ Accessories ⇨ Communications ⇨ Remote Desktop Connection. You will be prompted for a server name to connect to and login credentials. Once logged in, you install SQL Server as if you were sitting at the server console. To make this type of connection, the server would first need to allow access remotely.

Local Installation

Rather than go through each of the dialogs for the install, this section covers the more critical ones. Our test installs were from the MSDN Universal DVD. Microsoft Developer Network (MSDN) subscriptions allow developers to purchase much of Microsoft's operating system, servers, Office products, and more at a very attractive price and use them for development purposes. Our installations were done from this software source.

To get started, put in the CD or DVD. You may get an automatically started dialog or for Vista or Windows 2008 machines, you may have to run setup.exe because the splash screen may not open automatically. Once the dialog opens, you navigate to the correct version of SQL you wish to install. If you have to navigate on your own, you will eventually see Setup.exe in the Servers Directory of the version that you need. Run it.

Before the installation can begin, a number of prerequisites will be installed, such as the .NET Framework. After that, you'll be taken to the SQL Server Installation Center. Under the Installation page in the

Installation Center, select "New SQL Server stand-alone or add features to an existing installation." After that, the support files for the installation will run, which only takes a few minutes. Next, the installation wizard will ensure that your server setup functions, as shown in Figure 2-1. In this case, you can see that the there is a warning because the Windows Firewall port for SQL Server is not open, which would prevent users from accessing the instance.

> **Do not ignore anything that does not pass the check. Even warnings should be addressed now, not after you have completed what may be a partially successful install.**

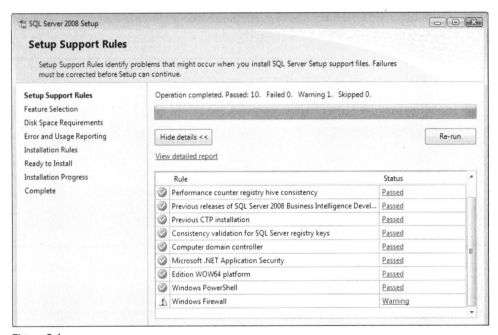

Figure 2-1

Next, choose the components you wish to install, as shown in Figure 2-2.

Your license for SQL Server will allow you to install all of the components on a single box. However, if you decide you wish to install the SQL Server Database Engine on one box, SQL Server Reporting Services on another box, and Analysis Services on a third box, that would require three licenses, not one. Licensing for Microsoft products changes over time and can become very complicated. Contact your vendor or a Microsoft representative to ensure that you are in compliance.

Several dialogs later, you will eventually get to the Server Configuration page. To make your collation-setting choice, click the Collation tab, shown in Figure 2-3. Keep in mind that you should have a good reason for changing it from the default.

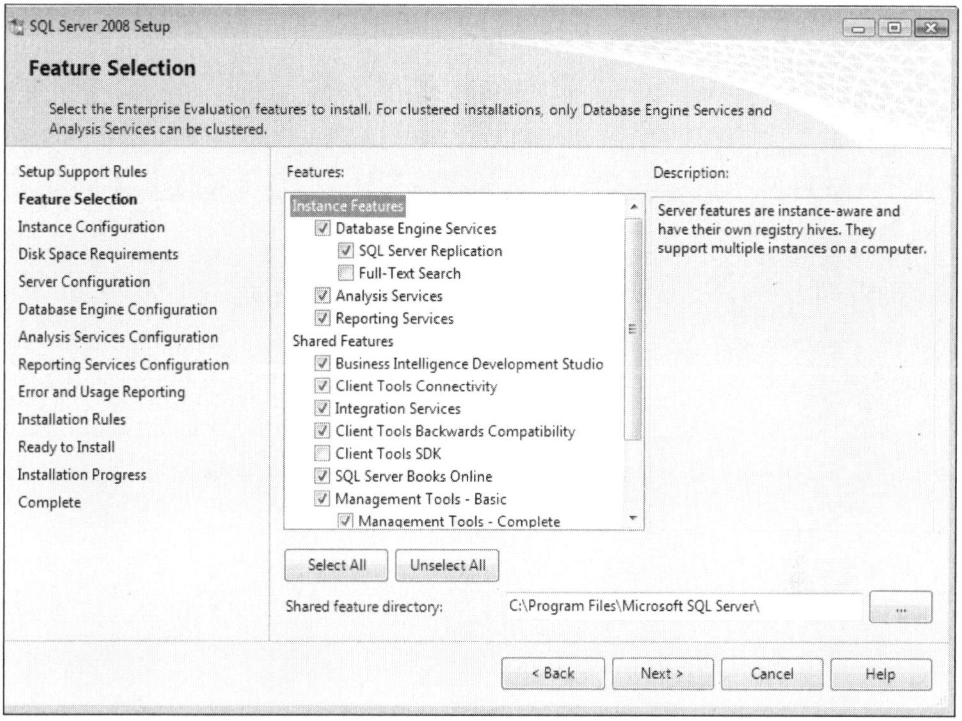

Figure 2-2

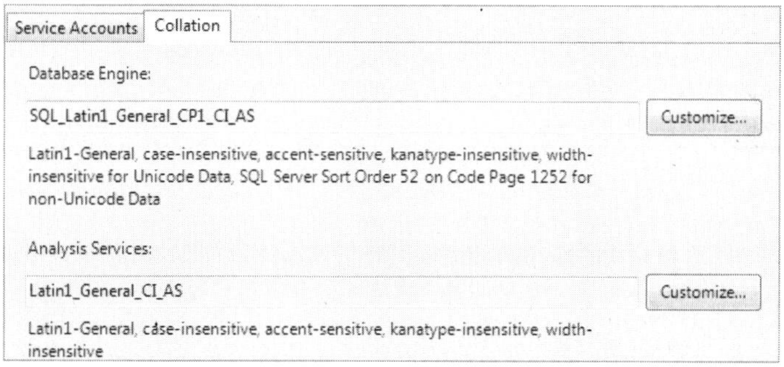

Figure 2-3

The next step in the process asks you to provision the sysadmin account. If your system is using Windows Authentication mode, you must have a Windows account that will act as your system administrator in SQL Server. The Account Provisioning tab shown in Figure 2-4 enables you to add a Windows accounts to the sysadmin role; you will not be able to proceed until you add a user.

You can also change the default directories for your data files in the Data Directories tab. For example, you can place tempdb on one drive, other system databases on another, and the user databases on a different drive.

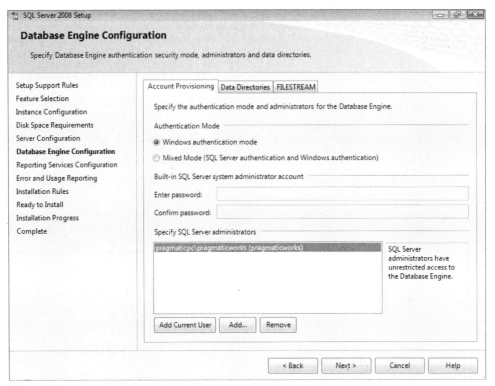

Figure 2-4

When you click Next, you'll be taken to the same type of screens for Analysis Services. After that, you'll jump to the Reporting Services configuration where the setup can use the typical installation to automatically configure Reporting Services.

After you provide all the information, you'll be taken to the Ready to Install screen where you are shown the status information about the install. Click Begin Install to start the installation with your specified configuration (Figure 2-5 shows the Installation Progress screen). If you encounter any problems during your install, you should check this screen to get those details. This information is stored in the `<SQL Install Directory>\100\Setup Bootstrap\LOG\<Date Stamp>` directory. You'll also see a link to the exact file on the final screen after the installation fails or succeeds. If you get into trouble and have to call Product Support Services (PSS), you will need to have these files ready.

Once your install is complete, be sure to check out your new server. Make sure you can log in, and do some work.

Where Are the Sample Databases?

SQL Server has two demonstration databases for SQL Server 2008. `AdventureWorks2008` is a transactional sample, and `AdventureWorksDW2008` is a data warehouse sample. These demo databases are not included on the setup media as they were with previous releases of SQL Server. To install them, download the sample databases from `www.codeplex.com/MSFTDBProdSamples` and run the quick setup after the SQL Server installation. Microsoft has moved the databases there to make it much easier for them to update the sample databases and allow for community participation.

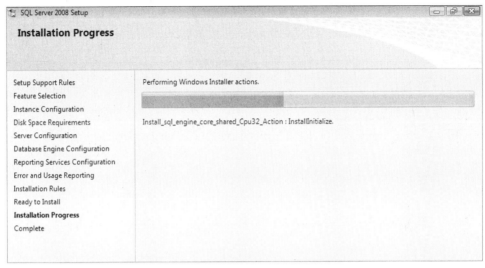

Figure 2-5

The familiar and comfortable `Pubs` and `Northwind` databases are not included on the SQL Server CD. Although `AdventureWorks` is a much more complete sample, you may wish to continue using the `Pubs` and `Northwind` databases on SQL Server 2008. You can download them from Microsoft's Web site (`www.microsoft.com/downloads/details.aspx?FamilyID=06616212-0356-46A0-8DA2-EEBC53A68034` at the time this was written). The file name is `SQL2000SampleDB.msi`. Download and extract this file. By default it is placed in the `C:\SQL Server 2000 Sample Databases` directory. Included are instructions that explain the install process, which is very simple.

Installing Analysis Services

We are not going to go through the screens for installing Analysis Services because they're pretty much self-explanatory. However, you should be aware of a few details.

Suppose you want to install a default instance of SQL Server 2008 Analysis Services on a box that already has an instance of SQL Server 2000 Analysis Services. SQL Server 2000 Analysis Services does not support named instances, so if you have SQL Server 2000 Analysis Services on your install box, you must upgrade the SQL Server 2000 Analysis Services install to a SQL 2008 named instance. Then you can install another instance of SQL Server 2008 as the default instance. You'll learn more about Analysis Services in Chapter 7.

Remember that SQL Server 2008 Analysis Services does not support SQL collations. You can get weird behavior if your Database Engine collation is a SQL Server collation and Analysis Services is a Windows collation.

Burning in the System

Before you move a system into common use, you should "burn it in." This means that you should stress the server. It is not unusual for a server to work in production for months or years with a hardware problem that existed at the time the server was deployed. Many of these failures will not show up when the server is under a light load but will become immediately evident when the server is pushed hard.

Several years ago, using SQL Server 6.5, I would get a 605 corruption error, which forced me to restore the database that had the error. When the restore was complete, I'd run my DBCCs and get a clean result. Within a week I'd get another 605 error and have to stay up late in the evening restoring the same server. After significant frustration with this recurring problem, I discovered that I had a disk controller failing only near 100 percent utilization. This is exactly the kind of problem that burning in your system is intended to expose prior to production. It's much easier to fix hardware before it goes live.

A second use of some of these tools is to compare the I/O throughput of your new system to your requirements or to the performance of an older system. While many tools are available, you can get two of them from Microsoft. One tool is called SQLIO, which is a disk subsystem benchmark tool. Microsoft provides this with no warranty and no support, but it is still a good tool to use. It is available from `www.microsoft.com/downloads`; search for SQLIO.

The second tool is SQLIOStress. You can download it from `http://support.microsoft.com/?kbid=231619` or search for SQLIOStress in Microsoft downloads. This tool simulates the I/O patterns of SQL Server, although it does so directly, without using your SQL install. It simulates write-ahead logging, page inserts and splits, checkpoints, read-ahead, sorts, hashes, backup scans, and many other scenarios. In addition, it does over 150 verification and validation checks. I would not put a server into use without using this tool. When you use it, you must identify a data and log file. Be sure you use the same data and log file locations you will be using when you create your databases, so you will be testing the right areas of your I/O subsystem.

Neither of these tools depends on SQL Server being installed, so you can do this burn-in either before or after the SQL install.

Post-Install Configuration

Now that you have your SQL Server components installed, you will probably need to do some additional configuration. Beginning with SQL Server 2005, Microsoft and the world have taken a more serious approach to security. In the past, almost everything was enabled by default. We have learned that it is better to leave most things turned off, so you must make a decision to implement the features and capabilities you need. Microsoft calls this "secure by default."

In SQL Server 2008, the Surface Area Configuration tool, which was used to enable given features in SQL Server 2005, has been discontinued. The following table shows how to perform tasks that used to be performed by Surface Area Configuration in a new manner.

Settings and Component Features	How to Configure
Protocols, and connection and startup options	Use SQL Server Configuration Manager.
Database Engine features	Use Declarative Management Framework.
SSAS features	Use the property settings in SQL Server Management Studio.
SSRS features	Edit the `RSReportServer.config` configuration file.

SQL Server Configuration Manager

The SQL Server Configuration Manager tool enables you to specify SQL Server Services options and whether the service starts automatically or manually. You can also stop and start services here, as the Service Manager in the toolbar no longer appears in SQL Server 2000. This program also includes a couple of very helpful features. Although I have not mentioned it before, I am sure you already know that SQL Server 2008 installs items for the Database Engine in strangely named directories: `MSSQL10.MSSQLSERVER` (Database Engine), `MSAS10.MSSQLSERVER` (SSAS), and `MSRS10.MSSQLSERVER` (SSRS). The word `MSSQLSERVER` would be replaced with your instance name and `MSSQLSERVER` represents the default instance name. How can you find out which of these directories belongs to a particular instance? You can find this in the registry, of course, but this is one of the things you can use the SQL Server Configuration Manager for. It will tell you many of the properties of the service. Double-click on one of the services and select the Advanced tab, shown in Figure 2-6. There you will find a lot of good information, including version information.

You may use this tool to set up the services, change service accounts, and auto-start services. You can also choose which network protocols SQL Server will listen on. This can be found in the SQL Server 2008 Network Configuration node. This node also enables you to import certificates for Secure Sockets Layer (SSL) encrypted communication.

The replacement for the Client Connectivity setup in SQL Server 2000 is located here as well, in the SQL Native Client Configuration node. You may choose which protocols the client uses and the order in which they will be used. You may also set up server aliases here. A server may listen on named pipes and TCP/IP. If you wish to force your client to use a specific protocol when communicating with a specific server, you may set up an alias for that.

SQL Server Management Studio

Once your instance is installed, you should visit SQL Server Management Studio and complete any configuration or tuning changes you wish to make. Most of the items you change are based on performance considerations and are covered later in the book. Among the items you may wish to consider changing are the following:

- ❑ **Processor section:** Number of processors

- ❑ **Memory Section:** Minimum and maximum memory

- ❑ **Database Section:** You may wish to set the default location for new data and log files. This is used when someone issues a create database command without specifying file locations.

- ❑ **Permissions Section:** Some sites require that only database admins have admin access, which means that operating system administrators should not have SQL admin capability. The default install adds a login for the administrators group on the local server. This login has SQL Server sysadmin permissions. Practically speaking, this means you cannot prevent any local administrator from having sysadmin permission for SQL. All they have to do is add themselves to the local administrator group, which is set by default. This is true for any login in SQL Server that has sysadmin privileges. Local server admins merely have to add themselves to the group, and they will have sysadmin privileges again. In some shops, usually smaller ones, this is not a problem; but if you want to exclude local server admins from having SQL privileges, delete the Builtin/Administrators login. Then add only specific logins for your SQL administrators, adding them to the sysadmin group.

Figure 2-6

tempdb

tempdb has taken on more responsibility than it had in the past. Historically, tempdb has been used for internal processes such as some index builds and table variable storage, as well as temporary storage space by programmers. The following is a partial list of some of the uses for tempdb:

- ❑ Bulk load with triggers
- ❑ Common table expressions

- ❏ DBCC operations
- ❏ Event notifications
- ❏ Indexes, including SORT_IN_TEMPDB, partitioned index sorts, and online index operations
- ❏ Large object type variables and parameters
- ❏ Multiple active result set operations
- ❏ Query notifications
- ❏ Row versioning
- ❏ Service Broker

The location and attributes of tempdb have always been important. This is even truer now. Therefore, always ensure that it is using Simple Recovery mode.

You also want to ensure that enough space has been preallocated to handle most operations. You do this by setting the file size to an appropriate value. Even though autogrow should be enabled, autogrow operations are expensive and time consuming. Think of autogrow as an emergency growth operation. When you enable autogrow, choose a file-growth increment sufficiently large so that autogrow operations do not have to occur frequently. Microsoft recommends a file-growth increment of 10 percent of the tempdb data file size, with a maximum of 6GB. File-growth operations can be slow, causing latch timeouts. The length of file-growth operations should be less than two minutes.

Use instant database file initialization if possible. Normally, SQL Server will write zeros into a data file to overwrite any data left on the disk from a preexisting file. This operation occurs under the following conditions:

- ❏ Creating a database.
- ❏ Adding log files or data files to an existing database.
- ❏ Increasing the size of a file (including autogrowth).
- ❏ Restoring a database or filegroup.

Instant file initialization claims disk space without overwriting with zeros. This enables initialization, and in this case tempdb autogrowth, to occur much faster. Log files must still be initialized with zeros, so they cannot be initialized instantly.

Instant file initialization applies globally on all instances that use the same service account. This setting applies to all databases on the instance, not just to tempdb. It occurs automatically on Windows XP Professional and Windows Server 2003 or later, when the SQL Server Service account has been granted the SE_MANAGE_VOLUME_NAME privilege or "Perform volume maintenance tasks" in Vista or Windows 2008. Windows administrators can set this feature by adding the SQL Server Service account to the Perform Volume Maintenance Tasks local security policy, as shown in Figure 2-7. You can get there from Control Panel ➪ Administrative Tools ➪ Local Security Policy.

Note a security issue related to using instant initialization. If files are not initialized to zeros, then old data will be visible on reused areas of disk, which may be a security risk. You could drop a filegroup for one database and add a filegroup and files on the same drive to another database. If these newly added files are not initialized, they will still contain the information from their previous use. Of course, an intruder would have to open the files directly and get the information, but it is doable. You can prevent this by ensuring that the physical files have the appropriate discretionary access control list (DACL) or are simply not using instant initialization.

If you use instant file initialization and later turn it off, the existing files are not affected. They still contain the original data. Only newly created or expanded files will be initialized with zeros.

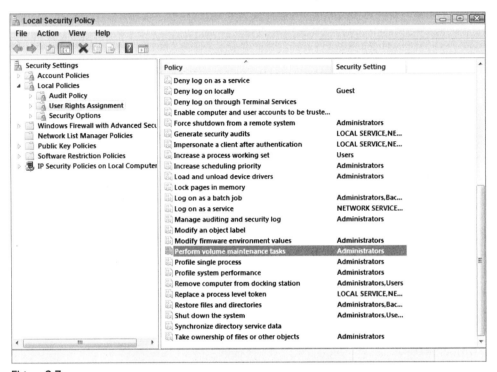

Figure 2-7

You should use multiple files in `tempdb` to ensure that `tempdb` operations can take advantage of all the I/O bandwidth available. One file per processor is best, but don't create more than two files per processor. Too many files simply increase the overhead and cannot be used simultaneously. (Dual-core CPUs count as two processors.) Ensure that each file is the same size. SQL Server 2008 continues to use the proportional fill algorithm from prior releases. This helps ensure the round-robin use of all files.

Finally, place `tempdb` on a fast I/O subsystem, using striping if multiple disks are available, and on a different drive from your user databases.

Back It Up

After you have made all of your configuration changes, now would be a good time to do your initial backups, create your disaster-recovery plans, and get things going. Backups are discussed more thoroughly in Chapter 18.

Uninstalling SQL Server

To uninstall SQL Server 2008, select Control Panel ⇨ Add/Remove Programs. If you wish to remove the entire instance, select Remove. If you wish to drop some of the services for the instance, but not all of them, select Change.

You can also use the Add/Remove Programs feature of the Control Panel to add or drop SQL Server components from an existing instance.

Uninstalling Reporting Services

When you uninstall Reporting Services, you need to do manual cleanup on some items, as described in this section. Before the uninstall, though, you need to gather some information. Make sure you know which databases are being used by this instance of Reporting Services. You can obtain this information from the Reporting Services Configuration tool. Discover which directory this instance of Reporting Services is installed in by running SQL Server Configuration Manager. You also need to discover which directory the Reporting Services usage and log files are using. To do this, run the Error and Usage Report Settings, in the All Programs ⇨ Microsoft SQL Server 2008 ⇨ Configuration Tools section, as shown in Figure 2-8.

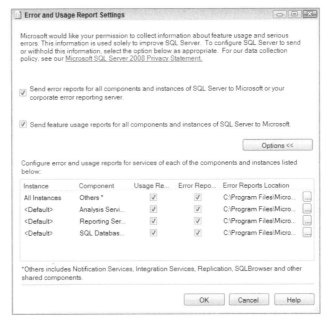

Figure 2-8

Dropping the ReportServer and ReportServerTempDB Databases

The Reporting Services uninstallation leaves the `ReportServer` and `ReportServerTempDB` databases so that you can reinstall another instance of Reporting Services and reuse the data. Note that these are the default database names, so ensure that you are dropping the appropriate databases. You should also make sure that no other instance of Reporting Services is using these databases. A Reporting Services server farm deployment would have many instances of Reporting Services sharing the same database. These instances would likely be on different servers as well. Once you are sure, just drop the databases.

Dropping the Remaining Directories

The normal uninstall also leaves all of the Reporting Services log files. The default location is the RS install directory or the alternate location you discovered earlier. To delete them, simply delete the appropriate directories.

Uninstalling Analysis Services

Uninstalling Analysis Services is much like uninstalling Reporting Services, in that you need to do some manual cleanup. Once again, you should gather some information prior to the uninstall. Discover which directory this instance of Analysis Services is installed in by running SQL Server Configuration Manager. Also discover which directory the Analysis Services usage and log files are using by running the Error and Usage Report Settings in the All Programs ⇨ Microsoft SQL Server 2008 ⇨ Configuration Tools section.

Although the normal uninstall does not leave any databases behind, it does leave all of the Analysis Services log files. The default location is the Analysis Services install directory or the alternate location you discovered previously. To delete them, simply delete the appropriate directories.

Uninstalling the SQL Server Database Engine

As with the other service, log files are not deleted when you uninstall the SQL Server Database Engine. To delete them, simply delete the appropriate directories.

You may have to remove the MS SQL Server Native Client separately, and you may find that the 100 directory remains and must be removed manually as well. If you have no other instances of SQL Server on your machine, instead of deleting only the 100 directory, you can delete the entire MS SQL Server directory under Program Files.

The .NET Framework 3.5 is also left on the machine. If you wish to remove it, do so from the Add/Remove Programs feature of the Control Panel, but make sure no other applications are using it.

The PSS group is currently working with the development group to define a manual uninstall process. This would be used when you have problems in the middle of a normal uninstall. You might find yourself stuck (you can't install and you can't uninstall). If you find yourself in a situation where SQL Server is installed, you wish to uninstall, and there is no SQL 2008 entry in Add/Remove Programs, run the following program from the command line and see if it brings up the Add/Remove Program GUI:

```
"C:\Program Files\Microsoft SQL Server\100\Setup Bootstrap\ARPWrapper.exe"
Remove
```

For all other issues where you are only partially installed and can't successfully uninstall or install, call PSS. Microsoft PSS warns against trying to manually hack the instance out of the registry.

For instance-level collation settings, unless you have a specific reason to pick a particular nondefault collation, use the default. Some valid reasons might be application requirements, compatibility requirements, or company policy. The most important thing is to have a consistent collation on all servers in a particular environment or you'll run into collation-conflict issues when consolidating, moving databases around between QA and production, and so on. One caveat is that on a U.S. English server, SQL Server will default to SQL_Latin1_General_CP1_CI_AS, while on a U.K. or other non-U.S. English server, it will install with Latin1_General_CI_AS. In an environment that could have both, it would be best to pick one of the two collations and stick with it.

Common Installation Issues

In writing this chapter we contacted the Product Support Services (PSS) group in Dallas, Texas. They let us know some of the most common installation issues that they have been receiving calls about for years, which we share with you in this section.

Installing Client Tools from a Network Share

There is a common problem many users run into when they try to install the SQL Server client tools from a fileshare copied from the install CD. They get the following error:

```
There was an unexpected failure during the setup wizard. You may review
the setup logs and/or click the help button for more information.
SQL Server Setup failed. For more information, review the Setup log file in
%ProgramFiles%\Microsoft SQL Server\100\Setup Bootstrap\LOG\Summary.txt.
```

When you go to the CORE(local).Log, you find the following information:

```
Running: InstallToolsAction.10 at: 2008/0/18 11:35:13
Error: Action "InstallToolsAction.10" threw an exception during execution.  Error
information reported during run:
Target collection includes the local machine.
Fatal Exception caught while installing package: "10"
      Error Code: 0x80070002 (2)
Windows Error Text: The system cannot find the file specified.   Source File Name:
sqlchaining\sqlprereqpackagemutator.cpp
Compiler Timestamp: Tue Aug  9 01:14:20 2008
      Function Name: sqls::SqlPreReqPackageMutator::modifyRequest
Source Line Number: 196

---- Context ---------------------------------------------
sqls::InstallPackageAction::perform

WinException caught while installing package. : 1603
      Error Code: 0x80070643 (1603)
Windows Error Text: Fatal error during installation.   Source File Name:
packageengine\installpackageaction.cpp
Compiler Timestamp: Fri Jul  1 01:28:25 2008
      Function Name: sqls::InstallPackageAction::perform
Source Line Number: 167

---- Context ---------------------------------------------
sqls::InstallPackageAction::perform
```

When you install from a network share, you must copy the contents of the two SQL Server install CDs to fileshares. There should be a share named *Servers*, which contains CD#1, and a share called *Tools*, which contains the contents for CD#2. These CDs are not marked clearly, and you may not copy CD#2 to the Tools share. The error we just showed you occurs as a result of this failure. Both of these fileshares should be under the same parent. Once you have copied CD#2 to the Tools folder, start setup again.

Admin Tools Not Installed by Default on Remote Cluster Nodes

To fix this, you must rerun setup on each of the secondary nodes to get the admin tool installed everywhere. Cluster installation is covered in Chapter 20.

Minimum Configuration Warning

SQL Server can install and run with the advertised 512MB RAM minimum, but it needs approximately 768MB of virtual memory. In other words, setup will fail spectacularly on a machine with just 512MB memory and no swap file. You need to temporarily create a swap file of at least 256MB (or add RAM).

Troubleshooting a Failed Install

SETUP.EXE compresses all the log files for each execution of setup into a single CAB file.

It is possible for setup to fail prior to creating the CAB file. If this is the case, the files will still exist singly.

The CAB files will be in the following directory:

```
"%ProgramFiles%\Microsoft SQL Server\100\Setup Bootstrap\LOG\Files
```

The format of the CAB file name is as follows:

```
SQLSetup[XXXX]_[Machine]_logs.CAB
```

The XXXX in the file name is a number incremented each time setup is run. You will be looking for the most recent CAB file. If setup fails, here are the initial troubleshooting steps PSS recommends:

1. The first and best place to get information is via the Web. Google for the error number. In addition, go specifically to the Microsoft Knowledge Base and search for the error number there.

2. The setup installs the components, each in its own MSI. The status of each of these installations is included in the Summary.txt file. Get it from the most recent SQLSetup[XXXX]_[Machine]_logs.cab. Each of the component installs should have a summary that looks like the following:

```
-----------------------------------------------------------------
Machine        : AMDF2002
Product        : Microsoft SQL Server 2008 Data Transformation Services
```

```
Product Version: 10.00.xxxx
Install        : Successful
Log File       : D:\Program Files\Microsoft SQL Server\100\Setup
Bootstrap\LOG\Files\SQLSetup0003_AMDF2002_DTS.log
-----------------------------------------------------------------
```

3. You are looking for the first MSI install that failed. Search for `Install: Failed`. The error number and message here may be sufficient to identify the cause of the failure. Use the error number and message you find to search for a resolution. If you need additional details, use the log file named in the summary. Look in this file for the component that failed. For the preceding summary, the log file is `SQLSetup0003_AMDF2002_DTS.log`. Search for `Return Value 3` in the Windows Installer log. The message you are looking for is usually just above this message, the first time it occurs.

4. If the `Summary.txt` file does not exist or does not have a failed component, check the datastore dump file (`SQLSetup[XXXX]_[Machine]_Datastore.XML`). It may have more error details. You are looking for `SetupStateScope`. The error information, identified as `Watson*` properties, should be in this node.

5. The next place to check is the Core(Local) and Core(Patched) log. The file name for this log is `SQLSetup0001_>srvr>_Core(Local).log`. Search it for errors. You are in the neighborhood where PSS will likely need to assist with the interpretation.

6. Is this a cluster install? If so, search the Task Scheduler log on the failing node. The filename is `%WINDIR%\Tasks\SchedLgU.TXT`. Look for `TaskScheduler` error references. In a clustered SQL Server 2008 setup, the Task Scheduler service is used to launch setup on the remote nodes. To help you find this log, go to Control Panel ⇨ Scheduled Tasks, and then select View Log under the Advanced drop-down menu. This will open the log in Notepad, and you can select File ⇨ Save As to keep a copy. Look for `Access Denied` errors in the log. These indicate a known Windows bug. As a workaround to the `Access Denied` bug, log off any active sessions on the remote node before running setup again.

7. Of course, search the Knowledge Base for any errors you discover in these logs.

If you call PSS with a setup issue, they'll want that CAB file (plus other system logs).

Summary

Installing SQL Server is generally quite easy. Ensure that you are using an enterprise-compatible collation and that you have chosen appropriate service accounts. Remember that SQL Server is secure by default. This means that you have to turn on the security features by using Management Studio, SQL Server Configuration Manager, or policies such as Database Mail. If you will be upgrading, there is some good advice coming up in Chapter 3.

3

Upgrading SQL Server 2008 Best Practices

Chapter 2 covers performing a new installation of SQL Server 2008. In this chapter, we discuss upgrading SQL Server from a previous version. First, we cover reasons for upgrading to SQL Server 2008. We then discuss the pros and cons of various upgrade strategies, and you learn about the various tools available to help mitigate risk during the upgrade process. We discuss SQL Server 2008 behavior changes and discontinued features that you need to know about before upgrading. To wrap up, we explain how to use the new Policy-Based Management that can be used to enable and disable features and functionality. By the end of the chapter, you will have learned everything you need to know in order to perform a successful upgrade to SQL Server 2008.

Why Upgrade to SQL Server 2008?

With the release of SQL Server 2008, Microsoft enhanced numerous features in the areas of scalability, reliability, availability, and security. Among the many benefits that these new features and capabilities provide are the following:

❑   Lower IT costs through improved scalability enhancements.

❑   High availability options that include data mirroring with compression and automatic page repair.

❑   Reduced SQL Server management with the Policy-Based Management.

❑   Better online database operation support.

❑   Improved manageability for larger databases.

❑   Stronger security with auditing and encryption.

❑   Accelerated deployment of line-of-business applications.

❑   Advanced business intelligence solutions for faster decision making.

As you'll see throughout this book, significant enhancements have been introduced throughout the product. During the development cycle, there were four pillars of focus for the product: dynamic development, beyond relational, pervasive insight, and enterprise data platform. For the database administrator, the enterprise data platform pillar had the following goals:

❑   **Availability and security advancements:** Enhanced high-availability options include database mirroring, server clustering, peer-to-peer replication, fine-grained online repairs, dynamic management views, backup and restore, data auditing, pluggable CPU, and many other improvements in the areas of online operations. These features ensure that SQL Server 2008 is available for your enterprise. Also, the SQL Server 2008 security initiative included enhancements, such as support for transparent data encryption, password-policy enforcement, fine-grained security control, user-schema separation, and improved auditing capabilities.

❑   **Continued focus on manageability:** SQL Server Management Studio is the integrated management toolset for relational and business intelligence technologies. This toolset is based on the Visual Studio 2008 Integrated Development Environment (IDE), which enables enhanced collaboration capabilities through the use of projects for storing code such as stored procedures. SQL Server 2008 also enhanced its ability to self-optimize and load balance its workload across processors. The dynamic management view (DMV), along with support for dedicated admin connection (DAC), ensures that administrators can get the information that they need to manage their environment under any conditions. More-over, SQL Server 2008 introduces Policy-Based Management, a policy-based architecture that enables DBAs to describe, monitor, and enforce desired system configurations.

❑   **Performance and scalability:** Performance and scalability enhancements have been intro-duced through technologies, such as parallel query table partitions, data compression, backup compression, query optimization modes, Resource Governor, snapshot isolation, and support for dynamic Address Windowing Extensions (AWE) memory. Enhancements in the area of buffer-pool management also ensure that the right data is in the data cache. SQLOS is the improved abstraction layer that provides SQL Server 2008 with the ability to scale, including thread scheduling, memory management, and I/O management on any technology platform. This capability empowers you with the technical and business flexi-bility to solve unique problems in a way that will best meet your needs.

Risk Mitigation — The Microsoft Contribution

As with all previous versions of SQL Server, the SQL team took extraordinary steps to ensure that the quality of SQL Server 2008 was as high-grade as possible. The specific steps of the software engineering cycle are beyond the scope of this book, but we highlight a few points here, consid-ered public knowledge, about the daily build process. We also touch on a few points about how *Trustworthy Computing* improves this process. Ever since the January 2002 memo from Bill Gates on Trustworthy Computing, security procedures have been incorporated into every software develop-ment process.

Today, a daily process produces x86, x64, and Itanium versions of SQL Server 2008 code (called *builds*) that have gone through a battery of tests. This process is utilized for both the development of new releases and the development of service packs for SQL Server 2008. These tests are a convergence of in-house build tests, customer-captured workloads, and Trustworthy Computing processes. Microsoft Research worked on bringing innovations to Microsoft's products. For example, on the SQL Server 2008 release, these innovations were in the areas of data compression and transparent data encryption enhancements. In the areas of software development, the Microsoft Research team is an essential contributor to the software engineering and testing processes. They improve the test harness with enhancements in several areas, including threat modeling, testing efficiencies, and penetration analysis.

In addition, many customer-captured workloads are also part of the software testing harness. These workloads are acquired through an assortment of programs such as the Customer Playback program and various lab engagements, including SQL Server 2008 compatibility labs.

The daily builds are tested against this gathered information, and out of this process come performance metrics, security metrics, and bugs. Bugs are subsequently filed, assigned, prioritized, and tracked until resolution. Once a bug has been fixed, its code goes through security testing as part of the software-engineering process. This happens before the code is checked back into the software tree for the next testing cycle.

Independent Software Vendors and SQL Community Contributions

Starting with SQL Server 2005 and continuing with SQL Server 2008, the concept of community technology preview (CTP) was adopted. The December 2004 CTP (2004) was the first of seven such releases. The decision to adopt this snapshot in time of code (or build) resulted in over 326,000 CTP downloads, providing unprecedented access to updated code to both independent software vendor (ISV) and SQL community testing. This type of access to beta code was leveraged as a means of identifying additional bugs, conducting additional testing of software fixes, and driving additional improvements based on community feedback.

Upgrading to SQL Server 2008

The installation guidelines are covered in Chapter 2, so we focus this section mainly on upgrade strategies and considerations for the SQL Server 2008 database component.

A smooth upgrade requires a good plan. When you devise an upgrade plan, you need to break down the upgrade process into individual tasks. This plan should have sections for pre-upgrade tasks, upgrade tasks, and post-upgrade tasks:

❑   Your *pre-upgrade tasks* should take into consideration SQL Server 2008 minimum hardware and software requirements. You should have an inventory of your applications that access the server, database-collation requirements, server dependencies, and legacy-systems requirements such as data-access methods. Your list should include database consistency checks and backup of all databases. Plans should be in place for testing the upgrade process and applications. You should have a thorough understanding of backward-compatibility issues and have workarounds or fixes identified. You should also use the SQL Server 2008 Upgrade Advisor, as described later in this chapter, to assist in identifying and resolving these issues.

❑ The *upgrade execution process* should be a smooth execution of your well-documented and rehearsed plan. To reiterate the importance of this step, make sure you make a backup of all the databases before you execute the upgrade process.

❑ *Post-upgrade tasks* should consist of reviewing the upgrade process, bringing the systems back online, monitoring, and testing the system. Specific database maintenance will also need to be performed before releasing the system to the user community. These and other recommended steps are outlined later in the chapter. We recommend that you run your database in backward-compatibility mode after the upgrade to minimize the amount of change to your environment. The database-compatibility mode should be updated as part of a follow-up upgrade process along with enabling new SQL Server 2008 features.

As part of deciding your upgrade strategy, we will discuss both the in-place (upgrade) and side-by-side migration methods for upgrading.

In-Place Upgrading

The in-place server upgrade is the easier of the two options. This is an all-or-nothing approach to upgrading, meaning that once the upgrade is initiated, there is no simple rollback procedure. This type of upgrade has the added requirement of greater upfront testing to avoid using a complex back-out plan. The benefit of this approach is that you don't have to worry about users and logins remaining in sync, and database connectivity changes will not be required for applications. In addition, SQL Server Agent jobs will be upgraded during the upgrade process.

Here's a high-level scenario of an in-place upgrade based on Figure 3-1. First, install the prerequisite files on your system. Before upgrading to SQL Server 2008, your server needs, at a minimum, .NET Framework 2.0, SQL Server 2000 with Service Pack 4, or SQL Server 2005 with Service Pack 2. The next step is to run the System Configuration Checker (SCC). The SCC examines the destination computer for conditions that would prevent an upgrade from completing, such as not meeting the minimum hardware or software requirements. If such a condition is found, setup will be aborted and the SQL Server 2008 components will be uninstalled. Once verified, the SQL Server setup program is able to lay the 2008 bits and backward-compatibility support files on disk while SQL Server 2005 (or 2000) is still available to users. However, planning to upgrade a server while users are online is not recommended. The setup program takes the server offline by stopping the existing SQL Server services. The 2008-based services assume control of the master database and the server identity. At this point, the SQL Server service takes over the databases and begins to update them while not allowing users back into the environment. When a request for data occurs in a database that has only been partially updated, the data associated with this request is updated, processed, and then returned to the user. The next step is to kick off the uninstall procedure for the old binaries. This step occurs only if no remaining SQL Server 2005 or 2000 instances are on the server. Finally, SQL Server Agent jobs are upgraded.

If you would like to change editions as a part of your upgrade, there are some limitations that you must be aware of. SQL Server 2005 Enterprise, Developer, Standard, and Workgroup editions can be upgraded to different editions of SQL Server 2008. SQL Server 2005 Express Editions can only be upgraded to the

Express edition of SQL Server 2008. If this is of interest to you, see SQL Server 2008 Books Online (BOL) for the topic "Version and Edition Upgrades," under the section "Upgrading to SQL Server 2008."

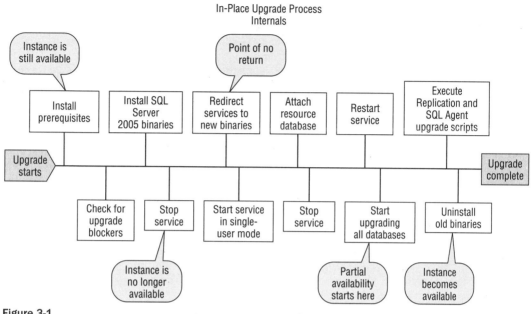

Figure 3-1

Side-by-Side Upgrade

In a side-by-side upgrade, SQL Server 2008 is installed either along with SQL Server 2005 (or 2000) as a separate instance or on a different server. You may want to select this option as part of a hardware refresh or migration to a new platform, such as Itanium or x64. Because of the backup and restore times involved in a back-out scenario, if you have a sizable database, this is definitely the option to go with.

As part of this method, you can simply back up the databases from the original server and then restore them to the SQL Server 2008 instance. Another option is to manually detach your database from the old instance and reattach it to the new instance. You can also leverage the Copy Database Wizard to migrate your databases to the new server. Although this approach provides for the best recovery scenario, it has additional requirements beyond those of the in-place upgrade, such as maintaining the original server name, caring for application connectivity, and keeping users and their logins in sync. If SQL Profiler traces are part of your upgrade testing, maintaining the database IDs is also important.

In-Place Upgrade versus Side-By-Side Upgrade Considerations

The following table shows a summary of the two upgrade methods:

Process	In-Place Upgrade	Side-by-Side Upgrade
Number of resulting instances	One	Two
Number of SQL Servers involved	One	More than one
Data file transfer	Automatic	Manual
SQL Server instance configuration	Automatic	Manual
Supporting upgrade utility	SQL Server setup	Various migration and data transfer methods

You should consider numerous factors before selecting an upgrade strategy. Your strategy should include the need for component-level upgrade, the ability to roll back in case of failure, the size of your databases, and the need for partial upgrade. For many of you, top priorities will be whether you will be able to upgrade to new hardware, facilitate a change of strategy such as a server consolidation, and manage a small server outage window for the upgrade.

Side-By-Side Upgrades

The arguments in favor of a side-by-side upgrade are as follows:

❑ More granular control over upgrade component-level process (database, Analysis Services, and others).

❑ Ability to run SQL Servers side-by-side for testing and verification.

❑ Ability to gather real matrix for upgrade (outage window).

❑ Rollback strategy as original server is still intact.

❑ Ability to upgrade platforms from a 32-bit to 64-bit server.

❑ Best for very large databases, as restore time could be sizable.

The arguments against a side-by-side upgrade are as follows:

❑ Additional hardware may be required for instance upgrade or additional physical server for physical server upgrade.

❑ Does not preserve SQL Server 2005 (or 2000) functionality.

❑ Issue of instance name for connecting applications.

Space requirement on the Storage Area Network (SAN), Especially for Every In-Place Upgrades

The advantages of an in-place upgrade are as follows:

❑ Fast, easy, and automated (best for small systems).

❑ No additional hardware required.

❑ Applications retain same instance name.

❑ Preserves SQL Server 2005 (or 2000) functionality automatically.

The disadvantages of an in-place upgrade are as follows:

❑   Downtime incurred because the entire server is offline during upgrade.

❑   No support for component-level upgrades.

❑   Complex rollback strategy.

❑   Backward-compatibility issues must be addressed for that SQL instance.

❑   In-place upgrade is not supported for all SQL Server components.

❑   Very large databases require substantial rollback time.

Pre-Upgrade Checks

To ensure that you have a successful upgrade to SQL Server 2008, here are a few housekeeping tips. Ensure that all system databases are configured to autogrow and that they have adequate hard-disk space. Make certain that all startup stored procedures are disabled, as the upgrade process will stop and start services on the SQL Server instance being upgraded. Now that you understand the strategies for upgrading to SQL Server 2008, it's time to look at the upgrade tools available to assist in this process.

SQL Server Upgrade Advisor

If you want to take advantage of the lessons other SQL Server users have already learned about upgrading, the SQL Server 2008 Upgrade Advisor is the tool for you. This tool is based on early adopters' feedback and internal lab-testing feedback. The SQL Server 2008 Upgrade Advisor is a free download available as part of the Microsoft SQL Server 2008 Feature Pack at `www.microsoft.com/downloads/details.aspx?FamilyId=C6C3E9EF-BA29-4A43-8D69-A2BED18FE73C` and is also available as part of the SQL Server 2008 installation media for all editions. The purpose of this tool is to identify known upgrade issues and provide guidance for workarounds or fixes for the identified issues on a per-server components' basis. Microsoft worked hard on this tool as a risk-mitigation effort to empower SQL Server 2005 and SQL Server 2000 users to upgrade to SQL Server 2008. So, whether you are running Analysis Services, Integration Services, DTS packages, Notification Services, Analysis Services, Reporting Services components, or a combination of components, the Upgrade Advisor tool can help.

Installing the SQL Server 2008 Upgrade Advisor

The Upgrade Advisor is a relatively simple tool to use. It can be found in the "Prepare" section of the default screen of the installation CD/DVD. It can also be found at `www.microsoft.com/sql`. Select the download section on the left side of the page, and then select SQL Server 2008. The Welcome screen for the Upgrade Advisor is shown in Figure 3-2. Be sure to select "Check for updates," as upgraded versions of this tool are available online.

The tool is constantly being updated to reflect the lessons learned by the DBAs who updated before you. Although the `SQLUASetup.msi` file itself is about 5.6MB, it will require installation of the .NET Framework 2.0, which can be downloaded through the Windows Update service or from MSDN. There are also x64 and Itanium versions of the tool and .NET framework that you can choose to install. Alternately, you can choose to install a single instance and version of the tool to test servers across your enterprise. This option supports a zero-footprint interrogation with read-only access to servers.

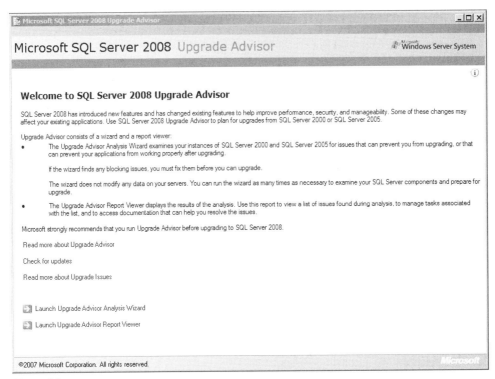

Figure 3-2

This tool is read-intensive and should be tested on a test server to evaluate the potential impact on your systems.

The installation process is straightforward; the only option is to select the location where you would like to install the tool. The default install path is *<your location>*:\Program Files\Microsoft SQL Server 2008 Upgrade Advisor. At the time of this writing, there are four incremental releases of this Upgrade Advisor with a total of 20 additional rules from the original release, for a grand total of 103 rules. These rules represent conditions, situations, or known errors that could affect your upgrade to SQL Server 2008.

Using the Upgrade Advisor

Once installed, the Upgrade Advisor presents you with two choices: Launch the Upgrade Advisor Analysis Wizard or Upgrade Advisor Report Viewer. Launch the Upgrade Advisor Analysis Wizard to run the tool. As shown in Figure 3-3, you simply select a server and the component(s) to analyze for upgrade, or you can click the Detect button, which starts the inspection process that selects the components installed on your system.

After you select the components for testing, the next decision is to select the databases that you would like to have evaluated for upgrade, as shown in Figure 3-4. The best part of this process is that you have the option to analyze SQL Profiler trace and SQL batch files to help make this a comprehensive analysis. That is, by adding these files to the evaluation process, Upgrade Advisor is evaluating not only the database but its trace workload and SQL scripts as well. All you have to do is select the path to the directory where your trace file(s) or your batch file(s) is located.

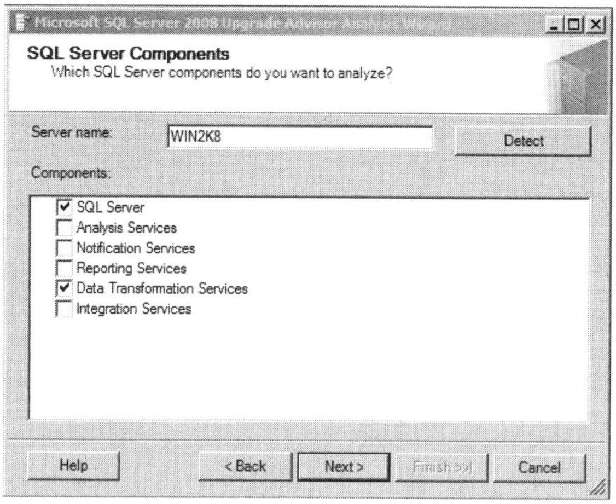

Figure 3-3

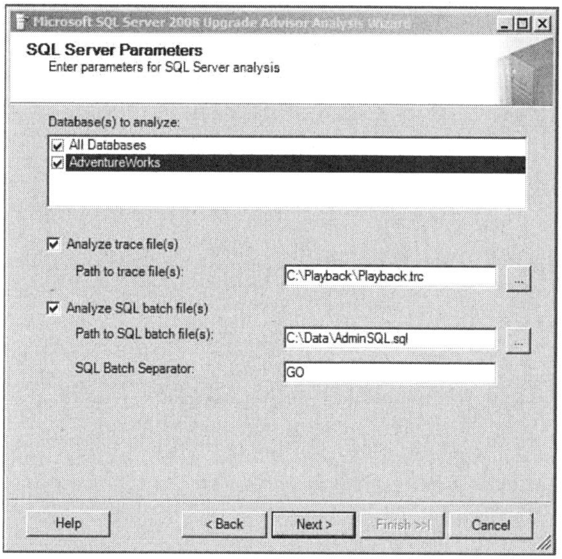

Figure 3-4

After you have completed configuration of the components that you want to evaluate, you will be prompted to begin the analysis. If you have any questions during the configuration steps, the Help button brings up an Upgrade Advisor-specific Book Online (UABOL) that is rich in information and guides you through the options. As the component-level analysis completes, a green, yellow, or red dialog box will indicate the outcome of the test.

Once the test is completed, you can view the discovered issues via the Upgrade Advisor Report Viewer. The reports themselves, as shown in Figure 3-5, are presented in an interface similar to a Web browser. The information can be analyzed by filtering the report presented by server, instance or component, or issue type. How to interpret the results of this report is discussed later in this chapter.

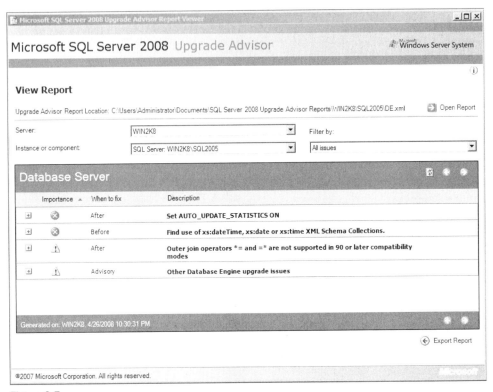

Figure 3-5

Scripting the Upgrade Advisor

If you have a server farm or if you just prefer scripting, a command-line capability is also available. With the `UpgradeAdvisorWizardCmd` utility, you can configure the tool via an XML configuration file and receive results as XML files. The following parameters can be passed to the `UpgradeAdvisorWizardCmd` utility:

❑   Command-line Help

❑   The configuration path and file name

❑   The SQL Server login and password for either SQL Server or Notification Services (if SQL Server authentication is being used, rather than Windows authentication).

❑   An optional flag to indicate whether to output reports in a comma-separated value (CSV) format.

All capabilities and parameters discussed in the wizard section are exposed through the configuration file. The results from a command-style interrogation can still be viewed in the Report Viewer, via XML documents or Excel if you used the CSV option. For example, the following XML document from Upgrade Advisor reflects the choices of analyzing all databases, Analysis Services, and DTS packages on a server named SQL08Demo and an instance named SQL2K5:

```
<Configuration>
  <Server>WIN2K8</Server>
```

```
        <Instance>SQL2005</Instance>
    <Components>
        <SQLServer>
            <Databases>
                <Database>*</Database>
            </Databases>
        </SQLServer>
    </Components>
</Configuration>
```

You can modify the file in an XML editor such as Visual Studio and save the file with a new file name. Then, you can use the new file as input to the command line of Upgrade Advisor. For example, the following displays the command prompt entry required to run the command line of Upgrade Advisor using Windows authentication. The configuration file already contains names for a remote server named SQL08Demo and an instance named SQL2K5, and the PATH environment variable contains the path to the Upgrade Wizard:

```
    C:\>UpgradeAdvisorWizardCmd -ConfigFile "SQL2K5Config.xml"
```

You can also install or remove the Upgrade Advisor application via the command prompt. From there you can control the install process with or without the UI. You can also configure the install path and process-logging options.

For more information on the Upgrade Advisor's configuration files, see the Upgrade Advisor Help section "UpgradeAdvisorWizardCmd Utility."

Resolving Upgrade Issues

The Upgrade Advisor's report contains a wealth of information. The key is to understand how this information is presented, what needs to be resolved, and when. As you see in Figure 3-5, the first column indicates the importance of a finding or a recommendation, the second column tells you when it needs to be addressed, and the Description column tells you about the issue. The recommended way to approach this analysis is to first categorize the information by "Importance" and "When to fix" the items. Specifically, the sum of the indicators should dictate whether issues should be addressed before or after the upgrade process. The following table provides our recommendations of when to address these issues.

Importance	When to Fix	Our Recommendation
Red	Before	Resolve Before Upgrade
Red	Anytime	Resolve Before Upgrade
Red	After	Resolve After Upgrade
Yellow	Anytime	Resolve After Upgrade
Yellow	After	Resolve After Upgrade
Yellow	Advisory	Resolve After Upgrade

Issues that have been flagged with an "Importance" of "Red," and "When to Fix" of "Before" or "Anytime" should be addressed before an upgrade process. Typically, these issues require remediation because of SQL Server 2008 functionality changes. The remaining issues can usually be resolved after the upgrade process because they either have a workaround within the upgrade process or will not affect it at all.

If you expand the error in question, additional information appears, as shown in Figure 3-6.

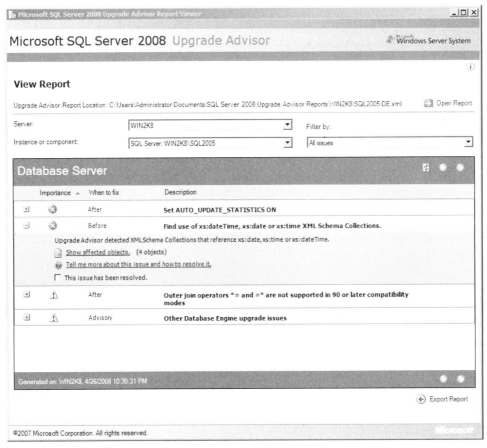

Figure 3-6

The "Show affected objects" link shows the exact objects flagged by the Upgrade Advisor process as affected, while the "Tell me more about this issue and how to resolve it" link takes you to the corresponding section of the Upgrade Advisor Books Online (UABOL). The UABOL describes the conditions and provides guidance regarding corrective action to address the issue. The UABOL is a true gem, as it provides guidance for problem resolution in areas beyond the scope of the tools (such as replication, SQL Server Agent, and Full-Text Search).

The "This issue has been resolved" checkmark is for your personal tracking of the issues that have been resolved. This metadata checkmark is in place to support remediation processes by allowing the report to be viewed by filtered status of resolved issues or pre-upgrade (unresolved) issues.

If you then prefer command line scripting, the viewer is nothing more than an XSLT transformation applied to the XML result file located in your My Documents\SQL Server 2008 Upgrade Advisor Reports\ directory. Individual component results and configuration files can be found in each server's name-based directories. You can even export viewer-based reports to other output formats such as CSV or text.

SQL Server 2008 Upgrade Assistant

If you feel comfortable with the content we have covered so far, feel free to skip to the "Post-Upgrade Checks" section of this chapter. In this section, we discuss a tool that offers a more detailed upgrade analysis, the SQL Server 2008 Upgrade Assistant (SSUA).

SQL Server Upgrade Assistant was first developed for use in the SQL Server 2005 application-compatibility lab engagements run as part of the Microsoft Ascend (SQL 2005 customer training) and Touchdown (SQL 2005 partner training) programs. The purpose of these labs was to help customers analyze their SQL Server 2000 or (7.0) applications to understand the impact of upgrading to SQL Server 2005 and to provide guidance on any changes that may be necessary to successfully migrate both their database and their application. The labs helped improve the quality of SQL Server 2005 by running upgrades and performing impact analysis on real customer workloads against SQL Server 2005. The labs themselves were run by Microsoft personnel and staffed by partners such as Scalability Experts. Nearly 50 labs were run worldwide, and hundreds of SQL Server 2000 applications were tested using this tool. A new version of SSUA was developed specifically for SQL Server 2008; you can download it free from www.scalabilityexperts.com/default.asp?action=article&ID=43.

From a conceptual standpoint, the difference between this tool and Upgrade Advisor is that SSUA naturally encompasses the essence of a true upgrade and testing methodology. By reviewing the results of a SQL Server 2005 (or 2000) workload against the results of the same workload being run against SQL Server 2008, you can identify upgrade blockers and application-coding changes that may be required. For SQL Server 2008, the SSUA tool supports upgrading from SQL Server 2005 and 2000.

We will walk you through an overview of this process and then provide details of the steps contained in the SSUA, which you can see in Figure 3-7. By using the SSUA, you will back up all databases and the users and capture a subset of production workload. You will then restore the databases and users you just backed up and process the workload you captured. The goal of this is to develop a new output file, also known as a *baseline*. You will then upgrade the test server to SQL Server 2008 and rerun the workload to capture a SQL Server 2008 reference output for comparison.

Capturing the Environment

You should establish your baseline by running DBCC CheckDB on each database and by backing up all SQL Server 2005 (or 2000) systems and user databases from your server. Following this step, you need to start capturing your trace file to avoid gaps in the process. When you capture a trace file, it needs to be a good representation of the workloads that characterize your environment. To do this, it might be necessary to create an artificial workload that better represents the workloads of the application over time. While capturing the trace file, it's a good idea to avoid multi-server operations such as linked server calls or bulk-copy operation dependencies. Be aware that there is a performance cost of 6 to 10 percent while tracing. The sum of the trace files and database backups represent a repeatable and reusable workload called a *playback*.

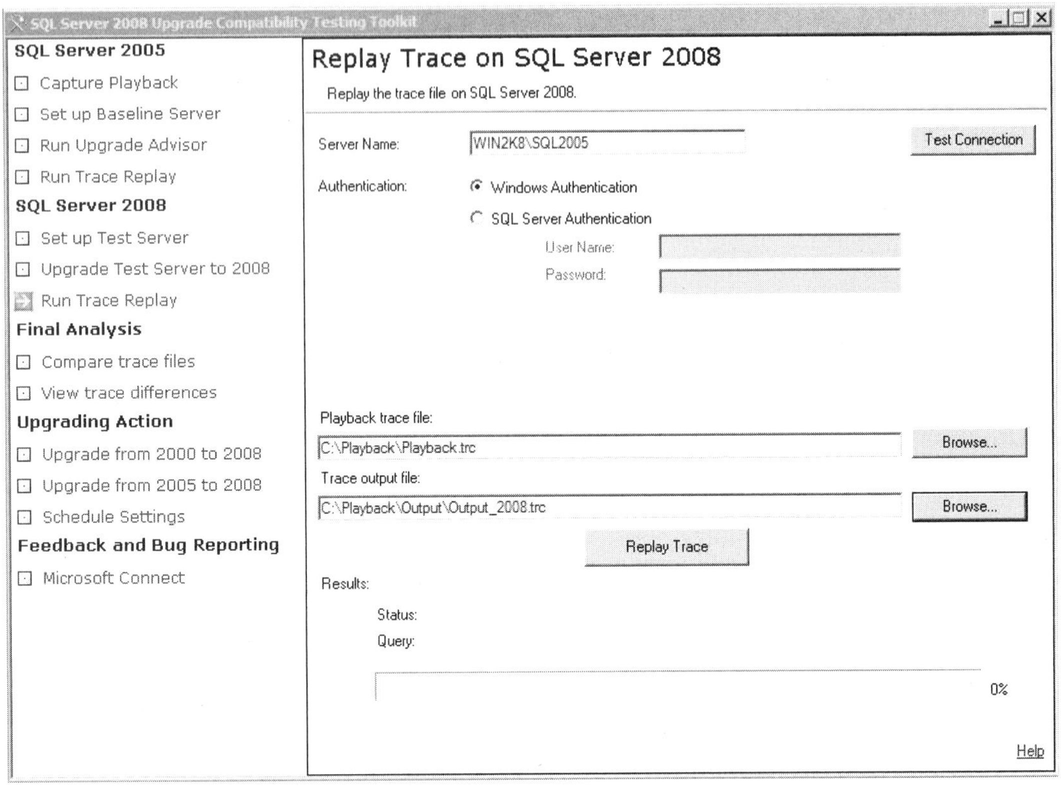

Figure 3-7

Setting Up the Baseline Server

Now that you have captured the playback, you can set up the baseline system that will be used for the remainder of the test. This server should be loaded with SQL Server 2005 SP2 (or 2000 SP4), with the minimum requirement for upgrading to 2008. In reality, it should be identical to the source system in collation and patching level. The tool will then check your server for this matching. If necessary, you will be prompted to patch or rebuild the master database. It will then restore your databases in the correct order so that your DB IDs are matched to production (this also includes padding the DB creation process to accomplish this). Finally, SSUA will recreate your logins and ensure that the IDs match production, as all of this is necessary to run the trace file. The next step in the process is to run the Upgrade Advisor as described earlier in this chapter. Once the environment has been remediated, you can then proceed to the next step of replaying the trace.

Running the SQL Profiler Trace

When you run the trace, first the statistics will be updated on all databases. The replay tool then uses the API and runs all of the queries within the trace file in order. The thing to keep in mind with this tool is that it is single-threaded replay, but it's possible that blocking can occur. If the trace appears to run very slowly or stop, you may want to check on SQL Server blocking; and if it does not clear up by itself, you will need to kill the blocking processes. The output from this step generates a trace-output file for comparison in the final analysis.

Upgrading to SQL Server 2008

Now you are ready to upgrade to SQL Server 2008. You have two options. You can use SSUA to restore the state of the SQL Server 2005 (or 2000) to its baseline and then upgrade in-place to SQL Server 2008, or you can migrate the SQL 2005 (or 2000) databases to an existing SQL Server 2008 instance. The thing to remember here is that you are not measuring performance metrics, so these servers don't have to be identical. You are measuring workload behavior between two versions of SQL Server. After restoring the baseline on a SQL Server 2008 platform, you will go through the "Running the SQL Profiler Trace" step again but this time on SQL Server 2008. The output from this step generates the other trace-output file for comparison in the final analysis.

Final Analysis

After completing all of these processes, you can get to the final steps of comparing the output files by filtering and comparing all batches in both trace files for discrepancies. The Report Viewer shows one error condition at a time by showing the last correct step, the error step, and the next correct sequences of the batch files. Once a condition has been identified, it can be filtered from the error-reviewing process to enable the DBA to focus on identifying new error conditions. After the SQL Server 2008 upgrade is completed, change the database compatibility mode to 10 and run your application to validate that it works in SQL Server 2008 compatibility mode. This ensures that there are no application behavior differences when your application is running on the database compatibility mode of 10.

Backward Compatibility

This section covers major product changes, classified in one of three categories: unsupported, discontinued, or affecting the way SQL Server 2000 or 2005 behaves today. Although the Upgrade Advisor tool will highlight these conditions if they are relevant to your environment, you should read this section to familiarize yourself with these changes.

Unsupported and Discontinued Features

From time to time, to move a technology forward, trade-offs have to be made. From SQL 2000 to SQL 2005 to SQL Server 2008, the following features are no longer available:

- ❑ English Query is no longer included; don't look for it on your installation media.
- ❑ `isql.exe` and `rbuildm.exe` are no longer present. You will have to use `sqlcmd.exe` and `setup.exe` instead if you need to rebuild the master database or the registry.
- ❑ The Northwind and Pubs databases have been replaced by the AdventureWorks2008 and AdventureWorksDW2008 databases. These new sample databases are intended to be more like real-life databases. If you want Northwind or Pubs sample databases, they are available at `www.microsoft.com/downloads/details.aspx?familyid=06616212-0356-46a0-8da2-eebc53a68034`.
- ❑ The allow updates option of `sp_configure` is still present but not functional.
- ❑ The metadata component of SQL Server 2000 DTS repository is deprecated as a feature. As part of the upgrade, the DTS packages will be migrated to the file system, and the specific tables will be present in `msdb` after upgrade.

- ❏ SQL Server Surface Area Configuration is no longer available. This functionality is primarily supported by the Policy-Based Management covered later in this chapter.

- ❏ Notification Services is no longer available.

SQL Server 2008 Deprecated Database Features

These features are no longer available as of the SQL Server 2008 release or the next scheduled release of the product. The following are some of the features scheduled for deprecation; it is recommended that you try to replace these features over time with the recommended items:

- ❏ Use `Backup Database` and `Restore Database` instead of the `Dump Database` or `Dump Transaction` and `Load Database` or `Load Transaction` (`Load Headeronly`) statements. These statements are available today for backward compatibility only.

- ❏ In the area of security, use "Execute As" instead of `SETUSER` in statements. `SETUSER` statements are available today for backward compatibility. The following stored procedures are also scheduled for deprecation: `sp_addalias`, `sp_dropalias`, `sp_addgroup`, `sp_changegroup`, `sp_dropgroup`, and `sp_helpgroup`. It is recommended that you familiarize yourself with the new security model and leverage role-based security.

- ❏ For a very long time, Microsoft has advised not to use system tables, as they are subject to change. With this release, most known (documented or undocumented) system tables have been omitted. References to a few popular system tables have been preserved through the use of views such as `sysusers` (`sys.sysusers`). The remainder, including `syslocks`, have been discontinued. Therefore, the instruction `Select * from syslocks` will return the following results:

  ```
  Msg 208, Level16, Stat 1, Line 1
  Invalid object name 'syslocks'.
  ```

  Refer to the SQL Server 2008 Books Online section "Querying the SQL Server System Catalog" for information on accessing the system tables through the catalog views.

Other SQL Server 2008 Changes Affecting Behavior

The behavior changes in these features could adversely affect migration to SQL Server 2008:

- ❏ Ensure that you have set `AUTO_UPDATE_STATISTICS ON` before you upgrade any databases. Otherwise, the database statistics will not be updated as part of the upgrade to SQL Server 2008. This will most likely cause suboptimal query plans.

- ❏ Unlike the SQL Server 2000 behavior, the max server memory option in SQL Server 2008 will not take advantage of the available memory beyond its limit. If your setting is too low, you will simply get an "insufficient system memory" error. This will happen despite memory availability beyond the max server memory setting.

- ❏ In SQL Server 2008, the query governor cost limit option works by setting it to a value other than 0 means that you have enabled a server-wide query timeout value measured in seconds.

- ❏ SQL Server 2008 does not support Banyan VINES, Multiprotocol, AppleTalk, or NWLink IPX/SPX. MDAC versions 2.6 or earlier are not supported, because they do not support named instances.

❑   SQL Server 2008 does not support the creation or upgrade of databases on compressed drives. Once updated, read-only databases or filegroups can be placed on NTFS compressed drives. They must, however, be set to READ_WRITE permission prior to going through the upgrade process.

With the exception of the Model database, after the upgrade process, all databases remain in backward-compatibility mode.

❑   Additional space will be required for data and log files; to maintain user objects and permissions; and for metadata information for LOB objects on a column basis. If your database also contains full-text catalog, additional space is needed in order for the full-text document ID map to be stored in the data file.

Set database log and data files to autogrow *during the upgrade process.*

❑   Before upgrading to SQL Server 2008, use the sp_dropextendedproc and sp_addextendedproc stored procedures to reregister any extended stored procedure that was not registered with full pathname.

❑   It is a good idea to allocate additional space or to have plenty of space for tempdb to grow during the upgrade process. Overall guidance for tempdb is covered in greater detail in Chapter 14.

tempdb *is responsible for managing temporary objects, row versioning, and online index rebuilds.*

❑   Disable all trace flags before upgrading to SQL Server 2008. The possibility exists that the trace-flag functionality either will be different in SQL server 2008 or will not exist. After the upgrade process, you should work with Microsoft Support to determine which (if any) of your trace flags are still required.

In SQL Server 2008, trace flags are now deterministic and can be set at the local or global level based on additional arguments (the default behavior is local).

❑   Migrate to database mail. If you happen to like SQL mail, the good news is that as long as you have Outlook 2002 (or greater) as a mail client, you will be able to upgrade to SQL Server 2008.

SQL Server 2008 database mail does not have a requirement for the Outlook mail client.

For additional behavior changes, see SQL Server 2008 Books Online.

SQL Server Component Considerations

In this section, we discuss individual components, along with any respective considerations that should be evaluated during an upgrade process. Components not covered here are covered in their respective chapters.

Upgrading Full-Text Catalog to SQL Server 2008

During the upgrade process, all databases with Full-Text Catalog are marked Full-Text disabled. This is because of the potential time involved in rebuilding the catalog. Before you upgrade your Full-Text Search environment, you should familiarize yourself with some of the enhancements. In the area of manageability and scalability, Full-Text Search has been integrated into each SQL Server 2008 instance. Full-Text Search now supports XML data types, XML indexes, and XML queries. Full-Text Catalogs are now a fully integrated part of the database backup and restore process. This functionality is also supported in the database attach and detach processes. I also recommend reading SQL Server 2008 Books Online to learn about additional behavior changes (for example, running the Full-Text action against `master` and `tempdb` is no longer supported).

Upgrading Reporting Services

Upgrading to Reporting Services 2008 is supported from Reporting Services 2005 SP2 and Reporting Services 2000 SP2. Reporting Services 2008 will support a Report database on SQL Server 2008 or SQL Server 2005, but not on SQL Server 2000. Moreover, Reporting Services 2008 no longer requires IIS. Prior to upgrading, run the SQL Server 2008 Upgrade Advisor and follow its recommendations, guidance on possible mitigation options, and steps. Then, before executing the upgrade, back up the database, applications, configurations files, and the encryption key.

There are two ways to upgrade Reporting Services:

❑ **In-place upgrade:** This can be accomplished by executing the SQL Server 2008 `setup.exe`; select the older Reporting Services, and it will be upgraded with Reporting Services 2008. This has the same advantages and disadvantages described earlier with in-place upgrade. The risk with this is that it is an all-or-nothing approach, difficult to roll back except by reinstalling it again.

❑ **Side-by-side upgrade:** With this option, the Reporting Services 2008 instance is installed in the same physical server along with the older version of Reporting Services or on a separate physical server. After the Reporting Services 2008 instance is installed, the report content is migrated either individually or in bulk, using one of the following options: Redeploy the reports using SQL Server 2008 Business Intelligence Development Studio; use `rs.exe` to extract and deploy the reports; or use Report Manager. Reports from SQL Server 2000, SP1, SP2, and SQL Server 2005, SP1, and SP2 are supported.

Published reports and snapshot reports, as well as Dundas-supported reports without any custom code, will be upgraded. After upgrading Reporting Services 2008, redeploy any custom extensions and assemblies, test the applications on Reporting Services 2008 after it is fully operational, and then remove any unused applications and tools from the previous version.

Upgrading Analysis Services

Analysis Services 2000 and 2005 can be upgraded either in-place or side-by-side to Analysis Services 2008, with the same advantages and disadvantages discussed earlier. There are customers who have upgraded or migrated from Analysis Services 2000 to either 2005 or 2008 as is and are pleased with performance. However, because Analysis Services has been significantly redesigned from the 2000 version, we recommend that you redesign your Analysis Services 2000 cubes to take advantage of Analysis Services 2008, as it includes many features and performance enhancements that a simple migration or upgrade will not take full advantage of:

❑ Data Source Views encapsulates schema metadata and enables logically defining relationships among tables and named calculations.

❑ Dimensions are based on more flexible attribute hierarchies.

❑ Cubes support perspectives, measure groups, report actions, KPI, parent-child, multiple fact tables, translations, and proactive caching.

The Analysis Services 2008 Migration Wizard will do its "best attempt" to redesign an Analysis Services 2000 database to the new features. Often, the Migration Wizard is used to first migrate a database to Analysis Services 2008, and the database is redesigned afterwards. Both in-place and side-by-side upgrade use the database Migration Wizard, shown in Figure 3-8. You can execute the wizard manually from the command line by using `migrationwizard.exe`, or access it from SQL Server 2008 Management Studio by right-clicking Analysis Services and choosing Migrate Database from the drop-down menu. An Analysis Services 2005 database will upgrade directly to Analysis Services 2008.

Figure 3-8

Upgrading DTS to SQL Server 2008 Integration Services (SSIS)

This section focuses on the challenges of DTS 2000 packages. First, understand that SSIS is a new ETL tool. Other than in a few areas for the purpose of backward compatibility, most DTS code has no direct equivalence to SSIS. As part of an upgrade scenario, DTS will continue to run as is using `dtsrun.exe`, included in the SQL Server 2008 installation media. SQL Server 2000 runtime and backward-compatibility tools can be installed to facilitate this as a part of an upgrade process. If you are doing an install on new hardware, you can get the DTS Designer Components (2000 runtime) or backward-compatibility components from the SQL Server 2008 download site (Feature Pack). The DTS Designer Components enable developers and DBAs to manage and edit DTS packages and components in a SQL Server 2008 environment. The SQL Server Backward Compatibility package includes all of the DTS Designer Components and additional support for SQL-DMO, DSO, and SQL VDI technologies. These components emulate SQL Server 2000 SP4 functionality.

The DTS 2000 packages will continue to run in a mixed environment. For example, packages can call each other via DTS API from one version to the other. In our experience, most DTS 2000 packages continue to run at plus or minus 10 percent of their original performance level. To achieve the promise of SQL Server Integration Services, you will most likely need to redesign your existing DTS packages. Microsoft provides the means to migrate your existing packages from the command line via DTSMigrationWizard.exe or from applications such as Business Intelligence (BI) Development Studio and SQL Server 2008 Management Studio. These wizards, such as the Package Migration Wizard shown in Figure 3-9, are only available in the Standard, Enterprise, and Developer editions of the product.

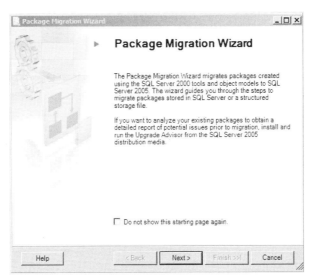

Figure 3-9

These wizards provide a "best attempt style" migration; that is, the wizard will do a task-for-task migration. Complex tasks that cannot be converted are encapsulated in a 2000 construct as part of the package migration. To avoid errors with the migration of your DTS packages, you should validate them with the Upgrade Advisor tool, covered earlier in this chapter. Neither Upgrade Advisor nor the DTS Migration Wizard can process SQL Server 7.0 packages that have not been saved to disk. To make things worse, SQL Server 7.0 packages must be upgraded to SSIS completely, because they cannot be maintained with the 2000 runtime after upgrade.

Figure 3-10 shows a SQL Server 2000 instance managed by SQL Server 2008 Management Studio. The Northwind Orders Schema package is stored locally and can be found nested in the Data Transformation Services folder, which is in the Legacy folder that can be found under the Management folder, see Figure 3-13.

As an example, we'll walk through migrating this simple DTS 2000 package. This package builds four dimensions and a fact table from the Northwind database. With the exception of the "Time Dimension," which relies on a Visual Basic script to parse out levels of a time dimension, this package is simple in nature.

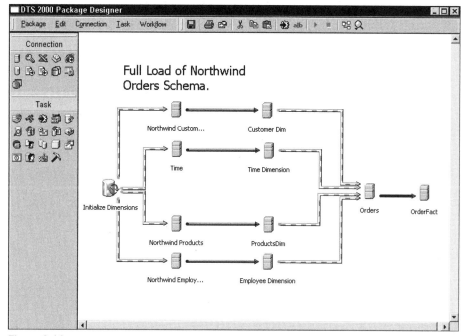

Figure 3-10

From the Management Studio environment, right-click the Northwind Orders Schema package and select the Migrate option. The first step of the Migration Wizard asks for the source of the package or packages — specifically, which SQL Server or directory they reside in. In this example, the file resides on a SQL 2000 Server. The wizard then asks you to select a destination location for the migrated package, as shown in Figure 3-11. Two options are available: a SQL Server destination or a DTS file.

Select a local SQL Server 2008 instance as the destination. The next step presents you with a list of the packages that reside on the source server, as shown in Figure 3-12. After selecting the lone package, enter the location of the error log to be captured for the migration process. Note that only copies of the original packages are actually migrated, the original packages are left functional and intact.

> *Other than maintenance packages and simple import/export wizard-based packages, authoring of packages is no longer supported on the server side. All packages (SSIS or DTS) must be authored in the BI Development Studio and imported to the production server from development.*

Finally, you'll see a summary screen of all your previous choices, enabling you to do a final check of everything. With the next click, the process of migrating a copy of the actual package is kicked off. Figure 3-13 identifies the migrated package shown in the SQL Server 2008 Integration Services instance. Meanwhile, the original package remains intact as part of the SQL Server 2000 instance.

We opted to do the migration from the SQL Server 2008 Management Studio to make a point: The packages are independent of each other and fully functional. The ideal place to perform this migration would have been in the BI Development Studio. To accomplish this, you would have started a new SSIS project and selected a migration option. The steps for the migration would have been identical from that point on. The BI Development Studio is the ideal location for the migration because it provides the capability to edit the package after migration. Although SSIS is not covered here, we briefly discuss the concepts to provide some context. SSIS is presented in greater detail in the Business Intelligence chapters of the book: Chapters 6, 7, and 8. An SSIS package is made up of one control-flow construct (or container) and one or many data-flow constructs (or containers). The control flow is more of a process construct made up of tasks such as FTP, e-mail, Sequence Containers, and Data Flow Tasks. The Data Flow Task is a pipeline-transformation construct optimized to transform the data from process to process (or task to task) all in-flight. Tasks that perform actions such as sorting, aggregation, data-type conversions, and conditional splits make up the data-flow pipeline. Figure 3-14 shows a control-flow view of the migrated package.

Figure 3-11

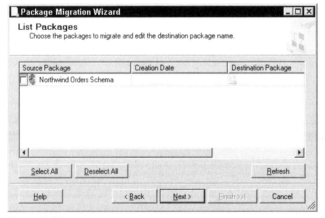

Figure 3-12

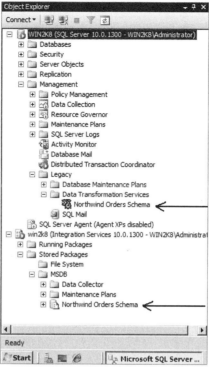

Figure 3-13

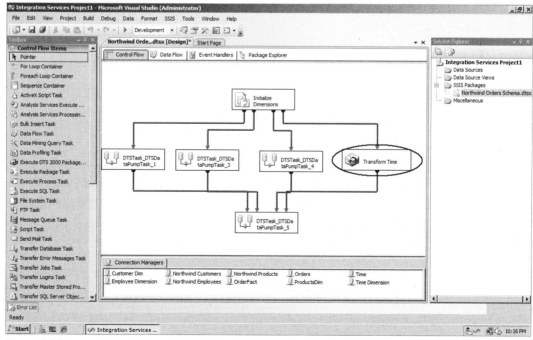

Figure 3-14

As part of the migration, each of the DTS pipeline tasks is transformed into a distinct task. This creates a total of six tasks: one Execute SQL task for the truncate tables statements, a data-flow task for each of the pipeline tasks (one per dimension), and one to load the fact table. The highlighted component called "Transform Time" is the "Time Dimension" that we earlier mentioned could not be migrated because of the use of Visual Basic. If you edit this task, you'll be presented with properties about it. The cool thing to remember here is that this task now has the capabilities of a SQL Server 2008 environment, meaning that you can take advantage of feature-like expressions by wrapping this task as part of a looping transform or a Sequence Container. To see the actual task, all you have to do is to edit it again, and it will be presented in a DTS 2000 environment, as shown in Figure 3-15.

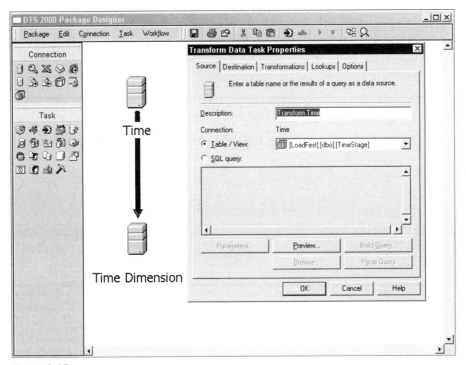

Figure 3-15

Remember that although the SSIS team tried to preserve the look and feel of DTS, the tool has been completely redesigned from the ground up. SSIS is not included as a feature of Express; all existing packages now have to be managed by another edition. If you try to save a DTS package in the Meta Data repository after applying SP4, you'll find that this feature is no longer supported. So, it's now official: SQL server 2000 Meta Data Services is a deprecated feature. To learn more about SSIS, read SQL Server 2008 Books Online, or see *Professional SQL Server 2008 Integration Services* (Wrox, 2008).

The following table offers a feature comparison between DTS and SSIS.

DTS 2000 Tasks	SSIS Tasks
ActiveX Script Task	ActiveX Script Task
Analysis Services Processing Task	None
Bulk Insert Task	Bulk Insert Task
Copy SQL Server Objects Task	Transfer SQL Server Objects Task
Custom Tasks	None
Data Driven Query Task	None
Data Mining Prediction Task	Data Mining Query Task
Dynamic Properties Task	None
Execute Package Task	Execute DTS 2000 Package Task
Execute Process Task	Execute Process Task
Execute SQL Task	Execute SQL Task
File Transfer Protocol Task	FTP Task
Message Queue Task	Message Queue Task
ParallelDataPump Task	None
Send Mail Task	Send Mail Task
Transfer Data (Data Pump) Task	Data Flow Task
Transfer Databases Task	Transfer Database Task
Transfer Error Messages Task	Transfer Error Messages Task
Transfer Jobs Task	Transfer Jobs Task
Transfer Logins Task	Transfer Logins Task
Transfer Master Stored Procedures Task	Transfer Master Stored Procedures Task
Connection Objects	Connection Managers
Error Handling	None
Global Variables	Package Variables
Package Logging	None
Package Passwords	None
Precedent Constraints	Precedent Constraints
Text Annotations	None

If you have SSIS 2005 packages, they can be updated to the new SSIS 2008 packages format. An SSIS Package Upgrade Wizard is accessible in several ways: from the drop-down menu of SQL Server 2008 Business Intelligence Development Studio under Project ⇨ Upgrade All Packages; by right-clicking on the SSIS packages in the Solution Explorer; from SQL Server Management Studio, where you can connect to the Integration Services; or from the command line by executing SSISUpgrade.exe. Figure 3-16 shows the wizard.

Figure 3-16

Log Shipping

Unlike SQL Server 2005, SQL Server 7.0 and 2000 log-shipping sessions cannot be directly upgraded. SQL Server 2000 implemented log shipping through xp_sqlmaint, which is no longer available in SQL Server 2008. Because of this, you will have to either reconfigure these sessions after upgrading to SQL Server 2008 or evaluate a different option. Refer to Chapter 19 for available upgrade options and details.

Failover Clustering and Data Mirroring

Failover clustering has undergone a few modifications that make the upgrade process a bit more complex. You will not be able to downgrade your cluster from SQL Server 2000 Enterprise Edition to SQL Server 2008 Standard Edition. Upgrading your existing cluster is discussed in detail in Chapter 20. Upgrading database mirroring is discussed in detail in Chapter 17.

Upgrading to 64-bit

Upgrading from a SQL Server 2000 32-bit or SQL 2005 32-bit to SQL Server 2008 x64-bit platform is not supported. Although running SQL Server 2000 32-bit with Service Pack 4 or SQL Server 2005 32-bit on a Windows x64-bit subsystem is supported, upgrading this configuration to an SQL Server 2008 x64-bit environment is not supported. Side-by-side migration is the only supported upgrade path for migrating databases from a 32-bit to x64-bit platform.

Post-Upgrade Checks

The information in the following sections is really about product behaviors that have surprised a lot of people. Paying attention to this information will ensure that you do not need to place a call to Microsoft Premier Support.

Poor Query Performance After Upgrade

A possible reason for poor query performance after upgrading to SQL Server 2008 is that the old statistics are considered outdated and cannot be used by the query optimizer. For most situations, this should not be an issue as long as you have enabled the auto-update statistics and autocreate statistics options. This enables statistics to be automatically updated by default when needed for query compilation. It is important to keep in mind that the statistics built from these features are only built from data sampling. Therefore, they can be less accurate than statistics built from the entire dataset. In databases with large tables, or in tables where previous statistics were created with fullscan, the difference in quality may cause the SQL Server 2008 query optimizer to produce a suboptimal query plan.

> *Anytime an index is created, the statistics that are part of that dataset are based on fullscan. In SQL Server 2005 and SQL Server 2008, they are created at index-creation time.*

To mitigate this issue, you should update the statistics immediately after upgrading to SQL Server 2008. Using `sp_updatestats` with the `resample` argument will rebuild statistics based on an inherited sampling ratio for all existing statistics. Typically, that ends up being a full sample for index-based statistics, and sampled statistics for the rest of the columns. An additional benefit that could be gained from this process is that if the data is less than 8MB (the new minimum sampling size), the statistics will also be built with fullscan.

Since we are already discussing statistics, I will take the opportunity to go over a few improvements in this area. Beginning with SQL Server 2005, there have been numerous additions to the statistics that SQL Server collects. This enables the optimizer to better evaluate the resources needed and the cost of different methods for getting information from tables or indexes. Although this process is a bit more expensive, the benefits far outweigh the costs. For example, multicolumn statistics are possible. You can use the following sample code to have a quick look at this feature:

```
USE AdventureWorksDW2008
go
sp_helpstats 'dbo.DimCustomer', 'ALL'
GO

-- Create a multi-column statistics object on DimCustomer.
CREATE STATISTICS FirstLast ON dbo.DimCustomer(FirstName,LastName)
GO

-- Validate that multi-column statistics created on DimCustomer.
sp_helpstats 'dbo.DimCustomer', 'ALL'
GO
```

```
DROP STATISTICS dbo.DimCustomer.FirstLast
GO

-- Create a multi-column index and a multi-column statistic is
-- also created on table DimCustomer
CREATE INDEX demo_firstlast ON dbo.DimCustomer (FirstName,LastName);
GO

-- Drop a multi-column index and a multi-colum statistic will
-- also be dropped from table DimCustomer
DROP INDEX demo_firstlast ON dbo.DimCustomer
GO
```

Autocreate statistics can only create single-column statistics.

Statistics were added for large-object support, such as images, text, and the `varchar(max)` or `varbinary(max)` data types. Improvements have also been introduced in the area of computed columns. Statistics can now be manually or automatically created. In addition, autocreate statistics can generate statistics on computed columns if they are needed. Along with support for date correlation across multiple tables, string-summary statistics have also been added — specifically, string-summary statistics to assist with `'Like'` operators by maintaining frequency-distribution information. The date-correlation optimization feature supports faster join queries across tables when correlated between date-time columns. Statistics on partitioned tables are maintained at the table level, not at the partition level. There have also been improvements in the compilation and recompilation logic. Minimal sample size has been increased to 8MB. Improvements in the optimizer resulted in better selectivity of the statistics to be evaluated for a particular operation and in the evaluation process as part of these operations.

There are numerous additional statistical enhancements that the optimizer has to take into consideration beyond the ones mentioned here. The reason I am discussing this is twofold. First, the default sampling for creating statistics on a table is 1 percent, and there are times when that will not be enough. Therefore, it is recommended that you either update the sample to 10 to 20 percent or, if time allows, go for a full sampling (with fullscan) for tables that approach 100 million rows. Second, the behavior change associated with this enhancement is a longer compilation time, which ultimately can result in a more efficient execution plan. Although the cost of compilation is higher, it is well justified, as the resulting compiled plan is leveraged by the subsequent queries in delivering much faster query results.

For these reasons, if your application uses mostly dynamic SQL, it could see overall performance degradation. But don't worry; the SQL Server team implemented features such as simple and forced parameterization to assist in these scenarios. The role of these features is to parameterize dynamic queries by creating execution plans that can be leveraged by similar queries. The goals of these features are to minimize the parse and compilation times. The benefits will vary from workload to workload. Understanding these features and selecting and applying the correct feature (simple or forced parameterization) will help you mitigate the incremental cost.

Updating Usage Counters

In previous versions of SQL Server, the values for the table and index row counts and page counts could become incorrect. These inaccuracies may cause incorrect space-usage reports returned by the `sp_spaceused` system stored procedure. To correct invalid row or page counts, it's recommended that you run `DBCC UPDATEUSAGE` on all databases following the upgrade. This issue has been resolved in SQL Server 2005 and later. Databases created on SQL Server 2008 should never experience incorrect counts; however, databases upgraded to SQL Server 2008 may contain invalid counts.

SQL Server Configuration Manager

The Surface Area Configuration (SAC) tool has been discontinued in SQL Server 2008 and most of the functionality available in the Surface Area Configuration for Services and Connections has been replaced by the SQL Server Configuration Manager. At the server level, there are behavioral changes between SQL Server 2005 and 2008. First, we recommend familiarizing yourself with the SQL Server Configuration Manager. It is one of the four menu options available when you choose Configuration Tools under the Microsoft SQL Server 2008 directory. As Figure 3-17 shows, it offers three options: the SQL Server Services, SQL Server Network Configuration, and the SQL Native Client Configuration.

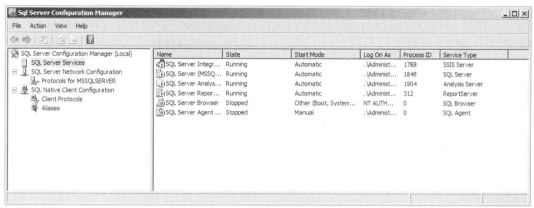

Figure 3-17

This interface enables you to configure, start, stop, and pause all the SQL Server component services installed. From there you can also select the client protocol and aliases for the SQL Server instances. In addition, you can choose whether the SQL Server protocols allowed will be TCP/IP, Named Pipes, VIA, Shared Memory, or a combination.

The user and password for the SQL Server services should be changed from the SQL Server Configuration Manager, rather than the Windows services, as it will apply permissions appropriate for the SQL services — for example, registry permissions.

Banyan VINES, Multiprotocol, AppleTalk, and NWLink IPX/SPX protocols are no longer supported.

Policy-Based Management

As mentioned, the Surface Area Configuration (SAC) tool has been discontinued in SQL Server 2008 and the Surface Area Configurations for features has been replaced by Policy-Based Management. SQL Server 2008 reduces management time for the database administrator by delivering a Policy-Based Management solution that provides the capability to define policies that can be applied to SQL Servers, databases, and other objects. The Policy-Based Management is accessible from SQL Server 2008 Management Studio, and all of the policy components can be found under its Management folder. Here's a crash course on the terminology of Policy-Based Management:

❏　**Policy:** A condition and the expected behavior that is enforced for one or more targets. It can be enabled or disabled.

❑ **Facet:** A set of logical properties that model the behavior and characteristics of the targets; for example, the Surface Area Configuration facet contains the behavior and characteristics to lock down the SQL Server.

❑ **Target:** An entity to manage; for example, a SQL Server instance, a database, a table, or other database objects.

❑ **Category:** A user-defined category to better help manage policies, such as a Best Practices category.

❑ **Condition:** This expresses the state of the allowed values for a facet.

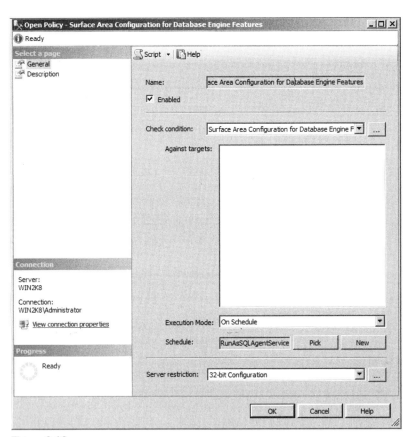

Figure 3-18

A policy can be enforced by four possible execution modes:

❑ **On Demand:** The policy is directly executed by a user, under the user security credentials.

❑ **On Change Prevent:** Automated mode that uses DDL triggers to prevent a policy violation.

❑ **On Change Log Only:** Automated mode that uses the event notification to evaluate whether a change has occurred, and logs policy violations.

❑ **On Schedule:** Automated mode that uses the SQL Server Agent to schedule and periodically evaluate a policy, and logs policy violations.

The Policy-Based Management is stored in the msdb database and the PolicyAdministratorRole role controls all policies in the SQL Server.

One of the predefined, disabled policies is the Surface Area Configuration for Database Engine Features. This policy uses the Surface Area Configuration facet that controls which features are enabled to reduce the surface area of the SQL Server. The policy objects are located under the Management folder of the SQL Server 2008 Management Studio. Open the Policies folder and right-click the Surface Area Configuration for the Database Engine Features option. From this window, shown in Figure 3-18, you would need to enable the policy, as it is disabled by default. Set up an Execution Mode, SQL Agent schedule (for On Schedule), and Server restrictions to filter on the SQL Server to run this policy, and then click OK. For more detailed information, click Help for SQL Server 2008 Books Online.

If you want to change a condition from False to True for the policy, go to the Management folder, open the Conditions folder, and right-click the Surface Area Configuration for the Database Engine Features condition, as shown in Figure 3-19. The Facet Properties window is shown in Figure 3-20.

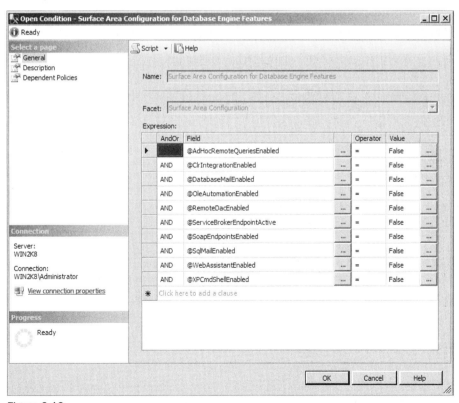

Figure 3-19

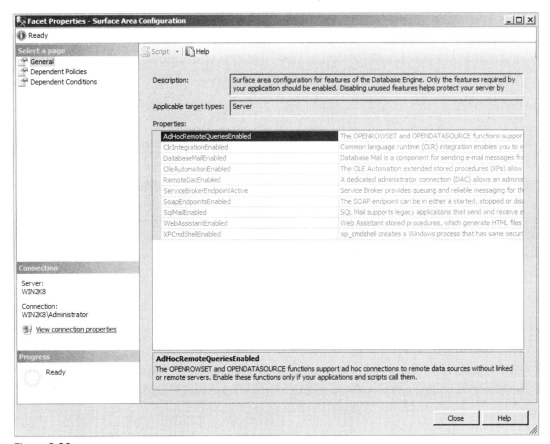

Figure 3-20

As part of upgrading to SQL Server 2008, you should evaluate whether features that you have installed should be turned on or off. This will help reduce your area of exposure to potential threats, both external and internal.

Moreover, the policy can be exported to an XML file and imported to other SQL Servers for policy evaluations. Additionally, a policy can be applied to a Local Server or Central Management Server Group. To achieve that, follow these steps:

1. First, export the policy as shown in Figure 3-21.

2. Using the Registered Servers window, create a Local Server or Central Management Server Group.

3. From the Server Group, open the Evaluate Policies window. From Choose Source, select the exported XML policy file.

4. Click the *Evaluate* button, which will run the policy on the Server Group, as shown in Figure 3-22.

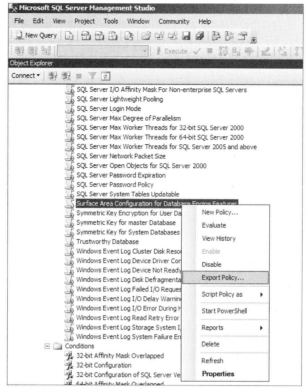

Figure 3-21

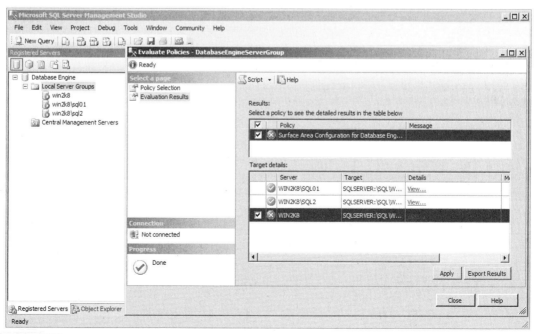

Figure 3-22

During the policy evaluation shown in Figure 3-22, a condition was out of compliance; therefore, a red X icon was displayed. Notice that the *Apply* button is enabled, allowing you to reset to compliance of the policy. After that, the *Export Results* button enables saving an XML result file of this policy evaluation. For a more detailed discussion on SQL Server 2008's Policy-Based Management feature, see Chapter 10.

Summary

In this chapter, we covered the compelling reasons for upgrading to SQL Server 2008. We reviewed strategies and tools such as the SQL Server 2008 Upgrade Assistant and the SQL Server 2008 Upgrade Advisor, which can be leveraged during the upgrade. Then, we discussed the upgrade process, which includes the pre-upgrade, the actual upgrade, and the post-upgrade steps for a successful upgrade. Several deprecated features were identified, along with features whose behavior changes could also affect your upgrade. In addition, we discussed how you can leverage the new Policy-Based Management to replace the Surface Area Configuration tool functionality and reduce management time for the database administrator. Now that we have done the groundwork for a successful upgrade, let's jump into SQL Server 2008.

Managing and Troubleshooting the Database Engine

With the server now installed or upgraded, the next thing you need to do is configure it for your environment. In this chapter, you will learn how to configure your SQL Server instance. After configuring the instance, you will learn how to manage the instance with Management Studio and a number of stored procedures or dynamic management views (DMVs). The chapter also covers how to monitor connections on your SQL Server and how to troubleshoot problems. This chapter assumes you already know the basics of Management Studio navigation and focuses on what you need to know as a database administrator (DBA). Many other chapters in this book cover various aspects of Management Studio, so those points are not duplicated here (backing up your database, for example, is covered in Chapter 18).

Configuration Tools

Now that you have SQL Server installed, or have upgraded to SQL Server 2008, it probably isn't configured exactly for your needs out of the box. In SQL Server 2008, Microsoft has chosen to increase the out of the box security of SQL Server dramatically by turning off features after installation, thereby reducing the software footprint. The features turned off vary based on the edition of SQL Server. For example, TCP/IP is disabled in Developer Edition by default, and every edition has CLR integration turned off. This makes the environment more usable for you as an administrator, as features you don't care about are not crowding your administration screen. It also reduces the options that a hacker can use to penetrate your system.

SQL Server Configuration Manager

The SQL Server Configuration Manager configures the SQL Server services much like the Services applet in the control panel, but it has much more functionality than the applet. For example, the program can also change what ports SQL Server listens on and what protocols each instance uses. You can open the program (see Figure 4-1) from Start ⇨ All Programs ⇨ Microsoft SQL Server 2008 ⇨ Configuration Tools ⇨ SQL Server Configuration Manager.

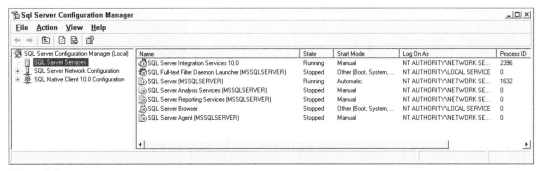

Figure 4-1

Select SQL Server Configuration Manager ⇨ SQL Server Services to configure the various SQL Server services. To configure an individual service such as SQL Server, double-click the service name to open the service Properties page. In the Log On tab, you can configure which account starts SQL Server. We recommend that you start SQL Server with a regular domain user account with minimal rights. The account should not have the privilege to Log on Locally, for example. There is no reason for the account to be a local or domain administrator in SQL Server 2008.

In addition, create a non-expiring password so your SQL Server doesn't fail to start when the password expires. If the SQL Server services do not need to communicate outside the instance's machine, you could start the service with the Local System account, but the account may have more local rights than you want. (We talk more about this in Chapter 9.)

> *We recommend using the Configuration Manager to change Services attributes instead of the Windows Services dialogs in the Administrative Tools area. The SQL development team puts special "SQL smarts" in Configuration Manager that do not exist in the Windows Administrative Tools area. Logins used as service accounts require minimum permission levels that are granted automatically when you use the Configuration Manager.*

On the Service tab, you can specify whether you'd like the service to start automatically, manually, or be disabled. If you go to the Advanced tab (shown in Figure 4-2) for each service, you can configure the more interesting options. For example, here you can turn off Customer Feedback Reporting. This feature enables Microsoft to receive utilization reports from your SQL Server. Even if you wanted to do this, in most production environments your SQL Server may not be able to send the report, due to a lack of Internet access from production servers.

Checking the Error Reporting option in the Advanced tab will e-mail Microsoft whenever a critical error has occurred. The minimal information is sent over a secure HTTPS protocol. Alternatively, you may also wish to send these errors to your own internal Corporate Error Reporting (CER) system, which is a product that you can download from Microsoft.

On the SQL Server 2008 Network Configuration page in the Configuration Manager, you can see a list of network protocols that SQL Server is listening on by instance. If you wish to turn a protocol on or off, you can do so by right-clicking the protocol and selecting Enable or Disable. By enabling only the Shared

Memory protocol, only clients that are running on the same computer can connect to your instance of SQL Server.

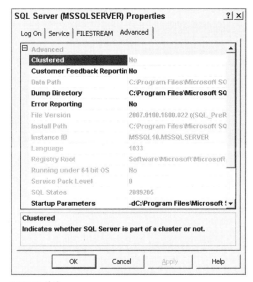

Figure 4-2

Dedicated Administrator Connection

Imagine you get a call informing you that a server is not responding. You go to SSMS to connect to the server to see what is going on. Your connection request waits, and waits, and then times out. You cannot get connected, you cannot debug, you cannot see anything. Is this when you simply stop and restart SQL Server? Maybe not — let's just start killing connections from Activity Monitor. Then try to connect — no luck again. Perhaps it's going to be a tough day.

The problem is that sometimes limited resources on the server can prevent additional connections. SQL Server 2005 added something to help you out in this very situation. The Dedicated Administrator Connection (DAC) enables you to connect and do your work on almost all occasions.

SQL Server listens for the DAC connection on a dynamically assigned port. The error log includes an entry containing the port number. A connection can be made on this port only by sysadmin role members from SSMS or the sqlcmd tool.

To connect to the DAC using SSMS, you add a prefix to the server name. For example, if the server name is Prod, then connect to server admin:Prod. You merely add the prefix admin: to the server name.

To connect using sqlcmd, use the -A option as follows:

```
sqlcmd -SProd -E -A -d master
```

Use the hyphen (-) instead of the slash (/) for the parameters in sqlcmd. *Also note that all of the parameters are case sensitive, so use the same case as the documentation.*

On clustered instances, Microsoft recommends that you enable a remote admin connection using `sp_configure`. You may then need to connect using the TCP address and DAC port number, which you can find in the error log:

```
Sqlcmd -S<serveraddress>,<DacPort>
```

If you are connecting locally using the IP address, you would use the Loopback Adapter address, as in the following example:

```
Sqlcmd -S127.0.0.1,1434
```

Configuration Servers and Server Groups

Although SQL Server administration is generally easier than some other database management systems (DBMSs), SQL Server DBAs often have to administer a larger number of servers than do other DBAs. There is still plenty of work to do. Something as simple as adding a new login or setting some server option can take a lot of time when you must do it on 50 servers.

SQL Server 2008 has a new feature intended to ease our lives — central management servers and server groups. This feature enables you to run T-SQL scripts and apply policy-based management (PBM) policies to a group of servers at the same time. PBM is covered in Chapter 10, but we will look at executing T-SQL on multiple servers right now.

You may execute T-SQL on a group of servers and have the results aggregated into a single result set or have each result set kept separately. When you aggregate the result sets, you have the option to include an extra column that indicates from which server each row is returned. You can use this tool to do any multi-server administration and much more. If you have common error tables on each server, you can query them all in a single statement — think of the possibilities!

These capabilities are part of SQL Server Management Studio (SSMS). In the Registered Servers dialog of SSMS, you may notice a Central Management Servers tree item. You must first register a central management server. Simply right-click and select Register Central Management Server. You can choose a configuration server from the resulting dialog. This server keeps metadata and does some of the background work for you.

After you have created a central management server, you can create server groups, and add server registrations to groups under the registration server. Once you have your servers set up, you may right-click anything — from the registration server to server groups or individual servers in groups — and select New Query, Object Explorer, or Run Policy. You then choose New Query, add T-SQL, and run the query against all of the servers in the group.

Create groups of servers based on common management needs. Maybe you organize your servers based on environment — Prod, System Test, QA, and so on; or perhaps you organize your servers based on functions — Human Resources, Customer, Inventory, and so on. This is going to be a good thing.

Two items to note about your registration server:

❑   It may not be a registered group under itself.

❑   All queries are executed using trusted connections.

To set options for multi-server result sets, select Tools ⇨ Options ⇨ Query Results ⇨ SQL Server ⇨ Multi-server results.

SQL Server Surface Area Configuration

SQL Server 2005 shipped with a nice little tool that aggregated security-related settings, called the SQL Server Surface Area Configuration tool (SQL SAC). It enabled the DBA to administer the surface area, or determine how open the SQL Server install would be. You could turn on and off services, allow the Dedicated Admin account, CLR integration, and Mail, to name a few things. This tool has been dropped from SQL Server 2008. The individual items can still be configured from their original locations. Using `sp_configure` and SQL Server Configuration Manager will enable you to configure most of the items formerly in SQL SAC.

Startup Parameters

SQL Server has an array of switches you can use to troubleshoot or enable advanced settings for the Database Engine. You can do this by setting the switches for the service or by running SQL Server from a command prompt. One tool you can use to change the SQL Server service's startup parameters so it uses the switch every time is SQL Server Configuration Manager. In the SQL Server 2008 Services page, double-click SQL Server (MSSQLServer by default but it may vary depending on your instance name) and go to the Advanced tab. Add any switches you wish using the Startup Parameters option, separated by semicolons (see Figure 4-3).

The second way to start SQL Server is by running `sqlservr.exe` from the command prompt. The file is located by default in the `C:\Program Files\Microsoft SQL Server\MSSQL10.MSSQLSERVER\MSSQL\Binn` directory. You can then turn on any nondefault parameters you wish by adding the switch after `sqlservr.exe`, as shown in Figure 4-4. This is generally the preferred way to start your SQL Server in a one-off debug mode, as you won't leave any settings intact that you may not want. You can stop the SQL Server by using the Ctrl+C combination or by closing the command prompt window.

Never start SQL Server this way for normal use; after you log off the machine, your command prompt will close, stopping SQL Server.

The syntax for the `sqlserver` runtime is as follows:

```
SQLServr.exe [-dmaster_file_path] [-lmaster_log_path]
        -eerror_log_path] [-sinstance_name][-c] [-f]
        [-gmemory_to_reserve] [-h] [-kcheckpoint Speed in MB/sec)
        [-m] [-n] [-Ttrace#] [-ttrace#] [-x]
        [-ystack dump on this error] [-B] [-K]
```

The startup options are very useful in troubleshooting a problem or for solving quick, one-off problems. Rather than describe every switch in this section, we instead cover the ones you are likely to find yourself using most frequently. For example, you can change which master database the SQL Server is using by using the -d and -l switches:

```
SQLServr.exe -d C:\temp\TempMasterDB.mdf -lC:\temp\TempMasterLog.ldf
```

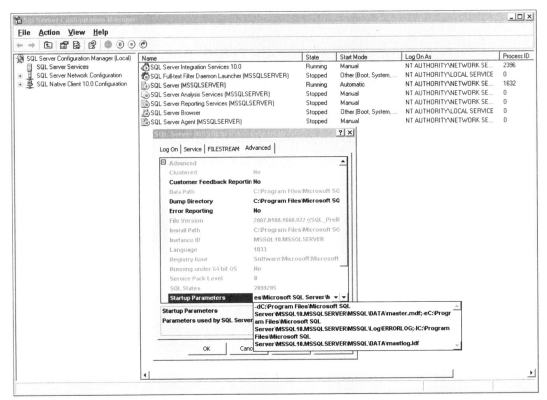

Figure 4-3

The -d switch specifies the database file, and the -l switch specifies the log file. This may be useful if you want to use a temporary configuration of the master database that may not be corrupt. Another useful switch is the -T, which enables you to start given trace flags for all the connections for a SQL Server instance. This can be used, for example, to turn on a trace flag to monitor deadlocks in your SQL Server instance (note that the "T" is uppercase):

```
SQLServr.exe -T1204
```

SQL Server also includes a lowercase trace flag option: SQLServr.exe -t1204. *This should only be used when directed by Microsoft Product Support Services (PSS) because using this flag sets other internal trace flags only used by PSS.*

> If you try to start an instance of SQL Server while it is already running, you will get a bunch of errors. When SQL runs against a master file, it opens the file exclusively to prevent another instance from writing to the same file. One of the errors will tell you that a file is in exclusive use or not available. No harm is done when this occurs.

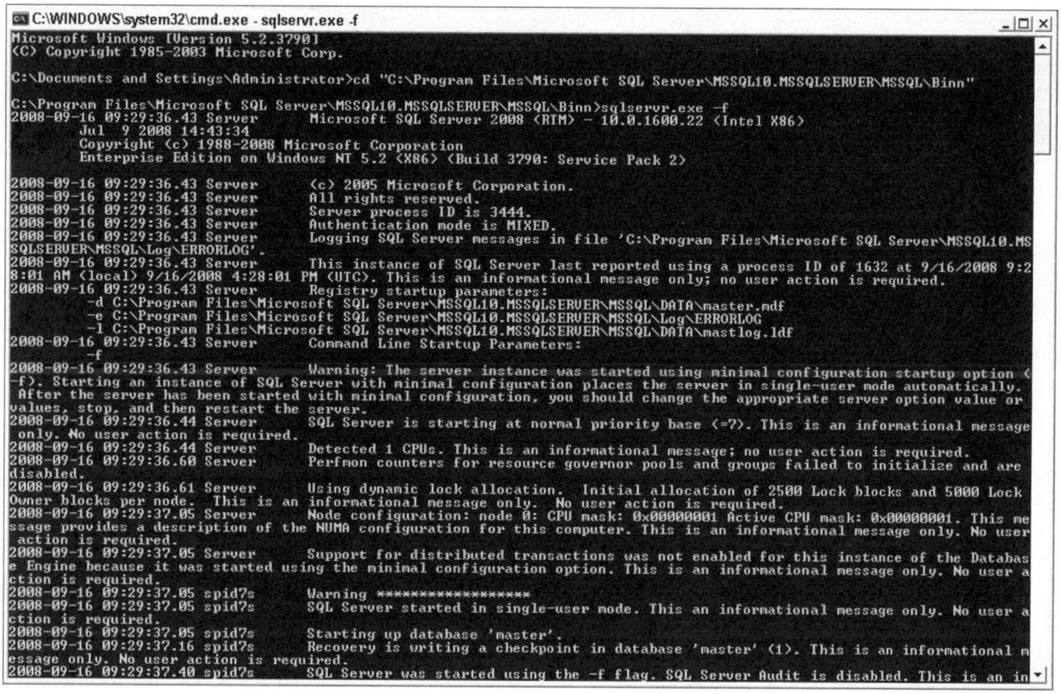

Figure 4-4

You will learn much more about trace flags later in this chapter.

The -f switch places SQL Server in minimal mode and only allows a single connection. By placing SQL Server in minimal mode, SQL Server starts with a minimum configuration, suspends the CHECKPOINT process and startup stored procedures, and remote connections are not allowed. This can be used to correct a configuration option that was set inappropriately, such as setting a memory option larger than the physical memory on the server. In such a case, SQL Server would fail to start. You could start it from the command prompt with the -f option, correct the memory setting, and then restart SQL normally. Another use of this option is to repair startup stored procedures. An administrator may have defined a startup stored procedure that is causing a problem which prevents SQL Server from starting. You can place SQL Server in minimal mode, remove or correct the startup stored procedure, and then start SQL Server again without the switch to repair the problem.

> Using SQL Server Configuration Manager, make sure you stop SQL Server Agent before placing SQL Server in single-user mode. Otherwise, SQL Server Agent will take the only available connection.

The -g switch is used to reserve additional memory outside SQL Server's main memory pool for use by extended stored procedures, OLE DB Providers used by distributed queries, and automation objects used by Transact SQL queries. The general recommendation is to *not* use this flag unless you see either of the following error messages in your SQL Server error log:

```
"Failed Virtual Allocate Bytes: FAIL_VIRTUAL_RESERVE <size>"
"Failed Virtual Allocate Bytes: FAIL_VIRTUAL_COMMIT <size>"
```

These messages indicate that SQL Server is trying to free up memory pool space to allocate the memory in this virtual memory area. In this case, you may wish to increase the amount of memory allocated to these objects by using the -g switch. If the -g switch is not used, the default of 256MB of memory is allocated to this area.

If you have a server that uses very few extended stored procedures, distributed queries, or automation objects, you may wish to use this switch with a value of less than 256 to reduce the amount of memory reserved for these objects. The memory would then be available for the general memory pool.

The -m switch puts SQL Server in single-user mode (sometimes called *master recovery mode*) and suspends the CHECKPOINT process, which writes data from disk to the database device. This switch is useful when you wish to recover the master database from a backup or perform other emergency maintenance procedures. Use of this switch also enables the capability to update system tables (sp_configure 'allow updates').

The -k switch, new to SQL Server 2008, is used to influence the checkpoint frequency. Currently, very little is documented about this switch. The -k switch forces the regeneration of the system master key if one exists. This should be used with extreme care, and only if directed by PSS. You can obtain the complete list of the switches by using the -? switch, as shown in the following example (complete details appear in the SQL Server documentation):

```
sqlservr.exe /?
```

Startup Stored Procedures

Startup stored procedures execute whenever the SQL Server instance is started. For example, you may have a startup stored procedure that e-mails you when the instance starts. You can also use startup stored procedures to create objects in tempdb and load them with data when SQL Server starts. These stored procedures run under the sysadmin server role, and only a sysadmin can create a startup stored procedure. Errors written out from the stored procedure are written to the SQL Server error log.

> **Make sure that you only do the examples in this section against a development server until you're certain you want to do this in production.**

1. By default, SQL Server does not scan for startup stored procedures. To enable it to do so, you must use sp_configure, as follows:

    ```
    sp_configure 'scan for startup procs', 1
    RECONFIGURE
    ```

2. The show advanced options setting must be turned on for the prior script to work:

```
sp_configure 'show advanced options', 1
RECONFIGURE
```

3. After you run this, you must restart the SQL Server instance to commit the setting. Try a simple example. First, create a table called SQLStartupLog in the master database that will log the time a SQL Server instance is started:

```
CREATE TABLE master.dbo.SQLStartupLog
(StartTime datetime)
GO
```

4. Create a stored procedure to log in to the table. Be sure to create this stored procedure in the master database. The following stored procedure will do the trick, logging the current date to the table:

```
CREATE PROC dbo.InsertSQLStartupLog
as
INSERT INTO master.dbo.SQLStartupLog
SELECT GETDATE()
```

5. You need to use the sp_procoption stored procedure to make the stored procedure a startup stored procedure. The sp_procoption stored procedure sets only one parameter. You must first specify the stored procedure you wish to set; the only available option name is startup, with a value of 1 (on) or 0 (off). Before running the following stored procedure, ensure that your SQL Server will scan for startup stored procedures:

```
sp_procoption @ProcName = 'master.dbo.InsertSQLStartupLog',
  @OptionName= 'startup',
  @OptionValue = 1
```

6. Stop and start your SQL Server instance and query the master.dbo.SQLStartupLog to see if the record was written. Before you leave this section, make sure that you disable the setting by running the following query:

```
sp_procoption @ProcName = 'master.dbo.InsertSQLStartupLog',
  @OptionName= 'startup',
  @OptionValue = 0

USE MASTER
GO
DROP TABLE master.dbo.SQLStartupLog
DROP PROC dbo.InsertSQLStartupLog
```

Rebuilding the System Databases

If one of your system databases becomes corrupted and your backups cannot be found, it may be time to rebuild the system databases. This will essentially reinstall the system databases and rid your system of anything that may be causing it to act unpredictably. The repercussion of this is that you must rein-stall any service packs; and all your user-defined databases, including the Reporting Services support database, will disappear. Additionally, any logins or server configurations will have to be redone.

Rebuilding your system databases should not be taken lightly. It is a high-impact technical decision that you make when no other good option exists. When you rebuild the system databases, the databases may appear to have disappeared, but their files are still in the operating system and can be reattached or restored. Reattaching the databases is generally the lowest-impact action.

To rebuild your system databases, locate your SQL Server installation media and go to a command prompt. From the command prompt, run `setup.exe` as if you were installing SQL Server, but you need to pass in a few new switches:

```
start /wait setup.exe /qn INSTANCENAME=<InstanceName> REINSTALL=SQL_Engine
```

The `/qn` switch suppresses any error or information messages and sends them to the error log. You will essentially see a blank screen for a few minutes before the database is finally rebuilt. You can append the `/qb` switch to see some of the messages. If you are reinstalling the system databases for the default instance, use `MSSQLSERVER` for your instance name.

The REBUILDDATABASE parameter allows you to choose which system databases you wish to rebuild. When rebuilding all databases, this parameter is unnecessary.

After the databases are rebuilt, you are returned to your default configuration and databases. You need to restore the master database (more on this in Chapter 18) or reattach each user-defined database and recreate the logins. The preferable option, of course, is to recover the master database from a backup. Then your logins and databases will automatically appear.

Management Studio

As you probably know by now, SQL Server Management Studio is where DBAs spend most of their time. This tool enables you to perform most of your management tasks and to run queries. It's a major evolution of Enterprise Manager (SQL Server 2000's management interface) and uses a light version of Visual Studio 2008. Because this is a professional-level book, we won't go into every aspect of Management Studio, but instead cover some of the more common and advanced features that you might like to use for administration.

Reports

One of the most impressive enhancements to the SQL Server management environment is the inte-grated reports that help a DBA in each area of administration. Standard reports are provided for server instances, databases, logins, and the Management tree item. Each runs as a Reporting Services report inside of SQL Server Management Studio. Server-level reports give you information about the instance of SQL Server and the operating system. Database-level reports drill into information about each database. You must have access to each database you wish to report on, or your login must have enough rights to run the server-level report.

New in SQL Server 2008 is the capability to write custom reports and attach them to many other nodes in the Object Explorer window.

Server Reports

You can access server-level reports from the Object Explorer window in Management Studio by right-clicking an instance of SQL Server and selecting Reports from the menu. A report favorite at the server level is the Server Dashboard, which is shown in Figure 4-5. The Server Dashboard report gives you a wealth of information about your SQL Server 2008 instance:

❑ What edition and version of SQL Server you're running.

❑ Anything for that instance that is not configured to the default SQL Server settings.

❑ The I/O and CPU statistics by type of activity (e.g., ad hoc queries, Reporting Services, and so on).

❑ High-level configuration information such as whether the instance is clustered or using AWE.

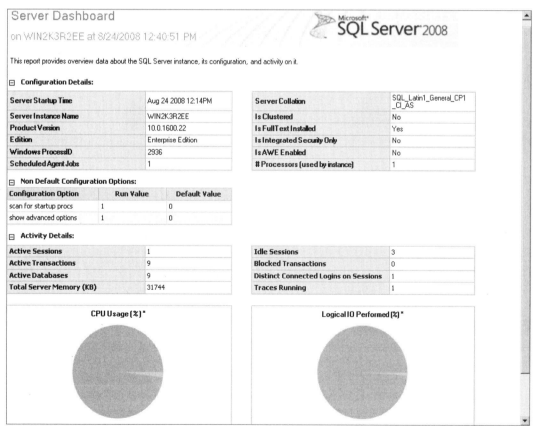

Figure 4-5

Most of the statistical information includes only data gathered since the last time you started SQL Server. For example, the Server Dashboard provides a few graphs that show CPU usage by type of query. This graph is not historical; it shows you the CPU usage only for the period of time that SQL Server has been online.

Database Reports

Database reports operate much like server-level reports. Select them by right-clicking the database name in the Object Explorer window in Management Studio. With these reports, you can see information that pertains to the database you selected. For example, you can see all the transactions currently running against a database, users being blocked, or disk utilization for a given database, as shown in Figure 4-6.

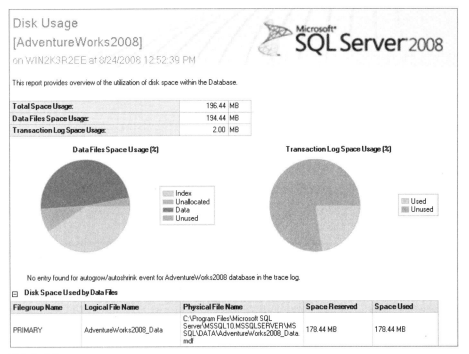

Figure 4-6

Configuring SQL Server

There are a few ways to configure your SQL Server. Earlier we used SQL Configuration Manager and `sp_configure`. These two tools help you turn on various features and services. Now we will look at other configuration options, and take a more detailed look at `sp_configure`. For the Database Engine, you have two main methods to configure the instance: the `sp_configure` stored procedure or the Server Properties screen. To access the Server Properties screen, right-click the Database Engine you want to configure in Management Studio and select Properties. Be careful before altering the configuration of your instance. Adjusting some of these settings could affect your instance's performance or security. This section describes a few of the more important settings, but more are covered throughout the book.

Using the Server Properties Screen

Using the Server Properties screen is much more user friendly than sp_configure, but it doesn't provide all the options available to you through sp_configure. The General tab in the Server Properties screen shows you information about your SQL Server instance that cannot be altered, such as the version of SQL Server you currently have installed and whether your instance is clustered. It also provides server information, such as the number of processors and amount of memory on the machine. Keep in mind that although your server may have 2GB of RAM available, that doesn't mean that all of that RAM is available to SQL Server.

On the Memory page of the Server Properties screen, you can see how much memory SQL Server is configured to use. By default, SQL Server is configured to use as much memory as the operating system and the edition of SQL Server allows it to consume. Typically, it is a good idea to set the minimum amount of memory that your instances will use in your environment. You can also turn on AWE from this screen. AWE enables SQL Server 32-bit machines to utilize more memory once you pass 4GB of RAM. (We talk much more about this feature in Chapter 11.)

Note the Configured Values and Running Values radio buttons at the bottom of the dialog. When you select Running Values, you will see the values that SQL Server is currently using. When you select Configured Values, you will see the values that SQL Server will use the next time it restarts. This is necessary because some values do not take effect until after a restart.

In the Processors page, you can restrict the SQL Server Engine to use named processors and assign some or all of those processors to I/O or threading operations. This is useful typically if you have multiple CPUs and more than one instance of SQL Server. You may have one instance use four processors and the other instance use the other four processors. In some cases, when you have a large number of concurrent connections to your SQL Server, you may wish to set the Maximum Worker Threads option. Configuring this to 0 (the default) enables SQL Server to automatically and dynamically find the best number of threads to allow on the processor. These threads are used for managing connections and other system functions such as performing CHECKPOINTs. Generally, leaving this setting alone will give you optimal performance.

You can select the SQL Server Priority option to force Windows to assign a higher priority to the SQL Server process. Tweaking this setting may be tempting, but you should only adjust it after thorough testing because it may starve other system threads. Use of this option is not generally recommended unless directed by PSS or some other SQL experts.

The Lightweight Pooling option should only be used on the rare occasion when the processor is highly utilized and context switching is extreme.

On the Security page, you can adjust whether your SQL Server accepts connections through SQL Server and Windows Authentication or Windows Authentication only. This same question is asked during setup of the instance, and this screen gives you another opportunity to change the setting. Under the Login Auditing section, you should always have at least Failed Logins Only selected. This enables SQL Server to audit when someone mistypes a password or is trying to force their way into the instance. (We talk much more about the other security settings on this page in Chapter 9.)

On the Connections page (shown in Figure 4-7), you can adjust the default connection properties. The Query Governor setting may be a bit misleading to the DBA. This setting tells SQL Server that if any SQL

Server query is estimated to take more than the specified number of seconds, it will be terminated prior to execution. You can adjust this setting without having to restart your instance, and it can be overridden at a connection level if the connection uses the following syntax and the command is run by a sysadmin:

```
SET QUERY_GOVERNOR_COST_LIMIT 120
```

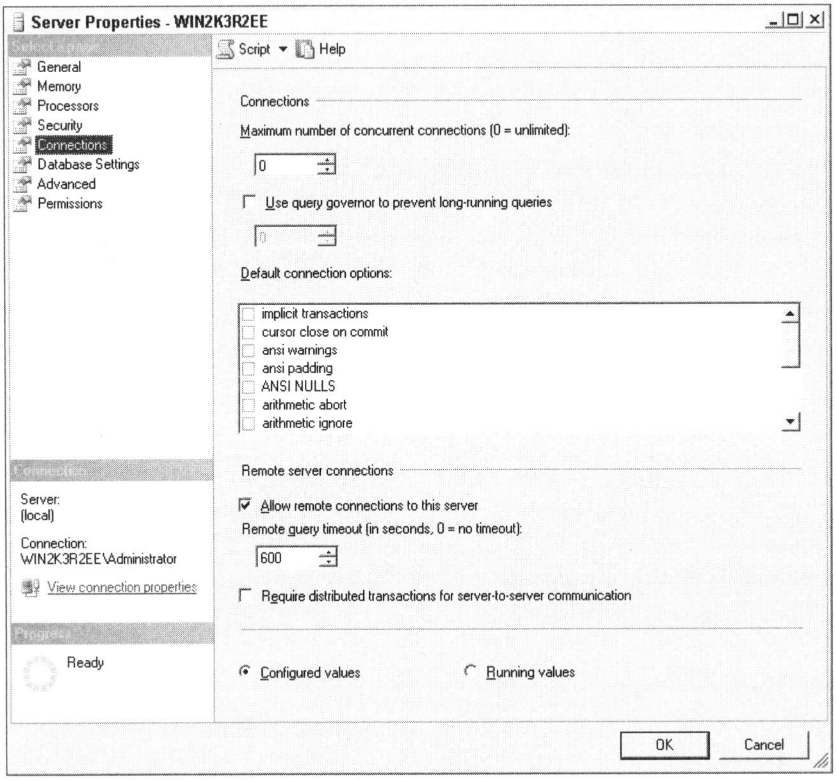

Figure 4-7

The preceding query specifies that SQL Server will allow queries to execute if they are estimated to use less than 120 seconds. If any query is sent to SQL Server that is estimated to take longer than this, the user's query will be cancelled, and he or she will receive the following error:

```
Msg 8649, Level 17, State 1, Line 4
The query has been canceled because the estimated cost of this query (200) exceeds
the configured threshold of 120. Contact the system administrator.
```

Because this setting is using the estimated cost of the query, it may not match the actual execution time. The query optimizer may estimate that a query will take two seconds to run, but in actuality it takes 45 seconds sometimes, based on system conditions. Using this option will *not* stop a query after it has begun executing, no matter how long it takes. I find this setting almost worthless, because it must be set to the largest possible good value. For example, if the largest expected nightly batch query could take 3,600 seconds, then you set it to 3600; otherwise, the nightly batch will fail. However, many queries will now be allowed to run that should be disallowed. The problem is that this is too indiscriminate, but there is light at the end of the tunnel. SQL Server 2008 added a wonderful new feature called Resource Governor, which gets us closer to what we really need. Resource Governor is covered in detail in Chapter 12.

In this screen, you can also set default connection options if someone has not explicitly defined connection settings. A good one possible option you may wish to set here would be SET NOCOUNT. This setting will prevent the "8 Rows Affected" message from being sent to the client if they do not request it. There is a small performance enhancement by doing this, as this message is an additional recordset sent from SQL Server and may be unneeded traffic.

You will not likely change many of the settings on the Database Settings page. The default index fillfactor of 0 is fine. You may change fillfactors for specific indexes, but probably not the default. This page also includes settings for how long you wait on a tape for backup (specify how long SQL Server will wait for a tape) and how long backups are kept before they expire (default backup media retention, in days). You may change them to suit your plan. I have rarely changed the default Recovery Interval (Minutes) option. Decide whether or not you plan to compress database backups and set the Compress Backup option accordingly. I highly recommend it. Details for these settings are covered in Chapter 18, but you should compress your backups.

The last setting on this page enables you to choose the default database and log file locations. The installation default setting places the log and data files on the same drive under the %System Drive%\Program Files\Microsoft SQL Server\MSSQL10.MSSQLSERVER\Data and Log directories. Unless this SQL Server install is for playing around, do not put your data and log files on the C drive.

A best practice is to separate data and logs on different drives. This enables you to get the most out of your RAID system and ensures proper recovery, as discussed in Chapter 11.

Using sp_configure

sp_configure is a stored procedure that enables you to change many of the configuration options in SQL Server. It hasn't changed in the last few versions of SQL Server, so we will not spend a lot of time on it. When you run the stored procedure with no parameters, it shows you the options and their current settings. By default, only the basic, or commonly used, settings are returned, of which there are 15. To see additional options, you need to configure the instance to display advanced options. You can do so by running sp_configure, as shown here:

```
sp_configure 'show advanced options', 1
RECONFIGURE
```

The change does not take effect until the RECONFIGURE command is issued. SQL Server does a check for invalid or not recommended settings when you use sp_configure. If you have provided a value that fails any of these checks, SQL Server warns you with the following message:

```
Msg 5807, Level 16, State 1, Line 1
Recovery intervals above 60 minutes not recommended. Use the RECONFIGURE WITH
OVERRIDE statement to force this configuration.
```

This gives you an opportunity to reconsider what may have been a bad choice, such as setting a memory option to more memory than exists on the box. The following code shows you how to issue the override for the setting:

```
EXEC sp_configure 'recovery interval', 90
RECONFIGURE WITH OVERRIDE
GO
```

Filtering Objects

SQL Server 2000 used an object model called DMO and SQL-NS to retrieve the list of objects for Enterprise Manager. If you had dozens or hundreds of objects to display, it would sometimes take minutes to display the list in Enterprise Manager because the old object models weren't built for showing that many objects. This became a problem when SQL Server implementations began to really scale and SQL Server was adopted by hosting providers and large enterprises that might have hundreds of databases on a single server.

Beginning with SQL Server 2005, Management Studio uses a new object model called SQL Server Management Objects (SMO), which scales much better than previous releases of the object model. For example, if you are in Management Studio, you can now expand the list of tables; and while you're waiting for the tree to expand, you can move on to the next task. Whenever the tables are fully ready to display, the menu expands and your task is not interrupted.

You can also filter objects easily, which is useful when you begin to have dozens of objects. To filter the objects in Management Studio, select the node of the tree that you wish to filter and click the Filter icon in the Object Explorer. The Object Explorer Filter Settings dialog (shown in Figure 4-8) will open, where you can filter by name, schema, or when the object was created. The Operator drop-down box enables you to select how you wish to filter, and then you can type the name in the Value column.

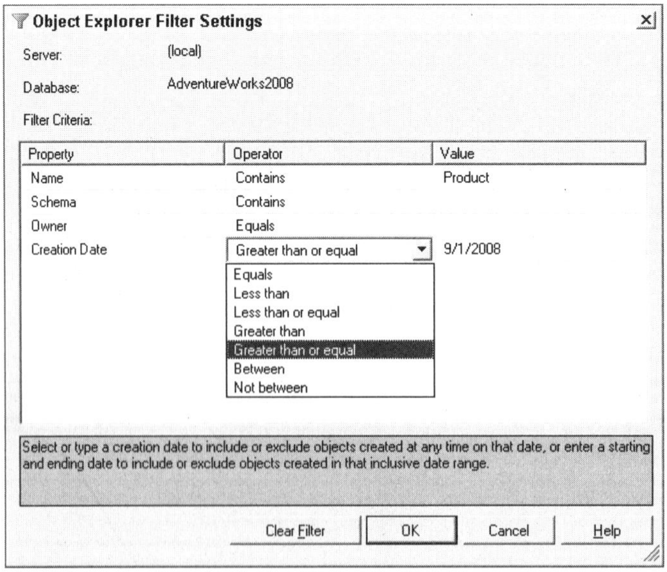

Figure 4-8

Error Logs

As you probably have already experienced, when something goes wrong with an application, the first thing to be blamed is typically the database. This leaves a DBA to disprove that it's his or her fault. The first thing the DBA does is typically connect to the server and look at the SQL Server instance error logs and then the Windows event logs.

In SQL Server 2008, you can quickly look through the logs in a consolidated manner using Management Studio. To view the logs, right-click SQL Server Logs under the Management tree and select View ⇨ SQL Server and Windows Log. This will open the Log File Viewer screen. From this screen, you can check and uncheck log files that you want to bring into the view. You can consolidate logs from SQL Server, Agent, Database Mail, and the Windows Event Files, shown in Figure 4-9.

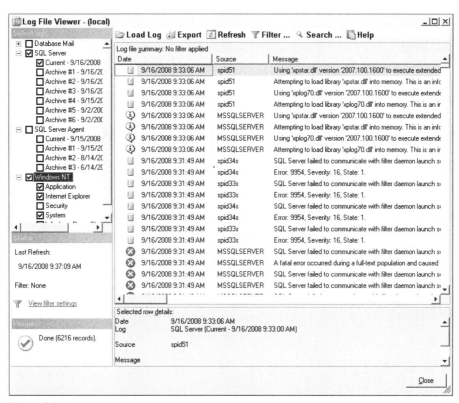

Figure 4-9

In some situations, you may want to merge the logs from several machines into a single view to determine what's causing an application problem. To do this, click the Load Log button and browse to your .LOG file. That file could be a Windows error log that's been output to .LOG format or a SQL log from a different instance. For example, you can use this to consolidate all the SQL logs from every instance on a single server to give you a holistic view of all the physical machines' problems.

Activity Monitor

The Activity Monitor gives you a view of current connections on an instance. The monitor can be used to determine whether you have any processes blocking other processes. To open the Activity Monitor in Management Studio, right click on the Server in the Object Explorer, then select Activity Monitor.

The tool is a fantastic comprehensive way to view who is connecting to your machine and what they're doing. Much improved over prior releases, the top section shows 4 graphs show processor time, waiting tasks, database io, and batch requests/sec –all commonly used performance counters for the server. There are 4 lists under the graphs, Processes, Resource Waits, Data File I/O, and Recent Expensive Queries. In all of these lists, you can also apply filters to show only certain hosts, logins, or connections using greater than a given number of resources. You can also sort by a given column by clicking on the column header.

On the Process Info page (shown in Figure 4-10), you can see each login connecting to your machine (also called a Server Process ID, or SPID). It's easy to miss how much information is in this window. You can slide left to right to see loads of important data about each connection. You'll find that most of the columns are very useful to you when debugging.

- ❑ **Session ID:** The unique number assigned to a process connected to SQL Server. This is also called a SPID. An icon next to the number represents what is happening in the connection. If you see an hourglass, you can quickly tell that the process is waiting on or is being blocked by another connection.

- ❑ **User Process Flag:** Indicates whether processes that are internal SQL Server processes are connected. These processes are filtered out by default. You can change the value to see the SQL Server internal processes by clicking the drop down and selecting the appropriate value.

- ❑ **Login:** The login to which the process is tied.

- ❑ **Database:** The current database context for the connection.

- ❑ **Task State:** Indicates whether the user is active or sleeping. (No, this doesn't mean the user is active or sleeping at his or her keyboard; it means that SQL Server keeps the connection active even though no activity is coming from the login until the user disconnects.)

- ❑ **Done:** Completed.

- ❑ **Pending:** The process is waiting for a worker thread.

- ❑ **Runnable:** The process has previously been active, has a connection, but has no work to do.

- ❑ **Running:** The process is currently performing work.

- ❑ **Suspended:** The process has work to do, but it has been stopped. Additional information about why the process is suspended may be found in the Wait Type column.

- ❑ **Command:** Shows the type of command currently being executed. For example, you may see SELECT, DBCC, INSERT, or AWAITING COMMAND here, to name a few. This won't show you the actual query that the user is executing, but it does highlight what type of activity is being run on your server. To see the actual command, select a row in this table, right click and choose Details.

❑ **Application:** The application that is connecting to your instance. This can be set by the developer in the connection string.

❑ **Wait Time (ms):** If the process is being blocked or waiting for another process to complete, this indicates how long the process has been waiting, in milliseconds; it will have a value of 0 if the process is not waiting.

❑ **Wait Type:** Indicates the event you are waiting on.

❑ **Wait Resource:** The text representation of the resource you are waiting on.

❑ **Blocked By:** The Session ID (SPID) that is blocking this connection.

❑ **Head Blocker:** A value of 1 means the Blocked By Session ID is the head of the blocking chain, otherwise 0.

❑ **Memory Use (KB):** The current amount of memory used by this connection. Number of pages in the Procedure cache attributed to this connection. Note this was reported in pages in prior releases.

❑ **Host:** The login's workstation or server name. This is a really useful item, but in some cases you may have a Web server connecting to your SQL Server, which may make this less important.

❑ **Workload Group:** The name of the Resource Governor workload group for this query.

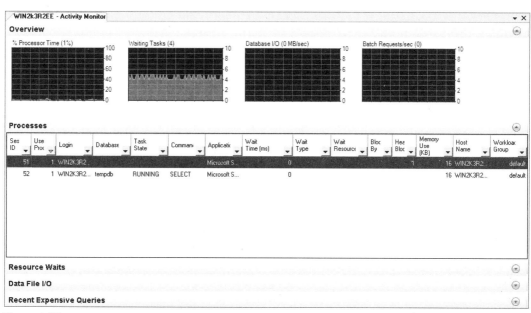

Figure 4-10

When you right click over the graph area, you can select Refresh to manually refresh the data. You can also click Refresh Interval to set the Activity Monitor to refresh automatically every 60 seconds (or whatever you define). The default refresh rate is 10 seconds. Don't set the refresh to anything too frequent, like every two seconds, as it can affect system performance, constantly running queries against the server.

```
By right-clicking any process, you can see the last query run with the connection,
trace the process using Profiler, or kill the connection.
```

The Locks by Process and Locks by Object that existed in prior versions no longer exists, but let's set up a locking condition and take a look at activity monitor. Run the following query in one query window while connected to the AdventureWorks2008 database and make sure you backup the Adventure-Works2008 database before performing these steps:

```
BEGIN TRAN
DELETE FROM Production.ProductCostHistory
WHERE ProductID = 707
```

Note that the query was intentionally not committed. In other words, there is a BEGIN TRAN command but no ROLLBACK or COMMIT command. This means that the rows inserted into Production.ProductCostHistory are still locked exclusively.

Next, without closing the first window, open a new query window and run the following query:

SELECT * FROM Production.ProductCostHistory

This query should hang up and wait on the Select from Production.ProductCostHistory, because the first transaction has the rows locked. Do not close either window. Note that at the top of each query window your session ID is displayed in parentheses, and at the bottom your login is displayed. If you cannot see the SPID in the tab at the top, hover your mouse over the tab, and a small window will popup showing the entire tab title, which includes the spid.While the query windows are open, go ahead and explore the Activity Monitor to see what these connections look like.

Open the Activity Monitor and note that one connection has a task state of suspended. This is the query that is trying to do the select. You can confirm this by comparing the session ID of the suspended session with the session ID of your query. Your wait type with be LCK_M_S, which means you are waiting on a shared lock for reading. If you hover the mouse over the Wait Resource column value, you will see more detailed information about the locks, including the object ids of the resources. In the Blocked By column, you will also see the session ID of the process that is blocking you, and it should match SPID of your first query. You have the option to kill the blocking process; to do so, select the row for the blocking process, right-click, and choose Kill Process.

The location of the Activity Monitor has moved in SQL Server Management Studio 2008. To open the Activity Monitor, open the Object Explorer, right-click on your server name, and select Activity Monitor.

While the locks still exist, let's take a look at a standard blocking report which comes with SQL Server 2008. In Object Explorer, right-click on your server name, select reports, then standard reports, and choose Activity –All Blocking Transactions. You will see the report shown in figure 4-12 below.

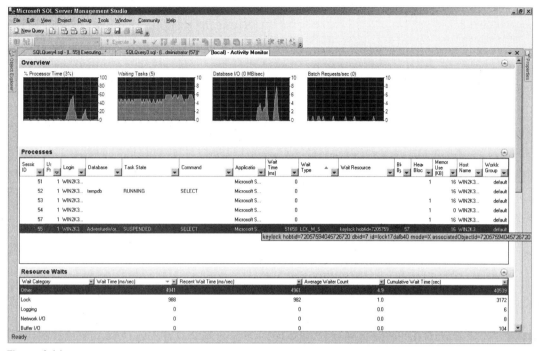

Figure 4-11

Figure 4-12

Now, back at the Activity Monitor, as you hover over the Wait Resource column, note the "mode = X".This mode means that there is an exclusive lock on that resource. An exclusive lock means that no one else is allowed to read the data cleanly. If you see a request mode of S, then SQL Server has granted a shared lock, which in most situations is harmless, and others are allowed to see the same data. A user can request a dirty read of the uncommitted data by adding a WITH (NOLOCK) clause:

```
SELECT *
FROM Production.ProductCostHistory
WITH (NOLOCK)
```

This query will return the data. Before you leave this section execute the following SQL in the query window which does the delete:

```
ROLLBACK TRAN
```

Monitoring Processes in T-SQL

You can also monitor the activity of your server via T-SQL. Generally, DBAs prefer this as a quick way to troubleshoot long-running queries or users who complain about slow performance. DBAs typically prefer T-SQL because the information you can retrieve is much more flexible than the Activity Monitor.

sp_who and sp_who2

The sp_who stored procedure also returns who is connecting to your instance, much like the Activity Monitor. You'll probably find yourself preferring the undocumented sp_who2 stored procedure, though, which gives you much more verbose information about each process. Whichever stored procedure you use, they both accept the same input parameters. For the purpose of this discussion, we go into more detail about sp_who2. Just keep in mind that sp_who shows a subset of the information.

To see all the connections to your server, run sp_who2 without any parameters. This displays the same type of information in the Activity Monitor. You can also pass in the parameter of 'active' to see only the active connections to your server:

```
sp_who2 'active'
```

You can also pass in the process ID, as shown here, to see the details about an individual process:

```
sp_who2 55
```

Although the example uses process ID 55, your process IDs may be different, and can be obtained from the Current Activity listing discussed earlier.

sys.dm_exec_connections

The sys.dm_exec_connections dynamic management view gives you even more information to help you troubleshoot the Database Engine of SQL Server. This DMV returns a row per session in SQL Server. Because it's a DMV, it's displayed as a table and allows you to write sophisticated queries against the view to filter out what you don't care about, as shown in the following query, which shows only user connections that have performed a write operation:

```
SELECT * FROM
sys.dm_exec_sessions WHERE is_user_process = 1
AND writes > 0
```

In addition to the information shown in the methods described earlier to view processes, this DMV indicates how many rows the user has retrieved since opening the connection, and the number of reads, writes, and logical reads. You can also see in this view the settings for each connection and what the last error was, if any.

DBCC INPUTBUFFER

DBCC INPUT BUFFER is a great DBCC command that enables you to see what SQL command an individual process ID is running. The command accepts only a single input parameter, which is the process id for the connection that you'd like to diagnose, as shown in the following query:

```
DBCC INPUTBUFFER (55)
```

The Eventinfo column returns the text of the last command from the connection. If you're running a batch that's particularly large, by default you would only see the first 256 characters in the query window:

```
EventType       Parameters EventInfo
--------------  ---------- ----------------------------------------------------
Language Event 0            begin tran delete from production.productcosthistory

(1 row(s) affected)
```

Here and in the following listings, your output may differ. The output shown here is provided only as an example of the type of results you may get.

Sys.dm_exec_sql_text

Sometimes you need the results of DBCC INPUTBUFFER in a tabular format. You can use the sys.dm_exec_sql_text dynamic management function to retrieve the text of a particular query. This can be used in conjunction with the sys.dm_exec_query_stats dynamic management view to retrieve the most poorly performing queries across all databases. The following query (which can be downloaded from this book's Web site at www.wrox.com) retrieves the number of times a query has executed, the average runtime by CPU and duration, and the text for the query:

```
SELECT TOP 10 execution_count [Number of Executions],
total_worker_time/execution_count AS [Average CPU Time],
Total_Elapsed_Time/execution_count as [Average Elapsed Time],
(SELECT SUBSTRING(text,statement_start_offset/2,
(CASE WHEN statement_end_offset = -1 then
LEN(CONVERT(nvarchar(max), text)) * 2
ELSE statement_end_offset
end -statement_start_offset)/2)
FROM sys.dm_exec_sql_text(sql_handle)) AS query_text
FROM sys.dm_exec_query_stats
ORDER BY [Average CPU Time] DESC
```

The sys.dm_exec_query_stats DMV also shows a great deal of other information that can be used. It shows you a line for each query plan that has been run. You can take the sql_handle column from this DMV and use it in the sys.dm_exec_sql_text function. Because this view is at a plan level, when someone changes some of the query's text, it shows the new query as a new line.

Trace Flags

Trace flags give you advanced mechanisms to tap into hidden SQL Server features and troubleshooting tactics. In some cases, they enable you to override the recommended behavior of SQL Server to turn on features such as network-drive support for database files. In other cases, trace flags can be used to turn on additional monitoring. There is a set of flags that help you diagnose deadlocks. To turn on a trace flag, use the DBCC TRACEON command, followed by the trace you'd like to turn on, as shown here:

```
DBCC TRACEON (1807)
```

To turn off the trace, use the DBCC TRACEOFF command. This command is followed by which traces you'd like to turn off (multiple traces can be separated by commas), as shown here:

```
DBCC TRACEOFF (1807, 3604)
```

When you turn on a trace, you are turning it on for a single connection by default. For example, if you turn on trace flag 1807, which helps diagnose deadlocks, you can diagnose deadlocks only in the scope of the connection that issued the DBCC TRACEON command. You can also turn on the trace at a server level by issuing the command followed by the -1 switch:

```
DBCC TRACEON (1807, -1)
```

Once you have turned on the traces, you're probably going to want to determine whether the trace is actually running. To do this, you can issue the DBCC TRACESTATUS command. One method to issue the command is to interrogate whether a given trace is running:

```
DBCC TRACESTATUS (3604)
```

This command would return the following results if the trace is not turned on:

```
TraceFlag Status Global Session
--------- ------ ------ -------
3604      0      0      0

(1 row(s) affected)
```

If you want to see all traces that apply to the connection, run the command with the -1 parameter:

```
DBCC TRACESTATUS (-1)
```

As shown in the following results of this query, two traces are turned on. Trace flag 1807 is turned on globally for every connection into the SQL Server, and trace flag 3604 is turned on for this session:

```
TraceFlag Status Global Session
--------- ------ ------ -------
1807      1      1      0
3604      1      0      1

(2 row(s) affected)
```

If no traces are turned on, you would receive only the following message:

```
DBCC execution completed. If DBCC printed error messages, contact your system
administrator.
```

Your instance of SQL Server should not have trace flags turned on indefinitely, unless you have been instructed by Microsoft Product Support to do so. When left to run all the time, trace flags may cause your instance to behave abnormally. Moreover, the flag you use today may not be available in a future release or service pack of SQL Server. If you are in debug mode, you can turn on a trace flag from the command prompt when starting SQL Server. As mentioned earlier in this chapter, you can also start a trace, when SQL Server starts, at the command prompt by calling the sqlservr.exe program and passing the -T switch after it.

We've mentioned a few trace flags here but not in any detail. As you proceed through this book, you'll see a number of other trace flags in practice. A favorite trace flag in your DBA toolbox, though, is certainly going to be the deadlock trace.

A deadlock is encountered when two or more connections, each with a resource locked, attempt to access the other's locked resource. Unless SQL Server intervenes, both will wait forever for the other's locked resource, so neither connection can make any progress. SQL Server chooses one of the connections as a deadlock *victim*. The victim's batch is aborted, its locked resources are freed, and a deadlock error appears to the client. The *survivor* continues with no errors. You'll learn much more about what deadlocks are and how they can affect your instance's performance in Chapters 6 and 7; for now, note that if you turn on trace flag 1204, anytime a deadlock is encountered, a message resembling the following is sent to the SQL Server error log:

```
Printing deadlock information
Wait-for graph

 Node:1

 RID: 8:1:89:0
    CleanCnt:2 Mode:X Flags: 0x2
 Grant List 0:
Owner:0x06F01340 Mode: X
  Flg:0x0 Ref:0 Life:02000000 SPID:100 ECID:0 XactLockInfo: 0x0C2C9578
SPID: 100 ECID: 0 Statement Type: SELECT Line #: 4
   Input Buf: Language Event: BEGIN TRAN
                             INSERT INTO Table2 Values(1)
                             Waitfor delay '00:00:10'
                             Select * from Table1
                             Rollback Tran
Requested by:
  ResType:LockOwner Stype:'OR'Xdes:0x0C2C9B88 Mode: S SPID:97 BatchID:0 ECID:0
   TaskProxy:(0x0B596354) Value:0x6f01420 Cost:(0/236)

 Node:2

 RID: 8:1:79:0
    CleanCnt:2 Mode:X Flags: 0x2
```

```
Grant List 0:

Owner:0x06F013A0 Mode: X
   Flg:0x0 Ref:0 Life:02000000 SPID:97 ECID:0 XactLockInfo: 0x0C2C9BB0
SPID: 97 ECID: 0 Statement Type: SELECT Line #: 4
   Input Buf: Language Event: BEGIN TRAN
                            INSERT INTO Table1 Values(1)
                            Waitfor delay '00:00:10'
                            Select * from Table2
                            Rollback Tran
Requested by:
   ResType:LockOwner Stype:'OR'Xdes:0x0C2C9550 Mode: S SPID:100 BatchID:0 ECID:0
TaskProxy:(0x0C178354) Value:0x6f01440 Cost:(0/236)
Victim Resource Owner:
ResType:LockOwner Stype:'OR'Xdes:0x0C2C9B88 Mode: S SPID:97 BatchID:0 ECID:0
TaskProxy:(0x0B596354) Value:0x6f01420 Cost:(0/236)
```

I took some liberties and formatted the log output so it would be easier to read.

This should indicate that you have a serious problem with a query or series of queries. It outputs the SPID (also referred to as *process id* from earlier sections) that blocked the other process (the victim). In this case, the victim was SPID 97 and the results of that query were lost, and you'd have to rerun the query.

Trace flag 1222 returns much more information than the 1204 trace flag to the error log, and it resembles an XML document (although it does not comply with an XSD). The results are very verbose, which is why you typically only see this enabled as a secondary step if the 1204 results were inadequate for solving the problem. The results of the trace flag's output would identify the victim and blocking queries and would resemble something like the following output from an error log:

```
Deadlock encountered ... . Printing deadlock information
Wait-for graph

Node:1

RID: 8:1:89:0                CleanCnt:2 Mode:X Flags: 0x2
Grant List 0:
Owner:0x06F01460 Mode: X     Flg:0x0 Ref:0 Life:02000000 SPID:100 ECID:0
XactLockInfo: 0x0C2C9578
SPID: 100 ECID: 0 Statement Type: SELECT Line #: 4
Input Buf: Language Event: BEGIN TRAN
                         INSERT INTO Table2 Values(1)
                         Waitfor delay '00:00:10'
                         Select * from Table1
                         Rollback Tran
Requested by:
   ResType:LockOwner Stype:'OR'Xdes:0x0C2C9B88 Mode: S SPID:97 BatchID:0 ECID:0
TaskProxy:(0x0B596354) Value:0x6f01420 Cost:(0/236)

Node:2

RID: 8:1:79:0                CleanCnt:2 Mode:X Flags: 0x2
Grant List 0:
```

```
      Owner:0x06F014A0 Mode: X        Flg:0x0 Ref:0 Life:02000000 SPID:97 ECID:0
XactLockInfo: 0x0C2C9BB0
SPID: 97 ECID: 0 Statement Type: SELECT Line #: 4
Input Buf: Language Event: BEGIN TRAN
                           INSERT INTO Table1 Values(1)
                           Waitfor delay '00:00:10'
                           Select * from Table2
                           Rollback Tran
Requested by:
ResType:LockOwner Stype:'OR'Xdes:0x0C2C9550 Mode: S SPID:100 BatchID:0 ECID:0
TaskProxy:(0x0C178354) Value:0x60bc7a0 Cost:(0/236)

Victim Resource Owner:
ResType:LockOwner Stype:'OR'Xdes:0x0C2C9B88 Mode: S SPID:97 BatchID:0 ECID:0
TaskProxy:(0x0B596354) Value:0x6f01420 Cost:(0/236)
deadlock-list

deadlock victim=process6572c70
 process-list
   process id=process6572c70 taskpriority=0 logused=236 waitresource=RID: 8:1:89:0
waittime=655 ownerId=28614 transactionname=user_transaction lasttranstarted=2008-
03-20T11:12:05.430 XDES=0xc2c9b88 lockMode=S schedulerid=1 kpid=3512
status=suspended spid=97 sbid=0 ecid=0 priority=0 trancount=1
lastbatchstarted=2008-03-20T11:12:05.430 lastbatchcompleted=2008-03-20T10:59:31.807
clientapp=Microsoft SQL Server Management Studio - Query hostname= WIN2K3R3EE
hostpid=3568 loginname= WIN2K3R3EE \wsnyder isolationlevel=read committed (2)
xactid=28614 currentdb=8 lockTimeout=4294967295 clientoption1=671090784
clientoption2=390200
executionStack
 frame procname=adhoc line=4 stmtstart=136 stmtend=178
sqlhandle=0x020000001f6096282ce91ac70887d37a98cbdc6991a7a81c
Select * from Table2
inputbuf
BEGIN TRAN
INSERT INTO Table1 Values(1)
Waitfor delay '00:00:10'
Select * from Table2
Rollback Tran

process id=process6572aa8 taskpriority=0 logused=236 waitresource=RID: 8:1:79:0
waittime=4491 ownerId=28601 transactionname=user_transaction lasttranstarted=2008-
03-20T11:12:01.610 XDES=0xc2c9550 lockMode=S schedulerid=1 kpid=2608
status=suspended spid=100 sbid=0 ecid=0 priority=0 trancount=1
lastbatchstarted=2008-03-20T11:12:01.610 lastbatchcompleted=2008-03-20T10:59:31.807
clientapp=Microsoft SQL Server Management Studio - Query hostname=WIN2K3R3EE
hostpid=3568 loginname= WIN2K3R3EE \wsnyder isolationlevel=read committed (2)
xactid=28601 currentdb=8 lockTimeout=4294967295 clientoption1=671090784
clientoption2=390200

executionStack

frame procname=adhoc line=4 stmtstart=136 stmtend=178
sqlhandle=0x020000008ee94419c818f3378d75e8f905e77fc3e20b9171
Select * from Table1
```

```
inputbuf
BEGIN TRAN
INSERT INTO Table2 Values(1)
Waitfor delay '00:00:10'
Select * from Table1
Rollback Tran
resource-list
ridlock fileid=1 pageid=89 dbid=8 objectname=tempdb.dbo.Table2
id=lock6085c80 mode=X associatedObjectId=72057594038910976
owner-list
  owner id=process6572aa8 mode=X
waiter-list
  waiter id=process6572c70 mode=S requestType=wait
  ridlock fileid=1 pageid=79 dbid=8 objectname=tempdb.dbo.Table1
id=lock6085c40 mode=X associatedObjectId=72057594038845440
owner-list
 owner id=process6572c70 mode=X
waiter-list
 waiter id=process6572aa8 mode=S requestType=wait
```

The output also gives you other verbose information that can be used to debug your instance, such as the user name of the victim or deadlocking process and other connection information.

Getting Help from Support

Whenever you get stuck on a SQL Server issue, generally you call the next layer of support. Whether that next layer is Microsoft or a vendor, a number of new tools are available to communicate with that next layer of support. The SQLDumper.exe and SQLDiag.exe programs can be used to help you better communicate with support to give them an excellent picture of your environment and problem while you reproduce the error.

SQLDumper.exe

Beginning in SQL Server 2000 SP3, SQLDumper.exe was included to help your SQL Server perform a dump of its environment after an exception occurs. A support organization such as Microsoft's Product Support Services (PSS) may also request that you execute the program on demand while you have a problem such as a hung server.

If you wish to create a dump file on demand, you need the Windows process ID for the SQL Server instance. There are a few ways you can obtain this ID. You can go to Task Manager, look in the SQL Server log, or go to SQL Server Configuration Manager, covered earlier in the chapter. On the SQL Server 2008 Services page of Configuration Manager, you can see each of the SQL Server services and the process ID.

By default, SQLDumper.exe can be found in the C:\Program Files\Microsoft SQL Server\100\Shared directory, as it is shared across all the SQL Server instances installed on a server. This directory may vary, though, based on where you installed the SQL Server tools. To create a dump file for support, go to a command prompt and access the C:\Program Files\Microsoft SQL Server\100\Shared directory. As with many command-line utilities, you can see the options by running the following command, and get more details about them from the SQL Server documentation:

```
SQLdumper.exe /?
```

Once there, you can create a full dump or a minidump. A full dump is much larger than a minidump. If a minidump is less than a megabyte, a full dump may run 110MB on your system. To create a full dump, use the following command:

```
Sqldumper.exe <ProcessID> 0 0x1100
```

The <ProcessID>is the Process ID of your SQL instance. This will output the full dump to the same directory that you're in. The file name will be called SQLDmpr0001.mdmp if this is the first time you've run the SQLDumper.exe program. Filenames are sequentially named after each execution. You won't be able to open the dump file in a text editor like Notepad. Instead, you need advanced troubleshooting tools such as Visual Studio or one of the PSS tools. A more practical dump would be a minidump, which contains most of the essential information the support needs. To create a minidump, use the following command:

```
Sqldumper.exe <ProcessID> 0 0x0120
```

You can view the SQLDUMPER_ERRORLOG.log file to determine whether there were any errors when you created the dump file or whether a dump has occurred. You need to be a local Windows administrator to run SQLDumper.exe or be logged in with the same account that starts the SQL Server service.

SQLDiag.exe

A tool that's slightly less of a black box than SQLDumper.exe is SQLDiag.exe. If you're experienced with SQL Server 2000, you may be familiar with a tool called PSSDiag.exe, which produced SQL and Windows trace files as well as system configuration logs. SQLDiag.exe has replaced this tool and has added many new features to the old PSS tool. The new tool consolidates and collects information about your system from several sources:

- ❏ Windows System Monitor (sysmon)
- ❏ Windows event logs
- ❏ SQL Server Profile traces
- ❏ SQL Server error logs
- ❏ Information about SQL Server blocking
- ❏ SQL Server configuration information

Because SQLDiag.exe gathers so much diagnostic information, you should only run it when you're requested to or when you're trying to prepare for a call with support. The SQL Server Profiler trace files alone can grow large quickly, so prepare to output these files to a drive that has a lot of space. The process also uses a sizable amount of processing power as it runs. You can execute the tool from a command prompt or as a service; and you can use the /? switch to be shown what switches are available.

SQLDiag.exe can take a configuration file as input. By default, this file is called SQLDiag.Xml, but you can pass in a different file name. If a configuration XML file does not exist, one will be created called ##SQLDiag.XML. This file can be altered to your liking and then later distributed as SQLDiag.XML.

Now that you know what SQLDiag.exe can do, follow this example to use the tool against a local development server. If you cannot get in front of the server, you will have to use a support tool such as Terminal

Services to remote into a server, as you can't point SQLDiag.exe at a remote instance. To run the tool, go to a command prompt. Because the SQL install adds the appropriate directory to the PATH environment variable, you won't have to go to the individual directory where the file is located. Instead, for the purpose of this example, go to the C:\Temp directory or something similar to that on a drive that has more than 100MB available.

The default location for the executable file is C:\Program Files\microsoft sql server\100\tools\Binn \SQLDIAG.EXE, but you can alter that to a new location with the /O switch. In this example, type the following command (note the lack of spaces after the + sign):

```
sqldiag /B +00:03:00 /E +00:02:00 /OC:\temp /C1
```

This command instructs SQLDiag.exe to begin capturing trace information in three minutes from when you press enter, and run for two minutes. This is done with the /B and /E switches. These two switches can also be used to start and stop the diagnostic at a given 24-hour clock time. The command also tells SQLDiag.exe to output the results of the traces and logs to the C:\temp directory, and the /C switch instructs the tool to compress the files using Windows compression. If you were running this in your environment, you would wait until you were instructed by SQLDiag.exe (in green text on your console) to attempt to reproduce the problem. In the figure below, I allowed SQLDiag to collect to the default directory. The results look something like what is shown in Figure 4-13.

Figure 4-13

Enter Control C, when you wish to terminate the collection of data. With the SQLDiag.exe now complete, you can go to the C:\temp directory to zip the contents up and send them to Microsoft. In the directory, you'll find a treasure chest of information for a support individual, including the following:

❑   ##files.txt — A list of files in the C:\Program Files\Microsoft SQL Server\100\Tools\binn directory, with their creation date. This can be used to determine whether you're running a patch that support has asked to be installed.

❑   ##envvars.txt — A list of all the environment variables for the server.

❑   SERVERNAME__sp_sqldiag_Shutdown.OUT — A consolidation of the instance's SQL logs and the results from a number of queries.

❑   `log_XX.trc` — A series of Profiler trace files of very granular SQL Server activities being performed.

❑   `SERVERNAME_MSINFO32.TXT` — A myriad of details about the server system and hardware.

These files are not only useful to support individuals. You may want to consider running this on a regular basis to establish a baseline of your server during key times (before patches, monthly, or whatever your metric is). If you decided to do this, you wouldn't want the Profiler part of `SQLDiag.exe` to run for more than a few seconds. You can gather useful baseline information if the tool is run in snapshot mode periodically. This mode performs the same functions just described but exits immediately after it gathers the necessary information. The following command uses the `/X` switch to run `SQLDiag.exe` in snapshot mode, and the `/N` switch (with 2 as the option) to create a new directory for each run of `SQLDiag.exe`:

```
sqldiag /OC:\temp\baseline /X /N 2
```

The first directory created is called `baseline_0000`, and each new one is named sequentially after that. Many corporations choose to run this through SQL Agent or Task Manager on the first of the month or before key changes to have an automatic baseline of their server and instance.

Summary

In this chapter, you learned some of the key concepts for managing and troubleshooting your SQL Server. You learned how to configure your server using SQL Server Configuration Manager and Management Studio. We also covered how to monitor the connections in your server using the Activity Monitor, and some of the key stored procedures and DMVs. Last, you learned how to use some troubleshooting tools such as trace flags, `SQLDumper.exe`, and `SQLDiag.exe` to send valuable information to your next tier in support or to create a baseline. With the key concepts out of the way, we can now drill into more specific management areas, such as security. In Chapter 5, you will learn much more about automating your SQL Server processes.

5

Automating SQL Server

Much of the work that a database administrator does is repetitive: backing up databases, rebuilding indexes, and checking for file sizes and disk-space availability. Responding to events such as the transaction log being full or being out of disk space may also be part of daily life for some DBAs. The problem grows rapidly with the number of servers you must administer. Automating this work is more than a convenience; it is a requirement for enterprise systems.

Two features in SQL Server 2008 come to the rescue of the DBA — maintenance plans, and SQL Server Agent.

Maintenance plans enable you to automate the routine maintenance activities for a database, Backups, database integrity checks, and index maintenance tasks can now all be automated with maintenance plans. The Maintenance Plan Wizard makes it easy to create maintenance plans by answering simple questions.

SQL Server Agent enables you to manually create a schedule of jobs to be run on a SQL Server, further enhancing the ability of the DBA to automate routine activities.

Maintenance Plans

Maintenance plans are a quick and easy way to automate routine maintenance tasks in SQL Server. They are no more than a user interface on top of regular SQL Server Agent jobs. However, the tasks in a plan aren't equivalent to job steps, as maintenance plans are built using SQL Server Integration Services (SSIS), and these are then run as a single SSIS job step in a job that maps to the maintenance plan name. For routine maintenance tasks they may be all that you need to automate on many SQL Servers.

There are two ways to create maintenance plans. The quick and easy way is to use the Maintenance Plan Wizard, and the manual way is to use the Maintenance Plan Designer.

Maintenance Plan Wizard

This section walks you through the steps of creating a backup using the Maintenance Plan Wizard:

1. The first step is to launch the Wizard, which lives on the context menu on the Maintenance Plans node in the Object Explorer in SQL Server Management Studio. Selecting the Maintenance Plans Wizard menu item will launch the first page of the Wizard.

    I usually opt to not show this page again, and then select Next. This brings up the Select Plan Properties page, where you can set some of the Plan options.

2. On this page, as shown in Figure 5-1, you specify a name and description for the plan and select the scheduling options. For the example in this chapter, stick with the default settings and create a manually scheduled plan.

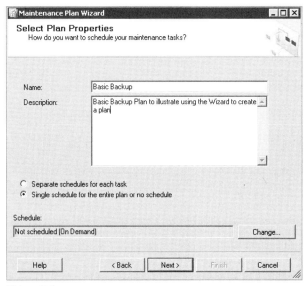

Figure 5-1

3. Select Next to move on to the Select Maintenance Tasks screen where you will choose the tasks you want the plan to perform. For this example select the Back Up Database (Full) option, as shown in Figure 5-2.

4. Select Next to move to the Select Maintenance Task Order screen shown in Figure 5-3. If you selected multiple tasks on the previous page, you can reorder them here to run in the order you want. In this example you only have a single task, so click Next.

5. In this example, the next page is the Define Back Up Database (Full) Task screen, shown in Figure 5-4. On this page you select the details for the backup task. If you had selected a different task on the Select Maintenance Tasks screen, you would have to supply the details for that task. In the case of multiple tasks, this step presents a separate page for each task you selected in your plan.

6. Figure 5-5 shows the dialog where you can select the databases you want to back up. In this case I have selected just one database to back up.

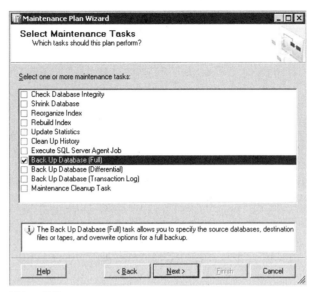

Figure 5-2

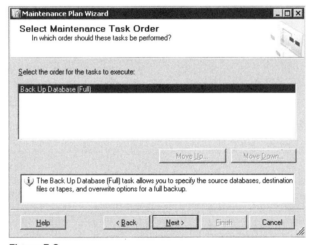

Figure 5-3

7. On the next page (shown in Figure 5-6), you select the reporting options for the plan: write a log to a specific location, send an e-mail, or both.

8. Select Next to go to the final page of the wizard, where you can confirm your selections (see Figure 5-7).

Click Finish to create your plan. While the plan is being created, a status page will show you the progress on each step of the plan's creation, as shown in Figure 5-8.

The new plan will now show up in the Object Explorer under the Maintenance Plans node, and can be manually run by using the menu from that node.

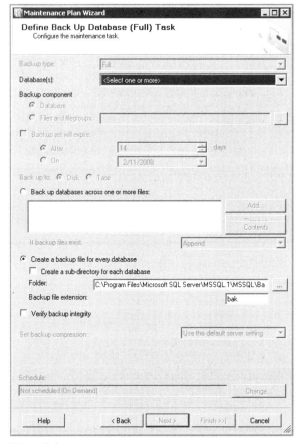

Figure 5-4

You will have noticed along the way that the Maintenance Plan Wizard can perform only a limited number of tasks, but these are some of the most important routine maintenance activities on the server. Using this wizard enables you to automate many of the essential tasks needed on a SQL Server.

If you want to explore more details about the plan you just created, look at the job created for this plan under the SQL Server Agent node, under the Jobs node. The job will be named *<Your plan name>*.subplan_1, so in this example the job name is Basic Backup.Subplan_1.

Maintenance Plan Designer

Now that you've used the Wizard to create a basic backup job, it's time to learn how to use the Designer to achieve the same task:

1. The starting point is the same; right-click on the Management Node in Object Explorer, and this time select the New Maintenance Plan item. This will open the New Maintenance Plan dialog, which you can see in Figure 5-9. Enter a new plan name, **Basic Backup 2**, so you don't conflict with the plan created using the Wizard. Click OK.

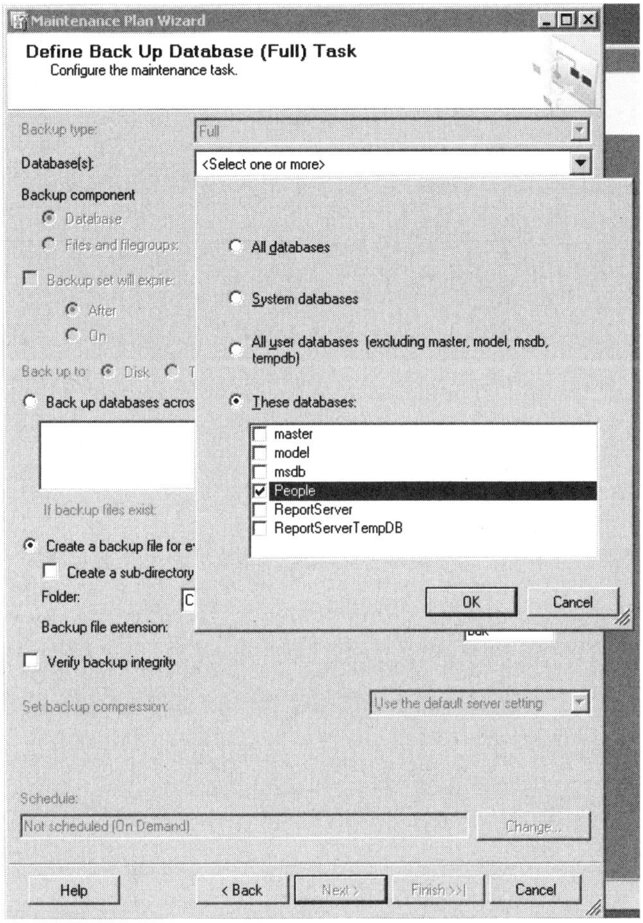

Figure 5-5

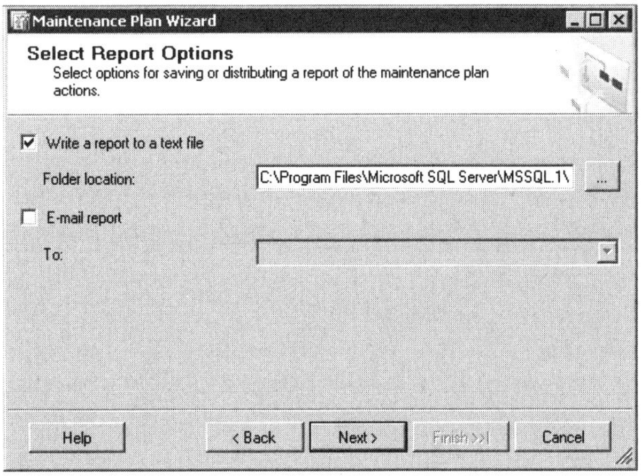

Figure 5-6

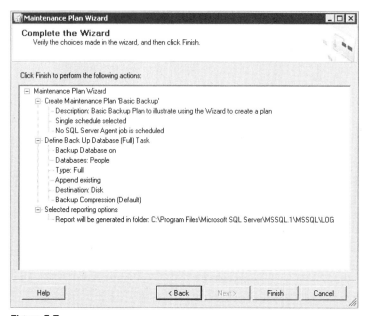

Figure 5-7

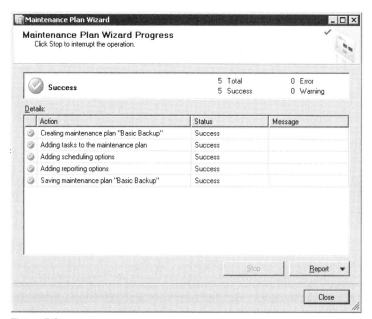

Figure 5-8

Figure 5-9

Figure 5-10 shows the Plan Designer dialog that will appear. You will see two new windows inside Management Studio. The Maintenance Plan Tasks toolbox appears as a pane below the Object Explorer. The Plan Designer window appears on the right side of the screen.

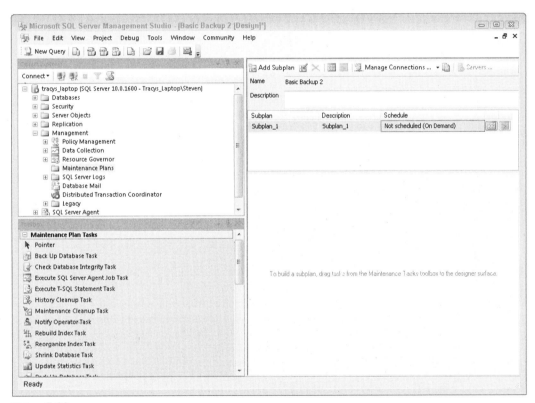

Figure 5-10

2. To create the basic backup task, click on the Back Up Database Task in the toolbox and drag it onto the designer's surface. After doing this your designer will look like Figure 5-11.

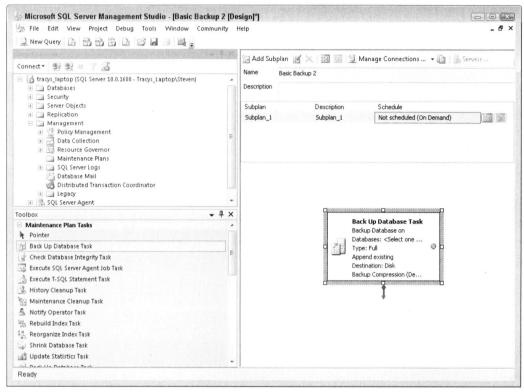

Figure 5-11

3. At this point you have created the basic Backup task, but haven't defined what the backup task needs to do. To specify the same parameters as you did when using the Wizard, you need to edit the properties of the Back Up Database Task. To do this, double-click the task on the designer. This will open the task properties screen, shown in Figure 5-12.

4. This is the same dialog you completed using the Wizard, so select the same database to back up, and the same options you selected when using the Wizard. When you have finished making those changes, click OK to return to the designer. This time you will notice that the Back Up Database Task no longer has the red warning sign, but now looks like Figure 5-13 (indicating the database you selected).

5. To create the plan you have just designed, merely save it. This will create the plan and the corresponding SQL Server Agent SQL Server Agent job.

You can use the Plan Designer at any time to edit the plan's properties.

SQL Server Agent

When a Maintenance Plan does not cover all the automation you require on a SQL Server, or anytime you need to do more than you can with a Maintenance Plan, using SQL Server Agent directly is the way to go.

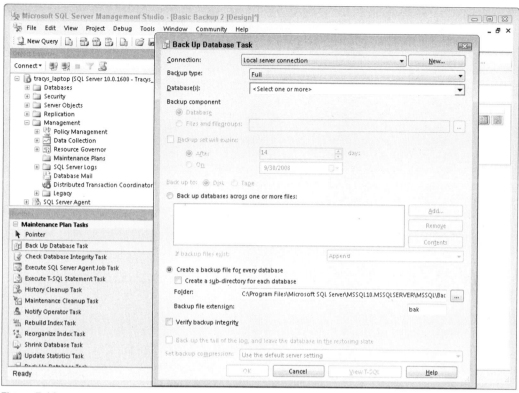

Figure 5-12

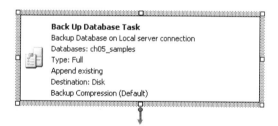

Figure 5-13

Automation Components

There are four basic components of SQL Server Agent, each of which we discuss in the following sections:

❑   **Jobs:** Defines the work to be done.

❑   **Schedules:** Defines when the job will be executed.

❑   **Alerts:** Enables you to set up an automatic response or notification when an event occurs.

❑   **Operators:** The people who can be notified regarding job status and alerts.

> By default, the SQL Server Agent service is not running, and the service is set to manual after the install of SQL Server. If you are going to be using this in production, be sure to use SQL Server Configuration Manager to set the Start Mode of this service to Automatic.
>
> You should never use the Services Console in the Administrative Tools folder to manage SQL Server Services. As clearly indicated in SQL Server Books Online, using the Services Console to manage SQL Server services is unsupported.

Jobs

As with Maintenance Plans, a basic reason to use SQL Server Agent is to schedule work to be done automatically, such as backing up a database. A SQL Server Agent job contains the definition of the work to be done. The job itself doesn't do the work, but is a container for the job steps, which is where the work is done. A job has a name, a description, an owner, and a category; and a job can be enabled or disabled. Jobs can be run in several ways:

❑   By attaching the job to one or more schedules.

❑   In response to one or more alerts.

❑   By executing sp_start_job.

❑   Manually via SQL Server Management Studio.

Job Steps

A job consists of one or more job steps. The job steps are where the work is actually done. Each job step has a name and a type. Be sure to give your jobs and job steps good descriptive names that will be useful when they appear in error and logging messages. You can create a number of different types of job step:

❑   **ActiveX Script:** Allows you to execute VBScript, JScript, or any other installable scripting language

❑   **Operating System commands (CmdExec):** Allows you to execute command prompt items. You can execute bat files or any of the commands that would be contained in a bat or cmd file.

❑   **SQL Server Analysis Services command:** Allows you to execute an XML for Analysis (XMLA) command. This must use the Execute method, which enables you to select data as well as administer and process Analysis Services objects.

❑   **SQL Server Analysis Services Query:** Allows you to execute a Multidimensional Expression (MDX) against a cube. MDX queries enable you to select data from a cube.

❑   **SQL Server SSIS Package Execution:** Allows you to do everything you need to do without going outside the environment. You can assign variable values, configurations, and anything else you need to execute the package. This is a nice improvement and certainly a time saver.

❑   **Transact-SQL Script (T-SQL):** Allows you to execute T-SQL scripts. T-SQL scripts do not use SQL Server Agent Proxy accounts, described later in this chapter. If you are not a member of the sysadmin fixed-server role, the T-SQL step will run using your user credentials within the database. When members of the sysadm fixed-server role create T-SQL job steps, they may specify that the job step should run under the security context of a specific database user. If they specify a database user, the step executes as the specified user; otherwise, the step will execute under the security context of the SQL Server Agent Service account.

The GUI for T-SQL security can be confusing. Although there is a Run As: drop-down on the first page of the Job Step Properties dialog where you set up job steps, this is not where you set the security for T-SQL steps. The Run As: drop-down here is used to specify security contexts for other types of steps. To set security for your T-SQL step, click the Advanced tab. At the bottom of the dialog is a Run as User drop-down. Set the T-SQL user security context here.

There are other job step types that you do not usually create yourself, although it is possible to do so. These jobs, with their associated steps, are usually created by setting up replication. The process of setting up replication defines jobs that use these step types, although there is nothing to prevent you from using these step types when needed:

❑   Replication Distributor

❑   Replication Merge

❑   Replication Queue Reader

❑   Replication Snapshot

❑   Replication Transaction Log Reader

Each job step runs under a *security context*. The security contexts for other types of job steps are described later in this chapter.

There is some control of flow related to job steps as well. You may specify an action for when the step succeeds and when the step fails. These actions can be one of the following:

❑   Quit the job, indicating success.

❑   Quit the job, with failure.

❑   Go to another job step.

You may also require that the job step be retried before it is failed. You may specify the number of retry attempts and the retry interval, in minutes. A job step will be retried the number of times you specify in the Retry Attempts field before it executes the On Failure control of flow. If the Retry Interval in Minutes field has been set, the step will wait for the specified time period before retrying. This can be useful when there are dependencies between jobs. For example, you may have a job step that does a bulk insert from a text file. The text file is placed into the proper directory by some other process, which may run late. You could create a VBScript job step that checks for the presence of the input file. To test for the file every 10 minutes for 30 minutes, you would set the retry attempts to 3 and the Retry Interval to 10.

When you create a job, you can place it into a job category. There are several predefined job categories, including [Uncategorized (Local)] and Database Engine Tuning Advisor. You can also create your own job categories. Each job can be in only one category. From the Object Explorer Window of SQL Server Management Studio, open the SQL Server Agent item in the tree view and right-click the Jobs Node, and from the menu select Manage Job Categories. The dialog box shown in Figure 5-14 will appear.

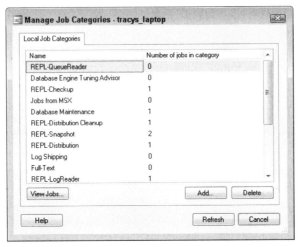

Figure 5-14

As trivial as it might seem, give some thought to organizing your jobs before creating your categories. You may be surprised how quickly the number of jobs on your server grows, making it difficult to find the correct job.

Job Step Logging

Each time a job is run, job history is created. Job history tells you when the job started, when it completed, and if it was successful. Each job step may be configured for logging and history as well. All of the logging setup for a job step is on the Advanced Tab of the job step properties. To append the job step history to the job history, check the "Include the step output in history" checkbox.

You may also choose to have the information logged to dbo.sysjobstepslogs in msdb. To log to this table, check the "Log to table" checkbox. To include step history from multiple job runs, also check the "Append output to existing entry in table." Otherwise, you will only have the most recent history.

Job steps executed by sysadmin role members may also have the job step history written to a file. Enter the file name in the Output File textbox. Check the "Append output to existing file" checkbox if you do not wish to overwrite the file. Job steps executed by others can only log to dbo.sysjobstepslogs in msdb.

Anytime you refer to network resources such as operating system files, ensure that the appropriate proxy account has the correct permissions. In addition, always use the UNC name for files, so the job or its steps are not dependent on directory maps. This is an easy place to get into trouble between the test and production environments if you are not very careful.

In addition to the logging capabilities described so far, output from T-SQL, Analysis Services Steps, and CMDExec steps can be written to a separate output file.

By default, SQL Server stores only 1,000 rows in its Job History Log, and a maximum of 100 for any one job. The Job History Log is a rolling log, so the oldest records are deleted to make room for newer job history. If you have a lot of jobs, or jobs that run frequently, the Job History Log can soon become full and start deleting old records. If you need to change the size of the log, you can do so under the SQL Server Agent properties, as shown in Figure 5-15.

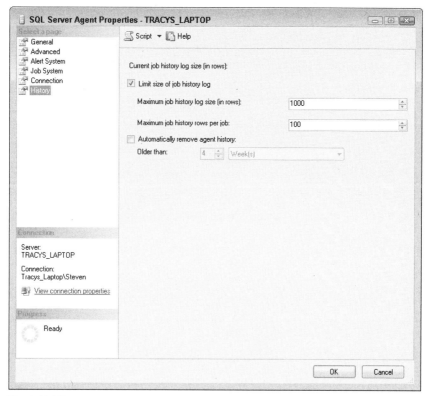

Figure 5-15

Job Notifications

You can configure SQL Server Agent to notify you when a job completes, succeeds, or fails. In the Job Properties dialog, choose Notifications to see the dialog box shown in Figure 5-16.

A job can send a notification via e-mail, pager, and Net Send.

> *Windows Messenger Service must be running on the server where SQL Server Agent is running to send notifications via Net Send. You can send a message to any workstation or user that can be seen from the SQL Server Agent server.*

As Figure 5-16 shows, there is a line in the dialog box for each of the delivery methods. Place a check beside the delivery method you want; you may choose multiple methods. Each option has a drop-down menu that enables you to choose an operator to notify. An operator enables you to define the e-mail address for the delivery. (Operator setup is described later in this chapter.) Then choose the event that should trigger the notification. It can be when the job completes, when the job fails, or when the job succeeds.

You may not wish to be notified at all for some jobs. However, for mission-critical jobs, you might wish to be e-mailed always when the job completes, and perhaps paged and notified through Net Send if the job fails, so you will know immediately.

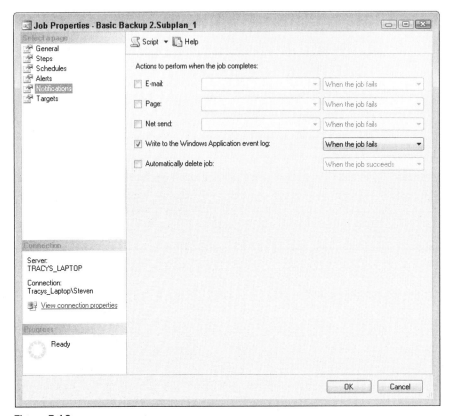

Figure 5-16

Schedules

One of the big benefits of SQL Server Agent is that you can have your jobs scheduled. You can schedule a job to run at any of these times:

❑ When SQL Server Agent starts.

❑ Once, at a specified date and time.

❑ On a recurring basis.

❑ When the CPU utilization of your server is idle.

You can define when the CPU is idle by setting up the Idle CPU Condition in SQL Server Agent Properties on the Advanced tab. You can define a minimum CPU utilization and a duration. When the CPU utilization is less than your definition for the duration you specify, CPU idle schedules are triggered.

Once your schedule is created, you can associate it with one or more jobs. A job can also have multiple schedules. You may wish to create a schedule for nightly batching and another for end-of-month processing. A single job can be associated with both schedules. If a scheduled job is triggered when the job is already running, that schedule is simply skipped.

To create a schedule in Management Studio, select SQL Server Agent, right-click Jobs, and choose Manage Schedules. The scheduler is particularly easy to use. You can easily create a schedule that runs on the last weekday of every month. (It is very convenient not to have to figure out which day is the last day of the month.)

The naming of a schedule can be a problem. Should the schedule name reflect *when* the schedule runs or *what* kind of work it includes? We suggest using both: Name regularly recurring jobs "per minute," "hourly," "midnight," and so on. For business-related schedules, you might create a schedule named "Accounts Payable End of Month" or "Bi Weekly Payroll Cycle." The reason for including business names is a matter of convenience. For example, you can disable a schedule; when you do so, that schedule no longer causes jobs to run. If you name many schedules based on business processes and someone instructs you not to run the payroll cycle yet, you can simply disable the associated schedule.

I have never had occasion to create a schedule to run when SQL Server Agent starts, but there might be some cleanup you wish to do, or you might wish to be notified when the system restarts; this would be the place to do so.

There are times when CPU idle jobs are worthwhile. If the CPU is not otherwise busy, you can get some batch-related work done. Be careful, however; if you have many jobs scheduled for CPU idle, they will begin to run quickly, and you can overpower your system. Be prudent with the number of jobs of this type that you schedule.

One item that is sorely lacking in SQL Server Agent's arsenal is the capability to link jobs together so that one begins as the other ends. You can make this happen by adding a final step in one job that executes the second job, but that puts all of the navigation inside job steps. It shouldn't be there. It should be outside at the job level. Some third-party tools do a good job of this. However, if you wish to do it on your own, it is likely to be difficult to maintain.

Operators

An operator is a SQL Server Agent object that contains a friendly name and some contact information. Operators can be notified on completion of SQL Server Agent jobs and when alerts occur. (Alerts are covered in the next section.) You may wish to notify operators who will fix problems related to jobs and alerts, so they may go about their business of supporting the business. You may also wish to automatically notify management when mission-critical events occur, such as failure of the payroll cycle.

You should define operators before you begin defining alerts. This enables you to choose the operators you wish to notify as you are defining the alert, saving you some time. To create a new operator, expand the SQL Server Agent Node in the Object Explorer in SQL Server Management Studio. From there, right-click on Operators and select New Operator. The New Operator dialog shown in Figure 5-17 will appear, where you can create a new operator.

The operator name must be unique and fewer than 128 characters.

For e-mail notifications, you can provide an e-mail address. You may provide multiple e-mail addresses separated by semicolons. This could also be an e-mail group defined within your e-mail system. If you wish to notify many people, it is better to define an e-mail group in your e-mail system. This enables you to change the list of people notified without having to change every job.

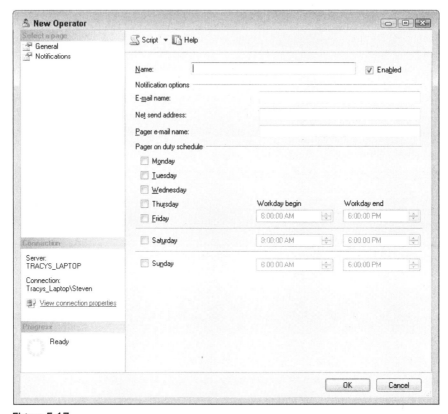

Figure 5-17

For pager notifications, you also provide an e-mail address. SQL Server Agent does not know anything about paging. You must have purchased paging via e-mail capabilities from a third-party provider. SQL Server Agent merely sends the e-mail to the pager address. Your pager software does the rest. Some pager systems require additional configuration characters to be sent around the Subject, CC, or To line. This can be set up in SQL Server Agent Configuration, covered at the end of this chapter.

Notice that there is a Pager on Duty Schedule associated with the Pager E-mail Name. This applies only to pagers. You can set up an on-duty schedule for paging this operator and then set this operator to be notified regarding an alert or job completion. When the job completes or the alert occurs, the operator will only be paged during his or her pager on-duty schedule.

You can also use Net Send to notify an operator. When Net Send is used, you must provide the name of the workstation for this operator, and a Message dialog box will pop up on his or her workstation. This is the least safe way of notifying, because the operator may not be at his or her desk.

Scheduling Notifications

Jobs allow you to notify a single operator for each of the three send types: e-mail, pager, and Net Send. Notifications from alerts allow you to notify multiple operators. This provides you with the capability to do some very nice things. For example, you can create an operator for each shift (First Shift Operators, Second Shift Operators, and Third Shift Operators), set up a group e-mail and a group page address for each of the shifts, set up the pager-duty schedule to match each shift's work schedule, and add all three operators to each alert. If an alert set up like this occurs at 2:00 A.M., then only the third-shift operators will be paged. If the alert occurs at 10:00 A.M., then only the first-shift operators will be paged.

There are several limitations of the schedule. Notice that the weekday schedule must be the same every day, although you can specify a different schedule for Saturday and Sunday. There is a big opportunity here for an enterprising individual. There is nothing to indicate company holidays or vacations. It would be really nice to be able to specify company holidays and let the schedule use the weekend schedule instead of the weekday schedule. It would also be nice to allow operators to specify vacation days that would be integrated into the system. You can disable operators, perhaps because they are on vacation, but you cannot schedule the disablement in advance. There are lots of opportunities for an add-in. Microsoft has maintained this limitation with essentially no improvements since SQL 7.0.

You can tell if a job, alert, or operator is disabled without having to go into the properties of the object. Management Studio tags disabled objects for SQL Server Agent with a small red down arrow. In Figure 5-18, one operator is enabled, and one operator is disabled.

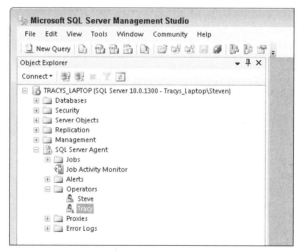

Figure 5-18

To use e-mail or pager notifications, Database Mail must be set up and enabled, and SQL Server Agent must be configured to use it. For pager notifications, you must have a third-party pager notification system. To use Net Send, Windows Messaging Service must be running on the same server as SQL Agent.

Failsafe Operator

What happens if an alert occurs and no operator is on duty, according to their pager on-duty schedule? Unless you specify a failsafe operator, no one would be notified. The failsafe operator is a security measure that enables an alert notification (not job notification) to be delivered for pager notifications (not e-mail or Net Send) that could not be sent.

Failures to send pager notifications include the following:

❑ None of the specified operators are on duty.

❑ SQL Server Agent cannot access the appropriate tables in msdb.

The failsafe operator is only used when *none* of the specified pager notifications could be made or msdb is not available. For example, suppose you have a long job that begins. The msdb database then fails for some reason, although SQL Server is still running, as is SQL Server Agent. The job needs to do a pager notification, but the sysoperators and sysnotifications tables in msdb are not available. SQL Server Agent will read the registry and obtain the failsafe operator information and send the page.

If you have three pager operators associated with a specific alert, and one of them is notified but two of them failed, the failsafe operator will *not* be notified.

You can indicate whether the failsafe operator will be notified using any or all of the three notification methods. Don't get confused here. A failsafe operator will only be notified if a pager notification cannot be successfully delivered. However, the failsafe operator in this case can be notified via e-mail, pager, Net Send, or a combination of these methods. Since the failsafe operator is a security mechanism, you may not delete an operator identified as failsafe. First, you must either disable the failsafe setup for SQL Agent, or choose a different failsafe operator. Then you can delete the operator.

You can disable an operator defined as failsafe. Disabling this operator will prevent any normal alerts or job notifications from being sent but will not restrict this operator's failsafe notifications.

Alerts

An *alert* is a predefined response to an event. An event can be any of the following:

❑ SQL Server event.

❑ SQL Server performance condition.

❑ Windows Management Instrumentation (WMI) event.

An alert can be created as a response to any of the events of these types. The following responses can be triggered as the result of an event alert:

❑ Start a SQL Server Agent job.

❑ Notify one or more operators.

You may only notify one operator for each notification type for job completion, but you may notify a list of operators for alerts.

To create an alert, open the New Alert dialog (see Figure 5-19) by selecting New Alert from the context menu on the Alerts Node under the SQL Server Agent node in SQL Server Management Studio.

When you create an alert, you give it a name. Ensure that this name tells you something about what is going on; it will be included in all messages. Names like "Log Full Alert" or "Severity 18 Alert on Production" might be useful.

You then choose the event type on which the alert is based, as shown in Figure 5-19. SQL Server events and SQL Server performance condition events are covered in this section; WMI events are outside the scope of this book, so are not addressed here.

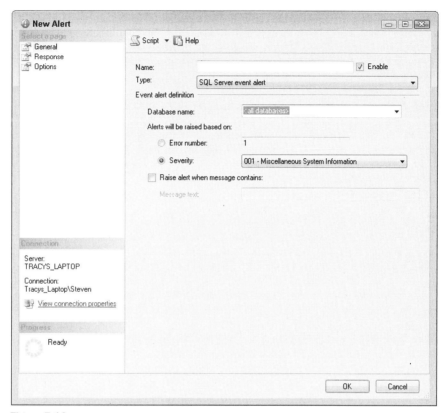

Figure 5-19

SQL Server Event

The SQL Server event alerts are based mainly on error messages. You can create an alert based on a specific error message number or on an error's severity. You might create an alert on error message number 9002 (log file full) or 1105 (out of disk space) message. An alert can be fired for any particular database or all databases. You may only care to get this alert when the Production database transaction log is full, not when the other test and development databases run out of log space. In this case, choose the Production database in the Database name drop-down list. I wish this drop-down were a multiselect, but it is not. If you wish to alert on two databases but not all of them, you have to create two separate alerts.

It is very common to set up 9002 alerts for your important databases to notify you if the database is out of log space. By the time your users call on the phone, you can tell them you are already aware of the problem and are working on it.

You can also choose to create an alert on a specific error-severity level. Each error message has an error-severity level. Severity 19 and above are fatal server errors. You may wish to create an alert for each of the severity levels between 19 and 25, so you can be notified of fatal SQL errors in any database.

What happens if you create an alert on a message that has a severity level of 16, and then create another alert of all severity-16 messages? When both the message number and message severity are covered in two separate alerts, only the message number alert will fire. You can think of the severity-level alert as a backup. Alerts defined on specific message numbers will fire when the message occurs. For all other error messages for that severity, the severity-level alert will fire as needed. This is a nice implementation.

You cannot create two message-level or severity-level alerts with the same message or severity level and the same database. For example, suppose you create an alert on message number 50001 for AdventureWorks2008 and another alert on message number 50001 for <all databases>. In this case, when the error message occurs in AdventureWorks2008, the alert for AdventureWorks 2008 will fire, not the <all databases> alert. The <all databases> alert will fire for a message number 50001 that occurs in any database other than AdventureWorks2008. The lesson here is that the most local handling of an event is the one that fires.

You may also create an alert that has an additional restriction on the text of the message. You can create an alert as before, but check the box "Raise alert when message contains:" and enter a text string in the textbox. The alert will then fire only on messages that include the specified text. For example, you could create an event that fires when the text "Page Bob" is included in the error message. Then applications could raise user errors that cause the alert to occur, paging Bob. This is a great way to amuse your friends and annoy Bob. The same principle as before applies: If a message with matching text is sent, the associated alert fires. The more general alert will fire if there is no text match.

SQL Server alerts work by watching the operating system application event log. If the event is not logged, the alert will not fire. The application log might be full, or the error might not be logged. You can create error messages with the sp_addmessage stored procedure. You may specify whether the message is logged or not. For example, you can create a simple message using the following SQL:

```
sp_addmessage 50001,16 ,'MESSAGE', @with_log =  'TRUE'
```

The preceding message has a message number of 50001 and a severity level of 16. You can then create alerts to test your system. Set these alerts to use e-mail as the response. To test the alert, use the following code:

```
Raiserror(50001,16,1)with log
Select * from msdb.dbo.sysmail_allitems
```

Raiserror sends the error message. Notice the included text with log. This is not necessary, because this message is always logged. You can cause an error message to be logged using the Raiserror command if you have the appropriate permissions.

The second statement displays all of the mail items. Scroll to the bottom of the list to check for the mail notification that has been attached as a response to the alert.

SQL Server Performance Condition

When you install SQL Server, a collection of Windows Performance Monitor counters is also installed. The Windows Performance Monitor tool enables the operations staff to monitor the performance of the server, including CPU utilization, memory utilization, and much more. When SQL Server is installed, an additional collection of monitor counters is added to enable DBAs to monitor the performance and status of SQL Server instances. You can create an alert on a condition based on any of these SQL Server counters.

You cannot create SQL Server alerts on counters that are not specifically for SQL Server, such as CPU utilization. However, the Performance Monitor tool gives you the capability to set alerts for these other non-SQL Server counters.

A SQL Server performance condition alert is shown in Figure 5-20.

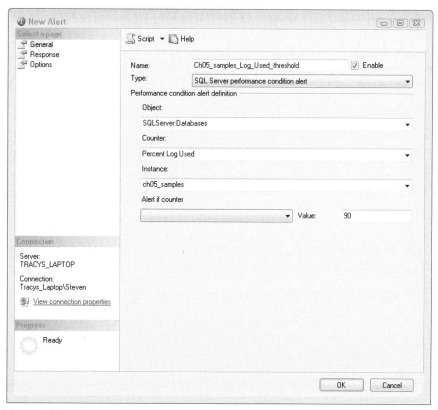

Figure 5-20

Performance counters are grouped according to their objects. For instance, the Databases object contains the counters associated with a specific database, such as Percent Log Used and Transactions/sec. The

`Buffer Manager` object includes counters specific to buffer management. You choose the object, and then the counter for which you wish to create an alert.

You cannot create multicounter alerts. For example, you cannot create an alert that fires when Percent Log Used is greater than 80 and Transactions/sec is greater than 100. You must choose to alert on a single counter.

The next choice you make is in the Instance textbox. When you choose `Databases` objects, the Instance textbox will contain the list of databases. You select the database on which to create the alert.

Next is the Alert If Counter box. You can alert if the counter falls below, becomes equal to, or rises above a value you specify. You specify the value in the Value textbox.

You have seen how you can create an alert to notify you when the transaction log becomes full. That is really a little too late, although better than no alerts at all. It would be much better to know when it looks like the log may become full but before it actually does. To do this, create a performance condition alert on the Percent Log Used counter for the `Databases` object for the database you are interested in. Choose when the counter rises above some safe limit, probably 80 to 95 percent. You will then be notified before the log is full. You will need to adjust this actual value so that you are not notified too quickly. If you have set up your log to be what you believe is large enough, then you might instead wish to notify on autogrowths.

Alert Responses

As you already know, you can respond to an alert by starting a SQL Server Agent job or notifying one or more operators. You set this up on the Response tab of the Create Alert dialog box. To execute a job, all you must do is check the checkbox and choose an existing job or create a new job. To notify an operator, check the appropriate box, and select the operators you wish to notify by choosing one or more of the notification methods. For alerts, it is really nice to have an operator for each shift you must cover, with the pager on duty set up appropriately, as discussed in the "Operators" section earlier in the chapter.

As you think about how you might best use this in your enterprise, imagine a scenario such as the transaction log getting full. You could set up a performance alert to notify operators when the log is actually full and run a job that grows the log. You could set up an alert that backs up the log when it becomes 70 percent full, and create another that backs up the log again when it is 80 percent full.

The scenario might play out as follows. You are having lunch and your pager goes off, notifying you that the log is 70 percent full. A job is run automatically that tries to back up the log to free space. In a couple of minutes you get a page telling you that the job completed successfully. After a few more potato chips, your pager goes off yet again — the log is now 80 percent full. The prior log backup did not free up any space. There must be a long-running transaction. The log backup job is run again, and you are notified upon its completion. You finish your lunch with no other pages. This means the last log backup freed up some space and you are now in good shape.

Your pager may have gone off again, telling you that the log is completely full and the job that automatically increases the log size has run. It's probably time for you to get back to work, but the automation you have brought to the system has already been fighting this problem while you ate your lunch, notifying you of each step. With some thoughtful consideration, you might be able to account for many planned responses such as this, making your life easier and operations tighter.

The Alert Options page in the Create Alert dialog box enables you to do several things:

- Specify when to include more detailed information in the notification.
- Add information to the notification.
- Delay the time between responses.

Sometimes the error text of the message might be long. Additionally, you may have a limit on the amount of data that can be presented on your devices. Some pagers limit you to as few as 32 characters. You should not include the error text for those message types that cannot handle the extra text, which are most commonly pagers.

The dialog includes a large textbox labeled "Additional notification message to send." You can type any text here and it will be included in the notification message. Perhaps something like "Get up, come in, and fix this problem immediately" might be appropriate. Perhaps "Remember that when you come in on weekends or at night to fix a problem, you receive a $300 bonus, so don't feel bad" might even be better.

At the bottom of the page, you can set a delay between responses. The default value for this is 0. Imagine a scenario where an alert goes off many times during a very short period. Perhaps a program is repeatedly executing raiserror or a performance condition alert is going wild. The performance condition alerts that run because of limited resources are especially vulnerable to this problem. You run low on memory, which causes an alert or job to run, which uses memory. This causes the alert to fire again, using more memory, repeatedly. You are paged repeatedly as well. Being notified that the transaction log is getting full 20 times a second is no more useful than hearing about it every five minutes. To remedy this problem, set your preferred delay between alerts, in minutes and seconds. When the alert occurs, it will be disabled for your specified delay time. Then it will be automatically enabled again. If the condition occurs again, the process starts all over again. This is a setting that you might find very useful from time to time.

You can right-click any of the SQL Server Agent objects and create a script that can drop or create the object. If you wish the same object to exist on many servers, you can script it out, change the server name, and load it onto a different server. This would mean you would have to keep operators, jobs, alerts, and proxies in sync between multiple servers, which could be painful and error prone. Multiserver jobs are covered later in the section "Multiserver Administration."

Event forwarding can also simplify your life when you administer many servers. Event forwarding is also covered in the "Multiserver Administration" section later in the chapter.

SQL Server Agent Security

SQL Server Agent security is more fine-grained than ever. In this section, we cover not only the service account, but also security issues such as who can create, see, and run SQL Server Agent jobs. What security do job steps run under? SQL Server 2008 allows multiple, separate proxy accounts to be affiliated with each job step. These proxy accounts are associated with SQL logins, which provide excellent control for each type of job step.

Service Account

The SQL Server Agent service account should be a domain account if you plan on taking advantage of Database Mail or require any network connectivity. The account should map to a login that is also a member of the sysadmin fixed-server role.

Access to SQL Agent

After the installation, only members of the sysadmin fixed-server role have access to SQL Server Agent objects. Others will not even see the SQL Server Agent object in the Object Explorer of Management Studio. To allow other users access to SQL Agent, you must add them to one of three fixed database roles in the msdb database:

- ❏ SQLAgentUserRole
- ❏ SQLAgentReaderRole
- ❏ SQLAgentOperatorRole

The roles are listed in order of increased capability, with SQLAgentOperator having the highest capability. Each higher role includes the permissions associated with the lower roles, so it does not make sense to assign a user to more than one role.

> *Members of the sysadmin fixed-server role have access to all of the capabilities of SQL Server Agent and do not have to be added to any of these roles.*

SQLAgentUserRole

Members of the user role have the most restricted access to SQL Server Agent. They can see only the Jobs node under SQL Server Agent and can only have access to local jobs and schedules that they own. They cannot use multiserver jobs, which are discussed later in this chapter. They can create, alter, delete, execute, start, and stop their own jobs and job schedules. They can view but not delete the job history for their own jobs. They can see and select operators to be notified on completion of their jobs and choose from the available proxies for their job steps.

SQLAgentReaderRole

The reader role includes all of the permissions of the user role. It can create and run the same things as a user, but this role can see the list of multiserver jobs, including their properties and history. They can also see all of the jobs and schedules on the local server, not just the ones they own. They can see only the Jobs node under SQL Server Agent as well.

SQLAgentOperatorRole

The operator role is the least restricted role and includes all of the permissions of the reader role and the user role. This role has additional read capabilities as well as execute capabilities. Members of this role can view the properties of proxies and operators. They can list the available proxies and alerts on the server as well.

Members of this role can also execute, start, or stop local jobs. They can enable or disable any job or operator, although they must use the sp_update_job and sp_update_schedule procedures to do so. They can delete job history for any job. The Jobs, Alerts, Operators, and Proxies nodes under SQL Server Agent are visible to this role. Only the Error Log node is hidden.

SQL Server Agent Proxies

A SQL Server Agent Proxy defines the security context under which different job steps run. In the case where the user who creates a SQL Server Agent job does not have permissions to access the resources needed by the job, the job creator can specify a proxy. The proxy contains the credentials of a Windows user account that does have access to the resources needed by the job.

For job steps that have a proxy specified, SQL Server Agent will impersonate the proxy account and run the job step while impersonating that user account.

SQL Server Agent Subsystems

The first step to making security finer-grained is to break up the objects on which security can be defined. Security is placed on each of the 11 SQL Server Agent subsystems. When you are adding a job step, they appear in the following order:

- ActiveX Script
- Operating System (CmdExec)
- Replication Distributor
- Replication Merge
- Replication Queue Reader
- Replication Snapshot
- Replication Transaction Log Reader
- Analysis Services Command
- Analysis Services Query
- SSIS Package Execution
- Transact SQL

The permissions for Transact SQL are not governed by proxy. Each user executes T-SQL under his or her own account. If you are a member of the sysadm group, you can choose any SQL login as the Run As Account.

All of the other subsystems use one or more proxies to determine permissions for the subsystem.

Proxies

Figure 5-21 shows the basic relationships among the parts.

Each subsystem has its own permissions. The following example shows the setup for permissions for the operating system (CmdExec) subsystem. The issue is, what operating-system permissions are used when someone executes a CmdExec job step? How can you allow multiple levels of permissions for different groups of users?

The proxy combines the permissions for the CmdExec step, as well as the users who may run under this proxy.

Credentials

The first thing you must do is create a credential. The easiest way to create a credential is in Management Studio: Expand Security, right-click on Credentials, and choose New Credential. You will be presented with a dialog box like the one shown in Figure 5-22.

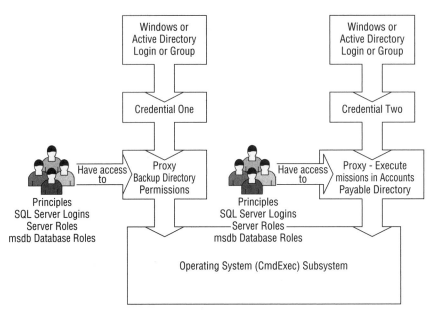

Figure 5-21

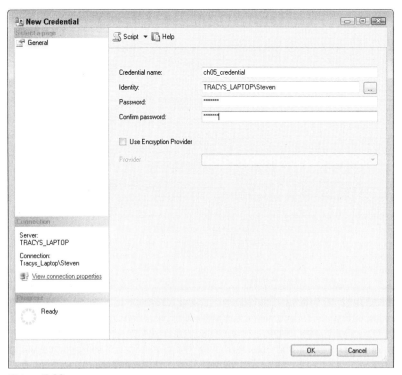

Figure 5-22

Give the credential a friendly name and associate it with a Windows login or group. You must also provide the password to complete the creation. The permissions associated with this login or group will be the permissions applied to the CmdExec job step.

> If your passwords time out on a regular basis, your job steps will begin to fail. You will have to reset the passwords for each credential or increase or drop the password expiration for the special accounts. These accounts should be created specifically for this and have the minimum security necessary for the job step to complete successfully.

Create Proxy

Now you can create your proxy. In Management Studio, expand SQL Server Agent, right-click Proxies, and choose New Proxy. You will get a New Proxy Account dialog box, shown in Figure 5-23.

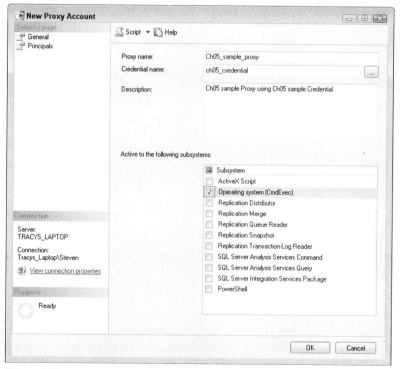

Figure 5-23

Give the proxy a name that provides information about its security level or its intended use. Then associate a credential with the proxy. The proxy will provide the permissions associated with its credential when it is used. Provide a more detailed description of what the proxy allows and how it should be used and when.

Then select the subsystems that can use the proxy. A proxy can be associated with many subsystems. Then you create a list of users (principles) who may use this proxy. This is done on the Principles page. A principle can be a Server Role, a SQL Login, or an msdb role.

Using Proxies

Now assume you have created the two proxies for the CmdExec subsystem as shown in Figure 5-21. Your SQL login is associated with both proxies. You wish to create a job that contains a CmdExec job step. When you add the job step, open the drop-down labeled Run As, which contains a list of all of the proxies you are allowed to use for your job step. Each proxy has its own permissions. Choose the proxy that contains the permissions you need for your job step, and you should be ready to go.

Configuring SQL Server Agent

Now that you have learned how things work in SQL Agent, you can take on the configuration task. You already know about many of the configurables, so now we will simply go through the dialogs with a brief description.

To start configuration, right-click the SQL Server Agent node in Management Studio and choose Properties. The General page will appear, as shown in Figure 5-24.

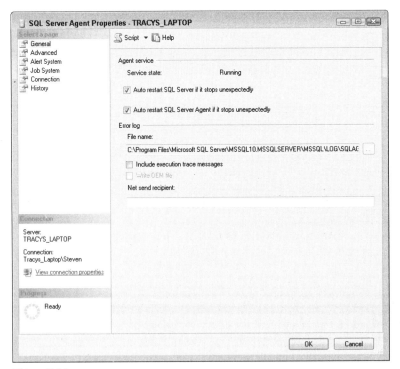

Figure 5-24

Make sure you check the two top checkboxes: "Auto restart SQL Server if it stops unexpectedly" and "Auto restart SQL Server Agent if it stops unexpectedly." The Service Control Manager will watch both of these services and automatically restart them if they fail.

We usually leave the error-log location at the default, but you can change it if you wish. If you need some additional logging, you can check "Include execution trace messages."

To get a Net Send when errors are logged, enter a workstation name in the Net Send Recipient textbox. Of course, Windows Messaging Service must be running on the server for Net Sends to occur.

Now choose the Advanced Page on the top left, which brings up the dialog shown in Figure 5-25.

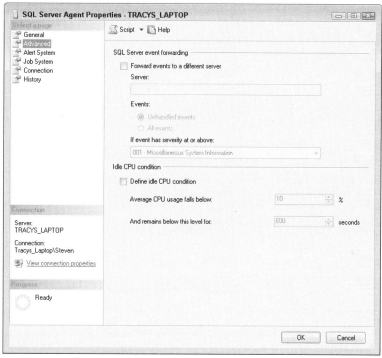

Figure 5-25

The top section, "SQL Server event forwarding," enables you to forward your events from one server to another. You can set up operators and alerts on a single server, and then have the other servers forward their events to the single server. If you plan on using this capability, you also need to understand how to use SQL Server Agent tokens, which are covered in the section "Using Token Replacement" later in this chapter.

If you want this server to forward its events, check the box labeled "Forward events to a different server." Then select the server name. You can forward all events or only unhandled events. An unhandled event is one that does not have an alert defined for it. You also select how severe the error must be before it will be forwarded. For example, you may not wish anything less than a severity 16 error (Miscellaneous User Error) to be forwarded. Whether or not you forward severity 16 errors depends on whether you have application-defined errors that specify notifications.

The second section is "Idle CPU condition." Recall that you can create a schedule that runs when the CPU becomes idle. This is where you define what *idle* means. The default is CPU utilization at less than 10 percent for 10 minutes.

The next page is for the Alert System, as shown in Figure 5-26.

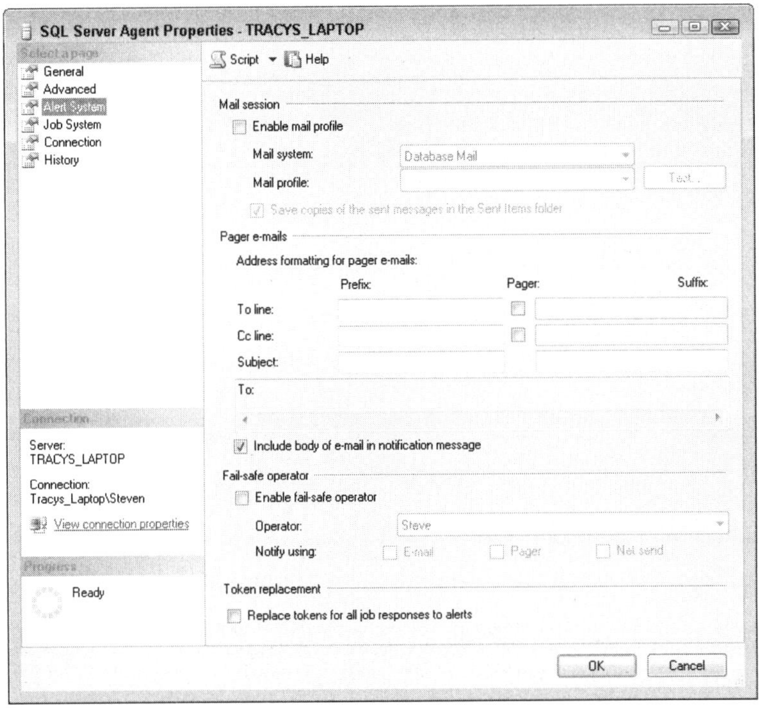

Figure 5-26

If you plan to use Database Mail or the older SQLMail, you do the setup here. Although you may have many mail profiles in Database Mail, SQL Server Agent will use only one profile. Choose the mail system and profile.

The second section is for pager e-mails. If your pager system requires special control characters in the To:, CC:, or Subject: line, you may add those characters here in front of the item (prefix) or after the item (suffix). As you make changes, you can see the effect in the small box below your data-entry section. You may also choose to include or exclude the body of the e-mail for pagers by indicating your selection in the appropriate checkbox.

The third section enables you to provide failsafe operator information. Please use this if you are doing any notifications. It is too easy to change a schedule in such a way that results in no one being notified, so don't get caught. Enable this section, choose an operator, and indicate how the failsafe messages should be delivered (by e-mail, pager, Net Send, or some combination of these).

The last checkbox enables you to specify whether or not you wish to have tokens replaced in jobs run from alerts. Details of token replacement are covered in the section "Multiserver Administration" later in this chapter.

The Job System page is next, as shown in Figure 5-27.

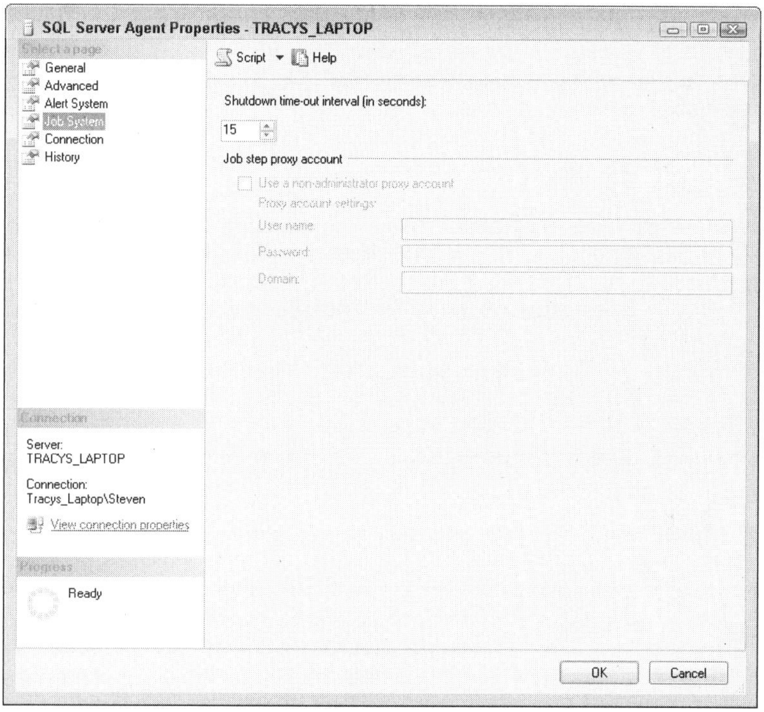

Figure 5-27

Suppose you are trying to shut down SQL Agent, and jobs are running. How long should SQL Server Agent wait for jobs to complete before killing them and shutting down? You specify that period in the Shutdown time-out interval (in seconds) list.

The second section is only available if you are administering a SQL Server 2000 Agent. This enables you to set the backwardly compatible non-administrator proxy. SQL 2000 only allowed one proxy. SQL Server 2005 and 2008 allow many proxies, so this is not necessary when administering SQL Server 2005 and 2008 Agents.

The Connection page is one that most users will not need. SQL Server Agent connects to SQL Server, by default, using the server name, default port, the SQL Server Agent Service account, and the highest-matching protocol between the client configuration and the protocols enabled for SQL Server. There are several circumstances where you may wish to alter these defaults:

❑   Your server has multiple network cards and you wish to specify a particular IP or port.

❑   You want to connect using a specific protocol (IP, for instance).

❑   You want SQL Server Agent to connect to the server using a login different from the service account login.

To accomplish this, you create an alias for the SQL Server, using Configuration Manager. Expand the SQL Native Client Configuration, right-click Aliases, and choose New Alias. Then set up the alias to suit your connectivity needs. Then, on the SQL Server Agent Connection page, enter the alias name and the connection information you want SQL Server Agent to use. Although SQL Server authentication is allowed, it is not recommended.

The last page is the History page, shown earlier in Figure 5-16. Carefully consider these settings. You can limit the size of the job history log to a fixed number of rows. That's easy and fine to do. The "Maximum job history rows per job" option is really a life saver, however. Imagine a job that runs repeatedly. It could be a job scheduled by a user to run every second, or it could be a job that runs from an alert that occurs repeatedly. In any case, the log entries from this job could fill up your entire job history, and you would have no history information for any other jobs. That could leave you in a tough spot if any other job needed debugging. This is exactly the situation that "Maximum job history rows per job" is intended to prevent. The default is 100 rows, but you can change it based on your needs.

SQL 2005 added the capability to remove older history rows even if the specified limit has not been reached. Simply check the box and set the age.

Database Mail

Database Mail was introduced with SQL Server 2005 and was a welcome replacement for SQLMail, although you may still use SQLMail if you wish. Database Mail and SQLMail enable you to notify operators via e-mail and to send e-mails via stored procedures.

SQLMail required Extended Messaging Application Programming Interface (MAPI) support, which could be problematic. Installing a new version of Office could cause SQLMail to fail, by installing a version of the MAPI driver that would be incompatible with SQLMail.

Database Mail is more secure, more reliable, and does not rely on MAPI. It uses Simple Mail Transfer Protocol (SMTP). It is cluster-aware, and allows automatic retry of failed e-mail messages as well as failover to another SMTP server, should the first become unavailable. Database Mail also enables you to set up multiple accounts and provide secured or public access to the accounts.

Database Mail is not available in the Express Edition of SQL Server.

Architecture

Database Mail is loosely coupled to SQL Server and is based on queuing, as shown in Figure 5-28. When an e-mail is sent, either by calling sp_send_dbmail or from SQL Server Agent notifications, security is checked. The e-mail is stored in a table in msdb, and a message is placed in the Service Broker message queue in msdb. This activates an external program, DatabaseMail.exe, located in the MSSQL\Binn directory. DatabaseMail.exe reads the message and sends the e-mail with any attachments to one or more SMTP mail servers. It then places a message in the status queue, containing the results of the send process. The status queue insert activates a stored procedure in msdb to update the status of the e-mail in msdb.

Security

For security reasons, Database Mail is disabled by default. You can enable and configure it using the Surface Area Configuration facet of policy-based management, by running the sp_configure stored procedure or by using the Database Mail Configuration Wizard.

Additionally, to send notifications via Database Mail from SQL Agent, SQL Server Agent must be configured to use Database Mail, as covered in the "SQL Server Agent Configuration" section of this chapter.

The external program, DatabaseMail.exe, must have network access to the SMTP servers. It runs using the security credentials for the SQL Server Service account. Therefore, the SQL Server Service account must have network access, and the SMTP servers must allow connections from the SQL Server computer. Database Mail supports Secure Sockets Layer (SSL) if it is required by the SMTP server.

> *Local System and Local Service do not have network access, and cannot be used as service accounts for SQL Server if you use Database Mail. Database Mail would not be able to connect to another computer (the SMTP server).*

To send Database Mail, you must either be a member of the sysadmin fixed-server role or be a member of the DatabaseMailUserRole in msdb. You can place a size limit on mail attachments and prohibit attachments with certain file extensions.

Configuration

To use Database Mail, you'll need to do some configuration. Specifically, you'll need to set up the Database Mail account, configure the mail procedure itself, and set up archiving.

Database Mail Account

A Database Mail account is a basic unit of configuration for Database Mail. An account contains the following configuration information:

❑ **"From" information for the e-mail messages:** All outgoing e-mail messages will indicate that they are from the account you provide here. This does not have to be a real e-mail account.

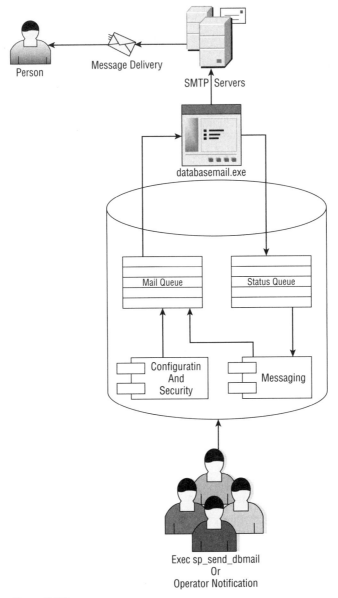

Figure 5-28

- ❑ **"Reply to" e-mail address:** If the recipient of one of these e-mails tries to reply, the reply will be sent to the e-mail address provided for this account.

- ❑ **SMTP connection information:** The SMTP Server name and port number are included in the account configuration. Database Mail supports encrypted and unencrypted messages.

Encryption is done via Secure Sockets Layer (SSL). Whether you wish the messages from this account to be encrypted is included in the account configuration.

❑ **E-mail retry configuration:** You may specify how many times to retry sending an e-mail and a wait period between retries.

❑ **E-mail size limits:** You may set a maximum size limit allowed for e-mails from this account.

❑ **Excluded attachment extension list:** You may provide a list of file extensions. Any attachment that has a file extension in the prohibited list will not be allowed.

❑ **Logging level:** You may specify how much logging should be done for this account.

If your SMTP Server requires a login, you may want to set up a specific local account, with minimum permissions, specifically for sending SMTP mail. The purpose of this account is to follow the principle of least privileges and should be used for no other purpose.

You may set up many accounts, but you should plan your implementation. For example, you may wish to have accounts for several different SMTP servers. This would enable you to automatically failover from one to another. This is done via profiles, which is covered in the next section. You may also wish to set up a special account that allows dangerous extensions or large attachments to be sent, and restrict that account to special users.

Another reason to set up multiple accounts is to provide different From and Reply to addresses. You may wish to do this for several departments in your company. For instance, you might set up an account named Accounts Payable that has a From address of AccountsPayable@mycompany.com and a Reply to address of IncomingAPEmail@mycompany.com. This reply address could be an e-mail group that sends to the accounts payable service reps at your company.

Setup

In this section, you will set up Database Mail. Use the Wizard by expanding Management in SQL Server Management Studio. Right-click Database Mail and choose Configure Database Mail.

Click through the introduction dialog box. The next box is the Select Configuration dialog box. Check the top radio button to indicate you are setting up Database Mail for the first time. Click Next.

If you haven't previously enabled Database Mail then you will receive a message box asking if you wish to enable the Database Mail feature. Choose yes and continue.

This brings you to the New Profile dialog box, shown in Figure 5-29.

To continue, you need to add at least one mail account. To add an account, click the Add button to display the New Database Mail Account dialog, shown in Figure 5-30. Here you provide the information needed to communicate with an SMTP server. Choose a name and description for this account.

E-mails sent from this account will be tagged from the e-mail address and display name that you set in this section. If the recipients reply to the e-mail, the reply will be sent to the address you supply in the Reply e-mail textbox. In the Server name textbox, you provide the name of the SMTP server.

This is usually in the form of `smtp.myserver.com`. You do not provide the complete URL, such as `http://smtp.myserver.com`. Database Mail does this for you. If you check the box labeled "This server requires a secure connection (SSL)," the URL created will be `https://smtp.myserver.com`. The default port number of 25 will do unless you have changed the SMTP port number.

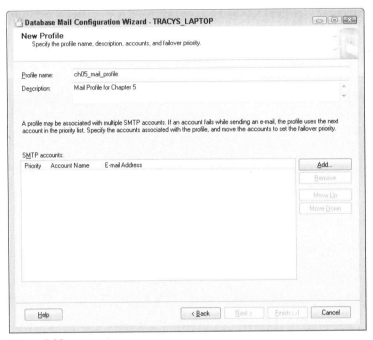

Figure 5-29

You provide the SMTP login information in the SMTP authentication section. Not all SMTP servers require authentication; some require only a known sender e-mail, and others require nothing. After supplying the needed information, click OK to return to the New Profile dialog, and then click Next.

The next page is the Manage Profile Security dialog, shown in Figure 5-31.

Here you set up public and private profiles. Check the Public checkbox next to a profile to make it public. You may also wish to set this as a default profile.

Click Next to move to the Configure System Parameters page. On this page you can change the values for system parameters such as retry attempts, maximum file size, and prohibited extensions, and set a logging level. The default values work well in most cases.

Clicking Next will take you to the Complete the Wizard page, where you have a last chance to confirm the selections you made before they are applied.

Clicking Finish applies the changes you made and displays progress and a completion report as each set of changes is made.

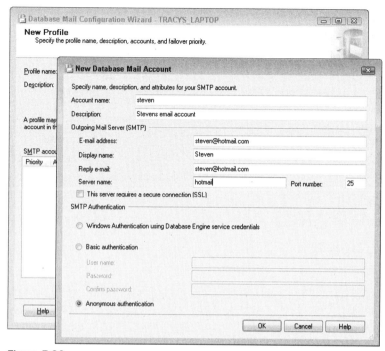

Figure 5-30

Figure 5-31

To ensure things are working properly, you should send a test e-mail. In SQL Server Management Studio, expand Management, right-click Database Mail, and choose Send Test E-Mail. You will be prompted to enter an e-mail address. Send the mail and wait for receipt.

Archiving

You can access mail information in the `sysmail_allitems` view. Attachments can be accessed via `sysmail_mailattachments`, and the mail log is in `sysmail_eventlog`. The tables under these views are not automatically maintained; they just get larger and larger. As a DBA, you will probably wish to do some maintenance. Microsoft provides stored procedures to delete items from these tables: `msdb.dbo.sysmail_delete_mailitems_sp` and `msdb.dbo.sysmail_delete_log_sp`. Each of these has two parameters: `@sent_before` and `@sent_status`.

`@sent_before` takes a `datetime` value and will delete all log or mail items with a time before the parameter time. When you do not specify a `sent_status`, all mail items that have a `send_request_date` prior to the parameter will be deleted, whether or not they have been sent, so be careful.

`@sent_status` can have values of `unsent`, `sent`, `failed`, or `retrying`. When you specify a `sent_status`, only the mail items that have a `sent_status` equal to the parameter will be deleted.

You may wish to archive this information prior to its deletion. Books Online will get you started with a small example that runs monthly and archives the month's mail, attachments, and logs into tables called, respectively, `DBMailArchive_<year>_<month>`, `DBMail_Attachments_<year>_<month>`, and `DBMail_Log_<year>_<month>`.

Multiserver Administration

There are several tactics within SQL Server 2008 that enable you to administer multiple servers more easily. The focus of these tactics is to centralize your administration. This can be done by forwarding events to a central event management server, which enables you to centralize alert handling. Another optimization is to use master and target servers to create jobs on a single master server and have the jobs run on multiple target servers.

Using Token Replacement

SQL Server 2008 has some really nice capabilities related to SQL Server Agent job tokens. A token is a string literal that you use in your job steps (T-SQL scripts, CMDExec job steps, or Active Script). Before the job runs, SQL Server Agent does a string replacement of the token with its value. Tokens are usable only in SQL Server Agent jobs.

One of the tokens is `(STRTDT)`. For example, you might add the following in a T-SQL job step:

```
PRINT 'Job Start Date(YYYYMMDD):' + $ESCAPE_SQUOTE(STRTDT))
```

If you capture the output, it should look like this:

```
Job Start Date(YYYYMMDD):20080923
```

Tokens are case sensitive.

The following is a list of tokens that can be used in any job:

- ❑ **(DATE):** Current Date (YYYYMMDD).
- ❑ **(INST):** Instance name of the SQL Server. This token is empty for the default instance.
- ❑ **(JOBID):** SQL Server Agent job ID.
- ❑ **(MACH):** Computer name where the job is run.
- ❑ **(MSSA):** Master SQLServerAgent service name.
- ❑ **(OSCMD):** Prefix for the program used to run CmdExec job steps.
- ❑ **(SQLDIR):** SQL Server's install directory. The default install directory is C:\Program Files\Microsoft SQL Server\MSSQL.
- ❑ **(STEPCT):** The number of times this step has executed. You could use this in looping code to terminate the step after a specific number of iterations. This count does not include retries on failure. This is updated on each step run during the job, like a real-time counter.
- ❑ **(STEPID):** The job step ID.
- ❑ **(SVR):** The server name of the computer running SQL Server, including the instance name.
- ❑ **(TIME):** Current time (HHMMSS).
- ❑ **(STRTTM):** The job's start time (HHMMSS).
- ❑ **(STRTDT):** The job's start date (YYYYMMDD).

The following is a list of tokens that can *only* be used in a job that has been started from an alert. If these tokens are included in a job started any other way, the job will throw an error:

- ❑ **(A-DBN):** Database name where the alert occurred.
- ❑ **(A-SVR):** Server name where the alert occurred.
- ❑ **(A-ERR):** Error number associated with the alert.
- ❑ **(A-SEV):** Error severity associated with the alert.
- ❑ **(A-MSG):** Message text associated with the alert.

The following token is available for use only on jobs run as the result of a WMI alert (see the "Using WMI" section later in the chapter).

- ❑ **(WMI(property)):** Provides the value for the WMI property named property. $(WMI(DatabaseName)) returns the value of the DatabaseName property for the WMI alert that caused the job to run.

You must use all of the tokens with escape macros. The purpose of this change is to increase the security related to the use of tokens from unknown sources. Consider the following token, which you might have included in a T-SQL job step:

```
Print 'Error message: $(A-MSG)'
```

The T-SQL job step runs as the result of a user error (`raiserror`). A malicious user could raise an error like this one:

```
Raiserror(''';Delete from dbo.Employee',16,1)
```

The error returned would be

```
';Delete from dbo.Employee
```

The print message would be

```
Print 'Error message:';Delete from dbo.Employee
```

You have just been attacked with a SQL injection attack. The delete statement will run if the T-SQL job step has permission.

Beginning with SQL Server 2005 SP1, you must add an escape macro. Since the `print` statement uses single quotes, a SQL injection attack would close out the single quote and then insert its own SQL. To prevent this attack, you could double-quote any quote that comes in via the token. The escape macro `ESCAPE_SQUOTE` does exactly that. It is used like this:

```
Print 'Error message: $(ESCAPE_SQUOTE(A-MSG))'
```

Continuing the example, you would end up with the following:

```
Print 'Error message:'';Delete from dbo.Employee
```

You would get an error due to the unmatched quote, and the step would fail; you would be safe.

The following is a list of escape macros:

- **$(ESCAPE_SQUOTE(token)):** Doubles single quotes (') in the replacement string.
- **$(ESCAPE_DQUOTE(token)):** Doubles double quotes (") in the replacement string.
- **$(ESCAPE_RBRACKET(token)):** Doubles right brackets (]) in the replacement string.
- **$(ESCAPE_NONE(token)):** The token replacement is made without changes. This is used for backward compatibility only.

You can also use these values directly if you ensure proper data types. The SQL script-looping job with tokens contains the following code that terminates a job step after it has executed five times. The top line converts the STEPCT token to an integer so it can be used in a comparison. Then the JOBID token for this job is converted to a binary 16 and passed to the `sp_stop_job` stored procedure, which can take the job ID of the job you wish to stop:

```
IF Convert(int,$(ESCAPE_NONE(STEPCT))) >5
  BEGIN
  DECLARE @jobid binary(16)
```

```
SELECT @jobid =Convert(Uniqueidentifier,$(ESCAPE_NONE(JOBID)))
EXEC msdb.dbo.sp_stop_job @job_id = @jobid
END
```

Imagine how you might use the alert-based tokens. You could create a SQL performance alert that fires when the <any database> transaction log becomes greater than 80 percent full. Create a job with a T-SQL step like this:

```
DECLARE @a varchar(100)
SELECT @a ='BACKUP LOG $(ESCAPE_SQUOTE(A-DBN))
  TO DISK = "\\UNCName\Share\$(ESCAPE_SQUOTE(A-DBN))\log.bak"'
SELECT @a
BACKUP LOG $(ESCAPE_SQUOTE(A-DBN))
  TO DISK = '\\UNCName\Share\\$(ESCAPE_SQUOTE(A-DBN))\log.bak'
```

where UNCName is the name of the server where you wish the backup to be stored and Share is the share on the server. Make sure the job runs when the alert occurs. If the alert fires for AdventureWorks 2008, the backup command will look like this:

```
BACKUP LOG AdventureWorks 2008 TO DISK = \\UNCName\Share\\AdventureWorks 2008\log.bak
```

You would have to create the directory first and grant appropriate permissions to the proxy you use. You could create a CMDExec step, which creates the directory on the fly. Now a single log backup job can back up any transaction log. You might improve this by adding the date and time to the file name.

Event Forwarding

Where events and alerts are concerned, you can create operators and alerts on a single system and then have the other systems forward their events to your central alert-handling SQL Server, which will respond to those alerts as necessary. The "Configuring SQL Server Agent" section of this chapter covers forwarding events.

You can set up operators on your master event management system. Create the jobs that will respond to the alerts. Then create alerts on the single master event management system to handle the event. The jobs you create can take advantage of SQL Server Agent tokens and know on which server and database the original event occurred.

Using WMI

Windows Management Instrumentation (WMI) is a set of functions embedded into the kernel of Microsoft Operating Systems and Servers, including SQL Server. The purpose of WMI is to allow local and remote monitoring and management of servers. It is a standards-based implementation based on the Distributed Management Task Force's (DMTF) Web-Based Enterprise Management (WBEM) and Common Information Model (CIM) specifications.

WMI is a big initiative and probably warrants an entire book of its own. What you need to know is that WMI has many events for SQL Server. Search for WMI to get you started in Books Online, and you will discover the many, many events. You can create alerts on these events. Included are Data Definition Language (DDL) events that occur when databases are created or dropped and when tables are created or dropped, for example.

WMI has a language to query these events called Windows Management Instrumentation Query Language (WQL). It is very much like T-SQL, and you will get comfortable with it immediately.

Browse Books Online for the kind of event you wish to monitor. Each event will have a list of attributes, just like a table has a list of columns. Using WMI, you can select the attributes from the event in an alert.

To create an alert, use SQL Serve Management Studio. In Object Explorer, open the SQL Server Agent tree node, right-click Alerts, and choose New Alert. In the Alert Type drop-down box, choose WMI Event Alert.

The namespace will be populated based on the server you are connected to and should look like this:

```
\\.\root\Microsoft\SqlServer\ServerEvents\SQL2008
```

The period (.) represents the server name, which you can change, such as \\MYSQLSERVER\. The last node should be MSSQLSERVER for a default instance and the *instance name* for named instances. In the preceding example, the instance I was running is called SQL2008.

In the textbox, you enter your WQL query, as shown here:

```
SELECT * FROM DDL_DATABASE_LEVEL_EVENTS
```

Or you could use this query:

```
Select TSQLCommand from DDL_DATABASE_LEVEL_EVENTS
```

To select only the TSQLCommand Attribute. There will be a pause when you click OK. If your namespace is incorrect, or the syntax or event/attribute names are incorrect, you will get a message immediately.

Then, in your job, you may use the WMI(attribute) event token — in this case:

```
Print '$(ESCAPE_SQUOTE(WMI(TSQLCommand)))'
```

To get events from a database, Service Broker notifications must be turned on for that database. To turn on Service Broker notifications for AdventureWorks2008, use the following syntax:

```
ALTER DATABASE AdventureWorks2008 SET ENABLE_BROKER;
```

If your alerts are occurring but the text replacement for the WMI token is not being done, you probably need to turn on the Service Broker for your database.

The service account that SQL Server Agent uses must have permission on the namespace and ALTER ANY EVENT NOTIFICATION *permissions. This will be done automatically if you use SQL Server Configuration Manager to set up accounts. However, to adjust these settings manually, from the Run prompt, type* **wmimgmt.msc**. *An administrative dialog will appear, allowing you to set up permissions.*

There is a test program for WMI on your server. To run it from the command line, type **WBEMTest**. It is installed in the WBEM directory of your Windows system directory.

Microsoft has an entire subsection of its Web site devoted to WMI. Just search for WMI on www.microsoft.com.

Multiserver Administration — Using Master and Target Servers

SQL Server enables you to set up a master server (MSX). The master server can send jobs to be run on one or more target servers (TSX). The master server may not also be a target server, receiving jobs from another master server. The target servers receive and run jobs from a single master server, in addition to their own local jobs. You may have multiple master servers in your environment, but a target server is associated with a single master server. This is a very simple two-level hierarchy; a server is a master server, a target server, or neither. The language used to describe the process is military in character: You *enlist* target servers to add them, and they *defect* to go away.

Setting up servers is easy. In SSMS, right-click the SQL Server Agent node, select Multiserver Administration, and choose Make This a Master. After the initial dialog box, you will see a box where you can provide the e-mail address, pager address, and Net Send location to set up a *master server operator*. This operator will be set up on the master server and all target servers. This is the *only* operator who can be notified from multiserver jobs.

The next dialog box enables you to choose all of the target servers. The list includes the servers that you have registered in SSMS. You may add additional registrations by clicking the Add Connection button. Choose the servers that you want to be targets of this master and click Next. SQL will check to ensure that the SQL versions of the master and targets are compatible. Close this dialog box. If the versions are not compatible, drop the target from the list and then continue. Later, you can upgrade the target or master, so the versions are the same.

Target servers must connect to the master server to share job status information. The next dialog box enables you to have the wizard create a login on the target, if necessary, and grant it login rights to the master server. Once you have completed the setup, you can refresh your SQL Server Agent nodes and see the change. There will be a note on the master server (MSX), as well as a note on the target server.

Now you can create jobs to be used at multiple target servers. Notice on the MSX that the Jobs node is divided into two sections: local jobs and multiserver jobs. Right-click multiserver jobs, and select New Job to create a simple job.

Now you can create jobs on the MSX server and have them run at one or many TSX servers. At this point, create a simple job. While doing this, be sure to go to the notifications page. The only operator you can notify is MSXOperator.

Creating multiserver jobs is a really nice way to manage a larger implementation without having to buy additional third-party products. No one on the TSX box can mess up your jobs, either. Use SSMS to connect to the target server as an administrator and look at the job properties for the job you just created and downloaded from the MSX. You can see the job, you can see the job history, and you can even run the job. You cannot delete the job, change the schedule, change the steps, or anything else. This job does not belong to you; it belongs to the MSX.

As you begin to think about how you might use this, be sure you consider the implications of a single job running on multiple servers. Any reference to directories, databases, and so on must be valid for all of the TSXs where this job runs. You can create a single backup share that all of the backups can use, for instance.

Since a job can start another job, you could also create a master job that has a single step that starts another job. This other job is created on each TSX and is specific to each TSX. This will allow you some customization, if necessary.

Back in SSMS, right-click the SQL Server Agent node on the master server, choose Multi Server Administration, and you can add target servers and manage target servers. Choose Manage Target Servers. In this dialog box, you can monitor the status of everything. When you create a job for a target server, the job is automatically downloaded to the target server. If the unread instructions count does not go down to 0, as shown in this figure, poll the target server. This will wake it up to accept the instructions.

You can also see the details of downloaded instructions by clicking the relevant tab. This will show you details of when jobs are downloaded and updated.

Using the Post Instructions button in the Target Server Status dialog, you can synchronize clocks between the servers, defect target servers, set polling intervals, and start jobs. You can also start the job directly from the Jobs node on the MSX or the TSX.

Job histories can be viewed on the MSX for the job, just like any other job, but you cannot see job-step details. To get the step details, view the job history from the TSX.

You can defect TSXs from the TSX SQL Server Agent node or from the Manage Target Servers dialog on the MSX. When all of the TSXs have been defected, the MSX is no longer an MSX.

Summary

Maintenance Plans are a great way to get started with automating common maintenance tasks.

SQL Server Agent provides many features and services to make your life easier. Just creating a few simple backup jobs that notify operators will automate many normal tasks. If you wish to get fancy, go ahead, but do some planning first, especially when considering multiserver jobs.

The pager notifications and the related on-duty schedules can be used for regular e-mail or pagers. This is a good way to ensure that the correct people are being notified. If you are going to have many operators for alert notifications, consider creating e-mail groups, and offload some of the notification work to your e-mail server. Start small, and take your time. As you get more comfortable with Maintenance Plans and SQL Server Agent, you can spread your wings and fly.

In the next chapter you will learn about SQL Server Integration Services.

6

Integration Services Administration and Performance Tuning

In keeping with the theme of focusing on how SQL Server 2008 changes the role of the DBA, in this chapter you learn how you can be better equipped as a DBA to maintain SQL Server's Business Intelligence components. The SQL Server 2008 Business Intelligence stack includes Integration Services (SSIS), Analysis Services (SSAS), and Reporting Services (SSRS). We focus on Integration Services and Analysis Services in this book, because these components require considerable understanding in order to manage successfully.

This chapter looks at the many and varied administrative tasks required for managing Integration Services. First, an overview of the Integration Services service is provided so that you can be more comfortable with and have a better understanding of the moveable parts that require the attention of an administrator. After getting comfortable with the architecture of Integration Services, you can focus on the administration of Integration Services, including configuration, event logs, and monitoring activity. Next, you'll gain an understanding of the various administrative tasks required of Integration Services packages, the functional component within SSIS, including creation, management, execution, and deployment. Last, you'll learn how to secure all of the Integration Services components.

> For more in-depth information about Integration Services, see *Professional SQL Server 2008 Integration Services*, by Brian Knight et al. (Wrox, 2008).

A Tour of Integration Services

Certainly the most important Business Intelligence change from SQL Server 2000 to 2008 is found in the component responsible for the movement and manipulation of data. The 2000 platform used Data Transformation Services (DTS), whereas the 2005 and 2008 platforms use Integration Services. The change in capabilities goes far beyond what a simple name change might imply, as

Integration Services was a complete ground-up rewrite of DTS. In fact, not a single code line from DTS remains within Integration Services today. You can learn more about upgrading from SQL Server 2000 DTS to SSIS in Chapter 3.

Integration Services is a solution that provides enterprise-level data integration and workflow solutions that have as their goal the extraction, transformation, and loading (ETL) of data from various sources to various destinations. SSIS includes a wide range of tools and wizards to assist in the creation of the workflow and data flow activities that you need to manage in these complex data-movement solutions.

Integration Services Uses

Before diving into the detailed components within Integration Services, you should understand some of the more common business scenarios that involve creating SSIS solutions.

One of the first scenarios is combining data from different sources stored in different storage systems. In this scenario, SSIS would be responsible for connecting to each data source, extracting the data, and merging it into a single dataset. In today's information systems topology, this is becoming increasingly common, as businesses' archive information that is not needed for regular operations but is invaluable to analyze business trends or meet compliance requirements. This scenario is also found when different parts of a business use different storage technologies or different schemas to represent the same data. In these cases, SSIS is used to perform the homogenization of the information. SSIS seamlessly handles multiple divergent data sources and the transformations that can alter data types, split or merge columns, and look up descriptive information that becomes powerful assets for these situations.

Another common scenario is the population and maintenance of data warehouses and data marts. In these business uses, the data volumes tend to be exceptionally large and the window of time in which to perform the extraction, transformation, and loading of the data tends to be rather short. SSIS includes the capability to bulk-load data directly from flat files in SQL Server, and has a destination component that can perform a bulk load into SQL Server. A key feature for large data volume and complex enrichment and transformation situations such as these is restartability. SSIS includes checkpoints to handle rerunning a package from a task or container within the control flow so that you can elegantly handle various types of errors that may occur during these complex data-loading scenarios.

Also important in data warehouse loads is the ability to source a particular destination from many different tables or files. In the database world, this is referred to as *denormalization*, and SSIS packages can easily merge data into a single dataset and load the destination table in a single process without the need to stage or land the data at each step of the process.

Lastly, we often require the management or partitioning of history within our data warehouses in order to review the state of activity at a certain point in time. This history management creates complex updating scenarios, and SSIS handles this with the assistance of the Slowly Changing Dimension Wizard. This wizard dynamically creates and configures a set of data transformation tasks used to manage inserting and updating records, updating related records, and adding new columns to tables to support this history management.

Often, businesses receive data from outside of their systems and need to perform data-quality routines to standardize and clean the data before loading it into their systems. SSIS can handle most data situations from heterogeneous databases or flat files. This is commonly the case when different areas of the business use different standards and formats for the information or when the data is being purchased, such as with address data. Sometimes the data formats are different because the platforms from which they originate differ from the intended destination. In these cases, SSIS includes a rich set of data-transformation tasks to perform a wide range of data-cleaning, converting, and enriching functions. You can replace values or get descriptions from code values by using exact or fuzzy lookups within SSIS. Identifying records that may be duplicates by using SSIS grouping transformations helps to successfully remove them before loading the destination.

The ability to dynamically adjust the data transformations being performed is a common scenario within businesses. Often, data needs to be handled differently based on certain values it may contain or even based upon the summary or count of values in a given set of records. SSIS includes a rich set of transformations that are useful for splitting or merging data based upon data values, applying different aggregations or calculations based on different parts of a dataset, and loading different parts of the data into different locations. SSIS containers specifically support evaluating expressions, enumerating across a set of information, and performing workflow tasks based on results of the data values.

Lastly, you commonly have operational administrative functions that require automation. SSIS includes an entire set of tasks devoted to these administrative functions. You can use tasks specifically designed to copy SQL Server objects or facilitate the bulk loading of data. You also have access in SSIS to a SQL Management Objects (SMO) enumerator to perform looping across your servers to perform administrative operations on each server in your environment. You can also schedule all of your SSIS packages and solutions using SQL Server Agent jobs.

The Four Main Parts of Integration Services

Integration Services consists of four main parts (see Figure 6-1):

- ❏   The SSIS service.
- ❏   The SSIS runtime engine and the runtime components.
- ❏   The SSIS object model.
- ❏   The SSIS data flow engine and the data flow components.

Integration Services Service

The component of architecture within Integration Services, responsible for monitoring packages as they execute and managing the storage of packages, is the SSIS service. Its primary job is to cache the data providers, monitor which packages are being executed, and monitor which packages are stored in the package store.

Integration Services Runtime Engine and Runtime Components

The SSIS runtime engine is responsible for saving the layout and design of the packages, running the packages, and providing support for all additional package functionality such as transactions, breakpoints, configuration, connections, event handling, and logging. The specific executables that make up this engine include packages, containers, and tasks. Three default constraints are found within SSIS: success, completion, and failure.

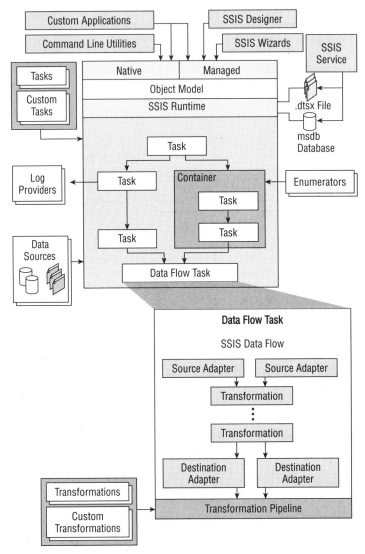

Figure 6-1

Integration Services Object Model

The managed application programming interface (API) used to access SSIS tools, command-line utilities, and custom applications is the SSIS object model. While we do not go into much detail about this object model, it is important to acknowledge it as a major component of Integration Services.

Integration Services Data Flow Engine and Data Flow Components

Within an SSIS package's control flow, a Data Flow Task creates instances of the data flow engine. This engine is responsible for providing the in-memory data movement from sources to destinations. Additionally, this engine performs the requested transformations to enrich the data for the purposes you specify. Three primary components make up the data flow engine: sources, transformations, and destinations. The *sources* provide connectivity to, and extract data from, a wide range of sources such as database tables or views, files, spreadsheets, and even XML files. The *destinations* permit the insert, update, and deletion of information on a similar wide range of destinations. Lastly, the *transformations* enable you to modify the source data before loading it into a destination using capabilities such as lookups, merging, pivoting, splitting, converting, and deriving information.

Project Management and Change Control

Clearly, one of the areas needing an entirely different mindset from the previous version of SQL Server involves how DBAs interact with the development team. The shared view of development by administrators and developers alike is enacted through the Business Intelligence Developer Studio (BIDS). With regard to Integration Services, the BIDS environment is how SSIS solutions and projects are created. Generally, the configuration of the BIDS solutions and projects is handled by the developers; however, administrators are called upon to help configure various aspects of these solutions. The administration and management of Integration Services is primarily performed within SQL Server Management Studio. Often, moving the Integration Services solutions from environment to environment means changing dynamic information within the package and setting up any information referenced by the packages. Examples of these elements include Package Configuration settings, referenced XML or configuration files, and solution data sources.

Note that that when a developer clicks Save or executes the package in BIDS, the old version of the package is immediately discarded. To remedy this, you should integrate the SSIS development environment into a source control system — such as Visual SourceSafe, for example. After such integration, when a package is saved you can always roll back to an earlier release of the package. You can use any type of source control system that integrates with Visual Studio 2008.

Administration of the Integration Services Service

Now that you have a better understanding of the parts of Integration Services, this section looks at the various administrative aspects of Integration Services, including the details needed to become comfortable working with the components. You'll start with a review of the Integration Services service and then look at various configuration elements of the service. Next, you'll look at how you can adjust properties of the SSIS service using either the Windows Services Snap-in or the SQL Server Configuration Manager. Understanding how you can modify Windows Firewall follows, and then you'll look at the management and configuration of event logs, and performance monitoring.

An Overview of the Integration Services Service

The Integration Services service is a Windows service used to manage SSIS packages. Accessed through SQL Server Management Studio, it provides the following management capabilities:

❑   Starting and stopping local and remote packages.

❑   Monitoring local and remote packages.

❑   Importing and exporting packages from different sources.

- ❑ Managing the package store.
- ❑ Customizing storage folders.
- ❑ Stopping running packages when service is stopped.
- ❑ Viewing the Windows Event Log.
- ❑ Connecting to multiple SSIS server instances.

To be very clear, you don't need this service for designing or executing packages. The primary purpose of this service is to manage packages within Management Studio. One side benefit to having the service running is that the SSIS Designer in Business Intelligence Developer Studio can use the service to cache the objects used in the designer, thus enhancing the designer's performance.

Configuration

The configuration of the Integration Services service includes viewing and possibly modifying the XML file responsible for the runtime configuration of the service, setting service properties using either the Windows Services Snap-in or SQL Server Configuration Manager, and, potentially, configuring Windows Firewall to permit access by Integration Services.

XML Configuration File

The `MsDtsSrvr.ini.xml` file responsible for the configuration of the Integration Services service is located in `<SQL Server Drive>\Program Files\Microsoft SQL Server\100\DTS\Binn` by default. You can also move this file to a new location by changing the `HKEY_LOCAL_MACHINE\SOFTWARE\Microsoft\Microsoft SQL Server\100\SSIS\ServiceConfigFile` registry key. This file includes settings for specifying whether running packages are stopped when the service is stopped, a listing of root folders to display in the Object Explorer of Management Studio, and settings for specifying which folders in the file system are managed by the service.

The configuration file name and location can be changed. This information is obtained by Management Studio from the Windows registry key `HKEY_LOCAL_MACHINE\SOFTWARE\Microsoft\MSDTS\ServiceConfigFile`. As with most registry key changes, you should back up the registry before making any changes, and you need to restart the service after making changes in order for them to take effect.

One example of a configuration change that must be made is when you connect to a named instance of SQL Server. The following example shows the modification for handling a named instance (`MyServerName\MyInstanceName`). This is because the default configuration for the SSIS service will always point to "`.`" and must be configured for a clustered or named instance.

```xml
<?xml version="1.0" encoding="utf-8"?>
<DtsServiceConfiguration xmlns:xsd="http://www.w3.org/2001/XMLSchema"
xmlns:xsi="http://www.w3.org/2001/XMLSchema-instance">
  <StopExecutingPackagesOnShutdown>true</StopExecutingPackagesOnShutdown>
  <TopLevelFolders>
    <Folder xsi:type="SqlServerFolder">
      <Name>MSDB</Name>
      <ServerName>MyServerName\MyInstanceName</ServerName>
    </Folder>
    <Folder xsi:type="File systemFolder">
      <Name>File System</Name>
```

```
        <StorePath>..\Packages</StorePath>
      </Folder>
    </TopLevelFolders>
  </DtsServiceConfiguration>
```

There isn't really a lot to configure in this file but it has some interesting uses. The first configuration line tells the packages how to react if the service is stopped. By default, packages that the service is running will stop upon the service stopping or being failed over. You could also configure the packages to continue to run until they complete after the service is stopped by changing the `StopExecutingPackagesOnShutDown` property to `False`:

```
    <StopExecutingPackagesOnShutdown>false</StopExecutingPackagesOnShutdown>
```

Other common configuration file change scenarios include adding additional paths from which to display packages other than the default SSIS package store path of `C:\Program Files\SQL Server\100\Packages` and creating a centralized folder structure for multiple servers by storing the service configuration file in a central fileshare.

Creating a Central SSIS Server

Many enterprise companies have so many packages that they decide to separate the service from SQL Server and place it on its own server. When you do this, you must still license the server just as if it were running SQL Server. The advantages of this are that your SSIS packages will not suffocate the SQL Server's memory during a large load and you have a central spot to manage. The disadvantages are that now you must license the server separately, and you add another layer of complexity when you're debugging packages. When you create a dedicated server you create a fantastic way to easily scale packages by adding more memory to your central server, but you also create an added performance hit, as all remote data must be copied over the network before entering the data flow buffer.

To create a centralized SSIS hub, you need only modify the `MsDtsSrvr.ini.xml` file and restart the service. The service can read a UNC path like `\\ServerName\Share` and it can point to multiple remote servers. Mapped drives are not recommended, as the account that starts the SSIS service would have to be aware of the drive and could create an unnecessary dependency on that account. In the following example, the service will enumerate packages from three servers, one of which is local and another that is a named instance. After restarting the service, you will see a total of six folders to expand in Management Studio. We cover the Management Studio aspect of SSIS in much more detail later in this chapter.

```
    <?xml version="1.0" encoding="utf-8" ?>
    <DtsServiceConfiguration xmlns:xsd="http://www.w3.org/2001/XMLSchema"
    xmlns:xsi="http://www.w3.org/2001/XMLSchema-instance">
      <StopExecutingPackagesOnShutdown>true</StopExecutingPackagesOnShutdown>
     <TopLevelFolders>
    <Folder xsi:type="SqlServerFolder">
      <Name>Server A MSDB</Name>
      <ServerName>localhost</ServerName>
      </Folder>
      <Name>Server B MSDB</Name>
      <ServerName>SQLServerB</ServerName>
      </Folder>
    <Folder xsi:type="File systemFolder">
      <Name>Server A File System</Name>
      <StorePath>P:\Packages</StorePath>
```

```
      </Folder>
  <Folder xsi:type="File systemFolder">
    <Name>Server B File System</Name>
    <StorePath>\\SQLServerB\Packages</StorePath>
    </Folder>
    </TopLevelFolders>
    </DtsServiceConfiguration>
```

Your next issue is how to schedule packages when using a centralized SSIS hub. You can schedule your packages through SQL Server Agent or through a scheduling system such as Task Scheduler from Windows. You're already paying for a license of SQL Server, so it's better to install SQL Server on your server and use Agent, as it gives you much more flexibility (you will see why later). You can also store configuration tables and logging tables on this SQL Server to centralize its processing as well. Both scheduling mechanisms are covered later in this chapter.

Each time you make a change to the configuration file, you need to stop and start the SSIS service, as described in the following sections. Now that you know how to configure the MsDtsSrvr.ini.xml file responsible for the configuration of the Integration Services service, you need to know how to set the service's properties.

Setting Service Properties Using the Windows Services Snap-In

As with any other Windows service, the Integration Services service has properties that dictate how it is to be started. Specifically, you can manage the following from the Windows Services Snap-in:

❑ Configure the startup type as Manual, Automatic, or Disabled.

❑ Request that the service is started, stopped, or restarted.

❑ Establish how the computer reacts to service failures.

❑ View or modify a listing of dependant services (none are set up by default).

To view and modify SSIS services properties using the Windows Services Snap-in, follow these steps:

1. Open the Services Snap-in from Control Panel ➪ Administrative Tools (or using the Category view from Performance and Maintenance ➪ Administrative Tools).

2. Locate and right-click SQL Server Integration Services in the list of services.

3. Select Properties to view the currently applied settings.

4. On the General tab, you can view or change the Startup type (Automatic, Manual, or Disabled). When set to either Manual or Automatic, you can change the Service status to Start, Stop, or Resume (see Figure 6-2).

5. On the Log On tab, you can view or alter the account used to start and run the service. By default, this runs under the NT AUTHORITY\NetworkService account.

6. On the Recovery tab, you can configure how the server responds to failures of the service by setting the First, Second, and Subsequent failures options to either Take No Action (the default), Restart the Service, Run a Program, or Restart the Computer (see Figure 6-3). You can also instruct the service to reset the failure count after a certain number of days.

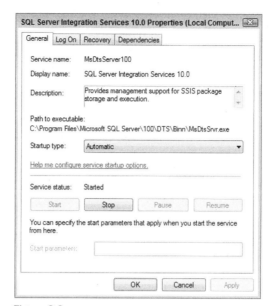

Figure 6-2

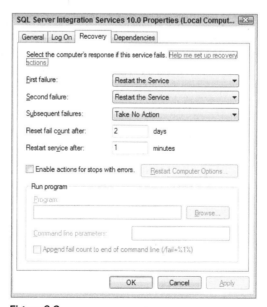

Figure 6-3

7. You can modify the list of services on which the SSIS service depends (none by default) and view the list of services dependent on the SSIS service (none by default) on the Dependencies tab.

Setting Service Properties Using SQL Server Configuration Manager

As with using the Windows Services Snap-in, you can also configure a limited set of Integration Services service properties using the SQL Server Configuration Manager. Specifically, you can both configure the logon information used by the service and establish the startup mode of the service.

Follow these steps to view and modify SSIS Services properties using the SQL Server Configuration Manager:

1. Open the SQL Server Configuration Manager from All Programs ➪ Microsoft SQL Server 2008 ➪ Configuration Tools.

2. On the list of services on the right side, right-click SQL Server Integration Services and select Properties.

3. On the Log On tab, you can view or alter the account used to start and run the service. By default, this runs under the NT AUTHORITY\NetworkService account.

4. On the Service tab, you can view or change the Startup type (Automatic, Manual, or Disabled).

Now that you are comfortable setting up the service properties for the Integration Services service using either the Windows Services Snap-in or the SQL Server Configuration Manager, you'll next learn how you can modify Windows Firewall to permit access to Integration Services.

Configuring Windows Firewall for Access

You'll probably find that your service requires modifications to be made to the Windows Firewall system in order to provide consistent access to Integration Services. The Windows Firewall system controls access to specific computer resources primarily by limiting access to preconfigured ports. You cannot modify the port number used by Integration Services, as it only works using port 135.

In addition to using the user interface mentioned in this section, you can also script out this process from the command line by running the following (note that the line has wrapped but everything should be on a single command when you type it):

```
netsh firewall add portopening protocol=TCP port=135 name="RPC (TCP/135)"
mode=ENABLE scope=SUBNET

netsh firewall add allowedprogram program="%ProgramFiles%\Microsoft SQL
Server\100\DTS\Binn\MsDtsSrvr.exe" name="SSIS Service" scope=SUBNET
```

Here's how to configure the Windows Firewall to permit Integration Services access:

1. Open the Windows Firewall from the Control Panel.

2. Select the Exceptions tab and click Add Program.

3. In the Add Program dialog, click Browse and select C:\Program Files\Microsoft SQL Server\100\DTS\Binn\MsDtsSrvr.exe. You should also, of course, use the Change Scope option in order to detail the computers that have access to the program by specifying a custom list of IP addresses, subnets, or both. The resulting exception is shown in the Windows Firewall dialog (see Figure 6-4).

4. Alternately, you can open the port instead of allowing the executable to have full reign of your network. To do this, click Add Port.

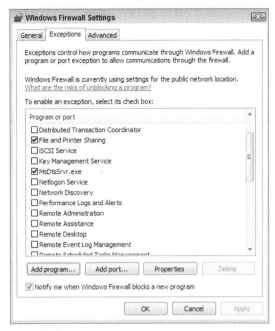

Figure 6-4

5. In the Add Port dialog, type a meaningful description like **RPC(TCP/135) Integration Services**, type **135** in the Port Number box, and select TCP as the protocol. You should also, of course, use the Change Scope option in order to indicate which computers have access to the port by specifying a custom list of IP addresses, subnets, or both.

That covers a substantial amount of the configuration required for the Integration Services service. Our next focus is event logging.

Event Logs

Integration Services records events raised by packages during their execution in logs. The SSIS log providers can write log entries to text files, SQL Server Profiler, SQL Server, Windows Event Log, or XML files. In order to perform logging, SSIS packages and tasks must have logging enabled. Logging can occur at the package, container, and task level, and you can specify different logs for packages, containers, and tasks.

To record the events raised, a log provider must be selected and a log added for the package. These logs can be created only at the package level, and a task or container must use one of the logs created for the package. Once you've configured the logs within packages, you can view them either using Windows Event Viewer or within SQL Server Management Studio.

To view SSIS event logs using the Windows Event Viewer:

1. Open the Event Viewer from Control Panel ➪ Administrative Tools (or use the Category view from Performance and Maintenance ➪ Administrative Tools).

2. Within the Event Viewer dialog, click Application.

3. After the Application snap-in is displayed, locate an entry in the Source column valued at SQLISService100 or SQLISPackage100. The SQLISPackage100 source logs would be generated from the package logs and the SQLISService100 source logs would be simple messages from the SSIS service.

4. Right-click the entry and select Event Properties to display descriptive information about the entry (see Figure 6-5).

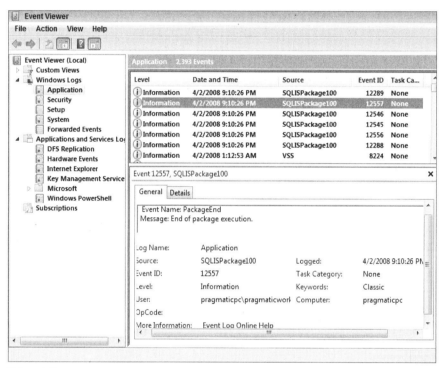

Figure 6-5

To view these events in SQL Server Management Studio:

1. Open Management Studio and connect to the target Integration Services server.

2. In Object Explorer, right-click Integration Services (the topmost node) and click View Logs.

3. Select SQL Server Integration Services from the Select Logs section.

4. You can see the details for an event displayed in the lower pane by clicking an event in the upper pane.

Monitoring Activity

Part of the performance monitoring of the Integration Services service includes configuring the logging of performance counters. These counters enable you to view and understand the use of resources consumed during the execution of SSIS packages. More specifically, the logging encompasses event-resource usage, while packages perform the Data Flow Tasks.

We begin by focusing on some of the more insightful counters, including Rows Read, Buffers in Use, and Buffers Spooled. The Rows Read counter provides the number of rows read from all data sources during package execution. The Buffers in Use counter details the number of pipeline buffers (memory pools) in use throughout the package pipeline. Lastly, the Buffers Spooled counter specifies the number of buffers used to handle the data flow processes. The Buffers Spooled counter is especially important because it is a good indicator of when your machine is running out of physical memory or running out of virtual memory during data flow processing. The importance of using buffers rather than spooling to disk is the difference between a package with 20 minutes execution time versus 20 hours in some cases. Each time you see a buffer spooled, a 10MB buffer has been written to disk.

One example of how these performance counters can be used includes ensuring that your server running the SSIS packages has enough memory. One of the bottlenecks in any transformation process includes input/output operations, whereby data is staged to disk during the transformations. Integration Services was designed to optimize system resources when transforming data between a source and destination, including attempting to perform these transformations in memory, rather than having to stage data to disk and incur I/O performance penalties. You should expect to see the value of the Buffers Spooled counter remain at zero (0) when only memory is being used during the transformation processes being performed by the SSIS packages. When you observe that the Buffers Spooled counter is normally valued higher than zero (0), it's a good indication that more memory is needed on the server processing the SSIS packages.

SQL Server Profiler enables you to analyze the data operations and query plans generated for various data flow pipeline activities. You can use this information to refine indexes or apply other optimization techniques to the data sources your SSIS solution is using. The SQL Server Profiler is covered in more detail in Chapter 13.

Administration of Integration Services Packages

Now that you've learned about the various aspects of Integration Services service administration, we'll now detail the main elements involved with the administration of SSIS packages. First you'll get an overview of SSIS package elements and administration, and then you'll look at various ways to create packages. Next, you'll look at the management of the developed SSIS packages. Once you understand how to create and manage packages, you'll move on to the deployment, execution, and scheduling of SSIS packages and solutions.

An Overview of Integration Services Packages

A package represents the main organizational and executable component of Integration Services. Packages include a collection of control flow tasks connected by precedence constraints used to manage the order of task execution, Data Flow Tasks that manage the complexities of moving data from sources to destinations with many transformation tasks in between, and event handlers responsible for communicating various information about the status of the package and its tasks.

In order to better understand the various package administrative functions, we'll start by discussing the flow of package creation or development. You start this process by designing a package using either the Import and Export Wizard or Business Intelligence Developer Studio. Next, you store these packages in either the file system or a SQL Server database (MSDB database, specifically) in order to facilitate reuse or later execution. Often, you will need to move packages from one storage location to another with the aid of tools such as the DTUtil command-line utility. Then, you run your packages using either the DTExec or DTExecUI utilities. Commonly, you will also need to schedule the execution of packages using the SQL Agent job scheduler. Lastly, you need to monitor the performance and status of packages using Management Studio.

Creating Packages

You can create Integration Services packages using the Import and Export Wizard or by creating a Business Intelligence Developer Studio Integration Services solution. We focus on using the Import and Export Wizard, as creation and development of packages within BIDS is more likely to be done by developers. Furthermore, many resources are available to assist in understanding how to create and develop packages within BIDS. As an administrator, you should understand how you can configure package templates for use by your team members.

Using the Import and Export Wizard to Create Packages

In your daily management of data, you often have to move or copy data to and from various data sources. Many times, these data management tasks are not in need of complex transformations or detailed workflow. These types of data management tasks are well suited for the Import and Export Wizard.

The key factor when considering using the Import and Export Wizard revolves around the data transformation capabilities you need before loading the destination or target. The Wizard only permits modifications such as setting the names, data types, and data type properties of the columns as they will be defined at the destination. Absolutely no column-level transformations are supported when using the Import and Export Wizard.

Mapping of data types from sources to destinations is managed by mapping files located by default in C:\Program Files\Microsoft SQL Server\100\DTS\MappingFiles. An example of one of these mapping files is the OracleClientToMSSql.xml mapping file, used to map Oracle data types to SQL Server data types. The following is a sample of the XML used to map the Oracle DATE data type to SQL Server's datetime data type:

```
<!-- DATE -->
<dtm:DataTypeMapping >
   <dtm:SourceDataType>
      <dtm:DataTypeName>DATE</dtm:DataTypeName>
   </dtm:SourceDataType>
   <dtm:DestinationDataType>
      <dtm:SimpleType>
         <dtm:DataTypeName>datetime</dtm:DataTypeName>
```

```
        </dtm:SimpleType>
      </dtm:DestinationDataType>
   </dtm:DataTypeMapping>
```

You can add mapping files to this directory to include new combinations of mappings that may not presently exist; and you can alter existing mapping files if they don't meet your needs. Note that after adding new or altering existing mapping files, you must restart the Import and Export Wizard or Business Intelligence Developer Studio in order to recognize these additions or modifications.

You can start using the Import and Export Wizard from the Business Intelligence Development Studio, from SQL Server Management Studio, or from a command prompt using the DTSWizard (`C:\ Program Files\Microsoft SQL Server\100\DTS\Binn`). The only difference in starting this wizard from BIDS is that the wizard cannot run the resulting package as the very last step; instead, the resulting package is saved as part of the solution in which the wizard was started.

You can start the Import and Export Wizard in a number of ways:

❑   In Management Studio, connect to a database server, and within the database node, right-click a database, select Tasks, and then select either Import Data or Export Data.

❑   In BIDS, open an SSIS solution, right-click the SSIS Packages Folder, and select SSIS Import and Export Wizard.

❑   Also in BIDS, click the Project ↪ SSIS Import and Export Wizard.

❑   From a command prompt, run DTSWizard.exe (`C:\Program Files\Microsoft SQL Server\100\DTS\Binn`).

Here's how to run the Import and Export Wizard to move data:

1.   Launch the Import and Export Wizard from Management Studio, BIDS, or the command prompt.

2.   On the Choose a Data Source page, select the location to copy the data from by setting up the data source (e.g., SQL Native Client, Excel, or Flat File) and the required information for that data source (e.g., Server Name, Authentication, and Database for a SQL Native Client). Alternately, if you selected to Export Data (within Management Studio), the source information is already preconfigured to include the server and database from which the wizard was launched.

3.   On the Choose a Destination page, select the location to copy the data to by setting up the data source and the required information for that data source. If you selected to Import Data (with Management Studio), the destination information is preconfigured to include the server and database from which the wizard was launched.

4.   On the Specify Table Copy or Query page, either copy the entire data source by selecting the option to ''Copy data from one or more tables,'' or you can specify that only a portion of the data source is copied by selecting the option to ''Write a query'' to specify the data to transfer. If you choose to write a query, on the Provide a Query Source page, you can either compose a SQL statement or browse for a SQL file to load and use to limit the data source records.

5. On the Select Source Tables and Views page, specify all the tables and views to be included unless you previously selected the option to write a query to specify the data, in which case only one table (the query) is available for selection.

6. Optionally, also on the Select Source Tables and Views page, you can configure various features that indicate such things as whether to optimize for many tables or run in a transaction.

7. Optionally, from the Select Source Tables and Views page, when copying tables or views that already exist in the destination, you may select Edit Mappings in order to configure things such as whether to delete or append data to an existing table or whether to enable identity inserts (see Figure 6-6).

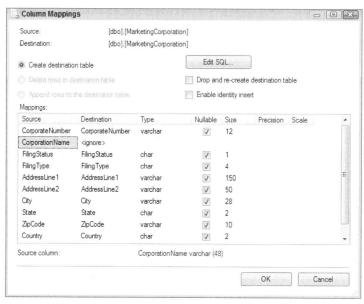

Figure 6-6

8. Optionally, from the Select Source Tables and Views page, when creating new tables or views that do not exist in the destination, you can select Edit Mappings to configure things such as whether to create destination tables or drop and recreate destination tables. You can also alter the destination mapping information for each column, including the name, data type, nullability, size, precision, and scale.

9. Lastly, if launched from Management Studio, on the Save and Execute Package page, you can choose to execute immediately and may optionally choose to save the SSIS package. When saving the package, you can save to SQL Server or to the file system, and you can configure the package-protection level to be applied to the saved package.

Creating and Using Package Templates

When you start a new Integration Services solution, the first thing you'll notice is that a package has already been included in the solution for your use. Although you cannot replace the default template that SSIS uses to generate this initial package (and any subsequent packages created by using the New SSIS Package command), you can design your own customized package or packages to be used as templates.

The primary benefits of creating these package templates include the following:

❑ Encapsulation of common package-design elements added to each package (such as logging or error handling).

❑ Productivity gained from inclusion of common package variables or package configurations.

❑ Enforcement of package-design standards such as annotations.

❑ Capability to override the SSIS package default protection level of `EncryptSensitiveWithUserKey`, which can be troublesome in multideveloper and deployment scenarios.

A common scenario in which you may decide to implement a custom package template is when your team decides that the default package-protection level should be `EncryptSensitiveWithPassword` in order to enable sharing development tasks among multiple DBAs or developers. By customizing and using a custom package template, rather than the default package that SSIS would create, you can ensure that this desired package-protection level is automatically selected. In another scenario, you may need to enforce common logging and error handling within your packages. The default SISS package does not contain any tasks to handle this functionality, but you can build it into your custom package template. Then, when used, each package automatically has this functionality built into the design.

Here's how you can designate an SSIS package as a template:

1. Create and save an SSIS package.

2. Copy the package file (`.dtsx`) you wish to use as a template to the `DataTransformationItems` folder. This folder is commonly located in `C:\Program Files\Microsoft Visual Studio 9.0\Common7\IDE\PrivateAssemblies\ProjectItems\ DataTransformationProject\DataTransformationItems`.

Once you have designated an SSIS package as a template, you can use it in Business Intelligence Developer Studio. Here's how you can use these templates to assist in SSIS package development:

1. Open an Integration Services project with Business Intelligence Developer Studio.

2. In Solution Explorer, right-click the solution or project (the topmost node) and select Add.

3. From the options displayed on the Add submenu, select New Item.

4. Within the Add New Item –Project Name dialog, select the package you want to use as a template and click Add.

Management

Once you have started to create packages, and solutions containing packages, you next need to focus on how these packages are managed. This section starts by reviewing how the Integration Services service can assist in managing packages. Next, we look at ways that you can configure Management Studio to meet your specific needs for managing packages. A brief tour of the DTUtil Package Management Utility is provided next, along with some details to assist with the importing and exporting of packages. We end with a review of package features that can be used in the package design and development stages to assist with the life-cycle management of packages and solutions.

Using Management Studio for Package Management

As discussed earlier in the "Integration Services Service" section, packages are managed primarily via Management Studio and its connection to the Integration Services service. Upon connecting to the service, you'll see two main folders: Running Packages and Stored Packages. The packages displayed are stored in either the msdb database sysssispackages table or the file system folders that are specified in the Integration Services service configuration file.

The main uses of Management Studio include monitoring running packages and managing the packages stored within the Integration Services environment. We'll now drill into some details surrounding these particular processes.

You can see information regarding currently executing packages within the Running Packages folder. Information about these packages is displayed on the Summary page, whereas information about a particular executing package can be obtained by clicking the package under the Running Packages folder and viewing the Summary page. You can stop the execution of a package listed within this folder by right-clicking the package and selecting Stop.

You can make changes to the storage of packages by adding custom folders and by copying packages from one type of storage to another using the Import and Export utilities. You can configure the logical folders displayed within the MSDB folder in Management Studio by altering the sysssispackagefolders table within the msdb database. The root folders in this table are those in which the parentfolderid column contains null values. You can add values to this table in order to add logical folders, bearing in mind that the folderid and parentfolderid columns are the keys values used to specify the folder hierarchy. Additionally, you can configure the default folders in the file system that Management Studio displays. This is discussed at length in the "XML Configuration File" section earlier in this chapter. Importing and exporting packages are discussed in the "Deployment" section of this chapter.

The main management tasks you can perform on packages within Management Studio include the following:

❑ Creating new Object Explorer folders to display packages saved in either the file system or SQL Server (msdb database sysssispackages table)

❑ Importing and exporting packages.

❑ Running packages.

❑ Deleting packages.

❑ Renaming packages.

Using the DTUtil Package Management Utility

Other than using Management Studio to manage packages, you also have the assistance of a command prompt utility named DTUtil. The primary reason it is important to understand DTUtil is that this utility permits you to manage packages using schedulers or batch files. As with using Management Studio, DTUtil enables you to copy, delete, move, sign, and even verify whether the server contains specified packages.

Using this utility, you include either the /SQL, /FILE, or /DTS options to specify where the packages that you want to manage are located. You use options (parameters) to specify particular behavior you want to use when running the utility. The options start with either a slash (/) or a minus sign (-) and can be added to the command line in any sequence.

You receive exit codes that let you know when something is wrong with your syntax or arguments or you simply have an invalid combination of options. When everything is correct, DTUtil returns exit code 0 and displays the message "The operation completed successfully." The following other exit codes may be returned:

- ❑ 1 — Failed.
- ❑ 4 — Cannot locate package.
- ❑ 5 — Cannot load package.
- ❑ 6 — Cannot resolve the command.

The following syntactical rules must be observed when you create the commands:

- ❑ Values for options must be strings and must be enclosed in quotation marks or contain no whitespace.
- ❑ Escaping single quotation marks in strings is done by enclosing the double-quoted string inside single quotation marks.
- ❑ Other than passwords, there is no case sensitivity.

One way you can use DTUtil is to regenerate package IDs for packages copied from other packages. Recall that when a copy of an existing package is made, the name and ID of the new package matches that of the copied package. You can use DTUtil along with the /I [D Regenerate] switch to regenerate the package IDs, and in some cases to correct corruption issues within your package. (Of course, to update multiple packages with just a single execution of DTUtil, you can create a batch file that can iterate through a given folder looking for all .dtsx (package) files and have DTUtil regenerate the package IDs.) If you wish to execute this command from within a batch file, use the following syntax from the directory containing the SSIS project:

```
for %%f in (<FilePath>\*.dtsx) do dtutil.exe /i /File %%f
```

By understanding the DTExec utility, you have a very powerful weapon to add to your package management arsenal.

Importing and Exporting Packages

Another common activity you need to understand as an administrator involves the ways in which you can move packages among the various storage locations and formats. The import and export functionality enables you to add or copy packages from one storage location and format to another storage location and format. Thus, not only can you add or copy the packages, but also change storage formats (e.g., from file system folders to the SQL Server msdb database).

Here's how you can import a package using the Integration Services Service from within Management Studio:

1. Open Management Studio and connect to an Integration Services server.

2. In Object Explorer, expand the Stored Packages folder and any subfolders to locate the folder into which you want to import a package.

3. Right-click the target folder and select Import Package.

4. On the Import Package dialog, select the package location from SQL Server, File System, or SSIS Package Store.

5. On the Import Package dialog, when the package location is SQL Server, specify the server, authentication type, user name, and password. When the package location is SSIS Package Store, specify the server.

6. Also on the Import Package dialog, click the Browse button next to Package path and select the package to import. From this screen, you can also change the package name to how it should appear in the new location, and specify the protection level of the package (see Figure 6-7).

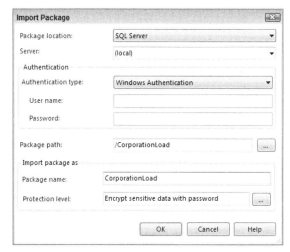

Figure 6-7

Using similar steps, you can export packages. The one notable difference is that you right-click the package to be exported and select Export, rather than right-click the target folder and select Import. Keep in mind that you can also perform these import and export operations using the DTUtil command-line utility.

Deployment

Once Integration Services packages and solutions have been developed either on local computers or on development servers, they need to be deployed to test on production servers. Usually, you start the deployment process once you have ensured that the packages run successfully within Business Intelligence Development Studio.

You deploy your packages or solutions via one of the following methods:

❑ Creating a package deployment utility and using the Package Installer Wizard.

❑ Using import or export package utilities in Management Studio.

❑ Saving or moving copies of packages in the file system.

❑ Executing the DTUtil Package Management Utility.

Often, the modifications made to your Integration Services solution will dictate which deployment method and tools to use. For example, if you modify only a single package out of a 30-package solution, using the import package utility within Management Studio or saving or moving copies of packages in the file system might be simpler than deploying the entire solution using the Package deployment utility and Package Installer Wizard.

You can further categorize these four options for deployment into automated and manual. Using a Package deployment utility in conjunction with the Package Installer Wizard would be best categorized as an automated deployment method, whereas the other options represent manual deployment methods. The following sections take a detailed look at each of these deployment methods.

Automated Package Deployment

A very common way to deploy packages involves using the Package deployment utility. This utility builds your SSIS packages, package configurations, and any supporting files into a special deployment folder located within the bin directory for the Integration Services project. In addition, this utility creates a special executable file named ProjectName.SSISDeploymentManifest and places it within this deployment folder. After creating the deployment utility, you then execute the manifest file to install the packages.

This deployment method relies upon two separate steps. First, you create a deployment utility that contains all the files needed for deployment. Second, you use the Package Installer Wizard to perform the deployment of these files to a target deployment server.

Using the Package Deployment Utility

The following steps walk you through using the Package deployment utility in order to deploy your Integration Services solution:

1. Open Business Intelligence Development Studio and an Integration Services solution.

2. Right-click your solution or project (the topmost node) in Solution Explorer and select Properties.

3. On the [*Solution/Project Name*] Property Pages dialog, select the Deployment Utility section.

4. Within the Deployment Utility section of the Property Pages dialog, set the value of the CreateDeploymentUtility to true (see Figure 6-8).

5. Optionally, you can configure the deployment to enable configuration changes by setting the AllowConfigurationChanges value to true. This option enables updating the configuration of key elements of your packages that would be machine or environment dependent, such as server names or database initial catalogs that are both properties of database connection managers.

6. Build your project as normal. The build process creates the `ProjectName`
    `.SSISDeploymentManifest` file and copies the packages to the `bin/Deployment` folder or
    whatever folder was specified for the `DeploymentOutputPath` on the project's Property Page
    in the Deployment Utility section.

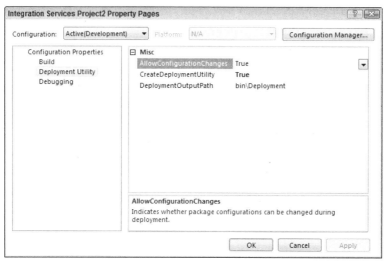

Figure 6-8

Because this utility copies all solution files as part of the process, you can deploy additional files, such as
a `Readme` file, with the project by simply placing these files in the Miscellaneous folder of the Integration
Services project.

Using the Package Installer Wizard

Once you have created a `SSISDeploymentManifest` file using the Package deployment utility, you
can install the packages by using the Package Installer Wizard, which can be started by clicking the
`SSISDeploymentMainfest` file. This wizard runs the `DTSInstall.exe` program and copies the packages
and any configuration to a designated location.

Using the Package Installer Wizard provides you with some really useful functionality that you either
can't find or is hard to achieve using the manual deployment methods. For example, you may choose
either a file-based or SQL-based deployment. Note that your file-based dependencies will always
be installed to the file system. Another important, as well as useful, capability of this deployment
process includes the ability to modify configurations for use on the target deployment server. This
enables you to update the values of the configuration properties, such as server name, as part of
the wizard.

These are the steps you need to take to ensure a successful deployment of your packages using the Package Installer Wizard:

1. Use Windows Explorer to browse to the file path location in which the SSISDeploymentManifest file was created (usually the solution or project location /bin/Deployment).

2. After creating the files within the Deployment folder, copy the Deployment folder and all its files to a target deployment server.

3. On the target deployment server, open the Deployment folder and double-click the SSISDeploymentManifest file in order to launch the Package Installer Wizard (DTSInstall.exe).

4. On the Deploy SSIS Packages page, select whether you want to deploy your packages to the file system or to SQL Server (see Figure 6-9). Optionally, you can also have the packages validated after they have been installed.

Figure 6-9

5. On the Select Installation Folder page, either provide a folder path for a file system deployment or provide a server name and the appropriate server credentials for a SQL Server deployment.

6. For a SQL Server deployment, on the Select Installation Folder page, provide a folder path for the package dependencies that will require storing within the file system.

7. Optionally, if the package includes configurations and you set the `AllowConfigurationChanges` value to `true` when the deployment manifest was created, the Configure Packages page will be displayed so that you can update the values for the configurations.

8. Optionally, if you requested validation of the packages, the Packages Validation page will be displayed so that you can review the validation results.

Manual Package Deployment

The previous sections outlined the use of the import or export package utilities, saving or moving copies of packages in the file system, and executing the DTUtil Package Management Utility as manual deployment methods. The primary difference among these deployment methods and using both the Package deployment utility and the Package Installer Wizard is that the manual methods require a better understanding of exactly what files need to be moved and where the files need to be located on the deployment target machine, and they offer no automated way to reconfigure some of the dynamic elements within the packages that often require modification when deploying to another machine (such as connection string server and initial catalog values).

Despite the lack of sophistication available when using these deployment methods, is some situations they are rather useful, if not better than the automated methods. One example of a situation in which they may prove to be a better fit is when you modify a single package in a solution containing 20 or more packages. Under the automated deployment method, the entire solution would be redeployed, whereas the manual methods could simply import, export, save, or move the single affected package. This has real benefits with some levels of testing, as you can isolate the impact of changing the one package without recertifying all the untouched packages just because they were redeployed over the older packages.

Import or Export Package Deployment

Earlier in the chapter, you looked at using the import and export functionality, which enables you to add or copy packages from one storage location and format to another storage location and format. One obvious use of this functionality is to deploy packages after development and testing have been completed.

An interesting benefit this approach may yield involves the capability of the import or export to change storage formats (e.g., from file system folders to the SQL server `msdb` database). This alteration of storage formats may be useful for disaster recovery, as a further safeguard for your Integration Services solutions, by saving them in various storage formats and locations.

File Save/Move Package Deployment

Probably the simplest way to get packages deployed involves copying them out of the Visual Studio project `bin` directory and placing them on the target server. This method does not have any of the more useful capabilities but it can work quite well for smaller-scale Integration Services solutions. One distinct capability missing from this deployment method is the ability to deploy to SQL Server.

DTUtil Package Deployment

As with using Management Studio, the DTUtil enables you to copy or move packages. As previously stressed in this chapter, the benefit of using the DTUtil is that the commands created can be scheduled or run later. Therefore, using these capabilities, you could schedule the deployment of your packages to another server simply by using DTUtil copy or move commands to move the modified packages to a target server.

The following example demonstrates how a DTUtil copy command can be used for deployment:

```
dtutil /DTS srcPackage.dtsx /COPY SQL;destPackage
```

Execution and Scheduling

Thus far, you have looked at ways to create, manage, and deploy Integration Services solutions. This section focuses on the ways in which you can execute and schedule execution of these solutions. As you have seen with other package and solution administrative tasks, the execution of packages can be performed using different tools. Specifically, you can execute packages from the following:

- ❑ Business Intelligence Development Studio.
- ❑ SQL Server Import and Export Wizard (when run from Management Studio).
- ❑ DTExec package execution command-line utility.
- ❑ DTExecUI package execution utility.
- ❑ SQL Server Agent jobs.

Which tool you should use often depends on factors such as in which stage of the package life cycle you are presently working. For example, the SSIS Designer within BIDS is a logical choice for package execution during development due to the features designed to assist in development (such as visually displaying package execution progress by changing the background color of tasks).

Running Packages in Business Intelligence Development Studio

Probably the first executions of packages will occur within BIDS, as this is the development environment used to create your Integration Services solutions. Within BIDS, you simply either right-click the package and then select Execute Package or press the F5 function key (or the Start button on the menu bar).

Running Packages with SQL Server Import and Export Wizard

When you use the Import and Export Wizard from Management Studio, you are given an option to execute the package immediately. This provides an opportunity to both relocate and execute packages in one administrative step.

Running Packages with DTExec

The\e primary use of DTExec is to enable you to run packages either from the command line, from a script, or using a scheduling utility. All configuration and execution features are available using this command. You can also load and run packages from SQL Server, the SSIS service, and the file system.

The following additional syntactical rules must be followed when you create these commands:

- ❑ All command options start with a slash (/) or a minus sign (−).
- ❑ Arguments are enclosed in quotation marks when they contain any whitespace.
- ❑ Values that contain single quotation marks are escaped by using double quotation marks within quoted strings.

The general syntax for the DTExec commands is as follows:

```
Dtexec /option value
```

Here's an example, which shows running the CaptureDataLineage.dtsx package:

```
Dtexec /FILE"C:\Program Files\Microsoft SQL Server\100\Samples\Integration
Services\Package Samples\CaptureDataLineage
Sample\CaptureDataLineage\CaptureDataLineage.dtsx" /CONNECTION
"(local).AdventureWorks2008";"\"Data Source=(local);Initial
Catalog=AdventureWorks2008;Provider=SQLNCLI.1;Integrated Security=SSPI;Auto
Translate=False;\""  /MAXCONCURRENT " -1 " /CHECKPOINTING OFF  /REPORTING
EWCDI
```

Whenever you execute a package using DTExec, one of the following exit codes may be returned:

- ❑ 0 — Successful execution
- ❑ 1 — Failed
- ❑ 3 — Canceled by User
- ❑ 4 — Unable to Find Package
- ❑ 5 — Unable to Load Package
- ❑ 6 — Syntax Not Correct

There are numerous options you can use to alter how the package execution is run. Some examples include /Decrypt, which sets the package password used to secure information within the package; and /Set, which you use to assign values to SSIS variables at runtime. The options are processed in the order in which they are specified. When using the /Set and /ConfigFile commands, the values are also processed in the order in which they are specified. Note that neither options nor arguments (except passwords) are case sensitive.

Running Packages with DTExecUI

You can configure the various options you need to run packages using the graphical equivalent to the DTExec utility: the DTExecUIutility. With the wizard that this utility uses to gather details regarding the package execution, you can better understand many of the options and see the syntax required to run the package execution.

You launch the DTExecUI utility by double-clicking a file with a .dtsx extension or from inside Management Studio by right-clicking on a package and selecting Run. You then select the options that you need to run the package along the left side of the utility pages, and configure the options in the main part of the page. When you are done, you can view the last page, which shows you the command line needed to execute the package with the options you selected (see Figure 6-10).

After you complete the various pages and review the command line that will be submitted, click the Execute button. This will submit the command line to the Integration Services engine by using the DTExecUI utility. Be careful when you use this utility in a 64-bit environment, because this utility runs in Windows on Win32, not on Win64. Thus, for 64-bit environments, you should use the 64-bit version of the DTExec utility at the command prompt or use SQL Server Agent.

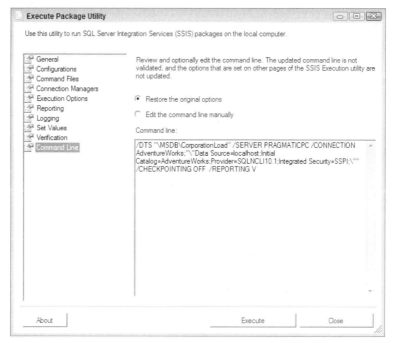

Figure 6-10

The main reason you should become more familiar with both the DTExec and DTExecUI utilities is that they are very useful for testing your packages and ultimately validating the proper command line that you may schedule using the SQL Server Agent.

Scheduling Execution with SQL Server Agent

Without a doubt, you will need the capability to automate the execution of your Integration Services packages. While many popular scheduling tools are available to accomplish this automation, here we look at how SQL Server Agent can assist in automating execution.

You start by creating a job and then including at least one step of the SQL Server Integration Services Packages type. You can also configure other job options. One option you may configure includes job notifications to send e-mail messages when the job completes, succeeds, or fails. Another job option you may configure includes job alerts to send notifications for SQL Server event alerts, performance condition alerts, or WMI event alerts.

Here's how to set up SQL Server Agent to execute a package:

1.   Open Management Studio and connect to a SQL Server.

2.   In Object Explorer, expand the SQL Server Agent.

3.   Within the SQL Server Agent section of Object Explorer, right-click the Jobs folder and select New Job.

4.   On the General page of the New Job dialog, provide a name, owner, category, and description for the job.

5. On the Steps page of the New Job dialog, click the New button along the bottom.

6. On the New Job Step dialog, provide a step name and select SQL Server Integration Services Packages type. In addition, configure the SSIS-specific tabbed sections with the information required to run your package. This SSIS section is almost identical to the options you provided when using the DTExecUI utility (see Figure 6-11). You have a package source that you set to SQL Server, file system, or SSIS package store. Next, you provide the package you wish to schedule. When you select the Command Line tab, you can review the detailed command line that will be submitted by the SQL Server Agent to execute the package. You may wish to compare this to the command-line values generated by the DTExecUI utility while you were testing package execution.

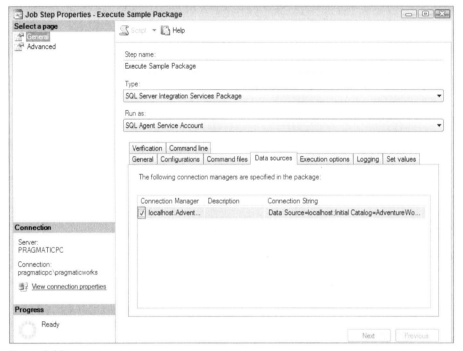

Figure 6-11

7. On the Advanced page of the New Job Step dialog, you can specify actions to perform when the step completes successfully, the number of retry attempts, the retry interval, and actions to perform should the step fail. After accepting the step configuration by pressing OK, the Step page of the New Job dialog will show your new step. After adding multiple steps, you can reorder the steps on this page.

8. After accepting the step configuration, from the New Job dialog you can optionally configure execution schedules, alerts, notifications, and target servers.

Applying Security to Integration Services

You have now looked at most of the important package administrative tasks, including creating, managing, deploying, and executing Integration Services solutions. Additionally, you have reviewed the major Integration Services service administrative tasks. This section describes the detailed security options available within Integration Services.

An Overview of Integration Services Security

Integration Services, like all of SQL Server, uses layers of security that rely upon different mechanisms to ensure the integrity of both the design of packages and the administration and execution of packages. SSIS security is found on both the client and the server, implemented with features such as the following:

- ❑ Package-protection levels to encrypt or remove sensitive information from the package.
- ❑ Package-protection levels with passwords to protect all or just sensitive information.
- ❑ Restricting access to packages with roles.
- ❑ Locking down file locations where packages may be stored.
- ❑ Signing packages with certificates.

Within packages, Integration Services generally defines sensitive data as information such as passwords and connection strings. You are not able to define what should and should not be considered sensitive by SSIS unless you do so within a custom-developed task.

Integration Services defines sensitive information as the following:

- ❑ Connection string password (Sensitive) or Whole connection string (All).
- ❑ Task-generated XML nodes tagged as sensitive by SSIS.
- ❑ Variables marked as sensitive by SSIS.

Securing Packages

The two primary ways in which you secure packages within Integration Services include setting package-protection levels and configuring appropriate database SSIS roles. The following sections look at these two security implementations.

Package Protection Levels

Many organizations have sensitive information in the SSIS package and want to control where that information resides within the organization. Your packages may contain passwords from your environment that if executed by the wrong individual may produce data files that could be sensitive.

These security concerns are addressed in Integration Services through the use of package protection levels. First, you can ensure that sensitive information that would provide details about where your information resides, such as connection strings, can be controlled by using `EncryptSensitive` package protection levels. Second, you can control who can open or execute a package by using `EncryptAll` package passwords.

The following package protection levels are at your disposal within Integration Services:

- ❑ Do not save sensitive.
- ❑ Encrypt (all/sensitive) with User Key.
- ❑ Encrypt (all/sensitive) with Password.
- ❑ Rely on server storage for encryption (SQL storage only).

The package protection levels are first assigned using Business Intelligence Development Studio. You can update these levels after deployment or during import or export of the package using Management Studio. In addition, you can alter the package protection levels when packages are copied from BIDS to any other location in which packages are stored. This is a nice compromise between development and administration, as developers can configure these levels to suit their rapid development requirements, and administrators can follow up and revise these levels to meet production security standards.

Database Integration Services Roles

If you deploy your packages to SQL Server (`msdb` database), you need to protect these packages within the database. Like traditional databases, this security is handled by using database roles. Three fixed database-level roles can be applied to the `msdb` database in order to control access to packages: `db_dtsadmin`, `db_dtsltduser`, and `db_dtsoperator`.

You apply these roles to packages within Management Studio, and these assignments are saved within the `msdb` database, in the `sysssispackages` table within the `readerrole`, `writerrole`, and `ownersid` columns. As the column names imply, you can view the roles that have read access to a particular package by looking at the value of the `readerrole` column, the roles that have write access to a particular package by looking at the value of the `writterrole` column, and the role that created the package by looking at the value of the `ownersid` column.

Follow these steps to assign a reader and writer role to packages:

1. Open Management Studio and connect to an Integration Services server.
2. In Object Explorer, expand the Stored Packages folder and expand the subfolder to assign roles.
3. Right-click the subfolder to assign roles.
4. In the Packages Roles dialog, select a reader role in the Reader Role list and a writer role in the Writer Role list.

You may also create user-defined roles if the default read and write actions for existing roles do not meet your security needs. In order to define these roles, you connect to a SQL Server instance and open the Roles node within the `msdb` database. In the Roles node, right-click the database roles and select New Database Role. Once a new role has been added to the `msdb` database, you must restart the `MSSQLSERVER` service before you can use the role.

These database Integration Services roles help to configure your `msdb` database `syssispackages` table with package security options for reading and writing to specific packages. By applying this level of security, you provide security at the server, database, and table levels. Again, the security discussed within this section only applies when you save your packages within SQL Server (`msdb` database). The next section explores the options for securing packages stored outside of SQL Server.

Saving Packages

When you develop packages, they are stored to the file system as XML files with a `.dtsx` file extension. In the "Deployment" section, you saw how you could move these files to your Integration Services server using import and export utilities, the `DTUtil` utility, or the Package Installer Wizard.

Without saving the packages and any related files (such as configuration files) within SQL Server (`msdb` database), you must apply the appropriate NTFS file permissions to secure these packages.

The next section explains how you should restrict access to computers running the SQL Server service because they can enumerate stored packages on local and remote locations.

Running Packages

After packages have been secured by using package protection and either database roles or file system security, you must limit access to currently running packages on your servers. Specifically, you need to manage who has rights to view the running packages and who can stop your executing packages.

The SQL Server service is used by Management Studio to determine and list currently executing packages. Only members of the Windows Administrators group are able to perform these actions. The service can also be used to enumerate folders and possibly even remote folders. These folders are where you store your packages, so it is important that you control access to computers running this service, and that you apply NTFS folder and file permissions to locations where you store your packages.

Package Resources

Having addressed the security needs of packages stored within SQL Server and stored within the file system, as well as managing access to running packages, we now turn to the various resources used by your packages.

You need to consider the following package resources:

❑ Configuration files
❑ Checkpoint files
❑ Log files

You must consider security for these resources, as they may contain sensitive information. For example, configuration files often contain login and password information for data sources used by your packages. Even if they do not contain sensitive information, you need to ensure that your packages can find and use them when they are executed. Another example are the checkpoint files used for restartability of packages. These checkpoint files save the current state information from the execution of packages, including the current values of any variables defined within the packages. Often, you use the variables to store information that may be deemed sensitive, so you should ensure that only appropriate staff is able to access these files. In any case, you can store these various files in SQL Server and use the database Integration Services roles for security, or you need to apply appropriate NTFS permissions.

Digital Signatures

As a last line of defense for ensuring successful usage of valid packages during execution, you can sign packages with certificates. After signing the packages, when you execute a package using a utility or program, the package signature is checked, and a warning may be issued, or the package may be prevented from executing should an invalid signature be determined. In order to ensure that this validation occurs, set the `CheckSignatureOnLoad` property for packages to `true`.

Summary

You are now familiar with many of the various administrative functions related to Integration Services. After getting a general introduction to Integration Services, you learned about important Integration Services administrative tasks such as managing the Integration Services service, including configuration, event logs, and monitoring activity. Next, you gained some insight into various administrative tasks required of Integration Services packages, including creation, management, execution, and deployment. Last, you learned how to implement security for all of the various Integration Services components. In Chapter 7 you will learn about similar administrative functions related to Analysis Services.

7

Analysis Services Administration and Performance Tuning

We continue our discussion of business intelligence administration and performance tuning by looking at how the DBA can perform Analysis Services administrative and performance tuning tasks. Our focus is the regular activities that a DBA may be called upon to perform, rather than the various details that may be performed by developers. First, you will take a quick tour of Analysis Services so that you have some common frame of reference for both the administrative and optimization aspects that are covered. Next, you'll look at the administration of the Analysis Server itself, including reviewing server settings and required services. You will also learn how to script various administrative activities such as moving an Analysis Services database from development to production and backing up an Analysis Services database. With that covered, you will review the management of the Analysis Services databases, including deployment, backup, restore, and synchronization, and then look at how you can monitor the performance of Analysis Services. Next is a look at administration of storage, including storage modes and configuring partitions, as well as the design of aggregations. With storage concepts in mind, you'll turn next to administration of processing tasks used to connect your designs with the data. Last, of course, you will learn how to configure security for Analysis Services.

> *A discussion of how to use Analysis Services from a developer's prospective is beyond the scope of this book, so we will not examine that issue here. If you're interested in learning more, see* Professional Microsoft SQL Server Analysis Services 2008 with MDX, *by Sivakumar Harinath et al. (Wrox, 2009).*

Tour of Analysis Services

To better understand the various touch points that you must manage as a DBA, we begin with a quick tour of Analysis Services. The primary value that Analysis Services brings to businesses is useful, important, and timely information that can be difficult or impossible to obtain from other sources (enterprise resource planning systems, accounting systems, customer relationship management systems, supply chain management systems, and so on). Analysis Services provides two distinct services that assist in supplying these business needs: Online Analytical Processing (OLAP) and data mining. With these services, Analysis Services differs from the more traditional Online Transaction Processing (OLTP) systems in that it is optimized for fast access to vast quantities of data, often spanning many years. Our focus is on the OLAP services provided.

The OLAP engine has to be optimized for lightning-quick data retrieval but also offers the following strategic benefits:

❑   Consolidated shared data access across multiple data sources that includes security at the most granular level and the ability to write back data.

❑   Rapid, unencumbered storage and aggregation of vast amounts of data.

❑   Multidimensional views of data that go beyond the traditional row and column two-dimensional views.

❑   Advanced calculations that offer better support and performance than RDBMS engine capabilities.

❑   Advanced data mining techniques to predict future activities based on the historical data in your database.

Where SSAS differs from traditional OLAP servers is that the 2008 release offers a Unified Dimensional Model (UDM) focused on unifying the dimensional and relational models. The relational model represents the standard model used by transaction processing systems. This relational model is generally optimized for data validity and storage optimization, rather than query performance. The dimensional model was developed specifically to address query performance — primarily by the denormalization of relational model schemas into a simpler model characterized by fewer joins and more user-friendly model elements (table and column names). Denormalization, as you might recall, is the process of optimizing the performance of a database by adding redundant data into a database table that would normally have been normalized or removed to additional tables.

Unified Dimensional Model Components

In the 2008 release of Analysis Services, the Unified Dimensional Model (UDM) is the cube. In simple terms, the UDM is a cube in Analysis Services that combines all the different elements of Analysis Services into a single view. Let's begin looking at the composition of the UDM:

❑   **Data source view:** At the heart of the UDM is the logical data schema that represents the data from the source in a familiar and standard manner. This schema is known as the data source view (DSV), and it isolates the cube from changes made to the underlying sources of data.

❑   **Dimensional model:** This model provides the framework from which the cube is designed. Included are the measures (facts) that users need to gain measurable insight into their business and the dimensions that users employ to constrain or limit the measurements to useful combinations of factors.

❑   **Calculations (expressions):** Often, a cube needs to be enhanced with additional calculations in order to add the necessary business value that it is expected to achieve. The calculations within the UDM are implemented by writing Multi Dimensional Expression (MDX) language code snippets. MDX is to the cube what SQL is to the database. In other words, MDX is what you use to get information from a cube to respond to various user requests.

❑ **Familiar and abstracted model:** Many additional features enhance the end-user analysis experience by making their reporting and navigation through the cube more natural. Again, like calculations, the model is often enhanced to include features not found in the data sources from which the cube was sourced. Features such as language translations, aliasing of database names, perspectives to reduce information overload, or Key Performance Indicators (KPIs) to quickly summarize data into meaningful measurements are all part of the UDM.

❑ **Administrative configuration:** With the cube designed and developed, the administrative aspects of the UDM come to the forefront. Often, administrative tasks such as configuring the security to be applied to the cube or devising a partitioning scheme to enhance both query and processing performance are applied to the UDM.

Analysis Services Architectural Components

Now that you understand the basics about the Unified Dimensional Model (UDM), let's turn to the various components that make up Analysis Services.

The Analysis Services server (msmdsvr.exe application) is implemented as a Microsoft Windows service and consists of security components, an XMLA listener, and a query processor (for MDX queries and DMX data-mining queries):

❑ **Query processor:** The query processor parses and processes statements similarly to the query processing engine within SQL Server. This processor is also responsible for the caching of objects, storage of UDM objects and their data, processing calculations, handling server resources, and managing transactions.

❑ **XMLA listener:** This listener component facilitates and manages communications between various clients and the Analysis Services server. The port configuration for this listener is located in the msmdsrv.ini file, which is located in the C:\Program Files\ Microsoft SQL Server\MSAS10.MSSQLSERVER\OLAP\Config folder by default. A value of 0 in this file under the <Port> tag simply indicates that SSAS is configured to listen on the default port of 2383 for the default instance of SSAS 2008, and 2382 for other instances of SSAS 2008.

SSAS 2008 named instances can use a variety of ports. The SQL Server Browser keeps track of the ports on which each named instance listens and performs any redirection required when a client does not specify the port number along with the named instance. We highly recommend that you use a firewall to restrict user access to Analysis Services ports from the Internet.

❑ **XML for Analysis:** XML for Analysis (XML/A) is a SOAP-based protocol used as the native protocol for communicating with SSAS. All client application interactions use XML/A to communicate with SSAS. This protocol is significant in that clients who need to communicate with SSAS do not need to install a client component, as past versions of Analysis Services required (such as Pivot Table Services). As a SOAP-based protocol, XML/A is optimized for disconnected and stateless environments that require time- and resource-efficient access. In addition to the defined protocol, Analysis Services also added extensions to support metadata management, session management, and locking capabilities. You have two different methods to send XML/A messages to Analysis Services: The default method uses TCP/IP, and an alternative is HTTP.

Administering Analysis Services Server

This section looks at some of the important administrative activities for the server instance of SSAS. SSAS usage is divided into two tools: Business Intelligence Development Studio (BIDS) for development, and Management Studio for administration. We start with a review of the configuration settings for the server in Management Studio, followed by detailing the services needed for SSAS to run, and end with an introduction to the Analysis Services Scripting Language (ASSL) and its use in performing administrative tasks.

These server properties are important for configuring the behavior of the SSAS server instance. To review and adjust the server properties, perform the following steps:

1. Open SQL Server Management Studio.

2. Connect to the Analysis Services server using the Object Explorer.

3. Right-click the server (the topmost node) and choose Properties. The dialog shown in Figure 7-1 appears.

By going to the Properties window, you can see dozens of properties that can help you tune your SSAS instance. You can see more properties by checking Show Advanced Properties. This section covers some of the most important properties to SSAS.

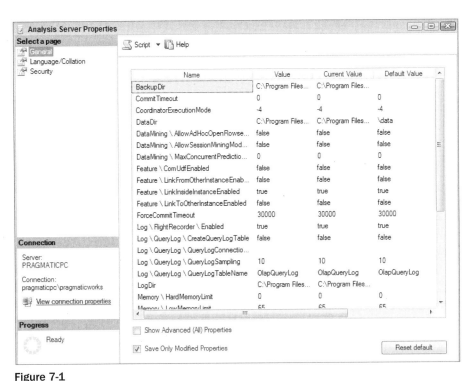

Figure 7-1

Lock Manager Properties

The lock manager properties are used to resolve deadlocking issues as they pertain to server behaviors in handling locking and timeouts. Of the three lock manager properties, only `DefaultLockTimeoutMS` should be altered without the guidance of Microsoft support. The `DefaultLockTimeoutMS` property defines the lock-request timeouts in milliseconds and defaults to none (−1).

Log Properties

The log properties control how and where logging takes place. Details related to error logging, exception logging, the flight recorder, query logging, and tracing are included in this property group. Some examples include the `QueryLog \ QueryLogConnectionString` and `QueryLog\QueryLogTableName` properties, which are used to direct the server to where the query logging is persisted (database and table). The `QueryLog \ QueryLogConnectionString` property specifies the SQL Server instance and database that will hold the Analysis Services query log. By default, once you specify this and set the `CreateQueryLog Table` property to True, SQL Server will begin to log every tenth query to the table. If you have an active Analysis Services instance, you may want to decrease this setting to every hundredth query.

This query log can later be used to tune your SQL Server by using a tool called Usage Based Optimization, whereby you tune the Analysis Services cube based on queries used in the past.

Memory Properties

The memory properties dictate how the server utilizes system memory resources. The `LowMemoryLimit` represents a threshold percentage of total physical memory, at which point the server will attempt to perform garbage collection for unused resources to free more resources. The default value is configured at 75 percent of total physical memory. The `TotalMemoryLimit` is used to tell the server how much of the total physical memory of the server hardware should be made available for use by Analysis Services. This limit is configured to 80 percent of all server memory by default.

> Only the **LowMemoryLimit** and the **TotalMemoryLimit** memory properties should be altered without the guidance of Microsoft support. Altering some of these settings could cause stability problems with your environment.

Network Properties

The network properties are used to control the network communication resources used by the server. Most notable are the settings that dictate whether the listener uses IPv4 or IPv6 protocols and whether the server will permit the use of Binary XML for requests or responses. In Windows 2008 and Windows Vista, IPv6 is enabled by default.

OLAP Properties

The OLAP properties control how the server will perform processing of the server objects (cubes, dimensions, and aggregations). Along with the processing properties, this section includes configuration properties for the way the server will process queries. Some of these query-processing properties are useful for simulating many testing scenarios. As an example, you could adjust the `IndexUseEnabled`,

`UseDataSlice`, and `AggregationUseEnabled` properties to benchmark different query-handling scenarios to determine whether some of these optimizations are providing the desired performance enhancement.

Security Properties

The security properties are responsible for controlling how the server handles permissions. Examples of these properties include `RequireClientAuthentication`, which is used to configure whether clients connecting to the server require authentication. By setting `BuiltInAdminsAreServerAdmins` to false, local server administrators are not implicitly given sysadmin rights to your SSAS instance. Note that both the local administrators and the service account are given escalated rights to Analysis Services by default because of this property.

Required Services

The core Windows services required by Analysis Services include SQL Server Analysis Services, SQL Server, SQL Server Agent, and SQL Server Browser. The role played by the first three services in supporting Analysis Services is readily apparent, but the SQL Server Browser service needs a bit of explanation. The SQL Server Browser service supports the Analysis Services redirector used when clients connect to named instances of Analysis Services.

All of these services are configured at the operating-system level via Administrative Tools ⇨ Services. As you would expect with configuring other services, the focus is on the logon account used by the service as the context in which to operate, the startup type used to indicate whether the service starts when the operating system starts, the recovery that indicates the actions taken by the service in the event of failure, and the dependencies that specify which other services are required for the service to function properly.

Commonly, the logon account used by any service should be one that has the least number of privileges required to function properly. More often than not, an account that has network rights is required, and this account would need to be granted access rights on the remote resources in addition to configuring the account to be used by the service.

Analysis Services Scripting Language

We'll now direct your attention to how many of your administrative tasks can be automated by using the built-in scripting language, Analysis Services Scripting Language, or ASSL. This language is based on XML and is what client applications use to get information from Analysis Services.

This scripting language has two distinct parts. The first part is used to define the objects that are part of the server, including the objects used to develop solutions (measures and dimensions). The other part is used to request the server to perform actions, such as processing objects or performing batch operations.

We focus on the scripting language components that help you manage the Analysis Services server. We start by looking at some examples of how you can use the language to process objects. Processing enables you to fill objects with data so they may be used by end users for business analysis. Some of the objects you can process include cubes, databases, dimensions, and partitions. To perform this processing using the scripting language, you use the language's `Process` command.

An example of a script that would process the AdventureWorks `Employee` dimension follows:

```
<Batch xmlns="http://schemas.microsoft.com/analysisservices/2003/engine">
<Parallel>
<Process xmlns:xsd="http://www.w3.org/2001/XMLSchema"
xmlns:xsi="http://www.w3.org/2001/XMLSchema-instance"
xmlns:ddl2="http://schemas.microsoft.com/analysisservices/2003/engine/2"
xmlns:ddl2_2="http://schemas.microsoft.com/analysisservices/2003/engine/2/2"
xmlns:ddl100_100="http://schemas.microsoft.com/analysisservices/2008/engine/10
0/100">
<Object>
<DatabaseID>Adventureworks DW</DatabaseID>
<DimensionID>Dim Employee</DimensionID>
</Object>
<Type>ProcessUpdate</Type>
<WriteBackTableCreation>UseExisting</WriteBackTableCreation>
    </Process>
  </Parallel>
</Batch>
```

Note that you can script many of the actions that you can configure in SQL Management Studio. For example, you can generate the example script shown here by right-clicking the AdventureWorks cube and selecting the Process Menu option. This will display the Process Cube dialog (see Figure 7-2). From this dialog, you click the Script button located along the top under the title bar and then select the location in which you want to generate the script.

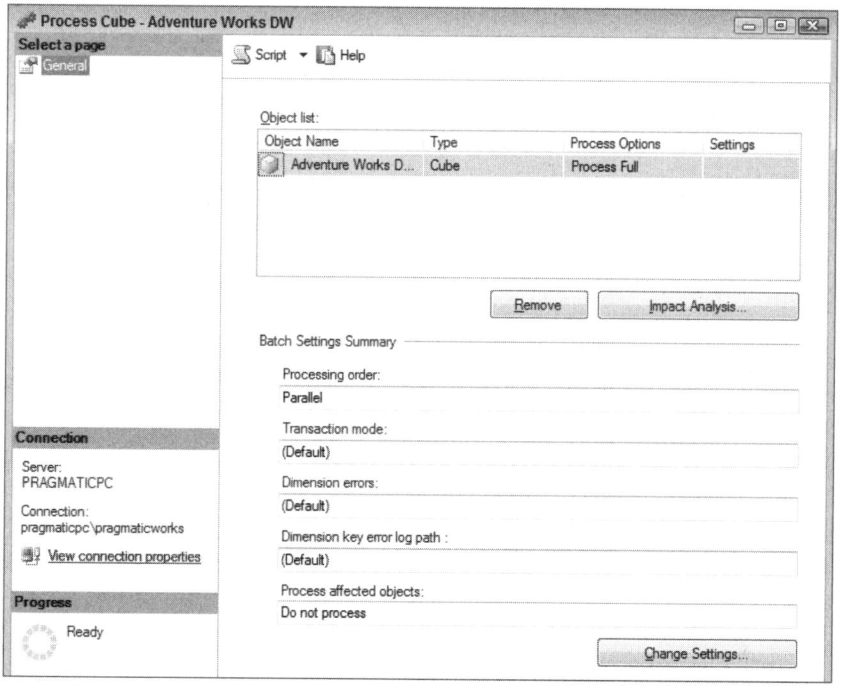

Figure 7-2

Don't worry about the options in this screen yet; they are discussed in the "Processing Analysis Services Objects" section.

Administering Analysis Services Databases

Now that you understand more about the Analysis Services server, we will look at the administrative tasks needed for the databases that will ultimately be deployed and run on the Analysis Services server. The primary tasks associated with managing the Analysis Services databases include deployment to the server, processing Analysis Services objects, performing disaster recovery activities such as backup and restore operations, and synchronizing databases to copy entire databases.

Deploying Analysis Services Databases

Obviously, without deployment there is no value to running an Analysis Services server. Through deployment of Analysis Services databases to the server, original and changed designs are applied to the server.

When performing administrative tasks, you can either use Management Studio to affect changes directly in a database in what is commonly referred to as *online mode*, or you can work within Business Intelligence Developer Studio to affect changes via a Build and Deploy process commonly referred to as *offline mode*.

More specific to database deployment, you have the following options:

- ❏ Deploy changes directly from Business Intelligence Developer Studio.
- ❏ Script changes and deploy from within Management Studio.
- ❏ Make incremental deployments using the Deployment Wizard.
- ❏ Process changes using the Synchronize Database Wizard.

Many of these options are useful only in very specific circumstances and as such are not given much attention in this chapter. The most useful and complete method of deploying the databases is to use the Deployment Wizard. Alternatively, the next best tool to assist with deployment is the Synchronize Database Wizard.

The main advantage of the Deployment Wizard is that it is the only deployment method that applies the database project definition to production and enables you to keep many of the production database configuration settings, such as security and partitioning. This is important because neither direct deployment from BIDS nor scripting from Management Studio permits the deployment to maintain existing configuration settings.

The main scenario in which the Synchronize Database Wizard is useful is when you are deploying changes from a quality-assurance or test environment into a production environment. This process copies the database and the data from one server to another while leaving it available for user queries. The advantage of this option cannot be understated: The availability of your database is maintained. This contrasts with other deployment options, which most likely will require additional processing of Analysis Services objects on the server after the deployment, and this process may require taking the database offline. You will look at synchronization later in this chapter.

The following steps show how the Deployment Wizard operates in order to understand how valuable it is for handling deployment:

1. Launch the Deployment Wizard from the Start menu under SQL Server 2008 ⇨ Analysis Services.

2. On the Specify Source Analysis Services Database page, enter a full path to an Analysis Services database (see Figure 7-3). This file should be provided to you by the SSAS developer, or you can find it under the SSAS project folder.

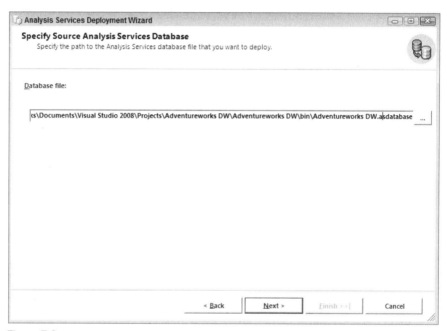

Figure 7-3

3. On the Installation Target page, indicate the server to which the database should be deployed, along with the desired database name (it defaults to the file name of the database).

4. On the Specify Options for Partitions and Roles page, indicate which configuration options (Partitions and Roles) should be maintained on the deployment target database and thus not overwritten by this deployment (see Figure 7-4). This screen would be especially useful if you have made changes in Management Studio to roles or partitions and did not want the developer's files to overwrite your own configuration.

5. On the Specify Configuration Properties page, select which configuration settings from the current configuration file (.configsettings) should be applied to the target database. These settings provide a very useful way to redirect items such as data source connection strings to point to production sources, rather than those used for development and testing. Note that the Retain checkboxes at the top provide an elegant way to manage updates of previous deployments, as they disable overwriting of both the configuration and the optimization setting (see Figure 7-5).

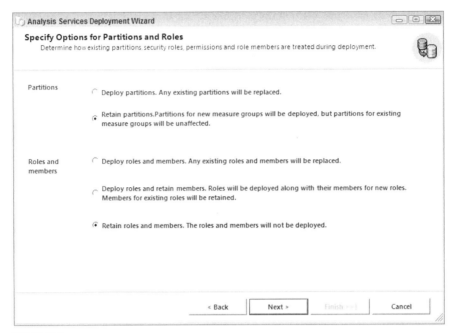

Figure 7-4

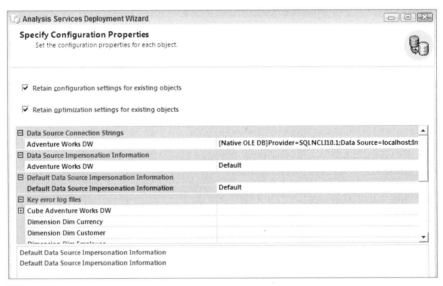

Figure 7-5

6. On the Select Processing Options page, enter the desired processing method and any writeback table options. To support a robust deployment, you may also select the option to include all processing in a single transaction that will roll back all changes should any part of the deployment fail. Note the Default processing method. This method enables Analysis

Services to review the modifications to be applied and determine the optimal processing needed (see Figure 7-6).

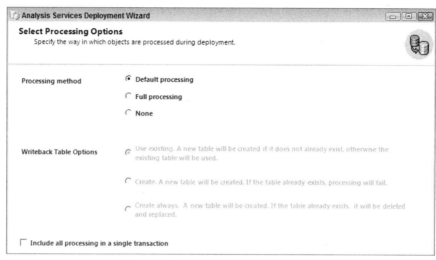

Figure 7-6

7. On the Confirm Deployment page is an option to script the entire deployment. This option is useful when either the person running the Deployment Wizard is not authorized to perform the actual deployment or the deployment needs to be scheduled so as not to interfere with other activities.

Processing Analysis Services Objects

Now that you understand how to deploy Analysis Services databases, you must add data to these objects by processing them. Additionally, if the cubes need to be updated to reflect development changes made after the initial deployment, you'll need to reprocess them. Last, when data sources have changes made to their information, you need to perform, minimally, an incremental reprocessing of the cube to ensure that you have up-to-date data within the Analysis Services solution. Note also that developers often build and test designs locally. These local cubes must first be deployed to the server before performing any processing.

The Analysis Services objects that require processing include measure groups, partitions, dimensions, cubes, mining models, mining structures, and databases. The processing is hierarchical — that is, processing an object that contains any other objects will also process those objects. For example, a database includes one or more cubes, and cubes contain one or more dimensions, so processing the database would also process all the cubes contained within that database and all the dimensions contained in or referenced by each of the cubes.

Processing Dimensions

Analysis Services processes dimensions by simply running queries that return data from the data source tables for the dimensions. This data is then organized into the hierarchies and ultimately into map files that list all of the unique hierarchical paths for each dimension. Processing dimensions can be optimized primarily through strategic indexes on the primary key and other key attributes.

Processing Cubes

The cube contains both measure groups and partitions and is combined with dimensions to give the cube a data definition. Processing a cube is done by issuing queries to get fact-table members and the related measure values such that each path of dimensional hierarchies includes a value.

Processing Partitions

Just as in database partitioning, the goal of Analysis Services partitioning is to improve query response times and administrator processing durations by breaking large data sets into smaller files — typically, by some sort of time slice. This processing is special in that you must evaluate your hardware space and Analysis Services data structure constraints. Partitioning is the key to ensuring that your query response times are fast and your processing activities are efficient.

Reprocessing

After deploying an Analysis Services database, many events create the need to reprocess some or all of the objects within the database. Examples of when reprocessing is required include object structural/schema changes, aggregation design changes, or refreshing object data.

Performing Processing

To perform processing of Analysis Services objects, you can either use SQL Server Management Studio or Business Intelligence Development Studio or run an XML for Analysis (XMLA) script. An alternative approach is to use Analysis Management Objects (AMO) to start processing jobs via programming tools.

When processing, note that as Analysis Services objects are being committed, the database will not be available to process user requests. That's because the processing commit phase requires an exclusive lock on the Analysis Services objects being committed. User requests are not denied during this commit process, but rather are queued until the commit is successfully completed. One alternative to processing your cube manually is called *proactive caching*. This is a more advanced option that incrementally gathers new data and loads the data into a new cached cube while queries are still happening in the original cube. As soon as the processing is complete, the new cube is opened to users and the old one is disposed.

Here's how to perform processing for an Analysis Services database from within SQL Server Management Studio:

1. Open Management Studio and connect to an Analysis Services server.

2. Right-click an Analysis Services database and select Process. The Process Database dialog appears, where you can configure the details of the processing (refer back to Figure 7-2).

3. Clicking the Impact Analysis button will give you an idea of the effect that performing the specified process will have on related objects. For example, by fully processing a dimension, all measure groups pointing to that dimension also need to be processed.

4. You can configure processing options such as the processing order by clicking Change Settings. Available options for the order include processing in parallel within a single transaction or processing sequentially within one or separate transactions. A very important

option is Process affected objects. This option controls whether all of the other objects that have dependencies on the database will also be processed (see Figure 7-7). A common architectural design employed in data warehousing involves the use of shared dimensions. These dimensions can be shared across the organization and allow for low maintenance and uniformity. The Process Affected Objects setting can therefore have a profound impact when you're using an architecture involving shared dimensions, as it may force reprocessing of many other databases in which the shared dimensions are used.

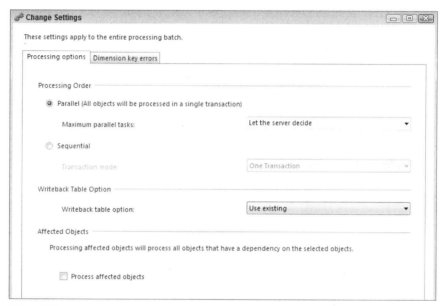

Figure 7-7

5. You can also configure very sophisticated dimension key error handling (see Figure 7-8). For example, you can configure the options to use a custom error configuration, which converts key errors to an unknown record, rather than terminating the processing. Additionally, you can specify error limits and what action to take when those limits have been exceeded. Last, you can choose to handle specific error conditions such as "key not found" or duplicate keys by reporting and continuing to process, by ignoring the error and continuing to process, and by reporting and stopping the processing.

Backing Up and Restoring Analysis Services Databases

Without question, performing backup and restore tasks are common functions within the domain of any DBA. A backup of the Analysis Services database captures the state of the database and its objects at a particular point in time to a file on the file system (named with an .abf file extension), while recovery restores a particular state of the database and its objects to the server from a backup file on the file system. Backup and recovery, therefore, are very useful for data recovery in case of problems with the database on the server in the future or simply to provide an audit of the state of the database.

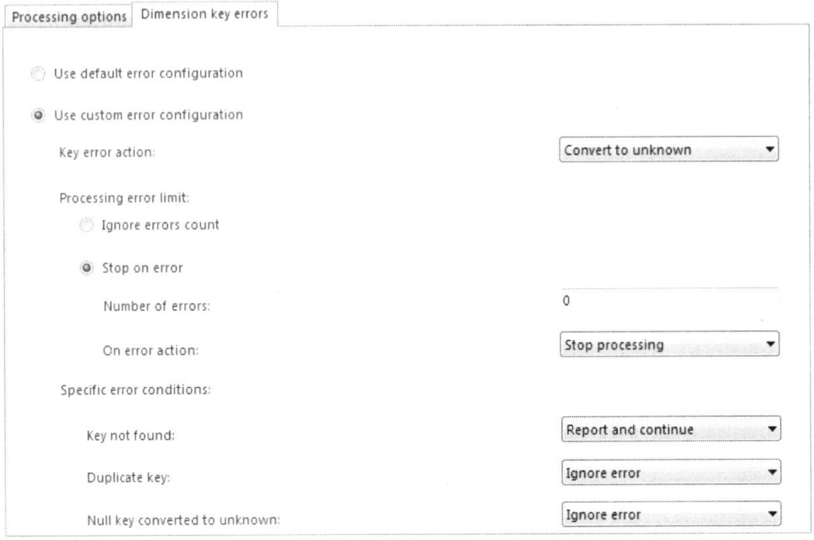

Figure 7-8

> The backups will back up only the Analysis Services database contents, not the underlying data sources used to populate the database. Therefore, we strongly suggest that you perform a backup of the data sources using a regular database or file system backup in conjunction with the Analysis Services backup to capture a true state of both the Analysis Services objects and their sources at or about the same point in time.

The information that the backup will include varies depending upon the storage type configured for the database. A detailed message displayed at the bottom of the Backup Database dialog clearly communicates the various objects included in a backup based on the type of storage. Although we cover storage options a bit later, you need to know that available options to be included in the backup are the metadata that defines all the objects, the aggregations calculated, and the source data used to populate the objects.

We'll now review what is involved in performing these functions for Analysis Services databases. Again, you can use Management Studio to assist with the setup and configuration of these tasks and script the results to permit scheduling:

1.   Open Management Studio and connect to an Analysis Services server.

2.   Right-click an Analysis Services database and select Backup. The Backup Database dialog appears, where you can configure the details of the backup, such as applying compression, where the backup file should be located, or whether the file should be encrypted (see Figure 7-9). We will cover storage types later, but you get a very clear statement of what information is part of the backup at the bottom of this dialog. Basically, the backup is

only backing up the Analysis Services information (partitions, metadata, source data, and aggregations) available to a database based on the storage type.

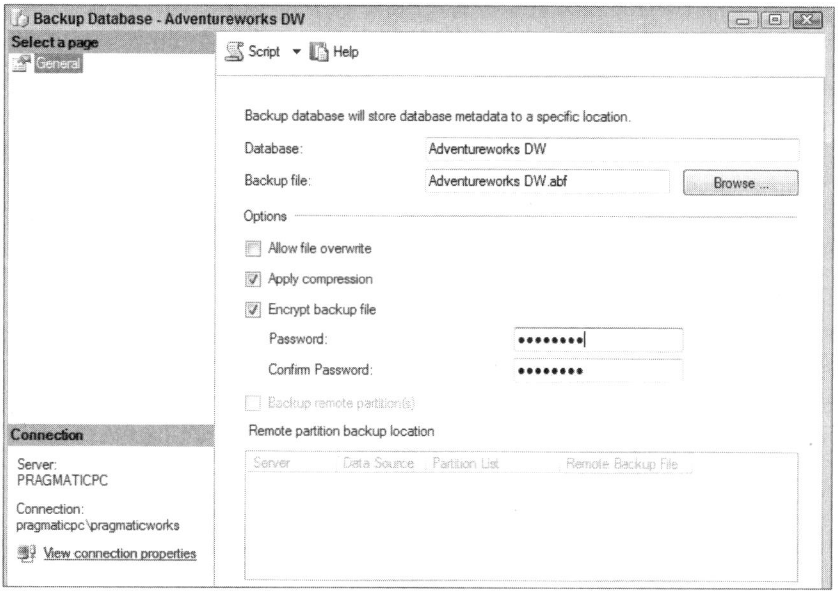

Figure 7-9

3. Optionally, you can script the backup by pressing the Script button along the top of the dialog. The resulting script looks like the following example (including, of course, a poor practice of including the password):

```
<Backup xmlns="http://schemas.microsoft.com/analysisservices/2003/engine">
  <Object>
    <DatabaseID>Adventureworks DW</DatabaseID>
  </Object>
  <File>Adventureworks DW.abf</File>
  <Password>password</Password>
</Backup>
```

Now that you have a backup of an Analysis Services database, it's time to turn your attention to recovery of Analysis Services databases. Recovery takes a previously created backup file (named with an .abf file extension) and restores it to an Analysis Services database. Several options are made available during this process:

❑   Using the original database name (or specifying a new database name).

❑   Overwriting an existing database.

❑   Including existing security information (or skipping security).

❑   Changing the restoration folder for each partition (except that remote partitions cannot become local).

Following are the steps needed to perform a recovery of the database:

1. Open Management Studio and connect to an Analysis Services server.

2. Right-click an Analysis Services database and select Restore. The Restore Database dialog appears, where you can configure the restoration details, such as including security or overwriting an existing database (see Figure 7-10).

3. Optionally, you can script the restore by clicking the Script button along the top of the dialog. The resulting script would look like the following example (including, again, a poor practice of including the password):

```
<Restore xmlns="http://schemas.microsoft.com/analysisservices/2003/engine">
  <File>C:\Program Files\Microsoft SQL
Server\MSAS10.MSSQLSERVER\OLAP\Backup\Adventureworks DW.abf</File>
  <DatabaseName>Adventureworks DW</DatabaseName>
  <AllowOverwrite>true</AllowOverwrite>
  <Password>password</Password>
  <DbStorageLocation
xmlns="http://schemas.microsoft.com/analysisservices/2008/engine/100/100">C:\
Program Files\Microsoft SQL Server\MSAS10.MSSQLSERVER\OLAP\Data\</DbStorageLocation>
</Restore>
```

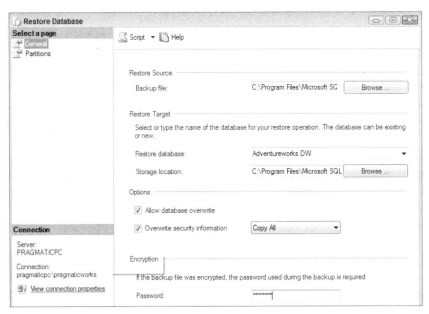

Figure 7-10

Synchronizing Analysis Services Databases

Another very important activity to perform involves synchronizing Analysis Services databases from one server to another. This is usually done as a mechanism for deploying from a test or quality-assurance server to a production server. This feature is attractive for this purpose because users can continue to browse the production cubes while the synchronization is taking place. When the synchronization completes, a user is automatically redirected to the newly synchronized copy of the database, and the older version is removed from the server. This differs greatly from what happens when you perform a deployment, as part of the deployment usually involves processing of dimensions and/or cubes. As you may recall, certain types of processing of Analysis Services objects require that the cube be taken offline, making it unavailable to users until the processing completes.

As with many other database tasks, the synchronization can be run immediately from the wizard, or the results of the selections can be saved to a script file for later execution or scheduling.

To synchronize an Analysis Services database between servers, follow these steps:

1. Open Management Studio and connect to the target Analysis Services server.

2. On this target server, right-click the databases folder and select Synchronize.

3. On the Select Databases to Synchronize page, specify the source server and database, and note that the destination server is hard-coded to the server from which you launched the synchronization.

4. If applicable, on the Specify Locations for Local Partitions page, the source folder displays the folder name on the server that contains the local partition, while the destination folder can be changed to reflect the folder into which you want the database to be synchronized.

5. If applicable, on the Specify Locations for Remote Partitions page, you can modify both the destination folder and server to reflect where you want the database to be synchronized. Additionally, if the location has remote partitions contained in that location that need to be included in the synchronization, you must place a check beside the Sync option.

6. On the Specify Query Criteria page, enter a value for the security definitions and indicate whether or not compression should be used. The security options include copying all definitions and membership information, skipping membership information but including the security definitions, and ignoring all security and membership details.

7. On the Select Synchronization Method page, you can either run the synchronization immediately or script to a file for later use in scheduling the synchronization.

Analysis Services Performance Monitoring and Tuning

Successful use of Analysis Services requires continual monitoring of how user queries and other processes are performing and making the required adjustments to improve their performance. The main tools for performing these tasks include the SQL Profiler, performance counters, and the Flight Recorder.

Monitoring Analysis Services Events Using SQL Profiler

Chapters 13 and 14 provide detailed coverage of how to use SQL Profiler, so here we focus on what is important about using this tool for monitoring your Analysis Services events. The capabilities related to using SQL Profiler for Analysis Services were vastly improved in the 2005 release and are now quite useful for this purpose. With SQL Server Profiler, you can review what the server is doing during processing and query resolution. Especially important is the ability to record the data generated by profiling to either a database table or file in order to review or replay it later to get a better understanding of what happened. You can also now either step through the events that were recorded or replay them as they originally occurred. Last, you can place the events side by side with the performance counters to spot trends affecting performance.

Our main focus here is tracing the Analysis Services server activity and investigating the performance of the MDX queries submitted to the server in order to process user requests for information.

The useful event categories include the following:

- ❑ Command events provide insight into the actual types of statements issued to perform actions.
- ❑ Discovery events detail requests for metadata about server objects, including the Discovery Server State events (such as open connections).
- ❑ Error and Warnings events.
- ❑ Notification events.
- ❑ Query events.

Because of all the detail that a trace returns, use the Column Filter button to display only the activities sent to a specific Analysis Services database.

Creating Traces for Replay

Traces are important because they enable you to determine various elements of status information for Analysis Services through certain counters. You start Performance Monitor by either selecting Performance in Administrative Tools from the Control Panel or by typing **PerfMon** at the command prompt. Two types of counters are used within Performance Monitor. The predefined counters measure statistics for your server and process performance, whereas user-defined counters are used to analyze events that may occur. There are also command-line tools such as LodCtr, LogMan, ReLog, TypePerf, and UnloadCtr to capture performance metrics.

Just as in the monitoring of other SQL services, the CPU usage, memory usage, and disk I/O rate are important counters to review in order to evaluate how Analysis Services is performing.

To get a better idea of how to configure these traces for replaying queries submitted to your Analysis Services server, start a trace by opening SQL Profiler and selecting File ➪ New Trace. When prompted, specify the Analysis Services server to connect to and configure trace properties to resemble what is shown in Figure 7-11.

To profile user queries, you have to ensure that the SQL Profiler is capturing the Audit Login event class, the Query Begin event class, and the Query End event class (see Figure 7-12. SQL server will be able to determine who was running the query and other session-specific information because you are including the Audit Login event class. The Query Begin and Query End event classes simply permit understanding what queries were submitted by reviewing the text of the query along with any parameters that would have been used during query processing.

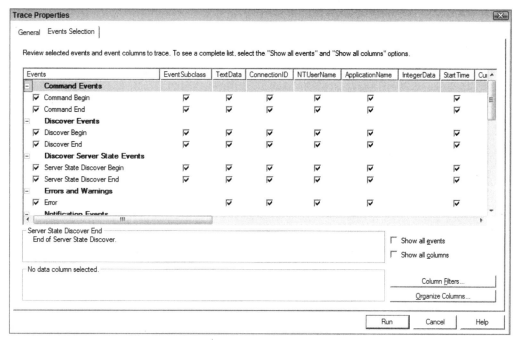

Figure 7-11

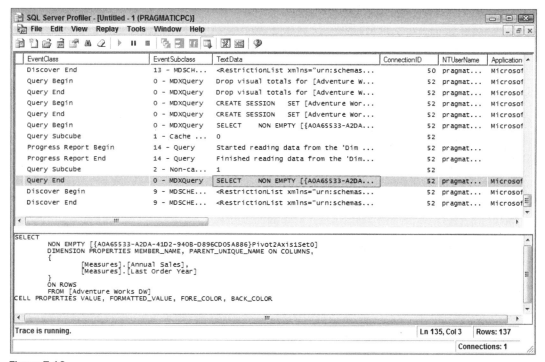

Figure 7-12

After you've set up the trace, you can start it. You can browse a cube within Management Studio to generate user activity involving the submission of queries to Analysis Services. The result in Profiler is a detailing of events along with the TextData recording the activities. For example, in Management Studio, you can add the Customer and Date dimensions while also requesting that Order Count and Average Sales Amount be displayed. This activity is all recorded with the Profiler, with the MDX statement recorded in the TextData column (see Figure 7-12).

Using Flight Recorder for After-the-Fact Analysis

As administrators, we are often disappointed when we cannot seem to find the cause of a particular problem. Mostly, we are stymied when we cannot reproduce reported problems. These situations arise as we attempt to recreate what happened to determine how things could have been handled differently to avoid the reported problem. Using the Flight Recorder, you may be able to replay the problem conditions that led to the reported problems. This Flight Recorder operates similarly to a tape recorder: It captures the Analysis Services server activity during runtime without requiring a trace. In fact, each time the server is restarted, a new trace file is automatically started. Additionally, the recorder is automatically enabled and can be configured using the Analysis Services Server Properties.

Here's how you can use the trace file created by the Flight Recorder to replay server activity:

1. Open SQL Server Profiler and open the trace file created by the Flight Recorder, by default located at `C:\Program Files\Microsoft SQL Server\MSAS10.MSSQLSERVER\OLAP\Log` and named `FlightRecorderCurrent.trc`.

2. Select Replay ⇨ Start on the toolbar.

3. On the Connect To Server dialog, enter the server name and authentication information.

4. On the Replay Configuration dialog, you can set up the desired playback features, such as replaying only statements issued to the server within a given time frame (see Figure 7-13).

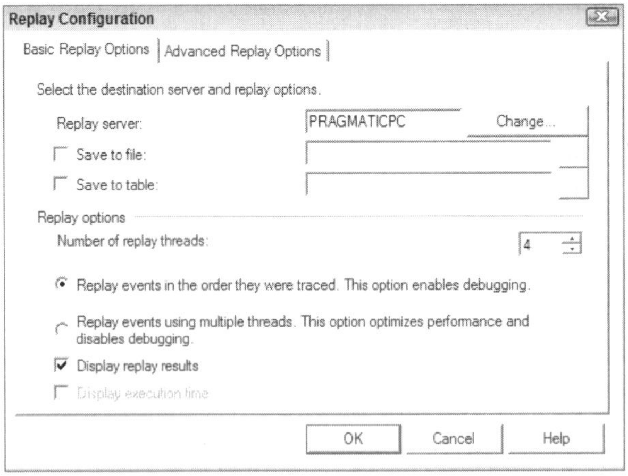

Figure 7-13

This replay is rather useful, as Analysis Services will begin to run the statements captured in the trace. Obviously, factors such as number of open connections and even the number of sessions that existed at the time of the original problem are important to consider when troubleshooting problems. When you replay the traces made by Flight Recorder, these factors are simulated on your behalf.

Management of Analysis Services Storage

One of the main reasons for using Analysis Services centers on performance with complex data retrieval. The design of the storage within Analysis Services, therefore, becomes very important when trying to achieve the query and processing performance expected. In order to understand storage design, this section first describes what modes of storage are available within Analysis Services. Next, you will look at the configuration of partitions. Last, you will learn how to design aggregations.

Storage Modes

Analysis Services permits configuring dimensions and measure groups using the following storage modes: Multidimensional OLAP (MOLAP), Relational OLAP (ROLAP), and Hybrid OLAP (HOLAP):

❑ **Multidimensional OLAP:** MOLAP storage mode is the most aggressive because it stores all the aggregations and a copy of the source data with the structure. Additionally, the structure stores the metadata required to understand the structure. The real benefit of this structure is query performance, as all information needed to respond to queries is available without having to access the source data. Periodic processing is required to update the data stored within the structure, and this processing can be either incremental or full. As a result, data latency is introduced with this storage mode. Also as a result of this structure, storage requirements become much more important due to the volume of information that the system requires.

❑ **Relational OLAP:** Indexed views within the data source of the ROLAP structure store the aggregations, while a copy of the source data is not stored within Analysis Service. With this mode, any queries that the query cache cannot answer must be passed on to the data source. That makes this storage mode slower than MOLAP or HOLAP. The benefit is that users can view data in real or near-real time, and because a copy of the source data is not being stored within the structure, the storage requirements are lower.

❑ **Hybrid OLAP:** As you might have guessed, the HOLAP storage mode is a combination of multidimensional OLAP and relational OLAP. This storage mode stores aggregations but does not store a copy of the source data. As a result, queries that access the aggregated values perform well, but those that do not, perform slower. Also as a result, this storage mode requires far less storage space.

Partition Configuration

When you need to configure partitions for your cubes, you have two primary tasks. First, you have the configuration of the storage of the partition, and second you have the optimization of the partition by configuring aggregations. The storage options, previously discussed, include MOLAP, HOLAP, or ROLAP. Aggregations are precalculated summaries of data, primarily employed so that query response time is made faster because the cube partition has prepared and saved the data in advance of its use.

You should understand that the configuration of storage in Analysis Services is configured separately for each partition of each measure group in a cube. This enables you to optimize your cube query strategies for each partition. An example would be to keep the current year's data in one partition optimized for more detailed and narrow queries, while keeping older data in another partition optimized for broader aggregated queries.

You configure your cube storage using either Business Intelligence Developer Studio or, after deployment, Management Studio. Often, it is not necessary for developers to be involved with partitioning or configuration of storage, so this is a better fit for using Management Studio. The downside is that the Visual Studio project will not be updated to reflect the current storage settings, and you must be very careful during deployment that your selections made in Management Studio are not overwritten. Specifically, you want to ensure that during deployment, when the Specify Options for Partitions and Roles page is displayed, you indicate that Partitions and Security should be maintained on the deployment target database and thus not overwritten by this deployment (refer to Figure 7-4).

When you deploy a cube for the first time, a measure group is set up to be entirely contained within a single partition, spanning the entire fact table used for the measures. With the Enterprise Edition, you can change that to define multiple partitions by setting the `StorageMode` property for each partition.

Here's how to set the storage options in SQL Server Management Studio:

1. Open Management Studio and connect to the target Analysis Services server.

2. In Object Explorer, right-click the cube that contains the partition and click Properties to set storage options. If you have more than one partition, right-click a partition and click Properties.

3. Select the Proactive Caching page.

4. Select the Standard Setting radio button to accept the default storage settings for the storage type specified by the slider bar. Now you may move the slider bar to change the storage type from MOLAP to HOLAP and to ROLAP (see Figure 7-14). For the purpose of this example, select Scheduled MOLAP and then click Options.

5. Clicking the Options button will display the Storage Options dialog, shown in Figure 7-15. This screen enables you to quickly configure how the cube will be processed automatically. If you check Enable Proactive Caching (available only in Enterprise Edition), the cube will be processed automatically. For scheduled MOLAP, check "Update the cache periodically" to automatically build the cube once a day. With proactive caching, the cube will remain online during the update. You can also have SSAS automatically detect changes in the underlying data warehouse and process as soon as the change is made, if you prefer to have more real-time analytics.

Designing Aggregations

Again, the primary role of aggregations is to precalculate summaries of the cube data so that user queries may be answered very fast. When a query is unable to use an aggregation, Analysis Services must query the lowest level of details it has stored and sum the values. Aggregations are stored in a cube in cells at the intersection of the selected dimensions.

Designing aggregations is all about trade-offs between space and user performance. Optimizing query performance via aggregations also increases the time it takes to process the cube. When you have few aggregations, the time required to process the cube and the storage space occupied by the cube is rather small, but the query response time may be slow because the query cannot leverage a precomputed summary (aggregate) and must instead rely upon having to retrieve data from the lowest levels within the cube and summarize at query time.

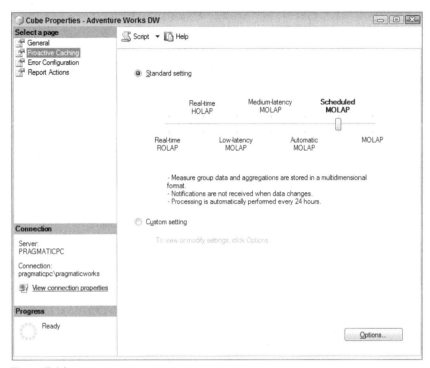

Figure 7-14

You design aggregations by determining which combination of attributes are often used by queries and could benefit from precalculation. You can begin this process by using the Aggregation Design Wizard, or after deployment you can use query usage statistics in conjunction with the Usage-Based Optimization Wizard. These methods obviously lend themselves to specific life-cycle usage. Developers would likely use the Aggregation Design Wizard to initially configure the aggregations prior to deployment, whereas administrators would opt to use the query statistics and the Usage-Based Optimization Wizard.

A good rule of thumb to start with is to optimize at a level of 20/80 and 80/20. When using the Aggregation Design Wizard, you are really not sure what the usage patterns will be, so optimizing to higher than a 20 percent performance increase would not be valuable. Conversely, when you have actual query statistics that clearly represent production usage patterns, you should optimize at about an 80 percent performance increase level. This in effect states that you want 80 percent of user queries to be answered directly from aggregations.

> *Details of the Aggregation Design Wizard are not covered here, as we assume that most administration of the aggregations will be performed in either Management Studio or BIDS using the Usage-Based Optimization Wizard.*

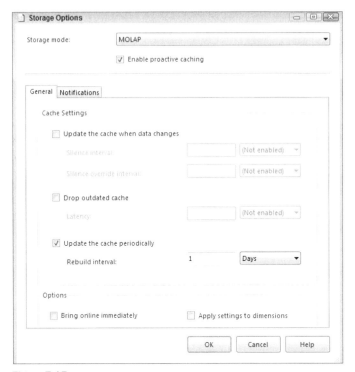

Figure 7-15

Before using the Usage-Based Optimization Wizard, you need to ensure that the query log is enabled and that it has been populated. You enable this log in Management Studio via the Analysis Services Server properties. The CreateQueryLogTable setting enables logging to a database table when true, while the QueryLogConnectionString specifies the database in which the logging will be stored. In addition, note the setting of the QueryLogSampling, as this determines which queries will be logged.

Once the Query Log has been enabled and is populated with query statistics, you can run the Usage-Based Optimization Wizard. Here are the steps needed to use this wizard:

1. Open Management Studio and connect to the target Analysis Services server.

2. Select the desired database, cube, and measure group.

3. Right-click the partitions folder and select Usage Based Optimization.

4. On the Select Partitions to Modify dialog, specify any partitions that are to be evaluated. You can either select all partitions for the measure group or you can select combinations of individual partitions.

5. On the Specify Query Criteria dialog, you can view query statistics for the selected measure group partition, including the total number of queries and the average response time for processing the queries. Optionally, you can set some limits to filter the queries that you would like the optimization to consider (see Figure 7-16), including an interesting option for filtering the queries by users. Presumably, one notable use of this option would be to enable you to ensure that your executives' queries are delivering the best response time.

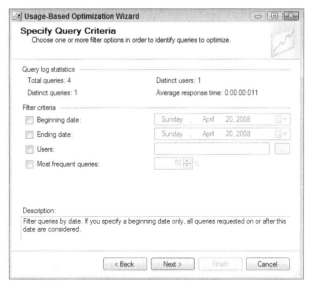

Figure 7-16

6.   On the Review the Queries That Will Be Optimized dialog, you can view the specific dimension member combinations under the client request column, the occurrences of those combinations, and the average duration of those combinations. At this point, you also have a column of checkboxes beside each row that enables you to indicate that you do not want some of the suggested queries optimized.

7.   Under the Review Aggregation Usage page, select the default options. This screen gives you full control over how each dimension is aggregated.

8.   Specify the counts of various cube objects on the Specify Object Counts dialog by clicking the Count button.

9.   On the Set Aggregations Options dialog, specify how long the aggregations should be designed. Options to consider include designing aggregations until a specified amount of storage has been used, until a specified percentage of performance gain has been reached, or until you decide to stop the optimization process (see Figure 7-17). Because you are basing this optimization on real query statistics, you should consider optimizing until a performance gain of about 30 percent has been attained. This translates loosely to optimizing 30 percent of the queries to use the aggregations, which is about 52KB.

10.   Last, you are presented with the Completing the Wizard dialog, which you can use to review the partitions affected by the aggregation design and to indicate whether or not you would like the affected partitions to be processed immediately.

In Profiler, you can see whether aggregations are being used easily on a query by query basis. In the Progress Report End event class, you'll see an aggregation being read, versus a partition, as shown in Figure 7-18.

You now have designed the storage of your Analysis Services cubes, set up partitions, and designed aggregations. In the next section, you will learn how to apply security to Analysis Services.

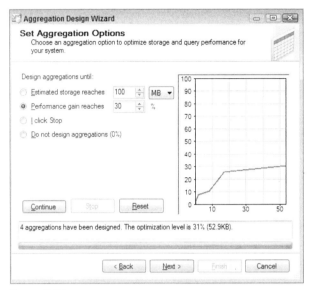

Figure 7-17

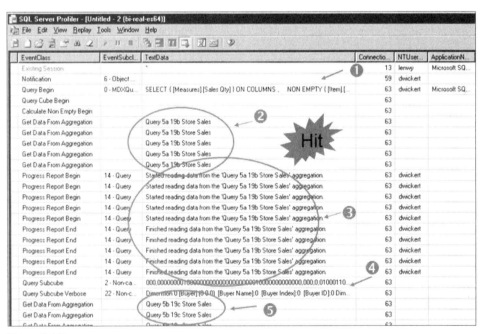

Figure 7-18

Applying Security to Analysis Services

Security within Analysis Services involves designing user permissions to selected cubes, dimensions, cells, mining models, and data sources. Analysis Services relies on Microsoft Windows to authenticate users, and only authenticated users who have rights within Analysis Services can establish a connection to Analysis Services.

After a user connects to Analysis Services, the permissions that user has within Analysis Services are determined by the rights assigned to the Analysis Services roles to which that user belongs, either directly or through membership in a Windows role. The two roles available in Analysis Services are server roles and database roles.

Server Role

The server role permits unrestricted access to the server and all the objects contained on the server. This role also allows its members to administer security by assigning permissions to other users. By default, all members of the Administrators local group are members of the server role in Analysis Services and have serverwide permissions to perform any task. You configure this access by using Management Studio, Business Intelligence Development Studio, or an XMLA script.

Here's how you add additional Windows users or groups to this Server role:

1. Open Management Studio and connect to an Analysis Services server.

2. Right-click the server node in Object Explorer and choose Properties.

3. On the Analysis Server Properties dialog, select the Security page. Note again that no users or groups are included automatically. Although it's not shown in the dialog, only members of the local Windows Administrators group are automatically assigned this server role.

4. Click the Add button and add users and groups with the standard Windows Select Users and Groups dialog.

5. After adding the users and groups, you can remove the local Administrators from the server role by selecting the General page and clicking the Show Advanced (ALL) Properties checkbox. Then set the `Security\BuiltinAdminsAreServerAdmins` property to false.

Database Role

Within Analysis Services, you can set up multiple database roles. Only the members of the server role are permitted to create these database roles within each database, grant administrative or user permissions to these database roles, and add Windows users and groups to these roles.

These database roles have no administrative capabilities unless they are granted Full Control, otherwise known as administrator rights, or a more limited set of administrator rights (such as Process the database, Process one or more Dimensions, and Read database metadata).

In summary, reading Analysis Services data is only available to members of the server role and members of a database role that have Full Control. Other users can get this access only if their database role expressly grants permissions to the objects in Analysis Services (dimensions, cubes, and cells).

You set up database roles using either Business Intelligence Developer Studio or Management Studio. In BIDS, you use the Role Designer, while in Management Studio you use the Create Role dialog. When Management Studio is used for setting up these roles, the changes do not require that you deploy the database, as they are made in online mode.

Here's how to add a database role to an Analysis Services database using Management Studio:

1. Open Management Studio and connect to an Analysis Services server.

2. Right-click the Roles folder located in one of the databases and select New Role.

3. On the Create Role dialog (see Figure 7-19), enter **Data Admin** as the role name and check the Full control (Administrator) checkbox.

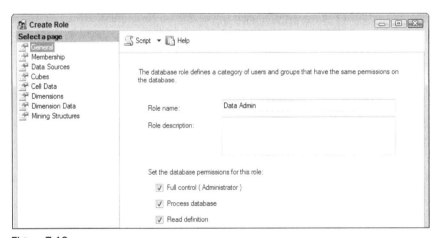

Figure 7-19

4. Select the Membership page and add a Windows user account.

If a developer redeploys the cube without your knowledge, your security may be overwritten. Once you change the settings, it's important to have the developer re-synch with the live server or use the Deployment Utility going forward.

Database Role Permissions

The easiest way to understand the granularity of permissions within Analysis Services is by reviewing the Create Role dialog's pages. Previously, when you added a new role, you assigned the Full Control (Administrator) database permissions. If you did not check that checkbox, you would have the ability to assign very granular permissions by using the various pages of the Create Role dialog.

The permissions form a sort of hierarchy in which the topmost permissions need to be assigned before any of the next lower-level permissions. This hierarchy includes Cubes, Dimensions, Dimension Data, and Cell Data. Analysis Services permits a database to include more than one cube, which is why you have that as a permission set for your roles. Within the cube, you have dimensions and measures. The measures are constrained by the various dimensions. Let's now look at some examples of assigning these permissions.

While reviewing the role permissions available, note two in particular that are regularly used to limit access to information: Dimensions and Dimension Data. These permit you to define what the user can see when browsing the cube. For example, you can configure security such that only staff in the Marketing department can use the Promotions dimension. Access permissions to an entire dimension are configured on the Dimensions page of the Create Role dialog (see Figure 7-20). You should understand that certain permissions require that other permissions be granted. In this example, you would have to ensure that the role for the Marketing department staff has been granted permissions to access the AdventureWorks cube.

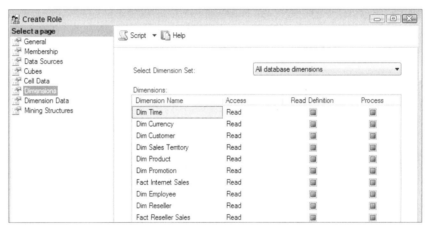

Figure 7-20

Once access has been modified for the dimensions, you have to define the specific attribute hierarchies and members within the dimension to which role members are allowed access. If you forget to do this, the role will not have permission to view any attribute hierarchies within the dimension, nor any of their members. For example, you can permit a regional sales manager access to the sales territories that he or she manages by selecting the Dimension Data page and selecting the AdventureWorks DW.Sales Territory from the Dimension combo box.

You may also encounter a security configuration that requires even more sophistication, and for that you have the Advanced tab on the Dimension Data page of the Create Role dialog. This tab enables the creation of very complex combinations of allowed and denied listings of dimension members, along with configuration of default members for your role. Here is where administrators may need to work with developers to understand the multidimensional expression language (MDX) syntax that would be required to configure these advanced security options.

Summary

We have covered a lot of ground in understanding the various administrative functions related to Analysis Services. After getting a general introduction to the elements that make up the Unified Dimensional Model (UDM) and looking at the high-level architecture of Analysis Services, we reviewed important server and database administrative tasks such as setting server configuration settings and deploying your databases. Next, you got some insight into performance monitoring and tuning. Then we turned our attention to storage administrative tasks such as configuring partitions or designing aggregations. Last, we reviewed the various security administration tasks such as creating database roles and assigning granular permissions to the roles. Now that you've learned about administering the Business Integration services, we'll move on in Chapter 8 to discussing how to administer the developer tools that SQL Server 2008 provides.

8

Administering the Development Features

Certain types of database applications development were not possible before SQL Server 2005 — for example, messages-based applications for a service-oriented type of architecture, or creating user-defined types in the database. Starting with SQL Server 2005 and continuing with SQL Server 2008, many programming features have been added, including Service Broker, CLR, and many enhancements in T-SQL. One of the most remarkable new technologies is Service Broker, which makes it possible to build database-intensive distributed applications. Service Broker implements a set of distributed communication patterns to add messaging capabilities to SQL Server applications. The other remarkable feature is the integration of the Common Language Runtime (CLR) component of the .NET Framework for Microsoft Windows with the SQL Server database engine. This integration enables developers to write procedures, triggers, and functions in any of the CLR languages, particularly Microsoft Visual C# .NET, Microsoft Visual Basic .NET, and Microsoft Visual C++. It also enables developers to extend the database with new types and aggregates.

In this chapter, we first explain how these new features work, and then show you how to administer them. We begin with Service Broker, and then move on to CLR integration.

Service Broker

SQL Service Broker is one of the best recent features in SQL Server 2005 because it makes it possible to write queuing and message-based applications. With Service Broker, database developers can write asynchronous applications to communicate between databases or servers and can easily build distributed, secure, and reliable applications. Service Broker can take care of all the communication and messaging, enabling the developer to focus on the core problem domain. In addition, because Service Broker is part of the database engine, it encompasses many additional qualities such as transaction consistency, reliability, and security.

Service Broker Architecture

Service Broker is designed around the basic functions of sending and receiving messages. It helps developers build asynchronous, loosely coupled applications in which independent components work together to accomplish a task. Service Broker is a framework and extension to T-SQL, and can create and use the components for building reliable and scalable message-based applications. The core of Service Broker architecture is the concept of a *dialog*, which is a reliable, persistent, bi-directional, ordered exchange of messages between two *endpoints*. An endpoint is the sender or receiver of a message. For example, in Figure 8-1, Initiator is one endpoint of a conversation and Target is the other endpoint. You will learn more about endpoints later in this chapter. Figure 8-1 shows the basic architecture of Service Broker (it includes a lot of terminology that is explained in the following sections).

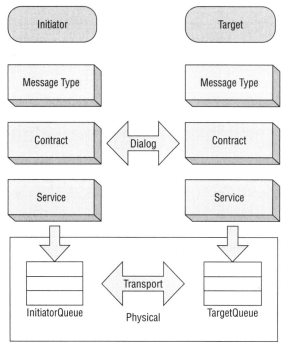

Figure 8-1

Message Type

A *message type* is a definition of the format of a message. The message type is an object in a database. *Messages* are the information exchanged between applications that use Service Broker. The message type object defines the name of the message and the type of data it contains. The following code shows the syntax for creating a message type:

```
CREATE MESSAGE TYPE message_type_name
    [ AUTHORIZATION owner_name ]
    [ VALIDATION = {  NONE
```

```
       | EMPTY
       | WELL_FORMED_XML
       | VALID_XML WITH SCHEMA COLLECTION schema_collection_name
    }
]
```

Permission for creating a message type defaults to members of the ddl_admin or db_owner fixed database roles and the sysadmin fixed server role. The REFERENCES permission for a message type defaults to the owner of the message type, members of the db_owner fixed database role, and members of the sysadmin fixed server role. When the CREATE MESSAGE TYPE statement specifies a schema collection, the user executing the statement must have REFERENCES permission on the schema collection specified.

Following are the arguments and their definitions for the CREATE MESSAGE TYPE statement:

❑   message_type_name: The name of the message type is just a SQL Server identifier. The convention is to use a URL for the name, but any valid name will suffice. By convention, the name has the form //<hostname/pathname/name— for example, //www.wrox.com/bookorder/purchaseorder. Although using a URL format is not required and it does not need to exist physically, it's generally easier to ensure uniqueness if you use a URL, especially when conversations span distributed systems. The message_type_name may be up to 128 characters.

❑   AUTHORIZATION owner_name: This argument defines the owner of the message type. The owner can be any valid database user or role. When this clause is omitted, the message type belongs to the user who executed the statement. If you execute the CREATE MESSAGE TYPE statement as either dbo or sa, owner_name may be the name of any valid user or role. Otherwise, owner_name must be the name of the current user, the name of a user for whom the current user has impersonate permission, or the name of a role to which the current user belongs.

❑   VALIDATION: This specifies how Service Broker validates the message body for messages of this type. When this clause is not specified, validation defaults to NONE. The possible values are as follows:

    ❑   NONE: The message is not validated at all. The message body may contain any data, including NULL.

    ❑   Empty: The message body must be NULL.

    ❑   WELL_FORMED_XML: When this clause is specified, the receiving endpoint will load the XML into an XML parser to ensure that it can be parsed. If the message fails the validation, it is discarded and an error message is sent back to the sender.

    ❑   VALID_XML WITH SCHEMA COLLECTION schema_collection_name: This clause validates the message against the schema_collection_name specified. The schema collection must be created in SQL Server before you use it here. The schema collection, added since SQL Server 2005, is an object that contains one or more XML schemas. Refer to the CREATE XML SCHEMA COLLECTION command in Books Online (BOL) for more information. If WITH SCHEMA COLLECTION schema_collection_name is not specified, the message will not be validated; however, the XML must still be well formed because anytime you specify WELL_FORMED_XML or VALID_XML, the message of that type is loaded into the XML parser when it is received.

The following is an example of creating a message type:

```
CREATE MESSAGE TYPE [//www.wrox.com/order/orderentry]
VALIDATE = WELL_FORMED_XML
```

The two XML validations load every message of that type into an XML parser when each message is received. If you have high message volume (maybe thousands of messages per second), each message passing through the XML parser will have an effect on performance. Therefore, avoid using XML validations when you have high message volume. If your application loads the message into a parser, it will be more efficient to handle parsing or validation in the application, rather than parse the message twice.

You can run the following query to view message types in the database in which you have created them:

```
SELECT * FROM sys.service_message_types
```

When you run this query, you will see default message types that are included in every SQL Server database installation. Later in the chapter, you will see some examples of using some of the default message types. These message types are an implicit part of every contract, which we'll discuss shortly, so any endpoint can receive instances of these message types.

You can ALTER or DROP a message type by using the following T-SQL command syntax:

```
ALTER MESSAGE TYPE message_type_name
   VALIDATION =
      {  NONE
       | EMPTY
       | WELL_FORMED_XML
       | VALID_XML WITH SCHEMA COLLECTION schema_collection_name
      }
```

Changing the validation of a message type does not affect messages that have already been delivered to a queue, which we'll discuss shortly. Permission to alter a message type defaults to the owner of the message type, members of the ddl_admin or db_owner fixed database roles, and members of the sysadmin fixed server role. When the ALTER MESSAGE TYPE statement specifies a schema collection, the user executing the statement must have REFERENCES permission on the schema collection specified.

The following example shows the syntax to drop a message type:

```
DROP MESSAGE TYPE message_type_name [, ... ... n]
```

Permission for dropping a message type defaults to the owner of the message type, members of the ddl_admin or db_owner fixed database roles, and members of the sysadmin fixed server role. Note that you can drop multiple message types. If you try to drop a message type when a contract is referencing the message type, you will get an error.

Contracts

As described earlier, Service Broker *contracts* define which message type can be used in a conversation. The contract is a database object. The following is the syntax for creating a contract:

```
CREATE CONTRACT contract_name
   [ AUTHORIZATION owner_name ]
      ( {   message_type_name SENT BY { INITIATOR | TARGET | ANY } | [ DEFAULT ] }
        [ , ... n]
      )
```

Permission for creating a contract defaults to members of the ddl_admin or db_owner fixed database roles and the sysadmin fixed server role. The REFERENCES permission for a contract defaults to the owner of the message type, members of the db_owner fixed database role, and members of the sysadmin fixed server role. The user executing the CREATE CONTRACT statement must have REFERENCES permission on all the message types specified unless the user executing the CREATE CONTRACT statement is a member of ddl_admin or db_owner, or the sysadmin role, because members of these roles have REFERENCES permission on all the message types by default.

The following list describes the arguments for the CREATE CONTRACT statement:

❑ contract_name: The name of the contract is just a SQL Server identifier. The convention is to use a URL, but any valid name will suffice. By convention, it has the form //hostname/pathname/name, so //www.wrox.com/bookorder/ ordercontract is an example of a valid contract name. Although using a URL format is not required, it's generally easier to ensure uniqueness if you use a URL, especially when conversations span distributed systems. The contract_name may be up to 128 characters.

❑ AUTHORIZATION owner_name: This argument is the same as it is in the message type.

❑ message_type_name: The name of the message type that this contract uses. You can have multiple message types per contract, as shown later in the example.

❑ SENT BY: This clause defines whether the message type can be sent by the initiator of the conversation, by the target of the conversation, or by either:

   ❑ INITIATOR: The initiator of the conversation can send the defined message type.

   ❑ TARGET: The target of the conversation can send the defined message type.

   ❑ ANY: The defined message type can be sent by either INITIATOR or TARGET.

❑ [DEFAULT]: If you query the sys.service_message_types catalog view, you will see a DEFAULT message type there.

The following code shows an example of creating a contract:

This is just an example to show the syntax; do not execute the code at this point.

241

```
CREATE CONTRACT [//www.wrox.com/bookorder/ordercontract]
(
[//www.wrox.com/order/orderentry] SENT BY INITIATOR
[//www.wrox.com/order/orderentryack] SENT BY TARGET
)
```

When a contract is created, at least one message type needs to be marked as SENT BY INITIATOR or SENT BY ANY. Obviously, a message type must exist before you create the contract. In addition, the message type and direction cannot be changed once the contract is defined, so you cannot alter the contract once you create it. If you have to change the message type, then you must first drop the contract if you have defined one for that message type. You can change the authorization only using the ALTER AUTHORIZATION statement.

Queue

We mentioned earlier that Service Broker performs asynchronous operations. In asynchronous processing, you send a request to do something and then you start doing something else; the system processes the request you made later. Between the time when you make the request and when the system process acts on it, the request must be stored somewhere. The place where these requests are stored is called the *queue*.

Service Broker implements queues via a *hidden table* in the database where the queue is defined. You cannot use normal T-SQL commands to manipulate the data in the queue, and you cannot use INSERT, DELETE, or UPDATE commands on queues. In addition, you cannot change the structure of the queue or create triggers on them. A read-only view is associated with every queue, so you can use a SELECT statement to see what messages are in the queue. The sender puts the message in the queue using T-SQL commands (commands that work on queues, which are described later). The transport layer moves that message reliably to the destination queue. The receiver application can then pull that message off the queue when it desires. The message from the initiator (first) queue is not deleted until that message has been successfully stored in a destination (second) queue, so there is no chance that the message will be lost in transit. Figure 8-2 shows how this works.

Assume that in Figure 8-2, Service Broker is delivering a message from the database InitiatorDB on InitiatorServer to TargetDB on TargerServer, which means a network is involved in delivering this message. Service Broker puts the messages that are to be sent over the network in a temporary queue, called transmission_queue, on the server, where the message is initiated. You can query this transmission_queue with the following select statement. Note that you won't see any row in the table if there is no message in the transit:

```
SELECT * FROM sys.transmission_queue
```

There is one such transmission_queue for each SQL Server instance. After a message is put into the transmission_queue, Service Broker sends the message over the network and marks that message as waiting for acknowledgment in the transmission_queue. When Service Broker receives the message from the TargetServer in the TargetDB queue, it sends an acknowledgment back to the InitiatorServer. When the InitiatorServer receives the acknowledgment message, it deletes the message from the transmission_queue. This process is called the *dialog*. We discuss the dialog and conversation later in this chapter. For now, just keep these terms in mind.

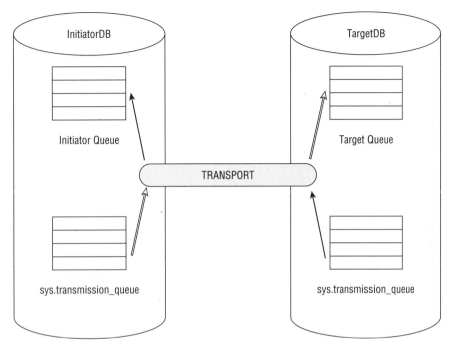

Figure 8-2

The following is the syntax to create a queue:

```
CREATE QUEUE queue_name
   [ WITH
      [ STATUS = { ON | OFF }  [ , ] ]
      [ RETENTION = { ON | OFF } [ , ] ]
      [ ACTIVATION
         (
           [ STATUS = { ON | OFF } , ]
              PROCEDURE_NAME = <procedure> ,
              MAX_QUEUE_READERS = max_readers ,
              EXECUTE AS { SELF | 'user_name' | OWNER }
         )
      ]
   ]
      [ ON { filegroup | [ DEFAULT ] } ]
```

The arguments to this statement are as follows:

❑   queue_name: The name of the queue that is created. This must be a SQL Server identifier. Because the queue is never referenced outside the database in which it is created, the URL-like syntax used for other Service Broker object names is not necessary for queue names.

❑   STATUS: When you create the queue, the STATUS parameter determines whether the queue is available (ON) or unavailable (OFF). If you don't specify the STATUS, the default value is ON. When the queue status is OFF, the queue is unavailable for adding or removing messages. When you deploy the application, it is a good idea to set the queue status to OFF so the application cannot submit the messages to the queue. Once the setup is done correctly, you can change this status to ON with the ALTER QUEUE statement, as you'll see shortly.

❑ RETENTION: When this parameter is OFF (the default setting), the message from the queue is deleted as soon as the transaction that receives the message commits. If RETENTION is ON, the queue saves all the incoming and outgoing messages until the conversation that owns the messages ends. This increases the size of the queue, which may affect the application's performance. You have to decide for your application requirements whether you need to retain the messages in the queue for a longer time or not. Later in the chapter you will look at an example that shows exactly what happens when RETENTION is either ON or OFF and when messages are deleted from the queue.

❑ ACTIVATION: We will talk about activation in detail later but for now it suffices to understand that this option specifies some information about a stored procedure to be executed when a message arrives in the queue:

   ❑ STATUS: If this parameter is ON, Service Broker activates (runs) the stored procedure specified in the PROCEDURE_NAME argument. If this parameter is OFF, the queue does not activate the stored procedure. You can use this argument to temporarily stop activation of the stored procedure to troubleshoot a problem with it. In addition, if you have made some changes to the activated stored procedure, it is good idea to change the STATUS to OFF before you deploy that stored procedure so that the next message in the queue will be processed by the modified stored procedure.

   ❑ PROCEDURE_NAME: This is the name of a stored procedure that is activated when a message arrives in the queue. The procedure has to be in the same database as the queue or be fully qualified. You will learn more about this later.

   ❑ MAX_QUEUE_READERS: This numeric value specifies the maximum number of instances of the stored procedure that the queue starts at the same time. The value of MAX_QUEUE_READERS must be a number between 0 and 32,767. Later, you will learn about the effect of setting this value too high or too low.

   ❑ EXECUTE AS: This specifies the database user account under which the activation stored procedure runs. If you specify a domain account, your SQL Server must be connected to the domain because at the time of activation, SQL Server checks for permission for that user. If this is a SQL Server user, SQL Server can check permission locally. If the value is SELF, the activation stored procedure will run under the context of the user creating this queue. If the value is 'user_name', the activation stored procedure will run under the context of the user specified here. The user_name parameter must be a valid SQL Server user. In addition, if the user creating the queue is not in the dbo or sysadmin role, then that user needs the IMPERSONATE permission for the user_name specified. See the "Securables and Object Permissions" section of Chapter 9 for more details on impersonation. If the value is OWNER, then the stored procedure executes as the owner of the queue. Keep in mind that the owners of the queue can be different from the one who is running the CREATE QUEUE command.

❑ ON { filegroup | [DEFAULT]: This specifies the SQL Server filegroup on which you want to create the queue. If your application is going to have a high volume of incoming messages, you may want to put your queue on a filegroup with a lot of disk space. If you don't specify this option, the queue is created on the default filegroup of the database in which you are creating the queue.

You can use the ALTER QUEUE command to change any of theses parameters. One additional parameter you can specify in ALTER QUEUE is to DROP the activation. That will delete all of the activation information associated with the queue. Of course, it will not drop the stored procedure specified in the PROCEDURE_NAME clause.

Permission for altering a queue defaults to the owner of the queue, members of the ddl_admin or db_owner fixed database roles, and members of the sysadmin fixed server role.

The following code shows the creation of a queue. Because it specifies the activation stored procedure name (through parameter PROCEDURE_NAME in the CREATE QUEUE statement) the activation procedure dbo.ProcessOrder must exist in the database before you run this statement. Do not run this statement yet, as this is just a code snippet to show how to create a queue. You will see a working example later in the "Service Broker Examples" section.

```
CREATE QUEUE dbo.acceptorder
WITH STATUS = ON
    ,RETENTION = OFF
    ,ACTIVATION (
                STATUS = ON
               ,PROCEDURE_NAME = dbo.ProcessOrder
               ,MAX_QUEUE_READERS = 5
               ,EXECUTE AS SELF
               )
```

Here's the code to alter the queue status:

```
ALTER QUEUE dbo.acceptorder WITH  STATUS = OFF, ACTIVATION (STATUS = OFF)
```

When you create a queue, you create an object of the type SERVICE_QUEUE. To view what queues exist in a database (keep in mind that the queue is for each database object, whereas sys.transmission_queue is for each SQL Server instance), you can use a SELECT statement as follows:

```
SELECT * FROM sys.service_queues
```

Three message queues are created as part of the SQL Server installation. If you want to view the contents of the queue, you can issue the following statement:

```
SELECT * FROM dbo.acceptorder
```

Services

To understand how services work, consider the postal service. When you want to send a letter to your friend, you write his or her address on the envelope before mailing it. In Service Broker world, that address on the envelope is called a *service*. A Service Broker service identifies an endpoint of a conversation, and that endpoint is a queue in a database. A service is associated with a list of contracts that is accepted by the service. Note that mapping a service to a contract is an optional step on the initiator. On the target, if you do not specify any contract, you won't be able to send any messages to the target.

Here is the syntax to create the service:

```
CREATE SERVICE service_name
   [ AUTHORIZATION owner_name ]
```

```
ON QUEUE [ schema_name. ]queue_name
[ ( contract_name | [DEFAULT] [ , ... n ] ) ]
```

The following list describes the arguments for the CREATE SERVICE statement:

- ❑ service_name: This is the name of the service to create.

- ❑ AUTHORIZATION: This is the same as discussed earlier in the message type section.

- ❑ queue_name: This is the name of the queue that receives the messages from this service.

- ❑ contract_name: This argument specifies a contract for which this service may be a target. If no contract is specified, then the service may only initiate a conversation.

The following code demonstrates how you create a service:

```
CREATE SERVICE orderentryservice
ON QUEUE acceptorder ([//www.wrox.com/bookorder/ordercontract])
```

You can query the catalog view SELECT * FROM sys.services to view the service defined in a database.

Now that you have an understanding of all the pieces of the architecture, Figure 8-3 shows the relationships among the metadata objects used by Service Broker.

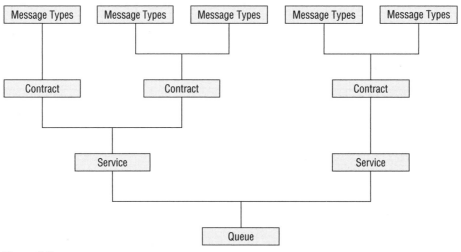

Figure 8-3

Service Broker Examples

Now you have enough information to write a small application. Although we have not covered some of the terms such as *activation* or *conversation*, we will do so as you go through the code.

Service Broker metadata names that are sent across the wire (e.g., message type, contract, service) are always case sensitive.

You'll start with a very simple example that involves Service Broker communication on the same server between two databases. (You will look at three examples; this first example illustrates how messaging and activation work in Service Broker. Don't worry about security in the first example.) The second example features a Service Broker application that communicates between two instances of SQL Server, and the third involves communication between two SQL Server instances with certificates and message encryption. Security is a major part of these examples.

> *Note that when you run examples between two instances of SQL Server and you are running SQL Server on Vista machines, Windows Firewall will block the connections between instances. You must add the TCP ports 1433, 5040, and 4040 to allow the TCP connections through the firewall.*

The first example assumes that you are the system administrator (sa) on the SQL Server. For now, our focus is on how Service Broker works, and not on which tricks you can do with it yet. Download the code for this chapter from this book's Web site at www.wrox.com. Open the Chapter 8 folder, followed by the `Sample1` folder, and double-click the `Sample1` solution file. It is assumed that you have SQL Server Management Studio (SSMS) installed where you open this file. Also make sure that you have installed the AdventureWorks2008 sample database for this example. You can read the "AdventureWorks Sample Databases" section in BOL to install that database.

In this example, you will send a message from the `Initiator` database, asking for the customer and product count, and receive that message on the `Target` database on the same SQL Server instance. The `Target` database will respond to that message with the customer and product count. The initiator database will store that count in a table and call it good.

You can find the `SetupInitiator.sql` script in the `Queries` folder in the `Sample1` solution. Let's go through the code in that file. Open the file and connect to your SQL Server instance. You will first set up the `InitiatorDB` and then the `TargetDB`. Do not run the script until after you have finished reading the explanation.

```
USE Master
GO

IF EXISTS(SELECT 1 FROM sys.databases WHERE name = 'InitiatorDB')
DROP DATABASE InitiatorDB
GO

CREATE DATABASE InitiatorDB;
GO

ALTER DATABASE InitiatorDB SET TRUSTWORTHY ON
GO

USE InitiatorDB
GO

SELECT Service_Broker_Guid, is_broker_enabled, is_trustworthy_on
FROM sys.databases
WHERE database_id = DB_ID()
GO
```

Create a brand-new database called `InitiatorDB` so that you don't interfere with other databases on your system. Notice that after creating the `InitiatorDB`, the next statement sets the TRUSTWORTHY bit to 1 for that database. If you are using certificate security with dialog encryption ON (explained later in the chapter), then setting the TRUSTWORTHY bit to ON is not necessary. The SELECT statement from the sys.databases catalog view will give you the Service_Broker_Guid, which is a unique Service Broker identifier for that database. The is_broker_enabled bit is set to 1 when you create a new database (not when you restore or attach from an existing database file). If this bit is 0, then message delivery in this database is not possible because Service Broker is not enabled in the database.

```
--------------------------------------------------------------------------------
--Create table to log what's happened.
--------------------------------------------------------------------------------
CREATE   TABLE dbo.ProcessHistory
(
 RowID int IDENTITY(1,1) NOT NULL
,Process varchar(60)  NOT NULL
,StatusDate datetime NOT NULL
,Status varchar(50) NULL
,MessageText xml NULL
,SPID int NULL
,UserName varchar(60) NULL
 CONSTRAINT PK_ProcessHistory PRIMARY KEY CLUSTERED(RowID)
)
```

This table was created to log information so you can view what has happened by looking at the rows in the table.

The interesting part starts here. As discussed earlier, the first thing you have to do when you create Service Broker objects is to create message types, as shown here:

```
--------------------------------------------------------------------------------
--First we have to create Message Types on InitiatorDB
--------------------------------------------------------------------------------
CREATE MESSAGE TYPE [//www.wrox.com/MTCustomerInfo/RequstCustomersCount]
VALIDATION = WELL_FORMED_XML
GO

CREATE MESSAGE TYPE [//www.wrox.com/MTCustomerInfo/ResponseTotalCustomers]
VALIDATION = WELL_FORMED_XML
GO

CREATE MESSAGE TYPE [//www.wrox.com/MTProductInfo/RequestProductsCount]
VALIDATION = WELL_FORMED_XML
GO

CREATE MESSAGE TYPE [//www.wrox.com/MTProductInfo/ResponseTotalProducts]
VALIDATION = WELL_FORMED_XML
GO
```

This code created four message types. Notice that we have used WELL_FORMED_XML as the validation for the message body for all message types. When the message is received, it will go through an XML parser for validation.

The message type [//www.wrox.com/MTCustomerInfo/RequstCustomersCount] is used when the initiator sends the message to the target to request the number of customers. Similarly, when the target replies with the number of customers, it uses the `[//www.wrox.com/MTCustomerInfo/ ResponseTotalCustomers]` message type.

The message type `[//www.wrox.com/MTProductInfo/RequestProductsCount]` is used when the initiator sends the message to the target to request the number of products. Similarly, when the target replies with the number of products, it uses the `[//www.wrox.com/MTProductInfo/ResponseTotalProducts]` message type.

We have not used the `AUTHORIZATION` clause in the `CREATE MESSAGE TYPE` statement, so the owner of these message types will be dbo, assuming you are sa on the SQL Server instance. Don't get confused about the message type. It tells Service Broker what to expect in the message body, including whether or not that message should be validated and how to validate it. In addition, based on the name of the message type, you can take some action.

The next bit of code creates a contract and binds the message types you created earlier to this contract (later you will see how the contract is used):

```
CREATE CONTRACT [//www.wrox.com/CTGeneralInfo/ProductCustomer]
(
    [//www.wrox.com/MTCustomerInfo/RequstCustomersCount] SENT BY INITIATOR
  , [//www.wrox.com/MTProductInfo/RequestProductsCount] SENT BY INITIATOR
  , [//www.wrox.com/MTCustomerInfo/ResponseTotalCustomers] SENT BY TARGET
  , [//www.wrox.com/MTProductInfo/ResponseTotalProducts] SENT BY TARGET
)
```

Notice the `SENT BY` clause. When `SENT BY` is set to `INITIATOR`, it means that only the initiator of the message can send the message of that type. When `SENT BY` is set to `TARGET`, only the target can send the message of that type.

You still need to create the stored procedure `CheckResponseFromTarget`, but ignore that here. For now, focus on the queue:

```
---------------------------------------------------------------------------
--Create queue to receive the message from target.
---------------------------------------------------------------------------
CREATE QUEUE dbo.ReceiveAckError
WITH STATUS = ON
    , RETENTION = OFF
    , ACTIVATION (
                STATUS = OFF
              , PROCEDURE_NAME = dbo.CheckResponseFromTarget
              , MAX_QUEUE_READERS = 5
              , EXECUTE AS SELF
                )
```

The queue `ReceiveAckError` will be used to receive the response from the target. When the target sends the reply to the original request from the initiator, that message goes in here. Notice that the queue `STATUS` is `ON`. When the status is `OFF`, the queue is unavailable for adding or removing messages. Also notice that the stored procedure `CheckResponseFromTarget` is executed when any message arrives in the queue `ReceiveAckError`. However, because the status of the `ACTIVATION` is set to `OFF`, the stored procedure will not be activated. The code specifies that a maximum of five instances of this stored procedure can be activated if necessary with the `MAX_QUEUE_READER` option. When you specify a stored procedure for activation, that stored procedure must exist before you create the queue; otherwise, the queue will not be created.

Now you need a service to which you can send, and from which you can receive, messages. Each service is bound to one, and only one, queue. When you send the message, you send the message to a service and not to the queue. The service puts the message into the queue:

```
CREATE SERVICE InitiatorService
ON QUEUE dbo.ReceiveAckError ([//www.wrox.com/CTGeneralInfo/ProductCustomer])
```

Notice that you specify the contract [//www.wrox.com/CTGeneralInfo/ProductCustomer] in the CREATE SERVICE statement. That means that only message types defined by this contract can be sent to this queue. This queue will not receive any other message types. Now run the SetupInitiator.sql script.

Open the SetupTarget.sql script. Notice that it looks similar to the SetupInitiator.sql script. You have created the same message types and the contract on TargetDB. The queue name is RequestQueue in the TargetDB, and the stored procedure activated when the message arrives is CheckRequestFromInitiator. You will understand the stored procedures CheckRequestFromInitiator and CheckResponseFromTarget very soon.

Next, run the SetupTarget.sql script on the same SQL Server where you have run the SetupInitiator.sql script. Your infrastructure is now ready to send your first message. At this point you may have some questions: How do you send the message? What happens when the message is sent? How will it be received?

Open the script SendMessageFromInitiator.sql and connect to the database InitiatorDB, which you created using the script SetupInitiator.sql. Following is the T-SQL code in the SendMessageFromInitiator.sql script:

```
USE InitiatorDB
GO

DECLARE @Conversation_Handle UNIQUEIDENTIFIER
       ,@SendMessage xml
       ,@MessageText varchar(255)

SET @MessageText =  'Request From Server: \\' + @@SERVERNAME
                  + ', DATABASE: ' + DB_NAME()
                  + ': ** Please send the total number of customers.'

SET @SendMessage = N'<message>'+ N'<![CDATA[' + @MessageText + N']]>' +
N'</message>'

BEGIN TRY
     BEGIN DIALOG CONVERSATION @Conversation_Handle
     FROM SERVICE [InitiatorService]
     TO SERVICE 'TargetService'
     ON CONTRACT [//www.wrox.com/CTGeneralInfo/ProductCustomer]
     WITH ENCRYPTION = OFF

     SELECT * FROM sys.conversation_endpoints
```

```
      WHERE conversation_handle = @Conversation_Handle;
      -------------------------------------------------------------
      SEND ON CONVERSATION @Conversation_Handle
      MESSAGE TYPE [//www.wrox.com/MTCustomerInfo/RequstCustomersCount]
      (@SendMessage);
      -------------------------------------------------------------
END TRY
BEGIN CATCH
    SELECT ERROR_NUMBER() AS ErrorNumber
         ,ERROR_MESSAGE() AS ErrorMessage
         ,ERROR_SEVERITY() AS ErrorSeverity
         ,ERROR_LINE() AS ErrorLine
END CATCH
```

Before you can understand the preceding code, you need to know what a conversation is. A *conversation* is a reliable, ordered exchange of messages. The core concept of Service Broker is the conversation.

Two kinds of conversations are defined in Service Broker architecture:

❑   **Dialog:** This is a two-way conversation between exactly two endpoints. An *endpoint* is a source or destination for messages associated with a queue; it can receive and send messages. A dialog is established between an initiator and target endpoint (refer to Figure 8-1). The initiator is just an endpoint that issues the BEGIN DIALOG command to start the dialog. After that, the initiator and the target are peers. The first message always goes from the initiator to the target. Once the target receives the first message, any number of messages can be sent in either direction.

❑   **Monolog:** This is a one-way conversation between a single publisher endpoint and any number of subscriber endpoints. Monologs are not available in SQL Server 2005 or 2008, though they will be included in future versions.

Each dialog has a conversation identifier to uniquely identify that dialog. It also has a sequence number to represent the sequencing of each message and to deliver the message in the correct order.

Service Broker normally delivers the messages exactly-once-in-order (EOIO). If you want to send messages according to the priority of the message, it's similar to priority mail through the postal service, whereby mail specified as next-day delivery or overnight delivery is delivered before regular mail. SQL Server 2008 introduces the concept of *conversation priorities* to do just that.

> **Normally, messages are delivered in the order they are received. If you want to change that normal behavior, then you have to specify the priority level. Messages with a higher priority level are typically sent or received before messages with lower priority level.**

We cover conversation priorities later in the chapter after the discussion about security considerations for Service Broker. It is important to understand how messages are delivered between two instances of SQL Server before looking at conversation priorities. Now you can begin to understand the T-SQL code. Before sending a message, you must create a dialog conversation. The command to do that is BEGIN DIALOG CONVERSATION. The arguments of this statement are as follows:

❑ @Conversation_Handle: When you run the BEGIN DIALOG statement, it returns the value of the type uniqueidentifier. The conversation handle is stored in the @Conversation_Handle variable. It is just a variable, so you can name it anything you like as long as the type of this variable is uniqueidentifier.

❑ Service: Because a dialog connects exactly two endpoints, you must specify both endpoints in the BEGIN DIALOG command. These endpoints are specified using service names. If a service is analogous to a postal address, then you need both a "from" address and a "to" address. That's what you need in BEGIN DIALOG. In this case, the "from" service is [InitiatorService] and the "to" service is 'TargetService'. Note the syntax: The "from" service name is in square brackets, and the "to" service is specified in quotes. The [InitiatorService] service is defined as the database InitiatorDB you created earlier, and the 'TargetService' is defined as the TargetDB created earlier. In this case, the message will go from database InitiatorDB to TargetDB.

❑ Contract: The contract defines the content of a dialog. In the CREATE CONTRACT statement, we have defined four message types.

❑ Encryption: We discuss this clause later in the section "Security Considerations for Service Broker." For now, set this to OFF.

Right after the BEGIN DIALOG statement is a SQL statement to select from the catalog view sys.conversation_endpoints. The effect of this statement is that every time you run the BEGIN DIALOG statement, a row is added to the sys.conversation_endpoints catalog view.

There are other clauses to the BEGIN DIALOG statement, but they are not covered here in order to keep the example simple. The only clause we need to discuss here is LIFETIME. The LIFETIME clause specifies the number of seconds that this dialog is allowed to live. If you don't specify this clause, the dialog lifetime is the maximum value of the int data type. We haven't specified the LIFETIME here because we are looking at how messaging works and we want the dialog to live longer while you examine the system view and the flow of the message. When you specify the LIFETIME to be 600 seconds, for example, if the dialog still exists after the lifetime expires (five minutes in this case), then an error will be returned to any statements that attempt to access it, and error messages are sent to both endpoints of the dialog. Note that the dialog doesn't go away when its lifetime expires. It remains in the sys.conversation_endpoints table in an error state until it is ended with the END CONVERSATION statement, described later.

Now take a look at the SEND statement. As described earlier, before sending a message, you must obtain a conversation handle. If you are the initiator of a conversation, you obtain a conversation handle by executing a BEGIN DIALOG command. The target of a conversation obtains a conversation handle from a RECEIVE statement. SEND has three parameters:

❑ A conversation handle associated with an open conversation.
❑ A message type that describes the contents of the message.
❑ The message body.

The message body in this case is contained in the variable @SendMessage. The message body of Service Broker queue is a varbinary(max) column, so a message body can contain up to two GB of binary data. That means when you send the message using the SEND command, it converts the message body to the varbinary(max) type. In this case, the variable @SendMessage, which is defined as an XML data type, is converted to varbinary(max) before SEND completes. Most SQL Server data types can be cast to or from varbinary(max), so you can send almost anything you want as a Service Broker message. If 2GB of data isn't enough, you can split large messages into 2GB pieces and reassemble them at the destination because Service Broker ensures that the message arrives in order. You can use the XML data type that converts implicitly to and from `varbinary(max)`, so using Service Broker with the XML data types is simple and straightforward.

You need to know one last thing before you run the script. The `BEGIN DIALOG` and `SEND` statements are inside a `while` loop to indicate how multiple threads of the activation stored procedure start, when you have several messages in a queue and one instance of the activation procedure cannot handle all those messages. For now, you will send only one message, so the variable `@NumberOfMessages` is set to 1.

You are now ready to run the script `SendMessageFromInitiator.sql`. Press Execute, which sends the message from the `InitiatorDB` database to the `TargetDB` database. Where did it go? It was shown earlier that when you send the message it goes to `sys.transmission_queue` first and then to the target queue (refer to Figure 8-2). That is true when the message is going over the network, but if you are sending the message on the same instance of the SQL Server, then the message is directly put into the target queue, which is `RequestQueue` in this case. If any error happens in that message transmission from initiator to target, you will see a row in the catalog view `sys.transmission_queue`, even if you are sending the message on the same instance of the SQL Server.

How did the message arrive at `RequestQueue` on the `TargetDB`? When you sent the message from the `InitiatorDB`, the `BEGIN DIALOG` statement specified the "to" service as `'TargetService'`, and when you created the `'TargetService'`, you specified the queue (or endpoint) as `RequestQueue`.

Now take a look at the message in the target queue. Open the script `ViewInfoOnTarget.sql` and run the following code from the script:

```
USE TargetDB
GO
SELECT Conversation_Handle, CAST(message_body as xml) AS message_body
    ,message_type_name, *
FROM dbo.RequestQueue WITH (NOLOCK)

SELECT Conversation_Handle, Conversation_ID, State_Desc
    ,Far_Service, *
FROM sys.conversation_endpoints
```

The output from this script is shown in Figure 8-4.

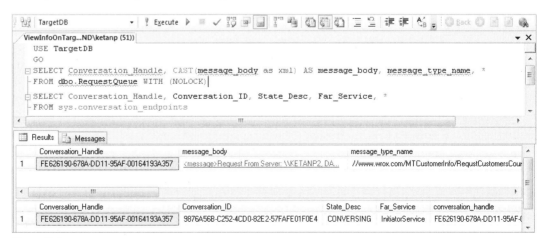

Figure 8-4

Notice that the messages in the queue are of the `varbinary` data type. The script converts the message into XML so you can read the content. You can also now see a row in the `sys.conversation_endpoints` catalog view. A `SELECT` statement is used to view the data in a queue.

Now you can retrieve the message from the `RequestQueue`. Open the script `ReceiveMessageOnTarget.sql`, which is shown here:

```
USE TargetDB
GO

DECLARE
    @message_type_name  nvarchar(256)
    ,@xmlmessage_body    xml
    ,@MessageFromTarget  varchar(255)
    ,@MessageText varchar(255)
    ,@conversation_handle UNIQUEIDENTIFIER

    ,@ErrorNumber int
    ,@ErrorMessage nvarchar(4000)
    ,@ErrSeverity int
    ,@ErrorLine int
    ,@comment nvarchar(4000)

    ,@ProcedureName varchar (60)
    ,@ResponseMessage xml
    ,@CustomerCount int
    ,@ProductCount int

    SET @ProcedureName = 'ManualMessageReceiveOnTarget'

BEGIN TRY
    BEGIN TRANSACTION
    -- Receive the next available message
    WAITFOR
    (
        RECEIVE TOP(1)
            @xmlmessage_body =  CASE WHEN validation = 'X'
                                    THEN CAST(message_body AS XML)
                                    ELSE CAST(N'<none/>' AS XML)
                                END
            ,@message_type_name = message_type_name
            ,@conversation_handle = conversation_handle
        FROM dbo.RequestQueue
    ), TIMEOUT 3000
    ---------------------------------------------------------------------------
    -- If we didn't get anything or if there is an error, bail out
    ---------------------------------------------------------------------------
    IF (@@ROWCOUNT = 0 OR @@ERROR <> 0)
    BEGIN
        ROLLBACK TRANSACTION
        GOTO Done
    END
    ELSE
    BEGIN
```

```
        IF @message_type_name = '//www.wrox.com/MTCustomerInfo/RequstCustomersCount'
        BEGIN

            ------------------------------------------------------------------------
            --- Your code to process the received message goes here.
            ------------------------------------------------------------------------

            ---Insert what we got into processhistory table.
            INSERT dbo.ProcessHistory(Process, StatusDate,  Status, MessageText, SPID,
UserName)
            SELECT @ProcedureName, GETDATE(),  'Success', @xmlmessage_body, @@SPID,
SUSER_NAME()

            SELECT @CustomerCount = COUNT(*)
            FROM AdventureWorks2008.Sales.Customer

                    SET @MessageText = 'Response From Server: \\'
                                        + @@SERVERNAME
                        + ', Database: ' + DB_NAME()
                        + ' ** Total Customers: '
                        + CAST(@CustomerCount AS varchar(15)) +  ' **'

            SET @ResponseMessage = N'<message>'
            + N'<![CDATA[' + @MessageText + N']]>' + N'</message>';

            SEND ON CONVERSATION @conversation_handle
            MESSAGE TYPE [//www.wrox.com/MTCustomerInfo/ResponseTotalCustomers]
            (@ResponseMessage)

            END CONVERSATION @conversation_handle

        END
        ELSE
        IF @message_type_name = '//www.wrox.com/MTProductInfo/RequestProductsCount'
        BEGIN

            ---------------------------------------------------
            --- Your code go here to process the received message.
            ---------------------------------------------------

            ---Let's insert what we got into processhistory table.
            INSERT dbo.ProcessHistory
(Process,StatusDate,Status, MessageText,SPID,UserName)
            SELECT @ProcedureName, GETDATE(),  'Success', @xmlmessage_body
                        ,@@SPID, SUSER_NAME()
            SELECT @ProductCount = COUNT(*)
            FROM AdventureWorks2008.Production.Product

            SET @MessageText = 'Response From Server: \\' + @@SERVERNAME
                        + ', Database: ' + DB_NAME()
                        + ' ** Total Products: '
                        + CAST(@ProductCount AS varchar(15)) +  ' **'

            SET @ResponseMessage = N'<message>'
            + N'<![CDATA[' + @MessageText + N']]>' + N'</message>';
```

```
            SEND ON CONVERSATION @conversation_handle
            MESSAGE TYPE [//www.wrox.com/MTProductInfo/ResponseTotalProducts]
            (@ResponseMessage)

            END CONVERSATION @conversation_handle

        END
        ELSE
        IF (@message_type_name
          = 'http://schemas.microsoft.com/SQL/ServiceBroker/EndDialog'
            OR @message_type_name
              = 'http://schemas.microsoft.com/SQL/ServiceBroker/Error')
          -- If the message_type_name indicates that the message is an error
          -- or an end dialog message, end the conversation.
        BEGIN

            END CONVERSATION @conversation_handle

            -----------------------------------------
            --- Your code go here to handle the error
            --- and do some type of notification (email etc)
            -----------------------------------------
            ---Let's insert what we got into processhistory table.
            INSERT dbo.ProcessHistory
            (Process, StatusDate,  Status, MessageText, SPID, UserName)
            SELECT @ProcedureName, GETDATE(), 'Error', @xmlmessage_body
                , @@SPID, SUSER_NAME()

        END
    END

    COMMIT TRAN

END TRY
BEGIN CATCH

    WHILE (@@TRANCOUNT > 0) ROLLBACK TRAN

    SELECT @ErrorNumber = ERROR_NUMBER(), @ErrorMessage = ERROR_MESSAGE()
                    ,@ErrSeverity = ERROR_SEVERITY()
                    , @ErrorLine = ERROR_LINE()

    SET @comment = 'Error Number: '+ CAST(@ErrorNumber AS varchar(25))
            + ', Error Message: ' + @ErrorMessage
            + ' Error Severity: ' + CAST(@ErrSeverity AS varchar(25))
            + ' Line Number: ' + CAST(@ErrorLine AS varchar(25))

    ---Let's insert what we got into processhistory table.
    INSERT dbo.ProcessHistory
    (Process, StatusDate, Status, MessageText, SPID, UserName)
    SELECT @ProcedureName, GETDATE(),  'Error', @comment, @@SPID, SUSER_NAME()

END CATCH

Done:
```

This code is exactly the same as the one in the stored procedure `CheckRequestFromInitiator` you created in the `SetupTarget.sql` script. You don't want to activate the stored procedure now and pick up the message because you won't know what happened. You need to know some things about the script first.

The command to retrieve a message from a queue is `RECEIVE`, and this is the only way you can retrieve the message from a queue. The `RECEIVE` command can pull one or more messages from a queue. In this case, the code is only pulling one message at a time, which is why `TOP (1)` appears in the `RECEIVE` statement. In the `FROM` clause of the `RECEIVE` statement, you have specified the name of the queue `RequestQueue`. You can also specify a `WHERE` clause in the `RECEIVE` statement, but it is not a full-featured `WHERE` clause. You can only specify a `conversation_handle` or `conversation_group_id`.

The basic `RECEIVE` command returns the messages available at the time the command executes. If the queue is empty, no rows are returned. In some cases, it might be more efficient to wait for messages to appear on the queue, rather than return immediately when the queue is empty. You can use the `WAITFOR` command with the `RECEIVE` command to force the `RECEIVE` command to wait for a message if the queue is empty. The following code shows the `WAITFOR` command:

```
WAITFOR
(
    RECEIVE TOP(1)
        @xmlmessage_body =  CASE WHEN validation = 'X'
                                 THEN CAST(message_body AS XML)
                                 ELSE CAST(N'<none/>' AS XML)
                            END
        ,@message_type_name = message_type_name
        ,@conversation_handle = conversation_handle
    FROM dbo.RequestQueue
), TIMEOUT 3000
```

The `TIMEOUT` clause specifies how many milliseconds the `RECEIVE` statement will wait for a message to appear on the queue before returning. In this case it will wait for three seconds.

The `RECEIVE` statement has three columns: `message_body`, `message_type_name`, and `conversation_handle`. The `message_body` contains the actual message, and the `message_type_name` contains the type of the message sent. If you look at the `SEND` statement in the `SendMessageFromInitiator.sql` script, you will see that you have sent a message of type `[//www.wrox.com/MTCustomerInfo/RequstCustomersCount]`. That's what appears in the `message_type_name` column. The last column is `conversation_handle`, which the target uses to send the message reply back to the initiator.

After the `RECEIVE` statement, the code checks the row count to ensure that it has received something, or to determine whether an error occurred. If it has not received anything, then you can take any action you like there. If it has received a message, then you want to take some action on that message. You use `message_type_name` in this case to decide what to do with the message. Because you are sending the message type `[//www.wrox.com/MTCustomerInfo/RequstCustomersCount]`, you'll want to count the number of customers. If you had received the message of type `//www.wrox.com/MTProductInfoRequestProductsCount`, you would have the count of the products. Your application may have some complex things to do instead of the simple `count(*)` you have here. You can call another stored procedure and pass parameters to that stored procedure to execute some tasks. In this case, the code has counted the number of customers, and you are ready to send the reply back to the initiator.

The next command is SEND, which we discussed earlier. Notice that here you don't perform the BEGIN DIALOG again. When you sent the message from the initiator, it created a row in the sys.conversation_endpoint view also. Because you are sending a message in the same conversation, you don't need to issue another BEGIN DIALOG, but you do need the conversation handle to send the message, which is why the target received the @conversation_handle in the RECEIVE command. After the SEND statement, you see END CONVERSATION @Conversation_Handle. The END CONVERSATION command ends the conversation and sends the message of type 'http://schemas.microsoft.com/SQL/ServiceBroker/EndDialog' on both sides of the dialog endpoint. In your application you can decide when you want to end the conversation, but it is very important that you do so. Otherwise, you will see thousands of rows in the sys.conversation_endpoints table after your application has run for a while, which is not good for application performance.

Once the target has received some information, the code has an INSERT statement to insert some information in the ProcessHistory table so you can later see what happened. Notice the BEGIN TRAN statement before the target receives the message and the COMMIT TRAN statement after successfully processing the message. You want to do that to maintain transaction consistency in the database. If something bad happens while you are processing the message, you may lose it. After the message is received from the queue, you cannot put it back without using BEGIN and COMMIT TRAN. Whether or not you need that in your application is up to you when you design it. If you cannot tolerate losing any messages, then consider using BEGIN and COMMIT TRAN.

Run the script ReceiveMessageOnTarget.sql now. After that, run the script ViewInfoOnTarget.sql in TargetDB. The output is shown in Figure 8-5.

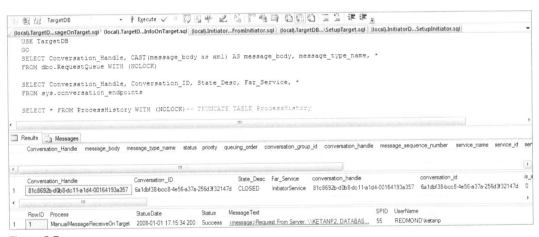

Figure 8-5

You probably noticed that after you ran the ReceiveMessageOnTarget.sql script, the message disappeared from the RequestQueue. You will still see a row in the conversation table with a state_desc of CLOSED. The state_desc is CLOSED because after the message was sent, the script issued END CONVERSATION. In addition, the message is inserted into the ProcessHistory table after it was received, so now the message is back on InitiatorDB with the customer count.

Before we receive the message from the queue ReceiveAckError in InitiatorDB, take a look at what's currently in the queue. Open the script ViewInfoOnInitiator.sql and run it. The output is shown in Figure 8-6.

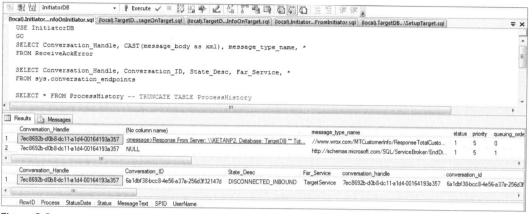

Figure 8-6

Two rows appear in the queue ReceiveAckError in InititatorDB: One is the customer count sent by the TargetDB, and the other is Service Broker end dialog message. The end dialog message appears because of the END CONVERSATION command you ran on the target after sending the message. Also notice that the state_desc column in sys.conversation_endpoint has the value DISCONNECTED_INBOUND. That's because the 'TargetService' has closed the conversation. You won't see any rows in the ProcessHistory table yet because you have not received the message from the queue yet.

Now you can receive the message from the ReceiveAckError queue. Open the script ReceiveMessageOnInitiator.sql. This script is very similar to ReceiveMessageOnTarget.sql. The difference is that the message_type_names you will see in this script are '//www.wrox.com/ MTCustomerInfo/ResponseTotalCustomers' and '//www.wrox.com/MTProductInfo/ ResponseTotalProducts'. In addition, the RECEIVE statement is receiving the message from the ReceiveAckError queue.

Now run the script ReceiveMessageOnInitiator.sql. After that, run the script ViewInfoOnInitiator .sql again. Note that you still see a row in the ReceiveAckError queue; that's because you have only run the ReceiveMessageOnInitiator.sql script once, so it receives only one message from the queue because you have set TOP (1) in the RECEIVE statement. Run the ReceiveMessageOnInitiator.sql script again, and then run the ViewInfoOnInitiator.sql script one more time. The output is shown in Figure 8-7.

Notice that the queue is now empty and that no rows exist in the sys.conversation_endpoints table. Make sure that you end the conversation. Whenever you do so, a row for that conversation is deleted from the sys.conversation_endpoints table. You will see two rows in the ProcessHistory table; one is the actual message from TargetDB, and the other is the result of END CONVERSATION.

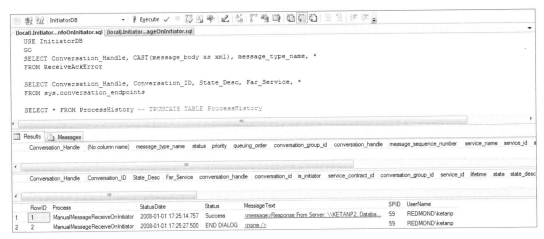

Figure 8-7

You ended the dialog in the script `ReceiveMessageOnInitiator.sql`, as shown here:

```
        IF (@message_type_name =
'http://schemas.microsoft.com/SQL/ServiceBroker/EndDialog')
            -- an end dialog message, end the conversation.
        BEGIN

            END CONVERSATION @conversation_handle

            ---Let's insert what we got into processhistory table.
            INSERT dbo.ProcessHistory(Process, StatusDate,  Status, MessageText, SPID,
UserName)
            SELECT @ProcedureName, GETDATE(),  'END DIALOG', @xmlmessage_body,'ID,
SUSER_NAME()

        END
```

Run the `ViewInfoOnTarget.sql` script again. Note that in the `TargetDB` `sys.conversation_endpoints` table, you still see a row even though you have ended the conversation. Those rows will be deleted by Service Broker after about 33 minutes.

You have just seen how the stored procedure is activated when a message gets into the queue. Activation is one of the most important things in a Service Broker application. Of course, it is not required, but activation is a tool to make it easier to write services that execute as stored procedures.

Activation

Service Broker *activation* is a unique way to ensure that the right resources are available to process Service Broker messages as they arrive on a queue. To use activation, you associate a stored procedure with a queue. The following is a section from the script `SetupTarget.sql`:

```
CREATE QUEUE dbo.RequestQueue
WITH STATUS = ON
```

```
        ,RETENTION = OFF
        ,ACTIVATION (
                     STATUS = ON
                     ,PROCEDURE_NAME = dbo.CheckRequestFromInitiator
                     ,MAX_QUEUE_READERS = 5
                     ,EXECUTE AS SELF
                     )
    GO
```

Similar code exists in `SetupInitiator.sql`, with a different queue name and `PROCEDURE_NAME`. One change we have made here is to set the `STATUS` parameter to `ON` in `ACTIVATION`. This is how you associate the stored procedure activation with a queue. This means that whenever a message arrives in a `RequestQueue` queue, an instance of the stored procedure `CheckRequestFromInitiator` will be started by Service Broker *only* if an instance of the stored procedure isn't already running. The `ACTIVATION STATUS` must be set to `ON` to activate a stored procedure when a message arrives in the queue.

When a message is written in the queue, the commit process (which writes the message row into the transaction log) checks to see whether a copy of the activation stored procedure is running. If not, the activation logic starts a stored procedure. When the activation logic finds that a stored procedure is already running, it also checks the number of arriving messages against the number of processed messages to determine whether the activated stored procedure is keeping up with the incoming message rate. If the rate of incoming messages is higher, then another copy of the stored procedure is started. This continues until either the activated stored procedures are able to keep up with incoming messages or the maximum number of stored procedure instances defined by the `MAX_QUEUE_READERS` parameter is reached. In this case, `MAX_QUEUE_READERS` is set to five, which means that no more than five instances of the stored procedure `CheckRequestFromInitiator` will be started at any given point in time.

If you have five messages in the `RequestQueue`, does that mean that five instances of `CheckRequestFromInitiator` will be started? It depends. When a stored procedure is configured for activation, it creates a queue monitor for the queue. When messages are added to the queue, after five seconds of inactivity, the queue monitor determines whether a stored procedure should be started. Suppose you sent four messages to the `RequestQueue`. Service Broker will start the first instance of the stored procedure `CheckRequestFromInitiator`. That leaves three messages waiting in the queue `RequestQueue` to be processed, but the queue monitor will not start another copy of `CheckRequestFromInitiator` unless the first message takes more than five seconds to process.

For example, assume that the first message is going to take more than five minutes; in that case, the queue monitor will start a second copy of `CheckRequestFromInitiator`. To process the third message, it may or may not start another instance of `CheckRequestFromInitiator`. When the third message is about to be processed, after waiting for five seconds, the queue monitor will check whether any of those instances has finished its work; if one has, the queue monitor uses whichever instance completed the work. If not, it starts a third instance of `CheckRequestFromInitiator`.

When stored procedures are started, they are owned by the queue monitor. If one throws an exception, the queue monitor catches it and starts a new copy. The queue monitor also ensures that when an activated stored procedure is not receiving any messages, no more copies are started.

You can see all the queue monitors configured in a SQL Server instance by running the following query:

```
SELECT * FROM sys.dm_broker_queue_monitors
```

Below is the output from the preceding query. You will see similar, but not exactly the same output, based on the number of queues defined in your database:

```
database_id queue_id     state     last_empty_rowset_time  last_activated_time     tasks_waiting
----------- ----------- --------- ----------------------- ----------------------- -------------
4           1627152842  INACTIVE  2008-07-01 16:53:45.040 2008-07-01 16:53:45.040 0
4           1040722760  INACTIVE  2008-07-01 16:53:45.040 2008-07-01 16:53:45.040 0
4           1659152956  INACTIVE  2008-07-01 16:53:45.040 2008-07-01 16:53:45.040 0
```

To find out which activated stored procedures are running in a SQL Server instance, execute the following query. You won't see any rows if no activated stored procedures are currently running.

```
SELECT * FROM sys.dm_broker_activated_tasks
```

So far in this example, you have received the messages from the queue manually by running the `ReceiveMessageOnTarget.sql` script on the `TargetDB`, and `ReceiveMessageOnInitiator.sql` on the `InitiatorDB`. Now try to receive messages using activated stored procedures. As you just learned, to activate a stored procedure on a queue, you have to associate the stored procedure with the queue, and the `ACTIVATION STATUS` must be `ON`. In the scripts `SetupInitiator.sql` and `SetupTarget.sql`, you associated the stored procedure with the queue, but the activation was not on, which is why you were receiving the messages manually. At this point, set the `ACTIVATION STATUS` to `ON` for both the initiator and target queues. Now follow these steps:

1. Open the `ActivateSPOnInitiator.sql` script and run it, which will set the `ACTIVATION STATUS` to `ON` for the `ReceiveAckError` queue. The stored procedure `CheckResponseFromTarget` will be activated when a message arrives in the queue.

2. Open the `ActivateSPOnTarget.sql` script and run it. That will set the `ACTIVATION STATUS` to `ON` for the `RequestQueue`. The stored procedure `CheckRequestFromInitiator` will be activated when a message arrives in the queue.

3. Now you are ready to send the message. Open the `SendMessageFromInitiator.sql` script and run it. What happens?

   ❑ The script has sent the message from `InitiatorDB` to `TargetDB` in the `RequestQueue`.

   ❑ The stored procedure `CheckRequestFromInitiator` was activated in `TargetDB`, which received the message and processed it (i.e., counted the number of customers in `AdventureWorks2008.Sales.Customer`), sent the response back to `InitiatorDB`, and then ended the conversation.

   ❑ The message came to the `ReceiveAckError` queue on `InitiatorDB`, and the stored procedure `CheckResponseFromTarget` was activated. The stored procedure received the message, put the result in `ProcessHistory`, and ended the conversation.

   You can see the content in the `ProcessHistory` table on `TargetDB` by running the script `ViewInfoOnTarget.sql`, and on `InitiatorDB` by running the script `ViewInfoOnInitiator.sql`.

4. Now take a look at multiple instances of the activation stored procedure in action. Open the `CheckRequestFromInitiator.sql` script and run it. This is the same stored procedure you

created in the `SetupTarget.sql` script with one small change — a `WAITFOR DELAY` of 20 seconds has been added:

```
        IF @message_type_name =
'//www.wrox.com/MTCustomerInfo/RequstCustomersCount'
        BEGIN


                ------------------------------------------------------------
                --- Your code to process the received message goes here.
                ------------------------------------------------------------

                ---Insert what we got into the processhistory table.
                INSERT dbo.ProcessHistory(Process, StatusDate,  Status, MessageText,
SPID, UserName)
                SELECT @ProcedureName, GETDATE(),  'Success', @xmlmessage_body,'ID,
SUSER_NAME()

                SELECT @CustomerCount = COUNT(*)
                FROM AdventureWorks2008.Sales.Customer

                SET @MessageText = 'Response From Server: \\' + @@SERVERNAME
                                    + ', Database: ' + DB_NAME() + ' ** Total Customers: '
                                    + CAST(@CustomerCount AS varchar(15)) + ' **'

                SET @ResponseMessage = N'<message>'+ N'<![CDATA[' + @MessageText + N']]>' +
N'</message>';

                WAITFOR DELAY '00:00:20';

                SEND ON CONVERSATION @conversation_handle
                MESSAGE TYPE [//www.wrox.com/MTCustomerInfo/ResponseTotalCustomers]
                (@ResponseMessage)

                END CONVERSATION @conversation_handle

        END
```

We added the delay to simulate the stored procedure doing some work so that when multiple messages arrive in the queue, the queue monitor will activate additional stored procedures.

5. Open the scripts `CheckResponseFromTarget.sql` and `CheckRequestFromInitiator.sql` and run them both.

6. Open the `SendManyMessages.sql` script and run it. This will send four messages to `TargetDB`. Figure 8-8 shows the output on `TargetDB` when you run the `ViewInfoOnTarget.sql` script after all the messages are processed.

Notice that the `RequestQueue` is empty because all the messages are processed. You can also see that all the conversations are `CLOSED`, because you ended the conversation with the `END CONVERSATION` statement. If you look at the `SPID` column in the third result set from `ProcessHistory`, you will see four distinct SPIDs there, which means that four instances of the stored procedure ran to process those four messages. The `StatusDate` column is also interesting: Note the delay of about five seconds before the next instance of `CheckRequestFromInitiator` was activated. That is what the queue monitor does.

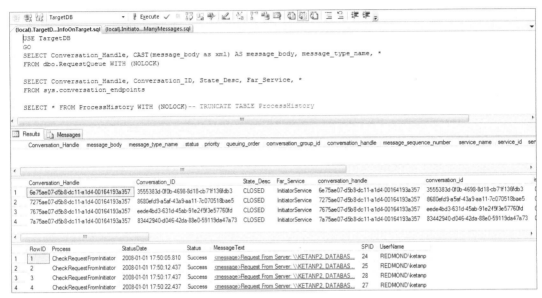

Figure 8-8

You will see similar output on `InitiatorDB` if you run the `ViewInfoOnInitiator.sql` script.

Because activation procedures run on background threads, there is no user connection on which they can report errors. Therefore, any error or `PRINT` output for an activated stored procedure is written to the SQL Server error log. When activation doesn't appear to be working, the first thing you want to look at is the SQL error log file.

Another interesting point to note here is that the reason you see multiple instances of `CheckRequestFromInitiator` is because you have a distinct `conversation_handle` for each message (see the second result set in Figure 8-8). That's because you issued the `BEGIN DIALOG` statement for each new message sent to the target. Take a look at the `SendManyMessages.sql` script:

```
WHILE (@Count < @NumberOfMessages)
BEGIN
    BEGIN TRY
        BEGIN DIALOG CONVERSATION @Conversation_Handle
        FROM SERVICE [InitiatorService]
        TO SERVICE 'TargetService'
        ON CONTRACT [//www.wrox.com/CTGeneralInfo/ProductCustomer]
        WITH ENCRYPTION = OFF;
```

```
                    SELECT * FROM sys.conversation_endpoints
                    WHERE conversation_handle = @Conversation_Handle;
                    -----------------------------------------------------------------
                    SEND ON CONVERSATION @Conversation_Handle
                    MESSAGE TYPE [//www.wrox.com/MTCustomerInfo/RequstCustomersCount]
                    (@SendMessage);
                    -----------------------------------------------------------------
            END TRY
            BEGIN CATCH
                SELECT ERROR_NUMBER() AS ErrorNumber
                      ,ERROR_MESSAGE() AS ErrorMessage
                      ,ERROR_SEVERITY() AS ErrorSeverity
                      ,ERROR_LINE() AS ErrorLine
                BREAK
            END CATCH

            SET @Count = @Count + 1
        END
```

The BEGIN DIALOG statement creates a new conversation handle for each message. If you move the BEGIN DIALOG before the WHILE loop, you will get only one conversation handle. In that case, no matter how many messages you send to the target, only one instance of CheckRequestFromInitiator will be created to process all the messages on the same conversation handle.

Conversation Groups

As just mentioned, in the previous example the SendManyMessages.sql script created a new conversation handle every time you sent the message with the SEND command. This means that only one message appears in each conversation group. If you query the sys.conversation_endpoints view after sending a bunch of messages with SendManyMessages.sql, you will notice that the conversation_handle column has distinct values in it. In this case, even though the messages may have arrived in the order they were sent, they will not necessarily be processed in that order. As shown, multiple instances of CheckRequestFromInitiator in TargetDB were processing messages, and there is no guarantee that the messages will be processed in the order in which they were received because you indicated that you don't care about the order by sending each message on a different conversation group.

Many messaging applications require that messages be processed in the exact order in which they are received. Although it is reasonably straightforward to ensure that messages are received in order, it is rather more difficult to ensure that they are processed in order. Consider an example in which an order entry application sends messages to credit card validation, inventory adjustment, shipping, and accounts receivable services on four different dialogs. These services may all respond, and it's possible that response messages for the same order may be processed on different threads simultaneously. That could cause a problem because if two different transactions are updating the order status simultaneously without being aware of each other, status information may be lost. To solve this type of problem, Service Broker uses a special kind of lock to ensure that only one task (one instance of the activation procedure) can read messages from a particular conversation at any given time. This special lock is called a *conversation group lock*.

To see how this works, open the Sample1 solution, and proceed through the following steps:

1. Run the scripts `CheckResponseFromTarget.sql` and `CheckRequestFromInitiator.sql`. These are the stored procedures that pick up the messages from the initiator and target queues, as explained earlier.

2. Run `ActivateSPOnTarget.sql` and `ActivateSPOnInitiator.sql`, which ensure that both queue status and activation are ON.

3. Open the script `SendMessageOnSameConvGroup.sql`. The code is as follows:

```
USE InitiatorDB
GO

DECLARE @Conversation_Handle UNIQUEIDENTIFIER
      ,@SendMessage xml
      ,@MessageText varchar(255)
      ,@Another_Conversation_Handle UNIQUEIDENTIFIER
      ,@conversation_group_id UNIQUEIDENTIFIER

SET @MessageText =  'Request From Server: \\' + @@SERVERNAME
             + ', DATABASE: ' + DB_NAME()
             + ': ** Please send the total number of customers.'

SET @SendMessage = N'<message>'+ N'<![CDATA[' + @MessageText + N']]>' +
N'</message>'

BEGIN DIALOG CONVERSATION @Conversation_Handle
FROM SERVICE [InitiatorService]
TO SERVICE 'TargetService'
ON CONTRACT [//www.wrox.com/CTGeneralInfo/ProductCustomer]
WITH ENCRYPTION = OFF;

----------------------------------------------------------------
SEND ON CONVERSATION @Conversation_Handle
MESSAGE TYPE [//www.wrox.com/MTCustomerInfo/RequstCustomersCount]
(@SendMessage);
----------------------------------------------------------------
SELECT @conversation_group_id = conversation_group_id
FROM sys.conversation_endpoints
WHERE conversation_handle = @Conversation_Handle;

BEGIN DIALOG CONVERSATION @Another_Conversation_Handle
FROM SERVICE [InitiatorService]
TO SERVICE 'TargetService'
ON CONTRACT [//www.wrox.com/CTGeneralInfo/ProductCustomer]
WITH RELATED_CONVERSATION_GROUP = @conversation_group_id
    ,ENCRYPTION = OFF;

SEND ON CONVERSATION @Another_Conversation_Handle
MESSAGE TYPE [//www.wrox.com/MTCustomerInfo/RequstCustomersCount]
(@SendMessage);
```

4. This code sends two messages on the same conversation group. When you send the first message, a conversation group is created by default. Before you send the second message,

you get the conversation group of the first message from the `sys.conversation_endpoints` table with the following script:

```
SELECT @conversation_group_id = conversation_group_id
FROM sys.conversation_endpoints
WHERE conversation_handle = @Conversation_Handle;
```

Then you send the second message on the same conversation group by using the `RELATED_CONVERSATION_GROUP` argument in the `BEGIN DIALOG` statement.

5.   Run the `SendMessageOnSameConvGroup.sql` script. Now open the script `ViewInfoOnInitiator.sql` and run it. Note that when you run `SELECT * FROM ProcessHistory`, the `SPID` column shows that only one SPID has worked on both response messages, which indicates that messages on the same conversation group can only be processed by a single thread.

You've now seen a basic example of how messaging works in Service Broker. You haven't yet sent a message from one SQL Server instance to another; nor have you sent a message with all the security features Service Broker provides for a secured application. The following section describes how security works in Service Broker. Then you will look at an example that sends a message from one SQL Server instance to another, which includes details about how to configure security for safe messaging.

Security Considerations for Service Broker

Configuring security is probably the most complex piece of Service Broker application. Nevertheless, Service Broker is designed to run enterprise applications in very secure environments. In fact, by default, Service Broker can only send messages within the database. Recall from the first example that in order to send the message to a different database on the same SQL Server instance, you had to set the `TRUSTWORTHY` bit to 1 for both databases.

Service Broker provides two distinct levels of security:

❑   **Transport security:** Secures the TCP/IP connection between two SQL Server instances on different servers

❑   **Dialog Security:** Secures each individual dialog between the two dialog endpoints. This ensures that the services exchanging the messages are who they say they are.

In cases where the highest level of security is required, using both transport and dialog security is appropriate. In addition, Service Broker uses regular SQL Server security to assign permission to users to enable them to create and use the various Service Broker objects such as message types, contracts, and services.

Transport Security

Transport security secures the TCP/IP connection. There are two parts to transport security: *authentication* (whereby the two instances of SQL server determine that they are willing to talk) and *encryption* of the data over the network. Note that authentication is not optional, but encryption is. In order for two SQL Server instances to exchange Service Broker messages, you must create an endpoint on each server using the `CREATE ENDPOINT` or `ALTER ENDPOINT` statements.

Service Broker offers two types of authentication: Windows and Certificate. Windows authentication uses the normal Windows authentication protocols — NTLM or Kerberos — to establish a connection between two endpoints. For simplicity, consider an endpoint an instance of SQL Server. Certificate-based authentication uses the TLS (Transport Layer Security) authentication protocol (SChannel) to authenticate the two endpoints. To establish either of these authentications, you have to use the CREATE ENDPOINT statement on each instance of the SQL Server. More details about this are discussed in the following sections.

Windows Authentication

Suppose you want two instances of SQL Server to exchange Service Broker messages. The first thing you have to do is create an endpoint on each SQL Server instance. At this point, you can start the second example and learn how to create endpoints. Open the folder Sample2 under the Chapter 8 folder and double-click the Sample2 solution file. You need two instances of SQL Server connected on the same domain.

Open the CreateEndPointOnInitiator.sql script and connect it to the initiator SQL Server. Be sure to change the Windows account name to the appropriate domain account in the GRANT CONNECT statement:

```
CREATE ENDPOINT InitiatorSSBEndPoint
STATE = STARTED
AS TCP(LISTENER_PORT = 5040)
FOR SERVICE_BROKER(AUTHENTICATION = WINDOWS, ENCRYPTION = REQUIRED)
```

You can create only one endpoint for Service Broker for each instance of SQL Server. This endpoint listens on a specific TCP port. In this example it is port 5040. The default port for Service Broker is 4022. You can specify any available port number between 1024 and 32767.

This script specifies WINDOWS for AUTHENTICATION, so Service Broker will use either NTLM or Kerberos depending on how your network is configured and how the endpoint is configured (Kerberos, NTLM, or both) in the endpoint configuration. Suppose you have two servers, InitiatorServer and TargerServer. If your SQL Server service account is "local system," in order to use Windows authentication, you have to make sure that your network has Kerberos authentication. If not, you will have to change the SQL Server service account to a domain user such as MYDOM\ketanp. If you have permission to run the SQL Server service under the "local system" account and your network does not have Kerberos, then you must use certificate-based authentication, which is covered in the section "Certificate-Based Authentication." For this exercise, we assume that you are running the SQL Server service using a domain account.

Run the CreateEndPointOnInitiator.sql script. Be sure to change the Windows account name to the appropriate domain account in the GRANT CONNECT statement. After you run the script, run the following SQL statement to view the TCP endpoint you just created:

```
SELECT * FROM sys.tcp_endpoints
```

Now open the CreateEndPointOnTarget.sql script. Be sure to change the Windows account name to the appropriate domain account in the GRANT CONNECT statement. Connect it to the target machine and run it. Now you have established endpoints on both ends.

The next step is to grant CONNECT permission to these endpoints so that remote machines can connect to them. To do that, first you have to add the login under which the SQL Server service runs on InitiatorServer to TargerServer, and vice versa.

Open the `AddRemoteLoginOnTarget.sql` script and connect to the `TargetServer` machine:

```
CREATE LOGIN [MYDOM\InitiatorLogin] FROM WINDOWS

GRANT CONNECT ON ENDPOINT::TargetSSBEndPoint TO [MYDOM\InitiatorLogin]
```

You are adding the account `MYDOM\InitiatorLogin` (which runs the SQL Server service on `InitiatorServer`) to `TargetServer`, and you are granting `CONNECT` permission on the endpoint you created on the `TargetServer` to this account. Please note that if you are using the "local system" service account to run the SQL Server, then the login name would be something like `[MYDOM\InitiatorServer$]`.

You need to perform a similar operation on the `InitiatorServer` machine to introduce the `MYDOM\TargetLogin` account and grant `CONNECT` permission. Open the `AddRemoteLoginOnInitiator.sql` script, connect to the `InitiatorServer` machine, and run it:

```
CREATE LOGIN [MYDOM\TargetLogin] FROM WINDOWS

GRANT CONNECT ON ENDPOINT::InitiatorSSBEndPoint TO [MYDOM\TargetLogin]
```

Again, if you are using the "local system" service account to run SQL Server, the login name would be something like `[MYDOM\TargetServer$]`.

If you are running the SQL Server service under the same domain account on both machines, you do not need to run the `AddRemoteLoginOnTarget.sql` and `AddRemoteLoginOnInitiator.sql` scripts.

You're done! You have set up the transport security using Windows authentication. You are not yet ready to send the message, however. First you need to understand certificate-based authentication.

Certificate-Based Authentication

In this section, we assume that you know what public and private keys are and how they work. If the endpoints are in different domains, Windows authentication can be complex and slow. In this case, you may choose to use certificate-based authentication. Each endpoint needs two certificates, one with its own private key and another with the opposite endpoint's public key. When one endpoint encrypts the data with the private key, it can only be decrypted with the corresponding public key at the opposite endpoint. The advantage of certificate-based authentication is that authentication only requires certificates. There is no need for the endpoints to contact a domain controller, as there is with Windows authentication, so the endpoints can be in different domains, which is one of the most compelling reasons to use certificates. For more information about how certificates work, please refer to the "Certificates and Service Broker" topic in BOL.

Now you'll use `Sample2` to create and install certificates on `InitiatorServer` and `TargerServer`. Open the script `CreateCertOnInitiator.sql` and connect to `InitiatorServer`:

```
USE MASTER
GO
IF NOT EXISTS(SELECT 1 FROM sys.symmetric_keys where name =
'##MS_DatabaseMasterKey##')
CREATE MASTER KEY ENCRYPTION BY PASSWORD = '23%&weq^yzYu2005!'
GO
```

```
IF NOT EXISTS (select 1 from sys.databases where
[is_master_key_encrypted_by_server] = 1)
ALTER MASTER KEY ADD ENCRYPTION BY SERVICE MASTER KEY
GO

IF NOT EXISTS (SELECT 1 FROM sys.certificates WHERE name = 'InitiatorDBCert')
CREATE  CERTIFICATE InitiatorDBCert
WITH SUBJECT = 'Initiator Server Certificate'
GO

BACKUP CERTIFICATE InitiatorDBCert TO FILE = 'C:\InitiatorDBCert.cer'
```

For simplicity, here we are using the certificate created by SQL Server, but other ways of creating and distributing certificates will work equally well.

You have created a master key in this script because when you create a certificate, you have to specify the encryption by password. If you don't specify it, the private key will be encrypted using the database master key. This script creates a certificate in the master database. The BACKUP CERTIFICATE statement backs up the public key certificate for this private key.

Now open the script CreateEndPointWithCertOnInitiator.sql and connect to InitiatorServer:

```
CREATE ENDPOINT InitiatorSSBEndPoint
STATE = STARTED
AS TCP(LISTENER_PORT = 5040)
FOR SERVICE_BROKER(AUTHENTICATION = CERTIFICATE InitiatorDBCert, ENCRYPTION =
REQUIRED)
```

This script creates an endpoint with CERTIFICATE authentication using the certificate you just created on InitiatorServer.

Do the same on TargetServer. Open CreateCertOnTarget.sql on TargetServer and run it. Then open CreateEndPointWithCertOnTarget.sql on TargetServer and run it.

So far, you have created certificates on both InitiatorServer and TargetServer and have associated the endpoint on each server with certificates. Now you have to introduce the endpoints to each other by exchanging the public keys. Copy the certificate you backed up using CreateCertOnInitiator.sql to TargetServer on C:\. Also copy the certificate backed up using CreateCertOnTarget.sql to InitiatorServer on C:\.

Once the certificates have been exchanged, all you have to do is associate them with a login that has CONNECT permission for the endpoint. Open the CreateLoginOnInitiator.sql script and connect to InitiatorServer:

```
CREATE LOGIN TargetServerUser WITH PASSWORD = '32sdgsgy^%$!'

CREATE USER TargetServerUser;

CREATE CERTIFICATE TargetDBCertPub  AUTHORIZATION TargetServerUser
FROM FILE = 'C:\TargetDBCert.cer'

GRANT CONNECT ON ENDPOINT::InitiatorSSBEndPoint TO TargetServerUser
```

This script creates a SQL Server login and creates a user in the master database. You are also importing the certificate you just copied from `TargetServer` and authorizing the user you created. At the end, you are granting `CONNECT` permission to the endpoint `InitiatorSSBEndPoint` to the user `TargetServerUser`. You still have to do the same on the `TargetServer`, so open the script `CreateLoginOnTarget.sql`, connect to `TargetServer`, and run it. You have now configured endpoints on both the `InitiatorServer` and `TargetServer` to use certificate-based authentication.

Our general recommendation is that if both endpoints are in the same Windows domain, then you should use Windows authentication; if both endpoints are in different domains, then you should use certificate authentication instead. These are recommendations, though, not rules.

Encryption

When you configured an endpoint on each SQL Server instance, you specified `ENCRYPTION = REQUIRED` in the `CREATE ENDPOINT` statement:

```
CREATE ENDPOINT InitiatorSSBEndPoint
STATE = STARTED
AS TCP(LISTENER_PORT = 5040)
FOR SERVICE_BROKER(AUTHENTICATION = WINDOWS, ENCRYPTION = REQUIRED)
```

By default, encryption is required for all transport connections. Along with authentication, all transport messages are checksummed and signed to ensure that the messages are not altered on the wire. Message encryption is required by default, so the endpoints you configured earlier will send the messages encrypted.

What if both endpoints are not configured with the same option in the `ENCRYPTION` clause? The clause has three options: `REQUIRED`, `SUPPORTED`, and `DISABLED`. The following table indicates whether data will be encrypted when endpoints are configured with different `ENCRYPTION` options.

EndpointA	EndpointB	Data Encrypted?
REQUIRED	REQUIRED	Yes
REQUIRED	SUPPORTED	Yes
DISABLED	DISABLED	No
DISABLED	SUPPORTED	No
SUPPORTED	SUPPORTED	Yes

When both endpoints of the dialog are in the same SQL Server instance — either in the same database or different databases (as in `Sample1`) in the same instance — encryption is never done. Service Broker message never leaves the server's memory, so there is no reason to encrypt it.

Routing

You are almost ready to send the message from `InitiatorServer` to `TargetServer`. Before we talk about dialog security, we need to introduce routing. This is a required component to send the messages between two instances of SQL Server. Routing isn't really related to the security configuration, but you need to know about it before you can send the message.

When messages are sent, Service Broker needs to know where to send them. A Service Broker *route* maps a service to a destination where messages can be sent. Four routes are involved in delivering a message to its destination:

1. When the SEND command is executed, a route from the local sys.routes table is used to determine where the message is sent.

2. When the message arrives at the destination SQL Server instance, a route from the sys.routes table in the msdb database is used to determine which database receives the message. Note that whenever a message comes from a remote SQL Server instance, it always goes to the msdb database first. Make sure that the is_broker_enabled bit is set to 1 in msdb; otherwise, your messages will not be delivered. Once the message has been successfully committed in the proper queue in the destination database, an acknowledgment is returned to the sender.

3. A route from the sys.routes table is used to determine where to send the acknowledgment message. When the message is sent from the sender, it always goes to the sys.transmission_queue table on the sender, and stays there until the receiver sends the acknowledgment that the message has been received. It is important that you specify the return route.

4. When the acknowledgment message arrives at the sender's SQL Server instance, a route in the msdb database is used to route the message to the sending service's queue in the sending database.

At this point, you need to create a route on InitiatorServer and a return route on TargetServer in order to send the messages between these two instances.

Open SetupInitiator.sql on InitiatorServer and run it, and then open SetupTarget.sql on TargetServer and run it. Both of these scripts are taken from Sample1. Now you can create the route and bind that route to a service. Open the CreateRouteOnInitiator.sql script and connect to InitiatorServer. Be sure to change the server name to whatever your target SQL Server name is before running this script:

```
USE InitiatorDB
GO
IF EXISTS(SELECT * FROM sys.routes WHERE name = 'RouteToTargetServer')
DROP ROUTE RouteToTargetServer
GO
CREATE ROUTE RouteToTargetServer
WITH
  SERVICE_NAME = 'TargetService'
 ,ADDRESS = 'TCP://TargetServer:5040'
```

Notice that the route is created in the database from which you are sending the message. In addition, the SERVICE_NAME specified is the TargetService, which is on the TargetServer in the TargetDB database. The ADDRESS argument specifies the name of the server, which is TargetServer, and the port on which it is listening. Remember that when you created the endpoint on TargetServer, you specified the port number. That's the port number you use here.

Now run the script `CreateRouteOnTarget.sql`.

Remember the `BEGIN DIALOG` statement you used to send the message? Here's part of it:

```
BEGIN DIALOG CONVERSATION @Conversation_Handle
FROM SERVICE [InitiatorService]
TO SERVICE 'TargetService'
ON CONTRACT [//www.wrox.com/CTGeneralInfo/ProductCustomer]
WITH ENCRYPTION = OFF
```

This tells Service Broker that the message is being sent to `TargetService`, but where is `TargetService`? Remember that Figure 8-2 shows the four points needed to deliver messages successfully. In this case, when the message is sent, Service Broker on `InitiatorServer` checks for routes in `sys.routes`. Because you have set `SERVICE_NAME = 'TargetService'` in the `CREATE ROUTE` statement, this indicates that the service resides on `TargetServer`, so the message will be sent to `TargetServer`. Then, on `TargetServer`, Service Broker checks the `msdb` database route table to determine which database the `TargetService` exists in, and sends the message to the `RequestQueue`, which is the endpoint for `TargetService`.

You have to create the route on `TargetServer` to complete the communication loop. Open the script `CreateRouteOnTarget.sql` Be sure to change the server name to whatever your target SQL Server name is before running this script. Connect to `TargetServer`:

```
USE TargetDB
GO
IF EXISTS(SELECT * FROM sys.routes WHERE name = 'RouteToInitiatorServer')
DROP ROUTE RouteToInitiatorServer
GO
CREATE ROUTE RouteToInitiatorServer
WITH
  SERVICE_NAME = 'InitiatorService'
,ADDRESS = 'TCP://InitiatorServer:5040'
```

Here you are defining the route to `InitiatorServer`, which resides on `InitiatorServer`.

Now you are ready to send the message. Open the `SendMessageFromInitiator.sql` script, connect to `InitiatorServer`, and run it. You can check the status on `TargetServer` using the `ViewInfoOnTarget.sql` script, and on `InitiatorServer` using `ViewInfoOnInitiator.sql`.

Two addresses have special meaning for Service Broker routes. When the route for a service name has an address of `LOCAL`, the message classifier looks for the service name in the local instance to find which queue to put the message in. The first priority is the current database where the route exists. If the service does not exist there, then the classifier checks the service list, which contains all the services that exist in the local SQL Server instance. The following SQL statement creates a local route:

```
CREATE ROUTE MyLocalRoute
WITH SERVICE_NAME = 'MyService'
     ,ADDRESS = 'LOCAL'
```

If you have services with the same name (in this case, `MyService`) in different databases on the local SQL Server instance, the classifier picks one of the services as the target service and sends the messages to that service. To avoid this, use the `BROKER_INSTANCE` parameter in the `CREATE ROUTE` statement to ensure that messages are delivered to the specific database (broker).

When you create a new database, you will find a route called AutoCreatedLocal in sys.routes. This route has no service name (remote_service_name column in sys.routes view) or broker identifier (broker_instance column in sys.routes view), and an address of LOCAL (address column in sys.routes view). Remember that in the first example in this chapter, you were sending messages from InitiatorDB to TargetDB without creating a route. AutoCreatedLocal is a wildcard route, so the message classifier uses this route for any service that does not have another route available. This route sends messages to local services, so in the first example in this chapter you were able to send the message to TargetService using AutoCreatedLocal. In a distributed application, it is better to drop this AutoCreatedLocal route, because without a wildcard route, you can be sure that messages only go where you intend them to go.

The other special address is called TRANSPORT. When you send the message to the target, you need the response from the target returned to the initiator, so a route must exist on the target to specify the address of the initiator in order to send the message back. Consider a scenario in which you want to send messages from 100 initiators to one target. You need 100 routes on the target to send the acknowledgment or messages back to the initiator. Instead, you can use a shortcut with the TRANSPORT address, so you just need to create one route on the target instead of 100. When messages are sent back from the target to the initiator, the classifier uses the service name from the dialog as an address.

Here's a short example. Suppose you want to send the message from InitiatorServer, which has an endpoint defined on port 4040, to TargetServer. On InitiatorServer, create this service:

```
CREATE QUEUE [InitiatorQueue]
CREATE SERVICE [TCP://InitiatorServer:4040/ResponseService]
ON QUEUE InitiatorQueue
```

When you send the message to TargetServer, you issue the BEGIN DIALOG statement as follows:

```
BEGIN DIALOG @Conversation_handle
FROM SERVICE [TCP://InitiatorServer:4040/ResponseService]
TO SERVICE 'TargetService'
ON CONTRACT 'AppContract'
```

You have already created the route on InitiatorServer. Now on TargerServer, create a wildcard route as follows:

```
CREATE ROUTE RouteToInitiatorServer WITH ADDRESS = 'TRANSPORT'
```

Now when the message needs to be sent back to InitiatorServer from TargetServer, because no specific route is created for the service [TCP://InitiatorServer:4040/ResponseService] on TargetServer, the classifier will look for a wildcard route with the TRANSPORT address and attempt to open a connection to TCP://InitiatorServer:4040. In this example, it will succeed, and the message will be returned successfully to InitiatorServer.

The biggest disadvantage of using TRANSPORT routes is that the address is hardcoded in the service name, so to move an application to another server you have to destroy all the existing dialogs to the service. You also have to re-create the service with a new server name in the address, and you must change your BEGIN DIALOG statement if you are not using dynamic SQL in BEGIN DIALOG. We don't recommend using this method of routing unless this disadvantage is acceptable in your environment.

Dialog Security

Dialog security is used to secure the dialogs from the initiator of the dialog to the target of the dialog. You have just learned that the data from one endpoint to another endpoint is encrypted by default, so why do you need dialog security? The difference is that dialog security works between dialog endpoints instead of transport endpoints (see Figure 8-9).

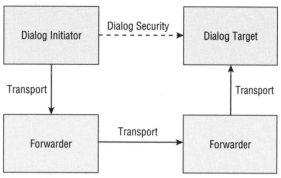

Figure 8-9

What are the Forwarder boxes in the diagram? Service Broker uses a concept of message forwarding, so a SQL Server instance can be configured to forward the messages using the following statement:

```
CREATE ENDPOINT ForwarderSSBEndPoint
STATE = STARTED
AS TCP(LISTENER_PORT = 5040)
FOR SERVICE_BROKER
(
    AUTHENTICATION = WINDOWS
  , MESSAGE_FORWARDING = ENABLED
  , MESSAGE_FORWARD_SIZE  = 40
)
```

This enables message forwarding and sets the maximum amount of memory to use for forwarding — in this case, 40MB. The messages on the forwarding server always stay in memory and aren't persisted in the database. In some scenarios, message forwarding is required. One of those scenarios is the case when two endpoints cannot connect directly, so some kind of gateway is needed to connect them. Please refer to the topic "Service Broker Message Forwarding" in BOL for more details about message forwarding.

Returning to Figure 8-9, when a message is initiated, it travels through two forwarders before it reaches the final destination. If you have used transport security, then you know that messages are decrypted and encrypted at each forwarder, so the message would be encrypted and decrypted three times en route. If you use dialog security instead, the messages going from the initiator to the target would be encrypted at the initiator and decrypted at the target, rather than at each forwarder. The extra overhead in the first case can cause significant delay and increase processing time. Dialog security has the advantage of encrypting and decrypting a message once, no matter how many Service Brokers the message is forwarded through, so if you have a message forwarder in your network, then you may want to use dialog security. If your network is secure enough that encryption on the wire is not required, or if transport security is sufficient, you may want to turn off dialog security. In the previous examples, you set `ENCRYPTION = OFF` in the `BEGIN DIALOG` statement. That's how you turn off dialog security.

Configuring dialog security is similar to configuring certificate-based authentication. Open the script `ConfigureDialogSecurityOnTarget.sql` and connect to `TargetServer`:

```
USE TargetDB
GO

IF NOT EXISTS(SELECT 1 FROM sys.symmetric_keys where name =
'##MS_DatabaseMasterKey##')
CREATE MASTER KEY ENCRYPTION BY PASSWORD = '23%&weq^yzYu2005!'
GO

IF NOT EXISTS (select 1 from sys.databases where
[is_master_key_encrypted_by_server] = 1)
ALTER MASTER KEY ADD ENCRYPTION BY SERVICE MASTER KEY
GO


--Create a USER TO own the TargetService.
IF NOT EXISTS(SELECT * FROM sys.sysusers WHERE name = 'TargetServiceOwner')
CREATE USER TargetServiceOwner WITHOUT LOGIN
GO

GRANT CONTROL ON SERVICE::TargetService TO TargetServiceOwner
GO

IF NOT EXISTS (SELECT 1 FROM sys.certificates WHERE name = 'TargetDBDialogCert')
CREATE  CERTIFICATE TargetDBDialogCert
AUTHORIZATION TargetServiceOwner
WITH SUBJECT = 'Target Server Certificate for Dialog Security'
GO

BACKUP CERTIFICATE TargetDBDialogCert TO FILE = 'C:\TargetDBDialogCert.cer'
```

This script creates a user and grants `CONTROL` permission on `TargetService` to that user. The script also creates a certificate and makes the `TargetServiceOwner` user the owner of that certificate. It also backs up the certificate to `C:\`. Note that you are creating a certificate in the database in which the service resides, not in the master database.

Now open the script `ConfigureDialogSecurityOnInitiator.sql` and connect to `InitiatorServer`:

```
USE InitiatorDB
GO

IF NOT EXISTS(SELECT 1 FROM sys.symmetric_keys where name =
'##MS_DatabaseMasterKey##')
CREATE MASTER KEY ENCRYPTION BY PASSWORD = '23%&weq^yzYu2005!'
GO

IF NOT EXISTS (select 1 from sys.databases where
```

```
[is_master_key_encrypted_by_server] = 1)
ALTER MASTER KEY ADD ENCRYPTION BY SERVICE MASTER KEY
GO


--Create a USER TO own the InitiatorService.
IF NOT EXISTS(SELECT * FROM sys.sysusers WHERE name = 'InitiatorServiceOwner')
CREATE USER InitiatorServiceOwner WITHOUT LOGIN
GO
--Make this user the owner of the InitiatorService.
ALTER AUTHORIZATION ON SERVICE::InitiatorService TO InitiatorServiceOwner
GO


IF NOT EXISTS (SELECT 1 FROM sys.certificates WHERE name = 'InitiatorDBDialogCert')
CREATE  CERTIFICATE InitiatorDBDialogCert
AUTHORIZATION   InitiatorServiceOwner
WITH SUBJECT = 'Initiator Server Certificate for Dialog Security'
GO


BACKUP CERTIFICATE InitiatorDBDialogCert TO FILE = 'C:\InitiatorDBDialogCert.cer'
```

This script creates a user and makes that user the owner of the `InitiatorService`. The script also creates a certificate and makes the `InitiatorServiceOwner` user the owner of that certificate. It also backs up the certificate to `C:\`, just as before.

Now copy the certificate `TargetDBDialogCert.cer` from `C:\` on `TargetServer` to `C:` on `InitiatorServer`. Similarly, copy the certificate `InitiatorDBDialogCert.cer` from `C:` on `InitiatorServer` to `C:` on `TargerServer`.

Now open the script `DialogImportCertOnInitiator.sql` and connect to `InitiatorServer`:

```
USE InitiatorDB
GO
--Create a USER TO own the TargetService.
IF NOT EXISTS(SELECT * FROM sys.sysusers WHERE name = 'TargetServiceOwner')
CREATE USER TargetServiceOwner WITHOUT LOGIN

--Import the certificate owned by above user
IF NOT EXISTS(SELECT * FROM sys.certificates WHERE name = 'TargetDBDialogCertPub')
CREATE CERTIFICATE TargetDBDialogCertPub
AUTHORIZATION TargetServiceOwner
FROM FILE = 'C:\TargetDBDialogCert.cer'
```

This script creates the user `TargetServiceOwner`, the same user you created on `TargetServer`. The script also imports the certificate that you copied from `TargetServer` and makes `TargetServiceOwner` the owner of that certificate.

Next, open the script `DialogImportCertOnTarget.sql` on `TargetServer`:

```
USE TargetDB
GO

IF NOT EXISTS(SELECT * FROM sys.sysusers WHERE name = 'InitiatorServiceOwner')
```

```
CREATE USER InitiatorServiceOwner WITHOUT LOGIN

--Import the certificate owned by above user
IF NOT EXISTS(SELECT * FROM sys.certificates WHERE name =
'InitiatorDBDialogCertPub')
CREATE CERTIFICATE InitiatorDBDialogCertPub
AUTHORIZATION InitiatorServiceOwner
FROM FILE = 'C:\InitiatorDBDialogCert.cer'

GRANT SEND ON SERVICE::TargetService TO InitiatorServiceOwner
```

This script does the same thing on `TargerServer` that you just did on `InitiatorServer`.

The last thing you have to do is create a REMOTE SERVICE BINDING to bind the user `TargetServiceOwner` you created on `InitiatorServer` to the TO SERVICE used in the BEGIN DIALOG command. The TO SERVICE in this case is `TargetService`. Open the `CreateRemoteBindingOnInitiator.sql` script and connect to `InitiatorServer`:

```
USE InitiatorDB
GO
IF NOT EXISTS(SELECT * FROM sys.remote_service_bindings WHERE name =
'ToTargetService')
CREATE REMOTE SERVICE BINDING ToTargetService
TO SERVICE  'TargetService'
WITH USER = TargetServiceOwner
```

Now the BEGIN DIALOG command knows which two certificates to use to authenticate the dialog: the private key certificate associated with the owner of the FROM SERVICE (user `InitiatorServiceOwner`) and the certificate owned by the user bound to the TO SERVICE (user `TargetServiceOwner`) with the REMOTE SERVICE BINDING.

You are now ready to send the first encrypted message to the `TargetServer`. Open the `SendMessageWithEncryption.sql` script. This script is similar to `SendMessageFromInitiator.sql` with the following small difference in the BEGIN DIALOG statement:

```
BEGIN DIALOG CONVERSATION @Conversation_Handle
FROM SERVICE [InitiatorService]
TO SERVICE 'TargetService'
ON CONTRACT [//www.wrox.com/CTGeneralInfo/ProductCustomer]
WITH ENCRYPTION = ON
```

You have turned on encryption, but how do you know the messages are encrypted? Run the script `SendMessageWithEncryption.sql`. Then open `ViewInfoOnTarget.sql`, connect to `TargetServer`, and run it.

Check the output of SELECT * FROM sys.conversation_endpoints. You will notice that the `outbound_session_key_identifier` and `inbound_session_key_identifier` columns in the `sys.conversation_endpoints` view have values other than 0, which indicates that the messages were encrypted.

Note than when you specify ENCRYPTION = OFF, it doesn't mean that encryption is disabled for a dialog. ENCRYPTION = OFF means that encryption is not required. If the TO SERVICE has the REMOTE SERVICE BINDING, the dialog will be secured even when ENCRYPTION = OFF is used. Change the ENCRYPTION = OFF statement in the script SendMessageWithEncryption.sql and run it. You will see that the messages are still encrypted.

If ENCRYPTION = ON is used and REMOTE SERVICE BINDING is not present, or the dialog security is not configured properly, the BEGIN DIALOG statement will fail.

With that under your belt, let's turn now to the conversation priorities topic introduced a little earlier.

Conversation Priorities

In SQL Server 2005, sending and receiving messages is handled on a first-come, first-served basis. In SQL Server 2008 you can set the priority for the conversations, which means messages from conversations that have high priority levels are typically sent or received before messages from conversations that have lower priority levels. You can set conversation priorities when you want certain types of messages to be processed first. For example, if you want certain users to run their reports first, you can set the priority high for their messages (queries) compared to other users, and Service Broker will process (run) those messages (queries) first.

Setting Conversation Priorities

The following example demonstrates the conversation priority:

1. Open the folder ConPriority under the Chapter 8 folder and double-click the ConPriority solution file. You need two instances of SQL Server connected to the same domain (as in Sample2). It is assumed that you understand how messages are delivered between two instances of SQL Server, as explained earlier in Sample2 in the section "Security Considerations for Service Broker."

2. Open the scripts CreateEndPointOnInitiator.sql and CreateEndPointOnTarget.sql. If you have already created Service Broker endpoints on your initiator and target servers (as explained in Sample2), then you can skip this step. Follow the instructions provided earlier in the "Windows Authentication" section to create the endpoints on the initiator and target server and grant the connect permission to these endpoints.

3. After you set up the endpoints, open the script CreateRouteOnInitiator.sql and connect to the initiator server. Change the server name (set the name to your target server) and run it. Similarly, open the script CreateRouteOnTarget.sql and connect to the target server. Change the server name (set the name to your initiator server) and run it. These scripts will create routes. For a detailed explanation of routing, refer to the "Routing" section earlier in this chapter.

4. Open the script SetupInitiator.sql and connect to the initiator server. (Each SQL statement in this script was explained earlier in the section "Service Broker Examples.") Run the script.

5. Open the script SetupTarget.sql, connect to the target server, and run it.

At this point, you have set up Service Broker and are ready to send the messages. Now you'll see how to set up conversation priorities. I have created two contracts and two services in the scripts SetupInitiator.sql and SetupTarget.sql, so that I can set a different priority for each contract.

6. Open the script ConPriorityInitiator.sql and connect to the initiator server. The first statement in the script is a directive to turn on the database option HONOR_BROKER_ PRIORITY:

```
--First the database option HONOR_PRIORITY must set to ON.
ALTER DATABASE InitiatorDB SET HONOR_BROKER_PRIORITY ON

-- Entry in Errorlog something like below.
--2007-12-28 11:28:28.360 spid51
--Setting database option HONOR_BROKER_PRIORITY to ON for database InitiatorDB.
```

> *In order for conversation priority to work, you must set the* HONOR_BROKER_PRIORITY *option to* ON *for that database.*

7. After you run this statement, you will see an entry in the SQL error log showing that the HONOR_BROKER_PRIORITY option for that particular database is turned on. Another way to see that is by running the following commands from the script ConPriorityInitiator.sql:

```
USE InitiatorDB
GO
SELECT is_honor_broker_priority_on, Service_Broker_Guid
    ,is_broker_enabled, is_trustworthy_on
FROM sys.databases
WHERE database_id = DB_ID()
GO
```

After you set the global database option to define priority for your conversations, you can then set the conversation priority at the contract or service level.

The following example shows the syntax to set up the conversation priority for a contract or a service:

```
CREATE BROKER PRIORITY ConversationPriorityName
FOR CONVERSATION
[ SET ( [ CONTRACT_NAME = {ContractName | ANY } ]
        [ [ , ] LOCAL_SERVICE_NAME = {LocalServiceName | ANY } ]
        [ [ , ] REMOTE_SERVICE_NAME = {'RemoteServiceName' | ANY } ]
        [ [ , ] PRIORITY_LEVEL = {PriorityValue | DEFAULT } ]
      )
]
```

> **Permission for creating a conversation priority defaults to members of the db_ddladmin or db_owner fixed database roles, and to the sysadmin fixed server role.**

ConversationPriority Name is the name for conversation priority. The name must be unique in the current database.

If SET is specified it must contain at least one criterion: CONTRACT_NAME, LOCAL_SERVICE_NAME, REMOTE_SERVICE_NAME, or PRIORITY_LEVEL. If SET is not specified, then the defaults are set for all three criteria. When you don't specify any SET option, it is like setting the priority for any conversation in that database with a default priority level of 5.

The PRIORITY_LEVEL is an integer literal from 1 (lowest priority) to 10 (highest priority). The default is 5.

You'll use the script ConPriorityInitiator.sql to create the priority. Don't run the script yet; let's take a look at it first. Recall that in the earlier script SetupInitiator.sql, you created two contracts, [//www.wrox.com/CTLPGeneralInfo/ProductCustomer] and [//www.wrox.com/CTHPGeneralInfo/ ProductCustomer]; and two services, InitiatorServiceLP and InitiatorServiceHP. Similarly, in SetupTarget.sql, you created the same contracts, plus two services, TargetServiceLP and TargetServiceHP. Note the addition of HP and LP in the names to indicate high priority and low priority conversations, respectively.

```
IF NOT EXISTS(SELECT * FROM sys.conversation_priorities
            WHERE name = 'LPFreeStuff')

CREATE BROKER PRIORITY LPFreeStuff
FOR CONVERSATION
SET(CONTRACT_NAME = [//www.wrox.com/CTLPGeneralInfo/ProductCustomer]
    ,LOCAL_SERVICE_NAME = InitiatorServiceLP
    ,REMOTE_SERVICE_NAME = 'TargetServiceLP'
    ,PRIORITY_LEVEL = 2
    )
```

This script defines the priority level of 2 for any conversation on contract [//www.wrox.com/ CTLPGeneralInfo/ProductCustomer], local service name InitiatorServiceLP, and remote service name TargetServiceLP. Remember that you don't have to specify all three options, although this example does. Here is another script:

```
IF NOT EXISTS(SELECT * FROM sys.conversation_priorities
            WHERE name = 'HPPayStuff')
CREATE BROKER PRIORITY HPPayStuff
FOR CONVERSATION
SET(CONTRACT_NAME = [//www.wrox.com/CTHPGeneralInfo/ProductCustomer]
    ,LOCAL_SERVICE_NAME = InitiatorServiceHP
    ,REMOTE_SERVICE_NAME = 'TargetServiceHP'
    ,PRIORITY_LEVEL = 8
    )
```

This script defines the priority level of 8 for any conversation on contract [//www.wrox.com/ CTHPGeneralInfo/ProductCustomer], local service name InitiatorServiceHP, and remote service name TargetServiceHP.

You have now defined two conversation priorities: LPFreeStuff (priority level = 2) and HPPayStuff (priority level = 8) in the InitiatorDB database.

Now run both of the preceding scripts. You can check whether these priorities were created or not using the following script, ConPriorityInfo.sql, with some details about the conversation priorities:

```
USE InitiatorDB
GO
SELECT scp.name AS priority_name
       ,ssc.name AS contract_name
       ,ssvc.name AS local_service_name
       ,scp.remote_service_name
       ,scp.priority AS priority_level
FROM sys.conversation_priorities AS scp
JOIN sys.service_contracts AS ssc
  ON scp.service_contract_id = ssc.service_contract_id
JOIN sys.services AS ssvc
  ON scp.local_service_id = ssvc.service_id
ORDER BY priority_name
         ,contract_name
         ,local_service_name
         ,remote_service_name
```

Using Priorities on the Initiator Endpoint

Now let's send some messages in order to consider some concepts of conversation priorities. Open the script SendMessageFromInitiator.sql and connect to the initiator server, but don't run the script yet. There are two parts to the script. Let's look at the first part:

```
------------------------------------------------------------------
----SEND LOW PRIORITY MESSAGES FIRST
------------------------------------------------------------------
USE InitiatorDB
GO

DECLARE @Conversation_Handle UNIQUEIDENTIFIER
       ,@SendMessage xml
       ,@MessageText varchar(255)

SET @MessageText =  'Request From Server: \\' + @@SERVERNAME
                    + ', DATABASE: ' + DB_NAME()
                    + ': ** Please send the total number of customers.'

SET @SendMessage = N'<message>'+ N'<![CDATA['
+ @MessageText + N']]>' + N'</message>'

BEGIN TRY
     BEGIN DIALOG CONVERSATION @Conversation_Handle
     FROM SERVICE [InitiatorServiceLP]
     TO SERVICE 'TargetServiceLP'
     ON CONTRACT [//www.wrox.com/CTLPGeneralInfo/ProductCustomer]
     WITH ENCRYPTION = OFF

     SELECT * FROM sys.conversation_endpoints
     WHERE conversation_handle = @Conversation_Handle;
     ------------------------------------------------------------------
     SEND ON CONVERSATION @Conversation_Handle
```

```
    MESSAGE TYPE [//www.wrox.com/MTCustomerInfo/RequstCustomersCount]
    (@SendMessage);
    ------------------------------------------------------------
END TRY
BEGIN CATCH
    SELECT ERROR_NUMBER() AS ErrorNumber
          ,ERROR_MESSAGE() AS ErrorMessage
          ,ERROR_SEVERITY() AS ErrorSeverity
          ,ERROR_LINE() AS ErrorLine
END CATCH
```

Starting with the BEGIN DIALOG section of the code, the conversation endpoints are created (see sys.conversation_endpoints view) when you run the BEGIN DIALOG statement.

Each conversation has two conversation endpoints: The initiator conversation endpoint associates one side of the conversation with the initiator service (InitiatorServiceLP in our case) and the initiator queue (ReceiveAckError in our case, from the SetupInitiator.sql script). The target conversation endpoint associates the other side of the conversation with the target service (TargetServiceLP in our case) and the queue (RequestQueue in our case, from the SetupTarget.sql script).

> Remember that Service Broker assigns conversation priority levels when conversation endpoints are created.

As soon as the BEGIN DIALOG statement is executed, Service Broker will assign the priority level 2 for this conversation. How does this occur? Service Broker first looks for a priority whose specified contract, local service, and remote service matches those used by the conversation endpoint. In our case, we have defined PRIORITY_LEVEL = 2 (see the script ConPriorityInitiator.sql) for the contract [//www.wrox.com/CTLPGeneralInfo/ProductCustomer], local service InitiatorServiceLP, and remote service TargetServiceLP, so Service Broker assigns priority level 2 because it found the match.

The following table describes how Service Broker assigns the priority level using match precedence:

Endpoint Contract	Endpoint Local Service	Endpoint Remote Service
Priority Contract	Priority Local Service	Priority Remote Service
Priority Contract	Priority Local Service	ANY
Priority Contract	ANY	Priority Remote Service
Priority Contract	ANY	ANY
ANY	Priority Local Service	Priority Remote Service
ANY	Priority Local Service	ANY
ANY	ANY	Priority Remote Service
ANY	ANY	ANY

Service Broker first looks for a priority whose specified contract, local service, and remote service matches those used by the conversation endpoint. If one is not found, Service Broker then looks for a priority with a contract and local service that matches those used by the endpoint, and where the remote service was specified as ANY. This continues for all the variations listed in the precedence table. If no match is found, then the endpoint is assigned the default priority of 5.

Now consider the second half of the script `SendMessageFromInitiator.sql`:

```
--------------------------------------------------------------------------
SEND HIGH PRIORITY MESSAGES NEXT
--------------------------------------------------------------------------
USE InitiatorDB
GO

DECLARE @Conversation_Handle UNIQUEIDENTIFIER
       ,@SendMessage xml
       ,@MessageText varchar(255)

SET @MessageText =  'Request From Server: \\' + @@SERVERNAME
                  + ', DATABASE: ' + DB_NAME()
                  + ': ** Please send the total number of customers.'

SET @SendMessage = N'<message>'+ N'<![CDATA['
+ @MessageText + N']]>' + N'</message>'

BEGIN TRY
      BEGIN DIALOG CONVERSATION @Conversation_Handle
      FROM SERVICE [InitiatorServiceHP]
      TO SERVICE 'TargetServiceHP'
      ON CONTRACT [//www.wrox.com/CTHPGeneralInfo/ProductCustomer]
      WITH ENCRYPTION = OFF


      SELECT * FROM sys.conversation_endpoints
      WHERE conversation_handle = @Conversation_Handle;
      -------------------------------------------------------------
      SEND ON CONVERSATION @Conversation_Handle
      MESSAGE TYPE [//www.wrox.com/MTCustomerInfo/RequstCustomersCount]
      (@SendMessage);
      -------------------------------------------------------------
END TRY
BEGIN CATCH
   SELECT ERROR_NUMBER() AS ErrorNumber
         ,ERROR_MESSAGE() AS ErrorMessage
         ,ERROR_SEVERITY() AS ErrorSeverity
         ,ERROR_LINE() AS ErrorLine
END CATCH
```

In this case, Service Broker assigns the conversation priority to 8. Now run the script and examine the results. Open the script `ViewInfoOnInitiator.sql` and connect to your initiator server and run it. Figure 8-10 shows the output.

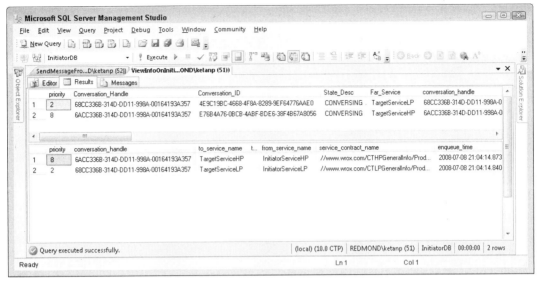

Figure 8-10

As you can see, the priorities are correctly assigned based on contract and service names. I disabled the queue `RequestQueue` on the target server, which explains why the messages are still in the `sys.transmission_queue` view on the initiator server, so that you can see what's going on. Now consider which message reaches the target server first, even though you enqueued (see the `enqueue_time` column in the preceding `sys.transmission_queue` output) the low-priority message first. Enable the queue `RequestQueue` on the target server so that the messages can reach the target server. Run the following script on the target server in the `TargetDB` database. You can find this statement at the bottom of the script in `SetupTarget.sql`:

```
ALTER QUEUE RequestQueue WITH  STATUS = ON, ACTIVATION (STATUS = OFF)
```

Now open `ViewInfoOnTarget.sql` and connect to the target server. Query the queue to see which message arrived first. The output is shown in Figure 8-11.

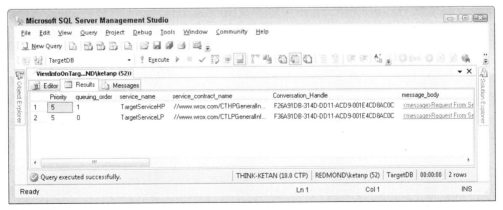

Figure 8-11

Notice the `queuing_order`, `service_name`, and `service_contract_name` columns in the output. As expected, the high-priority message arrived first (the `queuing_order` is low for the higher priority message, meaning it got into the queue first); but notice the `Priority` column output. The priority for both the messages is the same, the default of 5!

Remember: The priority level does not cross the instance of a SQL server.

Because we defined the priority level only on the initiator server, it was applied there when messages were sent. Service Broker coordinates priority levels across all of the transmission queues in an instance of the Database Engine on the initiator side. Service Broker first transmits messages from the priority 10 conversations in all of the transmission queues, then messages from priority 9 conversations, and so on. Priority levels are applied differently on initiator and target instances based on how they are defined.

Using Priorities on the Target Endpoint

Priorities can be defined on both the transmission side and the receiving side. You have not yet defined the priority level on the receiving side. Therefore, if you receive the message from the queue `RequestQueue`, Service Broker will dequeue (receive) the high-priority message first because it is the first message in the queue. But what if you want to dequeue the low-priority message first on the receiving side? You can define different conversation priority on the receiving side to receive that message first, as shown in the following example. Open the script `ConPriorityTarget.sql`, connect to the target server, and run it.

```
--SET Conversation Priorities for each Contract.

--First the database option HONOR_PRIORITY must set to ON.
ALTER DATABASE TargetDB SET HONOR_BROKER_PRIORITY ON

-- Entry in Errorlog something like below.
--2007-12-28 11:28:28.360 spid51
--Setting database option HONOR_BROKER_PRIORITY to ON for database TargetDB.
GO
USE TargetDB
GO


SELECT is_honor_broker_priority_on, Service_Broker_Guid
     ,is_broker_enabled, is_trustworthy_on
FROM sys.databases
WHERE database_id = DB_ID()
GO


USE TargetDB
GO


IF NOT EXISTS(SELECT * FROM sys.conversation_priorities
              WHERE name = 'LPFreeStuff')
CREATE BROKER PRIORITY LPFreeStuff
FOR CONVERSATION
SET(CONTRACT_NAME = [//www.wrox.com/CTLPGeneralInfo/ProductCustomer]
   ,LOCAL_SERVICE_NAME = TargetServiceLP
   ,REMOTE_SERVICE_NAME = 'InitiatorServiceLP'
   ,PRIORITY_LEVEL = 8
```

```
    )
GO

IF NOT EXISTS(SELECT * FROM sys.conversation_priorities
                WHERE name = 'HPPayStuff')
CREATE BROKER PRIORITY HPPayStuff
FOR CONVERSATION
SET(CONTRACT_NAME = [//www.wrox.com/CTHPGeneralInfo/ProductCustomer]
    ,LOCAL_SERVICE_NAME = TargetServiceHP
    ,REMOTE_SERVICE_NAME = 'InitiatorServiceHP'
    ,PRIORITY_LEVEL = 2
    )
```

Notice that you have assigned low priority on the receiving side to the message that came first. You have created priority levels on the receiving side, but these levels won't affect any existing in-transit conversation.

Before looking at conversation priority in action on the receiving side, let's clean up the queue on the receiving side first:

1. Open the script `ReceiveMessageOnTarget.sql` and connect to the target server. Run the script two times to receive those existing two messages you sent earlier.

2. Now send two messages from the initiator server. Open the script `SendMessageFromInitiator.sql` and connect to the initiator server and run it. Open the script `ViewInfoOnTarget.sql` and connect to the target server and run it. The output is shown in Figure 8-12.

Notice the output in the columns `Priority` and `queuing_order` and compare it with the output shown in Figure 8-11. Higher priority is now assigned to the message with the contract name `[//www.wrox.com/CTLPGeneralInfo/ProductCustomer]`. Therefore, if you retrieve the message from the queue, the high-priority message is retrieved first. You can run the script `ReceiveMessageOnTarget.sql` on the target server to check.

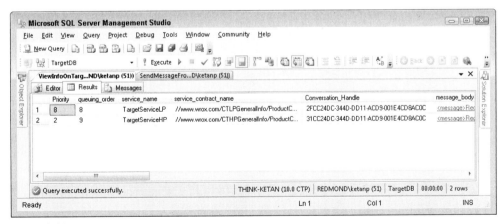

Figure 8-12

Reviewing Conversation Priorities

Let's summarize the concept of conversation priorities and how it operates:

❑ You have to set the HONOR_BROKER_PRIORITY database option to ON for conversation priority to work.

❑ You can create the conversation priorities using the CREATE BROKER PRIORITY statement, and alter conversation priorities using the ALTER BROKER PRIORITY statement.

❑ If you alter the conversation priority, any conversations already in transit won't be affected.

❑ The default conversation priority level is 5 for any conversation, whether you define the conversation priority in a database or not. The lowest conversation priority is 1, and the highest conversation priority is 10.

❑ When conversation priorities are defined, messages with high conversation priorities are read from the queue before messages with low conversation priorities.

❑ Conversation priorities do not cross an instance of SQL Server.

❑ Conversation priorities are defined separately on the transmission side and the receiving side.

❑ The HONOR_BROKER_PRIORITY database option must be set to ON for conversation priority to work. When this option is set to ON, conversation priorities will be applied to only those messages in the sys.transmission_queue. If the HONOR_BROKER_PRIORITY option for a database is set to OFF, then all messages will have the priority level set to 5, the default priority level.

❑ Conversation priorities are applied to messages that are in the transmission queue (sys.transmission_queue). Messages are placed in the transmission queue only if they are transmitted to a different SQL server instance or if any transmission error occurs. Therefore, if you send the message in the same instance of the SQL Server, no conversation priorities are applied because the messages are directly placed in the destination queue without going through the transmission queue.

❑ One transmission queue (sys.transmission_queue) exists for each database on a SQL Server instance. When SQL Server sends messages with conversation priorities defined to a different instance of SQL Server, they go through each transmission queue on the initiator instance and the messages start with a conversation priority of 10, then 9, and so on; so conversation priorities are applied for that instance.

❑ The RECEIVE statement is now aware of the conversation priority and retrieves messages based on priority levels for a particular conversation.

❑ The RECEIVE statement has a WHERE clause:

   ❑ When the RECEIVE statement executes without a WHERE clause, conversations with highest priority are retrieved first from the queue.

   ❑ When the RECEIVE statement executes with a WHERE clause, all the messages within that conversation group are retrieved from the queue, and from that conversation group all the messages with highest priority are retrieved, then the second-highest priority, and so on.

Administering Service Broker

Service Broker is integrated with the Database Engine, so administrating Service Broker application is a part of your day-to-day activities. This section describes the different tasks involved in administering a database that hosts a Service Broker application. Most administrative tasks are part of the normal administration of your database. Of course, there are some special things you have to do for a Service Broker application.

Installing Service Broker Application

You learned earlier that the key components to develop a Service Broker application are message types, contracts, queues, services, routes, endpoints, and stored procedures. When a development team provides the installation script for a Service Broker application, those scripts typically include T-SQL statements. A typical Service Broker application has an initiator, which resides on a server, and a target, which may reside on the same server in the same database, or in a different database, or even on a different server. Obviously, complex Service Broker applications may involve more than a couple of servers communicating with one another. In general, you should have separate scripts, for installation on the initiator and on the target.

Preparing the Databases

When messages are sent from one database to another, Service Broker uses a unique identifier to route the messages to the correct database. That unique identifier is called Service Broker *GUID*. The `Service_Broker_Guid` column in the `sys.databases` catalog view shows Service Broker identifier for each database. This identifier should be unique across all SQL Server instances on the same network to ensure proper message delivery.

Each database also has a setting for message delivery. The `is_broker_enabled` column in the `sys.databases` catalog view shows whether message delivery is enabled or disabled in a database.

Run the following T-SQL statement in the database in which you are going to install the application:

```
SELECT is_broker_enabled, Service_Broker_Guid
FROM sys.databases
WHERE database_id = DB_ID()
```

Make sure that the `is_broker_enabled` bit is set to 1 in order for the database to send and receive messages. If this bit is not 1, you can still install Service Broker application and even send messages, but you will see an error for that conversation in the `sys.transmission_queue` catalog view. In this case, the error message in the `transmission_status` column would be "The broker is disabled in the sender's database." There are two ways you can set this bit to 1. Both of the following commands require exclusive database access, so if you have users in the database in which you are running the command, you will be blocked by those connections:

```
ALTER DATABASE database_name SET NEW_BROKER
ALTER DATABASE database_name SET ENABLE_BROKER
```

The NEW_BROKER option activates Service Broker message delivery, creates a new Service Broker identifier for that database, and throws away any existing dialogs and messages. Therefore, you will see a different value in the `Service_Broker_Guid` column in the `sys.databases` view than what was shown before.

The ENABLE_BROKER option also activates Service Broker message delivery, but it preserves Service Broker identifier for that database, so you will see the same value in the `Service_Broker_Guid` column that was there before.

You will learn when to use these options, as well as DISABLE_BROKER and ERROR_BROKER_CONVERSATIONS, later in this section. When you create a brand-new database, this bit is set to 1 by default, so Service Broker message delivery is enabled by default in a newly created database.

If you are installing a Service Broker application for which more than one database is involved in the communication on the same instance of SQL Server, you have to set the is_trustworthy_on bit to 1 on the initiator database of the dialog. The is_trustworthy_on column in the sys.databases catalog view shows the bit value for each database. By default, this bit is 0 (OFF). You can run the following statement to set the bit to 1:

```
ALTER DATABASE database_name SET TRUSTWORTHY ON
```

This statement doesn't require exclusive database access. By default, when you restore or attach a database, this bit is set to 0 (OFF). Remember that in the first example in this chapter, you set this bit to 1 after creating the databases because that example sends and receives messages between two databases. For information on the TRUSTWORTHY bit, see "TRUSTWORTHY Database Property" in BOL.

Running the Scripts to Install the Application

Now that you have set up the database that is going to host Service Broker application, review the installation script provided by the development team. Of course, the code review should have happened long before the application was released for system test from development. As a best practice, you should have the queue STATUS OFF by default, and ACTIVATION STATUS OFF by default. As a part of the code review with the development team, notify them that you want to have these options as a part of the installation script, rather than you munging the installation scripts during deployment.

Another important consideration is that until installation is completed, you should not grant SEND permission to the queue. This enables you to complete the internal testing before your application users go wild. You and your team want to ensure that everything looks good before you give the green light. Consider creating a table that lists the objects for which you have to grant permission, and write a stored procedure to grant the permission on those objects. That way, if you have to change the permission on any object involved in your application, you don't have to start searching for those objects. All you have to do is add, change, or remove the object from the table and run the stored procedure to grant the permission. The installation script only inserts the objects in the table where you hold all the objects for your application. It will not grant any permission, but you will.

Be sure to keep the installation document up-to-date, because even though your development team has shown due diligence, it is hard to mimic the production environment in your development or test. While you are installing the application, you will certainly find something that is not in the installation document, so you want to ensure that you update the document right away.

Setting Permission on Service Broker Objects

In the section "Security Considerations for the Server Broker," we explained how to set up transport security using both Windows authentication and certificates. If your application involves more than one instance of SQL Server, consider creating a database principal for the application.

CONNECT Permission

Remote authorization is involved when more than one instance of SQL Server is involved in the application. To connect to a remote SQL Server, you have to grant CONNECT permission to the principal connecting to the remote instance.

If the initiator instance is running under a domain account, you have to add that domain account to the target instance and grant CONNECT permission:

```
GRANT CONNECT ON ENDPOINT::TargetSSBEndPoint TO [MYDOM\mssdev1]
```

You'll need to grant the same permission on the initiator instance, so that the target instance can connect to the initiator.

If the initiator instance is running under a "local system" account, then you have to add that machine account to the target instance and grant CONNECT permission:

```
GRANT CONNECT ON ENDPOINT::TargetSSBEndPoint TO [MYDOM\InitiatorMachine$]
```

You have to do the same thing on the initiator instance so the target instance can connect to the initiator. Keep in mind that in order for the machine account to be authenticated on the remote instance, you need Kerberos on your network. If Kerberos authentication is not available on your network, this method will not work. You would have to use certificates in that case.

If certificates are used for transport authentication, you have to grant the CONNECT permission on the endpoint on the initiator instance to the user who owns the certificate corresponding to the private key in the remote database.

See the scripts CreateLoginOnInitiator.sql and CreateEndPointWithCertOnInitiator.sql in Sample2.

```
GRANT CONNECT ON ENDPOINT::InitiatorSSBEndPoint TO TargetServerUser
```

You'll also have to do the same thing on the target instance. See the scripts CreateLoginOnTarget.sql and CreateEndPointWithCertOnTarget.sql in Sample2.

SEND Permission

When you send the message, you send it to a target service. You need SEND permission to send the message to a target service. The database principal that owns the initiating service must have SEND permission on the target service.

When you do not configure full-dialog security, you have to grant SEND permission on the target service as public, because the target service cannot verify the identity of the initiating service. Operations on behalf of the initiating service run as a member of the fixed database role public in the target database. This is called *anonymous dialog security*:

```
GRANT SEND ON SERVICE::TargetService TO PUBLIC
```

When you use FULL dialog security, you can establish the trust by exchanging the certificates that contain public keys, as discussed in the "Dialog Security" section earlier in this chapter. For better security, you should have a different user who has SEND permission to a service than the one who runs the activation on a queue tied to that service.

You don't need either of these steps if your dialog remains in the same SQL Server instance.

RECEIVE Permission

The user executing the BEGIN DIALOG, END CONVERSATION, MOVE DIALOG, RECEIVE, or GET CONVERSATION GROUP command must have RECEIVE permission on the queue associated with the FROM SERVICE. The following statement is an example of how you can grant RECEIVE permission on a RequestQueue:

```
GRANT RECEIVE ON dbo.RequestQueue TO [mydom\mssdev1]
```

In addition, if you have activation specified on a queue, the user specified in EXECUTE AS in ACTIVATION must have RECEIVE permission on the queue.

EXECUTE Permission

When you create a queue and define the ACTIVATION, you specify the stored procedure name and EXECUTE AS option there. The user you specify there must have permission to execute the stored procedure. Of course, if that stored procedure does some cross-database queries, you have to set those permissions too.

Notice that when you create the stored procedure and you have defined the EXECUTE AS clause with a user, the statements in that stored procedure will run under the defined security principal. Therefore, when a stored procedure is activated, it will be under the security context of the database principal you have specified in the CREATE QUEUE statement, and after that it will change the security context to the database principal you have specified in the CREATE PROCEDURE EXECUTE AS clause.

Managing Service Broker Queues

A Service Broker application that is running well will generally keep the queues fairly small. Make sure you have enough disk space available to handle any problems. The queue monitor will try to create enough instances of the activation procedure to process the incoming messages, and the transport layer does a good job of moving messages to their destination as efficiently as possible.

What if something goes wrong? If you have a lot of incoming messages in your application, a queue can get pretty big very quickly. Suppose your application has 1,000 messages coming in per second. If your network has to go down or your destination server is down for an hour, the sys.transmission_queue will have 4 million messages in it. You can have an SQL Server Agent job that monitors for a heavily used queue and a sys.transmission_queue to send an e-mail if the messages in the queue exceed a certain threshold.

You can also plan to put the queue on a separate filegroup so it's easy to maintain if it runs out of space. Try putting the queue on a separate filegroup by specifying the filegroup in the CREATE QUEUE statement, or use the ALTER QUEUE statement.

Finally, one of the best things you can do with a queue is use SELECT * FROM [queuename] to view what's in there.

Poison Message Handling

All transaction messaging systems have to deal with *poison messages*, which are messages that cannot be processed by the destination service. Any message containing data that can force the message processing transaction to roll back can become a poison message. Service Broker will detect the repeated rollbacks of messages, and disable the queue to keep a poorly handled message from becoming a poison message. When you design the application, make sure all messages are handled correctly, because only the application knows how to handle the messages — that is, whether to roll back or end the conversation.

Open `Sample1` to simulate a poison message and how to remove it from the queue. Open the script `PoisonMessageSimulate.sql` and run it. This will compile the stored procedure you created on `RequestQueue` again. Part of the code is reproduced here:

```
BEGIN TRY
    WHILE (1 = 1)
    BEGIN
        BEGIN TRANSACTION
        -- Receive the next available message
        WAITFOR
        (
            RECEIVE TOP(1)                      -- just handle one message at a time
                @xmlmessage_body =  CASE WHEN validation = 'X'
                                    THEN CAST(message_body AS XML)
                                    ELSE CAST(N'<none/>' AS XML)
                                END
                ,@message_type_name = message_type_name
                ,@conversation_handle = conversation_handle
            FROM dbo.RequestQueue
        ), TIMEOUT 3000
        -------------------------------------------------------------------------
        -- If we didn't get anything or if there is any error, bail out
        IF (@@ROWCOUNT = 0 OR @@ERROR <> 0)
        BEGIN
            ROLLBACK TRANSACTION
            BREAK
        END
        ELSE
        BEGIN
            IF @message_type_name =
//www.wrox.com/MTCustomerInfo/RequstCustomersCount'
            BEGIN

                ROLLBACK TRAN

            END
        END
    END --WHILE END here.
END TRY
```

The preceding script receives the message and rolls it back. This simulates a problem processing the message, so after the rollback the message goes back to the queue. This is detected by Service Broker, which disables the queue.

Run the script ActivateSPOnTarget.sql, which activates this stored procedure to run when the message arrives. Now open the SendMessageFromInitiator.sql script and run it. It will send the message to RequestQueue in the TargetDB database.

Now open the script RemovePoisonMessage.sql:

```
USE TargetDB
GO

SELECT name, is_receive_enabled
FROM sys.service_queues
GO
ALTER QUEUE RequestQueue WITH  ACTIVATION (STATUS = OFF)
GO
ALTER QUEUE RequestQueue
WITH STATUS = ON
GO

DECLARE
    @message_type_name  nvarchar(256)
    ,@xmlmessage_body     xml
    ,@MessageFromTarget  varchar(255)
    ,@MessageText varchar(255)
    ,@conversation_handle UNIQUEIDENTIFIER;

RECEIVE TOP(1)
    @xmlmessage_body = message_body
    ,@message_type_name = message_type_name
    ,@conversation_handle = conversation_handle
FROM dbo.RequestQueue

END CONVERSATION @conversation_handle
GO
SELECT name, is_receive_enabled
FROM sys.service_queues
GO
```

Because the queue is now disabled, you will see 0 in the is_receive_enabled column in the sys.service_queues catalog view for the RequestQueue.

First, you have to enable the queue, because when the queue is disabled, you cannot send or receive messages. After the queue is enabled, you receive the first message from the top of the queue, which is the one causing the problem. This assumes that only one message is processed at a time by the application. If this is not the case, the poison message could be any of the messages in the same conversation group as the message at the top of the queue. You can look at the SQL error log for more details about what's causing the message to fail.

You can also subscribe to the event called Broker_Queue_disabled, which will send the message to a designed queue when a queue is disabled. Here's how you can do that. Open the script PoisonMessageNotification.sql:

```
USE TargetDB
GO
CREATE QUEUE dbo.PoisonMessageNotification
```

```
GO
CREATE SERVICE ServicePoisonMessageNotification ON QUEUE
dbo.PoisonMessageNotification
([http://schemas.microsoft.com/SQL/Notifications/PostEventNotification])
GO
--below notification will send the message to queue
--when queue PoisonMessageNotification is disabled. The event
--generated is BROKER_QUEUE_DISABLED
CREATE EVENT NOTIFICATION PoisonMessageEvent
ON QUEUE RequestQueue
WITH FAN_IN
FOR BROKER_QUEUE_DISABLED
TO SERVICE 'ServicePoisonMessageNotification', 'current database'

GO
```

Now create a poison message on the `RequestQueue` as described earlier. Run the following script:

```
USE TargetDB
SELECT CAST(message_body as xml), * FROM PoisonMessageNotification
```

Note that an event was generated because the `RequestQueue` was disabled because of the poison message, and a message is put into the `PoisonMessageNotification` queue, which shows that `RequestQueue` is disabled. You can do whatever you like with that message in the `PoisonMessageNotification` queue, such as sending an e-mail. In fact, you can send the message to a different server, where you are probably monitoring other servers using the routing mechanism you learned about earlier.

This example also shows the power of Service Broker to provide you with event notifications in a Service Broker queue, enabling you to take action on that event. Refer to Books Online to see how event notification works.

Moving Service Broker Applications

Sometimes you need to move your application from one server to another. (Maybe you got lucky and management got you the biggest, latest-and-greatest hardware.) Usually you have to move the database where you are hosting Service Broker application to some other instance, and many aspects of the Server Broker application move with the database. Some aspects of the application must be recreated or reconfigured in the new location.

The stored procedures, users, certificates, and outgoing routes will move with the database, but some of the things you have to reconfigure on the new instance. If your Service Broker application sends messages across instances, you need to reconfigure the endpoint on each new instance. Of course, if the server you are moving the application to already has an endpoint configured, you do not need to do anything because endpoint and transport security apply at the server level, not at the database level. Make sure that the endpoint is configured according to your application requirement, though. For example, if your application requires transport security and the server to which you are moving the application doesn't have its endpoint configured with transport security, you will have to reconfigure it.

You must configure logins for any users that the application uses.

Most Service Broker databases have a database master key, but if you are using certificates for transport or dialog security, make sure you preserve the password for the master key you have created because you will need the password when you restore the database in the new location. Remember the script

`CreateCertOnInitiator.sql` and `ConfigureDialogSecurityOnInitiator.sql` where you created the master key with a password. You have to keep that password in a safe place.

If you have configured routing using `CREATE ROUTE`, and if you have specified the option called `BROKER_INSTANCE` in the statement, make sure that after you restore the database on a new location you use the `ALTER DATABASE database_name SET ENABLE_BROKER` statement to preserve the `BROKER_INSTANCE`. If you don't have that issue, or if you can reconfigure the route with a new initiator and target, you may use `ALTER DATABASE database_name SET NEW_BROKER`.

If you use `NEW_BROKER` in the `ALTER DATABASE` statement, it will clean up all the undelivered messages sitting in `sys.transmission_queue` and all the conversations in the `sys.conversation_endpoints` view. When you back up the database and restore it to a new location, make sure that application has finished processing all the messages; or if you have to process these messages after restoring to the new location, make sure that you do not use `ALTER DATABASE database_name SET NEW_BROKER`.

In addition, you should not change the `BROKER_INSTANCE` identifier when you attach a database for either of the following reasons:

- ❑ For recovery purposes
- ❑ To create a mirrored pair (see Chapter 17)

If you want to keep the same unique identifier for the database but ignore all the existing conversations (error them out), you have to use the following statement:

```
ALTER DATABASE database_name SET ERROR_BROKER_CONVERSATIONS
```

Also remember that the `msdb` database should always have the `is_broker_enabled` bit set to 1, especially if you have any incoming or outgoing Service Broker messages. You can run the following statement to check that:

```
SELECT name, is_broker_enabled FROM sys.databases WHERE name = 'msdb'
```

Finally, make sure that if you have any routes on your destination, they point back to the new server — otherwise, you will not get messages back to your new server.

Copying Service Broker Applications

The Development and Testing groups frequently refresh the environment with new data from production. In that case, as a DBA you provide a backup of the database. Most of the things discussed in the "Moving Service Broker Applications" section apply here as well, with some small changes.

Because the backup is a copy of the original application, be sure to change the unique identifier of that database using the following statement because Service Broker routing relies on a unique identifier in each database to deliver messages correctly:

```
ALTER DATABASE database_name SET NEW_BROKER
```

This is the one task you must not forget to do. In addition, change the routing on servers as described in the previous section.

If you are using the BROKER_INSTANCE option in CREATE ROUTE, we highly recommend that when you build an application, you store the route name in a table with a server name. (See the following table structure and stored procedure.) You should then write a stored procedure to retrieve the Broker_Instance from the sys.routes table, based on the route name you have stored in the table, to use in your application. That way, when you move or copy your application, you may have to drop and create the route, which may or may not have the same BROKER_INSTANCE, so you don't have to change your application at all.

```
CREATE TABLE ServerRoute
(
 ServerName varchar(50) NOT NULL
,RouteName varchar(100) NOT NULL
);

CREATE PROC GetRouteName
(
 @ServerName varchar(50)
,@Broker_Instance uniqueidentifier OUTPUT
)
AS
----------
SELECT @Broker_Instance = Broker_Instance
FROM sys.routes r
JOIN ServerRoute s
  ON s.RouteName = r.RouteName
 AND s.ServerName = @ServerName
----------
```

Replacing Expired Certificates

By default, certificates expire and become unusable. If you do not specify the expiration date in the CREATE CERTIFICATE statement, the expiration date is set to one year from when the certificate is created. When the certificate is about to expire, it must be replaced. To avoid disruptions, you must do this in the correct order. If you change the certificate at the endpoint, all connections to endpoints that do not have the new certificate will fail. However, the dialog won't fail, so when the certificate is replaced, it will continue from where it left off. To avoid this, create a new certificate and send the public key to all the remote connections. The remote Service Broker can associate this certificate with a user who represents the SQL Server instance whose certificate will be changed. Once all the remote endpoints have added the certificate to their users, you can change the local endpoint to the new certificate by using the ALTER ENDPOINT command.

Troubleshooting Service Broker Applications

You have learned how Service Broker works throughout this chapter. This section explains what to do when it doesn't work. You can use Dynamic Management Views (DMVs), catalog views, and the Profiler to troubleshoot the problems in a Service Broker application.

Design and Code Review

Because Service Broker may be a new technology to SQL DBAs and developers who have not worked with SQL Server 2005, we highly recommend that you do code review (if you are not doing one, start now!), and pay close attention to the following issues in the code review process so that any problems are resolved in the earliest stage of your application.

Not Handling All Message Types

You may sometimes wonder why, after sending a message of a particular type, nothing happens. You have probably forgotten to handle that message type in the stored procedure in which you receive the message. In addition to all the application message types, be sure to handle at least the following system message types:

- ❑ `[http://schemas.microsoft.com/SQL/ServiceBroker/Error]`
- ❑ `[http://schemas.microsoft.com/SQL/ServiceBroker/EndDialog]`

You can see how to handle these message types in one of the activation stored procedures we have created in `Sample1` or `Sample2`.

Not Dealing with Poison Messages

We discussed poison messages earlier in this chapter. Make sure you handle them; otherwise, Service Broker will disable the queue and your application will come to a halt.

Not Ending the Conversation

Remember that conversations persist in `sys.conversation_endpoints`, and they are not completely eliminated until both the initiator and the target have issued the `END CONVERSATION` command. When to end the conversation is totally up to your application, but make sure that you do so.

Service Broker Commands Outside of an Explicit Transaction

The key advantage of Service Broker is data integrity. When you receive messages from the queue with the `RECEIVE` command without a `BEGIN TRANSACTION` before the `RECEIVE`, your message will be deleted from the queue, which means that if something goes wrong while you are processing the message, you will not get the message back in the queue because you specified otherwise. If you do not see `BEGIN TRANSACTION` before the `RECEIVE` statement, carefully examine the logic to ensure that there is an active transaction. It may be that in your application you don't need the message after you receive it, in which case you can avoid `BEGIN TRANSACTION` before `RECEIVE`.

Using Catalog Views for Service Broker Metadata

Many catalog views are available to look at the metadata objects created for Service Broker, and some views to look at the data for Service Broker conversations. The following list shows the views you can use. You can refer to Books Online for each column in that metadata.

- ❑ `sys.service_message_types`
- ❑ `sys.service_contracts`
- ❑ `sys.service_contract_message_usages`
- ❑ `sys.services`
- ❑ `sys.service_contract_usages`

- ❑   sys.service_queues
- ❑   sys.certificates
- ❑   sys.routes
- ❑   sys.remote_service_bindings
- ❑   sys.service_broker_endpoints
- ❑   sys.tcp_endpoints
- ❑   sys.endpoints
- ❑   sys.databases

Not all of these views are for Service Broker, but they are related to Service Broker in some way. The following example queries should give you an idea about how you can use these views.

This query determines which Service Brokers are enabled in the current SQL Server instance:

```
SELECT name, is_broker_enabled, service_broker_guid, is_trustworthy_on
FROM sys.databases
```

The following query determines Service Broker endpoint state, port, connection authentication type, encryption algorithm, and whether forwarding is enabled or not:

```
SELECT se.name, te.port, se.protocol, se.state_desc,
se.is_message_forwarding_enabled, se.connection_auth as authentication_method,
se.encryption_algorithm_desc
FROM sys.service_broker_endpoints se
JOIN sys.tcp_endpoints te
  ON se.endpoint_id = te.endpoint_id
```

This query provides all the service names, along with their queues, and activation stored procedures and their status:

```
SELECT s.name AS Service, sq.Name AS Queue,
CASE WHEN sq.is_receive_enabled = 1 THEN 'Yes' ELSE 'No' END AS QueueActive,
ISNULL(sq.activation_procedure, 'N/A')
,CASE WHEN sq.is_activation_enabled = 1 THEN 'Yes' ELSE 'No' END  AS
Is_Activation_Enabled
FROM sys.services s
JOIN sys.service_queues sq
  ON s.service_queue_id = sq.object_id
```

This next query provides the queue and message types associated with that queue. This is helpful when you write the RECEIVE statement in the queue to ensure that you have covered all the message types for that queue:

```
SELECT sq.name AS Queue, mt.Name AS Message_Type_Name
FROM sys.service_queues sq
JOIN sys.services s
  ON s.service_queue_id = sq.object_id
JOIN sys.service_contract_usages scu
```

```
   ON s.service_id = scu.service_id
JOIN sys.service_contracts sc
   ON scu.service_contract_id = sc.service_contract_id
JOIN sys.service_contract_message_usages mtu
   ON mtu.service_contract_id = sc.service_contract_id
JOIN sys.service_message_types mt
   ON mt.message_type_id = mtu.message_type_id
GROUP BY sq.name, mt.Name
```

Using Catalog Views for Service Broker Data

The catalog views that expose the queue data and conversation endpoints are the most useful views. The two views most frequently used are sys.conversation_endpoints and sys.transmission_queue. In addition, to look at the data in the queue, you can always use SELECT * FROM [queuename], as mentioned earlier.

Take a look at the sys.conversation_endpoints and sys.transmission_queue views. The query shown in Figure 8-13 will give you the state of some of the dialogs in the sys.conversation_endpoints view. We have selected only a few columns here. For all the column descriptions, please refer to Books Online.

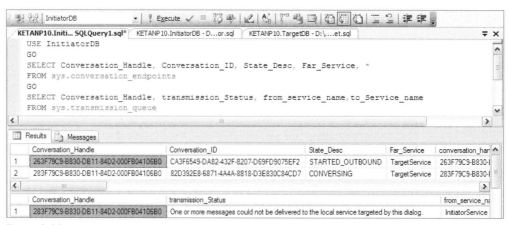

Figure 8-13

In Figure 8-13, the first result set (sys.conversation_endpoints) shows that the first dialog has State_Desc of STARTED_OUTBOUND, which means that the dialog on the initiator side has been started (with BEGIN DIALOG), but no messages have been sent on this dialog yet. The second row in that result set shows that a message has been sent (State_Desc is CONVERSING); but notice in the second result set (sys.transmission_queue) that the message is trying to send to a far service (TargetService), but it has failed because of some connection issue. Conversation_handle is the key column to find the related messages in the sys.conversation_endpoints and sys.transmission_queue views.

Together, both sys.conversation_endpoints and sys.transmission_queue provide valuable information in troubleshooting problems. Later in this chapter you will look at the most common errors you get in Service Broker communications, including their solutions using both of these views and the Profiler, described in the following section.

Dynamic Management Views

You can use some Service Broker–related DMVs to get information on activated tasks and queue_monitors:

- ❏ `sys.dm_broker_queue_monitors`: This DMV provides how many queue monitors you have in the current instance of SQL Server. For example, the query shown in Figure 8-14 will tell you when messages are being received in the queue, and how many sessions are waiting in a `RECEIVE` statement for this queue in the `TargetDB` database.

- ❏ `sys.dm_broker_activated_tasks`: This DMV returns a row for each stored procedure activated by Service Broker in the current instance of SQL Server. The query in Figure 8-15 will give you the number of stored procedures activated in the database `TargetDB` for each queue. Notice that five stored procedures are activated on `TargetQueue`.

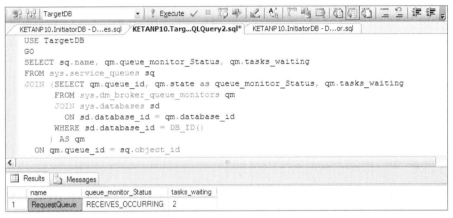

Figure 8-14

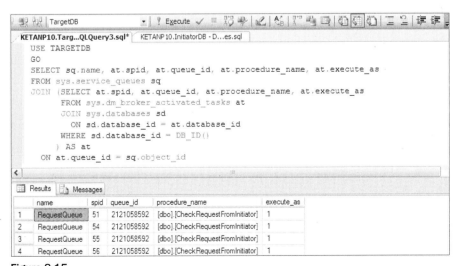

Figure 8-15

❑   `sys.dm_broker_connections`: Whenever Service Broker makes network connections, you will see rows in this DMV. If the connection is idle for 90 seconds, Service Broker closes the connection; otherwise, it keeps it open so messages can be sent using the same connection.

❑   `sys.dm_broker_forwarded_messages`: When a SQL Server instance is working as a message forwarder, you will see a row for each message in the process of being forwarded on a SQL Server instance.

Using SQL Profiler to View Service Broker Activities

Most of the activities in Service Broker happen in the background threads, and are not visible to the user. Often, when you issue BEGIN DIALOG and SEND the message, Service Broker does it successfully but you later realize that the message never reached the destination! You are left wondering why you are not getting any errors when you send the message. The message is on its way, but because you have forgotten to configure the route properly, or forgot to set some permission properly, Service Broker keeps trying to send the message repeatedly until it times out or you end the dialog.

Service Broker guarantees reliable message delivery, so it will keep trying in spite of failure and misconfigurations, which are required when you implement a highly reliable network application; but you are not going to get the errors reported back to your application when things go wrong. You have to determine for yourself what's going on behind the scenes. In most cases, the views described in the preceding section provide you with the necessary information to troubleshoot the problem, but sometimes you will need more information to diagnose an issue, and that's where you use *traces*.

Service Broker has several traces that provide enough information about internal performance to enable you to diagnose a problem. Figure 8-16 shows Service Broker events in the SQL Server Profiler Trace Properties window.

Figure 8-17 shows the trace of an event in which a message cannot be delivered to the remote server because the account that connects to the remote server doesn't have permission to connect on this endpoint.

This trace was run on the target instance, and the message here shows that the remote login Redmond\mssdev1 does not have connect permission on the endpoint of the target machine. Notice in Figure 8-17 the multiple error messages regarding "connection handshake failed" because Service Broker keeps trying to send the message. The first retry is after four seconds, and if that does not succeed, Service Broker resends exponentially up to 64 seconds (4, 8, 16, 32, and 64 seconds). When Service Broker reaches the maximum resend timeout (64 seconds), it will try once every 64 seconds (about once a minute).

In Figure 8-18, you can also see that the conversation is sitting on sys.transmission_queue on the initiator, so Service Broker will keep trying to send the message until it times out, the conversation is ended, or you fix the problem.

As you can see, the Profiler is a great tool for determining what's going in the background.

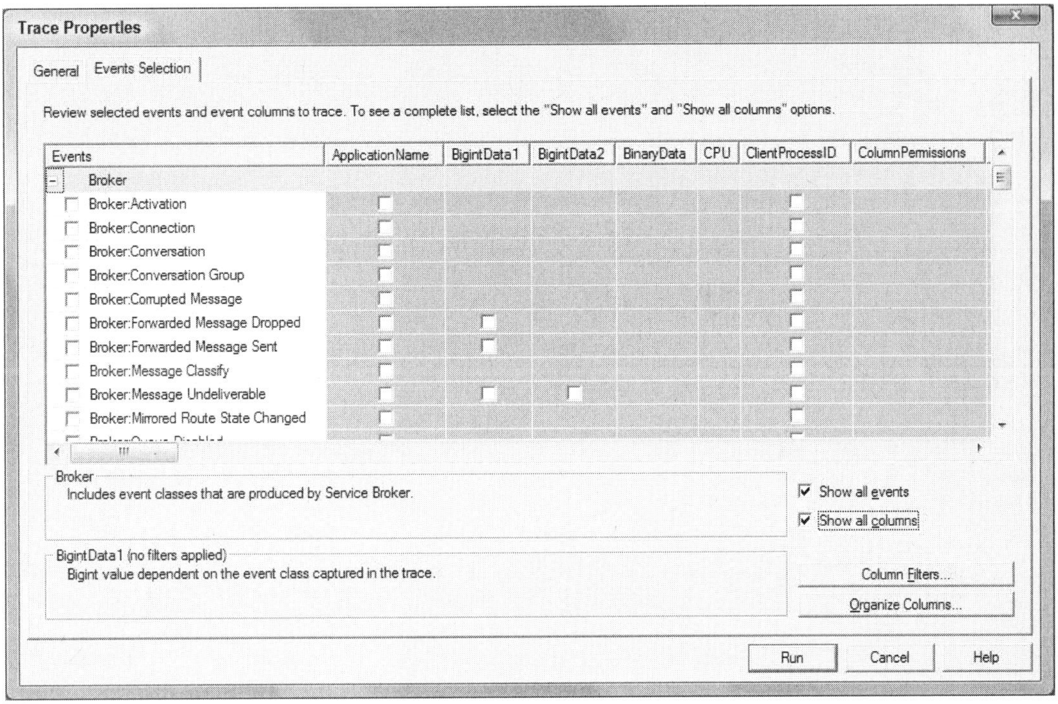

Figure 8-16

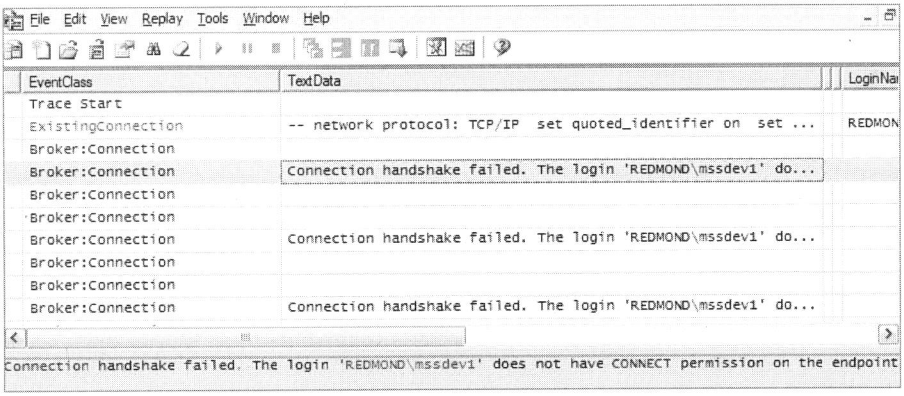

Figure 8-17

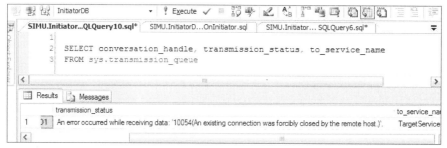

Figure 8-18

No Return Route

You have sent the message and you have verified that it reached the target, but you are expecting something from the target and that message never comes back to the initiator. If you trace the Message undeliverable event, you will see continuous duplicate message events, as shown in Figure 8-19.

EventClass	EventSubClass	D...	TextData
Trace Start			
Broker:Message Classify	1 - Local	4	
Broker:Conversation Group	1 - Create	7	
Broker:Conversation	12 - Dialo...	7	STARTED_INBOUND
Broker:Conversation	6 - Receiv...	7	CONVERSING
Broker:Remote Message Ack...	3 - Messag...	7	
Broker:Activation	1 - Start	7	
Broker:Message Classify	1 - Local	4	
Broker:Message Undeliverable	1 - Sequen...	7	This message could not be delivered because it is a d
Broker:Remote Message Ack...	3 - Messag...	7	
Broker:Message Classify	1 - Local	4	
Broker:Message Undeliverable	1 - Sequen...	7	This message could not be delivered because it is a d
Broker:Remote Message Ack...	3 - Messag...	7	
Broker:Conversation	1 - SEND M	7	CONVERSING

This message could not be delivered because it is a duplicate.

Figure 8-19

The issue here is that you have correctly defined the route to the target to ensure that messages are delivered from the initiator to the target, but you have not defined the route back to the initiator on the target. In Sample2, if you drop the route with DROP ROUTE in the TargetDB database, and then send the message from the initiator, you will be able to see this error in the Profiler if you connect it to your target instance.

Dropped Messages

When Service Broker cannot process a message, it drops it. Some of the reasons why messages are dropped include the following:

❑   The certificate in the message header doesn't exist, or it doesn't have the required permission, or public doesn't have send permission on the service.

❑   The service that sent the messages doesn't exist.

❑ The message or header is corrupt or has been altered.

❑ The XML message doesn't validate against the schema for the message type.

If you notice a lot of messages are piling up in `sys.transmission_queue`, you should use SQL Profiler to determine why messages are being dropped.

Conversation Endpoint Is Not in a Valid State for SEND

As soon as you send a message it is placed in the queue. If for some reason a message cannot be placed in the queue, you will see an error like the following:

```
Msg 8429, Level 16, State 1, Line 14
The conversation endpoint is not in a valid state for SEND. The current endpoint
state is 'ER'.
```

The most common cause of this error is that the conversation lifetime has expired, but it also happens when the conversation is ended by the far end (target server), or by some other error. If you want to produce this error, then run the following script after you've set up `Sample1` or `Sample2`:

```
USE InitiatorDB
GO

DECLARE @Conversation_Handle UNIQUEIDENTIFIER
      ,@SendMessage xml
      ,@MessageText varchar(255)

SET @MessageText = 'Request From Server: \\' + @@SERVERNAME
                + ', DATABASE: ' + DB_NAME()
                + ': ** Please send the total number of customers.'

SET @SendMessage = N'<message>'+ N'<![CDATA[' + @MessageText + N']]>' +
N'</message>'

BEGIN DIALOG CONVERSATION @Conversation_Handle
FROM SERVICE [InitiatorService]
TO SERVICE 'TargetService'
ON CONTRACT [//www.wrox.com/CTGeneralInfo/ProductCustomer]
WITH ENCRYPTION = OFF
    ,LIFETIME = 5

WAITFOR DELAY '00:00:07';


BEGIN TRY;

SEND ON CONVERSATION @Conversation_Handle
MESSAGE TYPE [//www.wrox.com/MTCustomerInfo/RequstCustomersCount]
(@SendMessage);

END TRY
BEGIN CATCH
   SELECT ERROR_NUMBER() AS ErrorNumber
        ,ERROR_MESSAGE() AS ErrorMessage
```

```
            ,ERROR_SEVERITY() AS ErrorSeverity
            ,ERROR_LINE() AS ErrorLine
    END CATCH
```

This script starts the dialog, but does not send the message until after seven seconds have passed. You specified the dialog lifetime in the LIFETIME clause to be five seconds, so you are not in a valid state to send the message on the expired conversation_handle.

Queue Disabled

If your application suddenly stops working, the first thing you want to check is queue status, using the following query:

```
SELECT name, CASE WHEN is_receive_enabled = 1 THEN 'Yes' ELSE 'No' END AS
QueueEnabled
FROM sys.service_queues
```

You can reenable the queue with the following query:

```
ALTER QUEUE ReceiveAckError WITH  STATUS = ON
```

In addition, make sure that activation is enabled if you have it. After you enable the queue, check the queue status again. If it is disabled again, you have a poison message on the queue. Read the "Poison Message Handling" section earlier in the chapter for details about detecting and handling poison messages.

Service Broker Is Disabled in a Database

If Service Broker is disabled in the database, your application can still send messages but they will not be delivered. This can be caused by restoring or attaching a database without the Service_Broker_Enabled option. Any message will sit in the sys.transmission_queue until Service Broker is enabled. Using the following, you can check whether the database is enabled for Service Broker or not:

```
SELECT name, CASE WHEN is_broker_enabled = 1 THEN 'Yes' ELSE 'No' END AS
Service_Broker_Enabled
FROM sys.databases
```

See the "Preparing the Databases" and "Moving Service Broker Applications" sections of this chapter for more details.

Could Not Obtain Information about Windows NT Group/User

When you log in under your domain account, if you are not connected to the domain, you will get the following error when you try to send the message:

```
Msg 15404, Level 16, State 19, Line 15
Could not obtain information about Windows NT group/user 'MYDOM\ketan', error code
0x54b.
```

Whenever SQL Server needs to authorize a user, it needs to connect to a domain controller if it doesn't have enough information cached for authorization. The only way to correct this problem is to connect to your domain.

Duplicate Routes

Suppose half the messages you send are lost somewhere. Maybe you forgot to drop a route that is not required and messages are being sent to that. For example, when you refresh your environment with test data, you have the old route, which is pointing to ServerX. After the refresh, you add another route to ServerY and forget to drop the route to ServerX. If Service Broker finds multiple routes to the same service, then it assumes that you want to do load balancing, and it divides the dialogs between the two servers. In this case, half the dialogs will go to ServerX even though you don't want them to go there. The solution is to drop the unnecessary route. You can also specify the BROKER_ID in the BEGIN DIALOG or CREATE ROUTE statement to prevent this, but as long as you are careful about dropping unnecessary routes, you will be fine.

Activation Stored Procedure Is Not Being Activated

Frequently, messages are not picked up from the queue, even though you know that you have defined the activation stored procedure on that queue. The first thing you should check is whether the activation status is ON or not using the following query:

```
SELECT name, CASE WHEN is_activation_enabled = 1 THEN 'Yes' ELSE 'No' END AS
ActivationEnabled
FROM sys.service_queues
```

You can enable the activation using the following query on a RequestQueue:

```
ALTER QUEUE RequestQueue WITH ACTIVATION (STATUS = ON)
```

If activation is enabled, it's possible that you don't have correct permission on the stored procedure for the user you have specified in the EXECUTE AS clause in the CREATE QUEUE statement. Look in the SQL error log: If that is the case, then you will see an error like this one:

```
The activated proc [dbo].[CheckResponseFromTarget] running on queue
InitiatorDB.dbo.ReceiveAckError output the following: 'EXECUTE permission denied
on object 'CheckResponseFromTarget', database 'InitiatorDB', schema 'dbo'.'
```

Grant proper permission on the stored procedure to avoid this error.

Performance Tuning Service Broker

If you think that Service Broker is not performing as well as expected, look for following things. Keep in mind that Service Broker uses SQL Server for all data storage, so all the factors that affect database performance affect Service Broker performance. Don't worry about the RECEIVE message from the queue, because that is a very well-tuned part.

Suppose you send a bunch of messages to a queue for which you have defined an activation stored procedure with MAX_QUEUE_READERS = 10, but you still see only one instance of that stored procedure running. That's happening because all those messages are on the same dialog. In that case, activation would not start an additional instance of the activation stored procedure because all of the messages have to be processed serially. If you want parallelism, you need more than one dialog. You have to use dialogs effectively. If you think that some tasks have to be processed serially, then group them in one dialog. Don't send the messages you want to be processed in parallel on the same dialog.

Not ending the conversation is another performance problem. You know that as soon as you issue BEGIN DIALOG an entry will be made to the sys.conversation_endpoints catalog. This will remain until you end the dialog with END CONVERSATION on both ends of the conversation. Do not assume that specifying LIFETIME in BEGIN DIALOG is sufficient to clear the rows from that catalog. If you forgot END CONVERSATION, you may see millions of rows in the sys.conversation_endpoints view if you have a very active service. Conversations are cached for performance, so millions of expired and useless conversations waste a lot of cache space. Without enough cache size available, these conversations are swapped out into tempdb, so tempdb will grow too. Too many conversations are not good because they use a lot of cache size, and too few conversations are not good either because you will get less parallelism, so make sure that you use conversation wisely in your application to get the best possible performance. Service Broker excels in many areas, including sending and receiving the messages in the queue, how quickly activation is initiated, and receiving from the queue.

Introduction to CLR Integration

In this section, we discuss what it means to be a .NET runtime host, deploying .NET assemblies, maintaining security for .NET assemblies, and monitoring performance. Also included is a short example demonstrating how to debug a .NET assembly. This section is not about how to write a cool .NET assembly, although we do create a small assembly to further your understanding of how it works. This section focuses on administration.

For more information on SQL Server Integration Services, see Professional SQL Server 2008 Integration Services, *by Brian Knight et al (Wrox, 2008); and to learn more about programming in SQL CLR, see* Professional SQL Server 2005 CLR Stored Procedures, Functions, and Triggers, *by Derek Comingore and Douglas Hinson (Wrox, 2007).*

SQL Server As .NET Runtime Host

A runtime host is defined as any process that loads the .NET runtime and runs code in the managed environment. The database programming model in SQL Server 2008 is significantly enhanced by hosting the Microsoft .NET Framework 3.5 Common Language Runtime (CLR). With CLR integration, also called SQL CLR, SQL Server enables .NET programmers to write stored procedures, user-defined functions, and triggers in any .NET-compatible language, particularly C# and VB.NET.

The .NET code that SQL Server runs is completely isolated from SQL Server itself. Of course, .NET code runs in the SQL Server process space, but SQL Server uses a construct in .NET called the *AppDomain (Application Domain)* to completely isolate all resources that the .NET code uses from the resources that SQL Server uses. The AppDomain protects SQL Server from all malicious use of system resources. Keep in mind that SQL Server manages its own thread scheduling; synchronization and locking; and, of course, memory management. There are other .NET hosts, such as ASP.NET and Internet Explorer, for which these tasks are managed by the CLR. There is no conflict of interest between SQL Server and CLR regarding which manages the resources. Obviously, SQL Server wins because reliability, security, and performance are of the utmost importance to SQL Server, and changes have been made in how the managed hosting APIs work, as well as in how the CLR works internally.

Figure 8-20 shows how SQL Server hosts, the CLR .NET hosts, want to have hooks into the CLR's resource management and allocations. They achieve that by calling ICLRRunTimeHost. These APIs call a shim DLL, MSCOREE.DLL, whose job is to load the runtime. The host (SQL Server) then can call

`ICLRHostRunTime::SetHostControl()`. This method points to the `IHostControl` interface, which contains the method `GetHostControl`, which the CLR can call to delegate tasks such as thread management and memory management to the host (SQL Server). SQL Server uses this interface to take control of some functions that the CLR calls down to the OS directly.

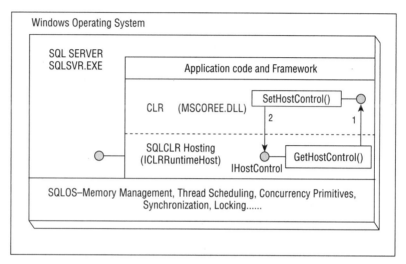

SQLCLR Hosting

Figure 8-20

The CLR calls SQL Server APIs for creating threads, both for running user code and for its own internal use. SQL Server uses a cooperative thread scheduling model, whereas managed code uses preemptive thread scheduling. In cooperative thread scheduling, the thread must voluntarily yield control of the processor, whereas in preemptive thread scheduling the processor takes control back from the thread after its time slice has expired. Some greedy managed code may not yield for a long time and may monopolize the CPU. SQL Server can identify those "runaway" threads, suspend them, and put them back in the queue. Some threads that are identified repeatedly as runaway threads are not allowed to run for a given period of time, which enables other worker threads to run.

Only one instance of the runtime engine can be loaded into the process space during the lifetime of a process. It is not possible to run multiple versions of the CLR within the same host.

Application Domains

In .NET, processes can be subdivided into execution zones called *application domains* (*AppDomains*) within a host (SQL Server) process. The managed code assemblies can be loaded and executed in these AppDomains. Figure 8-21 shows the relationship between a process and AppDomains.

SQL Server isolates code between databases by using AppDomains. This means that for each database, if you have registered an assembly and you invoke some function from that assembly, an AppDomain is created for that database. Only one AppDomain is created per database. Later you will look at some DMVs that you can use to obtain information about AppDomains.

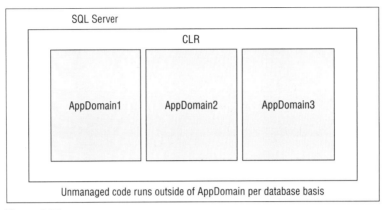

Figure 8-21

T-SQL versus CLR

It was mentioned earlier that you can write stored procedures, triggers, and functions using CLR-compatible languages. Does that mean DBAs need to take a crash course on C# or VB.NET? No, but you need to at least understand why code is returned in .NET languages versus T-SQL. You are the one who is going to run the production environments, so you need to be part of the decision regarding which set of tools is chosen for your application.

Data manipulation can be broadly categorized into two types: a declarative query language and a procedural query language. The declarative query language is composed of SELECT, INSERT, UPDATE, and DELETE statements; while a procedural language is composed of triggers, cursors, and WHILE statements. SQL CLR integration provides an alternative support to the procedural portion of T-SQL. Database applications should look to procedural programming when they cannot express the business logic needed with a query language. T-SQL is best when you perform set-based operations. It can take advantage of the query processor, which is best able to optimize the set operations. Do not write CLR code to start processing row-by-row operations, which you can do best with T-SQL in set operations. However, if your application requires performing complex calculations on a per-row basis over values stored in database tables, you can access the results from your table by first using SELECT and then by performing row-by-row operations using CLR code. Of course, there is a transition cost between the CLR and SQL layer, but if you are performing operations on high-volume data, the transition cost may be negligible.

Extended Stored Procedures versus CLR

To write server-side code with logic that was difficult to write in T-SQL, the only option prior to SQL Server 2005 was to write extended stored procedures (XPs). CLR integration in SQL Server 2005 and SQL Server 2008 now provides a more robust way to do those operations with managed code. The following list describes some of the benefits SQL CLR integration provides over extended stored procedures:

❑ **Granular control:** SQL Server administrators have little control over what XPs can or cannot do. Using the Code Access Security model, a SQL Server administrator can assign one of three permission buckets — SAFE, EXTERNAL_ACCESS, or UNSAFE — to exert varying degrees of control over the operations that managed code is allowed to perform.

❑ **Reliability:** There is no possibility of managed, user-code access violations making SQL Server crash, especially with SAFE and EXTERNAL_ACCESS assemblies.

❑ **New Data Types:** The managed APIs support new data types — such as XML, (n)varchar(max), and varbinary(max) — introduced in SQL Server 2005, while the Open Data Services (ODS) APIs have not been extended to support these new types.

These advantages do not apply if you register the assemblies with the UNSAFE permission set. Most extended stored procedures can be replaced, especially considering that Managed C++ is available as a coding option.

Enabling CLR Integration

By default, CLR integration is disabled. You cannot execute any .NET code until you intentionally change the configuration in SQL Server to allow CLR integration. You can do that using a T-SQL script.

Here are some things to remember before enabling CLR integration:

❑ By default, CLR integration is disabled. Only members of the sysadmin and serveradmin server role can change the setting using the sp_configure stored procedure. In addition, any user granted the server-level permission ALTER SETTINGS can perform this operation.

❑ After you enable CLR, you should monitor SQL Server for the following error messages in the error log: Failed Virtual Allocate Bytes: FAIL_VIRTUAL_RESERVE <size> and Failed Virtual Allocate Bytes: FAIL_VIRTUAL_COMMIT <size>. These error messages indicate that SQL Server is trying to allocate some memory from the SQL memory pool for extended stored procedures, DLL files, and automation objects. If you see such an error message, consider starting SQL Server with the -g option and specify reserving more memory outside of SQL memory pool. By default, the -g switch reserves 256MB of memory for extended stored procedures, DLL files, automation objects, and OLE DB providers.

❑ There is an advanced option called lightweight pooling. Setting that option to 1 (enabled) means that CLR execution is not supported. You must disable that option before you enable the CLR integration option using the 'clr enabled' sp_configure option.

The following T-SQL script will enable CLR integration:

```
sp_configure 'clr enabled', 1;
GO
RECONFIGURE;
GO
SELECT * FROM sys.configurations WHERE name = 'clr enabled'
```

You can disable CLR integration by setting the clr enabled option to 0. When you disable CLR integration, SQL Server stops executing all CLR routines and unloads all application domains.

You can check serverwide configuration using the catalog view sys.configurations. Look in the value_in_use column for the current configured value in the sys.configurations view.

Creating the CLR Assembly

In this section you will create a small C# table-valued function in order to demonstrate how to deploy an assembly, maintain security, and look for CLR objects in the database. The following code (provided in the folder `GetFileDetails`) will access the specified directory and list all the files and attributes as a tabular result set. This example also illustrates how impersonation works. If you don't have Visual Studio 2005 or Visual Studio 2008 installed, you can just take the compiled DLL from this book's Web site (www.wrox.com) and register that in the database, as shown later, or you can use the command we provide to compile the DLL from the `.cs` file using `csc.exe` (the C# compiler), which ships free with the .NET SDK. The following code will create a table-valued function:

```csharp
using System;
using System.Collections;
using System.Collections.Generic;
using System.Text;
using System.IO;
using Microsoft.SqlServer.Server;
using System.Data.SqlTypes;
using System.Security.Principal;

public class FileDetails
{

    [SqlFunction(DataAccess = DataAccessKind.Read, FillRowMethodName =
"FillFileRow"
    ,TableDefinition = "name nvarchar(4000), creationTime datetime, lastAccessTime
datetime, lastWriteTime datetime, isDirectory bit, isReadOnly bit, length bigint"
    )]
    public static IEnumerable GetFileDetails(string directoryPath)
    {
        try
        {
            DirectoryInfo di = new DirectoryInfo(directoryPath);
            return di.GetFiles();
        }
        catch (DirectoryNotFoundException dnf)
        {
            return new string[1] { dnf.ToString() };
        }
        catch (UnauthorizedAccessException ave)
        {
            return new string[1] { ave.ToString() };
        }
    }

    [SqlFunction(DataAccess = DataAccessKind.Read, FillRowMethodName =
    "FillFileRowWithImpersonation", TableDefinition = "name nvarchar(4000),
    creationTime datetime, lastAccessTime datetime, lastWriteTime datetime, isDirectory
    bit, isReadOnly bit, length bigint")]
    public static IEnumerable GetFileDetailsWithImpersonation(string directoryPath)
    {
        WindowsIdentity clientId = null;
        WindowsImpersonationContext impersonatedUser = null;
```

```
        clientId = SqlContext.WindowsIdentity;
        try
        {
            try
            {
                impersonatedUser = clientId.Impersonate();
                if (impersonatedUser != null)
                    return GetFileDetails(directoryPath);
                else return null;
            }
            finally
            {
                if (impersonatedUser != null)
                    impersonatedUser.Undo();
            }
        }
        catch
        {
            throw;
        }
    }
    public static void FillFileRow(object fileData, out SqlString name, out
SqlDateTime creationTime,
        out SqlDateTime lastAccessTime, out SqlDateTime lastWriteTime,
        out SqlBoolean isDirectory, out SqlBoolean isReadOnly, out SqlInt64 length)
    {
        FileInfo info = fileData as FileInfo;
        if (info == null)
        {
            name = "Error, directory list failed: " + fileData.ToString();
            creationTime = SqlDateTime.Null;
            lastAccessTime = SqlDateTime.Null;
            lastWriteTime = SqlDateTime.Null;
            isDirectory = SqlBoolean.Null;
            isReadOnly = SqlBoolean.Null;
            length = SqlInt64.Null;
        }
        else
        {
            name = info.Name;
            creationTime = info.CreationTime;
            lastAccessTime = info.LastAccessTime;
            lastWriteTime = info.LastWriteTime;
            isDirectory = (info.Attributes & FileAttributes.Directory) > 0;
            isReadOnly = info.IsReadOnly;
            length = info.Length;
        }
    }
    public static void FillFileRowWithImpersonation(object fileData,
        out SqlString name, out SqlDateTime creationTime,
        out SqlDateTime lastAccessTime, out SqlDateTime lastWriteTime,
        out SqlBoolean isDirectory, out SqlBoolean isReadOnly, out SqlInt64 length)
    {
        WindowsIdentity clientId = null;
```

```
                WindowsImpersonationContext impersonatedUser = null;

                clientId = SqlContext.WindowsIdentity;
                try
                {
                    try
                    {
                        impersonatedUser = clientId.Impersonate();
                        if (impersonatedUser != null)
                            FillFileRow(fileData, out name, out creationTime,
                                out lastAccessTime, out lastWriteTime, out isDirectory,
                                out isReadOnly, out length);
                        else
                        {
                            FillFileRow("Error: Impersonation failed!",
                                out name, out creationTime, out lastAccessTime,
                                out lastWriteTime, out isDirectory, out isReadOnly,
                                out length);
                        }
                    }
                    finally
                    {
                        if (impersonatedUser != null)
                            impersonatedUser.Undo();
                    }
                }
                catch
                {
                    throw;
                }
            }

        }
```

The preceding code has two main methods: GetFileDetails and GetFileDetailsWithImpersonation. The method GetFileDetails calls the method FillFileRow. The method GetFileDetailsWithImpersonation calls the methods FillFileRowWithImpersonation, GetFileDetails, FillFileRowWithImpersonation, and FillFileRow, in that order.

Later you will define two SQL TVFs called GetFileDetails and GetFileDetailsWithImpersonation. The function GetFileDetails will call the method GetFileDetails from this code. This method just gets the files list and other details such as creation time and last modified time using the SQL Server service account. The FillFileRow method gets this property and returns it to the SQL TVF. The SQL TVF function GetFileDetailsWithImpersonation calls the method GetFileDetailsWithImpersonation, which sets the impersonation to your login; and when it calls the GetFileDetails method, it uses your login identity, rather than the SQL Server service account. You'll see how to call these SQL TVF functions later.

Now you need to compile the code and create an assembly called GetFileDetails.dll. If you have Visual Studio 2005 or 2008, you can open the solution GetFileDetails.sln provided in the folder GetFileDetails. Build the project by clicking Build ⇨ Build GetFileDetails. That will create the GetFileDetails.dll file in the debug directory under the bin directory in your solution directory. You can deploy this assembly using Visual Studio 2005, but you will do that manually so that you know how to write T-SQL script to deploy the assembly in a database.

If you do not have Visual Studio 2005 or 2008, you can use the following command-line utility, `csc.exe`, to build `GetFileDetails.dll`:

```
C:\>C:\WINDOWS\Microsoft.NET\Framework\v2.0.50727\Csc.exe
/reference:C:\WINDOWS\Microsoft.NET\Framework\v2.0.50727\System.Data.dll
/reference:C:\WINDOWS\Microsoft.NET\Framework\v2.0.50727\System.dll /reference:C
:\WINDOWS\Microsoft.NET\Framework\v2.0.50727\System.Xml.dll /keyfile:c:\assembly
\keypair.snk /out:c:\assembly\GetFileDetails.dll /target:library C:\assembly\Get
FileDetails.cs
```

The `/out` parameter specifies the target location where `GetFileDetails.dll` will be created. The `/target` parameter specifies that this is a library (DLL). When you specify `GetFileDetails.cs`, you may have to specify the full path of the file if you are not in the directory where `GetFileDetails.cs` is located. In addition, the option `/keyfile` is used to sign the assembly. You will see why we use this option when you register the assembly.

Now that you have created the DLL, you need to deploy the assembly and associate it with SQL user-defined functions.

Deploying the Assembly

Managed code is compiled and then deployed in units called *assemblies*. An assembly is packaged as a DLL or executable (.exe). The executable can run on its own, but a DLL needs to be hosted in an existing application. You have created a DLL in this case because SQL Server will host it. You now have to register this assembly using the new DDL statement CREATE ASSEMBLY, like this:

```
CREATE ASSEMBLY assembly_name
[ AUTHORIZATION owner_name ]
FROM { <client_assembly_specifier> | <assembly_bits> [ , ... n ] }
[ WITH PERMISSION_SET = { SAFE | EXTERNAL_ACCESS | UNSAFE } ]
[ ; ]

<client_assembly_specifier> :: =
        '[\\computer_name\]share_name\[path\]manifest_file_name'
  | '[local_path\]manifest_file_name'

<assembly_bits> :: =
{ varbinary_literal | varbinary_expression }
```

The arguments of the CREATE ASSEMBLY statement are as follows:

❏   assembly_name: This is the name of the assembly, and must be unique within the database. It should be a valid SQL identifier.

❏   Authorization: This specifies the name of a user or role as an owner of the assembly. If you do not specify this, then the owner will be the user executing this statement.

❏   client_assembly_specifier: This is the location of the assembly being loaded, including the filename of that assembly. You can specify the local path or a network location (such as a UNC path). SQL Server does not load multimodule assemblies. If the assembly you are loading is dependent on other assemblies, SQL Server will look for those dependent assemblies in the same directory and load them with the same owner as the root-level assembly. The owner of the dependent assemblies must be the same as the owner of the root assembly. The user executing the CREATE ASSEMBLY statement must have read permission to the share where the file is located.

❑ assembly_bits: This is the list of binary values that make up the assembly and its dependent assemblies. The value is considered as the root-level assembly. The values corresponding to the dependent assemblies can be supplied in any order.

❑ PERMISSION_SET: Grouped into three categories, the code access security specifies what the assembly can do:

❑ SAFE: The assembly runs under the caller's security context. An assembly with this code access security cannot access any resources outside of the SQL Server instance. This is the default and the most restrictive permission you can set for an assembly.

❑ EXTERNAL_ACCESS: Assemblies created with this permission set can access external resources such as the file system, the network, environment variables, the registry, and more.

❑ UNSAFE: This permission extends the external_access permission set. This permission allows the assembly to call unmanaged code.

Security Notes

You have just learned about what code access security can be applied to an assembly, but this section provides a bit more detail about the various options.

SAFE is the most restrictive option and the default. If the assembly doesn't need access to external resources, then this is the permission you should use when you register the assembly.

You should use EXTERNAL_ACCESS whenever you need access to external resources. Keep in mind that when an assembly with this permission accesses external resources, it uses the SQL Server service account to do so. Therefore, make sure during the code review that impersonation is used while accessing the external resource. If impersonation is used, the external resources would be accessed under the caller's security context. Because this code can access external resources, before you register this assembly, you have to either set the TRUSTWORTHY bit in the database to 1, or sign the assembly, as you'll see later. The EXTERNAL_ACCESS assembly includes the reliability and scalability of the SAFE assembly.

We do not recommend using an UNSAFE assembly, because it could compromise SQL Server. It is no better than an extended stored procedure. You should have a very solid reason to use this option and should carefully examine what the assembly does, documenting it exactly. Keep in mind that when an assembly with this permission accesses external resources, it uses the SQL Server service account to do so.

The following table should help clarify how SQL Server applies rules for accessing resources outside of SQL Server when the assembly is created with either with the EXTERNAL_ACCESS or UNSAFE permission sets.

If the execution context	... Then
is SQL Server login ...	attempts to access external resources are denied and a security exception is raised.
corresponds to the Windows login and the execution context is the original caller ...	external resources are accessed under the SQL Server service account.
corresponds to the Windows login and the execution context is not the original caller ...	attempts to access external resources are denied and a security exception is raised.

Registering the Assembly

Now you are ready to register the assembly into a database. Open the solution Sample3.

Open and run the script CreateDB.sql. This will create a database called CLRDB. Next, open the script CreateAssembly.sql, shown here:

```
--------------------
USE CLRDB
GO
IF OBJECT_ID('GetFileDetails') IS NOT NULL
DROP FUNCTION [GetFileDetails];
GO
IF OBJECT_ID('GetFileDetailsWithImpersonation') IS NOT NULL
DROP FUNCTION [GetFileDetailsWithImpersonation];
GO
IF EXISTS (SELECT * FROM sys.assemblies WHERE [name] = 'GetFileDetails')
DROP ASSEMBLY [GetFileDetails];
GO
--------------------
USE master
GO
IF EXISTS (SELECT * FROM sys.server_principals WHERE [name] =
'ExternalAccess_Login')
DROP LOGIN ExternalAccess_Login;
GO
IF EXISTS (SELECT * FROM sys.asymmetric_keys WHERE [name] = 'ExternalAccess_Key')
DROP ASYMMETRIC KEY ExternalAccess_Key;
GO
CREATE ASYMMETRIC KEY ExternalAccess_Key
FROM EXECUTABLE FILE = 'C:\Assembly\GetFileDetails.dll'
GO
CREATE LOGIN ExternalAccess_Login FROM ASYMMETRIC KEY ExternalAccess_Key
GO
GRANT EXTERNAL ACCESS ASSEMBLY TO ExternalAccess_Login
GO
--------------------
USE CLRDB
GO
```

```
CREATE ASSEMBLY GetFileDetails
FROM  'C:\Assembly\GetFileDetails.dll'
WITH PERMISSION_SET = EXTERNAL_ACCESS;
GO
```

Make sure that the GetFileDetails.dll specified in the parameter EXECUTABLE FILE in CREATE
ASSEMBLY has the correct path to match your system. Before you register the assembly with SQL
Server, you must arrange for the appropriate permission. Assemblies with UNSAFE or EXTERNAL_ACCESS
permissions can only be registered and operate correctly if either the database TRUSTWORTHY bit is set
(ALTER DATABASE CLRDB SET TRUSTWORTHY ON), or the assembly is signed with a key, that key
is registered with SQL Server, a server principal is created from that key, and that principal
is granted the EXTERNAL_ACCESS or UNSAFE assembly permission. Here you'll use the latter
approach so that you can also see how you can sign the assembly and register it, because
the first approach is a simple matter of just setting the TRUSTWORTHY bit to ON. The latter
approach is also more granular, and therefore safer. Never register an assembly with SQL
Server (especially with EXTERNAL_ACCESS or UNSAFE permission) without thoroughly reviewing the source code of the assembly to ensure that its actions do not pose an operational or
security risk.

In the previous code, you created a login called ExternalAccess_Login from the asymmetric key
ExternalAccess_Key. When you created the assembly using the command-line option csc.exe, you
specified the /keyfile option. Because of that option, the assembly GetFileDetails.dll was signed.
You are now registering that key into SQL Server because in the CREATE ASYMMETRIC KEY statement
in this code you specified the EXECUTABLE FILE option to point to the signed DLL. You have granted
the EXTERNAL_ACCESS permission to ExternalAccess_Login. Then you create the assembly with the
CREATE ASSEMBLY command. The assembly is now registered in the CLRDB database. Remember that once
the assembly is registered in the database, you don't need the assembly file .dll, so you can move your
database from server to server without worrying about that file. Of course, you have to put the source
code from which you created the DLL into your source control so that if you need to modify anything in
the future, you will do that in the source. If you want to set the TRUSTWORTHY bit to 1 for the database,
you do not need to perform any of these steps except for creating the assembly.

Now open the CreateTVF.sql file and run it. The code is shown here:

```
USE CLRDB
GO

IF OBJECT_ID('GetFileDetails') IS NOT NULL
DROP FUNCTION GetFileDetails
GO
CREATE FUNCTION GetFileDetails(@directory nvarchar(256))
RETURNS
TABLE
(
 Name nvarchar(max)
,CreationTime datetime
,LastAccessTime datetime
,LastWriteTime datetime
,IsDirectory bit
,IsReadOnly bit
,Length bigint
)
```

```
AS EXTERNAL NAME [GetFileDetails].[FileDetails].[GetFileDetails]
GO


IF OBJECT_ID('GetFileDetailsWithImpersonation') IS NOT NULL
DROP FUNCTION GetFileDetailsWithImpersonation
GO
CREATE FUNCTION GetFileDetailsWithImpersonation(@directory nvarchar(256))
RETURNS
TABLE
(
 Name nvarchar(max)
,CreationTime datetime
,LastAccessTime datetime
,LastWriteTime datetime
,IsDirectory bit
,IsReadOnly bit
,Length bigint
)
AS EXTERNAL NAME [GetFileDetails].[FileDetails].[GetFileDetailsWithImpersonation]
GO
```

You are creating two table-valued functions (TVFs): `GetFileDetails` and `GetFileDetailsWithImpersonation`. The T-SQL function `GetFileDetails` calls the method `GetFileDetails` of the class `FileDetails` from the assembly `GetFileDetails`. The T-SQL function `GetFileDetailsWithImpersonation` calls the method `GetFileDetailsWithImpersonation` of the class `FileDetails` from the assembly `GetFileDetails`. Now you have mapped the T-SQL TVF to the methods in the assembly `GetFileDetails.dll`.

Now it's time to test these functions. Open the file `TestGetFileDetails.sql`. The code is shown here:

```
USE CLRDB
GO
DECLARE @TestDir nvarchar(256);
SELECT @TestDir = 'D:\test'

SELECT [Name], CreationTime, LastAccessTime, LastWriteTime,
   IsDirectory, IsReadOnly, Length
FROM GetFileDetails(@TestDir)

SELECT [Name], CreationTime, LastAccessTime, LastWriteTime,
   IsDirectory, IsReadOnly, Length
FROM GetFileDetailsWithImpersonation(@TestDir)
```

In the preceding script, you set the variable `@TestDir` to `'D:\test'` because you want to list all the files in the directory `D:\test`. You should set the permission on the directory `D:\test` so that only you have permission to that directory. If you have set the permission correctly, you will see the results shown in Figure 8-22 when you run the script.

The first function, `GetFileDetails`, fails with an Unauthorized Access exception. Because this assembly is registered with the `EXTERNAL_ACCESS` permission set, SQL Server uses the SQL Server service account to access the external resource; and because you set the permission on the directory `D:\test` so that only you can access it, the function failed. Of course, in this case the SQL Server service account is not running under the security context with which you have run the function.

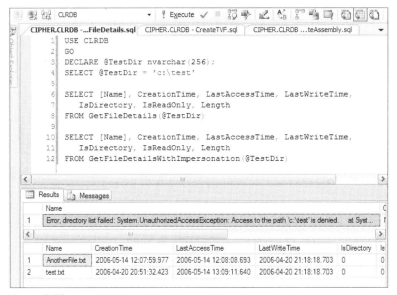

Figure 8-22

The second function, GetFileDetailsWithImpersonation, succeeded because you set the impersonation to the user who is connecting to SQL Server to execute the function. Now SQL Server will access the directory D:\test under the security context of the user executing the function, rather than the SQL Server service account.

ALTER ASSEMBLY

You can change the properties of an assembly or change the assembly code using the ALTER ASSEMBLY statement. Reload the assembly with the modified code and it will refresh the assembly to the latest copy of the .NET Framework module that holds its implementation, adding or removing files associated with it:

```
ALTER ASSEMBLY GetFileDetails
FROM '\\MyMachine\Assembly\GetFileDetails.dll'
```

If you decide that an assembly should only be called by another assembly and not from outside, you can change the visibility of the assembly as follows:

```
ALTER ASSEMBLY GetFileDetails
SET VISIBILTY = OFF
```

For full syntax details, you can refer to the topic "ALTER ASSEMBLY (Transact-SQL)" in BOL.

DROP ASSEMBLY

You can drop an assembly using the DROP ASSEMBLY statement. If the assembly is referenced by other objects, such as user-defined functions or stored procedures, then you cannot drop the assembly until you drop those dependent objects:

```
DROP ASSEMBLY GetFileDetails
```

There is a NO DEPENDENTS option to the DROP ASSEMBLY statement. If you don't specify this option, all the dependent assemblies will also be dropped:

```
DROP ASSEMBLY GetFileDetails WITH NO DEPENDENTS
```

Cataloging Objects

You can get information about different CLR objects, such as CLR stored procedures and CLR functions, using the queries described in the following sections.

Assemblies

The following are some queries from catalog views you can use to get more information on registered assemblies.

The sys.assemblies view gives you all the registered assemblies in the database:

```
SELECT * FROM sys.assemblies
```

The following view will give you all the files associated with the assembly:

```
SELECT a.Name AS AssemblyName, f.name AS AssemblyFileName
FROM sys.assembly_files f
JOIN sys.assemblies a
  ON a.assembly_id = f.assembly_id
```

The next view provides information about the assembly, its associated class, the methods in the class, and the SQL object associated with each assembly:

```
SELECT
 a.Name AS AssemblyName
,m.Assembly_Class
,m.Assembly_Method
,OBJECT_NAME(um.object_id) AS SQL_Object_Associated
,so.type_desc AS SQL_Object_Type
,u.name AS Execute_As_Principal_Name
FROM sys.assembly_modules m
JOIN sys.assemblies a
  ON a.assembly_id = m.assembly_id
LEFT JOIN sys.module_assembly_usages um
  ON um.assembly_id = a.assembly_id
LEFT JOIN sys.all_objects so
  ON so.object_id = um.object_id
LEFT JOIN sys.sysusers u
  ON u.uid = m.Execute_As_Principal_id
```

CLR Stored Procedures

This query will give you the CLR stored procedure and other details associated with it:

```
SELECT
 schema_name(sp.schema_id) + '.' + sp.[name] AS [SPName]
,sp.create_date
,sp.modify_date
```

```
 ,sa.permission_set_desc AS [Access]
FROM sys.procedures AS sp
JOIN sys.module_assembly_usages AS sau
  ON sp.object_id = sau.object_id
JOIN sys.assemblies AS sa
  ON sau.assembly_id = sa.assembly_id
WHERE sp.type = 'PC'
```

CLR Trigger Metadata

This query will give you the CLR trigger's details:

```
SELECT
 schema_name(so.schema_id) + '.' + tr.[name] AS [TriggerName]
,schema_name(so.schema_id) + '.' + object_name(tr.parent_id) AS [Parent]
,a.name AS AssemblyName
,te.type_desc AS [Trigger Type]
,te.is_first
,te.is_last
,tr.create_date
,tr.modify_date
,a.permission_set_desc AS Aseembly_Permission
,tr.is_disabled
,tr.is_instead_of_trigger
FROM sys.triggers AS tr
JOIN sys.objects AS so
  ON tr.object_id = so.object_id
JOIN sys.trigger_events AS te
  ON tr.object_id = te.object_id
JOIN sys.module_assembly_usages AS mau
  ON tr.object_id = mau.object_id
JOIN sys.assemblies AS a
  ON mau.assembly_id = a.assembly_id
WHERE tr.type_desc = N'CLR_TRIGGER'
```

CLR Scalar Function

The following query will give you the CLR scalar function:

```
SELECT
 schema_name(so.schema_id) + '.' + so.[name] AS [FunctionName]
,a.name AS AssemblyName
,so.create_date
,so.modify_date
,a.permission_set_desc AS Aseembly_Permission
FROM sys.objects AS so
JOIN sys.module_assembly_usages AS sau
  ON so.object_id = sau.object_id
JOIN sys.assemblies AS a
  ON sau.assembly_id = a.assembly_id
WHERE so.type_desc = N'CLR_SCALAR_FUNCTION'
```

CLR Table Valued Function

This query provides all CLR table-valued functions:

```
SELECT
 schema_name(so.schema_id) + N'.' + so.[name] AS [FunctionName]
,a.name AS AssemblyName
,so.create_date, so.modify_date
,a.permission_set_desc AS Aseembly_Permission
FROM sys.objects AS so
JOIN sys.module_assembly_usages AS sau
  ON so.object_id = sau.object_id
JOIN sys.assemblies AS a
  ON sau.assembly_id = a.assembly_id
WHERE so.type_desc = N'CLR_TABLE_VALUED_FUNCTION'
```

CLR User-Defined Aggregates

The following query returns the CLR user-defined aggregates:

```
SELECT
 schema_name(so.schema_id) + N'.' + so.[name] AS [FunctionName]
,a.name AS AssemblyName
,so.create_date
,so.modify_date
,a.permission_set_desc AS Aseembly_Permission
FROM sys.objects AS so
JOIN sys.module_assembly_usages AS mau
  ON so.object_id = mau.object_id
JOIN sys.assemblies AS a
  ON mau.assembly_id = a.assembly_id
WHERE so.type_desc = N'AGGREGATE_FUNCTION'
```

CLR User-Defined Types

This query provides a list of the CLR user-defined types:

```
SELECT
 st.[name] AS [TypeName]
,a.name AS [AssemblyName]
,a.permission_set_desc AS AssemblyName
,a.create_date AssemblyCreateDate
,st.max_length
,st.[precision]
,st.scale
,st.collation_name
,st.is_nullable
FROM sys.types AS st
JOIN sys.type_assembly_usages AS tau
  ON st.user_type_id = tau.user_type_id
JOIN sys.assemblies AS a
  ON tau.assembly_id = a.assembly_id
```

Application Domains

We talked earlier about application domains. This section looks at some DMVs that will give you more information about AppDomains in your servers. The following DMV provides information about all the AppDomains currently loaded, including their state:

```
SELECT * FROM sys.dm_clr_appdomains
```

Recall that an AppDomain is created for each database. An AppDomain has different states, described in the column *state* in the DMV sys.dm_clr_appdomains. The following list describes the different possible AppDomain states:

- ❑ E_APPDOMAIN_CREATING: An AppDomain is being created. After the AppDomain is created, you will see the following type of entry in the SQL error log:

    ```
    AppDomain 70 (InitiatorDB.dbo[runtime].69) created.
    ```

- ❑ E_APPDOMAIN_SHARED: An AppDomain is ready for use by multiple users. This is the state you will normally see after the AppDomain is loaded.

- ❑ E_APPDOMAIN_SINGLEUSER: An AppDomain is ready to be used by a single user to perform the DDL operations (such as CREATE ASSEMBLY).

- ❑ E_APPDOMAIN_DOOMED: An AppDomain is about to be unloaded, but cannot be yet because of some threads still executing in it.

- ❑ E_APPDOMAIN_UNLOADING: SQL is telling the CLR to unload the AppDomain, usually because an assembly is dropped or altered. You will see the following type of message in the SQL error log when this happens:

    ```
    AppDomain 70 (InitiatorDB.dbo[runtime].69) is marked for unload due to common
    language runtime (CLR) or security data definition language (DDL) operations.

    AppDomain 70 (InitiatorDB.dbo[runtime].69) unloaded.
    ```

- ❑ E_APPDOMAIN_UNLOADED: The CLR has unloaded the AppDomain. This is usually the result of an escalation procedure due to ThreadAbort, OutOfMemory, or an unhandled exception in user code. You will see an error message in the error log if any of these conditions occur before unloading the AppDomain.

- ❑ E_APPDOMAIN_ENQUEUE_DESTROY: An AppDomain is unloaded in the CLR and ready to be destroyed by SQL.

- ❑ E_APPDOMAIN_DESTROYM: An AppDomain is being destroyed by SQL.

- ❑ E_APPDOMAIN_ZOMBIE: An AppDomain has been destroyed, but all the references to it have not yet been cleaned up.

This view is helpful when the AppDomain in question is loaded, but it doesn't help much when the AppDomain is unloaded. The following query will give you all the states an AppDomain has gone through so you can see what exactly happened to it:

```
SELECT
 Timestamp
,rec.value('/Record[1]/AppDomain[1]/@address', 'nvarchar(10)') as Address
```

```
,rec.value('/Record[1]/AppDomain[1]/@dbId', 'int') as DBID
,d.name AS DatabaseName
,rec.value('/Record[1]/AppDomain[1]/@ownerId', 'int') as OwnerID
,u.Name AS AppDomainOwner
,rec.value('/Record[1]/AppDomain[1]/@type', 'nvarchar(32)') as AppDomainType
,rec.value('/Record[1]/AppDomain[1]/State[1]', 'nvarchar(32)')as AppDomainState
FROM (
       SELECT timestamp, cast(record as xml) as rec
       FROM sys.dm_os_ring_buffers
       WHERE ring_buffer_type = 'RING_BUFFER_CLRAPPDOMAIN'
       ) T
JOIN sys.sysdatabases d
  ON d.dbid = rec.value('/Record[1]/AppDomain[1]/@dbId', 'int')
JOIN sys.sysusers u
  on u.uid = rec.value('/Record[1]/AppDomain[1]/@ownerId', 'int')
ORDER BY timestamp DESC
```

Note that the DMV used in the sys.dm_os_ring_buffers query is not documented, so you should not rely on it for future releases of SQL Server. The DatabaseName column indicates which database the AppDomain belongs to and what stages it has gone through.

Performance Monitoring

You can use Windows System Monitor, DMVs, and SQL Profiler for SQL CLR performance monitoring.

System Monitor

You can use Windows System Monitor (PerfMon.exe) to monitor CLR activities for SQL Server. Use the counter in the .NET CLR group in System Monitor. Choose the sqlservr instance when you monitor CLR counters for SQL Server. Use the following counters to understand the health and activity of the programs running under the SQL-hosted environment:

❑   **.NET CLR Memory:** Provides detailed information about the three types of CLR heap memory, as well as garbage collection. These counters can be used to monitor CLR memory usage and to flag alerts if the memory used gets too large. If code is copying a lot of data into memory, you may have to check the code and take a different approach to reduce memory consumption, or add more memory.

❑   **.NET CLR Loading:** SQL Server isolates code between databases by using an AppDomain. This set of counters enables monitoring the number of AppDomains and the number of assemblies loaded in the system. You can also use some DMVs for AppDomain monitoring as described in the previous section.

❑   **.NET CLR Exceptions:** The Exceptions/Sec counter provides you with a good idea of how many exceptions the code is generating. The values vary from application to application because some-times developers use exceptions for some functionality, so you should monitor overtime to set the baseline and go from there.

SQL Profiler

SQL Profiler is not much use for monitoring the CLR because it has only one event for the CLR, called *Assembly Load*. This event tells you when an assembly is loaded with the message "Assembly Load Succeeded." If the load fails, it provides a message indicating which assembly load failed and some error code.

DMVs

The DMVs related to SQL CLR provide very useful information on CLR memory usage, which assemblies are currently loaded, the current requests waiting in CLR, and more. The following sections describe some queries that help in monitoring the CLR.

SQL CLR Memory Usage

You can find out how much memory SQL CLR is using, in KB, with the following query:

```
SELECT single_pages_kb + multi_pages_kb + virtual_memory_committed_kb
FROM sys.dm_os_memory_clerks WHERE type = 'MEMORYCLERK_SQLCLR'
```

The first column, `single_pages_kb`, is the memory allocated in the SQL buffer pool. The second column, `multi_pages_kb`, indicates the memory allocated by the SQL CLR host outside of the buffer pool. The third column, `virtual_memory_committed_kb`, indicates the amount of memory allocated by the CLR directly through bulk allocation (instead of heap allocation) through SQL server.

Note that you will see a second row with 0 if you don't have a NUMA (non-uniform memory access) system. In a NUMA system, each node has its own memory clerk, so in that case you would have to add the node totals to get the total memory usage.

Loaded Assemblies

The following query returns all the currently loaded assemblies:

```
SELECT
 a.name AS Assembly_Name
,ad.Appdomain_Name
,clr.Load_Time
FROM sys.dm_clr_loaded_assemblies AS clr
JOIN sys.assemblies AS a
  ON clr.assembly_id = a.assembly_id
JOIN sys.dm_clr_appdomains AS ad
  ON clr.appdomain_address = ad.appdomain_address
```

CLR Request Status

The following query returns the current request status in the SQL CLR:

```
SELECT session_id, request_id, start_time, status, command, database_id,
wait_type, wait_time, last_wait_type, wait_resource, cpu_time,
total_elapsed_time, nest_level, executing_managed_code
FROM sys.dm_exec_requests
WHERE executing_managed_code = 1
```

Time Spent in SQL CLR By a Query

The next query provides interesting statistics on a CLR query, such as execution count (how many times that query was executed), logical reads, physical reads, time elapsed, and last execution time:

```
SELECT
(SELECT text FROM sys.dm_exec_sql_text(qs.sql_handle)) AS query_text, qs.*
FROM sys.dm_exec_query_stats AS qs
WHERE qs.total_clr_time > 0
```

Finding the .NET Framework Version in SQL Server

If the .NET Framework is loaded you can use the following query to determine which .NET Framework version is used in SQL Server. (The .NET load is a lazy load in SQL Server. It is only loaded when any CLR assembly is called for the first time.)

```
SELECT value AS [.NET FrameWork Version]
FROM sys.dm_clr_properties
WHERE name = 'version'
```

If the .NET Framework is not loaded and you want to find out which .NET Framework version SQL Server is using, run the following query:

```
SELECT Product_Version AS [.NET FrameWork Version]
FROM sys.dm_os_loaded_modules
WHERE name LIKE N'%\MSCOREE.DLL'
```

Summary

With the SQL Server Service Broker, messaging is now deeply integrated into the Database Engine. Service Broker provides an excellent platform on which to build a reliable, scalable, and secure messaging system. You can base your service-oriented application on Service Broker, which adds reliability and fault tolerance to this approach. Service Broker also simplifies the design, construction, deployment, and servicing of service-oriented applications. With SQL Server 2008 you can now also define the conversation priority to send and receive messages in the order defined by your application. You have to set the HONOR_BROKER_PRIORITY option to 1 for the particular database in order for conversation priority to work. With Service Broker, you can build asynchronous applications using T-SQL language with reliable message transport. You have learned how to build the messaging application and how to administer it in this chapter.

With CLR integration, SQL Server has now become an application platform along with its usual Database Engine capabilities. You learned how to create an assembly and register it into SQL Server. You also learned how to set permission on assemblies and maintain them. The CLR's Framework class libraries are categorized according to degree of safety, which will alleviate some concerns DBAs have.

With the key concepts out of the way, you can now drill into more specific areas to manage, such as security. In Chapter 9, you will learn much more about securing your SQL Server.

Securing the Database Engine

In this chapter you learn how to use the security features of SQL Server 2008 to protect your SQL Server and the data it contains. While SQL Server security has generated entire books on the subject, it isn't too hard to learn the basics and tighten down your SQL Server 2008 system. This chapter focuses on those basics, such as implementing logins and users according to the principle of least privilege. This chapter also takes a look at additional security features built into the core engine, such as encryption, which debuted in SQL Server 2005 and has been enhanced in SQL Server 2008; the new audit features developed to help DBAs better meet regulatory compliance, such as with Sarbanes-Oxley; and what aspects of Policy-Based Management (covered in detail in Chapter 10) to use to increase the overall security of your SQL Server installation.

Security Principles

When it comes to securing any system, several security principles provide the best results. The ones we talk about with respect to securing your SQL Server are as follows:

- ❑ Principle of least privilege
- ❑ The CIA triad
- ❑ Defense in depth

The Principle of Least Privilege

The principle of least privilege is a security best practice which states that a person should be given only the rights he or she needs to do the job, and no more. The reasoning behind this is simple: If a person makes a mistake, the amount of damage that can be done is limited. If the person is malicious, or if a malicious person compromises another individual's account, granting the original person only the rights needed to do the job will limit the potential impact of an attack. In a classic scenario, suppose a user needs read access to a few tables in a database in order to create reports for the executive staff. The "easy" solution is to make the user a member of the db_datareader fixed database role. Unfortunately, this role gives read access to all tables and views in a database. Therefore, the user would have access to more data than he or she needs. Following the principle of least privilege, a database role should be created with SELECT permission granted against only the tables the user needs. The user should then be made a member of this new role.

The principle of least privilege also applies to applications, protocols, and services. For instance, it should be extended to service accounts, such as what SQL Server runs under, as well as the processes that run on a particular server or the connection mechanisms that are used. Consider telnet, for example. Telnet is a text-based remote access protocol that used to be very popular to manage servers such as Unix hosts. In the days when security wasn't as much of a concern as it is now, no one thought anything of using telnet to connect to a remote server and pass along their user name and password unencrypted. Today, protocols like telnet are more often than not a security liability; the functionality gained isn't worth the risk.

On Windows systems, remote access is usually done via Remote Desktop, an application such as the Microsoft SysInternals tool PSExec, or a third-party product such as Virtual Network Computing (VNC). As a result, the telnet server service is often disabled on Windows systems, if it's even installed. This follows the principle of least privilege. While some networking equipment such as routers and switches may still be managed using telnet (and even in these cases, secure protocols such as Secure Socket Shell (SSH) should be used if available), Windows administrators don't need it to manage servers. Because telnet is no longer needed to make a remote connection, it should not be active on the server.

Applying this to SQL Server, if you don't need SQL Server Analysis Services or SQL Server Reporting Services running on the same server as your main SQL Server engine, don't install them. Likewise, because SQL Server Reporting Services no longer requires IIS, unless your server is also serving up web applications, ensure that IIS is not installed with your SQL Server.

On a related note, you'll sometimes see in the SQL Server 2008 literature a reference to "least privileged authority." This is the application of the principle of least privilege to reduce the surface area for SQL Server, separate operating system and SQL Server functions where possible, not automatically enable certain security groups with full access to SQL Server, and so on.

The term surface area is taken from the mathematical concept of surface area but is used in the security realm to describe what is attackable or accessible in an application or system. For instance, if a Windows server has SQL Server and IIS installed, those two applications represent attackable points of the server. Compared to a server that has neither installed, it could be said that all else being equal, the server with SQL Server and IIS has a greater surface area than the second server.

The CIA Triad

Another security concept you should use for your planning is called the CIA triad (see Figure 9-1).

When talking about security, especially data security, the following three areas are core principles of our goals:

❑ **Confidentiality:** Data is not accessed by unauthorized people or in an unauthorized way.

❑   **Integrity:** Data is not modified by unauthorized people or in an unauthorized way.

❑   **Availability:** Data is available whenever needed by authorized people.

Figure 9-1

How you protect and lock down your SQL Servers affects all three principles. Confidentiality and integrity are logical when dealing with data. Availability, however, is also crucial to security. Inaccessible data doesn't do anyone any good, so your configuration must reflect how your customers will access the data. If this means putting a SQL Server in mixed mode so a web server can connect, this meets the availability principle.

Defense in Depth

Defense in depth is a relatively simple concept: When possible, use different security mechanisms to protect an asset so that should a single mechanism fail, additional safeguards are in place. For instance, consider your work PC. The following mechanisms are likely in place to protect your PC from some of the malicious attacks that might originate from the Internet:

❑   External router at the perimeter.

❑   Firewall at the perimeter.

❑   Personal firewall on the PC itself.

❑   Anti-virus software running on the PC.

❑   Patch management methodology and deployment software.

For instance, imagine a new attack using the NetBIOS protocol. NetBIOS is a standard communications means for PCs that must trust one another on a LAN or a WAN. It's not something that should be received from the Internet. Therefore, both the external router and the firewall should prevent NetBIOS traffic coming from the Internet. Your PC's personal firewall should realize that the IP address doesn't match the trusted network your PC resides on and prevent the traffic. Failing that, if Microsoft has released a security patch for the vulnerability being attacked, that patch management methodology and deployment software will have deployed the patch and updated your PC. Even if that didn't happen, once the attack is known, definitions downloaded by your anti-virus software should recognize the attack and stop it in its tracks.

Because five levels of protection are in place against this one type of attack, its chances of succeeding are extremely low. It would take the catastrophic failure of all five levels in order for your PC to become a victim of the attack.

Types of Attackers

When talking about attackers, there are typically three types to consider. The first are the merely curious. They poke around because they can. However, when they start hitting any sort of security, they stop. They aren't interested in breaking security for gain, they just want to "know what's behind the door." These represent the majority of folks. Good security practices quickly serve as a deterrent against this type of "attacker." The second are opportunistic, looking for low-hanging fruit (i.e., systems that are relatively easy to get into). With solid security practices, you deter them because they are looking for a payoff with minimal effort. Those of the third type are malicious, focused on breaking into your system. They will bring whatever resources they can to bear. If they are knowledgeable enough and persistent enough, they'll get through each layer of your security until they break through.

It is for this third type that monitoring and auditing really pay for themselves. Monitoring notifies you of suspicious activity. One little slip by the attacker and you're alerted that something is going on. This gives you the opportunity to catch them or shut them down entirely. Auditing helps you identify what the intruder accessed in the event that an attack was successful. Monitoring and auditing may also lead you to the attackers after the fact. Never neglect these aspects of a security architecture.

Creating a Secure Configuration

You could do everything right within the database to secure your organization's data, but if there are holes in the operating system or in the SQL Server configuration, an attacker can still get in and out with the data you've worked so hard to protect. Therefore, securely configuring your SQL Server's surface is critical to the overall security posture of your data. This section begins by looking at the new security features in SQL Server 2008, and then takes a look at how to deploy SQL Server securely, starting with the operating system.

New Security Features in SQL Server 2008

While SQL Server 2008 was intended to be more of an incremental upgrade from SQL Server 2005 than SQL Server 2005 was to SQL Server 2000, DBAs should take advantage of several new security features and enhancements to existing features in this release:

- ❑   Kerberos authentication through more than TCP/IP.
- ❑   Encryption enhancements:

  - ❑   Transparent data encryption
  - ❑   Extensible key management

- ❑   Auditing enhancements through the new `Audit` object.
- ❑   Security and surface area configuration through Policy-Based Management.

If you're familiar with SQL Server 2005's Surface Area Configuration (SAC) tool, that last enhancement may have caused a raised eyebrow. The Surface Area Configuration tool is not part of SQL Server 2008. Policy-Based Management handles all of the functions that SAC used to but enables you to apply them consistently across your SQL Server inventory by exporting and importing settings, rather than setting them manually per server. Chapter 10 covers Policy-Based Management in detail.

Operating System Security

In larger organizations, SQL Server DBAs aren't typically responsible for the overall server security where their SQL Servers run. However, even if you're among those who don't have that responsibility, you should look for several general things to ensure that the system administrators who support you are taking appropriate measures to secure the operating system (OS). While SQL Server interacts very closely with the OS, let's first look at those areas of Windows that you should consider unrelated to SQL Server itself, starting with security patches.

Patch Management

In July 2008, Microsoft announced the first security patches for SQL Server since July 2003. Called MS08-040, they applied to both SQL Server 2000 and SQL Server 2005. However, Microsoft rated the bulletin Important, not Critical. In the intervening five years between security vulnerability announcements, numerous operating system patches have been rated Critical. Therefore, the greatest vulnerability, with respect to the area of patch management, is likely going to come from an operating system lagging behind on security patches. Therefore, verify that your organization has a procedure for patch management and that it is properly and consistently followed. Subscribe to blogs such as the Microsoft Security Response Center blog (www.microsoft.com/security/msrc/) to remain aware of security threats related to reported vulnerabilities in order to determine how important a particular security update may be.

If you also wear the hat of the system administrator, you have an even greater responsibility to stay current. Attackers are now able to determine in a matter of days or even hours, via reverse engineering, what changes have been made in security updates. Because of the increased threat, Microsoft has made things relatively easy for the administrator with Automatic Updates built into the operating system. If you're not keen on receiving a patch as soon as it is released or if you need to track multiple servers for compliance, tools such as Windows Server Update Services (WSUS), which is free, enable you to manage patches, including when they are approved for deployment. By using Group Policy or by deploying the appropriate registry settings, you can control your servers to ensure they check in with your WSUS server and pull and deploy patches according to the schedule you define.

Administrators Group Management

Even though SQL Server 2008 does not add the BUILTIN\Administrators group to SQL Server with sysadmin rights, as in previous versions, the members of the local Administrators group for the server ultimately have a lot of control over SQL Server and can potentially affect availability, that third principle of the CIA triad, even if you have diligently restricted their access to the data. They have the capability to alter security, especially on local groups and NTFS locations, the importance of which is covered shortly. They also have the capability to stop and start services, including those related to SQL Server. In addition, they can override their access by starting SQL Server in single-user mode (though this would require bringing SQL Server down first), thereby violating confidentiality.

As a result, it's important to know who is a member of the local Administrators group on your SQL Servers. If you are charged with maintaining this group, ensure that only the people who need such rights are made members. Following the principle of least privilege is especially crucial in this area. You can verify who is a member of the Administrators group by using the Computer Management console (under Administrative Tools). Figure 9-2 shows an example of the members of the Administrators group being displayed using this tool.

> *To use Computer Management to connect to a server remotely, right-click Computer Management (Local) in the left pane (as shown in the background of Figure 9-2) and choose "Connect to another computer" from the pop-up menu.*

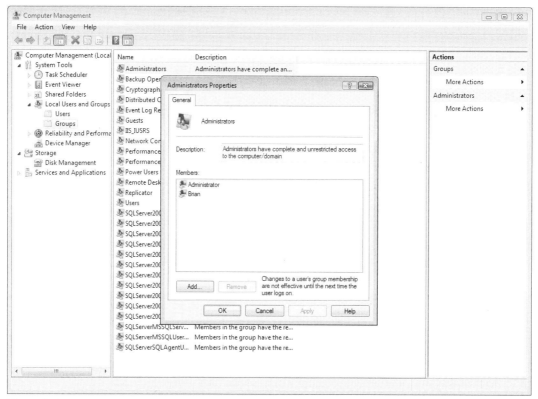

Figure 9-2

Managing Other Local Groups

Other groups you'll want to be concerned with are the Users group and the Remote Desktop Users group. The first, Users, typically determines who has local logon rights for the system. Usually you will see NT Authority\Authenticated Users. This corresponds to anyone the server can verify — in other words, any local users, any domain users, and any domain users from trusted domains. Remote Desktop Users is empty by default and unless you have a compelling reason to change this (e.g., you have DBAs who aren't granted local Administrative rights but who still need to manage SQL Server on the server), keep it that way. Administrators already have the capability to use Remote Desktop because of a setting within the Local Security Policy.

The reason to monitor who is a member of these groups is that someone who can log on locally or through remote desktop to your server has taken a giant step toward compromising your SQL Server, even if that person is able to log on without administrative rights. Typically, attackers try to get a login, any login, with access to a server and then proceed from there. The attacker will do reconnaissance and, if possible, attempt to do privilege escalation on an account or set of rights that allows the attacker some sort of administrative permissions over the system.

Looking at this from a patch management perspective, Microsoft tends to rate an operating system security patch as critical if a remote exploit is possible. However, it's not usual to see Microsoft rate a patch as important if there's only a local exploit or privilege escalation vulnerability. That's because it is assumed that you have adequately protected the ability to log on locally.

If you haven't guessed already, this is why security experts put such an emphasis on physical security. A user who can't get to the server can't log on locally. As a result, the local exploit that would allow such a user to gain administrative privileges can't be executed; and if you've taken care of physical security, the next step is to look at who has remote desktop access, because those local exploits tend to work through Remote Desktop, meaning you have to keep a careful eye on users who have the capability to connect to your server in such a manner.

Local Security Policy

The Local Security Policy snap-in, also found under Administrative Tools, shows and allows the configuration of security settings for the server. These settings should be of particular interest to the SQL Server DBA or system administrator supporting SQL Server because they control who can log on or connect to the server and how, who can shut down the server, and who can perform a couple of tasks that have some significant security ramifications.

> *On servers that are members of an Active Directory domain, some of these settings may not be changeable from the Local Security Policy snap-in. That's because those settings are affected by one or more Group Policies, which are policies set and stored at the Active Directory level. However, the Local Security Policy tool enables you to see those settings.*

Figure 9-3 shows the Local Security Policy snap-in. The policies you should monitor can be found by selecting Security Settings ➪ Local Policies ➪ User Rights Assignment.

Here is the list of policies to be checked periodically:

- ❑ Act as part of the operating system
- ❑ Allow log on locally
- ❑ Allow log on through Terminal Services
- ❑ Debug programs
- ❑ Deny log on locally
- ❑ Deny log on through Terminal Services
- ❑ Force shutdown from a remote system
- ❑ Shut down the system

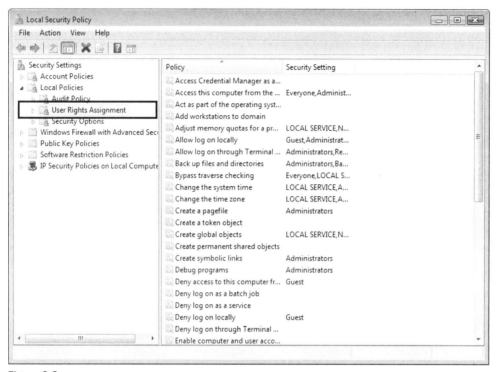

Figure 9-3

Let's look at the policies in more detail. You'll find them in the right pane of the Local Security Policy window. In cases where two policies are complementary, such as "Allow log on locally" and "Deny log on locally," they are combined because they must be considered together.

Act as part of the operating system

This right allows a user to impersonate another user without actually authenticating. That first user can then access all of the resources to which the second user has permission without the requisite user name/password check that would normally be expected. In Windows 2000, SQL Server needed this right, but in Windows XP and later it does not. In Windows 2000, this right was required if any user impersonation were to take place — hence the reason SQL Server needed it. In later versions of the operating system this is no longer required, so you should never see this populated on your SQL Server 2008 systems.

Allow log on locally/Deny log on locally

This policy permits what it says: logging on locally. Typically you'll see Guest, Administrators, Users, and Backup Operators permitted via this option, but then you'll see Guest in the Deny policy. All of these are local to the system and with the exception of Guest are groups whose membership you need to determine if you want to know exactly who has these rights. Solid physical security, as discussed earlier, ensures that not just any Tom, Dick, or Harriet can log on to your server and begin plying attacks against it from the benefit of the console.

Allow log on through Terminal Services/Deny log on through Terminal Services

This policy permits remote desktop connections for the users and groups listed. By default, you should see only Administrators and Remote Desktop Users here. This policy shouldn't be changed because any groups that need access should be made a member of the Remote Desktop Users group.

The Remote Desktop Users group is a special group that first appeared in Windows Server 2003. In Windows 2000, unless the server was set up in a special mode called Terminal Services in Application Mode, only members of the Administrators group could connect remotely. Application Mode introduces other complexities (e.g., additional licensing, additional steps for installing applications, etc.) and is intended for environments such as Citrix XenApp (formerly Citrix Presentation Server) where many users log on concurrently and run applications interactively on the server. Microsoft realized that there would be cases in which users need to connect to a server remotely but full administrative rights shouldn't be given, and where a server should not be configured in Application Mode. As a result, they created the Remote Desktop Users group. Administrators automatically have remote access through Remote Desktop, so you never need to place them in this special group. If you have cases where other users need such access, such as if your DBAs need Remote Desktop access to the servers on which SQL Server is installed, but the DBAs aren't local members of the local Administrators group, you can do that by ensuring that their Windows user accounts or Windows security groups containing their accounts are made members of the Remote Desktop Users group.

Debug programs

This policy permits a named user to connect a debugger to a process (such as the SQL Server service) or the kernel. This would allow, for instance, such a user to look at the memory contents of the process. Given the case of data within SQL Server, for example, a user granted this right would be allowed to look at the unencrypted data, thereby bypassing the encryption mechanisms intended to protect that data. By default, only the Administrators group is named, and this shouldn't change without a very strong reason. In production, no other groups or users should be added.

Force shutdown from a remote system/Shut down the system

This policy affects availability. A user who can bring the system down can render your SQL Server unavailable. Force shutdown from a remote system defaults to only Administrators. Shut down the system corresponds to who can shut down the system once logged on, and by default that list is Administrators, Backup Operators, and Users. Again, these defaults shouldn't be altered unless you have a compelling reason. One example would be if you have an operations group that doesn't have administrative rights. That may be a case to expand Force shutdown from a remote system. However, this is probably better done through a Group Policy Object (GPO) at the Active Directory level, rather than by touching individual servers.

Operating System Security and SQL Server

SQL Server 2008 is very specific with respect to how it interacts with Windows. Understanding what groups SQL Server uses and how they are used, the NTFS permissions on the various directories and files, and the rights needed by each service is important if you want to create as secure an installation as possible.

SQL Server–Related Security Groups

SQL Server 2008, like SQL Server 2005, uses security groups for file and registry permissions (with the exception of clustered SQL Servers on Windows Server 2008). Where the use of groups differs between

SQL Server 2005 and SQL Server 2008 is that in SQL Server 2008, these groups are only used for operating system operations (going back to that principle of least privilege). In SQL Server 2005, they were granted access into SQL Server as logins. Now the appropriate service account may be granted access, but the entire group is not granted access by default.

The groups related to the Database Engine are shown in the following table.

Service	Group Naming Convention
SQL Server	Default Instance: SQLServerMSSQLUser$*ComputerName*$MSSQLServer Named Instance: SQLServerMSSQLUser$*ComputerName*$*InstanceName*
SQL Server Agent	Default Instance: SQLServerSQLAgentUser$*ComputerName*$MSSQLServer Named Instance: SQLServerSQLAgentUser$*ComputerName*$*InstanceName*
Full-Text Search [if installed]	Default Instance: SQLServerFDHostUser$*ComputerName*$MSSQL10.MSSQLServer Named Instance: SQLServerFDHostUser$*ComputerName*$MSSQL10.*InstanceName*
SQL Server Browser	All Instances: SQLServerSQLBrowserUser$*ComputerName*
SQL Server Active Directory Helper	All Instances: SQLServerMSSQLServerADHelperUser$*ComputerName*

On a Windows XP/2003 installation, the appropriate service account will be a member of the security group; but for Windows Vista/Server 2008, because of service isolation, the service security identifier (SID), not the service account, is a member. You'll learn more about this in the next section, "Service Isolation in Windows Vista/Server 2008."

If you're dealing with a Windows Server 2003 cluster, you need to create domain groups for the services you are installing on the cluster. For instance, if you're installing only the Database Engine, you need a group for the SQL Server service and for the SQL Server Agent service. If you're also installing Analysis Services and Full-Text Search, you need separate groups for those services as well. Windows Server 2008 does not require the domain security groups for a clustered instance.

Service Isolation in Windows Vista/Server 2008

Starting with the Longhorn kernels, Windows services have their own SIDs, which can be used to grant or deny permissions against. The reason for this is simple: It ensures that just because two services happen to share the same service account, they cannot arbitrarily access each other's resources. Consider the case in which you have two SQL Server instances running on the same system. For convenience, both are running under the same domain user account. In prior versions of the operating system and/or prior versions of SQL Server, that domain user account would have access to the data files of both instances. That was the only option possible given the shared service account.

In SQL Server 2008 running on Windows Vista or Server 2008, that's no longer the case. The service itself can be assigned permissions, meaning the first instance, though running under the same service account as the second instance, can't access the second instance's data files. This is because SQL Server 2008 running on these operating systems isn't assigning the permission against the service account but rather against the service itself, albeit indirectly. For example, Figure 9-4 shows a specific example of the SQL Server service group for the named instance SQL2008. Notice that the member of the group is NT Service\MSSQL$SQL2008, the SQL Server service name for the named instance. On your own systems you should see something similar, but the exact member depends on the instance name of the SQL Server installed on that particular system.

Figure 9-4

Service isolation increases security by ensuring that the services do not access each other's resources, but remember to apply the principle of defense in depth. Even with service isolation, you should still use separate service accounts if possible to provide an additional layer of security.

SQL Server–Related Folders

With SQL Server 2005, Microsoft focused on increasing the file system security of the folders that SQL Server uses, and SQL Server 2008 is no different. The following table shows the different folders and what permissions are typically granted to them.

Folder	NTFS Permissions
Backup	Administrators *(Full Control)* CREATOR OWNER *(Full Control — subfolders and files only)* SQL Server service group *(Full Control)* SYSTEM *(Full Control)*
Binn	*(inherited from MSSQL parent folder)* Administrators *(Full Control)* CREATOR OWNER *(Full Control — subfolders and files only)* SQL Server service group *(Read and Execute)* SYSTEM *(Full Control)* Users *(Read and Execute)*

Folder	NTFS Permissions
DATA	Administrators *(Full Control)* CREATOR OWNER *(Full Control — subfolders and files only)* SQL Server service group *(Full Control)* SYSTEM *(Full Control)***Note:** *Data files themselves will have only the permissions for the Administrators and SQL Server service groups.*
FTData [if Full Text installed]	Administrators *(Full Control)* CREATOR OWNER *(Full Control — subfolders and files only)* SQL Server service group *(Full Control)* SYSTEM *(Full Control)*
Install	*(inherited from MSSQL parent folder)* Administrators *(Full Control)* CREATOR OWNER *(Full Control — subfolders and files only)* SQL Server service group *(Read and Execute)* SYSTEM *(Full Control)* Users *(Read and Execute)*
JOBS	Administrators *(Full Control)* CREATOR OWNER *(Full Control — subfolders and files only)* SQL Server Agent service group *(Full Control)* SYSTEM *(Full Control)*
Log	Administrators *(Full Control)* CREATOR OWNER *(Full Control — subfolders and files only)* Full Text service group *(if installed — List Folder/Read Data, Create Files/Write Data)* SQL Server Agent service group *(everything except Full Control, Delete [Folder], Change Permissions, and Take Ownership)* SQL Server service group *(Full Control)* SYSTEM *(Full Control)*
repldata [if applicable]	Administrators *(Full Control)* CREATOR OWNER *(Full Control — subfolders and files only)* SQL Server service group *(Full Control)* SYSTEM *(Full Control)*
Upgrade	*(inherited from MSSQL parent folder)* Administrators *(Full Control)* CREATOR OWNER *(Full Control — subfolders and files only)* SQL Server service group *(Read and Execute)* SYSTEM *(Full Control)* Users *(Read and Execute)*

The permissions specified are the minimum necessary for SQL Server to run and be supported. Therefore, although the folder permissions can be altered, you should not do so without good reason. An example scenario would be that of a SQL Server Agent job copying a backup file to a different location. In this situation, altering the Backup folder to allow read access to the SQL Server Agent service group would be appropriate.

Securing Data and Log Files

In SQL Server 2005, changing the permissions on the DATA folder had no effect on the data files that SQL Server placed within the folder. DBAs who attempted to gear processes around altered folder permissions found that SQL Server enforced a strict set of permissions on the individual files. SQL Server does this by breaking the permissions inheritance, meaning the data files do not acquire the permissions of the folder they are in. SQL Server assigns a specific set of permissions to each data file under its control: The Administrators group and local SQL Server service group are both granted Full Control, but no other permissions are granted..

Just as in SQL Server 2005, if a user altered the file permissions, SQL Server will change those permissions back the first time it accesses the data file after the permission change.

That said, it is still best to ensure that folder permissions are as restrictive as possible, as is the case with the DATA folder. If SQL Server is ever stopped, the permissions on the files could be changed by anyone who has Full Control rights over the folder. In fact, even if they don't have rights, if they are able to take ownership of the files, once they take ownership they could set the permissions to whatever they want. This effectively bypasses SQL Server's attempts to protect the files because SQL Server wouldn't be running and accessing the files at the time.

SQL Server 2008 does have a solution for situations like this when the data is "at rest," called Transparent Data Encryption (TDE), covered later in the chapter. However, TDE should not be relied upon exclusively to protect data files. Proper folder permissions are a must as well. Remember the security principle of defense in depth. If an attacker were to successfully disable TDE without your knowledge, those folder permissions, which provide an additional layer of security, could prevent the attacker from gaining access to the data files themselves even though the attacker succeeded in bypassing one of your security measures.

Securing Backup Files

Unlike data files, SQL Server does not alter the permissions on backup files. Wherever SQL Server creates a backup file, the new file inherits the permissions from the folder. Therefore, if the folder is insecure, the backup file will be vulnerable. Unless you're using a third-party product, or the database in question is protected using TDE, the data will be viewable to anyone who can read the backup file. Figure 9-5 shows an example of a backup from a database that does not have TDE enabled. If you look near the bottom of the image, you can see Test, Readable, No Security, and Backups. These are column values for one of the tables in the database that was backed up.

Although passwords on backups provide some security, they don't provide any sort of encryption. They exist solely to ensure that someone who doesn't know the password can't restore the backup. However, with a text or hex editor, an attacker could still extract the information from a backup file for malicious use, as Figure 9-5 demonstrates.

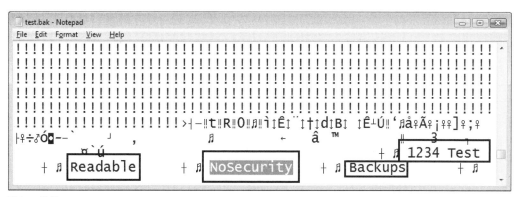

Figure 9-5

Using TDE on the database does ensure that the data in the backup is encrypted, just as it does for the data files. However, the advice is still the same: Ensure that the permissions on the folder(s) where you are storing your backups are as secure as possible. Again, practice defense in depth.

Surface Area Configuration

SQL Server 2005 introduced a new tool for DBAs called SQL Server Surface Area Configuration. It brought together into one place many of the features of SQL Server that a DBA would want to control in order to determine the security posture for a particular SQL Server. That's one of the problems with the tool: It works with one SQL Server instance at a time. For small shops with one or two SQL Servers, this isn't a big deal, but for large operations with many SQL Servers, the SQL Server Surface Area Configuration tool just wasn't efficient. Another problem with the tool is that it configured the settings once but there was no continuing enforcement. This meant that if someone made a change, such as enabling `xp_cmdshell` when it was originally disabled, there was no built-in and automated means to determine that the setting change had occurred and remedy the situation.

SQL Server 2008 strives to assist in managing either one server or many servers. As a result, the SQL Server Surface Area Configuration tool introduced in SQL Server 2005 is gone. Its function has been absorbed by *Policy-Based Management*, which is capable of checking and enforcing settings on one or many SQL Servers. Within Policy-Based Management, the facet to handle the aspects once managed by the SQL Server Surface Area Configuration tool is appropriately named Surface Area Configuration. Chapter 10 covers Policy-Based Management in detail.

Endpoints

Speaking of SQL Server surface area, let's talk about how to connect into SQL Server, a discussion that brings us to endpoints. An *endpoint* is simply a means of connecting to SQL Server. The term was introduced in SQL Server 2005 because this was the first version that gave us a lot of control over how connections could be made other than setting the protocols that were accepted.

Typical Endpoint Configuration

In most cases you will configure the protocols and, in the event of a TCP/IP endpoint, the port used. These are what are called TDS endpoints, because the Tabular Data Stream (TDS) protocol, the underlying communication protocol for SQL Server, is used to communicate with these endpoints. The SQL Server Configuration Manager handles the configuration of these TDS endpoints, of which there are four:

- ❑ Shared Memory
- ❑ Named Pipes
- ❑ TCP/IP
- ❑ VIA

You can see these endpoints within the SQL Server Configuration Manager by expanding SQL Server Network Configuration and clicking Protocols for *<Instance>* for the instance you want to manage (see Figure 9-6). The first option specifies whether or not you want to enable the protocol. Right-click the protocol in question and select Enable or Disable from the pop-up menu.

You can also set whether or not a protocol is enabled or disabled by selecting Properties from the pop-up menu or simply by double-clicking the protocol. The TCP/IP Properties dialog is shown in Figure 9-7. The Enabled option has a drop-down box from which you can simply select Yes or No.

If you need to configure the protocol in more detail, such as configuring the TCP port on which SQL Server will listen with respect to the TCP/IP protocol, simply click the IP Addresses tab. Figure 9-8 shows an example in which the TCP port has been statically set for port 5555 for all IP addresses.

Any endpoint changes that are made with regard to these protocols require the SQL Server service to be restarted. SQL Server reads the endpoint configuration only when the service first starts, so if you make a change, expect to receive an alert from the SQL Server Configuration Manager reminding you of this fact.

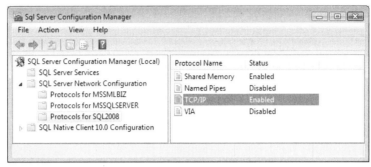

Figure 9-6

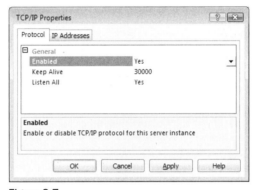

Figure 9-7

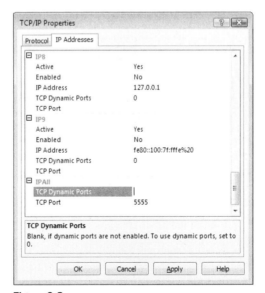

Figure 9-8

Other Endpoints

SQL Server 2008 also supports endpoints for database mirroring, Service Broker, and HTTP access. Endpoints for database mirroring and Service Broker are covered in detail in their respective chapters (Chapters 8 and 17). HTTP access is typically used to support the Simple Object Access Protocol (SOAP) and the concept of web services or native XML services. If you're not familiar with SOAP, SOAP uses XML to exchange messages, typically over the HTTP protocol. However, as of SQL Server 2008, HTTP/SOAP endpoints are considered deprecated.

Windows Authentication Changes in SQL Server 2008

Microsoft Windows 2000 introduced a new security protocol called Kerberos into the Windows environment. Prior to Windows 2000, the primary security protocol was NT LAN Manager (NTLM). Kerberos replaced it because it offered enhancements that raised the overall security level, such as time stamping and server verification. If a system is in an Active Directory domain, Kerberos authentication is possible (a Windows domain controller is required). Both SQL Server 2000 and SQL Server 2005 support the Kerberos protocol, albeit indirectly. They use the Windows Security Support Provider Interface (SSPI) to handle all Windows authentication. SSPI attempts to use Kerberos first and if that fails, it defaults to NTLM. However, even with off-loading Windows authentication in this manner to SSPI, SQL Server 2000 and SQL Server 2005 supported only Kerberos authentication for TCP/IP traffic.

In SQL Server 2008, Kerberos authentication support is also possible for the Named Pipes and Shared Memory protocols. Given the increased security due to using Kerberos over NTLM, Kerberos is recommended wherever possible. However, in order for Kerberos authentication to work, a *service principal name (SPN)* must be correctly configured in Active Directory. An SPN identifies the service in question so that when a client attempts to verify the server, the client finds the matching information in Active Directory. If the SPN is missing or incorrect, then the client won't use Kerberos to authenticate against the server.

In order for SQL Server to be able to create the SPN automatically, the SQL Server service must be running under a built-in account such as SYSTEM or NETWORK SERVICE, or it must be a member of the Domain Admins group in the Active Directory domain. Generally, however, the SQL Server service should run under a local or domain user account. In these cases, the SPN must be registered manually by a member of the Domain Admins group.

> *Manual SPN configuration is not typically the responsibility of a DBA, so it is outside the scope of this book. You can find instructions for setting up the SPN properly in Books Online or in the KB article "How to Use Kerberos Authentication in SQL Server." There is also an excellent white paper, "Troubleshooting Kerberos," on the Microsoft site that aids in any problems you might encounter. See* `http://technet.microsoft.com/en-us/library/cc728430.aspx`.

Identity and Access Control

Now that you understand the operating system configuration, how SQL Server uses the operating system security, the surface area configuration of SQL Server, and how to communicate with SQL Server via endpoints, it's time to talk about authenticating against SQL Server itself.

Quite simply, logins, as they are traditionally called, permit one to connect to SQL Server. Starting with SQL Server 2005, Microsoft began using the term *server principal* because of some confusion over the word *user*. In SQL Server nomenclature, *user* means a security principal within a database. In other words, for a particular database, if a login has access, it is mapped to a user. However, we tend to use the word user to refer to a person (such as an end-user) or a Windows user account. In an attempt to clear things up, Microsoft began using the term "server principals" where we would traditionally use the word "logins," and "database principals" where we would use the word "users."

> *You'll still see the older terms used. In fact, the T-SQL language uses* LOGIN *and* USER *to manage server and database principals, respectively.*

If you're still struggling over the difference between a login (server principal) and a user (database principal), imagine SQL Server as a building, perhaps a shopping mall, that requires a key for entrance. Logins are the equivalent of that key. Inside the mall, each individual store is locked and secured by its owner. If you have a key to open a particular store, then that key is a user for the database. Having a key to get into the mall doesn't mean you automatically have access to all of the stores within it.

Server Principals/Logins

We've established that logins allow you to connect to SQL Server. There are effectively three types of logins or server principals:

❑ Windows domain login

❑ Windows local login

❑ SQL Server login

A Windows domain or local login could refer to a particular Windows user, a Windows computer account (domain-level only), or a Windows security group.

Windows Authentication versus SQL Server Authentication

Though we've made a distinction between Windows domain and local logins, effectively there are two methods of authentication with respect to SQL Server: Windows authentication and SQL Server authentication. Windows authentication is the most secure solution for most environments, if you have the luxury of using this type of authentication. With Windows authentication, you grant the rights to the database to the Windows login. Where possible, Windows groups instead of individual Windows users should be used. This way, you create the login and assign rights only a single time, and the group delegates the user administration to the Active Directory administrator. This will simplify compliance with laws such as Sarbanes-Oxley because access to the database is controlled through a single mechanism.

The best thing about Windows authentication is that users have a single user name and password to remember. When users want to log in to the database, their Windows credentials are passed to the server automatically, so they are never prompted for a user name and password. Additionally, the domain policies that you set up for changing the user's login and lockouts apply automatically for SQL Server. You could also use domain policies to lock out the user during certain hours.

Conversely, there are some drawbacks to using Windows authentication. If your server is in a different domain than your users and the two domains don't trust each other, then you have to use SQL Server authentication. Another example is when you have a client, such as a web application, that is in a work-group. This is a common scenario for web servers that face the Internet. As of SQL Server 2005, SQL Server authentication enables you to lock out logins and force users to change their passwords. This is called *password policy enforcement*, and SQL Server will follow the password policy set on the system on which it is installed. If the SQL Server resides on a domain computer, that password policy is likely being passed down via a Group Policy object. You can check the existing password policy by looking in the Local Security Policy.

Creating the Login

To create a login in the Management Studio interface, connect to the server to which you wish to add the login click the Security group. Right-click on Logins and select New Login.

In SQL Server Management Studio for SQL Server 2005, you had only the options for Windows or SQL Server authentication. In SQL Server 2005, two more radio buttons are added: Mapped to Certificate and Mapped to Asymmetric Key. We'll look at those two new options in a bit under Logins with Certificates/Asymmetric Keys.

If you want Windows authentication, type the Windows local or domain user account name or the group to which you wish to grant access. Type the domain name first and then the user or group name, separated by a backslash, like this: *<DomainName>\<AccountName>*. Alternatively, you can search for the login by clicking Search. If you wish to add a SQL Server authenticated login, just select that radio button and type the login name and password.

> *Remember that passwords are case sensitive in SQL Server but user names aren't unless the SQL Server was installed with a case-sensitive collation. By default, SQL Server uses case-insensitive collations and therefore user names aren't case sensitive.*

If you have chosen to use SQL Server authentication, as shown in Figure 9-9, you have the option to enforce password policies and expiration. You can also force users to change their password the first time they connect. If you check Enforce Password Policy, the result varies based on the operating system that you have installed. This checkbox enforces the policy using the `NetValidatePasswordPolicy` API, which ensures that the password meets the following criteria by default:

❑ It must not contain all or part of the login name.

❑ It must be at least eight characters long.

❑ It must contain three of the following strong password options:

    ❑ Uppercase letters

    ❑ Lowercase letters

    ❑ Numbers 0–9

    ❑ Special characters such as ! or ^

In Windows XP, the criteria for passwords are weaker. The check ensures that your password is not blank and that it does not contain the login or computer name. The last check it makes ensures that your password does not contain any obvious words like "admin," "administrator," "password," "sa," or "sysadmin." If you type a weak password when setting up the login or when changing the password, you will receive the following error:

```
Msg 15118, Level 16, State 1, Line 1
Password validation failed. The password does not meet Windows policy requirements
because it is not complex enough.
```

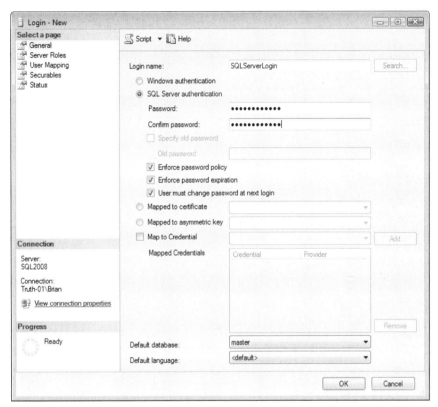

Figure 9-9

As a DBA, you can unlock a login by bringing up the status page for that login. The point of the account lockout feature is to deter hackers from performing a brute-force attack against your system whereby they work through a list of passwords, attempting to break yours. Previously in SQL Server 2000, you could log that you were being brute-force attacked but you couldn't do anything about it other than manually remove the login from access.

Back in the General page of the Login Properties screen, you can map a credential to the login. This is covered in more detail shortly (see the section on Credentials). However, if you have a credential already defined on the server, you can select it in the drop-down menu and then click Add to associate the credential with the login. In addition, you can set a default database for the login by selecting the database from the Default Database drop-down menu. Even though the default database is set to master by default, always make it a practice to change this database to the database in which the user spends most of his or her time. This makes it easier for your users, as they won't have to change databases after they log in to the server. It also helps keep clutter out of your master database. DBAs or users often connect to SQL Server and run a script that they think they're running against the proper database but in fact is running against the `master` database, potentially creating objects in that database by accident.

The downside to setting the database to something other than `master` is that if the login does not have access to the database you selected, the user will not be able to log in. For example, consider a user who connected by default to the database called `Reports`. If you were to delete the `Reports` database, or remove the user's access to the `Reports` database, that user would receive the following error:

```
Cannot connect to <instance name>
Cannot open user default database. Login failed.
Login failed for user '<user name>'. (Microsoft SQL Server, Error: 4064)
```

The last option on the General page is to set the login's default language; this will be set to the server's default language, but you can change that by selecting the new language from the drop-down box. This option essentially changes the error and informational messages that SQL Server returns to the user's native language (if available). The SQL Server tools will still have all their menus in English unless you have installed the multilingual SQL Server.

Defining Server Roles

Technically, you could click OK at this point and the login would be created. At this stage, though, the login has no rights to do anything in the SQL Server or in the database, as all you've provided is the key to the door. Click on the Server Roles page. Server roles give a user a right to perform a universal function across the entire server. For example, the `sysadmin` role is the equivalent of the "god" or "root" user. This role gives the user the rights to do anything he or she would like to do. If you have this option checked, there's no reason to check any other option because the `sysadmin` role trumps all other permissions, including explicit denial of rights. The accompanying table shows all the roles and the rights you give a user by checking each role.

Server Role	Rights Given
bulkadmin	Can run the BULK INSERT statement
dbcreator	Can create, alter, restore, and drop databases
diskadmin	Can manage the disk files
processadmin	Can terminate sessions connecting to your SQL Server
securityadmin	Can create logins and grant logins rights to a database. Can also reset passwords and alter the login.
serveradmin	Can shut down the SQL Server and alter the instance's configuration
setupadmin	Can add and remove linked servers
sysadmin	Can do anything on the server

Granting Database Rights

In the User Mappings page, you grant the login rights to the individual database. To do this, check each database to which you wish grant the login rights. Then, click the database role that you wish to give the user, if any. Once you check the database to assign the login rights to, the login is automatically granted access to the public role. The public role is a special role to which every user in the database belongs. As shown in Figure 9-10, when you assign the login rights to the database, user-defined roles appear in the role membership list below the list of databases, as in the role called Test. You'll learn much more about this in a moment when we cover roles. The list of system roles that appears gives users various rights to the database. As you check the database, you can also assign the user a default schema. This too is discussed later in this chapter in the "Users" section. The following table lists how these rights work.

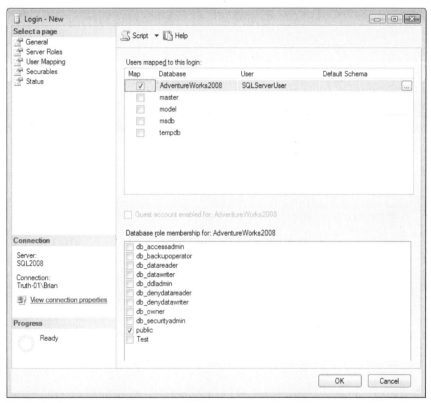

Figure 9-10

Database Role	Rights Given
db_accessadmin	Can add or remove access for a login
db_backupoperator	Can back up the specified database
db_datareader	Can read from every table in the database unless the access is explicitly denied
db_datawriter	Explicitly grants the user permission to run an UPDATE, DELETE, or INSERT statement for the database

Database Role	Rights Given
db_ddladmin	Can run any Data Definition Language (DDL) statement inside the database, including creating stored procedures or tables
db_denydatareader	Explicitly prevents the user from reading data
db_denydatawriter	Explicitly prevents the user from running an UPDATE, DELETE, or INSERT statement for the database
db_securityadmin	Can manage roles and permissions on objects
db_owner	Specifies a database administrator, who can perform any function

Defining Access to Server-Level Objects

Oftentimes, you need to delegate security to a login without giving overarching security such as sysadmin. For example, you may want a user to be able to run Profiler but not be a sysadmin, which you had to do in SQL Server 2000. You can do this in the Securables page of the Login dialog (shown in Figure 9-11), where you can secure to a very granular level on almost any type of server-level function that the login can perform.

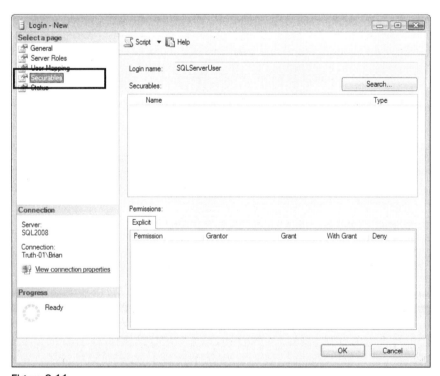

Figure 9-11

To grant or deny a login explicit rights, click Search and then select the type of object that you'd like to list in the bottom grid. For example, if you select All Objects of the Types, all securables will display. You could then check Grant or Deny to give rights to, or take rights away from, the login. You can also check With Grant. The With Grant option not only grants the login rights, but also allows the user to delegate those rights to someone else.

The Status Page

The final page is the Status page. On this page, you can unlock someone's login. You can also disable the login from accessing your system without having to delete the account. You cannot lockout someone's account as a sysadmin. This can be done only by the SQL Server instance. You can, however, unlock an account as a sysadmin by unchecking "Login is locked out."

Logins with T-SQL

Taking the same actions that you applied in Management Studio for creating a login, you can apply them by using T-SQL. It's often very important to know how to do these T-SQL commands in order to script a reproducible installation. Only the essential commands are covered in this section, rather than each minor detail. First, to create a login, use the CREATE LOGIN command, added in SQL Server 2005 to handle the additional options. To create a SQL Server authenticated login called LoginName, you can use the following syntax:

```
CREATE LOGIN LoginName WITH PASSWORD = 'StRonGPassWord1', CHECK_POLICY=ON,
CHECK_EXPIRATION=ON;
```

Ultimately, the CHECK_POLICY piece of this syntax (which checks the password's strength) is not required because it is on by default if not specified. The CHECK_EXPIRATION option, which enables the password to be expired, is not on by default and would be required if you wanted to enable the feature. To grant a Windows account access to your SQL Server, use the following syntax:

```
CREATE LOGIN [Domain\AccountName] FROM WINDOWS;
```

To add the login to a given server role, use the sp_addsrvrolemember stored procedure. The stored procedure accepts two parameters: the login name and the server role. The following example shows you how to add the login "MyLogin" to the sysadmin role:

```
EXEC sp_addsrvrolemember 'MyLogin', 'sysadmin';
```

Adding a login to a database role and a database as a user is discussed in the "Users" section of this chapter.

Another handy new function in SQL Server 2005 was the LOGINPROPERTY function. With this function, you can determine which properties are turned on for the given login. Developers can use these checks to build functionality into their applications to simplify the administration of an application's users. You can use the function with the following syntax:

```
LOGINPROPERTY ( 'login_name' ,
             { 'IsLocked' | 'IsExpired' | 'IsMustChange'
             | 'BadPasswordCount' | 'BadPasswordTime'
```

```
        | 'HistoryLength' | 'LockoutTime'
        | 'PasswordLastSetTime' | 'PasswordHash' }
```

For example, to determine whether the login name "MyLogin" must change passwords the next time he or she logs in, use the following code:

```
SELECT LOGINPROPERTY('MyLogin', 'IsMustChange');
```

If the login needed to be changed, a boolean 1 would be returned.

Understanding IDs and SIDs

When a login is created in SQL Server, behind the scenes it is assigned both an ID and a security ID (SID). For a Windows-based login, the SID comes from the SID of the account within Active Directory. For SQL Server–based logins, however, the ID and SID are generated by SQL Server. However, certain logins and fixed server roles have preassigned IDs and SIDs. For instance, the original sa account always as an ID of 1 and a SID of 0x01. You can see the IDs and SIDs for logins by executing the following query:

```
SELECT name, principal_id, sid
FROM sys.server_principals;
```

Within the database, you again have IDs and SIDs. If the database principal/user corresponds to a SQL Server login, then the SID in the database will match the SID for the login. As with logins, there are pre-created users and roles that have default IDs. For instance, the dbo user always has an ID of 1. The SIDs may be different, however. For instance, the SID for dbo always matches the login that owns the database. Therefore, if the original sa account owns the database, you'll see a SID of 0x01. You can see the IDs and SIDs for users in a particular database by running the following query in that database:

```
SELECT name, principal_id, sid
FROM sys.database_principals;
```

Logins with Certificates/Asymmetric Keys

In the discussion about creating a login we mentioned that you could assign a certificate or asymmetric key to a login using the GUI in Management Studio. This represents a change from SQL Server 2005. The reason to assign a certificate or asymmetric key is to perform code signing. At the present time, SQL Server does not support the use of a certificate or asymmetric key to connect to the server itself. If you wish to assign a certificate or asymmetric key to a login, the certificate or key must be present in the master database. Certificates and asymmetric keys in any other database are not usable in this manner.

The Security Hierarchy

Security can be confusing when you have a conflict between a explicit denial of rights conflicting with an explicit grant of rights. Granting access to an object or a role gives the user rights to a database unless the user has been denied that same access. The main point is that a denial of access always outweighs a grant of access, with the exception of the sysadmin role at a server. The other type of right that you can perform is a *revoke*. Revoke essentially removes any rights (grant or deny) from the user and is a neutral position.

For example, suppose that John has a login into SQL Server called DomainName\John. He is also a part of an Active Directory group called Accounting. John has been granted access to the Salary table, but the Accounting group has explicitly been denied access to that table. In this scenario, he would be denied access to the table. The following table takes this example a bit further and shows you what combinations of permissions would result in denial of access.

Accounting Group	John	Effective Rights for John
Granted access to table	Denied access to table	Denied
Denied access to table	Granted access to table	Denied
db_datareader	No rights	Read access to all tables
db_datawriter	db_denydatareader	Can write but not read
db_denydatareader	db_owner	Can do anything except read
db_denydatareader	sysadmin	Can do anything on server
Sysadmin	Denied all access from tables	Can do anything on server

In addition, note that a user granted rights to the db_datareader database role will not have rights to any stored procedures or functions. Typically, if you grant a user access to stored procedures, that user will not need access to the underlying tables — "typically" is used here because there are exceptions to the rule. The main exception is the case of dynamic queries inside the stored procedure. In that case, you need to grant access to the underlying tables. The way around this from a security perspective is context switching, covered momentarily.

BUILTIN\Administrators Login

Another special type of login that could pose some security issues for you is the BUILTIN\Administrators login. In prior versions of SQL Server this login was granted implicit sysadmin rights to your database server. This meant that anyone in the local Administrators group for the Windows machine had complete control over the SQL Server. As of SQL Server 2008, if you want BUILTIN\Administrators as a valid login to SQL Server, you must either add it during installation (in which case it will be a member of the sysadmin role) or grant it access manually later.

In some environments, having BUILTIN\Administrators with this level of access may be fine, but in most environments you don't want someone who is a Windows administrator to have access to sensitive data, such as salary information. This creates a challenge if you're trying to become HIPAA- or Sarbanes-Oxley–compliant too, as you have someone who was not explicitly given rights to become a sysadmin on your system. Also, keep in mind the principle of least privilege. In most cases, a system administrator will not need this sort of privilege within SQL Server. Therefore, if the principle is adhered to, only the rights needed will be granted.

If this is a problem for you, you're better off not adding the login. If it's present and you want to drop it, ensure that the SQL Server service accounts have a login to SQL Server, and have been given sysadmin rights. How these logins are granted access depends on your operating system. If you're running on Windows Vista or Windows Server 2008, you'll see the NT SERVICE\ <Service Name> specified. If you're running on Windows XP or Windows Server 2003, the service account for the service should be present. This differs from SQL Server 2005, which used the groups.

Granting Profiler Access

In SQL Server 2000, you had to be a sysadmin to use the Profiler application. This created a bottleneck for DBAs because that access was not granted lightly, and Profiler was sometimes the only tool that could be used to debug certain problems. Starting with SQL Server 2005, you can allow a login access to create a Profiler trace without having to give high-level authority by granting the user ALTER TRACE rights in the Securables page. You can also use the following syntax to grant them the right:

```
GRANT ALTER TRACE TO [LoginName]
```

Credentials

Credentials typically are used to map a SQL Server authenticated account to a Windows account. You can also use this feature to give an account access to items outside the SQL Server instance, such as a file share. This is used often in SQL CLR and, most importantly, to allow SSIS packages to impersonate Windows accounts when running. This is all done through setting up proxy accounts.

You can create a credential through Management Studio or through T-SQL. To create a credential in Management Studio, right-click on the Credentials folder in the Security tree and select New Credential. In the New Credential dialog, type a name for the credential, as shown in Figure 9-12, and select which Windows identity you'd like that credential to impersonate. Finally, type the password to protect the credential.

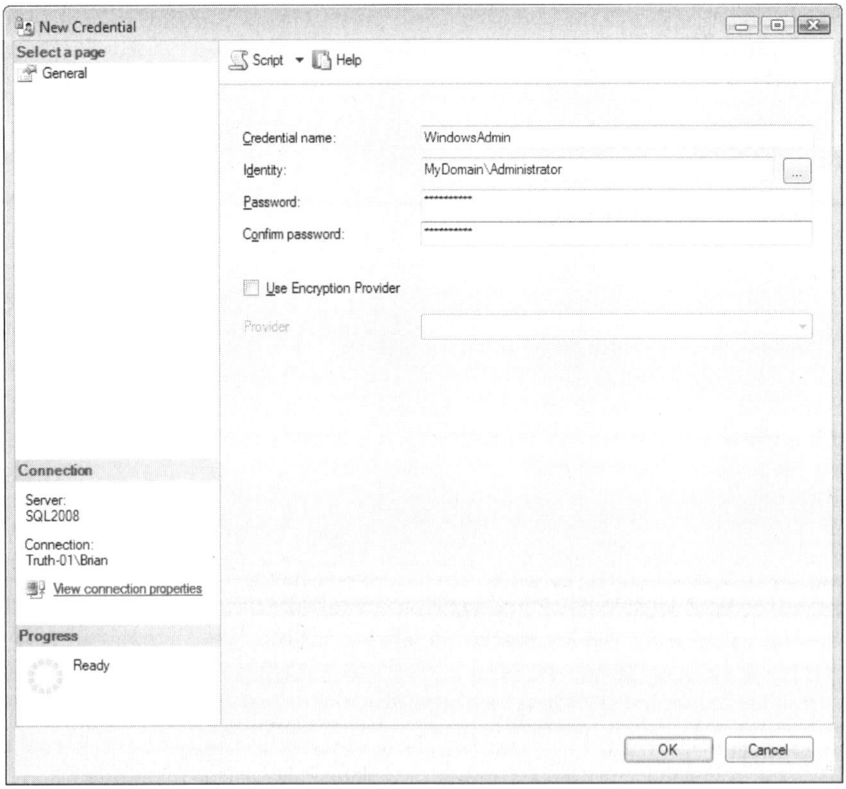

Figure 9-12

In T-SQL, use the CREATE CREDENTIAL T-SQL command to create a new credential. The IDENTITY keyword specifies which Windows account you wish to map the credential to, and the SECRET keyword specifies the password. To create the same credential created in Figure 9-12, use the following syntax:

```
CREATE CREDENTIAL [WindowsAdmin]
WITH IDENTITY = N'MyDomain\Administrator',
SECRET = N'password'
```

Users

When a login is granted access to a database, a user is created in the database with the same name as the login by default. The user is given specific rights to database roles or to granular objects inside the database, such as EXECUTE rights on a stored procedure. One method to create a user that was shown earlier was through the Login Properties dialog. In that dialog, you can go to the User Mappings page to check the databases to which you wish to add login and which roles you wish to assign to the user.

A person who's assigned to the db_owner database role in a database would not have access to the Login Properties dialog, though, unless he or she were a member of a specific server role, like sysadmin. The alternative way to do this that most DBAs prefer is to go to the individual database, right-click on the Users folder under Security, and select New User. The dialog shown in Figure 9-13 appears.

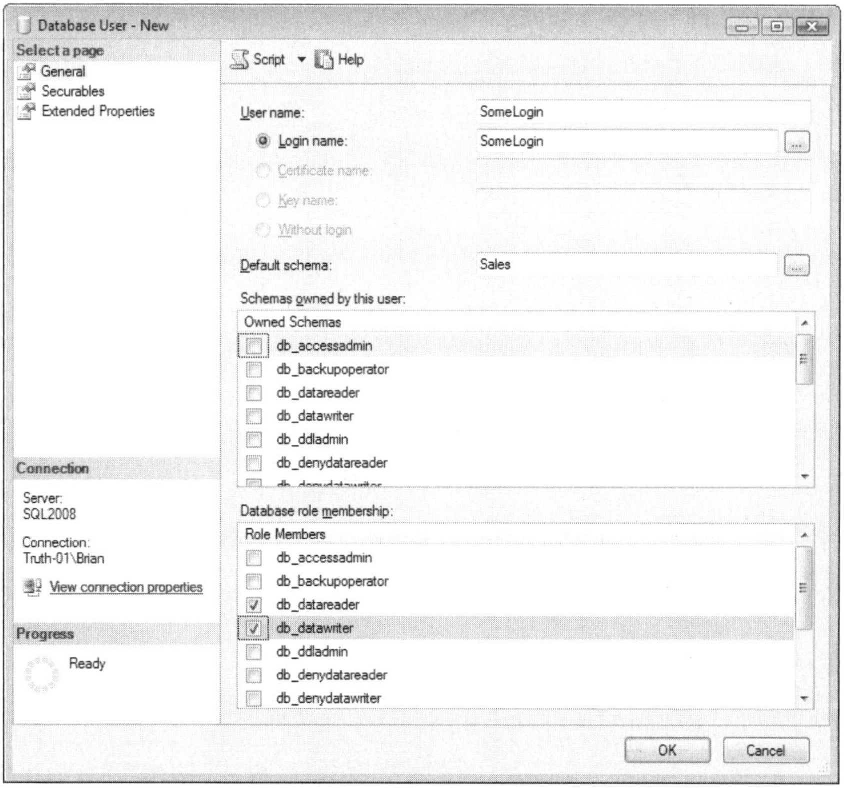

Figure 9-13

355

First, click the ellipsis button next to the right of the Login Name field. Select the login name that you wish to add to the database. Then, type the user name to which the login will be mapped. The Default Schema field specifies the schema that the user's objects will be created in and selected from. If you don't specify anything for this optional setting, the objects will be created with the user's name, like `UserName.TableName`. If you want the user to own a given schema, you can select them in the "Schemas Owned By User" grid by checking the checkbox beside the schema name. This is a new feature of Management Studio with SQL Server 2008. While you could select which schemas a user owned for an existing user in SQL Server 2005, you could not previously select schema ownership when you first created the user. Schemas are covered in detail later in this chapter. Finally, in this screen you must specify which database roles you wish the user to be a member of. Database roles were discussed in detail earlier in this chapter. If you've created user-defined database roles, they show up in this list as well.

Granular Permissions

Let's take a look at a quick common example. If you were to grant a user `db_datareader` and db_datawriter rights, that user would be able to read and write to any table in the database, but would not be able to execute stored procedures. Generally speaking, you want to have all your data access through stored procedures. There are numerous reasons for that, as covered in Chapters 6 and 7, and one of them is security. If you can encapsulate access through stored procedures, you can add auditing and guarantee that all access to your data will be done a certain way.

If the user had the rights to the database as shown in Figure 9-14, with no EXECUTE rights granted to the stored procedure, a user who tried to access any stored procedure would receive an error like the following:

```
Msg 229, Level 14, State 5, Procedure SelectSproc, Line 1
EXECUTE permission denied on object 'SelectSproc', database 'TicketSalesDB', schema
'dbo'.
```

If the user had stored procedure access, he or she would likely not need access to the underlying tables. There are exceptions to this related to dynamic queries. There are ways around that, however, by using context switching. To allow your users access to the stored procedures, you need to grant the user either access to each stored procedure or overarching rights to the database, but there is no database role for EXECUTE rights. The disadvantage to granting the user access to each stored procedure is it becomes a bit of a management headache. The disadvantage to granting overarching rights to every stored procedure is you may have stored procedures you don't wish the user to access.

For the purpose of this example, let's look at both situations. Typically, in an enterprise application environment, a DBA would grant a user access to each stored procedure individually. This is usually done when the Data Definition Language (DDL) is originally created.

For either example, go to the Securables tab of the Database User dialog and click Search. For the overarching permission, you would want to show the database securables. For individual rights to each stored procedure, you would want to display each stored procedure.

Both of these scenarios are shown in Figure 9-14. By selecting the database securable, you can select Execute from the Grant column, and the user will be able to execute any stored procedure in the database. If you were to select an individual stored procedure, you can select Execute to grant the rights to execute the single stored procedure. If you check the securable from the With Grant column, the user will be able to not only execute the stored procedure, but also give others rights to it as well.

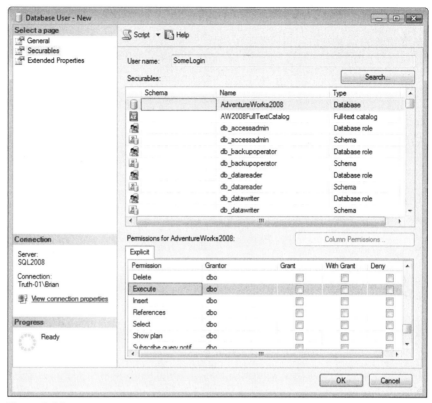

Figure 9-14

On a stored procedure, or almost any other database object, you may wish to enable certain securable actions. For example, if you want your developers to be able to see the schema in production but not alter it, you could grant them the View Definition permission and deny them Alter rights. The Control permission would enable a person to perform any action on the object, much as a db_owner does but at a granular level.

Roles

We have already discussed system database roles, but you can also create user-defined roles inside of your database. User-defined roles are essentially groups inside SQL Server for combining your users together. If you have gone through the trouble of granting the permissions for the users to only be able to access a select few stored procedures, you can use roles to ensure that every user thereafter will inherit those rights.

To do this, you essentially create the database role and then grant the rights to the role just as you do a user. When you grant new login rights to the database, you then assign them to the role with no other permissions. The user then inherits all rights given to him or her via the role.

Creating a role is simple in Management Studio. Right-click Database Roles under the database, click Security ⇨ Roles, and click New Role. Name the role and then specify who owns the role. You then go through the same screens discussed earlier in the "Users" section to specify what the role has permissions to do.

In T-SQL, you can use the CREATE ROLE DDL syntax to create a role. Simply name the role and then specify the owner of the role with the AUTHORIZATION keyword. Here's an example (of course, this example won't execute on your database unless you have a user named SalesManager):

```
CREATE ROLE [WebUsers] AUTHORIZATION [SalesManager]
```

Creating Users with T-SQL

To create a user through T-SQL, you can use the CREATE USER DDL. For example, if you wish to grant the login "LoginName" access to the database as a user named "LoginName," you could use the following syntax:

```
CREATE USER [LoginName] FOR LOGIN [LoginName]
```

The brackets around the login and user name permit the login to have spaces.

With the user now created, you will want to add the user to various roles. The most common roles to add a user to are db_datareader and db_datawriter, as you'll see. To do this through T-SQL, you would use the sp_addrolemember stored procedure, and then pass in the role you wish to add the user to followed by the user name. We prefixed each parameter with an N because each input parameter is a Unicode value. You can use sp_addrolemember to add the user to user-defined roles like the WebUsers role hypothetically created earlier in the previous section.

```
EXEC sp_addrolemember N'db_datawriter', N'LoginName'
EXEC sp_addrolemember N'db_datareader', N'LoginName'
EXEC sp_addrolemember N'WebUsers', N'LoginName'
```

Last, you can grant the user rights to various securables by using the GRANT statement. The syntax varies according to what you're trying to grant access to. The following three examples show how to grant the user access to create schemas and tables, and to execute the SprocName stored procedure:

```
GRANT CREATE SCHEMA TO [LoginName]
GRANT CREATE TABLE TO [LoginName]
GRANT EXECUTE ON SprocName to [LoginName]
```

The Guest User

The guest account is a special user in SQL Server that does not exist as a login. Essentially, if you grant the guest account access to your database, anyone who has a login into SQL Server will implictly have access to your database and be given any rights to which the guest account has been granted. Granting the guest account access to your database creates a security hole in your database, so this should never be done. The only databases that should ever have the guest account enabled are the master, msdb, and tempdb databases. These enable users access to create jobs, create temporary objects, and connect to SQL Server.

Schemas

Schemas were a feature in SQL Server 2000 that weren't emphasized much, but as of SQL Server 2005, they are an integral part of the Database Engine. Schemas enable you to group database objects into a logical group for security, ease of use, and manageability. They provide the same functionality as namespaces. Whether you have created custom schemas or not, it's a best practice to use schema names in your queries. If you were to query the Salary table in the HumanResources schema, it might look like this:

```
SELECT FirstName, LastName, Salary, StartDate, EndDate FROM HumanResources.Salary
```

Using this as an example, we would assume that the HumanResources schema contains information that should be considered more secure than data in other schemas, given the nature of Human Resources information. In SQL Server 2008, you can allow a user to see all tables in every schema with the exception of tables in the HumanResources schema. You could also give a user a schema that the user owned and could create tables within without interfering with the other tables in the database. This is because SQL Server considers both the schema and the object name when referring to objects. The user could create tables inside the schema that would therefore be considered by SQL Server to be named differently. Actually, SQL Server considers them separate objects altogether. The table Employees in the MyUser schema is a different table than the Employees table in the YourUser schema. If a schema is not specified, it is implicit that you want the default schema for that user. If you didn't specify a default schema when you created the user, SQL Server defaults the user to the dbo schema. In other words, using the defaults, if you query the Employees table without a schema name, you are executing a query against dbo.Employees.

Schema Example

This section presents an example that demonstrates how to use schemas to both compartmentalize your tables and secure them. First, create an empty database called SchemaExample. Next, create a login named SchemaExampleLogin and specify "P4ssw0rd!" for the password. Give the login public access to the SchemaExample database and make it the login's default database. Last, grant the login rights at a user-level in the SchemaExample database rights to create tables. You'll have to go to the User Properties dialog to do this, under the Securables page. You can use the steps covered in the "Login" section of this chapter to do this or you can use the following script:

```
USE [master]
GO
CREATE LOGIN [SchemaExampleLogin] WITH PASSWORD=N'P4ssw0rd!',
DEFAULT_DATABASE=[SchemaExample],
CHECK_EXPIRATION=ON,
CHECK_POLICY=ON
GO

USE [SchemaExample]
GO
CREATE USER [SchemaExampleLogin] FOR LOGIN [SchemaExampleLogin]
GRANT CREATE TABLE TO [SchemaExampleLogin]
```

You can download the preceding code from this book's Web site at www.wrox.com

With the preparation work now complete, it's time to create a schema. In Management Studio, connect to the SchemaExample database. Right-click Schemas under the Security tree and select New Schema. In the Schema-New dialog (shown in Figure 9-15), enter **TestSchema** for the schema name and make the schema owner the SchemaExampleLogin that you created earlier. Alternatively, you can use the CREATE SCHEMA syntax shown here to perform the same action:

```
CREATE SCHEMA [TestSchema] AUTHORIZATION [SchemaExampleLogin]
```

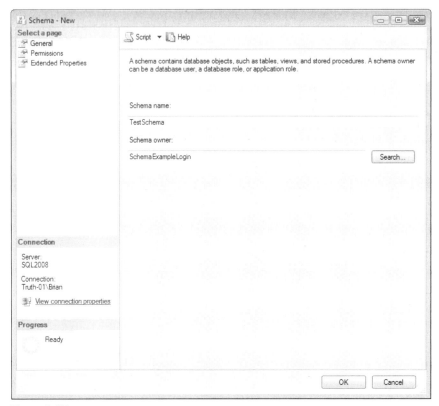

Figure 9-15

Now that the schema has been created, you can try to create a few tables using Management Studio and through T-SQL. Right-click on Tables in Management Studio under the `SchemaExample` database and select New Table. In the Table Designer, create one column called Column1 with an integer data type, as shown in Figure 9-16. Go to the Properties window of the Table Designer and select TestSchema from the Schema drop-down box. If the Properties window is not showing, select Properties Window from the View menu, or press F4. Also in the Properties window, type **TableDesignerTest** for the table name. Click Save and close the Table Designer.

You may need to save the table before modifying the properties.

In Management Studio, expand the Tables folder. (You may have to right-click and select Refresh to see the table.) You should see your newly created table there, and it should be entitled `TestSchema.TableDesignerTest`.

Next, open a new query while connecting with the login of SchemaExampleLogin, with "P4ssw0rd!" for the password. Ensure that the database that you're connected to is `SchemaExample`. Now try to create a simple test table by using the following syntax:

```
CREATE TABLE TestSchema.TestTable
(column1 int)
```

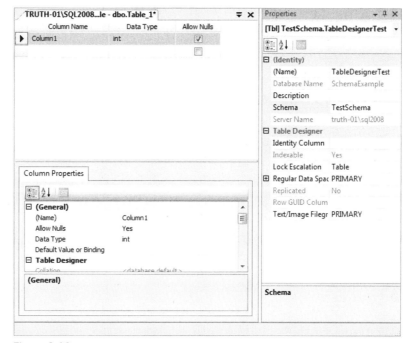

Figure 9-16

Next, try to create another table in the dbo schema by using the following syntax. Remember that because you didn't specify a schema in this syntax, the table will be created in the dbo schema:

```
CREATE TABLE TestTableProblem
(column1 int)
```

Because you don't have rights to create tables in the dbo schema, you will receive the following error message:

```
Msg 2760, Level 16, State 1, Line 1
The specified schema name "dbo" either does not exist or you do not have permission
to use it.
```

To create the table, you must explicitly grant the user rights to create the table in the dbo schema. To do this, use Management Studio to grant the user ALTER rights to the dbo schema in the Securables page. You can also use the following syntax to perform the same action. You need to be logged in as a user with higher authority to do this, though.

```
GRANT ALTER ON SCHEMA::[dbo] TO [SchemaExampleLogin]
GO
```

Once the user has been granted ALTER rights to the schema, that user will be able to create the table. This simple example shows how you can use schemas to control the user's access through grouping tables. Schemas are also handy from a usability perspective. If you name a table HumanResource.Contact, it's implicit that these are Human Resource contacts and not sales leads.

Changing Schemas

Once a schema has tables inside it, it cannot be dropped until all the objects have been moved out of it. SQL Server does not want to implicitly assume that you meant to move the tables from the `TestSchema` schema to the `dbo` schema. Instead of implicitly doing this, the command will fail until the administrator or owner explicitly moves the tables. The error the user would receive looks like the following (where `TableDesignerTest` is the first table in the schema):

```
Msg 3729, Level 16, State 1, Line 2
Cannot drop schema 'TestSchema' because it is being referenced by object
'TableDesignerTest'.
```

Nor can you drop any login or user that owns a schema. If you were to try to delete a user that owned a schema, you would receive an error like this:

```
Msg 15138, Level 16, State 1, Line 1
The database principal owns a schema in the database, and cannot be dropped.
```

The way around this is to create a new schema (or use an existing one) and move all the objects in the old schema to the new schema. You can do this by using the `ALTER SCHEMA` syntax followed by the `TRANSFER` keyword. The following syntax will create a new schema called `SecondSchema` and then move the `TestSchema` tables over to it (after which you could delete the empty schema):

```
CREATE SCHEMA SecondSchema
GO
ALTER SCHEMA SecondSchema TRANSFER TestSchema.TestTable
GO
ALTER SCHEMA SecondSchema TRANSFER TestSchema.TableDesignerTest
GO
```

User/Schema Separation

As shown when we created the `TestSchema` schema, every schema has an owner. This is a user in the database where the schema resides. Prior to SQL Server 2005, technically every database object, such as tables, views, and stored procedures, belonged to a schema, but that schema just signified who owned the object. For instance, if you saw `TestSchema.TestTable`, that meant there had to be a user in the database called TestSchema, and that user was the owner of `TestTable`. As of SQL Server 2005, that was no longer the case.

Now those objects truly belong to a schema; and the schema has an owner, but not the objects within the schema. At first glance this doesn't seem to accomplish much, but it has ramifications for a security feature called *ownership chaining*, which we'll look at in a following section with that title. It also meant that managing objects became a whole lot easier for DBAs.

Consider the situation in which multiple developers are working on objects in a database. Every developer has the capability to create and alter objects. In SQL Server 2000 and earlier, unless they were a member of either the `db_owner` or `db_ddladmin` roles, they could modify only the objects they owned. Imagine you have a developer, John, who has developed some 50 objects in the database. John is then reassigned to another project and should no longer have access to the database. You begin to revoke his access, but you realize he owns a lot of objects in the database. SQL Server won't let you drop his user account until you take care of the ownership problem; and you have no idea if anyone hard-coded a reference to `John.SomeTable` in their code. Suddenly this has become a major issue.

In SQL Server 2005 and 2008, objects are contained within a schema, and schemas are owned by users. When John first joined the project, you created a schema called `Silo4` because John was the fourth developer on the project. You set `Silo4` as his default schema and instructed him to develop all objects in `Silo4`, just as we did previously with `TestSchema`. John did just that, and now when John has to leave the project, you're in good shape. You can change the ownership of `Silo4` to another existing database user. Let's say Mary is going to pick up John's work. All you have to do is change the owner of `Silo4` from John to Mary and you can then proceed to drop John's user from the database.

Changing the Schema Owner

You can change the schema owner either through SSMS or through T-SQL. To change the owner through SSMS, right-click on the schema you want to modify under the Schemas tree, which is under the Security tree. Choose Properties from the pop-up menu. You can either manually enter the new Schema Owner and click OK or first search for the appropriate one, as shown in Figure 9-17.

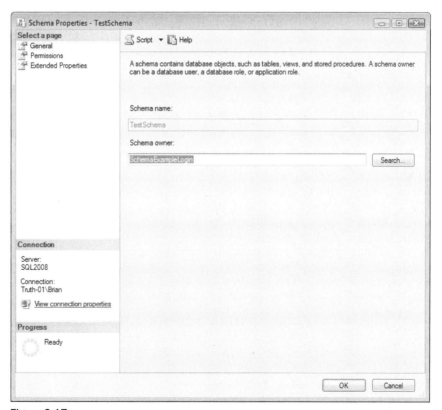

Figure 9-17

Changing the owner using T-SQL is as simple as the following:

```
ALTER AUTHORIZATION ON SCHEMA::TestSchema TO dbo
GO
```

This sets the `TestSchema` schema owner as `dbo`.

INFORMATION_SCHEMA and sys Schemas

Within SQL Server 2008 are two schemas that expose metadata information on database objects: `INFORMATION_SCHEMA` and `sys`. Prior to SQL Server 2005, metadata information was available to anyone with access to a particular database. This was during a "kinder, gentler era," when the information disclosed wasn't seen as a significant security vulnerability because no one was actively exploiting it.

However, given SQL injection techniques to try to wrestle out information about the structure of the database and similar attacks, Microsoft hardened the metadata views in SQL Server 2005. Now when you query them, SQL Server returns the information only on objects you have permission to access. To put this in perspective, recall the `HumanResources` schema. If a given user doesn't have access to the `HumanResources` schema or any objects in that schema, queries against any of the `INFORMATION_SCHEMA` or `sys` views will not return any information on these objects.

Securables and Object Permissions

We've touched on permissions several times in this chapter, but until now we've only scratched the surface. Let's look at SQL Server 2008's permission model in more detail. Starting with SQL Server 2005, the security model introduced the concepts of securables and scopes. Quite simply, a *securable* is any object you can assign permissions against. A *scope* is a securable that can contain other securables. For instance, the server securable corresponds to the SQL Server itself. It's a scope, too, though, because it contains endpoint, login, and database securables.

Ownership Chaining

If you look at some of the more basic securables, such as tables, views, and stored procedures, there's a security feature called *ownership chaining* that you need to be aware of. If one object refers to a second object, such as a stored procedure issuing a `SELECT` statement against a table, and both objects are in the same schema, an ownership chain is formed. When an ownership chain is in place, SQL Server will not check the security on the object being referred to. In other words, if the user is able to execute the stored procedure, SQL Server will not check to see whether the user can `SELECT` from the table when the user executes the stored procedure. SQL Server assumes that because both objects are in the same schema, the creator(s) intended for this type of access to happen from the stored procedure. If the user doesn't have `SELECT` permissions against the table, it doesn't matter. As long as the user is coming from an object in the same schema, the user is fine. However, if the user doesn't have `SELECT` permissions against that table and tries to hit it directly, there is no ownership chain; and in that case, SQL Server will check. Once it discovers the user doesn't have the appropriate permissions, it returns an error stating that.

Ownership chaining is not limited to only those objects within the same schema. That's just the simplest case to examine. Ownership chaining can happen across schemas if the schemas have the same owner, hence the name. For instance, if the `Sales` schema and the `Customers` schema were both owned by the same owner, a stored procedure in Sales could reference a table in Customers. This reference would create an ownership chain because both Sales and Customers have the same owner. Therefore, if a user had the permission to call the stored procedure in Sales, there wouldn't be a problem interacting with the table in Customers, even if the user didn't have permission to that table. The ownership chaining bypasses the security check. However, if the same user tried to query the table in Customers directly and didn't have permissions, the user would get an "access denied" message.

With respect to ownership chaining inside a database, note two cautions. One, ownership chaining is always on within a database. There isn't an option to turn it off. SQL Server assumes that if you have one object referring to another and they are either in the same schema or in schemas that share the same owner, you did this on purpose and the ownership chain was intended. Therefore, if someone developing in SQL Server isn't aware of ownership chaining, unintended consequences with respect to the security model could ensue. Two, when dynamic SQL is involved, ownership chaining breaks down. For instance, if a stored procedure issues a SELECT statement to a table but does it through EXEC() or sp_executesql, SQL Server handles that statement in a separate batch. Once SQL Server starts that second batch, the ownership chain is automatically broken. You'll learn how to overcome that shortly in the sections "Permission Context" and "EXECUTE AS Command."

Cross-Database Ownership Chaining

Taking ownership chaining one step further, it is possible for ownership chaining to occur across databases. There are a few caveats to this. The first is that the ownership of schemas is mapped back to the login level. For instance, a schema owned by the user John is mapped back to the login John. Where this really comes into play is a schema owned by the user dbo. This user maps to the actual owner of the database, so if the HR database is owned by HRLogin, then dbo maps back to login HRLogin. If the Sales database is owned by SalesLogin, then dbo maps back to the login SalesLogin. Though we might have a schema in each database owned by dbo, when we map it back to the logins, we see that the logins are entirely different. In this case, an ownership chain across databases would not be present. Now, if the owner of the Sales database were changed to HRLogin, then the logins would match up and an ownership chain has the potential to form.

The second caveat is that cross-database ownership chaining must be turned on either serverwide or for all databases in question. Therefore, if it were turned off at the server level (a recommended best practice is to keep it off) and either database had it turned off, it doesn't matter if the logins match up. An ownership chain will not be present.

The third and final proviso is that a login must have access to both databases. For instance, if the HR database has a stored procedure that references a table in the Sales database, if a user doesn't have access to both databases, none of the other conditions matter. For instance, let's say Mary has access to the HR database but not the Sales database. If she were to execute the stored procedure in HR, it would fail because she cannot enter the Sales database.

With all that said, it is strongly recommended you not activate cross-database ownership chaining on your user databases. The system databases master, msdb, and tempdb must have it on, but it does not have to be that way on user databases. In fact, the model database, which is cloned when a new database is created, must have cross-database ownership chaining turned off. You saw one potential issue with the case in which the owner of a database is changed, affecting ownership chaining. When cross-database ownership chaining is on, what may seem to be a simple change can result in a weakness in your security model. Therefore, the use of cross-database ownership chaining requires careful preparation and maintenance. Should you decide to turn it on, do so only at the database level and never serverwide, which isn't necessary.

Permission Context

Earlier, in the "Ownership Chaining" section, a classic security problem was raised: If it's a best practice to always use stored procedures, how do you handle dynamic SQL inside of a stored procedure? To illustrate this problem, let's use the same database and table from the previous section. In that example, you had a user named SchemaExampleLogin. This user did not have any rights to the dbo schema other than to add new tables into it. The user could not select from any table in the dbo schema, however. This is shown if you log in as SchemaExampleLogin and specify "P4ssw0rd!" for the password. Once logged in, attempt to query the dbo.TestTableProblem table:

```
SELECT * FROM dbo.TestTableProblem
```

You will receive the following error:

```
Msg 229, Level 14, State 5, Line 1
The SELECT permission was denied on object 'TestTableProblem', database
'SchemaExample', schema 'dbo'.
```

The best practice, as mentioned earlier, is not to grant the SchemaExampleLogin user access to the TestTableProblem table, but rather to create a stored procedure. This enables you to tightly control access to your tables through canned queries that you've already approved. (More benefits are listed in Chapters 6 and 7.) To fix the problem quickly, you could create a stored procedure as shown in the following example and grant SchemaExampleLogin the ability to execute it:

```
CREATE PROC DynamicSQLExample
AS

SELECT * FROM dbo.TestTableProblem
GO

GRANT EXECUTE ON DynamicSQLExample TO SchemaExampleLogin
GO
```

The stored procedure would then be called, returning the expected results:

```
EXEC DynamicSQLExample
```

Throughout the example in this section, you will need to flip back and forth from the lower privileged account SchemaExampleLogin to a database owner or sysadmin. Run the code that will create the stored procedures with the higher privileged account and the execution of the stored procedures with the SchemaExampleLogin user.

The problem crops up when you have a stored procedure with dynamic SQL. Dynamic SQL enables a T-SQL programmer to create a looser stored procedure that can order the data dynamically or select only certain columns. They should always be used sparingly because the query optimizer won't be able to give you the same optimized query plan as with a canned stored procedure. Typically, you see these types of queries with a search screen in an application, whereby a user may type any number of fields to search. You can alter the previous stored procedure as shown here to make it dynamic:

```
ALTER PROC DynamicSQLExample
@OrderBy Varchar(20)
AS

DECLARE @strSQL varchar(255)

SET @strSQL = 'SELECT * FROM dbo.TestTableProblem '
SET @strSQL = @strSQL + 'ORDER BY ' + @OrderBy
EXEC (@strSQL)
GO
```

Now, if you try to execute the stored procedure, like this

```
DynamicSQLExample 'column1'
```

you will see the same error that you saw before stating that you must have SELECT permission to the underlying table before you can run the stored procedure:

```
Msg 229, Level 14, State 5, Line 1
The SELECT permission was denied on object 'TestTableProblem', database
'SchemaExample',
schema 'dbo'.
```

The old way to solve this problem in SQL Server 2000 was to go ahead and grant the SchemaExampleLogin user more rights than you wanted and hope they exercised caution when selecting from the table. In SQL Server 2005, you can use context switching to impersonate another user for a short duration.

EXECUTE AS Command

Now that you know the previous problem, it is hoped that context switching will give you the best relief. Context switching temporarily gives the user executing the stored procedure higher rights, but only in the scope of the stored procedure's execution. As soon as the stored procedure has completed executing, the permissions are reverted back. You can also use context switching to troubleshoot permission problems. You can impersonate another login to see what problems they may be experiencing and try to reproduce the problem.

Context switching is done through the EXECUTE AS command. It's similar to the old SETUSER command, but SETUSER required that you be a sysadmin or db_owner to run. In its simplest form, the syntax would either state EXECUTE AS USER or EXECUTE AS LOGIN. As you can guess, this allows you to impersonate either a user or a login, respectively. In the previous example, you could create an additional user with very minimal rights to given tables that are needed. Then, you could impersonate that user in the stored procedure and revert back to the old permissions afterward. Some people like to create many new users for each type of access and then do impersonation based on the need.

Before you can do this type of context switching, though, the user you wish to impersonate must grant you access to do the impersonating. Otherwise, you would receive the following error anytime someone tried to run a query with context switching:

```
Msg 15517, Level 16, State 1, Procedure DynamicSQLExample, Line 5
Cannot execute as the database principal because the principal "dbo" does not
exist, this type of principal cannot be impersonated, or you do not have
permission.
```

To grant someone rights to impersonate your user, you can use the GRANT statement or go to the Securables page in the User Properties dialog. For example, to grant the SchemaExampleLogin user rights to impersonate the dbo account, use the following syntax:

```
GRANT IMPERSONATE ON USER::dbo TO SchemaExampleLogin;
```

This syntax would be a worst practice, as you're granting the user rights to impersonate a very sensitive account. The dbo user would have rights to do anything you would like inside the database. You should instead grant the user rights to impersonate a lower-privileged account. Because we have no other users for this example, the previous code will work fine temporarily.

The next step is to alter the previous stored procedure to enable context switching. You can see the EXECUTE AS statement in the following code, right before the SELECT statement. There is also quite a bit of debugging code in the stored procedure to show what context you're currently using. The USER_NAME function shows what login you're currently using. The USER_NAME function shows the user name that you're currently using, and the ORIGINAL_LOGIN function shows what your original login was before the context switch. The ORIGINAL_LOGIN function is a key function to use to help with auditing.

```
ALTER PROC DynamicSQLExample
@OrderBy Varchar(20)
AS

EXECUTE AS USER = 'dbo'
DECLARE @strSQL varchar(255)

SET @strSQL = 'SELECT * FROM dbo.TestTableProblem '
SET @strSQL = @strSQL + 'ORDER BY ' + @OrderBy
EXEC (@strSQL)
SELECT USER_NAME() as LoginNm,
USER_NAME() as UserNm,
ORIGINAL_LOGIN() as OriginalLoginNm;
GO
```

With the stored procedure now modified, go ahead and execute it again while logged in as SchemaExampleLogin:

```
DynamicSQLExample 'column1'
```

You should now see results from the query. The first result set should have Column1, but with no values. The second result set should contain the login and user names that you're impersonating.

After the stored procedure runs, rerun the following chunk of code to see what user you are currently impersonating:

```
SELECT USER_NAME() as LoginNm,
    USER_NAME() as UserNm,
    ORIGINAL_LOGIN() as OriginalLoginNm;
```

Note that now your user has reverted back to the SchemaExampleLogin. This shows that when you use context switching in a stored procedure, it reverts back as soon as the stored procedure completes running.

If you were to manually connect with the SchemaExampleLogin and run the following query, you can see another point:

```
EXECUTE AS USER = 'dbo'
GO
USE AdventureWorks2008
GO
```

When you're switching context to another user (not login), you will receive an error when trying to leave the database:

```
Msg 916, Level 14, State 1, Line 1
The server principal "SomeLogin" is not able to access the database
"AdventureWorks2008" under the current security context.
```

The solution, if you must do this, is to switch context to a login, not a user, as shown in the following code. You should not switch to a login context if only database-level items are needed. Otherwise, you may be giving the user more rights than are needed, and you may be opening yourself up to hackers. Use login context switching very sparingly.

```
EXECUTE AS login  = 'SomeLogin'
```

The keyword REVERT will revert the user's permissions back to the user's previous security context. If you have switched context multiple times, it will revert you back only a single switch, and you may have to issue REVERT several times before getting back to your original user. If you had switched context to a login and then began to use a different database, you would receive the following message when you tried to issue a REVERT command. This will force you to then go back to the original database to issue the REVERT.

```
Msg 15199, Level 16, State 1, Line 1
The current security context cannot be reverted. Please switch to the original
database where 'Execute As' was called and try it again.
```

Troubleshooting Permissions Issues

As you have seen throughout this chapter, if you don't configure permissions appropriately, it can be very tricky to troubleshoot. There is a new function that will help you figure out what permissions a given user has available before you have to dig through many screens in Management Studio. The function is `fn_my_permissions`, and it shows what permissions the caller has by default. For example, if you wish to see what access you have to the `TestSchema` schema, use the following syntax:

```
SELECT *
FROM fn_my_permissions('TestSchema', 'SCHEMA')
```

The second input parameter is the type of object, and the first parameter is the name of the specific object. To view what permissions you have to the `dbo.TestTableProblem` table, run the following syntax. If nothing is returned, either you have typed the wrong input parameter or you have no permissions. The input parameter `OBJECT` applies for all the basic database objects (tables, stored procedures, views, and so on).

```
SELECT *
FROM fn_my_permissions('dbo.TestTableProblem', 'OBJECT')
```

You can also find out what permissions a user has to the server by passing in the parameter of `SERVER` with an input parameter of `NULL` for the first parameter. In addition, use context switching to see what permissions someone else has when you are trying to debug a problem, as shown here:

```
EXECUTE AS Login = 'SomeLogin'
SELECT *
FROM fn_my_permissions(NULL, 'SERVER')
REVERT
```

Finally, if you're trying to determine whether you can impersonate someone else, you can use the input parameter of `USER` and pass in the user name. The same applies for the parameter of `LOGIN`:

```
SELECT * FROM fn_my_permissions('SchemaExamplelogin', 'USER');
```

Encryption

A common request in the days of SQL Server 2000 was for a way to encrypt data inside columns. Industries such as health care and banking have to encrypt their sensitive data. With the advent of laws like Sarbanes-Oxley, all publicly owned companies must encrypt sensitive data such as social security numbers or passwords. Developers would typically push the functionality into the application, rather than attempt to write an extended stored procedure. Each application then would have its own logic for the encryption and decryption. Beginning with SQL Server 2005, the functionality is built into the core Database Engine and can be used with minimal effort. SQL Server 2008 goes a step further with transparent data encryption, which can encrypt the data without any reworking of application or database code.

Setting Up an Encryption Methodology

The first question that security individuals ask when encrypting data is where do you want to store the keys for encryption? Essentially, the key is what allows encryption and decryption of the data to occur. SQL Server stores a hierarchy of keys. The top of the hierarchy is the service master key, an asymmetric key protected by the Windows Data Protection API. Beneath that, each database can have a master key that protects all the individual keys that can be created. In addition, SQL Server 2008 now supports external keys with the Extensible Key Management (EKM) module. You'll look at EKM later in the section "Extensible Key Management (EKM)." This section explains how to create and manage all the keys and certificates within SQL Server itself.

Encryption in SQL Server 2008 is done by first creating a master key in the database, typically using a certificate or asymmetric key, which is encrypted by the database master key, and then creating an individual symmetric key to do the data encryption, which is itself encrypted by the certificate or asymmetric key. Last, you use a series of functions to encrypt the data. The preceding sentence was worded very carefully because there is not a switch in the Table Designer that you can use to encrypt a column. Instead, you encrypt the data as it goes into the table using built-in system functions.

In SQL Server 2008, two types of encryption keys can be used: symmetric and asymmetric. Symmetric key encryption uses the same key to encrypt and decrypt the data. While this is less secure, it performs much faster, up to a thousand times faster, than asymmetric key encryption, which uses a different key for encryption and decryption. With asymmetric key encryption, you basically lock the door with one key and then pass out a different key to anyone who needs to open the door. With symmetric encryption, you essentially put the same key under the doormat and allow everyone to use it. You should never hand this key to anyone because it's the only one to the house. If you're wondering what the difference is between a certificate and an asymmetric key, the answer is: not much. A certificate is technically an asymmetric key, but there is a standard, X.509, that defines the format for a certificate. As a result, certificates can be backed up to a file. However, functionality and strength with regard to encryption are effectively the same within SQL Server.

As mentioned earlier, there is a noticeable performance degradation when encrypting and decrypting data. It's not nearly as noticeable with symmetric key encryption, though. There is a compromise to keeping your data secure with both types of keys. That solution enables you to encrypt your session key with the asymmetric key and then encrypt your data with the symmetric key. This is the methodology used by Encrypting File System and HTTPS. Because of the slight performance problem, you should never encrypt all of your columns in a table. For example, typically there's little reason to encrypt the data in a FirstName or Gender column.

Walking through an example will demonstrate how data is encrypted and decrypted. This example can be downloaded from this book's Web site at www.wrox.com. First, create a fresh database called EncryptionExample. Create a login named LowPrivLogin with a password of Encryptdemo08. Next, grant the login access to the EncryptionExample database. You can perform all of these steps through the Management Studio interface or by using a few lines of code:

```
CREATE DATABASE [EncryptionExample]
GO

CREATE LOGIN LowPrivLogin WITH PASSWORD = 'Encryptdemo08'
GO

USE EncryptionExample
GO

CREATE USER LowPrivLogin FOR LOGIN LowPrivLogin
GO
```

Create a table in the dbo schema that you'll use throughout this example. The table will hold fake credit card information. Notice that the credit card number is stored as a variable binary column. This is because you're going to use this column to store encrypted data.

```
CREATE TABLE dbo.CustomerCreditCards
        (CustomerID INT PRIMARY KEY,
         CardNumber varbinary(256))
```

To create the key, you cannot use the Management Studio GUI; you have to use T-SQL. You can use Management Studio to delete the key, but that's the only functionality that's available under the Security tree for a given database. First, create a master key for the database by using the CREATE MASTER KEY syntax:

```
CREATE MASTER KEY ENCRYPTION BY PASSWORD = 'EncryptionExampleMasterKey08$'
```

Next, you want to protect your other keys with a certificate. While logged in as a dbo, run the CREATE CERTIFICATE statement that follows. The subject is not needed, but it's handy metadata that can tell an administrator the purpose of the key. Remember the name of the certificate, because you're going to use it later.

```
CREATE CERTIFICATE [CertSymmetricKey]
    WITH SUBJECT = 'User defined subject. This key will protect the secret data.'
```

With the certificate now created, create a symmetric key using the CREATE KEY syntax as shown below. This syntax accepts a number of algorithms, including triple DES, AES 128, and RC4, to name just a few. There are ten algorithms in all, including several variations of the same. The new addition from SQL Server 2005 is TRIPLE_DES_3KEY, which uses a larger key (192-bit) than TRIPLE_DES (128-bit). Note that in the following syntax, the key is protected with the CertSymetricKey certificate. There are other ways of doing this as well. For example, you could encrypt the symmetric key with a password or another key.

```
CREATE SYMMETRIC KEY [SecretSymmetricKey]
    WITH ALGORITHM = TRIPLE_DES --AES_128 Fine too
    ENCRYPTION BY CERTIFICATE [CertSymmetricKey]
```

Encrypting the Data

You now are ready to begin encrypting your data. For the purpose of this example, remain logged in as a dbo account that created the keys. If you do not have access to the keys, you will not be able to see data. We'll cover that aspect of encryption momentarily.

First, use the symmetric key that was created earlier by issuing the OPEN SYMMETRIC KEY syntax. You specify the key name and indicate that you wish to decrypt the key with the certificate that you created earlier. This key will remain open until your session expires or you issue the CLOSE statement:

```
OPEN SYMMETRIC KEY [SecretSymmetricKey]
    DECRYPTION BY CERTIFICATE [CertSymmetricKey]
```

The next code block is a little more complex, but not too bad. In this block you get a unique GUID for the symmetric key that was created earlier by using the key_guid function. If you did not have permission to access the key, it would return NULL and be caught by the error trap later in the block of code. The entire point of retrieving the GUID is that it's required for the encryptbykey function later in the code block. This function is actually what does the encryption in our case. You pass to that function the GUID for the key and the data you wish to encrypt.

```
DECLARE @Key_Guid AS UNIQUEIDENTIFIER
SET @Key_Guid = key_guid( 'SecretSymmetricKey')
IF( @Key_Guid is not null )

BEGIN
INSERT INTO dbo.CustomerCreditCards
VALUES ( 1, encryptbykey( @Key_Guid, N'4111-1234-1234-5678'))

INSERT INTO dbo.CustomerCreditCards
VALUES ( 2, encryptbykey( @Key_Guid, N'4111-9876-7543-2100'))

INSERT INTO dbo.CustomerCreditCards
VALUES ( 3, encryptbykey( @Key_Guid, N'4111-9876-7543-2100'))


END
ELSE
BEGIN
  PRINT 'Error retrieving key GUID'
END
```

This will insert three encrypted credit card numbers. If you were to select against the table, you would see that the data for that column is all in binary:

```
SELECT * FROM dbo.CustomerCreditCards
```

If you wish to decrypt the data, one of the functions you can use is the decryptbykey function, shown in the following code. This will use the key you opened earlier to decrypt the data. If the key that was opened matches the key that encrypted the data, then you will be able to see the data unencrypted.

```
SELECT CustomerId,
       convert( NVARCHAR(100), decryptbykey( CardNumber )) as 'CardNumber'
    FROM dbo.CustomerCreditCards
GO
```

To close the key, use the CLOSE syntax, naming the key that you wish to close:

```
CLOSE SYMMETRIC KEY SecretSymmetricKey
```

At this point, the data that was viewed earlier will return NULL. Verify this by rerunning the same SELECT statement that you ran previously with the decryptbykey syntax. This is also the behavior if you try to open the wrong key to view the data or if you don't have permission to use the key. It works for you in this example because you have dbo rights to the database. With the data encrypted, only users who have access to your certificiate and the key would be able to see the data. To grant a user rights to see the data, you would have to use the syntax shown here (replace username with a valid user):

```
GRANT CONTROL on certificate::[CertSymetricKey]
  TO [username]
go
GRANT VIEW DEFINITION on symmetric key::[SecretSymmetricKey]
  TO [username]
```

This may be more permissions than you would be willing to permanently hand out to a user. The method here is to grant these rights only to a given account and temporarily escalate the rights to the user by using the EXECUTE AS statement.

Creating a Helper Function Example

For usability, you may decide to create a function to help users decrypt the data. You can use context switching to give the user rights to the certificate and key for a short amount of time. In the following function, you use the decryptbykeyautocert function to combine the OPEN SYMMETRIC KEY and decryptbykey functionality:

```
CREATE FUNCTION dbo.udfDecryptData ( @InputValue VARBINARY(256))
RETURNS NVARCHAR(20)
WITH EXECUTE AS 'DBO'
AS
BEGIN
RETURN convert( NVARCHAR(50), decryptbykeyautocert( cert_id( 'CertSymmetricKey' ),
null, @InputValue ))
END
```

For the purpose of this example, you'll allow the LowPrivLogin you created earlier access to the function and the credit card data by using the following code:

```
GRANT EXECUTE ON [dbo].[udfDecryptData] TO [LowPrivLogin]
GRANT SELECT ON [dbo].[CustomerCreditCards] TO [LowPrivLogin]
```

You're now ready to use the function. Either sign off as the dbo user and sign back in as the LowPrivLogin, or use the EXECUTE AS syntax that follows to simulate the user. The following code should look much like the SELECT statement used earlier, but now you're using the user-defined function you created:

```
EXECUTE AS USER = 'LowPrivLogin'
SELECT CustomerId,
       dbo.udfDecryptData( CardNumber ) as 'CardNumber'
    FROM dbo.CustomerCreditCards
REVERT
```

This will display the data unencrypted, and you would simply need to grant users rights to the function to enable them to see the data. As you can imagine, this does open a slight can of worms though, as it makes the data a little too easy to decrypt, but you did add layers of security and obscurity.

Column-Level Permissions

While you're encrypting data, you may find a table with data like your credit card data, whereby users should be able to see all columns except the credit card number. If this is the case, you have the option to protect data at a column level. To deny rights to an individual column, use the DENY SELECT statement. If you take the earlier example and deny the LowPrivLogin rights to the CardNumber column in the dbo.CustomerCreditCards table, it would look like the following code:

```
DENY SELECT (CardNumber) on dbo.CustomerCreditCards  to LowPrivLogin
```

If the LowPrivLogin attempted to pull the `CustomerID` column out of the table, he would experience no problem. The minute he tried a larger query, as shown below, he would have a permission problem:

```
EXECUTE AS USER = 'LowPrivLogin'
SELECT CustomerId,
       CardNumber
    FROM dbo.CustomerCreditCards
REVERT
```

This would return the following error. Any `SELECT *` statement would also fail with the same error.

```
Msg 230, Level 14, State 1, Line 2
The SELECT permission was denied on the column 'CardNumber' of the object
'CustomerCreditCards", database 'EncryptionExample', schema 'dbo'.
```

Transparent Data Encryption (TDE)

If you went through the sample code in the previous section, you were probably struck by how involved it was. The encryption options are quite extensive, enabling you to develop a solution that can meet most of your needs. But for an existing application, it could be quite costly to retrofit an encryption solution in this manner. In addition, what if you need to encrypt a large part of or even the entire database? In this case we're keeping track of performing a lot of "little" encryption/decryption calls. This results in a complex solution where the chances of making a mistake become increasingly likely.

Enter Transparent Data Encryption, a new feature in SQL Server 2008. With Transparent Data Encryption, SQL Server keeps the entire database encrypted on disk and performs the decrypt in memory. Because it's handling the entire database, the encryption is completely transparent and seamless to applications which use the database. When the data is "at rest" — in other words, when SQL Server isn't actively using the database, all of the data contained within is encrypted. As a result, should an attacker copy the data files, they'll find that the data they now have is unreadable and unusable. The same is true for any native backups taken by SQL Server. They, too, contain the data in encrypted form.

Enabling TDE

In order to use TDE, the first thing you must do is create a database master key for the master database, if you haven't already done so:

```
USE master
GO

CREATE MASTER KEY ENCRYPTION BY PASSWORD = '2008TDEexample'
```

With the database master key created in the master database, the next step is to create a certificate. This certificate will in turn be used to create what is known as a *database encryption key* within the database itself. You could use an asymmetric key, but it can't be backed up to a file in the event of a recovery. The database we want to encrypt is `AdventureWorks2008`. Therefore, let's ensure that our certificate reflects that in name and subject:

```
CREATE CERTIFICATE CertForAdventureWorks2008
WITH SUBJECT = 'Certificate for AdventureWorks2008 TDE'
GO
```

Because we're using a certificate, we can go ahead and back it up in the event that we'll need it in a recovery situation. We want to export it with the private key as well because SQL Server needs the private key to decrypt a database encryption key encrypted by the certificate:

```
BACKUP CERTIFICATE CertForAdventureWorks2008
  TO FILE = 'CertForAdventureWorks2008.cer'
    WITH PRIVATE KEY ( FILE = 'CertForAdventureWorks2008.key' ,
    ENCRYPTION BY PASSWORD = '2008TDEexample' )
GO
```

If no path is specified, SQL Server will write the files to the DATA directory. The certificate file, key file, and password are all critical. You want to ensure that all of this information is stored securely, preferably in an off-site location as well. Now that we have the certificate backed up, the next step is to create the database encryption key:

```
USE AdventureWorks2008
GO

CREATE DATABASE ENCRYPTION KEY
WITH ALGORITHM = AES_256
ENCRYPTION BY SERVER CERTIFICATE CertForAdventureWorks2008
GO
```

This brings us to the last step, which is to turn on TDE:

```
ALTER DATABASE AdventureWorks2008
SET ENCRYPTION ON
GO
```

SQL Server will use background threads in order to accomplish the encryption. Once they are done, your database is fully encrypted!

> After you've enabled TDE, keep in mind that SQL Server is able to decrypt by using the database encryption key. However, it decrypts the database encryption key using the certificate. We initially didn't create the certificate using the password option because the certificate must be encrypted by the database master key of the master database in order for SQL Server to be able to use it. Therefore, if at some point you alter the certificate to use a password, the next time SQL Server starts, it will not be able to open the certificate, which means it won't be able to open the database encryption key and the database will be unreadable. The moral of the story is to be careful how you handle certificates used for TDE. If you do something SQL Server doesn't expect, your data will be unavailable.

Restoring a Database Encrypted by TDE

If you're faced with restoring a database encrypted by TDE to the same server, as long as you didn't do anything with the certificate used to encrypt the database encryption key, there's nothing more to worry about. You can go about your normal mechanism for database recovery. If, however, you're restoring to a different server, be sure to create the certificate first using the files created when you backed up the certificate. Without the certificate installed, you will not be able to successfully restore the database.

Extensible Key Management (EKM)

One of the challenges when dealing with encryption is how to handle and protect the keys. SQL Server 2005 largely put that in the hands of SQL Server, with the exception of the fact that you can specify encryption of the keys using passwords. However, from an audit perspective, this may be considered an issue because the keys are located with the data. For instance, if you grab the right database backups, it's possible to recover the data because you have both the data and the keys used to encrypt said data.

The obvious solution is to use some sort of hardware device or software module that contains keys separate from SQL Server. This isn't a new idea — smart cards and the like have been around for a long time. However, SQL Server 2008 is the first version of SQL Server to support these types of mechanisms. In SQL Server, this support is called *Extensible Key Management*. It is available with the Enterprise Edition of SQL Server 2008 (and specially licensed editions such as Developer and Evaluation Editions that demonstrate the Enterprise Edition feature set).

We won't cover the details of an EKM implementation because each vendor is likely to have a slightly different take on it given the names of the keys and the like. However, before any EKM solution can be used, SQL Server must first be configured to permit EKM providers. This is done by using `sp_configure`:

```
sp_configure 'show advanced', 1
GO
RECONFIGURE
GO
sp_configure 'EKM provider enabled', 1
GO
RECONFIGURE
GO
```

SQL Server Audit

SQL Server 2008 Enterprise Edition introduces increased auditing capabilities through the use of SQL Server Audit. SQL Server Audit can track and log events that occur at the server level or the database level automatically. It does this through an `Audit` object.

Creating an Audit

An `Audit` object is a collection of one more individual actions or a group of actions to be tracked. For instance, you can configure an `Audit` object to track all failed logins. It writes all the events to a location you specify: the Application event log, the Security event log, or to a file.

You can create an `Audit` object using either Management Studio or T-SQL. To do this using SSMS, start by right-clicking on the Audits folder under the Security tree and selecting New Audit. You'll next need to give the `Audit` object a name and specify where it will write its information to. Give it the name Audit-FailedLogins and set it to write to a file. Specify the path where you want the file stored, as shown in Figure 9-18. Click OK to create the `Audit` object and you should now see it appear under the Audits folder. Create a second `Audit` object called Audit-EmployeeQueries. We'll use it to track SELECT statements issued against the `HumanResources.Employee` table in the `AdventureWorks2008` database.

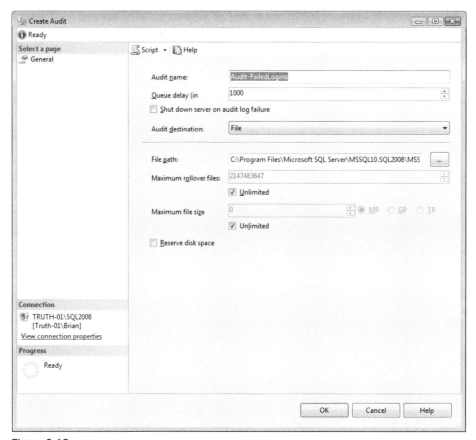

Figure 9-18

If you want to create an audit using T-SQL, you can do so by using the CREATE SERVER AUDIT command. The following query creates the Audit-EmployeeQueries object, as you just did in Management Studio. In this particular case, you're telling it to write to the Log directory of a SQL Server instance named SQL2008.

```
CREATE SERVER AUDIT [Audit-EmployeeQueries]
TO FILE
(FILEPATH = N'C:\Program Files\Microsoft SQL Server\MSSQL10.SQL2008\MSSQL\Log\');
```

When creating an Audit object via T-SQL, you must do so from the master database. Otherwise, SQL Server will return an error indicating that a server audit can't be created in a user database and the operation must be performed in the master database..

Creating and Enabling a Server Audit Specification

Once you've created the Audits, the next step is to create the appropriate Audit Specifications. An Audit Specification tells an Audit object what to track. In the case of the Audit-FailedLogins, we need to create a specification that looks for failed logins. To do so, right-click the Server Audit Specifications folder under the Security tree. Give the specification the name ServerAuditSpec-FailedLogins.

In the drop-down beside Audit, choose Audit-FailedLogins. This will assign this particular specification against that Audit object. Finally, underneath Audit Action Type, select FAILED_LOGIN_GROUP from the drop down. Figure 9-19 shows an example of this. This will cause this specification to track all failed logins. Click OK and the Server Audit Specification is created and assigned to the proper Audit object. You should see it appear under the Server Audit Specifications folder. Right-click on ServerAuditSpec-FailedLogins and select Enable Server Audit Specification.

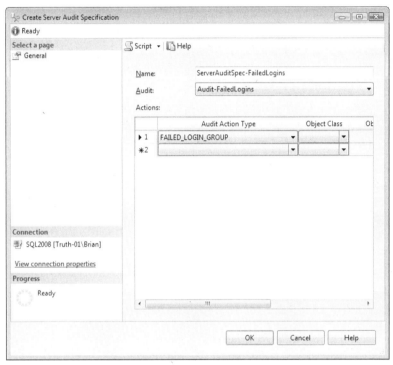

Figure 9-19

With the Server Audit Specification created, enabled, and associated with the proper Audit object, the next step is to enable the Audit object itself. Right-click the Audit-FailedLogins Audit object and select Enable Audit. You're now tracking failed logins to the file folder you specified. To test that it's working, create a new Database Engine query and specify that the authentication is SQL Server authentication. Enter some dummy text for the login and leave the password blank. Click Connect to generate the failed login. Cancel the login attempt and again right-click on Audit-FailedLogins. This time select View Audit Logs. You should see an entry for LOGIN FAILED, as shown in Figure 9-20.

To create the Server Audit Specification, use the CREATE SERVER AUDIT SPECIFICATION command. For instance, here's the T-SQL version of what we did in Management Studio:

```
CREATE SERVER AUDIT SPECIFICATION [ServerAuditSpec-FailedLogins]
FOR SERVER AUDIT [Audit-FailedLogins]
ADD (FAILED_LOGIN_GROUP)
WITH (STATE = ON)
GO
```

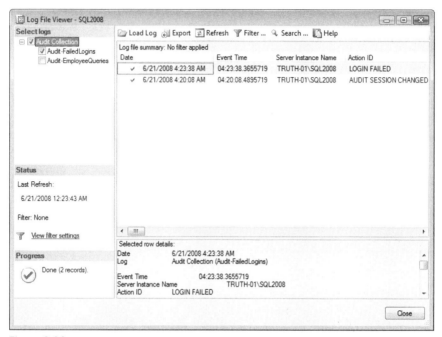

Figure 9-20

Creating and Enabling a Database Audit Specification

Now that you've created a `Server Audit` that monitors a `Server Audit Specification`, let's tackle a `Database Audit Specification`. Expand the `AdventureWorks2008` database and right-click Database Audit Specifications under the Security tree for the database. Choose New Database Audit Specification. Give it the name DatabaseAuditSpec-EmployeesTable. Select Audit-EmployeeQueries for the Audit. Under Audit Action Type choose `SELECT`. For the Object Class, chose `OBJECT`. Click on the ellipses for Object Name. In the dialog window, enter **[HumanResources].[Employee]** and click OK. Under Principal, click the ellipses and enter **[public]**. This enables you to track all users who issue a `SELECT` query against the `HumanResources.Employee` table. You should see something similar to Figure 9-21. Click OK. The Database Audit Specification should now appear under the folder. Right-click on it and select Enable Database Audit Specification. Navigate down to the Audit folder and right-click Audit-EmployeeQueries and select Enable Audit.

You can verify that the `Audit` object is working by executing a query against `HumanResources.Employee` and then viewing the audit log for Audit-EmployeeQueries. You should see a row for `SELECT`; and if you look at the details, you should see the actual query and the login/user who executed the query.

The T-SQL command to create a `Database Audit Specification` is `CREATE DATABASE AUDIT SPECIFICATION`. Here's the T-SQL command that creates the same specification you created in SSMS:

```
USE [AdventureWorks2008]
GO
```

```
CREATE DATABASE AUDIT SPECIFICATION [DatabaseAuditSpec-EmployeesTable]
FOR SERVER AUDIT [Audit-EmployeeQueries]
ADD (SELECT ON OBJECT::[HumanResources].[Employee] BY [public])
WITH (STATE = ON)
GO
```

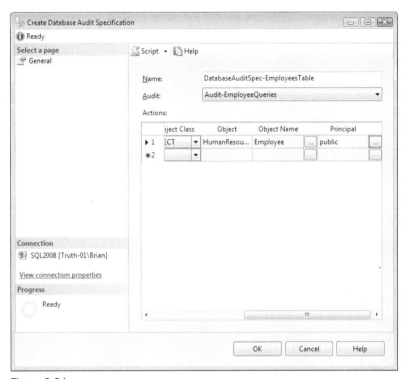

Figure 9-21

Summary

In this chapter, you learned how to secure your data and your Database Engine. We covered many ways to secure your data, whether through granular security or roles. Another mechanism assumes the attacker can get the sensitive data, but prevents the attacker from reading it due to encryption. Now that you know how to protect your SQL Server data, the next chapter explains how to enforce SQL Server configuration using Policy-Based Management.

10

Change Management

The challenges faced by database administrators have changed drastically since the early days of SQL Server. Laws like Health Insurance Portability and Accountability Act (HIPAA) and Sarbanes-Oxley have made a DBA's job much more structured because of their compliance requirements. In this chapter, you learn how to create projects for your SQL scripts and how to integrate those into Visual Source Safe, Microsoft's source control management system. You also learn how to monitor for unauthorized changes by using Policy-Based Management and how to script database management actions using PowerShell.

Creating Projects

Visual Studio projects are generally a foreign concept to DBAs because the idea originated in the programming world. Using the hierarchy of Visual Studio, you create a *solution*, which can contain many *projects*, which can contain many files for the project. For example, you may have a solution called LoanApplication that contains two projects: one for your C# program and another for the DDL to create the database. In the business intelligence world, these solutions help you group all the related files, such as SSRS reports, SSAS cubes, and the SSIS packages to load the data.

Inside Management Studio, you can also create projects to hold your scripts and connections for easy access. When you double-click a script, it automatically implements the connection associated with the script. By placing script files in a project, you also can store files easily in Source Safe. This enables you to check code in and out, allowing for a collaborative development environment wherein only one DBA can be editing the code at one time. We'll discuss this requirement later in this chapter, but version controlling your scripts is often a requirement for change management. You could also check all of your administrative scripts into Source Safe and share them with other administrators.

To create a project in Management Studio, select File ➪ New ➪ Project, and then select SQL Server Scripts as your project template. Call the project ProjectExampleScripts and name the solution AdminBookExamples (see Figure 10-1).

When you click OK, a new solution and project are created. Three folders are created in the project: Connections, Queries, and Miscellaneous. Your database connections will reside in the Connections folder, and all of the queries that you'd like to keep together in the project will be in the Queries folder. The Miscellaneous folder holds files that don't have a .SQL extension but that you'd like to keep in the project, such as a readme.txt file that may describe instructions for using the project.

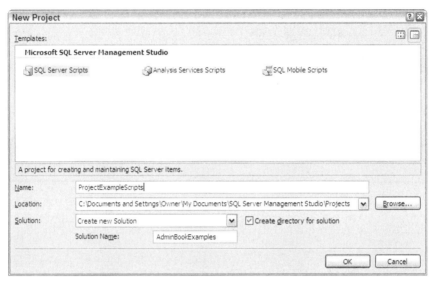

Figure 10-1

If you have a tool such as Visual Source Safe installed, you'll see a checkbox for automatically checking the solution into Source Safe upon creation. Any source management solution that is supported by Visual Studio will also work with SQL Server Management Studio.

Creating a Connection

Follow these steps to create a connection:

1. Right-click the Connections folder and select New Connection.

2. When the Connect to Server dialog opens, type your normal server connection information and how you wish to authenticate.

3. On the Connection Properties tab (shown in Figure 10-2), select AdventureWorks2008 for the Connect to database option. Note that you can also set the default protocol here if it differs from your preferred default.

   When you click OK, the connection is created in the Connections folder.

There are other ways to create this connection. If you create a query first, you'll be prompted for a connection prior to query creation. This also creates a connection in the Connections folder and typically is the easier way to create the connection.

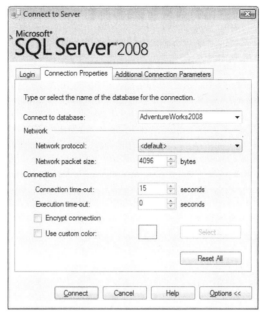

Figure 10-2

Creating a Project Query

The Queries folder holds all the queries for your project. To create a query in the project, follow these steps:

1. Right-click the Queries folder and select New Query. You will be prompted to confirm the connection. The default query name is SQLQuery1.sql.

2. Type whatever you wish in the Query window and select File ⇨ Save.

3. Rename the query SampleQuery1.sql by right-clicking it and selecting Rename. Click Save All to save the queries and the project.

With the query now saved, you're ready to begin using it. Close the Query window and double-click the query file again. Note that this time, the query opens automatically and does not prompt you for a connection. You can see what connection is associated with the query by right-clicking it and selecting Properties. You can then continue to add queries until your project is complete.

Again, generally the main point of creating an entire project and solution is to have integration with a source control system. If you are using a source control system such as Source Safe, each time you add or delete a new script, the project control files are checked out. Individual files are checked out automatically as you open and edit them.

Policy-Based Management

After a few publicly held companies collapsed dramatically in 2002, the U.S. government enacted a law called Sarbanes-Oxley, which demanded, among other things, specific IT accountability practices. One of the major requirements of the law was that companies have a good change management process and that they know who installed a schema change into production and when the installation occurred. Compliance with this statute required companies nationwide to spend hundreds of millions of dollars on new software to monitor changes and ensure good IT practices. Of course, they had the best motivation to be in compliance — if they weren't, they would be in violation of the law.

Part of those millions of dollars spent was on monitoring software for SQL Server to watch for unauthorized changes. In this section, you'll learn how to use Policy-Based Management, SQL Server 2008's own built-in suite of auditing tools, to detect and in some cases prevent unauthorized changes to your SQL Server infrastructure. Policy-Based Management is the first tool a DBA has to detect or prevent unauthorized or unexpected changes to a system. You use PowerShell to resolve such issues in a scalable and predictable way.

Policy-Based Management Overview

The first questions most DBAs ask when the SQL development team rolls out a new feature are "What does it do?" and "Why should we care?" Policy-Based Management enables a DBA to declare her *intent* regarding how a specific server should act and then apply that intent to one or more target servers. The original name for this feature was "Declarative Management Framework," which is even more confusing than "Policy-Based Management" until you see how the feature actually works. The short answer to "What does it do?" is that it allows for declarative, scalable, and repeatable SQL Server management.

Policy-Based Management starts with an item called a *facet*. Facets expose individual elements of the SQL Server system so they can be evaluated and compared to compliance criteria. The list of facets is loosely based on the objects in the SQL Server Management Object (SQL-SMO) hierarchy, which is the underlying object model for SQL Server Management Studio. Most facets are derived from combinations or subsets of SMO objects and other server state information. Facets present properties relevant to regular SQL Server management tasks.

For example, the Database Maintenance facet exposes several properties essential to the maintenance of individual databases, yet there is not a corresponding SMO object implementing this facet. Facets do not map directly to SMO objects, nor do they correspond to SQL Server Management Studio elements. Facets are a completely new representation of the SQL Server internal state.

Facets are presented in alphabetical order, making them easy to find. SQL Server Management Studio organizes the SMO objects in hierarchical order, which makes more sense as part of a GUI. Facet properties correspond to properties or combinations of properties of the underlying SMO objects. For example, a StoredProcedure object has facets for the nineteen different properties shown in Figure 10-3.

Properties can be compared using a combination of AND and OR logic to define a desired state. This end state is referred to as a *condition*. Conditions, which are always expressed as a Boolean value, are used to detect and optionally enforce desired configurations. One key limitation of a condition is that it can check the properties of only a single facet at a time. This is why the same property may appear in multiple facets. For example, Database Status appears in the Database Facet and the Database Maintenance Facet because it is necessary to completely evaluate conditions in both areas.

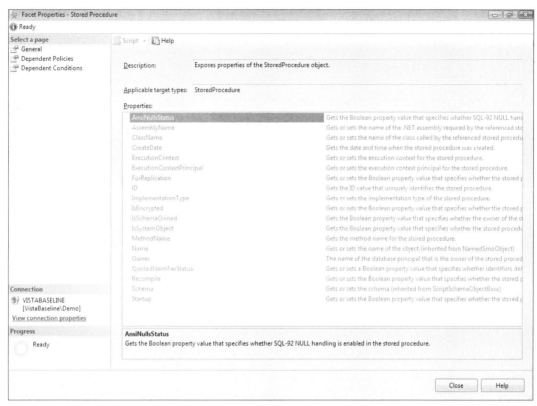

Figure 10-3

Policy-Based Management Step By Step

One of the first challenges a DBA faces when inheriting a system is figuring out the backup and restore strategy. Because DBAs tend to inherit systems far more often than they develop them from scratch, rapidly learning about these systems is critical to a DBA's ability to meet the fundamental requirements of his or her position. One of the more common problems a DBA inherits is a *runaway log file*. This is a situation in which a database is in FULL recovery mode yet has no active log backups. The first sign of trouble many database professionals see is when end users complain about a "log full" error on their application. By that point the problem is usually too far gone to fix easily. In addition, although it may seem self-evident, note that just because you've fixed one problem database does not mean there is not another one lurking somewhere else. Finally, if your developers can create databases, you may end up with another "log full" situation recurring without your knowledge, even if you have checked and repaired every single server and database.

Clearly, detecting "log full" situations is important. Being able to check all your systems at once as easily as you check a single system would be great. Without policies, a DBA has to manually check every system and every database or write a script and a mechanism to apply that script to every system. Scripts often miss new databases or must be very complex to iterate over all the databases and servers in a system. Policies enable you to do this quickly, easily, and repeatedly.

Example: Using Policy-Based Management to Identify Log Bloat Candidates

After deciding exactly what you want to accomplish, you can then declare your goal via conditions, and execute it using policies. Your *intent* in this example is to find all databases in FULL Recovery that have not had a successful log backup within the past three days. The facet you will use to implement this goal is the Database Maintenance facet. You will compare two properties of this facet in a single condition. TRUE (or pass) means the database is okay; FALSE (or fail) means you have a problem that needs to be addressed.

1. In SQL Server Management Studio, drill down to create a new condition (see Figure 10-4).

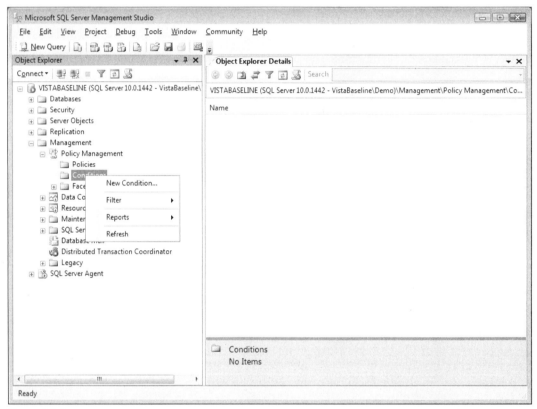

Figure 10-4

2. Name the condition Log Bloat Candidates.

The Facet you will work with is Database Maintenance.

The two properties you want to evaluate are Recovery Model and LastLogBackupDate (see Figure 10-5).

Success (Boolean TRUE) for either comparison is sufficient to "pass," so use OR to tie them together. You can extend an existing condition by evaluating more properties to create more complex conditions using any combination of AND and OR logic. Again, all the properties have to come from the same facet, which is why some properties appear in more than one facet. Comparisons are done using T-SQL syntax, not VBScript, C#, or any other computer language. Because DBAs will be implementing Policy-Based Management, T-SQL is the most natural syntax to use. Native T-SQL syntax also helps with the implementation details.

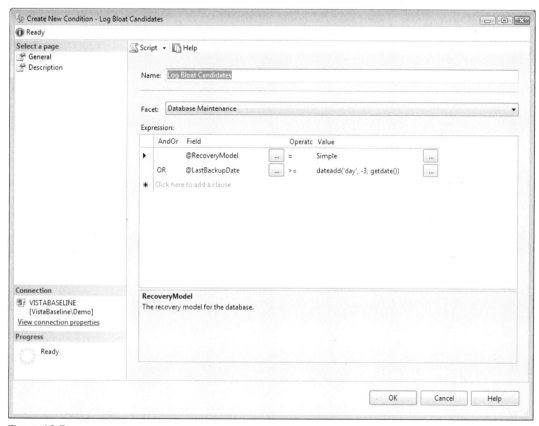

Figure 10-5

You can now create a policy and apply it to a *Target* via an *Evaluation Mode*. Log Bloat Candidates is a good name, so we'll use it again for the policy. Right-click Policies and select New Policy to open the Create New Policy dialog. Fill in the Policy Name field and select the Log Bloat Candidates condition. Leave the Evaluation Mode at On demand and the Server restriction at None (see Figure 10-6).

Now that you have created a complete policy, you can evaluate it against the local server in On Demand mode. SSMS connects to the target server, checks the conditions, and reports the answer. In SQL Server Management Studio, right-click on the policy you just created and select Evaluate. The results are shown in Figure 10-7.

As shown in the figure, the Admin database was configured incorrectly and does not have a log backup, yet it is in full recovery. Because this is your own utility database, you already know you can resolve the situation by changing the recovery model to SIMPLE. For other cases, you would have to check the recoverability specified in the appropriate database service level agreement and make your changes accordingly.

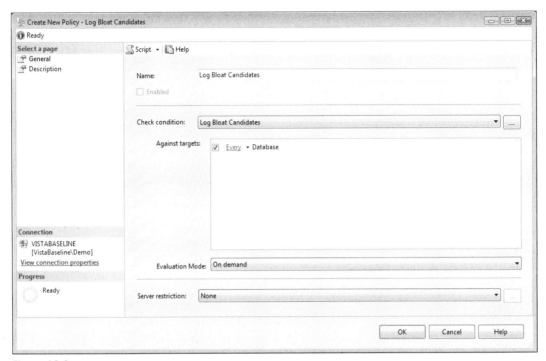

Figure 10-6

This seems like a lot of work for something you could find out with a couple of clicks in Management Studio. You could also write a script to do the same thing, checking some system views and the MSDB database, although that would have taken a bit longer to write than creating the policy. This demo system has only a few user databases, but note that every database on this server was checked. With large numbers of databases on a single server, you already have the first bit of scalability.

The next step in scalability is to use an item called a *Central Management Server*. A Central Management Server is the mechanism a DBA uses to apply actions, including policies, to one server and have those actions repeated across a designated list of servers. Setting up a Central Management Server is no more challenging than using the Registered Server list in SQL Server Management Studio. It even looks similar (see Figure 10-8).

The difference between the two registration types is that when you save the credentials for member servers, you are telling the Central Management Server how to connect to those systems as well as storing connection information in SQL Server Management Studio.

When you apply the policy to the Central Management Server, you are actually applying it across all the servers in the evaluation group. You can also use the Central Management Server to execute T-SQL commands across multiple servers at the same time.

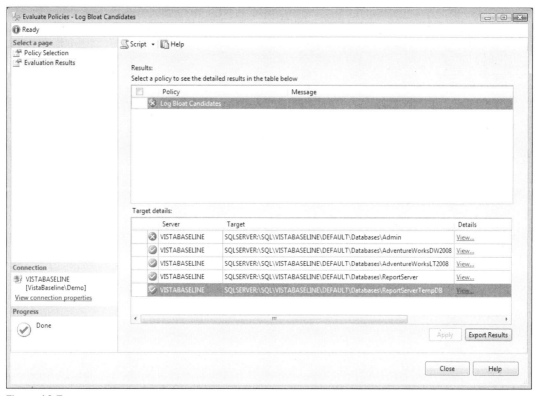

Figure 10-7

One final element and your Policy-Based Management story is complete. You need these actions to be repeatable. There are a couple of ways to make this happen. You can implement the policy using the On-Change: Log evaluation mode or the Scheduled evaluation mode. On Change is not appropriate for this scenario because a new database will never have a log backup, nor will a database that has just been changed to FULL recovery mode. Besides, a brand-new database very seldom causes problems with log bloat; the databases that are left alone for lengthy periods of time are the ones that present problems. A scan once a day is sufficient to alert you to any problem, with plenty of time to fix it before users ever notice anything.

For this example you did not use any additional conditions to limit the target servers and databases to which your policy applies. While a policy can implement one and only one condition, additional conditions can be created and used as filters to determine a valid set of target objects for a given policy.

Therefore, your final Log Bloat Candidate policy applies to all of your servers, runs automatically every day, and alerts you when it finds a database in FULL recovery with no log backup within the past three days. All you have to do is remember to add any new servers to the Central Management Server when you deploy them. Declarative, scalable, and repeatable server management is now a reality.

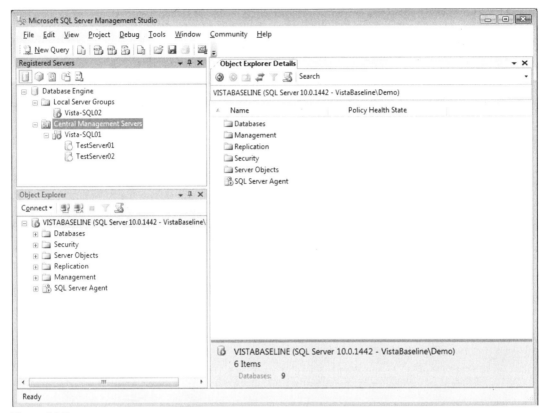

Figure 10-8

Scripting Policy-Based Management

Earlier in this chapter we mentioned creating a solution in SQL Server Management Studio for SQL administrative scripts. That discussion and the previous section naturally lead to a question: Can you create source-managed scripts of your policies? As with pretty much any action since SQL 2005, the answer is yes, you can create a script. Here is the script for the condition from the earlier example:

```
Declare @condition_id int
EXEC msdb.dbo.sp_syspolicy_add_condition @name=N'Log Bloat Candidates',
@description=N'', @facet=N'IDatabaseMaintenanceFacet', @expression=N'<Operator>
  <TypeClass>Bool</TypeClass>
  <OpType>OR</OpType>
  <Count>2</Count>
  <Operator>
    <TypeClass>Bool</TypeClass>
    <OpType>EQ</OpType>
    <Count>2</Count>
    <Attribute>
      <TypeClass>Numeric</TypeClass>
      <Name>RecoveryModel</Name>
```

```
    </Attribute>
    <Function>
      <TypeClass>Numeric</TypeClass>
      <FunctionType>Enum</FunctionType>
      <ReturnType>Numeric</ReturnType>
      <Count>2</Count>
      <Constant>
        <TypeClass>String</TypeClass>
        <ObjType>System.String</ObjType>
        <Value>Microsoft.SqlServer.Management.Smo.RecoveryModel</Value>
      </Constant>
      <Constant>
        <TypeClass>String</TypeClass>
        <ObjType>System.String</ObjType>
        <Value>Simple</Value>
      </Constant>
    </Function>
  </Operator>
  <Operator>
    <TypeClass>Bool</TypeClass>
    <OpType>GE</OpType>
    <Count>2</Count>
    <Attribute>
      <TypeClass>DateTime</TypeClass>
      <Name>LastBackupDate</Name>
    </Attribute>
    <Function>
      <TypeClass>DateTime</TypeClass>
      <FunctionType>DateAdd</FunctionType>
      <ReturnType>DateTime</ReturnType>
      <Count>3</Count>
      <Constant>
        <TypeClass>String</TypeClass>
        <ObjType>System.String</ObjType>
        <Value>day</Value>
      </Constant>
      <Constant>
        <TypeClass>Numeric</TypeClass>
        <ObjType>System.Double</ObjType>
        <Value>-3</Value>
      </Constant>
      <Function>
        <TypeClass>DateTime</TypeClass>
        <FunctionType>GetDate</FunctionType>
        <ReturnType>DateTime</ReturnType>
        <Count>0</Count>
      </Function>
    </Function>
  </Operator>
</Operator>', @is_name_condition=0, @obj_name=N'', @condition_id=@condition_id
OUTPUT
Select @condition_id

GO
```

Experienced readers will notice the large chunk of XML in the middle of the script. XML was introduced as a data type in SQL 2005. Now SQL Server manageability starts to embrace XML in server operations. Given that a condition is an arbitrary combination of facet comparisons, XML provides the perfect means of describing such an entity. Understanding XML and other rich data types is an essential DBA skill going forward, both for operations-oriented DBAs and development-focused DBAs. *Beginning XML Databases* by Gavin Powell (Wrox, 2006) is an excellent resource for the DBA who wants to learn XML.

The policy script looks like this:

```
Declare @object_set_id int
EXEC msdb.dbo.sp_syspolicy_add_object_set @object_set_name=N'Log Bloat
Candidates_ObjectSet', @facet=N'IDatabaseMaintenanceFacet',
@object_set_id=@object_set_id OUTPUT
Select @object_set_id

Declare @target_set_id int
EXEC msdb.dbo.sp_syspolicy_add_target_set @object_set_name=N'Log Bloat
Candidates_ObjectSet', @type_skeleton=N'Server/Database', @type=N'DATABASE',
@enabled=True, @target_set_id=@target_set_id OUTPUT
Select @target_set_id

EXEC msdb.dbo.sp_syspolicy_add_target_set_level @target_set_id=@target_set_id,
@type_skeleton=N'Server/Database', @level_name=N'Database', @condition_name=N'',
@target_set_level_id=0


GO

Declare @policy_id int
EXEC msdb.dbo.sp_syspolicy_add_policy @name=N'Log Bloat Candidates',
@condition_name=N'Log Bloat Candidates', @policy_category=N'', @description=N'',
@help_text=N'', @help_link=N'', @schedule_uid=N'00000000-0000-0000-0000-
000000000000', @execution_mode=0, @is_enabled=False, @policy_id=@policy_id OUTPUT,
@root_condition_name=N'', @object_set=N'Log Bloat Candidates_ObjectSet'
Select @policy_id


GO
```

This script contains no XML. Because a policy contains one and only one condition, all its elements are deterministic and can be mapped to a well-defined set of parameters. Not everything new has to be difficult.

Policy-Based Management Implementation

Experienced DBAs often ask an extra question beyond just "What does it do?" They want to know "How does it work?" You need to know if the actual implementation of a feature is complete, secure, and scalable before you bet your systems (and your job) on it.

We have already covered the On-Demand and Scheduled modes in the earlier examples. These run directly from SQL Server Management Studio and from the SQL Agent, respectively. This leaves us with the On-Change modes to delve into. On-Change is precisely what the name implies: It captures a change event inside a target SQL Server and either logs the change event or prevents the change from occurring. SQL Server Policy-Based Management uses DDL triggers to either log or rollback a change event to implement On-Change policy evaluation.

On-Change only works for deterministic event-driven events in which something changes inside the SQL Server. The earlier example for Log Bloat Candidates is not suitable for On-Change because there is no event to capture. You could catch the change in recovery model. A backup that does *not* happen is not an event and therefore cannot be captured.

Policy-Based Management is a big toolkit for managing SQL Server infrastructure. As with any new toolkit in SQL, Microsoft supplies a predefined set of policies. These policies have to be imported to each server (or to a Central Management Server) in order to use them. These policy scripts are located in the C:\Program Files\Microsoft SQL Server\100\Tools\Policies\DatabaseEngine\1033 folder on default-installed English-language SQL Servers. There are other folders containing example policies for Analysis Services and for Reporting Services. We will use one of the Database Engine example policies to demonstrate how On-Change:Prevent actually works. From SQL Server Management Studio, right-click Policies and select Import Policy. Open the file explorer (next to the File Name field) and browse to the list of sample policies (see Figure 10-9). Choose the one named SQL Server Password Policy and click Next to complete the import process.

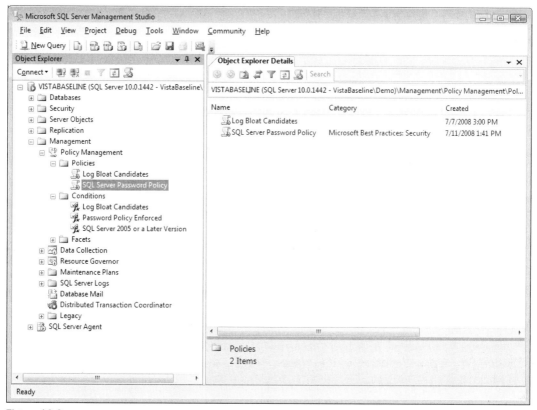

Figure 10-9

When you import a policy, you also import the underlying conditions for that policy. In this example, two conditions are necessary for this policy. The SQL Server 2005 or a Later Version condition acts as a filter to limit the policy to SQL Server versions that support the necessary feature. The SQL Password Policy was introduced in SQL 2005. The other condition is the actual test to see whether SQL Server passwords are required to follow the host system's Windows Password Policy. Password policy is a fundamental element of many compliance frameworks, so this is highly useful.

If you try to modify the evaluation mode of this policy to On-Change: Prevent, you will get an error stating that the condition SQL Server 2005 or a Later Version is not valid for that evaluation mode. This makes a lot of sense. While a major version change is certainly an event you can capture, it is not one that can be rolled back inside a trigger. For this example, you will remove the Server Restriction condition from the policy and test only the Password Policy Enforced Condition against an SQL Server 2008 system. Once the Server Restriction is removed, change the evaluation mode to On-Change: Prevent. You have one more step to have this policy lock down the server. Right-click the policy in the Object Explorer window and select Enable.

Now, just to prove policies are an absolute override on the server, try to remove the Password Policy on the SA login. You can select and deselect the option on the Login Properties page for the SA login without problems, but when you try to write the changes back to the server you get the error message shown in Figure 10-10.

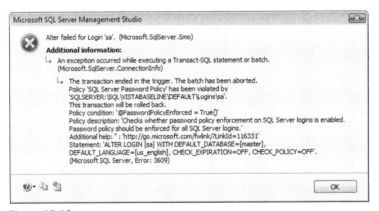

Figure 10-10

Let's examine this error in detail. First, you see that an Alter Login statement failed. Keep reading and you see that the transaction ended in the trigger. You also see who attempted to violate the policy and that the statement was ended by a trigger. You get detailed information on the exact policy and condition that was violated. Finally, you see the exact statement that violated the policy. This same error information is returned regardless of what client application executes the command.

The specific trigger used to evaluate a policy in On-Change mode may be a DDL trigger or a server trigger, depending on the specific facet used to build the condition. The following sections detail exactly how to create such triggers should you need to build your own version of Policy-Based Management.

DDL Trigger Syntax

The syntax for a DDL trigger is much like a DML trigger, but with a DDL trigger, instead of monitoring an INSERT statement, you would monitor a CREATE event, for example. The generic syntax looks like this:

```
CREATE TRIGGER <trigger_name>
ON { ALL SERVER | DATABASE }
[ WITH <ddl_trigger_option> [ , ... n ] ]
{ FOR | AFTER } { event_type | event_group } [ , ... n ]
AS { sql_statement  [ ; ] [ ... n ] | EXTERNAL NAME < method specifier >  [ ; ] }
```

Most of this syntax you probably recognize from DML triggers, so we'll focus mostly on the DDL-specific syntax. There are two scopes you can specify in a DDL trigger: ALL_SERVER or DATABASE. As the names imply, the ALL_SERVER scope monitors all server-level events, and the DATABASE option monitors database-level events.

The other important configurable part of the syntax is after the FOR clause. After the FOR clause, you specify what you'd like to monitor in the database or on the server with the DDL trigger option. This varies depending on what level of DDL trigger you have. The upcoming sections will break down these examples.

Database Triggers

Database DDL triggers are executed when you create, drop, or alter an object at a database level, such as a user, table, stored procedure, Service Broker queue, or view, to name a few. If you want to trap all database DDL events, you would use the trigger option in the earlier mentioned syntax of FOR DDL_DATABASE_LEVEL_EVENTS. The events are hierarchical, and the top-level database trigger types are shown in the following list. Under the trigger types mentioned in the list, you can get much more granular. For example, rather than trap all events when any type of table event occurs, you can narrow it down to only raise the DDL event when a table is dropped by using the DROP_TABLE trigger option.

- ❏ DDL_TRIGGER_EVENTS
- ❏ DDL_FUNCTION_EVENTS
- ❏ DDL_SYNONYM_EVENTS
- ❏ DDL_SSB_EVENTS
- ❏ DDL_DATABASE_SECURITY_EVENTS
- ❏ DDL_EVENT_NOTIFICATION_EVENTS
- ❏ DDL_PROCEDURE_EVENTS
- ❏ DDL_TABLE_VIEW_EVENTS
- ❏ DDL_TYPE_EVENTS
- ❏ DDL_XML_SCHEMA_COLLECTION_EVENTS

- ❏   DDL_PARTITION_EVENTS

- ❏   DDL_ASSEMBLY_EVENTS

To create a trigger that would audit for any stored procedure change, deletion, or creation, you could use a CREATE TRIGGER statement like the following:

```
CREATE TRIGGER ChangeWindow
ON DATABASE
FOR DDL_PROCEDURE_EVENTS
AS
-- Trigger statement here
```

As mentioned earlier, you can create granular triggers on certain events by using the event type after the FOR keyword. For example, to monitor for any DROP TABLE, CREATE TABLE, or ALTER TABLE statement issued, you could use the following code:

```
CREATE TRIGGER ChangeWindow
ON DATABASE
FOR CREATE_TABLE, DROP_TABLE, ALTER_TABLE
AS
-- Trigger statement here
```

Finally, you can monitor all changes by using the DDL_DATABASE_LEVEL_EVENTS event type:

```
CREATE TRIGGER ChangeWindow
ON DATABASE
FOR DDL_DATABASE_LEVEL_EVENTS
AS
-- Trigger statement here
```

An important function in your DDL trigger toolbox is the EVENTDATA() system function. The EVENTDATA() system function is raised whenever a DDL trigger is fired at any level; it outputs the event type, the user who executed the query, and the exact syntax the user ran. The function outputs this data in XML format, as shown here:

```
<EVENT_INSTANCE>
  <EventType>CREATE_USER</EventType>
  <PostTime>2006-07-09T12:50:16.103</PostTime>
  <SPID>60</SPID>
  <ServerName>BKNIGHT</ServerName>
  <LoginName>BKNIGHT\Owner</LoginName>
  <UserName>dbo</UserName>
  <DatabaseName>AdventureWorks</DatabaseName>
  <ObjectName>brian</ObjectName>
  <ObjectType>SQL USER</ObjectType>
  <DefaultSchema>brian</DefaultSchema>
  <SID>q7ZPUruGyU+nWuOrlc6Crg==</SID>
  <TSQLCommand>
    <SetOptions ANSI_NULLS="ON" ANSI_NULL_DEFAULT="ON" ANSI_PADDING="ON"
QUOTED_IDENTIFIER="ON" ENCRYPTED="FALSE" />
    <CommandText>CREATE USER [brian] FOR LOGIN [brian] WITH DEFAULT_SCHEMA
=
```

```
[dbo]</CommandText>
  </TSQLCommand>
</EVENT_INSTANCE>
```

You can then either pull all the data from the EVENTDATA() function and log it into a table as an XML data type, or pull selective data out using an XPath query. To do an XML XPath query in SQL Server, you would specify the path to the XML node. In DDL triggers, the key elements from the EVENTDATA() function are as follows:

- ❑   EventType: The type of event that caused the trigger.
- ❑   PostTime: The time the event occurred.
- ❑   SPID: The SPID of the user who caused the event.
- ❑   ServerName: The name of the instance on which the event occurred.
- ❑   LoginName: The login name that performed the action that triggered the event.
- ❑   UserName: The user name that performed the action that triggered the event.
- ❑   DatabaseName: The name of the database in which the event occurred.
- ❑   ObjectType: The type of object that was modified, deleted, or created.
- ❑   ObjectName: The name of the object that was modified, deleted, or created.
- ❑   TSQLCommand: The T-SQL command that was executed to cause the trigger to be run.

To pull out selective data, you could use code like the following to do an XPath query. You would first pass in the fully qualified element name, like /EVENT_INSTANCE/TSQLCommand, and the [1] in the following code means to pull out the first record. Because there is only one record in the EVENTDATA() function, you always pull the first record only. The EVENTDATA() function is only available to you in the scope of the trigger. If you were to run the following query outside the trigger, it would return NULL:

```
CREATE TRIGGER RestrictDDL
ON DATABASE
FOR DDL_DATABASE_LEVEL_EVENTS
AS

EXECUTE AS USER = 'DBO'

DECLARE @errordata XML
SET @errordata = EVENTDATA()

SELECT  @errordata
GO
```

You can use the ROLLBACK command in a DDL trigger to cancel the command that the user ran. You can also wrap this in a conditional IF statement to conditionally roll the statement back. Typically, though, you'll see that DDL triggers log that the event occurred and then potentially roll the command back if the user did not follow the correct change procedures.

We'll now walk through a complete example of how you could use DDL triggers to monitor for changes that occur in a database. The type of triggers that you're trying to monitor for are any database-level events, such as table or security changes. In the event of a change, you want to log that event into a table.

If the user is not logged in as the proper account, you want to roll the change back. This way, you can prevent users in the sysadmin role from making changes. The table that you want to log the change events into is called DDLAudit. To create the table, use the following syntax or you can download the complete example at www.wrox.com:

```
CREATE TABLE DDLAudit
(
    AuditID         int             NOT NULL identity
                                    CONSTRAINT DDLAuditPK
                                    PRIMARY KEY CLUSTERED,
    LoginName       sysname         NOT NULL,
    UserName        sysname         NOT NULL,
    PostDateTime    datetime        NOT NULL,
    EventType       varchar(100)    NOT NULL,
    DDLOp           varchar(2500)   NOT NULL
)
```

You're now ready to create the trigger to log into the table. Most SQL Server environments only allow changes to the database between certain maintenance window hours. You can use the following DDL trigger to prevent changes outside the 8:00 P.M. to 7:00 A.M. maintenance window. Changes made at any other time will be rolled back. If you are inside the maintenance window, the change will be logged to the DDLAudit table.

```
CREATE TRIGGER ChangeWindow
ON DATABASE
FOR DDL_DATABASE_LEVEL_EVENTS
AS

DECLARE @errordata XML
SET @errordata = EVENTDATA()

INSERT dbo.DDLAudit
        (LoginName,
         UserName,
         PostDateTime,
         EventType,
         DDLOp)
VALUES   (SYSTEM_USER, ORIGINAL_LOGIN(), GETDATE(),
    @errordata.value('(/EVENT_INSTANCE/EventType)[1]', 'varchar(100)'),
    @errordata.value('(/EVENT_INSTANCE/TSQLCommand)[1]', 'varchar(2500)') )

IF DATEPART(hh,GETDATE()) > 7 AND DATEPART(hh,GETDATE()) < 20
BEGIN

    RAISERROR ('You can only perform this change between 8PM and 7AM. Please try this
change again or contact Production support for an override.', 16, -1)
    ROLLBACK
END
```

Note that in this code, you trap the login that is being used as well as the original login to check for context switching (EXECUTE AS). With the trigger now created, test it by running a simple DDL, command such as the following:

```
CREATE table TriggerTest
(Column1 int)
```

If you executed this command after 7:00 A.M. and before 8:00 P.M., you would receive the following error, and the CREATE statement would roll back. If you looked at the tables in Management Studio, you should not see the TriggerTest table.

```
(1 row(s) affected)
Msg 50000, Level 16, State 1, Procedure ChangeWindow, Line 22
You can not perform this action on a production database. Please contact the
production DBA department for change procedures.
Msg 3609, Level 16, State 2, Line 2
The transaction ended in the trigger. The batch has been aborted.
```

If you were to run the statement before 7:00 A.M. or after 8:00 P.M., you would only see (1 row(s) affected), meaning that the change was logged, but you were able to successfully perform the action. You can test this by changing the server's time in Windows. After you try to create a few tables or make changes, select from the DDLAudit table to see the audited records.

There is little performance effect to this type of trigger because usually DDL events rarely happen. The trigger can be found in Management Studio by selecting the individual database, and then selecting Programmability ⇨ Database Triggers. You can create a script of the trigger to modify an existing trigger or you can delete the trigger by using Management Studio.

Of course, you are still going to want to occasionally run a DDL statement in production by overriding the trigger. To allow access, you need only temporarily turn off the trigger using the following syntax for database-level or server-level triggers:

```
DISABLE TRIGGER ALL ON DATABASE
GO
DISABLE TRIGGER ALL ON ALL SERVER
```

After the override, you can enable the triggers again by running the following syntax (you could replace the keyword ALL with the specific trigger name to enable or disable the individual trigger):

```
ENABLE TRIGGER ALL ON  DATABASE
GO
ENABLE Trigger ALL ON ALL SERVER;
```

Server Triggers

Server-level triggers operate the same way as database-level triggers, but they are monitors for server configuration, security, and other server-level changes. The following list shows the top-level events, but these too are hierarchical. For example, you can monitor any login changes, as you'll see in an upcoming example.

- ❑   DDL_DATABASE_EVENTS

- ❑   DROP_DATABASE

- ❑   DDL_ENDPOINT_EVENTS

- ❑   CREATE_DATABASE

- ❑   DDL_SERVER_SECURITY_EVENTS

- ❑   ALTER_DATABASE

We'll walk through another quick example. As mentioned in the last chapter, if you are in the sysadmin role, you can perform any function you wish on the server. With this DDL trigger, you can ensure that only a single login will be able to perform login-type events, such as creating logins. If anyone else tries to create, modify, or delete a login, it will be rolled back. Of course, you would have to implement additional security measures if this is your actual requirement, such as protecting the DDL trigger from change, but we've kept things simple for this example:

```
CREATE TRIGGER PreventChangeTrigger
ON ALL SERVER
FOR DDL_LOGIN_EVENTS

AS

IF SUSER_NAME() != 'BKNIGHT\OWNER'
BEGIN
  RAISERROR ('This change can only be performed by the server owner, Brian Knight.
Please contact him at extension x4444 to follow the procedure.', 16, -1)
ROLLBACK

END
```

If someone other than the BKNIGHT\OWNER login were to attempt a login change, they would receive the following error. You can issue a permission context switch (EXECUTE AS LOGIN) to test out the trigger in your development environment.

```
Msg 50000, Level 16, State 1, Procedure PreventChangeTrigger, Line 9
This change can only be performed by the server owner, Brian Knight. Please contact
him at extension x4444 to follow the procedure.
Msg 3609, Level 16, State 2, Line 1
```

The transaction ended in the trigger. The batch has been aborted.

DDL server triggers can be found in Management Studio under Server Objects ➪ Triggers. Like the database triggers, you can only script the trigger for modifications, and delete the trigger, from Management Studio.

Trigger Views

The Management Studio interface is still slightly lacking in what you can accomplish with DDL triggers, so a DBA must often go T-SQL as a management interface. One of the nice views that is available to show you all the database-level DDL triggers is sys.triggers; for server-level triggers, you can use sys.server_triggers. Between these two views, you can quickly see what views your server has installed on it with a query like this one:

```
SELECT type, name, parent_class_desc FROM sys.triggers
WHERE parent_class_desc = 'DATABASE'
UNION
SELECT type, name, parent_class_desc FROM sys.server_triggers
WHERE parent_class_desc = 'SERVER'
```

sqlcmd

PowerShell and `sqlcmd` are two complementary scripting environments for managing SQL Server. Each has its strengths and weaknesses, but together they provide a powerful toolkit for the script-friendly DBA. This section covers `sqlcmd`; PowerShell is covered in the section "Creating Change Scripts" later in this chapter.

Scripting Overview

Change management is all about creating a reproducible and auditable way to deploy and manage your changes. This is impossible to do properly by having a DBA execute T-SQL scripts through a Management Studio environment. Most non-Windows system administrators use shell scripts to create a repeatable change management process for their OS and database server environments. This accepted administrative practice has the broadest acceptance and the lowest risk. Scripting leverages native OS and application capabilities and works consistently regardless of the target system, at least outside the Windows environment. Just as experienced SQL DBAs have T-SQL script libraries, DBAs working with open-source and Unix-variant systems have shell script libraries that just keep getting larger as they collect more and more useful scriptlets. Now we have the same scripting capabilities on the Windows platform, only better.

In SQL 2005, we had the first major attempt to create a scripting environment that could cross the boundary between T-SQL and the outside world. `sqlcmd` is still a great mechanism for mixing SQL and operating system scripts for database schema deployments. (PowerShell, covered later in this chapter, takes this a step further, enabling us to script object behavior for scalable server configuration deployments.) The main way to create a repeatable change management system is by using `sqlcmd` files that encapsulate that T-SQL logic into a set of output logs. These logs provide an audit trail for your deployment activities. This way, you know that the change will deploy to each of your environments (test, QA, Production, etc.) and provide predictable results.

`sqlcmd` is a replacement for `isql` and `osql`. You can use either of two modes to execute a `sqlcmd` command: at a command line or in Management Studio. If you are an SQL Server 2000 DBA, the transition to `sqlcmd` will be an easy one; `sqlcmd` is very similar to `osql`, with some additional switches to simplify your daily job. You probably won't be familiar with executing `sqlcmd` commands from Management Studio, though. Using Management Studio to execute these types of commands gives you a great deal of control and replaces many of the old extended stored procedures such as `xp_cmdshell`. This section covers both solutions.

Executing sqlcmd from the Command Prompt

Executing `sqlcmd` from the command prompt enables you to run any query from a command prompt. More importantly, it allows you to wrap these queries into a packaged install batch file for deployments, making it easy for anyone to install the database. You can use many switches in `sqlcmd`, most of which have only a very specialized use. The following are some of the important switches (they are all case sensitive):

- ❏   `-U`: User name.
- ❏   `-P`: Password.

❏   -E: Use Windows authentication. If you use this switch, you will not need to pass in the -U and -P switches.

❏   -S: Instance name to connect to.

❏   -d: Database name to start in.

❏   -i: Input file that contains the query to run.

❏   -o: Output file to which you wish to log the output of the query.

❏   -Q: You can also pass in the query with the -Q switch instead of an input file.

We'll start with a few basic examples to demonstrate the commands you'll use on a regular basis.

Remember that you need to change the actual file save locations to something appropriate for your particular system.

1.   Create a new SQL file with Notepad or the text editor of your choice by typing the following query:

```
SELECT * FROM Purchasing.Vendor
```

Save the file as `C:\users\demo\documents\TestQuery.sql`.

2.   Go to a command prompt and type the following command:

```
sqlcmd -i c:\testquery.sql -S localhost -d AdventureWorks
```

The -i switch represents the input file that contains the file; the -S switch represents the server name to connect to; and the -d switch represents the database name. The query retrieves all the records from the Vendor table and displays them in the console window. If you do not specify a user name and password with the -U and -P switches, or the -E switch for Windows authentication, sqlcmd will default to Windows authentication.

A variation of this command is to use the -Q switch to pass the query to sqlcmd and then quit sqlcmd after the query is complete. The -q switch can also be used if you don't want to exit. The other variation in the following query is the use of the -o switch. The -o switch passes the results of the query to an output file and does not display anything in the console:

```
sqlcmd -Q "select * from purchasing.vendor" -d adventureworks -S localhost
-o C:\testoutput.txt
```

Another way to execute sqlcmd from a command prompt is by typing sqlcmd if you'd like to connect to your local instance, or by specifying the instance with the -S switch. You will then be presented with a 1> prompt, where you can type a query. If you want to execute an operating system command from the sqlcmd window, type !! in front of the command, like this:

```
1>!!dir
```

To execute an SQL command, type the command. After you press Enter, you will see a 2> and 3> prompt until you finally issue a GO statement to execute the batch. After the GO statement, the batch runs and the prompt resets to 1>.

That covers the basic commands, but to simplify matters, it would be great to have a set of commands that would execute each time you ran `sqlcmd`. An *initialization file* runs a series of commands after you execute `sqlcmd` but before control is handed off to the user.

To create an initialization file, follow these steps:

1. Create a T-SQL file called `C:\users\demo\documents\initexample.sql` with Notepad or another text editor.

   This file is going to run a series of commands after you first run `sqlcmd`. The `:setvar` statement can be used to set user variables that can be employed later in the script with the `$` sign. This example initialization script creates three variables. One holds the database name, one holds the 60-second timeout, and the last one holds the server name. You use the variables later in the script by using `$(variablename)`.

   ```
   :setvar  DBNAME AdventureWorksLT2008
   :setvar sqlcmdlogintimeout 60
   :setvar server "localhost"
   :connect $(server) -l $(sqlcmdlogintimeout)
   SELECT @@VERSION VersionofSQL;
   SELECT @@SERVERNAME as ServerName;
   ```

2. At a command prompt, type the following command to set the `sqlcmdini` environment variable:

   ```
   SET sqlcmdini=c:\users\demo\documents\initexample.sql
   ```

   This sets the environment variable for the user's profile. After you execute this, each time the `sqlcmd` program is executed, the `initexample.sql` script will execute before handing control to the user.

With the environment variable now set, just run `sqlcmd` from a command prompt (see Figure 10-11). After you run this, you will see the version of SQL Server and the server name before you're given control to run any query against the database.

Executing sqlcmd from Management Studio

While doing your day-to-day job, eventually you're going to find yourself wanting to integrate `sqlcmd` scripts into your regular T-SQL scripts, or someone may pass you a script that has `sqlcmd` integrated into it. To use this script in Management Studio's query environment, simply click the SQLCMD Mode icon in the Query window. If you try to execute `sqlcmd` syntax from within the Query window without being in SQLCMD mode, you will receive an error message like the following:

```
Msg 102, Level 15, State 1, Line 3
Incorrect syntax near '!'.
```

You can intermingle `sqlcmd` and T-SQL in the same script, and you can switch between script types easily as long as SQLCMD mode is enabled. Once enabled, any `sqlcmd` syntax will be highlighted in gray. You can also enable the mode each time a query is opened by going to Tools ⇨ Options in Management Studio. In the SQL Server page of the Query Execution group (shown in Figure 10-12), enable the option "By default, open new queries in SQLCMD mode." After you've enabled this option, any subsequent Query windows will be opened with the mode enabled.

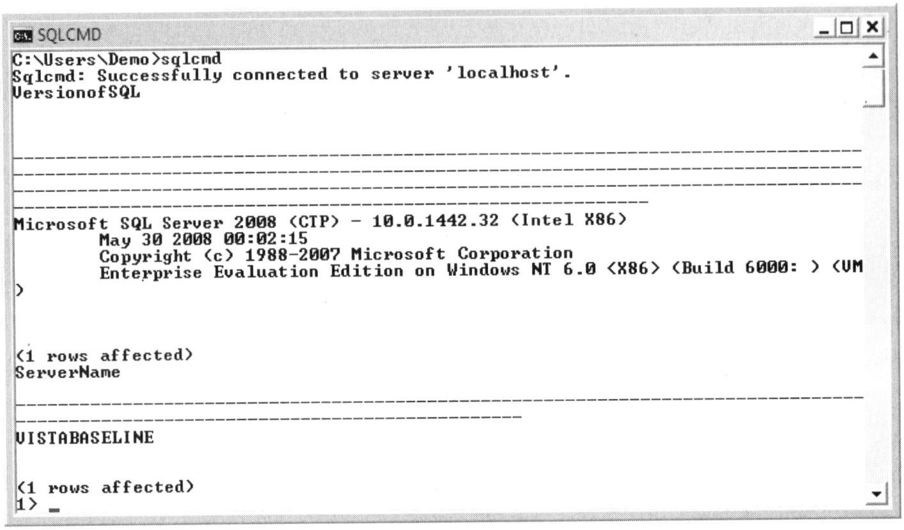

Figure 10-11

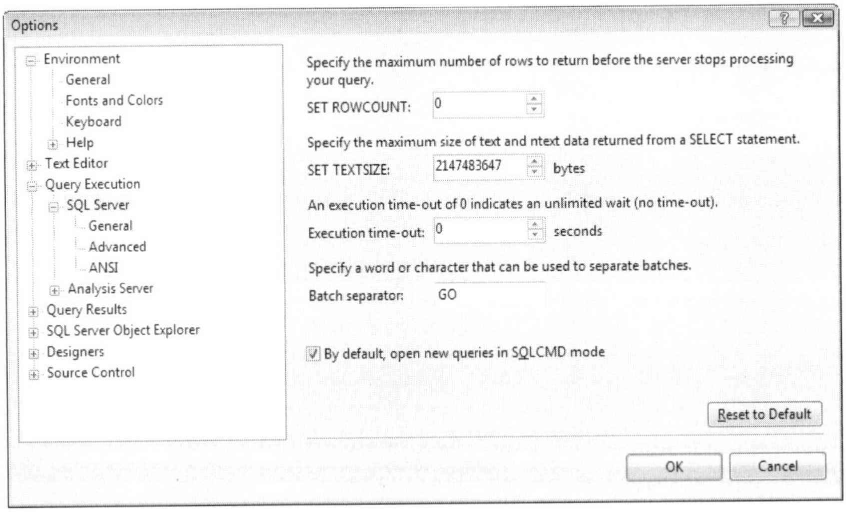

Figure 10-12

Using `sqlcmd` and T-SQL, you can connect to multiple servers from within the same script and run T-SQL statements. For example, the following script will log on to multiple servers and back up the `master` database of each server. The `:CONNECT` command is followed by the name of the instance to which you want to connect. This is a simple example, but it can be strengthened in a disaster recovery situation to do massive repairing of your databases or SQL Server instances.

Again, remember that you need to change the actual file save locations to something appropriate for your particular system.

```
:CONNECT localhost
BACKUP DATABASE master TO  DISK = N'C:\MSSQL\Backup\test.bak'

:CONNECT localhost\sql2k5test
BACKUP DATABASE master TO  DISK = N'C:\MSSQL\Backup\test2.bak'
```

You can also use the :SETVAR command inside sqlcmd to create a script variable. This variable enables you to set the variable either from within the :SETVAR command, as shown in the following code, or by passing it through the command prompt. The following example shows you how to set a variable called SQLServer to the value of Localhost. You then use that variable by using the variable name prefixed with a dollar sign and wrapping it in parentheses. Another variable called DBNAME is also created and used in the T-SQL backup command. As you can see, in sqlcmd you can mix T-SQL and sqlcmd easily, and the variables can intermix.

```
:SETVAR SQLServer Localhost
:CONNECT $(SQLServer)
:SETVAR DBNAME Master

BACKUP DATABASE $(DBNAME) TO  DISK = N'C:\MSSQL\Backup\test.bak'
```

Now modify the script slightly to look like the following, and then save it to a file called C:\InputFile.sql (place the file wherever is appropriate on your machine). This script will dynamically connect to a server and back up the master database:

```
:CONNECT $(SQLServer)
BACKUP DATABASE master TO  DISK = N'C:\MSSQL\Backup\test.bak'
```

With the script now saved, you can go to a command prompt and type the following command using the -v switch (again, all of these switches are case sensitive) to pass in the variable. In this case, you pass in the name localhost to the SQLServer variable:

```
sqlcmd -i c:\users\demo\documents\inputfile.sql -v SQLServer="localhost"
```

Creating Change Scripts

Creating change scripts is never a fun task for a DBA, but few things are more satisfying than a perfect deployment to four different environments. The only way to achieve this "perfect" deployment is to either invest a lot of time in writing a good script, like the one shown shortly, or invest in a tool.

There are many tools on the market to help a DBA package and deploy changes. For example, Red-Gate (www.red-gate.com) can compare two databases (test and production, for example) and package the change scripts to move production up to the same level. This same type of tool is available through many other vendors — ApexSQL, Idera, and Quest, to name a few. None of these tools eliminates human intervention entirely. You must have some interaction with the program to ensure that a change not meant to be deployed is not sent to production. The following sections address some specific tools for creating change scripts and deploying changes: Data Dude, PowerShell, and version tables.

Data Dude

Worth mentioning here is Visual Studio Team System for Database Professionals, also known as Data Dude. This Microsoft product aids in the complete change cycle. Visual Studio 2003 used to do this very well, but the deployment feature was removed in Visual Studio 2005 until the Team System version was released. The tool enables change detection and simple deployment to multiple environments. This is especially important in database deployment situations because developers rarely write comprehensive change scripts. Developers often "hand tweak" a data type or add a column that never makes it into the schema creation script. Data Dude compares the actual state of two databases and writes scripts to reconcile the two.

Think of your production system as version 1.0, and development as version 1.1. Script the production schema (or back it up as a baseline) and use it as the starting point. The scripts can then take the database to version 1.1, repeatedly and reliably. You can use the scripts to deploy to your quality testing environment and then use the exact same scripts to deploy to production. Because the output is T-SQL scripts, you can use Visual Source Safe (or the version management software of your choice) to have controllable versions of your database. As a bonus, Visual Studio Team System for Database Professionals creates the reverse scripts that take a version 1.1 database back down to version 1.0. Rollback has typically been an "Oops, let's restore" operation at best. Now it can be a predictable part of your deployment repertoire.

Another useful feature of Visual Studio Team System for Database Professionals is its ability to refactor a database. Refactoring can be as simple as changing a column name or as complex as breaking a column off into its own table. Many applications start with a field for "address," later needing "billing address," "shipping address," and "mailing address" fields. Data Dude not only enables such changes, but also updates every stored procedure and view that referenced the original column. You may have to make logic changes, but Data Dude does the heavy lifting of finding all the column references and updating where it can. Of course, that assumes all your data access code is in stored procedures and you don't do ad hoc SQL directly to the database tables. Following best design practices makes things easier in the long run in ways you cannot always predict.

PowerShell

Just as DBAs need to deploy database code changes reliably, they also need to deploy configuration changes in the same way. While T-SQL scripts can take you a good way down this path, something more is needed. PowerShell is that something. PowerShell is a new and largely backward-compatible scripting environment for Windows. It is shipped as a native feature in Windows Server 2008 and can be downloaded and installed on Windows Server 2003, Windows XP, and Windows Vista. While it is beyond the scope of this book to tell you everything about PowerShell, this section introduces some of the features that highlight just how useful it can be.

> *Professional Windows PowerShell Programming: Snap-ins, Cmdlets, Hosts, and Providers, by Arul Kumaravel et al. (Wrox, 2008), is an excellent in-depth guide to Windows PowerShell for readers who want a deeper look at the subject.*

PowerShell relies to a considerable degree on elements called *cmdlets* to do the heavy lifting. Cmdlets take an object model and present it like a disk drive. Of course, disk drives show up just as you would expect. Natively, PowerShell can traverse and explore event logs, registry hives, file systems, and pretty much anything else built into the Windows operating system. For SQL Server, the SQL Development team wrote a custom cmdlet that presents the SQL-SMO object model as a drive. The cmdlet also has some extra smarts regarding how it presents data to the console, just to make our jobs a bit easier.

We can start off with the server object and list its members (see Figure 10-13). One neat trick of PowerShell is that it has a built-in set of aliases that map its native verb-noun syntax into legacy commands. `dir` works just as well as `get-childitem`; and for the folks who believe that `ls` is the proper command for enumerating a folder, that works too. Note that the arguments for all commands must still be in PowerShell format. Trying to match that level of compatibility would have been impossibly complex.

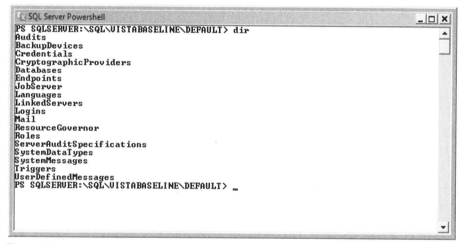

Figure 10-13

Because Server is an object, the cmdlet lists its properties and methods. If your current directory is a collection (folder), PowerShell will list all the members of the collection instead. You can `cd` to the database folder (collection) and list all the items in it (see Figure 10-14).

PowerShell is aware of the window size and adjusts the output format accordingly. In Figure 10-14, the SQL cmdlet stripped four columns from the output in order to fit the default PowerShell window size. A wider window will show more details, until the number of databases gets too large, at which point the cmdlet will switch to listing names only.

Like nearly everything else in Windows, PowerShell is case insensitive, at least regarding command and object names. If you are executing code against a case-sensitive SQL instance or database, any comparisons executed by the server will honor its collation rules.

PowerShell supports all the legacy DOS/command shell commands and is mostly syntax-compatible with Windows Scripting Host. The largest difference between PowerShell and most Unix-based shell environments is in how the pipe command (|) works. In Unix-based shells, the pipe command connects the text output of one command to the input of the next command. This often requires creative use of `grep` to parse the list and create meaningful input for the next command in the sequence. PowerShell passes .NET objects to the next command. Collections are automatically iterated over, and hierarchies can usually be traversed with the RECURSE option, provided the cmdlet supports that functionality. As of this writing, PowerShell is just getting started, but we believe it is the future for most Windows and Microsoft server platform management. It is the first truly universal Microsoft scripting environment.

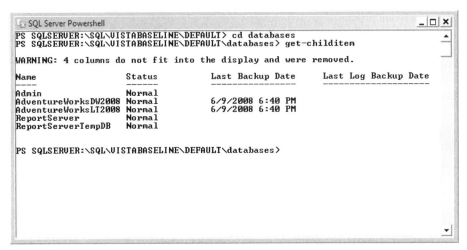

Figure 10-14

Version Tables

Another important practice when deploying changes is adding a version number to your changes, much as application developers do in their own version controlling. A table that we've used for years is the db_version table, which holds what version of the database is currently installed and what versions have been installed over the history of the database.

By looking in the change history, you can use the table to determine whether the DBA who deployed the change skipped a build of the database. If you jump from 2.0 to 2.2, you know you may have an issue. A version table can also be used in conjunction with the application's version number. For example, you may have a document specifying that version 2.1 of the application requires version 2.1.8 of the database. We've even had developers code the logic into the application at startup. If the application did not match the db_version table, then it would throw an error. The table's schema looks like the following. You can download this code, called db_version.sql, from this book's Web site at www.wrox.com.

```
if not exists (select * from sys.objects where object_id =
object_id(N'[dbo].[DB_VERSION]') and OBJECTPROPERTY(object_id, N'IsUserTable') = 1)
 BEGIN
CREATE TABLE [DB_VERSION] (
   [MajorVersion] [char] (5) NULL ,
   [MinorVersion] [char] (5) NULL ,
   [Build] [char] (5) NULL ,
   [Revision] [char] (5) NULL ,
   [OneOff] [char] (5) NULL,
```

```
    [DateInstalled] [datetime] NULL CONSTRAINT [DF__Version__DateIns__0876219E]
DEFAULT (getdate()),
    [InstalledBy] [varchar] (50) NULL ,
    [Description] [varchar] (255) NULL
) ON [PRIMARY]
END
```

For most environments, there are too many columns in this db_version table, but it was created as a catch-all, standard table. Every DBA who works at your company will know to go to the table, regardless of the application, to find the version. The version may match a document of known issues with the database. Typically, you may also find yourself creating views on top of the table to show you the last installed version. The following list describes a complete data dictionary for the table:

❑   MajorVersion: Major release of the application. In the application version it would be the following bolded number **(1.0.5.1)**.

❑   MinorVersion: Minor release of the application. In the application version it would be the following bolded number **(1.0.5.1)**.

❑   Build: Build number of the application. In the application version it would be the following bolded number **(1.0.5.1)**.

❑   Revision: Also called the minor service pack (or patch) position. This number also refers to bug fixes that are found in QA. For example, you may have numerous iterations of Portal 2.5.3 as you fix bugs. You could increment this number (Application Build 2.5.3.**2**, for the second iteration). In the application version it would be the following bolded number **(1.0.5.1)**.

❑   OneOff: In some cases, customization code may be required. For example, suppose Application A has a number of customized versions of Build 2.1.1. In those cases, you could have 2.1.1.0–**1** to indicate a customization (1 being for Client B, for example). This field is used in specialized situations only.

❑   DateInstalled: The date this application was installed in the environment. This is set to getdate() by default, which set it to the current date and time.

❑   InstalledBy: The name of the installer or creator of the service pack.

❑   Description: Description of the service pack. This can be used in an environment where multiple clients are sharing one database — for example, "Upgrade Application A 2.5.1.2 for Client B."

To insert it into the table, use the following syntax:

```
INSERT INTO DB_VERSION  SELECT 1, 5, 0, 2, NULL, getdate(),'Brian Knight','Script
to promote zip code changes'
```

Make sure that the deploying DBA knows she must place the lines of code to create the table and insert the version information into it at the top of each command file you create. A standard template script file with fill-in-the-blank fields makes this task easier and more consistent. A last use for the table is to run a check before you perform a database upgrade. Before applying the database install for version 1.1, you can run an IF statement against the table to ensure that version 1.0 is installed. If it isn't installed, you can throw an error and stop the script from executing.

Summary

This chapter described how to become compliant with best practices in change management. You learned that you can do this by monitoring for change using policies. You can also use Visual Studio to create database projects that integrate into Source Safe. The last key for creating a change management process is using `sqlcmd` and PowerShell for a smooth deployment by using scripts. In the next chapter, you will learn how to properly configure a server for optimum performance before installing SQL Server 2008.

11

Configuring the Server for Optimal Performance

The developer database administrator needs to know how to optimize performance to ensure that anything he or she designs will perform up to its potential. The developer DBA must ensure that the system will start its life performing well; and that as inevitable changes are made to the system throughout its life cycle, they are made in a way that enables the application to continue to perform. As the system grows in terms of data, users, and functionality, it needs to grow in ways that keep the system operating optimally.

Similarly, the production DBA needs to understand performance so that the system he or she maintains starts out performing well and then continues to do so throughout the system's life cycle. Several different elements factor into this, from getting the server set up correctly, to monitoring the system as it starts working, to implementing a full monitoring strategy to keep the system operating optimally.

The three most important aspects of delivering high performance around scalability, response time, reliability, and usability are as follows:

❑ Knowing what your system can deliver in terms of CPU, memory, input/output (I/O).

❑ Finding the bottlenecks.

❑ Knowing your target (how many, how fast).

This chapter discusses all of these issues and addresses the most pressing questions regarding performance and configuring a server.

What Every DBA Needs to Know about Performance

In this chapter, we lay out a lot of specific hardware recommendations that will enable you to improve the performance of your system. However, shaving milliseconds off of a transaction time isn't always worth the amount of time and hardware budget you spend to accomplish that goal. Frequently, good planning up front is worth more than clever optimization later. Always keep the following three things in mind: define your system performance targets, start tuning early, and focus on these performance requirements:

The Performance Tuning Cycle

Performance tuning is an iterative process and ideally starts at the beginning of the design process. Too often performance and optimization are tacked on at the end. Obtaining optimal performance starts with configuring the server, continues with designing an efficient schema and specifying optimized SQL statements, which leads to optimal index selection. The monitoring and analysis of performance can then feed back to any point in this process, right back to changes to server configuration or schema design. This system is illustrated in Figure 11-1.

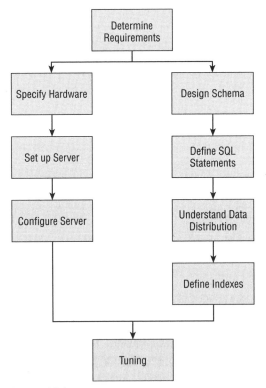

Figure 11-1

You start with your first best guess about how you think your application is going to work and what resources you think it's going to use and plan accordingly. Most often, it's only a best guess, as you really don't know yet exactly how the application is going to work.

In the case of a new application, you don't have an existing system to measure. In the best case, you will have some metrics from either an existing user base or management predictions regarding who the users will be, what they do on a daily basis, and how that would impact the new application.

In the case of an existing system that you are either moving to a new server or to which you are adding functionality, you can measure specific metrics on system resource usage, and use those as a starting point. Then you can add information about any new functionality. Will this increase the user base? Will it increase the processing load on the server? Will it change the data volume?

All this information enables you to make a good estimate of the new system's impact on resources. Even before you have implemented the new system, while testing is taking place, you have a great opportunity to start evaluating your estimates against the actual resource requirements and the performance you get from your test servers.

Defining Good Performance

The fundamental question that every DBA has to answer before refining a system is simple: Do we have good performance? Without either a specific target or some baseline to compare against, you will never know. Planning, sizing, testing, and monitoring will provide you with the information you need to be able to start answering this question. Identify your critical targets for CPU, memory, and I/O; create a baseline; and then after deploying, monitor your critical measurements.

For example, consider how performance requirements can vary in the case of an online store. Here, response time to users is critical to keep them shopping. On a database such as this, there are likely to be very clearly defined response times for the most important queries, and maybe a broad requirement that no query can take longer than two or three seconds. On a different database server delivering management reports on warehouse inventory levels, there may be an expectation that these reporting queries take some time to gather the right information, so response times as long as a few minutes may be acceptable, although there may still be some queries that have much shorter response time requirements. In yet another database the key performance criterion might be the time it takes to back up the database, or the time to load or unload data.

Along with the business stakeholders and users, define realistic requirements for the system and then proceed to address them. The key performance criteria might be defined as a very high-level requirement such as "no query must take longer than x seconds." In another system it might be that long-running operations must complete within a specific time window, such as backup must complete in an overnight window of x hours to meet the service level agreement (SLA).

Focus on What's Most Important

The final essential aspect of performance is being able to focus on what's really important — achieving the performance that users demand. You must know what you need to measure, how to measure it, and what the limitations of that measurement might be. Consider a typical system. The end users' experience is the net sum of all performance from their client machine through many layers to the database server and back again. Because the focus of this book is the DBA and SQL Server 2008, we are going to focus on measuring SQL Server 2008 performance, but it's worthwhile to have a basic understanding of the big picture, where DBAs fit in, and some of the tools and metrics that may have an impact on your system.

Figure 11-2 shows a schematic diagram of a typical web-based architecture. This schematic is typical of any enterprise customer using the Microsoft Windows Server System Reference Architecture to implement their enterprise solution. This may be the first time that many DBAs have looked at something like this and understood where their puzzle piece (that is, the database) fits into the big picture.

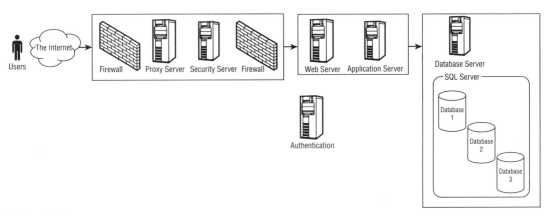

Figure 11-2

One of the first things you notice in the diagram is the number of elements in the bigger picture. When the user calls the help desk and complains of poor performance, finding the culprit involves a lot of possible candidates, so it is important to spend time identifying which piece of the complex system architecture might be guilty.

The important thing to take away from this exercise is an understanding of both the big picture and how to zero in on what's important for you. In this book we are interested in SQL Server, databases, and the server on which SQL Server runs.

What the Developer DBA Needs to Know about Performance

Good performance is built on a solid foundation, which for a SQL database is the schema. A well-designed schema will provide a solid foundation on which the rest of your application can be implemented. The rules to follow are less simple than traditional concepts such as "normalize to the nth form." Instead, they require that you have a solid understanding of the use of the system, including the usage pattern, the SQL statements, and the data. The optimal schema for an online transaction processing (OLTP) system may be less optimal for a decision support system (DSS), or for a data warehousing (DW) system.

Users

You first need to know who is going to use the system: how many users there will be, their concurrency, peak usage level, and what they are going to do. The users will usually fall into different groups based on either job function or feature usage. For an e-commerce-based system, for example, the user groups might be browsers, purchasers, order trackers, customers needing help, and others. For a sales analytics system, the user groups may be primarily analysts reading the data with report tools such as Performance-Point Server, Proclarity, or Excel, and perhaps running reporting for the sales team. For example, the e-commerce-based system is an OLTP database workload that is optimized for fewer and faster reads, updates and writes requests while the sales analytics system is a DSS database workload that is optimized for large table scans to generate reports.

SQL Statements

After determining the different groups of users, you need to understand what they do, which SQL statements will be run, and how often each of these is run for a user action. In the e-commerce example, a browser might arrive at the site, which invokes the home page, for example, requiring 20 or 30 different stored procedures to be executed. When users click on something on the home page, each action taken will require another set of stored procedures to be executed to return the data for the next page. So far it looks like everything has been read-only, but for ASP.NET pages there is the issue of session state, which may be kept in a SQL database. If that's the case, then you may already have seen a lot of write activity just to get to this stage.

Data

The final part of the picture is the data in the database. You need an understanding of the total data volume in each table, including how that data gets there and how it changes over time. For the e-commerce example, the main data elements of the site would be the catalog of items available for sale. For example, the catalog could come directly from the suppliers' Web sites through an Internet portal. Once this data is initially loaded, it can be refreshed with updates as each supplier changes their product line, and as prices vary. The overall volume of data won't change much unless you add or remove items or suppliers.

What will change, hopefully very quickly, will be the number of registered users, any click-tracking you do based on site personalization, the number of orders placed, the number of line items sold, and the number of orders shipped. Of course, you hope that you will sell a lot of items, which will result in a lot of new data growth every day.

A sound knowledge of the data, its distribution, and how it changes helps you find potential hot spots, which could be either frequently retrieved reference data, frequently inserted data, or frequently updated data. All of these could result in bottlenecks that might limit performance.

Robust Schema

An understanding of all the preceding pieces — users, SQL statements, and data — needs to come together to help implement a well-designed and well-performing application. If the foundation stone of your database schema is not solid, then anything you build on top of that unstable foundation is going to be unstable. Although you may be able to achieve something that's acceptable, you are unlikely to achieve an optimal solution.

How does all this information help you tune the server? You need to understand where the hot spots are in the data to enable the physical design to be implemented in the most efficient manner. If you are going through the process of designing a logical data model, you shouldn't care about performance issues. Only when you are ready to design the physical model do you take this information into account, and modify the design to incorporate your knowledge of data access patterns.

What the Production DBA Needs to Know about Performance

The production DBA's life is considerably different from that of the developer DBA, in that a production DBA is dealing with a system that someone else may have designed, built, and handed over, either as a new or an already running system. The production DBA may also face challenges with performance on very old systems running legacy applications on old outdated hardware. In this case, the scenario changes from designing an efficient system to making the system you have been given work as well as possible on that limited hardware.

The starting point for this process has to be an understanding of what the hardware can deliver; what hardware resources the system needs; and what are the expectations of the users in terms of user response time. The key elements of understanding the hardware are processor speed, type, and cache size. Next comes memory: How much is there? What is the bus speed? Then comes I/O: How many disks? How are they configured? How many NICs are there? Having answers to these questions is just the start.

The next step is determining how each component of the system is required to perform. Are there any performance-related service level agreements (SLAs)? If any performance guidelines are specified anywhere, are you meeting them, exceeding them, or failing them? In all cases, you should also know the trend. Have you been maintaining the status quo, getting better, or, as is most often the case, slowly getting worse?

The production DBA needs to understand all of this, and then know how to identify bottlenecks and resolve them to get the system performing at the required level again.

The tools that the production DBA uses to perform these tasks may include the following:

❑   **Task Manager:** Gives a quick, high-level view of server performance and use of resources

❑   **System Performance Monitor (or Reliability and Performance Monitor in Windows 2008 and Vista):** Provides a more detailed view of Windows server performance and per-instance SQL Server specific counters

❑   **SQL Profiler:** Enables captures of database workload traces, and identifies long-running transactions

❑   **SQL Server Management Studio:** Enables long-running transactions to be analyzed, and bottlenecks found and resolved

These tools are covered in more detail in Chapter 13.

Optimizing the Server

The rest of this chapter covers optimizing the server. This includes the hardware and operating system configuration to provide SQL Server with the best environment in which to execute. The three key resources that you should consider any time you discuss optimization or performance are the CPU, memory, and I/O.

Starting with the CPU, there aren't a lot of options to play with here other than the number and type of processors. The only real configuration option to consider once the server is mounted in the data center is whether it is enabled for hyperthreading — that is, should you turn hyperthreading on or off? Other than helping you make the right decision about hyperthreading, most of this part of the chapter focuses on understanding the different processor attributes so you can make the right purchasing decisions.

Memory has more options, and it's a lot easier to add or remove memory (RAM) than it is to change the number or type of processors in a server. When you initially configure the server, you should have some idea of how much memory you might need and understand the available configuration options. These options are primarily for non-uniform memory access (NUMA) systems. On a NUMA system, you will often have the choice of using *cell local memory* or *interleaved memory*. In Windows 2003 32-bit systems, a number of `boot.ini` settings can affect memory configuration. These are settings such as enabling physical address extensions (PAEs), which enables the Windows kernel to use the PAE version of the kernel, which in turn can take advantage of an additional four address lines on Intel processors that support PAE. The `boot.ini` file is not available on Windows 2008. In Windows 2008, at the command prompt, you need to execute the `BCDEDIT /SET PAE ForceEnable` command to activate PAE, and `BCDEDIT /SET IncreaseUserVA 3072` to activate 3GB.

`/3GB` and `/USERVA` are `boot.ini` settings that alter the way the operating system configures the 32-bit address space. I/O is, by far, the largest and most complex section of this chapter. In many ways I/O performance is perhaps the most important part of the server configuration to get right because everything you do lives on the disk. All the code you run in the operating system, SQL Server, and any other applications start off as files on the disk. All the data you touch in SQL Server lives on the disk. Data starts out life there, is read into memory, and then has to be written back to disk before it becomes a permanent change. Every change you make in SQL Server is written to the SQL log file, which lives on disk. All these factors make a good I/O configuration an essential part of any SQL Server system.

I/O configuration is actually too big a subject to cover in one chapter; it really requires a book of its own. This chapter introduces you to some of the I/O options available and then walks through several scenarios to provide some insight into how to make the right storage configuration decisions.

Before we start, it will be helpful to put each of the three server resources back into perspective in terms of their relative performance to each other. As you refer to this book in the future, you can easily pencil in the current start of processor, memory, and I/O performance to see how the relative speeds of different elements have changed.

An example of typical speeds and throughput for system resources is as follows:

❑ A CPU speed of 2 GHz results in 8GB/sec

❑ Memory speed of 500 MHz results in 2GB/sec

❑ Disk speed of 5 to 200MB/sec

Use the preceding numbers to do the math for throughput for a 10GB table:

❑ A 2 GHz CPU with a throughput of 8GB/sec would access 10GB of data in 1.2 seconds.

❑ 500 MHz memory with a throughput of 2GB/sec would access 10GB of data in 5 seconds.

❑ Disks with a throughput of 5MB/sec would access 10GB in 33 minutes.

Graphically, this might look something like what is shown in Figure 11-3.

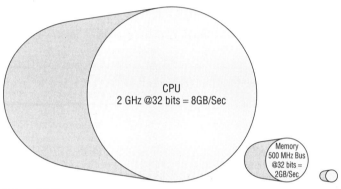

Figure 11-3

Given the relative difference between CPU speed and disk speed, unfortunately I can't draw the disk small enough, or the CPU big enough, to make this illustration to scale. The conclusion here is that disk access is much slower than memory access, which is slower than the CPU. The key, therefore, is to get as much data as you can into memory, and then as much of that onto the CPU as you can.

With SQL Server, there isn't much you can do to alter how much of your data is being operated on by the CPU; that's controlled by the developers who wrote SQL Server. What you can do, though, is obtain processors with larger caches, and at higher speeds. Add more memory of a faster speed, and design your storage subsystem to deliver the fastest performance possible within your requirements for speed, size, and cost.

Configuring Server Hardware

On most small- to medium-size servers, a common configuration for database servers is to make a BIOS change to enable hyperthreading, if based on your database testing you have determined that hyper-threading will provide a performance improvement for your scenario. Once this option is set, most of the remaining tasks are related to physically installing RAM, I/O adapters such as NICs, and disk adapters for SCSI or SATA. Moreover, review the vendors' documentation for any additional configuration options that they recommend.

On medium to large systems, you will find a variety of management software to help you configure, operate, and maintain the hardware. Most hardware vendors have their own version of this kind of software, offering a wide variety of capabilities and options.

On large enterprise systems such as the HP Superdome, NEC5800 Express, or Unisys ES7000 family, configuring the server hardware has entered a whole new dimension. On these larger enterprise systems, you will find a *management processor (MP)* within the server. The management processor, and its software interface, controls the hardware — from booting a hardware partition, to configuring a different hardware partition, to changing memory layout, to managing the power to different hardware components. The management processor handles all of these tasks.

The tasks that need to be achieved to manage all the large systems are very similar, but the way each hardware vendor implements its interface is unique, from the Java/Web site approach on Unisys to the Telnet-based command-line interface on HP and NEC systems.

Windows Server System Reference Architecture

Anytime you're thinking about building a new server, or are designing a new application, it is worthwhile to refer to the Windows Server System Reference Architecture (WSSRA) to find the latest Microsoft-recommended configurations and to determine whether a configuration exists that might match closely with what you want to do. If Microsoft has already built a server configuration that matches your requirements, then you can save a lot of time by reusing the work they have already done. The WSSRA is a reference architecture that contains prescriptive guidance for setting up servers for different roles in an enterprise.

Windows Server Catalog

The Windows Server Catalog (www.windowsservercatalog.com/) should be your first stop when considering purchasing any new hardware. If the new hardware isn't in the catalog, then it's not supported to run Windows Server 2008 (or Windows 2003) and won't be supported when running SQL Server either.

CPU

SQL Server 2008 operates in a very different environment than previous versions of SQL Server. When SQL Server 2000 was launched, a large server used for SQL Server may have had four to eight processors. Now SQL Server 2008 is able to run on the largest servers, with 64 cores, and up to 1TB of RAM running Windows Server 2008 or Windows 2003 Datacenter Edition. Currently, there is a bewildering array of processor options to consider when obtaining a new system. SQL Server 2008 can run on a wide variety of processors:

- ❏ 32-bit processors: x86
- ❏ 32-bit with 64-bit extension processors: x64
- ❏ 64-bit processors: IA64

What follows is a short introduction to these different processor families, along with a short discussion of some of the factors that influence making a decision about which processor you should use.

32-bit x86 Processors

A processor standard for more than a decade, an x86 processor can support up to 32 cores and can directly address 4GB of virtual address space where 2GB is assigned to a Windows process — for example, SQL Server — and 2GB is kept by the operating system. With the 3GB option, it can assign 3GB to a Windows process instead of 2GB. With the Address Windowing Extension (AWE), SQL Server can support up to 64GB. For SQL Server, AWE memory can only be used for data pages caching. Moreover, access to

421

AWE memory is slower than the virtual address memory. 32-bit systems are fast becoming a legacy platform, and have largely been replaced by 64-bit systems. Most newer servers available today support both 32-bit or x64. The reasons to consider running a server on a 32-bit system today are to support legacy applications that don't support 64-bit, or because SQL Server is running a database workload that doesn't require more than 3GB of RAM.

x64

x64 was originally introduced by AMD and implemented by Intel as EM64T. It requires Windows 2003 with SP1 or later. It is compatible with x86 machine code and will support 64-bit micro-code extensions. It can run SQL Server 2008 x64, delivering memory beyond 4GB and up to 1TB natively addressable and up to 64 cores without the need of physical address extension (PAE). Its processor clock speed is significantly faster than IA64 and it will run 32-bit applications natively. Moreover, it can run SQL Server 2008 32-bit, where it can deliver up to 4GB of virtual address space instead of 3GB RAM on x86. The x64 platform is the most popular server platform for database workloads, except for the very largest workloads.

IA64

This first 64-bit platform for Windows, also known as Itanium2, is incompatible with x86 machine code. It will execute x86 applications in Windows on Windows (WoW) emulation mode, but usually performs poorly. It is natively addressable up to 1TB of memory and 64 cores. Its processors have slower clock speed than the x64 or x86 processors but have large caches. SQL Server 2008 IA64 runs natively on this platform and can address all available memory without PAE. The IA64 platform is commonly deployed for the largest database workloads running on some of the largest IA64 servers.

If you're considering purchasing new servers today, you should seriously consider 64-bit processors, either x64 or IA64. The capability to increase memory beyond 4GB without resorting to PAE, and to greater than 64GB, means that a 64-bit system should be your first choice.

Choosing between x64 or IA64

The 64-bit architecture is becoming the new server standard, replacing the x86 architecture. The key factors when deciding between x64 and IA64 are cost, availability, scalability, and processor speed. It's always dangerous to generalize, but today most x64 processors have faster clock speeds than IA64 systems. The current state of processor clock speed is such that x64 processors are running at up to 3 GHz, whereas IA64 processors have been at 1.6 GHz for some time now, with no sign of an increase in the foreseeable future. However, processor speed alone can be misleading, as most IA64 processors have larger caches than x64 processors. The larger cache can help minimize the disadvantage of slower processor speeds. x64 processors are typically available in a wider range of servers than IA64 systems, which are increasingly only found in specialized machines, either high-performance workstations or very large, highly scalable systems from a few specialist vendors.

Both processors' architecture can address the maximum number of processors and memory supported by Windows but identifying which type is better for a particular database workload is not straightforward and likely requires benchmarking. My experience has been that when the numbers of processors and memory are equal on both systems, a database workload that is CPU-bound favors x64, and a database workload that is I/O bound (provided the I/O subsystem is not the bottleneck) will favor the IA64. Usually, x64 systems are less expensive and can run x86 applications. An additional consideration when considering the 64-bit processor architecture is the availability of drivers to support your legacy applications.

Hyperthreading

You want to answer two questions about hyperthreading. First, should you purchase processors that are hyperthreading capable? If you do, then the second question is whether you should run with hyperthreading enabled or disabled. This is a very difficult question to answer, and a one-size-fits-all approach will not work. Any answer must involve each customer testing for his or her individual system.

One of the most important factors when considering hyperthreading is to understand the maximum theoretical performance benefit that you might get from hyperthreading. Intel's documentation on hyperthreading reveals that the maximum theoretical performance gain from hyperthreading is 30 percent. Many customers running with hyperthreading enabled for the first time expect to see double the performance because they see two processors. You should understand that hyperthreading will only give you a maximum performance increase of 1.3 times nonhyperthreading performance at best, and in practice it may be closer to 1.1 to 1.15 times. This knowledge helps put any decision about hyperthreading back into perspective.

In some cases, hyperthreading, at least theoretically, won't provide any benefit. For example, in any database workload where the code is running a tight loop entirely from cache, hyperthreading won't provide any benefit because there is only a single execution engine. In some cases this scenario will result in degraded performance because the operating system will try to schedule activity on a processor that isn't physically there.

Another scenario in which hyperthreading can directly affect SQL Server performance is when a parallel plan might be chosen. One of the things a parallel plan does is split the work across the available processors with the assumption that each processor will be able to complete the same amount of work in the given time. In a hyperthreading-enabled scenario, any thread that's not currently executing will be stalled until the other thread on that processor completes.

No one can yet tell you whether hyperthreading will help or hurt your performance when running your workload. Plenty of theories abound about how it might impact different theoretical workloads, but no one has yet been able to come up with prescriptive guidance that definitively says turn it on here and turn it off over there. Unfortunately, that leaves customers with the burden of figuring it out for themselves. That said, however, there are a few things to consider that can help you make your decision.

First, the operating system can make a big difference. Windows 2000 wasn't hyperthreading aware, whereas Windows Server 2003 is, so expect to see better performance on Windows Server 2003 compared to Windows 2000. In addition, Windows Server 2003 Service Pack 1 added additional hyperthreading awareness, therefore run with Service Pack 1. As Windows 2000 is not hyperthreading aware, you probably want to be careful running with hyperthreading enabled, as it may actually reduce performance. Something else to consider is that hyperthreading itself has been evolving, and although there isn't any concrete evidence of changes in how it is implemented on different Intel processors, feedback from production deployments seems to indicate that it's getting better with each generation of processors. The point here is that hyperthreading on an older server may not perform as it would on a server with the very latest generation of processors.

Microsoft's licensing policy is the opposite of its competitors in that they license by the socket, not by the core or thread. This means that in some configurations it's possible for the operating system (and SQL

Server) to recognize up to eight processors (threads) and still run on a lower-end system SKU such as Windows Server 2003 Standard Edition and SQL Server 2008 Standard Edition.

Because it's so important to our discussion of hyperthreading, let's close this section by repeating the following: The maximum theoretical performance improvement with hyperthreading is only 30 percent compared to nonhyperthreaded applications. In practice, this will actually be a maximum of maybe just 10–15 percent. Moreover, for many customers this may be difficult to measure without performing a benchmark to compare it in their production and consistent database workload.

Cache

The reason modern processors need onboard cache is because the processor runs at 2 to 3 GHz, and main memory simply cannot keep up with the processor's appetite for memory. To try to alleviate this, processor designers added several layers of cache to keep recently used memory in small, fast memory caches so that if you need to reuse memory it might already be in cache. In addition, because of the way cache works, it doesn't just load the byte requested, but the subsequent range of addresses as well. The amount of memory loaded on each request is determined by the cache line size, and the processor's caching algorithm pre-fetch parameters.

The cache on modern processors is typically implemented as multiple layers, as L1, L2, and L3. Each subsequent layer is physically farther from the processor core, and is larger but slower until we are back at main memory. Some caches are general-purpose and hold copies of any memory such as L2 and L3. Other caches are very specific and hold only address lookups (TLB), data (L1 data), or instructions (instruction cache). Typically, L1 is smaller and faster than L2, which is smaller and faster than L3. L3 cache is often physically located on a separate chip, and so is farther from the processor core than L1 or L2, but still closer and faster than main memory.

Processor cache is implemented as a transparent look-through cache. This means that controlling functions on the chip manage the process of filling the cache and managing cache entries. At this point, we should consider some SQL Server specifics.

SQL Server 2008 is a more complex product than SQL Server 2005. Building in this additional complexity is achieved at the cost of additional lines of code, which results in additional bytes in the size of the final exe that is Sqlservr.exe. The exe for SQL Server 2005 is 28MB; the exe for SQL Server 2008 has grown and is now weighing in at 32MB. Moreover, simply starting the service requires more system resources. SQL Server 2005 runs in about 50MB of memory. You can easily see this by using the Task Manager and looking at the Mem Usage column for SQL Server. (The Mem Usage column provides an approximation of the working set for the process.) Connecting with SQLCMD and issuing a simple query, such as selecting a name from master..sysdatabases, adds another 0.5MB to that number. SQL Server 2008 uses around 60MB of memory just to start. On my test server, the Task Manager Mem Usage column reports 59,892KB. Connecting with SQLCMD and issuing the same command causes that to grow to over 64MB (64,232 KB).

All this increased complexity results in a lot more code to do the same operations in SQL Server 2008 than in SQL Server 2005. This manifests itself as an increase in sensitivity to cache size, so the smaller the cache, the slower you might run, and vice versa. In other words, if you have a choice between two processors running at the same speed, go for the one with the largest cache. Unfortunately, the increased cache usually comes at a cost. Whether that additional cost is worthwhile is very difficult to quantify. If you have the capability to run a benchmark on both processors, this is the best way to determine the potential improvement. Try to come up with a benchmark that delivers a specific metric that you can factor against the cost to deliver a clear indication of the cost/benefit of larger cache.

Note one qualification to the information presented in the preceding paragraph. SQL Server 2008 adds more complexity to how it determines the best plan for executing your query. You will see this in an increase in the time it takes to compile a query, and in most cases a reduction in the query execution time. This means that the first time a new query is run, there is a chance that it may actually take a bit longer to run than in SQL 2005, but future executions of the plan from cache will execute considerably faster.

This is an excellent reason to make use of any feature that enables you to reuse a plan. As long as SQL Server has taken all that time to figure out a fast way to get the data, reuse that plan as much as possible before it's removed from cache. This enables you to optimize for time. One sure way to fail to take advantage of this approach and worsen performance is to issue only ad hoc SQL statements, which ensures there is limited plan reuse. It also ensures that a greater amount of time is spent compiling statements that are rarely reused.

Multi-Core

One of the biggest challenges facing multi-processor system designers is how to reduce the latency caused by the physical limitations of the speed of light and the distance between processors and memory. One solution is to put multiple processors on a single chip. This is what a multi-core system does, and it provides more potential for better performance than a single-core system because of this reduced latency between processors and memory. The big question is, do you need a multi-core system?

The answer to this depends on how many processors you need and how much you are willing to pay. If you need an eight-processor system, you will get a faster comparable system for less money by purchasing a quad-socket dual-core system, rather than an eight-socket single-core system.

In most cases, a multi-core system will deliver 1.6 to 1.8 times the performance of a single-core system. This is pretty much in line with the performance of a dual-socket system, making it a very good option. For the latest information on this issue, check out what the hardware vendors are doing with their Transaction Processing Council numbers (see www.tpc.org). The TPC results are a great way to compare hardware, although some hardware vendors may not publish results for the systems you want to compare.

Another factor to consider is scalability. Rather than purchase a straightforward dual-socket, single-core system, you can purchase a dual-socket system with a single-core processor that is capable of being upgraded to dual-core processors in the future. This way, you can defer the expense of adding dual-core processors when you need to add more processing power.

Before continuing, it's worth defining some clear terminology here to avoid confusion when discussing multi-core systems:

❑   The **socket** is the physical socket into which you plug the processor. Before multi-core systems arrived, there used to be a direct one-to-one relationship between sockets and execution units.

❑   A **core** is equivalent to an execution unit, or what you would previously have considered to be a processor. With a multi-core processor there will be two or more of these per socket.

❑   A **thread** in this context is not the same as the thread you might create in your program, or the operating system threads; it is only relevant in the context of hyperthreading. A hyperthreading thread is not a new execution unit but a new pipeline on the front of an existing execution unit. See the section "Hyperthreading" for more details about how this is implemented.

Now let's look at a specific example to see what this actually means.

Figure 11-4 shows a single-socket, single-core processor with no hyperthreading, which results in one thread.

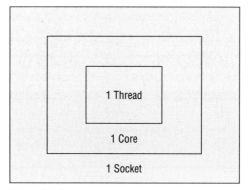

Figure 11-4

Figure 11-5 shows a single-socket, multi-core processor with hyperthreading, which results in four threads, licensed as one processor.

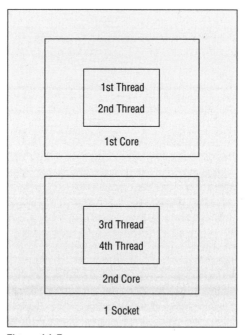

Figure 11-5

Figure 11-6 shows a dual-socket, dual-core processor with hyperthreading, which results in eight threads, licensed as two processors.

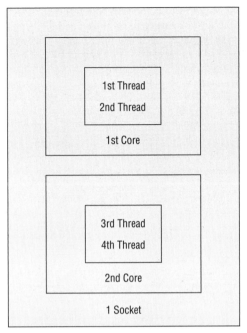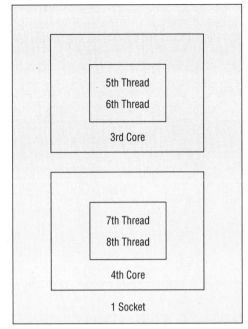

Figure 11-6

System Architecture

Another key purchasing decision has to be made regarding the machine architecture. For systems with up to eight processors there really isn't much choice. Single-socket, dual-socket, quad-socket, and even most eight-way systems are only available in a symmetric multi-processor (SMP) configuration. It's only when you move to 16-, 32-, or 64-way systems that you need to consider the options of SMP versus NUMA. This isn't something you actually need to configure, but rather something you should understand as an option when considering the purchase of one type of system versus another.

Symmetric Multi-Processing

A symmetric multi-processor (SMP) system is a system in which all the processors are connected to a system bus in a symmetric manner. All processors have to share access to system resources over a common system bus (see Figure 11-7). For most cases, this architecture works great for smaller systems in which the physical distance between resources is short, the number of resources is small, and the demand for those resources is small.

NUMA

NUMA stands for non-uniform memory access; this architecture is often also referred to as ccNUMA, meaning a cache-coherent version of NUMA. The main difference between an SMP system and a NUMA system is where the memory is connected to, and how processors are arranged on the system bus.

Whereas on an SMP system the memory is connected to all the processors symmetrically via a shared bus, on a NUMA system each group of four processors has its own pool of "local" memory. This has

427

the advantage that each processor doesn't pay a cost of going to a bus past more than four processors to access memory, provided the data it wants is in the local memory pool. If the data it wants is in the memory pool from another NUMA node, then the cost of accessing it is a little higher than on an SMP system. Therefore, one of the objectives with a NUMA system is to try to maximize the amount of data you get from local memory, as opposed to accessing memory on another node.

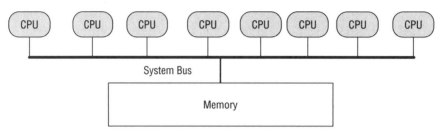

Figure 11-7

NUMA systems typically have a four-sockets-per-node configuration (see Figure 11-8) and implement multiple nodes up to the current system maximum of sixteen nodes. This fully populated configuration delivers a full 64 processors to the operating system.

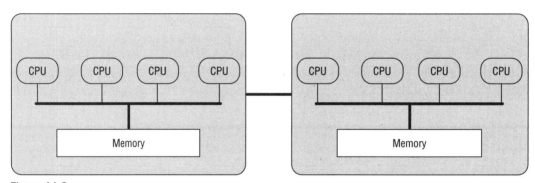

Figure 11-8

Smaller configurations that are any multiple of a four-socket node can usually be accommodated, allowing for highly configurable servers and highly scalable servers. For example, a company could start with a single four-socket node and scale up all the way to 16 four-socket nodes, for 64 sockets.

One of the problems with NUMA systems is that as they grow, the issues of maintaining cache coherency also grow, introducing management overhead. Another problem is that as the number of nodes increases, the chance of the data you want being local is reduced.

The operating system must also be NUMA-aware to schedule threads and allocate memory local to the node, which is more efficient than allocating nonlocal memory or scheduling a thread to run on a different node. Either of these actions incurs an overhead of node memory access, either to fetch data or to fetch the thread's data from the old node and transfer it to the new node. Intel Xeon and AMD Opteron use different architecture implementations to access memory. Intel uses a Front Side Bus (FSB) whereby the sockets are connected through the bus to the external controller to the memory; as a result, all sockets are equal distance to the memory. AMD uses an integrated memory controller on each socket to connect

428

to its local memory and the other sockets with their own memory by means of the HyperTransport link. This architecture is referred to as NUMA and the data latency depends on where the data requested by the CPU core is located in memory. For example, if the data is on a directly connected memory bank, access is very fast; if it is on a remote memory bank that is on another socket, it will incur some latency. While in the case of the Intel architecture, the FSB delivers equal-distance memory to each CPU core, the inefficiency with this approach is FSB contention, which Intel reduces by implementing larger caches.

Memory

This section looks at memory — specifically, memory on the server, including some of the issues associated with memory, the options you can use, and how they can impact the performance of the server. We'll start with a basic introduction to operating system memory, and then jump straight into the details of how to configure a server for different memory configurations.

Physical Memory

Physical memory is the RAM you install into the server. You are probably already familiar with the SIMMs and DIMMs that go into desktop PCs and servers. This is the *physical memory*, or *RAM*. This memory is measured in megabytes, gigabytes, or, if you are lucky, terabytes, as the latest editions of Windows Server 2003 Data Center Edition can now support systems with 1TB of RAM. Future editions of the operating system will increase this number as customers demand increasingly powerful systems to solve increasingly complex business problems.

Physical Address Space

The physical address space is the set of addresses that the processor uses to access anything on its bus. Much of this space is occupied by memory, but some parts of this address space are reserved for things such as mapping hardware buffers, and interface-specific memory areas such as video RAM. On a 32-bit processor, this is limited to a total of 4GB of addresses. On 32-bit Intel server processors with PAE, the address bus is actually 36 bits, which enables the processor to handle 64GB of addresses. You might assume that on a 64-bit processor the address bus would be 64 bits, but because there isn't a need for systems that can address 18 exabytes of memory yet, or the capability to build a system that large, manufacturers have limited the address bus to 40 bits, which is enough to address 1TB.

Virtual Memory Manager

The Virtual Memory Manager (VMM) is the part of the operating system that manages all the physical memory and shares it between all the processes that need memory on the system. Its job is to provide each process with the illusion that it has 4GB of virtual address space, and ensure that it has memory when it needs it, although the limited physical memory is actually shared between all the processes running on the system at the same time.

The VMM does this by managing the virtual memory for each process, and when necessary it will take back the physical memory behind virtual memory, and put the data that resided in that memory into the page file so that it is not lost. When the process needs to use that memory again, the VMM retrieves the data from the page file, finds a free page of memory (either from its list of free pages or from another process), writes the data from the page file into memory, and maps the new page back into the processed virtual address space. The resulting delay or interruption is called a *page fault*.

On a system with enough RAM to give every process all the memory it needs, the VMM doesn't have to do much other than hand out memory and clean up after a process is done with it. On a system without enough RAM to go around, the job is a little more involved. The VMM has to do some work to provide each process with the memory it needs when it needs it. It does this by using the page file to store data in pages that a process isn't using, or that the VMM determines it can remove from the process.

The Page File

On a server running SQL Server, the objective is to try to keep SQL Server running using just the available physical memory. SQL Server itself goes to great lengths to ensure that it doesn't over-allocate memory, and tries to remain within the limits of the physical memory available.

Given this basic objective of SQL Server, in most cases there is limited need for a page file. The main reason for changing the default size of the page file is to aid in diagnosing a system crash. In the event of a system crash, the kernel uses the parameters defined in the system recovery settings to decide what to do. You want the kernel to write some kind of memory dump, and in order to do this the page file size must be large enough to hold the type of memory dump you asked for. In servers with less than 2GB of RAM, a full memory dump is acceptable, so you need a page file that's at least 2GB. On servers with more than 2GB of RAM, a full memory dump can become excessively large, so choosing a smaller dump, such as a kernel dump, makes more sense. The smallest memory dump you can create is a mini-dump. A mini-dump has a lot less information than a kernel memory dump, but in many cases it may still have enough data to enable a system crash to be identified and resolved. If not, then a kernel dump, or in some cases a live kernel debug, is needed to isolate the root cause of the system crash.

In some cases, SQL Server and the OS might not cooperate well on sharing the available memory, and you may start to see system warnings about low virtual memory. If this starts to occur, then ideally add more RAM to the server, reconfigure SQL to use less memory, or increase the size of the page file. It may be better to reconfigure SQL Server to remain within the available physical memory than it is to increase the size of the page file. Reducing paging will always result in better performance; but if paging occurs, for best performance, the page file should be on fast disks that have minimal disk usage activity, and the disks should be periodically defragmented to ensure that the page file is contiguous on the disks, reducing the disk head movement and increasing performance. The metric in the Windows System Monitor to measure page file usage is Paging file: %Usage, which should be less than 70 percent.

Page Faults

Page faults are generally bad for SQL Server, but not all page faults are the same. Some are unavoidable, and some have limited impact on performance, while others can cause severe performance degradation and are the kind we want to avoid.

SQL Server is designed to work within the available physical memory to avoid the bad kind of page faults. Unfortunately, the System Performance Monitor page fault counter doesn't indicate whether you are experiencing the benign or bad kind of page fault, which means it doesn't tell you whether you are experiencing good or bad performance.

Soft Page Faults

The most common kind of page fault you will experience is the *soft page fault*. These occur when a new page of memory is required. Anytime SQL Server wants to use more memory, it asks the VMM for another page of memory. The VMM then issues a soft page fault to bring that memory into SQL Server's virtual address space. This actually happens the first time SQL Server tries to use the page, and not when SQL Server first asks for it. For the programmers among you, this means that SQL Server is calling `VirtualAlloc` to commit a page of memory. The page fault only occurs when SQL Server tries to write to the page the first time.

Hard Page Faults

Hard page faults are the ones you want to try to avoid. A hard page fault occurs when SQL Server tries to access a page of its memory that has been paged out to the page file. When this happens, the VMM has to step in and take some action to get the needed page from the page file on disk, find an empty page of memory, read the page from disk, write it to the new empty page, and then map the new page into SQL Server's address space. All the while, the SQL Server thread has been waiting. Only when the VMM has replaced the missing page of memory can SQL Server continue with what it was doing.

Why Page Faults Are Bad

If you look back to the section "Optimizing the Server," which discusses the relative difference in speed between the CPU, memory, and disks, you can see that disk speeds can be as slow as 5MB/sec, whereas memory speeds are likely to be around 2GB/sec. Whenever a hard page fault occurs, the thread that incurs the hard page fault will be waiting for a relatively long time before it can continue. If the thread running your query incurs a series of hard page faults, then your query will appear to run very slowly.

The most common symptom of this is intermittently slow-running queries. The resolution is either to add more memory to the server, reduce the memory used by other applications on the server, or tune your SQL Server's SQL statements to reduce the amount of memory they consume.

System performance counters that identify page faults are Pages Input/sec (shows the rate of pages read), and Pages Output/sec (shows the rate of pages written). See Chapter 13 for a more detailed discussion of the performance counters.

Virtual Address Space

On a 32-bit system, each running process has a total of 4GB of virtual address space (VAS). Note two important things about this: It's virtual memory, not physical memory, and it's only space, not actual memory.

The 4GB of VAS is shared between the kernel and your process, split in the middle at address 0x7FFFFFFFh, with user-mode address space from 0x00000000h through 0x7FFFFFFFh, and the kernel from 0x80000000h to 0xFFFFFFFFh. However, if you enable /3GB or /USERVA, the memory boundary can be moved from 2GB up to 3GB.

This means that there is no memory in the virtual address space until you either ask for memory or try to load something. In both cases, the OS takes your request and fills in a block of virtual address space with actual memory. Note that the actual memory isn't guaranteed to always be there, as the VMM can take the memory away and put it into the page file. This behavior is completely transparent; you know nothing except that the next time you try to access that piece of memory, it's very slow because you have to wait for the VMM to read the page from the page file, put it back into a page of memory, and then map that page back into your virtual address space.

32-Bit System Memory Configuration

Several options with 32-bit systems have been introduced over the years as ways to get around the basic limitations of a 32-bit system — that is, a 4GB address space evenly divided into 2GB of user address space and 2GB of kernel address space.

Physical Address Extensions

Intel introduced a way to get around the 4GB limitation of a 32-bit address bus by physically extending the address bus to 36 bits. This extension is Physical Address Extensions (PAE). It enables a 32-bit operating system to access up to 64GB of memory.

PAE is also a flag you can set in the boot.ini file to tell the operating system to use the version of the kernel that can take advantage of those extra four bits of address bus, and it enables a 32-bit Windows system to use more than 4GB of memory.

In some scenarios you will end up running the PAE kernel even if you don't enable it in boot.ini. This is the case if you are running Windows 2003 Server Datacenter Edition, and the hardware is hot-swap-memory-enabled. In this case, because the server may have additional memory added at any time that could exceed the 4GB limit of 32-bit addresses, the OS always uses the PAE kernel, just in case it ever has to deal with more than 4GB of physical memory.

3GB

One way to increase the amount of memory a 32-bit process can use is to take some of the space assigned to the kernel and use it for user mode address space. You can do this by specifying either the /3GB or /USERVA options in the boot.ini file.

The /3GB option moves the boundary to be at 3GB, giving each process an additional 1GB of address space. This means that the kernel now only has 1GB of memory to use. Therefore, the operating system will be somewhat memory constrained; and depending on the system configuration, this may cause the OS to run out of memory space. Typically, having this option on does not cause any problems, but before implementing it in production, it is best to first validate it on your test environment to prevent potential downtime.

The /USERVA option enables you to specify a different amount of address space to be taken from the kernel. You can specify any value between 2GB and 3GB as the boundary between user and kernel address space. This has the same effect as the /3GB setting of increasing each process's virtual address space, and reducing the kernel's address space, and can have the same consequences if the kernel ends up running out of memory space.

One of the limitations of reducing the amount of memory available for the kernel is that it reduces the amount of memory available for the kernel to track physical memory. This is why when you enable /3GB or /USERVA, the OS is limited to using a maximum of 16GB of RAM. As a result, if your server has more than 16GB of RAM installed, you do not want to use /3GB or /USERVA.

AWE

Another way for a 32-bit process to use more memory is with Address Window Extensions (AWE). AWE is a Windows API that enables a 32-bit process to create a small window in its virtual address space and then use this to map physical memory directly into its virtual address space. This enables any 32-bit process to use more than 2 or 3GB of memory. SQL Server is a process that has been written to use the

Windows AWE APIs. You can enable this on 32-bit editions of SQL Server by setting the SQL Server configuration option AWE enabled to 1, as shown here:

```
execute sp_configure 'awe_enabled', 1
```

Given what we know about memory, and AWE, it would seem that there is no reason to use AWE on a 64-bit system. After all, a 64-bit system has enough address space to address as much memory as it needs, so why would you consider using AWE on a 64-bit system? In fact, you can't enable AWE in a 64-bit version of SQL; the option is disabled.

However, it turns out that there are some great reasons for using AWE to access your memory, even on a 64-bit system. The SQL Server team realized that on 64-bit systems they could improve overall performance by using AWE. They found that using AWE memory enables memory to be allocated a lot faster. In addition, there is a more direct route to the memory, so every access is slightly faster.

Because of this, they changed the way 64-bit SQL Server works: Although you can't enable AWE on a 64-bit system, if the account used to run SQL Server has the "lock pages in memory" privilege, then SQL Server will automatically use AWE to access buffer pool memory.

3GB or AWE?

This is a question you end up answering pretty frequently. A customer has a system with somewhere between 2GB and 4GB of RAM, and they want to know whether they should use /3GB, or AWE, or maybe both. One thing to remember is that this has to be a 32-bit operating system running 32-bit SQL Server 2008. In any other scenario, this question isn't relevant because SQL Server will have 4GB of virtual address space (32-bit SQL Server on an X64 OS), or it will have a virtual address space of 16 exabytes (64-bit SQL Server on a 64-bit OS).

The /3GB option enables SQL Server to use more memory for anything it needs. It can use the additional 1GB of virtual address space for the buffer pool, the procedure cache, or any other operation for which it needs memory.

AWE enables SQL Server to use more memory, but only for the buffer pool. In most cases this is what SQL needs more memory for, but in some special cases SQL Server may need more memory for the procedure cache, or connections, or something else that can't be allocated from the buffer pool.

These situations in which SQL Server can't use the extra memory for the buffer pool are very few and far between, but they do occur, so you need to know how to spot this situation. For more details, refer to Chapter 13, which includes ways to determine the amount of memory SQL Server is using for stored procedures versus the buffer pool.

64-bit Systems

This section applies to both x64 and IA64 systems. With x64 systems, you can install a 32-bit operating system. If you have installed a 32-bit operating system onto an x64 system, even though the processor is 64-bit capable, it's running as a 32-bit processor, so everything we said about 32-bit systems from the preceding section applies.

Each flavor of 64-bit operating system has a slightly different memory layout, and provides each process with a slightly different amount of virtual address space. This is currently 7,152GB for IA64, and 8,192GB with x64. Note that Windows Server 2003 SP1 currently supports a maximum of 1TB of physical memory.

What this means for SQL Server is that you don't have to worry about using PAE or /3GB as a workaround for the 2GB limit imposed by 32-bit Windows.

You do still have to consider AWE, though. This is because using AWE even in a 64-bit environment can provide you with a performance boost at startup, when you need to take memory, and during normal operation. Using memory through AWE enables SQL Server to take a number of shortcuts and avoid going through the VMM. For these reasons, on a 64-bit system, if the account used to run SQL Server has the "Lock pages in memory" privilege, then SQL Server will default to using AWE memory.

Memory Configuration Scenarios

Now that you understand the various memory options, this section examines the key scenarios and makes specific recommendations:

❑ **32-bit OS and SQL with less than 2GB of RAM:** This is the simplest case. There isn't enough memory to require you to use PAE, /3GB, /USERVA, or AWE.

❑ **32-bit OS and SQL with 2–4GB of RAM:** In this case, you don't need to use PAE, as you haven't exceeded the 32-bit address space limit. You might want to consider using /3GB, /USERVA, or AWE. This means either AWE or /3GB, not both, and the decision would depend on what the application is doing, which dictates what memory demands it will place on SQL Server.

If you find that your 32-bit SQL Server system needs to use more than 2 to 4GB of memory, then rather than struggle with PAE, AWE, and /3GB, you should really be considering moving to a 64-bit system, which will provide immediate relief for many of the challenges we have to overcome in a 32-bit environment.

❑ **Special case — 32-bit OS with 2–4GB of RAM:** Use 3GB/ USERVA or AWE? A frequently asked question for customers in this space is whether should they use AWE to get to memory above the 2GB limit, or use /3GB or /USERVA to give SQL Server more memory. We have asked many people in the SQL Server developer team, and PSS, this question, and it seems that they all have a different answer. However, after asking a few more pointed questions, the answer becomes a little clearer.

When SQL Server uses AWE memory, it can only be used by the buffer pool for data pages. In most cases this is just fine, as that's what you need the extra memory for. In a few very special cases, however, SQL Server needs to use the extra memory for other things, such as the stored procedure cache, the memory for user connections, or other internal memory that SQL Server needs to do its work. In these cases, SQL Server won't be able to use the extra memory if it's provided through AWE, so you would have to use /3GB.

❑ **Special Case — 32-bit OS with 4GB of RAM:** A couple of special cases aren't covered in the previous points. One of these is the odd situation that occurs when you actually try to fit 4GB of RAM into a 32-bit server. Initially this would seem to be pretty straightforward — after all, 4GB is the maximum amount of memory that a 32-bit operating system can address, so it should be just fine.

Unfortunately, the operating system uses some of that 4GB address space to do things such as map hardware into the address space, so before you even fit your first byte of RAM into the system, there is already a load of stuff there taking up some of your 4GB of available physical addresses. One of the biggest chunks of this memory is for mapping memory from video cards. On most server systems, there won't be a lot of memory here, but it's quite easy to take a reasonably mid-range workstation video card with 256 to 512MB of memory installed, slot that into a server, and disable the built-in video adapter in the BIOS setup. That's going to be another 256 to 512MB of your precious 4GB of addresses that have been eaten up by the video card's memory.

This means that the operating system can't fit your 4GB of memory into the available space. To actually be able to use all your 4GB of memory, you need to enable PAE. This is the bit that seems so strange at first, until you look at the math and realize that not only do you have to account for the RAM you install, but also for all those other areas of memory you never even thought about before. After you do the calculations, it becomes clear why you need to enable PAE to use all 4GB of RAM.

To see this for yourself, open the Device Manager, switch the view to Resource View, and then expand the Memory node. You will see a window similar to the one shown in Figure 11-9.

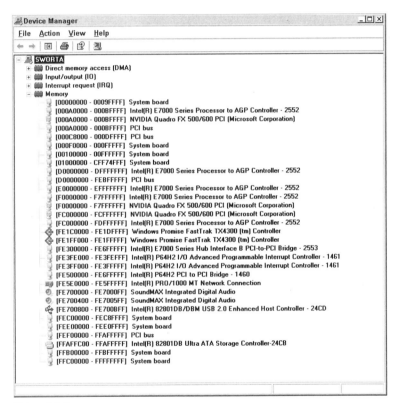

Figure 11-9

Initially this looks pretty confusing, but with a little explanation it starts to make more sense. The key to interpreting this window is to understand that most memory areas appear in this view multiple times. First there will be big chunks of memory allocated to the PCI bus. These areas are then duplicated in more detail, with specific memory allocations within each chunk of PCI bus memory. A good example of this is the area of memory shown in Figure 11-10.

In this figure you can see three things mapped into the memory at 000A0000–000BFFFF: two named AGP graphics controllers, and a third mapping for PCI bus. All this is indicating is that this is the AGP graphics aperture, that there are multiple AGP cards installed, and that this area of memory is on the PCI bus.

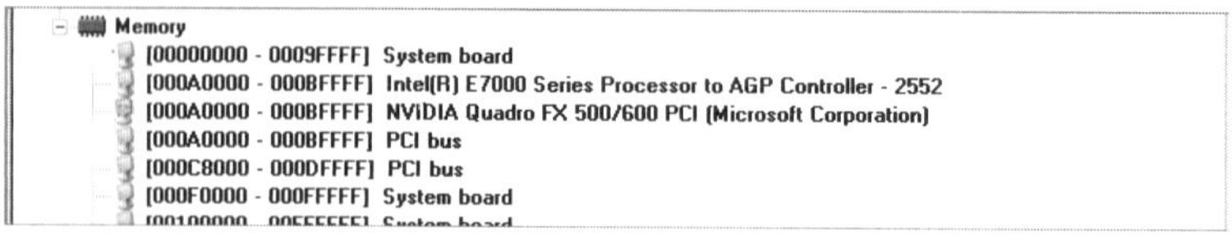

```
⊟ ▓ Memory
     ▓ [00000000 - 0009FFFF]  System board
     ▓ [000A0000 - 000BFFFF]  Intel(R) E7000 Series Processor to AGP Controller - 2552
     ▓ [000A0000 - 000BFFFF]  NVIDIA Quadro FX 500/600 PCI (Microsoft Corporation)
     ▓ [000A0000 - 000BFFFF]  PCI bus
     ▓ [000C8000 - 000DFFFF]  PCI bus
     ▓ [000F0000 - 000FFFFF]  System board
     ▓ [00100000 - 00FFFFFF]  System board
```

Figure 11-10

There is one more twist to this story. When enabling PAE as mentioned earlier, the BIOS must be able to map the physical memory into addresses above the 4GB limit. In some cases, the BIOS doesn't do this. In other cases, the hardware might not implement 36 address lines on the motherboard. Either of these reasons can prevent your server from mapping the additional memory above 4GB, preventing you from using a full 4GB of physical memory.

❑ **32-bit OS and SQL with 4 to 16GB of RAM:** In this case, you need PAE to enable the OS to access more than 4GB of RAM. You will also want to use AWE to enable SQL to access as much memory as possible. You might want to consider turning on /3GB as well.

❑ **32-bit OS and SQL with more than 16GB of RAM:** Again, you need to use PAE to enable the OS to access more than 4GB of RAM. You also need to enable AWE to allow SQL to use all the additional memory above 2GB. You can't use /3GB in this case because it would restrict your memory to just 16GB.

❑ **x64 system with 64-bit OS and 32-bit SQL with less than 4GB of RAM:** If your system is running on a 64-bit OS, you don't need PAE because the OS can already address up to 16 exabytes of memory. You don't need /3GB or /USERVA either, because on an x64 system every 32-bit process gets a full 4GB of user mode address space.

❑ **x64 system with 64-bit OS and 32-bit SQL with more than 4GB of RAM:** In this scenario, you still don't need PAE. You also don't need /3GB or /USERVA. What you do need is AWE, to enable SQL to use memory above 4GB. However, as you are running in a 32-bit process, although the server may have much more than 64GB of RAM available, your 32-bit process can only map a maximum of 64GB using AWE.

❑ **64-bit SQL on a 64-bit OS:** In this case, SQL Server, like every other 64-bit process, gets 7,152 to 8,192GB of memory space by default. If the "lock pages in memory" privilege is granted, SQL will use AWE as a more efficient way for it to access memory than through the OS VMM.

I/O

I/O encompasses both network I/O and disk I/O. In most cases with SQL Server, you are primarily concerned with disk I/O, as that's where the data lives. However, you also need to understand the effect that poor network I/O can have as a bottleneck to performance.

Configuring I/O for a server storage system is perhaps the place where you have the most options, and it can have the largest impact on the performance of your SQL Server system. When you turn off your computer, the only thing that exists is the data stored on your hard drive. When you turn the power on, the processor starts running, the OS is loaded, and SQL Server is started; all this happens by reading data and code from the disk.

This basic concept is true for everything that happens on a computer. Everything starts its life on the disk and has to be read from the disk into memory and from there through the various processor caches before it reaches the processor and can be used as either code or data. Any results the processor arrives at have to be written back to disk to persist any system event, e.g., shutdown, failure, maintenance, and so on.

SQL Server 2008 is very sensitive to disk performance, more so than many applications, because of the manner in which it manages large amounts of data in user databases. Many applications have the luxury of being able to load all their data from disk into memory and then being able to run for long periods of time without having to access the disk again. SQL Server strives for that model, as it is by far the fastest way to get anything done. Unfortunately, when the requested operation requires more data than can fit into memory, SQL Server has to do some shuffling around to keep going as fast as it can, and it has to start writing data back to disk so it can use that memory to generate some new results.

At some point in the life of SQL Server data, every piece of data that SQL server uses has to come from disk and must be written back to disk.

Network

Referring back to Figure 11-2, you can see that the network is a key component in any SQL Server system. The network is the link over which SQL Server receives all its requests to do something, and by which it sends all its results back to the client. In most cases, today's high-speed networks provide enough capacity to enable a SQL Server system to use all its other resources (CPU, memory, disk) to their maximum before the network becomes a bottleneck.

In some systems the type of work being done on the SQL Server is relatively small compared to the number of requests being sent to the server, or to the amount of data being returned to the client. In either of these cases, the network can be a bottleneck. Network bottlenecks can occur anywhere in the network. They can be on the NIC of the client, where the client is an application server that's serving the database server with hundreds of thousands of requests per second. Bottlenecks can occur on the fabric of the network between the NIC and the client (application server, Web server, or the user's workstation). This network fabric can consist of many pieces of network infrastructure, from the simplest system in which two machines are connected over a basic local area network to the most complex network interconnected systems in either the Internet or a global corporate WAN. In these larger more complex interconnected systems, much of the network can be beyond your control and may introduce bandwidth or latency issues outside of acceptable limits, but that we have no control over. In these cases you can do little more than investigate, document, and report your findings.

The parts of networking that we are going to examine here are those over which you may have direct control, and all are on the SQL Server system. We are making the assumption that the remainder of the network fabric is up to the job of supporting the number of requests received, and of passing the results back to the client in a timely manner.

It's beyond the scope of this book to go into the details of monitoring and tuning the network outside of the SQL Server system.

Disks

The other area of I/O is disk I/O. With earlier versions of SQL Server, disks were pretty simple, leaving you with limited options. In most cases you had a couple of disks at most to deal with. Large enterprise systems have long had the option of using Storage Area Network (SAN) or Network Attached Storage (NAS) storage, while medium to large business systems have been able to use external disk subsystems using some form of Redundant Array of Independent Drives (RAID), and most likely utilizing an SCSI interface that enables you to build disk subsystems with hundreds if not thousands of disks.

Take a moment to consider some of the basic physics involved in disk performance. It's important to understand the fundamental differences between different types of disks, as they explain differences in performance. This in turn helps you make an informed decision about what kind of disks to use. The following table demonstrates typical values, under ideal conditions, of the fundamental disk information.

Disk Rotational Speed	Rotational Latency	Track-to-Track Latency	Seek Time	Data Transfer Rate	Transfer Time for 8KB	Total Latency
5,400 RPM	5.5 ms	6.5 ms	12 ms	90MB/sec	88 >s	12.1 ms
7,200 RPM	4.1 ms	6.5 ms	10.7 ms	120MB/sec	66 >s	10.8 ms
10,000 RPM	3 ms	1.5 ms	4.5 ms	166MB/sec	48 >s	4.6 ms
15,000 RPM	2 ms	1.5 ms	3.5 ms	250MB/sec	32 >s	3.5 ms

Rotational latency is the time it takes the disk to make a half rotation. This figure is given for just half a rotation rather than a full rotation because on average the disk makes only a half rotation to find the sector you want to access. It is calculated quite simply as rotational speed in RPM divided by 60 (to give revolutions per second) and then divided by the number of rotations per second.

Track-to-track latency is the time it takes the disk head to move from one track to another. In the table, the number for 5,400 and 7,200 RPM disks is considerably slower than for the 10,000 and 15,000 RPM disks. This indicates that the slower disks are more likely to be ATA disks rather than SCSI disks. ATA disks have considerably slower internals than SCSI disks, which accounts for the considerable difference in price and performance between the two disk types.

Seek time is the magic number disk manufacturers publish, and it's their measure of rotational latency and track-to-track latency. This is calculated in the preceding table as the sum of rotational latency and track-to-track latency.

Data transfer rate is the average rate of throughput. This is usually calculated as the amount of data that can be read from a single track in one revolution, so for a modern disk with a data density of around 1MB/track, and for a 7,200 RPM disk, rotating at 120 revs per second, that equates to around 1MB per track at 120 revolutions per sec = 120MB/sec of data that can be read from the disk.

Transfer time for 8KB is the time it takes to transfer a given amount of data at that transfer rate. To see how long it takes to transfer an 8KB block, you simply divide the amount of data you want to move by the transfer rate, so 8KB/120MB = 66 micro secs (or >s)

Total latency for a given amount of data is the sum of rotational latency, track-to-track latency, and disk transfer time.

In the table you can clearly see that for a single 8KB transfer, the largest amount of time is spent moving the head to the right position over the disk's surface. Once there, reading the data is a tiny percentage of the time.

Latency limits the disk's ability to service random read requests. Sequential read requests will have an initial latency and are then limited by the disk's ability to read the data from the disk surface and get each I/O request back through the many layers, before reading the next sector from the disk's surface.

Disk write requests are often buffered to disk cache, which increases the SQL Server write performance but should only be used if the storage array implements a battery backup to protect that cache in case of a power failure. Otherwise, in a power failure, the database can become corrupted. Before using cache, check with your storage array vendor to verify that it has a battery backup and can guarantee writing the cache to disk in the event of a power failure. A typical storage array enables the cache to be configured as a range between read and write cache. As the database transaction log performs synchronous writes, it would benefit from having a greater amount of write cache assigned in the storage array.

Throughput in MB/sec is a measure of how many bytes the disk can transfer to or from its surface in a second. This is usually quoted as a theoretical number based on the disk's bus.

Throughput in IOs/sec is a measure of how many I/Os the disk can service per second. This is also typically quoted as a theoretical number based on the disk's bus.

The database workload determines which will have a greater impact on SQL Server performance, MB/sec throughput or I/Os/sec throughput. From a disk I/O point of view, an OLTP database workload that does small, random reads and writes will be gated by the I/Os/sec throughput. Such data requests ask for few rows per request per user (selects, deletes, inserts, or updates), and the disk's ability to seek the request data in the disk and return it determines the user's response time. Conversely, an OLAP or a reporting database with large sequential reads will be gated by the MB/sec throughput and will benefit most from reducing data fragmentation, making the data physically contiguous on disk. These are reads where the disk finds the starting disk data request and pulls data sequentially, and the disk capability to return the data helps determines the user's response time. However, in an OLAP and reporting database, the database workload not only typically returns more data per request than the OLTP, but the queries may be more complex and have more table joins, therefore requiring more system CPU work to deliver the final data dataset to the users. As a result, the user response time must include that in addition to the MB/sec throughput.

Storage Design

After all that talk about the different pieces of a storage system, it's time to get serious about figuring out how best to configure *your* storage system. This is a challenging task, so the following sections offer a set of guidelines, and then provide the details showing how you can figure this out for yourself.

No Silver Bullet in Storage Design

Simply put, there is no single simple way to configure storage that's going to suit every purpose. SQL Server systems can be required to do dramatically different things, and each implementation could require a radically different storage configuration to suit its peculiar I/O requirements.

Use the Vendors' Expertise

The vendors of each piece of hardware should be the people you turn to for expertise regarding how to configure their hardware. They may not necessarily know how to configure it best for SQL Server, however, so this is where you have to be able to convey SQL Server's requirements in a manner the hardware vendor will understand. This is best done by being able to quote specific figures for reads versus writes, sequential versus random I/O, block sizes, I/O's per second, MB/sec for throughput, and minimum and maximum latency figures. This information will help the vendor provide you with the optimal settings for their piece of the hardware, be it disks, an array controller, fiber, networking, or some other piece of the storage stack.

Every System Is Different

Each SQL Server system may have very different I/O requirements. Understand this and don't try to use a cookie-cutter approach to I/O configuration (unless you have already done the work to determine that you really do have SQL systems with the exact same IO requirements).

Simple Is Better

It is an age-old engineering concept that simpler solutions are easier to design, easier to build, easier to understand, and hence easier to maintain. In most cases, this holds true for I/O design as well. The simpler solutions invariably work faster, are more robust and reliable, and require less maintenance than more complex designs. Unless you have a very compelling, specific reason for using a complex storage design, keep it simple.

More Disks

More disks are invariably faster than fewer disks. For example, if you have to build a 1TB volume, it's going to deliver higher performance if it's built from a lot of small disks (ten 100GB disks) versus a few larger disks (two 500GB disks). This is true for various reasons. First, smaller disks are usually faster than larger disks. Second, you stand a better chance of being able to utilize more spindles to spread read and write traffic over multiple disks when you have more disks in the array. This gives you throughput that in some cases is the sum of individual disk throughput. For example, if those 100GB disks and 500GB disks all delivered the same throughput, which was, say 20MB/sec, then you would be able to sum that for the two 500GB disks to achieve just 40MB/sec. However, with the ten smaller disks, you would sum that to arrive at 200MB/sec, or five times more.

Faster Disks

Not surprisingly, faster disks are better for performance than slower disks. However, this doesn't just mean rotational speed, which is but one factor of overall disk speed. What you are looking for is some indicator of the disk's ability to handle the I/O characteristics of the workload you are specifically interested in. Unfortunately, disk manufacturers rarely, if ever, provide any information other than rotational speed and theoretical disk bus speeds. For example, you will often see a 10K or 15K RPM SCSI disk rated as being able to deliver a maximum throughput of 300MB/sec because it's on an SCSI 320 bus. However, if you hook up that disk and start running some tests using a tool such as SQLIO, the chances are good that for small-block-size, non-queued random reads, you will be lucky to get much more than 2–4MB/sec from that disk. Even for the fastest I/O types, large-block sequential I/O, you will be lucky to get more than 60–70 MB/sec. That's a long way from 300MB/sec. You can download the SQLIO Disk Subsystem Benchmark tool from www.microsoft.com/downloads/details.aspx?familyid=9A8B005B-84E4-4F24-8D65-CB53442D9E19.

Test

Testing is an absolutely essential part of any configuration, optimization, or performance tuning exercise. Too often we have spoken with customers who have been convinced that black is white based on absolutely nothing more than a gut feeling, or some half-truth overheard in a corridor conversation.

Until you have some test results in your hand, you don't truly know what the I/O subsystem is doing, so forget all that speculation, which is really nothing more than poorly informed guesswork, and start testing your I/O systems to determine what's really going on. IOMeter is a commonly used tool for I/O subsystem measurement and characterization to baseline an I/O subsystem. It is both a workload generator and a measurement tool that can emulate a disk or network I/O load. It can be found at www.iometer.org.

A commonly used disk performance metric is disk latency, which is measured by Windows System Monitor using the Avg Sec/Read, Avg Sec/Write, and Avg Sec/Transfer counters. Target disk latencies are as follows:

❑ Database Transaction Log, less than 5ms, ideally 0ms

❑ OLTP Data, less than 10ms

❑ Decision Support Systems (OLAP and Reporting) Data, less than 25ms

Once you have set up the system and tested it, you need to keep monitoring it to ensure that you are aware of any changes to the workload or I/O subsystem performance as soon as it starts. If you have a policy of monitoring, you will also build a history of system performance that can be invaluable for future performance investigations. Trying to track down the origins of a slow-moving trend can be very hard without a solid history of monitoring data. See Chapter 13 for more specifics on what and how to monitor.

Designing a Storage System

Now let's run through the steps you need to take when designing a storage system. The following sections introduce each of the different parts of a storage system, providing some guidance on key factors, and offering recommendations where they are appropriate.

The first questions you have to answer when designing a new storage system are about the disks:

❑ How many disks do you need?

❑ What size should they be?

❑ How fast should they be?

A Word About Space

The first thing you really need to determine is how much space you need. Once you have sized the data, you need to factor in index space, growth, room for backups, and recovery. All of these factors will increase the amount of space required.

How Many Disks

The number of disks you need is going to be driven by the amount of space you need, the performance you want, and how robust the storage needs to be. As an example, here are several alternative ways to build a 1TB disk subsystem:

❑ **Two 500GB SATA disks with a basic SATA controller:** This is the simplest and cheapest option. Use two of the latest 500GB disks. However, this is also the slowest option, and the least robust. With no redundancy, a loss of one disk results in the loss of the database.

❑ **Four 500GB SATA disks with a RAID 1 controller:** This is twice the cost of the previous system, and isn't much faster, but it provides a robust solution using a mirroring controller to provide redundancy.

❑ **Eight 250GB SATA disks with a RAID 1 controller:** This system is a robust step to improve performance. You've increased the number of disks by reducing their size. Using a striping controller, you can get some performance improvement by writing and reading from more disks at the same time with redundancy.

❑ **Sixteen 125GB SCSI disks with a RAID 1 controller:** Now you're starting to get into a more serious performance configuration with SCSI disks. This uses more, smaller disks, which will provide a significant performance improvement with redundancy.

With all of these configurations you need to be aware of other bottlenecks in the I/O path. The first thing to consider is the PC's bus bandwidth, and then the disk adapter's bus bandwidth. If your server is using a basic PCI bus, then this will likely be limited to around 200MB/sec, so anytime you need to do large sequential I/O to more than two to four disks, you may be limited by the PCI bus. Next is the disk bus. For example, with an SCSI 320 bus, you can max out the bandwidth with around six disks at about 260MB/sec. If you need a system able to deliver higher than 250MB/sec, then consider using an adapter with multiple channels.

Cost

Much as we would all like to have an unlimited budget, that's unlikely to be the case in most environments, so the ideal design will have to be modified to bring it in line with the available budget. This often results in less than optimal designs, but it's a necessary factor when designing any system.

Desired I/O Characteristics

The first thing you need to consider here are the I/O characteristics of the operations you are going to perform in SQL Server. This can be a complex issue to resolve, and in many cases the easiest way to determine this is through testing and monitoring of an existing system so that you can identify the exact types and volume of I/O that each major feature or function requires.

If you don't have an existing system, then you may be able to use the information in the following table as a guideline to get you started.

Operation	Random/ Sequential	Read/Write	Size Range
Create Database	Sequential	Write	512KB (only the log file is initialized in SQL Server 2008)
Backup Database	Sequential	Read/Write	Multiple of 64KB (up to 4MB)
Restore Database	Sequential	Read/Write	Multiple of 64KB (up to 4MB)
DBCC – CHECKDB	Sequential	Read	8KB–64KB
Alter Index - on - rebuild (Read Phase)	Sequential	Read	(see "Read Ahead" in Books Online)
Alter Index - on - rebuild (Write Phase)	Sequential	Write	Any multiple of 8KB up to 128KB
sys.dm_db_index_phyical_stats	Sequential	Read	8KB–64KB

To reduce storage cost, it is not necessary for all of the disk space you need to have the same storage characteristics. The SQL data, log, and `tempdb` files should be deployed onto the fastest, most robust storage you can afford, while space for backup and recovery and other repeatable tasks can be on slower and less robust storage.

In some cases, where your database is a copy of some other source system, you might decide to build the whole system on inexpensive, non-robust storage. In the event of a failure, you could rebuild the whole system from the source system. However, if your copy has an SLA that requires minimal downtime and doesn't allow for a full rebuild, even though the data is only a copy, you have to implement some form of robust storage so that you never have to take the unacceptable time of rebuilding from the source system.

RAID

As part of the "How many disks do you need?" question, you must consider the Redundant Array of Independent Drives (RAID) level you require, as this will influence the total number of disks required to build a storage system of a certain size and with the I/O characteristics you require:

- ❑ **Availability:** The first factor when thinking about RAID is the level of availability you need from the storage.

- ❑ **Cost:** An important part of any system is meeting the cost requirements. There's no point to specifying the latest greatest high-performance system if it costs 10, 100, or 1,000 times your budget.

- ❑ **Space:** Another major factor in combination with cost is how much physical space you need to provide.

- ❑ **Performance:** The performance of the storage is another major factor that should help you determine what level of RAID you should choose.

Mirroring

With RAID 1, one disk is mirrored onto another — meaning a minimum of two disks. This is fast, as reads can occur from both disks and writes incur minimal performance reduction. It provides redundancy from a disk failure but increases storage costs, as usage capacity is 50 percent of the available disk drives. For storage cost reasons, backups, data loads, and read-only database operations may not require this level of protection.

Striping with Mirroring

RAID 10 is a mirrored set in a stripped set with a minimum of four disks. This is the fastest arrangement; reads can occur from multiple disks, and writes incur minimal performance reduction. It also provides redundancy — it can survive more than one disk failure provided that the disk failures are not in the same mirrored set — but increases storage costs, as usage capacity is 50 percent of the available disk drives. Database systems that require the most I/O read/write performance and redundancy should be deployed on RAID 10. For storage cost reasons, backups, data loads, and read-only database operations may not require this level of protection.

Striping with Parity

Raid 5 is striping with parity with a minimum of three disks. During writes, it must calculate the data parity — for example, in a three disk array, it will write data across two disks and parity across the third disk. There is a performance penalty to calculating the parity, and therefore RAID 5 is not a good choice for databases that must handle a significant amount of writes. Another downside of RAID 5 is that in the event of a disk failure, performance can be seriously degraded while rebuilding the array with the new disk or if running with a failed disk, as parity needs to be calculated per each read to return the data. However, RAID 5 does not incur the performance reduction during reads. As a result, RAID 5 is efficient for predominantly read databases such as decision support systems (DSS). In addition, RAID 5 is more cost-effective than RAID 1 or RAID 10, as the disk space of one single drive is required for parity storage for each RAID 5 set, while for RAID 1 or RAID 10 it requires 50 percent of the disk space for redundancy.

RAID-Level Recommendations

You should use the fastest, most robust storage for SQL data files; the recommendation is to use striping with mirroring (RAID 10).

You should also use the fastest, most robust storage for SQL log files. Just like for SQL data files, the recommendation is to use striping with mirroring (RAID 10).

If you know your application is going to make extensive use of tempdb, use the fastest, most robust storage for tempdb. This might seem a little strange because the data in tempdb is always transitory, but the requirement for robustness comes from the need to keep the system running, not from a concern about losing data. If the rest of the system is using robust storage but tempdb isn't, then a single disk failure will prevent that SQL Server instance from running.

The operating system and SQL binary files can live on a simple mirror, although in many cases the time it takes to rebuild the OS and SQL may be within acceptable downtime, in which case a single disk will suffice.

For critical systems, the OS and SQL binary files should be on a mirrored disk array, but it only needs to be a single mirrored pair. OS and SQL binary files don't have high I/O requirements; they are typically read once when the application is loaded, and then not touched until new code paths need to be used, and then a few more 4KB random reads are issued. Therefore, these files don't require high-performance storage.

Isolation

Isolation is needed at several levels. You want to isolate the different types of I/O SQL Server generates to optimize each storage system. You don't want to mix the heavy random I/O generated by a high-volume OLTP system from the highly sequential write access to the log file.

At the same time, on a shared storage system such as a SAN, you want to ensure that your storage is isolated from the I/O generated by other systems using the same shared storage. Isolation is primarily concerned with the sharing of disks that results from virtualization on a SAN system, but the principle can also apply to other parts of the storage subsystem, specifically the ports, fiber, and switches that make up the SAN fabric.

Separating SQL Data from the Log

I/O to SQL data files is very different in nature from I/O to the SQL log file. SQL data traffic is random in nature with relatively larger block sizes, occasionally becoming large sequential I/O for large table scans. SQL log traffic is sequential in nature and is predominantly write until a checkpoint occurs, when you will see some read activity.

Because of this, it's important to separate SQL data files and log files onto separate physical disks. Doing this enables the heads on the log disks to track sequentially, matching the log write activity. The heads on the SQL data traffic will have a lot of seeks, as they need to get the next random disk block, but this won't impact log performance, nor will it be further randomized by having to intersperse random data reads and writes with sequential log writes.

Grouping Similar I/O Workloads

Going one step further, if you have multiple databases, or SQL instances, or tables within your database with very different access patterns, then wherever possible you should try to group similar I/O patterns together on the same set of physical disks. Identify read-only data access, write-only data access, and frequent read/write access, and then separate each group onto its own physical disks to improve performance and storage throughput.

Using tempdb

SQL Server 2008 makes much more extensive use of `tempdb` than previous versions, so it's very important to know how often you need to use this database. See Chapter 13 for more details on monitoring. If after monitoring you find that your system uses `tempdb` extensively, you should consider placing it on separate physical disks.

Another option considered by some users is placing `tempdb` on a RAM disk or other high-performance solid state disk. Because of the lightning-fast response times of these kinds of disks, this can provide a considerable performance boost for systems that make extensive use of `tempdb`.

> *Although it's okay to place* `tempdb` *on volatile disks such as RAM disks, it's not okay to put any other SQL files on these kinds of volatile storage. SQL Server has very specific requirements for its storage to ensure the integrity of data.*

`tempdb` is discussed in more detail in Chapter 2 and Chapter 12.

Large Storage System Considerations: SAN Systems

More and more SQL Server systems are using storage provided by an external storage array of some kind. Frequently, these large external systems are called a *SAN system*, but they could be NAS or some other storage array technology such as iSCSI. This terminology doesn't refer to the storage but to the technology used to connect your SQL Server to the box of disks on a network of some kind.

In the case of a SAN system, the network is a dedicated storage network, frequently built using fiber. For an iSCSI system, the network is an IP network (the IP part of TCP/IP) built with compatible network cards but using a private network dedicated to storage traffic. For a NAS system, the network is not dedicated; it is shared with all your other network traffic.

Any discussion on SQL Server storage configuration has to include information on the concepts involved in configuring an external storage array.

Disk Virtualization

SAN systems present many challenges when you are placing large numbers of fast, high-capacity disks in a single unit. One of these challenges is how to provide the fastest storage to the largest number of people. You know that to increase disk performance, you need to stripe across as many spindles as possible, but many users of the SAN may require as little as 250GB or less of storage. If your SAN system is filled with 76GB disks, you could deliver that 250GB using three or four disks. Unfortunately, delivering 250GB from just four disks isn't going to provide much performance. Step back and consider that the SAN itself may have as many as 140 of these 76GB disks. If you could take a small piece of a larger number of disks, you could build the same 250GB chunk of storage, but it would be much faster.

Now consider the situation in which you can take a 2GB chunk from each of those 140 76GB disks. When you combine all those 2GB chunks together, you end up with 280GB of raw disk space. After subtracting some system overhead, that would probably end up at around 250GB. Sure, you wasted a little bit of space for the overhead of managing 140 disks, but now you have a 250GB chunk of storage that has the potential to deliver I/O at the rate of the sum of 140 disks; or if each disk were capable of 50MB/sec for sequential 64K reads, you would have a combined I/O throughput of run around 7,000 MB/sec (7GB/sec). In practice, you won't get anywhere near that theoretical I/O rate, but you will see considerably higher I/O rates than you would if you just combined three or four disks.

Disk virtualization is a technique that SAN vendors use for doing this. All the large SAN vendors have their own unique method, but they are all based on the same basic concept: Slice each disk up into uniform slices, recombine these small slices into larger chunks of storage, and present these virtualized chunks to each application:

1. Start with a single disk, and create multiple slices on the disk.
2. Do the same thing across multiple disks.
3. Group a collection of these disk slices together using some level of RAID, and present it to the server as a logical unit number (LUN).

Logical Unit Numbers

When considering the logical unit numbers (LUNs) that the storage is going to present to the OS, you have to answer two questions. How big should each LUN be, and how many should you have? The starting point for answering these questions is determining how much storage you need. If you have differing storage requirements, then you also need to know how much of each different type you require. Different types of storage might range from high speed, high reliability for data and log; low speed, high reliability for archive data; high speed, low reliability for backup staging (before writing to tape); and low speed, low reliability for "other" storage that doesn't have tight performance criteria or present reliability concerns.

LUN Size

The next factor to be considered is LUN size. For a SAN-based system, or large local storage array, this equates to how big you make each chunk of storage to be presented to the operating system. These LUN-sized chunks of storage are how the OS sees the storage. By now, you may know from virtualization that the OS has no way of knowing how many disks, or how much from each disk, each LUN represents.

A number of factors can influence your decision regarding LUN size. For instance, you need to consider how the storage is going to be mounted in the OS. If you are going to mount each LUN as its own volume, then you can make them a little larger, although you need to remain far below the single-volume limit of 2TB. You want to stay well below this limit due to backup, restore, and startup times. On startup, the OS will run a basic check of each volume. Basically, the OS runs Check Disk (CHKDSK) at startup to validate each volume. If the volume is very large, then the time taken to run CHKDSK can become long — in some cases, very long — which can start to have a large impact on system startup time. For large enterprise servers with less than one server restart scheduled per year, this isn't a major problem, except when it's time to set everything up — installing the OS and drivers, and configuring the server. Many reboots may be required. If each reboot takes one or two hours, restarting the server eight or more times becomes a two- or three-day labor, rather than something you do while getting another coffee refill.

In most cases, the storage array vendor will have specific recommendations regarding how big each LUN should be. These recommendations are based upon their extensive experience with their storage systems, but be cautious here because much of the storage vendor's experience will have come from storage arrays, not running SQL Server, whose I/O requirements are completely different. Make sure the vendor understands the unique nature of the storage I/O characteristics you have for your system. On Windows 2003, the rule of thumb for performance is to make each LUN no larger than 1TB.

Number of LUNs

If there are no clear criteria that set an ideal size for each LUN, then there may be factors that dictate a specific number of LUNs. The simplest way to determine the number of LUNs you need is to divide the total storage volume required by the size of LUN you want, which gives you the "ideal" number of LUNs. That's not a very informed way of determining the number, however, and in many ways the calculation should start from the number of LUNs. The starting point for this is the storage vendor's recommendations. They should be able to provide guidance on how best to configure their storage, but, again, their expertise might not include experience with SQL Server.

Server Configuration

After spending a lot of time configuring the storage, you still have to configure the server. The main configuration options on the server are related to the number, placement, and configuration of the *host bus adapter (HBA)*, and then you're into the details of the operating system — specifically, the device manager and the file system. The HBA is the I/O interface that connects a host system to the SCSI bus or Storage Area Network (SAN). Moreover, HBA cards are available in a variety of different throughput, and some servers may have a limited number of faster PCI slots among all of their available PCI slots. You want to put the HBA in a PCI slot that will enable it to run at its maximum throughput. Check the server documentation.

Disk Adapters

The disk adapter is the interface card that you plug into the PCI bus inside your server to enable the PCI bus to connect to the ATA, SCSI, iSCSI, or fiber channel cabling required to connect to the disks. Several factors should be considered with disk adapters.

Number of Adapters

When determining the number of disk adapters, you first have to consider how many disks you need to support. On some interfaces, such as ATA and SCSI, there are physical limits to the number of disks allowed per bus: two disks per ATA bus (one master, one slave) and either 8 or 16 per SCSI bus (depending on which version of SCSI is in use). If you need an ATA-based system with eight disks, you need to have enough disk adapters to provide four ATA buses. If you need an SCSI-based system with 32 disks, and you are using a version of SCSI that supports 16 disks per bus, you would need two buses.

One adapter can provide more than one bus. You might find an ATA adapter that implements two or maybe four ATA buses, so your eight-disk system might only need a single adapter. In the case of SCSI adapters, many are multi-bus, so you should be able to deliver two SCSI buses from a single adapter card.

Multipath I/O (MPIO)

Microsoft Multipath I/O solutions use redundant physical path components — adapters, cables, and switches — to create logical "paths" between the server and the storage device. In the event that one or more of these components fails, causing the path to fail, multipathing logic uses an alternate path for I/O so that applications can still access their data.

Keeping a highly available solution requires redundancy in each component of the solution:

❑ Application availability through server clustering such as Microsoft Clustering Service provides redundancy among computers so that if a computer has a system failure, the running services — for example, SQL Server 2008 — will failover to another computer in that failover cluster. Microsoft Clustering Services is included with Windows 2003 Enterprise Edition and Windows 2003 Datacenter Edition. Moreover, multiple NIC card teaming can be implemented in case of a network card failure.

❑ Storage redundancy through RAID enables you to configure drives for performance and fault-tolerance to provide protection from a disk failure.

❑ Storage availability through multipathing enables multiple interfaces to the same storage unit (LUN) to deliver on the storage network components' redundancy. Multipathing manages the redundant I/O connections so that read/write requests are instantaneously rerouted in case of an I/O path failure. Microsoft MPIO in conjunction with the SAN vendor device-specific module (DSM) provides a tightly integrated Windows System multipathing solution that can be deployed in failover mode, whereby one I/O path is implemented as a failover partner to another, or it can be deployed in a dynamic load balancing mode whereby the I/O workload is balanced across all the available I/O paths based on an algorithm — for example, round-robin. Within either mode, if one path — for example, the fiber cable or the Host Bus Adapter (HBA) — were to fail, the I/O would continue through the surviving I/O paths.

Moreover, MPIO in dynamic load balancing mode enables you to performance scale the I/O across many HBAs, enabling more total throughput I/O to flow to the I/O subsystem. MPIO is supported in all Windows System processor architecture: X64, IA64, and X86. Furthermore, if the I/O subsystem is connected through the server by way of a fabric switch, then redundant fabric switches should be deployed to prevent it from becoming a single point of failure. For a high-throughput I/O subsystem and for redundancy, deploy MPIO.

Figure 11-11 shows an MPIO implementation. Following is a description of each of the common MPIO parameters:

❑ **LUN Identifier:** A value used by the DSM to identify a particular LUN

❑ **Drive Letter:** Assigned by the user

❑ **Disk Number:** Assigned by the MPIO framework for all DSM supported disks

❑ **Status:** Can be good or degraded

❑ **Number of Active Paths:** Number of active paths to the LUN

❑ **Load Balancing Policy:** Indicates the load balancing policy for the LUN, which can be as follows:

  ❑ Round Robin: The I/O requests are distributed across all active paths to the device in a round-robin manner.

  ❑ Shortest Queue Requests: Each I/O request is routed to the active path with the least number of outstanding requests.

  ❑ Shortest Queue Bytes: Each I/O request is routed to the active path with the least number of outstanding data bytes.

  ❑ Shortest Queue Service Time: Each I/O request is routed to the active path where the total outstanding time for pending I/O requests is the least.

  ❑ No Load Balance: All I/O requests are routed through a chosen active path.

❑ **ALB:** Indicates whether the adaptive load balance is enabled or disabled for the LUN

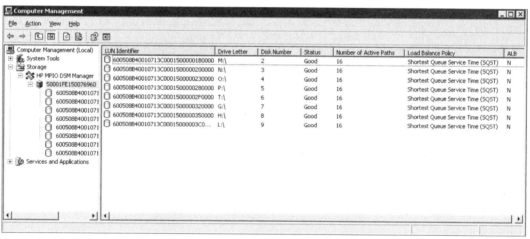

Figure 11-11

Placement

In larger servers, the physical placement of the adapter card in the PCI slots can have an impact on performance. There are two ways in which placement can affect performance. On a large system, the physical distance between the furthest PCI slot and the CPU can increase latency and reduce overall bandwidth.

On some systems, the PCI slots are not all of the same type. It is increasingly common for systems to have a few PCI-X or fast 64-bit PCI slots, with the remainder being slower slots. Placing a high-speed 64-bit, PCI-X, or PCI-Express disk adapter into a slow-speed PCI slot (some won't physically fit, but some will) can force the whole bus to run at a considerably slower speed than expected. Check the server documentation or ask the vendor to identify the faster PCI slots.

Firmware

Most disk adapters have firmware that can be upgraded. Even when you first purchase a new disk adapter, you should check the vendor's Web site to make sure you have the very latest firmware version. Vendors change their firmware to fix bugs, improve performance, and match specific drivers, so you must always confirm that you have the latest firmware to ensure optimal performance.

Drivers

Even though the disk adapter probably comes with drivers, there is a very good chance that they are outdated by the time you purchase the adapter, so even before installing anything you should check the vendor's Web site for the very latest signed drivers.

In most cases, only run the latest signed driver, because this is the one that has been through full certification testing. Sometimes the vendor's Web site will offer a new version of a driver that fixes a specific problem you are encountering, but which hasn't been signed yet. In this very specific case, it's acceptable to take the risk of using the unsigned driver, provided you understand that you may encounter system crashes as a result of unfound bugs. If this happens, then the unsigned driver should be removed or rolled back immediately while further troubleshooting is performed to determine the true cause of the system crash.

Configuration

Many disk adapters have options that can be set to change the way they work in different environments, or for different types of disks to which they may be attached. For ATA and SCSI adapters, this configuration is usually pretty minimal, unless the adapter includes RAID, which is another topic altogether. In most cases the configuration involves fiber channel options on HBAs. iSCSI adapters that are network interface cards (NICs) also have configuration options, but these are the same settings you may have used to configure any IP-based network adapter and were covered earlier in the material on NICs.

Partitioning

After installing the disks, you need to configure the disks themselves, and the first step with a new disk is to consider the disk partitions. What kind of partition do you want to create on the disk? There are two main options: a Master Boot Record (MBR) partition or a GUID Partition Table (GPT) partition. The MBR partition is older and has partition size and number of partition limitations; it is the type most commonly deployed. A GPT partition can be used for very large partitions and large number of partitions, but it has limitations on x86 platforms. Unless you have a specific requirement that forces the use of GPT, you should use an MBR partition.

Mounting Volumes

After you have partitioned the disks, you have to decide what kind of volumes you want. The choice here is between using a *basic volume* or a *dynamic volume*. We recommend using basic volumes unless you need specific features that only a dynamic volume can provide. If you are running in a clustered environment, there are limitations on using dynamic volumes. This may result in having to resize your LUNs, or using an alternate option such as mount points.

Start Sector Alignment

Start sector alignment is a topic that frequently comes up for discussion. When dealing with storage arrays, the value you use for start sector alignment is driven by the cache line size. You need to ensure that the start sector on the partition is aligned with the start of the cache line on the SAN. If you're not familiar with the intricacies of cache lines, ask your SAN vendor.

The value to use for start sector alignment is supplied by the storage vendor. After obtaining a value, check whether the vendor specified this in sectors (each sector is 512 bytes) or KB. The Start Sector Offset is set using either `diskpar` or `diskparT`. Note the difference, as one has a T at the end, the other doesn't. `diskpar` is the older tool. `diskparT` started shipping with Windows Server 2003 SP1. `diskpar` takes the disk offset as a number of clusters, whereas `diskparT` takes its offset as a number of KB. A value specified in `diskpar` of 64KB (clusters) results in a start sector offset of 32K. Using 32 (KB) in `diskparT /align` will also give you a 32K offset.

The disk alignment must be performed prior to copying the data to the partition, as it is a destructive process whereby all of the data in the partition is deleted during the copy. If you determine that this must be done after you have copied data into the partition, you need to move the data to a separate disk location prior to performing the disk alignment. Using `diskparT`, you first select the disk to align, after the disk is selected, and then run this command on the selected disk (see Figure 11-12):

```
Create partition primary align = <Vendor recommended Align value>
```

Figure 11-12

Windows 2008 automatically performs the sector alignment that would work for most storage devices. However, if the storage vendor recommends a different setting, or after further I/O testing a different setting is determined that would work better for a specific storage device, `diskparT` can be used to change it.

File Systems — NTFS versus FAT

This shouldn't even be an issue anymore: Always use NTFS. The reliability and security offered by NTFS and the speed and functional improvements of NTFS over FAT make it the only real choice for your file system.

NTFS Allocation Unit Size

Another topic that frequently comes up is the NTFS *allocation unit size*, also known as NTFS *cluster size*. In testing, we ran with SQL Server, and found that changing the NTFS cluster size has no impact on SQL performance. This is due to the small number and large size of the files that SQL uses. The recommendation that results from this is to continue to use an allocation unit size of 64K. Whatever you decide to use, test to confirm that you are getting the I/O characteristics you expected by using IOMeter.

Fragmentation

Any discussion on disks would not be complete without considering fragmentation. Fragmentation can occur in several forms with SQL Server:

❏   Internal fragmentation occurs when data gets old, i.e., it has been subject to many inserts, updates, and deletes. This is covered in Chapter 16.

❏   External fragmentation, which we are interested in here, can take two forms:

    ❏   Classic file fragmentation occurs when a file is created and the file system doesn't have enough contiguous disk space to create the file in a single fragment. You end up with a single file spread across multiple file fragments.

    ❏   Autogrow fragmentation is the fragmentation that occurs when you enable autogrow and the database size continuously grows with the addition of more files. These files may or may not have classic file fragmentation as well, but SQL Server has to manage multiple data and/or log files, which creates additional overhead. In some cases the number of files can be in the thousands.

One important point to consider here is that SQL database files don't become more fragmented once they have been created. If files are created when there isn't enough contiguous free space, they are created in multiple fragments. If the disk is defragmented (and the OS has enough space to fully defragment all files) right after the files are created, then the files are no longer fragmented, and won't ever become fragmented.

In the ideal scenario, you have dedicated disks for your SQL database files, and you can size each file correctly, create the files, and disable autogrow. In this situation, you start with clean disks, create one or two files that aren't fragmented, and they stay that way forever. That way, you only need to deal with internal fragmentation.

In the next scenario, you start from the previous situation but allow autogrow at some tiny size or percentage, so you end up adding hundreds or thousands of small files. In this case, those files may or may not be fragmented, depending on how much free space is available on the disk when each autogrow operation occurs. Your only solution here to remove the fragmentation is to schedule server downtime to rebuild each database using a few large files, sized correctly for the expected database growth, and then disable autogrow. This way, you resolve any disk fragmentation that occurs, and by disabling autogrow you prevent external fragmentation from ever occurring.

In the worst-case scenario, you don't have dedicated disks, you used the default database sizes, and enabled autogrow. Now you may have several problems to resolve. Your SQL database files are competing for I/O capacity with the OS, and anything else running on the server. Until you add dedicated disks for SQL Server this won't be resolved. In addition, you may also end up with a lot of file fragments, as each autogrow operation adds another data or log file. As each new file is created by autogrow, it might be fragmented over the disk surface. As more files are added and the disk fills up, the chance of creating fragmented files increases.

The best way to avoid problems is to follow these steps:

1.   Install the OS.

2.   Defragment the disk.

3. Install any applications (SQL Server).

4. Defragment the disk.

5. Create data and log files at maximum size.

6. Check for fragmentation and defragment if necessary.

7. Disable autogrow.

8. Routinely defragment the disk to clean up fragmentation caused by other applications. This preserves the free space should you ever need to add more SQL data or log files.

In most cases, the operating system's disk defragmenter does a great job and is all you need. In some cases, however, you may need to consider purchasing a third-party disk defragmentation utility.

Summary

This chapter covered a lot of ground — from introducing performance to the various resources you need to consider when configuring a server. We started by looking at the key things any DBA needs to know about performance, before discussing the performance-tuning process. Then we dug into the specifics of server hardware, looking at the different attributes of CPUs, memory, networks, and disk I/O.

The discussion on CPUs examined the different types of processors you might encounter and explained the differences and the various options available. The memory section looked at the different memory settings you might need to use and covered all the scenarios you might encounter, including how to set the server to enable SQL Server to utilize the available memory. The disk I/O section examined the many details involved in storage subsystem configuration. We looked at how to design a storage system and at some of the considerations necessary when working with large SAN systems. Finally, you learned how to configure the server side of the storage system.

In the next chapter you will learn how to optimize your T-SQL/SQL Server configuration.

12

Optimizing SQL
Server 2008

Since the inception of SQL Server 7.0, the database engine has been enabled for self-tuning and managing. With the advent of SQL Server 2008, these concepts have reached new heights. When implemented on an optimized platform (as described in Chapter 11) with a properly configured SQL Server instance that has also been well maintained, SQL Server 2008 remains largely self-tuning and healing. In this chapter we introduce and discuss the SQL Server 2008 technologies needed to accomplish this feat.

Application Optimization

The first order of business for scaling SQL Server 2008 on the Windows Server platform is optimizing the application. The *Pareto Principle*, which states that only a few vital factors are responsible for producing most of the problems in scaling such an application, is reflected in this optimization. If the application is not well written, getting a bigger hammer will only postpone your scalability issues, rather than resolve them. Tuning an application for performance is beyond the scope of this chapter.

The goal of performance tuning SQL Server 2008 is to minimize the response time for each SQL statement and increase system throughput. This will maximize the scalability of the entire database server by reducing network-traffic latency, and optimizing disk I/O throughput and CPU processing time.

Defining a Workload

A prerequisite to tuning any database environment is a thorough understanding of basic database principles. Two critical principles are the logical and physical structure of the data and the inherent differences in the application of the database. For example, different demands are made by an online transaction processing (OLTP) environment than are made by a decision support (DSS) environment. A DSS environment often needs a heavily optimized I/O subsystem to keep up with the massive amounts of data retrieval (or reads) it will perform. An OLTP transactional environment needs an I/O subsystem optimized for more of a balance between read and write operations.

In most cases, SQL Server testing to scale with the actual demands on the application while in production is not possible. As a preferred practice, you need to set up a test environment that best matches the production system and then use a load generator such as Quest Benchmark Factory or Idera SQLscaler to simulate the database workload of the targeted production data-tier environment. This technique enables offline measuring and tuning the database system before you deploy it into the production environment.

Further, the use of this technique in a test environment enables you to compartmentalize specific pieces of the overall solution to be tested individually. As an example, using the load-generator approach enables you to reduce unknowns or variables from a performance-tuning equation by addressing each component on an individual basis (hardware, database, and application).

System Harmony Is the Goal

Scaling an application and its database is dependent on the harmony of the memory, disk I/O, network, and processors, as shown in Figure 12-1. A well-designed system balances these components and should allow the system (the application and data tiers) to sustain a run rate of greater than 80 percent processor usage.

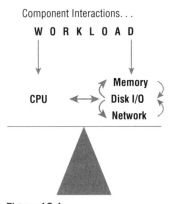

Figure 12-1

Of these resource components, a processor bottleneck on a well-tuned system (application\database), is the least problematic because it has the simplest resolution: Add more processors or upgrade the processor speed/technology.

The Silent Killer: I/O Problems

Customers often complain about their SQL Server performance and point to the database because the processors aren't that busy. After a discussion and a little elbow grease, frequently the culprit is an I/O bottleneck. The confusion comes from the fact that disk I/O is inversely proportional to CPU. In other words, over time, the processors are waiting for outstanding data requests that are queued on an overburdened disk subsystem. This section is about laying out the SQL Server shell or container on disk and configuring it properly to maximize the exploitation of the hardware resources. Scaling any database is a balancing act based on moving the bottleneck to the least affected resource.

SQL Server I/O Process Model

Windows Server 2003 or 2008 with SQL Server 2008 storage engine work together to mask the high cost of a disk I/O request. The Windows Server I/O Manager handles all I/O operations. The I/O Manager fulfills all I/O (read or write) requests by means of *scatter-gather* or asynchronous methods. For examples of scatter-gather or asynchronous methods, refer to SQL 2008 Books Online (BOL) under "I/O Architecture."

The SQL Server storage engine manages when disk I/O operations are performed, how they are performed, and the number of operations that are performed. However, the Windows operating system (I/O Manager Subsystem) performs the underlying I/O operations and provides the interface to the physical media. That is why we always recommend running SQL Server 2008 on the latest version of Windows. There are behavioral differences between Windows Server 2003, Windows Server 2003 with SP1, Windows Server 2003 R2, and Windows 2008 that SQL Server 2008 can take advantage of. For more Windows 2008 details, see `www.microsoft.com/windowsserver2008/en/us/product-information.aspx` and select "Editions" for edition specifics.

The job of the database storage engine is to manage or mitigate as much of the cost of these I/O operations as possible. For instance, the database storage engine allocates much of its virtual memory space to a data buffer cache. This cache is managed via cost-based analysis to ensure that memory is optimized to efficiently use its memory space for data content — that is, data frequently updated or requested is maintained in memory. This benefits the user's request by performing a logical I/O and avoiding expensive physical I/O requests.

Database File Placement

SQL Server stores its database on the operating system files — that is, physical disks or Logical Unit Numbers (LUNs) surfaced from a disk array. The database is made up of three file types: a primary data file (MDF), one or more secondary data file(s) (NDF), and transaction log file(s) (LDF).

Database file location is critical to the I/O performance of the DBMS. Using a fast and dedicated I/O subsystem for database files enables it to perform most efficiently. As described in Chapter 11, available disk space does not equate to better performance. Rather, the more, faster physical drives there are, or LUNs, the better your database I/O subsystem will perform. Data can be stored according to usage across data files and filegroups that span many physical disks. A *filegroup* is a collection of data files used in managing database data-file placement.

Reference data that is rarely updated or archived data can be placed in a read-only filegroup. This filegroup, along with additional read/write filegroups, can be part of an updatable database.

In SQL Server 2008, the use of MDF, NDF, and LDF file extensions is optional.

There are functional changes to `tempdb` to take into consideration when you are creating your primary data-file placement strategy.

tempdb Considerations

When SQL Server is restarted, tempdb is the only database that returns to the original default size of 8MB or to the predefined size set by the administrator, and it can then grow from there based on usage requirements. During the autogrow operation, threads can lock database resources during the database-growth operation, affecting server concurrency. To avoid timeouts, the autogrow operation should be limited to less than two minutes.

Beginning with SQL Server 2005 and continuing in SQL Server 2008, tempdb has added support for a whole new set of features. tempdb typically consists of a primary data and log files, but it also has two version stores. A version store is a collection of data pages that hold data rows required to support particular features that use row versioning. These two version stores are as follows:

❑   Row versions generated by data modification transactions in tempdb that use snapshot or read committed row versioning isolation levels

❑   Row versions in tempdb that are generated by data modification transactions for features such as online index operations, Multiple Active Result Sets (MARS), and AFTER triggers

As a result, placing the tempdb database on a dedicated and fast I/O subsystem will ensure good performance. As mentioned, the tempdb database supports user objects (such as temporary tables), internal objects (intermediate sort results), and functionality-based requirements on the version stores. A great deal of work has been performed on tempdb internals to improve scalability.

To manage tempdb space requirements, SQL Server 2008 needs to support the following features in tempdb:

❑   Query

❑   Triggers

❑   Snapshot isolation and read committed snapshots

❑   Multiple Active Result Sets (MARS)

❑   Online index creation

❑   Temporary tables, table variables, and table-valued functions

❑   DBCC Check

❑   Large Object (LOB) parameters

❑   Cursors

❑   Service Broker and event notification

❑   XML and Large Object (LOB) variable

❑   Query notifications

❑   Database mail

❑   Index creation

❑   User-defined functions

Consider reading BOL under "Capacity Planning for tempdb" for additional information and functionality details regarding tempdb usage.

We recommend that you do some type of capacity planning for `tempdb` to ensure that it's properly sized and can handle the needs of your enterprise system. At a minimum, we recommend the following:

1. Take into consideration the size of your existing `tempdb`.

2. Monitor `tempdb` while running the processes known to affect tempdb the most. The following query outputs the five executing tasks that make the most use of `tempdb`:

```
SELECT top 5 * FROM sys.dm_db_session_space_usage
ORDER BY (user_objects_alloc_page_count + internal_objects_alloc_page_count)
DESC
```

3. Rebuild the index of your largest table online while monitoring `tempdb`. Don't be surprised if this number turns out to be two times the table size, as this process now takes place in `tempdb`.

The following is a recommended query to monitor `tempDB` size. This query identifies and expresses `tempdb` space used, in kilobytes, by internal objects, free space, version store, and user objects:

```
select sum(user_object_reserved_page_count)*8 as user_objects_kb,
    sum(internal_object_reserved_page_count)*8 as internal_objects_kb,
    sum(version_store_reserved_page_count)*8  as version_store_kb,
    sum(unallocated_extent_page_count)*8 as freespace_kb
from sys.dm_db_file_space_usage
where database_id = 2
```

The output on your system depends on your database setup and usage. The output of this query on my system follows:

user_objects_kb	internal_objects_kb	version_store_kb	freespace_kb
256	640	0	6208

If any of these stores run out of space, `tempdb` *will run out of space and SQL Server will stop.*

Taking into consideration the preceding results, the following steps are recommended:

1. Pre-allocate space for `tempdb` files based on the results of your testing, but leave autogrow enabled in case `tempdb` runs out of space to prevent SQL Server from stopping.

2. Per SQL Server instance, as a rule of thumb, create one `tempdb` data file per CPU or processor core, all equal in size.

3. Make sure `tempdb` is in simple recovery model (this allows for space recovery).

4. Set autogrow to 10 percent.

5. Place `tempdb` on a fast and dedicated I/O subsystem.

6. Create alerts that monitor the environment by using SQL Server Agent or Microsoft System Center Operations Manager with SQL Knowledge Pack to ensure that you track for error 1101 or 1105 (`tempdb` is full). This is crucial because the server stops processing if it receives those errors. Right-click SQL Server Agent in SQL Server Management Studio and fill in the

dialog, as shown in Figure 12-2. Moreover, you can monitor the following counters using Windows System Performance Monitor:

❑ SQLServer:Databases: Log File(s) Size(KB) — Returns the cumulative size of all the log files in the database.

❑ SQLServer:Databases: Data File(s) Size(KB) — Returns the cumulative size of all the data files in the database.

❑ SQLServer:Databases: Log File(s) Used (KB) — Returns the cumulative used size of all log files in the database. A large active portion of the log in `tempdb` can be a warning sign that a long transaction is preventing log cleanup.

7. Use instant database file initialization. If you are not running the SQL Server (MSSQLSERVER) Service account with admin privileges, make sure that the SE_MANAGE_VOLUME_NAME permission has been assigned to the service account. This feature can reduce a 15-minute file-initialization process to about one second for the same process.

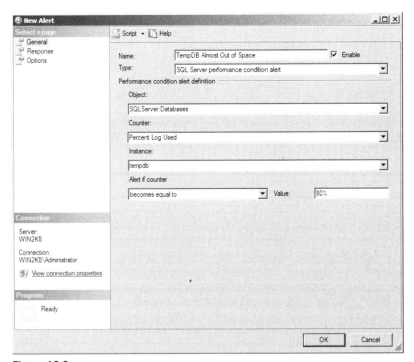

Figure 12-2

Another great tool is the `sys.dm_db_task_space_usage` DMV, which provides insight into `tempdb`'s space consumption on a per-task basis. Keep in mind that once the task is complete, the counters reset to zero. In addition, you should monitor the per disk Avg. Sec/ Read and Avg. Sec/ Write as follows:

❑ Less than 10 milliseconds (ms) = Very good

❑ Between 10–20 ms = Borderline

❑ Between 20–50 ms = Slow, needs attention

❑ Greater than 50 ms = Serious IO bottleneck

If you have very large `tempdb` usage requirements, read the Q917047, "Microsoft SQL Server I/O subsystem requirements for tempdb database" at `http://support.microsoft.com/kb/917047` or look in SQL Server 2008 Books Online (BOL) for "Optimizing tempdb Performance."

It is hoped that this section has impressed upon you that in SQL Server 2008, more capacity planning is required to optimize `tempdb` for performance.

Table and Index Partitioning

Simply stated, *partitioning* is the breaking up of a large object, such as a table, into smaller, manageable pieces. Partitioning has been around for a while. This feature received a lot of attention once it supported the ability to use constraints with views. This provided the capability for the optimizer to eliminate partitions (or tables) joined by a union of all statements on a view. These partitions could also be distributed across servers. This technology was introduced as a distributed partitioned view (DPV) during the SQL 7.0 launch.

SQL Server 2008 has the capability to partition database tables and their indexes over filegroups within a single database. This type of partitioning has many benefits over DPV, such as being transparent to the application (meaning no application code changes are necessary). Other benefits include database recoverability, simplified maintenance, and manageability.

Although we're discussing partitioning as part of this performance-tuning chapter, partitioning is first and foremost a manageability and scalability tool. In most situations, implementing partitioning also offers performance improvements as a byproduct of scalability. Several operations can be performed only on a partitioned table:

❑ Switch data into a partition

❑ Switch data out of a partition

❑ Merge partition range

❑ Split partition range

Partitioning is supported only in SQL Server 2008 Enterprise and Developer Editions.

These benefits are highlighted throughout this section.

Why Consider Partitioning?

For a variety of reasons, you may have very large tables. When these tables (or databases) reach a certain size, it becomes difficult to perform activities such as database maintenance, backup, or restore operations that consume a lot of time. Environmental issues such as poor concurrency due to a large number of users on a sizable table result in lock escalations, which translates into further challenges. If archiving the data is not possible because of regulatory compliance needs, independent software vendor (ISV) requirements, or cultural requirements, partitioning is most likely the tool for you. If you are still unsure whether or not to implement partitioning, run your workload through the Database Tuning Advisor (DTA), which will make recommendations for partitioning and generate the code for you. The DTA is covered in detail in Chapter 15, and can be found under the "Performance Tools" section of the Microsoft SQL Server 2008 program menu.

> *Partitioning is covered through the book's various chapters to ensure that details are presented in their appropriate contexts.*

Here is a high-level process for partitioning:

1. Create a partition function to define a data-placement strategy.

2. Create filegroups to support the partition function.

3. Create a partition scheme to define the physical data distribution strategy (map the function data to filegroups).

4. Create a table or index on the partition function.

5. Enjoy redirected queries to appropriate resources.

After implementation, partitioning will positively affect your environment and most of your processes. Make sure you understand this technology to ensure that every process benefits from it. The following lists presents a few processes that may be affected by partitioning your environment:

❑ Database backup and restore strategy (support for partial database availability).

❑ Index maintenance strategy (rebuild), including index views.

❑ Data management strategy (large insert or table truncates).

❑ End-user database workload.

❑ Concurrency:

  ❑ Parallel partition query processing — In SQL Server 2005, if the query only accessed one table partition, then all available processor threads could access and operate on it in parallel. If more than one table partition was accessed by the query, then only one processor thread was allowed per partition, even when more processors were available. For example, if you have an eight-processor server and the query accessed two table partitions, six processors would not be used by that query. In SQL Server 2008, parallel partition processing has been implemented whereby all available processors are used in parallel to satisfy the query for a partition table. The parallel feature can be enabled or disabled based on the usage requirements of your database workload.

  ❑ Table partition lock-escalation strategy.

❑ Enhanced distribution or isolated database workloads using filegroups.

Implementing Partitioning

As mentioned earlier, partitioning breaks a physical object, such as a large table, into multiple manageable pieces. A *row* is the unit on which partitioning is based. Unlike DPVs, all partitions must reside within a single database.

Creating a Partition Function

Simply stated, a *partition function* is your primary data-partitioning strategy. The first order of business is to determine your partitioning strategy. Identifying and prioritizing challenges is the best way to decide on a partitioning strategy. Whether it's to move old data within a table to a slower, inexpensive I/O subsystem, enhance database workload concurrency, or simply maintain a very large database, identifying and prioritizing is essential. Once you've selected your strategy, you need to create a partitioning function that matches that strategy.

Remember to evaluate a table for partitioning, as the partition function is based on the distribution of data (selectivity of a column and the range or breadth of that column). The range supports the number of partitions by which the table can be partitioned. There is a product limit of 1,000 partitions per table. This range should also match up with the desired strategy — for example, spreading out (or partitioning) a huge customer table by customer last name or by geographical location for better workload management may be a sound strategy. Another example of a sound strategy may be to partition a table by date for the purpose of archiving data based on date range for a more efficient environment.

> *User-defined data types, alias data types, timestamps, images, XML, varchar(max), nvarchar(max), or varbinary(max) cannot be implemented as partitioning columns.*

As an example, we will partition a trouble-ticketing system for a telephone company. When a trouble ticket is generated based on an outage, it is submitted to the database. At this point, many activities are initiated: Technicians are dispatched, parts are replaced or reordered, and service can be rerouted within the network. Service level agreements (SLAs) are monitored and escalations are initiated. All of these activities take place because of the trouble ticket. In this system, the activities table and ticketing table have hot spots, as shown in Figure 12-3.

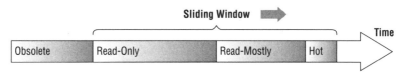

Figure 12-3

In Figure 12-3, the information marked as "Hot" is the new or recent data, and it is only relevant or of interest during the outage. The information marked as "Read-Only" and "Read-Mostly" is usually used for minor analysis during postmortem processes and then for application reporting. Eventually, the data becomes obsolete and should be moved to a warehouse. Unfortunately, because of internal regulatory requirements, this database has to be online for seven years. Partitioning this environment will provide sizable benefits. Under a *sliding-window* scenario (explained in the "Creating a Partition Scheme" section later in this chapter), every month (or quarter) a new partition would be introduced to the environment as a retainer for the current ("Hot") data for the tickets and activities tables. As part of this process, a partition with data from these tables that is older than seven years would also be retired.

As described earlier, there is a one-to-many relationship between tickets and activities. Although there are obvious size differences between these tables, it is important to put them through identical processes. This enables you to run processes that will affect resources shared by and limited to these objects. To mitigate the impact of doing daily activities such as backups and index maintenance on all this data, these tables will be partitioned based on date ranges. We will create a left partition function based on the ticketdate column, as outlined in the following (if you execute the preceding statement, remove the line break):

```
CREATE PARTITION FUNCTION
PFL_Years (datetime)
AS RANGE LEFT
FOR VALUES ('19991231 23:59:59.997', '20011231 23:59:59.997', '20031231
23:59:59.997', '20051231 23:59:59.997', '20061231 23:59:59.997')
```

SQL Server rounds time to .003 seconds, meaning that a time of .997 would be rounded up to 1.0 second.

❑   The boundary value '19991231 23:59:59.997' is the leftmost partition and includes all values less than or equal to '19991231 23:59:59.997'.

❑   The boundary value '20011231 23:59:59.997' is the second partition and includes all values greater than '19991231 23:59:59.997' but less than or equal to '20011231 23:59:59.997'.

❑   The boundary value '20031231 23:59:59.997' is the third partition and includes all values greater than '20011231 23:59:59.997' but less than or equal to '20031231 23:59:59.997'.

❑   The boundary value '20051231 23:59:59.997' is the fourth partition and includes all values greater than '20031231 23:59:59.997' but less than or equal to '20051231 23:59:59.997'.

❑   The boundary value '20061231 23:59:59.997' is the fifth partition and includes all values greater than '20051231 23:59:59.997' but less than or equal to '20061231 23:59:59.997'.

❑   Finally, the sixth partition includes all values greater than '20061231 23:59:59.997'.

The range partition function specifies the boundaries of the range. The `left` or `right` keyword specifies the interval of the boundary to which the value belongs. There can be no holes in the partition domain; all values must be obtainable. In this code sample, all transactions must fall within a date specified by the sample value range.

Creating Filegroups

You should create filegroups to support the strategy set by the partition function. As a best practice, user objects should be created and mapped to a filegroup outside of the primary filegroup, leaving the primary filegroup for system objects. This ensures database availability in the event of an outage that affects the availability of any filegroup outside of the primary filegroup.

To continue with this example exercise, you need to create filegroups CY00, CY02, CY04, CY05, CY06, and CY07 in the database before creating the partition scheme.

Creating a Partition Scheme

A partition scheme is what maps database objects such as a table to a physical entity such as a filegroup, and then to a file. There are definitely backup, restore, and data-archival considerations when making this decision. (These are discussed in Chapter 18.) The following sample code maps the partition functions or dates to individual filegroups. The partition scheme depends on the `PFL_Years` partition function to be available from the earlier example.

```
CREATE PARTITION SCHEME CYScheme
AS
PARTITION PFL_Years
TO ([CY00], [CY02], [CY04], [CY05], [CY06], [CY07])
```

This supports the placement of filegroups on individual physical disk subsystems. Such an option also supports the capability to move old data to an older, inexpensive I/O subsystem and to reassign the new, faster I/O subsystem to support "Hot" data (CY07). When the older data has been moved to the inexpensive I/O subsystem, filegroups can be marked as read-only. Once this data has been backed up, it no longer needs to be part of the backup process. SQL Server automatically ignores these filegroups as part of index maintenance.

The other option for a partition-function scheme enables the mapping of the partition scheme to map the partition function to a single filegroup. The following sample code maps the partition function to the default filegroup:

This code will fail if you have not created the PFL_Years *partition function.*

```
CREATE PARTITION SCHEME CYScheme2
AS
PARTITION PFL_Years
TO ([Default], [Default], [Default], [Default], [Default], [Default])
```

Partitioning enables the capability to delete or insert gigabytes of data on a 500+ GB partitioned table with a simple metadata switch (in seconds). The process utilized to accomplish this is called *sliding window*. On a nonpartitioned table, this process would take hours because of lock escalation and index resynchronization. However, using a partitioned table with the sliding-window process consists of three types of actions:

1. An empty target table or partitioned table is created outside of the source data partitioned table.
2. The source data partitioned table is switched with the empty target.
3. At the conclusion of this process, the data is now in the target and can be dropped.

This process could be repeated in reverse to insert a new partition with data into this source partitioned table as the repository for the "Hot" data. Again, the only impact to the source partitioned table is a brief pause while a schema-lock is placed during the partition swaps, which can take a few seconds. This switch process can only be performed on partitions within the same filegroup. Implementation details and best practices are covered later in this chapter and in upcoming chapters.

Creating Tables and Indexes

As the following code shows, the syntax for creating a table is accomplished as it has always been. The only exception is that it is created on a partition schema instead of a specific or default filegroup. SQL Server 2008 provides the capability to create tables, indexes, and indexed views on partition schemes. This supports the distribution of database objects across several filegroups. This is different from the existing capability to create an entire object within a filegroup (which is still available in SQL Server 2008).

```
CREATE TABLE [dbo].[Tickets]
(       [TiketID] [int] NOT NULL,
        [CustomerID] [int] NULL,
        [State] [int] NULL,
        [Status] [tinyint] NOT NULL,
        [TicketDate] [datetime] NOT NULL
        CONSTRAINT TicketYear
        CHECK ([TicketDate] >= '19991231 23:59:59.997'
AND [TicketDate] <= '20061231 23:59:59.997'))
ON CYScheme (TicketDate)
GO

CREATE TABLE [dbo].[Activities]
(       [TiketID] [int] NOT NULL,
        [ActivityDetail] [varchar] (255) NULL,
        [TicketDate] [datetime] NOT NULL,
        [ActivityDate] [datetime] NOT NULL
        CONSTRAINT ActivityYear
        CHECK ([ActivityDate] >= '19991231 23:59:59.997'
AND [ActivityDate] <= '20061231 23:59:59.997'))
ON CYScheme (TicketDate)
GO
```

The following sections cover two areas of best practices: index alignment and storage alignment.

Index Alignment

An aligned index uses an equivalent partition function and includes the same partitioning columns as its table (as shown in Figure 12-4). They actually don't have to use the identical partition function or scheme, but there has to be a one-to-one correlation of data-to-index entries within a partition.

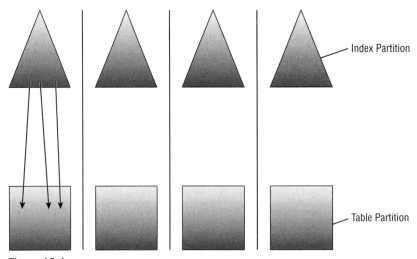

Figure 12-4

A benefit derived from index alignment is the ability to switch partitions in or out of a table with a simple metadata operation. In the trouble-ticket example, you would be able to programmatically add a new partition for the new month (or current month) and delete the outgoing month from the table as part of the seven-year cycle.

Storage Alignment

Index alignment is the first requirement of a storage-aligned solution. There are two options for storage alignment. The big differentiator is the ability to use the same partition scheme, or a different one, as long as both tables and indexes have an equal number of partitions. The first option, shown in Figure 12-5, demonstrates a storage-aligned solution with the index and relevant data in distinct and dedicated filegroups. If a query to compare data in CY04 and CY02 is executed on an aligned index and data, the query would be localized to the aligned environment. This would benefit users working in other table partitions isolated from the ongoing work within these two partitions.

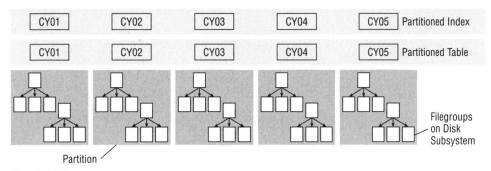

Figure 12-5

Figure 12-6 shows the same query executed on a different architecture. Because of the alignment of index and data, the query will still be localized but will run in parallel on both the relevant index and data partitions. This would still benefit users working in other partitions isolated from the ongoing work within these four partitions.

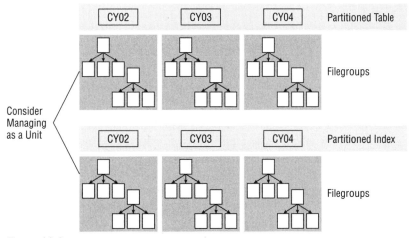

Figure 12-6

Additional benefits derived from storage alignment are partial database availability and piecemeal database restores. For instance, in the example scenario, the CY04 partition could be offline, and the application would still be processing trouble tickets. This would occur regardless of which partition went down, as long as the primary filegroup that contains the system-tables information (as is the best practice) and the partition that contains the current month's data are online. Considerations that will affect query parallelism of this environment are discussed later in the CPU Considerations section of this chapter.

Here is an example of a SQL script for partitioning operations on a table using the AdventureWorks2008 database. For simplicity in this example, all the partitions are placed on the primary file group, but in a real-life scenario, to achieve I/O performance benefits, partitions may be placed on different filegroups, which are then placed on different physical disk drives.

First, create the partition function:

```
USE AdventureWorks2008;

CREATE PARTITION FUNCTION [OrderDateRangePFN](datetime)
AS RANGE RIGHT
FOR VALUES (N'2001-01-01 00:00:00', N'2002-01-01 00:00:00',
N'2003-01-01 00:00:00', N'2004-01-01 00:00:00');
```

Then create the partition scheme:

```
CREATE PARTITION SCHEME [OrderDatePScheme]
AS PARTITION [OrderDateRangePFN]
TO ([Primary], [Primary], [Primary], [Primary], [Primary]);
```

For this example, you create two tables: SalesOrderHeader is the partitioned table and SalesOrderHeaderOLD is the nonpartitioned table. Load data into the SalesOrderHeader table. Then, create clustered indexes on both tables. Finally, a check constraint needs to be applied to the SalesOrderHeaderOLD table in order to allow the data to switch into the SalesOrderHeader partitioned table:

```
CREATE TABLE [dbo].[SalesOrderHeader](
 [SalesOrderID] [int] NULL,
 [RevisionNumber] [tinyint] NOT NULL,
 [OrderDate] [datetime] NOT NULL,
 [DueDate] [datetime] NOT NULL,
 [ShipDate] [datetime] NULL,
 [Status] [tinyint] NOT NULL
) ON [OrderDatePScheme]([OrderDate]);

CREATE TABLE [dbo].[SalesOrderHeaderOLD](
 [SalesOrderID] [int] NULL,
 [RevisionNumber] [tinyint] NOT NULL,
 [OrderDate] [datetime] NOT NULL  ,
 [DueDate] [datetime] NOT NULL,
 [ShipDate] [datetime] NULL,
 [Status] [tinyint] NOT NULL);

INSERT INTO SalesOrderHeader SELECT [SalesOrderID],[RevisionNumber],
```

```
[OrderDate],[DueDate],[ShipDate],[Status] FROM SALES.[SalesOrderHeader];

CREATE CLUSTERED INDEX SalesOrderHeaderCLInd
ON SalesOrderHeader(OrderDate) ON OrderDatePScheme(OrderDate);

CREATE CLUSTERED INDEX SalesOrderHeaderOLDCLInd ON
SalesOrderHeaderOLD(OrderDate);

ALTER TABLE [DBO].[SalesOrderHeaderOLD] WITH CHECK ADD CONSTRAINT
[CK_SalesOrderHeaderOLD_ORDERDATE] CHECK ([ORDERDATE]>=('2003-01-01
00:00:00') AND [ORDERDATE]<('2004-01-01 00:00:00'));
```

Before you start to do table partition operations, you should verify that you have data in the partitioned table and no data in the nonpartitioned table. The following query returns which partitions have data and how many rows:

```
SELECT $partition.OrderDateRangePFN(OrderDate) AS 'Partition Number', min(OrderDate)
AS 'Min Order Date', max(OrderDate) AS 'Max Order Date',count(*) AS 'Rows In
Partition' FROM SalesOrderHeader

GROUP BY $partition.OrderDateRangePFN(OrderDate);
```

Now, verify that no data has been inserted into the SalesOrderHeaderOLD nonpartitioned table; this query should return no data:

```
SELECT * FROM [SalesOrderHeaderOLD]
```

To simply switch the data from partition 4 into the SalesOrderHeaderOLD table, execute the following command:

```
ALTER TABLE SalesOrderHeader
SWITCH PARTITION 4 TO SalesOrderHeaderOLD;
```

To simply switch the data from SalesOrderHeaderOLD back to partition 4, execute the following command:

```
ALTER TABLE SalesOrderHeaderOLD
SWITCH TO SalesOrderHeader PARTITION 4;
```

To merge a partition range, execute the following command:

```
ALTER PARTITION FUNCTION OrderDateRangePFN()
MERGE RANGE ('2003-01-01 00:00:00');
```

You may want to split a partition range. The split range area should be empty of data because if data were available, SQL Server would need to physically (I/O) move the data across the range. For a large table, the data movement can take time and resources. Therefore, if the range is not empty, the split is not instantaneous. To split a range, you must add a new filegroup for the range before splitting it:

```
ALTER PARTITION SCHEME OrderDatePScheme NEXT USED [Primary];
ALTER PARTITION FUNCTION OrderDateRangePFN()
SPLIT RANGE ('2003-01-01 00:00:00');
```

Data Compression

SQL Server 2008 data compression brings enhancements in storage and performance benefits. Reducing the amount of disk space that a database occupies reduces the overall data files storage footprint and offers increase in throughput with the following:

❑   Better I/O utilization, as more data is read and written per page

❑   Better memory utilization, as more data will fit in the buffer cache

❑   Reduction in page latching, as more data will fit in each page

It is true that disk space is becoming less expensive. However, implementation of a high-performance database system requires a high-performing disk system or Storage Area Network (SAN) or Network Attached Storage (NAS) storage, which is not inexpensive. Additionally, this may require additional storage for high availability, backups, QA, and test environments. Overall, it lowers SQL Server 2008's total cost of ownership, making it more competitive.

Before implementing data compression, you must consider the trade-off between I/O and CPU. To compress and uncompress data requires CPU processing utilization, so it would not be recommended for a system that is CPU-bound. However, it would benefit a system that is more I/O-bound. Second, keep in mind that accessing the compressed data requires CPU processing work, and if this data is highly selected, there is a CPU performance penalty. Data compression makes most sense on data that is older and less queried. As a simple example, with a very large partitioned table, the older partitions that are less queried may be compressed while the highly volatile partitions are not. You can compress volatile data, but you must consider the costs versus benefits for your database workload, and the capacity of your hardware to support it with the goal of achieving the highest throughput.

> **Data compression is only available in SQL Server 2008 Enterprise and Developer Editions.**

You can use data compression on the following database objects:

❑   Tables (but not system tables)

❑   Clustered indexes

❑   Nonclustered indexes

❑   Index views

❑   Partitioned tables and indexes where each partition can have a different compression setting

Row Compression

SQL Server 2008 implements *row* and *page* data compression. The data compression ratio depends on the schema and data distribution, where compression stores fixed-value data types in a variable format — that is, a 4-byte column with a 1-byte value can be compressed to a 1-byte. A 1-byte column with a 1-byte value will have no compression, but NULL or 0 values take no bytes. Compression does take a few bits of metadata overhead to store per value. For example, an `Integer` data type column storing a 1-byte value will have a 75% compression ratio. To create a new compressed table with row compression, use the `CREATE TABLE` command, as follows:

```
USE AdventureWorks2008
GO
CREATE TABLE [Person].[AddressType_Compressed_Row](
 [AddressTypeID] [int] IDENTITY(1,1) NOT NULL,
 [Name] [dbo].[Name] NOT NULL,
 [rowguid] [uniqueidentifier] ROWGUIDCOL  NOT NULL,
 [ModifiedDate] [datetime] NOT NULL,
)
WITH (DATA_COMPRESSION=ROW)
GO
```

To change the compression setting of a table, use the `ALTER TABLE` command:

```
USE AdventureWorks2008
GO
ALTER TABLE Person.AddressType_Compressed_Row REBUILD
WITH (DATA_COMPRESSION=ROW)
GO
```

Page Compression

Page compression includes row compression, and then implements two other compression operations:

❏ **Prefix compression:** For each page and each column, a prefix value is identified that can be used to reduce the storage requirements. This value is stored in the Compression Information (CI) structure for each page. Then, repeated prefix values are replaced by a reference to the prefix stored in the CI.

❏ **Dictionary compression:** Searches for repeated values anywhere in the page, which are replaced by a reference to the CI.

When page compression is enabled for a new table, new inserted rows are row compressed until the page is full, and then page compression is applied. If afterward there is space in the page for additional new inserted rows, they are inserted and compressed; if not, the new inserted rows go onto another page. When a populated table is compressed, the indexes are rebuilt. Using page compression, non-leaf pages of the indexes are compressed using row compression. To create a new compressed table with page compression, use the following commands:

```
USE AdventureWorks2008
GO
CREATE TABLE [Person].[AddressType_Compressed_Page](
 [AddressTypeID] [int] IDENTITY(1,1) NOT NULL,
 [Name] [dbo].[Name] NOT NULL,
 [rowguid] [uniqueidentifier] ROWGUIDCOL  NOT NULL,
 [ModifiedDate] [datetime] NOT NULL,
)
WITH (DATA_COMPRESSION=PAGE)
GO
```

To change the compression setting of a table, use the ALTER TABLE command:

```
USE AdventureWorks2008
GO
ALTER TABLE Person.AddressType_Compressed_Page REBUILD
WITH (DATA_COMPRESSION=PAGE)
GO
```

Moreover, on a partitioned table or index, compression can be applied or altered on individual partitions. The following code shows an example of applying compression to a partitioned table and index:

```
USE AdventureWorks2008
GO

CREATE PARTITION FUNCTION [TableCompression](Int)
AS RANGE RIGHT
FOR VALUES (1, 10000, 12000, 16000);
GO

CREATE PARTITION SCHEME KeyRangePS
AS
PARTITION [TableCompression]
TO ([Default], [Default], [Default], [Default], [Default])
GO

CREATE TABLE PartitionTable
(KeyID int,
Description varchar(30))
ON KeyRangePS (KeyID)
WITH
(
DATA_COMPRESSION = ROW ON PARTITIONS (1),
DATA_COMPRESSION = PAGE ON PARTITIONS (2 TO 4)
)
GO

CREATE INDEX IX_PartTabKeyID
  ON PartitionTable (KeyID)
WITH (DATA_COMPRESSION = ROW ON PARTITIONS(1),
DATA_COMPRESSION = PAGE ON PARTITIONS (2 TO 4 ) )
GO
```

Table partition operations on a compression partition table have the following behaviors:

❑ **Splitting a partition:** Both partitions inherit the original partition setting.

❑ **Merging partitions:** The resultant partition inherits the compression setting of the destination partition.

❑ **Switching partitions:** The compression setting of the partition and the table to switch must match.

❑ **Dropping a partitioned clustered index:** The table retains the compression setting.

Additionally, data compression can be managed from SQL Server 2008 Management Studio in Object Explorer by choosing the table or index to data compress. For example, to compress a table, follow these steps:

1. Choose the table and then right-click. From the pop-up menu, choose Storage ➪ Manage Compression.

2. On the Data Compression Wizard that opens, click Next, and in the Select Compression Type dialog of the Data Compression Wizard, select the Compression type drop-down to change the compression (None, Row, or Page). Figure 12-7 shows the Select Compression Type dialog.

3. After making a Compression Type change, to see the estimated space savings, click the Calculate button. Then, click Next to complete the wizard.

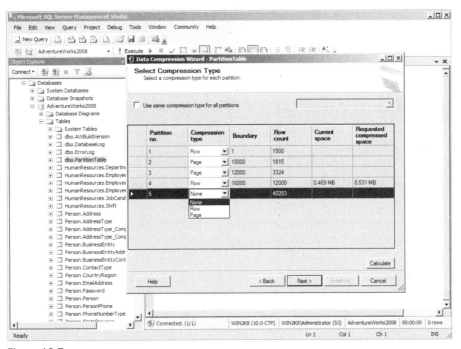

Figure 12-7

Estimating Space Savings

Prior to enabling data compression, you can evaluate the estimated compression cost savings. For example, if a row is more than 4KB and the whole value precision is always used of the data type, there may not be much compression savings. The `sp_estimate_data_compression_savings` stored procedure creates a sample data set in `tempdb` and evaluates the compression space savings, returning the estimated table and sample savings. It can evaluate tables, clustered indexes, nonclustered indexes, index views, and table and index partitions for either page or row compression. Moreover, this stored procedure can estimate the size of a compressed table, index, or partition in the uncompressed state. This stored procedure performs the same cost-saving calculation that was performed by the Data Compression Wizard shown in Figure 12-7 when clicking the Calculate button.

The syntax of the `sp_estimate_data_compression_savings` stored procedure follows:

```
sp_estimate_data_compression_savings
[ @schema_name = ] 'schema_name'
, [ @object_name = ] 'object_name'
, [@index_id = ] index_id
, [@partition_number = ] partition_number
, [@data_compression = ] 'data_compression'
[;]
```

In this code:

❑   `@schema_name` is the name of the schema that contains the object.

❑   `@object_name` is the name of the table or index view that the index is on.

❑   `@index_id` is the ID number of the index. Specify NULL for all indexes in a table or view.

❑   `@partition_number` is the partition number of the object; it can be NULL or 1 for nonpartitioned objects.

❑   `@data_compression` is the type of compression to evaluate; it can be NONE, ROW, or PAGE.

Figure 12-8 shows an example of estimating the space savings for the SalesOrderDetail table in the AdventureWorks2008 database using page compression.

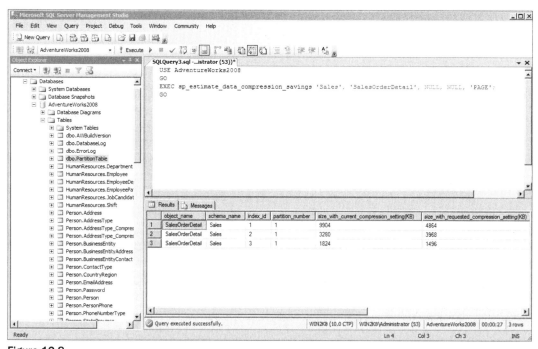

Figure 12-8

As for the result information:

- ❏ `index_id` identifies the object. In this case, 1 = clustered index (includes table); 2 and 3 are non-clustered indexes.
- ❏ `Size_with_current_compression_setting` is the current size of the object.
- ❏ `Size_with_requested_compression_setting` is the compressed size of the object

In this example, the clustered index, including the table, is 9904 KB but when page-compressed, it is 4864 KB, a space saving of 5040 KB.

Monitoring Data Compression

For monitoring data compression at the SQL Server 2008 instance level, two counters are available in the `SQL Server:Access Method` object:

- ❏ Page compression attempts/sec counts the number of page compression attempts per second.
- ❏ Pages compressed/sec counts the number of pages compressed per second.

Moreover, the `sys.dm_db_index_operational_stats` dynamic management function includes the `page_compression_attempt_count` and `page_compression_success_count`. Additionally, the `sys.dm_db_index_physical_stats` dynamic management function includes the `compressed_page_count`, which displays the number of pages compressed per object and per partition.

To identify compressed objects in the database, you can view the `data_compression` column (0 = No, 1 = Row, 2 = Page) of the `sys.partitions` catalog view. Additionally, from SQL Server 2008 Management Studio in Object Explorer, choose the table and right-click; then, from the pop-up menu choose Storage ⇨ Manage Compression for the Data Compression Wizard. For detailed information on data compression, refer to *Creating Compressed Tables and Indexes* in SQL Server 2008 Books Online.

Data Compression Considerations

When deciding whether to use data compression, keep the following items in mind:

- ❏ Data compression is available with SQL Server 2008 Enterprise and Developer Editions only.
- ❏ Enabling and disabling table or clustered index compression will rebuild all nonclustered indexes.
- ❏ Data compression cannot be used with sparse columns.
- ❏ Large objects (LOB) that are out-of-row are not compressed.
- ❏ Non-leaf pages in indexes are only compressed using row compression.
- ❏ Nonclustered indexes do not inherit the compression setting of the table.
- ❏ When you drop a clustered index, the table retains those compression settings.
- ❏ Unless specified, creating a clustered index inherits the compression setting of the table.

> **A word of caution for high availability systems: Changing the compression setting may generate extra transaction log operations.**

Memory Considerations and Enhancements

Since memory is fast relative to disk I/O, using this system resource effectively can have a large impact on the system's overall ability to scale and perform well. Most 32-bit systems available on the market today support Intel's 32-bit Intel (IA-32) microprocessor PAE, or *physical address extensions*, technology. This technology enables the operating system and application to address an amount of physical memory up to 32GB for Enterprise Edition (EE) and 64GB for Datacenter Edition. With the release of Windows Server 2003 Service Pack 1 of x64, and IA64 platforms, more physical accessible memory is supported. The platform of choice is shifting from 32-bit to 64-bit, and the hardware aspects of all of these issues are discussed in Chapter 11.

SQL Server 2008 memory architecture and capabilities vary greatly from those of previous versions of SQL Servers. Changes include the ability to consume and release memory-based, internal-server conditions dynamically using the AWE mechanism. In SQL Server 2000, all memory allocations above 4GB were static. Additional memory enhancements include the introduction of hierarchical memory architecture to maximize data locality and improve scalability by removing a centralized memory manager. SQL Server 2008 has resource monitoring, dynamic management views (DMVs), and a common caching framework. All of these concepts are discussed throughout this chapter.

Tuning SQL Server Memory

The following performance counters are available from the System Performance Monitor. The *SQL Server Cache Hit Ratio* signifies the balance between servicing user requests from data in the data cache and having to request data from the I/O subsystem. Accessing data in RAM (or data cache) is exponentially faster than accessing the same information from the I/O subsystem; thus, the desired state is to load all active data in RAM. Unfortunately, RAM is a limited resource. A desired cache hit ratio average should be well over 90 percent. This does not mean that the SQL Server environment would not benefit from additional memory. A lower number signifies that the system memory or data cache allocation is below desired size.

Another reliable indicator of instance memory pressure is the *SQL Server:Buffer Manager:Page-life-expectancy* counter. This counter indicates the amount of time that a buffer page remains in memory, in seconds. The ideal number should be above 300 seconds (or five minutes); anything lower signifies memory pressure. Be careful not to under-allocate total system memory, as it will force the operating system to start moving page faults to physical disk. A page fault is a phenomenon that occurs when the operating system goes to physical disk to resolve memory references. The operating system may incur some paging, but when excessive paging takes places, it uses disk I/O and CPU resources, which can introduce latency in the overall server, resulting in slower database performance. You can identify a lack of adequate system memory by monitoring the *Memory: Pages/sec performance* counter. It should be as close to zero as possible, as a higher value indicates that more hard-paging is taking place.

SQL Server 2008 has several features that should help with this issue. With Windows Server 2003, SQL Server 2008 has support for dynamic address windowing extensions (AWE) memory allocation, hot-add memory, a manager framework, and other enhancements. The SQL Server operating system (SQLOS) layer is the improved version of the User Mode Scheduler (UMS), now simply called *scheduler*. Consistent with its predecessor, SQLOS is a user-mode cooperative and on-demand thread-management system. An example of a cooperative workload is one that yields the processor during a periodic interval or while in a wait state, meaning that if a batch request does not have access to all of the required data for its execution, it will request its data and then yield its position to a process that needs processing time.

SQLOS is a thin layer that sits between SQL Server and Windows to manage the interaction between these environments. It enables SQL Server to scale on any hardware. This was accomplished by moving to a distributed model and creating an architecture that would foster locality of resources to aid in getting rid of global resource management bottlenecks. The challenge with global resource management is that in large hardware design, global resources cannot keep up with the demands of the system, slowing overall performance. Figure 12-9 highlights the SQLOS components that perform thread scheduling and synchronization, perform SQL Server memory management, provide exception handling, and host the Common Language Runtime (CLR).

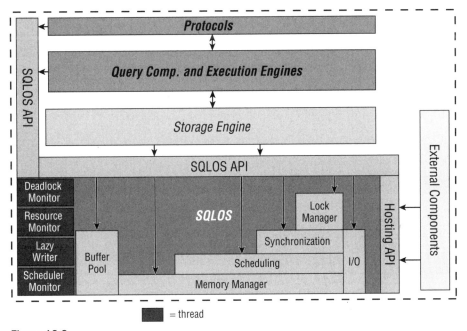

Figure 12-9

The goal of this environment is to empower the SQL Server platform to exploit all of today's hardware innovation across the X86, X64, and IA64 platforms. SQLOS was built to bring together the concepts of data locality, support for dynamic configuration, and hardware workload exploitation. This architecture also enables SQL Server 2008 to better support both Cache Coherent Non-uniform Memory Access (CC-NUMA), Interleave NUMA (NUMA hardware with memory that behaves like an SMP system), Soft-NUMA architecture (registry-activated, software-based emulated NUMA architecture used to partition a large SMP system), and large SMP systems, by affinitizing memory to a few CPUs.

The architecture introduces the concept of a *memory node*, which is one hierarchy between memory and CPUs. There will be a memory node for each set of CPUs to localize memory and its content to these CPUs. On an SMP architecture, a memory node shares memory across all CPUs, while on a NUMA architecture, there will be a memory node per NUMA node. As shown in Figure 12-10, the goal of this design is to support SQL Server scalability across all hardware architectures by enabling the software to adapt to or emulate various hardware architectures.

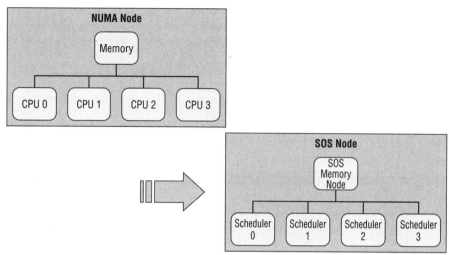

Figure 12-10

Schedulers are discussed later in this chapter, but for the purposes of this discussion, they manage the work being executed on a CPU.

Memory nodes share the memory allocated by Max Server Memory, setting evenly across a single memory node for SMP system and across one or more memory nodes for NUMA architectures. Each memory node has its own lazy writer thread that manages its workload based on its memory node. As seen in Figure 12-11, the CPU node is a subset of memory nodes and provides for logical grouping for CPUs.

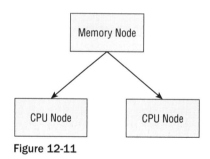

Figure 12-11

A CPU node is also a hierarchical structure designed to provide logical grouping for CPUs. The purpose is to localize and load-balance related workloads to a CPU node. On an SMP system, all CPUs would be grouped under a single CPU node, while on a NUMA-based system, there would be as many CPU nodes as the system supported. The relationship between a CPU node and a memory node is explicit. There can be many CPU nodes to a memory node, but there will never be more than one memory node to a CPU node. Each level of this hierarchy provides localized services to the components that it manages, resulting in the capability to process and manage workloads in such a way as to exploit the scalability of whatever hardware architecture SQL Server is running on. SQLOS also enables services such as dynamic affinity, load-balancing workloads, dynamic memory capabilities, Dedicated Admin Connection (DAC), and support for partitioned resource management capabilities.

SQL Server 2008 leverages the common caching framework (also part of SQLOS) to achieve fine-grain control over managing the increasing number of cache mechanisms (Cache Store, User Store, and Object Store). This framework improves the behavior of these mechanisms by providing a common policy that can be applied to internal caches to manage them in a wide range of operating conditions. For additional information about these caches, refer to SQL Server 2008 Books Online.

SQL Server 2008 also features a memory-tracking enhancement called the Memory Broker, which enables the tracking of OS-wide memory events. Memory Broker manages and tracks the dynamic consumption of internal SQL Server memory. Based on internal consumption and pressures, it automatically calculates the optimal memory configuration for components such as buffer pool, optimizer, query execution, and caches. It propagates the memory configuration information back to these components for implementation. SQL Server 2008 also supports dynamic management of conventional, locked, and large-page memory, as well as the hot-add memory feature mentioned earlier. SQL Server 2008 Standard Edition (32-bit) supports the AWE memory mechanism. The Windows policy Lock Pages in Memory is granted by default to the local administrative accounts but can be explicitly granted to other user accounts. To ensure that the AWE-enabled memory runs as expected, it needs this privilege to allow SQL Server to manage which pages are being flushed out of memory.

Hot-add memory provides the ability to introduce additional memory in an operational server without taking it offline. In addition to OEM vendor support, Windows Server 2003 and SQL Server 2008 Enterprise Edition are required to support this feature. Although a sample implementation script is provided in the following section, refer to BOL for additional implementation details.

Windows 2008 Hot-Add CPU

With Windows 2008 and SQL Server 2008, SQL Server supports hot-add CPU, whereby CPUs can be dynamically added while the server is online. The system requirements to support hot-add CPU are as follows:

❑ Hardware support for hot-add CPU.

❑ Supported by the 64-bit edition of Windows Server 2008 Datacenter or the Windows Server 2008 Enterprise Edition for Itanium-Based Systems operating system.

❑ Supported by SQL Server 2008 Enterprise Edition.

❑ SQL Server 2008 must not be configured for soft NUMA. For more information about soft NUMA, search for the following topics online: "Understanding Non-uniform Memory Access" and "How to Configure SQL Server to Use Soft-NUMA."

With these requirements met, to have SQL Server 2008 recognize the new dynamically added CPU, execute the RECONFIGURE command.

Configuring SQL Server 2008 for Dynamic Memory on an X86 Platform

Although some of these concepts are covered in Chapter 11, we reintroduce them here to bring all of the concepts discussed here together. PAE and 3GB technologies can be used independently or together. In Windows 2003, you use a switch in the boot.ini file to activate either feature. In Windows 2008, at the command prompt, you need to execute the BCDEDIT /SET PAE ForceEnable command to activate PAE, and `BCDEDIT /SET IncreaseUserVA 3072` to activate 3GB. The `boot.ini` file is not available on Windows Vista or Windows 2008.

This section provides guidelines on their use with SQL Server 2008. See the following table for clarification.

System Memory	Less than 4GB	More than 4GB	More than 16GB
/PAE	NO	YES	YES
/3GB	NO	YES	NO
AWE	NO	YES	YES

To activate the AWE mapped memory feature with the ability to lock pages in memory, follow these steps. After modifying the `boot.ini` file or using `BCDEDIT`, the database server requires a reboot to enable the PAE kernel. Then, AWE must be enabled in SQL Server with the `sp_configure` directive.

For Windows 2003, add the following entry to your `c:\boot.ini` file:

```
[boot loader]
timeout=30
default=multi(0)disk(0)rdisk(0)partition(1)\WINDOWS
[operating systems]
multi(0)disk(0)rdisk(0)partition(1)\WINDOWS="Microsoft
Windows 2003, Enterprise" /PAE /3GB /fastdetect
```

Windows may have c:\boot.ini as a hidden and read-only file.

For Windows 2008, run the following two `BCDEDIT` commands at the command prompt:

```
BCDEDIT /SET PAE ForceEnable
BCDEDIT /SET IncreaseUserVA 3072
```

Then, enable Lock Pages in Memory using the following procedure:

1. Click Start ⇨ Run, type **gpedit.msc**, and then click OK. The Group Policy window appears.
2. In the left pane, expand Computer Configuration, and then expand Windows Settings.
3. Expand Security Settings, and then expand Local Policies.
4. Click User Rights Assignment. The policies appear in the right pane.
5. In the right pane, double-click Lock Pages in Memory to see the Properties window, shown in Figure 12-12.
6. On the Local Security Setting tab, click Add User or Group.
7. In the Select Users or Groups dialog, add the SQL Server Service account that runs `Sqlservr.exe`, and then click OK.
8. Close the Group Policy window and restart the SQL Server service.

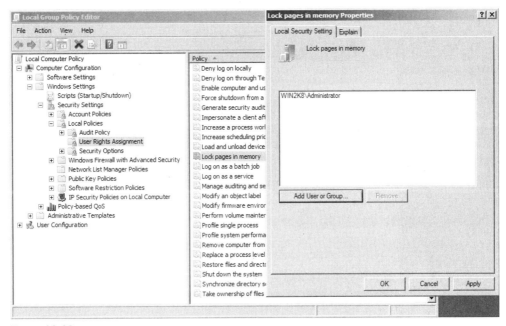

Figure 12-12

Next, issue the following `sp_configure` statements:

```
sp_configure 'show advanced options', 1;
RECONFIGURE;
GO
sp_configure 'awe enabled', 1;
RECONFIGURE;
GO
-- (8 GB)
sp_configure 'min server memory', 8192;
RECONFIGURE;
GO
-- (15 GB)
sp_configure 'max server memory', 15360;
RECONFIGURE;
GO
```

As configured above, SQL Server 2008 will not go beyond this upper limit setting even if memory is available and the system is under memory pressure. Ensure that you are setting the desired limit.

Next, configure your SQL Server for hot-add memory. In the SQL Server Configuration Manager, click SQL Server 2008 Services. In the right pane, right-click SQL Server service, and then click Properties. Select the advanced tab, and add ; -h in the Startup Parameters box. The semicolon is used as a separator for startup options. The SQL Server service must be rebooted to enable this feature.

A 500MB memory cost for this feature is reserved for administrative purposes.

Remember that when allocating SQL Server memory on a system with more than 16GB, Windows 2003 requires at least 2GB of available memory to manage the remaining memory. Therefore, when you start an instance of SQL Server with the AWE mechanism enabled, you should not use the default max server memory setting, but instead limit it to 2GB less than the total available memory. Additional information can be found in BOL, or refer to article Q283037.

AWE mapped memory cannot be managed or monitored through the task manager; this has to be accomplished through `sys.dm_os_memory_clerks` DMV:

```
select sum(awe_allocated_kb)/1024 as [AWE Allocated Memory in MB] from
sys.dm_os_memory_clerks
```

Removing memory from the database server requires a reboot.

64-bit Versions of SQL Server 2008

If your platform is IA64 or x64, you are in luck. SQL Server 2008 64-bit supports 1TB of RAM, and all of it is native addressable memory so there's no need for `/3GB` or `/PAE` switches in your `boot.ini` file. The mechanism used to manage AWE memory in 32-bit systems can be used to manage memory on 64-bit systems. Specifically, this mechanism is used to ensure that SQL Server manages what is flushed out of its memory. To enable this feature, the SQL Server service account requires the "Lock Pages in Memory" privilege.

Memory-Friendly Applications

You need to identify the type of application driving the database and verify that it can benefit from a large SQL Server data-cache allocation. In other words, is it memory friendly? Simply stated, a database that does not need to keep its data in memory for an extended length of time will not benefit from a larger memory allocation. For example, a call-center application in which no two operators handle the same customer's information and where no relationship exists between customer records has no need to keep data in memory, as data won't be reused. In this case, the application is not deemed memory friendly; thus, keeping customers' data in memory longer than required would not benefit performance. Another type of inefficient memory use occurs when an application stores excessive amounts of data, beyond what is required by an operation — for example, a table scan. This type of operation suffers from the high cost of data invalidation. Larger amounts of data than are necessary are read into memory, and thus must be flushed out.

Resource Governor

Resource Governor is a new SQL Server 2008 technology that limits the amount of resources that can be allocated to each database workload from the total resources available to SQL Server 2008. When enabled, Resource Governor classifies each incoming session and determines to which workload group the session belongs. Each workload group is then associated to a resource pool that limits those groups of workloads. Moreover, Resource Governor protects against runaway queries on the SQL Server and unpredictable workload execution, and sets workload priority. In order for Resource Governor to limit resources, it must be able to differentiate workloads. It does that as follows:

❑   Classifies incoming connections to route them to a specific workload group.

❑   Monitors resource usage for each workload group.

❑   Pools resources to set limits on CPU and memory to each specific resource pool.

❑   Identifies workloads and groups them together to a specific pool of resources.

❑   Sets workload priority within a workload group.

The constraints on Resource Governor are as follows:

❑   It applies only to the SQL Server Relational Engine and not to Analysis Services, Report Services, or Integration Services.

❑   It cannot monitor resources between SQL Server instances. However, Windows Resource Manager (part of Windows) can be used to monitor resources across Windows processes, including SQL Server.

❑   It can limit CPU bandwidth and memory.

❑   A typical OLTP workload consists of small and fast database operations that individually take a fraction of CPU time and may be too miniscule to enable Resource Governor to apply bandwidth limits.

The Basic Elements of Resource Governor

The main elements of Resource Governor include resource pools, workload groups, and classification support, explained in the following sections.

Resource Pools

The resource pools are the physical resources of the SQL Server. During SQL Server installation, two pools are created: *internal* and *default*. The resources that can be managed are min and max CPU and min and max memory. By default, the Resource Governor is disabled; to enable it, use the ALTER RESOURCE GOVERNOR RECONFIGURE command. It is disabled by the command ALTER RESOURCE GOVERNOR DISABLE.

The internal pool is used for SQL Server's own internal functions. It contains only the internal workload group; it cannot be altered, and it is not restricted.

The default pool is the predefined user resource pool. It contains the default workload group and can contain user-defined workload groups. It can be altered but cannot be created or dropped.

User-defined pools can be created using the CREATE RESOURCE POOL DDL statement or by using SQL Server Management Studio. Moreover, a pool can be modified by using the ALTER RESOURCE POOL command, and it can be deleted by using the DROP RESOURCE POOL command.

The following syntax creates a resource pool for Resource Governor:

```
CREATE RESOURCE POOL pool_name
[ WITH
        ( [ MIN_CPU_PERCENT = value ]
    [ [ , ] MAX_CPU_PERCENT = value ]
    [ [ , ] MIN_MEMORY_PERCENT = value ]
    [ [ , ] MAX_MEMORY_PERCENT = value ] )
]  [;]
```

Workload Groups

A workload group is a container for similar sessions according to the defined classification rules and applies the policy to each session of the group. It also contains two predefined workload groups: *internal* and *default*. The internal workload group relates to the internal resource pool and cannot be changed. The default workload group is associated with the default resource pool and is the group used when no session classification user-defined function exists, when a classification failure occurs, or when a classification user-defined function returns NULL.

The user-defined workload group can be created by using the CREATE WORKLOAD GROUP command, modified by using the ALTER WORKLOAD GROUP command, and dropped by using the DROP WORKLOAD GROUP command.

The following syntax creates a workload group for Resource Governor:

```
CREATE WORKLOAD GROUP group_name
[ WITH
    ( [ IMPORTANCE = { LOW | MEDIUM | HIGH } ]
            [ [ , ] REQUEST_MAX_MEMORY_GRANT_PERCENT = value ]
            [ [ , ] REQUEST_MAX_CPU_TIME_SEC = value ]
            [ [ , ] REQUEST_MEMORY_GRANT_TIMEOUT_SEC = value ]
            [ [ , ] MAX_DOP = value ]
            [ [ , ] GROUP_MAX_REQUESTS = value ] )
]
[ USING { pool_name | "default" } ] [ ; ]
```

You can apply seven configuration settings to a workload group:

❑   Maximum memory allocation per request

❑   Maximum CPU time per request

❑   Resource time-out per request

❑   Relative importance setting per request

❑   Workgroup limit per number of requests

❑   Maximum degree of parallelism

❑   A specific resource pool

Classification

Resource Governor supports classifying incoming connections into existing workload groups. It supports system-wide provided rules and user-defined rules using connection-specific attributes. In the absence of a user-defined classification function, it will use the default workload group. After the user-defined classification function is registered with Resource Governor, the function is executed for every new connection, and the connection is routed to one of the existing workload groups to be limited by the resource pool. Only one user-defined classification function can be designated as a classifier; and after registering it, it takes effect after an ALTER RESOURCE GOVERNOR RECONFIGURE command is executed.

Resource Governor uses connection-specific functions such as HOST_NAME(), APP_NAME(), SUSER_NAME(), SUSER_SNAME(), IS_SRVROLEMEMBER() and IS_MEMBER() to identify each connection.

Figure 12-13 shows the components of Resource Governor and their relationships.

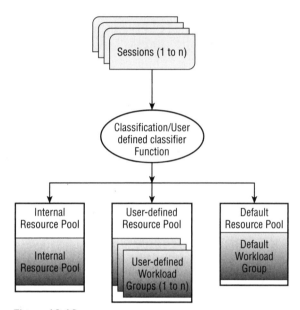

Figure 12-13

Following is a Resource Governor Implementation example that creates three resource pools to support the resource requirements for three different workload groups. First, create three resource pools: adhoc, reports, and admin requests:

```
USE Master;
BEGIN TRAN;
CREATE RESOURCE POOL poolAdhoc with
( MIN_CPU_PERCENT = 10, MAX_CPU_PERCENT = 30,
MIN_MEMORY_PERCENT= 15, MAX_MEMORY_PERCENT= 25);

CREATE RESOURCE POOL poolReports with
( MIN_CPU_PERCENT = 20, MAX_CPU_PERCENT = 35,
MIN_MEMORY_PERCENT= 15,  MAX_MEMORY_PERCENT= 45);

CREATE RESOURCE POOL poolAdmin with
( MIN_CPU_PERCENT = 15, MAX_CPU_PERCENT = 25,
MIN_MEMORY_PERCENT= 15,  MAX_MEMORY_PERCENT= 30);
```

Next, create three workload groups and associate them with the three resource pools:

```
CREATE WORKLOAD GROUP groupAdhoc using poolAdhoc;
CREATE WORKLOAD GROUP groupReports with (MAX_DOP = 8) using poolReports;
CREATE WORKLOAD GROUP groupAdmin using poolAdmin;
```

Create a user-defined classification function that identifies each new session and routes it to one of the three workload groups. Note that any request that cannot be identified by the user-defined classification function is directed to the default workload group:

```
CREATE FUNCTION rgclassifier_v1() RETURNS SYSNAME
WITH SCHEMABINDING
AS
BEGIN
    DECLARE @grp_name AS SYSNAME
      IF (SUSER_NAME() = 'sa')
          SET @grp_name = 'groupAdmin'
      IF (APP_NAME() LIKE '%MANAGEMENT STUDIO%')
          OR (APP_NAME() LIKE '%QUERY ANALYZER%')
          SET @grp_name = 'groupAdhoc'
      IF (APP_NAME() LIKE '%REPORT SERVER%')
          SET @grp_name = 'groupReports'
    RETURN @grp_name
END;
```

Next, the user-defined classification function needs to be registered to Resource Governor. Note that all of these operations have been inside an explicit transaction; that's a preventive measure so that in case of a user error, it can be rolled back. Additionally, only one user-defined classification function can be registered to the Resource Governor at any one time:

```
ALTER RESOURCE GOVERNOR WITH (CLASSIFIER_FUNCTION= dbo.rgclassifier_v1);
COMMIT TRAN;
```

Finally, to have these new changes take effect or to enable Resource Governor, run the following command:

```
ALTER RESOURCE GOVERNOR RECONFIGURE;
```

Using Resource Governor from SQL Server 2008 Management Studio

From inside SQL Server 2008 Management Studio in Object Explorer, Resource Governor is in the Management node. By default, Resource Governor is disabled. To enable it, right-click Resource Governor and then click Enable. Moreover, from Object Explorer inside the Management node, right-click Resource Governor and then click Properties to add, delete, or modify properties of the resource pools and workload groups or to add or remove a user-defined classification function and enable Resource Governor. From the Resource Governor Properties dialog, you can see that two resource pools, Internal and Default, with two corresponding workload groups, are visible. These are created by SQL Server 2008 during installation. Moreover, no classification function is available until one is created. If Resource Governor is enabled, it will use the default system-defined rules and the default pool, as configured in Figure 12-14.

After running the preceding Resource Governor script to create the three user-defined resource pools, workload groups, and the user-defined classification function; and after enabling the Resource Governor, the properties should match what is shown in Figure 12-15.

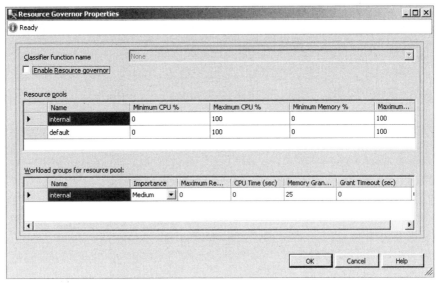

Figure 12-14

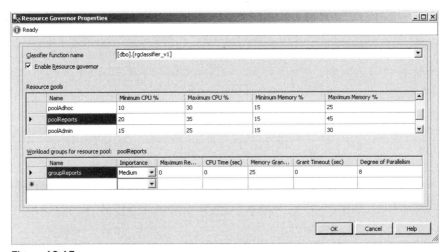

Figure 12-15

Monitoring Resource Governor

SQL Server 2008 includes two performance objects to collect workload group and pool statistics per each SQL Server instance:

❑ SQLServer:Resource Pool Stats for resource-specific statistics.

❑ SQLServer:Workload Group Stats for workload-specific statistics.

Moreover, there are Resource Governor Dynamic Management Views (DMVs) that return information specific to resource statistics, as indicated in the following table.

Resource Governor Dynamic Management Views	Description
sys.dm_resource_governor_configuration	For current in-memory configuration state
sys.dm_resource_governor_resource_pools	For resource pool state, configuration, and statistics
sys.dm_resource_governor_workload_groups	For workload group statistics and in-memory configuration

For more detailed information on Resource Governor, refer to SQL 2008 Books Online under "Resource Governor."

CPU Considerations

The challenge in building a large SMP is that because processors have increased performance through technology enhancements and the use of increasingly larger caches, the performance gains achieved through leveraging these caches are significant. Consequently, you need to cache relevant data whenever possible, to enable processors to have relevant data available and resident in their caches. Chip and hardware vendors have attempted to capitalize on this phenomenon through expansion of the processor and system cache.

As a result, new system architectures such as cellular multiprocessing (CMP), CC-NUMA, shown in Figure 12-16, and NUMA (non-cache coherent) are now available in the market. Although this has been successful, it has produced two challenges: the need to manage data locally and cache coherency.

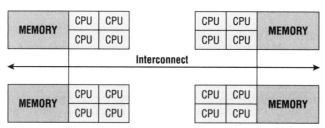

Figure 12-16

Data Locality

Data locality is the concept of having all relevant data locally available to the processor while it's processing a request. All memory within a system is available to any processor on any cell. This introduces the concepts of *near memory* and *far memory*. Near memory is the preferred method, as it is accessed by a processor on the same cell. As shown in Figure 12-17, accessing far memory is expensive because the request has to leave the cell and traverse the system interconnect crossbar to get the cell that holds the required information in its memory.

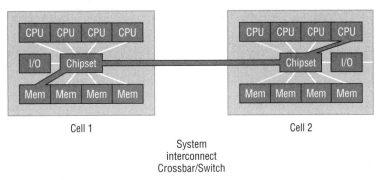

Cell 1   Cell 2

System
interconnect
Crossbar/Switch

Figure 12-17

The cost of accessing objects in far memory versus near memory is often threefold or more. If data locality is left unmanaged in a large SMP system, it can prevent an application from scaling due to data-locality issues. SQL Server 2000 SP4 (Post SP3 Quick Fix Engineering (QFE) available) first introduced innovations to better scale on this platform.

Cache Coherency

For reasons of data integrity, only one processor can update any piece of data at a time; other processors that have copies in their caches will have their local copy "invalidated" and thus must be reloaded. This mechanism is referred to as *cache coherency*. Cache coherency requires that all the caches are in agreement regarding the location of all copies of the data and which processor currently has permission to perform the update. Supporting coherency protocols is one of the major scaling problems in designing big SMPs, particularly if there is a lot of update traffic. This was better addressed with the introduction of NUMA and CMP architectures.

SQL Server 2008 has been optimized to take advantage of NUMA advancements exposed by both Windows and the hardware itself. As discussed in the "Memory Considerations and Enhancements" section, SQLOS is the technology that the SQL Server leverages to exploit these advances.

Affinity Mask

The affinity mask configuration option restricts a SQL Server instance to running on a subset of the processors. If SQL Server 2008 is running on a dedicated server, allowing SQL Server to use all processors will ensure best performance. In a server consolidation or multiple-instance environment, for more predictable performance, SQL Server may be configured on dedicated hardware resources that affinitize processors by SQL Server instance.

The benefits of hyperthreading in SQL Server workloads have been a matter of heated discussion. To ensure predictability of the environment, you may want to disable hyperthreading. When configuring SQL Server 2008, processor affinity should coincide with the number of processors or cores available to SQL Server. Hyperthreading is discussed in greater detail in Chapter 11.

If hyperthreading is enabled, be sure to set processor affinity on both logical processors on a physical processor to the same SQL Server instance.

SQL Server Processor Affinity Mask

SQL Server's mechanism for scheduling work requests is handled through a data structure concept called a *scheduler*. The scheduler is created for each processor assigned to SQL Server through the affinity mask configuration setting at startup. *Worker threads* (a subset of the max worker threads configuration setting) are dynamically created during a batch request and are evenly distributed between each CPU node and load-balanced across its schedulers (see Figure 12-18).

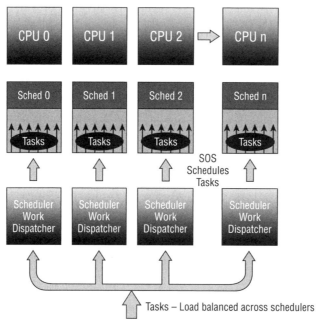

Figure 12-18

Incoming connections are assigned to the CPU node. SQL Server assigns the batch request to a task or tasks, and the tasks are managed across schedulers. At any given time, only one task can be scheduled for execution by a scheduler on a processor. A task is a unit of work scheduled by the SQL Server. This architecture guarantees an even distribution of the hundreds, or in many cases, thousands of connections that can result from a large deployment.

Default SQL Server Work Scheduling

The default setting for affinity mask is 0, which enables the Windows scheduler to schedule and move schedulers across any available processor within a CPU node to execute its worker threads. SQL Server 2008 in this configuration has its processes controlled and scheduled by the Windows scheduler. For example, suppose a client requests a connection and the connection is accepted. If no threads are available, then one is dynamically created and associated with a task. The work assignments from the scheduler to the processors are managed through the Windows scheduler, which has its work distributed among all processors within a CPU node. This is the preferred method of execution, as Windows load-balances the schedulers evenly on all processors.

SQL Server Work Scheduling Using Affinity Mask

The affinity mask configuration setting can be used to assign a subset of the available processors to the SQL Server process. SQL Server worker threads are scheduled preemptively by the scheduler. A worker thread will continue to execute on its processor until it is forced to wait for a resource, such as locks or I/O, to become available. If the time slice expires, the thread will voluntarily yield, at which time the scheduler selects another worker thread to begin execution. If it cannot proceed without access to a resource such as disk I/O, it sleeps until the resource is available. When access to that resource is available, the process is placed on the run queue before being put back on the processor. When the Windows kernel transfers control of the processor from an executing process to another that is ready to run, this is referred to as a *context switch*.

Context Switching

Context switching is expensive because of the associated housekeeping required to move from one running thread to another. Housekeeping refers to the maintenance of keeping the context or the set of processor register values and other data that describes the process state. The Windows kernel loads the context of the new process, which then starts to execute. When the process taken off the processor next runs, it resumes from the point at which it was taken off the processor. This is possible because the saved context includes the instruction pointer. In addition to this *user mode* time, context switching can take place in the Windows operating system (OS) for *privileged mode* time.

The total processor time is equal to the privileged mode time plus the user mode time.

Privileged Mode

Privileged mode is a processing mode designed for operating system components and hardware-manipulating drivers. It allows direct access to hardware and all memory. Privileged time includes time-servicing interrupts and deferred process calls (DPCs).

User Mode

User mode is a restricted processing mode designed for applications such as SQL Server, Exchange, and other application and integral subsystems. The goal of performance tuning is to maximize user mode processing by reducing privileged mode processing. This can be monitored with the *Processor: % Privileged Time* counter, which displays the average busy time as a percentage of the sample time. A value above 15 percent may indicate that a disk array is being heavily utilized or that there is a high volume of network traffic requests. In some rare cases, a high rate of privileged time might even be attributed to a large number of interrupts generated by a failing device.

Priority Boost

By enabling the Priority Boost option, SQL Server runs at a priority base of 13 in the Windows System scheduler, rather than its default of 7. On a dedicated server, this might improve performance, although it can also cause priority imbalances between SQL Server functions and operating system functions, leading to instability. Improvements in SQL Server and Windows make the use of this option unnecessary.

Priority boost should not be used when implementing failover clustering.

SQL Server Lightweight Pooling

Context switching can often become problematic. Preferably, context switching should be less than 1,000 per second per processor. The SQL Server Lightweight Pooling option provides relief for this by enabling tasks to use NT "fibers," rather than threads, as workers.

A *fiber* is an executable unit that is lighter than a thread and operates in the context of user mode. When lightweight pooling is selected, each scheduler uses a single thread to control the scheduling of work requests by multiple fibers. A fiber can be viewed as a "lightweight thread," which under certain circumstances takes less overhead than standard worker threads to context switch. The number of fibers is controlled by the Max Worker Threads configuration setting.

Max Degree of Parallelism (MAXDOP)

By default, the MAXDOP value is set to 0, which enables SQL Server to consider all processors when creating an execution plan. In some systems, based on application-workload profiles, it is recommended that you set this value to 1 (including for SAP and Siebel); this prevents the query optimizer from choosing parallel query plans. Using multiple processors to run a query is not always desirable in an OLTP environment, although it is desirable in a data warehousing environment.

> *In SQL Server 2008, you can assign query hints to individual queries to control the degree of parallelism.*

Partitioned table parallelism is also affected by the MAXDOP setting. Returning to the example used in the "Storage Alignment" section, a thread can be leveraged across each partition. Had the query been limited to a single partition, multiple threads would be spawned up to the MAXDOP setting.

Affinity I/O Mask

The affinity I/O mask feature, shown in Figure 12-19, was introduced with SP1 of SQL Server 2000. This option defines the specific processors on which SQL Server I/O threads can execute. The affinity I/O mask option has a default setting of 0, indicating that SQL Server threads are allowed to execute on all processors. The performance gains associated with enabling the affinity I/O mask feature are achieved by grouping the SQL threads that perform all I/O tasks (Non-data cache retrievals — specifically, physical I/O requests) on dedicated resources. This keeps I/O processing and related data in the same cache systems, maximizing data locality and minimizing unnecessary bus traffic.

When using affinity masks to assign processor resources to the operating system, either SQL Server processes (non-I/O) or SQL Server I/O processes, you must be careful not to assign multiple functions to any individual processor.

You should consider SQL I/O affinity when there is high privileged time on the processors that are not affinitized to SQL Server. For example, consider a 32-processor system running under load with 30 of the 32 processors affinitized to SQL Server, leaving two processors to the Windows OS and other non-SQL activities. If the *Processor: % Privileged* time is high (greater than 15 percent), SQL I/O affinity can be configured to help reduce the privileged-time overhead in the processors assigned to SQL Server.

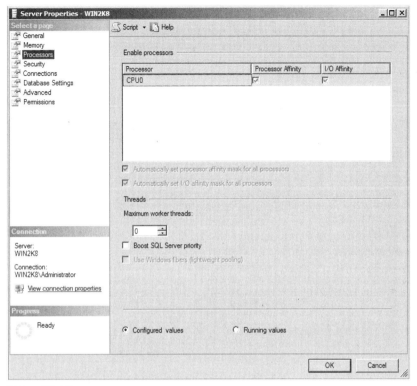

Figure 12-19

The following steps outline the SQL I/O affinity procedure for determining what values to set:

1. Add I/O capability until there is no I/O bottleneck (disk queue length has been eliminated) and all unnecessary processes have been stopped.

2. Add a processor designated to SQL I/O affinity.

3. Measure the CPU utilization of these processors under heavy load.

4. Increase the number of processors until the designated processors are no longer peaked. For a non-SMP system, select processors that are in the same cell node.

Max Server Memory

When max server memory is kept at the default dynamic setting, SQL Server acquires and frees memory in response to internal and external pressure. Starting with SQL Server 2005, dynamic AWE is supported. For SQL Server implementations based on Windows Server 2003, a max server memory setting is optional but recommended. For Windows 2000 implementations, the max server memory setting is strongly recommended.

Index Creation Memory Option

The index creation memory setting, shown in Figure 12-20, determines how much memory can be used by SQL Server for sort operations during the index-creation process. The default value of 0 allows SQL Server to automatically determine the ideal value. In conditions where index creation is performed on very large tables, pre-allocating space in memory enables a faster index-creation process.

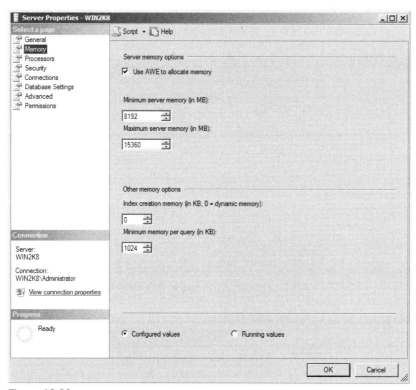

Figure 12-20

Note that once memory is allocated, it is reserved exclusively for the index-creation process, and values are set in KB of memory.

Minimum Memory per Query

You can use the Minimum memory per query option to improve the performance of queries that use hashing or sorting operations. SQL Server automatically allocates the minimum amount of memory set in this configuration setting. The default Minimum memory per query option setting is equal to 1024KB, as shown in Figure 12-20. It is important to ensure that the SQL Server environment has the minimum amount of query memory available. However, in an environment with high query-execution concurrency, if this setting is configured too high, SQL Server will wait for a memory allocation to meet the minimum memory level before executing a query.

Summary

Building on the hardware specifications you learned in Chapter 11, this chapter provided the necessary steps for setting and configuring SQL Server 2008. If these lessons are applied correctly, SQL Server 2008 is more than capable of autotuning itself to predictably provide the availability and performance to support the requirements of your enterprise. Chapter 13 discusses proactive monitoring of this environment, and Chapter 14 describes how to tune T-SQL code for the SQL Server environment.

13

Monitoring Your SQL Server

Effective monitoring of your SQL Server is the first step to an easy life as a DBA. Having good monitoring in place enables you to move from reactively dealing with events to proactively diagnosing problems and fixing them before your users are even aware there is a problem.

Many of the SQL Server administration guides available explain how to use Reliability and Performance Monitor (PerfMon), how to capture a Profiler trace using either SQL profiler or SQL Trace, or how to run a few dynamic management views (DMVs) to find blocking, or long-running, queries.

This chapter will teach you how to proactively monitor your SQL Server system so that you can prevent or react to events before the server gets to the point where users begin calling.

Here's a quick example. I recently took over an existing system after the DBA moved to a different team. This system ran well, but there was something that needed fixing every other day — transaction logs filling, `tempdb` out of space, not enough locks, filegroups filling up. Nothing major, just a slow steady trickle of problems that needed fixing. This is the DBA's death of 1,000 cuts. Your time is sucked away doing these essential maintenance tasks until you get to the point where you don't have time to do anything else.

After a few weeks of this, I managed to put some new monitoring in place and was able to make several proactive changes to resolve issues before anything broke. These changes weren't rocket science, they were simple things such as moving data to a new filegroup, turning on autogrow for several files and extending them to allow a known amount of growth, and rebuilding badly fragmented indexes that were reserving unneeded space. All this took considerably less time than dealing with the steady stream of failures and provided a greatly improved experience for the users of this system.

So what did I do to monitor this system? Nothing dramatic — just a few simple steps, mostly some T-SQL monitoring of tables, database and filegroup free space, index usage, and fragmentation. I did a few things to monitor resource usage and help find the key pain points. Once I understood the pain points I was able to take a few steps to get ahead of the curve on fixing things.

Now that you've seen the value in monitoring SQL, you will learn how to do this for yourself.

The Goal of Monitoring

The goal of monitoring databases is to see what's going on inside SQL Server — namely, how effectively SQL Server is using the server resources (CPU, Memory, I/O). You want this information so that you can see how well the system is performing. Capturing this data over time enables you to build a profile of what the system normally looks like: How much of what resource do you use for each part of the system's working cycle? From the data collected over time you can start to build a baseline of "normal" activity. That baseline enables you to identify abnormal activities that might lead to issues if left unchecked.

Abnormal activity could be an increase in a specific table's growth rate, a change in replication throughput, or a query or job taking longer than usual or using more of a scarce server resource than you expected. Identifying these anomalies before they become an issue that causes your users to call and complain makes for a much easier life. Using this data, you can identify what might be about to break, or where changes need to be made to rectify the root cause before the problem becomes entrenched.

Sometimes this monitoring is related to performance issues such as slow-running queries or deadlocks, but in many cases the data will point to something that you can change to avoid problems in the future.

This philosophy is about the equivalent of "an apple a day keeps the doctor away" — preventative medicine for your SQL Server.

Determining Your Monitoring Objectives

Before you start monitoring you must first clearly identify your reasons for monitoring. These reasons may include the following:

❑   Establish a baseline.

❑   Identify new trends before they become problems.

❑   Monitor database growth.

❑   Identify daily, weekly, and monthly maintenance tasks.

❑   Identify performance changes over time.

❑   Audit user activity.

❑   Diagnose a specific performance problem.

Establishing a Baseline

Monitoring is extremely important to help ensure the smooth running of your SQL Server systems. However, just monitoring by itself, and being able to determine the value of a key performance metric at any point in time, is not of great value unless you have a sound baseline to compare the metric against. Is

50 transactions per second good, mediocre, or bad? If the server is running at 75% CPU, is that normal? Is it normal for this time of day, on this day of the week, during this month of the year? With a baseline of the system's performance, you immediately have something to compare the current metrics against.

If your baseline shows that you normally get 30 transactions per second, then 50 transactions per second might be good; the system is able to process more transactions. However, it may also be an indication that something else is going on, which has caused an increase in the transactions. What your baseline looks like depends on your system, of course. In some cases it might be a set of Performance Monitor logs with key server resource and SQL counters captured during several periods of significant system activity, or stress tests. In another case, it might be the results of analysis of a SQL Profiler trace captured during a period of high activity. The analysis might be as simple as a list of the stored procedure calls made by a particular application, with the call frequency.

To determine whether your SQL Server system is performing optimally, take performance measurements at a regular interval over time, even when no problem occurs, to establish a server performance baseline. How many samples, and how long each needs to be, is determined by the nature of the workload on your servers. If your servers have a cyclic workload, the samples should aim to query at multiple points in several cycles to allow a good estimation of min, max, and average rates. If the workload is very uniform, then fewer samples over shorter periods can provide a good indication of min, max, and average rates. At a minimum, use baseline performance to determine the following:

- ❏ Peak and off-peak hours of operation.
- ❏ Query or batch response time.

Another consideration is how often the baseline should be recaptured. In a system that is rapidly growing, you may need to recapture a baseline frequently. I would suggest that when current performance has changed by 15–25 percent compared to the old baseline, it is a good point to consider recapturing the baseline.

Comparing Current Metrics to the Baseline

A key part of comparing current metrics to those in the baseline is determining an acceptable limit from the baseline outside of which the current metric is not acceptable and which flags an issue that needs investigating.

What is acceptable here depends on the application and the specific metric. For example, a metric looking at free space in a database filegroup for a system with massive data growth and an aggressive archiving strategy might set a limit of 20 percent free space before triggering some kind of alert. On a different system with very little database growth, that same metric might be set to just 5 percent.

You will have to make your own judgment of what is an acceptable limit for deviation from the baseline based on your knowledge of how your system is growing and changing.

What's New in Monitoring for SQL Server 2008

The SQL Server Books Online documentation on monitoring covers a couple of new topics, and all the old favorites on using System Monitor, SQL Profiler, and SQL Trace. The new monitoring features in SQL Server 2008 are Data Collection and SQL Server Extended Events.

Data Collection

If you've used the SQL Server Performance Dashboard Reports with SQL Server 2005 SP1, you'll find Data Collection in SQL Server 2008 to be like that on steroids.

It provides an extensible framework for collecting data, storing it in a data warehouse, and then building reporting on top of the data warehouse. Rather than being stuck with predefined reports, you have a very comprehensive monitoring framework. One of the other challenges with DMVs, the standard reports, and the Performance Dashboard reports is that they only provide a snapshot of current system execution, so you can't see what happened one second before or how things have changed over the last one second. Data Collection solves that problem because the Management Data Warehouse is now the repository of the data collected.

SQL Server Extended Events

Previous versions of SQL Server have had several levels of events available to monitor. You had the option of the full set of SQL events in Profiler and SQL Trace, and then there were the *notification events*, which are a reduced set of events based around DDL type events.

SQL Server 2008 introduces a new event framework — SQL Server Extended Events. These are user-definable events that are more tightly integrated with the Windows world of events through the Event Tracing for Windows (ETW) framework.

Choosing the Appropriate Monitoring Tools

Once you define your monitoring goals you should select the appropriate tools for monitoring. The following list describes the basic monitoring tools:

❑   **Performance Monitor:** Performance Monitor is a very useful tool that tracks resource use on Microsoft operating systems. It can monitor resource usage for the server and provide information specific to SQL Server either locally or for a remote server. It can be used to capture a baseline of server resource usage, or it can monitor over longer periods of time to help identify trends. It can also be very useful for ad hoc monitoring to help identify any resource bottlenecks responsible for performance issues. It can be configured to generate alerts when predetermined thresholds are exceeded.

❑   **SQL Profiler:** This tool is a graphical application that enables you to capture a trace of events that occurred in SQL Server. All SQL Server events can be captured by this tool into the trace. The trace can be stored in a file or written to a SQL Server table.

SQL Profiler also enables the captured events to be replayed. This makes it a very valuable tool for workload analysis, testing, and performance tuning. It can monitor a SQL Server instance locally or remotely. You can also use the features of SQL Profiler within a custom application, by using the Profiler system stored procedures.

❑   **SQL Trace:** SQL Trace is the T-SQL stored procedure way to invoke a SQL Server trace without having to start up the SQL Profiler application. It requires a little more work to set up, but it's a lightweight way to capture a trace; and because it's scriptable, it enables the automation of trace capture, making it very easy to repeatedly capture the same events.

❑ **Default trace:** Introduced with SQL Server 2005, the default trace is a lightweight trace that runs in a continuous loop and captures a small set of key database and server events. This can be very useful in diagnosing events that may have occurred when no other monitoring was in place.

❑ **Activity Monitor in SQL Server Management Studio:** This tool graphically displays the following information:

> ❑ Processes running on an instance of SQL Server
>
> ❑ Locks
>
> ❑ User activity
>
> ❑ Blocked processes

Activity Monitor works well for ad hoc monitoring, but not very well for trend analysis.

> *To open Activity Monitor in SQL Server Management Studio, connect to the server with Object Explorer, expand Management, and then double-click Activity Monitor.*

❑ **Dynamic management views:** Dynamic management views return server state information that can be used to monitor the health of a server instance, diagnose problems, and tune performance. This is one of the best tools added to SQL Server 2005 for ad hoc monitoring. These views provide a snapshot of the exact state of SQL Server at the point they are queried. This is extremely valuable, but you may need to do a lot of work to interpret the meaning of some of the data returned, as they often provide just a running total of some internal counter. This makes it necessary to add quite a bit of additional code to provide useful trend information.

❑ **Transact-SQL:** Some system stored procedures provide useful information for SQL Server monitoring, such as `sp_who`, `sp_who2`, `sp_lock`, and several others. These stored procedures are best for ad hoc monitoring, not trend analysis.

The rest of the chapter discusses these tools in detail.

Performance Monitor

Performance Monitor is an important tool because not only does it enable you to know how SQL Server is performing, it is also the tool that indicates how Windows is performing. Performance Monitor provides a huge set of counters. Probably no one understands all of them, so don't be daunted.

This section is not about how to use Performance Monitor (although later in this section you will learn about two very valuable tools, Logman, and Relog, that make using Performance Monitor a lot easier in a production environment). The focus in this chapter is on how you can use the capabilities of this tool to diagnose performance problems in your system. For general information about using Performance Monitor, look at the Vista or Windows Server 2008 documentation.

As mentioned, you need to monitor three server resources:

❑ CPU

❑ Memory

❑ I/O (primarily disk I/O, but in some cases network as well)

Monitor these key counters over a "typical" 24-hour period. Pick a typical business day, not a weekend or holiday, so you get an accurate picture of what's happening. You should also take into account any specific knowledge of your business and monitor for peaks of activity such as end of week, end of month, or other special activities.

CPU Resource Counters

Several counters show the state of the available CPU resources. Bottlenecks due to CPU resource shortages are frequently caused by problems such as more users than expected, one or more users running very expensive queries, or routine operational activities such as index rebuilding.

The first step to finding the cause of the bottleneck is to identify that the bottleneck is a CPU resource issue. The following counters will help you do this:

❑ **Object: Processor - Counter: % Processor Time:** This counter determines the percentage of time each processor is busy. There is a `_Total` instance of the counter that for multiprocessor systems measures the total processor utilization across all processors in the system. On multiprocessor machines, the `_Total` instance might not show a processor bottleneck when one exists. This can happen when queries are executing that run on either a single thread or fewer threads than there are processors. This is often the case on OLTP systems, or where MAXDOP has been set to less than the number of processors available.

In this case, a query can be bottlenecked on the CPU as it's using 100 percent of the single CPU it's scheduled to run on, or in the case of a parallel query as it's using 100 percent of multiple CPUs, but in both cases other idle CPUs are available that this query is not using.

If the `_Total` instance of this counter is regularly at more than 80 percent, that's a good indication that the server is reaching the limits of the current hardware. Your options here are to buy more or faster processors, or optimize the queries to use less CPU. See Chapter 11 for a detailed discussion on hardware.

❑ **Object: System - Counter: Processor Queue Length:** The processor queue length is a measure of how many threads are sitting in a ready state waiting on a processor to become available to run them. Interpreting and using this counter is a very advanced operating system performance-tuning option that is only needed when investigating complex multi-threaded code problems. For SQL Server systems, processor utilization will identify CPU bottlenecks much more easily than trying to interpret this counter.

❑ **Object: Processor - Counter: % Privileged Time:** This counter indicates the percentage of the sample interval when the processor was executing in kernel mode. On a SQL Server system, kernel mode time is time spent executing system services such as the memory manager, or more likely, the I/O manager. In most cases, privileged time equates to time spent reading and writing from disk or the network.

It is useful to monitor this counter when you find an indication of high CPU usage. If this counter indicates that more than 15–20 percent of processor time is spent executing privileged code, you may have a problem, most likely with one of the I/O drivers, or possibly with a filter driver installed by antivirus software scanning the SQL data or log files.

❑ **Object: Process - Counter: % Processor Time - Instance sqlservr:** This counter measures the percentage of the sample interval during which SQL Server is using the available processors. When the Processor % Processor Time counter is high, or you suspect a CPU bottleneck, look at this counter to confirm that it is SQL Server that is using the CPU, and not some other process.

❑ **Object: Process - Counter: % Privileged Time - Instance: sqlservr:** This counter measures the percentage of the sample that SQL Server is running in kernel mode. As with the previous counter, this counter is useful when investigating high CPU usage on the server to confirm that it is SQL Server that is using the processor resource, and not some other process.

Isolating Processor Bottlenecks

After determining that you have a processor bottleneck, the next step is to track down its root cause. This might lead you to a single query, a set of queries, a set of users, an application, or an operational task that is causing the bottleneck.

To further isolate the root cause, you need to dig deeper into what's running inside SQL Server. The tools described in the remainder of this chapter will help you do this.

The focus of this chapter is on monitoring. Once you've identified a processor bottleneck, consult the relevant chapter for details on how to resolve it. For hardware issues see Chapter 11; for SQL Server configuration, see Chapter 12; and for SQL Query tuning, see Chapter 14.

Disk Activity

SQL Server relies on the Windows operating system to perform I/O operations. The disk system handles the storage and movement of data on your system, giving it a powerful influence on your system's overall responsiveness. Disk I/O is frequently the cause of bottlenecks in a system. You need to observe many factors in determining the performance of the disk system, including the level of usage, the rate of throughput, the amount of disk space available, and whether a queue is developing for the disk systems. Unless your database fits into physical memory, SQL Server constantly brings database pages into and out of the buffer pool. This generates substantial I/O traffic. Similarly, log records need to be flushed to the disk before a transaction can be declared committed. SQL Server 2005 started to make considerably more use of `tempdb` and this hasn't changed with SQL Server 2008, so beginning with SQL Server 2005, `tempdb` I/O activity can also cause a performance bottleneck.

Many of these factors are interrelated. For example, if disk utilization is high, disk throughput might peak, latency for each I/O starts to increase, and eventually a queue might begin to form. These conditions will result in increased response time, causing performance to slow.

Several other factors can impact I/O performance, such as fragmentation and low disk space. Make sure you monitor for free disk space and take action when it falls below a given threshold. In general, the level of free space to raise an alert is when free disk space falls below 15–20 percent. Above this level of free space many disk systems will start to slow down because they have to spend more time searching for increasingly fragmented free space.

You should look at several key metrics when monitoring I/O performance:

❑ Throughput, IOPS: How many I/Os per second (IOPS) can the storage subsystem deliver?

❑ Throughput, MB/sec: How many MB/sec can the I/O subsystem deliver?

❑ Latency: How long does each I/O request take?

❑ Queue depth: How many I/O requests are waiting in the queue?

For each of these metrics you should also distinguish between read and write activity.

Disk Counters on NT 4.0 and Windows 2000

On NT 4.0, the disk performance counters are turned off by default. On Windows 2000, only the physical disk counters are enabled by default. If you are using either operating system you need to run the following commands to enable the counters that are disabled:

`diskperf -yv`

or

`diskperf -ye`(when monitoring RAID disks)

After running these commands, reboot the server to enable the changes. On later operating systems (Windows Server 2003, and Windows Server 2008), all the disk performance counters are enabled by default.

Physical versus Logical Disk Counters

What is the difference between the logical and physical disk counters? This is a common question. One way to think about this is that the logical disk counters are monitoring I/O where the I/O request leaves the application layer (or as the requests enter kernel mode), whereas the physical disk counters monitor I/O as it's leaving the bottom of the kernel storage driver stack. Figure 13-1 shows the I/O software stack and illustrates where the logical disk and physical disk counters are monitoring I/O.

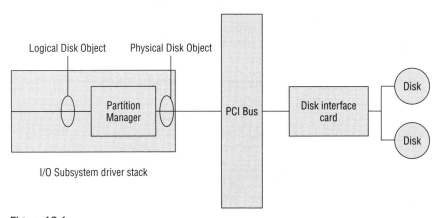

Figure 13-1

In some scenarios the logical and physical counters will provide the same results; in others they will provide different results.

The different I\O subsystem configurations that affect the values displayed by the logical and physical disk counters are discussed in the following sections.

Single Disk, Single Partition

Figure 13-2 shows a single disk with a single partition. In this case there will be a single set of logical disk counters and a single set of physical disk counters.

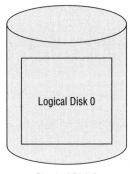

Physical Disk 0

Figure 13-2

This configuration works well in a small SQL Server configuration with a few disks, where the SQL data and log files are already spread over different disks.

Single Disk, Multiple Partitions

Figure 13-3 shows a single disk that is split into multiple partitions. In this case, there will be multiple instances of the logical disk counters, one per partition, and just a single set of physical disk counters.

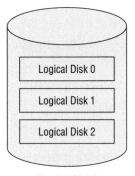

Physical Disk 0

Figure 13-3

This kind of configuration doesn't provide any performance advantages, but it does allow more accurate monitoring of I/O to the different partitions. If you place different sets of data onto different partitions, you can see how much I/O is going to each set by monitoring the logical disk counters.

An example of this might be to put SQL log files on one partition, tempdb data files on another partition, a filegroup for data on another partition, a filegroup for indexes on another partition, and backups on another partition.

In a small SQL Server environment with only a few disks, using this kind of configuration can result in more accurate monitoring of I/O.

Multiple Disks, Single Volume — Software RAID

Figure 13-4 shows multiple disks configured in a software RAID array and mounted as a single volume. In this configuration there is a single set of logical disk counters, and multiple sets of physical disk counters.

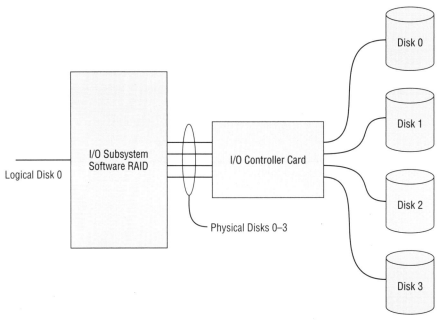

Figure 13-4

This configuration works well in a small SQL Server configuration where the hardware budget won't stretch to a RAID array controller, but multiple disks are available and you want to create a RAID volume spanning them.

Multiple Disks, Single Volume — Hardware RAID

Figure 13-5 shows a hardware RAID array. In this configuration, multiple disks are managed by the hardware RAID controller. The operating system only sees a single physical disk presented to it by the array controller card. The disk counters appear to be the same as the single disk, single partition configuration — that is, a single set of physical disk counters and a corresponding single set of logical disk counters.

The following counters provide information about how many I/O operations are being performed:

❑ **Object: Physical Disk - Counter: Disk Writes/Sec and Object: Physical Disk - Counter: Disk Reads/Sec:** These two counters show how many I/O operations have been performed per second over the sample interval. This information is very useful for determining whether the I/O subsystem is approaching capacity. It can be used in isolation to compare against the theoretical ideal for the I/O subsystem based upon the number and type of disks in the I/O subsystem. It is also very useful when compared against the I/O subsystem baseline to determine how close you are to maximum capacity.

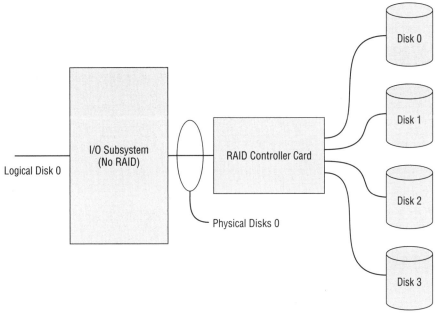

Figure 13-5

Use these counters in combination with throughput MB/Sec, and IO size to confirm that the type of IO is as expected, and that you are getting the expected throughput for the number and type of I/Os being issued.

Monitoring I/O Throughput - MB/Sec

The following counters provide information about how many MB/Sec are being read and written to and from the disk:

❑ **Object: Physical Disk - Counter: Disk Write Bytes/Sec and Object: Physical Disk - Counter: Disk Read Bytes/Sec:** These two counters show how many bytes per second are being transferred over the sample interval. This is an average over the sample period, so with long sample periods it may average out big peaks and troughs in throughput. Over a short sample period, this may fluctuate dramatically, as it sees the results of one or two larger I/Os flooding the I/O subsystem. This information is useful to determine whether the I/O subsystem is approaching its capacity.

As with the IOPS counters, it can be used in isolation to compare against the theoretical throughput for the number and type of disks in the I/O subsystem, but it is more useful when it can be compared against a baseline of the maximum throughput available from the I/O subsystem.

Monitoring I/O Latency

The following counters provide information on how long each read and write operation is taking:

❑ **Object: Physical Disk - Counter: Avg. Disk Sec/Write and Object: Physical Disk - Counter: Avg. Disk Sec/Read:** These two counters show average latency, or how long each I/O has taken. It is an average taken over every I/O issued during the sample period.

This information is extremely useful and can be used independently to determine how well the I/O subsystem is dealing with the current I/O load. Ideally, these counters should be below 5–10 mS (milliseconds). On larger Data Warehouse or Decision Support System systems, it is acceptable for the values of these counters to be in the range of 10–20 mS. Sustained values over 50 mS are an indication that the I/O subsystem is heavily stressed, and that a more detailed investigation of I/O should be undertaken.

These counters will show performance degradations before queuing will start. It should also be used with the following disk queue length counters to help diagnose I/O subsystem bottlenecks.

Monitoring I/O Queue Depth

The following counters provide information on the read and write queue depth:

❑ **Object: Physical Disk - Counter: Avg. Disk Write Queue Length and Object: Physical Disk - Counter: Avg. Disk Read Queue Length:** These two counters show the average queue depth over the sample period. Disk queue lengths greater than 2 indicate that there may be an I/O subsystem bottleneck.

Correctly interpreting these counters is more challenging when the I/O subsystem is a RAID array, or when the disk controller has built-in caching and intelligence. In these cases, the controller will have is own queue, which is designed to absorb and buffer, and effectively hide from this counter, any queuing going on at the disk level. For these reasons, monitoring these counters is less useful than monitoring the latency counters. If these counters do show queue lengths consistently greater than 2, it's a good indication of a potential I/O subsystem bottleneck.

Monitoring Individual Instances versus _Total

In multi-disk systems with several disks, monitoring all the preceding counters for all available disks provides a mass of fluctuating counters to monitor. In some cases, monitoring the _Total instance, which combines the values for all instances, can be a useful way to detect I/O problems. The scenario in which this doesn't work is when I/O to different disks has very different characteristics. In this case, the _Total instance will show a reasonably good average number although some disks may be sitting idle and others are melting from all the I/O requests they are servicing.

Monitoring Transfers versus Read and Write

One thing you may have noticed in the list of counters is that the transfer counters are missing. This is because the transfer counters average out the read and write activity; therefore, for a system that is heavy on one kind of I/O at the expense of the other (reads versus writes), the transfer counters do not show an accurate picture of what is happening.

In addition, read I/O and write I/O usually have very different characteristics, and different performance than the underlying storage. Monitoring a combination of two potentially very disparate values doesn't provide a meaningful metric.

Monitoring %Disk Counters

Another set of disk counters missing from this list are all the %Disk counters. While these counters can provide interesting information, there are enough problems with the results (e.g., the total percent can often exceed 100) that these counters don't provide a useful detailed metric.

If you can afford to monitor all the counters detailed in the preceding sections, you will have a much more complete view of what's going on with your system.

If you want a few simple metrics that provide a good approximate indication of overall I/O subsystem activity, then the %Disk Time, %Disk Read Time, and %Disk Write time counters can provide that.

Logman Script for I/O Counters

Logman is a command-line tool that enables the management of performance counter logs (see the "Logman" section later in the chapter for more details).

The following script will create a new counter log called IO Counters and collect samples for every counter detailed above, for all instances and with a five-second sample interval, and write the log to `c:\perflogs\IO Counters`, appending a six-digit incrementing sequence number to each log:

```
Logman create counter "IO Counters" -si 05 -v nnnnnn -o "c:\perflogs\IO
Counters" -c "\PhysicalDisk(*)\Avg. Disk Bytes/Read" " \PhysicalDisk(*)\Avg.
Disk Bytes/Write" "\PhysicalDisk(*)\Avg. Disk Read Queue Length"
"\PhysicalDisk(*)\Avg. Disk sec/Read" "\PhysicalDisk(*)\Avg. Disk sec/Write"
"\PhysicalDisk(*)\Avg. Disk Write Queue Length" "\PhysicalDisk(*)\Disk Read
Bytes/sec" "\PhysicalDisk(*)\Disk Reads/sec" "\PhysicalDisk(*)\Disk Write
Bytes/sec" "\PhysicalDisk(*)\Disk Writes/sec"
```

After running this script, run the following command to confirm that the settings are as expected:

```
logman query "IO Counters"
```

Isolating Disk Activity Created by SQL Server

We have discussed all the counters you should monitor to find disk bottlenecks. However, you may have multiple applications running on your servers, and it is very possible that they could cause a lot of disk I/O, or you may have memory bottlenecks in your system. You should isolate the disk activities created by SQL Server. Monitor the following counters to determine whether the disk activity is caused by SQL server:

❑ SQL Server: Buffer Manager: Page reads/sec

❑ SQL Server: Buffer Manager: Page writes/sec

Sometimes your application is too big for the hardware you have, and a problem that appears to be related to disk I/O may be resolved by adding more RAM. Make sure you do a proper analysis before making a decision. That's where trend analysis is very helpful because you can see how the performance problem evolved.

Is Disk Performance the Bottleneck?

With the help of the disk counters, you can determine whether you have disk bottlenecks in your system. Several conditions must exist in order for you to make that determination, including a sustained rate of disk activity well above your baseline, persistent disk queue length longer than two per disk, and the absence of a significant amount of paging. Without this combination of factors, it is unlikely that you have a disk bottleneck in your system.

Note here that sometimes your disk hardware may be faulty, and that could cause a lot of interrupts to the CPU. It is a processor bottleneck caused by a disk subsystem, which can have a systemwide performance impact. Make sure you consider this when you analyze the performance data.

> *If, after monitoring your system, you came to the conclusion that you have a disk bottleneck, you need to be able to resolve the problem. See Chapter 11 for more details on removing disk bottlenecks related to hardware issues, Chapter 12 for SQL Server configuration issues, and Chapter 14 for SQL query tuning.*

Memory Usage

Memory is perhaps the most critical resource affecting SQL Server performance. Without enough memory, SQL Server is forced to keep reading and writing data to disk to complete a query. Disk access is anywhere from 1,000 to 100,000 times slower than memory access, depending on exactly how fast your memory is.

Because of this, ensuring SQL Server has enough memory is one of the most important steps you can take to keep SQL Server running as fast as possible. Monitoring memory usage, how much is available, and how well SQL Server is using the available memory is therefore a vitally important step.

In an ideal environment, SQL Server will be running on a dedicated machine and sharing memory only with the operating system and other essential applications. However, in many environments, budget or other constraints mean that SQL will be sharing a server with other applications. In this case it is important to monitor how much memory each application is using and verify that everyone is playing well together.

Low memory conditions can slow the operation of the applications and services on your system. Monitor an instance of SQL Server periodically to confirm that the memory usage is within typical ranges. When your server is low on memory, paging — the process of moving virtual memory back and forth between physical memory and the disk — can be prolonged, resulting in more work for your disks. The paging activity might have to compete with other transactions being performed, intensifying disk bottleneck. Monitor the counters described in the following sections to identify memory bottlenecks.

SQL Server is one of the best behaved server applications available. When the operating system triggers the low memory notification event, SQL will release memory for other applications to use, actually starving itself of memory if another memory-greedy application is running on the machine. The good news is that SQL will only release a small amount of memory at a time, so it may take hours, and even days, before SQL will start to suffer. Unfortunately, if the other application desperately needs more memory, it can take hours before SQL frees up enough memory for the other application to run without excessive paging.

Object: Memory - Counter: Available Mbytes

This counter reports how many megabytes of memory are currently available for programs to use. It is the best single indication that there may be a memory bottleneck on the server.

Determining the appropriate value for this counter depends on the size of the system you are monitoring. If this counter routinely shows values less than 128MB, you may have a serious memory shortage.

On a server with 4GB or more of physical memory (RAM), the operating system will send a low memory notification when available memory reaches 128MB. At this point, SQL will release some of its memory for other processes to use.

Ideally, aim to have at least 256MB to 500MB of Available MBytes. On larger systems with more than 16GB of RAM, this number should be increased to 500MB to 1GB. If you have more than 64GB of RAM on your server, increase this to 1–2GB.

> *There is one case where values for this counter will not directly relate to how SQL Server is using memory: when the SQL Server configuration has been set to limit the maximum amount of memory that SQL Server can use. This is the* max_server_memory *option. See Chapters 11 and 12 for more details on this.*

Monitoring SQL Server Process Memory Usage

Having used the Memory Object, Available Mbytes counter to determine that there is a potential memory shortage, the next step is to determine which processes are using the available memory. As your focus is on SQL Server, you hope that SQL Server is using the memory. However, you should always confirm that this is the case.

The usual place to look for a process's memory usage is in the Process object under the instance for the process. For SQL Server, these counters are detailed in the following list:

❑ **Object: Process – Instance : sqlservr - Counter: Virtual Bytes:** This counter indicates the size of the virtual address space allocated by the process. Virtual address space (VAS) is used by a lot of processes that aren't related to memory performance. This counter is of value when looking for the root cause of SQL Server "out of memory" errors. If running on a 32-bit system, virtual address space is limited to 2GB (except when the /3GB switch is enabled). In this environment, if virtual bytes approaches 1.5GB to 1.7GB, that is about as much space as can be allocated. At this point the root cause of the problem is a VAS limitation issue, and the resolution is to reduce SQL Server's memory usage, enable AWE, boot using /3GB, or move to a 64-bit environment. To learn more about AWE, refer to Chapter 11.

This counter includes the AWE window, but it will not show how much physical memory is reserved though AWE.

❑ **Object: Process – Instance: sqlservr - Counter: Working Set:** This counter indicates the size of the working set for the SQL Server process. The working set is the total set of pages currently resident in memory, as opposed to being paged to disk. It can provide an indication of memory pressure when this is significantly lower than the Private Bytes for the process.

This counter does not include AWE memory allocations.

❑ **Object: Process – Instance: sqlservr –Counter: Private Bytes**: The Private Bytes counter tells you how much memory this process has allocated that cannot be shared with other processes — that is, it's private to this process. To understand the difference between this counter and virtual bytes, you just need to know that certain files loaded into a process's memory space — the EXE, any DLLs, and memory mapped files — will automatically be shared by the operating system. Therefore, Private Bytes indicates the amount of memory used by the process for its stacks, heaps, and any other virtually allocated memory in use.

It does not show anything about AWE memory.

Monitoring SQL Server AWE Memory

If your SQL Server is configured to use AWE memory, the regular process memory counters will not show how much memory SQL Server is actually using. In this scenario, you may see "AvailableMB," indicating that 15GB of the available 16GB of memory is in use, but when you add up the memory actually in use (the working set) for all running processes, it falls a long way short of the 15GB being used. This is because SQL Server has taken 12GB of memory and is using it through AWE.

In this case, the only way to see this AWE memory is to look at the SQL Server–specific counters that indicate how much memory SQL is using:

- ❏ **Object: SQL Server:Buffer Manager – Counter: Database Pages** — This counter shows the number of pages used by the buffer pool for database content.

- ❏ **Object: SQL Server:Buffer Manager – Counter; Target Pages** — This counter shows how many pages SQL Server wants to allocate for the buffer pool.

- ❏ **Object: SQL Server:Buffer Manager – Counter: Total Pages** — This counter shows how many pages SQL Server is currently using for the buffer pool.

- ❏ **Object: SQL Server:Memory Manager – Counter: Target Server Memory (KB)** — This counter shows how much memory SQL Server would like to use for all its memory requirements.

- ❏ **Object: SQL Server:Memory Manager – Counter: Total Server Memory (KB)** — This counter shows how much memory SQL Server is currently using.

Other SQL Server Memory Counters

The following is a list of some additional SQL Server memory counters. When looking at memory issues, these counters can provide more detailed information than the counters already described:

- ❏ **Buffer Cache Hit Ratio:** This counter is an indication of how many page requests were found in the buffer pool. It tends to be a little coarse in that 98 percent and above is good, but 97.9 percent might indicate a memory issue.

- ❏ **Free Pages:** This counter indicates how many free pages SQL Server has for new page requests. Acceptable values for this counter depend on how much memory you have available and the memory usage profile for your applications. Having a good baseline is very useful, as the values for this counter can be compared to the baseline to determine whether there is a current memory issue, or whether the value is part of the expected behavior of the system.

  This counter should be read in conjunction with the Page Life Expectancy counter.

- ❏ **Page Life Expectancy:** This counter provides an indication of the time, in seconds, that a page is expected to remain in the buffer pool before being flushed to disk. Values above 300 are generally considered okay. Values approaching 300 are a cause for concern. Values below 300 are a good indication of a memory shortage.

  Read this counter with the Free Pages counter. You should expect to see Free Pages drop dramatically as the page life expectancy drops below 300. Both are an indication of a memory bottleneck.

Scripting Memory Counters with Logman

Here is a Logman script that will create a counter log of the memory counters discussed in this section (see the "Logman" section later in the chapter for more information):

```
Logman create counter "Memory Counters" -si 05 -v nnnnnn -o
"c:\perflogs\Memory Counters" -c "\Memory\Available MBytes"
"\Process(sqlservr)\Virtual Bytes" "\Process(sqlservr)\Working Set"
"\Process(sqlservr)\Private Bytes" "\SQLServer:Buffer Manager\Database
pages" "\SQLServer:Buffer Manager\Target pages" "\SQLServer:Buffer
Manager\Total pages" "\SQLServer:Memory Manager\Target Server Memory (KB)"
"\SQLServer:Memory Manager\Total Server Memory (KB)"
```

Resolving Memory Bottlenecks

The easy solution to memory bottlenecks is to add more memory; but as we said earlier, tuning your application always comes first. Try to find queries that are memory intensive, such as queries with large worktables — such as hashes for joins and sorts — and see if you can tune them. You will learn more about tuning T-SQL queries in Chapter 14.

In addition, refer to Chapter 11 to ensure that you have configured your server properly. If you are running a 32-bit machine and after adding more memory you are still running into memory bottlenecks, then look into a 64-bit system.

Performance Monitoring Tools

There are a few tools that are well hidden in the command-line utilities that have shipped with Windows operating systems for some time now. Two of these that are extremely valuable when using Performance Monitor are Logman and Relog.

Logman

Logman is a command-line way to script performance monitoring counter logs. You can create, alter, start, and stop counter logs using Logman.

You have seen several examples earlier in this chapter of using Logman to create different counter logs. Here is a short command-line script file to start and stop a counter collection:

```
REM start counter collection
logman start "Memory Counters"
timeout /t 5
REM add a timout for some short period
REM to allow the collection to start
REM do something interesting here

REM stop the counter collection
logman stop "Memory Counters"
timeout /t 5
REM make sure to wait 5 to ensure its stopped
```

Complete documentation for Logman is available through the Windows help system.

Relog

Relog is a command-line utility that enables you to read a log file and write selected parts of it to a new log file.

You can use it to change the file format from blg to csv. You can use it to resample data and turn a very large file with a short sample period into a smaller file with a longer sample period. You can also use it to extract a short period of data for a subset of counters from a much larger file.

Complete documentation for Relog is available through the Windows help system.

Monitoring Events

Performance Monitor enables you to sample performance counters. Events are fired at the time of some significant occurrence within SQL Server. Using events enables you to react to the behavior at the time it occurs, and not have to wait until some later time. SQL Server generates many different events and has several tools available to monitor some of these events.

The following list describes the different features you can use to monitor events that happened in the Database Engine:

- ❑ **Default Trace:** Initially added in SQL Server 2005, this is perhaps one of the best kept secrets in SQL Server. It's virtually impossible to find any documentation on this feature. The default trace is basically a flight data recorder for SQL Server. It records the last 5MB of key events. The events it records were selected to be very lightweight, yet valuable when troubleshooting a critical SQL event.

- ❑ **SQL Trace:** This records specified events and stores them in a file (or files) that you can use later to analyze the data. You have to specify which Database Engine events you want to trace when you define the trace. There are two ways to access the trace data:

  - ❑ Using SQL Server Profiler, a graphical user interface

  - ❑ Through T-SQL system stored procedures

- ❑ **SQL Server Profiler:** This exploits all of the event-capturing functionality of SQL Trace, and adds the capability to trace information to or from a table, save the trace definitions as templates, extract query plans and deadlock events as separate XML files, and replay trace results for diagnosis and optimization. One of the most powerful options, and perhaps least understood, is using a database table to store the trace. Storing the trace file in a database table enables the use of powerful T-SQL queries to perform complex analysis of the events in the trace.

- ❑ **Event notifications:** These send information to a Service Broker service about many of the same events (not all) that are captured by SQL Trace. Unlike traces, event notifications can be used to perform an action inside SQL Server in response to events. Because event notifications execute asynchronously, these actions do not consume any resources defined by the immediate transaction, meaning, for example, that if you want to be notified when a table is altered in a database, then the ALTER TABLE statement would not consume more resources or be delayed because you have defined event notification.

- ❑ **SQL Server Extended Events:** These are new with SQL Server 2008 and extend the Event Notification mechanism, although they are built on the Event Tracing for Windows (ETW) framework. Extended Events are a different set of events from those used by Event Notifications and can be used to diagnose issues such as low memory conditions, high CPU use, and deadlocks. The logs created when using SQL Server Extended Events can also be correlated with other ETW logs using tracerpt.exe. See the topic on Extended Events in SQL Server Books Online for more references to information on using ETW and `tracerpt.exe`. For more details, see the section "SQL Server Extended Event Notification" later in this chapter.

There are number of reasons you want to monitor events that occur inside your SQL Server:

❑ **Find the worst-performing queries or stored procedures:** We have provided a trace template on this book's Web site at www.wrox.com, which you can import into your SQL Server Profiler to capture this scenario. We have included the Showplan Statistics Profile, Showplan XML, and Showplan XML Statistics Profile under Performance event groups. We included these events because after you determine the worst-performing queries, we are sure that you will want to see what query plan was generated by them. Just looking at the duration of the T-SQL batch or stored procedure does not get you anywhere. Consider filtering the trace data by setting some value in the `Duration` column to only retrieve those events that are longer than a specific duration so that you minimize your dataset for analysis.

❑ **Audit user activities:** You can create a trace with Audit Login events; and by selecting the `EventClass` (the default), `EventSubClass`, `LoginSID`, and `LoginName` data columns, you can audit use activities in SQL Server. You may add more events from the Security Audit event group or data columns based on your need. You may someday need this type of information for legal purposes in addition to your technical purposes.

❑ **Identify the cause of a deadlock:** We highly recommend that you set the startup trace flags for tracing deadlocks. SQL Trace doesn't persist between server cycles unless you use SQL Job to achieve this. You can use startup trace flag 1204 or 1222 (1222 returns more verbose information than 1204 and resembles an XML document) to trace a deadlock anytime it happens on your SQL Server. Refer to Chapter 4 to learn more about these trace flags and how to set them. To capture deadlock information using SQL Trace, you need to capture these events in your `trace: Start` with `Standard` trace template and add the Lock event classes (Lock: Deadlock graph, Lock: Deadlock, or Lock: Deadlock Chain). If you specify the Deadlock graph event class, SQL Server Profiler produces a graphical representation of the deadlock.

❑ **Collect a representative set of events for stress testing:** For some benchmarking, you want to reply to the trace generated. SQL Server provides the standard template `TSQL_Replay` to capture a trace that can be replayed later. If you want to use a trace to replay later, make sure that you use this standard template because in order to replay the trace, SQL Server needs some specific events captured, and this template does just that. Later in this chapter you will see how to replay the trace.

❑ **Create a workload to use for the Database Engine Tuning Adviser:** SQL Server Profiler provides a predefined `Tuning` template that gathers the appropriate Transact-SQL events in the trace output so it can be used as a workload for the Database Engine Tuning Advisor.

❑ **Take a performance baseline:** Earlier you learned that you should take a baseline and update it at regular intervals to compare with previous baselines to determine how your application is performing. For example, suppose you have a batch process that loads some data once a day and validates it, does some transformation, and so on, and puts it into your warehouse after deleting the existing set of data. After some time there is an increase in data volume and suddenly your process starts slowing down. You would guess that an increase in data volume is slowing the process down, but is that the only reason? In fact, there could be more than one reason. The query plan generated may be different — because the stats may be incorrect, because your data volume increased, and so on. If you have a statistic profile for the query plan taken during the regular baseline, with other data (such as performance logs) you can quickly identify the root cause.

The following sections provide details on each of the event monitoring tools.

The Default Trace

The default trace was introduced in SQL Server 2005. This trace is always on and captures a very minimal set of lightweight events. If after learning more about the default trace you decide you really do not want it running, you can turn it off using the following T-SQL code:

```
-- Turn ON advanced options
exec sp_configure 'show advanced options', '1'
reconfigure with override
go
-- Turn OFF default trace
exec sp_configure 'default trace enabled', '0'
reconfigure with override
go
-- Turn OFF advanced options
exec sp_configure 'show advanced options', '0'
reconfigure with override
go
```

The default trace logs 30 events to five trace files that work as a First-In, First-Out buffer, with the oldest file being deleted to make room for new events in the next `trc` file.

The default trace files typically live in the SQL Server log folder. Among the SQL Server Error log files you will find five trace files. These are just regular SQL Server trace files, so you can open them in SQL Profiler, or load them into a database table using the regular trace functions.

The key thing is to have some idea of what events are recorded in the default trace, and remember to look at it when something happens to SQL Server.

SQL Trace

As mentioned earlier, you have two ways to define the SQL Trace: using T-SQL system stored procedures and SQL Server Profiler. This section first explains the SQL Trace architecture; then you will study an example to create the server-side trace using the T-SQL system stored procedure.

Before we start, you need to know some basic trace terminology:

❑ **Event:** The occurrence of an action within an instance of the Microsoft SQL Server Database Engine or the SQL Server Database Engine, such as the Audit: Logout event, which happens when a user logs out of SQL Server

❑ **Data column:** An attribute of an event, such as the SPID column for the Audit:Logout event, which indicates the SQL SPID of the user who logged off. Another example is the ApplicationName column, which gives you an application name for the event.

> *In SQL Server, trace column values greater than 1GB return an error and are truncated in the trace output.*

❑ **Filter:** Criteria that limit the events collected in a trace. For example, if you are interested only in the events generated by the SQL Server Management Studio – Query application, you can set the filter on the `ApplicationName` column to SQL Server Management Studio – Query and you will only see events generated by this application in your trace.

❑   **Template:** In SQL Server Profiler, a file that defines the event classes and data columns to be collected in a trace. Many default templates are provided with SQL Server, and these files are located in the directory `\Program Files\Microsoft SQL Server\100\Tools\Profiler\Templates\Microsoft SQL Server\100`.

For even more terminology related to trace, refer to the Books Online section "SQL Trace Terminology."

SQL Trace Architecture

You should understand how SQL Trace works before looking at an example. Figure 13-6 shows the basic form of the architecture. Events are the main unit of activity for tracing. When you define the trace, you specify which events you want to trace. For example, if you want to trace the SP: Starting event, SQL Server will trace only this event (with some other default events that SQL Server always captures). The event source can be any source that produces the trace event, such as a T-SQL statement, deadlocks, other events, and more.

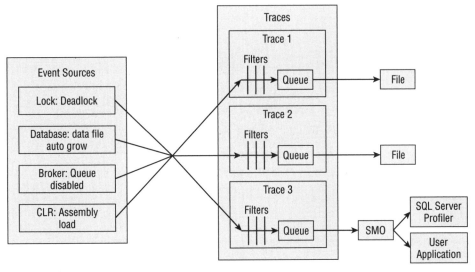

Figure 13-6

After an event occurs, if the event class has been included in a trace definition, the event information is gathered by the trace. If filters have been defined for the event class (e.g., if you are only interested in the events for `LoginName = 'foo'`) in the trace definition, the filters are applied and the trace event information is passed to a queue. From the queue, the trace information is written to a file or it can be used by Server Management Objects (SMO) in applications, such as SQL Server Profiler.

Creating a Server-Side Trace Using T-SQL Stored Procedures

If you have used SQL Profiler before, you know that creating a trace using it is very easy. Creating a trace using T-SQL system stored procedures requires some extra effort because it uses internal IDs for events and data column definitions. Fortunately, the `sp_trace_setevent` article in SQL Server Books Online

(BOL) documents the internal ID number for each event and each data column. You need four stored procedures to create and start a server-side trace:

❏ `sp_trace_create`: Creates a trace definition. The new trace will be in a stopped state.

❏ `sp_trace_setevent`: Once you define a trace using `sp_trace_create`, this stored procedure adds or removes an event or event column to a trace. `sp_trace_setevent` may be executed only on existing traces that are stopped (whose status is 0). An error is returned if this stored procedure is executed on a trace that does not exist or whose status is not 0.

❏ `sp_trace_setfilter`: Applies a filter to a trace. `sp_trace_setfilter` may be executed only on existing traces that are stopped. SQL Server returns an error if this stored procedure is executed on a trace that does not exist or whose status is not 0.

❏ `sp_trace_setstatus`: This modifies the current state of the specified trace.

Now you'll create a server-side trace. This trace will capture the events Audit Login and SQL: StmtStarting. It will capture the data columns `SPID`, `DatabaseName`, `TextData`, and `HostName` for the Audit Login event; and it will capture the data columns `ApplicationName`, `SPID`, `TextData`, and `DatabaseName` for the SQL: StmtStarting event.

You want to capture the trace data for the application SQL Server Management Studio – Query only. Save the trace data in a file located on some remote share. The maximum file size should be 6MB, and you need to enable file rollover so that another file is created when the current file becomes larger than 6MB. Finally, you want the server to process the trace data, and to stop the trace at a certain time.

Server-side traces are much more efficient than client-side tracing with SQL Server Profiler. Defining server-side traces using stored procedures is a bit hard but there is an easy way to do it, which we will look at soon.

Open the sample `SQLTrace-ServerSide` in the Chapter 13 folder found on this book's Web site at `www.wrox.com`. Open the file `CreateTrace.sql`, which is shown here:

```
-- Create a Queue
declare @rc int
declare @TraceID int
declare @maxfilesize bigint
declare @DateTime datetime

set @maxfilesize = 10
set @DateTime = '2008-06-28 14:00:00.000'
--------------------
-- The .trc extension will be appended to the filename automatically.
-- If you are writing from remote server to local drive,
-- please use UNC path and make sure server has write access to your network
share
exec @rc = sp_trace_create @traceid = @TraceID output
,@options = 2
,@tracefile = N'<SQL Server Drive>:\temp\trace\ServerSideTrace'
,@maxfilesize = @maxfilesize
,@stoptime  = @Datetime
,@filecount = NULL
if (@rc != 0) goto error
```

```
-- Set the events
declare @on bit
set @on = 1
exec sp_trace_setevent
 @traceid = @TraceID
,@eventid  = 14
,@columnid = 8
,@on = @on

exec sp_trace_setevent @TraceID, 14, 1, @on
exec sp_trace_setevent @TraceID, 14, 35, @on
exec sp_trace_setevent @TraceID, 14, 12, @on
exec sp_trace_setevent @TraceID, 40, 1, @on
exec sp_trace_setevent @TraceID, 40, 10, @on
exec sp_trace_setevent @TraceID, 40, 35, @on
exec sp_trace_setevent @TraceID, 40, 12, @on


-- Set the Filters
declare @intfilter int
declare @bigintfilter bigint

exec sp_trace_setfilter
 @traceid = @TraceID
,@columnid = 10
,@logical_operator = 1
,@comparison_operator = 6
,@value = N'SQL Server Management Studio - Query'

-- Set the trace status to start
exec sp_trace_setstatus @traceid = @TraceID, @status = 1

-- display trace id for future references
select TraceID=@TraceID
goto finish

error:
select ErrorCode=@rc

finish:
go
```

Now we'll take a look at this stored procedure. The `@traceid` parameter returns an integer that you must use if you want to modify the trace, stop or restart it, or look at its properties.

The second parameter, `@options`, lets you specify one or more trace options. A value of 1 tells the trace to produce a rowset and send it to Profiler. You can't use this option value if you capture to a server-side file. Typically, only Profiler-created traces have this option value. Traces that use the `sp_trace_create` stored procedure should never have an option value of 1, because this value is reserved for Profiler-defined traces. Because the value for the `@options` parameter is a bitmap, you can combine values by adding them together. For example, if you want a trace that enables file rollover and shuts down SQL Server if SQL Server can't write to the trace file, the option value is 6 (4 + 2). Note that not all option values can be combined (option value 8, by definition, doesn't combine with any other option value). In this case, the option value 2 means that when the trace file reaches the size specified by the value in the parameter `@maxfilesize`, the current trace file is closed, and a new file is created. All new records will be written to the new file; and the new file will have the same name as the previous file, but an integer will be appended to indicate its sequence. For details about other `@option` values, please refer to the `sp_trace_setevent` article in SQL Server Books Online.

In the `@tracefile` parameter, you can specify where you want to store the trace results: either a local directory (such as `N 'C:\MSSQL\Trace\trace.trc'`) or a UNC to a share or path (`N'\Servername\Sharename\Directory\trace.trc'`). The extension `.trc` is added automatically, so you don't need to specify that. Note that you cannot specify the `@tracefile` if you set the `@option` value to 8; in that case, the server will store the last 5MB of trace information.

You can specify the maximum size of the trace file before it creates another file to add the trace data using the `@maxfilesize` parameter, in MB. In this case we have specified 10MB, which means that once the trace file size exceeds 10MB, SQL Trace will create another file and start adding data there. We recommend using this option because if you create one big file, it's not easy to move it around; and if you have multiple files, then you can start looking at the older files while trace is writing to the new file. In addition, if disk space issues arise while gathering the trace data, you can move files to different drives or servers.

You can optionally specify the trace stop time using the `@stoptime` parameter, which is of the `datetime` type.

The `@filecount` parameter is used to specify the maximum number of trace files to be maintained with the same base filename. Please refer to Books Online for a detailed description of this parameter.

Now let's look at how to set up the events and choose the data columns for those events. The stored procedure `sp_trace_setevent` will do that job. The first parameter is the `traceid`, which you got from the `sp_trace_create` stored procedure. The second parameter, `@eventid`, is the internal ID of the event you are trying to trace. The first call of the stored procedure specifies 14, which is the Audit Login event. In the third parameter you have to specify which data column you want to capture for the event indicated. In this case, we have set `@columnid` to 8, which is the data column `HostName`. You have to call this stored procedure for each data column you want for a particular event. We called this stored procedure multiple times for `@eventid` 14 because we want multiple data columns. The last parameter is `@ON`, which is a bit parameter used to specify whether you want to turn the event on or off. As mentioned earlier, the `sp_trace_setevent` article in SQL Server Books Online documents the internal ID number for each event and each data column.

Once the event is established, you want to set the filter on it. You use the stored procedure `sp_trace_setfilter` to set the filter on a particular event and the data column. The article `sp_trace_setfilter` in BOL documents the internal ID number for the `@comparison_operator` and `@logical_operator` parameters. In this case, you want only the trace generated by the application name SQL Server Management Studio – Query.

To start the trace you have to use the stored procedure `sp_trace_setstatus`. You can specify the trace ID you want to take action on with the option 0, 1, or 2. Because we want to start the trace, we have specified 1. If you want to stop it, specify 0. If you specify 2, it closes the specified trace and deletes its definition from the server.

You're all set to run the server-side trace. Note that we have specified the `@datetime` option to stop the trace. You have to change the `datetime` value as your needs dictate. Make sure that if you specify the UNC path for the trace file, the SQL Server service account has write access to the share. Run the script now.

It seems like plenty of work to get these internal IDs right when you create the server-side trace. Fortunately, there is an easy way to create the server-side trace using SQL Server Profiler, as you'll see in a moment.

You can define all the events, data columns, filters, filenames (you have to select the option to save to the file, as you cannot store to a table when you create a server-side trace) and size using SQL Server Profiler and then click Run. After that, select File ⇨ Export ⇨ Script Trace Definition ⇨ For SQL Server and save the script. Now you have the script to create the server-side trace. You may have to check the @maxfilesize *option to ensure that it has the correct value if you have changed something other than the default, which is 5MB.*

When you define the server-side trace, you cannot store the trace result directly into the table. You have to store it into the file; later you can use a function, discussed next, to put the trace data into a table.

Retrieving the Trace Metadata

Now that you have defined the trace, you also need to understand how to get the information about the trace. There are built-in functions you can use to do that. The function fn_trace_getinfo (trace_id) is used to get the information about a particular trace. If you do not know the trace_id, specify DEFAULT as the function argument and it will list all the traces.

Run the following T-SQL. Be sure to change the trace_id parameter value to whatever trace_id you got when you ran the script CreateTrace.sql:

```
SELECT *
FROM fn_trace_getinfo (2)
```

Figure 13-7 shows the output.

Figure 13-7

In Figure 13-7, the Property 1 row contains the @options parameter value. A trace with a Property 1 value of 1 is most likely a trace started from Profiler. The Property 2 row contains the trace filename, if any. The Property 3 row contains the maximum file size, which is 10MB in this case; and the Property 4 row contains the stop time, which has some value for this trace. The Property 5 row shows the trace's status — in this case 1, which means that Trace is running.

The function fn_trace_geteventinfo() shows you the events and data columns that a particular trace captures, but the function returns the data with the event and data column IDs, instead of a name or explanation, so you must track down their meaning.

The function `fn_trace_getfilterinfo()` returns information about a particular trace's filters:

```
SELECT *
FROM fn_trace_geteventinfo (2)
```

Retrieving Data from the Trace File

There are two ways you can retrieve the trace data from the file: using the function `fn_trace_gettable` or with SQL Server Profiler. The function `fn_trace_gettable` is a table-valued function, so you can read directly from the file using this function and insert the data into a table to analyze:

```
SELECT * FROM fn_trace_gettable ( '<SQL Server Drive>:\temp\trace\ServerSideTrace
.trc' , DEFAULT)
```

You can also use `SELECT INTO` in this query to store the result in a table. We like to put the trace data into a table because then you can write a T-SQL statement to query the data. For example, the `TextData` column is created with the `ntext` data type. You can alter the data type to `nvarchar(max)` so that you can use the string functions. You should not be using the `ntext` or `text` data types anyway, because they will be deprecated in a future SQL Server release; use `nvarchar(max)` or `varchar(max)` instead. Note that even though the trace is running, you can still read the data from the file to which Trace is writing. You don't have to stop the trace for that. The only gotcha in storing the trace data into a table is that the `EventClass` value is stored as an `int` value and not as a friendly name. We have provided a script, `EventClassID_Name.sql`, that creates a table and inserts the `eventclassid` and its name into that table. You can then use this table to get the event class name when you analyze the trace result stored there. You can write a query like the following to do that, assuming that you have stored the trace result in the table `TraceResult`:

```
SELECT ECN.EventClassName, TR.*
FROM TraceResult TR
LEFT JOIN EventClassIdToName ECN
  ON ECN.EventClassID = TR.EventClass
```

SQL Server Profiler

SQL Server Profiler is a rich interface to create and manage traces and analyze and replay trace results. SQL Server Profiler shows how SQL Server resolves queries internally. This enables you to see exactly what Transact-SQL statements or multi-dimensional expressions are submitted to the server and how the server accesses the database or cube to return result sets.

If you do not know how to create a trace using Profiler, please refer to the BOL topic "Using SQL Server Profiler." This section explains how to use Showplan XML and how to correlate the trace events to Performance Monitor counters. This section also describes how to capture and replay the trace.

You can read the trace file created using a T-SQL stored procedure with SQL Profiler. To use SQL Profiler to read the trace file, just go to the File menu and open the trace file you are interested in.

In SQL Server 2008, the server reports both the duration of an event and CPU time used by the event, in milliseconds. In SQL Server 2005, the server reports the duration of an event in microseconds (one millionth of a second) and the amount of CPU time used by the event in milliseconds (one thousandth of a second). In SQL Server 2000, the server reported both duration and CPU time in milliseconds.

In SQL Server 2005, the SQL Server Profiler graphical user interface displays the Duration *column in milliseconds by default, but when a trace is saved to either a file or a database table, the* Duration *column value is written in microseconds. If you want to display the duration column in microseconds in SQL Profiler, go to Tools ⇨ Options and select the option "Show values in Duration column in microseconds (SQL Server 2005 only)."*

Showplan XML

You can get the query plan in an XML document and use this document later to generate the graphical query plan. Showplan output in XML format can be moved from one computer to another and thus rendered on any computer, even on computers where SQL Server is not installed. Showplan output in XML format can also be programmatically processed using XML technologies, such as XPath, XQuery, and so on. XML Showplan processing is supported in SQL Server 2005, which contains a built-in query evaluation engine for XPath and XQuery.

You can generate XML Showplan output using the following means:

❑   Select Display Estimated Execution Plan or Include Actual Execution Plan from the query editor toolbar in SQL Server Management Studio

❑   Use the Transact-SQL Showplan SET statement options SHOWPLAN_XML and STATISTICS XML.

❑   Select the SQL Server Profiler event classes Showplan XML, Showplan XML for Query Compile, and Showplan XML Statistics Profile for tracing.

❑   Use the sys.dm_exec_query_plan dynamic management view.

XML Showplans are returned in the nvarchar (max) data type for all of these methods except the last. XML Showplans are returned in the xml data type when you use this dynamic management view.

You can visit http://schemas.microsoft.com/sqlserver/2004/07/showplan/showplanxml.xsd for the XML Showplan schema or you can look in the directory where SQL Server is installed: \Program Files\Microsoft SQL Server\100\Tools\Binn\schemas\sqlserver\2004\07\showplan.

Chapter 14 explains how to read the query plan. Figure 13-8 shows what a query plan looks like in SQL Profiler when you choose the Showplan XML event. This event is under the Performance object. To see these additional events, you need to click the Events Selection tab and select the Show All Events option.

If you right-click on the Showplan XML event, you will see a menu item Extract Event Data. This saves the query plan with a .sqlplan extension. You can later open that file with SQL Server Management Studio or Profiler, and it will display the graphical plan exactly as shown in Figure 13-8. You can also use File ⇨ Export ⇨ Extract SQL Server Event in SQL Profiler to achieve the same results.

When you set up the trace using Profiler, if you choose Showplan XML or Showplan Statistics Profile or Showplan XML for Query Compile, a tab will show up in the Trace Properties dialog, shown in Figure 13-9.

Also shown in Figure 13-9 is a Deadlock XML option to store the deadlock graph in an XML document, which you can view later in SQL Management Studio or Profiler. This option is enabled only if you choose the Deadlock Graph event.

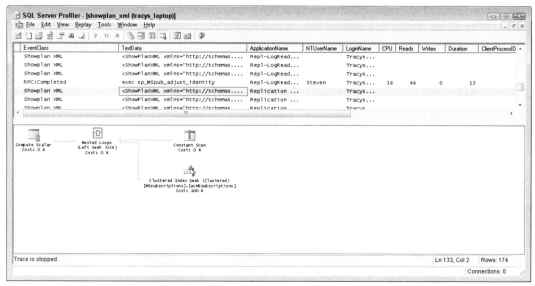

Figure 13-8

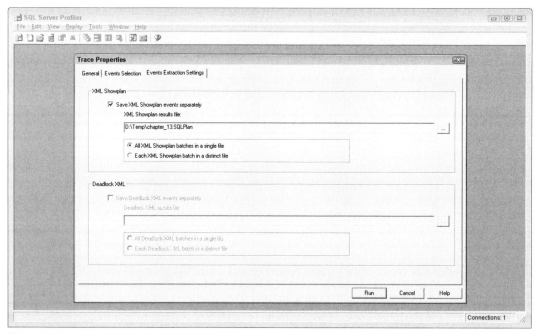

Figure 13-9

You can also use SET SHOWPLAN_XML ON before you execute the query, which will give you an estimated execution plan in XML without executing it. You can also use SET STATISTICS XML ON, which will give you an execution plan in XML format, as shown in Figure 13-10. Click the link in the XML Showplan to open an XML editor within SQL Server Management Studio.

If you want to see the graphical execution plan from this XML document, you can save the document with a .sqlplan extension. Open that file in SQL Server Management Studio and you will get the graphical execution plan. Figure 13-11 shows the graphical execution plan generated from the XML document.

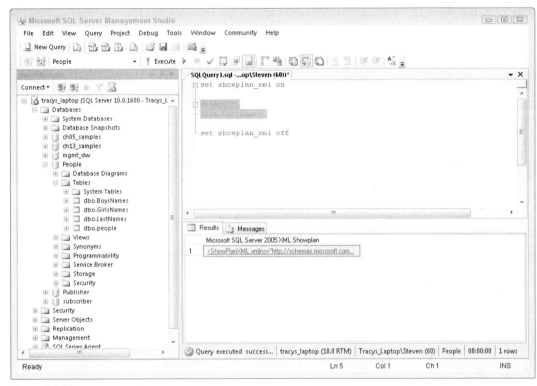

Figure 13-10

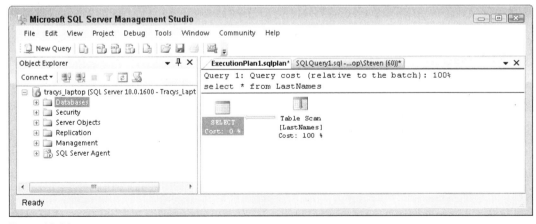

Figure 13-11

When the Showplan XML event class is included in a trace, the amount of overhead will significantly impede performance. Showplan XML stores a query plan that is created when the query is optimized. To minimize the overhead incurred, limit the use of this event class to traces that monitor specific problems for brief periods of time, and be sure to use the data column filter based on specifics you are going to trace.

Correlating a Trace with Windows Performance Log Data

In SQL Server 2005, a new feature was added to correlate the trace data with Performance Monitor log data based on the `StartTime` and `EndTime` data columns in the SQL trace file. If you have taken Trace and Performance Monitor data at the same time, you can relate the events that happened in SQL Server with the server activities such as processor time, disk activity, and memory usage. Figures 13-12 and 13-13 show an example of correlating trace and Performance Monitor log data.

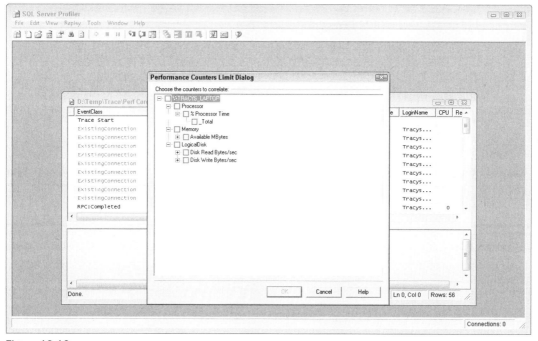

Figure 13-12

To bring up the performance data after you open a trace file, click File ⇨ Import Performance Data. That will bring up the dialog shown in Figure 13-12. Note that this option is not enabled unless you open a saved trace file. You can select the performance counters you are interested in and then click OK. That will bring the performance counters inside the Profiler to correlate the SQL Server activity during a specific time, as shown in Figure 13-13. Move the red vertical bar to select a particular time you are interested in to see what was happening at that time in SQL Server.

If you look at the peak value for a performance counter — for example, avg. disk queue length — that will bring up whatever query SQL Server was executing at the time. However, that doesn't mean the query caused the disk queue length to increase exactly at that time. It's possible that the query started a little earlier and is now requesting a lot of data from disk, which may be causing the average disk queue length to shoot up. In short, be careful before you jump to conclusions; make sure you look at the whole picture.

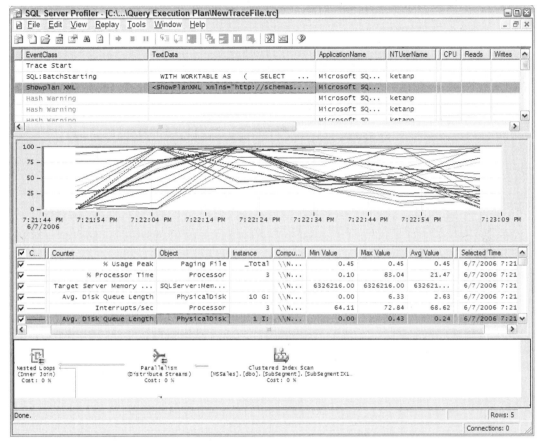

Figure 13-13

Replaying a Trace

Replay is the capability to save a trace and replay it later. This functionality enables you to reproduce the activity captured in a trace. When you create or edit a trace, you can save the trace to replay it later. Be sure to choose the predefined template called TSQL_Replay when you create the trace using SQL Profiler. SQL Server needs specific events and data columns to be captured in order to replay the trace later. If you miss those events and data columns, SQL Server will not replay the trace. Trace replay supports debugging by using the Toggle Breakpoint and the Run to Cursor options on the SQL Server Profiler Replay menu. These options especially improve the analysis of long scripts because they can break the replay of the trace into short segments so they can be analyzed incrementally.

The following types of events are ignored when you replay the trace:

❑   Traces that contain transactional replication and other transaction log activity. These events are skipped. Other types of replication do not mark the transaction log so they are not affected.

❑ Traces that contain operations involving globally unique identifiers (GUID). These events are skipped.

❑ Traces that contain operations on `text`, `ntext`, and `image` columns involving the `bcp` utility, the `BULK INSERT`, `READTEXT`, `WRITETEXT`, and `UPDATETEXT` statements, and full-text operations. These events are skipped.

❑ Traces that contain session binding: `sp_getbindtoken` and `sp_bindsession` system stored procedures. These events are skipped.

❑ SQL Server Profiler does not support replaying traces collected by Microsoft SQL Server version 7.0 or earlier.

In addition, some requirements must be met in order to replay the trace on the target server:

❑ All logins and users contained in the trace must be created already on the target and in the same database as the source.

❑ All logins and users in the target must have the same permissions they had in the source.

❑ All login passwords must be the same as those of the user who executes the replay. You can use the Transfer Login task in SSIS to transfer the logins to the target server on which you want to replay the trace.

❑ The database IDs on the target ideally should be the same as those on the source. However, if they are not the same, matching can be performed based on the database name if it is present in the trace, so make sure that you have the `DatabaseName` data column selected in the trace.

❑ The default database on the target server for a login should be the same as on the source when the trace was taken.

❑ Replaying events associated with missing or incorrect logins results in replay errors, but the replay operation continues.

Performance Considerations When Using Trace

SQL Server tracing incurs no overhead unless it captures an event, and most events need very few resources. Profiler becomes expensive only if you trace more than 100 event classes and capture all the data from those events. Normally, you will see a maximum of 5 percent to 10 percent overhead if you capture everything. Most of the performance hit results from a longer code path; the actual resources that the trace needs in order to capture event data aren't particularly CPU-intensive. In addition, to minimize the performance hit, you can define all your traces as server-side traces, avoiding the overhead of producing rowsets to send to the Profiler client.

Event Notifications

Event notifications are special database objects that send messages to the Service Broker service (see Chapter 8 for details on the Service Broker) with information regarding server or database events. Event notifications can be programmed against many of the same events captured by SQL Trace, but not all. Unlike creating traces, event notifications can be used to perform an action inside an instance of SQL Server in response to events. Later in this chapter you'll see an example that shows how to subscribe to those events and take actions if needed.

To subscribe to an event, you have to create the Service Broker queue that will receive the details regarding the event. In addition, a queue requires the Service Broker service in order to receive the message.

Then you need to create an event notification. You can create a stored procedure and activate it when the event message is in the queue to take a certain action. This example assumes you know how the Service Broker works, so be sure to read Chapter 8 if you don't already know about the Server Broker.

Event notifications are created at the server or database level.

We will create an event notification in a database whereby you will be notified when a new table is created. Open the project EventNotification using SQL Server Management Studio, and then open the CreateDatabase.sql script. This script creates a database called StoreEvent for the example. Run this script.

Next, open the CreateQueue.sql script, shown here:

```
USE StoreEvent
GO

--CREATE QUEUE to receive the event details.
IF OBJECT_ID('dbo.NotifyQueue') IS NULL
CREATE QUEUE dbo.NotifyQueue
WITH STATUS = ON
    ,RETENTION = OFF
GO

--create the service so that when event happens
--server can send the message to this service.
--we are using the pre-defined contract here.
IF NOT EXISTS(SELECT * FROM sys.services WHERE name =
'EventNotificationService')
CREATE SERVICE EventNotificationService
ON QUEUE NotifyQueue
([http://schemas.microsoft.com/SQL/Notifications/PostEventNotification])

IF NOT EXISTS(SELECT * FROM sys.routes WHERE name = 'NotifyRoute')

CREATE ROUTE NotifyRoute
WITH SERVICE_NAME = 'EventNotificationService',
ADDRESS = 'LOCAL';
GO
```

This script creates a queue in the StoreEvent database to store the event data when a table is created in the StoreEvent database. It creates a Service Broker service EventNotificationService such that SQL Server can send the message when a subscribed event happens. The route NotifyRoute will help route the message to a local SQL server instance. Run this script.

Now you need to create the event notification. Open the script CreateEventNotification.sql, shown here:

```
USE StoreEvent
GO
CREATE EVENT NOTIFICATION CreateTableNotification
ON DATABASE
FOR CREATE_TABLE
TO SERVICE 'EventNotificationService', 'current database' ;
```

This script creates an event notification called `CreateTableNotification` that notifies you when a table is created in the `StoreEvent` database.

Note that messages are sent from one service to another, as discussed in Chapter 8. In this case, you have created the target end of the service, which is `EventNotificationServer`; the initiator end of the service is SQL Server itself.

When a table is created in the `StoreEvent` database, you will get the message in the queue `NotifyQueue`, so create a table and run the following script to see what's in the queue:

```
SELECT CAST(message_body AS xml)
FROM NotifyQueue
```

Here is what the XML message in the queue looks like:

```
<EVENT_INSTANCE>
  <EventType>CREATE_TABLE</EventType>
  <PostTime>2008-09-23T21:53:14.463</PostTime>
  <SPID>56</SPID>
  <ServerName>CIPHER</ServerName>
  <LoginName>REDMOND\ketanp</LoginName>
  <UserName>dbo</UserName>
  <DatabaseName>StoreEvent</DatabaseName>
  <SchemaName>dbo</SchemaName>
  <ObjectName>TestTable1</ObjectName>
  <ObjectType>TABLE</ObjectType>
  <TSQLCommand>
    <SetOptions ANSI_NULLS="ON" ANSI_NULL_DEFAULT="ON" ANSI_PADDING="ON"
QUOTED_IDENTIFIER="ON" ENCRYPTED="FALSE" />
    <CommandText>CREATE TABLE TestTable1 (col1 int, col2 varchar(100), col3
xml)
</CommandText>
  </TSQLCommand>
</EVENT_INSTANCE>
```

You can take some action with this event if you create a stored procedure and have it activated when a message arrives in the queue. Refer to Chapter 8 for details on stored procedure activation.

You create the server-wide event in the same way. For a full list of the events for which you can be notified, you can query the `sys.event_notification_event_types` view. Please refer to the script `Metadata_EventNotification.sql` to get the catalog view list that stores the metadata about event notifications.

Note that you can also be notified for grouped events. For example, if you want to be notified when a table is created, altered, or dropped, you don't have to create three separate event notifications. You can use the group event called `DDL_TABLE_EVENTS` and just create one event notification to achieve the same thing. Another example is related to monitoring all the locking events using the event group `TRC_LOCKS`. When you create an event notification with this group, you can be notified about the following events: `LOCK_DEADLOCK`, `LOCK_DEADLOCK_CHAIN`, `LOCK_ESCALATION`, and `DEADLOCK_GRAPH`.

Please refer to the BOL topic "DDL Event Groups for Use with Event Notifications" for all the event groups.

Event notifications can be used to do the following:

- ❑ Log and review changes or activity occurring on the database or server.
- ❑ Perform an action in response to an event in an asynchronous, rather than synchronous, manner.

Event notifications can offer a programming alternative to DDL triggers and SQL Trace.

SQL Server Extended Event Notifications

SQL Server Extended Event notifications (XEvents) are a completely new feature for SQL Server 2008. They provide a deep insight into SQL Server internals and are designed to enable faster diagnosis of issues with SQL Server.

They provide the capability to act either synchronously or asynchronously to SQL Events and are designed to be extremely lightweight and highly scalable.

XEvent Objects

This section introduces the new objects in XEvents. The object hierarchy for XEvent objects is shown in Figure 13-14.

Module

The `Module` object is equivalent to the binary that contains the events. `Module` is equivalent to `SQLServr.exe`, or `MyDll.dll` if you were to write your own code and load it into SQLServer. The only place you will see the module is as an attribute of the package in the DMV `sys.dm_xe_packages`.

Package

A package is a container object within the module. The packages that come with SQL Server can be seen in the DMV `sys.dm_xe_packages` and are described in the following table.

Name	Description	capabilities_desc	module_address
package0	Default package. Contains all standard types, maps, compare operators, actions, and targets	utility	0x01000000
sqlos	Extended events for SQL operating system	NULL	0x01000000
sqlserver	Extended events for Microsoft SQL Server	NULL	0x01000000

As with modules, you won't be creating any packages unless you're writing your own code and creating your own new events.

Event

Events are the first "real" objects in the hierarchy. An event represents an occurrence of a significant activity within SQL Server. To get a better understanding of events, take a look at some of the events available. These can be found in the DMV sys.dm_xe_objects and have a type of 'event'. The following code will output a list of event types:

```
select name
from sys.dm_xe_objects
where object_type ='event'
order by name
```

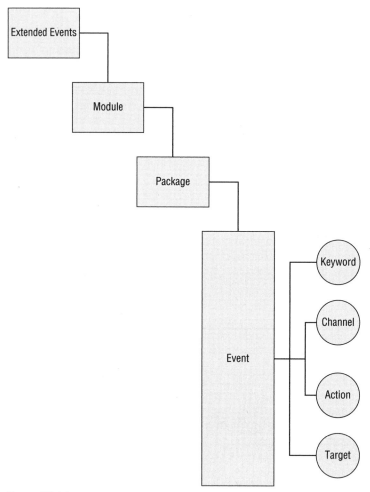

Figure 13-14

This returns a list of 254 different event types. A select few are listed here:

```
checkpoint_begin
checkpoint_end
database_transaction_begin
database_transaction_end
lock_acquired
lock_deadlock
lock_released
```

```
locks_lock_timeouts
locks_lock_timeouts_greater_than_0
locks_lock_waits
sp_statement_completed
sp_statement_starting
sql_statement_completed
sql_statement_starting
wait_info
wait_info_external
```

All events have two additional attributes: `Keyword` and `Channel`.

The `Keyword` for an event is a way of grouping events based on who fires the event, so keywords are memory, broker, server, and so on.

The `Channel` for an event reflects who might be interested in the event. There are just four channels in SQL Server 2008:

❏   debug

❏   analytical

❏   operational

❏   administration

To see the `Channel` and `Keyword` for the events requires that you join several of the XEvent DMVs, as in the following code:

```
select p.name as package_name
, k.event
, k.keyword
, c.channel
, k.description
from (
select c.object_package_guid as event_package
, c.object_name as event
, v.map_value as keyword
, o.description
from sys.dm_xe_object_columns as c inner join sys.dm_xe_map_values as v
  on c.type_name = v.name
  and c.column_value = v.map_key
  and c.type_package_guid = v.object_package_guid
inner join sys.dm_xe_objects as o
  on o.name = c.object_name
  and o.package_guid = c.object_package_guid
where c.name = 'keyword'
) as k inner join (
select c.object_package_guid as event_package
, c.object_name as event
, v.map_value as channel
, o.description
from sys.dm_xe_object_columns as c inner join sys.dm_xe_map_values as v
  on c.type_name = v.name
  and c.column_value = v.map_key
  and c.type_package_guid = v.object_package_guid
```

```
inner join sys.dm_xe_objects as o
  on o.name = c.object_name
  and o.package_guid = c.object_package_guid
where c.name = 'channel'
) as c
on
k.event_package = c.event_package and k.event = c.event
inner join sys.dm_xe_packages as p on p.guid = k.event_package
order by keyword
, channel
, event
```

The following table shows a few of the events, including their keywords and channels.

Package Name	Event	Keyword	Channel	Description
sqlserver	broker_activation_ task_aborted	broker	Admin	Broker activation task aborted
sqlserver	broker_activation_ task_started	broker	Analytic	Broker activation task started
sqlserver	change_tracking_ cleanup	change_tracking	Debug	Change Tracking Cleanup
sqlserver	app_domain_ ring_buffer_recorded	clr	Debug	AppDomain ring buffer recorded
sqlserver	cursor_manager_ cursor_end	cursor	Analytic	Cursor manager cursor end
sqlserver	checkpoint_begin	database	Analytic	Checkpoint has begun
sqlserver	database_started	database	Operational	Database started
sqlserver	deadlock_monitor_ state_transition	deadlock_monitor	Debug	Deadlock Monitor state transition
sqlserver	error_reported	errors	Admin	Error has been reported
sqlserver	trace_print	errors	Debug	Trace message published
sqlserver	assert_fired	exception	Debug	Assert fired
sqlos	dump_exception_ routine_executed	exception	Debug	Dump exception routine executed
sqlserver	sql_statement_ starting	execution	Analytic	SQL statement starting
sqlserver	databases_log_ file_size_changed	io	Analytic	Database log file size changed

Package Name	Event	Keyword	Channel	Description
sqlserver	file_read	io	Analytic	File read
sqlserver	flush_file_buffers	io	Debug	FlushFileBuffers called

Action

Actions are what we want to happen when an event fires. They are invoked synchronously on the thread that fired the event. The available events are stored in the DMV `sys.dm_xe_objects` with an `object_type = 'action'`:

```
select name
from sys.dm_xe_objects
where object_type = 'action'
order by name
```

This query can return 37 actions, some of which are listed here:

- ❑ attach_activity_id
- ❑ attach_activity_id_xfer
- ❑ callstack
- ❑ collect_cpu_cycle_time
- ❑ collect_system_time
- ❑ create_dump_all_thread
- ❑ create_dump_single_thread
- ❑ database_context
- ❑ database_id
- ❑ debug_break
- ❑ plan_handle
- ❑ session_id
- ❑ sos_context
- ❑ sql_text
- ❑ transaction_id
- ❑ tsql_stack

Predicate

A predicate is a filter that is applied to the event right before the event is published. A Boolean expression, it can be either local or global and can store state.

Predicates are stored in the DMV `sys.dm_xe_objects` and can be seen using the following T-SQL:

```
select name, description
from sys.dm_xe_objects
```

```
where object_type = 'pred_compare'
order by name
-- 111 rows

select name, description
from sys.dm_xe_objects
where object_type = 'pred_source'
order by name
-- 29 rows
```

A few of the pred_compare objects are shown in the following table.

Name	Description
divides_by_uint64	Whether a uint64 divides another with no remainder
equal_ansi_string	Equality operator between two ANSI string values
greater_than_equal_float64	Greater than or equal operator between two 64-bit double values
greater_than_i_sql_ansi_string	Greater than operator between two SQL ANSI string values
less_than_ansi_string	Less than operator between two ANSI string values
less_than_equal_i_unicode_string_ptr	Less than or equal operator between two UNICODE string pointer values
less_than_int64	Less than operator between two 64-bit signed int values
not_equal_ptr	Inequality operator between two generic pointer values

Some of the pred_source objects are listed in the following table.

Name	Description
Counter	Counts the number of times evaluated
cpu_id	Gets the current CPU ID
current_thread_id	Gets the current Windows thread ID
database_id	Gets the current database ID
node_affinity	Gets the current NUMA node affinity
partitioned_counter	Per-CPU partitioned counter. Value is aggregated and approximate.
scheduler_address	Gets the current scheduler address
scheduler_id	Gets the current scheduler ID
session_id	Gets the current session ID
system_thread_id	Gets the current system thread ID
task_address	Gets the current task address

Name	Description
task_elapsed_quantum	Gets the time elapsed since quantum started
task_execution_time	Gets the current task execution time
transaction_id	Gets the current transaction ID
worker_address	Gets the current worker address

Target

A target is a way of defining what you want to happen to the events you are monitoring. The thirteen targets defined for SQL Server 2008 are shown in the following table. Like the other XEvent objects, they can be found in the DMV sys.dm_xe_objects with an object_type = 'target'.

The following T-SQL code returns the list of targets from sys.dm_xe_objects:

```
select name, description
from sys.dm_xe_objects
where object_type = 'target'
order by name
```

Name	description
asynchronous_bucketizer	Asynchronous bucketizing target
asynchronous_file_target	Asynchronous file target
asynchronous_security_audit_event_log _target	Asynchronous security audit NT event log target
asynchronous_security_audit_file _target	Asynchronous security audit file target
asynchronous_security_audit_security _log_target	Asynchronous security audit NT security log target
etw_classic_sync_target	Event Tracing for Windows (ETW) Synchronous Target
pair_matching	Pairing target
ring_buffer	Asynchronous ring buffer target.
synchronous_bucketizer	Synchronous bucketizing target
synchronous_event_counter	Synchronous Counter target
synchronous_security_audit_event_log _target	Synchronous security audit NT event log target
synchronous_security_audit_file _target	Synchronous security audit file target
synchronous_security_audit_security _log_target	Synchronous security audit NT security log target

Event Session

The event session is where all the objects detailed earlier are brought together to actually do something. You create the event session to define which of those objects you want to use to perform your event capture.

Event sessions are created using the new for SQL Server 2008 DDL CREATE EVENT SESSION syntax. This one statement enables you to define all the objects you need to create a new event session. The only thing you cannot do is start the session. For transaction consistency, the session must be created first. Once it has been created, it can be started using the ALTER EVENT SESSION syntax:

```
ALTER EVENT SESSION <session name>  STATE = START
```

To see which sessions are currently active, use the following queries:

```
select *
from sys.dm_xe_sessions

select *
from sys.dm_xe_session_events
```

If you run these before creating an event session, they return no rows.

Catalog Views

There are several new catalog views in SQL Server 2008 that expose information about XEvents:

- ❏ server_event_sessions
- ❏ server_event_session_targets
- ❏ server_event_session_fields
- ❏ server_event_session_events
- ❏ server_event_session_actions

DMVs

You have already seen some of the new DMVs in action. For completeness, here is the full list:

- ❏ sys.dm_os_dispatcher_pools: Returns information about session dispatcher pools. Dispatcher pools are thread pools used by system components to perform background processing.
- ❏ sys.dm_xe_map_values: Returns a mapping of internal numeric keys to human-readable text.
- ❏ sys.dm_xe_object_columns: Returns the schema information for all the objects
- ❏ sys.dm_xe_objects: Returns a row for each object exposed by an event package. Objects can be one of the following:
  - ❏ **Events:** Indicate points of interest in an execution path. All events contain information about a point of interest.
  - ❏ **Actions:** Run synchronously when events fire. An action can append run-time data to an event.
  - ❏ **Targets:** Consume events, either synchronously on the thread that fires the event or asynchronously on a system-provided thread

❑ **Predicate sources:** Retrieve values from event sources for use in comparison operations. Predicate comparisons compare specific data types and return a Boolean value.

❑ **Types:** Encapsulate the length and characteristics of the byte collection, which is required in order to interpret the data

❑ `sys.dm_xe_packages`: Lists all the packages registered with the extended events engine

❑ `sys.dm_xe_session_event_actions`: Returns information about event session actions. Actions are executed when events are fired. This management view aggregates statistics about the number of times an action has run and the total run time of the action.

❑ `sys.dm_xe_session_events`: Returns information about session events. Events are discrete execution points. Predicates can be applied to events to stop them from firing if the event does not contain the required information.

❑ `sys.dm_xe_session_object_columns`: Shows the configuration values for objects that are bound to a session

❑ `sys.dm_xe_session_targets`: Returns information about session targets

❑ `sys.dm_xe_sessions`: Returns information about an active extended events session. This session is a collection of events, actions, and targets.

Monitoring with Dynamic Management Views and Functions

Dynamic management views (DMVs) and dynamic management functions (DMFs) are a godsend to the DBA. They provide plenty of information about server and database state. DMVs are designed to give you a window into what's going on inside SQL Server. They return server state information that you can use to monitor the health of a server instance, diagnose problems, and tune performance. There are two types of DMVs and functions:

❑ Server-scoped dynamic management views and functions

❑ Database-scoped dynamic management views and functions

All DMVs and functions exist in the `sys` schema and follow the naming convention `dm_*` and `fn*`, respectively. To view the information from a server-scoped DMV, you have to grant the SERVER VIEW STATE permission to the user. For database-scoped DMVs and functions, you have to grant the VIEW DATABASE STATE permission to the user. Once you grant the VIEW STATE permission, that user can see all the views; to restrict the user, deny the SELECT permission on the dynamic management views or functions that you do not want the user to access. The following example grants the VIEW SERVER STATE permission to the user Aish:

```
GRANT VIEW SERVER STATE TO [MyDom\Aish]
```

If you want the user `[MyDom\Aish]` to be restricted from viewing information in the view `sys.dm_os_wait_stats,` you need to DENY SELECT as follows:

```
DENY SELECT ON sys.dm_os_wait_stats TO [MyDom\Aish]
```

DMVs and functions are generally divided into the following categories:

- ❑ CLR-related dynamic management views
- ❑ I/O-related dynamic management views and functions
- ❑ Database mirroring–related dynamic management views
- ❑ Query notifications–related dynamic management views
- ❑ Database-related dynamic management views
- ❑ Replication-related dynamic management views
- ❑ Execution-related dynamic management views and functions
- ❑ Service Broker–related dynamic management views
- ❑ Full-Text-Search-related dynamic management views
- ❑ SQL Server OS–related dynamic management views
- ❑ Index-related dynamic management views and functions
- ❑ Transaction-related dynamic management views and functions

Rather than describe all the views here, we will look at examples for the common tasks a DBA would perform to monitor a SQL Server. For details about all the DMVs and functions, please refer to the Books Online topic "Dynamic Management Views and Functions."

Following are some of the scenarios in which you can use DMVs and functions. You can also open a sample DMV to get all the scripts. Here we will provide just a few examples, but in the sample DMV solution you will find many examples for monitoring your SQL Server.

What's Going on Inside SQL Server?

The following sections illustrate querying the DMVs to determine what is currently going on inside SQL Server.

Currently Running Queries

This query show the SQL text for currently running queries. It helps you find which queries are currently running and displays the SQL text for each currently running query. This is useful when you are trying to determine what is currently running in terms of T-SQL code, and not just SPIDs.

```
select r.session_id
  ,status
  ,substring(qt.text,r.statement_start_offset/2,
  (case when r.statement_end_offset = -1
  then len(convert(nvarchar(max), qt.text)) * 2
  else r.statement_end_offset end - r.statement_start_offset)/2)
  as query_text
  ,qt.dbid
  ,qt.objectid
  ,r.cpu_time
  ,r.total_elapsed_time
  ,r.reads
  ,r.writes
```

```
    ,r.logical_reads
    ,r.scheduler_id
from sys.dm_exec_requests r
cross apply sys.dm_exec_sql_text(sql_handle) as qt
where r.session_id > 50
order by r.cpu_time desc
```

Who Is Using Which Resources?

This query samples the DMVs over a 10-second interval and reports on the delta between the first and second sample:

```
-- Who is using all the resources?
select spid, kpid, cpu, physical_io, memusage, sql_handle, 1 as sample,
getdate() as sampleTime, hostname, program_name, nt_username
into #Resources
from master..sysprocesses

waitfor delay '00:00:10'

Insert #Resources
select spid, kpid, cpu, physical_io, memusage, sql_handle, 2 as sample,
getdate() as sampleTime, hostname, program_name, nt_username
from master..sysprocesses

-- Find the deltas
select r1.spid
, r1.kpid
, r2.cpu - r1.cpu as d_cpu_total
, r2.physical_io - r1.physical_io as d_physical_io_total
, r2.memusage - r1.memusage as d_memusage_total
, r1.hostname, r1.program_name, r1.nt_username
, r1.sql_handle
, r2.sql_handle
from #resources as r1 inner join #resources as r2 on r1.spid = r2.spid
    and r1.kpid = r2.kpid
where r1.sample = 1
and r2.sample = 2
and (r2.cpu - r1.cpu) > 0
order by (r2.cpu - r1.cpu) desc

select r1.spid
, r1.kpid
, r2.cpu - r1.cpu as d_cpu_total
, r2.physical_io - r1.physical_io as d_physical_io_total
, r2.memusage - r1.memusage as d_memusage_total
, r1.hostname, r1.program_name, r1.nt_username
into #Usage
from #resources as r1 inner join #resources as r2 on r1.spid = r2.spid
    and r1.kpid = r2.kpid
where r1.sample = 1
and r2.sample = 2
and (r2.cpu - r1.cpu) > 0
order by (r2.cpu - r1.cpu) desc

select spid, hostname, program_name, nt_username
, sum(d_cpu_total) as sum_cpu
```

```
, sum(d_physical_io_total) as sum_io
from #Usage
group by spid, hostname, program_name, nt_username
order by 6 desc

drop table #resources
drop table #Usage
```

Who Is Waiting?

This query, which shows the tasks that are currently waiting, uses the same sampling principle as the preceding query:

```
select *
, 1 as sample
, getdate() as sample_time
into #waiting_tasks
from sys.dm_os_waiting_tasks

waitfor delay '00:00:10'

insert #waiting_tasks
select *
, 2
, getdate()
from sys.dm_os_waiting_tasks

-- figure out the deltas
select w1.session_id
, w1.exec_context_id
,w2.wait_duration_ms - w1.wait_duration_ms as d_wait_duration
, w1.wait_type
, w2.wait_type
, datediff(ms, w1.sample_time, w2.sample_time) as interval_ms
from #waiting_tasks as w1 inner join #waiting_tasks as w2 on w1.session_id =
w2.session_id
and w1.exec_context_id = w2.exec_context_id
where w1.sample = 1
and w2.sample = 2
order by 3 desc

-- select * from #waiting_tasks

drop table #waiting_tasks
```

Wait Stats

This query samples the wait stats to see what has changed over the sample period:

```
select *, 1 as sample, getdate() as sample_time
into #wait_stats
from sys.dm_os_wait_stats

waitfor delay '00:00:30'
```

```
insert #wait_stats
select *, 2, getdate()
from sys.dm_os_wait_stats

-- figure out the deltas

select w2.wait_type
,w2.waiting_tasks_count - w1.waiting_tasks_count as d_wtc
, w2.wait_time_ms - w1.wait_time_ms as d_wtm
, cast((w2.wait_time_ms - w1.wait_time_ms) as float) /
cast((w2.waiting_tasks_count - w1.waiting_tasks_count) as float) as avg_wtm
, datediff(ms, w1.sample_time, w2.sample_time) as interval
from #wait_stats as w1 inner join #wait_stats as w2 on w1.wait_type =
w2.wait_type
where w1.sample = 1
and w2.sample = 2
and w2.wait_time_ms - w1.wait_time_ms > 0
and w2.waiting_tasks_count - w1.waiting_tasks_count > 0
order by 3 desc

drop table #wait_stats
```

Viewing the Locking Information

The following query will help you get the locking information in a particular database:

```
SELECT l.resource_type, l.resource_associated_entity_id
,OBJECT_NAME(sp.OBJECT_ID) AS ObjectName
,l.request_status, l.request_mode,request_session_id
,l.resource_description
FROM sys.dm_tran_locks l
LEFT JOIN sys.partitions sp
 ON sp.hobt_id = l.resource_associated_entity_id
WHERE l.resource_database_id = DB_ID()
```

Viewing Blocking Information

The following query returns blocking information on your server:

```
SELECT
t1.resource_type
,t1.resource_database_id
,t1.resource_associated_entity_id
,OBJECT_NAME(sp.OBJECT_ID) AS ObjectName
,t1.request_mode
,t1.request_session_id
,t2.blocking_session_id
FROM sys.dm_tran_locks as t1
JOIN sys.dm_os_waiting_tasks as t2
  ON t1.lock_owner_address = t2.resource_address
LEFT JOIN sys.partitions sp
  ON sp.hobt_id = t1.resource_associated_entity_id
```

Index Usage in a Database

The following query will give you index usage for the database in which you run the query. It creates a table and stores the results in that table so you can analyze it later. This query can be very helpful for determining which indexes are truly useful in your application and which are not. If certain indexes are not used, then you should consider dropping them because they take unnecessary time to create or maintain. The results stored in the second table, NotUsedIndexes, indicate which indexes are not used. Make sure you run these queries for several days, which will give you a better idea of the overall picture than looking at data for just one day. Keep in mind that dynamic management views are volatile, and whenever SQL Server is restarted, these views are initialized again.

```
-----------------------------------------------------------------------
IF OBJECT_ID('dbo.IndexUsageStats') IS NULL
CREATE TABLE dbo.IndexUsageStats
(
 IndexName sysname NULL
,ObjectName sysname NOT NULL
,user_seeks bigint NOT NULL
,user_scans bigint NOT NULL
,user_lookups bigint NOT NULL
,user_updates bigint NOT NULL
,last_user_seek datetime NULL
,last_user_scan datetime NULL
,last_user_lookup datetime NULL
,last_user_update datetime NULL
,StatusDate datetime NOT NULL
,DatabaseName sysname NOT NULL
)

GO
----Below query will give you index USED per table in a database.
INSERT INTO dbo.IndexUsageStats
(
 IndexName
,ObjectName
,user_seeks
,user_scans
,user_lookups
,user_updates
,last_user_seek
,last_user_scan
,last_user_lookup
,last_user_update
,StatusDate
,DatabaseName
)
SELECT
 si.name AS IndexName
,so.name AS ObjectName
,diu.user_seeks
,diu.user_scans
,diu.user_lookups
,diu.user_updates
,diu.last_user_seek
```

```
,diu.last_user_scan
,diu.last_user_lookup
,diu.last_user_update
,GETDATE() AS StatusDate
,sd.name AS DatabaseName
FROM sys.dm_db_index_usage_stats  diu
JOIN sys.indexes si
  ON diu.object_id = si.object_id
 AND diu.index_id = si.index_id
JOIN sys.all_objects so
  ON so.object_id = si.object_id
JOIN sys.databases sd
  ON sd.database_id = diu.database_id
WHERE is_ms_shipped <> 1
  AND diu.database_id = DB_ID()


----------------------------------------------------------------------
--This will store the indexes which are not used.
IF OBJECT_ID('dbo.NotUsedIndexes') IS NULL
CREATE TABLE dbo.NotUsedIndexes
(
 IndexName sysname NULL
,ObjectName sysname NOT NULL
,StatusDate datetime NOT NULL
,DatabaseName sysname NOT NULL
)

----Below query will give you index which are NOT used per table in a database.
INSERT dbo.NotUsedIndexes
(
 IndexName
,ObjectName
,StatusDate
,DatabaseName
)
SELECT
 si.name AS IndexName
,so.name AS ObjectName
,GETDATE() AS  StatusDate
,DB_NAME()
FROM sys.indexes si
JOIN sys.all_objects so
  ON so.object_id = si.object_id
WHERE si.index_id NOT IN (SELECT index_id
                          FROM sys.dm_db_index_usage_stats diu
                          WHERE si.object_id = diu.object_id
                            AND si.index_id = diu.index_id
                          )
  AND so.is_ms_shipped <> 1
```

View Queries Waiting for Memory Grants

The following query will indicate the queries that are waiting for memory grants. SQL Server analyzes a query and determines how much memory it needs based on the estimated plan. If memory is not available at that time, the query is suspended until the memory required is available. If a query is waiting for a memory grant, an entry will show up in the DMV sys.dm_exec_query_memory_grants:

```
SELECT
 es.session_id AS SPID
,es.login_name
,es.host_name
,es.program_name, es.status AS Session_Status
,mg.requested_memory_kb
,DATEDIFF(mi, mg.request_time
, GETDATE()) AS [WaitingSince-InMins]
FROM sys.dm_exec_query_memory_grants mg
JOIN sys.dm_exec_sessions es
  ON es.session_id = mg.session_id
WHERE mg.grant_time IS NULL
ORDER BY mg.request_time
```

Connected User Information

The following query will tell you which users are connected, and how many sessions each of them has open:

```
SELECT login_name
, count(session_id) as session_count
FROM sys.dm_exec_sessions
GROUP BY login_name
```

Filegroup Free Space

The following T-SQL indicates how much free space remains in each filegroup. This is very valuable when your database uses multiple filegroups.

```
-- Find the total size of each Filegroup
select data_space_id, (sum(size)*8)/1000 as total_size_MB
into #filegroups
from sys.database_files
group by data_space_id
order by data_space_id

-- FInd how much we have allocated in each FG
select ds.name, au.data_space_id
, (sum(au.total_pages) * 8)/1000 as Allocated_MB
, (sum(au.used_pages) * 8)/1000 as used_MB
, (sum(au.data_pages) * 8)/1000 as Data_MB
, ((sum(au.total_pages) - sum(au.used_pages) ) * 8 )/1000 as Free_MB
into #Allocations
from sys.allocation_units as au inner join sys.data_spaces as ds
    on au.data_space_id = ds.data_space_id
group by ds.name, au.data_space_id
order by au.data_space_id
```

```
-- Bring it all together
select f.data_space_id
, a.name
, f.total_size_MB
, a.allocated_MB
, f.total_size_MB - a.allocated_MB as free_in_fg_MB
, a.used_MB
, a.data_MB
, a.Free_MB
from #filegroups as f inner join #allocations as a
on f.data_space_id = a.data_space_id
order by f.data_space_id

drop table #allocations

drop table #filegroups
```

Query Plan and Query Text for Currently Running Queries

Use the following query to find out the query plan in XML and the query text for the currently running batch for a particular session. Make sure that you are using a grid to output the result in SQL Server Management Studio. When you get the result, you can click the link for the XML plan, which will open an XML editor inside Management Studio. If you want to look at the graphical query plan from this XML plan, save the XML plan with the .sqlplan extension and then open that file in SQL Server Management Studio, where you will see the graphical execution plan. Here is the query:

```
SELECT
 er.session_id
,es.login_name
,er.request_id
,er.start_time
,QueryPlan_XML = (SELECT query_plan FROM
sys.dm_exec_query_plan(er.plan_handle))
,SQLText = (SELECT Text FROM sys.dm_exec_sql_text(er.sql_handle))
FROM sys.dm_exec_requests er
JOIN sys.dm_exec_sessions es
  ON er.session_id = es.session_id
WHERE er.session_id >= 50
ORDER BY er.start_time ASC
```

Memory Usage

The following query will indicate the memory used, in KB, by each internal SQL Server component:

```
SELECT
 name
,type
,SUM(single_pages_kb + multi_pages_kb) AS MemoryUsedInKB
FROM sys.dm_os_memory_clerks
GROUP BY name, type
ORDER BY SUM(single_pages_kb + multi_pages_kb) DESC
```

Monitoring Logs

Another aspect of monitoring that is frequently overlooked is monitoring the various log files available. SQL Server writes its own error log, and then there are the Windows Event logs, and you may find events logged in the Application, Security, or System Event logs.

Traditionally, the SQL Server and Windows Event logs have been viewed separately. The SQL Server Management Studio Log File viewer enables you to combine both sets of logs into a combined view.

For SQL Server 2008, the Log File viewer has been revised and now includes a hierarchical view of events where appropriate.

Monitoring the SQL Server Error Log

The SQL Server Error log can contain a lot of very useful information. It is definitely the place to go looking for deadlock information once the relevant deadlock trace flags have been enabled.

Anytime a significant event issue occurs, the first place to search for additional information should be the SQL Server Error Log.

Monitoring the Windows Event Logs

Three Windows event logs may hold entries of relevance to a SQL Server event:

❑ Application event log

❑ Security event log

❑ System event log

These event logs should be another place that you go to look for information about any issues that arise with SQL Server.

Management Data Warehouse

New to SQL Server 2008 is the Management Data Warehouse and Data Collection. This is a new framework for data collection, storage, and reporting that for SQL Server 2008 will be the start of an entirely new architecture due to roll out over the next few releases of SQL Server.

For SQL Server 2008, you get the basics of Data Collection, a few Data Collection sets, the Management Data Warehouse, and some reports.

Now for some of the basic concepts:

❑ **Data provider:** A data provider is a source of data to be captured. SQL Server 2008 has four data providers:

   ❑ SQL Trace

   ❑ Performance Monitor Counters

❑ T-SQL

❑ Query Activity

❑ **Collection item:** A collection item is a specific item of data to be collected. This might be a single performance monitor counter, a SQL Trace event, or a T-SQL query of a DMV.

❑ **Collection set**: A collection set is a logical grouping of collection items that are collected together. This might be all the performance counters monitoring disk I/O, or all the SQL trace events to look for long-running queries.

❑ **Management Data Warehouse (MDW)**: The Management Data Warehouse is where the items in each collection set are stored. It is the repository of historical data that you have collected.

❑ **Target servers**: The target servers are the systems that you want to monitor. Ideally, the MDW should be on a separate server. If it's on one of the target servers, you run the risk of recording activity about the data collection, rather than the target server you are really interested in.

❑ **Data collection process**: Data collection is performed by a series of SQL Agent jobs running SSIS packages that perform the data collection. Data is then captured based on the schedule defined for each collection set. It is then cached and only written to the MDW when the current buffer is full. This helps optimize I/O to the MDW.

You should expect to consume between 200–400MB/day for each server being monitored. These figures come from using the basic set of data collection sets, with 200MB per day for an idle server and 400MB per day for a busy server.

System Data Collection Sets

Three system data collection sets ship with SQL Server 2008:

❑ **Disk Usage:** The Disk Usage system collector set collects disk usage performance counters. It is very helpful for monitoring disk usage. The collected data is cached, and then uploaded to the warehouse every six hours, where it is retained for 90 days.

❑ **Query Activity:** The Query Activity system collection set captures query activity on the target server. It collects data from the server every 15 minutes, and helps you identify the most interesting queries running on a server without having to run a Profiler trace. It captures the top three queries from several different resource usage categories.

❑ **Server Activity:** The Server Activity system collection set collects a set of performance counters. Wait Statistics, Scheduler, Performance Counters, and Memory counters are collected every 60 seconds. The active sessions and requests are collected every 10 seconds. The data is uploaded to the warehouse every five minutes and is deleted from the warehouse after 14 days.

Viewing Data Collected by the System Data Collection Sets

Along with the system data collection sets is a set of reports that displays the history collected in the Management Data Warehouse for each of these data collection sets. To access these reports in SQL Server Management Studio, open Object Explorer and select Management ⇨ Data Collection ⇨ System Data Collection Sets. Under the System Data Collection Sets node you will see the three system data collection sets listed. To see the reports, right-click on a data collection set node (e.g., Disk Usage), select the reports item from the menu, and then select Reports ⇨ Historical ⇨ Disk Usage Summary. Figure 13-15 shows this navigation path.

The Disk Usage report is displayed, showing the history of disk usage data stored in the Management Data Warehouse. It will look something like the report shown in Figure 13-16.

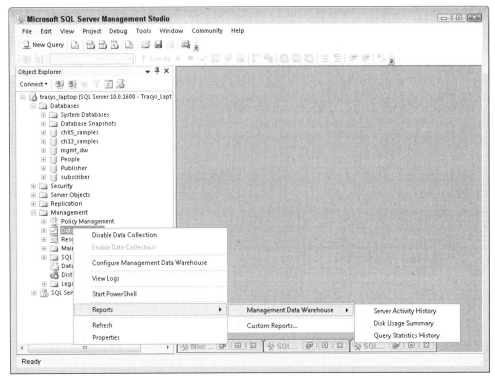

Figure 13-15

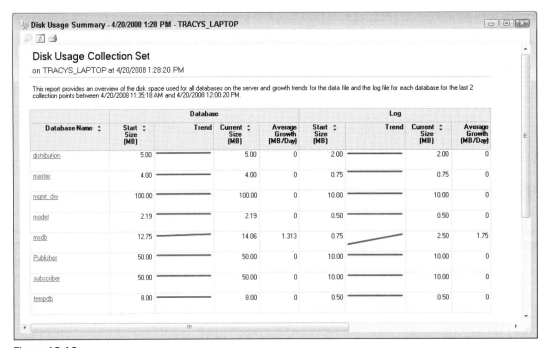

Figure 13-16

Click on a database name to see the detailed report for that database, as shown in Figure 13-17.

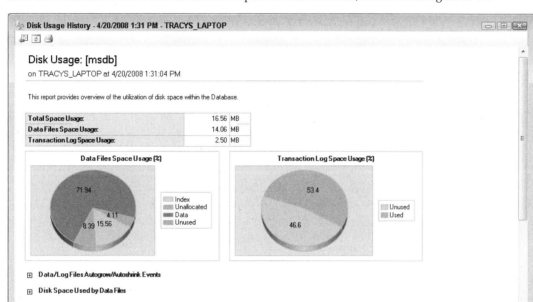

Figure 13-17

Creating Your Own Data Collection Set

After seeing the system data collection sets, the next step is to set up your own custom data collection sets. Currently, there is no wizard or easy user interface to handle this process, so you need to write T-SQL to execute the steps required. Fortunately, there are only a couple of simple steps. The hardest part is determining what data you want to collect, where it needs to come from, and what schedule you want to capture the data on.

For this example you are going to create a custom collection set to execute a T-SQL query that queries the max ID from an example table that has a high insertion rate. This information enables you to report on insertion rates over a period of time.

You first need to create the sample table, which can live in either an existing database or a new database that you create. In this example, the T-SQL to create a 50MB database in the default location is included with the table-creation code. The steps needed to complete this are described along with the code.

1.   Create the sample database and table:

```
CREATE DATABASE [ch13_samples] ON  PRIMARY
( NAME = N'ch13_samples'
, FILENAME = N'C:\Program Files\Microsoft SQL
  Server\MSSQL10.MSSQLSERVER\MSSQL\DATA\ch13_samples.mdf'
, SIZE = 51200KB
, MAXSIZE = UNLIMITED
, FILEGROWTH = 1024KB )
LOG ON
```

```
( NAME = N'ch13_samples_log'
, FILENAME = N'C:\Program Files\Microsoft SQL
Server\MSSQL10.MSSQLSERVER\MSSQL\DATA\ch13_samples_log.ldf'
, SIZE = 10240KB
, MAXSIZE = 2048GB
, FILEGROWTH = 10%)
GO

create table Sales (
ID int identity (1,1) not null,
sku int not null,
quantity int not null
)
go

-- insert some sales
insert sales (sku, quantity) values (1,1)
```

2. Create the collection set to get the max (id) every hour, and keep this for 45 days in the Management Data Warehouse:

```
-- Create the collection set
-- Make sure this runs in msdb as thats where the DC SPs live.
use msdb
GO

-- Find the uid for the schedule we want to use which is every 60 minutes
declare @schedule_uid uniqueidentifier
select @schedule_uid = (select schedule_uid
  from sysschedules_localserver_view
    where name=N'CollectorSchedule_Every_60min')

-- Create a new custom collection set
declare @collection_set_id int
exec dbo.sp_syscollector_create_collection_set
    @name = N'Sample insertion rate',
    @schedule_uid = @schedule_uid,  -- 60 minutes
    @collection_mode = 1, -- Set collection mode to non cached,
ie collection and upload are on the same schedule
    @days_until_expiration = 45, -- Keep data for 45 days
    @description = N'Sample max(id) so we can
determine hourly insertion rates',
    @collection_set_id = @collection_set_id output

select @collection_set_id as collection_set_id

declare @paramters xml
declare @collection_item_id int
declare @collection_type_uid uniqueidentifier

-- Create the XML parameters for the collection item
select @paramters = convert(xml,
    N'<TSQLQueryCollector>
        <Query>
            <Value>select max(id) as max_id from sales</Value>
```

```
        <OutputTable>max_sales_id</OutputTable>
    </Query>
    <Databases>
        <Database>Ch13_samples</Database>
    </Databases>
</TSQLQueryCollector>')

-- Find the Collector type we want to use which is TSQL
select @collection_type_uid  = collector_type_uid
from syscollector_collector_types
where name = 'Generic T-SQL Query Collector Type'

-- Create the new collection item
exec dbo.sp_syscollector_create_collection_item
    @collection_set_id = @collection_set_id,
    @collector_type_uid = @Collection_type_uid,
    @name = 'Sales max ID',
    @frequency = 60,
    @parameters = @paramters,
    @collection_item_id = @collection_item_id output;

-- report the ID that just got created
select @collection_item_id as collection_item_id

-- start the collection set
exec dbo.sp_syscollector_start_collection_set
    @Collection_set_id = @collection_set_id
```

Now you have created a new custom snapshot that contains the max ID from the sales table, sampled over time. This will enable you to report on the growth of records in the sales table.

Examining the Data You Collected

The data collected is stored in the Management Data Warehouse. For the preceding example, there is now a new custom snapshot table created, called `custom_snapshots.max_sales_id`, as shown in Figure 13-18.

Note that the table you created has some additional columns, not defined in the data you selected for the snapshot. These are `database_name`, `collection_time`, and `snapshot_id`. In addition, the collection time is stored in a `datimeoffset` column. This is a new data type in SQL Server 2008, and when queried returns the date/time as a UTC time.

Here is the T-SQL to retrieve the data stored by the collection set you just created:

```
-- Find the data we recorded
-- Switch to the MDW
use mgmt_dw
go

-- Query the custom snapshot
select *
from custom_snapshots.max_sales_id
```

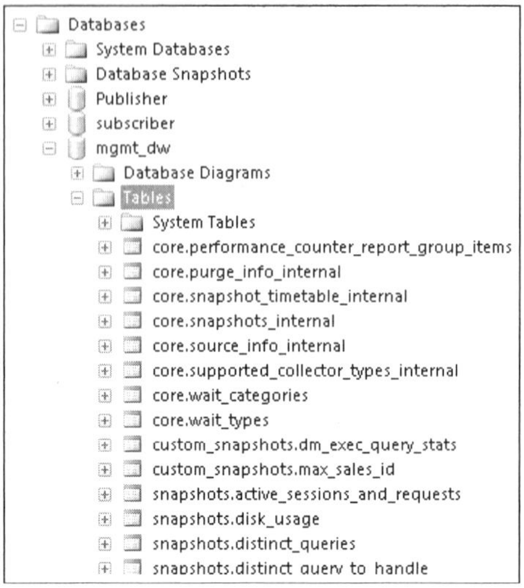

Figure 13-18

The following table shows the results of this query after the collector has been running for a few minutes with no inserts to the table.

max_id	database_name	collection_time	snapshot_id
1	Ch13_samples	9/23/2008 1:59:44 AM +00:00	93
1	Ch13_samples	9/23/2008 2:00:21 AM +00:00	97

To fully leverage the data stored in the Management Data Warehouse, consider creating SQL Server Reporting Services reports to display the data.

Summary

Monitoring SQL Server regularly and gathering the performance data is the key to identifying performance problems. In this chapter you have learned how to use Performance Monitor and which counters to monitor, as well as how to use SQL Profiler and SQL Trace to capture selected SQL Server events. You learned about the Default Trace, the different types of activity displayed by the Activity Monitor, and how to query dynamic management views. You also took a look at extended events, data collection, and the Management Data Warehouse. In the next chapter you will learn more about performance tuning T-SQL.

14

Performance Tuning T-SQL

Performance tuning T-SQL is very interesting, but also quite frequently frustrating. It is interesting because there is so much involved in tuning that a knowledge of the product's architecture and internals plays a very large role in doing it well. Of course, knowledge alone is not sufficient without the right tools, which you will learn about in this chapter. If you have tuned a query and reduced its runtime, you may have jumped up and down with excitement, but sometimes you cannot achieve that result even after losing sleep for many nights. In this chapter you will learn how to gather the data for query tuning, the tools for query tuning, the stages a query goes through before execution, and how to analyze the execution plan. It is very important to understand which stages a query passes through before actually being executed by the execution engine, so we'll start with physical query processing.

Physical Query Processing

SQL Server performs two main steps to produce the desired result when a query is fired. As you would guess, the first step is query compilation, which generates the query plan; and the second step is the execution of the query plan. The compilation phase in SQL Server 2008 goes through three steps: parsing, algebrization, and optimization. In SQL Server 2000, there was a *normalization* phase, which was replaced with the algebrization piece in SQL Server 2005. The SQL Server team has spent much effort to re-architect and rewrite several parts of SQL Server. Of course, the goal is to redesign logic to serve current and future expansions of SQL Server functionality. Having said that, after the three steps just mentioned are completed, the compiler stores the optimized query plan in the plan cache. The execution engine takes over after that; it copies the plan into its executable form and, of course, executes the steps in the query plan to produce the desired result. If the same query or stored procedure is executed again, the compilation phase is skipped and the execution engine uses the same cached plan to start the execution.

You can see this in action with an example. The goal is to determine whether the stored procedure plan is reused or not. The example also uses SQL Profiler and the dynamic management view (DMV) sys.dm_exec_cached_plans to examine some interesting details. In order to determine whether a compiled plan is reused or not, you have to monitor the events SP:CacheMiss,

`SP:CacheHit`, and `SP:CacheInsert` under the Stored Procedures event class. Figure 14-1 shows these stored procedure plan compilation events in SQL Profiler.

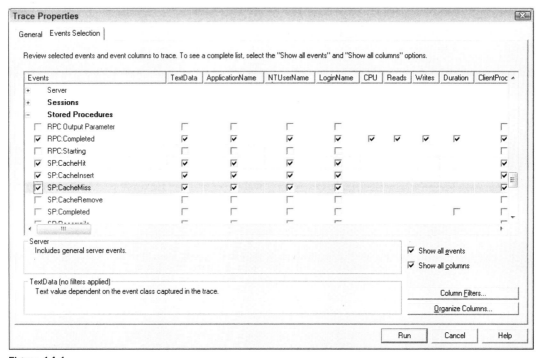

Figure 14-1

Download the sample code for this chapter from this book's Web page at `www.wrox.com`. Open the sample solution `QueryPlanReUse` and then open the script `ExecuteSP.sql`. Connect to the SQL Server on which you have the AdventureWorks2008 database.

> **Don't do this exercise on a production server!**

Compile the stored procedure `TestCacheReUse` in AdventureWorks2008. The code is as follows:

```
USE AdventureWorks2008
GO
IF OBJECT_ID('dbo.TestCacheReUse') IS NOT NULL
    DROP PROC dbo.TestCacheReUse
GO
CREATE PROC dbo.TestCacheReUse
AS

SELECT BusinessEntityID, LoginID, JobTitle
FROM HumanResources.Employee
```

```
WHERE BusinessEntityID = 109
GO
```

Connect the SQL Profiler to your designated machine and start it after selecting the events, as shown in Figure 14-1. Now execute the stored procedure `TestCacheReUse` as follows:

```
USE AdventureWorks2008
GO
EXEC dbo.TestCacheReUse
```

Note that in SQL Server Profiler you will find the `SP:CacheMiss` and `SP:CacheInsert` events, as shown in Figure 14-2

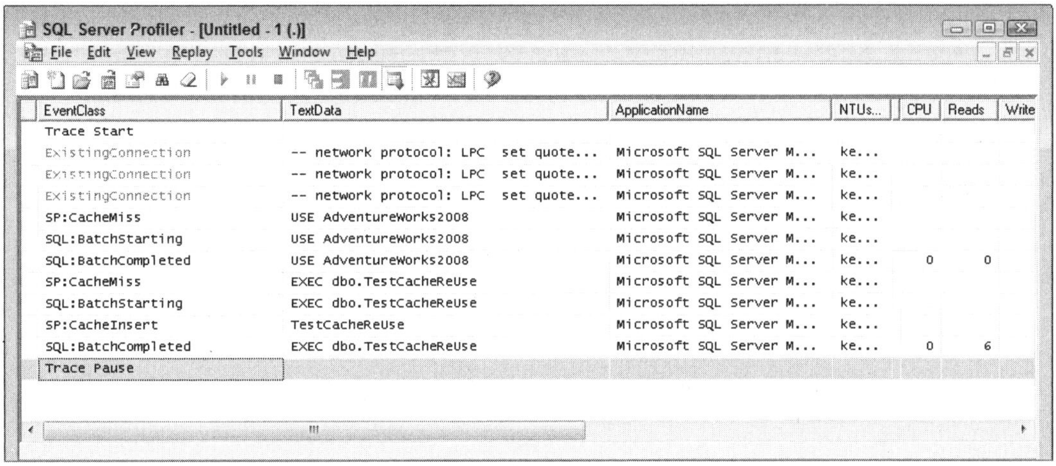

Figure 14-2

As shown in Figure 14-2, the `SP:CacheMiss` event indicates that the compiled plan is not found in the plan cache. The stored procedure plan is compiled and inserted into the plan cache indicated by `SP:CacheInsert`, and then the procedure `TestCacheReUse` is executed.

Execute the same procedure again. This time SQL Server 2008 finds the query plan in the plan cache, as shown in Figure 14-3.

As shown in Figure 14-3, the plan for the stored procedure `TestCacheReUse` was found in the plan cache, which is why you see the event `SP:CacheHit`.

The DMV `sys.dm_exec_cached_plans` also provides information about the plans that are currently cached, along with some other information. Open the script `DMV_cachePlanInfo.sql` from the solution `QueryPlanReUse`, shown here (note that the syntax in the following query is valid only when the database is in level 90 compatibility mode):

```
SELECT  bucketid, (SELECT Text FROM sys.dm_exec_sql_text(plan_handle)) AS
SQLStatement, usecounts
,size_in_bytes, refcounts
```

```
FROM sys.dm_exec_cached_plans
WHERE cacheobjtype = 'Compiled Plan'
  AND objtype = 'proc'
```

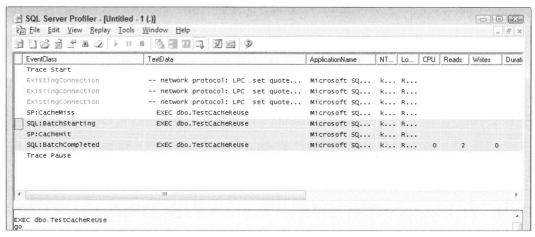

Figure 14-3

Run this script; you should see output similar to what is shown in Figure 14-4.

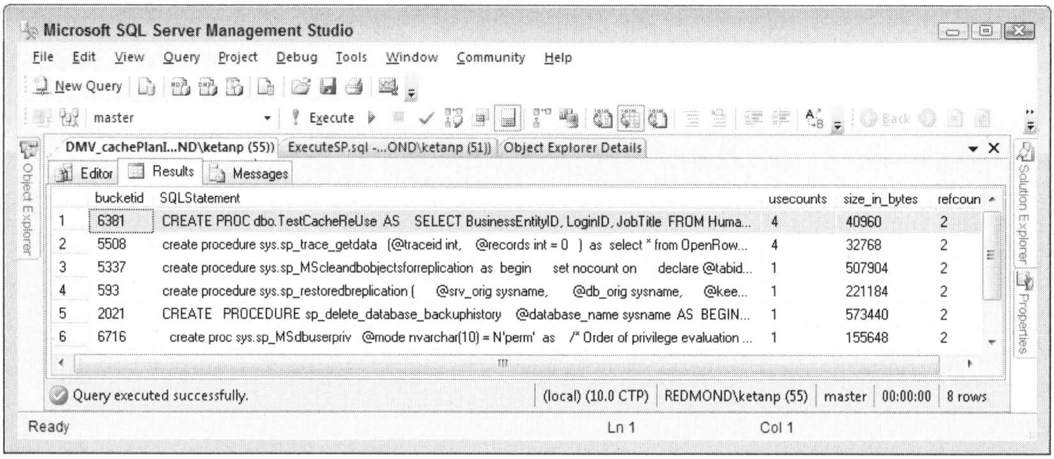

Figure 14-4

In this script, we used the dynamic management function (DMF) `sys.dm_exec_sql_text` to get the SQL text from `plan_handle`. In Figure 14-4, you can see that the compiled plan for the stored procedure `TestCacheReUse` that you executed earlier is cached. The column `UseCounts` in the output shows how many times this plan has been used since its inception. The first inception of the plan for this stored procedure was created when the `SP:CacheInsert` event happened, as shown in Figure 14-2. You can also see the number of bytes consumed by the cache object in Figure 14-4. In this case, the cache plan for the stored procedure `TestCacheReUse` has consumed 40KB in the plan cache. If you run `DBCC FREEPROCCACHE` now, and then run the query in the `DMV_cachePlanInfo.sql` script, you will notice that the rows returned are 0 because `DBCC FREEPROCCACHE` cleared the procedure cache.

If you use `WITH RECOMPILE` in the stored procedure `TestCacheReUse(CREATE PROC TestCacheReUse WITH RECOMPILE AS ... )` and run the stored procedure, the plan will not be cached in the procedure cache because you are telling SQL Server 2008 (with the `WITH RECOMPILE` option) not to cache a plan for the stored procedure, and to recompile the stored procedure every time you execute it. Use this option wisely, because compiling a stored procedure every time it executes can be very costly, and compilation eats many CPU cycles.

Compilation

As discussed earlier, before a query, batch, stored procedure, trigger, or dynamic SQL statement begins execution on SQL Server 2008, the batch is compiled into a plan. The plan is then executed for its effects or to produce results. The flowchart in Figure 14-5 displays the steps in the compilation process in SQL Server 2008.

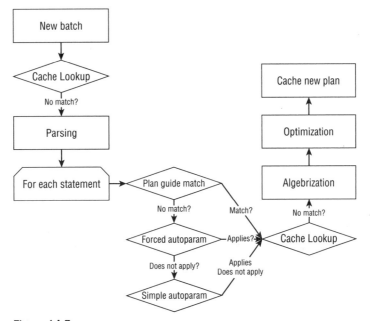

Figure 14-5

When a batch starts, the compilation process tries to find the cached plan in the plan cache. If it finds a match, the execution engine takes over. If a match is not found, the parser starts parsing (explained later in this section). The plan guide match feature (introduced with SQL Server 2005) determines whether an existing plan guide for a particular statement exists (you will learn how to create the plan guide later). If it exists, it uses the plan guide for that statement for execution. (The concepts of *forced autoparam* and *simple autoparam* are described later in the chapter.) If a match is found, the parse tree is sent to the algebrizer (explained later in this section), which creates a logical tree for input to the optimizer (also explained later in this section). The plan is then cached in the plan cache. Of course, not all the plans are cached; for example, when you create a stored procedure with WITH RECOMPILE, the plan is not cached.

Often, the cache plan needs to be recompiled because it is not valid for some reason. Suppose that a batch has been compiled into a collection of one or more query plans. SQL Server 2008 checks for validity (correctness) and optimality of that query plan before it begins executing any of the individual query plans. If one of the checks fails, the statement corresponding to the query plan or the entire batch is compiled again, and a possibly different query plan is produced. Such compilations are known as *recompilations*.

Note that when a batch is recompiled in SQL Server 2000, all of the statements in the batch are recompiled, not just the one that triggered the recompilation. In SQL Server 2005 or 2008, if a statement in a batch causes the recompilation, then only that statement is recompiled, not the whole batch. This *statement-level recompilation* has some advantages. In particular, it results in less CPU time and memory use during batch recompilations, and obtains fewer compile locks. In addition, if you have a long stored procedure, then you do not need to break it into small chunks just to reduce compile time (as you would probably do in SQL Server 2000).

Reasons for recompilation can be broadly classified in two categories:

- ❑ Correctness
- ❑ Plan optimality

Correctness

If the query processor decides that the cache plan would produce incorrect results, it will recompile that statement or batch. There are two possible reasons why the plan would produce incorrect results, related to schemas of objects and SET options.

Schemas of Objects

Your query batch could be referencing many objects such as tables, views, user-defined functions (UDFs), or indexes; and if the schemas of any of the objects referenced in the query has changed since your batch was last compiled, your batch must be recompiled for statement-correctness reasons. Schema changes could include many things, such as adding an index on a table or in an indexed view, or adding or dropping a column in a table or view.

In SQL Server 2005 or 2008, manually dropping or creating a statistic on a table causes recompilation. Manually updating statistics does not change the schema version. This means that queries that reference the table but do not use the updated statistics are not recompiled. Only queries that use the updated statistics are recompiled.

Batches with unqualified object names result in non-reuse of query plans. For example, in "SELECT * FROM MyTable", MyTable may legitimately resolve to Aish.MyTable if Aish issues this query and she owns a table with that name. Similarly, MyTable may resolve to Joe.MyTable. In such cases, SQL Server 2008 does not reuse query plans. If, however, Aish issues "SELECT * FROM dbo.MyTable", there is no ambiguity because the object is uniquely identified, and query plan reuse can happen. (See the uid column in sys.syscacheobjects. It indicates the user ID for the connection in which the plan was generated. Only query plans with the same user ID are candidates for reuse. When uid is set to -2, it means that the query does not depend on implicit name resolution, and can be shared among different user IDs.)

SET Options

Some of the SET options affect query results. If the setting of a SET option affecting plan reuse is changed inside of a batch, a recompilation happens. The SET options that affect plan reusability are ANSI_NULLS, ANSI_NULL_DFLT_ON, ANSI_PADDING, ANSI_WARNINGS, CURSOR_CLOSE_ON_COMMIT, IMPLICIT_TRANSACTIONS, and QUOTED_IDENTIFIER.

These SET options affect plan reuse because SQL Server performs *constant folding*, evaluating a constant expression at compile time to enable some optimizations, and because the settings of these options affect the results of such expressions.

> To avoid SET option–related recompilations, establish SET options at connection time, and ensure that they do not change for the duration of the connection.

The following example demonstrates how SET options cause recompilation. Open the script RecompileSetOption.sql from the solution QueryPlanReUse:

```
USE AdventureWorks2008
GO

IF OBJECT_ID('dbo.RecompileSetOption') IS NOT NULL
    DROP PROC dbo.RecompileSetOption
GO

CREATE PROC dbo.RecompileSetOption
AS
SET ANSI_NULLS OFF

SELECT s.CustomerID, COUNT(s.SalesOrderID)
FROM Sales.SalesOrderHeader s
GROUP BY s.CustomerID
HAVING COUNT(s.SalesOrderID) > 8
GO


EXEC dbo.RecompileSetOption      -- Causes a recompilation
GO
EXEC dbo.RecompileSetOption      -- does not cause a recompilation
GO
```

By default, the SET ANSI_NULLS option is ON, so when you compile this stored procedure it will compile with SET ANSI_NULLS ON. Inside the stored procedure, you have set ANSI_NULLS to OFF, so when you begin executing this stored procedure, the compiled plan is not valid and will recompile with SET ANSI_NULLS OFF. The second execution does not cause a recompilation because the cached plan is compiled with "ansi_nulls" set to OFF.

Plan Optimality

SQL Server 2008 is designed to generate the optimal query execution plan as data changes in your database. As you know, data distributions are tracked with statistics (histograms) in the SQL Server 2008 query processor. The table content changes because of INSERT, UPDATE, and DELETE operations. Table contents are tracked *directly* using the number of rows in the table (cardinality), and *indirectly* using statistics on table columns (we explain this in detail later in the chapter). The query processor checks the threshold to determine whether it should recompile the query plan or not, using the following formula:

```
[ Colmodctr (snapshot) - Colmodctr (current) ] >= RT
```

In SQL Server 2005 and 2008, the table modifications are tracked using `Colmodctr` (explained shortly). In SQL Server 2000, the counter was `Rowmodctr`. The `Colmodctr` is stored for each column, so changes to a table can be tracked with finer granularity in SQL Server 2005 and later. Note that `Rowmodctr` is available in SQL Server 2005 and later, but it is only there for backward compatibility.

In this formula, `colmodctr (snapshot)` is the value stored at the time the query plan was generated, and `colmodctr (current)` is the current value. If the difference between these counters as shown in the formula is greater or equal to RT (recompilation threshold), then recompilation happens for that statement. RT is calculated as follows for permanent and temporary tables. Note that n refers to a table's cardinality (the number of rows in the table) when a query plan is compiled.

For a permanent table, the formula is as follows:

```
If n <= 500, RT = 500
If n > 500, RT = 500 + 0.20 * n
```

For a temporary table, the formula is as follows:

```
If n < 6, RT = 6
If 6 <= n <= 500, RT = 500
If n > 500, RT = 500 + 0.20 * n
```

For a table variable, RT does not exist. Therefore, recompilations do not happen because of changes in cardinality to table variables. It is interesting to note that if you are using a table variable and you add a large number of rows, the query plan generated may be not optimal if you have already cached the plan before adding the large number of rows.

The following table shows how the `colmodctr` is modified in SQL Server 2005 and later because of different data manipulation language (DML) statements.

Statement	colmodctr
INSERT	All `colmodctr` + = 1 (`colmodctr` is incremented by 1 for each column in the table for each insert.)
DELETE	All `colmodctr` + = 1
UPDATE	If the update is to non-key columns, `colmodctr`+ = 1 for all of the updated columns. If the update is to key columns, `colmodctr`+ = 2 for all of the columns.
BULK INSERT	Like n INSERTs. All `colmodctr` + = n (n is the number of rows bulk inserted).
TABLE TRUNCATION	Like n DELETEs. All `colmodctr` + = n (n is the table's cardinality).

Tools and Commands for Recompilation Scenarios

You can use the following tools to observe or debug the recompilation-related events.

SQL Profiler

Capture the following events under the event classes `Stored Procedure` and `TSQL` to see the recompilation events. Be sure to select the column `EventSubClass` to view what caused the recompilation:

- ❑ `SP:Starting`
- ❑ `SP:StmtCompleted`
- ❑ `SP:Recompile`
- ❑ `SP:Completed`
- ❑ `SP:CacheInsert`
- ❑ `SP:CacheHit`
- ❑ `SP:CacheMiss`

You can also select the `AutoStats` event under the `Performance` event class to detect recompilations related to statistics updates.

Sys.syscacheobjects Virtual Table

Although this virtual table exists in the `resource` database, you can access it from any database. Note that the `resource` database was first introduced in SQL Server 2005. The `resource` database is a read-only database that contains all the system objects included with SQL Server 2008. SQL Server 2008 system objects, such as `sys.objects`, are physically persisted in the `resource` database, but they logically appear in the `sys` schema of every database. The `resource` database does not contain user data or user metadata.

The `cacheobjtype` column of this virtual table is particularly interesting. When `cacheobjtype` = `"Compiled Plan"`, the row refers to a query plan. When `cacheobjtype` = `"Executable Plan"`, the row refers to an execution context. Note that each execution context must have its associated query plan, but not vice versa. The `objtype` column indicates the type of object whose plan is cached (e.g., `"proc"` or `"Adhoc"`). The `setopts` column encodes a bitmap indicating the SET options that were in effect when the plan was compiled. Sometimes multiple copies of the same compiled plan (that differ in only their `setopts` columns) are cached in a plan cache. This indicates that different connections are using different sets of SET options (an undesirable situation). The `usecounts` column stores the number of times a cached object has been reused since the time the object was cached.

DBCC FREEPROCCACHE

The `DBCC FREEPROCCACHE` command clears the cached query plan and execution context. We recommend using this *only* in a development or test environment. Avoid running it in a production environment.

DBCC FLUSHPROCINDB (db_id)

The `DBCC FLUSHPROCINDB (db_id)` command is the same as `DBCC FREEPROCCACHE` except it clears only the cached plan for a given database. The recommendation for use is the same as `DBCC FREEPROCCACHE`.

Parser and Algebrizer

Parsing is the process of checking the syntax and transforming the SQL batch into a parse tree. Parsing includes, for example, whether a nondelimited column name starts with a digit or not. Parsing does not check whether the columns you have listed in a WHERE clause actually exist in any of the tables you have listed in the FROM clause. That is taken care of by the *binding* process (algebrizer). Parsing turns the SQL text into logical trees. One logical tree is created per query.

The *algebrizer* component was added in SQL Server 2005. This component replaced the *normalizer* in SQL Server 2000. The output of the parser — a parse tree — is the input to the algebrizer. The major function of the algebrizer is *binding*, so sometimes the entire algebrizer process is referred as *binding*. The binding process checks whether the semantics are correct. For example, if you are trying to JOIN table A with trigger T, then the binding process will error this out even though it may be parsed successfully. Other tasks performed by the algebrizer are covered in the following sections.

Name Resolution

The algebrizer performs the tasks of checking whether every object name in the query (the parse tree) actually refers to a valid table or column that exists in the system catalog, and whether it is visible in the query scope.

Type Derivation

The algebrizer determines the type for each node in the parse tree. For example, if you are issuing a UNION query, the algebrizer figures out the type derivation for the final data type. (The columns' data types could be different when you are unioning queries.)

Aggregate Binding

The algebrizer binds the aggregate to the host query and makes its decisions based on query syntax. Consider the following query in the AdventureWorks2008 database:

```
SELECT s.CustomerID
FROM Sales.SalesOrderHeader s
GROUP BY s.CustomerID
HAVING EXISTS(SELECT * FROM Sales.Customer c
WHERE c.TerritoryID > COUNT(s.SalesPersonID))
```

In this query, although the aggregation is done in the inner query that counts the ContactID, the actual operation of this aggregation is performed in the outer query.

For example, in the query plan shown in Figure 14-6, you can see that the aggregation is done on the result from the SalesOrderHeader table, although the aggregation is performed in the inner query. The outer query is converted something like this:

```
SELECT COUNT(s.SalesPersonID)
FROM Sales.SalesOrderHeader s
GROUP BY s.SalesPersonID
```

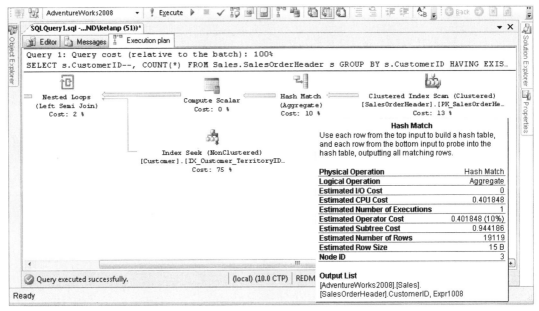

Figure 14-6

Grouping Binding

This is probably the obvious one. Consider this query:

```
SELECT s.CustomerID, SalesPersonID, COUNT(s.SalesOrderID)
FROM Sales.SalesOrderHeader s
GROUP BY s.CustomerID, s.SalesPersonID
```

If you do not add the CustomerID and SalesPersonID columns in the GROUP BY list, the query will error out. The grouped queries have different semantics than the nongrouped queries. All non-aggregated columns or expressions in the SELECT list of a query with GROUP BY must have a direct match in the GROUP BY list. The process of verifying this via the algebrizer is known as *grouping binding*.

Optimization

Optimization is probably the most complex and important piece to processing your queries. The logical tree created by the parser and algebrizer is the input to the optimizer. The optimizer needs the logical tree, metadata about objects involved in the query, such as columns, indexes, statistics, and constraints, and hardware information. The optimizer uses this information to create the compiled plan, which is made of physical operators. Note that the logical tree includes logical operators that describe *what to do*, such as "read table," "join," and so on. The physical operators produced by the optimizer specify algorithms that describe *how to do*, such as "index seek," "index scan," "hash join," and so on. The optimizer tells SQL Server 2008 how to exactly carry out the steps in order to get the results efficiently. Its job is to produce an efficient execution plan for each query in the batch or stored procedure. Figure 14-7 shows this process graphically.

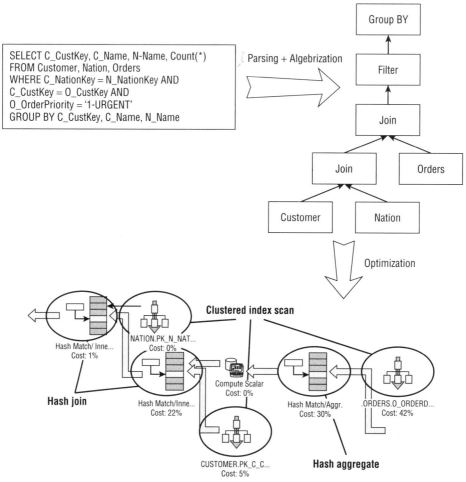

SELECT C_CustKey, C_Name, N-Name, Count(*)
FROM Customer, Nation, Orders
WHERE C_NationKey = N_NationKey AND
C_CustKey = O_CustKey AND
O_OrderPriority = '1-URGENT'
GROUP BY C_CustKey, C_Name, N_Name

Parsing + Algebrization

Group BY

Filter

Join

Join   Orders

Customer   Nation

Optimization

Clustered index scan

NATION.PK_N_NAT...
Cost: 0%

Hash Match/ Inne...
Cost: 1%

Hash join

Hash Match/Inne...
Cost: 22%

Compute Scalar
Cost: 0%

Hash Match/Aggr.
Cost: 30%

.ORDERS.O_ORDERD...
Cost: 42%

CUSTOMER.PK_C_C...
Cost: 5%

Hash aggregate

Figure 14-7

As shown in Figure 14-7, parsing and the algebrizer describe "what to do," and the optimizer describes "how to do it." SQL Server's query optimizer is a cost-based optimizer, which means it will create a plan with the least cost. Complex queries may have millions of possible execution plans, so the optimizer does not explore them all, but tries to find a plan that has a cost reasonably close to the theoretical minimum, because it has to come up with a good plan in a reasonable amount of time. Keep in mind that the lowest estimated cost doesn't mean the lowest resource cost. The optimizer chooses the plan to get the results quickly to the users. Suppose the optimizer chooses a parallel plan for your queries that uses multiple CPUs, which typically uses more resources than the serial plan but offers faster results. Of course, the optimizer cannot always come up with the best plan, which is why we have a job — for query tuning.

Optimization Flow

The flowchart in Figure 14-8 explains the steps involved in optimizing a query. These steps are simplified for explanation purposes. We don't mean to oversimplify the state-of-the-art optimization engine written by the SQL Server development team.

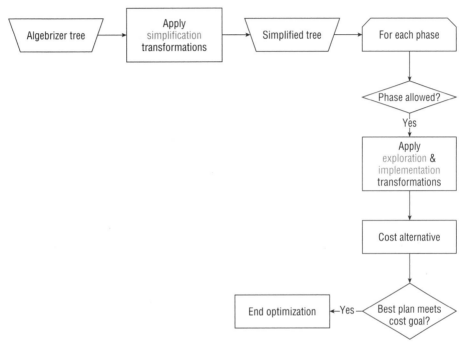

Figure 14-8

As shown in Figure 14-8, the input to the optimizer is a logical tree produced by the algebrizer. The query optimizer is a transformation-based engine. These transformations are applied to fragments of the query tree. Three kinds of transformation rules are applied: simplification, exploration, and implementation. The following sections discuss each of these transformations.

Simplification

The simplification process creates an output tree that is better than the input tree. For example, it might push the filter down in the tree, reduce the group by columns, or perform other transformations. Figure 14-9 shows an example of simplification transformation (filter pushing).

In Figure 14-9, you can see that the logical tree on the left has the filter after the join. The optimizer pushes the filter further down in the tree to filter the data out of the Orders table with a predicate on O_OrderPriority. This optimizes the query by performing the filtering early in the execution.

Figure 14-10 is another example of the simplification transformation (aggregate reduction). It includes reducing the number of group by columns in the execution plan.

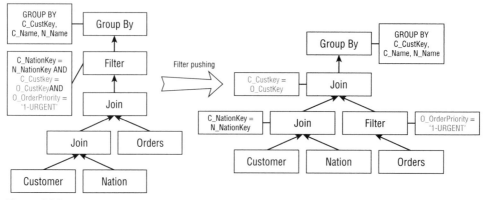

Figure 14-9

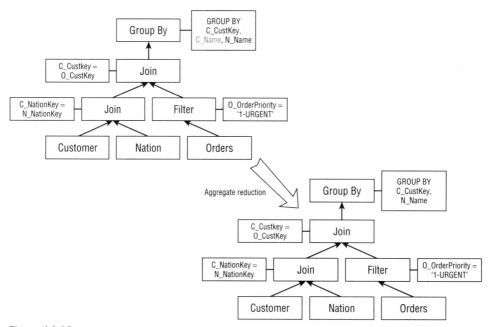

Figure 14-10

Figure 14-10 shows that the C_Name column is removed from the Group By clause because it contains the column C_Custkey (refer to Figure 14-7 for the T-SQL statement), which is unique on the Customer table, so there is no need to include the C_Name column in the Group By clause. That's exactly what the optimizer does.

Exploration

As mentioned previously, SQL Server uses a cost-based optimizer implementation. Therefore, the optimizer will look at alternative options to come up with the cheapest plan (see Figure 14-11). It makes a global choice using the estimated cost.

Figure 14-11

The optimizer explores the options related to which table should be used for inner versus outer. This is not a simple determination because it depends on many things, such as the size of the table, the available indices, and operators higher in the tree. It is not a clear choice like the examples you saw in the simplification transformation.

Implementation

The third transformation is implementation. Refer to Figure 14-12 for an example.

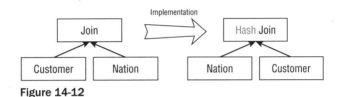

Figure 14-12

As explained earlier, the implantation transforms the "what to do" part into the "how to do" part. In this example, the JOIN logical operation is transformed into a HASH JOIN physical operation. The query cost is derived from physical operators based on model-of-execution algorithms (I/O and CPU) and estimations of data distribution, data properties, and size. Needless to say, the cost also depends on hardware such as the number of CPUs and the amount of memory available at the time of optimization.

Refer back to Figure 14-8. If the optimizer compared the cost of every valid plan and chose the least costly one, the optimization process could take a very long time, and the number of valid plans could be huge. Therefore, the optimization process is divided into three *search phases*. As discussed earlier, a set of transformation rules is associated with each phase. After each phase, SQL Server 2008 evaluates the cost of the cheapest query plan to that point. If the plan is cheap enough, then the optimizer stops there and chooses that query plan. If the plan is not cheap enough, the optimizer runs through the next phase, which has an additional set of rules that are more complex.

The first phase of the cost-based optimization, Phase 0, contains a limited set of rules. These rules are applied to queries with at least four tables. Because JOIN reordering alone generates many valid plans, the optimizer uses a limited number of join orders in Phase 0 and it considers only hash and loop joins in this phase. In other words, if this phase finds a plan with an estimated cost below 0.2 (internal cost unit), the optimization ends there.

The second phase, Phase 1, uses more transformation rules and different join orders. The best plan that costs less than 1.0 would cause optimization to stop in this phase. Note that until Phase 1, the plans are nonparallel (serial query plans). What if you have more than one CPU in your system? In that case, if the cost of the plan produced in Phase 1 is more than the *cost threshold for parallelism* (see sp_configure for this parameter; the default value is 5), then Phase 1 is repeated to find the best parallel plan. Then the cost of the serial plan produced earlier is compared with the new parallel plan, and the next phase, Phase 2 (the full optimization phase), is executed for the cheaper of the two plans.

Tuning Process

There is always room for tuning, but it is very important that you have enough data to start with. Therefore, you need to take a baseline of the system's performance and compare against that baseline so that you know where to start. Chapter 13 has details on getting the baseline. Just because a process is slow doesn't mean that you have to start tuning SQL statements. There are many basic things you need to do first, such as configure the SQL Server 2008 database, and make sure `tempdb` and the log files are on their own drives. It is very important to get the server configuration correct. See Chapters 11 and 12 for details about configuring your server and database for optimal performance. There is also a white paper on `tempdb` that we recommend you read as well. This document is for SQL Server 2005, but it's useful for SQL Server 2008 as well: `www.microsoft.com/technet/prodtechnol/sql/2005/workingwithtempdb.mspx`.

Don't overlook the obvious. For example, suppose you notice that performance is suddenly pretty bad on your server. If you have done a baseline and that doesn't show much change in performance, then it is unlikely that the sudden performance change was caused by an application in most cases, unless a new patch for your application caused some performance changes. In that case, look at your server configuration and see if that changed recently. Sometimes you merely run out of disk space, especially on drives where your page files reside, and that will bring the server to its knees.

We assume here that you already know what clustered and nonclustered indexes are, including how they work and how they are physically structured, and what a heap is.

Database I/O Information

Normally, an enterprise application has one or two databases residing on the server, in which case you would know that you have to look into queries against those databases. However, if you have many databases on the server and you are not sure which database is causing a lot of I/O and may be responsible for a performance issue, you have to look at the I/O activities against the database and find out which causes the most I/O and stalls on I/O. The DMF called `sys.dm_io_virtual_file_stats` comes in handy for this purpose.

You can use the following script to find out this information. The script is provided in the subfolder `DatabaseIO` in the sample folder for this chapter, which you can download from this book's Web site at `www.wrox.com`.

```
-- Database IO analysis.
WITH IOFORDATABASE AS
(
SELECT
 DB_NAME(VFS.database_id) AS DatabaseName
,CASE WHEN smf.type = 1 THEN 'LOG_FILE' ELSE 'DATA_FILE' END AS DatabaseFile_Type
,SUM(VFS.num_of_bytes_written) AS IO_Write
,SUM(VFS.num_of_bytes_read) AS IO_Read
,SUM(VFS.num_of_bytes_read + VFS.num_of_bytes_written) AS Total_IO
,SUM(VFS.io_stall) AS IO_STALL
FROM sys.dm_io_virtual_file_stats(NULL, NULL) AS VFS
JOIN sys.master_files AS smf
```

```
    ON VFS.database_id = smf.database_id
   AND VFS.file_id = smf.file_id
GROUP BY
 DB_NAME(VFS.database_id)
,smf.type
)
SELECT
 ROW_NUMBER() OVER(ORDER BY io_stall DESC) AS RowNumber
,DatabaseName
,DatabaseFile_Type
,CAST(1.0 * IO_Read/ (1024 * 1024) AS DECIMAL(12, 2)) AS IO_Read_MB
,CAST(1.0 * IO_Write/ (1024 * 1024) AS DECIMAL(12, 2)) AS IO_Write_MB
,CAST(1. * Total_IO / (1024 * 1024) AS DECIMAL(12, 2)) AS IO_TOTAL_MB
,CAST(IO_STALL / 1000. AS DECIMAL(12, 2)) AS IO_STALL_Seconds
,CAST(100. * IO_STALL / SUM(IO_STALL) OVER() AS DECIMAL(10, 2)) AS IO_STALL_Pct
FROM IOFORDATABASE
ORDER BY IO_STALL_Seconds DESC
```

Figure 14-13 shows sample output from this script.

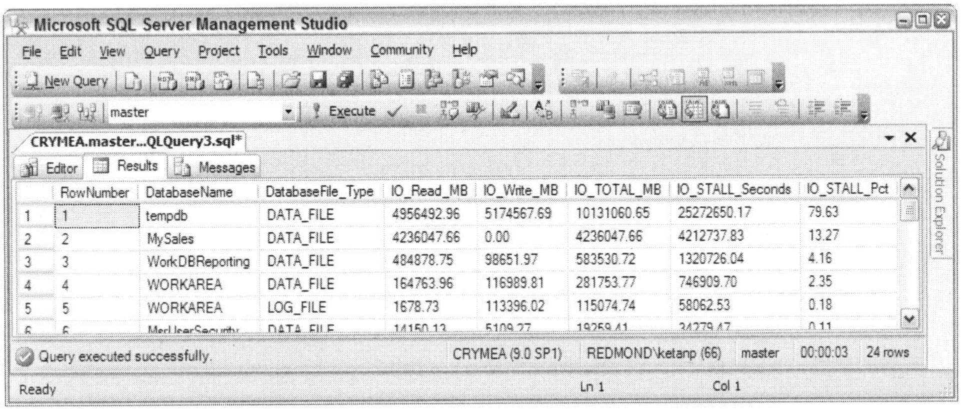

Figure 14-13

Keep in mind that the counters show the value from the time the instance of SQL Server is started, but it gives you a good idea of which database is getting hammered. In this example, you can see that tempdb is being hit hard, but that is not your primary application database, so look at the following row and you'll see that the MySales database is next. It's likely that queries against the MySales database are causing the heavy tempdb usage. This query will give you a good starting point to further investigate the process level (stored procedures, ad-hoc T-SQL statements, etc.) for the database in question.

Next you will look at how to gather the query plan and analyze it. You will also learn about the different tools you need in this process.

Working with the Query Plan

Looking at the query plan is the first step to take in the process of query tuning. The SQL Server query plan comes in different flavors: textual, graphical, and, with SQL Server 2008, XML format. *Showplan* is the term used to describe any of these query plan flavors. Different types of Showplans have different information. SQL Server 2008 can produce a plan with operators only, with cost information, and with XML format some additional runtime details. The following table summarizes the various Showplan formats.

Plan Contents	Text Format	Graphical Format	XML Format
Operators	`SET SHOWPLAN_TEXT ON`	N/A	N/A
Operators and estimated costs	`SET SHOWPLAN_ALL ON`	Displays the estimated execution plan in SQL Server Management Studio	`SET SHOWPLAN_XML ON`
Operators + estimated cardinalities and costs + runtime information	`SET STATISTICS PROFILE ON`	Displays the actual execution plan in SQL Server Management Studio	`SET STATISTICS XML ON`

Estimated Execution Plan

This section describes how to get the *estimated* execution plan. In the next section you will learn how to get the *actual* execution plan. There are five ways you can get the estimated execution plan: SET SHOWPLAN_TEXT, SET SHOWPLAN_ALL, SET SHOWPLAN_XML, a graphical estimated execution plan using SQL Server Management Studio (now on SSMS), and SQL Trace. The SQL Trace option is covered in a separate section at the end of the chapter; the other options are described in the following sections.

SET SHOWPLAN_TEXT and SET SHOWPLAN_ALL

We start with a simple query to demonstrate how to read the query plan. Open the script SimpleQueryPlan.sql from the Queryplans solution in the sample folder for this chapter. The code for the query is shown here:

```
USE AdventureWorks2008
GO
SET SHOWPLAN_TEXT ON
GO
SELECT sh.CustomerID, st.Name, SUM(sh.SubTotal) AS SubTotal
FROM Sales.SalesOrderHeader sh
JOIN Sales.Customer c
  ON c.CustomerID = sh.CustomerID
JOIN Sales.SalesTerritory st
  ON st.TerritoryID = c.TerritoryID
GROUP BY sh.CustomerID, st.Name
HAVING SUM(sh.SubTotal) > 2000.00
GO
SET SHOWPLAN_TEXT OFF
GO
```

When you SET the SHOWPLAN_TEXT ON, the query will not be executed; it just produces the estimated plan. The textual plan is shown here.

The output tells you that there are seven operators: Filter, Hash Match (Inner Join), Hash Match (Aggregate), Clustered Index Scan, Merge Join, Clustered Index Scan, and Index Scan. They are shown in bold in the query plan.

```
StmtText
----------------------------------------------------------------------------
|--Filter(WHERE:([Expr1006]>(2000.00)))
       |--Hash Match(Inner Join,
HASH:([sh].[CustomerID])=([c].[CustomerID]))
              |--Hash Match(Aggregate, HASH:([sh].[CustomerID])
DEFINE:([Expr1006]=SUM(
                     [AdventureWorks2008].[Sales].[SalesOrderHeader].[SubTotal] as
                     [sh].[SubTotal])))
              |     |--Clustered Index Scan(OBJECT:(
                     [AdventureWorks2008].[Sales].[SalesOrderHeader].
                     [PK_SalesOrderHeader_SalesOrderID] AS [sh]))
              |--Merge Join(Inner Join,
MERGE:([st].[TerritoryID])=([c].[TerritoryID]),

RESIDUAL:([AdventureWorks2008].[Sales].[SalesTerritory].[TerritoryID] as

[st].[TerritoryID]=[AdventureWorks2008].[Sales].[Customer].[Territory
ID] as
                     [c].[TerritoryID]))
                  |--Clustered Index Scan(OBJECT:(
                     [AdventureWorks2008].[Sales].[SalesTerritory].
                     [PK_SalesTerritory_TerritoryID] AS [st]), ORDERED FORWARD)
                  |--Index Scan(OBJECT:(
                     [AdventureWorks2008].[Sales].[Customer].
                     [IX_Customer_TerritoryID] AS [c]), ORDERED FORWARD)
```

I suggest that you use SSMS to view the plan output because the formatting here doesn't look that good. You can run this query in the AdventureWorks2008 database. Note that in this plan all you have is operators' names and their basic arguments. For more details on the query plan, other options are available, which we will explore soon.

To analyze the plan you read branches in *inner levels* before outer ones (bottom to top), and branches that appear in the *same level* from top to bottom. You can tell which branches are inner and which are outer based on the position of the pipe (|) character. When the plan is executed, the general flow of the rows is from the top down and from right to left. An operator with more indentation produces rows consumed by an operator with less indentation, and it produces rows for the next operator above, and so forth. For the JOIN operators, there are two input operators at the same level to the right of the JOIN operator, denoting the two row sets. The higher of the two (in this case, Clustered Index Scan on the object Sales.SalesTerritory) is referred to as the *outer table* (so Sales.SalesTerritory is the outer table) and the lower (Index Scan on the object Sales.Customer) is the *inner table*. The operation on the outer table is initiated first, and the one on the inner table is repeatedly executed for each row of the outer table that arrives to the join operator. Please note that the join algorithms are explained in detail later.

Now you can analyze the plan for the query. As shown in the plan, the hash match (inner join) operation has two levels: hash match (aggregate) and merge join. Now look at the merge join. The merge join has two levels: The first is the clustered index scan on Sales.Territory, and the index scanned on this object is PK_SalesTerritory_TerritoryID. We will cover index access methods in more detail a little later in the chapter. That is the outer table for the merge join. The inner table `Sales.Customer` is scanned only once because of the merge join, and that physical operation is done using an index scan on index `IX_Customer_TerritoryID` on the `sales.Customer` table. The merge join is on the `TerritoryID`, as per the plan `Merge Join(Inner Join, MERGE:([st].[TerritoryID]) = ([c].[TerritoryID])`. Because the `RESIDUAL` predicate is present in the merge join, all rows that satisfy the merge predicate evaluate the residual predicate, and only those rows that satisfy it are returned.

Now the result of this merge join becomes the inner table for hash match (inner join): `Hash Match (Inner Join, HASH:([sh].[CustomerID]) = ([c].[CustomerID]))`. The outer table is the result of `Hash Match (Aggregate)`. You can see that the `CustomerID` is the hash key (`HASH:([sh].[CustomerID]`) in the hash aggregate operation. Therefore, the aggregation is performed and, as per the query, the `SUM` operation is done on the column `SubTotal` from the `Sales.SalesOrderHeader` table (defined by the `DEFINE:([Expr1006]`). Now the `Hash Match (Inner join)` operation is performed on `CustomerID` (the result of the merge join) repeatedly for each row from the outer table (the result of `hash match [aggregate]`). Finally, the filter is applied on column SubTotal using the filter physical operator with the predicate (`WHERE:([Expr1006]>(2000.00))`) to only get rows with SubTotal > 2000.00.

> *The merge join itself is very fast, but it can be an expensive choice if sort operations are required. However, if the data volume is large and the desired data can be obtained presorted from existing B-tree indexes,* `Merge Join` *is often the fastest available join algorithm. In addition,* `Merge Join` *performance can vary a lot based on one-to-many or many-to-many joins.*

In the query file, we have set the `SET SHOWPLAN_TEXT OFF` following the query. This is because `SET SHOWPLAN_TEXT ON` is not only causing the query plan to show up, it is also turning off the query execution for the connection. The query execution will be turned off for this connection until you execute `SET SHOWPLAN_TEXT OFF` on the same connection. The `SET SHOWPLAN_ALL` command is similar to `SET SHOWPLAN_TEXT`. The only difference is the additional information about the query plan produced by `SET SHOWPLAN_ALL`. It adds the *estimated* number of rows produced by each operator in the query plan, the estimated CPU time, the estimated I/O time, and the total cost estimate that was used internally when comparing this plan to other possible plans.

SET SHOWPLAN_XML

The `SET SHOWPLAN_XML` feature was added in SQL Server 2005 to retrieve the Showplan in XML form. The output of the `SHOWPLAN_XML` is generated by a compilation of a batch, so it produces a single XML document for the whole batch. You can open the `ShowPlan_XML.sql` file from the solution `QueryPlans` to see how you can get the estimated plan in XML. The query is shown here:

```
USE AdventureWorks2008
GO
SET SHOWPLAN_XML ON
GO
SELECT sh.CustomerID, st.Name, SUM(sh.SubTotal) AS SubTotal
FROM Sales.SalesOrderHeader sh
JOIN Sales.Customer c
  ON c.CustomerID = sh.CustomerID
JOIN Sales.SalesTerritory st
  ON st.TerritoryID = c.TerritoryID
GROUP BY sh.CustomerID, st.Name
HAVING SUM(sh.SubTotal) > 2000.00
GO
```

```
SET SHOWPLAN_XML OFF
GO
```

When you run this query in Management Studio, you will see a link in the result tab. Clicking the link opens the XML document inside Management Studio. You can also save that document with the extension .sqlplan. When you open that file using Management Studio, you will get a graphical query plan. The graphical plan from the XML document generated by this query is shown in Figure 14-14.

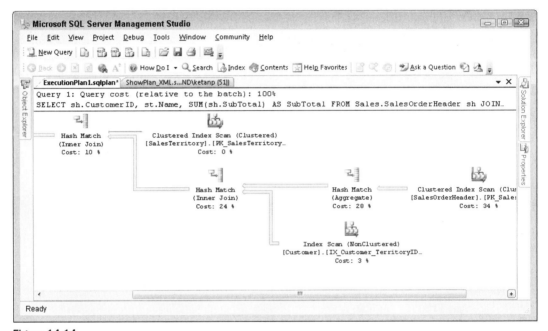

Figure 14-14

XML is the richest format of the Showplan. It contains some unique information not available in other Showplan formats. The XML Showplan contains the size of the plan in cache (the CachedPlanSize attributes), and parameter values for which the plan has been optimized (the Parameter sniffing element). When a stored procedure is compiled for the first time, the values of the parameters supplied with the execution call are used to optimize the statements within that stored procedure. This process is known as *parameter sniffing*. Also available is some runtime information, which is unique to the XML plan and is described further in the section "Actual Execution Plan" later in this chapter.

You can write code to parse and analyze the XML Showplan. This is probably the greatest advantage it offers, as this task is very hard to achieve with other forms of the Showplan.

Refer to the white paper at http://msdn.microsoft.com/en-us/library/ms345130.aspx for information on how you can extract the estimated execution cost of a query from its XML Showplan using CLR functions. You can use this technique to ensure that users can submit only those queries costing less than a predetermined threshold to a server running SQL Server, thereby ensuring it is not overloaded with costly, long-running queries.

Graphical Estimated Showplan

You can view a graphical estimated plan in Management Studio. To access the plan, either use the shortcut key Ctrl+L or select Query ⇨ Display Estimated Execution plan. You can also select the button indicated in Figure 14-15.

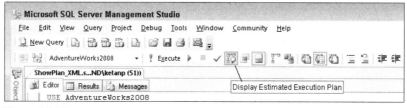

Figure 14-15

If you use any of these options to display the graphical estimated query plan, it will display the plan as soon as compilation is completed because compilation complexity can vary according to the number and size of the tables. Right-clicking the graphical plan area in the Execution Plan tab reveals different zoom options and properties for the graphical plan.

Actual Execution Plan

This section describes the options you can use to get the actual execution plan (SET STATISTICS XML ON|OFF, SET STATISTICS PROFILE ON|OFF) using the graphical actual execution plan option in Management Studio. You can get the actual execution plan using SQL Trace as well; see the section "Gathering Query Plans for Analysis with SQL Trace" later in this chapter.

SET STATISTICS XML ON|OFF

There are two kinds of runtime information in the XML Showplan: *per SQL statement* and *per thread*. If a statement has a parameter, the plan contains the parameterRuntimeValue attribute, which shows the value of each parameter when the statement was executed. The degreeOfParallelism attribute shows the actual degree of parallelism. The degree of parallelism shows the number of concurrent threads working on the single query. The compile time value for degree of parallelism is always half the number of CPUs available to SQL Server unless there are two CPUs in the system. In that case, the value will be 2 as well.

The XML plan may also contain warnings. These are events generated during compilation or execution time. For example, missing statistics are a compiler-generated event. One important feature in SQL Server 2008 (originally added in SQL Server 2005) is the USE PLAN hint. This feature requires the plan hint in XML format so you can use the XML Showplan. Using the USE PLAN hint, you can force the query to be executed using a certain plan. For example, suppose you found out that a query was running slowly in the production environment but faster in the pre-production environment. You also found out that the plan generated in the production environment is not optimal for some reason. In that case, you can use the better plan generated in the pre-production environment and force that plan in the production environment using the USE PLAN hint. For more details on how to implement it, please refer to the Books Online (BOL) topic "Using the USE PLAN Query Hint."

SET STATISTICS PROFILE ON|OFF

We like the SET STATISTICS PROFILE ON|OFF option better than the previous option, and we always use it for query analysis and tuning. Run the query from earlier, using the script Statistics_Profile.sql in the QueryPlans solution. The code is shown here. If you don't want to mess with your Adventure-Works2008 database, you can back up and restore the AdventureWorks2008 database with a different name. If you do that, be sure to change the USE *DatabaseName* line in the script. Here is the code:

```
USE AdventureWorks2008
GO
SET STATISTICS PROFILE ON
GO
SELECT p.name AS ProdName, c.TerritoryID, SUM(od.OrderQty)
FROM Sales.SalesOrderDetail od
JOIN Production.Product p
  ON p.ProductID = od.ProductID
JOIN Sales.SalesOrderHeader oh
  ON oh.SalesOrderID = od.SalesOrderID
JOIN Sales.Customer c
  ON c.CustomerID = oh.CustomerID
WHERE OrderDate >= '2004-06-09'
  AND OrderDate <= '2004-06-11'
GROUP BY p.name, c.TerritoryID
GO
SET STATISTICS PROFILE OFF
```

After you run the query you will get output similar to what is shown in Figure 14-16.

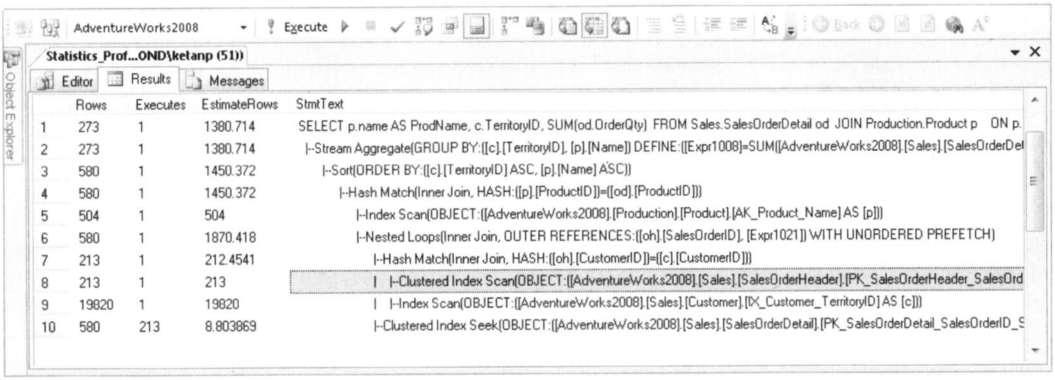

Figure 14-16

The four most important columns in the output of SET STATISTICS PROFILE are Rows, EstimateRows, Executes, and, of course, the StmtText. The Rows column contains the number of rows actually returned by each operator. Now read the plan. We can't fit the whole plan on the page, so run this query on your test machine and look at the output on your screen as you follow along. Start from the inner level, bottom to top. Look at lines (or row numbers) 8 and 9. They are at the same level as the hash match (line 7), so line 8 is the clustered index scan on index `PK_SalesOrderHeader_SalesOrderID` on the table `SalesOrderHeader`. This is outer table for the hash match. It scans the clustered index in range, as shown here, although you can't see the entire example in Figure 14-16:

```
WHERE:([AdventureWorks2008].[Sales].[SalesOrderHeader].[OrderDate] as
[oh].[OrderDate]>='2004-06-09 00:00:00.000' AND
[AdventureWorks2008].[Sales].[SalesOrderHeader].[OrderDate] as [oh].[OrderDate]<=
'2004-
06-11 00:00:00.000'))
```

The entire table is scanned for the `WHERE` clause on the `OrderDate` column. The estimated rows from this operator are 213, which shows in the `EstimatedRows` column. The output of this operator are the `SalesOrderID` and `CustomerID` columns (not shown in Figure 14-16). Notice that the smaller table (`SalesOrderHeader` — the table itself is not smaller, but because we have criteria on the `OrderDate` the result set is smaller) is on the outer side of the hash match because the hash key, `CustomerID` in this case, is stored in memory after that hash, and fewer hashes is better because it requires less memory. Therefore, if you see a hash join in your query and you notice that the outer side table's result set is bigger than the inside table, there may be some plan issue, the supporting indexes don't exist, or the statistics are outdated on these tables, which led the optimizer to estimate an incorrect number of rows. We will look at different index access methods and join algorithms a little later in the chapter.

Now the `Sales.Customer` table is scanned on the nonclustered index `IX_Customer_TerritoryID` for `CustomerID` (see line 9) for the hash match. Why does the optimizer choose the nonclustered index `IX_Customer_TerritoryID` on the `Sales.Customer` table for scanning `CustomerID` when it has a clustered index on `CustomerID`? Look at the query for this example. You have selected the `TerritoryID` column from the `Customer` table, and because the leaf level in the nonclustered index also has a clustering key (`CustomerID`) in this case, the nonclustered index `IX_Customer_TerritoryID` has necessary information (`TerritoryID` and `CustomerID`) at its leaf level for this query. Remember that the leaf level of a nonclustered index has fewer pages than a clustered index of leaf pages (because leaf pages of a clustered index hold the actual data row), so traversing the nonclustered index in this case would cause less I/O (because it needs to access fewer pages). As you can see, the hash match operation has produced 213 rows (see the `Rows` column for the actual rows produced).

Now let's move up. The hash match (line 7) and clustered index seek (line 10) are at the same level as the nested loop inner join (line 6). The result of the hash match physical operation was 213 rows and the output columns were `SalesOrderID` and `TerritoryID` (line 7). You have a join on the `Sales.SalesOrderDetail` table on the `SalesOrderID` column, so the `SalesOrderID` from the hash match operation is now the outer side of the nested loop join; and the clustered index seek on `PK_SalesOrderDetail_SalesOrderID_SalesOrderDetailID` in the `Sales.SalesOrderDetail` table is the inner side of the nested loop. The nested loop will look into the inner table for each row from the outer table. Therefore, for 213 `SalesOrderIDs` (the output of the hash match in line 7), there will be 213 clustered index seeks performed on the index `PK_SalesOrderDetail_SalesOrderID_SalesOrderDetailID`.

You can see that line 10 indicates 213 in the `Executes` column, which means that the clustered index on the `Sales.SalesOrderDetail` table was sought for 213 times, and 580 rows were qualified because of this operation (see the `Rows` column in line 10). As a result, the nested loop physical operation has produced 580 rows (see line 6).

Moving up again, the hash match operation (line 4) has two levels: the index scan on the Product table (line 5) and a nested loop (line 6). The unordered nonclustered index scan on the index AK_Product_Name on the Product table is performed and a hash key is created on the ProductID. Because the Product table has 504 rows, this operation produces 504 rows (see the Rows column in line 5). The inner table (the result of the nested loop join) is probed on the ProductID (remember that the OutputList of the nested loop operation produces columns [od].[OrderQty], [od].[ProductID], and [c].[TerritoryID]). Therefore, the result of the hash match operation is 580 rows (line 4).

Moving up, note the Sort operation in line 3. Why is sorting required when you have not asked for it? Because you asked for GROUP BY (a logical operation); and if the optimizer chooses the Stream Aggregate physical operation, then it requires the input to be sorted, which is why you are seeing the Sort operation. The sort is done on TerritoryID and Name in ascending order.

> Sort *is a STOP and GO operator. Nothing will come out (to left side of operator) of the* Sort *operator until all the input rows are processed, so* Sort *is usually slow. If you don't need sorted data, never add the* ORDER BY *clause. In this case, because we asked for* GROUP BY*, we get* ORDER BY *for free because of the stream aggregate, so the data is already sorted.*

Let's move up once again. In line 2, the stream aggregate operation is a result of GROUP BY. This operator removes duplicate rows. The number of rows produced by this operator is 273 (the Rows column in line 2). In other words, 307 duplicate rows (580 minus 273) were removed by this operation. In this stream aggregation, the physical operation is chosen by the optimizer. If the optimizer had chosen the hash aggregate option, the Sort operation would have been omitted because hash aggregation doesn't require sorted input. That's it — the result is returned.

Graphical Actual Execution Plan

You can use Management Studio to view the graphical actual execution plan. Again, either use the shortcut Ctrl+M, select Query ⇨ Include Actual Execution plan, or select the button indicated in Figure 14-17.

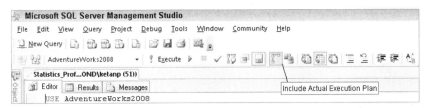

Figure 14-17

If you use any of these options to display the graphical actual query plan, nothing will happen. After query execution, the actual plan is displayed in a separate tab.

Join Algorithms

You saw earlier the different types of joins in the query plans. Here we discuss the physical strategies SQL Server 2008 can use to process joins. Before SQL Server 7.0, there was only one join algorithm, called *nested loops.* Since version 7.0, SQL Server 2008 supports *hash* and *merge join* algorithms. This section describes each of them and explains the conditions under which each provides better performance.

Nested Loop or Loop Join

The nested loop join, also called *nested iteration*, uses one join input as the outer input table (shown as the top input in the graphical execution plan; see Figure 14-18) and the other input as the inner (bottom) input table. The outer loop consumes the outer input table row by row. The inner loop, executed for each outer row, searches for matching rows in the inner input table. You can use the Join.sql script from the QueryPlans solution for the following exercises. The following query is an example that produces a nested loop join:

```
--Nested Loop Join

SELECT C.CustomerID, c.TerritoryID
FROM Sales.SalesOrderHeader oh
JOIN Sales.Customer c
  ON c.CustomerID = oh.CustomerID
WHERE c.CustomerID IN (10,12)
GROUP BY C.CustomerID, c.TerritoryID
```

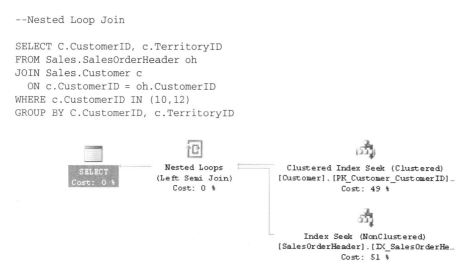

Figure 14-18

A nested loop join is particularly effective if the outer input is small and the inner input is preindexed and large. In many small transactions, such as those affecting only a small set of rows, indexed nested loop joins are superior to both merge joins and hash joins. In large queries, however, nested loop joins are often not the optimal choice. Of course, the presence of a nested loop join operator in the execution plan doesn't indicate whether it's an efficient plan or not. A nested loop join is the default algorithm, so it can always be applied if another algorithm does match the specific criteria. For example, the "requires join" algorithm must be *equijoin* (the join condition is based on the equality operator).

In the example query, a clustered index seek is performed on the outer table Customer for CustomerID 10 and 12, and for each CustomerID, an index seek is performed on the inner table SalesOrderHeader. Therefore, Index IX_SalesOrderHeader_CustomerID is sought two times (one time for CustomerID 10 and one time for CustomerID 12) on the SalesOrderHeader table.

Hash Join

The hash join has two inputs like every other join: the *build input* (outer table) and the *probe input* (inner table). The query optimizer assigns these roles so that the smaller of the two inputs is the build input. A variant of the hash join (hash aggregate physical operator) can do duplicate removal and grouping, such as SUM (OrderQty) GROUP BY TerritoryID. These modifications use only one input for both the build and probe roles.

The following query is an example of a hash join, and the graphical execution plan is shown in Figure 14-19:

```
--Hash Match

SELECT p.Name As ProductName, ps.Name As ProductSubcategoryName
FROM Production.Product p
JOIN Production.ProductSubcategory ps
  ON p.ProductSubcategoryID = ps.ProductSubcategoryID
ORDER BY p.Name,  ps.Name
```

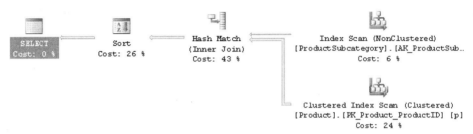

Figure 14-19

As discussed earlier, the hash join first scans or computes the entire build input and then builds a hash table in memory if it fits the memory grant (in Figure 14-19, it is the `Production.ProductSubCategory` table). Each row is inserted into a hash bucket according to the hash value computed for the hash key, so building the hash table needs memory. If the entire build input is smaller than the available memory, all rows can be inserted into the hash table (you will see what happens if there is not enough memory shortly). This build phase is followed by the probe phase. The entire probe input (in Figure 14-19, it is the `Production.Product` table) is scanned or computed one row at a time, and for each probe row (from the `Production.Product` table), the hash key's value is computed, the corresponding hash bucket (the one created from the `Production.ProductSubCategory` table) is scanned, and the matches are produced. This strategy is called an *in-memory hash join*.

If you're talking about the AdventureWorks2008 database running on your laptop with 1GB of RAM, you won't have the problem of not fitting the hash table in memory. In the real world, however, with millions of rows in a table, it's possible there won't be enough memory to fit the hash table. If the build input does not fit in memory, a hash join proceeds in several steps. This is known as a *grace hash join*. In this hash join strategy, each step has a build phase and a probe phase. Initially, the entire build and probe inputs are consumed and partitioned (using a hash function on the hash keys) into multiple files. Using the hash function on the hash keys guarantees that any two joining records must be in the same pair of files. Therefore, the task of joining two large inputs has been reduced to multiple, but smaller, instances of the same tasks. The hash join is then applied to each pair of partitioned files. If the input is so large that the preceding steps need to be performed many times, multiple partitioning steps and multiple partitioning levels are required. This hash strategy is called a *recursive hash join*.

SQL Server always starts with an in-memory hash join and changes to other strategies if necessary.

Recursive hash joins (or *hash bailouts*) cause reduced performance in your server. If you see many Hash Warning events in a trace (the Hash Warning event is under the Errors and Warnings event class), update statistics on the columns that are being joined. You should capture this event if you see that you have

581

many hash joins in your query. This will ensure that hash bailouts are not causing performance problems on your server. When good indexes on join columns are missing, the optimizer normally chooses the hash join.

Merge Join

The merge join relies on sorted input and is a very efficient algorithm if both inputs are available sorted (see Figure 14-20):

```
SELECT oh.SalesOrderID, oh.OrderDate, od.ProductID
FROM Sales.SalesOrderDetail od
JOIN Sales.SalesOrderHeader oh
  ON oh.SalesOrderID = od.SalesOrderID
```

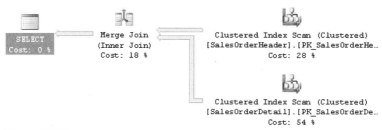

Figure 14-20

With a *one-to-many merge join*, a merge join operator scans each input only once, which is why it is superior to other operators if the predicate is not very selective. For sorted input, the optimizer can use a clustered index. If a nonclustered index is covering the join and select columns, the optimizer would probably choose that option because it has fewer pages to fetch.

A *many-to-many merge join* is little more complicated. A many-to-many merge join uses a temporary table to store rows. If there are duplicate values from each input, one of the inputs will have to rewind to the start of the duplicates as each duplicate from the other input is processed.

In this query, both tables have a clustered index on the SalesOrderID column, so the optimizer chooses a merge join. Sometimes the optimizer chooses the merge join, even if one of the inputs is not presorted by an index, by adding a sort to the plan. The optimizer would do that if the input were small. If the optimizer chooses to sort before the merge, check whether the input has many rows and is not presorted by an index. To prevent the sort, you have to add the required indexes to avoid a costly operation.

Index Access Methods

This section describes different index access methods. You can use this knowledge when you tune the query and decide whether it is using the correct index access method or not, and take the appropriate action.

In addition, you should make a copy (Backup and Restore) of the AdventureWorks2008 database on your machine so that if you drop or create indexes on it, the original AdventureWorks2008 database remains intact. When you restore the database, call it AdWork2 for these examples.

Table Scan

A table scan involves a sequential scan of all data pages belonging to the table. Run the following script in the AdWork2 database:

```
SELECT * INTO dbo.New_SalesOrderHeader
FROM Sales.SalesOrderHeader
```

After you run this script to make a copy of the SalesOrderHeader table, run the following script:

```
SELECT SalesOrderID, OrderDate, CustomerID
FROM dbo.New_SalesOrderHeader
```

Because this is a heap, this statement causes a table scan. If you want, you can always get the actual textual plan using SET STATISTICS PROFILE ON. Figure 14-21 displays the graphical plan.

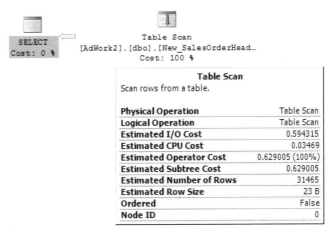

Table Scan	
Scan rows from a table.	
Physical Operation	Table Scan
Logical Operation	Table Scan
Estimated I/O Cost	0.594315
Estimated CPU Cost	0.03469
Estimated Operator Cost	0.629005 (100%)
Estimated Subtree Cost	0.629005
Estimated Number of Rows	31465
Estimated Row Size	23 B
Ordered	False
Node ID	0

Figure 14-21

In a table scan, SQL Server uses Index Allocation Map (IAM) pages to direct the disk arm to scan the extents belonging to the table according to their physical order on disk. As you might guess, the number of logical reads would be the same as the number of pages for this table.

SET STATISTICS IO ON|OFF

Let's look at the STATISTICS IO output for the example query. This is a session-level setting. STATISTICS IO provides you with I/O-related information for the statement you run.

SET STATISTICS IO *is set at runtime and not at parse time. This is an important tool in your query-tuning arsenal, as disk I/Os are normally a bottleneck on your system, so it is very important to identify how many I/Os your query generates and whether they are necessary or not.*

```
DBCC DROPCLEANBUFFERS
GO
SET STATISTICS IO ON
GO
```

```
SELECT SalesOrderID, OrderDate, CustomerID
FROM dbo.New_SalesOrderHeader
GO
SET STATISTICS IO OFF

Table 'New_SalesOrderHeader'. Scan count 1, logical reads 799, physical reads 0,
read-ahead reads 798, lob logical reads 0, lob physical reads 0, lob read-ahead
reads 0.
```

The scan count tells you how many times the table was accessed for this query. If you have multiple tables in your query, you will see statistics showing I/O information for each table. In this case, the New_SalesOrderHeader table was accessed once.

The logical reads counter indicates how many pages were read from the data cache. In this case, 799 reads were done from cache. Please note that the logical reads number may be a little different on your machine. As mentioned earlier, because of the whole table scan, the number of logical reads equals the number of pages allocated to this table. You can also run the following query to verify the number of pages allocated to the table. Note the resulting number in the dpages column:

```
SELECT dpages, *
FROM sys.sysindexes
WHERE ID = OBJECT_ID('New_SalesOrderHeader')
```

The physical reads counter indicates the number of pages read from the disk. It shows 0 for the preceding code. Does that mean that there were no physical reads from disk? No; keep reading.

The read-ahead reads counter indicates the number of pages from the physical disk that were placed into the internal data cache when SQL Server guesses that you will need them later in the query. In this case, this counter shows 798, which means that many physical reads. Both the physical reads and read-ahead reads counters indicate the amount of physical disk activity.

The lob logical reads, lob physical reads, and lob read-ahead reads are the same as the other reads, but these counters indicate reads for the large objects — for example, if you read a column with the data types varchar(max), nvarchar(max), xml, or varbinary(max). Note that when T-SQL statements retrieve lob columns, some lob retrieval operations might require traversing the lob tree multiple times. This may cause SET STATISTICS IO to report higher than expected logical reads.

Clearing Caches

The first statement in the preceding example query is DBCC DROPCLEANBUFFERS. In a query-tuning exercise, this command is very handy to clear the data cache globally. If you run the query a second time but comment out the DBCC DROPCLEANBUFFERS statement first, the read-ahead reads counter will be 0, which means that the data pages you have asked for are already in the data cache (buffer pool). In your query-tuning exercises, make sure that when you run your query a second time after making some changes, you clear the data cache so that you get correct I/O information, and so does the query runtime.

The other important command to clear the plan cache (not data cache) is DBCC FREEPROCCACHE. It will clear the execution plan from cache globally.

If you want to clear the execution plans for a particular database, you can run the following undocumented command:

```
DBCC FLUSHPROCINDB(<db_id>)
```

> **Please do not run these commands in your production system because clearing the cache will obviously have a performance impact. When you do query-tuning in your development/test environment, be aware of this effect.**

Clustered Index Scan (Unordered)

Try creating a clustered index on the New_SalesOrderHeader table. A clustered index is structured as a balanced tree (all indexes in SQL Server 2008 are structured as balanced trees). A *balanced tree* is one in which "no leaf is much farther away from the root than any other leaf" (adopted from www.nist.gov/dads/HTML/balancedtree.html). Different balancing schemes allow different definitions of "much farther" and different amounts of work to keep them balanced. A clustered index maintains the entire table's data at its leaf level (a clustered index is not a copy of the table's data; it *is* the data).

Let's run a query to see the effect of adding a clustered index. Run the following script, which is available in the QueryPlans solution as IndexAccess.sql:

```
CREATE CLUSTERED INDEX IXCU_SalesOrderID ON New_SalesOrderHeader(SalesOrderID)
```

Now run this script:

```
DBCC DROPCLEANBUFFERS
GO
SET STATISTICS IO ON
GO
SELECT SalesOrderID, RevisionNumber, OrderDate, DueDate
FROM New_SalesOrderHeader
GO
SET STATISTICS IO OFF
```

The results of Statistics IO is shown here, and the query plan is shown in Figure 14-22:

```
Table 'New_SalesOrderHeader'. Scan count 1, logical reads 805, physical reads 1,
read-ahead reads 801, lob logical reads 0, lob physical reads 0, lob read-ahead
reads 0.
```

As shown in the Statistics IO output, the number of pages read was 805 (logical reads), which is the same as the table scan (a little more because the leaf level in a clustered index also contains unique row information, and a link to the previous and next page in a doubly linked list, so more space is required to hold that information). Even though the execution plan shows a clustered index scan, the activities are the same as the table scan, so unless you have a predicate on a clustered index key, the whole clustered index will be scanned to get the data, which is the same as a table scan. You can also see in Figure 14-22, in the information box of the clustered index scan operators, that the scan was not ordered

(Ordered = False), which means that the access method did not rely on the linked list that maintains the logical order of the index. Let's see what happens if we create a covering nonclustered index on the table.

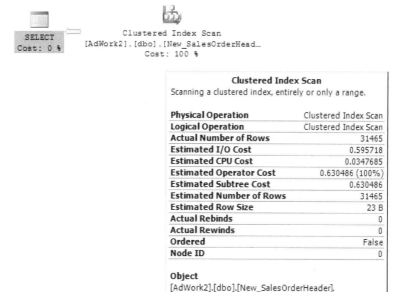

SELECT
Cost: 0 %

Clustered Index Scan
[AdWork2].[dbo].[New_SalesOrderHead...
Cost: 100 %

Clustered Index Scan	
Scanning a clustered index, entirely or only a range.	
Physical Operation	Clustered Index Scan
Logical Operation	Clustered Index Scan
Actual Number of Rows	31465
Estimated I/O Cost	0.595718
Estimated CPU Cost	0.0347685
Estimated Operator Cost	0.630486 (100%)
Estimated Subtree Cost	0.630486
Estimated Number of Rows	31465
Estimated Row Size	23 B
Actual Rebinds	0
Actual Rewinds	0
Ordered	False
Node ID	0
Object	
[AdWork2].[dbo].[New_SalesOrderHeader]. [IXCU_SalesOrderID]	

Figure 14-22

Covering Nonclustered Index Scan (Unordered)

A covering index means that a nonclustered index contains all the columns specified in a query. Let's look at this using the same query used in the previous example:

```
CREATE NONCLUSTERED INDEX IXNC_SalesOrderID ON New_SalesOrderHeader(OrderDate)
INCLUDE(RevisionNumber, DueDate)
GO
DBCC DROPCLEANBUFFERS
GO
SET STATISTICS IO ON
GO
SELECT SalesOrderID,RevisionNumber, OrderDate, DueDate
FROM New_SalesOrderHeader
GO
SET STATISTICS IO OFF
```

This script creates a nonclustered index on the OrderDate column. Notice the INCLUDE clause with the column names RevisionName and DueDate. The INCLUDE feature, introduced in SQL Server 2005, enables you to specify the non-key columns to be added to the leaf level of the nonclustered index. The RevisionName and DueDate columns are included because your query needs these columns. The nonclustered index is chosen for this operation so that the data can be served directly from the leaf level of the nonclustered index (because the nonclustered index has the data for these included columns). See the CREATE INDEX topic in BOL for details on the INCLUDE clause. The statistics I/O information for the query is shown here:

```
Table 'New_SalesOrderHeader'. Scan count 1, logical reads 96, physical reads 1,
read-ahead reads 94,
lob logical reads 0, lob physical reads 0, lob read-ahead reads 0.
```

The query plan is shown in Figure 14-23.

	Index Scan
[AdWork2].[dbo].[New_SalesOrderHead...	
Cost: 100 %	

| Index Scan | |
Scan a nonclustered index, entirely or only a range.	
Physical Operation	Index Scan
Logical Operation	Index Scan
Actual Number of Rows	31465
Estimated I/O Cost	0.0720139
Estimated CPU Cost	0.0347685
Estimated Operator Cost	0.106782 (100%)
Estimated Subtree Cost	0.106782
Estimated Number of Rows	31465
Estimated Row Size	28 B
Actual Rebinds	0
Actual Rewinds	0
Ordered	False
Node ID	0
Object	
[AdWork2].[dbo].[New_SalesOrderHeader].	
[IXNC_SalesOrderID]	

Figure 14-23

As you can see from the statistics I/O result, only 96 logical reads were done to fulfill this query. Notice that the results returned by the clustered index query and the covering nonclustered index query are identical (number of columns and number of rows), but there were 805 logical reads in the clustered index and only 96 logical reads in the nonclustered scan because the nonclustered index has covered the query and served the data from its leaf level.

The clustered index leaf level contains the full data rows (all columns), whereas the nonclustered index has only one key column and two included columns. That means the row size is smaller for a nonclustered index, and the smaller row size can hold more data and requires less I/O.

Clustered Index Scan (Ordered)

An ordered clustered index scan is also a full scan of the clustered index, but the data is returned in order by the clustering key. This time, run the same query as before, but ordered by the SalesOrderID column:

```
DBCC DROPCLEANBUFFERS
GO
SET STATISTICS IO ON
GO
SELECT SalesOrderID,RevisionNumber, OrderDate, DueDate
FROM New_SalesOrderHeader
ORDER BY SalesOrderID
GO
SET STATISTICS IO OFF
```

The statistics I/O information is as follows:

```
Table 'New_SalesOrderHeader'. Scan count 1, logical reads 805, physical reads 1,
read-ahead reads 808,
lob logical reads 0, lob physical reads 0, lob read-ahead reads 0.
```

The query plan is shown in Figure 14-24.

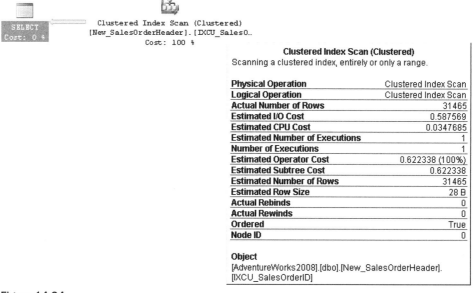

Clustered Index Scan (Clustered)
Scanning a clustered index, entirely or only a range.

Physical Operation	Clustered Index Scan
Logical Operation	Clustered Index Scan
Actual Number of Rows	31465
Estimated I/O Cost	0.587569
Estimated CPU Cost	0.0347685
Estimated Number of Executions	1
Number of Executions	1
Estimated Operator Cost	0.622338 (100%)
Estimated Subtree Cost	0.622338
Estimated Number of Rows	31465
Estimated Row Size	28 B
Actual Rebinds	0
Actual Rewinds	0
Ordered	True
Node ID	0

Object
[AdventureWorks2008].[dbo].[New_SalesOrderHeader].
[IXCU_SalesOrderID]

Figure 14-24

As you can see, the query plan is the same as the one in Figure 14-22, but here we have Ordered = True. The statistics IO information is also the same as the unordered clustered index scan. Note that unlike the unordered clustered index scan, the performance of the ordered clustered index scan depends on the fragmentation level of the index. *Fragmentation* is out-of-order pages, which means that although Page 1 appears after Page 2 according to the linked list, *physically* Page 2 comes before Page 1. The percentage of fragmentation is greater if more pages in the leaf level of the index are out of order with respect to the total number of pages. Moving the disk arm sequentially is always faster than random arm movement, so if the fragmentation is higher than for ordered data, there will be more random arm movement, resulting in slower performance.

If you do not need the data sorted, do not include the ORDER BY *clause.*

Also note that even though you have a covering nonclustered index, the optimizer did not choose it this time (as in Figure 14-23) because you asked that the data be sorted on the SalesOrderID column (which is obviously not sorted on the leaf level of the nonclustered index).

Covering Nonclustered Index Scan (Ordered)

If you run the previous query with OrderDate in the ORDER BY clause, the optimizer would choose the covering nonclustered index. The query plan would be exactly the same as shown in Figure 14-23, except that you would see Ordered = True in the information box. The statistics IO information is also the same as for the non-ordered covering nonclustered index scan. Of course, an ordered index scan is not only used when you explicitly request the data sorted; the optimizer can also choose to sort the data if the plan uses an operator that can benefit from sorted data.

Nonclustered Index Seek with Ordered Partial Scan and Lookups

To demonstrate this access method, you first have to drop the clustered index on the New_SalesOrderHeader table. Now run the following script:

```
DROP INDEX New_SalesOrderHeader.IXCU_SalesOrderID
GO
DBCC DROPCLEANBUFFERS
GO
SET STATISTICS IO ON
GO
SELECT SalesOrderID,RevisionNumber, OrderDate, DueDate
FROM New_SalesOrderHeader
WHERE OrderDate BETWEEN '2001-10-08 00:00:00.000' AND '2001-10-10 00:00:00.000'
GO
SET STATISTICS IO OFF
```

The statistics IO looks like this:

```
(25 row(s) affected)
Table 'New_SalesOrderHeader'. Scan count 1, logical reads 27, physical reads 3,
read-ahead reads 0, lob logical reads 0, lob physical reads 0, lob read-ahead reads
0.
```

The query execution plan is shown in Figure 14-25.

Remember that you don't have a clustered index on this table. This is called a *heap*. In the query, you have requested the SalesOrderID, RevisionNumber, OrderDate, DueDate, and SalesOrderNumber columns, and added a predicate on the OrderDate column. Because of the predicate on the key column in the IXNC_SalesOrderID index, the optimizer chooses this index and looks for all the rows that have the OrderDate specified in the WHERE clause. This index also has all the columns at its leaf level except for SalesOrderID. To find the SalesOrderID column value, SQL Server 2008 performs RID lookups of the corresponding data row for each key. As each key is found, SQL Server 2008 can apply the lookup. In addition, because this is a heap table, each lookup translates to a single page read. Because there are 25 rows qualified by the WHERE clause, there will be 25 reads for data row lookup. If you look at the statistics IO information, there are 27 logical reads, which means that out of those 27 logical reads, 25 are the result of the RID lookup. You can probably guess that most of the cost in this query is in the RID lookup, which is also evident in the query plan, which shows that the cost of the RID lookup operation is 94 percent. Lookups are always random I/Os (as opposed to sequential), which are more costly. When seeking many times, however, SQL Server often sorts to make I/Os more sequential.

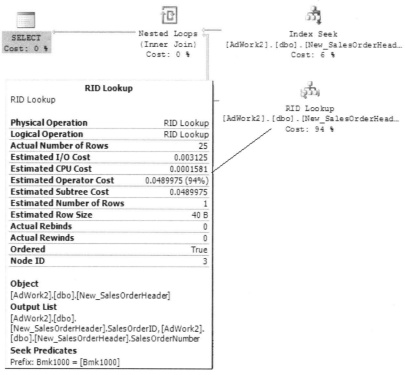

Figure 14-25

This query plan was an RID lookup on a heap. Create your clustered index and run the same query again:

```
CREATE CLUSTERED INDEX IXCU_SalesOrderID ON New_SalesOrderHeader(SalesOrderID)
GO
DBCC DROPCLEANBUFFERS
GO
SET STATISTICS IO ON
GO
SELECT SalesOrderID,RevisionNumber, OrderDate, DueDate, SalesOrderNumber
FROM New_SalesOrderHeader
WHERE OrderDate BETWEEN '2001-10-08 00:00:00.000' AND '2001-10-10 00:00:00.000'
GO
SET STATISTICS IO OFF
```

The following code shows the statistics IO output for this query:

```
(25 row(s) affected)
Table 'New_SalesOrderHeader'. Scan count 1, logical reads 77, physical reads 4,
```

```
read-ahead reads 0, lob logical reads 0,
lob physical reads 0, lob read-ahead reads 0.
```

Figure 14-26 shows the query plan for this query.

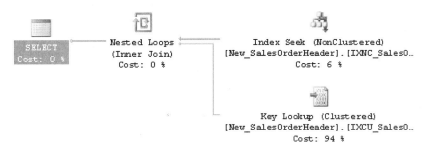

Figure 14-26

The query plans in Figure 14-25 and Figure 14-26 are almost identical except that in Figure 14-26 a clustered index is sought for each row found in the outer reference (the nonclustered index). Once again, you can see in Figure 14-26 that the clustered index seek incurs most of the cost (94 percent) for this query, but note the `statistics IO` information for the two queries. The logical reads in the clustered index seek query plan are a lot higher than those in the RID lookup plan. Does that mean that a clustered index on the table is not so good? No. This index access method is efficient only when the predicate is highly selective, or a point query. *Selectivity* is defined as the percentage of the number of rows returned by the query out of the total number of rows in the table. A *point query* is one that has an equals (=) operator in the predicate. Because the cost of the lookup operation is greater, the optimizer decided to just do the clustered index scan. For example, if you change the `WHERE` clause in the query to `WHERE OrderDate BETWEEN '2001-10-08 00:00:00.000' AND '2001-12-10 00:00:00.000'`, then the optimizer would just do the clustered index scan to return the result for that query. Remember that the *nonleaf* levels of the clustered index typically reside in cache because of all the lookup operations going through it, so you shouldn't concern yourself too much about the higher cost of the query in the clustered index seek scenario shown in Figure 14-26.

Clustered Index Seek with Ordered Partial Scan

This is a simple one. The optimizer normally uses this technique for range queries, in which you filter based on the first key column of the clustered index. Run the following query:

```
DBCC DROPCLEANBUFFERS
GO
SET STATISTICS IO ON
GO
SELECT SalesOrderID,RevisionNumber, OrderDate, DueDate, SalesOrderNumber
FROM New_SalesOrderHeader
WHERE SalesOrderID BETWEEN 43696 AND 45734
GO
SET STATISTICS IO OFF
```

The `statistics IO` output is as follows:

```
(2039 row(s) affected)
Table 'New_SalesOrderHeader'. Scan count 1, logical reads 56, physical reads 1,
```

read-ahead reads 53,
lob logical reads 0, lob physical reads 0, lob read-ahead reads 0.

The query plan is shown in Figure 14-27.

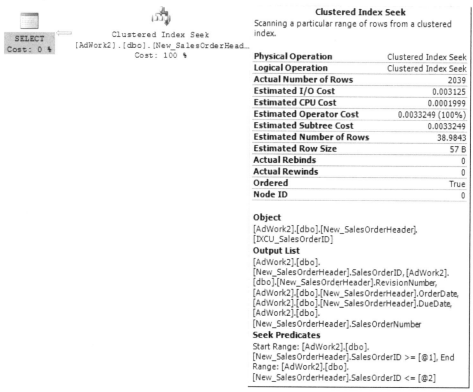

Clustered Index Seek	
Scanning a particular range of rows from a clustered index.	
Physical Operation	Clustered Index Seek
Logical Operation	Clustered Index Seek
Actual Number of Rows	2039
Estimated I/O Cost	0.003125
Estimated CPU Cost	0.0001999
Estimated Operator Cost	0.0033249 (100%)
Estimated Subtree Cost	0.0033249
Estimated Number of Rows	38.9843
Estimated Row Size	57 B
Actual Rebinds	0
Actual Rewinds	0
Ordered	True
Node ID	0

Object
[AdWork2].[dbo].[New_SalesOrderHeader].
[IXCU_SalesOrderID]
Output List
[AdWork2].[dbo].
[New_SalesOrderHeader].SalesOrderID, [AdWork2].
[dbo].[New_SalesOrderHeader].RevisionNumber,
[AdWork2].[dbo].[New_SalesOrderHeader].OrderDate,
[AdWork2].[dbo].[New_SalesOrderHeader].DueDate,
[AdWork2].[dbo].
[New_SalesOrderHeader].SalesOrderNumber
Seek Predicates
Start Range: [AdWork2].[dbo].
[New_SalesOrderHeader].SalesOrderID >= [@1], End
Range: [AdWork2].[dbo].
[New_SalesOrderHeader].SalesOrderID <= [@2]

Figure 14-27

This index access method first performs a seek operation on the first key (43696 in this case) and then performs an ordered partial scan at the leaf level, starting from first key in the range and continuing until the last key (45734). Because the leaf level of the clustered index is actually the data rows, no lookup is required in this access method.

Look at Figure 14-28 to understand the I/O cost for this index access method. To read at least a single leaf page, the number of seek operations required is equal to the number of levels in the index.

How do you find the level in the index? Run the INDEXPROPERTY function with the IndexDepth property:

```
SELECT INDEXPROPERTY (OBJECT_ID('New_SalesOrderHeader'), 'IXCU_SalesOrderID',
'IndexDepth')
```

In this case, the index depth is 3, and of course the last level is the leaf level where the data resides. As shown in Figure 14-28, the cost of the seek operation (three random reads in this case, because that is the depth of the index) and the cost of the ordered partial scan within the leaf level to get the data (in this case 53, according to the read-ahead reads) add up to 56 logical reads, as indicated in the `statistics IO` information. As you can see, an ordered partial scan typically incurs the bulk of the query's cost because it involves most of the I/O to scan the range (53 in this case). As mentioned earlier, index fragmentation plays an important role in ordered partial scan operations, so when there is high fragmentation in the index, the disk arm needs to move a lot, which results in degraded performance.

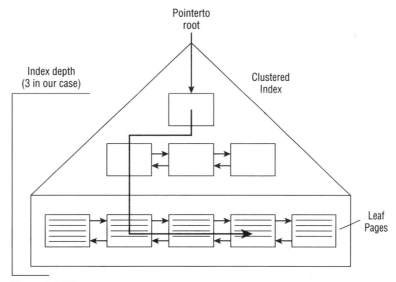

Figure 14-28

Note that this plan is called a *trivial plan*, which means that there is no better plan than this, and the plan does not depend on the selectivity of the query. As long as you have a predicate on the `SalesOrderID` columns, no matter how many rows are sought, the plan will always be the same *unless* you have a better index that the plan chooses in this case. Try adding the following index on this table. Then run the query again and see what happens and why. Notice which index is chosen by the optimizer, and the number of logical reads compared to that in Figure 14-27:

```
CREATE NONCLUSTERED INDEX IXNC_SalesOrderID_2 ON New_SalesOrderHeader(SalesOrderID,
OrderDate)
INCLUDE(RevisionNumber, DueDate, SalesOrderNumber)
```

Now drop the index after you are done with the exercise:

```
DROP INDEX New_SalesOrderHeader.IXNC_SalesOrderID_2
```

Note that you cannot keep adding indexes on your table, because maintaining those indexes is not free. Maintaining a balance tree is a costly operation because of the physical data movement involved when you modify data. Proceed cautiously and analyze the cost of adding indexes for data modification operations, especially on an OLTP system.

Fragmentation

This section elaborates on the topic of index fragmentation covered earlier. There are two types of fragmentation: *logical scan fragmentation* and *average page density*. Logical scan fragmentation is the percentage of out-of-order pages in the index in regard to their physical order, rather than their logical order, in the linked list. This fragmentation has a substantial impact on ordered scan operations like the one shown in Figure 14-27. This type of fragmentation has no impact on operations that do not rely on an ordered scan, such as seek operations, unordered scans, or lookup operations.

The average page density is the percentage of pages that are full. A low percentage (fewer pages full) has a negative impact on the queries that read the data because these queries end up reading more pages than they could, were the pages better populated. The upside of having free space in pages is that insert operations in these pages do not cause page splits, which are very expensive. In short, free space in pages is bad for a data warehouse type of system (more read queries), whereas it is good for an OLTP system that involves many data modification operations.

Rebuilding the indexes and specifying the proper fill factor based on your application will reduce or remove the fragmentation. You can use the following DMF to find out both types of fragmentation in your index. For example, to find out the fragmentation for indexes on the New_SalesOrderHeader table, run the following query:

```
SELECT *
FROM sys.dm_db_index_physical_stats (DB_ID(),
OBJECT_ID('dbo.New_SalesOrderHeader'), NULL, NULL, NULL)
```

Look for the avg_fragmentation_in_percent column for logical fragmentation. Ideally, it should be 0, which indicates no logical fragmentation. For average page density, look at the avg_page_space_used_in_percent column. It shows the average percentage of available data storage space used in all pages.

> DBCC SHOWCONTIG was another way to get this information in SQL Server 2000. DBCC SHOWCONTIG will be deprecated in the next release of SQL Server, so do not use it. You can use the sys.dm_db_index_physical_stats view instead.

SQL Server 2005 added a feature to build the indexes online — an ONLINE option is added to the CREATE and ALTER INDEX statements. This feature enables you to create, drop, and rebuild the index online. See Chapter 15 for more details. The following is an example of rebuilding the index IXNC_SalesOrderID on the New_SalesOrderHeader table:

```
ALTER INDEX IXNC_SalesOrderID ON dbo.New_SalesOrderHeader REBUILD WITH (ONLINE =
ON)
```

Statistics

Microsoft SQL Server 2008 collects statistics about individual columns (single-column statistics) or sets of columns (multi-column statistics). Note that a histogram is only collected for the leading column. The query optimizer uses these statistics to estimate the selectivity of expressions, and thus the size of intermediate and final query results. Good statistics enable the optimizer to accurately assess the cost of different query plans and choose a high-quality plan. All information about a single statistics object is stored in several columns of a single row in the sysindexes table, and in a statistics binary large object (statblob) kept in an *internal-only* table.

If, in your execution plan, you note a large difference between the estimated row count and the actual row count, the first thing you should check are the statistics on the join columns and the column in the WHERE clause for that table (be careful with the inner side of loop joins; the row count should match the estimated rows multiplied by the estimated executions). Make sure that the statistics are current. Check the UpdateDate, Rows, and Rows Sampled columns (DBCC SHOW_STATISTICS). It is very important that you keep up-to-date statistics. You can use the following views and command to get details about statistics.

To see how many statistics exist in your table you can use the sys.stats view. To view which columns are part of the statistics, use the sys.stats_columns view. To view the histogram and density information, you can use DBCC SHOW_STATISTICS. For example, to view the histogram information for the IXNC_SalesOrderID index on the New_SalesOrderHeader table, run the following command:

```
DBCC SHOW_STATISTICS ('dbo.New_SalesOrderHeader', 'IXNC_SalesOrderID')
```

Data Modification Query Plan

When you execute data modification plans, the plan has two stages. The first stage is read-only, and determines which rows need to be inserted, updated, or deleted. It generates the data stream to describe the changes. For INSERT statements you will have column values, so the data stream contains the column values. DELETE statements have key column(s), and UPDATE statements have both data streams, the changed columns' values and the table key. If you have foreign keys, the plan includes performing constraint validation. It also maintains indexes; and if any triggers exist, it fires these triggers as well.

There are two maintenance strategies for INSERT, UPDATE, and DELETE statements: per-row and per-index. Consider the following DELETE query, which has a per-row query plan:

```
DELETE FROM New_SalesOrderHeader
WHERE OrderDate = '2001-07-01 00:00:00.000'
```

The query plan is shown in Figure 14-29.

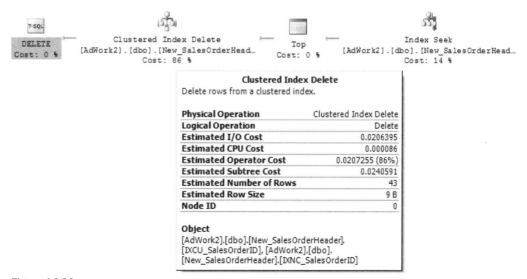

Figure 14-29

With a per-row plan, SQL Server 2008 maintains the indexes and the base table together for each row affected by the query. The updates to all nonclustered indexes are performed in conjunction with each row update on the base table. Note that the base table could be a heap or a clustered index. If you look at the Clustered Index Delete information box in Figure 14-29, in the Object information you will notice that both the clustered index and the nonclustered index are listed, which indicates that the indexes are maintained with a per-row operation.

Because of the short code path and update to all indexes and tables together, the per-row update strategy is more efficient in term of CPU cycles.

Now consider another query plan with the following query. The change in this query is to the WHERE clause (changed to < =). We're using the Sales.SalesOrderHeader table to produce the plan for this example:

```
DELETE FROM Sales.SalesOrderHeader
WHERE OrderDate < '2003-07-01 00:00:00.000'
```

The query plan is shown in Figure 14-30. Note that this figure shows only part of the plan because there are so many indexes on this table in the AdventureWorks2008 database. Run the statement in SSMS to see the full query plan.

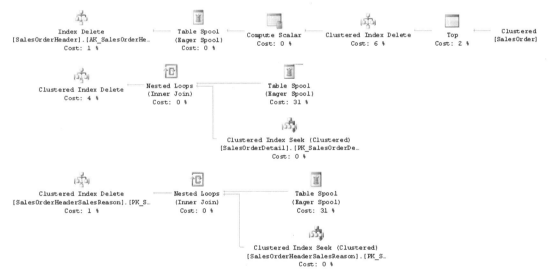

Figure 14-30

This query plan is performing per-index maintenance. The plan first deletes qualifying rows from the clustered index, and at the same time it builds the temporary spool table containing the clustering key values for the other nonclustered indexes that must be maintained. SQL Server 2008 reads the spool data as many times as the number of nonclustered indexes on the table. The sort operator between the index delete operator and the spool operator indicates that SQL Server 2008 sorts the data according to the key column of the index it is about to delete so that the index pages can be accessed optimally. The sequence operator enforces the execution order of each branch. SQL Server 2008 updates the indexes one after another from the top of the plan to the bottom.

As shown in the query plan, per-index maintenance is more complicated; but because it maintains individual indexes after sorting the key (`Sort` operator), it never visits the same page again, saving in I/O. Therefore, when you are updating many rows, the optimizer usually chooses the per-index plan.

Your disk configuration is also important in designing write/read-intensive operations. See Chapter 11 for more information.

Inserting, Updating, and Deleting with MERGE

In SQL Server 2008, you can perform `INSERT`, `UPDATE`, and `DELETE` operations in a single statement using `MERGE`. The `MERGE` syntax enables you to join a data source with a target table or view, and then perform multiple actions based on the results of that join. `MERGE` statements provide the capability to efficiently perform multiple DML operations against a single target table based on a source table. Following is the basic syntax for a `MERGE` T-SQL statement. For details on the syntax, please refer to SQL Server BOL.

```
[ WITH <common_table_expression> [, ... n] ]
MERGE
    [ TOP ( expression ) [ PERCENT ] ]
    [ INTO ] target_table [ WITH ( <merge_hint> ) ] [ [ AS ] table_alias ]
    USING <table_source>
    ON <merge_search_condition>
    [ WHEN MATCHED [ AND <clause_search_condition> ]
        THEN <merge_matched> ]
    [ WHEN NOT MATCHED [ BY TARGET ] [ AND <clause_search_condition> ]
        THEN <merge_not_matched> ]
    [ WHEN NOT MATCHED BY SOURCE [ AND <clause_search_condition> ]
        THEN <merge_matched> ]
    [ <output_clause> ]
    [ OPTION ( <query_hint> [ , ... n ] ) ]
;
```

As you can see, a single statement combines multiple DML actions (`INSERT`/`UPDATE`/`DELETE`) on a target table, and it operates on a join between a target (recipient of the DML) and a source (provider of the data).

Take a look at the `MERGE` clause.

When target and source are both matched (`WHEN MATCHED` clause from `MERGE` syntax), the `MERGE` clause is used as follows:

❑ Row exists in both source and target

❑ Equivalent to `source INNER JOIN target`

❑ Valid actions: `UPDATE` or `DELETE`

When the target is not matched (`WHEN NOT MATCHED [ BY TARGET ]`) clause from `MERGE` syntax), the `MERGE` clause is used as follows:

❑ Row exists in source but not in target

❑ Equivalent to `source LEFT OUTER JOIN target`

❑ Valid action: `INSERT`

When the source is not matched (WHEN NOT MATCHED BY SOURCE clause from MERGE syntax), the MERGE clause is used as follows:

❑   Row exists in target but not in source

❑   Equivalent to source RIGHT OUTER JOIN target

❑   Valid actions: UPDATE or DELETE

Let's look at an example using MERGE. After you understand how MERGE works, we will look into performance considerations using MERGE versus INSERT/UPDATE/DELETE DML.

Open the script MergeSample.sql from the MERGE folder provided with the downloads for this chapter. Here is the code:

```
-----------------------
use tempdb
go
-----------------------
IF OBJECT_ID('Stocks') IS NOT NULL
DROP TABLE Stocks
GO

CREATE TABLE Stocks
(
 Symbol varchar(10) NOT NULL
,Quantity int NOT NULL CHECK(Quantity > 0)
)

CREATE UNIQUE CLUSTERED INDEX IXU_Stocks ON Stocks(Symbol)
-----------------------
IF OBJECT_ID('Trades') IS NOT NULL
DROP TABLE Trades
GO

CREATE TABLE Trades
(
 Symbol varchar(10) NOT NULL
,DeltaQuantity int NOT NULL
)

CREATE UNIQUE CLUSTERED INDEX IXU_Trades ON Trades(Symbol)
-----------------------
INSERT Stocks VALUES('MSFT', 20), ('GOOG', 5);
INSERT Trades VALUES('MSFT', 10), ('GOOG', -5), ('INTEL', 8);
-----------------------
MERGE Stocks s
USING Trades t
  ON s.Symbol = t.Symbol
WHEN MATCHED AND (s.Quantity + t.DeltaQuantity = 0) THEN
    DELETE -- delete stock if entirely sold
WHEN MATCHED THEN
-- delete takes precedence on update
    UPDATE SET s.Quantity = s.Quantity + t.DeltaQuantity
```

```
WHEN NOT MATCHED THEN
    INSERT VALUES (t.Symbol, t.DeltaQuantity)
OUTPUT $action,  inserted.Symbol AS NewSymbol, deleted.Symbol AS DeletedSymbol;


-------------------------
SELECT * FROM Stocks
SELECT * FROM Trades
-------------------------


Go
DROP TABLE Stocks
DROP TABLE Trades
```

This code creates two tables, Stocks and Trades, and inserts some rows in the tables as shown. Let's focus on MERGE statement. The MERGE keyword is followed by the target table Stocks, and the USING keyword is followed by the source table Trades. We are joining on Symbol, which is a unique key on both tables. The first WHEN condition says that if MATCHES (meaning Symbol exists in both tables; MSFT and GOOG in this case) and source table (Trades) quantity plus target table (Stocks) quantity sums to be zero (i.e., adding the quantity of GOOG symbols in the Stocks and Trades tables is zero), THEN DELETE that row. As a result of this condition, the row with the GOOG symbol will be deleted from the target table Stocks. The second WHEN condition says that WHEN MATCHED (if Symbol exists in both tables), then UPDATE the quantity of source from target. As a result of this second condition, the value of the MSFT symbol in the target table (Stocks) is updated to 30. In the final WHEN condition, if the target table doesn't have Symbol but the source table has it, then INSERT the new values. As a result, the symbol INTEL will be added to the target table Stocks. Running the MERGE statement returns the following results:

```
$action      NewSymbol   DeletedSymbol
----------   ---------   -------------
DELETE       NULL        GOOG
INSERT       INTEL       NULL
UPDATE       MSFT        MSFT
```

You will see this result because of the OUTPUT keyword specified in the MERGE statement. SQL Server 2008 includes a powerful extension to the INSERT statement that enables it to consume rows returned by the OUTPUT clause of nested INSERT, UPDATE, DELETE, or MERGE statements. As you can see, the GOOG row is deleted from the Stocks table, a new row with the INTEL symbol is inserted into the Stocks table, and a row with the symbol MSFT is updated. Normally you don't want to have the OUTPUT keyword if you are modifying or deleting thousands of rows in a table unless the result of MERGE is a source of input to an INSERT statement.

As shown in the example, you can have multiple WHEN MATCHED conditions in the MERGE statement. If so, the first clause must be accompanied by an AND <search_condition> clause. In this case, the search_condition is (s.Quantity + t.DeltaQuantity = 0). For any given row, the second WHEN MATCHED clause is only applied if the first is not. If there are two WHEN MATCHED clauses, then one must specify an UPDATE action and one must specify a DELETE action. The MERGE statement can have only one WHEN NOT MATCHED clause, and at most two WHEN NOT MATCHED BY SOURCE clauses.

Merge Performance

Looking at the preceding MERGE statement, you might assume that because you can do all the DML operations (INSERT/UPDATE/DELETE) in a single statement, rather than run INSERT/UPDATE/DELETE individually, it should make MERGE faster. This is not always true. Here are some things you should consider when using MERGE:

❑ In general, join performance is optimal if the source and target have an index on join keys, and at least one is unique.

❑ If the source and target are of similar size, then merge join is the most efficient query plan because both tables are scanned once and there is no need to sort the data.

❑ If the source is much smaller than the target, then a nested loop join is preferable since seeking target is more efficient if performed in sorted order. However, performance will be optimal only if the source join keys are unique.

❑ New OPENROWSET (BULK ...) hints allow high-performance bulk merge scenarios because ordering and uniqueness of join keys guarantee efficient performance without sorts and unnecessary data copies. See BOL for details on OPENROWSET syntax. Following is an example of how you can implement MERGE using the OPENROWSET (BULK ...) option:

```
MERGE Sales AS T
USING OPENROWSET(BULK 'C:\SalesDir\SalesData.txt',
                FORMATFILE ='C:\SalesDir\SalesData.fmt',
                ORDER (SaleID) UNIQUE
                ,ROWS_PER_BATCH = 100000
) AS S(SaleID, SaleTotal, DateModified)
  ON T.SaleID = S.SaleID
WHEN MATCHED THEN
   UPDATE SET SaleTotal = S.SaleTotal
            ,DateModified = S.DateModified
WHEN NOT MATCHED THEN
   INSERT (SaleID, SaleTotal, DateModified)
   VALUES (SaleID, SaleTotal, DateModified);
```

Query Processing Enhancements on Partitioned Tables and Indexes

Before you look further into this topic, you may want to refer to the section "Partition Tables and Indexes" in Chapter 15 for a better understanding of partitioned tables.

SQL Server 2008 improves query processing performance on partitioned tables for many parallel plans, changing the way parallel and serial plans are represented. It also enhances the partitioning information provided in both compile-time and run-time execution plans to help you better understand what's going on in the query plan.

Partitioned tables and indexes are supported only in SQL Server Enterprise, Developer, and Evaluation editions.

Partition-Aware Seek Operation

Let's look at an example to understand the partition-aware SEEK operation. Suppose you have a table called Sales with columns WeekID, GeographyID, ProductID, and SalesAmount. This table is partitioned on `WeekID`, which means each partition contains sales for a week. Suppose also that this table has a clustered index on `GeographyID`. Now you want to perform a query like the following:

```
SELECT * FROM Sales WHERE GeographyID = 4 AND WeekID < 10
```

The partition boundaries for table `Sales` are defined by the following partition function:

```
CREATE PARTITION FUNCTION myRangePF1 (int) AS RANGE LEFT FOR VALUES (3, 7, 10);
```

In SQL Server 2008, when the query optimizer starts processing this query it inserts `PartitionID` (which is hidden to represent the partition number in a partitioned table) as a leading column in the SEEK or SCAN operation. The query optimizer will look at the clustered index on `GeographyID` with composite columns, with `PartitionID` as the leading column (`PartitionID, GeographyID`). First, SQL Server 2008 figures out which partitions it needs to look at during the first-level SEEK operation. In this case, because this table is partitioned on `WeekID`, and the predicate in the query is `WeekID < 10`, SQL Server 2008 will find all the partitions that have `WeekID` less than 10 first (see Figure 14-31). In this case, SQL Server 2008 finds three partitions that have `WeekID` less than 10, so it performs a second-level SEEK operation within those three partitions to find the records that have `GeographyID = 4`.

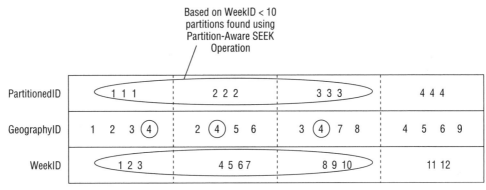

Figure 14-31

Parallel Query Execution Strategy for Partitioned Objects

SQL Server 2008 has implemented new way to use parallelism to improve query performance when you access the partitioned table. If the number of threads is less than the number of partitions, the query processor assigns each thread to a different partition, initially leaving one or more partitions without an assigned thread. When a thread finishes executing on a partition, the query processor assigns it to the next partition until each partition has been assigned a single thread. This is the only case in which the query processor reallocates threads to other partitions.

If the number of threads is equal to the number of partitions, the query processor assigns one thread to each partition. When a thread finishes, it is *not* reallocated to another partition.

What if SQL Server 2008 has more threads than the number of partitions it actually needs to access in order to get the data? Consider the example in Figure 14-31. You have data in three partitions and SQL

Server has 10 threads to access the partitions. SQL Server will use all the available threads to access those partitions, but how will it assign those threads to each partition? It assigns three threads to each partition, and the remaining thread is assigned to one partition. Therefore, out of three partitions, two will have six threads working on them (three threads each), and one partition will have four threads working on it. If you have only one partition to access, then all the available threads will be assigned to that partition — in this case, 10. Keep in mind that when a thread finishes its execution, it is not reassigned to another partition.

Remember the following key points to get better query performance on partitioned tables when you are accessing large amounts of data:

❑ Use more memory to reduce I/O cost if your performance data proves that your system is I/O bound.

❑ Take advantage of the fact that multicore processors are on a commodity server, as SQL Server 2008 can also use it for parallel query processing capabilities.

❑ Make sure you have a clustered index on partitioned tables so that the query processor can take advantage of index scanning optimizations done in SQL Server 2008.

❑ If you are aggregating a large amount of data from a partitioned table, make sure you have enough `tempdb` space on your server. See the article "Capacity Planning for tempdb" in BOL for more information on how to monitor `tempdb` space usage.

Execution Plans for Partitioned Heaps

As mentioned earlier, `PartitionID` is always a leading column to seek for a particular partition or range of partitions, even if the partitioned table is a heap. In SQL Server 2008, a partitioned heap is treated as a logical index on the partition ID. Partition elimination on a partitioned heap is represented in an execution plan as a `Table Scan` operator with a `SEEK` predicate on partition ID. The following example shows the Showplan information provided:

```
|-- Table Scan (OBJECT: ([db].[dbo].[Sales]),
    SEEK: ([PtnId1001]=[Expr1011]) ORDERED FORWARD)
```

As you can see, even if it looks like a table scan, it still seeks on `PartitionID`.

Gathering Query Plans for Analysis with SQL Trace

Earlier you examined the query plans with different option such as `SET STATISTICS PROFILE ON` and `SET STATISTICS XML ON`. This technique does not work when you want to gather the query plans in your production environment. You have to use SQL Trace to get the query plan for analysis. The download files for this chapter include the trace file `QueryPlanAnalysis.tdf`, which you can import into your SQL Trace to gather data for query plan analysis. You can create a server-side trace from this template. See Chapter 13 for details about how to create server-side traces and import the trace data into a database table. We recommend that you create a server-side trace so that you don't miss any events. In addition, import the data into a database table for analysis, rather in SQL Profiler, because SQL Profiler doesn't offer as many options to play with data.

The template for query plan gathering in your environment is in the folder for this chapter. The trace template name is `QueryPlanAnalysis.tdf`. Please make sure that you set filters for your criteria to gather the data, because the file size will grow very quickly. In addition, depending on whether you prefer a textual execution plan or XML, you can check one of the events Showplan Statistics Profile or Showplan XML Statistics Profile.

Summary

In this chapter you learned how query parsing, compiling, and optimization are done in SQL Server 2005. You also learned how to read the query plan. Keep in mind that when you read the query plan (using STATISTICS PROFILE, for example) the most important columns you want to look at are Rows, Executes, and EstimatedRows. If you see a big discrepancy between Rows (the actual row count) and EstimatedRows, remove that small query from your main query and start your analysis there. Note that we are not suggesting that every performance problem with a query stems from bad statistics or cardinality estimations. In the real world, where users are less experienced, most performance problems result from user errors (lack of indexes and such). Check the statistics on the columns in the JOIN and WHERE clauses.

You also learned about the different index access methods and join algorithms. Normally, I/O is the slowest process, so your goal in query tuning is to reduce the number of I/Os and balance the data modification operation (in an OLTP system), and for that knowledge of index access methods and join algorithms is vital. Tuning is not easy, but with patience and attention to details, we are sure that you will get to the root of the problem. Of course, make sure that your server and disk configuration are done properly. You have also learned in this chapter about new features on SQL Server 2008, such as the MERGE and the query-processing enhancements on partitioned tables and indexes. Now that you know about configuring your server, optimizing SQL Server, and tuning queries, you can move on to learn about indexing your database in the next chapter.

Indexing Your Database

Indexes are the solution to many performance problems, but may be the root of so many more. A good understanding of indexes is essential for the survival of any DBA; yet as with most things in SQL Server, each new version brings about change, and many new features. In this chapter we begin by reviewing the new index-related features in SQL Server 2008, and then touch on the basics to make sure you have a full understanding of indexing before going into the details of those new indexing features.

As with most things in SQL Server, the ultimate reference is Books Online, so we won't be duplicating the reference material available there. What we will do is try to make sense of it, and put that information into a context you can use. This chapter does not cover the internal details of indexes, so it doesn't include a detailed discussion of the new allocation unit types.

Noteworthy Index-Related Features in SQL Server

This section first highlights the index-related features new in SQL Server 2008, and then reviews the many indexing features that were first added in SQL Server 2005 and continue to shine in SQL Server 2008.

What's New for Indexes in SQL Server 2008

SQL Server 2008 offers several new index-related features:

❑   **Filtered indexes and statistics:** In SQL Server 2008, you can use a predicate to create filtered indexes and statistics on a subset of rows in the table. Prior to SQL Server 2008, indexes and statistics were created on all of the rows in the table. Now you have a WHERE predicate in the index or statistics you create to limit the number of rows when you create a index or stats. Filtered indexes and statistics are especially suitable for queries that select from well-defined subsets of data; columns with heterogeneous categories of values; and columns with distinct ranges of values.

❑ **Compressed storage of tables and indexes:** SQL Server 2008 supports on-disk storage compression in both row and page format for tables, indexes, and indexed views. Compression of partitioned tables and indexes can be configured independently for each partition. Chapter 12 covers this topic in detail.

❑ **Spatial indexes:** SQL Server 2008 introduces support for spatial data and spatial indexes. Spatial data in this context represents geometric objects or physical location. SQL Server supports two spatial data types: geography and geometry. A *spatial column* is a table column that contains data of a spatial data type, such as `geometry` or `geography`. A *spatial index* is a type of extended index that enables you to index a spatial column. SQL Server uses the .NET CLR (Common Language Runtime) to implement this data type. Refer to the topic ''Working with Spatial Indexes (Database Engine)'' in Books Online (BOL) for details.

Index Features from SQL Server 2005

SQL Server 2005 added so many new features that it was an absolute garden of delight for any DBA, but at the same time it could be challenging to find the exact information you needed. This section highlights the index-related features that were introduced in SQL Server 2005 and are now incorporated into SQL Server 2008, and provides a very brief overview of each.

❑ **Partitioned tables and indexes:** Beginning with SQL Server 2005, you can create tables on multiple partitions, and indexes on each partition. This enables you to manage operations on very large datasets, such as loading and unloading a new set of data, more efficiently by indexing just the new partition, rather than having to re-index the whole table. You will find a lot more information about partitioned tables and indexes later in this chapter.

❑ **Online index operations:** Online index operations were added as an availability feature in SQL Server 2005. They enable users to continue to query against a table while indexes are being built or rebuilt. The main scenario for using this new feature is when you need to make index changes during normal operating hours. The new syntax for using online index operations is the addition of the `ONLINE = ON` option with the `CREATE INDEX`, `ALTER INDEX`, `DROP INDEX`, and `ALTER TABLE` operations.

❑ **Parallel index operations:** Parallel index operations are another useful feature from SQL Server 2005. They are available only in Enterprise Edition, and only apply to systems running on multiprocessor machines. The key scenario for using this feature is when you need to restrict the amount of CPU resources that index operations consume. This might be either for multiple index operations to coexist, or more likely when you need to allow other tasks to complete while performing index operations. They enable a DBA to specify the `MAXDOP` for an index operation. This is very useful on large systems, enabling you to limit the maximum number of processors used in index operations. It's effectively a `MAXDOP` specifically for index operations, and it works in conjunction with the server-configured `MAXDOP` setting. The new syntax for parallel index operations is the `MAXDOP = n` option, which can be specified on `CREATE INDEX`, `ALTER INDEX`, `DROP INDEX` (for clustered indexes only), `ALTER TABLE ADD` (constraint), `ALTER TABLE DROP` (clustered index), and `CONSTRAINT` operations.

❑ **Asynchronous statistics update:** This is a performance `SET` option — `AUTO_UPDATE_STATISTICS_ASYNC`. When this option is set, outdated statistics are placed on a queue and are automatically updated by a worker thread later. The query that generated the autoupdate request will continue before the stats are updated. Note that asynchronous statistics updates cannot occur if any data definition language (DDL) statements such as `CREATE`, `ALTER`, or `DROP` occur in the same transaction.

❑ **Full-text indexes:** Beginning with SQL Server 2005, Full-Text Search supports the creation of indexes on XML columns. It was also upgraded to use MSSearch 3.0, which includes additional performance improvements for full-text index population. It also means that there is now one instance of MSSearch for each SQL Server instance.

❑ **Non-key columns in nonclustered indexes:** With SQL Server 2005 and SQL Server 2008, non-key columns can be added to a nonclustered index. This has several advantages. It enables queries to retrieve data faster, as the query can now retrieve everything it needs from the index pages without having to do a bookmark lookup into the table to read the data row. The non-key columns are not counted in the limits for the nonclustered index number of columns (16 columns), or key length (900 bytes). The new syntax for this option is INCLUDE (`Column Name`,...), which is used with the CREATE INDEX statement.

❑ **Index lock granularity changes:** In SQL Server 2005, the CREATE INDEX and ALTER INDEX T-SQL statements were enhanced by the addition of new options to control the locking that occurs during the index operation. ALLOW_ROW_LOCKS and ALLOW_PAGE_LOCKS specify the granularity of the lock to be taken during the index operation.

❑ **Indexes on XML columns:** This type of index on the XML data in a column enables the Database Engine to find elements within the XML data without having to shred the XML each time.

❑ **Dropping and rebuilding large indexes:** The Database Engine was modified in SQL Server 2005 to treat indexes occupying over 128 extents in a new, more scalable way. If a drop or rebuild is required on an index larger than 128 extents, then the process is broken down into logical and physical stages. In the logical phase, the pages are simply marked as deallocated. Once the transaction commits, the physical phase of deallocating the pages occurs. The deallocation takes place in batches, occurring in the background, thereby avoiding taking locks for a long period of time.

❑ **Indexed view enhancements:** Indexed views have been enhanced in several ways. They can now contain scalar aggregates, and some user-defined functions (with restrictions). In addition, the query optimizer can now match more queries to indexed views if the query uses scalar expressions, scalar aggregates, user-defined functions, interval expressions, and equivalency conditions.

❑ **Version store:** The *version store* is a major enhancement in SQL Server 2005 and 2008. It provides the basis for the row versioning framework that is used by Online Indexing, MARS (Multiple Active Result Sets), triggers, and the new row-versioning-based isolation levels.

❑ **Database Tuning Advisor:** The Database Tuning Advisor (DTA) replaced SQL Server 2000's Index Tuning Wizard (ITW). DTA now offers the following new features:

  ❑ **Time-bound tuning:** Enables you to limit the amount of time spent analyzing a workload. The more time spent, the better the analysis, but the higher the load on the system.

  ❑ **Tune across multiple DBs:** You can tune workloads that run across multiple databases.

  ❑ **Tune a broader class of events and triggers:** The DTA adds the capability to tune using workloads with a larger range of events than was possible with the ITW.

  ❑ **Tuning log:** The DTA writes a log of any events it is unable to tune, along with the reason.

  ❑ **What-if analysis:** The DTA enables you to specify a theoretical server configuration in an input XML file, and provides tuning recommendations for the given workload based on the theoretical server configuration. This enables you to model how changing the server configuration will change the tuning required for optimal performance. Unfortunately, using this option requires manually editing an XML configuration file.

❑ **More control over tuning options:** The DTA adds more options to control tuning recommendations.

❑ **XML file support:** Support for input and output XML files. The input file enables you to provide a different server configuration. The output file enables you to store the DTA recommendations in an XML file. Again, in most cases using this and other XML file–based features requires manual editing of the XML file.

❑ **Partitioning support:** One of the DTA tuning options is the capability to ask for partitioning recommendations.

❑ **Offloading tuning load to lower-spec hardware:** The DTA uses just the metadata and statistics from a server to perform its tuning analysis. Because it doesn't need all the data as well, it can easily be run on lower-spec hardware without affecting the quality or speed of delivery of the tuning recommendations. However, during the tuning process, the test server must have access to the production server so that metadata about the server configuration can be captured.

❑ **Db_owners can now play too:** With ITW, only members of the sysadmin role could execute the wizard. With DTA, members of the db_owners role have the rights to get the same recommendations. Note that the first time DTA is run, it must be run by a member of the sysadmin role before a member of the db_owners role can use it.

Sample Database

For this chapter and the example walkthroughs, we looked at the various sample databases available; and after playing with most of them we decided that a simpler case would work just as well, be easier for readers to reproduce in their own environment, and be simpler to use to illustrate how each feature works.

Open the SQL Server solution file People.ssmssln under the downloads folder for this chapter on the book's website at www.wrox.com.

You can either build the People database using following steps or restore the People database from the backup file People.bak provided in the People folder. To build the People database:

1. Open the script 1_CreateDatabase.sql. The FILENAME option in the CREATE DATABASE statement has the path C:\mssql\Data. Make sure that you create these folders before running the script or adjust it to the correct path according to your system. Now run the script 1_CreateDatabase.sql.

2. Open the script 2_CreateTables.sql and run it. This script will create four tables: People, BoysNames, GirlsNames, and LastNames.

3. Open the script 3_MakeNames.sql and run it. This script creates the stored procedure MakeNames, which is used in the next step to populate some data. This procedure has two arguments. The first is the number of names to insert (the default is 100). The second indicates which type of name to insert: a male name (''B'' for Boys), a female name (''G'' for Girls), or the default, a last name (''L'' for LastNames).

4. Open the script `4_Exec_MakeNames.sql` and run it. This script will populate data in the tables `BoysNames`, `GirlsNames`, and `LastNames`.

5. Open the script `5_InsertPeople.sql` and run it. It will create the stored procedure `InsertPeople`.

6. Open the script `6_MakePeople.sql` and run it. It will create the stored procedure `MakePeople`.

7. Now open the script `7_Exec_MakePeople.sql` and run it. Note that this step may take a while to execute. This script uses data from the tables `BoysNames`, `GirlsNames`, and `LastNames` and then performs some calculations to determine the rest of the data to be inserted into the `People` table. When you run the stored procedure with default parameters, the `People` table will be populated with 19,998 rows.

For clarity, here are the four tables you just created:

```
use People
go

IF OBJECT_ID('dbo.People') IS NULL

create table dbo.People
(
 personID uniqueidentifier DEFAULT NEWSEQUENTIALID(),
 firstName varchar(80) not null,
 lastName varchar(80) not null,
 DOB datetime not null,
 DOD datetime null,
 sex char(1) not null
)
go

IF OBJECT_ID('dbo.BoysNames') IS NULL
create table dbo.BoysNames
 (
 ID int identity(0,1) not null,
 Name varchar(80) not null
 )
go

IF OBJECT_ID('dbo.GirlsNames') IS NULL
create table dbo.GirlsNames
 (
 ID int identity(0,1) not null,
 Name varchar(80) not null
 )
go

IF OBJECT_ID('dbo.LastNames') IS NULL
create table dbo.LastNames
 (
 ID int identity(0,1) not null,
 Name varchar(80) not null
 )
go
```

The sample workload consists of a key table called `People`.

There are two ways to insert rows in the `People` table. The first is used to randomly distribute data over the time period of the database. This simulates an existing dataset distributed over a time period. This insert procedure does random number lookups to find a male and female first name, and then a last name. It then randomly generates a date of birth for a date between today and 110 years ago. Then, with all this new data, two rows are inserted into the `People` table: one `male`, one `female`. This is the data load procedure that can be run to initially populate the `People` table.

The other data insert procedure is used primarily for the partitioning example, and is called `births`. This procedure does the same male and female name lookup, but then inserts two records using the current date/time as the DOB. This simulates inserting new records into one end of the table. You will look at this procedure soon in the section "Partitioned Tables and Indexes."

The update part of the workload consists of several procedures. One is called `Marriage`, which finds a male entry and a female entry from the `People` table, creates a match, and updates the female last name to match the male last name in the `People` table. Another stored procedure is called `Death`. This finds the oldest record based on the earliest date of birth (DOB) in the `People` table and sets its date of death (DOD) to be the current date/time for that record in the `People` table.

All the individual procedures also have other procedures that call them in a loop to make it easier to apply a load to the system. These looping procedures are called `Do<something>`, where *something* is either `Births`, `Deaths`, or `Marriages`.. The `Do<something>` procedures take two arguments, both of which are defaulted. The first argument is the number of times to call the underlying procedure (defaults to 10,000 for `DoBirths` and `DoMarriages` and 1,000 for `DoDeaths`). The second argument specifies how frequently to report stats on the number of inserts, and the time taken (defaults to 500 for `DoBirths` and `DoMarriages` and 100 for `DoDeaths`).

Now that you have a good understanding of the sample database `People`, you will use this database and the scripts provided to explore the topics in the rest of the chapter.

Partitioned Tables and Indexes

Now we'll get started digging into the details of some of these awesome features. First you'll learn why you would need to use each feature, and then how you should use it. Along the way, you'll discover more about what partitioned tables and indexes are and how you use them.

Why Use Partitioned Tables and Indexes?

Partitioned tables are a way to spread a single table over multiple partitions, and while doing so each partition can be on a separate filegroup. There are several reasons for doing this:

❑ **Faster and easier data loading:** If your database has a very large amount of data to load, you might want to consider using a partitioned table. By "a very large amount of data," we don't mean a specific amount of data, but any case in which the load operation takes longer than is acceptable in the production cycle. A partitioned table enables you to load the data to an empty table that's not in use by the "live" data, so it has less impact on concurrent live operations.

Clearly, there will be an impact on the I/O subsystem, but if you also have separate filegroups on different physical disks, even this has a minimal impact on overall system performance.

Once the data is loaded to the new table, you can perform a switch to add the new table to the live data. This switch is a simple metadata change that executes very quickly; that is why partitioned tables are a great way to load large amounts of data with limited impact to users who are touching the rest of the data in the table.

❏ **Faster and easier data deletion or archival:** For the very same reasons, partitioned tables also help you to delete or archive data. If your data is partitioned on boundaries that are also the natural boundaries on which you add or remove data, then the data is considered to be *aligned*. When your data is aligned, deleting or archiving data is as simple as switching a table out of the current partition, after which you can unload or archive it at your leisure.

There is a bit of a catch to this part: With archiving, you often want to move the old data to slower or different storage. The switch operation is so fast because all it does is change metadata; it doesn't move any data around, so to actually move the data from the filegroup where it lived to the old, slow disk archival filegroup, you actually have to move the data, but you are moving it when the partition isn't attached to the existing partitioned table. Therefore, although this may take quite some time, it will have minimal impact on any queries executing against the live data.

❏ **Faster queries:** We're sure the opportunity to get faster queries has you very interested. When querying a partitioned table, the query optimizer can eliminate searching through partitions that it knows won't hold any results. This is referred to as *partition elimination*. This works only if the data in the partitioned table or index is aligned with the query. That is, the data has to be distributed among the partitions in a way that matches the search clause on the query. You will learn more details about this as we cover how to create a partitioned table.

SQL Server 2008 offers some improvements for parallel query processing enhancements on partitioned tables and indexes. Refer to the section "Query Processing Enhancements on Partitioned Tables and Indexes" in Chapter 14 for details on this topic.

❏ **Sliding windows:** A *sliding window* is basically what we referred to earlier in the discussion about adding new data and then deleting or archiving old data. What we did was fill a new table, switch it into the live table, and then switch an existing partition out of the live table for archival or deletion. It's kind of like sliding a window of new data into the current partitioned table, and then sliding an old window of data out of the partitioned table.

Prerequisites for Partitioning

Before you get all excited about partitioned tables, you should remember that partitioning is available only with SQL Server 2005 and later Enterprise Edition. There are also some expectations about the hardware in use, in particular the storage system, although these are implicit expectations, and you can store the data anywhere you want. You just won't get the same performance benefits you would get if you had a larger enterprise storage system with multiple disk groups dedicated to different partitions.

Creating Partitioned Tables

When you decide to create a partitioned table for the first time, you can get pretty lost in the documentation for partition functions, range left versus range right, partition schemes, and how to actually create something that would work, so we'll walk you through the steps in this process.

Creating a Partitioned Table from an Existing Table

Open the `PeoplePartition.ssmssln` solution, included with the download files for this chapter, to work through the following exercises. Suppose that you're starting out with an existing table and you want to turn it into a partitioned table. You will use the `People` table, in this case converting it to a partitioned table. You will also use the database backup file `PeoplePartition.bak` provided with this solution and restore it to use for this example.

Open the script `RestoreDatabase.sql`. This script will restore the database with the name `PeoplePartition` and set the recovery mode to `simple` for this database. The code for the restore script is as follows:

> *Be sure to change the* FROM DISK *path to the correct file location of* `PeoplePartition.bak` *and be sure to change the file location for the* MOVE *option to represent the correct path on your system.*

```
USE master
GO

RESTORE DATABASE [PeoplePartition]
FROM  DISK = N'C:\Samples\PeoplePartition\PeoplePartition.bak'
WITH  FILE = 1,
 MOVE N'PeoplePartition' TO N'C:\mssql\Data\PeoplePartition.mdf'
,MOVE N'PeoplePartition_log' TO N'C:\mssql\Data\PeoplePartition_1.LDF'
,NOUNLOAD
,REPLACE
,STATS = 10
GO
----------------------------
```

Run this script. This will restore the database named `PeoplePartition`.

You face a bit of a limitation in that you can't spread the table over multiple filegroups, as that would require you to physically move all the data around, so this system partitions a table onto a partition scheme on a single set of filegroups.

The `partition` function is the function that determines how your data is split between partitions. Creating a partition function is the first step in creating a partitioned table or index. Before creating a `partition` function, you need to determine which column you are going to use to partition the data in the table. In this case you will use the DOB column in the `People` table. (As another example, suppose you have a fact table, `Sales`, which has sales for each `FiscalMonth`. You could use `FiscalMonth` as a partition column.)

Open the script `Partitions_1.sql` but don't run it yet. The following code is for a partition function that splits a table called `People` into multiple partitions based on the DOB column:

```
USE PeoplePartition
GO

CREATE PARTITION FUNCTION [PeopleRangePF1] (datetime)
AS RANGE RIGHT FOR VALUES
(  '01/01/1900', '01/01/1910', '01/01/1920'
  ,'01/01/1930', '01/01/1940', '01/01/1950'
```

```
      ,'01/01/1960', '01/01/1970', '01/01/1980'
      ,'01/01/1990', '01/01/2000', '01/01/2005'
      ,'01/01/2006'
   );
   GO
```

Take a look at the parameter passed to CREATE PARTITION FUNCTION statement. This parameter specifies the data type of the column used for partitioning. You could pass any data type (for your partitioned column) except text, ntext, image, xml, timestamp, varchar(max), nvarchar(max), varbinary(max), alias data types, or CLR user-defined data types. In this case you are using the DOB column from the People table, which is of datetime type, so you are passing datetime as the value for this parameter.

In SQL Server 2005, when you specify datetime or smalldatetime as the data type in this function, the literal values provided with the VALUE parameter are evaluated, assuming that us_english is the language for that session. Starting with SQL Server 2008, this behavior is deprecated. It is recommended that you specify the literal values for the datetime or smalldatetime data type using *yyyymmdd* format, or you can convert these literals to a specific date/time format on your server. You can select the language setting for the instance using SELECT @@LANGUAGE TSQLand determine the date/time format.

Look at the AS RANGE [LEFT|RIGHT] FOR VALUES parameter in this function. The values specified in this parameter define the range of values each partition will hold. Consider the first two values specified here, '01/01/1900 ' and '01/01/1910 '. The first partition will contain all the dates *before* January 1, 1900. The second partition will contain all the dates *starting* with January 1, 1900 and *before* January 1, 1910. The boundary conditions here are defined by LEFT RANGE or RIGHT RANGE. The statements about what each partition will contain are true because we have specified RIGHT RANGE. If we had specified LEFT RANGE, the first partition would contain all the dates *on or before* January 1, 1900; the second partition would contain all the dates *after* January 1, 1900 and *on or before* January 1, 1910, and so on. If you don't specify the RANGE LEFT or RANGE RIGHT, the default will be LEFT. You don't have to specify these values in order. If they are not in order, SQL Server will order them before creating the function.

How many VALUES have you specified in this function? 13. How many partitions will be created? 14. The number of partitions created is always the number of values specified in the CREATE PARTITION FUNCTION VALUES parameter +1. You can create a maximum of 1,000 partitions for a partitioned table, which means you can specify 999 values in this function.

Now run the script Partitions_1.sql.

The second step is to create the partition scheme. Open the script Partitions_2.sql, shown here, but don't run it yet:

```
USE PeoplePartition
GO

--DROP PARTITION SCHEME [PeoplePS1]
CREATE PARTITION SCHEME [PeoplePS1]
AS PARTITION [PeopleRangePF1] TO
(
   [PRIMARY], [PRIMARY], [PRIMARY]
 , [PRIMARY], [PRIMARY], [PRIMARY]
 , [PRIMARY], [PRIMARY], [PRIMARY]
```

```
 , [PRIMARY], [PRIMARY], [PRIMARY]
 , [PRIMARY], [PRIMARY]
 );
 GO
```

This is pretty simple syntax. The main thing you need to look out for is the exact number of partitions to be created. This partition function created 13 boundaries, so you need to have 13 +1 = 14 partitions to hold the data.

Now run the script Partitions_2.sql.

Because you are partitioning an existing table, you have to keep all the data on the existing filegroup. For cases where you need to physically move the data to different filegroups, see the details in the section "Deleting Data from the Partitioned Table" later in this chapter about how to move data around most efficiently.

The third step is applying the partition by creating a clustered index on the partition scheme. As the comment says, you already have data in your table, so now you have to spread it across the partitions, which you do by using a clustered index.

Open the script Partitions_3.sql:

```
USE PeoplePartition
GO
-- we already have data in the table, so we have to
-- partition it using a clustered index
CREATE CLUSTERED INDEX cix_people ON People (dob)
ON PeoplePS1 (DOB)
Go
```

The fourth and final step is to check the system metadata to confirm that you have partitioned correctly. Open the script Partitions_4.sql:

```
USE PeoplePartition
GO
--  this will tell us how many entries there are in each partition?
SELECT $partition.PeopleRangePF1(dob) AS [Partition Number], count(*) AS total
FROM dbo.People
group by $partition.PeopleRangePF1(dob)
order by $partition.PeopleRangePF1(dob)
compute sum (count(*))
```

The purpose of the script is to list the number of partitions and the number of rows contained in each partition. The $partition function returns the partition number for a specified partition function.

Run the Partitions_4.sql script now. Your results will differ from the following if you have different data in the table:

```
Partition Number total
---------------- -----------
10               19998
11               19998
13               19998
```

```
sum
-----------
59994
```

The sum of 59994 shows the total number of rows in the partitioned table People. It also shows that partition numbers 10, 11, and 13 contain all the rows. Here is the explanation of the rows sitting in different partitions: Partition number 10 contains rows for DOB on or after '01/01/1980' and before '01/01/1990'. Partition number 11 contains rows for DOB on or after '01/01/1990' and before '01/01/2000'. Partition number 13 contains rows for DOB on or after '01/01/2005' and before '01/01/2006'.

Adding New Data to the Partitioned Table

Now that your table is partitioned, you need a way to add new data offline, and to switch that new data into the partitioned table. The first step creates a table to hold all the new data to be loaded. The table NewPeople needs an identical structure to the partitioned table — number of columns, data types, indexes, constraints, and so on.

Open the script Partitions_5.sql, but don't run it yet. Here is the partial code from this script:

```
USE PeoplePartition
GO

-- Now go create a new People table to hold any births after 7/11/2006
-- MUST BE IDENTICAL to People
create table NewPeople (
 [personID] [uniqueidentifier] NULL DEFAULT (newsequentialid()),
 [firstName] [varchar](80) NOT NULL,
 [lastName] [varchar](80) NOT NULL,
 [DOB] [datetime] NOT NULL,
 [DOD] [datetime] NULL,
 [sex] [char](1) NOT NULL
) on [PRIMARY]  -- Must be on the same filegroup as the target partition.
```

You will use this table to load that and later switch this data into the partitioned table.

Run the script now. It should create the NewPeople table.

Now you need to populate the NewPeople table, using the following steps:

1. Open the script Partitions_Birth.sql and run it.

2. Open the script Partitions_DoBirths.sql and run it. This script contains the code to insert data into the NewPeople table.

3. Open the script Exec_Partitions_DoBirths.sql and run it. The script will take a few seconds to execute. This script inserts 19,998 rows into the NewPeople table.

You're now ready to move to the next step of creating a clustered index to match the partitioned index. Open the script Partitions_6.sql but don't run it yet. As mentioned earlier, the structure of the table you are switching into the partitioned table should match the structure of the partitioned table exactly, so you need to create the clustered index on the DOB column, and add the CHECK constraint on the DOB column. The CHECK constraint on the new table ensures that the data matches the partition function boundary you are just about to set up. Following is the portion of the code from the file Partitions_6.sql that performs these tasks. Copy the following code from the file and run it:

```
USE PeoplePartition
GO
-- create the index on the new table.
create clustered index cix_NewPeople on NewPeople(dob)

-- create a check constraint on the source table
-- to enforce the integrity of the data in the partition
-- and to make the structure identical with People table.

ALTER TABLE NewPeople
ADD CONSTRAINT [CK_DOB_DateRange]
CHECK ([DOB] >= '01/01/2007');
GO
```

Creating the clustered index takes quite some time, but it doesn't affect your live system performance because it's not connected in any way to the live People table.

Now you can start making changes to the live partition to prepare it for the new set of data you want to load. The first step here is to alter the partition scheme to specify where the new partition is going to live. This has to be on the same filegroup as the new table you just filled up. In this case, this is easy, as everything is on PRIMARY anyway. In a production system with multiple filegroups, this could be one of the empty filegroups available. For more details on using multiple filegroups, see the section "Partitioning a Production System" coming up shortly. Here is the relevant code from the file Partitions_6.sql. Copy this portion of the code from the file and run it:

```
-- alter the partition scheme to ready a
-- new empty partition

ALTER PARTITION SCHEME PeoplePS1
NEXT USED [PRIMARY];
GO
```

The next step is to create the new partition boundary in the partition function. This is done by using an ALTER PARTITION function statement. In this case, you have a RANGE RIGHT function, your new data is for 01 January 2007, and you want all the new data to be in the new partition, so using RANGE RIGHT, you specify the boundary as 01 January 2007 as explained earlier when you created the partitioned function. Following is the relevant code from Partitions_6.sql. Copy this portion of the code and run it:

```
 ALTER PARTITION FUNCTION PeopleRangePF1()
SPLIT RANGE ('01/01/2007');
GO
```

Now you are ready to switch the new data in the table NewPeople into the partitioned table People. First, you want to count the number of rows in the NewPeople table and make sure that after the switch you get the same number of rows. To do that, run the following lines from the Partitions_6.sql file:

```
 select count (*) from NewPeople
 -----------
 19998
```

Now you can apply the switch and move all those people into the new partition. Here is the code from file `Partitions_6.sql` to switch the `NewPeople` table into the partitioned table `People`. Copy these code lines from the file and run it:

```
ALTER TABLE NewPeople
SWITCH TO People PARTITION 15;
GO
```

The switch runs very quickly, so you check how many people are in each table. First check to see how many people are now in the `NewPeople` table:

```
select count (*) from NewPeople
-- this table is now empty
```

As expected, the table is empty; and it is hoped that all records in the `NewPeople` table are in the partitioned table in the new partition. Open the script `Partitions_4.sql` and run it. The following code shows the script and the output:

```
USE PeoplePartition
GO
--  this will tell us how many entries there are in each partition?
SELECT $partition.PeopleRangePF1(dob) AS [Partition Number], count(*) AS total
FROM dbo.People
group by $partition.PeopleRangePF1(dob)
order by $partition.PeopleRangePF1(dob)
compute sum (count(*))

Partition Number total
---------------- -----------
10               19998
11               19998
13               19998
15               19998

sum
-----------
79992
```

Querying the partitioned table, we now have a partition 15 with 19,998 people in it. As you can see, it was relatively easy to slide in a new partition.

Deleting Data from the Partitioned Table

After a new set of data that represents a new day, week, or month of data has been added to your table, you also need to move out the old data, either deleting it or archiving it somewhere. The first step in this process is to create a new table for the data. This must be an empty table, and must have the exact same structure as the partitioned table. In addition, it must be on the same filegroup as the partition you are going to remove. Open the file `Partitions_7.sql` to do this exercise. Here is the relevant portion of the code from this file:

```
USE PeoplePartition
GO
-- Now go slide out the oldest partition.
```

```
-- Step one, we need a table to put the data into
create table OldPeople (
  [personID] [uniqueidentifier] NULL DEFAULT (newsequentialid()),
  [firstName] [varchar](80) NOT NULL,
  [lastName] [varchar](80) NOT NULL,
  [DOB] [datetime] NOT NULL,
  [DOD] [datetime] NULL,
  [sex] [char](1) NOT NULL
) on [PRIMARY]   -- Must be on the same filegroup as the source partition!

-- we need a clustered index on DOB to match the partition

create clustered index cix_OldPeople on OldPeople(dob)
go
```

Copy this portion of the code and run it. Note that you don't need a check constraint on this table, as it's moving out of the partition, not into it.

Now that you have the table and clustered index to match the partitioned table and index, you can execute the switch to move out a set of data. This is done using the ALTER TABLE switch statement again, but note that now the syntax has changed a little: You have to specify partition numbers. Copy the following code from the Partitions_7.sql file and run it:

```
-- now go switch out the partition
ALTER TABLE People
SWITCH partition 10
TO OldPeople -- No partition here as we are switching to a NON partitioned table
GO
```

That was remarkably easy and amazingly fast. Now check how many rows are in each partition again. Open the script Partitions_4.sql and run it again to check the data in the partitioned table People:

```
USE PeoplePartition
GO
--   this will tell us how many entries there are in each partition?
SELECT $partition.PeopleRangePF1(dob) AS [Partition Number], count(*) AS total
FROM dbo.People
group by $partition.PeopleRangePF1(dob)
order by $partition.PeopleRangePF1(dob)
compute sum (count(*))


Partition Number total
---------------- ----------
11               19998
13               19998
15               19998

sum
----------
59994
```

Now count the number of rows in the OldPeople table. Copy the following lines from the file Partitions_7.sql and run it. As you can see, 19,998 rows were in partition number 10, and that many rows are now in the OldPeople table:

```
SELECT COUNT(*) FROM OldPeople -- 19998
```

Remember that earlier when you built the NewPeople table and switched that table to the People partitioned table, you had data in four partitions, 10, 11, 13, and 15. You can see that partition 10 is no longer part of the partitioned table after you switched out that partition to the OldPeople table, and that the rows from that partition are now in the OldPeople table.

You could also run the following code, provided in the file Partitions_7.sql, to see which partition has how many rows. I have selected only a few columns from the sys.partitions view. Copy this code and run it. The output is shown here. Your output may be a little different if you have inserted some rows in other partitions:

```
SELECT partition_id, partition_number, rows
FROM sys.partitions
WHERE object_id = OBJECT_ID('People')
ORDER BY partition_number

--Result of the above query.
 partition_id        partition_number rows
-------------------- ---------------- --------------------
 72057594039042048   1                0
 72057594039107584   2                0
 72057594039173120   3                0
 72057594039238656   4                0
 72057594039304192   5                0
 72057594039369728   6                0
 72057594039435264   7                0
 72057594039500800   8                0
 72057594039566336   9                0
 72057594040221696   10               0
 72057594039697408   11               19998
 72057594039762944   12               0
 72057594039828480   13               19998
 72057594039894016   14               0
 72057594040025088   15               19998
```

You could also merge a partition using the ALTER PARTITION MERGE RANGE function. This drops the partition and merges any values in that partition to an existing partition.

Copy the following code from the file Partitions_7.sql and run it. Running this code will remove partition number 10 and renumber the partitions from 1 to 14, leaving you with 14 partitions instead of 15:

```
ALTER PARTITION FUNCTION PeopleRangePF1()
MERGE RANGE ('01/01/1980');
GO
```

Now copy the following code from the file `Partitions_7.sql` and run it. The output is shown here:

```
SELECT partition_id, partition_number, rows
FROM sys.partitions
WHERE object_id = OBJECT_ID('People')
ORDER BY partition_number

--Result of the above query.
partition_id          partition_number rows
--------------------  ---------------- --------------------
72057594039042048     1                0
72057594039107584     2                0
72057594039173120     3                0
72057594039238656     4                0
72057594039304192     5                0
72057594039369728     6                0
72057594039435264     7                0
72057594039500800     8                0
72057594039566336     9                0
72057594039697408     10               19998
72057594039762944     11               0
72057594039828480     12               19998
72057594039894016     13               0
72057594040025088     14               19998
-----------------
```

That was all pretty easy, but you aren't quite done yet. You have moved the old partition data out of the partitioned table but it's still on the same filegroup consuming fast, expensive disk resources. You want the data to be on the old, slow, cheap disks for archival, or in some location ready to be backed up and deleted.

To do this, you need to physically move the data from one filegroup to another. There are several ways you can do this, but the fastest and most efficient is to use a `select into`. This is straightforward, but you do have to be a little careful about altering the default filegroup if anyone else might be creating objects in the database while you are doing your data movements. You need to complete three steps here:

1. Alter the default filegroup to be the archival filegroup.
2. Select into a new table.
3. Alter the default filegroup back.

Open the file `MoveDataToArchiveFG.sql` and take a look, but don't run the script yet. You don't have the filegroup and file to archive the data from the PRIMARY filegroup. Copy the following code from `MoveDataToArchiveFG.sql` and run it:

```
USE PeoplePartition
GO
SELECT name, is_default
FROM sys.filegroups
GO
--Output from above script.
name      is_default
------------------
PRIMARY   1
```

Next you need to create a filegroup in the database `PeoplePartition` and then create the data file in that filegroup to archive the data. Copy the following code from the file `MoveDataToArchiveFG.sql`. Be sure to modify the `FILENAME` option in the `ALTER DATABASE` statement to specify the correct path before you run the script. After copying the code, run it:

```
--------------------------------------------
USE master
GO

ALTER DATABASE People
ADD FILEGROUP People_Archive
GO


--------------------------------------------
ALTER DATABASE PeoplePartition
ADD FILE
(
 NAME = 'PeoplePartition_Archive'
,FILENAME = 'C:\MSSQL\Data\PeoplePartition_Archive.ndf'
,SIZE = 10
)
TO FILEGROUP PeoplePartition_Archive
GO
--------------------------------------------
```

You have now added the filegroup and the data file for that filegroup. Now you'll modify this new filegroup to be the `DEFAULT` filegroup. Copy the following code from `MoveDataToArchiveFG.sql` and run it:

```
--------------------------------------------
USE master
GO

ALTER DATABASE PeoplePartition
MODIFY FILEGROUP [PeoplePartition_Archive] DEFAULT
GO
```

You can now use the following script in the file `MoveDataToArchiveFG.sql` to check that the filegroup `PeoplePartition_Archive` is now the default. Copy this code and run it:

```
--------------------------------------------
USE PeoplePartition
GO
SELECT name, is_default
FROM sys.filegroups
GO

--output from above script.
name                     is_default
------------------------ ----------
PRIMARY                  0
PeoplePartition_Archive  1
--------------------------------------------
```

In a real production system you probably won't be creating your database files on the C: *drive. You have both the* PRIMARY *and* PeoplePartition_Archive *filegroups on the* C: *drive for illustrative purposes but they should be on different drives in a real-world scenario.*

Now you are ready to archive the OldPeople table to this new filegroup. Copy the following code from MoveDataToArchiveFG.sql and run it:

```
USE PeoplePartition
GO
-- Move the data to new filegroup.
SELECT * INTO Archive2PeoplePartition
FROM OldPeople
```

Technically, you can delete the data from the OldPeople table after this, but you can leave it alone here, as this is just an example.

Next, modify the DEFAULT filegroup back to PRIMARY so that whenever you create a new object, by default it will go to the PRIMARY filegroup. Copy the following code from the file MoveDataToArchiveFG.sql and run it:

```
USE master
GO

ALTER DATABASE PeoplePartition
MODIFY FILEGROUP [PRIMARY] DEFAULT
GO
```

You can now run the following code from MoveDataToArchiveFG.sql to see the filegroup for each object in the People database:

```
--------------------------------------------
USE PeoplePartition
GO
-- Lets go check which filegroup all our objects are on
SELECT
 object_name(i.object_id) as ObjectName
,i.name as indexName
, f.name as filegroupName
FROM sys.indexes as i
JOIN sys.filegroups as f
  ON i.data_space_id = f.data_space_id
WHERE i.object_id > 100


/*
--output from above script.
--output from above script.
ObjectName                           indexName                  filegroupName
------------------------------------ -------------------------  --------------
GirlsNames                           NULL                       PRIMARY
LastNames                            NULL                       PRIMARY
NewPeople                            cix_NewPeople              PRIMARY
OldPeople                            cix_OldPeople              PRIMARY
```

```
Archive2People                      NULL                     PeoplePartition_Archive
queue_messages_1977058079           queue_clustered_index    PRIMARY
queue_messages_1977058079           queue_secondary_index    PRIMARY
queue_messages_2009058193           queue_clustered_index    PRIMARY
queue_messages_2009058193           queue_secondary_index    PRIMARY
queue_messages_2041058307           queue_clustered_index    PRIMARY
queue_messages_2041058307           queue_secondary_index    PRIMARY
filestream_tombstone_2073058421     FSTSClusIdx              PRIMARY
filestream_tombstone_2073058421     FSTSNCIdx                PRIMARY
syscommittab                        ci_commit_ts             PRIMARY
syscommittab                        si_xdes_id               PRIMARY
BoysNames                           NULL                     PRIMARY
*/
```

As you can see, the `Archive2People` filegroup is now on the `PeoplePartition_Archive` filegroup.

Partitioning a Production System

The examples covered so far help to show how you can implement a sliding window scenario, but they gloss over some of the finer details that are going to be key points on a production system. One of the main issues on a production system is that you will have multiple filegroups matched to different physical storage.

The only place this affects any of what you've seen so far is when you're creating and altering the partition scheme. Rather than the example already shown, you would create a partition scheme using something like the following:.

This is just for illustration purposes. You don't need to execute this code. If you do, of course, you will get an error.

```
CREATE PARTITION SCHEME [PeoplePS1]
AS PARTITION [PeopleRangePF1]
TO ([FileGroup1], [FileGroup2], [FileGroup3] );
GO
```

Here, each of your partitions would go to a different filegroup.

When you create filegroups, you need to ensure that you have enough filegroups not just for the live table, but also for new data and for the old data before it's moved to archival storage or deleted. Therefore, you need filegroups for at least the number of live partitions, plus two more: one for the new data and one for the old data.

An alternative physical layout might have multiple partitions sharing the same filegroup. The exact details of laying out physical disks is beyond the scope of this chapter, but is touched on in Chapter 11.

Partitioning and the Database Tuning Advisor

The Database Tuning Advisor (DTA) will provide partitioning recommendations if you ask it to. To do this you need to change the tuning options on the Tuning Options tab. Under the section titled Partitioning Strategy to Employ, change the default setting of No Partitioning to Full Partitioning. The other thing you need to do is determine what kind of queries to tune. It's no good using your INSERT, DELETE, or SWITCH queries, as DTA isn't really interested in them, so you have to tune the SELECT statements that go against the nonpartitioned table. The DTA isn't interested in INSERT, DELETE, or SWITCH statements because it can't improve their performance by adding indexes, so it ignores them and looks only at statements it can tune, i.e., SELECT statements.

If the table is big enough, and the queries would benefit from partitioning, the DTA will provide scripts to create the partition function, the partition scheme, and the clustered index. Here is an example of a DTA partitioning recommendation we received from a different database. The underlying table has 57,000,000 rows, and uses 1.8GB of data space and 3.6GB of index space:

```
CREATE PARTITION FUNCTION [_dta_pf__2533](int) AS RANGE LEFT FOR VALUES (103863552,
196930103, 203421423, 246065168, 269171113, 269702979, 270375078, 273695583,
276447808, 280951053, 298459732, 298855583, 299375843, 299810346, 301474640)

CREATE PARTITION SCHEME [_dta_ps__8258] AS PARTITION [_dta_pf__2533] TO ([PRIMARY],
[PRIMARY], [PRIMARY], [PRIMARY], [PRIMARY], [PRIMARY], [PRIMARY], [PRIMARY],
[PRIMARY], [PRIMARY], [PRIMARY], [PRIMARY], [PRIMARY], [PRIMARY], [PRIMARY],
[PRIMARY])

CREATE NONCLUSTERED INDEX [_dta_index_myTable_6_741577680_23810504_K1_K2_K3] ON
[dbo].[myTable]
(
  [Col1] ASC,
  [Col2] ASC,
  [Col3] ASC
)WITH (SORT_IN_TEMPDB = OFF, DROP_EXISTING = OFF, IGNORE_DUP_KEY = OFF, ONLINE =
OFF) ON [_dta_ps__8258]([Colx])
```

Filtered Indexes and Filtered Statistics

As mentioned previously, filtered indexes and filtered statistics are new features in SQL Server 2008. Filtered indexes or stats can take a WHERE predicate to indicate which rows are to be indexed. Obviously, you are indexing only a portion of rows in a table, which means you can only create a nonclustered filtered index. If you try to create a filtered clustered index, SQL Server will return a syntax error. Here is the syntax to create the filtered index:

This is not the complete CREATE INDEX syntax, but rather a portion to indicate the WHERE predicate required to create the filtered index. Refer to the topic "CREATE INDEX (Transact-SQL)" in BOL for the complete syntax.

```
CREATE [ UNIQUE ] [ CLUSTERED | NONCLUSTERED ] INDEX index_name
    ON <object> ( column [ ASC | DESC ] [ , ... n ] )
    [ INCLUDE ( column_name [ , ... n ] ) ]
    [ WHERE <filter_predicate> ]
```

Why do you need a nonclustered index with subset of data in a table? A well-designed filtered index can offer the following advantages over full-table indexes:

❑ **Improved query performance and plan quality** — If the index is deep (more pages because of more data), traversing an index takes more I/O and results in slow query performance. If you have a very large table and you know that there are more user queries on a well-defined subset of data, then creating a filtered index will make queries run faster, as less I/O will be performed because the number of pages is less for the smaller amount of data in that filtered index. More-over, stats on the full table may be less accurate compared to filtered stats with less data, which also helps improve query performance.

❑ **Reduced index maintenance costs** — Maintaining a filtered index is less costly than maintaining a full index because of smaller data size. Obviously, it reduces the cost of updating statistics too because of the smaller size of the filtered index. As mentioned earlier, you have to know your user queries and what kind of data they query often to create a well-defined filtered index with a subset of that data. If the data outside of the filtered index is modified frequently, then it won't cost anything to maintain the filtered index. That enables you to create many filtered indexes when the data in those indexes is not modified frequently.

❑ **Reduced index storage costs** — Less data, less space. If you don't need a full-table nonclustered index, creating a smaller dataset for a nonclustered filtered index takes less disk space. In addi-tion, creating filtered indexes versus one large nonclustered index will not increase your storage requirements by much.

There are some considerations you should keep in mind to effectively use filtered indexes. As with any other indexes you create, you have to analyze your workload for specific user queries. You still have to understand your application and determine which user queries rely on specific subsets of data. Examples of data that have well-defined subsets are columns with mostly null values, columns with heterogeneous categories of values, and columns with distinct ranges of values.

For example, suppose you have a column with null and non-null values and your user queries mostly ask for non-null values as the WHERE predicate. If your table is large, you should consider creating a filtered nonclustered index on this column, which contains only non-null values. That way, the size of the index will be smaller, and you will have less index maintenance cost. In addition, because of less data in that index, you will have fewer I/Os and your queries will also be faster.

In general, the Database Engine and tools provide the same support for filtered indexes that they provide for nonclustered full-table indexes, considering filtered indexes as a special type of nonclustered indexes.

The following table provides information about tools and features that fully support, do not support, or have restricted support for filtered indexes.

Tool/Feature	Level of Support for Filtered Indexes	Description
Missing Indexes	Do not support	This feature suggests missing indexes for user queries to improve performance. It will not suggest any missing filtered Indexes.
DTA	Fully supported	The DTA will recommend filtered indexes.
Online Index Operation	Fully supported	You can do online index operations on filtered indexes.
Table Hints	Supported with restrictions	You could use a filtered index as table hints. Some restrictions are applied. Refer to the topic "Filtered Index Design Guidelines" in BOL for details.

Tool/Feature	Level of Support for Filtered Indexes	Description
ALTER INDEX	Fully supported	You can use the CREATE INDEX WITH DROP_EXISTING option to do this.
XML Indexes	Not supported	You cannot create filtered XML indexes.
Full-Text Indexes	Not supported	You cannot create full-text filtered indexes.
IGNORE_DUP_KEY option of CREATE INDEX	Not supported	You cannot use this option in a CREATE INDEX statement when you create filtered indexes.

You can use the following metadata query to get information about the filtered indexes:

```
SELECT * FROM sys.indexes WHERE has_filter = 1
```

You can also query the sys.sql_expression_dependencies view to see the dependency information on a filtered index:

```
SELECT * FROM sys.indexes WHERE has_filter = 1
```

Filtered statistics also work like filtered indexes. The SQL Server Database Engine automatically creates and maintains filtered statistics for filtered indexes. These filtered statistics are more accurate than full-table statistics because they cover only the rows in the filtered index. Filtered indexes use the default sampling rate for creating filtered statistics. When you create filtered statistics with the CREATE STATISTICS statement, you can choose the sampling rate.

Index Maintenance

A number of problems can occur with indexes over time as data changes in the underlying table. As rows are inserted, deleted, and updated, the distribution of data through the index can become unbalanced, with some pages becoming fully packed, leading to additional results causing immediate page splits. Other pages can become very sparsely filled, causing many pages to be read to access a few rows of data. These problems can be easily overcome with some simple index maintenance.

The first thing you need to do is implement some monitoring to figure out when the indexes are getting to the stage where they need attention. The second step is figuring out which of the various options for index maintenance you should use to clean up the index.

Monitoring Index Fragmentation

SQL Server 2000 used DBCC showcontig to monitor index fragmentation. With SQL Server 2005 and later editions, you have a new function, sys.dm_db_index_physical_stats. The syntax for this function is detailed in full in BOL, so here's a look at running it with our People sample database:

```
use People
go

SELECT *
```

```
FROM sys.dm_db_index_physical_stats
  (
  DB_ID('People'),
  OBJECT_ID('People'),
  NULL,
  NULL ,
  'DETAILED'
  )
go
```

The results provide a lot of information, but there are just a few things you really want to focus on. In fact, to get the information you need on the level of fragmentation, you can use the following query:

```
SELECT index_id, index_level, avg_fragmentation_in_percent
FROM sys.dm_db_index_physical_stats
  (
  DB_ID('People'),
  OBJECT_ID('People'),
  NULL,
  NULL ,
  'DETAILED'
  )
go
```

What you are looking for is any level of index where the avg_fragmentation_in_percent is higher than 0, although low single digits are also acceptable. In the case of the People table, I dropped and recreated the table, created the indexes, and then loaded 200,000 rows. After executing these steps the results don't look so good, and they show a high level of index fragmentation. Please note that your results may differ:

```
index_id    index_level avg_fragmentation_in_percent
----------- ----------- ----------------------------
1           0           98.6089375760737
1           1           96.4285714285714
1           2           0
6           0           1.38666666666667
6           1           57.1428571428571
6           2           0
7           0           98.3564458140729
7           1           100
7           2           0
8           0           99.1496598639456
8           1           98.4375
8           2           0
9           0           98.4857309260338
9           1           88.8888888888889
9           2           0
10          0           98.772504091653
10          1           40
10          2           0
```

In this case, you would probably want to clean the indexes up a bit, as described in the following section.

Cleaning Up Indexes

Now that you know you have fragmented indexes, you have three options for cleaning them up. The first and most comprehensive is to drop and recreate the indexes. This is the most intrusive, as each index needs to be dropped and then recreated. When an index is dropped, it is not available for use. Moreover, the drop and create operations are automatic, so the table is locked while this is happening, and not available for use. The second option is to use the statement ALTER INDEX REORGANIZE, which was first added in SQL Server 2005. This statement replaces DBCC INDEXDEFRAG. The third option is to use the other statement, ALTER INDEX REBUILD, which replaces DBCC DBREINDEX.

If you have the luxury and time to take the table offline, you should use the first option, and drop and recreate the indexes. If you need to keep the table online, and want a less intrusive option, you should use either of the ALTER INDEX options. Both ALTER INDEX options are online, enabling the table to remain available during the index maintenance operation. The more online of the two is ALTER INDEX REORGANIZE, but it doesn't do as comprehensive a job with the index. We'll run each option on the badly fragmented index and see how well it does.

We'll start with ALTER INDEX REORGANIZE. After running the command

```
alter index all on people reorganize
```

the index fragmentation now looks as follows (your results may differ):

```
index_id    index_level avg_fragmentation_in_percent
----------- ----------- ----------------------------
1           0           0.960960960960961
1           1           96.4285714285714
1           2           0
6           0           1.38740661686233
6           1           57.1428571428571
6           2           0
7           0           2.53968253968254
7           1           100
7           2           0
8           0           1.9639407598197
8           1           98.4375
8           2           0
9           0           2.031144211239
9           1           88.8888888888889
9           2           0
10          0           2.45464247598719
10          1           40
10          2           0
```

It's an improvement. You aren't back to the level you could be, but it was fast.

Now try the next option, ALTER INDEX REBUILD:

```
alter index all on people rebuild
```

After running this command, the indexes look as follows (again, your results may differ):

index_id	index_level	avg_fragmentation_in_percent
1	0	0
1	1	11.7647058823529
1	2	0
6	0	0
6	1	0
6	2	0
7	0	0
7	1	0
7	2	0
8	0	0
8	1	12.5
8	2	0
9	0	0
9	1	0
9	2	0
10	0	0
10	1	0
10	2	0

It's pretty easy to see the large improvement in this over the results from REORGANIZE.

Finally, do the big one, and drop and recreate the indexes. After doing this, the indexes look like the following (your results may differ):

index_id	index_level	avg_fragmentation_in_percent
1	0	0
1	1	0
1	2	0
6	0	0
6	1	0
6	2	0
7	0	0
7	1	0
7	2	0
8	0	0
8	1	12.5
8	2	0
9	0	0
9	1	0
9	2	0
10	0	0
10	1	0
10	2	0

That's a quick look at index maintenance. What we haven't done is monitor the impact that the fragmentation might have had on queries. We will look into that in the next section.

Database Tuning Advisor

It used to be that the DBA had to spend a lot of time reviewing the database design, learning about data distribution, finding and examining in detail the main queries, and then manually tuning indexes to try to find the best set of indexes to suit individual queries. With the DTA, that slow and laborious process is no longer needed. You can use the DTA to tune individual queries as they are being developed, and to tune entire workloads as they become available.

The DTA does this either by analyzing individual queries from SQL Management Studio, or with a SQL Server Profiler trace file. The workload should contain at least one example of each query called, but it doesn't need to contain repeated calls to the same procedure, as you would expect to see in a trace from a production system. This is because the DTA only tunes each unique query; it isn't going to look at the interaction of all the queries in the result set and provide a balanced set of indexes to suit a mix of INSERT, UPDATE, and DELETE statements. It simply looks at each query and provides recommendations to improve that query, so the DBA still has some work to do in deciding which indexes to implement to get the best compromise between insert, update, and delete performance.

Now we'll jump straight into using the DTA to create some indexes.

Using the DTA to Tune Individual Queries

Imagine the following scenario: As a developer DBA, you are writing queries for a new database that has no queries and you want to create an initial set of indexes. You need a database with data in it, and that data has to be representative of the final data distribution. In the sample workload, you'll examine the index recommendations with three levels of data in the target tables.

For the exercise in this section, open the solution file PeopleDTA.ssmssln from the folder PeopleDTA in the download files. I have also provided a PeopleDTA.bak database backup file in the PeopleDTA folder. Restore that database with the name PeopleDTA and set the recovery mode to simple for this database. You can find the restore script named RestorePeopleDTA.sql in this solution. The code for the restore script is as follows:

> *Be sure to change the* FROM DISK *path to the correct file location of* PeopleDTA.bak, *and change the file location for the* MOVE *option to represent the correct path on your system.*

```
USE master
GO

RESTORE DATABASE [PeopleDTA]
FROM  DISK = N'C:\Samples\PeopleDTA\PeopleDTA.bak'
WITH  FILE = 1,
 MOVE N'People' TO N'C:\mssql\Data\PeopleDTA.mdf'
,MOVE N'People_log' TO N'C:\mssql\Data\PeopleDTA_1.LDF'
,NOUNLOAD
,REPLACE
,STATS = 10
GO
------------------------------
ALTER DATABASE [PeopleDTA] SET RECOVERY SIMPLE
GO
```

Run it. After the database is restored, you can run the following script to truncate the few tables. The script is provided in the `RestorePeopleDTA.sql` file so just copy the following lines from the code and run them:

```
USE PeopleDTA
GO

TRUNCATE TABLE People
```

Next, you need to insert and update data in the listed tables, and then run the DTA to get some statistics. The following table shows the numbers of rows in each table where you'll run the DTA for the `InsertPeople` query.

	Insert	Update 1
People	0	1,000,000
BoysNames	100	100
GirlsNames	100	100
LastNames	2,000	2,000

Before starting to run the DTA, you need to figure out how to determine the effectiveness of each of the DTA recommendations. DTA will give you its expectation of performance improvement, but you should check its effectiveness for yourself, so you need some way to measure before and after performance.

We've chosen to use three metrics for this. The first is the insert time for each row. To get this you can use a simple stored procedure that calls the `Insert` stored procedure multiple times and reports how many rows it inserted and the insert rate at predetermined intervals. The second metric is the output of the `statistics IO`. You can gather this data using SQL Server Management Studio, by turning on the Query option for `Statistics IO`. The third metric is statistics time which displays the number of milliseconds required to parse, compile, and execute each SQL statement.

Before you start tuning, capture your starting metrics. To ensure that you get consistent results, you also need to capture a cold time and several warm times, and then average the warm times.

One other thing you'll look at in this example is the wait time during query execution. You can only do this if you run the procedure in a tight loop, because unless the query is very slow-running, you won't be able to capture the instantaneous results you need to see any waits; but by running in a tight loop, you can sample the wait stats repeatedly and thereby stand a good chance of seeing what the query is waiting on.

The examples shown in the figures in this chapter were run on a Lenovo 645DD2 Dual-Core CPU @ 2.2 GHz laptop with 4GB of RAM, and a single 150GB hard drive. Note that your results may vary depending on the machine on which you run this workload.

Start off by capturing stats for the `Exec_InsertPeople` stored procedure with an empty `People` table. To ensure that the server is in a cold state, use the following commands before each cold run to flush memory to disk, and make sure you get a full stored procedure compile cycle on the first run. This is much faster than restarting SQL Server every time, and it provides good repeatable results:

```
dbcc dropcleanbuffers
dbcc freeproccache
```

Open the script `Exec_InsertPeople.sql`, which includes the following code, and run it:

```
USE PeopleDTA
GO

dbcc dropcleanbuffers
dbcc freeproccache
GO

SET STATISTICS TIME ON
SET STATISTICS IO ON
GO

-- Cold run
EXEC dbo.InsertPeople
GO

-- First Warm run
EXEC dbo.InsertPeople
GO

-- Second Warm run
EXEC dbo.InsertPeople
GO

-- Third Warm run
EXEC dbo.InsertPeople
GO


SET STATISTICS TIME OFF
SET STATISTICS IO OFF
GO

-- we ran the SP to insert 2 people 4 times, so we should have 8 people in the DB
SELECT COUNT(*)
FROM People

GO
```

Following are the partial results of executing this script. You should see four sections in the results on your system: Cold run, first warm run, second warm run, and third warm run. The full result is not presented here. Please use your query results in SQL Server Management Studio to follow the explanation.

```
DBCC execution completed. If DBCC printed error messages, contact your system
administrator.
DBCC execution completed. If DBCC printed error messages, contact your system
administrator.

 SQL Server Execution Times:
    CPU time = 0 ms,  elapsed time = 0 ms.
SQL Server parse and compile time:
    CPU time = 0 ms, elapsed time = 0 ms.
--------------------Cold run----------------
```

```
    SQL Server Execution Times:
       CPU time = 0 ms,  elapsed time = 0 ms.
    SQL Server parse and compile time:
       CPU time = 16 ms, elapsed time = 58 ms.

    SQL Server Execution Times:
       CPU time = 0 ms,  elapsed time = 0 ms.
    Table 'BoysNames'. Scan count 1, logical reads 1, physical reads 0, read-
    ahead reads 0,
    lob logical reads 0, lob physical reads 0, lob read-ahead reads 0.

    SQL Server Execution Times:
       CPU time = 0 ms,  elapsed time = 9 ms.
    Table 'GirlsNames'. Scan count 1, logical reads 1, physical reads 0, read-
    ahead reads 0,
    lob logical reads 0, lob physical reads 0, lob read-ahead reads 0.

    SQL Server Execution Times:
       CPU time = 0 ms,  elapsed time = 1 ms.
    Table 'LastNames'. Scan count 1, logical reads 16, physical reads 2, read-
    ahead reads 10,
    lob logical reads 0, lob physical reads 0, lob read-ahead reads 0.

    SQL Server Execution Times:
       CPU time = 0 ms,  elapsed time = 1 ms.

    SQL Server Execution Times:
       CPU time = 0 ms,  elapsed time = 0 ms.
    Table 'BoysNames'. Scan count 1, logical reads 1, physical reads 0, read-
    ahead reads 0,
    lob logical reads 0, lob physical reads 0, lob read-ahead reads 0.

    SQL Server Execution Times:
       CPU time = 0 ms,  elapsed time = 0 ms.
    Table 'GirlsNames'. Scan count 1, logical reads 1, physical reads 0, read-
    ahead reads 0,
    lob logical reads 0, lob physical reads 0, lob read-ahead reads 0.

    SQL Server Execution Times:
       CPU time = 0 ms,  elapsed time = 0 ms.
    Table 'LastNames'. Scan count 1, logical reads 16, physical reads 0, read-
    ahead reads 0,
    lob logical reads 0, lob physical reads 0, lob read-ahead reads 0.

    SQL Server Execution Times:
       CPU time = 0 ms,  elapsed time = 0 ms.
    Table 'People'. Scan count 0, logical reads 1, physical reads 0, read-
    ahead reads 0, lob
    logical reads 0, lob physical reads 0, lob read-ahead reads 0.

    SQL Server Execution Times:
       CPU time = 0 ms,  elapsed time = 1 ms.
    Table 'People'. Scan count 0, logical reads 1, physical reads 0, read-
    ahead reads 0, lob
    logical reads 0, lob physical reads 0, lob read-ahead reads 0.
```

633

```
SQL Server Execution Times:
  CPU time = 0 ms,  elapsed time = 1 ms.

SQL Server Execution Times:
  CPU time = 16 ms,  elapsed time = 72 ms.
SQL Server parse and compile time:
  CPU time = 0 ms, elapsed time = 0 ms.
```

This is some very useful information. Looking at both the cold and warm run outputs, you can see that they are both pretty fast, with a cold run elapsed time of 76 ms and a warm run elapsed time of 3 ms.

Looking at the cold run stats and focusing on the number of physical reads, you can see that there were a total of two physical reads, both for LastNames table. There was one logical read for the BoysName table and one logical read for the GirlsNames table.

The warm run stats show that there were no physical reads, only logical reads. The parse and compile time was also greatly reduced to zero. This tells us that the query didn't need recompiling, which is good because that saves a lot of time each time it's called. The warm run stats also show that it's taking about 30 to 40 ms for each insert.

Given that we are only issuing two physical reads to execute the query, and that repeated calls don't invoke additional physical reads, it's going to be hard to improve performance by further reducing these already low numbers. It's also going to be hard to see any small time-based improvements when the time taken is already so short, at just 30–40 milliseconds.

To make it easier to observe small changes in performance, you need to execute the queries hundreds or thousands of times, and then look at the overall stats for a very large number of executions. This helps to highlight any small changes.

To do this, open the file Exec_MakePeople-1.sql and run it. The following code is taken from the file and shows the result of the execution of this script. Note that the results on your machine may vary a little.

```
USE PeopleDTA
GO

EXEC dbo.MakePeople @People = 5000, @ReportInterval = 1000

/*
--output from above script.

-----------------------------------------------------------------
Inserted 2000 people in 1496mS at a rate of 1336.9 per Second
-----------------------------------------------------------------
Inserted 2000 people in 1356mS at a rate of 1474.93 per Second
-----------------------------------------------------------------
Inserted 2000 people in 1356mS at a rate of 1474.93 per Second
-----------------------------------------------------------------
Inserted 2000 people in 1340mS at a rate of 1492.54 per Second
-----------------------------------------------------------------
Inserted 2000 people in 1513mS at a rate of 1321.88 per Second

*/ .
```

The inserts are going fast enough that you are getting between 1,300 and 1,500 inserts per second.

Now you should see what you are waiting on. To do that, open the file `MakePeople-WaitType.sql`. The code for this follows, but don't run it yet:

```
--- before running this make sure to run the editor in SQLCMD mode by
--- selecting "SQLCMD mode" from Query menu.
!!sqlcmd /S(local) /E /d PeopleDTA /Q "exec MakePeople 10000, 1000"
```

Be sure to change the `/S` parameter to provide the correct machine name if you are not running on your local machine. Once you open the file, use the SQLCMD mode functionality that comes with SQL Server Management Studio (SSMS) to run this from the command prompt. To do this from the Query menu, select the SQLCMD mode option — but don't run the code yet.

Now open the file `WatchWaitType.sql`, shown next, to watch the inserts you are waiting for:

```
set nocount on
while 1 > 0
begin
   select spid, kpid, blocked, waittime, lastwaittype, waitresource
   from master..sysprocesses
   where program_name = 'SQLCMD'
   waitfor delay '00:00:00.05'
end
```

Next, run the `MakePeople-WaitType.sql` script and then run the `WatchWaitType.sql` script. The following code shows a portion of the output from the `WatchWaitType.sql` script. This will give you the `LastWaitType` (which is `WRITELOG`) because of the `INSERT` into the `People` table in the `InsertPeople` stored procedure, which is called by the `MakePeople` stored procedure. You will see substantial output because the script is running in the loop, but the purpose here is to see the wait type:

```
/*
--partial output from above query.
spid   kpid   blocked waittime              lastwaittype     waitresource
------ ------ ------- -------------------- --------------- -------------
53     6728   0       1                    WRITELOG

spid   kpid   blocked waittime              lastwaittype     waitresource
------ ------ ------- -------------------- --------------- -------------
53     6728   0       0                    WRITELOG

spid   kpid   blocked waittime              lastwaittype     waitresource
------ ------ ------- -------------------- --------------- --------------
53     6728   0       1                    WRITELOG

spid   kpid   blocked waittime              lastwaittype     waitresource
------ ------ ------- -------------------- --------------- -------------
53     6728   0       0                    WRITELOG

*/
```

Not surprisingly, on such a simple insert on a very basic slow disk, most of the time is spent waiting on the log write. The information here tells you that most of the stats are meaningless except for the raw write rate that results from the `Exec_MakePeople-1.sql` script.

One final check before going on to the DTA is to take a look at the output of `showplan_text` to see what the query plan looks like. You can then compare this with the query plan after applying any recommendations from the DTA and see how it changes.

Open the script `Exec_InsertPeople-2.sql`, shown here:

```
USE PeopleDTA
GO

dbcc dropcleanbuffers
dbcc freeproccache
GO

SET SHOWPLAN_TEXT ON
GO

EXEC dbo.InsertPeople
GO

SET SHOWPLAN_TEXT OFF
```

Run the script to look at the execution plan. The output is substantial because the SHOWPLAN_TEXT option is ON. The complete output is provided inside the same script file as a comment. Following are the key elements of interest:

```
|--Table Scan(OBJECT:([PeopleDTA].[dbo].[BoysNames]))
|--Table Scan(OBJECT:([PeopleDTA].[dbo].[GirlsNames]))
|--Table Scan(OBJECT:([PeopleDTA].[dbo].[LastNames]))
```

This shows that you are using a table scan to get the names from the lookup tables `BoysNames`, `GirlsNames`, and `LastNames`. On `BoysNames` and `GirlsNames` this works just fine because the tables are so small, but this isn't so optimal on `LastNames`, a table that has 2,000 rows and occupies seven or eight database pages.

Now see what the DTA recommends for you. Running the DTA against the sample query is simple. Open the file `Exec_InsertPeople-3.sql` in a new query window. Right-click somewhere in the window and select Analyze Query in Database Engine Tuning Advisor, as shown in Figure 15-1.

This brings up the Database Engine Tuning Advisor (see Figure 15-2).

You need to change two things before you click the Start Analysis button. First, change the database for workload analysis from `master` to `PeopleDTA`. Second, select the database you want to tune — in this case, `PeopleDTA`. Now you are ready to start the analysis session by clicking the Start Analysis button. When you start the analysis session, the DTA adds a new Progress tab and updates its analysis progress.

When the analysis is complete, the DTA adds two more tabs: Recommendations and Reports.

For the insert query, the DTA has recommended that you create a clustered index on the `LastNames` table, as shown in Figure 15-3. This will reduce the number of reads in the `LastNames` table.

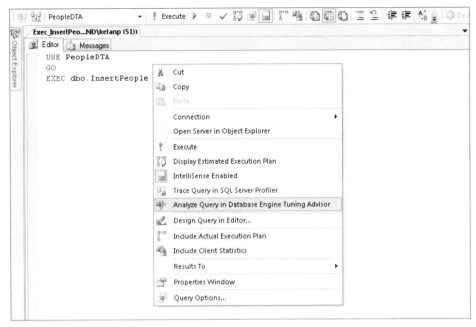

Figure 15-1

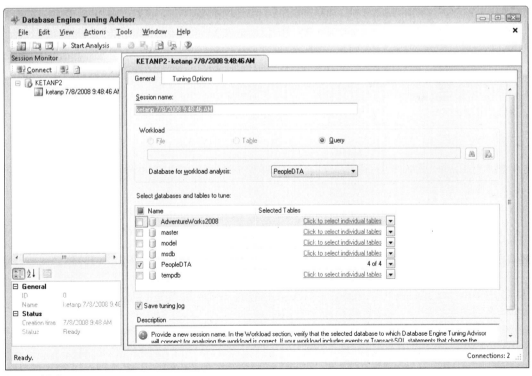

Figure 15-2

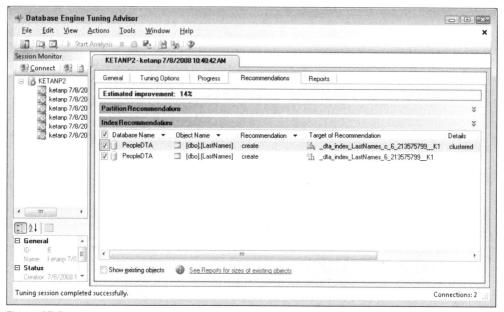

Figure 15-3

Implement this recommendation by selecting Apply Recommendations from the Actions menu in the Database Tuning Advisor window. Start by looking at the stats time and I/O after adding the clustered and nonclustered index on the LastNames table.

Open the script Exec_InsertPeople-4.sql and run it. The following is abbreviated stats output, showing just the key areas that have changed:

```
--------------------Cold run-----------------

SQL Server Execution Times:
   CPU time = 0 ms,  elapsed time = 0 ms.
SQL Server parse and compile time:
   CPU time = 0 ms, elapsed time = 40 ms.

SQL Server Execution Times:
   CPU time = 0 ms,  elapsed time = 0 ms.
Table 'BoysNames'. Scan count 1, logical reads 1, physical reads 0, read-ahead
reads 0, lob logical reads 0, lob physical reads 0, lob read-ahead reads 0.

SQL Server Execution Times:
   CPU time = 0 ms,  elapsed time = 8 ms.
Table 'GirlsNames'. Scan count 1, logical reads 1, physical reads 0, read-ahead
reads 0, lob logical reads 0, lob physical reads 0, lob read-ahead reads 0.

SQL Server Execution Times:
   CPU time = 0 ms,  elapsed time = 1 ms.
```

```
Table 'LastNames'. Scan count 1, logical reads 4, physical reads 0, read-ahead
reads 0, lob logical reads 0, lob physical reads 0, lob read-ahead reads 0.

SQL Server Execution Times:
   CPU time = 0 ms,  elapsed time = 61 ms.
SQL Server parse and compile time:
   CPU time = 0 ms, elapsed time = 0 ms.

--------------------1st Warm run-------------

 SQL Server Execution Times:
   CPU time = 0 ms,  elapsed time = 0 ms.
SQL Server parse and compile time:
   CPU time = 0 ms, elapsed time = 0 ms.

 SQL Server Execution Times:
   CPU time = 0 ms,  elapsed time = 0 ms.
Table 'BoysNames'. Scan count 1, logical reads 1, physical reads 0, read-ahead
reads 0, lob logical reads 0, lob physical reads 0, lob read-ahead reads 0.

 SQL Server Execution Times:
   CPU time = 0 ms,  elapsed time = 0 ms.
Table 'GirlsNames'. Scan count 1, logical reads 1, physical reads 0, read-ahead
reads 0, lob logical reads 0, lob physical reads 0, lob read-ahead reads 0.

 SQL Server Execution Times:        •
   CPU time = 0 ms,  elapsed time = 0 ms.
Table 'LastNames'. Scan count 1, logical reads 4, physical reads 0, read-ahead
reads 0, lob logical reads 0, lob physical reads 0, lob read-ahead reads 0.

 SQL Server Execution Times:
   CPU time = 0 ms,  elapsed time = 1 ms.

 SQL Server Execution Times:
   CPU time = 0 ms,  elapsed time = 2 ms.
```

There are two differences between these stats and the earlier pre-indexed stats. Now that you are using the clustered index on LastNames, the number of logical reads is reduced dramatically, from 16 down to 4. In addition, when the table is first read on the cold run, now it is being read in using a read-ahead, which brings the whole table into memory much more quickly than if you use a regular table scan as you did before indexing.

You can run the Exec_InsertPeople-2.sql script to see the SHOWPLAN_TEXT output as well. Here is the relevant section from the plan output. As you can see when the insert runs, it uses the clustered index on the LastNames table:

```
StmtText
------------------------------------------------------------------------------
      |--Clustered Index
Seek(OBJECT:([PeopleDTA].[dbo].[LastNames].[_dta_index_LastNames_c_7_21575115__K1]),
```

This shows that you are in fact using the newly added clustered index. Now see how much this affects the execution of the query (remember that before you were able to achieve 1,300–1,500 inserts per second). Open the script `Exec_MakePeople-1.sql` and run it again:

```
----------------------------------------------------------
Inserted 2000 people in 1416mS at a rate of 1412.43 per Second
----------------------------------------------------------
Inserted 2000 people in 1263mS at a rate of 1583.53 per Second
----------------------------------------------------------
Inserted 2000 people in 1246mS at a rate of 1605.14 per Second
----------------------------------------------------------
Inserted 2000 people in 1546mS at a rate of 1293.66 per Second
----------------------------------------------------------
Inserted 2000 people in 1526mS at a rate of 1310.62 per Second
```

This shows that the rate of insertion has increased to 1,600 per second. That's quite an improvement for adding a clustered index.

One final thing to check. You can run the scripts `MakePeople-WaitType.sql` and `WatchWaitType.sql` as you did earlier:

```
spid   kpid   blocked waittime          lastwaittype
54     5804   0       0                 WRITELOG
54     5804   0       0                 WRITELOG
54     5804   0       0                 WRITELOG
54     5804   0       0                 WRITELOG
```

No surprises there: It's still the log that's limiting insert performance.

Indexes for Updates

Next you want to tune the update query. Start that by capturing some metrics about the query's performance. Before doing that, however, fill the `People` table a bit by writing a couple of million rows. You need that many rows in order to get a full set of results for the `Marriage` query, which pulls out the top 1,000 rows for a given date range.

Open the script `Exec_InsertPeople-5.sql` and run it. It will truncate the `People` table and fill up with 1,000,000 rows. After that, you can start capturing metrics around the raw query performance again. Open the query `Exec_Marriage.sql` that calls the `Marriage` stored procedure and that updates the `LastName` column in the `People` table. Here is the code:

```
USE PeopleDTA
GO
EXEC dbo.Marriage
```

Here are the results of the cold run and two warm runs, edited to remove the many extra rows, and with some additional formatting for clarity:

```
--------------------Cold run----------------
SQL Server Execution Times:
   CPU time = 0 ms,  elapsed time = 0 ms.
```

```
Table 'People'. Scan count 4, logical reads 7053, physical reads 15, read-ahead
reads 1101, lob logical reads 0, lob physical reads 0, lob read-ahead reads 0.
Table 'Worktable'. Scan count 1, logical reads 5, physical reads 0, read-ahead
reads 0, lob logical reads 0, lob physical reads 0, lob read-ahead reads 0.

 SQL Server Execution Times:
   CPU time = 124 ms,   elapsed time = 755 ms.

(1 row(s) affected)

 SQL Server Execution Times:
   CPU time = 0 ms,   elapsed time = 0 ms.

 SQL Server Execution Times:
   CPU time = 0 ms,   elapsed time = 1 ms.

 SQL Server Execution Times:
   CPU time = 0 ms,   elapsed time = 1 ms.

 SQL Server Execution Times:
   CPU time = 623 ms,   elapsed time = 2287 ms.
 SQL Server parse and compile time:
   CPU time = 0 ms, elapsed time = 1 ms.
```

This shows that the cold run took 2,287 ms to complete.

The warm run looks like this:

```
-------------------1st Warm run------------
 SQL Server Execution Times:
   CPU time = 0 ms,   elapsed time = 0 ms.
Table 'People'. Scan count 4, logical reads 7053, physical reads 0, read-ahead
reads 0, lob logical reads 0, lob physical reads 0, lob read-ahead reads 0.
Table 'Worktable'. Scan count 1, logical reads 5, physical reads 0, read-ahead
reads 0, lob logical reads 0, lob physical reads 0, lob read-ahead reads 0.

 SQL Server Execution Times:
   CPU time = 125 ms,   elapsed time = 107 ms.

(1 row(s) affected)

 SQL Server Execution Times:
   CPU time = 0 ms,   elapsed time = 0 ms.

 SQL Server Execution Times:
   CPU time = 0 ms,   elapsed time = 1 ms.

 SQL Server Execution Times:
   CPU time = 0 ms,   elapsed time = 0 ms.

 SQL Server Execution Times:
   CPU time = 140 ms,   elapsed time = 133 ms.
 SQL Server parse and compile time:
   CPU time = 0 ms, elapsed time = 0 ms.
```

There was a significant improvement between the cold and warm runs, which took 133 ms, down to the reduction in compilation time and the faster access, as the tables are now mostly loaded into memory. This is shown in the reduction in read-ahead reads between the cold and warm runs.

This procedure is taking between 2.2 seconds for a cold run and 0.1 second for a warm run, so it should be much easier to see any improvement that the DTA can make. However, we'll still run it in a loop and see what the average update rate is over a longer period of executions.

Open the script `Exec_DoMarriage.sql`, shown here, and run it:

```
USE PeopleDTA
GO

EXEC dbo.DoMarriages @People = 50, @ReportInterval = 5
```

This stored procedure calls the `Marriage` stored procedure, which in turn actually updates the `LastName` column in the `People` table. Run the script to see the following results:

```
----------------------------------------------------------
Married 10 people in 436mS at a rate of 22.9358 per Second
----------------------------------------------------------
Married 10 people in 373mS at a rate of 26.8097 per Second
----------------------------------------------------------
Married 10 people in 376mS at a rate of 26.5957 per Second
----------------------------------------------------------
Married 10 people in 360mS at a rate of 27.7778 per Second
----------------------------------------------------------
Married 10 people in 390mS at a rate of 25.641 per Second
----------------------------------------------------------
Married 10 people in 360mS at a rate of 27.7778 per Second
----------------------------------------------------------
Married 10 people in 360mS at a rate of 27.7778 per Second
----------------------------------------------------------
Married 10 people in 360mS at a rate of 27.7778 per Second
----------------------------------------------------------
Married 10 people in 350mS at a rate of 28.5714 per Second
----------------------------------------------------------
Married 10 people in 360mS at a rate of 27.7778 per Second
```

The results show that the query is taking between 22 and 28 updates per seconds to execute, so it should be relatively easy to see any performance improvement.

Before running the DTA, let's take a quick look at the wait types. Run the command again and run the monitoring code and capture the `waittypes` from `sysprocesses`. The output should look something like this:

spid	kpid	blocked	waittime	lastwaittype
52	4212	0	546	LOGMGR_RESERVE_APPEND
52	4212	0	0	SOS_SCHEDULER_YIELD

There was a pretty even split between these two wait types. SQL Server Books Online explains what each of the wait types means. Look these up either by searching on the wait type or by searching for `sys.dm_os_wait_stats`. The `LOGMGR_RESERVE_APPEND` occurs when you are waiting to see whether truncating the log gives you enough space to write the current log record. In this case, the database was configured with the `simple` recovery model, and the log file is on a very slow disk, so expect to see a lot of log-related waits.

`SOS_SCHEDULER_YIELD` occurs when a task voluntarily yields the scheduler and has to wait for a new quantum. These are quite different from the wait types in the insert query, which is expected because the update has a very different characteristic than the insert.

Now see what the DTA has to say about this workload. This time we'll show you how to run the DTA against a workload. The next step here is to set up SQL Server Profiler to capture a trace file, which is covered in Chapter 13. Remember two key things when setting up SQL Serve Profiler for this trace: use the Tuning template, and ensure that the files are set to roll over, although the overall file size will be trivial.

Open the file `Exec_Marriage_1.sql`. Once the Profiler is set up and the trace is running, run the script. When it is completed, stop the trace, which saves the file. Now you have a workload trace file on disk, and you can start the DTA and use it to tune the workload. You can launch the DTA from SQL Server Management Studio or the Profiler from the Tools menu. Launch the DTA and connect to your SQL Server. If you have been following through the earlier sections, you will see the earlier trace sessions in the left pane of the DTA, as shown in Figure 15-4.

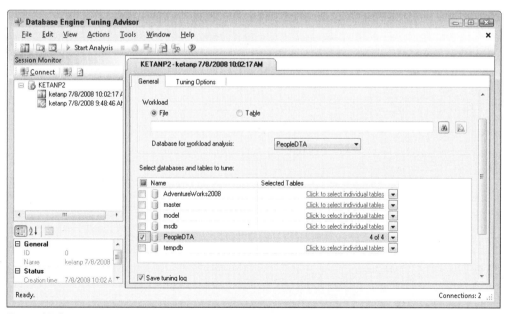

Figure 15-4

This is another part of the DTA that is worth briefly mentioning. Each of your tuning sessions is saved, so you can go back and review what you asked the DTA to tune, and the recommendations it made. However, if you just use the default session names, as we have been doing, then the tuning session names don't really have a lot of meaning, and pretty soon it's difficult to know what each session was for. Therefore, we suggest that you come up with a naming scheme that makes sense to you. This will help you find the session you're looking for in the future.

After setting the database to be PeopleDTA in both the drop-down selection and the list of databases to tune (refer to Figure 15-4), you need to tell the DTA that you want to tune a file, and where the file is. Either type in the file name and full path, or use the Browse button (the binoculars icon) to select the trace file you just created, as shown in Figure 15-5.

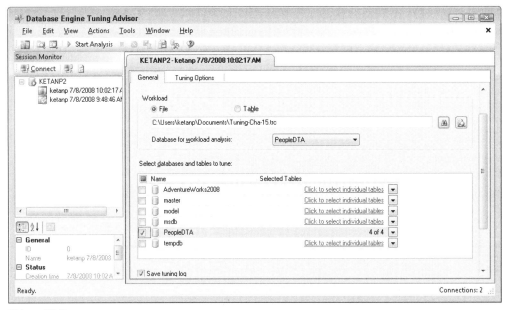

Figure 15-5

Now you can start the analysis session by clicking Start Analysis again and see what results the DTA has for you this time, as shown in Figure 15-6.

This time the DTA has two recommendations, and reckons it can improve things by approximately 97 percent. To take a closer look at what you can do with these recommendations, just scroll the recommendations window way over to the right to find the Definition column. If you hover over this a ToolTip pops up, telling you to click on the link to get a T-SQL script of the recommendations. Doing so reveals a script like the one shown in Figure 15-7.

You can now copy this script either to the clipboard and from there into a file, or directly into SQL Server Management Studio to be executed. Alternately, after taking a look at the recommendations, you can have the DTA run them for you by selecting Apply Recommendations from the Actions menu.

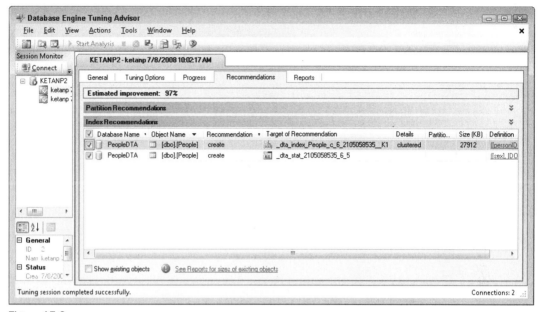

Figure 15-6

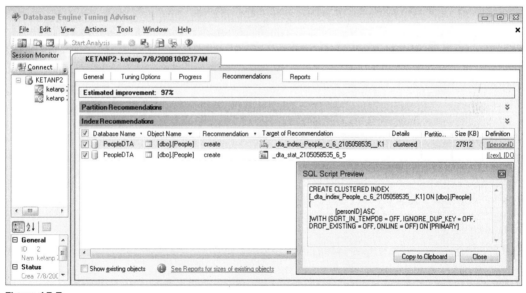

Figure 15-7

Before doing that, take a look at some of the other information in the Reports tab. This area of the DTA holds a lot of useful information about what the DTA did and why. In the simple case we have been working with here, most of the interesting information is on the Statement cost reports. Start with the first report in the list, shown in Figure 15-8.

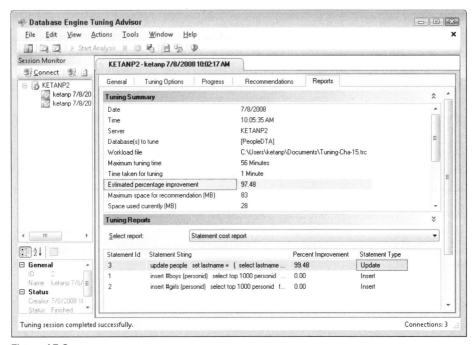

Figure 15-8

This shows the various statements in the workload, and the estimated improvement that the DTA expects to gain from the recommendation. In this case, all of the improvement comes from the update statement, which the Tuning report believes will be improved by approximately 97 percent.

To apply the changes, simply let the DTA make them. When you select Apply Recommendations, the DTA asks whether you want to run the script now or schedule it for some time in the future. Choose to make the changes right away so you can see the immediate impact. While it's executing, the DTA shows the status of the changes, as shown in Figure 15-9.

Now that it's done, go back and run the script Exec_Marriage.sql to see how fast your queries are running. Start with the output of stats I/O and stats time. Running the same script again now gives you the following results.

This is the cold run:

```
SQL Server Execution Times:
    CPU time = 0 ms,  elapsed time = 0 ms.
Table 'People'. Scan count 2, logical reads 9, physical reads 0, read-ahead reads
0, lob logical reads 0,
lob physical reads 0, lob read-ahead reads 0.
Table 'Worktable'. Scan count 1, logical reads 5, physical reads 0, read-ahead
```

```
reads 0,
lob logical reads 0, lob physical reads 0, lob read-ahead reads 0.

 SQL Server Execution Times:
   CPU time = 0 ms,  elapsed time = 51 ms.

(1 row(s) affected)

 SQL Server Execution Times:
   CPU time = 0 ms,  elapsed time = 0 ms.

 SQL Server Execution Times:
   CPU time = 0 ms,  elapsed time = 1 ms.

 SQL Server Execution Times:
   CPU time = 0 ms,  elapsed time = 1 ms.

 SQL Server Execution Times:
   CPU time = 265 ms,   elapsed time = 626 ms.
SQL Server parse and compile time:
   CPU time = 0 ms, elapsed time = 0 ms.
```

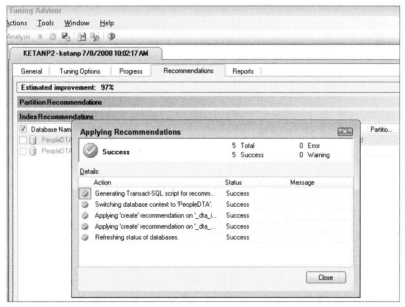

Figure 15-9

The cold run time was 2,287 ms before and now it is 626 ms. Excellent improvement.

This is the result for the warm run:

```
SQL Server Execution Times:
   CPU time = 0 ms,  elapsed time = 0 ms.
Table 'People'. Scan count 2, logical reads 9, physical reads 0, read-ahead reads
```

```
 0,
lob logical reads 0, lob physical reads 0, lob read-ahead reads 0.
Table 'Worktable'. Scan count 1, logical reads 4, physical reads 0, read-ahead
reads 0,
lob logical reads 0, lob physical reads 0, lob read-ahead reads 0.

 SQL Server Execution Times:
   CPU time = 0 ms,  elapsed time = 0 ms.

(1 row(s) affected)

 SQL Server Execution Times:
   CPU time = 0 ms,  elapsed time = 0 ms.

 SQL Server Execution Times:
   CPU time = 0 ms,  elapsed time = 1 ms.

 SQL Server Execution Times:
   CPU time = 0 ms,  elapsed time = 1 ms.

 SQL Server Execution Times:
   CPU time = 16 ms,  elapsed time = 15 ms.
SQL Server parse and compile time:
   CPU time = 0 ms, elapsed time = 0 ms.
```

The warm runtime was 133 ms; after tuning it is reduced to 15 ms.

Open the script `Exec_DoMarriage.sql` and run it again to see what the update takes:

```
------------------------------------------------------------
Married 10 people in 156mS at a rate of 64.1026 per Second
------------------------------------------------------------
Married 10 people in 76mS at a rate of 131.579 per Second
------------------------------------------------------------
Married 10 people in 76mS at a rate of 131.579 per Second
------------------------------------------------------------
Married 10 people in 63mS at a rate of 158.73 per Second
------------------------------------------------------------
Married 10 people in 140mS at a rate of 71.4286 per Second
------------------------------------------------------------
Married 10 people in 63mS at a rate of 158.73 per Second
------------------------------------------------------------
Married 10 people in 80mS at a rate of 125 per Second
------------------------------------------------------------
Married 10 people in 106mS at a rate of 94.3396 per Second
------------------------------------------------------------
Married 10 people in 93mS at a rate of 107.527 per Second
------------------------------------------------------------
Married 10 people in 80mS at a rate of 125 per Second
```

That's pretty remarkable; you have gone from 22 to 28 updates per second to almost 158 (max) updates per second. Note that the results on your machine may vary a bit because of the machine configuration.

Now check the waits again:

```
spid   kpid   blocked waittime              lastwaittype
58     4688   0       859                   LOGMGR_RESERVE_APPEND
```

This time the waits are predominantly this one wait type.

Reassessing Inserts after Adding Update Indexes

Now go back and measure the impact the update indexes have had on the `Exec_InsertPeople.sql` procedure. You haven't done anything else to the `insert` procedure, but the `update` procedure added a clustered index to the `People` table so now the `insert` procedure has to contend with the additional overhead of index maintenance, inserting new records, and splitting index pages. You can run `Exec_InsertPeople.sql` to find out how much slower this makes the inserts, and how it changes what you are waiting on.

The only obvious change here is that you can see that you are now doing an insert into a clustered index table versus the heap you were inserting into before. You can also see how this has changed the insert rate when you run `Exec_MakePeople-1.sql`.

Too Many Indexes?

One final scenario we are going to look at is how the DTA informs you when you have too many indexes. To make this obvious, we'll add a whole stack of other indexes to the four tables in this scenario, run the DTA against the `insert` and `update` procedures, and see what it indicates about indexes you aren't using.

Open the script `BadIndexes.sql`. This code will create some unnecessary indexes. Now run the script, shown here:

```
-- Create Bad indexes
use people
go

create clustered index cix_boysnames on BoysNames ( ID, Name)
go
create index ix_boysnames_id on BoysNames (id)
go

create index ix_boysnames_name on BoysNames (name)
go

create clustered index cix_girlsnames on GirlsNames ( ID, Name)
go
create index ix_Girlsnames_id on GirlsNames (id)
go
create index ix_Girlsnames_name on GirlsNames (name)
go

create clustered index cix_LastNames on LastNames ( ID, Name)
go
```

```
create index ix_Lastnames_id on LastNames (id)
go
create index ix_Lastnames_name on LastNames (name)
go

create clustered index cix_people on people(firstname)
go
create index ix_people_id on people(personid)
go
create index ix_people_dob on people(dob)
go
create index ix_people_lastname on people(lastname)
go
create index ix_people_dod on people(dod)
go
create index ix_people_sex on people(sex)
go
```

Open the file Exec_MakePeople-1.sql and run it. Here are the results of running the query (your results may vary a bit):

```
-----------------------------------------------------------
Inserted 2000 people in 6900mS at a rate of 289.855 per Second
-----------------------------------------------------------
Inserted 2000 people in 1903mS at a rate of 1050.97 per Second
-----------------------------------------------------------
Inserted 2000 people in 1403mS at a rate of 1425.52 per Second
-----------------------------------------------------------
Inserted 2000 people in 1246mS at a rate of 1605.14 per Second
-----------------------------------------------------------
Inserted 2000 people in 1436mS at a rate of 1392.76 per Second
```

These results show that insert performance has dropped dramatically. The worst batch is at only 289 inserts per second. The wait stats show that you are still waiting on the log write, although you are clearly spending a lot more time in index maintenance and reading extra pages The stats I/O time indicates that you are incurring a few extra reads on the BoysNames and GirlsNames tables, but otherwise there isn't a great difference in the stats. The showplan indicates that there is an index scan on both BoysNames and GirlsNames, rather than the single-page table scan that was there before. This is what accounts for the extra page reads:

```
|--Index Scan(OBJECT:([People].[dbo].[BoysNames].[ix_boysnames_name]))
|--Index Scan(OBJECT:([People].[dbo].[GirlsNames].[ix_Girlsnames_name]))
|--Index Scan(OBJECT:([People].[dbo].[lastNames].[ix_Lastnames_name]))
```

In addition, you are no longer using a useful clustered index on LastNames, but have to use the non-clustered index, which results in an extra page read required on every LastNames access. Overall the performance degradation isn't that great. On a system with a faster disk it might be considerably higher.

Now see what the DTA has to say about all these extra indexes. You can use the trace file you captured earlier of the Exec_Marriage_1.sql trace, but you'll have to change the DTA options. Open the DTA and select the trace file you used earlier. Select the Tuning Options tab, and under the section titled "Physical

Design Structures (PDS) to keep in database'' change the default selection from Keep All Existing PDS to Do Not Keep Any Existing PDS. You can have the DTA advise you about additional indexes as well by keeping the same options selected under the PDS section, or you can have the DTA just show you which indexes to remove. For now, ask the DTA to examine the existing indexes and to recommend additional indexes if it finds any, as shown in Figure 15-10.

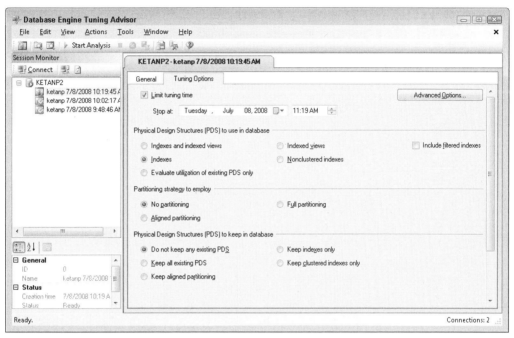

Figure 15-10

Now that you have done that, you can start the analysis session and see what results the DTA provides. The results, shown in Figure 15-11, indicate that the DTA has easily found the bad indexes. It is recommending that you drop 12 of them, and in their place create one new index on the People table.

Tuning a Workload

Tuning a whole workload is just as easy. The biggest challenge with tuning a workload is when creating the trace file of the workload in the first place, as you must determine what to put into the trace file. We did that earlier using a trace file (refer to Figure 15-4).

A note of caution when tuning a workload: the DTA makes recommendations based on the cost estimates for each part of the workload. In a workload with a variety of queries, the DTA focuses on the big gains, and may therefore miss recommendations for some of the smaller queries. Because of this, it's still worthwhile to tune individual queries after applying recommendations for the whole workload.

A good example of this is when the DTA didn't recommend indexes on the LastNames table when tuning the workload. When you tuned just the Exec_InsertPeople-3.sqlprocedure, the DTA was able to see

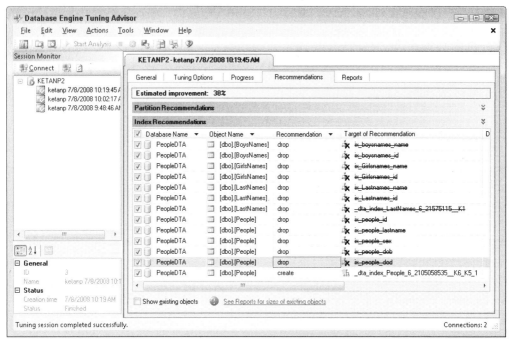

Figure 15-11

enough of an improvement to recommend indexes. Figure 15-3, shown earlier, indicates the recommendations the DTA comes up with for the LastNames table when tuning the Exec_InsertPeople-3.sql procedure.

Summary

This chapter started by looking at all the new index-related features in SQL Server 2008. From there we examined the details of partitioning, looking at how to set up partitioning, and covering the three main scenarios for partitioning: creating a partition from an existing table, adding a new partition, and deleting an old partition. Next we took a look at index fragmentation and how the commands for this have changed since SQL Server 2000. Finally, we looked at the Database Tuning Advisor, including comprehensive coverage of the various options and how to assess the value of the DTA's recommendations. The next chapter looks at replication.

16

Replication

Today's enterprise needs to distribute its data across many departments and geographically dispersed offices. SQL Server replication provides ways to distribute data and database objects among its SQL Server databases, databases from other vendors such as Oracle, and mobile devices such as Pocket PC and point-of-sale terminals. Along with log shipping, database mirroring, and clustering, replication provides functionalities that satisfy customers' needs for load balancing, high availability, and scaling.

This chapter introduces you to the concept of replication, explaining how to implement basic snapshot replication, and noting things to pay attention to when setting up transactional and merge replication.

Replication Overview

SQL Server replication closely resembles the magazine publishing industry, so we'll use that analogy to explain its overall architecture. Consider *National Geographic*. The starting point is the large pool of journalists writing *articles*. From all the available articles, the editor picks which ones will be included in the current month's magazine. The selected set of articles is then published in a *publication*. Once a monthly publication is printed, it is shipped out via various distribution channels to subscribers all over the world.

In SQL Server replication, similar terminology is used. The pool from which a publication is formed can be considered a database. Each piece selected for publication is an *article*; it can be a table, a stored procedure, or another database object. Like a magazine publisher, replication also needs a *distributor* to deliver publications, keep track of delivery status, and maintain a history of synchronization to maintain data consistency. Depending on the kind of replication model you choose, articles from a publication can be stored as files in a folder to which both publisher and subscriber(s) have access, or transactions within articles can be committed on subscribers synchronously or asynchronously. Regardless of how publications are delivered, replication always needs a distributor database to keep track of delivery status. Depending on the capacity of the publication server, the distributor database can be on the same server as the publisher or on other dedicated or nondedicated servers.

Conceptually, however, there are differences between SQL Server replication and a magazine publishing business. For example, in some replication models, a subscriber or subscribers can update articles and have them propagated back to the publisher or other subscribers. In the peer-to-peer replication model, each participant of replication acts both as publisher and subscriber, so that changes made in different databases will be replicated back and forth between multiple servers.

> *This chapter does not cover programming replication using Replication Management Objects (RMO). RMO is a managed code-programming model for SQL Server replication. All the steps and processes discussed in the chapter can be programmed using RMO. For more information on RMO, we recommend you go through sample applications and code samples from Books Online.*

Replication Types

Several different replication models are in use for SQL Server 2008:

- ❑ Snapshot replication

- ❑ Transactional replication

- ❑ Merge replication

- ❑ Peer-to-peer replication

- ❑ Oracle Publishing replication

These are described in more detail in the following sections.

Snapshot Replication

As its name implies, snapshot replication takes a snapshot of a publication and makes it available to subscribers. When the snapshot is applied on the subscribing database, the articles in the subscriber, such as tables, views, and stored procedures, are dropped and recreated. Snapshot replication is a one-shot deal; there is no continuous stream of data from the publisher to the subscriber. The data on the publisher at the time the snapshot is taken is applied to the subscriber.

Snapshot replication is best suited for fairly static data, when it is acceptable to have copies of data that are out of date between replication intervals, or when article size is small. For example, suppose you have lookup tables to maintain zip codes. Those tables can be good snapshot replication candidates in most cases because they are typically static.

Transactional Replication

Transactional replication, as its name implies, replicates each transaction defined in the article being published. To set up transactional replication, a snapshot of the publisher is taken and applied to the subscriber as a one-shot deal to create the same set of data. Once the snapshot is taken, the Log Reader agent reads all the transactions that occur against the articles being published and records them in the distribution database. The transactions are then applied to each subscriber according to the subscription's configuration.

Transactional replication allows for faster data synchronization with less latency. Depending on how it is set up, this data synchronization can occur in nearly real time, so it is useful for cases where you want incremental changes to happen at the subscriber quickly.

Merge Replication

Merge replication is usually used when there is no constant network connectivity among publishers and subscribers. It enables sites to work fairly autonomously and merge the changes to the data when they are next online. It needs a snapshot to initialize the replication, after which subsequent changes are tracked with triggers.

One side effect of merge replication is the possibility of conflicts when offline changes are merged in. Merge replication will automatically resolve these in the Merge agent using the conflict resolver model chosen when the publication was created. If you don't want to use automatic conflict resolution, you can configure the publication for interactive conflict resolution.

When the publication is configured for interactive conflict resolution, each conflict must be manually resolved. This can be done using the Interactive Resolver user interface.

Other "Types" of Replication

The following two options are often considered additional types of replication, but they are not really separate replication types:

- ❑ **Peer-to-peer replication:** Peer-to-peer replication is not its own type, but is a subtype of transactional replication. In peer-to-peer replication, each publisher owns a subset of the total set of rows in an article. It publishes its own rows, to which each of its peers subscribe, and it subscribes to the other rows from each of its peers. More details about peer-to-peer transactional replication appear later in this chapter.

- ❑ **Oracle Publishing:** SQL Server 2000 enabled the capability to subscribe to data published from an Oracle database. Using Oracle Publishing, you can subscribe using either snapshot or transactional replication, but not merge replication.

Replication Components

This section introduces the key components of SQL Server replication, which are grouped into the following areas: replication roles, replication data, replication agents, and replication internal components.

Replication Roles

There are three key roles in replication:

- ❑ **Publisher:** The publisher is the server, or database instance, that is the source, or master, for the articles being published.

- ❑ **Distributor:** The distributor is the intermediary in the act of publishing and subscribing, and in some types of replication is the medium whereby the data gets from the publisher to the subscriber. The distributor is a database that can live on either the publishing server, its own dedicated server, or the subscriber.

- ❑ **Subscriber:** The subscriber is the server, or database instance, that is the destination, or slave, for the articles being published. In some replication models the subscriber can also be a publisher, either for the articles being received, when the data is being sent onto another subscriber, of the same set of data in the updating subscriber model, or for another set of articles in a peer-to-peer model.

Replication Data

There are three key components to replication data: articles, publications, and subscriptions:

- ❑ **Article:** An article is the smallest set of data that can be configured for replication. It can consist of a table, a view, or a stored procedure, and can have additional restrictions on the rows and columns that will be included in each article.

- ❑ **Publication:** A publication is a grouping of articles that will be published together. Using a publication enables the replication of logically grouped articles to be managed together, rather than having to manage each article individually.

- ❑ **Subscription:** A subscription is a request to receive data from one or more publications. It can add additional constraints to the publication regarding how and when the data is distributed.

Replication Agents

SQL Server Agent jobs are a key component of replication. A number of SQL Agent jobs are created by replication:

- ❑ **Snapshot agent:** The Snapshot agent is a SQL Agent Job that takes and applies the snapshot either for setting up transactional or merge replication or for a snapshot replication.

- ❑ **Log Reader agent:** The Log Reader agent is the SQL Agent job that reads the transaction log on the publisher and records the transactions for each article being published into the distribution database.

- ❑ **Distribution agent:** The Distribution agent is the SQL Agent job that reads the transactions written to the distribution database and applies them to the subscribing databases.

- ❑ **Merge agent:** The Merge agent is the SQL Agent job that manages activities of merge replication.

- ❑ **Other agents:** You may come across quite a few other SQL Agent Jobs, as described in the following list:
    - ❑ Queue Reader agent
    - ❑ History agent
    - ❑ Distribution cleanup
    - ❑ Expired subscriptions cleanup
    - ❑ Replication agents checkup
    - ❑ Reinitialize failed subscriptions agent

Replication Enhancements in SQL Server 2008

There are several changes to replication for SQL Server 2008:

- ❑ Peer-to-peer transactional replication can now detect conflicts during synchronization. You add nodes to peer-to-peer replication without having to stop and flush every node. A new peer-to-peer replication topology wizard enables the configuration of many tasks.

❑ Replication Monitor has several new usability enhancements. Most Replication Monitor grid displays have been enhanced to support the user configuration of columns, sorting, and filtering. The Common Jobs tab for the Publisher node has been renamed to Agents, and provides a one-stop location for managing all replication SQL Agent Jobs. The Warnings and Agents tab for the Publication node has been split into a Warnings tab and an Agents tab.

❑ Transactional replication has enhanced support for partitioned tables, as it now enables the use of the SWITCH PARTITION statement.

Replication Models

There are quite a few different ways that replication can be set up. This section covers some of the most common replication topologies. These can be considered the basic building blocks, and from these considerably more complex topologies can be constructed.

Single Publisher, One or More Subscribers

This is perhaps the simplest topology to use with a single publishing database, with one or more subscription databases. This topology might be used where you need to keep a hot standby system, or distribute data from a central office to multiple field offices. Figure 16-1 shows the basic structure of this topology with the distributor on the publishing server.

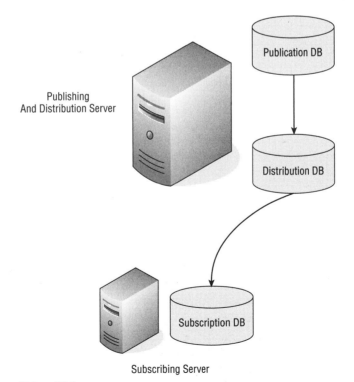

Figure 16-1

Figure 16-2 shows a more advanced option with a separate server for the distribution database. Use this option when you need more performance at the distributor than you can get from a single server acting as the publisher and distributor.

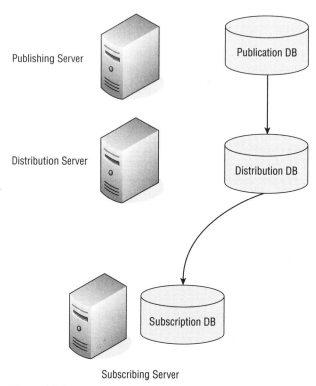

Publishing Server

Publication DB

Distribution Server

Distribution DB

Subscription DB

Subscribing Server

Figure 16-2

Figure 16-3 shows the next variant, with multiple subscription databases.

Multiple Publishers, Single Subscriber

In a Point of Service (POS) application, it is often necessary to send data from the many POS terminals in a store to a central system either in the store or at head office where the individual transactions can be consolidated. The replication topology to use for this is a multiple publisher, single subscriber model. Figure 16-4 shows this topology.

Multiple Publishers Also Subscribing

In a Customer Resource Management (CRM) application it might be necessary to have an address book that contains all contacts, and that is updated locally. One way to do this is to have each branch office publish any updates made at that office, and also subscribe to the updates made by all other branch offices. Figure 16-5 shows how this could be achieved.

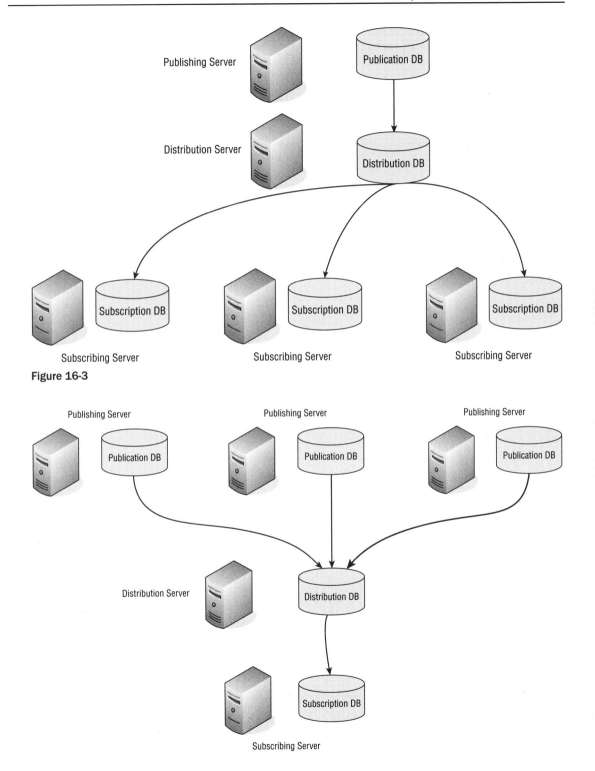

Figure 16-3

Figure 16-4

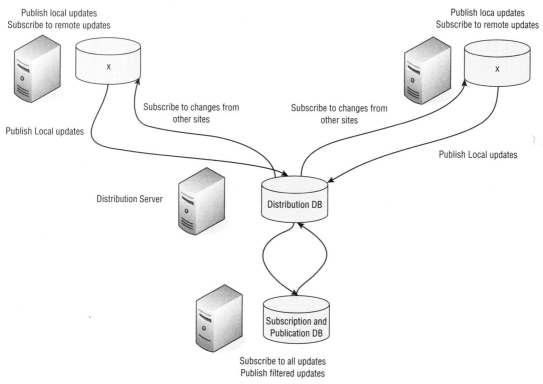

Figure 16-5

An alternative approach might be to use peer-to-peer replication.

Updating Subscriber

An alternative approach for the CRM application mentioned in the previous section might be to use an *updating subscriber*. In this topology, the master copy of the contacts is held at a central location. This would be published to all branch offices. Any changes at the branch offices are then updated back to the publisher using the Updating Subscriber feature built into replication.

Figure 16-6 shows the updating subscriber topology.

Peer-to-peer

Yet another way to implement the CRM application is to use peer-to-peer replication. Peer-to-peer replication doesn't have the concept of a master copy of the data; instead, each instance owns its own set of rows and receives any updates made at the other instances.

Figure 16-7 shows a peer-to-peer topology. Peer-to-peer replication is covered in detail as a replication type later in the chapter.

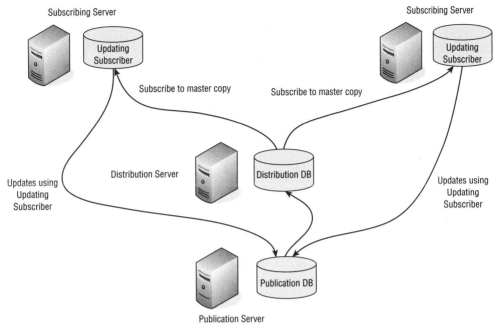

Figure 16-6

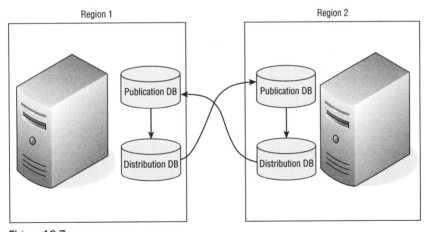

Figure 16-7

Implementing Replication

With so much terminology involved, replication can be confusing and misleading initially. In this section, you'll go through an exercise to set up snapshot replication.

You shouldn't have trouble setting up snapshot replication. Transactional and merge replication is similar. We will review the major differences right after snapshot replication setup.

The Setup

To keep things simple, you will create two new databases in this replication example: a new database called `Publisher` that will be the publisher, and a new database called `Subscriber` that will be the subscriber. For the purposes of this example, you will create a sales schema, and in that schema create a single table, `Cars`. You will then insert a small set of rows into that table. The scenario is based on a car company that sells fuel-efficient hybrid cars in the United States, China, and Sweden. You'll set up snapshot replication between database servers in the U.S. and China to refresh data. Furthermore, you can set up transactional replication between database servers in the U.S. and Sweden. The data can also be used to set up merge replication. Use the following script to create the table and insert some relevant data:

```
-- Make sure we are in the Publisher database
Use Publisher
Go

-- Create the new Sales schema
Create Schema Sales
Go

-- Create the Cars table
CREATE TABLE Sales.Cars
(ProdID INT PRIMARY KEY,
ProdDesc varchar(35),
Country varchar(7),
LastUpdate smalldatetime
)
Go

-- Insert rows into the Cars table

insert Sales.Cars (prodid, proddesc, country, lastupdate)
values (1, 'ProEfficient Sedan', 'US', getdate())

insert Sales.Cars (prodid, proddesc, country, lastupdate)
values (2, 'ProEfficient Van', 'US', getdate())

insert Sales.Cars (prodid, proddesc, country, lastupdate)
values (3, 'JieNeng Crossover', 'China', getdate())

insert Sales.Cars (prodid, proddesc, country, lastupdate)
values (4, 'Jieneng Utility', 'China', getdate())

insert Sales.Cars (prodid, proddesc, country, lastupdate)
values (5, 'EuroEfficient Wagon', 'Sweden', getdate())

insert Sales.Cars (prodid, proddesc, country, lastupdate)
values (6, 'EuroEfficient Pickup', 'Sweden', getdate())
```

Replication can be implemented through both GUI wizard pages and scripting. If you are new to replication, we recommend that you go through the GUI and property pages through SQL Server Management Studio first. Best of all, Management Studio enables you to generate SQL scripts at the end of processes, which you can save to a file and edit for other deployment.

You must implement a distributor before you can create publications and subscribe to publications, so you'll create the distributor first. A distributor is needed for all types of replications.

Setting Up Distribution

As mentioned earlier, a distributor consists of a distribution database (where replication history, status, and other important information will be stored) and a shared folder (where data and articles can be stored, retrieved, and refreshed). In addition, you need to find out the domain name and account that will be used during the process to run various replication agents, such as the Snapshot agent, Log Reader agent, and Queue Reader agent. That is not necessary here, though, because you can choose to impersonate the SQL Server Agent account. That is good for testing and learning, but when you put things into production, a dedicated domain account is recommended for security reasons.

Here is a step-by-step process to follow:

1. Using SQL Server Management Studio, connect to the distributor server. Expand the server in Object Explorer.

2. Right-click Replication, and select Configure Distribution.

3. At the Welcome screen, click Next. You will see the Distributor screen, where you pick which server will be used as the distributor.

4. Click Next. The Snapshot Folder screen appears, where you are asked to enter the snapshot folder. Because the snapshot folder will be accessed by subscribers, a network path is needed.

5. After you pick the snapshot folder, move to the Distribution Database screen shown in Figure 16-8, where you configure the name of the distribution database (distribution, in this example), and the folder locations for the database and log files. Click Next to continue.

Figure 16-8

6.   The next page is the Publishers screen, shown in Figure 16-9, where you set the list of servers that can use this distribution database.

Figure 16-9

7.   Figure 16-10 shows the Wizard Actions screen, where you can define what the wizard will do. The options here are to configure the distribution database or create scripts. If you want to create scripts, select both options.

Figure 16-10

8. The next page of the wizard displays a list of actions SQL Server will perform. At this point, confirm that the list of actions is what you expect. If it's not, go back and fix the settings that are incorrect. If it is correct, select Finish to have the wizard execute the actions you selected.

    You will see a screen indicating the progress the wizard has made at executing the actions you selected.

9. Figure 16-11 shows the wizard actions completed successfully. If any errors are reported, investigate and resolve each one before attempting to rerun the wizard.

Figure 16-11

After executing the wizard you are able to browse to the new distribution database using the Server Explorer in Management Studio. The new distribution database appears under System Databases, as shown in Figure 16-12.

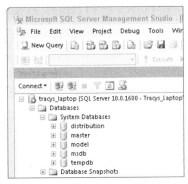

Figure 16-12

As you can see, setting up a distributor is not a difficult task. A distribution database is created. In addition, as mentioned earlier, SQL Server Agent plays a very important role in setting up replication. If you expand the SQL Server Agent in Object Explorer, and open the Jobs folder, you'll see that a number of new jobs were created for the replication.

Implementing Snapshot Replication

By now, you know that all replication needs publication, distribution, and subscription. Now that you've set up the distribution, you can use that for the replication exercise later in this chapter. As with any replication, you need to create a publication before subscribers can subscribe to it, so that is what you'll do next.

Setting Up Snapshot Publication

Once again, you will use Management Studio to accomplish the setup, and you can elect to have everything scripted at the end of the process:

1. Within Management Studio, while connected to the server where the publication database resides, expand the Replication folder. Right-click Local Publications and select New Publication.

2. You will see the Publication Wizard welcome screen; click Next. On the Publication Database screen, you will be asked to pick a database for publication. Pick Publisher as your database to create a publication, and click Next.

3. Figure 16-13 shows the Publication Type screen where you select the type of replication. In this case, select Snapshot publication. Click Next to continue.

4. Next is the Articles screen, where you select the tables in this article. By default, nothing is selected, so you have to either select all tables or expand the Tables node and pick the tables you want to publish.

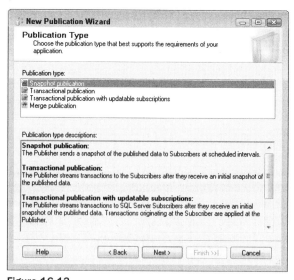

Figure 16-13

Expand the Tables item; then select the Cars table you created earlier for publication and its children, as shown in Figure 16-14. You can see that the Cars table under the sales schema is selected. If necessary, you can pick and choose columns of the table for publication by unchecking the box next to the column name. We won't use this feature here, but it can be useful in certain scenarios.

Figure 16-14

Also note that you can set properties of articles that you choose to publish. These properties affect how the article is published and some behaviors when it is synchronized with the subscriber. Don't change the default properties here, but note that they too can be very useful.

Click Next to continue.

5. On the Filter Table Rows page, the wizard will give you an option to filter out rows. Click the Add button to display the Add Filter page.

6. As mentioned earlier, because you want to replicate data to the Chinese market, you need to filter the cars by country, as shown in Figure 16-15.

   After you click OK, the filter will be applied. This returns you to the previous screen, which now has a filter defined, as shown in Figure 16-16.

7. Figure 16-17 shows the Snapshot Agent screen, where you are asked to define how the snapshot should be created, and when it should be scheduled to run. In this case, don't schedule it; you will invoke it manually by running a SQL Server Agent job yourself. Click Next to continue.

8. The next screen is the Snapshot Agent Security screen, where you can specify the accounts to be used to run the publication. As mentioned earlier, different replication models call for different agents to be run. For security purposes, on the next screen define the account under which the agents run. Click the Security Settings button to configure the account.

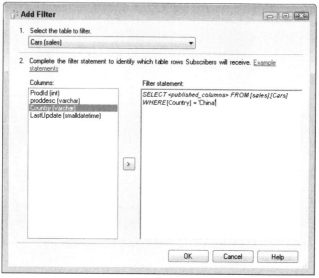

Figure 16-15

Figure 16-16

It is convenient to have a dedicated domain account with a secure password that doesn't need to be changed very often for this purpose. However, if you don't have that access, you can choose to impersonate the SQL Server Agent account for this exercise. It is best to have a dedicated account. Enter the account details on the Snapshot Agent Security screen, shown in Figure 16-18. Once the account is set, click OK.

Figure 16-17

Figure 16-18

9. Figure 16-19 shows the Wizard Actions screen, where you can specify whether you want the wizard to create the publication or script the creation. Now you are almost done with this publication. At this stage you can choose to create the publication and/or generate scripts.

10. The next screen is the wizard action confirmation screen. Review the actions specified here, and if anything is incorrect go back and fix it. When everything is correct, click Finish to have the wizard execute the actions you selected.

Figure 16-19

11. Figure 16-20 shows the confirmation screen indicting that that the wizard has executed all actions correctly. If any errors are reported, investigate and resolve them before attempting to execute the actions again.

Figure 16-20

The rest of the process is pretty similar to the distributor creation documented earlier. Once you click Finish, the snapshot publication will be created. Again, you can use Object Explorer to see the publication and SQL Server jobs created during this process.

At this point no files or folders have been created, and the snapshot has not been created, as no one is subscribed to the snapshot. To get SQL Server to do anything further, you have to subscribe to the new publication. Once there is a subscriber, SQL Server will create all the necessary files. You can find these in the shared folder defined when the distributor was set up earlier. The default location is `C:\Program Files\Microsoft SQL Server\MSSQL10.MSSQLSERVER\MSSQL\ReplData`. If you specified a different location during setup, you can always get the current location by expanding the Replication node in SQL Server management Studio Object Explorer, expanding Local Publications, and selecting the relevant publication. Right-click and select properties. On the Snapshot page you will see a section titled "Location of snapshot files" that shows you the current location.

Setting Up a Subscription to the Snapshot Publication

Now that a snapshot publication is created, you can subscribe to it from a different server:

1. Connect to the subscription server using SQL Server Management Studio, and expand the Replication node in Object Explorer. Right-click Local Subscription and select New Subscriptions.

2. You will see the welcome screen of the New Subscription Wizard. Click Next to choose the publication you want to subscribe to.

    Select <Find SQL Server Publisher ... > from the drop-down list. You will see the typical Connect to Server window that is common in SQL Server Management Studio. Connect to the server where you set up the snapshot publication earlier, and click Connect. You will see the Publication screen shown in Figure 16-21. Expand the database (Publisher) and select the Cars publication. Click Next to continue.

Figure 16-21

3. The next screen is the Distribution Agent Location screen, where you select the location for the distribution agents to execute. This can be either at the distributor for a push subscription

or at the subscriber for a pull subscription. Make your subscription a push subscription and click Next.

4. The next screen is the Subscribers screen, where you can set the subscriber properties. If you want to add additional subscribers, you can do so on this page as well. Select Next to move to the next screen.

5. Figure 16-22 shows the Distribution Agent Security screen, where you will see the familiar screen used for setting agent security settings. This is similar to the step in which you set up the domain account for the Snapshot agent. Click the ellipsis (. . .) to set up the security options. If you want to specify a different domain account for Distribution Agent Security, you need to fill out account information here.

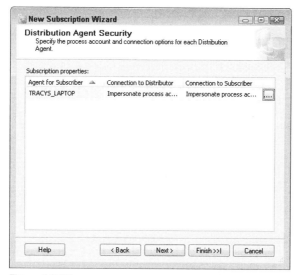

Figure 16-22

6. Specify the synchronization schedule. Because this is just your first test example, make it simple and set it to run on demand. Click the drop-down and select "Run on demand only." Click Next to continue.

7. Figure 16-23 shows the Initialize Subscriptions screen, where you specify when the snapshot is initialized. Check the box to select initialization; and in the drop-down, choose to initialize immediately.

8. Next is the Wizard Actions screen shown earlier (refer to Figure 16-19), where you can choose to create the subscription and/or script the creation. Make your selection and click Next to continue.

9. From the confirmation screen that appears, confirm that the actions are as you expect. If not, then go back and fix anything before executing the wizard actions you selected. When you are satisfied, click Finish to execute the actions.

10. The next screen indicates that the wizard has successfully completed the actions selected. If this step shows any errors, investigate and resolve before attempting to rerun the wizard.

Figure 16-23

Verifying Snapshot Replication

So far, the setup is pretty simple, but how do you know it actually works? You can conduct some tests here to make sure it does indeed work properly:

1. Connect to the publication server and verify the records there:

```
1> :connect MyPublisher
Sqlcmd: Successfully connected to server 'MyPublisher'.
1> use publisher
2> go
Changed database context to 'publisher'.
1> select * from Sales.Cars
2> go
ProdID      ProdDesc                                  Country LastUpdate
----------- ----------------------------------------- ------- -------------------
          1 ProEfficient Sedan                        US      2008-06-14 15:33:00
          2 ProEfficient Van                          US      2008-06-14 15:33:00
          3 JieNeng Crossover                         China   2008-06-14 15:33:00
          4 JieNeng Utility                           China   2008-06-14 15:33:00
          5 EuroEfficient Wagon                       Sweden  2008-06-14 15:33:00
          6 EuroEfficient Pickup                      Sweden  2008-06-14 15:33:00

(6 rows affected)
```

2. Now connect to the subscription server. You've already initialized the subscription, so you will only see cars for the Chinese market:

```
1> :connect MySubscriber
Sqlcmd: Successfully connected to server 'MySubscriber'.
1> use subscriber
```

```
2> go
Changed database context to 'subscriber'.
1> select * from Sales.Cars
2> go
ProdID      ProdDesc                                    Country LastUpdate
----------- ------------------------------------------- ------- -------------------
          3 JieNeng Crossover                           China   2008-06-14 15:33:00
          4 JieNeng Utility                             China   2008-06-14 15:33:00

(2 rows affected)
```

3. Now suppose you made some changes to cars for the Chinese market and upgraded JieNeng Crossover to JieNeng Crossover LE at the publication server:

```
1> :connect MyPublisher
Sqlcmd: Successfully connected to server 'MyPublisher'.
1> use publisher
2> go
Changed database context to 'publisher'.
1> update Sales.Cars set proddesc = 'JieNeng Crossover LE' where prodid = 3
2> go

(1 rows affected)
```

4. You've updated records at the publisher, so you need to take a new snapshot by running the SQL Server Agent jobs. In Object Explorer, expand the SQL Server Agent Jobs folder, right-click the "MYPUBLISHER-publisher-ChinaCars-1" job, and select Start Job from the context menu.

5. Because you implemented a pull subscription, you need to go to the subscriber and run the job to refresh this snapshot. Open Object Explorer on the subscriber, expand the SQL Server Agent Jobs folder, right-click the job, and select Start Job from the context menu.

6. Now ensure that the data is indeed refreshed:

```
1> :connect MySubscriber
Sqlcmd: Successfully connected to server 'mySubscriber'.
1> use subscriber
2> go
Changed database context to 'subscriber'.
1> select * from Sales.Cars
2> go
ProdID      ProdDesc                                    Country LastUpdate
----------- ------------------------------------------- ------- -------------------
          3 JieNeng Crossover LE                        China   2008-06-14 15:33:00
          4 JieNeng Utility                             China   2008-06-14 15:33:00

(2 rows affected)
```

Implementing Transactional and Merge Replication

Procedurally, setting up transactional and merge replication is very similar to the snapshot replication discussed earlier. We do not discuss detailed step-by-step instructions here. Instead, we note some differences and things you need to pay attention to.

The typical transactional replication is not too different from snapshot replication. One major component added is the Log Reader agent. This agent tracks all changes made to the article so it can be propagated to the subscriber. As a result, the load on the distribution database is higher than with snapshot replication, which means you need to keep a closer eye on it, especially the log file of the distribution database.

If you implement transactional publication with updateable subscription, changes at the subscriber are applied back to the publisher. To enable this, SQL Server adds one additional column in tables included in the publication to track changes. This column is called `MSrepl_tran_version` and is a unique identifier column. Therefore, code such as

```
insert into Sales.Cars values (9, 'English Car', 'UK', getdate())
```

will fail because it does not have a column list. As a result, the application of that code needs to be updated. To fix that, the column list that corresponds to the values in parentheses must be provided right after the table name.

For transactional replication with updatable subscription, a linked server is used among SQL Server publishing and subscribing databases. The linked server uses MS DTC (Distributed Transaction Coordinator) to coordinate transactions; therefore, MS DTC on the publisher must be enabled to accept remote connections.

For merge replication, all articles must have a unique identifier column with a unique index and the `ROWGUIDCOL` property. If they don't have it, SQL Server will add one for you. Just like transactional replication with updateable subscription, an `INSERT` statement without the column list will fail.

Additional agents are used for transactional and merge replication, such as the Log Reader agent and Queue Reader agent. The agents require a domain account to run under. The domain account can be their own or shared with other agents. How you choose to implement that depends on your company's security policy.

For merge replication, you can choose to synchronize data over HTTPS.

Peer-to-Peer Replication

Peer-to-peer is a type of transactional replication. Unlike the traditional replication types, it provides a headless topology, whereby there are multiple publishers and one or more subscribers. In peer-to-peer replication, every participant is both a publisher and a subscriber. It is suitable for cases in which user applications need to read or modify data at any of the databases participating in the setup. It provides an interesting alternative for load-balancing and high-availability scenarios. Note that this feature is available only in the Enterprise Edition of SQL Server 2008. Oracle calls this kind of replication "multimaster," whereas DB2 calls it "update anywhere."

Keep the following in mind when evaluating and setting up peer-to-peer replication:

❑ It is designed for a small number of participating databases. A good rule-of-thumb number is less than 10. If you use more than that, you could encounter performance issues.

❑ Unlike merge replication, peer-to-peer replication does not handle conflict resolution.

❑ Peer-to-peer does not support data filtering. That would defeat its purpose because everybody is an equal partner here for high availability and load balancing.

❑ Applications can scale out read operations across multiple databases, and databases are always online. Participating nodes can be added or removed for maintenance.

❑ As mentioned, peer-to-peer replication is available only in Enterprise Edition; however, for your testing purposes, it is available in Developer Edition of SQL Server 2008.

From an implementation standpoint, the process is very similar to the replication types discussed earlier. However, there are a few things that you need to pay attention to:

1. To start out, the easiest approach is to begin with one database, back it up, and restore it on all other participating databases. This way, you start from a clean and consistent slate.

2. All replications need a distributor, so it needs to be ready before you start setting up peer-to-peer replication.

3. After the distributor is set, you need to create a publication just like a regular transactional replication publication. However, do not create the initial snapshot or schedule the Snapshot agent at the Snapshot Agent screen. In addition, you need to ensure that the publication name is the same across all participating servers. Otherwise, peer-to-peer setup will fail.

4. After the publication is created, you need to modify a property in the Subscription Options page to set the publication as peer-to-peer. Note that this is a one-way change, and once the publication is set to peer-to-peer you can't change it back.

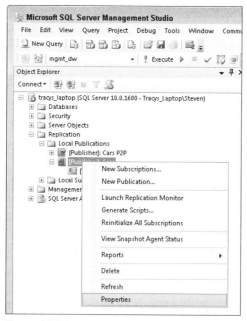

Figure 16-24

5. Access the Publication Properties page by selecting the publication in Management Studio and right-clicking on it. This will display the context menu, as shown in Figure 16-24. Click Properties to display the page.

6. From the Publications Properties page, select the Subscription Options tab (see Figure 16-25).

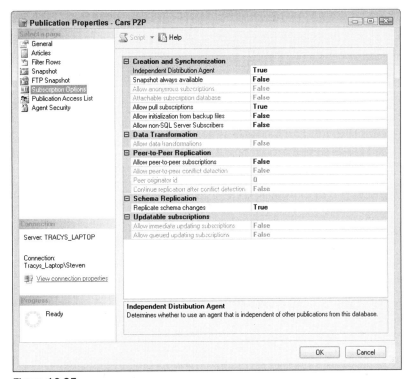

Figure 16-25

You will see a section here for peer-to-peer replication. Note that the setting for "Allow peer-to-peer subscriptions" is set to False. Change this to True, as shown in Figure 16-26, and when you select OK the publication will be enabled for peer-to-peer.

7. Now you can proceed with the rest of the setup by right-clicking the publication and selecting Configure Peer-to-Peer Topology, as shown in Figure 16-27. Again, you can see this only after Subscription Options is modified. This feature is only available in SQL Server 2008 Enterprise Edition.

8. Follow the remaining screens to complete the wizard, selecting the appropriate options as discussed earlier in the setup for snapshot replication. Most of the options are similar to typical replication setup. One difference is that this process asks you to add peers, rather than subscribers, as you did with the other types of replication.

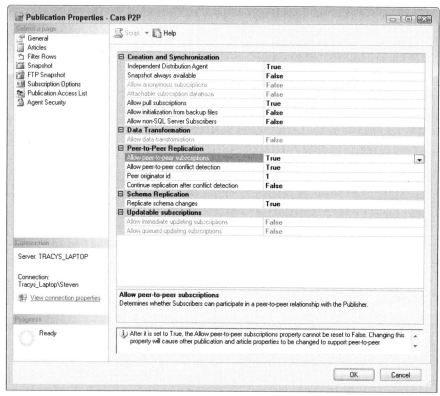

Figure 16-26

Figure 16-27

Scripting Replication

The preferred interface for managing replication is the graphical interfaces provided in SQL Server Management Studio in the various replication wizards. However, many DBAs will want to be able to create a script that can be checked into a source code control system such as Visual Source Safe or Visual Studio Team Foundation Server.

To script replication, you have two options. You can use either the various replication wizards, which provide a scripting option, or SQL Server Management Studio and script individual objects.

The scripts can be saved into your source code control system, where they can be version controlled and used to deploy a replication configuration to development, test, QA, pre-production, and production systems. See Chapter 10 for more information on using Visual Studio Team Server Database Edition (VSTS DB Pro) and Team Server Source Control (TSSC).

Monitoring Replication

This section discusses three tools for monitoring replication: Replication Monitor, Performance Monitor, and the replication-related DMVs.

Replication Monitor

Replication Monitor is built into SQL Server Management Studio. It shows the status of replication and can be used to make configuration changes. It will also show the current latency and the number of commands outstanding. It does not show the transaction or command rates; nor does it show any history of what happened at any time before the current snapshot of data was read.

You can invoke the Replication Monitor from Management Studio. Expand a publishing server and right-click the Replication folder to launch it, as shown in Figure 16-28.

To look at subscription status, double-click any entry of the All Subscriptions tab to bring up a window where you can easily view reports and the status of publication to distribution, distribution to subscription, and undistributed commands. It is a user-friendly tool that provides a good overview of all your replication status information.

Tracer tokens are a way to measure the current performance of replication. The Tracer Tokens tab is shown in Figure 16-29. You can think of a tracer token as a dummy record that the Replication Monitor uses to gauge the performance of your replication model. It can give you a pretty good idea of latency among your publisher, distributor, and subscriber.

Performance Monitor

Several replication-related Performance Monitor objects and counters can be monitored in SQL Server:

- ❑ **SQLServer:Replication Agent:** Has just a single counter, Running, that shows the number of replication agents running on this server.
- ❑ **SQL Server:Replication Log Reader:** Shows the statistics for the Log Reader, with counters for Commands per second, Transactions per second, and Latency.

❑ **SQL Server:Replication Dist.:** Shows the statistics for the distributor with the same counters as for the Log Reader.

❑ **SQL Server:Replication Merge:** Shows the statistics for the Merge agent, with counters for Conflicts per second, Downloaded changes per second, and Updates per second.

❑ **SQL Server:Replication Snapshot:** Shows the statistics for the Snapshot agent, with counters for Delivered commands per second and Delivered transactions per second.

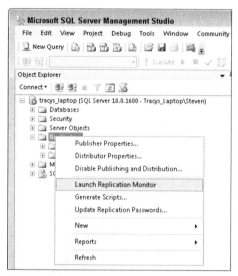

Figure 16-28

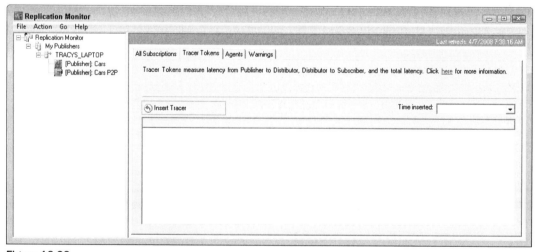

Figure 16-29

When considering which performance counters to use, your replication type is the key factor to consider. For snapshot replication, look at the Replication Snapshot counters. For merge replication, look at the Replication Merge counters. For transactional replication, look at the Replication Log Reader and Replication Dist. counters.

Here is some more information on the counters you should monitor for transactional replication:

❑ **Object: SQL Server:Replication Log Reader - Counter: LogReader:Delivered Cmds/Sec** and **Tx/Sec** — These two counters are repeated for each publication; they display the commands or transactions read per second and indicate how many commands or transactions are being read by the Log Reader per second. If this counter increases, it indicates that the Tx rate at the publisher has increased.

❑ **Object: SQL Server:Replication Dist. - Counter: Dist:Delivered Cmds/Sec** and **Tx/Sec** — These two counters are repeated for each subscription, and display the commands or transactions per second being delivered to the subscriber. If this number is lower than the Log Reader delivered number, it is an indication that commands may be backing up on the distribution database. If it is higher than the Log Reader rate and there is already a backlog of commands, it might indicate that replication is catching up.

Replication DMVs

There are four replication-related DMVs in every SQL Server database:

❑ `sys.dm_repl_articles` — Contains information about each article being published. It returns data from the database being published and returns a row for each object being published in each article. The syntax is as follows:

```
select *
from sys.dm_repl_articles
```

❑ `sys.dm_repl_schemas` — Contains information about each table and column being published. It returns data from the database being published and returns one row for each column in each object being published. The syntax is as follows:

```
select *
from sys.dm_repl_schemas
```

❑ `sys.dm_repl_tranhash` — Contains information about the hashing of transactions. The syntax is as follows:

```
select *
from sys.dm_repl_tranhash
```

❑ `sys.dm_repl_traninfo` — Contains information about each transaction in a transactional replication. The syntax is as follows:

```
select *
from sys.dm_repl_traninfo
```

These DMVs show information about what is being published from a specific database. They will not help you monitor what's going on with replication. For that, you have to either run the `sp_replcounters` system stored procedure (discussed in the next section) or go digging into the distribution database. It's much easier to just execute the `sp_replcounters` stored procedure than go digging into the inner workings of replication in the MSDB or distribution databases, although it may not have all the information you want to monitor. If you do need more information, you need to search the distribution database. This is currently undocumented territory, but a good place to start is the source code for the replication stored procedures. Use these to begin determining where the data you want is located, and take it from there.

sp_replcounters

The `sp_replcounters` replication system stored procedure returns information about the transaction rate, latency, and first and last log sequence number (LSN) for each publication on a server. Run it on the publishing server. Calling this stored procedure on a server that is acting as the distributor or subscribing to publications from another server will not return any data.

Here is an example of the output of this stored procedure. Please note that the results have been split over two lines for clarity.

database	replicated transactions	replication rate trans/sec	replication latency (sec)
Publisher	178	129.0323	0.016

replbeginlsn	replnextlsn
0x0002FACC003458780001	0x0002FACC003459A1003D

Summary

This chapter covered the details of replication. You learned about the various types of replication — snapshot, transactional, and merge — and the different topologies that can be used with replication. You learned how to monitor replication using the Replication Monitor, the Performance Monitor, and the relevant performance counters, and about some of the replication DMVs and system stored procedures.

Along with log shipping, database mirroring, and clustering, SQL Server 2008 provides many features to satisfy customers needs for load balancing, high availability, disaster recovery, and scaling.

In the next chapter you learn about database mirroring.

17

Database Mirroring

Database mirroring is a reliable, high-availability solution in SQL Server 2008. Maximizing database availability is a top priority for most DBAs. It is hard to explain the pain a DBA goes through when a database goes down; you're unable to get it right back online, and at the same time you're answering pointed questions from your manager. Database mirroring will come to the rescue in certain scenarios, which we explain in this chapter. It will help you get the database back online with automatic or manual failover to your mirror database, adding another alternative to the SQL Server 2008 arsenal. This chapter explains database mirroring concepts, shows you how to administer the mirrored database, and provides an example demonstrating how to implement database mirroring. We also discuss the database snapshot, which you can use with database mirroring to read the mirrored databases.

Overview of Database Mirroring

Database mirroring is a high-availability solution at the database level, implemented on a per-database basis. To maximize database availability, you need to minimize planned as well as unplanned downtime. Planned downtime is very common, such as changes you have to apply to your production system, hardware upgrades, software upgrades (security patches and service packs), database configuration changes, or database storage upgrades. These all require your database or server to be unavailable for short periods of time if everything goes as planned. Unplanned downtime can be caused by hardware failures such as storage failure, by power outages, by human error, or by natural disasters, all of which can cause the production server or data center to be unavailable.

Figure 17-1 illustrates a number of mirroring concepts, which we'll discuss in detail.

Database mirroring involves two copies of a single database, residing on separate instances of SQL Server, usually on different computers. You can have separate instances of SQL Server 2008 on the same computer, but that would most likely not fit your high-availability requirements other than for testing purposes. At any given time, only one copy of the database is available to clients. This copy of the database is known as the *principal database*. The SQL Server that hosts this principal database is known as the *principal server*. Database mirroring works by transferring and applying the stream of database log records to the copy of the database. The copy of the database is known as the *mirror database*. The SQL Server that hosts this mirror database is known as the *mirror server*. The principal and mirror servers are each considered a *partner* in a database mirroring *session*. As you would guess, a given server may assume the role of principal for one database and the role of mirror for another database. Database mirroring applies every database modification (DML, DDL, and so on) made to the principal database to the mirror database, including physical and logical database changes such as database files and indexes. For automatic failover, a third server called the *witness* is required. We will discuss the witness server later.

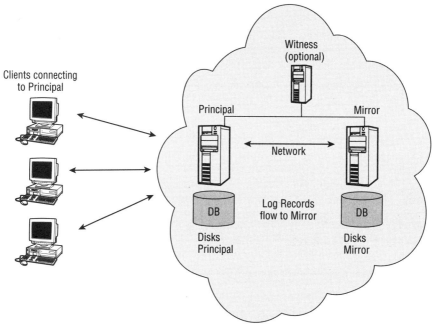

Figure 17-1

Database mirroring helps minimize both planned and unplanned downtime as follows:

❑   It provides ways to perform automatic or manual failover for mirrored databases.

❑   It keeps the mirrored database up-to-date with the production database, either synchronously or asynchronously. You can set these operating modes for database mirroring, which we will discuss shortly.

❑   It enables the mirrored database to be in a remote data center, to provide a foundation for disaster recovery.

You cannot mirror the master, msdb, tempdb, *or* model *databases. You can mirror multiple databases from a SQL Server instance, though. You cannot re-mirror the mirror database. Mirroring does not support a principal database having more than one mirrored partner.*

Operating Modes of Database Mirroring

We mentioned that to keep the mirror database up-to-date, database mirroring transfers and applies the stream of database log records on the mirror database. It is important to understand which *operating mode* database mirroring is configured in. The following table outlines the operating modes of database mirroring.

Operating Mode	Transaction Safety	Transfer Mechanism	Quorum Required	Witness Server	Failover Type
High Performance	OFF	Asynchronous	No	N/A	Forced failover only (with possible data loss). This is a manual step.
High Safety **without** automatic failover	FULL	Synchronous	Yes	No	Manual or forced
High Safety **with** automatic failover	FULL	Synchronous	Yes	Yes	Automatic or manual

There are three possible operating modes for a database mirroring session. The exact mode of the operation is based on the transaction safety setting and whether the witness server is part of the mirroring session.

When you set up database mirroring, you have to decide whether you want the principal database and mirror database to be in sync at all times for full data safety or whether you can live with some data loss in case of principal failure. You have two options: SAFETY FULL or SAFETY OFF. These options are part of the ALTER DATABASE statement when you set up database mirroring, as described later. As you know, in SQL Server 2008, data changes are first recorded in the transaction log before any changes to the actual data pages are made. The transaction log records are first placed in the database's log buffer in memory and then flushed to the log file on the disk (referred to as "hardening the transaction log") as soon as possible.

If you choose SAFETY FULL, you are setting up database mirroring in *high-safety mode* (also known as *synchronous mirroring mode*). As the principal server hardens (flushes the log buffer to disk) log records of the principal database to disk, it also sends log buffers to the mirror. The principal then waits for a response from the mirror server. The mirror responds to a commit when it has hardened those same log records to the mirror's transaction log. The commit is then reported to the client. Synchronous transfer guarantees that all transactions in the mirror database's transaction log will be synchronized with the principal database's transaction log, so that the transactions are considered safely transferred. Figure 17-2 shows the sequence of events when SAFETY is set to FULL.

Keep in mind that it is guaranteed that you won't lose data and that both the principal and mirror will be in sync as long as the transaction is committed successfully. There is some performance impact here because the transaction is not committed until it is hardened to the transaction log on the mirror server. There will be a slight increase in response time and a reduction in transaction throughput because the principal server has to wait for an acknowledgment from the mirror that the transaction is hardened to the mirror transaction log. How long that delay might be depends on many factors, such as server capacity, database workload, network latency, application architecture, disk throughput, and more. An application with a lot of small transactions will have more impact on response time than one with long transactions, because transactions wait for acknowledgment from the mirror, and the wait time adds proportionately more to the response time of short transactions.

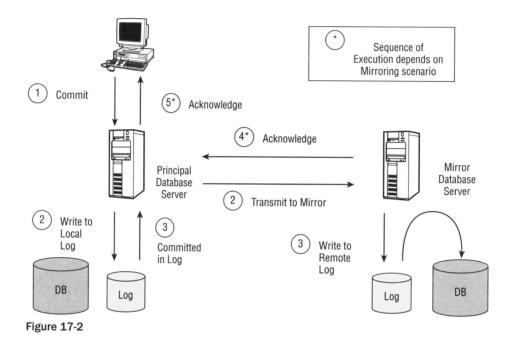

Figure 17-2

If you choose the SAFETY OFF option, you are setting up database mirroring in high performance mode, or asynchronous mirroring mode. In this mode, the log transfer process is the same as in synchronous mode, but the principal does not wait for acknowledgment from the mirror that the log buffer is hardened to the disk on a commit. As soon as step 3 in Figure 17-2 occurs, the transaction is committed on the principal. The database is synchronized after the mirror server catches up to the principal server. Because the mirror server is busy keeping up with the principal server, if the principal suddenly fails, you may lose data. In this operating mode, there is minimal impact on response time or transaction throughput, as it does not wait for the mirror to commit.

Note three important terms here, which are discussed further later in the chapter:

- ❑ **Send queue:** While sending the log records from the principal to the mirror, if the log records can't be sent at the rate at which they are generated, a queue builds up at the principal. This is known as the *send queue*. The send queue does not use extra storage or memory. It exists entirely in the transaction log of the principal. It refers to the part of the log that has not yet been sent to the mirror.

- ❑ **Redo queue:** While applying log records on the mirror, if the log records can't be applied at the rate at which they are received, a queue builds up at the mirror. This is known as the *redo queue.* Like the send queue, the redo queue does not use extra storage or memory. It exists entirely in the transaction log of the mirror. It refers to the part of the hardened log that remains to be applied to the mirror database to roll it forward. Mostly, a single thread is used for redo, but SQL Server 2008 Enterprise Edition implements *parallel redo* — that is, a thread for every four processing units (equivalent to four cores).

❑   **Stream compression:** When transferring data across the partners, data mirroring uses stream data compression, which reduces network utilization and can achieve at least a 12.5 percent compression ratio. In the data mirror scenario, the principal compresses the data before sending it to the mirror and the mirror uncompresses the data before applying it. This will slightly increase the CPU utilization on both the principal and the mirror to compress and uncompress the data, while reducing network utilization. It is especially useful for database workloads that incur a great deal of data modification throughout the day, reducing the amount of network resources that data mirroring uses.

Database Mirroring Example

Now that you understand transaction safety, you can look at an example to better understand the operating modes and other mirroring concepts. You will need to designate three SQL Server instances for this example: one principal server, one mirror server, and one witness server. In this example, you will set up high-safety mode with automatic failover. This example assumes that all three SQL server instances are on the network and are running under the same domain account, which is administrator on the SQL Server instance and has access to the other SQL Server instances. Moreover, you need the AdventureWorks2008 sample database that is available with SQL Server 2008.

Preparing the Endpoints

We discuss endpoints in great detail in Chapter 8. You can refer to the "Transport Security" section in that chapter for details. In order for database-mirroring partners to connect to each other, they must trust each other, which is established by means of Transmission Control Protocol (TCP) endpoints. Therefore, on each partner you have to create the endpoint using the T-SQL statement `CREATE ENDPOINT` and grant the connect permission on these endpoints using the `GRANT CONNECT ON ENDPOINT` statement. The endpoint concept is exactly the same as discussed in Chapter 8, so the rules are the same. The only difference is that instead of creating an endpoint for Service Broker, you are creating an endpoint for database mirroring here. The security rules are the same; you can use either Windows authentication or certificates for authentication. This example uses certificates so that you can learn how to use them for transport authentication. Windows authentication is very easy to establish, so we leave that for you as a separate exercise.

You can find all the example scripts for this chapter on this book's Web site at `www.wrox.com`, but you need to make a few modifications before running the scripts.

First, for data mirroring to work, the TPC/IP protocol has to be enabled. Use the SQL Server Configuration Manager to verify that the TCP/IP protocol is enabled. Second, in the principal, mirror, and witness, create a new folder at a location of your choosing to store the data mirror example.

Note the use of `<your folder>` to refer to the created folder in the scripts in this chapter. You need to change this to match your folder name.

Next, create the certificates on each partner server. Connect to the principal server and execute the `CreateCertOnPrincipal.sql` script:

```
USE MASTER
GO
IF NOT EXISTS(SELECT 1 FROM sys.symmetric_keys where name =
'##MS_DatabaseMasterKey##')
CREATE MASTER KEY ENCRYPTION BY PASSWORD = '23%&weq^yzYu3000!'
GO

IF NOT EXISTS (select 1 from sys.databases where
[is_master_key_encrypted_by_server] = 1)
ALTER MASTER KEY ADD ENCRYPTION BY SERVICE MASTER KEY
GO

IF NOT EXISTS (SELECT 1 FROM sys.certificates WHERE name = 'PrincipalServerCert')
CREATE  CERTIFICATE PrincipalServerCert
WITH SUBJECT = 'Principal Server Certificate'
GO

BACKUP CERTIFICATE PrincipalServerCert TO FILE = '<your folder>
\PrincipalServerCert.cer'
```

For simplicity, we are using the certificates created by SQL Server 2008, but there are other ways to create and distribute certificates, which will work equally well here. The BACKUP CERTIFICATE statement backs up the public key certificate for this private key.

Now create the endpoint on the principal server. Connect to the principal server and execute the `CreateEndPointOnPrincipal.sql` script:

```
--Check If Mirroring endpoint exists
IF NOT EXISTS(SELECT * FROM sys.endpoints WHERE type = 4)
CREATE ENDPOINT DBMirrorEndPoint
STATE = STARTED AS TCP (LISTENER_PORT = 5022)
FOR DATABASE_MIRRORING ( AUTHENTICATION = CERTIFICATE PrincipalServerCert,
                         ENCRYPTION = REQUIRED
                         ,ROLE = ALL
                         )
```

This code created the endpoint DBMirrorEndPoint, and you have specified the Principal ServerCert certificate to use for authentication. You also specified ROLE = ALL, which indicates that this server can act as either the principal, mirror, or witness server. If you want this server to act only as the witness, you can specify WITNESS as a parameter. You can also specify the PARTNER option, which indicates that the server can act as either the principal or the mirror, but not the witness.

Now create the certificates on both the mirror and the witness servers. Connect to the mirror server and execute the `CreateCertOnMirror.sql` script:

```
USE MASTER
GO
IF NOT EXISTS(SELECT 1 FROM sys.symmetric_keys where name =
'##MS_DatabaseMasterKey##')
```

```
CREATE MASTER KEY ENCRYPTION BY PASSWORD = '23%&weq^yzYu3000!'
GO

IF NOT EXISTS (select 1 from sys.databases where
[is_master_key_encrypted_by_server] = 1)
ALTER MASTER KEY ADD ENCRYPTION BY SERVICE MASTER KEY
GO

IF NOT EXISTS (SELECT 1 FROM sys.certificates WHERE name = 'MirrorServerCert')
CREATE  CERTIFICATE MirrorServerCert
WITH SUBJECT = 'Mirror Server Certificate'
GO

BACKUP CERTIFICATE MirrorServerCert TO FILE = '<your folder>\MirrorServerCert.cer'
```

Next, while connected to the mirror server, execute the `CreateEndPointOnMirror.sql` script:

```
--Check If Mirroring endpoint exists
IF NOT EXISTS(SELECT * FROM sys.endpoints WHERE type = 4)
CREATE ENDPOINT DBMirrorEndPoint
STATE=STARTED AS TCP (LISTENER_PORT = 5023)
FOR DATABASE_MIRRORING ( AUTHENTICATION = CERTIFICATE MirrorServerCert,
                         ENCRYPTION = REQUIRED
                        ,ROLE = ALL
                       )
```

Connect to the witness server and execute the `CreateCertOnWitness.sql` script:

```
USE MASTER
GO
IF NOT EXISTS(SELECT 1 FROM sys.symmetric_keys where name =
'##MS_DatabaseMasterKey##')
CREATE MASTER KEY ENCRYPTION BY PASSWORD = '23%&weq^yzYu3000!'
GO

IF NOT EXISTS (select 1 from sys.databases where
[is_master_key_encrypted_by_server] = 1)
ALTER MASTER KEY ADD ENCRYPTION BY SERVICE MASTER KEY
GO

IF NOT EXISTS (SELECT 1 FROM sys.certificates WHERE name = 'WitnessServerCert')
CREATE  CERTIFICATE WitnessServerCert
WITH SUBJECT = 'Witness Server Certificate'
GO

BACKUP CERTIFICATE WitnessServerCert TO FILE = '<your folder>\WitnessServerCert.cer'
```

Finally, while connected to the witness server, execute the `CreateEndPointOnWitness.sql` script:

```
--Check If Mirroring endpoint exists
IF NOT EXISTS(SELECT * FROM sys.endpoints WHERE type = 4)
CREATE ENDPOINT DBMirrorEndPoint
STATE=STARTED AS TCP (LISTENER_PORT = 5024)
```

```
FOR DATABASE_MIRRORING ( AUTHENTICATION = CERTIFICATE WitnessServerCert, ENCRYPTION
= REQUIRED
                         ,ROLE = ALL
                         )
```

Because all the partners can talk to each other, each partner needs permission to connect to the others. To do that, you have to create logins on each server and associate the logins with certificates from the other two servers and grant connect permission to that user on the endpoint.

First, copy the certificates created in the previous scripts with the BACKUP CERTIFICATE command to the other two servers. For example, copy the certificate PrincipalServerCert.cer on the principal from the new folder you created earlier to the similar folders on both the witness and mirror servers.

Connect to the principal server and execute the Principal_CreateLoginAndGrant.sql script:

```
USE MASTER
GO

--For Mirror server to connect
IF NOT EXISTS(SELECT 1 FROM sys.syslogins WHERE name = 'MirrorServerUser')
CREATE LOGIN MirrorServerUser WITH PASSWORD = '32sdgsgy^%$!'

IF NOT EXISTS(SELECT 1 FROM sys.sysusers WHERE name = 'MirrorServerUser')
CREATE USER MirrorServerUser;

IF NOT EXISTS(SELECT 1 FROM sys.certificates WHERE name = 'MirrorDBCertPub')
CREATE CERTIFICATE MirrorDBCertPub  AUTHORIZATION MirrorServerUser
FROM FILE = '<your folder>\MirrorServerCert.cer'

GRANT CONNECT ON ENDPOINT::DBMirrorEndPoint TO MirrorServerUser
GO

--For Witness server to connect
IF NOT EXISTS(SELECT 1 FROM sys.syslogins WHERE name = 'WitnessServerUser')
CREATE LOGIN WitnessServerUser WITH PASSWORD = '32sdgsgy^%$!'

IF NOT EXISTS(SELECT 1 FROM sys.sysusers WHERE name = 'WitnessServerUser')
CREATE USER WitnessServerUser;

IF NOT EXISTS(SELECT 1 FROM sys.certificates WHERE name = 'WitnessDBCertPub')
CREATE CERTIFICATE WitnessDBCertPub  AUTHORIZATION WitnessServerUser
FROM FILE = '<your folder>\WitnessServerCert.cer'

GRANT CONNECT ON ENDPOINT::DBMirrorEndPoint TO WitnessServerUser
GO
```

This script creates two users on the principal server: MirrorServerUser and WitnessServerUser. These users are mapped to the certificates from the mirror and the witness. After that, you granted connect permission on the endpoint, so now the mirror and the witness server have permission to connect to the endpoint on the principal server. Perform the same steps on the mirror server and witness server.

Next, connect to the mirror server and execute the Mirror_CreateLoginAndGrant.sql script. Finally, connect to the witness server and execute the Witness_CreateLoginAndGrant.sql script.

Now you have configured the endpoints on each server, using certificates. If you want to use the Windows authentication, the steps to configure the endpoints are a bit easier than using certificates. Simply do the following on each server (this example is for the principal):

```
IF NOT EXISTS(SELECT * FROM sys.endpoints WHERE type = 4)
CREATE ENDPOINT DBMirrorEndPoint
STATE = STARTED AS TCP (LISTENER_PORT = 5022)
FOR DATABASE_MIRRORING ( AUTHENTICATION = WINDOWS, ROLE = ALL)

GRANT CONNECT ON ENDPOINT::DBMirrorEndPoint TO
[MyDomain\MirrorServerServiceAccount]
GO

GRANT CONNECT ON ENDPOINT::DBMirrorEndPoint TO
[MyDomain\WitnessServerServiceAccount]
GO
```

Of course, you have to change the logins appropriately. In Windows authentication mode, each server uses the service account under which it is running to connect to the other partners, so you have to grant connect permission on the endpoint to the service account of SQL Server 2008. Additionally, you can use SQL Server 2008 Management Studio to configure data mirroring with Windows authentication. Right-click the database you want to mirror and choose Tasks ⇨ Mirror. A wizard will start, as shown in Figure 17-3. Click the Configure Security button, which will take you through the steps to configure database mirroring. The wizard tries to use 5022 as the default TCP port for database mirroring, but you can change it if you want.

You need only one mirroring endpoint per server; it doesn't matter how many databases you mirror. Be sure to use a port that is not used by other endpoints. You can specify any available port number between 1024 and 32767.

Do not reconfigure an in-use database mirroring endpoint (using ALTER ENDPOINT). The server instances use each other's endpoints to learn the state of the other systems. If the endpoint is reconfigured, it might restart, which can appear to be an error to the other server instances. This is particularly important in high-safety mode with automatic failover, where reconfiguring the endpoint on a partner can cause a failover to occur.

Preparing the Database for Mirroring

Before you can set up the data mirroring, you need a database to work with. We will use the `AdventureWorks2008` database for this example. Note that the database must use the recovery model of FULL:

```
-- As a reminder you will need to set the database Recovery model to FULL
-- recovery in order to establish mirroring.
ALTER DATABASE AdventureWorks2008 SET RECOVERY FULL
```

Connect to the principal server and execute the `BackupDatabase.sql` script:

```
--Take a full database backup.
BACKUP DATABASE [AdventureWorks2008] TO DISK = N'<your folder>
\AdventureWorks2008.bak'
WITH FORMAT, INIT, NAME = N'AdventureWorks2008-Full Database Backup',STATS = 10
GO
```

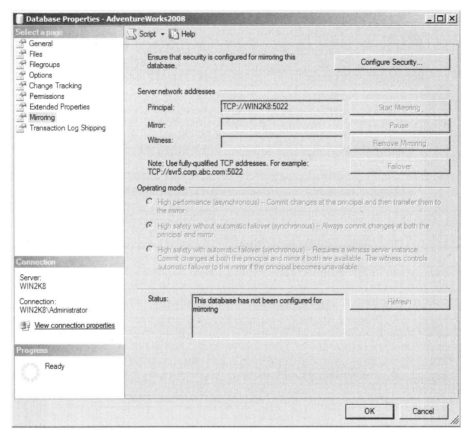

Figure 17-3

Using this script, back up `AdventureWorks2008` using a full database backup. Next, restore this database on your designated mirror server with the `NORECOVERY` option for the `RESTORE DATABASE` statement. The following script assumes that the backup of the principal database exists in the folder you created earlier on the mirror server.

Connect to the designated mirror server and execute the `RestoreDatabase.sql` script:

```
--If the path of the mirror database differs from the
--path of the principal database (for instance, their drive letters differ),
--creating the mirror database requires that the restore operation
--include a MOVE clause. See BOL for details on MOVE option.

RESTORE DATABASE [AdventureWorks2008]
FROM DISK = '<your folder>\AdventureWorks2008.bak'
WITH
 NORECOVERY
,MOVE N'AdventureWorks2008_Data' TO N'<your folder>\AdventureWorks2008_Data.mdf'
,MOVE N'AdventureWorks2008_Log' TO N'<your folder>\AdventureWorks2008_Log.LDF'
```

This code restores the database `AdventureWorks2008` in `NORECOVERY` mode on your mirror server; the `NORECOVERY` option is required. Now that you have a database ready to be mirrored, you should understand what it takes to do initial synchronization between the principal and mirror servers.

To establish the mirroring session, the database name must be the same on both principal and mirror; and before you back up the principal database, make sure that the database is in `FULL` recovery model.

Initial Synchronization between Principal and Mirror

You have just backed up and restored the `AdventureWorks2008` database for mirroring. Of course, mirroring a database the size of `AdventureWorks2008` does not simulate a real-life scenario by any means. In real life, you might mirror a production database with hundreds of thousands of MB. Therefore, depending on the database's size and the distance between the servers, it may take a long time to copy and restore the database on the mirror. During this time, the principal database may have produced many transaction logs. Before you set up mirroring, you must copy and restore all these transaction logs with the `NORECOVERY` option on the mirror server. If you don't want to bother copying and restoring these transaction logs on the mirror, you can suspend the transaction log backups (if you have a SQL job to do backup transaction logs, you can disable that job) until the database on the mirror is restored and the database mirroring session is established (you will learn that very soon). After the database mirroring session is established, you can resume the transaction log backup on the principal server again. It is very important to understand that in this approach, because you have stopped the transaction log backups, the transaction log file will grow, so make sure you have enough disk space for transaction log-file growth.

In order for the database mirroring session to be established, both databases (principal and mirror) must be in sync, so at some point you have to stop the transaction log backup on your principal. Decide when you want to do it: before backing up the full database and restoring on the mirror server or after backing up the full database. In the first case, you have to plan for transaction-file growth; and in the second case, you have to copy and restore all the transactions logs on the mirror before you establish the mirroring session.

If you are mirroring a very large database, it is going to take a longer time to back up and then restore it on the mirror server. To minimize the performance impact on the principal server, try to plan mirroring setup during low-activity periods on your system. On a highly active system you may want to increase the time between each transaction log backup so that you have a smaller number of logs to copy and restore on the mirror, although this increases the database's data loss exposure in case of a principal failure. If you have very minimal database activities, you can stop taking transaction log backups on the principal, back up the database on the principal, restore on the mirror, establish the mirroring session, and then restart the transaction log backup job on the principal.

Establishing the Mirroring Session

Now you'll create some database activities in the `AdventureWorks2008` database before you establish the mirroring session so you understand practically what we have just discussed.

Connect to the principal server and execute the `ModifyData.sql` script. This script updates data into the `AdventureWorks2008.person.address` table.

Connect to the principal server and execute `BackupLogPrincipal.sql`:

```
USE MASTER
GO
BACKUP LOG AdventureWorks2008 TO DISK = '<your folder>\AdventureWorks2008.trn'
```

That will back up the transaction log of `AdventureWorks2008`. Now the `AdventureWorks2008` databases on the principal and the mirror are *not* in sync. See what happens if you try to establish the mirroring session between these two databases.

Connect to the mirror server and execute the `SetupMirrorServer.sql` script (this will run successfully):

```
USE MASTER
GO
ALTER DATABASE AdventureWorks2008
SET PARTNER = 'TCP://YourPrincipalServer:5022'
```

Now connect to the principal server and execute the `SetupPrincipalServer.sql` script:

```
USE MASTER
GO
ALTER DATABASE AdventureWorks2008
SET PARTNER = 'TCP://YourMirrorServer:5023'
```

This script will fail on the principal with the following message:

```
Msg 1412, Level 16, State 0, Line 1
The remote copy of database "AdventureWorks2008" has not been rolled forward to
a point
in time that is encompassed in the local copy of the database log.
```

This shows that the database on the mirror server is not rolled forward enough to establish the mirroring session, so now you have to restore the transaction log that you backed up on the principal server to the mirror server with `NORECOVERY` mode in order to synchronize the mirror with the principal. Connect to the mirror server and execute the `RestoreLogOnMirror.sql` script:

```
USE MASTER
GO
RESTORE LOG AdventureWorks2008
FROM DISK = '<your folder>\AdventureWorks2008.trn'
WITH NORECOVERY
```

This script assumes that you have copied the transaction log in the `C:\` drive on the mirror server. If you put the transaction log somewhere else, substitute that folder location and then run the script. Now the principal and mirror databases are in sync.

Connect to the mirror server and execute the `SetupMirrorServer.sql` script again. Then connect to the principal server and execute the `SetupPrincipalServer.sql` script. It should succeed now, and you have just established the mirroring session.

Note that the order in which you execute these scripts is important:

1. Connect to the mirror server and execute `SetupMirrorServer.sql`.

2. Connect to the principal server and execute `SetupPrincipalServer.sql`.

When you establish the mirroring session, the transaction safety is set to FULL by default, so the mirroring session is always established in high-safety operating mode *without* automatic failover.

When you execute the `SetupPrincipalServer.sql` or `SetupMirrorServer.sql` scripts, you may get the following type of error:

```
2008-08-20 17:53:16.630 spid15s     Database mirroring connection error 4 'An
error occurred while receiving data: '64(The specified network name is no longer
available.)'.' for 'TCP://YourMirrorServer:5022'. 2008-08-20 17:55:13.710 spid15s
Error: 1443, Severity: 16, State: 2.
```

It's possible that the firewall on the mirror or principal server is blocking the connection on the port specified.

High-Safety Operating Mode with Automatic Failover

You have established the mirroring session in high-safety operating mode *without automatic failover*. Now you want to change it to *automatic failover*. This means that if the principal database (or the server hosting it) fails, the database mirroring will failover to the mirror server, and the mirror server will assume the principal role and serve the database. However, you need a third server, the witness, for automatic failover to the mirror. The witness just sits there as a third party and is used by the mirror to verify that the principal is really down, providing a "2 out of 3" condition for automatic failover. No user action is necessary to failover to the mirror if a witness server is present.

Witness Server

If you choose the SAFETY FULL option, you have an option to set up a witness server (refer to Figure 17-1). We discuss how to set up a witness server soon. The presence of the witness server in high-safety mode determines whether you can perform automatic failover or not when the principal database fails. Note that automatic failover will happen when the following conditions are met:

❑ Witness and mirror are both connected to the principal when the principal is failing (going away).

❑ Safety is set to FULL.

❑ Mirroring state is synchronized.

You must have a separate instance of SQL Server other than the principal and mirror servers to fully take advantage of database mirroring with automatic failover. You can use the same witness server to participate in multiple, concurrent database mirroring sessions.

Now you'll establish the witness server in your example. Connect to either the principal or mirror server and execute the `SetupWitnessServer.sql` script:

```
USE MASTER
GO
ALTER DATABASE AdventureWorks2008
SET WITNESS = 'TCP://YourWitnessServer:5024'
```

Yes, you must connect to either the principal or the mirror to execute this script. When you execute the script, both the principal and the mirror servers must be up and running. You have now established a witness server, which will provide automatic failover support.

The witness server is optional in database mirroring and only if you want automatic failover.

The Quorum

When you set up the witness server, a *quorum* is required to make the database available. A quorum is a relationship between two or more connected server instances in a database mirroring session.

Three types of quorums are possible:

❑ **Full:** Both partners and witness are connected.

❑ **Partner-to-partner:** Both partners are connected.

❑ **Witness-to-partner:** A witness and one of the partners are connected.

A database that thinks it is the principal in its data mirroring session must have at least a partial quorum to serve the database. You will learn more about quorums later in the chapter.

High-Safety Operating Mode without Automatic Failover

High safety without automatic failover is the default operating mode set when you establish database mirroring. In this operating mode, a witness is not set up, so automatic failover is not possible. Because the witness server is not present in this operating mode, the principal doesn't need to form a quorum to serve the database. If the principal loses its quorum with the mirror, it still keeps serving the database.

High-Performance Operating Mode

By default, the SAFETY is ON when you establish the mirroring session, so to activate the high-performance operating mode you have to turn the safety OFF:

```
USE Master
ALTER DATABASE AdventureWorks2008 SET PARTNER SAFETY OFF
```

There is minimal impact on transaction throughput and response time in this mode. The log transfer to the mirror works the same way as in high-safety mode, but because the principal doesn't wait for hardening the log to disk on the mirror, it's possible that if the principal goes down unexpectedly, you may lose data.

You can configure the witness server in high-performance mode, but because you cannot do automatic failover in this mode, the witness will not provide any benefits. Therefore, don't define a witness when you configure database mirroring in high-performance mode. You can remove the witness server by running the following command if you want to change the operating mode to high performance with no witness:

```
USE Master
ALTER DATABASE AdventureWorks2008 SET WITNESS OFF
```

If you configure the witness server in a high-performance mode session, the enforcement of quorum means the following:

❑ If the mirror server is lost, then the principal must be connected to the witness. Otherwise, the principal server takes its database offline until either the witness server or the mirror server rejoins the session.

❑ If the principal server is lost, then forcing failover to the mirror requires that the mirror server be connected to the witness.

The only way you can failover to the mirror in this mode is by running the following command on the mirror when the principal server is disconnected from the mirroring session. This is called *forced failover*. See the table presented earlier in this chapter for the different failover types. We discuss this further later in the chapter.

```
USE MASTER
ALTER DATABASE AdventureWorks2008 SET PARTNER FORCE_SERVICE_ALLOW_DATA_LOSS
```

The forced failover causes an immediate recovery of the mirror database, which may cause data loss. This mode is best used for transferring data over long distances (for disaster recovery to a remote site) or for mirroring an active database for which some potential data loss is acceptable. For example, you can use high-performance mode for mirroring your warehouse. Then you can use a database snapshot (discussed later in this chapter) to create a snapshot on the mirror server to enable a reporting environment from the mirrored warehouse.

Database Mirroring and SQL Server 2008 Editions

Now that you understand the operating modes of database mirroring, the following table summarizes which features of database mirroring are available in which SQL Server 2008 editions.

Database Mirroring Feature	Enterprise Edition	Developer Edition	Standard Edition	Workgroup Edition	SQL Express
Partner (principal or mirror)	✓	✓	✓		
Witness	✓	✓	✓	✓	✓
Safety = FULL	✓	✓	✓		
Safety = OFF	✓	✓			
Available during UNDO after failover	✓	✓	✓		
Parallel REDO	✓	✓			

The Workgroup and SQL Express editions can only be used as a witness server in a mirroring session. Some other features mentioned later in this chapter require either the Enterprise or Developer edition. If you want to use high-performance operating mode, you need the Enterprise or Developer edition.

SQL Server 2008 may use multiple threads to roll forward the log in the redo queue on the mirror database. This is called *parallel redo*. This feature is available only in the Enterprise or Developer editions. Note that if the mirror server has fewer than five CPUs, SQL Server only uses a single thread for redo. Parallel redo is optimized by using one thread per four CPUs.

Database Mirroring Catalog Views

In the example so far, you have set up the mirroring session but you still haven't learned how to get information about the mirroring configuration. Therefore, before continuing with failover scenarios and other topics, we'll explain how you can get that information. The following sections describe the catalog views you can use to get information about database mirroring. It would be redundant to mention each and every column in database mirroring catalog views here, as SQL Server 2008 Books Online describes them well. Our goal here is to show you when and how you should use these views.

sys.database_mirroring

The most important view to monitor mirroring state, safety level, and witness status (when present) is sys.database_mirroring. See the following query, which you can execute on either partner (principal or mirror), and you will get the same results:

```
SELECT
 DB_NAME(database_id) AS DatabaseName
,mirroring_role_desc
,mirroring_safety_level_desc
,mirroring_state_desc
,mirroring_safety_sequence
,mirroring_role_sequence
,mirroring_partner_instance
,mirroring_witness_name
,mirroring_witness_state_desc
,mirroring_failover_lsn
,mirroring_connection_timeout
,mirroring_redo_queue
FROM sys.database_mirroring
WHERE mirroring_guid IS NOT NULL
```

You will use this query often once you establish the mirroring session. If you run this query after you establish the mirroring session in the example scenario, you will see output similar to the following. We have put the result in a table for ease of reading. Of course, some values will be different based on your server names, and so on.

Metadata Column in Select List	Principal Values: YourPrincipalServer	Mirror Values: YourMirrorServer
DatabaseName	AdventureWorks2008	AdventureWorks2008
mirroring_role_desc	PRINCIPAL	MIRROR
mirroring_safety_level_desc	FULL	FULL
mirroring_state_desc	SYNCHRONIZED	SYNCHRONIZED
mirroring_safety_sequence	1	1
mirroring_role_sequence	1	1
mirroring_partner_instance	WIN2K8\Mirror	WIN2K8
mirroring_witness_name	TCP://WIN2K8:5024	TCP://WIN2K8:5024
mirroring_witness_state_desc	CONNECTED	CONNECTED
mirroring_failover_lsn	66000000034200001	66000000034200001
mirroring_connection_timeout	10	10
mirroring_redo_queue	NULL	NULL

Some values in the preceding table are self-explanatory, but others require some additional explanation:

❏ mirroring_safety_sequence gives a count of how many times the safety has changed (from FULL to OFF and back) since the mirroring session was established.

❏ mirroring_role_sequence gives a count of how many times failover has happened since the mirroring session was established.

❏ mirroring_failover_lsn gives the log sequence number of the latest transaction that is guaranteed to be hardened to permanent storage on both partners. In this case, because there is very little database activity, both of these numbers are the same if you use the ModifyData.sql script in a WHILE loop (if you change the script, be sure not to use an infinite loop!).

❏ mirroring_connection_timeout gives the mirroring connection timeout, in seconds. This is the number of seconds to wait for a reply from a partner or witness before considering them unavailable. The default timeout value is 10 seconds. If it is null, then the database is inaccessible or not mirrored.

❏ mirroring_redo_queue displays the maximum amount of the transaction log to be redone at the mirror in megabytes when the mirroring_redo_queue_type is not set to unlimited. When the maximum is reached, the principal transaction log temporarily stalls to enable the mirror to catch up; therefore, it can limit the failover time. When the mirroring_redo_queue_type is set to unlimited which is the default, data mirroring does not inhibit the redo_queue.

sys.database_mirroring_witnesses

If you have a witness established for your mirroring session, then sys.database_mirroring_witnesses returns data mirroring information:

```
SELECT * FROM sys.database_mirroring_witnesses
```

You can execute this query on the witness server to list the corresponding principal and mirror server names, the database name, and the safety level for all the mirroring sessions for which this server is acting as a witness. You will get multiple rows from this query if the same witness server is acting as a witness for more than one mirroring session.

❏   role_sequence_number column displays how many times failover has happened between mirroring partners since the mirroring session was established.

❏   is_suspended column displays whether database mirroring is suspended or not. If this column value is 1, then mirroring is currently suspended.

sys.database_mirroring_endpoints

The following query returns information about database mirroring endpoints such as port number, whether encryption is enabled or not, authentication type, and endpoint state:

```
SELECT
  dme.name AS EndPointName
 ,dme.protocol_desc
 ,dme.type_desc AS EndPointType
 ,dme.role_desc AS MirroringRole
 ,dme.state_desc AS EndPointStatus
 ,te.port AS PortUsed
 ,CASE WHEN dme.is_encryption_enabled = 1
        THEN 'Yes'
        ELSE 'No'
  END AS Is_Encryption_Enabled
 ,dme.encryption_algorithm_desc
 ,dme.connection_auth_desc
FROM sys.database_mirroring_endpoints dme
JOIN sys.tcp_endpoints te
  ON dme.endpoint_id = te.endpoint_id
```

This query uses the sys.tcp_endpoints view because the port information is not available in the sys.database_mirroring_endpoints catalog view.

Database Mirroring Role Change

In the example so far, you have learned how to establish the database mirroring session. You must have noticed that if you try to query the AdventureWorks2008 database on your mirror server, you get an error like the following:

```
Msg 954, Level 14, State 1, Line 1
The database "AdventureWorks2008" cannot be opened. It is acting as a mirror database.
```

You cannot access the mirrored database, so how do you switch the roles of the mirroring partners? There are three ways you can failover to the mirror server as described in the table earlier in this chapter. The failover types depend on which transaction safety is used (FULL or OFF) and whether a witness server is present or not.

Automatic Failover

Automatic failover is a database mirroring feature in high-availability mode (SAFETY FULL when a witness server is present). When a failure occurs on the principal, automatic failover is initiated. Because you have set up database mirroring in high-availability mode with a witness server, you are ready to do automatic failover. The following events occur in an automatic failover scenario:

1. **The failure occurs:** The principal database becomes unavailable. This could be the result of a power failure, a hardware failure, a storage failure, or some other reason.

2. **The failure is detected:** The failure is detected by the mirror and the witness. Note that both partners and witness continually ping each other to identify their presence. Of course, it is more than just a simple ping, detecting things such as whether the SQL Server is available, whether the principal database is available, and so on. A timeout is specified for the ping, which is set to 10 seconds by default when you set up the database mirroring session. You can change the timeout by using the following command:

   ```
   ALTER DATABASE <db_name> SET PARTNER TIMEOUT <value_in_seconds>
   ```

   If the principal does not respond to the ping message within the timeout period, it is considered to be down, and failure is detected. You should leave the default setting for timeout at 10 seconds, or at least do not change it to less than 10 seconds, because under heavy load and sporadic network conditions, false failures may occur and your database will start failing over back and forth.

3. **A complete redo is performed on the mirror:** The mirror database has been in the restoring state until now, continuously redoing the log (rolling it forward onto the database). When failure is detected, the mirror needs to recover the database. In order to do that, the mirror needs to redo the remaining log entries in the redo queue.

4. **The failover decision is made:** The mirror now contacts the witness server to form a quorum and determines whether the database should failover to the mirror. Note here that in the high-safety mode with automatic failover, the witness must be present for automatic failover. The decision takes about 1 second, so if the principal comes back up before step 3 is complete, that failover is terminated.

5. **The mirror becomes the principal:** The redo continues while the failover decision is being made. After both the witness and the mirror have formed a quorum on the failover decision, the database is recovered completely. The mirror's role is switched to principal, recovery is run (this involves setting up various database states and rolling back any in-flight system transactions and starting up rollback of user transactions); and then the database is available to the clients, and normal operations can be performed. Undo of the user transactions continues in parallel (that holds some locks) until it is completed.

6. **Undo:** There may be uncommitted transactions, the transactions sent to the mirror while the principal was available but not committed before the principal went down in the transaction log of the new principal, which are rolled back.

Normally, the time taken to failover in this operating mode is very short, usually seconds, but that mostly depends on the redo phase. If the mirror is already caught up with the principal before the principal has gone down, the redo phase will not introduce time lag. The time to apply the redo records depends on the redo queue length and the redo rate on the mirror. Note that the failover will not happen if the `mirroring_state` is not synchronized. There are some performance counters available, which are examined in the "Performance Monitoring Database Mirroring" section, later in this chapter. From these counters, you can estimate the time it will take to apply the transaction log for the redo queue on the mirror server.

To measure the actual time, you can use the SQL Profiler to trace the event. See Chapter 13 to learn more about running traces with SQL Profiler, which we will use here to measure the actual time it takes to failover:

1. Open SQL Profiler.

2. Connect to the mirror server.

3. Choose the Database Mirroring State Change event under the Database events group.

4. Choose the `TextData` and `StartTime` columns.

5. Start the trace.

6. Stop the SQL Server service on the principal server. Soon, automatic failover will happen.

Two columns in the trace are of interest: `TextData` provides the description of the database mirroring state change event. `StartTime` represents the timestamp at which time the event took place. Figure 17-4 shows the SQL Profiler trace of the events.

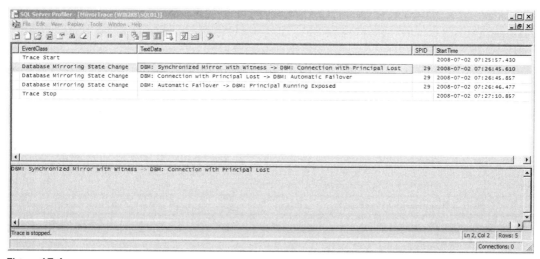

Figure 17-4

In the event Synchronized Mirror with Witness, the mirror informs the witness server that the connection to the principal is lost, which is the step 4 event in Figure 17-2. Then the mirror fails over and is running exposed, which means that the partner is lost. You will also see a message similar to the following in the mirror server SQL error log:

```
The mirrored database "AdventureWorks2008" is changing roles from "MIRROR" to
"PRINCIPAL" due to Auto Failover.
```

Note that in the `StartTime` column the actual failover time for this automatic failover was approximately seven seconds.

The length of the failover depends upon the type of failure and the load on the database. Under load, it takes longer to failover than in a no-load situation. In addition, a manual failover takes a little more time compared to automatic failover. You will see messages similar to the following in the SQL error log:

```
The mirrored database "AdventureWorks2008" is changing roles from "MIRROR" to
"PRINCIPAL" due to Failover from partner.
Starting up database 'AdventureWorks2008'.
Analysis of database 'AdventureWorks2008' (9) is 81% complete (approximately 0
seconds
remain).
Analysis of database 'AdventureWorks2008' (9) is 100% complete (approximately 0
seconds
remain).
Recovery of database 'AdventureWorks2008' (9) is 0% complete (approximately 30
seconds
remain). Phase 2 of 3.
Recovery of database 'AdventureWorks2008' (9) is 16% complete (approximately 17
seconds
remain). Phase 2 of 3.
13 transactions rolled forward in database 'AdventureWorks2008' (9).
Recovery of database 'AdventureWorks2008' (9) is 16% complete (approximately 17
seconds
remain). Phase 3 of 3.
Recovery of database 'AdventureWorks2008' (9) is 100% complete (approximately 0
seconds
remain). Phase 3 of 3.
```

The additional steps during analysis and recovery of the database cause the manual failover to take longer.

When the failover happens, the clients need to be redirected to the new principal server. We discuss that in the section "Preparing the Mirror Server for Failover," along with other tasks you have to do on the mirror server to prepare it for failover and take on the database workload.

Manual Failover

In a manual failover, you are making a decision to switch the roles of the partners. The current mirror server becomes the new principal, and the current principal becomes the new mirror. For manual failover, the SAFETY must be set to FULL. It doesn't matter whether you have a witness server set up or not. You can use the following command for manual failover:

```
ALTER DATABASE AdventureWorks2008 SET PARTNER FAILOVER
```

You have to run this command on the principal server in order to successfully failover. In addition, the `mirroring_state` must be synchronized in order for failover to succeed. If it is not synchronized, you will get the following message when you try to execute the failover command on the principal:

```
Msg 1422, Level 16, State 2, Line 1
The mirror server instance is not caught up to the recent changes to database
"AdventureWorks2008". Unable to fail over.
```

Now you can try a manual failover using your data mirroring servers. Open the `Database MirroringCommands.sql` script. When you performed automatic failover earlier, we had you stop the original principal SQL Server service. Make sure you start that service back up before the manual failover, because both the mirror and principal must be up and running for this step.

If you want to see what's happening behind the scenes, you can start SQL Profiler, connect it to the mirror server, and select the event Database Mirroring State Change under the Database event group. Then run the trace. Two columns in the trace are of interest: `TextData` and `StartTime`. Moreover, if you want to see activities on the principal, you can start another instance of SQL Profiler and connect it to the principal.

Now connect to your principal server and execute the following command:

```
ALTER DATABASE AdventureWorks2008 SET PARTNER FAILOVER
```

You can also use SQL Server 2008 Management Studio to execute a manual failover as follows: Right-click the principal database and select Tasks ⇨ Mirror to access the dialog shown in Figure 17-5. Click the Failover button to get a failover confirmation dialog. Click OK again.

You can use manual failover for planned downtime, as discussed in the section "Preparing the Mirror Server for Failover" later in this chapter.

Forced Failover

For forced failover, you need to execute the following command on the mirror server.

> **Be cautious about using this command, as you risk data loss by running it.**

```
ALTER DATABASE AdventureWorks2008 SET PARTNER FORCE_SERVICE_ALLOW_DATA_LOSS
```

When you run this command, the mirror should not be able to connect to the principal; otherwise, you will not be able to failover. If your principal is up and running and the mirror can connect to it when you try to run the command, you will get the following error message:

```
Msg 1455, Level 16, State 2, Line 1
The database mirroring service cannot be forced for database "AdventureWorks2008"
because the database is not in the correct state to become the principal database.
```

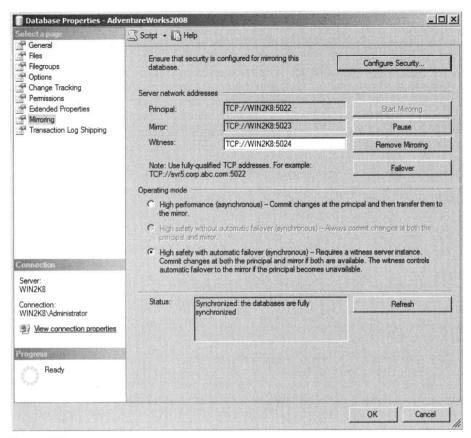

Figure 17-5

Now try this exercise using your data mirroring servers. Because you have set up the database mirroring in full-safety mode with automatic failover, you first need to remove it. Open the `DatabaseMirroringCommands.sql` script and execute the following command on either the principal server or the mirror server:

```
ALTER DATABASE AdventureWorks2008 SET WITNESS OFF
```

Then execute the following command on the principal server:

```
ALTER DATABASE AdventureWorks2008 SET SAFETY OFF
```

Now the database `AdventureWorks2008` is set with `SAFETY OFF` with no witness, and you can force a failover. You'll have to simulate the scenario whereby the mirror server cannot form a quorum (cannot connect) with the principal server. To achieve that, stop the SQL Server service on the principal and execute the following command on the mirror server:

```
ALTER DATABASE AdventureWorks2008 SET PARTNER FORCE_SERVICE_ALLOW_DATA_LOSS
```

This command now forces the `AdventureWorks2008` database on the mirror server to recover and come online. The `mirroring_state` (`sys.database_mirroring`) doesn't matter (synchronized or not) in this case because it is a forced failover, which is why you may lose data.

Now see what happens if you bring the original principal server (the one on which you stopped the SQL Server service) back online. After bringing the server online, the mirroring session will be suspended. You can execute the `sys.database_mirroring` catalog view in the `MirroringCatalogView.sql` script to view the mirroring state by connecting to either the principal server or the mirror server. To resume the mirroring session, execute the following command from the `DatabaseMirroringCommands.sql` script on either the principal or the mirror:

```
ALTER DATABASE AdventureWorks2008 SET PARTNER RESUME
```

Database Availability Scenarios

So far we have talked about database mirroring operating modes and how to failover in different operating modes. This section describes what happens to the database availability of clients when the server is lost. The server might be lost not only because the power is off but also because of a communication link failure or some other reason; the point is that the other server in the mirroring session cannot communicate. Several different scenarios exist. To keep matters clear, we use three server names in this section: ServerA (principal), ServerB (mirror) and ServerC (witness).

Principal Is Lost

If the principal server is lost, the failover scenario depends on the transaction safety (FULL or OFF) and whether a witness is present.

Scenario 1: Safety FULL with a Witness

This scenario was covered in the automatic failover section. In this scenario, the mirror forms a quorum with the witness because the principal is lost. Automatic failover will happen (of course, certain conditions must be met, as mentioned earlier), the mirror becomes the new principal server, and the database will be available on the new principal.

In this situation, before the failure ServerA was the principal, ServerB was the mirror, and ServerC was the witness. ServerA now fails. After failover, ServerB becomes the principal and serves the database. However, because there is no mirror server after failover (because ServerA is down), ServerB is running exposed, and the mirroring state is `DISCONNECTED`. If ServerA becomes operational, then it automatically assumes the mirror role, except for the fact that the session is suspended until a `RESUME` is issued.

If `SAFETY` is `FULL` and you have configured a witness, in order to serve the database, at least two servers need be available to form a quorum. In this scenario, if ServerA fails, then ServerB becomes the principal and serves the database; but now if ServerC (witness) goes down, ServerB will not be able to serve the database.

Scenario 2: Safety FULL without a Witness

In this operating mode, `SAFETY` is `FULL`, but automatic failover is not possible. Therefore, if ServerA (principal) fails, the database is unavailable to the clients. You need to manually perform several steps to force the database to become available again.

In this situation, before the failure, ServerA was the principal, ServerB was the mirror, and there was no witness. ServerA is now lost, so the database is unavailable to clients. In order to make the database available, you need to execute the following commands on the mirror:

```
ALTER DATABASE <database_name> SET PARTNER OFF
RESTORE DATABASE <database_name> WITH RECOVERY
```

These commands will bring the database on ServerB online, making it available again. When ServerA comes online, you have to reestablish the mirroring session.

There is another option here, whereby you do not have to reestablish the mirroring session. Execute the following command on ServerB (which is still the mirror after ServerA becomes unavailable):

```
ALTER DATABASE <database_name> SET PARTNER FORCE_SERVICE_ALLOW_DATA_LOSS
```

That will bring the database online on ServerB, which becomes the principal server. When ServerA comes online, it automatically assumes the mirror role. However, the mirroring session is suspended, meaning no transaction logs will be sent from ServerB to ServerA. You need to resume the mirroring session by starting to send the transaction logs from ServerB to ServerA by executing the following command:

```
ALTER DATABASE <database_name> SET PARTNER RESUME
```

For larger databases, performing the backup and restore to reestablish the mirroring session can take some time.

Whether you choose to break the mirroring session or force failover, you lose any transactions that were not sent to the mirror at the time of failure.

Scenario 3: SAFETY OFF

When SAFETY is OFF, the witness doesn't add any value, so we recommend that you not configure a witness in that case. If ServerA (principal) is lost in this scenario, the database becomes unavailable. Then you have to force failover for the database to become available again.

In this scenario, before the failure, ServerA was the principal and ServerB was the mirror. ServerA now fails and the database is not available to clients. You can manually failover to ServerB by using the following command:

```
ALTER DATABASE <database_name> SET PARTNER FORCE_SERVICE_ALLOW_DATA_LOSS
```

However, the SAFETY is OFF, so any transactions that were not received by the mirror at the time of the principal failure will be lost. Therefore, manual failover with SAFETY is OFF involves acknowledging the possibility of data loss. When ServerA becomes operational again, it automatically assumes the mirror role, but the mirroring session is suspended. You can resume the mirroring session again by executing the following command:

```
ALTER DATABASE <database_name> SET PARTNER RESUME
```

Mirror Is Lost

If the mirror fails, then the principal continues functioning, so the database continues to be available to the clients. The mirroring state is DISCONNECTED, and the principal is running exposed in this case. You can use the sys.database_mirroring catalog view to see the mirroring state on the principal server.

When the mirror goes down, you have to be a little careful and take steps to ensure that the principal continues to serve the database without any issue. When the mirror goes down, the mirroring state is changed to DISCONNECTED, and as long as the state is DISCONNECTED the transaction log space cannot be reused, even if you back up the transaction log. If your transaction log files keep growing and reach their maximum size limit, or your disk runs out of space, the complete database comes to a halt.

You have some options here:

1. Make sure you have plenty of disk space for the transaction log to grow on the principal and be sure to bring the mirror server online before you run out of disk space.

2. Break the database mirroring session using the following command: ALTER DATABASE <database_name> SET PARTNER OFF

   The issue here is that when your mirror server becomes operational, you have to reestablish the mirroring session by a backup and restore of the principal database and by performing the steps mentioned in the previous example. For a large database, the backup and restore operations can take some time, consider the following step.

3. Break the database mirroring session using the following command: ALTER DATABASE <database_name> SET PARTNER OFF

   Make a note of the time when the mirror went down, and make sure the job that backs up the transaction log is running on the principal. When the mirror comes back online, apply all the transaction logs on the mirror database. The first transaction log you should apply is the one you backed up after the mirror went down. Be sure to apply the transaction log on the mirror database with the NORECOVERY option. That way, you don't have to back up the entire database and restore it on the mirror. Of course, you have to perform other steps to reestablish the mirroring session because the session was broken.

Witness Is Lost

If the witness is lost, the database mirroring session will continue functioning without interruption, and the database will be available. Automatic failover will not happen. When the witness comes back online, it automatically joins the mirroring session, of course, as a witness. With SAFETY FULL, if the witness is lost and then the mirror or the principal is lost, the database becomes unavailable to the clients.

Mirror and Witness Are Lost

Assuming that you have configured the mirroring session with a witness, if the mirror server is unavailable, the principal will continue and the database is available, but it is running exposed. If the witness is also lost, then the principal becomes isolated and cannot serve the clients. Even though the principal database is running, it is not available to the clients because it cannot form a quorum. If you try to access the database, you will get the following message:

```
Msg 955, Level 14, State 1, Line 1
Database <database_name> is enabled for Database Mirroring, but neither the partner
nor witness server instances are available: the database cannot be opened.
```

With both the mirror and the witness lost, the only way you can bring the database online to serve clients is by breaking the mirroring session with the following command on the principal:

```
ALTER DATABASE <database_name> SET PARTNER OFF
```

Once the mirror becomes available, you can reestablish the mirroring session. To do so, you may have to back up and restore the database on the mirror, but if you want to avoid that step, refer to the third option in the "Mirror Is Lost" section. Once the witness becomes available, it can join in again as a witness, but you must establish the mirroring session with the mirror first, as shown earlier.

Monitoring Database Mirroring

There are different ways to monitor database mirroring, based on what information you want to track. For basic information about the database mirroring state, safety level, and witness status, you can use catalog views. Refer to the "Database Mirroring Catalog Views" section earlier in this chapter for more details about catalog views. To monitor the performance of database mirroring, SQL Server 2008 provides a set of System Monitor performance objects. There is also a GUI "Database Mirroring Monitor" available with SQL Server 2008 Management Studio, which you can access if your database is mirrored. We discuss both the key System Monitor counters and the GUI in this section.

Monitoring Using System Monitor

The object SQL Server: Database Mirroring has plenty of counters to monitor database mirroring performance. You can use these counters to monitor the database mirroring activities on each partner, and the traffic between them, as shown in Figure 17-6. You can do this for each database instance, so if you are mirroring more than one database on a server, select the database you want to monitor from the list box. The key counters are described in the following sections.

Counters for the Principal

The following System Monitor counters are used on the principal server:

❑ **Log Bytes Sent/Sec:** The rate at which the principal is sending transaction log data to the mirror

❑ **Log Send Queue KB:** The total kilobytes of the log that have not been sent to the mirror server yet. As the transaction log data is sent from the principal to the mirror, the Log Send Queue is depleted, growing again as new transactions are recorded into the log buffer on the principal.

❑ **Transaction Delay:** The delay (in milliseconds) spent waiting for commit acknowledgment from the mirror. This counter reports the total delay for all the transactions in process at the time.

You can determine the average delay per transaction by dividing this counter by the Transactions/Sec counter. For high-performance mode, this counter is zero because the principal doesn't wait for the mirror to harden the transaction log to disk.

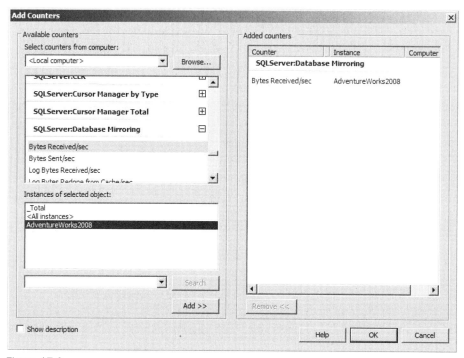

Figure 17-6

You can do a simple exercise using the ModifyData.sql script to get a feel for how this counter reports on the transaction delay:

1. Start the System Monitor and add this counter on your principal.

2. On the principal, execute the ModifyData.sql script and note the average for this counter. It should show a value greater than 0.

3. On the principal, execute this command:

```
ALTER DATABASE AdventureWorks2008 SET SAFETY OFF
```

This puts database mirroring in high-performance mode.

4. Execute the ModifyData.sql script again. You should now notice that this counter is 0.

❏ **Transaction/Sec:** You will find this counter in the SQL Server: Databases object, which measures database throughput and shows how many transactions are processed in a second. This counter gives you an idea of how fast the log file will grow if your mirror is down, the mirror state is DISCONNECTED, and you need to expand the log file. Be sure to choose the database instance you are interested in for this counter.

❑ **Log Bytes Flushed/Sec:** This counter is under the SQL Server: Databases object, which indicates how many bytes are written to disk (log hardening) per second on the principal. This is the log-generation rate of your application. These are also the bytes sent to the mirror when it is flushed to the disk on the principal. In normal operating conditions, the Log Bytes Flushed/Sec and Log Bytes Sent/Sec counters should show the same value. If you refer to Figure 17-2, the activity labeled 2 happens at the same time, which is exactly what the System Monitor indicates.

Counters for the Mirror

The following System Monitor counters are on the mirror server under the object SQL Server: Database Mirroring:

❑ **Redo Bytes/Sec:** The rate at which log bytes are rolled forward (replayed) to the data pages, per second, from the redo queue

❑ **Redo Queue KB:** This counter shows the total KB of the transaction log still to be applied to the mirror database (rolled forward). You will learn later how to calculate the estimated time the mirror takes to redo the logs using this counter and the Redo Bytes/Sec counter. The failover time depends on how big this queue is and how fast the mirror can empty this queue.

❑ **Log Bytes Received/Sec:** The rate at which log bytes are received from the principal. If the mirror can keep up with the principal to minimize the failover time, then ideally the Log Bytes Received/Sec and Redo Bytes/Sec counter will show the same *average* value, which means that the Redo Queue KB is zero. Whatever bytes the principal sends are immediately rolled forward to the data pages on the mirror and there is no redo left, so the mirror is ready to failover right away.

From a DBA standpoint, we would like to know approximately how far the mirror is behind the principal; and once the mirror catches up, how long would it take to redo the transaction log so that it can failover. A calculation is required, described in a moment, but you can also use the Database Mirroring Monitor that ships with SQL Server 2008 and can give you all this information readily. First the calculation.

To calculate the estimated time for the mirror to catch up (in seconds) with the principal, you can use the Log Send Queue counter from the principal and the Log Bytes Received/Sec counter on the mirror. Moreover, you can use the Log Bytes Send/Sec counter on the principal instead of Log Bytes Received/Sec on the mirror. Use their average values and calculate as follows:

```
Estimated time to catch up (in seconds) = (Log Send Queue)/(Log Bytes Received
/sec)
```

To calculate the estimated time for the mirror to replay the transaction log (redo) in order to get ready for failover, you can use the Redo Queue KB counter (this counter gives you KB value, so convert it to bytes) and the Redo Bytes/Sec counter on the mirror. Use their average values and calculate as follows:

```
Estimated time to redo (in seconds) = (Redo Queue)/(Redo Bytes/sec)
```

Monitoring Using Database Mirroring Monitor

The SQL Server 2008 database mirroring development team came up with this powerful tool to monitor the database mirroring activities that make the DBA's life easier. You can access this tool by running sqlmonitor.exe from the command prompt and then selecting Go ⇨ Database Mirroring Monitor, or you can right-click any user database in Object Explorer in SQL Management Studio on any registered SQL Server 2008 server and select Tasks ➪ Launch Database Mirroring Monitor. You can monitor all your mirroring sessions from here.

You have to register the mirrored database in the Database Mirroring Monitor before you can use it. To do so, click Action ➪ Register Mirrored Database, and follow the wizard. You can give the wizard either the principal server name or the mirror server name; it will figure out the other partner. Figure 17-7 shows the Database Mirroring Monitor with a registered mirrored database.

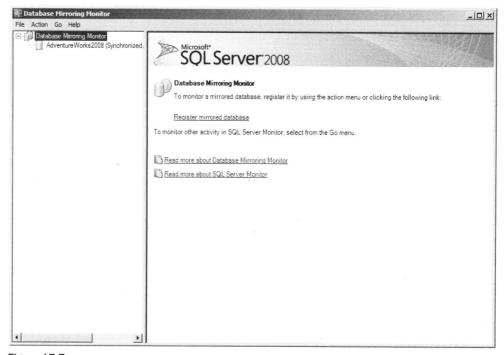

Figure 17-7

You can monitor the key counters mentioned in the previous section using this GUI. You can also set alerts for these counters to receive an e-mail or take an action if any counter exceeds a set threshold, as covered later.

If you set up mirroring using the SQL Server 2008 Management Studio, it creates the SQL job called Database Mirroring Monitor Job, which runs every one minute by default to refresh these counters. This data is stored in the msdb.dbo.dbm_monitor_data table. You can change the job schedule if desired. If you set up database mirroring using the scripts provided here, you can create the SQL job using the following command to refresh the counters:

```
sp_dbmmonitoraddmonitoring [ update_period ]
```

By default, the [update_period] is one minute. You can specify a value between 1 and 120, in minutes. If you don't create this job, just press F5 when you are on the Database Mirroring Monitor screen. It will call the `sp_dbmmonitorresults` stored procedure to refresh the data (adding a row for new readings) in the `msdb.dbo.dbm_monitor_data` table. Actually, `sp_dbmmonitorresults` calls another stored procedure in the `msdb` database called `sp_dbmmonitorupdate` to update the status table and calculate the performance matrix displayed in the UI. If you press F5 more than once in 15 seconds, it won't refresh the data again in the table.

Take a look at the Status screen details in Figure 17-7. The Status area is where the server instance names, their current role, mirroring state, and witness connection status (if there is a witness) comes from the `sys.database_mirroring` catalog view. If you click the History button, you will get a history of the mirroring status and other performance counters. The mirroring status and performance history is kept for seven days (168 hours) by default in the `msdb.dbo.dbm_monitor_data` table. If you want to change the retention period, you can use the `sp_dbmmonitorchangealert` stored procedure, like this:

```
EXEC sp_dbmmonitorchangealert AdventureWorks2008, 5, 8, 1
```

This example changes the retention period to eight hours for the `AdventureWorks2008` database. You can refer to SQL 2008 Books Online for a description of this stored procedure.

❑ **Principal Log: Unsent Log:** This counter provides the same value as the Log Send Queue KB counter on the principal. Unsent Log reads the last value, so if you want to compare the Performance Monitor and this counter, look at its last value. You can run the script `ModifyData.sql` from earlier in the chapter after suspending the mirroring session using the following command:

```
ALTER DATABASE AdventureWorks2008 SET PARTNER SUSPEND
```

You will see this counter value start to go up.

❑ **Principal Log: Oldest Unsent Transaction:** This counter gives you the age, in hh:mm:ss format, of the oldest unsent transaction waiting in the Send Queue. It indicates that the mirror is behind the principal by that amount of time.

❑ **Principal Log: Time to Send Log (Estimated):** The estimated time the principal instance requires to send the log currently in the Send Queue to the mirror server. Because the rate of the incoming transaction can change, this counter can only provide an estimate. This counter also provides a rough estimate of the time required to manually failover. If you suspend the mirroring, you will notice that this counter shows a value of "Infinite," which means that because you are not sending any transaction logs to the mirror, the mirror will never catch up.

❑ **Principal Log: Current Send Rate:** This counter provides the rate at which the transaction log is sent to the mirror, in KB/Sec. This is the same as the Performance Monitor counter Log Bytes Sent/Sec. The counter Current Send Rate provides the value in KB, whereas the counter Log Bytes Sent/Sec provides the value in bytes. When Time to Send Log is infinite, this counter shows a value of 0 KB/Sec because no log is being sent to the mirror server.

❑ **Principal Log: Current Rate of New Transaction:** The rate at which new transactions are coming in per second. This is the same as the Transaction/sec counter in the `Database` object.

❑ **Mirror Log: Unrestored Log:** This counter is for the mirror server. It provides the amount of log in KB waiting in the Redo Queue yet to be restored. This is the same as the Redo Queue KB counter for the mirror server. If this counter is 0, the mirror is keeping up with the principal and can failover immediately if required.

713

❑ **Mirror Log: Time to Restore Log:** This counter provides an estimate, in minutes, of how long the mirror will take to replay the transactions waiting in the Redo Queue. You saw this calculation earlier; this is the estimated time that the mirror requires before failover can occur.

❑ **Mirror Log: Current Restore Rate:** The rate at which the transaction log is restored into the mirror database, in KB/Sec

❑ **Mirror Committed Overhead:** This counter measures the delay (in milliseconds) spent waiting for a commit acknowledgment from the mirror. This counter is the same as the Transaction Delay on the principal. It is relevant only in high-safety mode. For high-performance mode, this counter is zero because the principal does not wait for the mirror to harden the transaction log to disk.

❑ **Time to Send and Restore All Current Log (Estimated):** This counter measures the time needed to send and restore all of the log that has been committed at the principal at the current time. This time may be less than the sum of the values of the Time to Send Log (Estimated) and Time to Restore Log (Estimated) fields, because sending and restoring can operate in parallel. This estimate does predict the time required to send and restore new transactions committed at the principal while working through backlogs in the Send Queue.

❑ **Witness Address:** The fully qualified domain name of the witness, with the port number assigned for that endpoint

❑ **Operating Mode:** The operating mode of the database mirroring session. It can be one of the following:

   ❑ High performance (asynchronous)

   ❑ High safety without automatic failover (synchronous)

   ❑ High safety with automatic failover (synchronous)

Setting Thresholds on Counters and Sending Alerts

You can set warnings for different mirroring thresholds so that you receive alerts based on the threshold you have set. Figure 17-8 shows the Warnings tab of the Database Mirroring Monitor. There are different warnings for which you can set thresholds.

You can set an alert using SQL Server 2008 Management Studio for this event. For a detailed look at how to set alerts, refer to Chapter 5. We will give you a quick summary of how to set them here. Start by clicking the Set Thresholds button on the Warnings tab, which opens the dialog shown in Figure 17-9.

Here, you can set the threshold for counters on both the principal and mirror servers individually so that you can either keep the thresholds the same or vary them based on your requirements. For this example, select the checkbox for the first warning, "Warn if the unsent log exceeds the threshold," and set the threshold value to 100KB, just for the principal server.

Next, under the Alert folder in SQL Server Agent in SQL Server 2008 Management Studio, add a new alert. You will see a dialog similar to the one shown in Figure 17-10. Type the alert name and select the database name for which you need this alert — in this case, AdventureWorks2008. SQL Server will raise the error when the threshold you set is exceeded. Enter 32042 for the error number. Refer to the section "Using Warning Thresholds and Alerts on Mirroring Performance Metrics" in SQL 2008 Books Online to get the error numbers for other events. Now click Response on the left pane and fill out the operator information to specify who will receive the alert when the threshold is exceeded.

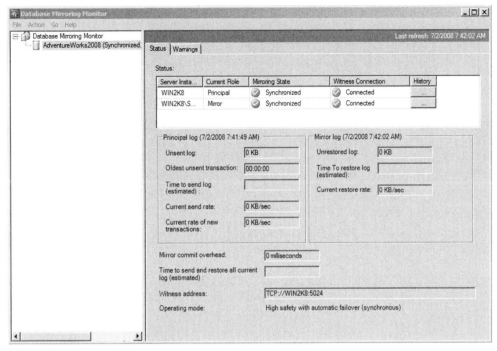

Figure 17-8

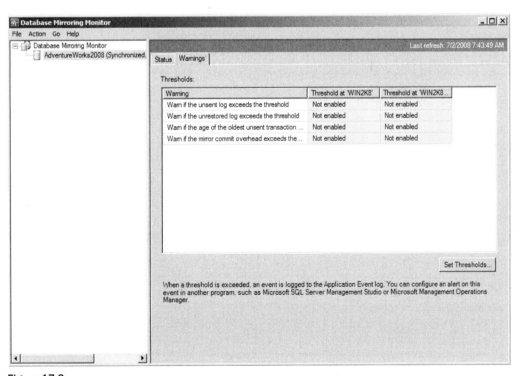

Figure 17-9

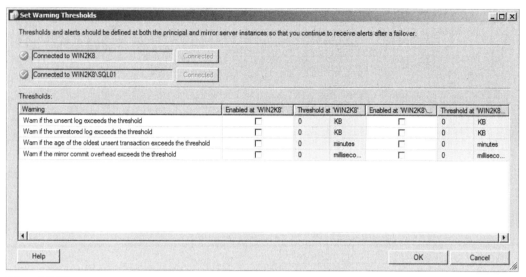

Figure 17-10

On the principal, you can test this alert by suspending database mirroring using the following command:

```
ALTER DATABASE AdventureWorks2008 SET PARTNER SUSPEND
```

The log will not be sent to the mirror and the Unsent Log counter will start increasing. When it reaches the threshold of 100KB, you should get the alert. You'll look at an example demonstrating how to set up the database mirroring event change (suspended, synchronizing, synchronized) and send a notification in the section "Mirroring Event Listener Setup."

Monitoring Using SQL Profiler

You will find the Database Mirroring State Change event under the Database event class of SQL Profiler in SQL Server 2008. This event records all the database mirroring state changes (suspended, synchronizing, synchronized, and so on) that occur on the server.

Troubleshooting Database Mirroring

Database mirroring errors typically occur at two main points: during setup and at runtime. This section covers each of these separately.

Troubleshooting Setup Errors

You may get the following error while setting up database mirroring:

```
2006-08-20 17:53:16.630 spid15s    Database mirroring connection error 4'An
error occurred while receiving data: '64(The specified network name is no longer
available.)'.' for 'TCP://yourMirrorServer:5023'. 2006-08-20 17:55:13.710 spid15s
Error: 1443, Severity: 16, State: 2.
```

It may be that the firewall on the mirror server or the principal server is blocking the connection on the specified port. Check whether the firewall is blocking that communication port.

Similarly, you may get the following error while setting up database mirroring on the principal server:

```
Msg 1412, Level 16, State 0, Line 1
The remote copy of database "AdventureWorks2008" has not been rolled forward to
a point
in time that is encompassed in the local copy of the database log.
```

This indicates that the database on the mirror server is not rolled forward enough to establish the mirroring session. You may have backed up some transaction logs while backing up and restoring the database, so you have to restore these transaction logs to the mirror server with the NORECOVERY option to synchronize the mirror with the principal. See the RestoreLogOnMirror.sql script for an example.

Make sure that the SQL Server service accounts on each server are trusted and that the user account under which the SQL Server instance is running has the necessary connect permissions. If the servers are on nontrusted domains, make sure the certificates are correct. Refer to the "Preparing the Endpoints" section earlier in this chapter for details regarding how to configure the certificates.

Ensure that the endpoint status is started on all partners and the witness. You can use the MirroringCatalogView.sql script, which is included in the download for this chapter. Check the EndPointStatus column and ensure that the value is STARTED.

Make sure you aren't using a port used by another process. The port number must be unique per server, not per SQL Server instance. You can use any port number between 1024 and 32767. Use the MirroringCatalogView.sql script to view the port information under the PortUsed column.

Verify that the encryption settings for the endpoints are compatible on the principal, mirror, and witness. You can check the encryption setting using MirroringCatalogView.sql. Look for the script that selects from the sys.database_mirroring_endpoints catalog view, and check the IS_ENCRYPTION_ENABLED column. This column has a value of either 0 or 1. A value of 0 means encryption is DISABLED for the endpoint, and a value of 1 means encryption is either REQUIRED or SUPPORTED.

Make sure you have identified the correct fully qualified names of the partners and witness (if any) in the ALTER DATABASE command.

Troubleshooting Runtime Errors

If your database mirroring setup is done correctly and you get errors afterward, the first thing you want to look at is the sys.database_mirroring catalog view. Check the status of the mirroring state. If it is SUSPENDED, check the SQL error log for more details. You may have added a data file or log file on the principal for which you do not have the exact same path on the mirror, which will cause a Redo error to occur on the mirror, causing the database session to be suspended. You will see an error similar to the following in the mirror server error log:

```
Error: 5123, Severity: 16, State: 1.
CREATE FILE encountered operating system error 3(The system cannot find the path
specified.) while attempting to open or create the physical file
'<your folder>\AdventureWorks2008_1.ndf'.
```

If that is the case, create the folder on the mirror and then resume the mirroring session using the following command:

```
ALTER DATABASE AdventureWorks2008 SET PARTNER RESUME
```

If you have added the file and you do not have that drive on the mirror, you have to delete that file from the principal. If pages are allocated on the file, you need to empty the file before you can delete it. Then resume the mirroring session again.

If you cannot connect to the principal database even though your server is online, it is most likely because safety is set to FULL, and the principal server cannot form a quorum because both the witness and mirror are lost. This can happen, for example, if your system is in high-safety mode with the witness, and the mirror and witness have become disconnected from the principal. You can force the mirror server to recover, using the following command on the mirror:

```
ALTER DATABASE AdventureWorks2008 SET PARTNER FORCE_SERVICE_ALLOW_DATA_LOSS
```

After that, because both the old principal and the witness are not available, the new principal cannot serve the database, so turn the SAFETY to OFF using the following command:

```
ALTER DATABASE AdventureWorks2008 SET PARTNER SAFETY OFF
```

Ensure that there is sufficient disk space on the mirror for both redo (free space on the data drives) and log hardening (free space on the log drive).

Automatic Page Repair

On SQL Server 2008 Enterprise and Developer Editions, data mirroring can automatically correct error numbers 823 and 824, which are caused by data *cyclic redundancy check (CRC)* errors raised while the server is reading a page. When a mirror partner is unable to read a page, it asynchronously requests a copy from its partner; if the page requested is successfully applied, the page is repaired and the error is resolved. During the repair, the actual data is preserved. Note that it does not repair control type pages, such as allocation pages. The page repair operation varies depending on whether the principal or mirror is requesting the page.

Principal Request Page

The principal identifies a page read error, marks the page with an 829 error (restore pending), inserts a row into the suspect_pages table in MSDB with the error status, and requests the page from the mirror. If the mirror is successful in reading the page, it returns the page to the principal who applies it. After the page is repaired, the principal marks the page as restored — that is, event_type = 5 in the suspect_pages table. Then any deferred transactions are resolved.

Mirror Request Page

The mirror identifies a page read error, marks the page with an 829 error (restore pending), and inserts a row into the suspect_pages table in MSDB with the error status. It requests the page from the principal and sets the mirror session in a SUSPENDED state. If the principal is successful in reading the page, it returns the page to the mirror. After the page is applied at the mirror, the mirror resumes the data mirroring session and marks the page as restored in the suspect_pages table — that is, event_type = 5.

A sys.dm_db_mirroring_auto_page_repair catalog view included in SQL Server 2008 displays corrupted pages in the data mirroring environment. This catalog view returns a maximum of 100 rows per database of every automatic page repair attempt; as it reaches this maximum, the next entry replaces the oldest entry. Execute this with the following command:

```
SELECT * FROM sys.dm_db_mirroring_auto_page_repair
```

Most of the columns returned are self-explanatory, but two may require some explanation. The error_type column indicates errors encountered that are to be corrected. The page_status column indicates where the program is in the process of repairing that page.

Preparing the Mirror Server for Failover

When you set up mirroring, your intentions are clear that in the event of failover, the mirror takes on the full load. In order for the mirror to be fully functional as a principal, you have to do some configurations on the mirror server. Please note that database mirroring is a database-to-database failover solution only; the entire SQL Server instance is not mirrored. If you want to implement full SQL Server instance failover, then consider Windows failover clustering. We compare different high-availability technologies in the section "Database Mirroring and Other High-Availability Solutions."

Hardware, Software, and Server Configuration

Your mirror server hardware should be identical (CPU, memory, storage, and network capacity) to that of the principal if you want your mirror server to handle the same load as your principal. You may argue that if your principal is a 16-way, 64-bit server with 32GB of RAM, having identical mirror hardware is a costly solution if your principal is not going down often and such expensive hardware is sitting idle. If your application is not critical, then you may want to have a smaller server just for failover and taking the load for some time, but I would argue that if the application is not that critical, you do not have such extensive hardware on the primary either.

Moreover, with such huge hardware, the process on the server must be very heavy, so if you failover, your mirror should be able to handle that load even if it is for a short time. In addition, you have to consider the business cost versus the hardware cost and then make the decision. You can also use your mirror server for noncritical work so that while it is a mirror, it can be used for some other work. Of course, you have to plan that out properly to make good use of your mirror server. Provided that your database server performance characteristics can be supported within the virtual server maximum performance capacity, data mirroring can be deployed on virtual servers.

Make sure that you have the same operating system version, service packs, and patches on both servers. Obviously, during a rolling upgrade (as discussed in "Database Availability During Planned Downtime"), service packs and patch levels can be temporarily different.

You need to have the same edition of SQL Server on both partners. If you are using a witness, then you don't need the same edition on it. You can use a smaller server for the witness because it doesn't carry any actual load — it is only used to form a quorum. Of course, the availability of the witness server is critical for automatic failover. Refer to the table in the section "Database Mirroring and SQL Server 2008 Editions" for more details on which editions support which database mirroring features.

Make sure you have an identical directory structure for the SQL Server install and database files on both the partners. If you add a database file to a volume/directory and that volume/directory does not exist on the mirror, the mirroring session will be suspended immediately.

On both principal and mirror, make sure that all the SQL Server configurations are identical (e.g., `tempdb` size, trace flags, startup parameters, memory settings, degree of parallelism).

Logins and their permissions are very important. All SQL Server logins on the principal must also be present on the mirror server; otherwise, your application will not be able to connect in the event of failover. You can use SQL Server 2008 Integration Services, with the "Transfer logins" task, to copy logins and passwords from one server to another. (Refer to the section "Managing Changing Roles" in Chapter 19 for more information.) Moreover, you still need to set the database permission for these logins. If you transfer these logins to a different domain, then you have to match the security identifier (SID) — that is, the unique name that Windows uses to identify a specific user name or group.

On the principal, many other objects may exist and be needed for that application. You have to transfer all these objects (e.g., SQL jobs, SQL Server Integration Services packages, linked server definitions, maintenance plans, supported databases, SQL Mail or Database Mail settings, and DTC settings) to the mirror server.

If you are using SQL Server authentication, you have to resolve the logins on the new principal server after failover. You can use the `sp_change_users_login` stored procedure to resolve these logins. Note that `sp_change_users_login` cannot be used with a SQL Server login created from Windows.

Be sure to have a process in place so that when you make any changes to any configuration on the principal server, you repeat or transfer the changes on the mirror server.

Once you set up your mirror, failover the database and let your application run for some time on the new principal, because that is the best way to ensure that all the settings are correct. Try to schedule this task during a slow time of the day, and deliver the proper communication procedures prior to testing failover.

Database Availability During Planned Downtime

There are two ways you can configure the mirroring session as far as transaction safety is concerned: SAFETY FULL and SAFETY OFF. This section describes the steps for both of these options and explains how to use the "rolling upgrade" technique to perform a software and hardware upgrade while keeping the database online for applications.

Safety Full

Assuming that you have configured the mirroring session with SAFETY FULL, if you have to perform software and hardware upgrades, perform the following steps in order:

1. Perform the hardware and software changes on the mirror server first. If you have to restart the SQL Server 2008 or the server itself, you can do so. As soon as the server comes back up again, the mirroring session will be established automatically and the mirror will start synchronizing with the principal. Note that the principal is exposed while the mirror database is down, so if you have a witness configured, make sure that it is available during

this time; otherwise, the principal will be running in isolation and will not be able to serve the database, because it cannot form a quorum.

2. Once the mirror is synchronized with the principal, you can failover using the following command:

```
ALTER DATABASE <database_name> SET PARTNER FAILOVER
```

The application will now connect to the new principal. We will talk about application redirection when the database is mirrored in the section "Client Redirection to the Mirror." Open and in-flight transactions during failover will be rolled back. If that is not tolerable for your application, you can stop the application for the brief failover moment and restart the application after failover completes.

3. Now perform the hardware or software upgrade on your old principal server. When you are done with upgrades and the database becomes available on the old principal, it will assume the mirror role, the database mirroring session will be established automatically, and it will start synchronizing.

4. If you have a witness set up, perform the hardware or software upgrade on that server.

5. At this point, your old principal is acting as a mirror. You can fail back to your old principal now that all your upgrades are done. If you have identical hardware on the new principal, you may leave it as is so that you don't have to stop the application momentarily; but if your hardware is not identical, consider switching back to your original principal.

Safety Off

If you have configured the database mirroring with SAFETY OFF, you can still use the "rolling upgrade" technique by following these steps:

1. Perform the hardware and software changes on the mirror first. See the preceding section for more details.

2. On the principal server, change the SAFETY to FULL using this command:

```
ALTER DATABASE <database_name> SET SAFETY FULL
```

Plan this activity during off-peak hours to reduce the mirror server synchronization time.

3. Once the mirror is synchronized, you can perform the failover to the mirror.

4. Perform the hardware and software upgrade on the old principal. Once the old principal comes back up, it will assume the mirror role and start synchronizing with the new principal.

5. Once synchronized, you can fail back to your original principal.

If you are using mirroring just to make a redundant copy of your database, you may not want to failover for planned downtime, as you may not have properly configured all the other settings on the mirror, as described in the section "Hardware, Software, and Server Configuration." In that case, you have to take the principal down for upgrade, and the database will not be available.

SQL Job Configuration on the Mirror

For identical configuration on both the principal server and the mirror server, you also have to synchronize SQL jobs on your mirror server as mentioned earlier. When the database is the mirror, you do not want these SQL jobs to run. You have some options regarding how to do that:

❑ Disable the jobs and enable them manually when the database becomes the principal. However, as a DBA, you do not want to manually manage these jobs, so this is not a good option.

❑ Have some logic in the SQL job steps that checks for the database mirroring state and runs the next step only if the database mirroring state is principal.

❑ Listen for the database mirroring change event when the database becomes the principal and execute a SQL job that enables all the SQL jobs you want to run. Stop or disable these jobs again when the event is fired, indicating that the database state has changed to mirror. We describe how to listen to these database mirroring state change events in the section "Mirroring Event Listener Setup," later in the chapter.

Database TRUSTWORTHY Bit on the Mirror

If you restore the database, the TRUSTWORTHY bit is set to 0 automatically, so when you set up database mirroring, this bit is set to 0 as soon as you restore your database on your mirror server. If your application requires this bit to be 1, in case of failover, your application will not work because this bit is set to 0 on the mirror, which is now the new principal. To avoid this, when you set up database mirroring, once it is set up correctly, failover to the mirror and set this bit to 1 using the following command:

```
ALTER DATABASE <database_name> SET TRUSTWORTHY ON
```

Then optionally fail back to your original principal.

Client Redirection to the Mirror

In SQL Server 2008, if you connect to a database that is being mirrored with ADO.NET or the SQL Native Client, your application can take advantage of the drivers' ability to automatically redirect connections when a database mirroring failover occurs. You must specify the initial principal server and database in the connection string and optionally the failover partner server. There are many ways to write the connection string, but here is one example, specifying ServerA as the principal, ServerB as the mirror, and AdventureWorks2008 as the database name:

```
"Data Source=ServerA;Failover Partner=ServerB;Initial Catalog=AdventureWorks2008;
Integrated
Security=True;"
```

The failover partner in the connection string is used as an alternate server name if the connection to the initial principal server fails. If the connection to the initial principal server succeeds, the failover partner name is not used, but the driver will store the failover partner name that it retrieves from the principal server in the client-side cache.

Assume a client is successfully connected to the principal, and a database mirroring failover (automatic, manual, or forced) occurs. The next time the application attempts to use the connection, the ADO.NET or

SQL Native Client driver will detect that the connection to the old principal has failed and will automatically retry connecting to the new principal as specified in the failover partner name. If successful, and a new mirror server is specified for the database mirroring session by the new principal, the driver will retrieve the new partner failover server name and place it in its client cache. If the client cannot connect to the alternate server, the driver will try each server alternately until the login timeout period is reached.

The advantage of using the database mirroring client support built into ADO.NET and the SQL Native Client driver is that you do not need to recode the application, or place special codes in the application, to handle a database mirroring failover.

If you do not use the ADO.NET or SQL Native Client automatic redirection, you can use other techniques that enable your application to failover. For example, you could use network load balancing (NLB) to redirect connections from one server to another while remaining transparent to the client application that is using the NLB virtual server name. On failover, reconfigure NLB to divert all client applications using the database to the new principal by tracking the mirroring state change event to; then change the NLB configuration to divert the client applications to the new principal server. Additionally, consider writing your own redirection code and retry logic. Moreover, the Domain Name System (DNS) service provides a name-to-IP resolution that can be used to redirect clients to the new principal server. Provided that the administrator has access to the DNS server either by script or by using the Windows DNS management tool to modify the IP address to redirect client applications during a failover, DNS acts as the cross-reference for the client applications, as they will continue to connect to the same name; after the DNS modification, it redirects the database request to the new principal server.

Mirroring Multiple Databases

You can mirror multiple databases on the same server, as discussed earlier. You can either use the same server for a mirror partner or use a different mirror server for each database. I recommend using the same mirror server for mirroring multiple databases from a principal server. That way, maintenance is reduced, and the system is less complex; otherwise, you have to perform all the steps mentioned in ''Hardware, Software, and Server Configuration'' on each mirror server.

If you want to use the database mirroring feature with database dependencies, especially with high-safety and automatic failover, you have to be careful when you design your application. Consider a scenario in which your application is using two databases, DB1 and DB2, on a server called ServerA. Now you have set up database mirroring for both of these databases to your mirror server, ServerB, with automatic failover. Suppose a failover occurs with only DB1 (perhaps because of a disk failure on the disk where DB1 resides or a sporadic network issue that could cause the mirroring session of one database to time out); and because of the automatic failover, the database fails over to the mirror ServerB. Therefore, ServerB will be the principal for database DB1, and ServerA the principal for database DB2. Where would your application connect? Even though both databases are available, your application may not function correctly. This could also happen if you manually failover one database and not the other.

An application that relies on multiple databases is not a good candidate for a high-safety with automatic failover scenario. You can probably have high-safety mode *without* automatic failover and specify an alert when mirroring state changes so that you can manually failover all the databases or have a SQL job that does that for you.

Additionally, remember that you cannot mirror a system database. Moreover, make sure that you do not mirror too many databases on a single server, or it may affect server and application performance.

Because of resource constraints, on a 32-bit server you do not want to mirror more than 10 databases per SQL Server instance. Use System Monitor counters and the Database Mirroring Monitor to understand how your servers are performing.

Database Mirroring and Other High-Availability Solutions

Database mirroring is another weapon in the arsenal of SQL Server high-availability solutions. SQL Server 2008 provides at least four high-availability solutions. Of course, each solution has some overlaps with the others, and each has some advantages and disadvantages:

- ❑ **Failover clustering:** This is a typical solution for high availability with a two-node Windows failover cluster with one SQL Server instance. Clustering is discussed in more detail in Chapter 20.

- ❑ **Database mirroring:** For this discussion, we consider the high-safety mode with a witness.

- ❑ **Log shipping:** SQL Server 2008 has built-in log shipping. Log shipping is discussed in detail in Chapter 19.

- ❑ **Transactional replication:** For comparison purposes, we'll consider a separate distribution server with a single subscriber server as a standby if the publisher fails.

Let's compare database mirroring with these other technologies.

Database Mirroring and Clustering

Obviously, the most distinct difference between database mirroring and a Window failover cluster solution is the level at which each provides redundancy. Database mirroring provides protection at the database level, as you have seen, whereas a cluster solution provides protection at the SQL Server instance level.

As discussed in the section "Mirroring Multiple Databases," if your application requires multiple database dependencies, clustering is probably a better solution. If you need to provide availability for one database at a time, mirroring is a good solution and has many advantages compared to clustering — for example, ease of configuration.

Unlike clustering, database mirroring does not require proprietary hardware and does not have a single failure point with the shared storage. Database mirroring brings the standby database online faster than any other SQL Server high-availability technology and works well in ADO.NET and SQL Native Access Client for client-side redirect.

Another important difference is that in database mirroring, the principal and mirror servers are separate SQL Server instances with distinct names, whereas a SQL Server instance on a cluster gets one virtual server name and IP address that remains the same no matter which node of the cluster is hosting that SQL Server instance.

You cannot use database mirroring within a cluster, although you can consider using database mirroring as a method for creating a hot standby for a cluster SQL Server 2008 database. If you do, be aware that because a cluster failover is longer than the timeout value on database mirroring, a high-availability mode mirroring session will react to a cluster failover as a failure of the principal server. It would then put the cluster node into a mirroring state. You can increase the database mirroring timeout value by using following command:

```
ALTER DATABASE <database_name> SET PARTNER TIMEOUT <integer_value_in_seconds>
```

Database Mirroring and Transactional Replication

The common process between database mirroring and transactional replication is reading the transaction log on the originating server. Although the synchronization mechanism is different, database mirroring directly initiates I/O to the transaction log file to transfer the log records.

Transactional replication can be used with more than one subscriber, whereas database mirroring is a one-database-to-one-database solution. You can read nearly real-time data on the subscriber database, while you cannot read data on the mirrored database unless you create a database snapshot, which is a static, point-in-time snapshot of the database.

Database Mirroring and Log Shipping

Database mirroring and log shipping both rely on moving the transaction log and restoring it. In database mirroring, the mirror database is constantly in a recovering state, which is why you cannot query the mirrored database. In log shipping, the database is in standby mode, so you can query the database if the log is not being restored at the same time. In addition, log shipping supports the bulk-logged recovery model, while mirroring supports only the full recovery model.

If your application relies on multiple databases for its operation, you may want to consider log shipping for failover. Sometimes it is a little bit tedious to set up log shipping going the other way once a failover has occurred, whereas mirroring is easy in that aspect.

You can use log shipping and mirroring together. You can use log shipping to ship the log to a remote site for disaster recovery and have a database-mirroring, high-availability configuration locally.

In the high-performance mode, there is a potential for data loss if the principal fails and the mirror is recovered using a forced failover recovery. If you are log shipping the old principal, and the transaction log file of the old principal is undamaged, you can make a "tail of the log" backup from the principal to get the last set of log records from the transaction log. If the standby log-shipping database has had every other transaction log backup applied to it, you can then apply the "tail of the log" backup to the standby server and not lose any of the old principal's data. You can then compare the data in the log-shipping standby server with the remote database and potentially copy missing data to the remote server.

Mirroring Event Listener Setup

In this section, we provide steps you can use to take some action when the database mirroring session changes state (for example, from disconnected to synchronizing or from synchronized to suspended). You can perform the following steps to configure an alert for mirroring state change events and take some action on these events.

Right-click the Alert folder under SQL Server Agent in SQL Server 2008 Management Studio and select New Alert. The dialog shown in Figure 17-11 will appear.

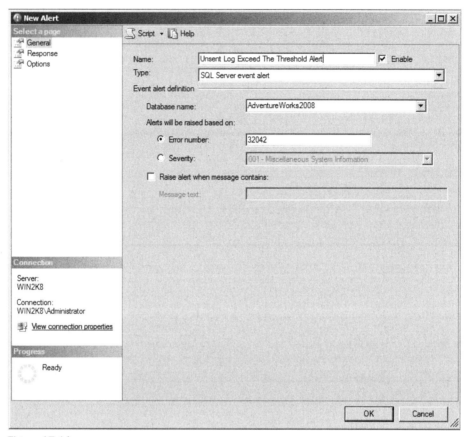

Figure 17-11

Type the name of the event and select the event type "WMI event alert" from the drop-down menu. The namespace is automatically filled out for you. In the query field, type the following query:

```
SELECT * FROM DATABASE_MIRRORING_STATE_CHANGE
```

In this example, the alert is fired for all database mirroring state change events for all the databases mirrored on this server. If you want to be alerted about a specific database mirroring state change event for a specific database, you can add a WHERE clause to the SELECT statement:

```
SELECT * FROM DATABASE_MIRRORING_STATE_CHANGE WHERE State = 8 AND
DatabaseName = 'AdventureWorks2008'
```

This statement will only listen for the "automatic failover" state change (state = 8) for the AdventureWorks2008 database. The following table lists all the database mirroring state change events so that you can use it to build the WHERE clause to listen to specific events.

State	Name	Description
0	Null Notification	This state occurs briefly when a mirroring session is started.
1	Synchronized Principal with Witness	This state occurs on the principal when the principal and mirror are connected and synchronized and the principal and witness are connected. For a mirroring configuration with a witness, this is the normal operating state.
2	Synchronized Principal without Witness	This state occurs on the principal when the principal and mirror are connected and synchronized but the principal does not have a connection to the witness. For a mirroring configuration without a witness, this is the normal operating state.
3	Synchronized Mirror with Witness	This state occurs on the mirror when the principal and mirror are connected and synchronized and the mirror and witness are connected. For a mirroring configuration with a witness, this is the normal operating state.
4	Synchronized Mirror without Witness	This state occurs on the mirror when the principal and mirror are connected and synchronized but the mirror does not have a connection to the witness. For a mirroring configuration without a witness, this is the normal operating state.
5	Connection with Principal Lost	This state occurs on the mirror server instance when it cannot connect to the principal.
6	Connection with Mirror Lost	This state occurs on the principal server instance when it cannot connect to the mirror.
7	Manual Failover	This state occurs on the principal server instance when the user fails over manually from the principal, or on the mirror server instance when a forced service is executed at the mirror.
8	Automatic Failover	This state occurs on the mirror server instance when the operating mode is high safety with automatic failover (synchronous) and the mirror and witness server instances cannot connect to the principal server instance.
9	Mirroring Suspended	This state occurs on either partner instance when the user suspends (pauses) the mirroring session, or when the mirror server instance encounters an error. It also occurs on the mirror server instance following a forced service command. When the mirror comes online as the principal, mirroring is automatically suspended.
10	No Quorum	If a witness is configured, this state occurs on the principal or mirror server instance when it cannot connect to its partner or to the witness server instance.
11	Synchronizing Mirror	This state occurs on the mirror server instance when there is a backlog of unsent log. The status of the session is Synchronizing.
12	Principal Running Exposed	This state occurs on the principal server instance when the operating mode is high safety (synchronous) and the principal cannot connect to the mirror server instance.
13	Synchronizing Principal	This state occurs on the principal server instance when there is a backlog of unsent log. The status of the session is Synchronizing.

Now select the Response page, shown in Figure 17-12. This dialog enables you to specify what you want SQL Server 2008 to do if the event occurs. In Figure 17-12, you want to execute the SQL job TestEventChange when a database mirroring state change event occurs to notify you both by e-mail and page. Moreover, you can go to the Options page, where you can specify an additional message. Click OK. You are now all set to receive the alert when the database mirroring process changes its state.

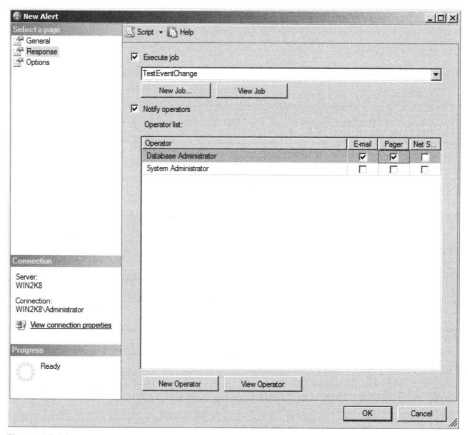

Figure 17-12

In the TestEventChange SQL job, you can actually add the following script to store the history of database mirroring state change events in a table. You should create this table first in some other database, such as msdb:

```
CREATE TABLE dbo.MirroringStateChanges
(
 EventTime varchar(max) NULL
,EventDescription varchar(max) NULL
,NewState int NULL
,DatabaseName varchar(max) NULL
)
```

Add the following script as a job step to insert into this table:

```
INSERT INTO dbo.MirroringStateChanges
(
 [EventTime]
,[EventDescription]
,[NewState]
,[DatabaseName]
)
VALUES
(
 $(ESCAPE_NONE(WMI(StartTime)))
,$(ESCAPE_NONE(WMI(TextData)))
,$(ESCAPE_NONE(WMI(State)))
,$(ESCAPE_NONE(WMI(DatabaseName)))
 )
```

You can change the database mirroring state using the ALTER DATABASE command to test this alert. Additionally, the database mirroring state change is logged to Event Viewer under the Application events as something like the following:

```
The mirrored database "AdventureWorks2008" is changing roles from "MIRROR" to
"PRINCIPAL" due to Failover from partner
```

Database Snapshots

As you have probably figured out by now, the mirror database is in NORECOVERY mode, so you cannot query the mirror database. If you want to read data from the mirror database to be used for reporting, SQL Server 2008 (Enterprise Edition and Developer Edition) has a feature called Database Snapshots, first introduced in SQL Server 2005. A database snapshot is a point-in-time, read-only, static view of a database (the source database). This feature comes in handy for reading the mirror database. Multiple database snapshots can exist but they always reside on the same SQL Server instance as the database. Each database snapshot is transactionally consistent with the source database at the point in time of the snapshot's creation. A snapshot persists until it is explicitly dropped by the database owner.

Using this feature, you can create a snapshot on the mirror database. Then, you can read the database snapshot as you would read any other database. The database snapshot operates at a data-page level. Before a page of the source database is modified for the first time after the database snapshot, the original page is copied from the source database to the snapshot file. This process is called a *copy-on-write* operation. The snapshot stores the original page, preserving the data records as they existed when the snapshot was created. Subsequent updates to records in a modified page on the source database do not affect the data contents of the snapshot. In this way, the snapshot preserves the original pages for all data records that have ever been modified since the snapshot was taken. Even if you modify the source data, the snapshot will still have the same data from the time when it was created. (See the topic "Database Mirroring and Database Snapshots" in SQL Server 2008 Books Online for more information.)

The following example shows how to create a snapshot on the AdventureWorks2008 database:

```
CREATE DATABASE AdventureWorks2008_Snapshot ON
(NAME = AdventureWorks2008, FILENAME = '<your folder>\ADW_Mirroring_
```

```
snapshot_Data1.SS')
AS SNAPSHOT OF AdventureWorks2008
```

Because new data changes will be continuous on the mirrored database, if you want to read more recent data not in the database snapshot after you have created it, you need to drop the database snapshot and recreate it. You can drop the snapshot in the same manner as you would drop a database:

```
DROP DATABASE AdventureWorks2008_Snapshot
```

Generating a database snapshot has some performance impact on the mirror server, so please evaluate the impact if you want to create many snapshots on multiple databases on a server. Most important, from a database mirroring perspective, having too many snapshots on a mirror database can slow down the redo and cause the database to fall more and more behind the principal, potentially resulting in huge failover times.

In addition, prepare an area of disk space as big as the size of the source database, because as data changes on the source database, the snapshot will start copying the original pages to the snapshot file, and it will start growing. Additionally, you may want to evaluate SQL Server replication as an alternative reporting solution.

Summary

Database mirroring provides a database redundancy solution using the log-transfer mechanism. The transaction log records are sent to the mirror transaction log as soon as the log buffer is written to the disk on the principal. Mirroring can be configured in either high-performance mode or high-safety mode. In high-safety mode, if the principal fails, the mirror server automatically becomes a new principal and recovers its database. Understanding application behavior in terms of log-generation rate, number of concurrent connections, and size of transactions is important in achieving the best performance. Network bandwidth plays a very important role in a database mirroring environment. When used with a high-bandwidth and low-latency network, database mirroring can provide a reliable, high-availability solution against planned and unplanned downtime. In Chapter 18, you'll explore the details of the backup and recovery options that SQL Server 2008 provides.

18

Backup and Recovery

Data is a critical asset for an organization to maintain information about its customers, inventory, purchases, financials, and products. Over the course of many years, organizations amass information to improve the daily customer experience, as well as to leverage this information to support strategic decisions. Downtime is unacceptable and can be costly for the organization; for example, without their databases, a stock brokerage house cannot take stock orders and an airline cannot sell tickets. Every hour the database is down can add up to millions of dollars of business opportunities lost. To keep their business activities going, organizations deploy high-availability solutions, such as failover clustering, data mirroring, and log shipping, so that when a database server fails, they can continue to run their business on a standby database server. All of these topics are covered in other chapters in this book.

In addition, a *storage area network (SAN)* system is protected by fault-tolerant disk arrays; and to protect it from a local disaster, businesses normally have a *disaster recovery plan* to handle scenarios, such as when the site where the organization does its business is down and it needs to quickly redeploy the data center to continue to serve customers.

While a high-availability solution tries to keep the business data online, a database backup plan is crucial to protect the business data asset. If there is a data-error problem and the database is unrecoverable, the DBA can use the database backup to recover the database to a consistent state. Moreover, the better database backup strategy will reduce the amount of data loss in case of certain kinds of errors encountered during the course of the daily database activities. In this chapter, we first present an overview of backup and restore. Then we walk you through planning and developing a backup plan, managing backups, and performing restores. We also discuss data archiving and disaster recovery planning.

Types of Failure

A variety of failures can bring down your database. Anything from a user error to a natural disaster could take your database offline. Your backup and recovery plan needs to account for the possibility of these failures and more.

Hardware Failure

Hardware is more reliable than it has been in the past. However, components can still fail, including the CPU, memory, bus, network card, disk drives, and controllers. A database system on a high-availability solution can mitigate a hardware failure such that if one database server fails, SQL Server will failover to the standby database server that includes fault-tolerant disk arrays and perhaps redundant I/O controllers. All of this helps keep the database online. However, high-availability solutions cannot protect against a faulty controller or a disk that causes I/O failures and corrupts the data.

> *Use SQLIOSim to help identify the optimal disk configuration or troubleshoot I/O faults. SQLIOSim replaces SQLIOStress in prior releases. You can get more information or download SQLIOSism from* http://support.microsoft.com/default.aspx?scid=kb;en-us;231619.

User Error

A common user error is not including a restrictive WHERE clause during an update or delete operation and modifying more rows than expected or intended. As a preventive measure, users should start data modifications inside a BEGIN TRANSACTION, and then they can verify that the correct number of rows were updated before executing a COMMIT TRANSACTION. If the data modification was not performed inside a transaction, the data will be permanently changed, and the user would have no capability to undo the changes. Then, to recover the data, a DBA needs to restore from backup.

> *While some third-party tools have been able to read the transaction log and restore transactions and groups of transactions, currently I do not believe any of them can accurately read the SQL 2008 logs. Perhaps by the time you read this, some of these tools will be updated. Because these tools can read and report everything inside the transaction log, they can also be used for auditing purposes. Lumigent (*www.lumigent.com*) makes Log Expolorer, and ApexSQL(*www.apexsql.com*) makes a tool called ApexSql Log.*

Application Failure

The user application may contain a bug that causes unwanted data modifications. To prevent this possibility, the application should go through a strict QA process to uncover any such bugs. However, there is no guarantee that an undetected bug may not cause unwanted data modifications in the future. Once the bug is detected and corrected, the DBA may need to recover the database from backup or possibly using a log explorer utility. The process is to identify the time that the problem occurred and to recover to that point in time.

Software Failure

The operating system can fail, as can the relational database system. A software driver may be faulty and causing data corruption; for example, the I/O hardware controller may be functioning correctly, but the software driver may not be. One preventive measure is to keep the system current with service packs and patches, including security patches. The DBA may choose any of the following patch-management solutions: automatic updates from Microsoft Update, Windows Server Update Services, SMS, or a partner solution to keep the servers updated. Unfortunately, some of these updates may require a reboot either to SQL Server or to the Windows OS that causes some planned downtime, but planned downtime can be mitigated by a high-availability solution to fail over to the standby database server. Choose a maintenance time frame when there is lowest user activity; identify the patches that require a reboot ahead of time and apply them at one time whenever possible to enable only a single reboot. Record each software driver version and check the vendor Web site for the most current updates. Additionally, the driver must be approved for the computer hardware and the Windows version. Having a supported and updated driver version can make a significant performance difference to the hardware device.

> *Test your patches in advance, so you know they work. Then you can apply them all at once. You will know from your testing if a reboot is required. This should occur during a "planned" maintenance period. If you are using clusters, you may failover, apply patches, and reboot one server while the other is still providing access. That way, users won't see any interruption in service.*

Too Much Privilege

Sometimes applications are using SQL Server logins that have more privilege than necessary. That is, instead of restricting security to just what the application needs, it is faster and easier to just grant DBO or sysadmin security. As a result, the application with this privilege may delete data from the wrong table because of either a bug or a user accidentally using a free-form query window. To reduce this risk, give application users only the database permissions required to do their work, and restrict sysadmin and DBO permissions only to users who need it and have the experience to know how to use it.

> *DBA, this also applies to you. It is fairly common for DBAs to type in a quick update to fix some problem. Just as you press the key to execute the query, you realize that you have made a huge mistake but are powerless to stop the execution. That sinking feeling that you have really messed things up happens quickly. To avoid this, you should have a regular-privilege account as well as your high-privilege account. Use your regular account for routine activity, switching to your high-privilege account only when necessary. This also raises your awareness, enabling you to avoid mistakes. I often place a yellow sticky note on my monitor when I am using the privileged account on the production servers to remind me to be careful.*

Local Disasters

An unexpected disaster can devastate an area, resulting in an inoperable or completely destroyed data center. In such cases, you need to relocate the data center, and that is where disaster planning comes into play: to quickly bring up the new data center and reopen for business. Depending on the disaster, data loss may occur because the location is inaccessible, and you may be unable to extract the last few data records. To reduce the exposure from a local disaster, a company can set up a disaster recovery site by means of data mirroring, a geographically dispersed failover cluster, log shipping, or SAN replication.

> *Although there are other disk storage technologies, such as NAS and DAS, Microsoft recommends the use of SAN.*

Making Plans

You (or your company) should have a plan for high-availability, backup/recovery, and disaster recovery. There may be a plan for each, or they may all be included in a single document. In a small company, by default this task may fall directly on your shoulders. For larger companies, you may be part of a team that plans for these events. In all cases, a risk/benefit analysis must be done. You must consider the likelihood of the event occurring, the cost of the downtime and other potential costs associated with the event, and the cost of the solution. Your first job will be the research and documentation regarding the risks, costs, and benefits. Management will then decide which events to plan for and make the risk decision. My point here is that the DBA is *not* the risk decision-maker — that's management's job. However, it *is* your job to ensure that management understands the issues and that a decision is made. It is then your job to implement whatever plan is necessary and to test the plan on a regular basis.

In this section you will learn the basics of a backup/recovery plan and a disaster recovery plan. Of course, entire books cover each of these subjects, so consider this a basic introduction. High-availability is not covered.

Backup/Recovery Plan

You or your team has primary responsibility for the backup/recovery plan, including the following:

- ❑ Analyze business requirements.
- ❑ Categorize databases by recovery criteria.
- ❑ Document the plan.
- ❑ Validate, implement, and test the plan.
- ❑ Establish a failed backup notification policy.
- ❑ Maintain the plan.

Analyze Business Requirements

First you must gather some requirements for your plan. You need to have answers to the following questions:

- ❑ **Who are the stakeholders/owners for each application or database?** You need to determine the people from whom you should ask questions. You must also identify the decision-makers who can approve your final plan.

- ❑ **What is the purpose for this database?** Knowing a database's purpose, such as whether it is for a data mart, a data warehouse, or the general ledger accounting database, gives you great insight into what might be necessary for your plan.

- ❑ **What is the acceptable downtime for the application/database in the case of an error, such as a disk drive error?** You ask this question because it takes time to restore the database when a problem has occurred. Knowing the answer helps you design a backup/restore plan that works within the downtime constraints.

  Often the first answer to this question is, "There is no acceptable downtime." People may not initially understand the costs associated with their answers. However, when you associate costs with the options, you begin to get closer to the real need. Keep in mind that this is an iterative process as you communicate with management and business users.

  You may also need to get several answers, depending on business cycles. For instance, while finance is closing the monthly books, the cost of any downtime is extremely high. During the rest of the month, the cost of downtime is much less. You may choose to implement a different plan during month-end close than you do during the rest of the month. This might include more frequent log backups, or you may choose to implement a single plan that meets the strictest requirements. In either case, document everything.

It may be that this question should be broken down into two questions: What is the cost of downtime? How much cost is reasonable for the business to absorb?

❑   **What data changes and how often?** You ask this question to determine what type of backups are necessary. Maybe data changes during nightly batch only, and is read during the rest of the day. Maybe some tables change very frequently, but others are historical. Maybe there are numerous updates but they occur on a very small number of rows, while the rest of the database is read-only.

If the database is already in production, looking at the transaction log growth will provide some useful information also.

❑   **How much data loss is acceptable?** This is another tricky question, one that might take a long time to answer. What is the value of the data? What harm would befall the company if this data or part of it became lost? When thinking about this subject, you must also consider any regulatory requirements, as well. Some data must be kept available for a certain period of time. Some businesses may have a very low tolerance for data loss, while others may tolerate a great deal of data loss. It depends not only on the value of the data, but also how much risk the business is willing to accept. You must also consider non-SQL Server options, as well. For example, maybe the business cannot accept any loss of customer orders, but customer orders are entered manually and a paper copy is kept. If yesterday's orders were lost, someone could re-enter the data. This might be a preferable solution — or not. The point is to consider all your business options, not just SQL Server backup/restore.

The answer to this question may change over time. As business processes change or as the business grows, the business requirements change. Therefore, your backup/restore plan may need to change. Review the requirements with the business on a regular basis that you deem reasonable. Document each review.

❑   **What is the size and growth of the database?** If this database has not been implemented, you are not likely to get great information, but get the best you can. For all implemented databases, your normal monitoring procedures will provide this information. You should also work in concert with any project teams who are developing new projects around this database, which may change the answers to this and any of the other questions.

❑   **What is the maintenance window for this database?** Certain maintenance tasks that must be done on the database affect the online response. Items such as Database Console Commands (DBCCs), index maintenance, and, potentially, backups are among these items. Your plan must ensure that your work stays within the maintenance window.

❑   **What are the budget constraints for this database?** Often, there is no specific answer to this question. Instead, evaluating the the risks and the costs will be a negotiation process with the business. However, if there is a specific budget, you certainly need to know what it is.

❑   **What is the notification plan for this database?** When errors occur for which you must restore, who should be notified? How will they be notified? In addition, how will you know when a database error occurs?

Categorize Databases by Recovery Criteria

If you have many databases, you can do yourself a favor by categorizing the databases into groups. Then you can have a plan for each group. You might categorize by the following criteria:

- ❏ **Criticality:** Is this database mission-critical?
- ❏ **Size:** Large databases need more time for backup/restore than small databases. However, you can mitigate the time with filegroup backups or other interim measures. Filegroup backups are covered later in this chapter.
- ❏ **Volatility:** Databases with a larger volume of data change need a different plan than inactive databases.

Name the groups something useful, like the following:

- ❏ Mission-Critical with High Activity
- ❏ Mission-Critical with Low Activity
- ❏ Non-Critical

For each category, choose the following:

- ❏ **Recovery model:**
  - ❏ Minimize data loss.
  - ❏ Maximize performance of bulk load operations.
  - ❏ Minimize maintenance costs.
- ❏ **Backup plan:** All groups need a periodic full database backup. Depending on the category and recovery model, you choose between differential backups, file/filegroup backups, and log backups. You also choose whether or not to use compression and which backup media to use.
- ❏ **Backup frequency:** How often will each of the backups be executed?
- ❏ **Backup security policy:** For tape media, what is the rotation policy? How will you implement offsite storage? Will you use passwords and encryption on your backups?

> **Password protection on backups is weak and will be removed in the next edition of SQL Server. Do not use password-protected backups.**

Document the Disaster Recovery Plan

You will have already created at least one document and probably two others. The first is the requirements document from your business interviews. The second is the document that describes the database categorization. In addition, you need a document that includes the following information:

- ❏ Contact list
- ❏ Decision tree
- ❏ Recovery success criteria

- ❏ Location of keys, backups, software, hardware
- ❏ Infrastructure documentation

You should have a *contact list* of management people who can declare and activate the emergency call-out. All necessary contact information should be available. The procedures for responding should be documented (such as who calls whom).

You should also have a contact list for everything else. This list should include vendors, technicians, off-site storage people, service people, parts suppliers, transportation companies, and so on — everyone! The list should also include backups when primaries cannot be contacted.

Departments should have fallback operational procedures, although this might not be in your documents. It is more likely this would be in departmental documentation. However, both plans should sync and make sense when put together.

The *decision tree* specifies what you need to do based on the circumstances. You may have a separate decision tree for disaster recovery than the one you use for normal recovery. When a disaster strikes and mission-critical processes are down, things can get very stressful. The decision tree prompts you, so you mostly just follow the plan, instead of making on-the-fly mistakes. The decision tree must be logical, clear, and easy to understand and follow, as you will be using it under duress.

The decision tree should classify database loss scenarios, such as natural disasters — e.g., hurricane, earthquake, and so on — that can affect a wide area. You may not be able to rely on locally held backups, software, or hardware. The tree will cover single-location loss — power loss, fire, explosion; you may be able to recover to a site close to the affected location.

The specific decision tree for your purposes should include normal recovery scenarios, such as single server/data corruption or single database loss, disk drive, controller, memory failure, user error, and application failure. You should work to recover the missing data quickly, while not affecting other systems.

Another item you might include in your decision tree is loss of performance or service. In these cases, the database is not damaged but inaccessible or slow. You should be able to debug and correct this quickly.

You may also include security failures, whereby the database health is okay, but security is compromised due to malicious software, individual access, virus attack, and so on. You should be able to discover security breaches and protect data.

The *recovery success criteria* can be layered and may include service level agreements (SLAs). Perhaps the first level of success means that a certain application is online within x amount of time. A second level or completion level might be that all processes that use the database are available. Be sure you understand and document this criteria; you are likely to be measured by it.

Your documentation should include everything you need to get the job done. The location of keys or key-holders and the ability to contact and arrange for offsite storage people to deliver backups is important. Hardware, or access and prompt response of hardware people, as well as software support and/or availability of the software disks is also necessary. You should also have easy access to the levels of software, service packs, and driver levels for your server.

Any other infrastructure documentation you might need should also be included, such as naming conventions, DNS, or network information — anything you need to get the job done.

The decision tree should prioritize recovery steps. Thinking about these steps will enable you to make a plan that minimizes downtime and maximizes parallel work between all the players who need to be involved.

The decision tree should identify the most critical databases so recovery can be completed in the best order for the business. Don't forget about dependencies between databases also.

Critical processes should be identified in the decision tree: SSIS, SSAS, SQL Agent, ETL processes, and so on. What should be done for each of these processes? For instance, you might need to stop a process scheduler until the restore is complete.

List recovery steps in the correct order based on business needs. Don't assume you will be able to think calmly and make the best decisions on-the-fly when bad things are happening. Make all of the basic decisions in advance, and when the bad thing happens, engage your brain, but follow the documented process.

Validating, Implementing, and Testing the Plan

This is often not nearly as difficult as getting the proper information from the business, so don't worry. If you can get the true needs of the business, then you can usually implement your backup/restore plan simply. Of course, no plan is good if it doesn't work, and you won't know whether it works until you test it.

The people who need to implement this plan should practice it. This includes setting up secondary servers, completing the restores, and making the applications/data available. You should simulate failures as well, and practice the responses to them. Simulated failures might be loss of the most recent full backup or a transaction log. You should consider that the restore sight might be in a different time zone, or a database might be much, much larger than it used to be. What happens if key people do not respond or your contact list is inaccurate? What if access cards no longer work or keys are not available?

Failed Backup Notification Policy

Because the success of your plan depends on successful backups, you need a plan to receive notification when backups fail.

You also need to ensure that backups are usable. Validate the backups, as shown later. You should also use DBCC commands to ensure that you are backing up a healthy database. Additionally, the database backups should occur after other normal maintenance tasks, such as database shrinking and index maintenance. This is because when you have to restore from a database backup, you are restoring a database ready to go and not a database in need of additional maintenance.

Maintaining the Plan

There are four steps to successfully maintaining the plan:

❑   **Communicate the plan:** For effective communication, the documentation should be publicly available within your company; and IT, the business users, and management should be informed of its content and location.

❑   **Establish a policy to periodically rehearse the plan:** Your policy should call for periodic rehearsal of the plan. Some companies carry out a drill every other year; others do this annually.

You might have a complete companywide call out once a year and an IT test more frequently. In any case, you must test the plan on a schedule. Infrastructure changes and software and hardware updates, can all conspire to make your plan unusable. You may have worked very hard to do all of the steps up to this point, and you may have done them all perfectly, but when disaster strikes, you will be measured solely by your ability to actually recover, not by how fine a plan you may have. Rehearsal is the only way to guarantee success.

❏   **Establish a policy to periodically validate the plan:** The policy to periodically validate the plan centers around the changing business environment. The business may have changed processes, or the ability or willingness to absorb risk, or some other factor that may have invalidated your plan. You should revalidate the information you gathered from the business and reassess your plan on a scheduled basis. Additionally, be aware of new projects and how they may affect your planning.

❏   **Revise the plan as needed:** The last requirement is to keep the plan up-to-date. Revisit the plan, and revise whenever needed. It is fairly common to come up with a plan and then let it grow stale on the shelf. This often renders the plan useless or, even worse, dangerous to use.

Overview of Backup and Restore

Before you can effectively formulate a backup and restore plan, you need to know how backup and recovery works on a mechanical level. SQL Server 2008 has several different backup and recovery processes that you can use, depending on the needs of your organization. This section examines how backup and recovery work and helps you choose the best plan for your needs.

How Backup Works

Database backup is a procedure that safeguards your organization's investment to reduce the amount of data loss. A database backup is the process of making a point-in-time copy of the data and transaction log into an image on either disks or tapes. SQL Server 2008 implements versatile backup processes that can be used separately or together to produce the optimal backup strategy required by an organization. Moreover, SQL Server 2008 can perform the database backup while it is online and available to users. Additionally, it supports up to 64 concurrent backup devices. The following types of backup are available:

❏   **Full backup:** This is a copy of all data in the database, including the transaction log. Using this backup type, you can restore the database to the point in time when the backup was taken. It is the most basic of the backups and is often required prior to any of the other backup types. When restoring from a full database backup, all of the database files are restored without any other dependencies, the database is available, and it is transactionally consistent.

❏   **Partial backup:** This is a way to back up only those parts of the database that are changing. This reduces the size of the backup and the time it takes to backup and restore. It is a copy of the primary filegroup and read/write filegroups. To take advantage of this type of backup, you need to group together the tables that change into a set of filegroups and the tables that are static or history in a different set of filegroups. The filegroups containing historical data will be marked read/write or read-only. A partial backup normally includes the primary filegroup and read-write filegroups, but read-only filegroups can optionally be included. A partial backup can speed up the backup process for databases with large read-only areas. For example, a large database may have archival data that does not change, so there is no need to back it up every time, which reduces the amount of data to back up.

❑ **File/filegroup backup:** This is a copy of files or filegroups of a database. This method is typically used for very large databases for which it is not feasible to do a full database backup. A transaction-log backup is needed with this backup type if the backup includes read/write files or filegroups. The challenge is maintaining the files, filegroups, and transaction-log backups, because larger databases have many files and filegroups. It also requires more steps to restore the database.

> *A table and all of its indexes must be backed up in the same backup. SQL Server checks for this and sends an error when this rule is violated. In order to take advantage of file/filegroup backups, you may need to plan the location of your indexes with the backup plan in mind.*

❑ **Differential backup:** This is a copy of all the data that has changed since the last full backup. The SQL Server 2008 backup process identifies each changed extent and backs it up. Differentials are cumulative: If you do an entire backup on Sunday night, the differential taken on Monday night includes all of the changes since Sunday night. If you take another differential on Tuesday night, it will include all of the changes since Sunday night. When restoring, you would restore the last full database backup, then the more recent differential backup. Then you would restore any transaction-log backups since the last differential. This can mean quicker recovery. Whether differentials are good for you depends on what percentage of rows change between full database backups. As the percentage of rows changed approaches the number of rows in the database, the differential backup gets closer to the size of an entire database backup. When this occurs, it is often better to get another full database backup and start a new differential.

Another benefit of using differentials is realized when a group of rows is changed repeatedly. Remember that a transaction log backup includes each change that is made. The differential backup includes only the last change for a row. Imagine a database that keeps track of 100 stock values. The stock value is updated every minute. Each row is updated 1,440 times per day. Consider a full database backup on Sunday night and transaction-log backups during the week. At the end of the day Friday, restoring from all of the transaction logs would mean that you have to replay each change to each row. In this case, each row would be updated 7,200 times (1,440 times/day times 5 days). When you include 100 stocks, the restore would have to replay 720,000 transactions. If you had done a differential backup at the end of each day, you would only have to replace the 100 rows. The differential keeps the most recent version only; and in some situations, it can be a great solution.

❑ **Partial differential backup:** This works the same as a differential backup but is matched to data from a partial backup. It is a copy of all extents modified since the last partial backup. To restore requires the partial backup.

❑ **File differential backup:** This is a copy of the file or filegroup of all extents modified since the last file or filegroup backup. A transaction-log backup is required after this backup for read/write files or filegroups. Moreover, after the restore, you need to restore the transaction log as well. Using the file backup and file differential backup methods increases the complexity of the restore procedures. Furthermore, it may take longer to restore the complete database.

❑ **Copy-only backup:** This can be made for the database or transaction log. The copy-only backup does not interfere with the normal backup restore procedures. A normal full database backup resets the differential backups made afterward, whereas a copy-only backup does not affect the next differential backup; it will still contain the changes since the last full backup. A copy-only backup of the transaction log does not truncate the log or affect the next normal transaction log backup. Copy-only backups are useful when you wish to make a copy of the database for testing or development purposes without affecting the restore process. Copy-only backups are not supported in SSMS and must be done via T-SQL.

The transaction log in SQL Server 2008 is a main component for a transactional relational database system that maintains the ACID properties for transactions: atomicity, consistency, isolation, and durability. SQL Server 2008 and earlier versions implement the write ahead logging (WAL) protocol, which means that the transaction-log records are written to a stable media prior to the data being written to disk and before SQL Server 2008 sends an acknowledgment that the data has been permanently committed. A stable media is usually a physical disk drive, but it can be any device which guarantees that on restart the data will not be lost. On a storage area network (SAN), which may have a built-in cache, instead of writing the transaction log directly to physical disk drives, in a power failure, the SAN must certify that it implements a battery backup to provide ample time to write all cached I/O to physical disk drives before it powers down. Additionally, SAN vendors often mirror their built-in cache for redundancy. The transactional relational database system expects the data to be available on restart; if it is not, it will identify the database as corrupted because the data consistency of the database cannot be determined.

In addition, when a data modification occurs, SQL Server 2008 generates a new log sequence number (LSN) used on restart to identify the consistency of the data while performing database recovery. Additionally, the LSN is used when restoring the transaction log; SQL Server 2008 uses it to determine the sequences of each transaction log restored. If, for example, a transaction-log backup is not available, that is known as a *broken log chain*, and it will prevent a transaction-log recovery past that point. Backing up the transaction log to point-in-time recovery is a critical part of a backup strategy. A DBA can perform three types of transaction-log backup:

❑ **Pure transaction-log backup:** This is when there have not been any bulk-logged operations performed on the database. That is, every data modification performed is represented in the transaction log. The database recovery model can be in Full or Bulk-Logged mode, provided that no bulk-logged operation has been performed. This is the most common transaction-log backup type, as it best protects the data and provides the capability to recover to a point in time.

❑ **Bulk transaction-log backup:** This is when bulk-logged operations have been performed in the database, so point-in-time recovery is not allowed. To improve performance on bulk operations — that is, to reduce transaction logging — the database can be set in the bulk-logged recovery model whereby only the allocation pages are logged, not the actual data modifications in the transaction log. During a transaction-log backup, SQL Server extracts and includes the bulk-logged data inside the transaction-log backup to allow recoverability.

> *There is no syntax difference between the pure transaction log backup and the bulk transaction log backup. SQL Server works automatically to back up whatever is available and necessary. We include this information to help you understand the difference between the recovery models.*

❑ **Tail transaction-log backup:** This is a transaction-log backup that you make after the database has been damaged. Imagine you take a full database backup every night and do transaction-log backups on the hour. Your data files are corrupted at 1:30 P.M. Your last log backup occurred at 1:00 P.M., so you can recover until that time. What about the transactions that occurred between 1:00 P.M. and 1:30 P.M.? The transaction log disk is still good, but you cannot do a normal transaction log backup now because the database is not accessible. The tail transaction-log backup enables you to do a final transaction log backup, even when the database is unavailable to capture the transactions between 1:00 P.M. and 1:30 P.M. That way, you are able to restore up to 1:30 P.M. Whew — what a save! The biggest risk here is forgetting to do the backup. When you have confirmed that you must go through a restore, do this backup first.

> *This cannot be performed if the database is in the bulk-logged recovery model and bulk operations have been performed, because the transaction-log backup would need to retrieve the data modifications for the bulk operations from the data files, which are not accessible.*

Another available backup option is to detach the database or shut down SQL Server and use the OS to copy the database files to a backup device. To back up the database files, you would detach the database like this:

```
EXEC MASTER.dbo.sp_detach_db @dbname = N'AdventureWorks2008',
@keepfulltextindexfile=N'TRUE'
```

To restore, you would attach the database files like this:

```
EXEC MASTER.dbo.sp_attach_db @dbname = N'AdventureWorks2008',   @filename1 =
N'C:\Program
Files\Microsoft  SQL  Server\MSSQL10.MSSQLSERVER  \MSSQL\Data\AdventureWorks2008_Data
.mdf',   @filename2 =
N'C:\Program
Files\Microsoft SQL Server\MSSQL10.MSSQLSERVER
\MSSQL\Data\AdventureWorks2008_log.ldf' ;
```

The drive letter "C" as well as the rest of the file location should be changed to reflect the directory where your data files are stored. The example uses the default location for data files.

If you attach an encrypted database, the database owner must open the master key of the database by using the following command:

```
OPEN MASTER KEY DECRYPTION BY PASSWORD = '<password>'
```
Microsoft recommends you enable automatic decryption of the master key by using the following command:

```
ALTER MASTER KEY ADD ENCRYPTION BY SERVICE MASTER KEY
```

Backup Compression

A new feature in SQL 2008 enables the backup files to be stored in compressed form. This may achieve both shorter backup times and smaller files containing the backup. The trade-off you are making is increased CPU usage to do the compression, in exchange for less I/O due to the smaller files. Generally, the result of backup compression is greatly reduced backup times. Whether or not you will benefit from using compression is relative to the availability or scarcity of CPU and I/O resources, as well as the degree of compression obtained.

You can determine the state of your system by looking at the following:

❑　Windows performance monitor counters for your disks.

❑　SQL Server performance counters:

    ❑　SQLServer:Backup Device ➪ Device Throughput Bytes/sec.

    ❑　SQLServer:Databases ➪ Backup/Restore Throughput/sec.

The capability to compress backups is a feature of SQL Server 2008 Enterprise, and any edition of SQL Server 2008 or later can read and restore using compressed backups.

Backup media beginning with SQL Server 7 used a media format called Microsoft Tape Format (MTF). This is the same format that Windows Operating System backups used, enabling SQL Server backups to coexist on the same media with Windows backups. This was especially convenient for users with a single tape drive. Beginning with SQL 2008, compressed backups must use a different media format, which is incompatible with Windows backups. This leads to some restrictions regarding the use of backup compression:

❑ Compressed and uncompressed backups cannot coexist in the same media set.

❑ Prior versions of SQL Server cannot read compressed backups.

❑ NT backups and compressed backups cannot coexist in the same media set.

If you violate one of these restrictions, SQL Server returns an error.

A new server-level configuration option, backup compression default, enables your default backups to be either compressed or uncompressed. You can set this option via `sp_configure` and from SSMS. Backup compression is turned off by default. You may override the default using the `with compression` or `with no_compression` option in the `backup` T-SQL command or using the Backup dialogs in SSMS or the Database Maintenance Plan Wizard.

Log backup compression for the primary database in log shipping is always dependent on the default backup compression value.

How much compression you achieve depends on several factors:

❑ Databases that are compressed will not see additional compression in backups.

❑ Encrypted data does not compress as well as unencrypted data.

❑ Character data types compress better than other data types.

❑ Greater levels of compression are achieved when a page has multiple rows in which a column contains the same value.

How Restore Works

Restore brings back the database in case of a failure and is a major function of a transactional relational database system. When a DBA restores a database, three restore phases must happen.

Restore versus Recovery

The terms *restore* and *recovery* are often confused and misused. Restore is what occurs when you use the RESTORE T-SQL command to get a database back.

Recovery is a process that brings a database into a consistent state. This means that committed transactions are applied to disk (redo phase) and transactions that are begun but not yet committed are rolled off (undo phase). The result is a database that contains only committed transactions — a consistent state.

Each time the server is started, an automatic recovery process runs. At startup, you do not know how SQL Server last stopped. It could have been a clean shutdown, or a power outage could have brought the server down. In the case of the power outage, there may have been transactions that were begun but not yet completed. Recovery does the work necessary to ensure that committed transactions are included and not yet committed transactions are removed.

The last step in a restore process that you begin is also recovery. The RESTORE command enables you to specify when recovery runs. If recovery has not yet run, you may restore a differential or continue to restore transaction logs. Once recovery has run, no more log restores may occur, and the database is brought online.

In the *copy phase*, the database image is created and initialized on disk, and then the full backup is copied. That can be followed by any differential and transaction-log backups. These are done via the RESTORE T-SQL command.

After the full backup has been applied and any differential and transaction logs have been restored, the DBA allows recovery to run. During the recovery process, SQL Server performs both a *redo phase* and an *undo phase*. During the *redo phase*, all committed transaction records that were in the transaction log but not in the data files are written to the data files. The WAL protocol guarantees that the transaction records that were committed have been written to the transaction-log stable media. Then, during the redo, SQL Server evaluates the transaction-log records and applies the data modifications to the data files in the database.

The duration of the redo phase depends on how many data modifications SQL Server 2008 performed, which depends on what SQL Server was doing at the time of the failure and the recovery interval setting. For example, if SQL Server 2008 just finished updating 10 million rows from a table and committed the transaction but was unexpectedly shut down right after, during recovery it would have to redo those data modifications to the data. The SQL Server 2008 recovery interval setting influences recovery time according to how many dirty pages are kept in memory before the checkpoint process must write them to stable media. By default, the recovery interval is set to 0, which means that SQL Server keeps less than a minute of work that is not yet written to the data files. With that setting, during recovery, there is minimal redo work before the database becomes available for users. The higher the recovery interval value, the longer the recovery may take.

After the redo phase is the *undo phase*, where any transactions that did not complete are rolled back. Depending on the amount of work and the length of the transactions at the time before shutdown, this phase can take some time. For example, if the DBA was in the middle of deleting 10 million rows, SQL Server 2008 is required to roll back all those rows during recovery. SQL Server 2008 does make the database available to users while in the undo phase, but users should expect some performance impact while in the redo phase.

Comparing Recovery Models

Understanding the recovery models is essential to developing an effective backup strategy. The recovery model determines how the transaction log is managed by SQL Server 2008. The model you choose depends on the backup/restore plan you have for a database. In the *full recovery model*, the transaction log records all data modifications, makes available all database recovery options, and implements the highest data protection but uses the most transaction-log space. This recovery model can be used with all database backup operations, it is capable of point-in-time recovery, and it enables backing up the transaction log. Most OLTP production systems and mission-critical applications that require minimal data loss should use this recovery model.

The first transaction log backup cannot be completed until after a full database backup has been done.

The *bulk-logged recovery model* performs minimal logging for certain database operations, including bulk import operations, such as BCP, BULK INSERT, SELECT INTO, CREATE INDEX, ALTER INDEX REBUILD, and DBCC DBREINDEX. Instead of logging every modification for these database operations, it logs the extent allocations and flags the changed extents. As a result, these operations execute faster, as they are minimally logged, but it presents possible data-loss risks for recovery. A transaction-log backup copies everything in the transaction log, checks the extents flagged as changed, and copies them from the data files into the log backup. Additionally, after a bulk-logged operation, point-in-time recovery using transaction-log backup is disallowed.

Consider the same scenario presented earlier. The database is using the bulk-logged recovery model. The full database backup occurred at 1:00 P.M. A transaction log backup occurs at 1:30 P.M. Then a bulk-logged database operation is performed. Next, the physical drives containing the data files fail at 2:00 P.M. You would not be able to recover up to 2:00 P.M. because the transaction-log backup would need to access the data files to retrieve the data modifications performed during the bulk-logged operations. You could not perform a tail-log backup. As a result, data will be lost and you can only recover up to 1:30 P.M.

When you do bulk operations in this mode, you are at risk of losing data until you complete a log backup after the bulk operations. The data loss in this scenario can be minimized with some bulk-logged database operations by implementing shorter transactions performing transaction-log backups during and immediately after the bulk-logged operations. Oftentimes, this recovery model is used when the DBA is performing bulk-logged operations and then switches back to full after the bulk-logged operation completes, in order to improve the performance for bulk operations. Additionally, this model is commonly used in an OLAP or Report database for which there are nightly bulk data loads. A backup is taken, and afterward no data is modified during the day, so if the data is lost because of a failure, it can be restored from backup.

The *simple recovery model* implements minimal logging, just like the bulk-logged recovery model, except that it keeps the transaction-log records only until the next checkpoint process occurs, writing the dirty changes to the data files. Then the checkpoint process truncates the transaction log. Transaction-log backups are not allowed; therefore, point-in-time recovery is not available. Typically, this recovery model is used for development or test servers, where data loss is acceptable and data can be reloaded. Moreover, this model may be used by an OLAP and Reporting database for which there may be only a nightly data load and then a full or differential backup is performed. With this model, if the database were to fail during the data load, you would have to start from the beginning, unless a full or differential backup was taken during the process. In addition, if a DBA switches from one of the other recovery models to this one, the transaction-log continuity is broken, as it truncates the transaction log. In addition, during the time that the database is in this recovery mode, the database is more exposed to potential data loss.

Transactional replication, log shipping, or data mirroring is not allowed in the simple recovery model, as there is no transaction log.

Choosing a Model

Choosing the best recovery model depends on the amount of acceptable data loss, the database's read and write daily activities, and how critical that database is to the daily business of your organization.

Choose the full recovery model for a mission-critical database to keep data loss to a minimum because it is fully logged; and in case of damaged data files, the tail transaction log can be backed up and used to restore the database to a given point in time. Therefore, OLTP production systems usually use the full recovery model, except when the database is modified nightly, as is sometimes the case with OLAP or Reporting databases.

You can use the bulk-logged recovery model to increase bulk operations' performance because it does minimal logging. For example, you could do a nightly bulk operation and then switch back to full recovery. The bulk-logged model will fully log, as is the case with the full recovery model, except for the bulk operations. Therefore, you could use bulk-logged recovery as a permanent recovery model, except it poses a risk of data loss. As long as there are no bulk-data operations, the DBA can back up the transaction log; but oftentimes, unknown to the DBA, the tail transaction-log backup recovery may no longer be available if a bulk operation has been performed. To guard against someone doing bulk operations without a database backup and to reduce that data risk, you should switch to bulk-logged only when a bulk operation needs to be performed. Bulk-logged can be a permanent recovery model in an OLAP or Report database where there is no daily modification activity, as there is limited data loss risk if the databases are backed up right after any nightly data load. There is no chance of data loss throughout the day, as nothing would have changed. In addition, some data loss may be acceptable, as the OLAP and Reporting databases can be reloaded from the OLTP data source whenever needed.

The simple recovery model acts like the bulk-logged model, except that it does not save the transaction log; instead, the checkpoint process truncates it. Therefore, no one has to maintain the transaction log. This recovery model is commonly used for development, read-only, and test systems for which transaction-log backups are not required. If there is data loss, a new copy of the data can be reloaded from the OLTP data source. If the DBA switches to this recovery model from one of the others, the transaction-log continuity is broken because there is no way to back up the transaction log. In this recovery model, there is no point-in-time recovery because the DBA cannot back up the transaction log. Therefore, any restore would be from the previous full, and any differential, backups.

Switching Recovery Models

SQL Server 2008 provides complete flexibility to switch among the recovery models. However, be aware of the limitations when switching among them, as switching can result in data loss during recovery. The following list outlines the limitations of switching recovery models:

❑ **Switching from full to bulk-logged:** Because bulk-logged database operations may be performed, a transaction-log backup is recommended at a minimum, so that the DBA can recover to this last transaction log if the tail transaction log is not available. To change to this recovery model, use this command:

```
ALTER DATABASE < db_name> SET RECOVERY BULK_LOGGED
```

❑ **Switching from full to simple:** Because the transaction-log continuity is broken by this recovery model, a transaction-log backup is recommended, at minimum, before the switch. After the recovery model switch, transaction-log backups and point-in-time recovery are disallowed. To change to this recovery model, use the following command:

```
ALTER DATABASE < db_name> SET RECOVERY SIMPLE
```

❑ **Switching from bulk-logged to full:** Because bulk-logged database operations may have been performed and to minimize potential data loss if the tail transaction log is not accessible, a transaction-log backup is recommended after the switch. To change to this recovery model, use the following command:

```
ALTER DATABASE < db_name> SET RECOVERY FULL
```

❑ **Switching from bulk-logged to simple:** In this recovery model there is a greater chance of data loss in case of a database failure, so at a minimum, a transaction-log backup is highly recommended before the switch. To change to this recovery model, use the following command:

```
ALTER DATABASE < db_name> SET RECOVERY SIMPLE
```

❑ **Switching from simple to full:** To enable the full recovery model to start to apply transaction-log backups, a full, differential, file, or filegroup backup is required after the switch. To change to this recovery model, use the following command:

```
ALTER DATABASE < db_name> SET RECOVERY FULL
```

❑ **Switching from simple to bulk-logged:** To enable the bulk-logged recovery model to start to apply transaction-log backups, a full, differential, file, or filegroup backup is required after the switch. To change to this recovery model, use the following command:

```
ALTER DATABASE < db_name> SET RECOVERY BULK_LOGGED
```

The recovery model is configured for each database. You can also switch the recovery model from SQL Server Management Studio by opening the Database Properties and choosing Options, as shown in Figure 18-1.

Verifying the Backup Images

With any backup solution, a critical operation is verifying the backup images that they will restore. Often, a DBA may be meticulously doing backups, but along the way the database becomes corrupted, and every backup from that point on is not usable. Plan on doing periodic restores to verify recoverability. Additionally, perform database consistency checks to validate the database structures. Use the RESTORE VERIFYONLY T-SQL command to perform validation checks on the backup image. It does not restore the backup, but it performs validation checks, including the following:

❑ Confirms the backup set is readable
❑ Page ID
❑ If the backup was created WITH CHECKSUMS, then it will validate it
❑ Checks destination devices for sufficient space

However, the RESTORE VERIFYONLY command does not completely guarantee that the backup is restorable. That is why you need a policy to randomly restore a backup to a test server. RESTORE VERIFYONLY simply provides another level of validation. Here's the syntax:

```
RESTORE VERIFYONLY FROM <backup_device_name>
```

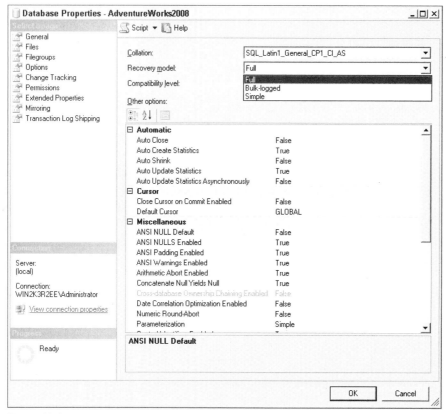

Figure 18-1

An example resulting message is the following:

```
The backup set on file 1 is valid.
```

RESTORE VERIFYONLY *does not work on database snapshots. If you are planning to revert (restore) from a database snapshot, then use* DBCC CHECKDB *to ensure that the database is healthy.*

For higher reliability, to guard against a malfunctioning backup device that may render the entire backup unrecoverable, use mirroring of backup sets for redundancy. They can be either disk or tape and have the following restrictions:

❑ Backup devices must be identical.

❑ To create a new, or extend an existing, backup, the mirror backup set must be intact. If one is not present, the media backup set cannot be used.

❑ To restore from a media backup set, only one of the mirror devices must be present.

❑ If one mirror of the media backup set is damaged, no additional mirroring can performed on that media backup set.

For example, use the following command to use a backup device mirroring on the `AdventureWorks2008` database:

```
BACKUP DATABASE AdventureWorks2008

TO TAPE = '\\.\tape0', TAPE = '\\.\tape1'

MIRROR TO TAPE = '\\.\tape2', TAPE = '\\.\tape3'

WITH FORMAT, MEDIANAME = 'AdventureWorks2008Set1'
```

Backing Up History Tables

SQL Server 2008 maintains the backup history for the server in the `MSDB` database in a group of tables from which it can identify the backup available for a database. In the Restore dialog, SQL Server presents the restores available for the database. The tables are as follows:

❑ `Backupfile`: A row for each data or log file backed up.

❑ `Backupfilegroup`: A row for each filegroup in a backup set.

❑ `Backupmediafamily`: A row for each media family.

❑ `Backupmediaset`: A row for each backup media set.

❑ `Backupset`: A row for each backup set.

A media set is an ordered collection of all tapes or disks from all devices that took part in the backup. A media family is a collection of all backup media on a single device that took part in the backup. A media backup is a tape or disk device used for backup.

The following three backup information statements return information from the history backup tables:

❑ RESTORE FILELISTONLY: Returns a list of database and log files in a backup set from the `backup file` table:

```
RESTORE  FILELISTONLY FROM AdventureWorks2008_Backup
```

❑ RESTORE HEADERONLY: Returns all the backup header information for all the backup sets in a device from the `backupset` table:

```
RESTORE  HEADERONLY FROM AdventureWorks2008_Backup
```

❑ RESTORE LABELONLY: Returns information about the backup media of a backup device from the `backupmediaset` table:

```
RESTORE LABELONLY FROM AdventureWorks2008_Backup
```

RESTORE HEADERONLY, RESTORE FILELISTONLY, RESTORE VERIFYONLY and RESTORE LABLELONLY do not actually restore anything, and therefore are completely safe to run. They only provide information. I wish they were named something different, so that RESTORE could be reserved for use only in that serious situation when you are changing things.

Permissions Required for Backup and Restore

SQL Server provides granular permission for both backup and restoring a database. A Windows or SQL Server authenticated user or group can be given permission to perform the backup and restore operations. To have permission to back up a database, a user must have at minimum the following permissions:

- ❑ Server role: `none`
- ❑ DB role: `db_backupoperator`

To restore a database, a user must have at minimum the following permissions:

- ❑ Server role: `dbcreater`
- ❑ DB role: `db_owner`

Backing Up System Databases

SQL Server 2008 system databases are critical to the operation of each SQL Server instance. These databases are not often modified, but they contain important information that needs to be backed up. After creating a new SQL Server 2008 instance, develop a backup plan to perform a full backup of the system databases, except for `tempdb`. SQL Server 2008 recreates `tempdb` every time it is restarted, as it does not contain any data to recover. Backing up these system databases takes only minutes, so there is no excuse for not having a proper backup. I often schedule these backups nightly and do extra backups to my local hard drive before and after any changes I make. That keeps me safe until the current night's normal backup.

Master

The master database contains the login information, metadata about each database for the SQL instance. Moreover, it contains SQL Server configuration information. For example, the database is altered every time you do the following:

- ❑ Add, remove, or modify a database level setting.
- ❑ Add or delete a user database.
- ❑ Add or remove a file or filegroup in a user database.
- ❑ Add, remove, or modify a login's security.
- ❑ Modify a SQL Server 2008 serverwide configuration.
- ❑ Add or remove a logical backup device.
- ❑ Configure distributed queries or remote procedure calls (RPC).
- ❑ Add, modify, or remove a linked server or remote login.

Although these modifications occur infrequently, when they do, consider doing a full database backup. If a backup is not performed, you stand to lose the modifications if a previous backup of the master is restored. Moreover, as a precautionary measure, before and after adding any service pack or hotfix, perform a new backup of the master database.

MSDB

The msdb database contains SQL jobs, backup jobs, schedules, operators, and backup and restore histories and can contain Integration Services packages and other items. If you create a new job or add a new Integration Services package and msdb were to fail, the previous backup would not contain these new jobs and would need to be recreated.

tempdb

tempdb cannot be backed up. Because it is recreated every time SQL Server 2008 is restarted, no data in it needs to be recovered.

Model

Typically, the model database changes even less frequently than the other system databases. Model is the template database used when a new database is created. If you want a certain database object to be present in every new database, such as a stored procedure or table, place it in Model. In these cases, it should be backed up; otherwise, any Model modifications will be lost and need to be recreated. Additionally, keep scripts of any changes you make to the model, just to add another layer of safety.

Full-text Backup

Full-text search performs fast querying of unstructured data using keywords based on the words in a particular language. It is primarily used to search char, varchar, and nvarchar fields. Prior to querying, the full-text index must be created by a population or crawl process, during which full-text search performs a breakdown of the keywords and stores them in the full-text index. Each full-text index is then stored in a full-text catalog. Then a catalog is stored in a filegroup. Unlike previous versions of SQL Server, in SQL Server 2008, a full backup includes the full-text indexes. In SQL 2005, full-text indexes were part of a catalog that existed in a filegroup, with a physical path and was simply treatedas a database file. SQL 2008 treats all of the catalog as a virtual object–simply a collection of full-text indexes. Full-text indexes are now stored and treated like other indexes for the purpose of backups. To backup all of the full-text indexes, you must discover the files which contain any full-text index, then backup the file or filegroup.

The following query returns the list of all filegroups in the current database that contain any full-text index:

```
SELECT DISTINCT Name FROM sys.filegroups f INNER JOIN sys.fulltext_indexes i
   ON f.data_space_id = i.data_space_id
```

Since SQL 2005 treated full-text indexes as a filegroup, an upgrade will create a new filegroup and place the upgraded full-text indexes into the filegroup. The purpose of this is to maintain the same IO performance characteristics for full-text indexes that existed in SQL 2005.

The end result is that backups for full-text indexes are completely incorporated into the standard backup architecture. You can place full text indexes on separate filegroups, Primary filegroup, or allow them to live in the same filegroup as the base table This improvement makes administration easier than in prior releases.

Planning for Recovery

To mitigate the risk and extent of data loss, one of the DBA's most important tasks is database backup and planning for recovery. You need to develop a backup plan that minimizes data loss and is able to be implemented within the maintenance window of time allowed. Choose the best SQL Server backup capabilities to achieve the preferred backup plan, one that meets the continuity and data loss requirements for the business. You must also set up the backup procedure and monitor it every day to ensure that it is working successfully. That includes validating that the database backup will restore properly.

An organization may be current with its backups and assume that it has the necessary backups to restore the database, only to find that the database was corrupted and some of the recent database backups will not restore. Cases like these can go undiscovered for months until someone needs to restore a database and finds out that it is not recoverable. To reduce this risk, run the database-consistency checks against each database and design a process to test the recoverability of the database backup. Additionally, send database backups offsite to protect them in case of a local disaster, but keep local copies of recent backups in case you need to perform a quick restore.

Another critical task is disaster recovery planning. If the organization data center were to be completely destroyed, you should be able to quickly deploy a new data center with minimum data loss and minimum business disruption. Disaster recovery planning is not complete until a team periodically simulates a data center failure and proceeds through the test drill to deploy a new data center.

Recoverability Requirements

Any backup planning should start with the end goal in mind: the recoverability requirements. We have already covered the planning, but here are a few more things you might also consider:

❑ Perhaps only part of the database must be online. You can consider a piecemeal restore to reduce your restore time, especially on larger databases for which a restore can take a long time. Determine what parts of the database must be available and arrange the data into filegroups so that you can recover the most critical filegroups first. Archived data or reporting data is less critical and can be recovered last.

❑ The organization may allocate newer, redundant hardware and RAID array with a high-availability solution to mitigate downtime. A company might also consider faster and more backup devices to quickly restore the database.

❑ Determine how easy or difficult it would be to recreate lost data for each database. For some databases, data can be easily recreated by extracting data from another system or from flat-file data loads. Typically, decision-support databases use ETL tools to extract data; for example, if some unrecoverable data loss occurred, the ETL tool can be executed to reload the data.

❑ What is the acceptable downtime in a media failure, such as a failed disk drive? As disk technology continues to become less expensive, most organizations deploy databases on a fault-tolerant disk array that reduces the exposure of one of the disk drives failing, causing the database to become unavailable. For example, on a RAID 5 set, loss of a single drive will cause a noticeable performance slowdown. If a second drive in the same RAID 5 were to fail, the data would be lost. To mitigate this risk, have spare drives in the disk array system and get a service-level agreement from the hardware provider to deliver and install the drives. Another common scenario is a department inside the organization deploying a database in a less than ideal hardware environment. With time, the database becomes mission critical to that department, but it lives under the DBA's radar with no accountability. The DBA should attempt to identify all database sources within the organization and develop a recovery plan.

❏   Determine which databases have any external dependencies on other databases, requiring both databases to be restored in order for users to be able to perform their daily activity. Determine whether there is any linked server(s), external application(s), or mainframe connectivity on which a database has dependencies.

❏   Identify the available hardware that can be allocated for redeployment and where it is located.

❏   Identify the staff required for backup, restore, and disaster recovery. They need to understand the disaster recovery procedures and where they fit in these procedures. Record when all staff members are available, their contact numbers, the chain of communication, and the responsibility of each member. Determine the chain of command and find out, if the lead is unavailable, whether backup members have the expertise to carry out the duties for backup, restore, and disaster recovery. Find out the expertise of the staff and what additional training they might need to support the environment. Identify any training classes that may be beneficial.

❏   Finally, document any information about stored SQL jobs, linked servers, and logins that may be needed when the database is restored onto another database server.

Data Usage Patterns

Part of your recovery plan should include analyzing how your data is used in a typical scenario. Determine for each database how often the data is modified. You'll require different backup strategies for a database that may have a data load once a day than for others that may be read-only or some that change every minute. Separate the tables that are modified from read-only tables. Each type can be placed on different filegroups and a backup plan developed around it.

Identify the usage pattern of the databases during the day to determine the backup strategy to use. For example, during high activity, a DBA may schedule more frequent differential or transaction-log backups, while full backups may be performed during off-peak hours.

Determine the disk space used by the transaction log during peak times and the log's performance. For example, during peak times, the transaction log may fill the available disk drive allocated to it. Moreover, during peak times, the number of disks allocated for the transaction log may not be adequate to sustain the database's performance. The database recovery model setting affects both disk space and performance.

For a database in the full recovery model, consider switching to bulk-logged mode during bulk operations to improve performance, as that will incur minimal transaction logging. Prior to the start of the bulk operations, you should at minimum perform a transactional or differential backup to guard against the risk of a data-drive failure when the tail transaction log may not be accessible.

Maintenance Time Window

Sometimes, the backup strategy is dictated by the maintenance time window available to perform database defragmentation, backups, statistics updates, and other maintenance activities. To keep enhancing the customer experience, organizations are demanding more timely information and giving customers greater access to information, and customers are more dependent on having this information. This creates a challenge to create the best customer experience, mitigate the risk of data loss, and enable quick restores if the database system fails.

The task of the DBA is to find the best backup strategy to meet the organization's business requirements. Usually, the maintenance time window is limited. SQL Server 2008 implements various backup options that can be used in combination to meet these requirements. The following are some of the challenges you face when designing a backup strategy:

❑ Available backup time may be limited in a mission-critical, highly available database. Organizations often have service-level agreements and must finish their maintenance by a certain time when users are back on the system. If the backup takes longer, it may delay other database activities, which might not finish by the time users log in to the system, costing a company opportunity loss.

❑ There may be a large number of databases to back up during the maintenance time window. You can try to optimize your time for all available backup media by performing concurrent backups within the capacity of the database server.

❑ A growing database puts pressure on the maintenance window. Additional backup devices, higher-performance database servers, and faster I/O may be needed to relieve the pressure. Sometimes the maintenance time window can be increased, but oftentimes it cannot. You may need to consider a SAN copy solution to speed the backup process.

❑ Other database activities are likely performed on all of the databases in the database server (e.g., database-consistency checking, defragmentation, update statistics, and perhaps data loads). As the database grows, these other activities may take longer to perform, too.

❑ Software updates, security patches, service packs, and database structure updates may need to fit within this maintenance time window.

❑ Full-text catalogs may need to be processed.

❑ As more organizations see the benefit of decision-support systems such as SQL Server Analysis Services, the analysis services database may need to be processed during this time.

As a result, any solution needs to address and balance the following goals:

❑ A backup strategy that can be accomplished within the allocated maintenance time window

❑ A restore strategy based on the backup strategy that requires the minimum number of steps and complexity to recovery the databases

❑ Minimal to no data loss

❑ A backup strategy that is the least expensive to maintain and manage

To meet these requirements, a small database can use a full database backup every night. However, as the database becomes larger, that may not be possible. A good next step is to perform a full database backup on the weekend and nightly full differential backups. As the database becomes larger, consider moving read-only and read/write data to different filegroups, and then use full partial backups during the weekend and partial differential backups at night. As the database continues to grow, consider nightly backup of individual files. A file backup solution is more difficult to maintain, and another preferred solution for these larger databases may be a SAN copy operation. It is a more expensive solution, but for large databases it can better meet the backup and restore requirements with the fewest steps and highest availability.

Also consider how the database is to be used. If the database is mission critical, apply redundancy around the hardware, such as a failover cluster solution with fault-tolerant disk drives. Identify what level of data loss the company can afford and plan to back up the transaction log to meet the time requirement. Also use the full recovery model so that you can get recovery to the point of failure.

The other important component is the number of steps required to restore the database and the amount of time required. The more steps required, the higher the probability that something may not work or one of the backup images may be unavailable. When a database failure occurs, the goal is to restore it as fast as possible.

Other High-Availability Solutions

When your database has been deployed in a high-availability solution, such as failover clustering, log shipping, or data mirroring, it may require additional backup considerations:

❑ In log shipping, the transaction log is backed up by the log-shipping process. No other transaction-log backup should be permitted, as that will break the log chain and prevent any additional transaction log restores on the standby server. If that occurred, you would need to reconfigure log shipping.

❑ In data mirroring, if the mirror server is down, the principal server transaction log queues all modifications to be sent to the mirror in the transaction log. The transaction log cannot be truncated past the point where it has not sent data modifications to the mirror server.

❑ A failover cluster is a single database, so there are no special considerations. However, if the failover cluster is integrated with log shipping or data mirroring, the transaction-log limitations already mentioned apply.

❑ Any use of replication requires you to make a detailed backup recovery plan that includes the synchronization of the source database, the distribution database, and the subscribers.

In transaction replication, if the subscriber is down, the transaction log cannot be truncated past the point where it has not replicated those data modifications to the subscriber server.

Developing and Executing a Backup Plan

SQL Server 2008 provides two methods for planning and executing backups. You can use either the graphical interface of Management Studio or the T-SQL backup commands. This section covers both of these methods.

Using SQL Server 2008 Management Studio

SQL Server 2008 Management Studio (SSMS) exposes backup management capabilities for a DBA to either develop a scheduled maintenance plan or directly perform a backup. Before you start, decide the destination for the backup image. It can be a backup location such as a directory path with a file name or a separate backup device.

If you're using a backup device, first you need to create a logical device that defines where SQL Server will copy the backup image. From SQL Server 2008 Management Studio, select Server Objects ⇨ Backup Devices ⇨ New Backup Device. You'll see the dialog shown in Figure 18-2. There are two destination options:

❑ **Tape:** Requires that a local tape drive be present on the database server.

❑ **File:** Requires a valid disk destination.

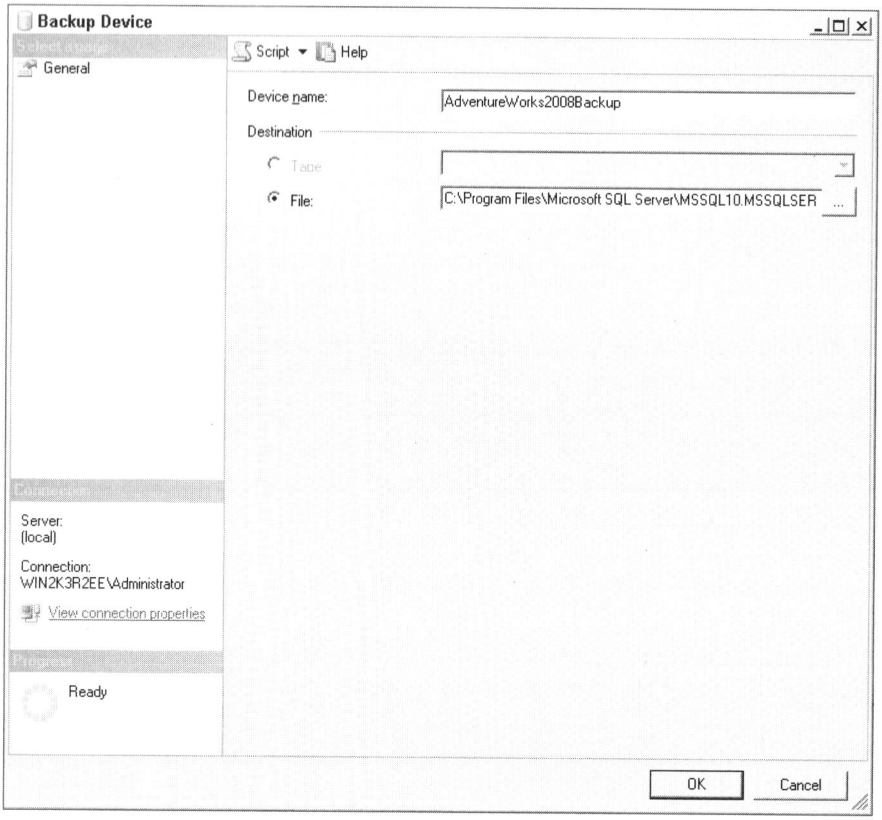

Figure 18-2

I prefer not to use backup devices when backing up to disk, because the location is hard-coded. Instead, create unique backup file names that include the database name, the backup type, and some date/time information to make the name unique. This is much more flexible than using a backup device. To perform a database backup from SQL Server 2008 Management Studio, select the database you want to back up, right-click, and choose Tasks ⇨ Backup. The Back Up Database dialog appears, as shown in Figure 18-3.

In the Source area of this dialog, configure the following:

❑ **Database:** Choose the database to back up.

❑ **Recovery model:** This value is grayed out, as it cannot be changed. Notice that this is in full recovery model. If it were simple recovery model, the transaction log could not be backed up, as the transaction log is truncated by the checkpoint process and files, and filegroup backups would not be available, except for read-only files or filegroups.

❑ **Backup type:** Choose among Full, Differential, or Transaction Log.

❑ **Copy Only Backup:** Allows you to do a backup that does not affect the transaction chain or truncate the log.

❑   **Backup component:** Choose from the following options:

   ❑   **Database:** Backs up the database.

   ❑   **Files and filegroups:** Backs up files or filegroups. This option presents a dialog from which you can choose one or more files or filegroups.

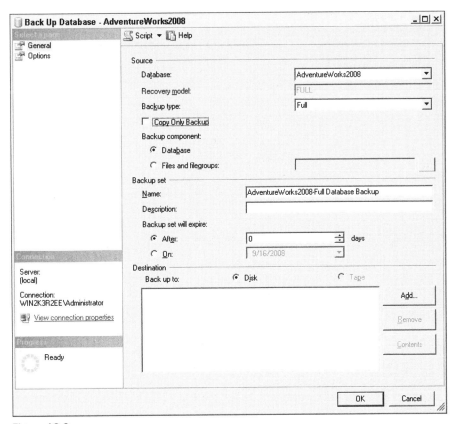

Figure 18-3

In the Backup Set area of this dialog, configure the following:

❑   **Name:** Give the backup set a name for easier identification. This name will distinguish the backup from others in the backup device.

❑   **Description:** Provide an optional description for this media set.

❑   **Backup set will expire:** Configure these options based on your business's retention policy; this guards against SQL Server's backup process overwriting the backup set.

❑   **After:** This determines the number of days, from 0 to 99,999, after which the set can be over-written. Zero is the default, which means the set never expires. You can change the serverwide default by choosing SQL Server Properties ⇨ Database Settings. Change the default backup media retention (in days).

❑ **On:** Specify a date on which the backup set will expire.

SQL Server 2008 supports up to 64 backup devices. In the Destination area of this dialog, configure the following:

❑ **Disk:** Specify a full valid destination path with a file name or a disk backup device.

❑ **Tape:** Specify a tape drive or a tape backup device. The tape drive must be local to the database server.

Clicking the Contents button shows the media set or media family of the device selected.

While in the Back Up Database dialog, select the Options page to see the dialog shown in Figure 18-4.

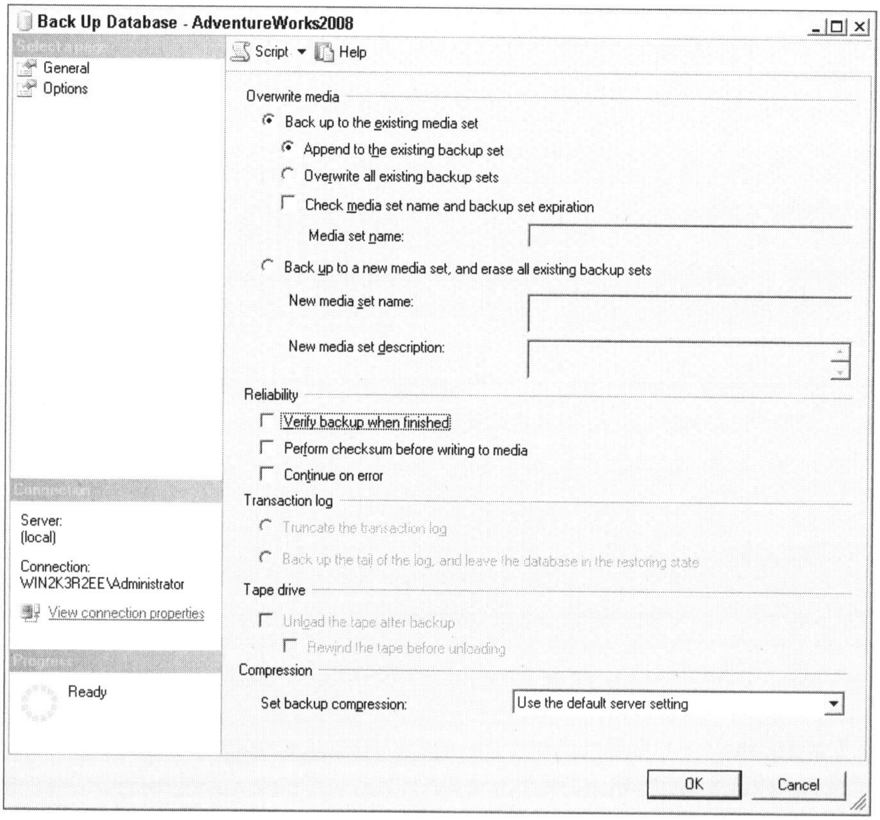

Figure 18-4

In the Overwrite Media section, you can choose to back up to the existing media set, in which case you have to configure these options:

- ❏ **Append to the existing backup set:** Preserves the existing backups by appending to that media set. This is the default.

- ❏ **Overwrite all existing backup sets:** Erases all the existing backups and replaces them with the current backup. This overwrites all existing backup sets unless the "Check media set name and backup set expiration" box is checked.

Alternately, you can choose to back up to a new media set and erase all existing backup sets, which erases all backups in the media and begins a media set, according to your specifications.

The Reliability section of this dialog has two checkboxes that are both good recommended practices, as a backup is of no value if it is not recoverable:

- ❏ **Verify backup when finished:** After the backup finishes, SQL Server confirms that all volumes are readable.

- ❏ **Perform checksum before writing to media:** SQL Server does a checksum prior to writing to media, which can be used during recovery to verify that the backup was not tampered with. Note that there is a performance penalty with this operation.

- ❏ **Continue on Error:** Backup should continue to run after encountering an error such as a page chechksum error or torn page.

The Transaction Log section of this dialog contains options that apply only during transaction-log backups:

- ❏ **Truncate the transaction log:** During normal transaction-log backups, it is common practice to manage the size of the transaction log and to truncate it after it has been backed up to a backup media.

- ❏ **Back up the tail of the log and leave the database in the restoring state:** This option is useful when the data files of the database are not accessible (e.g., the physical drives have failed but the transaction log in separate physical drives is still accessible). As a result, during database recovery, apply this as the last transaction-log backup to recover right to the point of failure.

The Tape Drive section of the dialog contains tape drive instructions to rewind and unload the tape.

The Compression section of this dialog enables you to specify one of three compression options for the backup:

- ❏ Use the default server setting
- ❏ Compress backup
- ❏ Do not compress backup

Click OK and the backup process executes.

Database Maintenance Plans

Another approach to executing the backup plan is to develop database maintenance plans for each database, schedule them, and have SQL Server e-mail you a backup history report. Some people love the database maintenance plans, while others hate them due to some inconsistencies in prior versions. I have always used them for small shops.

The purpose of the database maintenance plan is ease of use and reuse. A database maintenance plan includes many of the normal maintenance things you must do for a database, grouped all together, executed on a schedule, with history and reporting — it is nice. You can create a plan manually or use the Wizard, which steps you through a series of dialogs.

In response to feedback regarding prior versions of the database maintenance plan feature, SQL Server 2008 implemented, and SQL 2008 continues an all-new, and much more flexible, maintenance plan interface. Prior versions implemented special stored procedures that did the work. Beginning in SQL Server 2005, maintenance plans are SSIS packages. In the past, each maintenance item had its own schedule, independent of the other tasks. For instance, you may have scheduled DBCC to run at 1:00 A.M. and the database backups to begin at 3:00 A.M. The plan works well for a while, but as databases grow, the DBCC task runs until 4:00 A.M., overlapping the backup schedule. Using SSIS tasks and precedents, you can now have backups begin only after the DBCCs finish — a real improvement.

> To create a Maintenance Plan, the server configuration option Agent XPs must be turned on using sp_configure.

To create maintenance plans for one or more databases from SQL Server 2008 Management Studio, choose the Management folder ➪ Maintenance Plans and then right-click and choose New Maintenance Plan. After naming the maintenance plan, you'll be taken to the maintenance plan design screen:

1. Choose the Back Up Database Task and drag it to the designer.

2. Right-click on the Back Up Database Task and choose Edit to open the Backup Database Task dialog, as shown in Figure 18-5.

3. In the Connection field, choose Local Server Connection, or, if this maintenance plan is to back up databases on another server, choose New Connection and provide the connection information.

4. In the Database(s) field, choose one or more databases. You can choose more than one database if they have identical backup requirements.

5. In the Backup Component field, choose either Database or Files and Filegroups. If you choose Files and Filegroups, you need to specify which files or filegroups to back up.

6. You may optionally choose an expiration date for the backup set. This prevents accidental overwrites.

7. In the Back Up To field, choose either Disk or Tape.

8. You can choose a list of hard-coded files to backup your databases to or have the maintenance plan create an automatically named backup file for each database.

    a. If you choose Back Up Databases Across one or More Files:

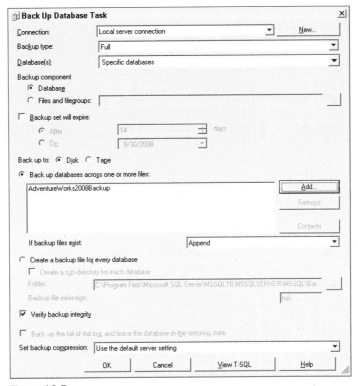

Figure 18-5

1.   Click the Add button to configure the backup location. For disk, provide the full path to the file name or the disk backup device. For tape, provide the tape location or the tape backup device. You can use more than one file or backup device. If more than one is chosen, all the databases will be backed up across them, up to the 64 backup devices that SQL Server supports.

2.   On the If Backup Files Exist field, select whether to append to the existing backup file or to overwrite; the default is Append.

b.   If you choose Create a Backup File for Every Database:

1.   Choose the "Create a backup file for every database" option.

2.   Select the root directory for the backups.

3.   Choose a backup file extension.

9.   Click the Verify Backup Integrity checkbox as a recommended practice.

10.   For transaction log backups, you can optionally choose to backup the tail of the log.

11.   In the Set Backup Compression field, specify whether the backup should be compressed.

12.   Click OK.

13. Click the Reporting and Logging button on the Maintenance Plan [Design] Menu tab and choose how to receive the backup history report. If you choose e-mail, Database Mail must be configured. Moreover, a SQL Server Agent Operator must be configured to e-mail the report. Then click OK.

14. Click the Schedule button and set up the schedule for this maintenance plan.

When you allow a maintance plan to create a backup file for each database, it creates a file formatted as 'AdventureWorks2008_backup_2008_09_01_090243_2394128' for the AdventureWorks2008 database. This include the backup type and date and time of the backup. This is very good. The down side of using this option is that you get a single backup file and cannot get the performance benefits of a multi-file backup.

You can include additional backup database tasks for other database backups with various backup requirements. For example, one Back Up Database Task may be performing full database backups on several databases, another may be performing differential backups, while another may be performing filegroup backups. They will share the same schedule.

Earlier in this chapter you organized your databases into categories, based on the backup/restore needs. You could create maintenance plans that satisfy the needs of each category. Then, when a new database is created on that server, you simply categorize it, adding it to the appropriate maintenance plan.

When the maintenance plan is complete, it is automatically scheduled as a SQL job in SQL Agent.

Using Transact-SQL Backup Commands

All the backup commands using SQL Server 2008 Management Studio and all functionality are available directly using T-SQL. Here are some examples of the syntax:

1. Create a logical backup device for the `AdventureWorks2008` database backup:

```
EXEC sp_addumpdevice 'disk', 'AdventureWorks2008Backup',
'C:\BACKUP\AdventureWorks2008.bak';
```

Your drive letters may be different, so you may have to change the file name reference. Note also that if you use a file share, you should use the UNC name instead of a shared drive letter, as shown here: \myserver\myshare\Backup\AdventureWorks2008.bak.

2. Create a full `AdventureWorks2008` database backup:

```
BACKUP DATABASE AdventureWorks2008 TO AdventureWorks2008Backup;
```

3. Create a full differential backup:

```
BACKUP   DATABASE   AdventureWorks2008   TO   AdventureWorks2008Backup
WITH DIFFERENTIAL;
```

4. Create a tail transaction-log backup. This type of backup is only used after a database failure when the transaction logs are still available:

```
BACKUP LOG AdventureWorks2008 TO tailLogBackup WITH NORECOVERY;
```

The prior tail lob backup assumes you have created a new backup device called tailLogBackup.

A best practice would avoid the use of the backup device with disk files. The following commands reflect that practice:

1. Create a backup file name for the `AdventureWorks2008` database backup:

```
DECLARE @devname varchar(256)
SELECT @devname = 'C:\BACKUP\AdventureWorks2008 _Full_'+ REPLACE
(REPLACE(CONVERT(Varchar(40), GETDATE(), 120),'-','_'),':','_') + '.bak';
```

2. Create a full `AdventureWorks2008` database backup:

```
BACKUP DATABASE AdventureWorks2008 TO DISK = @devname;
```

3. Create a backup file name for the `AdventureWorks2008` differential backup:

```
DECLARE @devname varchar(256)
SELECT @devname = 'C:\BACKUP\AdventureWorks2008 _Differential_' + REPLACE
(REPLACE(CONVERT(Varchar(40), GETDATE(), 120),'-','_'),':','_') + '.bak';
```

4. Create a full differential backup:

```
BACKUP DATABASE AdventureWorks2008 TO DISK = @devname    WITH DIFFERENTIAL;
```

5. Create a backup file name for the `AdventureWorks2008` database backup:

```
DECLARE @devname varchar(256)

SELECT @devname = 'C:\BACKUP\AdventureWorks2008 _Log_' + REPLACE
(REPLACE(CONVERT(Varchar(40), GETDATE(), 120),'-','_'),':','_') + '.bak';
```

6. Create anormal transaction log backup:.

```
BACKUP LOG AdventureWorks2008 TO DISK = @devname;
```

When using disk files, place each backup in its own backup file and name the file appropriately. The name should include the unique database name (which might include some server part, if you have databases named the same in several servers), backup type, and date information. The preceding examples use yyyy_mm_dd hh_mm_ss as the date part. It is not unusual to create a stored procedure or user-defined function (UDF) that accepts parameters and returns the name of the backup file.

Do not use mapped drive letters in your backup file names. If backing up to files on file shares, use the UNC name. Mapped drive letters may vary depending on who is logged in to the physical server. You can create permanent mapped drive letters, but UNC names are preferred.

Managing Backups

Managing your backups is another important DBA task. The better your maintenance procedure, the faster and more accurately the backups will be identified and quickly restored. Meticulously running backups does little good if the backups cannot be identified or, worse, were lost or overwritten. The following tips should help your backup management program:

❑ Descriptively label all the backups to prevent overwriting or misplacing a backup.

❑ Set up a retention policy to prevent a tape or disk backup from being overwritten. These may be dictated by corporate policy, government regulations, cost, space, or logistics.

❑ Tapes can go bad, so set up a reuse policy. Define how many times a tape may be reused before throwing it away. This adds a tape cost, but a worn tape can stop a successful restore.

❑ Set up a storage location where the backups can easily be organized, found, and accessed. For example, if you're not available and someone else needs to perform the restore, that person must be able to get to the location and correctly identify the backups. You should also keep a copy of the backups stored offsite in a location where they will be protected from a local disaster. This offsite location should allow 24-hour access in case you need a backup. Moreover, keep a copy of the more recent backups locally in case they are quickly needed for a restore.

❑ The backup storage location should be secured such that unauthorized individuals do not have access to sensitive data. Furthermore, for the most sensitive data, use SQL Server 2008 column-level encryption.

❑ You must backup and maintain any encryption keys used with databases that are encrypted. These keys must be backed up again when the accounts (commonly the service account or machine account) change. These certificates *must* be maintained or the database will not be restorable or the data will not be accessible.

❑ Set up a logistical procedure to promptly move a copy of each backup to the offsite location to prevent it from being destroyed in a disaster.

Backup and Restore Performance

As stated previously, SQL Server 2008 supports 64 backup devices. It will use multiple backup devices in parallel to back up and restore for faster throughput. The backup devices should be on a different controller from the database for better throughput. For disk devices, consider the RAID level used for fault tolerance and performance. Work with the SAN or disk array vendor to get their recommendations for the solution. A combination of full, differential, and transaction-log backups will improve performance.

Some of the largest database systems may use SAN Snapshot Disk technology supported by many SAN vendors for faster backup and restore (see Figure 18-6). It is configured as a three-way mirror whereby the business continuity volume (BCV) is data synchronized and then split from the mirror set. The disadvantage of this solution is the cost of the SAN hardware and software to implement it. The advantages of this solution are as follows:

❑ Nearly instant and low-impact backups, as the disk split occurs instantaneously

❑ Nearly instant database restore. In a restore, the BCV can be reintroduced and attached to SQL Server for instant restore while it is data synchronizing the others in the mirror set.

❑ It keeps the system online and available almost continuously with minimal impact to SQL Server, as the data synchronization occurs on the SAN level.

❑ It enables you to mount the BCV disks on another SQL Server to perform conventional backups and consistency checks.

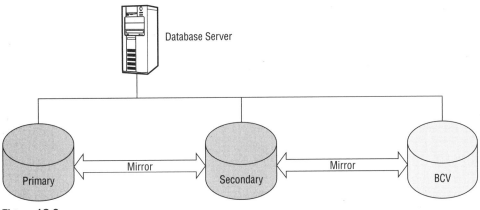

Figure 18-6

Performing Recovery

This section explains the various methods of recovery, through both Management Studio and T-SQL. You will also learn how to restore the system databases.

Restore Process

It is a DBA's task to ensure that backups are consistently taken and validated in order to restore. Each backup sequence is labeled and stored to enable quick identification to restore a database.

Instant File Initialization

Versions prior to SQL Server 2005 required file initialization by filling the files with zeros to overwrite any existing data inside the file for the following SQL Server operations: creating a database; adding files, logs, or data to an existing database; increasing the size of an existing file; and restoring a database or filegroup. As a result, for a large database, file initialization would take significant time. Beginning with SQL Server 2005, however, data files can use instant file initialization, provided that the SQL Server service account is assigned to the Windows SE_MANAGE_VOLUME_NAME permission, which can be done by assigning the account to the Perform Volume Maintenance Tasks security policy. Instant file initialization reduces the time required to create a database or perform other tasks by initializing the new file areas with zeros.

Instant file initialization works only on Windows XP and Windows 2003 and later versions. In addition, the transaction-log file cannot be instant-file initialized.

Full Database Restore

A full restore contains the complete backup image of all the data in all the files and enough of the transaction log to enable a consistent restore of committed transactions and uncommitted transactions. A full restore can be the base restore for differential and transaction-log restores to bring the database to a certain point in time. During the full restore, choose whether you want to overwrite the current database, whether the database should be left in operation mode, or whether to allow additional restores, such as differential backups or transaction logs. You also need to choose "with move" if the database files are to be moved to a different directory location or file name. Then perform the full database restore, followed by all differential and transaction-log backups. The advantage of this process is that it recovers the database in fewer steps and is online for user access. However, it is slow; you need a maintenance window to perform it.

A full differential restore image contains all extents that have been modified since the last full backup. Typically, it is smaller and faster than a full backup image, provided there is not a high turnover of modification activity. A differential restore is commonly used to augment the full restore. During the restore, the full backup is restored, the database is left in NORECOVERY mode, and the differential restore is performed.

Partial Database Restore

A partial restore image contains the primary filegroup, all the read/write filegroups, and any read-only filegroups specified. A filegroup is read-only if it was changed to read-only prior to its last backup. A partial restore of a read-only database contains only the primary filegroup. This kind of backup is typically used when a database has read-only filegroups and, more important, large read-only filegroups that can be backed up to save disk space.

A partial differential backup image contains changes in the primary filegroup and any changes to read/write filegroups. Restoring a partial differential requires a partial backup image.

Transaction-Log Restore

As mentioned previously, a mission-critical database reduces data-loss exposure by performing periodic transaction log backups. The transaction-log restore requires a full database backup, a file backup, or a filegroup backup as its base. Then you apply the differential restores and next apply all transaction-log backups in sequence, with the oldest first, to bring the database to a point in time — either by completing all the transaction-log restores or by stopping at a specific point. For example, you can restore the database to a point before a certain error by using one of the following transaction-log restore options:

❑   With Stopat: Stop the transaction restore at the specified time.

❑   With Stopatmark: Stop the transaction-log restore at the marked transaction.

❑   With Stopbeforemark: Stop the transaction-log restore before the marked transaction.

You can insert a transaction-log mark in the transaction log by using the WITH MARK option with the BEGIN TRANSACTION command. During each mark, a row is inserted into the logmarkhistory table in msdb after the commit completes. Normally, restoring to a point in time requires that you specify the exact time for the restore point. Perhaps a batch process went awry and you wish to restore the database to the point immediately prior to the beginning of the batch process. What time did the batch process begin? That is hard to determine unless you have some sort of log-reading utility. This is where logmarks are helpful.

For the first transaction in the batch process, add a logmark with a unique name for the batch. That way, if you need to restore to the beginning of the batch, you can restore to the logmark — easy.

An example of a transaction-log restore sequence might be as follows:

1. Restore the full database with NORECOVERY.

2. Restore any differential backups with NORECOVERY.

3. Restore each transaction log with NORECOVERY. You can use the STOP clause to restore the database to a point in time.

4. If you have the tail transaction log, restore it. Then set the database to RECOVERY.

After the database is recovered, no additional restores can be performed without starting over.

File/Filegroup Restore

This is also called a piecemeal restore. You first restore the primary filegroup using the PARTIAL keyword. Then, the remaining filegroups can be restored. Each filegroup, when consistent, can be brought online while the other filesgroups are begin restored. This allows the DBA to make parts of the database available more quickly, without having to wait on the entire database restore. The following is an example of restoring a database in piecemeal by filegroup, starting with the Primary filegroup:

```
RESTORE   DATABASE  AdventureWorks2008  FILEGROUP='PRIMARY'  FROM  AdventureWorks2008_
Backup
WITH PARTIAL, NORECOVERY;
RESTORE DATABASE AdventureWorks2008 FILEGROUP=' AdventureWorks20082 ' FROM
AdventureWorks2008_Backup  WITH NORECOVERY;
RESTORE LOG AdventureWorks2008 FROM AdventureWorks2008_Backup WITH NORECOVERY;
RESTORE LOG AdventureWorks2008 FROM AdventureWorks2008_Backup WITH NORECOVERY;
RESTORE LOG AdventureWorks2008 FROM AdventureWorks2008_Backup WITH NORECOVERY;
RESTORE LOG AdventureWorks2008 FROM TailLogBackup WITH RECOVERY;
```

The Filegroup AdventureWorks20083, which is read/write, is recovered next:

```
RESTORE DATABASE AdventureWorks2008 FILEGROUP=' AdventureWorks20083' FROM
AdventureWorks2008_Backup WITH NORECOVERY;
RESTORE LOG AdventureWorks2008 FROM AdventureWorks2008_Backup WITH NORECOVERY;
RESTORE LOG AdventureWorks2008 FROM AdventureWorks2008_Backup WITH NORECOVERY;
RESTORE LOG AdventureWorks2008 FROM TailLogBackup2 WITH RECOVERY;
```

The Filegroup AdventureWorks20084, which is read-only, is restored last and does not require transaction logs, as it is read-only:

```
RESTORE DATABASE AdventureWorks2008 FILEGROUP=' AdventureWorks20084 ' FROM
AdventureWorks2008_Backup WITH RECOVERY;
```

File and filegroup backups require that the recovery model is either full or bulk-logged to enable transaction-log backups, unless the database is read-only.

This example is appropriate when you place many backups in a single device. If you put each backup in its own file, then you must use the file names in the RESTORE commands.

Database Snapshot Restore

SQL Server 2005 and 2008 support database snapshots whereby a read-only, point-in-time copy of the database can be taken. The snapshot file, when taken, contains no data, because it uses the "copy on first write" technology. As the database is modified, the first time a value is modified, the old value is placed in the snapshot file. This type of Restore is not intended for restore of media failures. It is generally used when you wish to make a series of changes to the database, then revert back to the original version prior to the changes. If the changes are minimal, this can occur very quickly. A common use for this is when testing—make changes during the test, then revert to the original version. A restore from snapshot returns the database to the point in time when the snapshot was taken. There are limitations to snapshots, as well. Blobs, read-only or compressed filegroups, offline files, and multiple snapshots prevent you from being able to revert using a snapshot.

To create a database snapshot, use the following syntax:

```
CREATE DATABASE AdventureWorksDW2008_dbss9AM ON ( NAME = AdventureWorksDW2008_Data,
FILENAME =
```

'C:\Program Files\Microsoft SQL Server\MSSQL10.MSSQLSERVER\MSSQL\Data\Adventure WorksDW2008_dataTo restore from a snapshot, use this syntax:

```
USE MASTER
USE MASTER
```

RESTORE DATABASE AdventureWorksDW2008 FROM DATABASE_SNAPSHOT = 'AdventureWorksDW2008_dbss9AM';Page Restore

Beginning with SQL 2005, there has been a much-improved page-level reporting structure available. Page errors are now logged in the suspect_pages table in MSDB. Along with the ability to log page errors, the SQL team has provided the DBA with the ability to restore suspect pages. SQL 2008 Enterprise can restore pages while the database remains online and available, even the filegroup and file that contains the suspect pages. Other versions of SQL Server only allow offline restore of suspect pages.

Only data pages can be restored, which excludes allocation pages, full-text indexes, the transaction log and the database and file boot pages. Page restore also does not work with bulk-logged recovery model.

The restoration process for page restore is just like that of a file restore, except you provide the page numbers you wish to restore. The syntax is:

```
RESTORE DATABASE <dbname>
PAGE = '<file:page>, ... '
FROM <backup file or device>
WITH NORECOVERY
```

You then restore any differential, then log backups with NORECOVERY. Then you create a normal log backup and restore it:

```
BACKUP LOG <dbname> TO <filename>
RESTORE LOG <dbname> FROM <filename> WITH RECOVERY
```

You can identify suspect pages from the suspect_pages table in msdb, the sql error log, sql event traces, some DBCC commands, and Windows Management Instrumentation (WMI) provider for server events. Page restores can be a great thing–the ability to restore pages quickly without having to restore the whole database. This is especially useful when you have hardware failures like controller or disk drive intermittent failures.

History Tables Restore

The msdb database maintains restore metadata tables, which are restored as part of msdb database restore:

❑   restorefile — Contains one row for each restored file, including files restored indirectly by filegroup name

❑   restorefilegroup — Contains one row for each restored filegroup

❑   restorehistory — Contains one row for each restore operation

SQL Server Management Studio Restore

To restore a database from SQL Server 2008 Management Studio, choose the Database folder, right-click the database of your choice, and choose Tasks ➪ Restore. The Restore Database dialog, shown in Figure 18-7, exposes the restore capability.

In addition to database restore, also available from the same restore menu are files and filegroups and transaction log restores.

In the Restore Database dialog, in the Destination for Restore area, select from the following options:

❑   **To database:** Choose the name of an existing database or type the database name.

❑   **To a point in time:** For a transaction log restore, choosing a stop time for the restoration is equivalent to STOPAT in the Restore Log command. A point in time is commonly used when a database is being restored because of a user or application data modification error and you have identified the time when the error occurred. Therefore, you want to stop the restoration before the error. This option is not possible for the Simple recovery model, because the transaction log is truncated.

In the Source for Restore area of this dialog, choose between the following options:

❑   **From database:** The name of the database to restore; this information is retrieved from the backup history tables in msdb.

❑   **From device:** Choose either the backup device or the backup file name to restore from. This may be used when restoring a database onto another SQL Server 2008 instance and there is no restore data in the backup tables in msdb.

Next, select the backup sets to restore from the list at the bottom of the dialog. When selecting the restore source, it populates this field with the backup sets available for the database. It also provides an option to choose which backup sets to restore.

From the Restore Database dialog, select the Options page, and you'll be taken to the dialog shown in Figure 18-8.

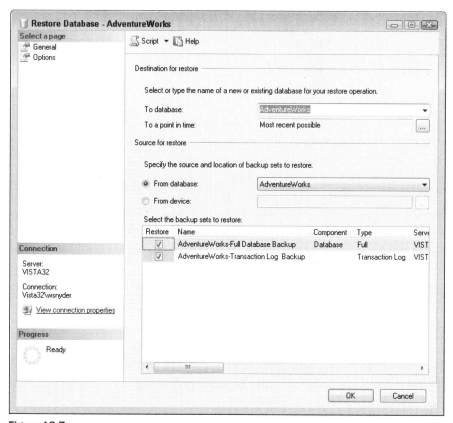

Figure 18-7

The Restore Options section of this dialog has the following options:

❑ **Overwrite the existing database:** This checkbox is used when the database you wish to restore already exists in the SQL Server instance. Checking this box this will overwrite the existing database; this is equivalent to the REPLACE option in the Restore Database command.

❑ **Preserve the replication settings:** Use this checkbox when you're restoring a publisher database; it's equivalent to the PRESERVE_REPLICATION option in the Restore Database command.

❑ **Prompt before restoring each backup:** Use this checkbox when you're swapping tapes that contain backup sets.

❑ **Restrict access to the restored database:** Use this checkbox when you need to perform additional database operations or validation before allowing users to access the database. This option limits database access to members of db_owner, dbcreator, or sysadmin and is equivalent to the RESTRICTED_USER option in the Restore Database command.

❑ **Restore the database files as:** Here you can choose to restore the database in another directory and with a different file name. For example, if a new database copy has been created in the same directory, you need to change the file name of the restored database. This is equivalent to the MOVE option in the Restore Database command. If the file names are not changed, SQL Server generates the following error:

```
Restore failed for Server 'Server1'.
(Microsoft.SqlServer.SmoExtended)System.Data.SqlClient.SqlError:
Exclusive access could not be obtained because the database is in
use.(Microsoft.SqlServer.Smo)
```

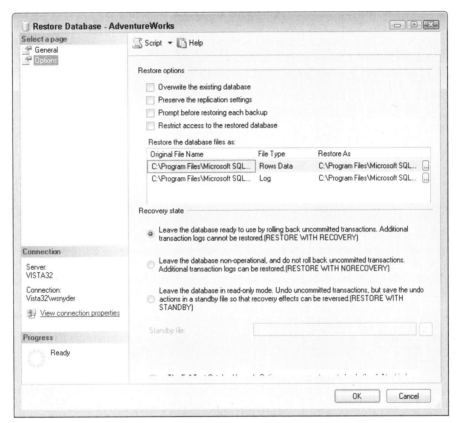

Figure 18-8

In the Recovery State section of this dialog, select one of these options:

❑ **Restore with RECOVERY:** The default setting recovers the database, which means that no more backup images can be restored and the database becomes available to users. If additional backup images need to be restored, such as a full database restore followed by several transaction logs, the recovery should be performed after the last step, because after recovery, no additional backup images can be restored without starting the restore over. This is equivalent to the WITH RECOVERY option in the Restore Database command.

❑ **Restore with NORECOVERY:** After a backup image is restored, the database is not recovered to enable additional backup images to be applied, such as a database differential or a transaction log backup. Moreover, the database is not user accessible while in NORECOVERY. This state is used on the mirror server in data mirroring and is one of the states available on the secondary server in log shipping. This is equivalent to the WITH NORECOVERY option in the Restore Database command.

❏   **Restore with STANDBY:** After a backup image has been restored, the database is left in a state in which it allows additional backup images to be restored while allowing read-only user access. In this state, in order for the database to maintain data consistency, the undo and uncommitted transactions are saved in the standby file to allow preceding backup images to commit them. Perhaps you're planning to apply additional backup images and want to validate the data before each restore. Oftentimes, this option is used on the secondary server in log shipping to allow users access for reporting. This is equivalent to the WITH STANDBY option in the Restore Database command.

T-SQL Restore Command

All the restore commands using SQL Server 2008 Management Studio and all functionality are available directly from T-SQL. For example, to conduct a simple restore of a full database backup, use this syntax:

```
RESTORE DATABASE [AdventureWorks2008] FROM  DISK ='
C:\Program
Files\Microsoft SQL Server\MSSQL10.MSSQLSERVER \MSSQL\Backup\AdventureWorks2008.bak'
```

The following is a more complex example of a database restore using a full database, differential, and then transaction-log restore, including the STOPAT option, enabling the DBA to stop the restore at a point in time before a data modification that caused an error. As a good practice, the STOPAT option has been placed in all the transaction-log backups. If the stop date is in the previous transaction-log backup, it stops there. Otherwise, if the stop date has been passed over, the restore process has to be started again.

```
--Restore the full database backup
RESTORE DATABASE AdventureWorks2008 FROM AdventureWorks2008Backup
    WITH NORECOVERY;
--Restore the differential database backup
RESTORE DATABASE AdventureWorks2008 FROM AdventureWorks2008Backup
    WITH NORECOVERY;
-- Restore the transaction logs with a STOPAT to restore to a point in time.
RESTORE LOG AdventureWorks2008
    FROM AdventureWorks2008Log1
    WITH NORECOVERY, STOPAT = 'Nov 1, 2008 12:00 AM';
RESTORE LOG AdventureWorks2008
    FROM AdventureWorks2008Log2
    WITH RECOVERY, STOPAT = 'Nov 1, 2008 12:00 AM';
```

Databases that use transparent encryption automatically have their backups encrypted with the same key. When you restore these backups, the server encryption key must also be available. No key — no access to the data. The encryption keys must be saved for as long as the backups.

Restoring System Databases

The cause of the master database failure determines the procedure to follow in order to recover it. For a failure that necessitates the installation of a new SQL Server 2008 instance, if you have a copy of the most recent master full database backup, follow these steps:

1. Install the new SQL Sever 2008 instance.

2. Start the SQL Server 2008 instance.

3. Install service packs and hotfixes.

4. Stop the SQL Server agent; if you don't, it may take the only single-user connection. Additionally, shut down any other services that may be accessing the SQL Server instance, as that may take the only connection.

5. Start the SQL Server 2008 instance in single-user mode. There are several ways to set SQL Server 2008 to single user mode: by using SQL Server Configuration Manager, executing the SQL Server binary from the command line, or, from Windows Services, locating the SQL Server service. In all cases, add the -m startup parameter to set SQL Server 2008 to single user mode, then restart. The recommended approach is to go to SQL Server Configuration Manager, under SQL Server 2008 Services, and locate the SQL Server instance. Stop that SQL service. Then, on the Advanced tab, add the -m startup parameter to the service and restart the SQL service, as shown in Figure 18-9.

6. Use SQLCMD or an administration tool to log on to the SQL Server 2008 instance with a system administrator account. Restore the master database by executing the following command:

```
RESTORE DATABASE [MASTER] FROM  DISK =
N'C:\Program
Files\Microsoft SQL Server\MSSQL10.MSSQLSERVER\MSSQL\Backup\master.bak'
```

If SQL Server will not start because the master database is corrupted and a current master backup is not available, the master database has to be rebuilt. Execute the SQL Server 2008 setup.exe to repair the system databases.

The rebuildm.exe *application, available in SQL Server 2000, has been discontinued.*

After the rebuild and SQL Server 2008 starts, if a current copy of the master database backup is available, set the SQL Server 2008 instance in single-user mode and restore it, according to the previous instructions. If a current master database backup is not available, any modifications to the master database (e.g., login security, endpoints, or linked server) will be lost and need to be redeployed.

Additionally, setup.exe creates a new msdb and model during the system database rebuild. If a current copy of model and msdb are available, restore them. If not, all modifications performed to model and msdb will need to be redeployed.

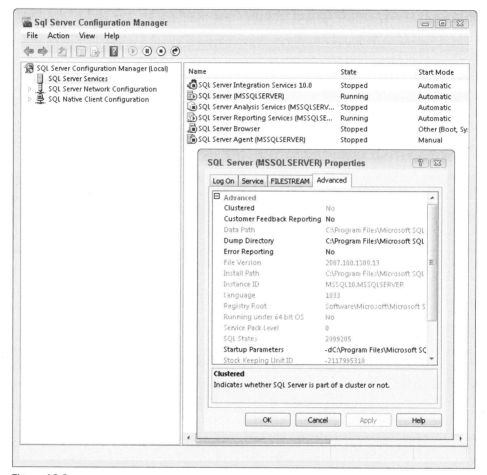

Figure 18-9

The syntax to rebuild the master database is as follows:

```
start /wait setup.exe /qn INSTANCENAME=<InstanceName> REINSTALL=SQL_Engine
```

Then attach the user databases.

If only the model or msdb databases are damaged, you can restore them from a current backup. If a backup is not available, then you have to execute Setup.exe, which recreates all the system databases. Typically, model and msdb reside in the same disk system with the master, and if a disk-array failure occurred, most likely all three would be lost. To mitigate disk failure, consider using a RAID array where master, model, and msdb reside. tempdb do not need to be restored, as it is automatically recreated by SQL Server at startup. tempdb is a critical database and is a single point of failure for the SQL Server instance; as such, it should be deployed on a fault-tolerant disk array.

Archiving Data

Archiving a large amount of data from very large tables can be challenging. For example, selecting millions of rows from a billon-row table, copying them, and then deleting them is a long-running delete process that may escalate to a table lock and reduce concurrency, which is not acceptable, unless no one will be using the table. A commonly used procedure is to periodically delete a small number of rows to improve table concurrency, as the smaller number of rows may take page locks and use an index for faster access, completing faster.

An efficient procedure to archive large amounts of data is to use a sliding time window table partitioning scheme. There are two approaches to this solution: using SQL Server 2008 data partitioning or using a partitioned view.

SQL Server 2008 Table Partitioning

SQL Server 2008 supports table partitioning, whereby a table can be carved into as many as 1,000 pieces, with each residing on its own filegroup. Each filegroup can be independently backed up.

Let's look at a partitioning example in which each partition contains one month's data. With table partitioning, a new empty partition is created when the next monthly data becomes available. Then the oldest partition can be switched out into a table and moved to an archive table monthly. The basic steps to create a table partition are as follows:

1. Create a partition function that describes how the data is to be partitioned.
2. Create a partition schema that maps the pieces to the filegroups.
3. Create one or more tables using the partition scheme.

The following is an example of creating a partition table using a monthly sliding window:

```
--Create partition function
CREATE PARTITION FUNCTION [OrderDateRangePFN](datetime)
AS RANGE RIGHT
FOR VALUES (N'2009-01-01 00:00:00', N'2009-02-01 00:00:00', N'2009-03-01 00:00:00',
N'2009-04-01 00:00:00');
--Create partition scheme
CREATE PARTITION SCHEME [OrderDatePScheme]
AS PARTITION [OrderDateRangePFN]
TO ([filegroup1], [filegroup2], [filegroup3], [filegroup4], [filegroup5]);
--Create partitioned table SalesOrderHeader
CREATE TABLE [dbo].[SalesOrderHeader](
   [SalesOrderID] [int] NULL,
   [RevisionNumber] [tinyint] NOT NULL,
   [OrderDate] [datetime] NOT NULL,
   [DueDate] [datetime] NOT NULL,
   [ShipDate] [datetime] NULL,
   [Status] [tinyint] NOT NULL
) ON [OrderDatePScheme]([OrderDate]);
```

This example places each partition on a different filegroup. Splitting and merging partitions requires data movement. You can achieve high-speed splits and merges without table locking or reducing concurrency if you place the partitions on the same filegroup. When partitions are on the same filegroup, switching out a partition or merging is only a schema change and occurs very quickly. There are several other smaller restrictions for high-speed partitioning, but the filegroup restriction is the more important.

Partitioned View

This technique has been available since earlier versions of SQL Server. It uses a partition view to group independent, identical tables together (for example, a new table for each month). Here is the procedure:

1. Create individual, identical tables with a check constraint to limit the data that can reside in each.

2. Create a view to unite all of these tables together.

3. Load the data through the partition view. SQL Server evaluates the table constraint to insert the data in the correct table.

4. Before the next date period, create a new table with the date period constraint and include it as part of the view definition. Then load the current data through the view.

5. To archive, remove the oldest table from the view definition and then archive it. Each table can be placed in its own filegroup and backed up individually.

This technique does not have the 1,000-partition limitation, but it requires more management, as each table is independent and managed.

Disaster Recovery Planning

Disaster recovery requires considerable planning. A local disaster can cause severe financial loss to the organization. To reduce this, the organization must be able to quickly execute the disaster recovery (DR) plan to bring its systems online. It requires a robust disaster recovery plan and periodic DR drills to ensure that everything will work as planned. Often, organizations have well-intended disaster recovery plans, but they have never tested them for readiness; then, in a real disaster, the plan does not go smoothly. DR planning is based on the specific organization's business requirements, but there are some general areas that need to be addressed to put any plan into action.

Use project management software, such as Microsoft Project, whereby people, resources, hardware, software, and tasks and their completion can be input to provide a systematic approach to managing the tasks, resources, and critical paths. Then develop a checklist of detailed steps for recovery.

Disaster recovery solutions with Windows failover clusters are commonly used to provide hardware redundancy within the data center site and can be configured across data centers by using a more expensive SAN solution to deploy a geographically dispersed Windows failover cluster. Moreover, log shipping and data mirroring can both be inexpensively deployed as disaster recovery solutions. Another solution is SAN replication to maintain a copy of the data in the remote location. Certain organizations have a standby disaster recovery solution available to take over all operations or, at the very least, the mission-critical operations. A few of these organizations failover to the disaster recovery site periodically to validate that their plan will work in a real disaster. Others may not have a disaster recovery plan but an agreement with another organization that offers disaster recovery.

You need hardware at the remote site, and if it is not already available, you need a plan to acquire the hardware required to bring the organization online quickly. Document the current hardware that will be needed. For computers, consider the number of CPUs and speed, hyperthreading, dual-core, 64-bit, local disk drive capacity, RAID level, and the amount of physical memory required. Preferably, try to acquire the exact hardware to minimize surprises. For the SAN or disk arrays, consider the disk space requirements, the number of LUNs required, the RAID level, and the SAN cache. For the network, acquire a similar network infrastructure to maintain the same performance. Some questions to ask include the following:

- ❏ How quickly can these computers be made available? Who will deliver or pick up the hardware?
- ❏ Will the computers be preconfigured, or will the DR team need to configure them? Who will provide the expertise, and what is the availability for that staff resource?
- ❏ Will the SAN be preconfigured with the LUNs and RAID levels, or will the DR team need to configure it? Who will provide the expertise, and what is the availability for that staff resource?
- ❏ Who will acquire the network equipment, and who will have the expertise to set it up and configure it?
- ❏ Will the DR site have Internet access — to download service packs, hotfixes, and for e-mail?

Make a detailed list of all software required, any hotfixes, and service packs. Take an inventory of how each is going to be available to the DR team. Make sure that the software is at the required version level and that licensing keys are available and valid. Determine who is responsible to make available the software and the contact information for that staff member. If the software is in a certain location, know who has the physical keys and what access they have. In this scenario, 24/7 access is required. In the event of a disaster, you need a list of staff resources to be contacted, which must be current and therefore periodically updated. Know who is responsible to maintain this list and where will it be found during a disaster. You also need to know the chain of command and who is onsite and offsite.

Who will be onsite to execute the plan? Create a detailed plan of the roles required and who will fill those roles. Ensure that there is a backup resource in case a staff resource is missing. How will the staff get to the DR site? Determine how many are needed in each role and who will be the overall project manager or lead to escalate any issues. Who will have the passwords? What logins are required to make the systems available for business?

As mentioned previously, the DR site must be accessible 24/7 and conveniently located. As larger DR deployment can take days to execute, the site should have beds for staff to take naps and easy access to food and transportation. Identify who has the key to access the remote site; if that person is not available, who is the designated replacement? Can resources remotely access the site if they must work from a remote location, and what is required to have remote access turned on? Are the backups for all the databases available at the DR site, or who is responsible to bring them there? If that staff resource is unavailable, who is the designated replacement?

To ensure that the DR plan will work during a real disaster and to reduce loss, as a best practice, periodically simulate a disaster drill and put the DR planning in action to identify any steps that were not taken into account, how quickly the organization can be expected to be online again, and areas that can be streamlined to speed the process. Most important, ensure that the plan will execute as expected, smoothly and quickly. To get the most effect from this simulated scenario, everyone should approach it as if it were a real disaster and take all actions exactly as planned.

Summary

Backup and recovery are the last defenses to recover an organization data asset when everything else fails. The backup and restore functionality must be able to guarantee that many years of customer information, buying patterns, financial data, and inventory can be recovered. SQL Server 2008 is a scalable and highly available RDBMS solution supporting some of the largest databases with the highest number of concurrent users running mission-critical applications. These key backup and restore functionalities ensure that it can support a larger database with less management.

19

SQL Server 2008 Log Shipping

Log shipping is an SQL Server technique that became available several releases ago. In log shipping, the database transaction log from one SQL Server is backed up and restored onto a secondary SQL Server, where it is often deployed for high-availability, reporting, and disaster-recovery scenarios. Beginning with SQL Server 2005, log shipping has been enhanced to continue to deliver business continuity and to be one of the high-availability solutions to maintain a warm standby. Using log shipping, the secondary server will be the warm standby used for failover. SQL Server 2008 adds the performance increase that is gained by compressing the backup and log files.

For many years, organizations have depended on log shipping for their business continuity, as it is a low-cost, efficient, and simple solution to deploy. It takes advantage of the transaction-log backup and restore functionalities of SQL Server. The two log-shipping SQL Servers can be located next to each other for high availability or across a distance for disaster recovery. The only distance requirement for the two SQL Servers is that they share connectivity that enables the secondary SQL Server to copy the transaction log and restore it. In this chapter, you will learn about log-shipping architecture and deployment scenarios. We will discuss how to configure log shipping and the various scenarios for switching roles between the primary and secondary servers. You will also learn how to troubleshoot your log-shipping setup and how to integrate log shipping with other high-availability solutions.

Log Shipping Deployment Scenarios

This section describes different scenarios in which log shipping is deployed: as a warm standby server to maintain a backup database copy in the same physical location to protect from a primary server failure; as a disaster recovery solution whereby the two servers are geographically separated in case the local area where the primary server resides suffers from a disaster; or as a reporting solution whereby the secondary server is used to satisfy the reporting needs.

Log Shipping to Create a Warm Standby Server

A common log-shipping scenario is as a warm standby server whereby the log-shipping secondary server is located close to the primary server. If the primary server goes down for planned or unplanned downtime, the secondary server takes over and maintains business continuity. Then, the DBA may choose to failback when the primary server becomes available. Sometimes, log shipping is used instead of Windows failover clustering, as it is a less expensive solution; for example, clustering requires a shared disk system that an organization may not own. Clustering also requires Windows failover-cluster compatible hardware that appears in the Hardware Compatibility List. Log shipping does not have such hardware requirements, so an organization may already own hardware that is not failover-cluster compatible that can be used for log shipping.

> *Unlike clustering, log shipping failover is always a manual process. This means you must initiate and monitor the status of the failover process. When you use Windows Clustering for SQL Server, the monitoring and failover is done automatically. When you determine that you must fail over to the secondary log shipping server, the execution of the steps can be manual or automated. If you choose automation, then you must create scripts that do part of the work on your behalf. Examples of these scripts are covered later.*

Moreover, in log shipping, the primary and secondary databases exist on separate servers. This is a shared-nothing physical environment. Windows failover clustering uses one shared disk system with a single copy of your database on the shared disk, which could become corrupted. It is simple to configure a warm standby server with log shipping because it uses the dependable transaction log backup, operating system copy file, and transaction log restore. In most warm standby scenarios, you should configure the log-shipping jobs to execute at a shorter interval to maintain the secondary server closely in sync with the primary server, to reduce the amount of time to switch roles, and to reduce data loss. Additionally, to further limit data loss, if the active portion of the primary server's transaction log is available, the secondary server would be restored to the point in time of the failed primary server.

However, in some situations, the active portion of the transaction log may not be available, or some transaction log files that were in transit may not have made it to the secondary server, causing some data loss. In a typical role-switch scenario, you would recover all in-transit transaction logs and the active portion of the transaction log before recovering the secondary server. Users would also need to be redirected, because log shipping, unlike Windows failover clustering, has no automatic user redirect.

Another difference between log shipping and clustering is that clustering is a server solution. All databases on the server are clustered. Log shipping is done per database. You can even log ship from one database to another on the same server. If you need high availability for all of the databases on a server, you can achieve it using either clustering or log shipping. If you choose log shipping, you have to set it up for each database on the server. If you want some, but not all, of the databases on a server to be highly available, log shipping would be your choice.

Log Shipping As a Disaster Recovery Solution

An organization may have a local high-availability solution, perhaps around Windows failover clustering, but then deploy log shipping to a secondary server at a remote location to protect from a power grid failure or local disaster. The challenges with this scenario are that the network bandwidth must have the capacity to support log shipping large log files to the remote location. Moreover, in the event of a disaster, there is a potential that some of the files may be in transit and may not make it to the secondary server. Even if the bandwidth supports log shipping comfortably, during a disaster the bandwidth may be constrained by other activity that will slow down the file transfers. That means the possibility of data loss. For mission-critical applications for which you want to minimize any data loss, you may need to choose another solution.

Even in the best scenario, remember that the databases are kept in sync using the transaction logs. The amount of data which might be at risk during a disaster is the data which is included in the transaction log. By comparison, database mirroring can send transactions to be sync'd as soon as the transaction commits, without waiting for a transaction log backup. Using log shipping, you may need to accept a greater amount of data loss because of a missing log file, or an inaccessible backup log folder. If the transaction log files in the backup folder or the active transaction log are not accessible, such as in a disaster where the primary server cannot be restarted because of a power grid failure, you may be able to stitch the primary server's active transaction log and transaction log files together by using a third-party transaction log analyzer in order to identify transactions that did not make it across and manually apply them. However, your availability or recovery plan should not depend on these log analyzers. The transaction log files backed up by the backup job should be archived to provide point-in-time recovery of the primary server (if, for example, a user error modifies some data that needs to be recovered). Moreover, archiving the transaction logs along with a full database backup offers another disaster recovery option when needed. To control when the transaction log files are deleted so that the OS backup program can back up these files on its own schedule, set the "Delete files older than" option to a time period great than that of the OS backup program schedule. This option is found in the Transaction Log Backup Settings. For example, if the OS backup is scheduled to run every night, set the "Delete files older than" option to at least keep the files there until the OS backup completes.

Log Shipping As a Report Database Solution

In certain scenarios, it may be feasible to use the secondary server's database for production reporting, provided that the database recovery mode is STANDBY. However, there are several inherent disadvantages to using this server for reporting. The restore process needs exclusive access to the database while restoring; if users are running reports, the restore process will fail to restore and the job will wait for the next restore interval to try again. Log shipping alerts may trigger, sending an alert that the secondary server has fallen behind. Moreover, at the time of role-switching, there may be transaction logs that have not been applied because reporting prevented it, which increases the role-switching time as these transaction logs are applied. However, log shipping can be configured to disconnect users who are in the database to restore the transaction logs, but longer-running reports may be kept from completing in that case. As an example, if you have the restore run every 10 minutes, but you have a report which takes 30 minutes complete. The report would never run to completion because log shipping would kill the connection every 10 minutes. To improve the chances that the report will run to completion, the restore job interval would have to be longer, which makes the secondary server fall further behind. Additionally, the data for the reports will not be current; and the secondary server's database schema cannot be optimized for reporting, because it is read-only. For example, if particular indices are beneficial to the report database, the indices need to be created in the primary server's database, which may suffer from having the additional indices.

For these reasons, using log shipping for reporting has several challenges and does not make a good reporting solution for some environments. For occasional reporting, provided the organization can live with these challenges, you can certainly use log shipping for reporting. A better report solution may be transactional replication, which provides concurrency, granularity, and near real-time synchronization, with the added flexibility to allow modification of the database schema.

In my opinion, the fact that log shipping must have exclusive access to the database is a big disadvantage. If you apply logs every hour, then any currently running report must be killed before the log can be applied. This kind of partial access infuriates users, and has caused me to bypass the use of log shipping for reporting purposes many times. However, if you can live with this issue, then it is an excellent solution.

Log-Shipping Architecture

The basic log-shipping architecture is shown in Figure 19-1. The architecture requires three servers: a *primary server*, a *secondary server* (also known as the *standby server*), and an optional *monitor server*.

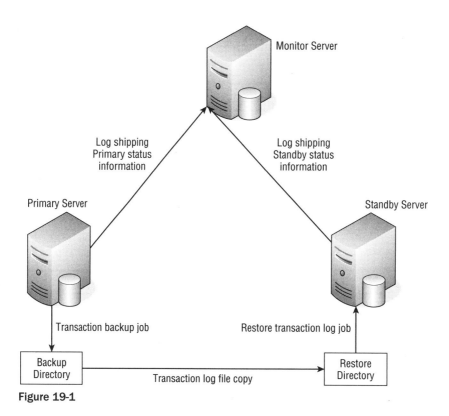

Figure 19-1

Primary Server

The primary server is the production server to which users connect and do work. It holds the SQL Server 2008 instance that needs to be protected in case of hardware failure, software error, natural disaster, or user-induced errors. In log shipping, the primary server is configured to execute a SQL Agent job to back up the transaction log to a file. For log shipping to function, the server must be using the database recovery models of either *Bulk Logged* or *Full*. (See the Database Properties using SQL Server 2008 Management Studio.)

Secondary Server

The secondary server is the backup SQL Server 2008 instance that maintains a copy of the primary server database. The secondary server uses the SQL Agent to copy the transaction-log file from the backup folder where it was placed by the primary server's transaction-log backup to restore it. The secondary server is configured with two SQL Agent jobs: one to copy the transaction-log file from the shared backup folder and the other to restore the transaction log. For log shipping to function, the secondary server must be using the database recovery models of either Bulk Logged or Full. This server should have similar performance specifications to those of the primary server, to maintain a consistent user experience during failover.

Monitor Server

Having a monitor server as part of log shipping is optional but recommended. The monitor server should be a different physical server to prevent it from becoming a single point of failure from the primary or secondary server. When the monitor server participates in log shipping, it manages the jobs that produce monitoring information, such as the last time the transaction log was backed up on the primary server, the last transaction log that was restored on the secondary server, and the time deltas between the processes. The monitor server will also send alerts to page or e-mail the operator when log-shipping thresholds are crossed. A single monitor server can monitor multiple log-shipping environments. Without a monitor server, the primary and secondary servers assume the monitoring duties.

Log Shipping Process

SQL Agent is used on the participating servers to execute the processes that implement log shipping. There are three main processes:

1. **Back up the transaction log on the primary server.** A SQL Agent job on the primary server backs up the transaction log at a user-configurable time interval to a file in a backup folder. By default, the file name is time-stamped to provide uniqueness — for example, databasename_yyyymmddhhmmss.trn. By default, the backup job is named LSBackup_databasename, and it executes an operating system command to back up the transaction log:

   ```
   "C:\Program Files\Microsoft SQL Server\100\Tools\Binn\sqllogship.exe"
   -Backup 0E5D9AA6-D054-45C9-9C6B-33301DD934E2 -server SQLServer1
   ```

2. **Copy the transaction log to the secondary server.** A SQL Agent job on the secondary server uses UNC or a shared drive to access the backup folder on the primary server to copy the transaction-log file to a local folder on the secondary server. By default, the copy job is named LSCopy_servername_databasename, and it executes an operating system command to copy the transaction-log file:

   ```
   "C:\Program Files\Microsoft SQL Server\100\Tools\Binn\sqllogship.exe"
   -Copy F2305BFA-B9E3-4B1C-885D-3069D0D11998 -server SQLServer2
   ```

3. **Restore the transaction log on secondary server**. A SQL Agent job on the secondary server restores the transaction log on the secondary server. To restore the transaction log, the database must be in either Standby or NORECOVERY mode. The default restore job name is `LSRestore_servername_databasename`, and it executes an operating system command to copy the transaction-log file:

```
"C:\Program Files\Microsoft SQL Server\100\Tools\Binn\sqllogship.exe"
-Restore F2305BFA-B9E3-4B1C-885D-3069D0D11998 -server SQLServer2
```

Most of the log-shipping objects can be found in MSDB. *For more information, see SQL Server 2008 Books Online.*

System Requirements

The servers that participate in log shipping must meet the minimum SQL Server 2008 hardware requirements; see Microsoft SQL Server 2008 Books Online. Additionally, certain hardware infrastructure requirements are necessary to deploy log shipping.

Network

The log-shipping SQL Servers must be networked such that the primary server has access to the backup folder, and the secondary server has access to copy the transaction-log files from the backup folder and into its local folder. In addition, the monitor server must be able to connect to both the primary and secondary servers. To improve copying the transaction-log file in a very active log-shipping environment, place the participating servers on their own network segment and use an additional network card dedicated to log shipping. Log shipping will function with any feasible network speed, but on a slow network the transaction-log file transfer will take longer, and the secondary server will likely be further behind the primary server.

Identical Capacity Servers

The primary and secondary servers should have identical performance capacity so that in a failover, the secondary server can take over and provide the same level of performance and user experience. Additionally, some organizations have service-level agreements (SLA) to meet. The SLA may require that you provide the same performance during failover as you would normally, requiring your secondary server to have the same capacity as the primary. Some businesses allow the secondary server to be much smaller. You should understand the specific requirements of your business, and configure the secondary server appropriately.

Storage

To mitigate the risk of storage failure becoming a single point of failure, the primary and secondary servers should not share the same disk system. Unlike a Windows failover cluster that requires a shared-disk infrastructure, log shipping has no such requirements. In a disaster recovery scenario configuration, the primary and secondary servers would be located at a distance from each other and would be unlikely to share the same disk system. Moreover, when identifying the performance specification for the disk systems, consider the log-shipping I/O activities.

Monitor Server

The monitor server should be on separate hardware from the primary or secondary servers to prevent a failure that could bring down the monitor server and lose monitoring capabilities. The monitor server incurs low activity as part of log shipping and may be deployed on another production server. Additionally, a single monitor server can monitor more than one log-shipping environment.

Software

Three SQL Server editions are supported for log shipping:

- ❑ SQL Server 2008 Enterprise Edition.
- ❑ SQL Server 2008 Standard Edition.
- ❑ SQL Server 2008 Workgroup Edition.

The log-shipping servers should have identical case-sensitivity settings, and the log-shipping databases must use either the full or bulk-logged recovery model.

Deploying Log Shipping

Before you can begin the log-shipping deployment process, you need to do some initial configuration. Then you have a choice regarding how you want to deploy: using the SQL Server 2008 Management Studio or using T-SQL scripts. Typically, a DBA uses SQL Server 2008 Management Studio to configure log shipping and then generates SQL scripts for future redeployment. We cover both procedures here.

Initial Configuration

To configure your network for log shipping, first create a backup folder that the primary server can access; share it, and ensure that it is accessible by the secondary server. For example, you could use the folder c:\primaryBackupLog, which is also shared as a UNC path: \\primaryserver\primaryBackupLog. The primary server's SQL Agent account must have read and write permission to the folder, and the secondary server's SQL Agent account or the proxy account executing the job should have read permission to this folder.

Next, create a destination folder on the secondary server, such as c:\secondaryBackupDest. The secondary server's SQL Agent account or the proxy account executing the job must have read and write permission to this folder.

The recovery model for the log-shipped database must be set to either Full or bulk_logged There are two ways to set the recovery model: with Management Studio or with a T-SQL command. Using Management Studio, open the Database Properties window and select Options. From the Recovery model drop-down, choose the recovery model, as shown in Figure 19-2.

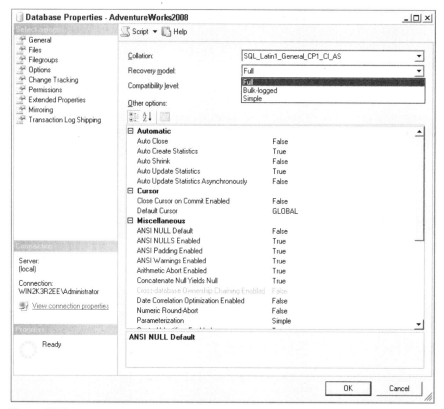

Figure 19-2

To use T-SQL, open a SQL query window and use the `ALTER DATABASE` command to change the recovery model. For example, to change the `AdventureWorks2008` database to `Full`, use this T-SQL:

```
USE master;
GO
ALTER DATABASE AdventureWorks
SET RECOVERY FULL;
GO
```

Deploying with Management Studio

To deploy log shipping with Management Studio, start by opening the database to be configured and select the database properties; then select Transaction Log Shipping. Click the checkbox that reads "Enable this as a primary database in a log shipping configuration," as shown in Figure 19-3.

Next, click the Backup Settings button. The Transaction Log Backup Settings dialog will appear, shown in Figure 19-4.

Here, you need to provide the network path to the backup folder and the local path if the folder is local to the primary server. If the folder is local to the primary server, log shipping will use the local path.

Remember that the SQL Server service and the SQL Agent account or its proxy running the backup job must have read and write permission to this folder. If possible, this folder should reside on a fault-tolerant disk system so that if a drive is lost, all the transaction log files are not lost.

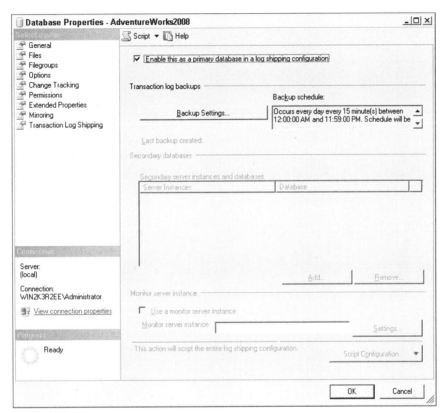

Figure 19-3

Transaction-log backup files that have been applied and are older than the value in the "Delete files older than" field are deleted to control the folder size containing older transaction backup log files. However, for an additional level of protection, if the business requires point-in-time recovery, leave the files there until the OS backup program backs them up to another storage device, provided that a full database backup is also available to apply these transaction logs. The default setting is 72 hours.

For the "Alert if no backup occurs within" field, the value you choose should be based on the business requirements. For example, the amount of data your organization can stand to lose determines the transaction backup interval setting or how critical the data is. The alert time also depends on the transaction backup interval setting. For example, if the business requires a highly available secondary server whereby the transaction log is backed up every couple of minutes, this setting should be configured to send an alert if the job fails to run within that interval. The default setting is one hour.

Click the Schedule button to display the Job Schedule Properties page and set up a schedule for the transaction-log backup job. The important setting is the Occurs Every field, which defaults to 15 minutes. This setting can be configured to once every minute for higher availability. However, the time interval should be appropriately set to allow the previous transaction-log backup job to complete. This value helps determine the degree to which the primary and secondary servers are in sync. When you're done here, click OK on the Job Schedule Properties page; then click OK in the Transaction Log Backup Settings dialog to return to the Database Properties page for Transaction Log Shipping.

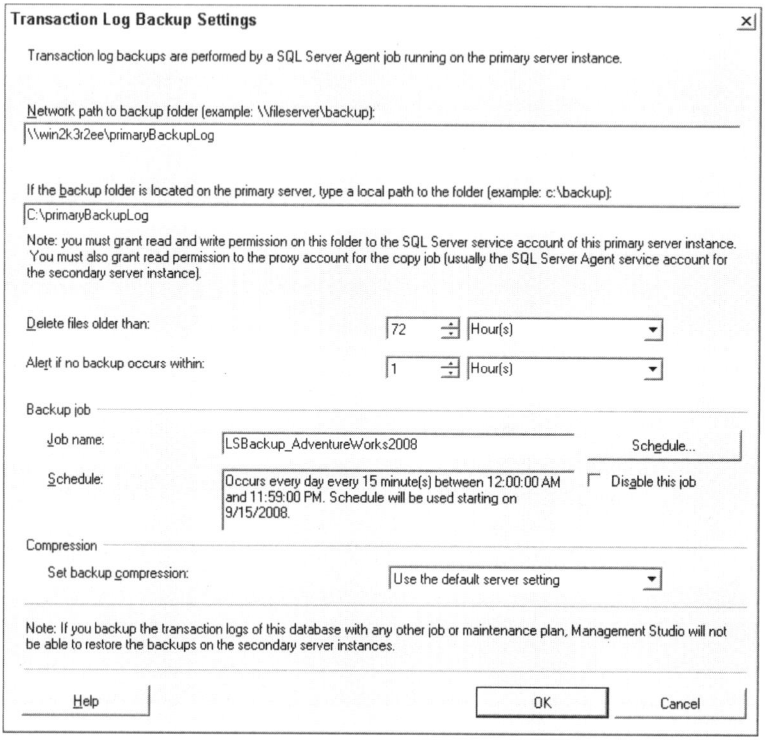

Transaction Log Backup Settings

Transaction log backups are performed by a SQL Server Agent job running on the primary server instance.

Network path to backup folder (example: \\fileserver\backup):

`\\win2k3r2ee\primaryBackupLog`

If the backup folder is located on the primary server, type a local path to the folder (example: c:\backup):

`C:\primaryBackupLog`

Note: you must grant read and write permission on this folder to the SQL Server service account of this primary server instance. You must also grant read permission to the proxy account for the copy job (usually the SQL Server Agent service account for the secondary server instance).

Delete files older than: `72` Hour(s)

Alert if no backup occurs within: `1` Hour(s)

Backup job

Job name: `LSBackup_AdventureWorks2008`   Schedule...

Schedule: `Occurs every day every 15 minute(s) between 12:00:00 AM and 11:59:00 PM. Schedule will be used starting on 9/15/2008.`   ☐ Disable this job

Compression

Set backup compression: `Use the default server setting`

Note: If you backup the transaction logs of this database with any other job or maintenance plan, Management Studio will not be able to restore the backups on the secondary server instances.

Help   OK   Cancel

Figure 19-4

Click Add to display the Secondary Database Settings dialog and set up a secondary (standby) server, as shown in Figure 19-5.

Here, click Connect and choose the Secondary Server instance. Then choose an existing database or a new database name. On the Initialize Secondary Database tab, there are three options to choose from for the secondary database. They answer the question "Do you want the Management Studio to restore a backup into the secondary database?

❑ **Yes, generate a full backup of the primary database and restore it into the secondary database (and create the secondary database if it does not exist):** The Restore Options setting enables you to set the database folder locations for the data and the log files. If this is not set, the default database locations are used.

❑ **Yes, restore an existing backup of the primary database into the secondary database (and create the secondary database if it does not exist):** The Restore Options setting enables you to set database folder locations for the data and the log files. You also specify the network location of the backup file you wish to restore.

❑ **No, the secondary database is initialized:** The option means that the database has already been created. The transaction logs preceding the database restore must be available to enable log shipping to work. For example, the log sequence number (LSN) of the primary server and the secondary server databases must match. Also, the secondary database must be in either NORECOVERY or STANDBY mode to allow additional transaction-log files to be applied.

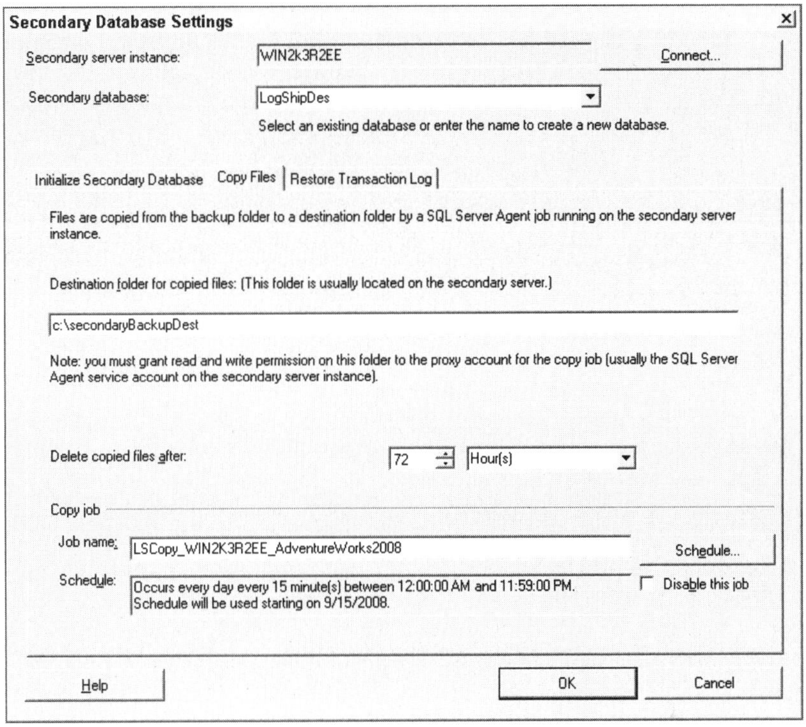

Figure 19-5

If you have Management Studio restore the secondary database from the primary backup, the database file path and name created will be the same as the primary database. Management Studio provides you the opportunity to specify path names in the dialog box by clicking on the Restore Options button. Make sure you use the Restore Options button to provide the data and log file names and paths for the secondary database. You cannot change the file names however. Management Studio will only handle the simple cases. For the example in this book I had both the primary and secondary database on the same server. I created the secondary database LogShipDest with the same file names as those for the AdventureWorks2008 database, but placed them in a different directory. I then used the Restore Options button to name the file paths for the LogShipdest database.

On the Copy Files tab, choose the Destination folder for the copied files directory (e.g., c:\secondaryBackupDest). The SQL Agent account or the proxy executing the copy job must have read and write permissions to this folder. The "Delete copied files after" option controls the folder size after the transaction log is restored on the secondary server's database. Any files older than the specified time are deleted. The default is 72 hours.

Click the Schedule button to set up a schedule for the transaction-log-file copy job. The important setting is the Occurs Every field, which defaults to 15 minutes. Click OK when you're done to return to the Secondary Database Settings page.

Click the Restore Transaction Log tab. You have two options for the "On Database state when restoring backups" field:

- ❏ **No recovery mode:** The secondary database is left in NORECOVERY mode, which allows the server to restore additional transactional-log backups but doesn't allow user access.

- ❏ **Standby mode:** The secondary database allows read-only operations to be performed in the database, such as reporting. However, as mentioned previously, the restore process needs exclusive access to the secondary database; if users are accessing the database, the restore process cannot complete.

For the "Delay restoring backups at least" setting, the default is 0 minutes. Typically, you would change this setting if your organization wants to keep the secondary database around in case of a primary database's data corruption. This delay may prevent the secondary database from restoring the corrupted transaction-log file.

The "Alert if no restore occurs within" setting defaults to 45 minutes and should be set to the tolerance level of the business. An alert can be a symptom of a serious error on the secondary database that prevents it from accepting additional transaction-log restores. Look in the history of the restore job; the default name is LSRestore_ServerName_PrimaryDatabaseName and is found under SQL Agent jobs on the secondary server. Additionally, look in the Windows Event Viewer for any additional information. You can also copy and paste the restore job command into a SQL command window, which provides additional error information to help diagnose the problem.

Click OK on the Secondary Database Settings page when you're done. To add another secondary server instance, click Add and follow the same steps to add another secondary server.

To add a monitor server, from the Transaction Log Shipping page of the primary database properties, click "Use a monitor server instance." Then click Settings. A separate monitor instance from either the primary or secondary server is recommended so that a failure of the primary or secondary server won't bring down the monitor server.

On the Log Shipping Monitor Settings page, click Connect and then choose a monitor server instance for this log-shipping environment. The account must have sysadmin role permissions on the secondary server. In the "By impersonating the proxy account of the job or Using the following SQL Server login" field, choose how the backup, copy, and restore jobs connect to this server instance to update MSDB job history information. For integrated security, the jobs should connect by impersonating the proxy account of the SQL Server Agent running the jobs or by SQL Server login.

The Delete History After field controls the amount of history data held in MSDB; the default is 96 hours. How long you should hold history depends on your business-retention requirements and your available disk space. The default value is fine for most deployments unless you plan to perform data analysis over time; then you should change the default.

When you're done, click OK on the Log Shipping Monitor Settings page. Then click OK on the Database Properties to finish setting up the Log Shipping Configuration.

Deploying with T-SQL Commands

Another deployment option is to use the actual T-SQL commands to configure log shipping. Even if you choose to use the SQL Server Management Studio to configure log shipping, saving the generated command script enables you to quickly reconfigure the server to expedite a disaster recovery scenario while avoiding any user-induced errors. The following T-SQL commands are equivalent to the steps you took in SQL Server Management Studio.

On the primary server, execute the following stored procedures in the MSDB:

- ❑ `master.dbo.sp_add_log_shipping_primary_database`: Configures the primary database for a log-shipping configuration; this configures the log-shipping backup job.
- ❑ `msdb.dbo.sp_add_schedule`: Creates a schedule for the log-shipping configuration.
- ❑ `msdb.dbo.sp_attach_schedule`: Links the log-shipping job to the schedule.
- ❑ `msdb.dbo.sp_update_job`: Enables the transaction-log backup job.
- ❑ `master.dbo.sp_add_log_shipping_alert_job`: Creates the alert job and adds the job ID in the `log_shipping_monitor_alert` table. This stored procedure enables the alert notifications.

On the secondary server, execute the following stored procedures:

- ❑ `master.dbo.sp_add_log_shipping_secondary_primary`: Sets up the primary information, adds local and remote monitor links, and creates copy and restore jobs on the secondary server for the specified primary database.
- ❑ `msdb.dbo.sp_add_schedule`: Sets the schedule for the copy job.
- ❑ `msdb.dbo.sp_attach_schedule`: Links the copy job to the schedule.
- ❑ `msdb.dbo.sp_add_schedule`: Sets the schedule for the restore job.
- ❑ `msdb.dbo.sp_attach_schedule`: Links the restore job to the schedule.
- ❑ `master.dbo.sp_add_log_shipping_secondary_database`: Sets up secondary databases for log shipping.
- ❑ `msdb.dbo.sp_update_job`: Enables the copy job.
- ❑ `msdb.dbo.sp_update_job`: Enables the transaction-log restore job.

Back on the primary server, execute this stored procedure in the MSDB:

- ❑ `master.dbo.sp_add_log_shipping_primary_secondary`: Adds an entry for a secondary database on the primary server.

Monitoring and Troubleshooting

Log shipping has monitoring capabilities to identify the progress of the backup, copy, and restore jobs. For example, a job that has not made any progress is likely an indication that something is wrong and needs further analysis. If one of the jobs has failed, you can go to the SQL Agent job history and the Windows Event Viewer to identify the error message and correct it. Monitoring also helps to determine whether the backup, copy, or restore jobs are out of sync with the secondary server.

There are two approaches to monitoring the log-shipping process: using the Transaction Log Shipping Status report or executing the `master.dbo.sp_help_log_shipping_monitor` stored procedure. Either method can help you determine whether the secondary server is out of sync with the primary server, and the time delta between the two. You can also determine which jobs are not making any progress and the last transaction-log backup, copy and, restore file name processed on the secondary server.

Log shipping also alerts jobs that check if a preset threshold has been exceeded by executing the `sys.sp_check_log_shipping_monitor_alert` stored procedure. If the threshold has been exceeded, the stored procedure raises an alert. You can choose to modify the log-shipping alert jobs to capture the alert and notify you using SQL Agent.

If a monitor server is deployed as part of log shipping, there will be one alert on the monitor server that reports on the transaction-log backup, copy file, and restore transaction log. If not, the primary server manages the alert job for the transaction-log backup, and the secondary server manages the alert job for the copy file and restore transaction log. If the monitoring server is present, the primary and secondary servers will not deploy alert jobs.

The following is an example error that results if the transaction-log backup process has exceeded the preset threshold of 30 minutes:

```
Executed as user: NT AUTHORITY\SYSTEM. The log shipping primary database
SQLServer1.AdventureWorks2008 has backup threshold of 30 minutes and has not
performed a backup log operation for 60 minutes. Check agent log and log shipping
monitor information. [SQLSTATE 42000](Error 14420). This step failed.
```

The next example shows an error that results if the restore transaction-log process has exceeded the preset threshold of 30 minutes:

```
Executed as user: NT AUTHORITY\SYSTEM. The log shipping secondary database
SQLServer2.AdventureWorks2008 has restore threshold of 30 minutes and is out of
sync. No restore was performed for 60 minutes. Restored latency is 15 minutes. Check
agent log and log shipping monitor information. [SQLSTATE 42000](Error 14421).
The step failed.
```

As an example, you can set up an alert so that when error 14420 or 14221 is raised, SQL Agent sends an alert to the operator.

Monitoring with Management Studio

The Transaction Log Shipping Status report displays monitoring information from Management Studio. The report executes the `sp_help_log_shipping_monitor` stored procedure. When executed on the primary server, it reports on the transaction-log backup details; when executed on the secondary server, it reports on the copy and transaction-log restore details. When the monitor server is configured, the report executed from the monitor server produces a consolidated report of the transaction-log backup, copy, and transaction-log restore details in one report. To access the Transaction Log Shipping Status report:

1. Connect to the primary, secondary, or monitor server. The monitor server is the most useful option because it has the consolidated log-shipping detail data.
2. If the Object Explorer is not visible, select View ➪ Object Explorer.
3. Right-click the server node in the Object Explorer and select Reports ➪ Standard Reports ➪ Transaction Log Shipping Status.

Figure 19-6 shows an example of a Transaction Log Shipping Status report executed from the monitor server, showing the details for all log-shipping activities with alerts.

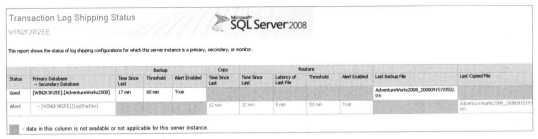

Figure 19-6

Monitoring with Stored Procedures

Executing the `sp_help_log_shipping_monitor` stored procedure in the `master` database from a SQL query window will produce log-shipping status details, similar to the Transaction Log Shipping Status report. If you execute it from the primary server, it returns detailed information on the transaction-log backup job. If you execute it from the secondary server, it returns information on the copy and transaction-log restore jobs. If it is executed from the monitor server, it returns a consolidated detail result of the transaction-log backup, copy, and transaction-log restore, as the monitor server is visible to all log-shipping processes.

For additional log-shipping operational and troubleshooting detail information, the log-shipping tables can be queried using the log-shipping stored procedures found in the MSDB database. For more information, see SQL Server 2008 Books Online.

Troubleshooting Approach

As mentioned previously, log shipping consists of three basic operations: backing up the transaction log, copying the file, and restoring the transaction log. Troubleshooting this process is simply a matter of identifying which operation is not functioning. You can use the log-shipping monitoring capabilities to identify the problem. For example, if the restore transaction-log file is showing that no new files have been restored in the last 60 minutes, you need to look at the secondary server first.

Look at the log-shipping job history under the SQL Agent and the Windows Event Viewer to determine the actual error message. For example, if the copy file job is failing, it may be that the network is down. If the restore transaction-log job is failing, it may be that the server is unavailable or that users are using the database if the database is in standby mode.

Moreover, be aware that changing the database recovery model to `Simple` will break log shipping because the transaction log is truncated instead of backed up. At that point, you would need to reconfigure log shipping. If you have saved the log-shipping configuration scripts, the reconfiguration should be fairly simple. Additionally, there should not be any other transaction-log backup operation outside of log shipping, because that will break log shipping, as the log chain will not match on the secondary server.

Managing Changing Roles

For business continuity, a high-availability solution must allow smooth role-switching between the current primary and secondary servers. To accomplish this goal, log shipping requires that certain dependencies are available on the secondary server, because the scope of log shipping is at the database level. Any object outside of the log-shipped database will not be maintained by log shipping. For example, SQL Server logins are contained in the master database, and SQL jobs are contained in msdb. Therefore, these dependencies and others need to be systematically maintained by other procedures to enable users to connect to the secondary server after it becomes the new primary server. Furthermore, a process needs to be developed to redirect the application to the new primary server.

Synchronizing Dependencies

Log shipping applies changes that occur inside the log-shipping database but it does not maintain any outside dependencies. Moreover, log shipping cannot be used to ship system databases. Newly added logins, new database users, jobs, and other dependencies that live in other databases are not synchronized by log shipping. In a failover scenario, when users attempt to log in to the secondary server's database, they will not have a login there. Moreover, any jobs configured on the primary server will not be present either; and if the primary server uses linked servers to access a remote SQL Server, then the database operations would fail because they would not be able to find the linked server. Therefore, you need to identify the outside dependencies that the log-shipping database uses, and develop a plan to make these resources available during the failover. The following sections describe common log-shipping dependencies and their solutions.

Login and Database Users

Because SQL Server logins and new database users are created on the primary server and its database, you need to develop a process to synchronize these users with the secondary server and database to prevent login-access issues in a failover scenario. This synchronization process works best if you set it up as a SQL job that runs at certain scheduled intervals. In a planned failover, you should run these SQL jobs before failover to update the secondary server with the current access information. Here are the steps:

1. To develop an Integration Services (SSIS) package to Transfer logins, open SQL Server Business Intelligence Development Studio and Start a new Integration Services project.

2. In the Solution Explorer, name the project SSIS Transfer Logins, and rename the SSIS Package to Transfer Logins.

3. Click on the Toolbox and drag the Transfer Logins Task into the package.

4. Right-click the Transfer Logins Task and choose Edit.

5. Click Logins. You'll see the dialog shown in Figure 19-7.

6. For SourceConnection, enter a new connection to the primary server.

7. For DestinationConnection, enter a new connection for the secondary server.

8. For LoginsToTransfer, choose AllLoginsFromSelectedDatabases.

9. For `DatabasesList`, choose the log-shipping database.

10. In the Options section, in the `IfObjectExists` entry, choose what to do if the login exists, such as `FailTask`, `Override`, or `Skip`. If the secondary server is hosting other databases, you may encounter duplicate logins.

11. Save the package, and choose Build ➪ Build SSIS Transfer Logins to compile the package.

12. From Microsoft SQL Server 2008 Management Studio, connect to the Integration Services of the primary server.

13. Under Stored Packages, choose MSDB, right-click, and choose Import Package.

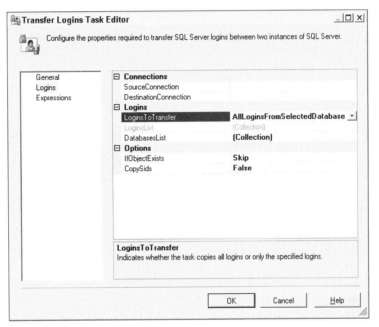

Figure 19-7

The next step is to create a new SQL Agent job on the primary server and rename it "Sync Secondary Server Access Information." This job will synchronize the logins from the primary server to the secondary servers and execute the new SSIS Transfer Logins package. You will use Bulk Copy Program (BCP) to copy the logins:

1. Create a step named BCP Syslogins with these characteristics:

   ❑ **Type:** Operating system.

   ❑ **Run As:** SQL Agent Service (the account needs sysadmin permission to execute this command, and needs read/write permission on the folder from which it copies the file).

   ❑ **Command:** BCP Master.sys.syslogins out c:\login1\syslogins.dat /N /S <Server_Name> -T.

2. Create a step named Copy Syslogins with these characteristics:

- ❑ **Type:** Operating system.
- ❑ **Run As:** SQL Agent Service (the account needs read access to the source folder and read/write access to the destination folder).
- ❑ **Command:** `COPY c:\login1\syslogins.dat \\SecondaryServer\login2`.

3. Create a step named Transfer Logins Task with these characteristics:

- ❑ **Type:** Operating system.
- ❑ **Run As:** SQL Agent Service (the account needs sysadmin permission to execute this command).
- ❑ **Command:** `DTEXEC /sq <Package_Name> /Ser <Server_Name>`.

Next, create a new SQL Agent job on the secondary server called "Resolve Logins Job." This job resolves the logins on the secondary server once the secondary database has been recovered. The SQL Server Agent service account or a proxy account must have the sysadmin role to run this job.

4. Create a step named Resolve Logins with these characteristics:

- ❑ **Type:** Transact-SQL script (T-SQL)
- ❑ **Command:** `EXEC sp_resolve_logins @dest_db = '<Database_Name>', @dest_path = 'c:\login2\', @filename = 'syslogins.dat';`

If you intend to use this method of tracking logins, you should probably run this task every night. Otherwise, a serious primary server failure could still leave you in trouble.

SQL Agent Jobs

The Integration Services Transfer Jobs Task can be used to synchronize jobs from the primary server to the secondary server. Create a package using SQL Server Business Intelligence Studio, and choose the Transfer Jobs Task. Provide the connection information and the jobs to transfer. Then compile and import the package into SQL Server 2008 or execute it as an SSIS file system. However, it is better to develop a SQL Agent job to periodically synchronize the secondary server.

Other Database Dependencies

Make a list of all dependencies on which the log-shipping database depends. These can be distributed queries/linked servers, encrypted data, certificates, user-defined error messages, event notifications and WMI events, extended stored procedures, server configuration, full-text engine, permissions on objects, replication settings, Service Broker applications, startup procedures, triggers, CLR procedures, and database mail. Develop a plan to synchronize these to the secondary server.

Switching Roles from the Primary to Secondary Servers

At some point the primary server will die. The secondary server will then assume the role of the primary server. This is called *role switching*. There are two potential types of role switches: planned failover and unplanned failover. A planned failover is most likely when the DBA needs to perform some type of maintenance, usually scheduled at a time of low business activity or during a maintenance window — for example, switching roles to apply a service pack on the primary server. An unplanned failover is when the DBA switches roles for business continuity because the primary server becomes unavailable.

Planned Failover

For a planned failover, find a time when the primary server is less active. It is likely that the secondary server will not have restored all of the transaction logs from the primary server, and transaction logs will be in the process of being copied across by the SQL Agent job that the restore SQL Agent job has not completed. Additionally, the active transaction log may contain records that have not been backed up. To completely synchronize the secondary server, the active transaction log must be restored on the secondary server. The steps to do that are as follows:

1. Stop and disable the primary server transaction log backup job.

2. Manually copy all transaction-log backups that have not been copied from the primary server backup folder to the secondary server folder. Then restore each transaction log in sequence to the secondary server. A different option is to execute the log-shipping copy and restore jobs to restore the remainder of the transaction logs. Then use the log-shipping monitoring tool or report to verify that the entire set of transaction-log backups has been copied and restored on the secondary server.

3. Stop and disable the secondary server's copy and restore jobs.

4. Execute the Sync Secondary Server Access Information job and then disable it.

5. Back up the active transaction log from the primary to the secondary server with `NORECOVERY`:

   ```
   USE MASTER;
   BACKUP LOG <Database_Name> TO DISK =
   'C:\primaryBackupLog\<Database_Name>.trn'
   WITH NORECOVERY;
   ```

   This accomplishes two goals:

   ❑ It backs up the active transaction log from the primary server and restores it to the secondary server to synchronize the secondary database.

   ❑ It changes the old primary server database to `NORECOVERY` mode to allow transaction logs from the new primary server to be applied without initializing the database by a restore, as the log chain would not have been broken.

6. Copy the backup files to the secondary server. On the secondary server, restore the unapplied active transaction log(s) and then recover the database:

   ```
   RESTORE LOG <Database_Name>
   FROM DISK ='c:\secondaryBackupDest\Database_name.trn'WITH RECOVERY
   ```

7. If the active transaction log is not accessible, the database can be recovered without it:

   ```
   RESTORE DATABASE <Database_Name>  WITH RECOVERY;
   ```

8. On the new primary server, execute the Resolve Logins job to synchronize the logins. The secondary server's database becomes the primary server's database and will start to accept data modifications.

9. Redirect all applications to the new primary server.

10. Configure log shipping from the new primary server to the secondary server. The secondary server (the former primary server) is already in NORECOVERY mode. During log-shipping configuration, in the Secondary Database Settings dialog box, choose "No, the secondary database is initialized."

11. When you finish configuring log shipping, the new primary server will be executing the transaction-log backup job, and the secondary server will be copying and restoring the transaction-log files. Set up and enable all SQL jobs that were synchronizing from the old primary server (e.g., to synchronize the logins and database users to the old primary server).

Unplanned Role Change

If the primary server is unavailable, some data loss is probable. For example, the active transaction log may not be accessible, or the last transaction-log backup may not be reachable. Therefore, you have to verify that the last copy and restore transaction logs have been restored by using the log-shipping monitoring and reporting functions. If the active transaction-log backup is accessible, it should be restored to bring the secondary server in synchronization with the primary server up to the point of failure. Then restore the secondary database with RECOVERY.

After assessing the damage and fixing the old primary server, you will most likely need to reconfigure log-shipping configuration because the active transaction log may not have been accessible, or the log chain may have been broken. When you configure log shipping, in the Secondary Database Settings dialog, choose either to restore from a previous database backup or to generate a new database backup to restore. You may choose to switch roles to promote the original primary server.

Switching Between Primary and Secondary Roles

After performing the steps to switch the primary and secondary roles in a planned role change whereby the Log Shipping jobs have been deployed to both primary and secondary servers, you can switch between primary and secondary servers by following these steps:

1. Stop and disable the primary server's transaction-log backup job.

2. Verify that all the transaction-log backups have been copied and restored, either manually or by executing the SQL jobs to do that.

3. Execute the Sync Logins job.

4. Stop and disable the transaction-log copy and restore jobs on the secondary server.

5. Back up the active transaction log on the primary server with NORECOVERY.

6. Restore the active transaction-log backup on the secondary server.

7. Restore the secondary server's database with RECOVERY.

8. Execute the Resolve Logins job.

9. Enable the transaction-log backup on the new primary server to log-ship to the secondary server.

10. Enable the secondary server transaction-log copy and restore jobs.

11. Enable synchronization of the logins and database users.

12. Enable any other SQL jobs.

Redirecting Clients to Connect to the Secondary Server

Log shipping does not provide any client-redirect capability. After switching roles, the client connections need to be redirected to the secondary server with minimal disruptions to users. The approach you choose may depend on the infrastructure and who controls it. Additionally, the number of clients that need to be redirected, the required availability of the application, such as a service level agreement (SLA), and the application activity may all play a factor in the decision. At minimum, users will experience a brief interruption as the client applications are redirected. The following sections discuss a few common approaches to redirecting client connections to the secondary server.

Application Coding

The application can be developed as failover aware with the capability to connect to the secondary server either with automatic retry or by manually changing the server name. The application logic would connect to the primary server first, but if it is unavailable, and after the retry logic has run unsuccessfully, the application can attempt to connect to the secondary server after it has been promoted to a primary server. After the secondary database has been recovered, however, it may not necessarily be ready to serve user requests. For example, you may need to run several tasks or jobs first, such as running the Resolve Logins task.

After database recovery, the database may need to be put into single-user mode to prevent other users from connecting while you perform tasks or jobs. Therefore, the application logic must be able to handle this situation where the primary server is no longer available and the secondary server is not yet accessible. It would be nice for applications to provide an option to connect to the primary or secondary server. If this were available then you could simply inform users which server to use.

Network Load Balancing

Use a network load balancing solution, either Windows Network Load Balancing (NLB) or a hardware solution whereby the application connects using the load balancing network name or IP address, and the load balancing solution directs the application to the database server. Therefore, in a failover scenario, the application continues to connect to the network load balancing network name or IP address, while the load balancer is updated manually or by script with the new primary server network name and IP address. Then clients are redirected. NLB is included with certain versions of Microsoft Windows. Configuration is straightforward, and it acts as the cross-reference to direct applications to the current primary server.

Domain Name Service (DNS)

DNS provides name-to-IP address resolution and can be used to redirect clients to the new primary server. If you have access to the DNS server, you can modify the IP address to redirect client applications after a failover, either by script or by using the Windows DNS management tool. DNS acts as a cross-reference for the client applications, because they will continue to connect to the same name, but the DNS modification will redirect the database request to the new primary server.

SQL Client Aliasing

This method may be less favorable if many client applications connect directly to the database server, because the alias would have to be created at each client computer, which may not be feasible. It is more feasible if the client applications connect to a Web or application server that then connects to the database server. Then the SQL client alias would have to be applied on the Web or application server, and all the clients would be redirected to the new primary server. To configure aliasing, go to the SQL Server Configuration Manager, under the SQL Native Client Configuration.

Database Backup Plan

A full database backup copies all the data and the transaction log to a backup device, which is usually a tape or disk drive. It is used in case of an unrecoverable failure so that the database can be restored to that point in time. A full database restore is also required as a starting point for differential or transaction-log restores. The backup should be stored offsite so that the database is not lost in the event of a disaster.

A differential database backup copies all modified extents in the database since the last full database backup. An *extent* is a unit of space allocation that consists of eight database pages that SQL Server uses to allocate space for database objects. Differential database backups are smaller than the full database backup, except in certain scenarios where the database is very active and every extent is modified since the last full backup. To restore from a differential database backup, a full database backup is required prior to the differential backup.

Full or differential database backup operations will not break log shipping, provided no transaction-log operations are performed that change it. Note several considerations with backup operations using log shipping, however:

❑ The database backup process and transaction-log backup cannot be run concurrently. Therefore, in a large, active database for which the database backup can take some time, the transaction log may quickly grow, causing the secondary server to become out of sync, as it is not receiving the transaction-log restores in the same timely manner until the database backup completes.

❑ Another transaction-log backup cannot be performed in addition to log shipping, because that breaks the log chain for the log-shipping process. SQL Server will not prevent an operator from creating additional transaction-log backup jobs on a log-shipping database.

❑ A transaction-log backup that truncates the transaction log will break the log chain, and log shipping will stop functioning.

❑ If the database is changed to the `simple` recovery model, the transaction log will be truncated by SQL Server and log shipping will stop functioning.

Integrating Log Shipping with Other High-Availability Solutions

Log shipping can be deployed along with other Microsoft high-availability solutions (e.g., in a Windows failover cluster, where it maintains a remote disaster recovery site if the local Windows failover cluster becomes unavailable). Moreover, it can be deployed with data mirroring to maintain a remote site if the data-mirroring pair becomes unavailable. Log shipping can also be deployed with replication to maintain a highly available replication publisher.

SQL Server 2008 Data Mirroring

Log shipping can be integrated with a SQL Server 2008 data mirroring solution. For example, an organization may deploy local data mirroring and log shipping from the principal server to a remote location. This would be applicable because data mirroring cannot have more than two partners; therefore, if an organization wants to protect its data investment by using local data mirroring for high availability but requires a business continuity plan for disaster recovery, it can deploy log shipping from the primary server to a remote secondary server. However, during a data-mirroring role switch, log shipping will not automatically switch roles, and manual steps must be taken to enable the former mirror, which is now the principal, to start to log ship its transaction log to the secondary server by deploying log shipping from the new principal server.

Windows Failover Clustering

Log shipping can be deployed to ship a database from inside a Windows failover SQL cluster to a remote location for disaster recovery. For example, in a local disaster whereby the Windows failover cluster is not available, log shipping will offer business continuity at the remote location. Unless an organization is deploying a geographically dispersed Windows failover cluster, the cluster nodes are located near each other and can both be down in a local disaster. In a cluster environment, the backup folder and BCP folder should be set up as a cluster resource and should be in the same cluster group with the SQL Server that contains the log-shipping database. That way, in a cluster-failover scenario, the backup folder will failover with the log-shipping SQL Server to be accessible by the other Windows failover cluster node. Additionally, any configuration and data files in that Windows failover cluster that the other cluster node needs to access should be set up as a cluster resource included in the log-shipping SQL Server cluster group.

For example, if you choose to execute the SSIS Transfer Logins Task package from a file instead of storing it in SQL Server, that folder should be included as a cluster resource to make it available to all cluster nodes. A folder can be set up as a cluster resource by first creating it. Then, using the cluster administrator, create a new resource and choose Shared Folder. Make sure that it is placed in the same group with the SQL Server that contains the log-shipping database. Inside the Windows failover cluster, SQL Server can be made to depend on the folder. For example, if the folder is not yet online, SQL Server will wait for that resource. The decision to make something a dependency is based on whether the resource must be available before SQL Server starts. For example, if the backup folder for the transaction-log files is not available, should SQL Server wait? Probably not, because a database that is up and serving users is more important than the transaction-log backup.

SQL Server 2008 Replication

In a replication topology where the SQL Server 2008 publisher is the data consolidator, it is a single point of failure. All of the subscribers connect to the publisher to receive data updates. If the publisher fails, then replication stops until the publisher can be brought online again. Log shipping has been used as a high-availability solution to protect the publisher from becoming a single point of failure. In this configuration, the primary server is the publisher, which log ships its transaction log to a secondary server. In addition, in order for replication to continue to work after the role switch, the primary and secondary server configurations must be identical. For transactional replication, to prevent the subscribers from having data that has not been shipped to the secondary server, the primary server should be configured with backup, whereby a transaction is not replicated to the subscribers until a transaction-log backup has been performed.

This does introduce a latency penalty whereby the subscribers are not quite real time, as replication needs to wait for log shipping. This latency can be reduced by decreasing the interval to perform the transaction-log backup. Without sync with backup, there is a possibility that the subscriber's data may not match with the publisher during a log-shipping role switch and data loss may occur. In merge replication, after the role switch, the merge publisher may be able to synchronize any changes lost during the role switch by merge replicating with each subscriber. A more common high-availability solution to prevent a single point of failure for the publisher is to configure a Windows failover cluster so that in case of a failure, replication fails over to the other cluster node. Log shipping is supported by transactional and merge replication.

Removing Log Shipping

Before deleting the log-shipping database, remove log shipping from it. When you remove log shipping, all schedules, jobs, history, and error information are deleted. Recall that there are two ways to remove log shipping: with Management Studio and with T-SQL. You may want to script the log-shipping configuration before deleting to quickly redeploy log shipping in the future.

Removing Log Shipping with Management Studio

To use Management Studio to remove log shipping, follow these steps:

1. Choose the primary database properties.

2. Under Select a Page, choose Transaction Log Shipping.

3. Clear the checkbox marked "Enable this as a primary database in a log shipping configuration," and click OK.

4. You can also choose to remove a secondary server from the primary server's database properties. Under Secondary Databases, choose the secondary server instance and click Remove.

5. To remove a monitor server instance, uncheck the "Use a monitor server instance" checkbox.

Removing Log Shipping with T-SQL Commands

To remove log shipping with T-SQL, issue this command on the primary server:

```
Use Master;
sp_delete_log_shipping_primary_secondary  @primary_database, @secondary_server,
@secondary_database;
```

This command deletes secondary information on the primary server from the `Msdb.dbo.log_shipping_primary_secondaries` table:

On the secondary server, issue this command:

```
Use Master;
sp_delete_log_shipping_secondary_database @secondary_database;
```

This command deletes the secondary information on the secondary server and its jobs by executing the `sys.sp_delete_log_shipping_secondary_database_internal` stored procedure:

Back on the primary server, issue this command:

```
Use Master;
sp_delete_log_shipping_primary_database @database;
```

This command deletes the log-shipping information from the primary server and its jobs, removes monitor info and the monitor, and deletes the `msdb.dbo.log_shipping_primary_databases` table:

Then, if desirable, you can delete the secondary database.

Log-Shipping Performance

On the primary server, to continue to meet performance requirements while concurrent users are accessing the log-shipping system, consider placing the log-shipping backup directory on a separate disk drive from the database. Backup compression also improves performance. As part of ongoing administration, monitor the I/O performance counters for any bottlenecks (e.g., average queue length higher than two for each physical drive). Do database administration activities such as index defragmentation during a period of lower activity, because depending on the level of fragmentation, the transaction-log file will be larger and take longer to back up, which can affect users. To keep the secondary server more closely in sync with the primary server, maintain shorter transactions.

> Log shipping uses the default settings for backup compression on the server. Whether a log is compressed depends on the Backup Compression default setting.

To ensure fast recovery in a role switch, the secondary server should have identical capacity to the primary server. This enables it to stay in sync with the primary server. Also, in a role switch, the secondary server will be able to provide the same performance experience that users expect. Similarly, separate the file copy directory from the database; and, as part of ongoing administration, monitor I/O performance counters. Furthermore, monitor network bandwidth to ensure that there is capacity to move the transaction-log file in a timely manner.

Upgrading to SQL Server 2008 Log Shipping

SQL Server 2005 log shipping cannot be directly upgraded to SQL Server 2008, as the log-shipping procedures have changed. Therefore, when upgrading a SQL Server 2005 instance, the log-shipping process stops functioning. There are three common approaches to upgrading log shipping.

Minimum Downtime Approach

The minimum downtime approach requires that the secondary server be upgraded in place using the setup program to SQL Server 2008 first. This will not break log shipping, because SQL Server 2005 transaction logs can be applied to SQL Server 2008. Afterward, a planned failover takes place whereby the role-switch procedures are followed and users are redirected to the secondary server, which has been promoted. After the role switch and after users are redirected, stop and disable the log shipping jobs. The newly upgraded SQL Server 2008 primary server cannot log-ship to the old primary server running SQL Server 2005.

Complete an in-place upgrade on the old primary server using the SQL Server 2008 setup program and leave it as the secondary server. Configure SQL Server 2008 log shipping from the new primary server to the secondary server using the same log-shipping shared folders used by SQL Server 2005. Additionally, in the Secondary Database Settings, on the Initialize Secondary Database page, choose "No, the Secondary database is initialized." SQL Server 2008 log shipping will then start shipping the transaction log. If you prefer, switch the roles back to the original primary server.

With Downtime Approach

With the downtime approach, the primary and secondary servers will not be available during the upgrade, as both are upgraded in place using the setup program. Use this method if you have allocated downtime to upgrade the SQL Server 2005 servers. This is the simpler approach, as it does not involve going through the failover process. Verify that the secondary server is in sync with the primary server by applying all the transaction-log backups and the active transaction log from the primary server. Stop and disable the log-shipping jobs; then do an in-place upgrade on the secondary server, followed by an upgrade to the primary server. Configure SQL Server 2008 log shipping using the same shared folders. Additionally, in the Secondary Database Settings, on the Initialize Secondary Database page, choose "No, the Secondary database is initialized." SQL Server 2008 log shipping will start shipping the transaction log without having to take a database backup and restore on the secondary server.

Deploy Log Shipping Approach

The deploy log shipping approach is more feasible when the log-shipping databases are small and can quickly be backed up, copied, and restored on the secondary server. It is similar to the downtime approach, but instead of verifying and waiting for synchronization of the secondary database, after the upgrade and during the SQL Server 2008 log-shipping configuration, you can choose "Yes, generate a full backup of the primary database" on the Initialize Secondary Database page. The log-shipping process will perform a database backup on the primary server and restore the backup onto the secondary server to start the log shipping.

Summary

Log shipping is a simple, inexpensive, dependable SQL Server high-availability solution with a long track record. As a disaster recovery solution, it has been deployed to maintain a secondary server over a distance for business continuity to protect from a local disaster, power-grid failure, and network outages. Log shipping can ship the log anywhere in the world. Its only limitation is the network bandwidth capacity to transfer the transaction log file in a timely manner. It can be combined with a reporting solution when an organization requires point-in-time reporting, rather than real time. Moreover, it has been deployed as an alternative to Windows failover clustering to provide a local, high-availability solution, where it is less expensive to implement because it does not require a shared disk system.

The main challenge in deploying log shipping is that it does not provide any automatic client redirect; therefore, an operator needs to have an approach for it. In addition, the role switch requires some user intervention to ensure that all of the transaction logs have been restored to the secondary server. Switching the roles back also requires some manual intervention. Another challenge is that log shipping is at the user database level and does not copy new logins, database users, SQL jobs, Integration Services, or DTS packages from the primary server. However, using Integration Services' Tasks and SQL Agent jobs, it can be accomplished.

Many organizations have used log shipping very successfully by scripting all the processes such as role switching, login synchronization, and client redirects, and are quickly able to failover with minimal manual downtime. Furthermore, as log shipping involves two or more physical separate servers that do not have any shared components like a Windows failover cluster, you can achieve patch-management independence whereby one server is patched, the roles are switched, and then the other server is patched.

Data mirroring is a new high-availability technology that may eventually replace log shipping. However, log shipping is a time-tested, high-availability solution that many large, strategic customers with mission-critical applications depend on every day to provide local disaster recovery.

20

Clustering SQL
Server 2008

Most DBAs don't think of their job as an adventure, but after installing their first SQL Server 2008 cluster, they may want to reconsider. Unlike most aspects of the DBA's job, the task of installing, configuring, and administering a SQL Server 2008 cluster really can be an adventure, with the attendant excitement and danger lurking in the most unexpected places; and, as in most adventure stories, the outcome is uncertain.

You might think we're telling you can't just follow a bunch of steps and get clustering going for your company. Actually, you can, but the problem is that literally hundreds of steps must be executed correctly and in the right sequence. This can be a challenge. You'll find, though, that after doing a cluster once, it will be very easy to repeat the process.

To rephrase this for emphasis: If you want to have a successful SQL Server 2008 cluster, you will need to spend time on the following tasks:

❑ Studying all aspects of clustering and mastering all of its intricacies.

❑ Researching hardware and software configurations to identify what will work best for your organization.

❑ Configuring hardware.

❑ Configuring the operating system.

❑ Configuring SQL Server 2008.

❑ Testing

❑   Documenting

❑   Administering and troubleshooting the production SQL Server 2008 cluster.

If all of this hard work and attention to detail doesn't scare you away, you are ready to read this chapter as the first step of your adventure.

With this chapter's tried-and-true information, you will be able to successfully install, configure, and administer a SQL Server 2008 cluster installation. You will learn how clustering works and whether it's the right solution for your organization. You'll learn how to choose between upgrading an old cluster and building a new one; how to plan for clustering, including hardware and the operating system; and how to install a SQL Server cluster. Finally, you'll learn how to maintain and troubleshoot an operating SQL Server cluster. While it is possible to cluster a geographically remote data center with Windows 2008, this chapter focuses on clusters that are geographically close and in the same network.

If you don't have a storage area network (SAN) or the hardware to create these examples with us, consider using a virtual PC solution. You can then download Internet Small Computer Systems Interface (ISCSI) target software such as StarWind by Rocket Division (www.rocketdivision.com) to simulate shared disk arrays for the cluster. Regardless of the cluster, disk configuration is one of the most challenging pieces of the puzzle, and ISCSI does make this slightly less challenging. However, you may pay a performance price if your network is not calibrated properly.

Clustering and Your Organization

Many DBAs seem to have difficulty understanding exactly what clustering is. What do we (and Microsoft) mean when we refer to SQL Server 2008 clustering? Here's a good working definition:

Microsoft SQL Server 2008 clustering is a high-availability option designed to increase the uptime of SQL Server 2008 instances. A SQL Server 2008 cluster includes two or more physical servers, called *nodes*, identically configured. One is designated as the *active node*, on which a SQL Server 2008 instance is running in production, and the other is an *inactive node*, on which SQL Server is installed but not running. If the SQL Server 2008 instance on the active node fails, the inactive node becomes the active node and continues SQL Server 2008 production with minimal downtime.

This definition is straightforward and to the point, but it has a lot of implications that are not so clear, and this is where many clustering misunderstandings arise. One of the best ways to more fully understand what clustering can and cannot do is to drill down into the details.

What Clustering Can Do

The benefits of using SQL Server 2008 clustering are very specific. Clustering is designed to boost the availability of physical server hardware, the operating system, and the SQL Server services. Should any of these aspects fail, an instance of SQL Server 2008 fails. If any of these three fails, another server in a cluster can automatically be assigned the task of taking over the failed SQL Server 2008 instance, keeping downtime to a minimum.

The use of clusters can help reduce downtime when you're performing maintenance on cluster nodes. For example, if you need to change hardware on a physical server or add a new service pack to the operating system, you can do so one node at a time. First, you would upgrade the node that is not running an active SQL Server 2008 instance. Next, you would manually failover from the production node to the now upgraded node, making it the active node. Then you would upgrade the currently inactive node. Once it is upgraded, you would fail back to the original node. This cluster feature helps to reduce the overall downtime caused by upgrades.

What Clustering Cannot Do

The list of what clustering cannot do is much longer than the list of what it can do, and this is where the misunderstandings start for many people. This list is long because of the many myths about clustering. Clustering is just one part of many required parts to ensure high availability. In many ways, it is not even the most important part; it is just one of the many pieces of the puzzle. Other aspects of high availability, such as the power supply, are actually much more important. Without power, the most sophisticated cluster hardware in the world won't work. If all of the pieces of the puzzle are not in place, spending a lot of money on clustering may not be a good investment. We talk about this more in the section "Getting Prepared for Clustering."

Some DBAs believe that clustering will reduce downtime to zero. This is not the case. Clustering can mitigate downtime, but it can't eliminate it. For example, the failover itself causes an outage lasting from 30 seconds to a few minutes while the services are stopped on one node and started on the other node.

Nor is clustering designed to intrinsically protect data. This is a great surprise to many DBAs. Data must be protected using other options, such as backups, log shipping, or disk mirroring. In actuality, the same database drives are being shared, albeit not seen at the same time, by all servers in the cluster, so corruption in one would carry over to the others.

Clustering is not designed for load balancing either. Load balancing is the act of having many servers act as one, spreading your load across many servers simultaneously. Many DBAs, especially those who work for large commercial Web sites, think that clustering provides load balancing between the nodes of a cluster. This is not the case. Clustering only helps boost the uptime of SQL Server 2008 instances. If you need load balancing, then you must look for a different solution.

Clustering can require expensive hardware and software. It requires certified hardware and the Enterprise or Datacenter versions of the operating system and SQL Server 2008 Standard or Enterprise edition. Many organizations cannot cost-justify this expense. Clustering was designed to work within the confines of a data center, not over geographic distances (geoclusters) in Windows 2003. In Windows 2008, this restriction is lifted and geoclusters are a possibility. Because of this, clustering is not a good solution if you want to failover to another data center located far from your production data center.

As you will quickly become aware as you read this chapter, SQL Server 2008 clustering is not for beginning DBAs. Clustering requires DBAs to be highly trained in hardware and software, and DBAs with clustering experience command higher salaries.

Although SQL Server 2008 is cluster aware, not all front-end applications that use SQL Server 2008 as the back end are cluster aware. For example, even if the failover of a SQL Server 2008 instance is relatively seamless, a front-end application may not be as smart. Many applications require that users exit and then restart the front-end application after a SQL Server 2008 instance failover, and users may lose the data on their current screen.

Choosing SQL Server 2008 Clustering for the Right Reasons

When it comes right down to it, the only justification for a SQL Server 2008 cluster is to boost the high availability of SQL Server instances, but this justification makes sense only if the following are true:

- ❑ The cost (and pain) of being down is more than the cost of purchasing the cluster hardware and software and maintaining it over time.

- ❑ You have in place the capability to protect your data. Remember that clusters don't protect data.

- ❑ You don't need to be able to failover to a geographically remote data center unless you have a Microsoft certified third-party hardware and software solution. SQL Server 2008, out of the box, does not support geographically remote clustering.

- ❑ You have in place all the necessary peripherals required to support a highly available server environment (e.g., backup power and so on).

- ❑ You have qualified DBA staff to install, configure, and administer a SQL Server 2008 cluster.

If all of these things are true, your organization qualifies as a candidate for installing a SQL Server 2008 cluster, and you should proceed; but if your organization doesn't meet these criteria, and you are not willing to put them into place, you are most likely wasting your time and money with a SQL Server 2008 cluster and would probably be better off with an alternative, high-availability option, such as one of those discussed next.

Alternatives to Clustering

SQL Server 2008 clustering is just one of many options available to help ensure the high availability of your SQL Server 2008 instances, and high-availability solutions consist of multiple layers of solutions to ensure uptime. This section takes a brief look at alternatives to clustering, starting with the least expensive and easy-to-implement options and then looking at the more expensive and harder-to-implement options.

Warm Backup Server

A *warm backup* refers to having a spare physical server available that you can use as your SQL Server 2008 server should your production server fail. Generally speaking, this server will not have SQL Server 2008 or any database backups installed on it. This means that it will take time to install SQL Server 2008, restoring the databases and repointing applications to the new server, before you are up and running again. It also means that you may lose some of your data if you cannot recover the transaction logs from the failed production server and you have only your most recent database backups to restore from.

If being down a while or possibly losing data is not a major concern, having a warm backup server is the least expensive way to ensure that your organization stays in business should your production SQL Server 2008 server fail.

Hot Backup Server

The major difference between a warm backup server and a hot backup server is that your spare server (the "hot" one) will have SQL Server 2008 preinstalled and a copy of the most recent database backups on it. This means that you save a lot of installation and configuration time, getting back into production sooner than you would with the use of a warm backup server. You still need to repoint your database applications, and you may lose some of your data should you not be able to recover the transaction logs from the failed server.

Log Shipping

Log shipping is one step beyond what a hot backup server can provide. In a log-shipping scenario, you have two SQL Servers, as with the hot backup server. This includes the production server and a spare. The spare also has SQL Server 2008 installed. The major difference between a hot backup server and log shipping is that log shipping adds the capability not only to send database backups from the production server to the spare server automatically, but also to send database transaction logs and automatically restore them. This means there is less manual work than with a hot backup server, and less chance for data loss, as the most data you might lose would be the equivalent of one transaction log. For example, if you create transaction logs every 15 minutes, in the worst case you would lose only 15 minutes of data.

Log shipping is covered in detail in Chapter 19.

Replication

Many experts include SQL Server 2008 replication as a means of increasing high availability, but we are not among them. Although replication is great for moving data from one SQL Server to one or more SQL Servers, it's not a good high-availability option. It is much too complex and limited in its ability to easily replicate entire databases to be worth the effort of spending any time trying to make it work in failover scenarios.

Replication is covered in detail in Chapter 16.

Database Mirroring

Database mirroring is new to SQL Server 2008 and in many ways is a very good alternative to SQL Server 2008 clustering. Like clustering, database mirroring can be used to automatically failover a failed instance of SQL Server 2008 to a spare server, on a database-by-database basis. The biggest difference between clustering and database mirroring is that data is actually protected, not just the SQL Server 2008 instance. In addition, database mirroring can be done over long distances, does not require specially certified hardware, is less expensive than clustering, requires less knowledge to set up and manage, and is fully automatic, like clustering. In many cases, database mirroring is a much better choice than clustering for high availability.

Database mirroring is covered in detail in Chapter 17.

Third-Party Clustering Solutions

Microsoft is not the only company that offers a clustering solution for SQL Server 2008. Several third-party companies also offer solutions. In general, these options are just as expensive and complex as Microsoft's clustering option, offering few, if any, benefits beyond what Microsoft offers.

What to Do?

While we hope that this brief rundown has helped you clarify your options, it is not enough information for you to make a good decision. If the best solution is not self-evident, then you need to spend a lot of time researching the preceding options before you can really determine what is best for your organization.

Clustering: The Big Picture

If you're going to get involved with clustering, you need to know how it works, including clustering configuration options.

How Clustering Works

Clustering is a complex technology with a lot of messy details. To avoid scaring you too much too soon, we'll take a look at the big picture of how clustering works. In this section, we take a look at active and passive nodes, the shared disk array, the quorum, public and private networks, and the virtual server. Finally, we explain how a failover works.

Active Nodes versus Passive Nodes

Although a SQL Server 2008 cluster can support up to eight nodes, clustering actually occurs between only two nodes at a time because a single SQL Server 2008 instance can run on only a single node at a time; and should a failover occur, the failed instance can failover to another individual node only. This adds up to two nodes. Clusters of three or more nodes are used only where you need to cluster multiple instances of SQL Server 2008. We discuss larger clusters later in this chapter.

In a two-node SQL Server 2008 cluster, one of the physical server nodes is considered the *active* node, and the second one is the *passive* node. It doesn't matter which of the physical servers in a cluster is designated as active or passive, but it is easier from an administrative point of view to simply assign one node as the active and the other as the passive. This way, there is no confusion about which physical server is performing which role at the current time.

When we refer to an active node, we mean that this particular node is currently running an active instance of SQL Server 2008 and that it is accessing the instance's databases, which are located on a shared data array.

When we refer to a passive node, we mean that this particular node is not currently running the production load and is not accessing the instance's databases. When the passive node is not in production, it is in a state of readiness; if the active node fails and a failover occurs, it can automatically go into production and begin accessing the instance's databases located on the shared disk array. In this case, the passive node then becomes the active node, and the formerly active node becomes the passive node (or the failed node, if a failure occurs that prevents it from operating).

Later in this chapter, we will at two different types of SQL Server 2008 cluster configurations: active/passive and active/active.

Shared Disk Array

Unlike nonclustered SQL Server 2008 instances, which usually store their databases on local disk storage, clustered SQL Server 2008 instances store data on a shared disk array. By *shared*, we mean that both nodes of the cluster are physically connected to the disk array, but only the active node can access the instance's databases. To ensure the integrity of the databases, both nodes of a cluster never access them at the same time.

Generally speaking, a shared disk array is a SCSI- or fiber-connected RAID 5 or RAID 10 disk array housed in a stand-alone unit, or it might be a SAN. This shared array must have at least two logical partitions. One partition is used for storing the clustered instance's SQL Server databases, and the other is used for the quorum. In a SAN, it is recommended that you align each LUN (logical grouping on the SAN) with a physical disk in Windows.

The Quorum

When both nodes of a cluster are up and running, participating in their respective roles (active and passive), they communicate with each other over the network. For example, if you change a configuration setting on the active node, this configuration change is automatically and very quickly sent to the passive node and the same change is made, thereby ensuring synchronization.

As you might imagine, though, it is possible to make a change on the active node, but before the change is sent over the network and made on the passive node (which becomes the active node after the failover), the active node fails, and the change never gets to the passive node. Depending on the nature of the change, this could cause problems, even causing both nodes of the cluster to fail.

To prevent this from happening, a SQL Server 2008 cluster uses a *quorum*. A quorum is essentially a log file, similar in concept to database logs. Its purpose is to record any change made on the active node; and should any change recorded there not get to the passive node because the active node has failed and cannot send the change to the passive node over the network, the passive node, when it becomes the active node, can read the quorum file to find out what the change was and then make the change before it becomes the new active node. If the state of this drive is compromised, your cluster may be in a damaged state.

In order for this to work, the quorum file must reside on the *quorum drive*. A quorum drive is a logical drive on the shared array dedicated to the function of storing the quorum.

Public and Private Networks

Each node of a cluster must have at least two network cards to be a fully supported installation. One network card will be connected to the public network, and the other network card will be connected to a private network.

The public network is the network to which the SQL Server 2008 clients are attached, which is how they communicate to a clustered SQL Server 2008 instance.

The private network is used solely for communications between the nodes of the cluster. It is used mainly for the *heartbeat signal*. In a cluster, the active node puts out a heartbeat signal, which tells the other nodes in the cluster that it is working. Should the heartbeat signal stop, a passive node in the cluster becomes aware that the active node has failed and that it should at this time initiate a failover so that it can become the active node and take control over the SQL Server 2008 instance.

The Virtual Server

One of the biggest mysteries of clustering is how clients know when and how to switch communicating from a failed cluster node to the new active node. The answer may be surprising: They don't. That's right — SQL Server 2008 clients don't need to know anything about specific nodes of a cluster (such as the NETBIOS name or IP address of individual cluster nodes). This is because each clustered SQL Server 2008 instance is given a virtual name and IP address, which clients use to connect to the cluster. In other words, clients don't connect to a node's specific name or IP address but instead to a virtual name and IP address that stays the same no matter what node in a cluster is active.

How a Failover Works

Although a failover can occur for many reasons, we look here at the case when the power stops for the active node of a cluster and the passive node has to take over. This will provide a general overview of how a failover occurs.

Assume that a single SQL Server 2008 instance is running on the active node of a cluster and that a passive node is ready to take over when needed. At this time, the active node is communicating with both the database and the quorum on the shared array. Because only a single node at a time can be communicating with the shared array, the passive node is not communicating with the database or the quorum. In addition, the active node is sending out heartbeat signals over the private network, and the passive node is monitoring them so it can take over if they stop. Clients are also interacting with the active node via the virtual name and IP address, running production transactions.

Now assume that, for whatever reason, the active node stops working because it is no longer receiving any electricity. The passive node, which is monitoring the heartbeats from the active node, notices that it is not receiving the heartbeat signals. After a predetermined delay, the passive node assumes that the active node has failed and initiates a failover. As part of the failover process, the passive node (now the active node) takes over control of the shared array and reads the quorum, looking for any unsynchronized configuration changes. It also takes over control of the virtual server name and IP address. In addition, as the node takes over the databases, it has to perform a SQL Server startup, using the databases, just as if it were starting from a shutdown, going through a database recovery.

The time this takes depends on many factors, including the speed of the system and the number of transactions that might have to be rolled forward or back during the database recovery process. Once the recovery process is complete, the new active node announces itself on the network with the virtual name and IP address, which enables the clients to reconnect and begin using the SQL Server 2008 instance with minimal interruption.

Clustering Options

Up to this point, we have been talking about simple two-node clusters running a single instance of SQL Server 2008. In fact, this is only one of many options you have when clustering SQL Server 2008. This section takes a look at these options.

Active/Passive versus Active/Active

The examples so far have described what is called an *active/passive cluster*. This is a two-node cluster in which there is only one active instance of SQL Server 2008. Should the active node fail, the passive node takes over the single instance of SQL Server 2008, becoming the active node.

In order to save hardware costs, some organizations like to configure what is called an active/active cluster. This is also a two-node cluster, but instead of only a single instance of SQL Server 2008 running, there are two instances, one on each physical node of the cluster. In this case, should one instance of

SQL Server 2008 fail, the other active node takes over, which means the remaining node must run two instances of SQL Server 2008 instead of one.

The advantage of an active/active cluster is that you make better use of the available hardware. Both nodes of the cluster are in use instead of just one, as in an active/passive cluster. The disadvantage is that when a failover occurs, both SQL Server 2008 instances are running on a single server, which can hurt the performance of both instances. To help overcome this problem, both of the physical servers can be oversized in order to better meet the needs of both instances should a failover occur. Chances are good, however, that the perfect balance will not be met and there will be some performance hit when failing over to a secondary server. In addition, if you have an active/active cluster running two instances of SQL Server 2008, each instance needs its own logical disk on the shared array. Logical disks cannot be shared among instances of SQL Server 2008.

If you need two SQL Server 2008 clustered instances, you have three options:

- ❑ Two active/passive clusters
- ❑ One active/active cluster
- ❑ One three-node cluster (more on this shortly)

Which should you choose? If you want to be conservative, chose two active/passive clusters because they are easier to administer and provide more redundancy; also, they won't cause any application slowdown should a failover occur.

If you want to save hardware costs and don't mind potential application slowdowns and the added complexity of this option, use an active/active cluster.

If you think you will be adding more clustered SQL Server 2008 instances in the future and don't mind the complexity of large clusters, consider a multinode cluster.

Multinode Clusters

The number of nodes supported for SQL Server 2008 clustering depends on which version of the software you purchase, along with which version of the operating system you intend to use.

Purchasing the Right Software

One of the reasons it is very important to research your clustering needs is that they directly affect what software you need, along with licensing costs. Here are your options:

- ❑ Windows Server 2008 Enterprise Edition (32-bit or 64-bit) and SQL Server 2008 Standard Edition (32-bit or 64-bit). Supports up to two-node clustering.
- ❑ Windows Server 2008 Enterprise Edition (32-bit or 64-bit) and SQL Server 2008 Enterprise Edition (32-bit or 64-bit). Supports up to eight-node clustering.
- ❑ Windows Server 2008 Datacenter Edition (32-bit or 64-bit) and SQL Server 2008 Enterprise Edition (32-bit or 64-bit). Supports up to eight-node clustering.

If you need only a two-node cluster, you can save a lot of money by purchasing Windows Server 2008 Enterprise Edition and SQL Server 2008 Standard Edition. If you want more than two clustered nodes, your licensing costs will escalate quickly but there are some features that have been withheld in the Standard Edition of SQL Server to slow the failover.

What about Windows 2003 Server? Can you cluster SQL Server 2008 with it? Yes, you can, but given the increased stability of clustering in Windows 2008 over Windows 2003, we recommend using Windows 2008.

Number of Nodes to Use

Like most things in clustering, there are no clear-cut answers to how many nodes your cluster should use. Before we try to offer some advice in this area, let's first discuss how multinode clustering works.

As covered earlier, in a two-node cluster, an instance of SQL Server 2008 runs on the active node, while the passive node is currently not running SQL Server 2008, but is ready to do so when a failover occurs. This same principle applies to multinode clusters.

For example, let's say that you have a three-node cluster. In this case, two of the nodes would be active, running their own individual instances of SQL Server 2008, and the third physical node would act as a passive node for the other two active nodes. If either of the two active nodes failed, the passive node would take over.

Let's look at the other extreme: an eight-node cluster. In this case, you could have seven active nodes and one passive. Should any of the seven active nodes fail, then the passive node would take over after a failover.

The advantage of larger nodes is that less hardware is used for failover needs. For example, in a two-node cluster, 50 percent of your hardware is used for redundancy; but if you are using an eight-node cluster, only 12.5 percent of your cluster hardware is used for redundancy.

On the downside, using only one passive node in a multinode cluster assumes that no more than one of the active nodes will fail at the same time; or if they do, the failed-over nodes will run slowly on the single node. Conversely, if you want, a multinode cluster can have more than one passive node. For example, you could have six active nodes and two passive nodes. Besides these risks, multinode clusters are more complex to manage than two-node clusters, in addition to being very expensive in terms of hardware and software licensing costs.

Ultimately, deciding how many nodes your cluster should have depends on your needs (how many SQL Server 2008 instances do you need to cluster?), along with your budget, your in-house expertise, and your level of aversion, if any, to complexity. Some companies have many different SQL Server instances they need to cluster, but choose to use multiple two-node active/passive clusters instead of a single multinode cluster. It is often best to just keep things as simple as possible.

Clustering Multiple Instances of SQL Server on the Same Server

Up to this point, we have made the assumption that a single instance of SQL Server 2008 will run on a single physical server, but this is not a requirement. In fact, SQL Server 2008 Enterprise Edition can run up to 50 instances on a single clustered physical server, and SQL Server 2008 Standard Edition can run up to 16 instances. But is this a good idea? Not in the world we live in.

The purpose of clustering is to boost high availability; it is not to save money. Adding multiple instances to a cluster adds complexity, and complexity *reduces* high availability. Cluster multiple instances of SQL Server 2008 on the same physical node at your own risk.

Upgrading SQL Server Clustering

If your company is like most, it probably already has some older version SQL Server clusters in production. If so, you need to decide how to upgrade them to SQL Server 2008. Your available options include the following:

- ❏ Don't upgrade.
- ❏ Perform an in-place SQL Server 2008 upgrade.
- ❏ Rebuild your cluster from scratch, and then install SQL Server 2008 clustering.

This section considers each of these options.

Don't Upgrade

This is an easy decision. Not upgrading is simple and doesn't cost anything. Just because a new version of SQL Server comes out doesn't mean you have to upgrade to it. If your current SQL Server cluster is running fine, why change it? You are just asking for potential new problems where you have none now, and you will have new costs.

On the other hand, if your current SQL Server cluster is not fine, you have the perfect reason to upgrade. SQL Server 2008 offers many new benefits, and they may solve the problems your current cluster is experiencing. However, don't automatically assume this is the case. Before you upgrade, do the research to determine whether the new features of SQL Server 2008 will actually resolve your problems. If not, sticking with what you know may be the best choice.

Upgrading Your SQL Server 2008 Cluster In-Place

Before we begin talking about how to upgrade a current cluster to a SQL Server 2008 cluster, we first need to discuss what operating system you are currently running. If you are on Windows Server 2008 with the latest service pack, you are in good shape and an in-place upgrade to SQL Server 2008 should not be a problem. If, however, you are running Windows 2003 Server and you also want to go to Windows 2008, then you should seriously consider rebuilding your server nodes so that they are running at the latest operating system level.

The logic behind this is that if you are going to all the trouble to upgrade to SQL Server 2008, you should be running on the latest operating system; otherwise, you aren't taking advantage of the latest technology and the benefits it brings to high availability. Therefore, if you are still running Windows Server 2003 (or earlier), we strongly recommend that you don't upgrade in place. And don't even think about upgrading the operating system in place, and then upgrading to SQL Server 2008 in place. You are just asking for trouble.

Rebuilding Your Cluster from Scratch

Rebuilding your cluster from scratch is a good idea if any one of the following conditions exists:

- ❏ You need to upgrade your current hardware (it is either old or underpowered).
- ❏ You need to upgrade the operating system.

❏   The current cluster installation is unstable.

❏   You have disdain for upgrading software in place and prefer a fresh install.

If you do decide to upgrade from scratch, you have to decide whether you will install onto new hardware or use your old hardware. If you install on new hardware, you have the convenience of building the cluster, and testing it, at your own pace, while the current cluster is still in production. This helps to ensure that you have done an outstanding job and at the same time relieves some of the stress that you will experience if you have to reuse your old hardware and then rebuild the cluster during a brief and intense rebuild.

If you don't have the luxury of acquiring new hardware, you have to identify a good time when your system can be down while the rebuild occurs. This could range from a 4-hour period to a 12-hour period, depending on your particular circumstances. Besides the time your cluster will be down, there is also the added risk of unexpected problems. For example, you might make an installation mistake halfway through the upgrade and have to start over. Because of the uncertainty involved, you should first estimate how much time you think the upgrade will take under good circumstances, and then double that estimate as the size of your requested window of downtime. This way, your users are prepared for the worst.

Whether you upgrade using new hardware or old hardware, you have to consider two additional issues. One, will you reuse your current virtual server name and IP address or select new ones? Two, how will you move your data from the old cluster to the new cluster?

The clients that access your current SQL Server cluster do so using the cluster's virtual name and IP address. If you want the clients to continue using the same virtual name and IP address, you need to reuse the old virtual name and IP address in the new cluster. This is the most common approach because it is generally easier to change a single virtual name and IP address than to reconfigure dozens, if not hundreds, of clients that access the cluster.

If you are upgrading using old hardware, reusing the former virtual name and IP address is not an issue because the old cluster is brought down and then the new one is put up, so there is never a time when the virtual name and IP address are on two clusters at the same time (which won't work).

If you upgrade by using new hardware, you need to assign a virtual name and IP address for testing, but you won't be able to use the old ones because they are currently in use. In this case, you need to use a temporary virtual name and IP address for testing; and when you are ready for the actual changeover from the old cluster to the new cluster, you need to follow these general steps:

1.   Secure your data.

2.   Remove SQL Server clustering from the old cluster or turn off the old cluster.

3.   On the new cluster, remove SQL Server 2008 clustering, and then reinstall it using the virtual name and IP address of the old cluster.

4.   Restore the data.

Uninstalling SQL Server 2008 clustering and then reinstalling it with the old virtual name and IP address is a pain but doesn't take a long time. Besides, this is the only way to change the virtual name or IP address of a SQL Server 2008 cluster install.

How you move the data from the old cluster to the new cluster depends somewhat on whether you are using old hardware or new hardware.

If you are using old hardware, all you have to do is back up the system and user databases and then detach the user databases. Rebuild the cluster without deleting the backups or detached databases. When the cluster is rebuilt, restore the system databases and reattach the detached databases. This, of course, assumes that the databases will remain in their current location. If you need to move the databases, then you need to follow the next option.

If you are moving to new hardware, or will be moving the location of the databases on old hardware, you should first do full backups of the system and user databases, and then detach the user databases. Next, move these to the new server or new location. Then when the cluster is rebuilt, restore the system databases and reattach the user databases.

> There isn't space here to include all the gory details, such as what happens if the drive letter changes, and so on. The key to success is to plan all of these steps and, if possible, perform a trial run before you do an actual cutover.

Backout Plan

No matter how you decide to upgrade to SQL Server 2008 clustering, you need to have a backout plan. Essentially, a backout plan is what you do if your upgrade fails. We can't tell you exactly what to do for a backout plan, because we don't know your particular circumstances, but we do know that you need such a plan if the upgrade fails. Therefore, as you plan your upgrade, consider how the plan could fail, and come up with options to get you back in business should things not go well. Your job could depend on how good your backout plan is. Typically, a backout plan consists of reinstalling SQL Server, restoring the system and user databases, and incurring at least a few hours of outage.

Which Upgrade Option Is Best?

Speaking from personal experience, we always prefer to upgrade by rebuilding clusters from scratch on new hardware. This is the easiest, fastest, least risky, and least stressful way. Unfortunately, you may not have this option for whatever reasons management gives you. In this case, you have to work with what you have been given. The key to a successful upgrade is a lot of detailed planning, as much testing as possible, and, of course, having a great backout plan.

Getting Prepared for Clustering

When it comes to SQL Server 2008 clustering, the devil is in the details. If you are not familiar with this expression, you will be by the time you complete your first SQL Server 2008 clustering installation. If you take the time to ensure that every step is done correctly and in the right order, your cluster installation will be smooth and relatively quick and painless; but if you don't like to read instructions, instead preferring the trial-and-error approach to computer administration, then expect to face a lot of frustration and a lot of time installing and reinstalling your SQL Server 2008 cluster, as not paying attention to the details is something you will later regret.

The best way to ensure a smooth cluster installation is to create a very detailed, step-by-step plan for the installation, down to the screen level. Yes, this is boring and tedious, but it forces you to think through every option and how it will affect your installation and your organization (once it is in production). In addition, such a plan will come in handy the next time you build a cluster, and will be great documentation for your disaster recovery plan. You do have a disaster recovery plan, don't you?

Preparing the Infrastructure

Before you even begin building a SQL Server 2008 cluster, you must ensure that your network infrastructure is in place. Here's a checklist of everything required before you begin installing a SQL Server 2008 cluster. In many cases, these items are the responsibility of others on your IT staff, but it is your responsibility to ensure that all of these are in place before you begin building your SQL Server 2008 cluster:

- ❑ Your network must have at least one Active Directory server, and ideally two for redundancy.

- ❑ Your network must have at least one DNS server, and ideally two for redundancy.

- ❑ Your network must have available switch ports for the public network cards used by the nodes of the cluster. Be sure they are manually set to match the manually set network card settings used in the nodes of the cluster. In addition, all the nodes of a cluster must be on the same subnet.

- ❑ You must have secure IP addresses for all the public network cards. Windows 2008 does support DHCP but we recommend that you use static IPs.

- ❑ You must decide how you will configure the private heartbeat network. Will you use a direct network card–to–network card connection, or use a hub or switch?

- ❑ You need to secure IP addresses for the private network cards. Generally, use a private network subnet such as 10.0.0.0–10.255.255.255, 172.16.0.0–172.31.255.255, or 192.168.0.0–192.168.255.255. Remember, this is a private network seen only by the nodes of the cluster. Again, Windows 2008 allows DHCP to claim these IP addresses.

- ❑ Ensure that you have proper electrical power for the new cluster servers and shared array (assuming they are being newly added to your data center).

- ❑ Ensure that battery backup power is available for all the nodes in your cluster and your shared array.

- ❑ If you don't already have one, create a SQL Server service account to be used by the SQL Server services running on the cluster. This must be a domain account, with the password set to never expire.

- ❑ If you don't already have one, create a cluster service account to be used by the Windows Clustering service. This must be a domain account, with the password set to never expire.

- ❑ Create three global groups, one each for SQL Server Service, SQL Server Agent Service, and SQL Server Analysis Services. You will need these when you install SQL Server 2008 on a cluster.

- ❑ Determine a name for your virtual cluster (Clustering Services) and secure a virtual IP address for it. This name will be used for management of the cluster after it is created.

- ❑ Determine a name for your virtual SQL Server 2008 cluster and secure a virtual IP address for it. This will be the name that clients will connect to.

❏   If your server nodes have AMP/ACPI power-saving features, turn them off. This includes network cards, drives, and other components. Their activation can cause a failover.

You will learn more about most of these as we go over the installation process.

Preparing the Hardware

Based on our experience building clusters, the hardware presents the thorniest problems, often taking the most time to research and configure. Part of the reason for this is that there are many hardware options, some of which work, some of which don't. Unfortunately, there is no complete resource you can use to help you sort through this. Each vendor offers different hardware, and the available hardware is always changing, along with new and updated hardware drivers, making this entire subject a moving target with no easy answers. In spite of all this, here is what you need to know to get started on selecting the proper hardware for your SQL Server 2008 cluster.

Finding Your Way Through the Hardware Jungle

This section describes the basic hardware you need for a SQL Server cluster. To keep things simple, we only refer to a two-node active/passive cluster, although these same recommendations apply to multi-node clusters. The following are our personal minimum recommendations. If you check out Microsoft's minimum hardware requirements for a SQL Server 2008 cluster, they will be somewhat less. We also highly suggest that each node in your cluster be identical. This can avoid a lot of installation and administrative headaches.

The minimum specifications for the server nodes should be the following:

❏   Dual CPUs, 2 GHz or higher, 2MB L2 Cache (32-bit or 64-bit)

❏   2GB or more RAM

❏   Local mirrored SCSI drive for the application drive (RAID 10 or 5 will also work) (C:), 9GB or larger

❏   SCSI DVD drive

❏   SCSI connection for local SCSI drive and DVD drive

❏   SCSI or fiber connection to shared array or SAN or shared ISCSI drives

❏   Redundant power supplies

❏   Private network card

❏   Public network card

❏   Mouse, keyboard, and monitor (can be shared)

The shared array should have a SCSI-attached RAID 5 or RAID 10 array with an appropriate high-speed SCSI connection. With Microsoft clustering, SCSI is supported only if you have a two-node cluster. If you want to cluster more than two nodes, you must use a fiber-attached disk array or SAN; or you may have a fiber-attached RAID 5 or RAID 10 array with an appropriate high-speed connection; or you may use a fiber-attached SAN storage array with an appropriate high-speed connection (generally a fiber switch).

Because this chapter is about SQL Server 2008 clustering, not hardware, we won't spend much time on hardware specifics. If you are new to clustering, contact your hardware vendor for specific hardware recommendations. Keep in mind that you will be running SQL Server 2008 on this cluster, so ensure that whatever hardware you select meets the needs of your predicted production load.

Preparing the Hardware

As a DBA, you may not be the one who installs the hardware. In any case, here are the general steps most people follow when building cluster hardware:

1. Install and configure the hardware for each node in the cluster as if it will be running as a stand-alone server. This includes installing the latest approved drivers and firmware.

2. Once the hardware is installed, install the operating system and the latest service pack, along with any additional required drivers.

3. Connect the node to the public network. To make things easy, name the network used for public connections "network."

4. Install the private heartbeat network. To make things easy, name the private heartbeat network "private."

5. Install and configure the shared array, ISCSI targets, or SAN. For ISCSI targets, you will need to purchase a third-party tool to host the disks. An inexpensive solution that we used when writing this book was StarWind (`www.rocketdivision.com`).

6. Install and configure the SCSI or fiber cards in each of the nodes and install the latest drivers. In Windows 2008, you can also use ISCSI. In this case, you'll need to set up the ISCSI initiators to connect to the drives.

7. One at a time, connect each node to the shared array, ISCSI drive, or SAN, following the instructions for your specific hardware. It is critical that you do this one node at a time. In other words, only one node at a time should be physically on and connected to the shared array or SAN and configured. Once that node is configured, turn it off and turn the next node on and configure it, and so on, one node at a time. If you do not follow this procedure, you risk corrupting the disk configuration on your nodes, requiring you to start over again.

8. After connecting each node to the shared array, ISCSI, or SAN, use Disk Administrator to configure and format the drives on the shared array. You need at least two logical drives on the shared array. One is for storing your SQL Server databases, and the other one is for the quorum drive. The data drive must be big enough to store all the required data, and the quorum drive must be at least 500MB (which is the smallest size that an NTFS volume can efficiently operate). When configuring the shared drives using Disk Administrator, each node of the cluster is required to use the same drive letter when referring to the drives on the shared array or SAN. For example, you might want to assign your data drive as drive "F:" on all the nodes, and assign the quorum drive letter "Q:" on all the nodes.

9. Once all of the hardware is put together, test, test, and test again, ensuring that there are no problems before you begin installing clustering services. While you may be able to do some diagnostic hardware testing before you install the operating system, you will have to wait until after installing the operating system before you can fully test the hardware.

Once all of the hardware has been configured and tested, you are ready to install Windows 2008 clustering, which is our next topic.

Clustering Windows Server 2008

Before you can install SQL Server 2008 clustering, you must first install Windows Server 2008 failover cluster services. Once it is successfully installed and tested, then you can install SQL Server 2008 clustering. In this section, we take a high-level, step-by-step approach to installing and configuring Windows 2008 clustering.

Before Installing Windows 2008 Clustering

Before you install Windows 2008 clustering, you need to perform a series of important steps. This is especially important if you didn't build the cluster nodes, as you want to ensure everything is working correctly before you begin the actual cluster installation. Once they are complete, then you can install Windows 2008 clustering. Here are the steps you must take:

1. Ensure that all the nodes are working properly and are configured identically (hardware, software, and drivers).

2. Confirm that each node can see the data and quorum drives on the shared array or SAN. There are other quorum options but we'll start here for our installation. Try writing a file to the disk to ensure that the other nodes can see the file.

3. Verify that none of the nodes have been configured as a domain controller or that you have multiple domain controllers in your environment or any other critical services such as Exchange running on them.

4. Verify that all drives are NTFS and are not compressed.

5. Ensure that the public and private networks are properly installed and configured.

6. Ping each node in the public and private networks to ensure that you have good network connections. Also ping the domain controller and DNS server to verify that they are available.

7. Verify that you have disabled NetBIOS for all private network cards.

8. Verify that there are no network shares on any of the shared drives.

9. If you intend to use SQL Server encryption, install the server certificate with the fully qualified DNS name of the virtual server on all nodes in the cluster.

10. Check all of the error logs to ensure that there are no unpleasant surprises. If there are, resolve them before proceeding with the cluster installation.

11. Add the SQL Server and Clustering service accounts to the Local Administrators group of all the nodes in the cluster.

12. Verify that no anti-virus software has been installed on the nodes. Anti-virus software can reduce the availability of clusters and must not be installed on them. If you want to check for possible viruses on a cluster, you can install the software on a non-node and then run scans on the cluster nodes remotely.

13. Verify that the Windows Cryptographic Service Provider is enabled on each of the nodes.

14. Verify that the Windows Task Scheduler service is running on each of the nodes.

These are a lot of things to check, but each is very important. If skipped, any one of these steps could prevent your cluster from installing or working properly.

Installing Windows Server 2008 Clustering

Now that all of your nodes and shared array, ISCSI device, or SAN is ready, you are ready to install Windows 2008 failover clustering. This section describes the process from beginning to end.

To begin, you must enable the clustering feature for each of the Windows 2008 node candidates. In Windows 2003 Server, this feature was enabled by default, but in 2008 the decision was made to reduce the surface area of Windows by disabling the feature by default. To enable the failover clustering feature, open the Add Features Wizard from the Server Manager. Check Failover Clustering and the wizard will complete the installation for you (shown in Figure 20-1). This doesn't actually cluster your machines, but will install the necessary components on your machine to manage the cluster and do the failover. This step needs to be repeated on each node participating in the cluster.

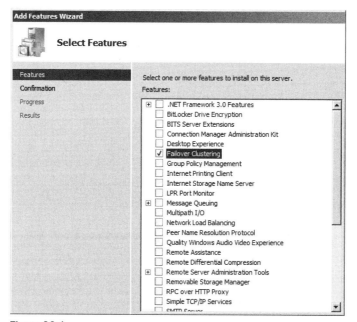

Figure 20-1

Running Validate

Before you create the cluster, you want to validate that the nodes are running on supported hardware and that you're in an ideal environment. To do this, open the Failover Cluster Management tool and click Validate a Configuration. This will open the Validate a Cluster Configuration Wizard, which runs a full diagnosis of your cluster prior to the installation. The fantastic thing about this wizard is that it can also be used after installation of the cluster to ensure you still meet the cluster hardware requirements and that all the hardware is in proper working condition.

> *If you pass the validation in this wizard, Microsoft will support you. Gone are the days of looking over a long matrix list to determine whether you will be supported on a given hardware platform!*

Once you're in the Validate a Configuration Wizard, you will be asked which nodes or potential nodes you wish to test. Enter each of them into the list and click Next. You will then be asked what types of tests you want to run. The tests will then begin to run and you'll get a visual confirmation as the validation tests moves from step to step if you passed, as shown in Figure 20-2. If you fail a test, do not install the cluster, even though you can override the test and still cluster the nodes. If you review the report, you'll see a component-by-component evaluation of your configuration to determine whether your hardware is suitable.

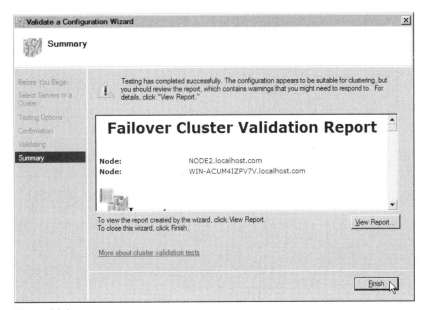

Figure 20-2

Viewing the report is as easy as clicking the View Report button. Doing so takes you to an HTML report, a very granular report about each of your hardware components and whether they're cluster approved.

Installing the Clustered Nodes

Windows 2008 clustering has changed substantially since Windows 2003. To put it to you differently, clustering has been so simplified, we've been able to shorten this chapter by ten pages! This is mainly because you can now cluster all nodes at once in a simple wizard that asks you two questions. If you've clustered in Windows 2003, you will be jumping out of your seat, as we were, when you see the steps to clustering in Windows 2008:

1. Click the Create a Cluster button from within the Failover Cluster Management tool. This opens the Create Cluster Wizard. The first internal screen after the welcome screen asks you which nodes will participate in the cluster. Type in each node and click Add as shown in Figure 20-3. Don't worry, more nodes can be added later.

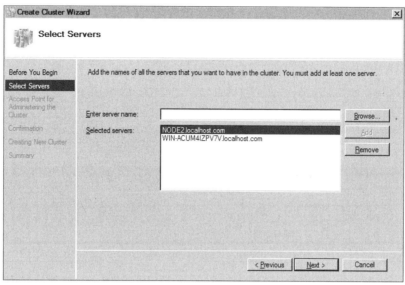

Figure 20-3

2. Assign the Windows cluster an IP address and specify which network you want the cluster to use, as shown in Figure 20-4. In the example in the figure, you can see that Windows2008Cluster was the Windows cluster name used for management. That name is too long for NetBIOS and would be shortened for customers using that network protocol.

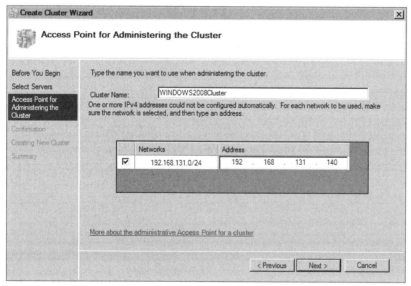

Figure 20-4

You're done! The cluster will begin to be created and configured (see Figure 20-5) and you will be notified when the build process is done. This is a much shorter process than it was in Windows 2003; it took no more than two minutes on our test environment.

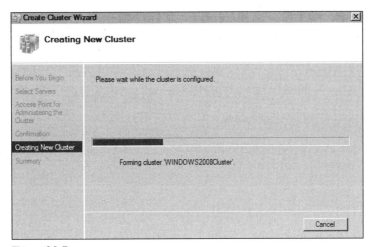

Figure 20-5

Configuring Windows Server 2008 for Clustering

Before you install SQL Server 2008, there is one small step you need to perform, and that is to prepare the cluster for SQL Server. In the previous section, we clustered Windows but we didn't tell Windows which drives will be used in the cluster. This is because Microsoft now deploys a minimalist approach to clustering during the installation, doing the absolute minimum it needs to get you clustered and then allowing you to add the necessary components later.

From the Failover Cluster Management tool, click the Storage shortcut under Navigate. Then, click Add Disk from the Actions pane. Add any disks that you want to be visible to SQL Server and click OK (see Figure 20-6). If you cannot see your disks here, they are already added as a disk resource or the disk is not visible to all nodes in the cluster. This might indicate that the masking is incorrect in your SAN or there's a communication problem of some sort.

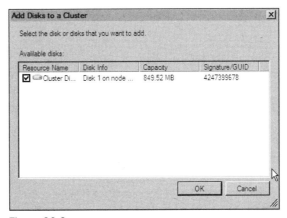

Figure 20-6

Clustering SQL Server 2008

Believe it or not, the procedure to install a SQL Server 2008 instance onto a cluster is one of the easiest parts of getting your SQL Server 2008 cluster up and running. The SQL Server 2008 setup program is used for the install, and it does the heavy lifting for you. All you have to do is make a few (but critically important) decisions, and then sit back and watch the installation take place. In fact, the setup program even goes to the trouble to verify that your nodes are all properly configured; and if not, it will suggest how to fix any problems before the installation begins.

When the installation process does begin, the setup program recognizes all the nodes, and once you give it the go-ahead to install on each one, it does so, all automatically. SQL Server 2008 binaries are installed on the local drive of each node, and the system databases are stored on the shared array you designate.

The next section shows the step-by-step instructions for installing a SQL Server 2008 instance in a cluster. The assumption for this example is that you will be installing this instance in a two-node active/passive cluster. Even if you will be installing in a two-node active/active or a multinode cluster, the steps in this section are applicable. The only real difference is that you have to run SQL Server 2008 setup for every instance you want to install on the cluster, and you have to specify a different logical drive on the shared array.

Clustering SQL Server

To begin installing your SQL Server 2008 cluster, you need the installation medium (CD or DVD). You can either install it directly from the media, or copy the install files from the media to the current active node of the cluster, and run the setup program from there.

To begin the installation, do the following:

1. Run `Setup.exe`. The prerequisites components (which you learned about in Chapter 2) will install first. It is a good idea to run these prerequisites on each of the nodes prior to clustering, as doing so will save time and enable you to debug visually if something goes wrong during the installation. We won't go over each step of the actual SQL Server installation because this has been covered in Chapter 2. Instead, we cover only the differences from a normal nonclustered installation.

2. Once you get to the SQL Server Installation Center, click "New SQL Server failover cluster installation." Note in this screen you can also add new nodes to the cluster after the installation, as shown in Figure 20-7.

    For the most part, the cluster installation is exactly the same as the regular SQL Server installation with the exception of just a few screens. When you get to the Setup Support Rules page, you'll notice a number of new rules that are checked (see Figure 20-8). For example, a check is made to determine whether MSDTC is clustered. While SQL Server will work without MSDTC clustered, some features such as distributed transactions for linked servers or SSIS will not work without it clustered.

3. In the Instance Configuration dialog, specify a virtual name for your SQL Server instance, as shown in Figure 20-9. This is the name that all of your applications will connect to in their connection strings. The name of the directory where your program files will go is also based on this name by default.

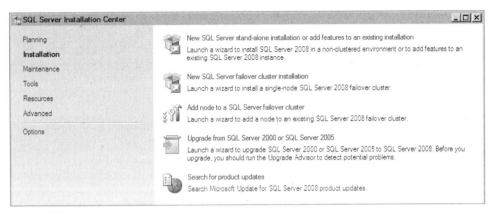

Figure 20-7

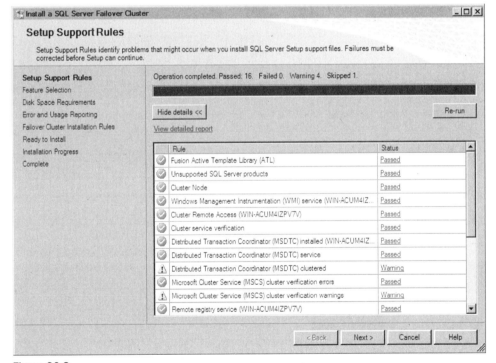

Figure 20-8

4. Specify the cluster resource group that will group all of your SQL Server resources, such as your network name, IP, and SQL Server services, as shown in Figure 20-10.

A nice improvement over SQL Server 2005 is that you can have SQL Server use multiple drives in a cluster during the installation. In SQL Server 2005, you had to configure this behavior afterward, and you weren't allowed to back up to another disk other than the main SQL Server disk until you fixed the dependencies. In SQL Server 2008, simply check which clustered drive resources you'd like SQL Server to be able to access, as shown in Figure 20-11.

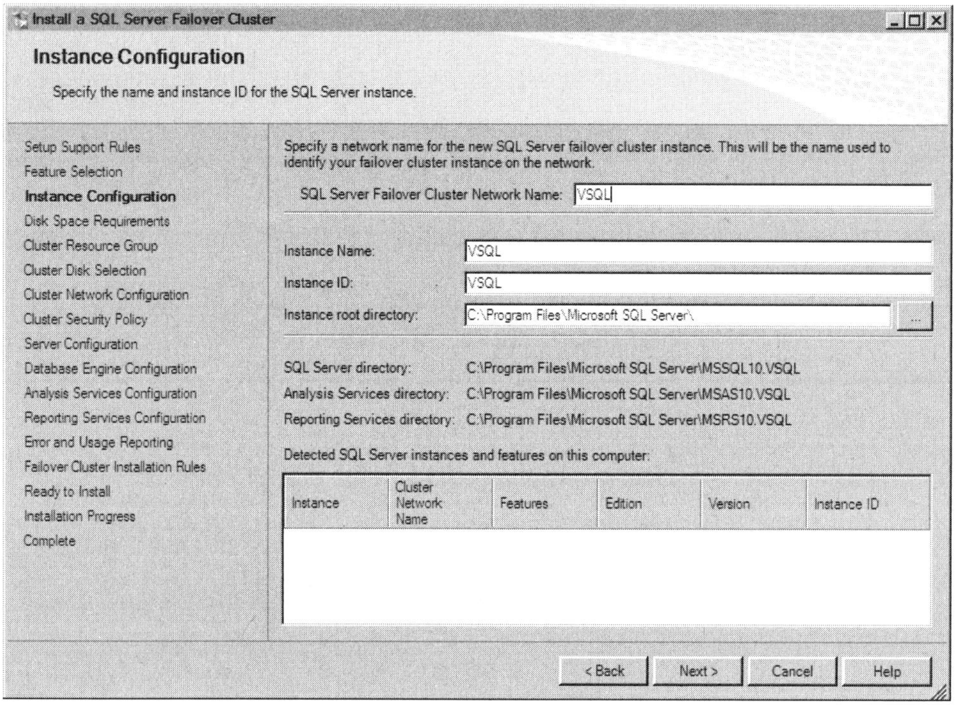

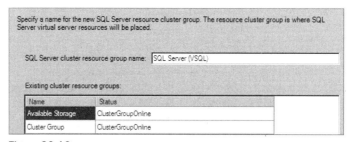

Figure 20-9

Figure 20-10

5. With the drive configuration complete, specify the network that SQL Server will use to communicate with clients, and provide an IP address for each of the networks. This IP address should have been obtained earlier from a network administrator. Notice in Figure 20-12 that Windows 2008 can now use DHCP.

6. The last clustering dialog, shown in Figure 20-13 , asks which domain or local groups will be able to manage the stated service. Creating a custom group for this is now optional; you can just specify that the service security IDs (SIDs) will be used there instead.

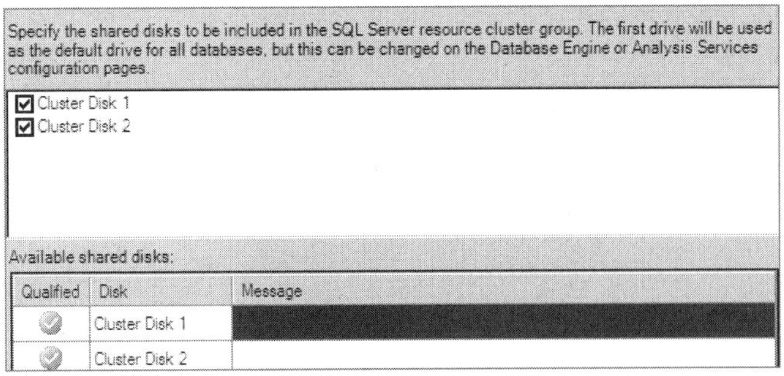

Specify the shared disks to be included in the SQL Server resource cluster group. The first drive will be used as the default drive for all databases, but this can be changed on the Database Engine or Analysis Services configuration pages.

☑ Cluster Disk 1
☑ Cluster Disk 2

Available shared disks:

Qualified	Disk	Message
✅	Cluster Disk 1	
✅	Cluster Disk 2	

Figure 20-11

Specify the network settings for this failover cluster:

☑	IP Type	DHCP	Address	Subnet Mask	Network
☑	IPv4	☐	192.168.131.158	255.255.255.0	Cluster Network 1
☑	IPv6	☑			Cluster Network 1

Figure 20-12

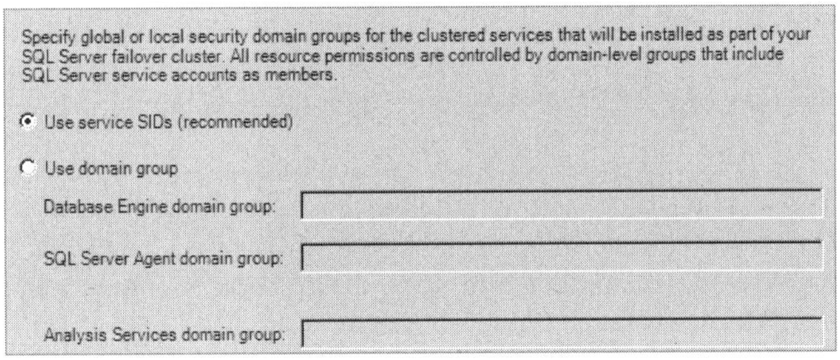

Specify global or local security domain groups for the clustered services that will be installed as part of your SQL Server failover cluster. All resource permissions are controlled by domain-level groups that include SQL Server service accounts as members.

◉ Use service SIDs (recommended)

○ Use domain group

Database Engine domain group: [   ]

SQL Server Agent domain group: [   ]

Analysis Services domain group: [   ]

Figure 20-13

The installation will then proceed to copy the files to all the nodes and run the scripts. Additionally, all the cluster resources will be created and configured. You can see this process occur in the Failover Cluster Management tool.

Installing the Service Pack and Hot Fixes

Once you have installed SQL Server 2008 clustering, your next step is to install the latest SQL Server 2008 service pack and hot fixes, which can be downloaded from Microsoft's Web site. Installing a service pack or hot fix is fairly straightforward because it is cluster aware. Once the service pack or hot fix setup program is started, it detects that you have a cluster and will upgrade all nodes simultaneously. After setup is complete, you may need to reboot your servers and failover the nodes. Generally, once you have run the service pack, you should reboot the active node first. Once it has rebooted, reboot the passive node. This way, failover and failback are automatic.

Test, Test, and Test Again

After you have installed SQL Server 2008 clustering on your nodes, you need to thoroughly test the installation, just as you did after first installing Windows 2008 clustering. However, not only do you want to test SQL Server 2008 clustering, you also want to test how your clients "react" to failovers. Because of this, the following testing section is very similar to the one you previously read but has been modified to meet the more complex needs of the additional client testing you need to do.

The following is a series of tests you can perform to verify that your SQL Server 2008 cluster, and its clients, works properly during failover situations. After you perform each test, verify whether you get the expected results (a successful failover), and be sure you check the Windows log files for any possible problems. If you find a problem during one test, resolve it before proceeding to the next test.

Preparing for the Testing

As with your previous cluster testing, identify a workstation that has the Failover Cluster Management Tool on it, and use this copy of the tool for interacting with your cluster during testing.

Now for the hard part. Essentially, you need to test each client that will be accessing your SQL Server 2008 cluster. In other words, you want to test to see what will happen to each client should a failover occur. Some client software deals with clustering failovers automatically, while others choke and die. The only way to know for sure is to test them.

To do so, first identify all the client applications, which might be one product, or a dozen products. Each of these products has to be configured to access the virtual server name (and IP address) on the new SQL Server instance. In addition, in order for the clients to work, you need to have the appropriate databases restored or installed on the new cluster. Yes, this is a lot of work, but it's necessary if you want a highly available clustering solution you can count on.

Once you have at least one copy of each of your client applications connected to the SQL Server 2008 instance, you are ready for testing. Keep in mind that while testing, you are testing multiple things, including the Windows 2008 cluster, the SQL Server 2008 cluster, and the client applications.

Moving Groups Between Nodes

The easiest test to perform is to use Failover Cluster Management Tool to manually move the cluster and SQL Server resource groups from the active node to a passive node, and then back again. To do this, go to the resource group that has SQL Server, select Move This Service, and specify where you'd like to move the group. This initiates the move of the resources groups from your active node to the designated passive node.

Once this happens, check the Failover Cluster Management Tool and each of the client applications. Each should continue to operate as if no failover had occurred. The Failover Cluster Management Tool should pass this test easily. The clients are another story. You must check each client to see if it continues to work as before. If not, you need to determine why not, which is not always easy. Most clients that stop working after a failover will reconnect if you exit and restart the client.

Once the group has been successfully moved from the active node to a passive node, use the same procedure to move the group back to the original node; and as before, check the Failover Cluster Management Tool, the clients, and the event logs to see if there were any problems. If you have Cluster Service or SQL Server 2008 problems because of the test failover, you need to resolve them before proceeding. If you have a client problem, you can continue with your testing and try to resolve it later. In most cases, if a client fails this first test, it will fail all of the tests.

Manually Failing Over Nodes By Turning Them Off

Turn off the active node. Once this happens, watch the failover in the Failover Cluster Management Tool and the clients. As before, check for any problems. Next, turn on the node and wait until it boots back up successfully. Then turn off the now current active node. Again, watch the failover in the Failover Cluster Management Tool and the clients, and check for problems. Turn the node back on when done.

Manually Failing Over Nodes by Breaking the Public Network Connections

Unplug the public network connection from the active node. This will cause a failover to a passive node, which you can watch in the Failover Cluster Management Tool and the clients. Check for any problems. Now plug the public network connection back into the server and unplug the public network connection from the now active node. This will cause a failover to the current passive node, which you can watch in the Failover Cluster Management Tool. Watch the failover in the Failover Cluster Management Tool and the clients, and check for problems. Once the testing is complete, plug the network connection back into the server.

Manually Failing Over Nodes by Breaking the Shared Array Connection

From the active node, remove the shared array connection. This will cause a failover that you can watch in the Failover Cluster Management Tool and applications. Check for any problems. Next, reconnect the broken connection from the now active node and remove the shared array connection. Watch the failover in the Failover Cluster Management Tool and the clients, and check for problems. When done, reconnect the broken connection.

If you pass all of these tests the first time, it will be a near-miracle, but miracles do happen. If you run into problems, resolve them before continuing.

Maintaining the Cluster

After you have your SQL Server 2008 cluster up and running (and tested), you are ready to put it into production. This may involve creating new databases, moving databases from older servers to this one, setting up jobs, and so on. In most cases, managing SQL Server 2008 on a cluster is the same as managing it on a noncluster. The key thing to keep in mind is that whenever you access your cluster with any of your SQL Server 2008 administrative tools, such as Management Studio, you will be accessing it using its virtual name and IP address; but if you are using any of the operating system tools, such as System Monitor, you need to point these directly to the node in question (which is usually the active node).

In most cases, as a DBA, you probably will be administering SQL Server 2008 using Management Studio, but sometimes you need to access the individual nodes of the cluster. If you have easy access to the cluster, you can always log on locally; if you prefer remote administration, you can use Terminal Services to access the nodes.

When DBAs begin to administer their first cluster, they get a little confused as to where SQL Server 2008 is actually running. Keep in mind that a clustered instance of SQL Server 2008 (even in a multinode cluster) consists of only two nodes: the active node and the passive node. At any one time, an instance of SQL Server 2008 is running on the active node only, so when you need to look at the nodes directly, generally you want to look at the active node. If you don't know which node is currently active, you can find out by using the Failover Cluster Management Tool.

When you log in to the active node (or connect to it remotely using Terminal Services) and then bring up Windows Explorer (a routine task), you will be able to see the SQL Server data drives and the quorum drive; but if you log on to the passive node, you will not be able to see the SQL Server data drives or the quorum drive. This is because drives can be accessed from only a single node at a time. Conversely, if you check the event logs on either the active or passive nodes, you will see that they are virtually identical, with events from both nodes displayed. Event logs are replicated between the active and passive nodes.

If you access your cluster through Terminal Services, be aware of a couple of odd behaviors. For example, if you use Terminal Services to connect to the cluster using the virtual cluster name and IP address, you will be connecting to the active node, just as if you used Terminal Services to connect to the active node directly (using its virtual name and IP address); but if a failover should occur and you are using Terminal Services to access the cluster using the virtual cluster name and IP address, Terminal Services gets a little confused, especially if you are using Windows Explorer. For example, you may discover that your data and quorum drives no longer appear to be accessible, even though they really are. To resolve this problem, log out of Terminal Services and reconnect after a failover.

Troubleshooting Cluster Problems

Troubleshooting cluster-related issues is not for the faint of heart or the beginner. It requires a lot of fortitude, persistence, experience, and a support contract with Microsoft Technical Support. The problem is that clustering is very complex and involves your node hardware, shared array, hardware drivers, operating system, clustering services, and SQL Server 2008. Any problem you are having could be caused by any one of them, and identifying the exact cause of a problem is often difficult.

Another reason cluster troubleshooting is difficult is that the feedback you get, in the form of messages or logs, is not always accurate or complete, assuming you get any feedback at all; and when you do get feedback, the resources for identifying and remedying problems are minimal.

Because of all of this, if you have a cluster, you should plan to purchase Microsoft Technical Support for your cluster. This is a very good investment, and one that will pay for itself. We have used Microsoft Technical Support many times, and in most cases they have been able to help. You don't need to automatically call support as soon as you have a problem; always try to identify and resolve problems on your own if you can. But at some point, especially if your cluster is down and you need help getting it back up, you need to be able to recognize when you can't resolve the problem by yourself and when you need outside help.

In this section we have included some general advice to get you started when you need to identify and resolve cluster-related problems.

How to Approach Clustering Troubleshooting

In the discussion about how to install clustering in this chapter, we repeatedly emphasized the importance of performing a task, testing, and if everything is working OK, then proceeding with the next step. This methodical approach is to help you more easily identify what is causing the problem as soon as possible after it happens. For example, if things are working correctly, then you perform a task and test what you did and the task you performed fails, you can fairly assume that what you just did is directly or indirectly responsible for the problem, making problem identification easier. If you don't perform regular testing and don't notice a problem until after many tasks have been performed, then identifying the cause of a problem or problems is much more difficult. Therefore, the best way to troubleshoot problems is to perform incremental testing. This also makes it much easier if you have a detailed installation plan that you can follow, helping you to ensure that you are performing all the necessary steps (including testing at appropriate places).

Doing It Right the First Time

You can save a lot of troubleshooting problems by preventing them. Here's how:

❑ Be doubly sure that all of the hardware for your nodes and shared array is on Microsoft's cluster compatibility list.

❑ Be sure that you are using the latest hardware and software drivers and service packs.

❑ Create a detailed installation plan that you can use as your guide for the installation and for disaster recovery should the need arise.

❑ Learn as much as you can about clustering before you begin your installation. Many cluster problems are user-created because the person responsible guessed instead of knowing for sure what he or she was doing.

Gathering Information

To help identify the cause of a problem you often need a lot of information. Unfortunately, the information you need may not exist, or it may be scattered about in many different locations, or it may be downright misleading. In any event, to troubleshoot problems, you need to find as much information as you can.

Use the following guidelines and resources when gathering information to troubleshoot a cluster problem:

❑ Know what is supposed to happen. If you expect a specific result, and you are not getting it, be sure that you fully understand what is supposed to happen, and exactly what is happening. In other words, know the difference between the two.

❑ Know what happened directly before the problem occurred. This is much easier if you test incrementally, as described earlier.

❑ Know whether the problem is repeatable. Not all problems can be easily repeated, but if they can, the repetition can provide useful information.

❑ Take note of any onscreen error messages. Be sure that you take screen captures of any messages for reference. Some DBAs have the habit of clicking OK after an error message without recording its exact content. Often, the exact content of a message is helpful if you need to search the Internet to learn more about it.

❑ There are a variety of logs you may be able to view, depending on how far along you are in the cluster setup process. These include the three operating system logs: the cluster log (located at `c:\windows\cluster\cluster.log`); the SQL Server Setup log files (located at

`%ProgramFiles%\Microsoft SQL Server\100\Setup Bootstrap\LOG\Summary.txt`); and the SQL Server 2008 log files.

❑ If the error messages you identify aren't obvious (are they ever?), search for them on the Internet, including newsgroups.

The more information you can gather about a problem, the better position you are in to resolve the problem.

Resolving Problems

Sometimes a problem is obvious and the solution is obvious. If that's the case, you are lucky. In many other cases, the problem you have may or may not be obvious, but the solution is not obvious. In these cases, we have found that instead of wasting a lot of time trying to identify and fix a problem, the easier and quicker solution is to reinstall your cluster from scratch.

Many cluster problems are due to the complexity of the software involved, and it is often much faster to just rebuild the cluster from scratch, including the operating system. This is especially true if you have tried to install cluster services or SQL Server 2008 clustering and the setup process aborted during setup and did not uninstall itself cleanly.

When you are building a new cluster, rebuilding it to resolve problems is usually an option because time is not an issue, but suppose you have a SQL Server 2008 cluster in production and it fails so badly that neither node works and you don't have time to rebuild it. What do you do? You bring in Microsoft.

Working with Microsoft

Operating a SQL Server 2008 cluster without having a Microsoft Technical Support contract is like operating a car without insurance. You can do it, but if you have any unexpected problems, you will be sorry you went without.

Generally, there are two main reasons you would need to call Microsoft Technical Support for clustering issues. One, it's a noncritical issue that you just can't figure out for yourself. In this case, you will be assigned an engineer, and over a period of several days, you will work with that engineer to resolve your problem. This often involves running an application provided by Microsoft to gather information about your cluster so the engineer can diagnose it.

The second reason to call is because your production cluster is down and there are no obvious solutions to getting it back up quickly. Generally, in this case, we recommend you call Microsoft Technical Support as soon as you can to get the problem ticket started. In addition, you must emphasize to the technical call screener (the first person who answers the phone) and the engineer you are assigned to that you are facing a production down situation and that you want to declare a *critical situation*, or *critsit*. This tells Microsoft that your problem is top priority and you will get special service. When you declare a critsit, the person on the phone may try to dissuade you from doing so because it causes a chain of events to happen within Microsoft Technical Support that they prefer to avoid; but if your production cluster is down, you need to emphasize the serious nature of your problem and tell them that you want to open the critsit. You may have to repeat this several times so that that the nature of your problem is fully understood. If it is, you will get immediate help with your problem until your cluster is back up and running.

Summary

Although this chapter is long, it still represents only the tip of the iceberg when it comes to covering everything the DBA should know about SQL Server 2008 clustering. In addition to reading this chapter, you should read all of the clustering articles in SQL Server 2008 Books Online, and any additional information you can find on Microsoft's Web site and elsewhere on the Internet. As we said at the beginning of this chapter, clustering is an adventure, and after reading this chapter, we are sure you now agree.

Index

32-bit systems (x86), 432–433, 479–482
/3GB option, 432, 433, 479, 480
AWE, 432, 433, 476, 480, 481, 482
PAE, 432, 476, 479, 480
memory nodes, 477, 478
Memory: Pages/sec performance **counter,**
476
memory usage **query, 547**
memory-friendly applications, 482
MERGE, 24
INSERT/UPDATE/DELETE operations with,
597–599
performance, 599–600
Merge agent jobs, 656
merge joins, 573, 574, 582
many-to-many, 582
one-to-many, 582
merge replication, 655, 674–675
message types, 238–240
Microsoft Data Access Components. *See*
MDAC
Microsoft Operations Manager Pack, 23
Microsoft Security Response Center blog, 333
Microsoft SQL Server 2008. *See* **SQL Server**
2008
Microsoft System Center Operations Manager,
459
Microsoft Visual Studio 2008. *See* **Visual**
Studio 2008
middleware, 32
minimum configuration warning (SQL Server
install), 60
minimum memory per query option, 494
MinorVersion, 411
Mirror Committed Overhead, 714
mirror database, 684
Mirror Log: Current Restore Rate, 714
Mirror Log: Time to Restore Log, 714
Mirror Log: Unrestored Log, 713
mirror request page, 718–719
mirror server, 684
preparing, for failover, 719–723
mirroring. *See* **database mirroring**
mirroring_connection_timeout, 699
mirroring_failover_lsn, 699

mirroring_redo_queue, 699–700
mirroring_role_sequence, 699
mirroring_safety_sequence, 699
missing indexes feature, 625
model database, 7, 8
backing up, 751
Module object, 531
modules, 531
money (data type), 13
monitoring, 497–554. *See also* **performance**
monitoring
baseline and
current metrics compared to, 499
establishing, 498–499
data compression and, 475
database mirroring, 709–716
%Disk counters, 509
event monitoring, 514–539
reasons for, 515–516
tools for, 514–515
goal of, 498
index fragmentation, 626–627
individual instances *v._*Total, 508
I/O latency, 508
I/O queue depth, 508
I/O throughput-MB/sec, 507
log monitoring, 548
SQL Server Error log, 548
Windows event logs, 548
MDW and, 548–554
new features in, 499–500
objectives, identifying, 498
replication, 679–682
Resource Governor and, 487–488
security and, 332
SQL Server process memory usage, 511–512
standard reports and, 500, 547
tools for, 500–501. *See also specific*
monitoring tools
Activity Monitor, 501
Data Collection, 500, 548, 549
Default Trace, 501, 514, 516
DMFs, 539–547
DMVs, 501, 539–547
event notifications, 515, 529–531

simplification transformation (query optimization), 567–568
single publisher, one or more subscribers (replication model), 657–658
64-bit systems
  IA64 processors, 422
  memory configuration, 433–434, 479
  memory configuration scenarios
    64-bit SQL on a 64-bit OS, 436
    x64 system with 64-bit OS and 32-bit SQL with less than 4GB of RAM, 436
    x64 system with 64-bit OS and 32-bit SQL with more than 4GB of RAM, 436
  SQL Server 2008 and, 88–89
  x64 processors, 422
sliding window, 463, 465, 611
smalldatetime, 14, 15
smallint, 12
smallmoney, 13
SMO (SQL Server Management Objects), 23, 112, 386
SMP (symmetric multi-processor) systems, 427
snapshot agent, 656
Snapshot agent jobs, 656
snapshot replication, 654, 666–674
snapshots, database, 729–730
SOAP (Simple Object Access Protocol), endpoints (deprecated), 25, 343
sockets, 425
soft page faults, 430–431
solutions v. projects (Visual Studio), 383. See also projects
Sort operation, 579, 597
sort order, collations and, 42–43
Source Safe, Visual, 383, 384, 385, 408, 412, 679
space savings, from data compression, 473–475
sp_addsrvrolemember, 351
spatial indexes, 25, 606
spatial libraries, advanced, 25
spatial services (SQL Server 2008), 25
spatial support, standards-based, 25
SP:CacheHit, 556, 557

SP:CacheInsert, 556, 557
SP:CacheMiss, 555, 556, 557
sp_configure, 111–112, 481
SPN (service principal name), 344
sp_replcounters replication system stored procedure, 682
sp_trace_create, 517, 520
sp_trace_setevent, 517, 520
sp_trace_setfilter, 518, 520
sp_trace_setstatus, 518, 520, 521
sp_who, 118
sp_who2, 118
SQL client aliasing, 800
SQL CLR. See CLR integration
SQL CMD, 23
SQL community testing, 65
SQL, dynamic. See dynamic SQL
SQL Native Client, 6
SQL Profiler, 23, 418, 500
  Analysis Services events and, 223–224
  bottlenecks and, 354
  CLR integration performance monitoring with, 325
  database mirroring and, 716
  recompilations and, 563
  Service Broker activities and, 302–307
SQL Server
  Agent. See SQL Server Agent
  Analysis Services. See Analysis Services
  Audit. See Audit
  authentication. See authentication
  automating. See Maintenance Plans; SQL Server Agent
  collations. See collations
  Configuration Manager. See Configuration Manager
  Database Engine. See Database Engine
  editions. See editions
  Extended Events. See XEvents
  Integration Services. See Integration Services
  I/O process model. See I/O
  Management Objects. See SMO
  Management Studio. See Management Studio
  monitoring. See monitoring
  as .NET runtime host. See .NET runtime host